Children – The Modern Law

Children – The Modern Law

Fourth Edition

ANDREW BAINHAM
of the Middle Temple, Barrister
Tenant at 14 Gray's Inn Square
University Reader in Family Law and Policy
Formerly Fellow of Christ's College Cambridge

STEPHEN GILMORE
of Lincoln's Inn, Barrister
Senior Lecturer in Law
King's College London

With contributions by

Neville Harris
of Gray's Inn, Barrister
Professor of Law
University of Manchester

Kathryn Hollingsworth
Professor of Law
University of Newcastle

Family Law

Published by Family Law
A publishing imprint of Jordan Publishing Limited
21 St Thomas Street
Bristol BS1 6JS

British Library Cataloguing-in-Publication Data

A catalogue record for this book is available from the British Library.

ISBN 978 1 84661 498 9

Typeset by Letterpart Limited, Caterham on the Hill, Surrey CR3 5XL

Printed in Great Britain by CPI Antony Rowe, Chippenham and Eastbourne

DEDICATION

IN MEMORY OF GWEN BAINHAM (1914–2010)
MOTHER, GRANDMOTHER, GREAT-GRANDMOTHER
AND SCHOOLTEACHER
WHO HAD A LIFELONG LOVE OF CHILDREN

PREFACE

Eight years is a long time in family law. The changes which have taken place since the last edition was published in 2005 have been many and various.

Radical changes to the law of parentage introduced by the Human Fertilisation and Embryology Act 2008 have widened the categories of legal parents. As well as fuelling the debate about whether parenthood is primarily biological or social, these developments have provoked new questions about the gender-specific status of 'mother' or 'father' and indeed whether children should be limited to two parents.

The law on child support was amended by the Child Maintenance and Other Payments Act 2008 and the Welfare Reform Act 2012, changing how child support is calculated, extending enforcement mechanisms, whilst at the same time effecting a notable shift towards the promotion of private ordering.

The private law in the Children Act 1989 was significantly amended by the Children and Adoption Act 2006 to reflect the growing importance attached to contact between parents and children following relationship breakdown. These provisions, designed to facilitate and if necessary enforce contact, are about to be supplemented by a controversial legislative statement of the importance to children of the continuing involvement of both parents when the Children and Families Bill 2013 is enacted. The same legislation will abolish the principal private law orders for residence and contact and replace them with a generic 'child arrangements order'. The new order will cover much of the same ground, but the intention is to avoid the loaded terminology and imbalance in the parents' positions which the current orders are thought to embody.

Overshadowing all these changes, important though they are, is the substantial withdrawal of legal aid in April 2013 from private law cases. Henceforth the implication is that, with limited exceptions, such disputes are not really the business of the law but are more appropriate for resolution outside the courts. Even where they do reach the courts the sense is that parents locked in dispute, apart from the affluent, will have to go it alone without the assistance of lawyers. Time will tell whether any of this is an improvement on what went before or whether it is more calculated to promote the best interests of children.

There have also been extensive developments in the case law since the last edition. The House of Lords in *Re G (Children)* [2006] UKHL 43 and the Supreme Court in *Re B* [2009] UKSC 5 have both considered what, if any, priority should be given to 'natural parents' who get into disputes with others (and some may think that the guidance given is less than clear). Other important decisions at the highest level have considered specific aspects of the private law. In *Holmes-Moorhouse v London Borough of Richmond Upon Thames* [2009] UKHL 7 the House of Lords gave guidance on the courts' approach to shared residence. Several leading decisions have addressed the growing phenomenon of international child abduction, clarifying the impact of the ECtHR's jurisprudence on interpretation of the Hague Convention (*Re D (Abduction: Rights of Custody)* [2006] UKHL 51 [2007] 1 FLR 961; *Re E (Children) (Abduction: Custody Appeal)* [2011] UKSC 27, [2011] 2 FLR 758; *Re S (A Child) (Abduction: Rights of Custody)* [2012] UKSC 10, [2012] 2 FLR 442), and the meaning of 'habitual residence' (*Re A (Children)* [2013] UKSC 60, [2013] 1 FLR 1041); and the Court of Appeal has delivered significant decisions on the related issue of permission to relocate from the jurisdiction (*K v K (Relocation: Shared Care Arrangement)* [2011] EWCA Civ 793, [2012] 2 FLR 880, and *Re F (Child: International Relocation)* [2012] EWCA Civ 1364, [2013] 1 FLR 645).

The public law has also not escaped legislative attention, with enactment since the last edition of the Children Act 2004 and the Children and Young Persons Act 2008 (restructuring, and making further provision for, the delivery of social work services to children), and the Childcare Act 2006 (regulating child-minding and childcare provision). The intended reforms in the Children and Families Bill 2013 have the potential for changing the landscape of the public law. The attempt to impose a rigid six month time limit for care proceedings, again subject to only limited exceptions, along with a strident insistence that expert evidence be 'necessary', will change the face of these proceedings in a way which many of those who are well-informed do not think will be for the better. The same can be said of the provisions which would reduce the courts' scrutiny of the care plan and which unashamedly give a push to adoption as the 'officially preferred' solution for long-term substitute care.

The case law on care proceedings has proved equally controversial. The House of Lords or Supreme Court has several times been called upon to consider the difficult evidential questions involved in child protection (*In re B (Children) (Care Proceedings: Standard of Proof) (CAFCASS intervening)* [2008] UKHL 35, [2009] AC 11; *In re S-B (Children) (Care Proceedings: Standard of Proof)* [2009] UKSC 17, [2010] 1 AC 678; *In re J (Children)* [2013] UKSC 9; and *In re B (A Child)* [2013] UKSC 33). The balance between adequate child protection and maintaining family integrity can appear almost impossible to strike properly where someone in a child's household is a possible perpetrator of proven harm to another child in the past. The principles enunciated by the Supreme Court have divided commentators, including the authors of this book.

In the criminal justice sphere, reforms continue to be made to the treatment of children in conflict with the law though these are not (yet) quite as extensive as those set out in earlier editions of this book. Nonetheless, important changes have been instigated through legislation (for example, new sentences, forms of diversion and changes to the system of remand), judicial decision (including, most recently, the protections available to 17 year olds detained and questioned by the police) and in policy and practice. Perhaps most significantly since the last edition of this book was published, the numbers of children being brought into the youth justice system and sentenced to custody have dropped massively. There is also a much greater focus on the rights of children in trouble with the law.

Of great importance to children's development, and enshrined in a fundamental human right, education is a field marked by almost constant legal change. Areas receiving particular attention in chapter 17 include special educational needs (including the important reforms under the Children and Families Bill), the school curriculum, discipline, truancy and the raising of the 'participation age', and important judicial rulings on matters such as sex education and the wearing of religious dress or symbols by school pupils. This is a field in which children's independent rights have tended to be overshadowed by those of their parents and carers but, as the chapter shows, they are belatedly receiving a degree of recognition.

As can be seen from the foregoing brief summary, in under a decade the landscape of child law has altered significantly. To accommodate these changes we have made considerable changes to the structure of the book.

The previous edition addressed international child law issues in its final chapter. This was never intended to relegate international issues merely to an 'add-on'. Now, however, international perspectives are such a feature of how we must all think about child law across all subject matter that they cannot be left to a final chapter. We have now, therefore, incorporated international provisions, where relevant, into the body of other chapters. The developments in the area of international child abduction are such that we felt that it now warrants a separate chapter of its own. Previous editions had structured the private law relating to children around chapters addressing the married, unmarried, and social family respectively. However, in light of the major changes since enactment of the Children Act 1989 to the law on parentage/parenthood and parental responsibility, and to the law relating to same sex couples, such an arrangement is clearly no longer appropriate nor efficient. We have now, therefore, introduced three chapters respectively addressing in general the issues of parentage, parental responsibility, and private law disputes concerning children. Adoption is now used primarily as a means of ensuring a permanent, stable placement for children who have been taken into care, and we now therefore discuss the law of adoption, together with special guardianship and other modes of permanency planning for children, later in the book than in previous editions, after the discussion of care and supervision orders.

The extensive developments in the law are reflected in the growing size of editions of this book. While the first two editions ran to about 600 pages, this latest edition fights just shy of 1000. Keeping pace with the volume of legislative and case law developments has presented us with an ongoing challenge. However, we have sought to do our best to state the law as at 1 September 2013 and, where possible, have managed to incorporate some later references.

Andrew Bainham
Stephen Gilmore
September 2013

ACKNOWLEDGMENTS

This is the fourth edition of *Children – The Modern Law* but the first to which my co-author Stephen Gilmore has contributed. I feel delighted and fortunate that Stephen, one of our leading family law commentators, has agreed to join me. It is only right that I should acknowledge that he has undertaken the lion's share of the extensive up-dating which was required for this new edition. While both of us accept responsibility for the whole book, I have been primarily responsible for chapters 1, 3, 7 and 16 while Stephen has been principally responsible for chapters 2, 4, 5, 6, 8, 9, 10, 11, 12 and 13. We have both contributed directly to chapter 14. I should also acknowledge that chapter 1, though significantly up-dated since the first edition in 1993, still bears the hallmark of the historical scholarship of Stephen Cretney who wrote the original chapter.

When I wrote the first edition twenty years ago, my conception was to try to produce a book which ranged beyond the conventional boundaries of 'mainstream family law'. Children have a place in society as well as in families and it seemed important to me that a textbook on children law should reflect this. In particular an attempt should be made to cover the crucially important areas of education and criminal justice. The difficulty has always been that these are vast specialisms in their own right, demanding specialist attention. Both Stephen and I were therefore delighted when Neville Harris and Kathryn Hollingsworth, leading commentators on education law and juvenile justice respectively, were willing to join us and to contribute chapters which greatly enrich this new edition. Kathyrn would like to thank Ann Sinclair for her research assistance.

I thank the staff at Jordans for their support in producing this latest edition and for their commitment to the book over the last twenty years. Thank you also to Tracy Robinson for all her kind patience and assistance with the manuscript at proof stage.

My own contribution to this edition has been informed in places by recent practice at the Family Bar. I want to thank Brenda Hale, Alan Ward, Clive Lewis and John Spencer for their support of my application to be Called. I also thank my two former pupil supervisors, Nicholas Yates of 1 Hare Court and Jane Rayson of 4 Paper Buildings for their kindness and generosity towards me. I cannot thank enough Sarah Forster and all my friends and colleagues at 14 Gray's Inn Square for making it possible for me to enjoy this Indian summer at the Bar – and in London's friendliest family law chambers! Special thanks go to my former student, Sally Gore, who in an interesting role reversal has taught me some of the things I needed to know quickly as a fledgling junior tenant.

Last but not least, my greatest debt is to my wife Hsin-Ping and our two children, James and Erin, both born since the last edition was published. I thank Hsin-Ping for her support in producing this edition. More especially, without her drive and enthusiasm I would not have been called to the Bar or returned to practice and would have missed out on one of life's truly fascinating experiences.

Andrew Bainham
14 Gray's Inn Square
Family Law Chambers

Two decades ago I purchased the first edition of Andrew Bainham's *Children The Modern Law*. The book sparked my particular interest in child law, and ultimately led to my career as an academic specialising in that field. Andrew Bainham was then at the University of East Anglia, and I was accepted for the LL.M in Family Law and Family Policy there. By a happy coincidence, one of my fellow students on the LL.M course was Greg Woodgate, who is now the publisher of Family Law titles within Jordan Publishing. When we arrived in Norwich for our course, Andrew had just moved to become a Fellow of Christ's College, Cambridge, which was a great disappointment to us, but students on the course still benefited greatly from the scholarship contained in *Children The Modern Law*.

So Andrew's invitation to co-author the fourth edition of this book has a special significance for me, and it is a great privilege and pleasure to be associated with this title, and to work with Andrew, Greg and the team at Jordan Publishing. I should like to thank Andrew for his encouragement and his patient understanding of the difficulties involved in completing a book of this sort, and for reading and commenting on the various chapters that I updated. Grateful thanks are also owed to Professor Marilyn Freeman who kindly provided me with very useful materials on international child abduction, and to my colleague, Dr Sandy Steel, who generously shared with me his knowledge of the law on tortious liability of local authorities.

Finally, I should like to thank my wife, Penny, and my children, Libby and Tom, for their forbearance during the writing of the book. They could not have been more delighted that the manuscript was finally completed on the day we set off for our recent summer holiday!

Stephen Gilmore
Somerset House, London
The Feast of St Augustine, Patron Saint of Brewers and Printers, 2013

CONTENTS

Part II
Children and Families

PART III
Children and Local Authorities

Chapter 10
Local Authority Support for Children and Families

Chapter 13
Permanence for Children: Adoption and Special Guardianship   **651**

Part IV
Children and Society

Chapter 15
Children and the Criminal Law

TABLE OF CASES

References are to page numbers.

TABLE OF STATUTES

References are to page numbers.

TABLE OF STATUTORY INSTRUMENTS

References are to page numbers.

TABLE OF ABBREVIATIONS

CA 1989/the Children Act	Children Act 1989
CAFCASS	Children and Family Court Advisory and Support Service
CAO	child assessment order
CDA 1998	Crime and Disorder Act 1998
CJEU	European Court of Justice
CPS	Crown Prosecution Service
CSA 1991	Child Support Act 1991
CSO	child safety order
DBS	Disclosure and Barring Service
DCSF	Department for Children, Schools and Familes
DFE	Department for Education
DfEE	Department for Education and Employment
DfES	Department for Education and Skills
DPP	Director of Public Prosecutions
DTO	detention and training order
DWP	Department for Work and Pensions
ECHR	The European Convention for the Protection of Human Rights and Fundamental Freedoms
ECtHR	European Court of Human Rights
EHCP	education, health and care plan
EMA	educational maintenance allowance
EPO	emergency protection order
ESO	education supervision order
EYFS	Early Years Foundation Stage
FAO	family assistance order
FLA 1996	Family Law Act 1996
FPR	Family Procedure Rules 2010, SI 2010/2955
GAL	guardian ad litem
HFEA 1990	Human Fertilisation and Embryology Act 1990
HFEA 2008	Human Fertilisation and Embryology Act 2008
HMCI	Her Majesty's Chief Inspector of Schools
HRA 1998	Human Rights Act 1998
IAP	independent appeal panel
ICACU	International Child Abduction and Contact Unit

IEP	individual education plan
LASCH	local authority secure children's home
LEA	local education authority
LGO	Local Government Ombudsman
MACR	minimum age of criminal responsibility
MCA 1973	Matrimonial Causes Act 1973
MHA 1983	Matrimonial Homes Act 1983
MIAM	mediation information and assessment meeting
MoJ	Ministry of Justice
NYAS	National Youth Advocacy Service
NCSC	National Care Standards Commission
NSPCC	National Society for the Prevention of Cruelty to Children
Ofsted	Office for Standards in Education
PACE 1984	Police and Criminal Evidence Act 1984
PCC(S)A 2000	Powers of Criminal Courts (Sentencing) Act 2000
PCO	parental compensation order
PHSE	personal health and social education
PRO	parental responsibility order
QCA	Qualification and Curriculum Authority
RE	religious education
SEN	special educational needs
SENCO	special educational needs co-ordinator
SRE	sex and relationships education
STC	secure training centre
UNCRC	United Nations Convention on the Rights of the Child
VAA	voluntary adoption agencies
YJB	Youth Justice Board
YOI	youth offender institution
YOT	youth offending team
YRO	youth rehabilitation order

Part I

BACKGROUND AND SOURCES OF CHILDREN LAW

Part I of the book aims to introduce the student to the historical evolution, sources and fundamental principles of the law affecting children. Chapter 1 sketches the profound historical and demographic changes which have influenced the attitude of society towards children, and which provide the context in which legal change has occurred.

Chapter 2 is concerned with the two most important sources of children law domestically and internationally. Part I of the chapter focuses on the Children Act 1989, its basic principles and underlying philosophies. There is no question that the Act constitutes the single most important source of children law. Even where it does not have direct application, its influence is nonetheless likely to be pervasive. Part II of the chapter examines some of the more important Articles and principles set out in the United Nations Convention on the Rights of the Child (UNCRC). This is, equally clearly, the most important international source, not only influencing the development of domestic laws but also the interpretation of other international conventions affecting children.

Chapter 1

CHILDREN AND THE LAW: A DEMOGRAPHIC AND HISTORICAL SKETCH

CHILDHOOD: WHAT IS A CHILD?

The concept of 'childhood' is both a social and legal construct. It is not an immutable classification, and who may be regarded as a 'child' by a particular society, or under the law of that society, is liable to revision and re-evaluation.[1] This most obviously occurred in England in 1969 when the status of childhood, or more accurately 'minority',[2] was redefined with the reduction in the age of majority from 21 to 18.[3] The effect of this was to regard as adults many young people previously denied this status. Yet the position is more complex than this. Children of various ages below majority nonetheless have legal capacity to take certain actions and decisions so that, to that limited extent, they might be viewed as equivalent to 'adults' for some purposes and 'children' for others.[4] It should also be remembered that, although the expression 'child' is apposite to include all those aged from one day to 17 years and 364 days, there is a great deal of practical difference, in terms of the kinds of problems the law has to resolve, between the position of a newborn baby and that of a 17-year-old approaching majority.

A 'child' is normally defined as a 'person' below the age of majority, and this is the position taken in the Children Act 1989 and in the UNCRC.[5] This inevitably gives rise to definitional difficulties at either end of the spectrum

---

[1] On the changing historical conceptions of childhood, see P Ariès *Centuries of Childhood* (Jonathan Cape, 1979) and I Pinchbeck and M Hewitt *Children in English Society* Vol I (Routledge and Kegan Paul, 1969) and Vol II (1973). See also MDA Freeman *The Rights and Wrongs of Children* (Frances Pinter, 1983), ch 1, and *The Moral Status of Children* (Martinus Nijhoff, 1997), ch 2. For a volume of essays explaining ideas of childhood in different legal contexts see J Fionda (ed) *Legal Concepts of Childhood* (Hart Publishing, 2001). For an explanation of the relationship between the sociology of childhood and children's rights see M Freeman 'The Sociology of Childhood and Children's Rights' (1998) *International Journal of Children's Rights* 433.

[2] The term 'minor' includes both 'children' and 'young persons' who have been distinguished for certain purposes, especially in connection with juvenile justice, in English law. Scots law, until comparatively recently, drew a distinction between 'minors' and 'pupils'.

[3] Family Law Reform Act 1969, s 1, following the recommendations of the Latey Committee. See the *Report of the Committee on the Age of Majority* (1967) (Cmnd 3342).

[4] The age of 16 years is particularly important in this respect, since children who have attained this age have a significant number of legal capacities in common with adults.

[5] A child is defined, subject to limited qualifications relating to financial support, as 'a person

since there may be legitimate disagreement about when precisely personhood (and hence childhood) begins and when childhood ends.

The beginning of childhood

The beginning of childhood raises directly the status of the foetus or unborn child. English law generally takes the position that personhood is established at birth and not before. This is the assumption underlying much of the criminal law governing offences against the person, which depends on the child having achieved a separate existence from the mother.[6]

The criminal law and the law of tort do offer certain protection to the foetus or unborn child but not on the basis that it is a 'child'. A good example is the case of *Attorney-General's Reference (No 3 of 1994)*[7] in which the Court of Appeal held that the doctrine of transferred malice could in principle apply where a defendant stabbed a pregnant woman causing the premature birth and subsequent death of her child. The defendant could be liable for the murder or manslaughter of the child on the basis of his intention to cause injury to the mother since, before birth, the foetus might be taken to be *part* of the mother. The House of Lords rejected the Court of Appeal's analysis on the basis that a foetus is 'neither a distinct person separate from its mother nor merely an adjunct of the mother' but 'a unique organism'. While holding that the doctrine of transferred malice could not be invoked so as to found a conviction for murder the House contrived to find a basis for liability in manslaughter. It held that it was a sufficient mens rea for constructive manslaughter that the defendant had intended to commit an act which was unlawful and which all sober and reasonable people would have recognised as creating a risk of harm to some other person. It was unnecessary to show that the person who died was the intended victim. Although a foetus was not a living person, the possibility of a dangerous act directed at a pregnant woman causing harm to the child to whom she subsequently gave birth made it permissible on public policy grounds to regard that child as within the scope of the defendant's mens rea when committing the unlawful act.[8]

Much the same view is taken in the USA, where the unborn child is not regarded as a person under the Constitution.[9] It does not follow that no legal

---

under the age of eighteen' (s 105(1) of the Children Act). In the UNCRC, 'a child means every human being below the age of eighteen years unless, under the law applicable to the child, majority is attained earlier' (Art 1).

6   See, generally, D Ormerod *Smith and Hogan: Criminal Law* (13th edn, Butterworths, 2011), especially at pp 492–493, and chapter 15 below.

7   [1996] 2 WLR 412 (CA) and [1997] 3 WLR 421 (HL).

8   For commentary, see J Keown 'Homicide by Prenatal Assault Revisited' [1998] CLJ 240.

9   *Roe v Wade* 410 US 113 (1973). For a discussion of some of the Canadian cases, see Alison Diduck 'Child Protection and Foetal Rights in Canada' (1993) 5 JCL 133. See also the decision of the Scottish Court of Session in *Kelly v Kelly* [1997] 2 FLR 828.

protections should be extended to the foetus but merely that, if they are, they are not based on the status of childhood or personhood.[10]

The issue has caused particular difficulty where a local authority wishes to take early action to protect a newborn baby from potentially inadequate or irresponsible parents. Here, it has been held that a foetus may not be made a ward of court and, by analogy, could not be the subject of an exercise of the inherent jurisdiction more generally.[11] On the other hand, it was held before the Children Act 1989 that the authority might intervene immediately following birth, and might found its intervention largely, if not exclusively, on the mother's behaviour towards her unborn child while pregnant.[12]

Under the Children Act 1989, intervention will now be based on the prospective element in the threshold test of 'significant harm' which applies in care proceedings. An alternative where the expectant mother is herself a minor would be, with leave, to use the inherent jurisdiction of the High Court. In one case this was used to authorise a caesarean section to be performed on a 17-year-old crack cocaine addict, and thereafter to detain her for medical treatment, using reasonable force if necessary, in a maternity ward.[13]

However, much more importantly than this, there is nothing to prevent the authority from making the mother's unborn child the subject of a child protection plan before commencing proceedings and achieving a degree of supervision over the pregnancy and birth in that way. Such plans are habitually produced by local authorities especially where, as is often the case, the mother has had successive previous children removed from her care. The authority will then often formally issue proceedings within days of the birth usually seeking an interim care order. Such cases often result in a compromise whereby a mother and baby placement is found while assessments of the mother's parenting capacity are carried out at the interim stage of care proceedings.

Another effect of drawing the line for childhood at birth is to prevent the status of parenthood, and the legal responsibilities which go with it, from coming into being until that point. Thus, the prospective father of an unborn child has no legal standing to prevent the mother from undergoing an abortion.[14]

---

[10] A useful and well-balanced discussion of the role of the law in regulating pregnancy is to be found in E Sutherland 'Regulating Pregnancy; Should We and Can We?' in E Sutherland and A McCall Smith (eds) *Family Rights: Family Law and Medical Advance* (Edinburgh University Press, 1990), at p 100. For a detailed examination of parental responsibility towards a child before birth, see M Brazier 'Parental responsibilities, foetal welfare and children's health' in C Bridge (ed) *Family Law Towards the Millennium: Essays for PM Bromley* (Butterworths, 1997), ch 8.

[11] *Re F (In Utero)* [1988] Fam 122.

[12] *D (A Minor) v Berkshire County Council* [1987] 1 All ER 20. Whether such early intervention is justified as a matter of policy is a contentious issue. See chapter 12 below.

[13] *A Metropolitan Borough Council v DB* [1997] 1 FLR 767.

[14] *Paton v British Pregnancy Advisory Service Trustees* [1979] QB 276, upheld by the ECtHR in *Paton v United Kingdom* (1980) 3 EHRR 408 and *C v S* [1987] 1 All ER 1230.

The end of childhood

The end of childhood can also be problematic. The existence of an age of
majority and the attainment of adulthood suggests, prima facie, a termination
of the legal significance of the parent–child relationship and the disabilities of
minority. Yet it is undeniably true that many young adults remain in the
parental home, and some degree of factual dependency will often continue to
exist.[15] This has caused acute difficulties in the case of mentally incapacitated
young adults who, in reality, are as dependent on their parents as are young
children. Thus, the cessation of parental responsibility and the wardship
jurisdiction at majority had left the courts struggling to find a legal basis for
protective action where, for example, a sterilisation operation was thought
necessary.[16] The Court of Protection now, however, enjoys an extensive
jurisdiction to protect the welfare of vulnerable adults under the Mental
Capacity Act 2005.

In certain limited respects, the relationship of parent and child endures for life,
particularly for the purposes of succession. It was also the case that a few legal
disabilities endured beyond majority, such as that relating to the holding of
public offices, which was dependent on attaining the age of 21.[17] This has,
however, now been reduced to 18 by the Electoral Adminstration Act 2006. It
was, until 1994, also true that private acts of buggery between consenting males
were lawful only if the parties had attained 21, but the requisite age was
reduced to 18 in that year[18] and then to 16 by the Sexual Offences
(Amendment) Act 2000 to bring it in line with the age of consent for
heterosexual intercourse.[19] It remains generally the case that applicants for
adoption should have attained the age of 21, subject to certain qualifications
which apply to married couples or civil partners adopting together.[20] It should
also be noted that a perceived benefit of adoption is that membership of the
new adoptive family endures for life since a new relationship of parent and
child is created and with it a new network of lasting kinship relations. Although
we may cease to be dependent on our parents when we become adults, we
nonetheless remain 'their children'.

---

[15] Legal liability can sometimes remain with parents to provide financial support for adult
children who have left home and are in advanced education, and in some jurisdictions there is,
conversely, liability on adult children to support their parents. See *B v B (Adult Student:
Liability to Support)* [1998] 1 FLR 373, and chapter 9 below.

[16] See *T v T* [1988] Fam 52 and *Re F (Mental Patient: Sterilisation)* [1990] AC 1, discussed in
chapter 8 below. See also on the contact issue *Re C (Mental Patient: Contact)* [1993] 1 FLR
940. Cases involving judicially authorised caesarean sections raise at the same time issues about
the protection of the foetus and paternalistic interventions in relation to adults. See *Norfolk
and Norwich Healthcare (NHS) Trust v W* [1996] 2 FLR 613 and *Re MB (Medical Treatment)*
[1997] 2 FLR 426. The leading authority is *St George's Healthcare National Health Service
Trust v S* [1998] 3 All ER 673 and chapter 8 below.

[17] Representation of the People Act 1949.

[18] Criminal Justice and Public Order Act 1994, s 143, amending Sexual Offences Act 1967,
s 12(1).

[19] See further chapter 15 below.

[20] Adoption and Children Act 2002, s 50. See further chapter 13.

HISTORICAL BACKGROUND

The law reflects changing social and cultural attitudes and assumptions, and this is particularly true of family law. The history of those changes is a fascinating subject of study which, in recent years, has attracted much scholarly writing.[21] Considerations of space make it impossible to give even a brief summary of this research in this book, but it may be helpful for the reader to have a sketch of a number of key areas, such as the rules governing legal decision-taking within the family, the role of the State from the Elizabethan

---

[21] The history of family law in England is the subject of a seminal work by Stephen Cretney. See S Cretney *Family Law in the Twentieth Century: A History* (Oxford University Press, 2003). Specifically on the aspects of family law relating to children, see Part IV – 'Children, the Family and the State'. Another useful introduction is to be found in WR Cornish and G de N Clark *Law and Society in England 1750–1950* (Sweet & Maxwell, 1989) (particularly chs 5 and 6); and both AH Manchester *A Modern Legal History of England and Wales 1750–1950* (Butterworths, 1980) and RH Graveson and FR Crane (eds) *A Century of Family Law 1857–1957* (Sweet & Maxwell, 1957) are valuable. RA Houlbrooke *The English Family 1450–1700* (Longman, 1984) is a study from a modern perspective, as is L Stone *The Family, Sex and Marriage in England, 1500–1800* (Weidenfeld & Nicolson, 1977). Reference may also usefully be made to the standard, if now dated, general legal history texts: F Pollock and FW Maitland *The History of English Law before the Time of Edward I* (Cambridge University Press, 1898); and Sir William Holdsworth *A History of English Law* (Methuen, 1966). For a scholarly collection of essays examining the problems of family law reform from an historical perspective, see S Cretney *Law, Law Reform Reform and the Family* (Clarendon, 1998). For an evaluation of the achievements and failings of the twentieth century from the perspective of children's rights see M Freeman 'The End of the Century of the Child?' (2000) 53 *Current Legal Problems* 505. An authoritative volume of essays on the development of family law and policy in the United States and England is S Katz, J Eekelaar and M Maclean (eds) *Cross Currents* (Oxford University Press, 2000). For an assessment of the state of family law at the beginning of the twenty-first century, see S Cretney (ed) *Family Law – Essays for the New Millenium* (Family Law, 2000). See also, more recently, G Douglas and N Lowe (eds) *The Continuing Evolution of Family Law* (Jordans, 2009).

The most accessible general social history is probably I Pinchbeck and M Hewitt *Children in English Society* Vol I (Routledge, 1969) and Vol II (1973) – although this work is not universally admired: see PEH Hair 'Children in Society 1850–1980' in T Barker and M Drake (eds) *Population and Society in Britain 1850–1980* (Batsford, 1982), at p 57. The evolution of public policy is traced in J Packman *The Child's Generation: Child Care Policy in Britain* (2nd edn, Blackwell, 1981). For an authoritative study of the history of social policies for children, see H Hendrick *Child Welfare: England 1872–1989* (Routledge, 1994). A more discursive and international approach is taken in P Ariès *Centuries of Childhood* (Jonathan Cape, 1962). Demographic factors are addressed in P Laslett and R Wall (eds) *Household and Family in Past Time: Comparative Studies in the Size and Structure of the Domestic Group over the Last Three Centuries in England, France, Serbia, Japan and Colonial North America, with further materials from Western Europe* (Cambridge University Press, 1972); EA Wrigley and RS Schofield *The Population History of England 1541–1871, A Reconstruction* (Cambridge University Press, 1989); and in J Eekelaar and D Pearl (eds) *An Aging World – Dilemmas and Challenges for Law and Social Policy* (Clarendon Press, 1989). For more specialist works, see L deMause (ed) *The History of Childhood* (Harper & Row, 1975); and L Pollock *A Lasting Relationship: Parents and Children over Three Centuries* (Fourth Estate, 1987). Useful comparative demographic material is to be found in the *Proceedings* of the *Seminar on present demographic trends and lifestyles in Europe* (Council of Europe, 1991).

Stimulating general works include J Weeks *Sex, Politics and Society: The Regulation of Sexuality Since 1800* (Longman, 1981); J Donzelot *The Policing of Families* (Hutchinson, 1980) and JE Goldthorpe *Family Life in Western Societies: a Historical Sociology of Family Relationships in Britain and North America* (1987).

Poor Law through the child protection measures of the late nineteenth century down to the development of child-centred services as part of the post-Second World War Welfare State, and the development of legal procedures designed to shield children from the worst consequences of the breakdown of their parents' relationships. These historical developments must be seen in the context of rapidly changing demographic factors, and a brief account of the most relevant data therefore follows.

Demographic factors: children and families[22]

The first issue relates to the proportion of children in the population and to the size of family units in which they are reared. There are two conflicting trends to note: on the one hand the number of live births[23] has fallen sharply since the early twentieth century[24] albeit recovering somewhat in recent years, but on the other hand there has been a dramatic improvement (paradoxically most marked in the Second World War)[25] in infant mortality rates. The proportion of the population represented by children aged under 16 years in the UK fell from 23.5 per cent (25 per cent boys and 22 per cent girls) in 1961 to 20 per cent in 2000 (21 per cent boys and 19 per cent girls). By 2009 this figure had fallen to 18.7 per cent. It is projected to remain around this level to 2026 before falling to 18.0 per cent in 2031.[26]

---

[22] See generally C Gibson 'Changing Family Patterns in England and Wales' in S Katz, J Eekelaar and M Maclean (eds) *Cross Currents* (Oxford University Press, 2000).

[23] The number of children in Britain probably increased decade by decade from the mid-eighteenth century to the early twentieth century: see PEH Hair 'Children in Society 1950–1980' in T Barker and M Drake (eds) *Population and Society in Britain 1850–1980* (Batsford, 1982); and, generally, EA Wrigley and RS Schofield *The Population History of England, 1541–1871, A Reconstruction* (Cambridge University Press, 1989).

[24] In the first decade of the twentieth century the average number of live births was approximately 1.1 million each year, but – after the 'baby boomer' years of the 1960s when, once again, more than a million live births were recorded – the number in the 1980s and 1990s stabilised at around a figure of 750,000 annually. There were 669,000 births in the UK in 2001 and it was predicted that the number of births would remain reasonably constant over the next 40 years: *Social Trends* 33 (2003), Tables 1.7 and 1.8. In fact there has been a steady recovery in the birth rate in recent years (thought in part to be attributable to an increase in births to mothers not born in the UK). There were 772, 200 live births recorded in 2007, up 3 per cent on 2006 and up 15 per cent on 2001: *Social Trends* 39 (2009), Figure 1.8. In 2009 there were 790,000 live births, a marginal decrease of 0.5 per cent on the 2008 figure: *Social Trends* 41 (2011) 'Population', figure 1. In 2010 the figure had declined to 723, 165 but increased again slightly in 2011 to 723, 913: *ONS Statistical Bulletin*, 17 October 2012.

[25] In 1901 the rate of infant mortality approached 160 for every 1,000 live births, but by 1961 it had fallen to 22.1 for every 1,000 live births. In 1991 the rate had fallen to 7.4: *Population Trends* 70 (1992), Table 8. By 1996 it had fallen yet further to 6.1: *Population Trends* 90 (1997), Table 8. The downward trend is continuing and by 2001 the figure had dropped to 5.5: *Population Trends* 108 (2002), Table 2.1. By 2007 it was just 4.8: *Social Trends* 39 (2009), Table 7.5. In 2011 infant mortality was at 4.1 per 1,000 live births, the lowest figure ever recorded for England and Wales: ONS, *Statistical Bulletin*, 20 November 2012.

[26] *Social Trends* 32 (2002), Table 1.3. *Social Trends* 41 (2011), 'Population', Table 3.

An ageing population and its impact

The life expectancy of a boy born in 1901 was 45 years and of a girl born that year 49 years; the life expectancy of a boy born in 2004 was almost 77 years and that of a girl over 81 years.[27] This significant improvement means that young people form a much smaller proportion of the population. In 2007, for the first time, the proportion of the population aged under 16 dropped below the proportion over state pension age.[28] The proportion of the population which is of pensionable age has risen sharply and can be expected to continue to rise: in 1961, 4 per cent of the people in the UK were aged 75 or over: by 2000 the figure was 7 per cent (5 per cent men and 9 per cent women) and those aged over 65 represented 15.6 per cent of the population. It is estimated that the proportion of those aged 65 and over will rise to 22.3 per cent by 2031 with those aged over 75 making up 11.7 per cent.[29] The fastest growing sub-group of the population are the 'oldest old', now regarded as those aged over 90 years. This group increased threefold between 1971 and 2007 (to 1 per cent of the female population and 0.4 per cent of the male population). It is projected that by 2031 about 2.1 percent of the female population and 1.4 of the male population may comprise the oldest old.[30]

These changes have had (and will continue to have) a dramatic effect on the composition and size of kinship groups.[31] Whereas the modern child expects to know both his parents throughout his childhood and some at least of his grandparents, eighteenth-century children often knew none of their grandparents, frequently knew only one of their parents, and not uncommonly knew neither of their parents.[32] So the modern child is much more likely to have at least the possibility of knowing his or her parents, grandparents and siblings. But, in fact, the family unit has become much smaller. Whereas the typical mid-Victorian family contained four or more children (and it was not uncommon to find families with up to 10 children), by 1991 only 5 per cent of households had three or more dependent children and by 2000 this had fallen further to 4 per cent.[33] Figures for 2008 show a further fall to just 3 per cent.[34] This trend towards a much smaller functioning family unit is reinforced by the increase in the number of single-parent families. The percentage of all

---

[27] *Social Trends* 33 (2003), Chart 7.1 and *Social Trends* 39 (2009), Table 7.2.

[28] *Social Trends* 39 (2009), Table 1.2.

[29] *Social Trends* 32 (2002), Table 1.3. *Social Trends* 41 (2011), 'Population', Table 3.

[30] *Social Trends* 39 (2009), Figure 1.3.

[31] For a collection of essays exploring evolving notions and practices of kinship in contemporary Britain and the interrelationship of kinship, law and social policy see F Ebtehaj, B Lindley and M Richards (eds), *Kinship Matters* (Hart Publishing, 2006).

[32] Hair 'Children in Society 1850–1980' in Barker and Drake (above), at p 44.

[33] The figures for the proportion of households with one or two dependent children was of course much higher at 20 per cent in 1991 and 19 per cent in 2001: *Social Trends* 32 (2002), Table 2.2.

[34] The proportion of households with one or two dependent children has also fallen further to 18 per cent: *Social Trends* 41, 'Households and Families' (2011), Table 2.

dependent children living in lone-parent families trebled to reach 22 per cent between 1972 and 2001[35] with the great majority of the parents being lone mothers rather than lone fathers.[36]

Divorce, remarriage and step-children

There are, on latest figures, between 115,000–120,000 divorces each year in England and Wales[37] and a very large number of children who experience the divorce of their parents; in 1983 it was estimated[38] that one in five children would experience a parental divorce by the time the child was 16 years of age. More than one half (51 per cent) of couples divorcing in England and Wales in 2007 had at least one child under 16.[39] Although the total of children experiencing parental divorce has declined between 1989 and 2009 from 216,000 to almost 154,000, it will be seen that the numbers are still very significant.[40] Many divorcing parents remarry[41] and in 1990 there were more than 40,000 births within marriage to women who had remarried. This figure had, however, sharply declined to 32,600 by 1996.[42] There was a further significant decline to 23,900 by 2001.[43] Such children will have kinship links with more than one family. The law's response to this phenomenon has not always been consistent.[44] Concern has also been expressed about the difficulties which children and parents encounter in keeping in contact after the

---

[35]   *Social Trends* 32 (2002), Table 2.16.
[36]   Around 9 out of 10 live with single mothers: *Social Trends* 39 (2009), Table 2.4. But the majority – 78 per cent in the Spring of 2002 – of dependent children still live in a household headed by a couple: *Social Trends* 33 (2003), Table 2.4. This proportion has remained largely stable: *Social Trends* 39 (2009), Table 2.4.
[37]   After many years in which the total numbers of divorces had been increasing, between 2003 and 2009 there was a steady downward trend in England and Wales. In 2008 there were 121,700 divorces falling by 6.4 per cent to 113, 900 in 2009. *Social Trends* 41 (2011), 'Households and Families', Figure 4.
[38]   J Haskey 'Children of Divorcing Couples' in *Population Trends* 31 (1983).
[39]   *Social Trends* 39 (2009), at p 20. Of these, 20 per cent were under five years old and 63 per cent were under eleven.
[40]   *Social Trends* 41 (2011), 'Households and Families', Figure 4. The decrease is thought to be partly attributable to the decline in the number of divorces and partly to the reduction in the average number of children involved in each divorce.
[41]   Remarriages increased by about one-third between 1971 and 1972 following the liberalisation of divorce brought about by the Divorce Reform Act 1969. Since then the number of remarriages has remained fairly constant. In 2000 there were 126,000 remarriages for one or both partners – about 40 per cent of all marriages that year: *Social Trends* 33 (2003), Figure 2.10. This proportion continued to remain fairly constant: *Social Trends* 39 (2009), Table 2.11. There has however been a recent increase in the proportion of first marriages and a corresponding decrease in the proportion of remarriages, doubtless reflecting the declining numbers of divorces. Provisional estimates for 2009 showed that 35 per cent of marriages were remarriages for one or both parties. *Social Trends* 41 (2011), 'Households and Families', Figure 2.
[42]   *Population Trends* 70 (1992), Table 11 and *Population Trends* 90 (1997), Table 11.
[43]   *Population Trends* 108 (2002), Table 3.3.
[44]   The Children Act 1975 introduced provisions intended to discourage the use of legal adoption by couples wishing to integrate children of a previous relationship into their family, while the Children Act 1989 is more neutral on the issue as is the Adoption and Children Act 2002: see chapter 13 below and generally J Masson et al *Mine, Yours or Ours?* (1983).

breakdown of the parents' relationship[45] although there have been some important studies in recent years which challenge the orthodox view that divorce is necessarily harmful for children, and which focus instead on the *quality* of parental relationships both before and after divorce in the new social situation of increasingly fragmented households.[46] Step-parental relationships are one aspect of the wider debate about social parenthood in its many different manifestations.

Births outside marriage

Perhaps the most striking of all the demographic changes which have occurred since the end of the Second World War is the dramatic increase in the proportion of births which take place outside marriage. In 1961 there were 48,500 live births in England and Wales outside marriage (ie some 6 per cent of all births);[47] but by 1996 there were 232,700, representing well over one-third (35.8 per cent) of all births and by 2000 the figure of 238,600 constituted almost 40 per cent of the total.[48] This trend has continued and is showing no sign of abating. By 2007, figures from the Office for National Statistics revealed that 343,200 babies were born outside marriage, some 44.4 per cent of the total and by 2010 this had risen yet further to 47.2 per cent.[49] Moreover, there are significant regional variations. In Wales, for example, there is already a more than fifty-fifty chance of being born to unmarried parents.[50] It nonetheless remains the case that the dominant form of family is centred on marriage with 62 percent of all dependent children living with married parents in 2011.[51]

These figures are all the more remarkable in the light of the fact that a large number of pregnancies are now legally terminated by abortion. In 1991 over 167,000 legal abortions were carried out on residents in England and Wales (the great majority on unmarried women) and in 1996 the figure was just under 167,000.[52] Around one-third of pregnancies outside marriage are terminated by an abortion.[53] In fact the percentage of all pregnancies terminated by abortion has remained relatively constant over the last decade at between 19 and

---

[45] See, generally, MPM Richards and M Dyson *Separation, Divorce and the Development of Children: a Review* (1983).

[46] See generally chapter 5. See also C Smart and B Neale *Family Fragments?* (Polity Press, 1999). The question of why some children survive these family transitions better than others is explored in J Pryor and B Rodgers *Children in Changing Families: Life After Parental Separation* (Blackwell, 2001). For a study which examines children's own perspectives of family life after divorce see C Smart, B Neale and A Wade *The Changing Experience of Childhood: Families and Divorce* (Polity, 2001).

[47] *Population Trends* 70 (1992), Table 10.

[48] *Population Trends* 90 (1997), Table 10 and *Population Trends* 108 (2002), Table 3.2.

[49] ONS, *Statistical Bulletin*, 10 July 2012.

[50] Figures for 2005 indicated that 52 per cent of babies born in Wales were born outside marriage. *Social Trends* 37 (2007).

[51] ONS, *Statistical Bulletin, Families and Households*, 1 November 2012.

[52] *Population Trends* 70 (1992), Table 16 and *Population Trends* 90 (1997) Table 17.

[53] *Social Trends* 32 (2002), Chart 2.11.

22 per cent.[54] Although a high proportion of lone-parent families are headed by a single woman,[55] it should not be assumed that the child born outside marriage is likely to be brought up in a one-parent household: in 2001 more than three-quarters of all births outside marriage were registered jointly by both parents, and three-quarters of these parents were parents living at the same address.[56] This proportion has continued to rise so that by 2005 joint registrations had increased to 84 per cent. The figures for 2009 were 86.6 per cent joint registrations of which 65.7 per cent were by parents living at the same address.[57] Teenage mothers account for a significant proportion of births outside marriage and of births registered without details of the father. In 2000 almost 9 in 10 live births to women aged under 20 in England and Wales occurred outside marriage. Just over one-quarter (27 per cent) of births to teenage mothers were registered solely by the mothers and recent research has established a link between sole registration and social exclusion.[58] 39 per cent of sole registrants were shown to be aged 20 or younger and sole registrant mothers were likely to be poor and have low levels of educational attainment.[59]

It seems that to some extent social reality and legal institutions in this area have not been so closely related as is often assumed. Research has revealed, for example, that many cohabiting, but unmarried, fathers were quite unaware of the legal position that they lacked parental responsibility in the legal, as opposed to social, sense in relation to their children.[60] The legal and social positions have now been brought much closer together by the radical reform introduced by the Adoption and Children Act 2002 which confers automatic parental responsibility on the man registered as the father of the child of an unmarried mother.[61]

The Welfare Reform Act 2009 takes this policy further and contains provisions designed to increase the proportion of joint registrations and indeed to

---

[54]   *Population Trends* 108 (2002), Table 4.1 and *Social Trends* 39 (2009), at p 22. It was 21.0 per cent in 2009, down from 21.8 per cent in 2008. *Social Trends* 41 (2011), 'Households and Families' Table 8.

[55]   Almost ten times as many as are headed by a man, although there has been a noteworthy increase in the number of single-parent households headed by men in recent years. In 1999 18 per cent of all households with dependent children were headed by women and just 1 per cent by men. Later figures indicated 20 per cent by women and 2 per cent by men: *Social Trends* 32 (2002), Table 2.17. In 2012 there were 2.0 million lone parents in the UK with dependent children. Such families constituted 26 per cent of all families with dependent children. 91 per cent were headed by women and 9 per cent by men. ONS, *Statistical Bulletin, Families and Households* November 1, 2012.

[56]   *Social Trends* 33 (2003), Figure 2.18.

[57]   Green Paper, *Joint birth registration: promoting parental responsibility*, Cm 7160 (DWP, 2007), para 37 and Figure 1; *Social Trends* 41 (2011).

[58]   *Social Trends* 32 (2002), at p 47 and Chart 2.14. And see J Graham, C Creegan, M Barnard, A Mowlam and S McKay, *Sole and joint birth registration: exploring the circumstances, choices and motivations of unmarried parents* (Department for Work and Pensions Research Report No 463, 2007).

[59]   Green Paper, supra note 57, paras 41–42.

[60]   See R Pickford *Fathers, Marriage and the Law* (Family Policy Studies Centre for the Joseph Rowntree Foundation, 1999).

[61]   See chapter 4.

establish, subject to exemptions, a norm of joint registration by both parents. This is designed in part to combat the effects of social exclusion and to encourage the acceptance of parental responsibility by more fathers. The effect of this reform can be expected to be that, as joint registrations modestly increase and sole registrations correspondingly decrease, a yet higher proportion of unmarried, biological fathers will acquire parental responsibility and with it what might be viewed as a full parental status. These questions are closely related to the issue of the status of legitimacy and its concomitant illegitimacy which we discuss in chapter 3.

Social parenting

One phenomenon already alluded to by implication is that very large numbers of children are now raised in, or move between, households[62] in which one or more parental figures are not their biological parents. We noted above the high incidence of remarriage and step-parenthood. Although numerically much less significant, at least some children are also now in the households of civil partners;[63] civil partnership being a relatively recently created formal legal status for partners of the same sex approximating to, but not legally identical to, marriage.[64] A 'social' child may become a 'child of the family' in relation to these formalised relationships and this can have significance for the purposes of family provision and financial support.[65] Many children also live in households in which one of their biological parents cohabits *informally* with a partner whether of the opposite or same sex. In 2006 the lowest number of marriages was recorded since 1895.[66] In contrast, cohabitation is on the increase and the proportion of dependent children living with cohabiting couples increased from 8 per cent to 15 per cent between 1997 and 2010.[67]

Very many children are also raised by substitute carers, whether or not related to them, where for whatever reason their natural parents are unable or unwilling to discharge their parental responsibilities. In the year ending March 2008, for example, 23,000 children started to be looked after by local authorities, 17,300 of whom were placed with foster parents.[68] This figure has

---

[62] For a useful treatment of the movement of children between different households see M Maclean and J Eekelaar, *The Parental Obligation: A Study of Parenthood across Households* (Hart Publishing, 1997).

[63] Less than 1 per cent of dependent children lived in civil partner or same-sex cohabiting couple families in 2012. The Office of National Statistics currently takes the view that the percentages are not sufficiently robust to be published. ONS, *Statistical Bulletin, Households and Families*, 1 November 2012.

[64] Though marriage itself is soon likely to be available to same-sex partners if the Marriage (Same Sex Couples) Bill 2013 is enacted.

[65] See chapter 9. But note that the concept of 'child of the family' does not extend to social parenting in *informal* partnerships, whether opposite or same sex, though arguably it should given the high incidence of the latter.

[66] *Social Trends* 39 (2009), Figure 2.10.

[67] Ibid, Table 2.4. and *Social Trends* 41 (2011), 'Households and Families' Table 4.

[68] *Social Trends* 39 (2009), Table 2.21.

sharply increased to 28,220 children for the year ended 31 March 2012. This represents an increase of 21 per cent on the 2008 figures.[69]

This increasing diversity in household composition and parenting arrangements has given rise to new debates about what legal status should be given to these many parent-substitutes who are involved in discharging parenting functions.[70] More fundamentally, there is now a serious definitional question about what exactly a parent is, socially and legally.[71] There is also an important issue about gender. The advent of same-sex parenting, along with other recent developments, has now raised the question whether there is any longer (if there ever was) a distinctive role and status for 'mothers' or for 'fathers', or whether society and the law should concentrate instead on the gender-neutral concept of 'parent'. As we shall see, this latter approach appears to have commended itself to Parliament in relation to same-sex parentage in both the Adoption and Children Act 2002[72] and the Human Fertilisation and Embryology Act 2008.[73]

THE CHILD AS A LEGAL PERSON

All legal systems give parents or other adults powers in respect of the upbringing of children, but the extent of those powers differs from time to time and from place to place. In England, Blackstone (writing in the eighteenth century) accepted that the power of parents over their children was derived from the need to enable a parent more effectually to perform his duty to the child (although he also saw parental rights as being, to some extent, a recompense for the care and trouble taken by the parent in the faithful discharge of his duties).[74] Blackstone also pointed out that the assessment of the scope of parental power varied from time to time and from nation to nation:

> 'the ancient Roman laws gave the father a power of life and death over his children; upon this principle, that he who gave has also the power of taking away. Moreover a son could not acquire any property of his own during the life of his father, but all his acquisitions belonged to the father, or at least the profits of them for his life.'

Parental power in English law was still 'sufficient to keep the child in order and obedience';[75] and Blackstone's description of the eighteenth-century parent's right bears extended citation. The parent (he said):

> '… may lawfully correct his child, being under age, in a reasonable manner: for this is for the benefit of his education. The consent or concurrence of the parent to the

---

[69] Department for Education, *First Statistical Release, 20/2012*, September 25 2012.
[70] We explore this question in chapter 5.
[71] We explore this question in chapter 3.
[72] See chapter 9.
[73] See chapter 3.
[74] Blackstone *Commentaries on the Laws of England* (4th edn, 1770) Book 1, ch 15, section 2.
[75] Ibid.

marriage of his child under age, was also directed by our ancient law to be obtained ... and this is also another means, which the law has put into the parent's hands, in order the better to discharge his duty; first, of protecting his children from the snares of artful and designing persons; and, next, of settling properly in life, by preventing the ill consequences of too early and precipitate marriages. A father has no other power over his son's estate, than as his trustee or guardian; for, though he may receive the profits during the child's minority, yet he must account for them when he comes of age. He may indeed have the benefit of his children's labour while they live with him, and are maintained by him: but this is no more than he is entitled to from his apprentices or servants. The legal power of a father (for a mother, as such, is entitled to no power, but only to reverence and respect) over the persons of his children ceases at the age of 21: for they are then enfranchised by arriving at years of discretion, or that point which the law has established (as some must necessarily be established) when the empire of the father, or other guardian, gives place to the empire of reason. Yet, until that age arrives, this empire of the father continues even after his death; for he may by his will appoint a guardian to his children. He may also delegate part of his parental authority during his life, to the tutor or schoolmaster of his child; who is then *in loco parentis*, and has such a portion of the power the parent committed to his charge, viz. that of restraint and correction, as may be necessary to answer the purposes for which he is employed.'

Legal power and social reality

Although it is difficult to make any confident assessment of the way in which parental authority was exercised in times past,[76] there is ample evidence that the right to a child's services was widely regarded as being an economically valuable asset. As recently as 1921,[77] it was said to be 'no uncommon thing, when a child has reached an age at which it can work and earn wages, for parents who have habitually neglected it and left it to be brought up by a relative or even a stranger, to claim it back simply in order to take its earnings'; and there is some evidence that child stealing – not a crime until 1814 – was sometimes practised by those who wanted a cheap supply of labourers for trades such as chimney sweeping and prostitution.[78]

At the upper end of the socio-economic scale, it appears that parents and guardians did not hesitate to exercise parental rights in respect of matters such as education. In one of the (comparatively few) reported cases,[79] a young man of 16 was told by the court that the guardian was the best judge of his education, and that, since the boy had no reasonable complaint against the master at Eton, he would be compelled to return there if he did not go voluntarily. And even in the latter part of the nineteenth century the courts were reluctant to give any real weight to a child's views. In *Re Agar-Ellis*,[80] the

---

[76] See, generally, I Pinchbeck and M Hewitt *Children in English Society* (Routledge, 1973) Vol 2, chs 12 and 13.
[77] See *Report of the Committee on Child Adoption* (1921) (Cmnd 1254), at para 13.
[78] I Pinchbeck and M Hewitt (above), at p 360.
[79] *Hall v Hall* (1749) 3 Att 721.
[80] (1883) 23 ChD 317.

parents of a 16-year-old girl were separated. The father exercised his legal right[81] to take his daughter away from her mother, to send her to boarding school and to have her looked after by clergymen and others during the holidays, moving from one lodging to another. The court refused an application for the daughter to spend the holiday with her mother and, indeed, for the mother to have any access to her. It was said that in the absence of any fault on the father's part the court had no jurisdiction to interfere with the father's legal right to control the custody and education of his daughter.

The father's exclusive entitlement to parental authority

As already seen, in Blackstone's time, parental authority was vested exclusively in a child's father: the mother was not entitled to any power with respect to the child, but 'only to reverence and respect'.[82] One of the most remarkable features of the development of English law is that this remained the underlying principle of the law until 1973. Only in that year did Parliament enact that, in relation to the legal custody or upbringing of a minor, and in relation to his property or the application of income therefrom, a mother was to have the same rights and authority as the law had previously allowed to a father.[83] The fact that, for so long, a mother had no legal rights in respect of a legitimate[84] child may prompt the reader to ask how far the law is, in reality, relevant in practical terms. How many mothers, fathers, or children born before 1973, were aware of the legal position which denied the mother any parental authority? How far did this rule of law affect their behaviour?[85] Perhaps the reality is that the denial of parental authority to a mother was rarely noticed in the functioning family, but this is not to say that the 1973 reform was irrelevant. Although such things may be difficult to measure, the law presumably has some impact on attitudes and, in any event, it is, no doubt, important that the law should reflect a position which is defensible, both socially and morally. It may be argued, for example, that it is important for the law to assert the principle of contact between parents and children even if enforcement of contact is difficult or even impossible.

Erosion of the father's legal rights

The evolution of the law is of more pressing practical significance in cases in which the parental relationship is no longer harmonious, and very slowly – but then at an increasing pace – nineteenth century parliaments began to allow the courts to intervene between father and mother in such cases. It was no longer regarded as acceptable that mothers who had separated from adulterous or cruel husbands should be deprived of the care of their children, and even

---

[81]   On parental 'rights' in the modern law, see chapter 7 below.

[82]   Blackstone *Commentaries on the Laws of England* (4th edn, 1770), at p 453.

[83]   Guardianship Act 1973, s 1(1).

[84]   The position in respect of an illegitimate child was different: see chapter 4 below.

[85]   As noted above, similar questions were raised in relation to unmarried fathers who lacked parental responsibility. See Pickford (above).

denied any form of contact with them; or for the children to be handed over to complete strangers, or perhaps even to the father's mistress.[86]

Talfourd's Act

The first legislative interference with the father's virtually absolute right to have the possession of his children and to deny the mother any contact with them was the Custody of Infants Act 1839, which empowered the court to make orders giving custody of any child up to the age of seven to the mother and to make orders giving her access to her children during their infancy.[87]

The Matrimonial Causes Act 1857

The introduction of judicial divorce by the Matrimonial Causes Act 1857 required the legislature to consider the consequences of granting a decree of divorce both in respect of financial matters and in respect of the upbringing of the parties' children; and the Act gave the court a wide discretion in judicial separation, nullity or divorce proceedings to make such orders with respect to the custody, maintenance and education of the children of the marriage 'as it may deem just and proper'.[88] The Act also empowered the divorce court to direct that proper proceedings be taken for placing such children under the protection of the Court of Chancery.[89] The Act thus accepted – for the first time – the important principle that, whenever there were matrimonial proceedings, a father's rights might be overridden by the court, and it also gave effect to the view that the child of divorced (or legally separated) parents might need the ongoing supervision, available in wardship, of all important steps in his or her life.[90]

Later Victorian legislation[91]

The extensive discretion conferred on the court by the divorce legislation was not easy to reconcile with the restrictive approach underlying the Custody of

---

[86]   See *R v de Manneville* (1804) 5 East 221 and *de Manneville v de Manneville* (1804) 10 Ves 52 in which a father forcibly took an eight-month-old unweaned baby from the house in which it was living with the mother; and see *R v Greenhill* (1836) 4 Ad&E 624 where the Court of King's Bench ordered Mrs Greenhill to hand over her three small daughters (all under six years of age) to their father, notwithstanding the fact that he had been guilty of considerable cruelty to the wife and children and intended to hand the children over to the care of his mistress. When Mrs Greenhill refused to comply with the order she was committed to prison for contempt of court.

[87]   The Act, known as Talfourd's Act, was promoted by Serjeant Talfourd, a lawyer with experience of some remarkable cases, and the parliamentary proceedings were protracted and bitter: see I Pinchbeck and M Hewitt *Children in English Society* Vol 2, at pp 371–375 and, generally, as to the scope and objects of the Act, see *Warde v Warde* (1849) 2 Ph 786. The Act was restrictively interpreted: see *Re Halliday* (1853) 17 Jur 56; *Shillito v Collett* (1860) 8 WR 683; *Re Winscom* (1865) 2 H&M 540.

[88]   Matrimonial Causes Act 1857, s 33.

[89]   Ibid.

[90]   For the wardship jurisdiction, see pp 645 et seq below.

[91]   The text deals only with legislation conferring powers on the superior courts, but the last

Infants Act 1839: on divorce or judicial separation, the court had a complete discretion, but in other cases its discretion was greatly circumscribed. Not without difficulty and hesitation it came to be accepted that a wide discretion vested in the courts was necessary in cases relating to the upbringing of children; and the Custody of Infants Act 1873 empowered the court[92] to give custody of a child up to the age of 16 (rather than seven) to the mother. That Act also removed the bar established by the Custody of Infants Act 1839 against access or custody petitions by an adulterous mother; and it provided that no agreement contained in a separation deed should be held to be invalid by reason only of its providing that the father of an infant should give up the custody or control of the infant to the mother. But the parties were not to be allowed to oust the court's powers, since the Custody of Infants Act 1873 provided that the court should not enforce any agreement if it was of the opinion that it would not be for the benefit of the infant to give effect thereto.[93]

Father rules from beyond the grave: guardianship

At common law, a father's parental authority survived his death: a father could appoint a testamentary guardian[94] for his child, and the guardian then, effectively, stepped into the position of the father on the father's death. The mother had no right to interfere with the exercise of the testamentary guardian's authority.[95] But the principles underlying the statutes passed in 1839, 1857 and 1873 made it 'difficult to accept that in a free country a widowed mother might be robbed of her young children, even if they were babes in arms, by a stranger appointed guardian by her late husband against her wishes or by her late husband's distant relative whom she had never seen'.[96] A vigorous public campaign eventually lead to the enactment of the Guardianship of Infants Act 1886 which provided[97] that, on the death of the father of an infant, the mother, if surviving, should be the infant's guardian, either alone (when no guardian had been appointed by the father) or jointly with any guardian appointed by the father. The 1886 Act also empowered the

---

quarter of the nineteenth century also saw the creation of the magistrates' jurisdiction – for long particularly significant in the case of the working classes. The Matrimonial Causes Act 1878, s 4, provided that when a husband was convicted of assault the court might order that the legal custody of any children of the marriage under the age of 10 years be given to the wife (although no order was to be made in favour of a wife proved to have committed adultery). The Summary Jurisdiction (Married Women) Act 1895 greatly extended the magistrates' powers.

92   The Court of Chancery.
93   See, for example, the notorious case of *Re Besant* (1878) 11 ChD 508, in which the court overrode a provision in a deed of separation made between a Church of England clergyman and his wife. The mother (the founder of the ethical code known as theosophy) had written works which the Court of Appeal considered 'disgusting to decent English men and women, a violation of morality, decency and womanly propriety', and had proselytised on behalf of her atheistical beliefs, and the court directed that custody of the daughter be given to the father. For the background, see R Dinnage *Annie Besant* (1986).
94   Under the Tenures Abolition Act 1660, as amended by the Wills Act 1837.
95   *Talbot v Earl of Shrewsbury* (1840) 4 My&Cr 672 at 683.
96   See I Pinchbeck and M Hewitt *Children in English Society* Vol 2, at p 381.
97   Section 2.

court to appoint a guardian or guardians to act jointly with the mother where no guardian had been appointed by the father, or where the guardians or guardian appointed by him had died or refused to act.

Freestanding custody applications

The problem of guardianship and abuse of paternal power were the matters which precipitated the enactment of the Guardianship of Infants Act 1886, but in conceptual terms that Act can today be seen as having a far greater significance. The reality is that the Act destroyed the concept of the family as a domestic kingdom ruled by the father. This was done by conferring on the court – which for this purpose included the county court as well as the High Court[98] – an unrestricted power on the mother's application to make such order as it thought fit regarding the custody of an infant and the right of access, thereto, of either parent, 'having regard to the welfare of the infant, and to the conduct of the parents, and to the wishes as well of the mother as of the father'.[99] It was no longer necessary to bring any other issue (such as the termination of the partners' marriage) before the court if either parent wanted the court to assume jurisdiction to deal with the upbringing of children; it was sufficient that either parent wanted the court to deal with the questions of custody and access.

The unfit parent

The Guardianship of Infants Act 1886 also[100] gave the divorce court power to include, in decrees of divorce and judicial separation, a declaration that one spouse was unfit to have the custody of the children. The person declared unfit lost the right to custody or guardianship of the child which he or she would otherwise have had on the death of the other parent; but, in theory at least, a declaration of unfitness did not mean that the parent was to be deprived of all contact with the child, nor did it debar the unfit parent from seeking and being given custody or access.[101]

The family and outsiders

The 1886 legislation – the substance of which remained on the statute book until the enactment of the Children Act 1989 – gave effect to the principle that

---

[98]   Section 9.

[99]   The Act also provided that the court could alter, vary or discharge such orders on the application of either parent or, after the death of either parent, on the application of a guardian appointed under the Act.

[100]   Section 7.

[101]   *Re A & B* [1897] 1 Ch 786 at 795. A modern manifestation of the unfitness question is the debate about whether the behaviour of some parents is so bad that there should be power to deprive them of parental responsibility. As the law stands only the unmarried father, but not married parents or the unmarried mother, may have parental responsibility removed by the court. Step-parents, civil partners and second female parents may however have the parental responsibility they have acquired later removed by court order. See Children Act 1989, ss 4, 4ZA and 4A and chapter 4 below.

the child's welfare should be the determining factor in disputes between parents over their child's upbringing, but the position was very different when the dispute was between the parents and an outsider – typically a foster parent who had provided a home for a destitute child. In particular, parents often sought to reclaim a boy or girl of an age to earn wages from one of the children's homes established by the philanthropist Dr Barnardo[102] in an attempt to provide vagrant and destitute children with care, training and a sound upbringing, according to the tenets of evangelical protestantism; and these parents were not deterred by the fact that Barnardo required the parents of those whom he 'rescued' to renounce all claim to the child.[103] On a number of occasions, Barnardo was ordered to return children to the legal parents;[104] but, in due course, Parliament responded to what was seen to be a scandalous situation. In the words of Lord Herschell:

> 'When a parent has abandoned or deserted his child, has cared nothing for it, and has left it to be cared for by others, it is outrageous that he should be allowed to go before a Court and say, although I have neglected every duty which I owed my child, and although to deliver up to me now would be most disastrous for the child, still I have a legal right to the custody of the child, that custody I will have, and you must give it to me ... All that this legislation proposes to do so is that where the court is satisfied that a parent has so behaved as to disentitle him to the custody of the child it shall have power to refuse its writ to procure the delivery of that child back to the parent.'

The Custody of Children Act 1891 (which remained on the statute book until repealed by the Children Act 1989) empowered the court in its discretion to decline to issue a writ of habeas corpus or make an order for the production of a child if the court considered that the parent had abandoned or deserted the child, or that he had otherwise so conducted himself that the court should refuse to enforce his right to the custody of the child. More generally, the Act provided[105] that the court should not make an order for the delivery of a child to a parent who had abandoned or deserted the child, or who had allowed the child to be brought up by another person at that person's expense (or by the poor law guardians) for such a length of time and under such circumstances as to satisfy the court that the parent was 'unmindful of his parental duties', unless the parent had satisfied the court that 'having regard to the welfare of the child' the parent was a fit person to have the custody of the child.

Religion: the first recognition of children's rights?

Perhaps the most remarkable provision of the Custody of Children Act 1891, however, was that dealing with religious education. Some, at least, of the

---

[102] For a comprehensive account, see G Wagner *Barnardo* (Weidenfeld & Nicolson, 1979), ch 13. See also J Rose *For the Sake of the Children: Inside Dr Barnardo's* (1988).

[103] Such an agreement was without legal effect.

[104] See *R v Barnardo* (1889) 23 QBD 305, (1890) 24 QBD 283, [1891] 1 QB 194; *Barnardo v McHugh* [1891] AC 388; *Barnardo v Ford* [1892] AC 326.

[105] Section 3.

Barnardo cases were prompted by parents being brought to believe that the child's spiritual health was at risk by reason of the religious teaching given in the Barnardo homes; and, in an attempt to allay fears on this score, the Act provided[106] that a court denying a parent custody of his child might, nevertheless, take such steps as it thought fit to secure that the child be brought up 'in the religion in which the parent had a legal right to require that the child should be brought up'. To this extent, the parental right to control the child's spiritual upbringing was firmly reasserted, even though the parental right to have the physical care of the child was removed; but – remarkably for legislation of the period – it was also provided that nothing in the legislation should interfere with or affect the power of the court to consult the *wishes of the child* in considering what order ought to be made, or diminish the right which the child possessed to the exercise of the child's own free choice. It can plausibly be argued that this – little noted – provision marks the first statutory recognition of the child's legal right to autonomy.

The role of the Court of Chancery: wardship

The Court of Chancery exercised the prerogative jurisdiction of the Crown over infants; and it would, in so doing, apply the principle that the primary consideration was the child's welfare.[107] However, the court was reluctant to override the wishes of the father;[108] and, in practice,[109] it would at this time only act in cases in which it had the means of applying property for the use and maintenance of the children concerned.[110] Indeed, the promoters of the Custody of Children Act 1891 sought to explain the necessity for legislation by arguing that legislation would give to the poorer child the same protection as

---

[106] Section 4.

[107] For a modern evaluation of the wardship jurisdiction see N Lowe 'Inherently disposed to protect children: the continuing role of wardship' in R Probert and C Barton (eds) *Fifty Years in Family Law: Essays for Stephen Cretney* (Intersentia, 2012) 161.

[108] 'It is not the benefit of the infant as conceived by the court, but it must be the benefit to the infant having regard to the natural law which points out that the father knows far better as a rule what is good for his children than a Court of Justice can': see *Re Agar-Ellis* (1883) 24 ChD 317 at 337–338, per Bowen LJ. A similar approach was taken nearly a century later by Lord Templeman in *Re KD (A Minor) (Access: Principles)* [1988] 2 FLR 139 at 141 (HL): 'The best person to bring up a child is the natural parent. It matters not whether the parent is wise or foolish, rich or poor, educated or illiterate, provided the child's moral and physical health are not endangered'. An even more recent example is provided by Waite LJ in *Re T (Wardship: Medical Treatment)* [1997] 1 FLR 502 at 514: '... in the last analysis the best interests of every child include an expectation that difficult decisions affecting the length and quality of its life will be taken for it by the parent to whom its care has been entrusted by nature'. In practice today, however, the courts are prepared to override even the strongly held, religiously inspired and reasonably held convictions of parents if the welfare of the child, as perceived by the court, demands intervention. The leading authority is now *Re A (Children) (Conjoined Twins: Surgical Separation)* [2000] 4 All ER 961. See further chapter 8.

[109] Although not in theory: see generally NV Lowe and RAH White *Wards of Court* (2nd edn, Barry Rose/Kluwer, 1986), at p 3.

[110] See *Wellesley v Duke of Beaufort* (1827) 2 Russ 1 at 21, per Lord Eldon.

that traditionally given by the Court of Chancery to wealthier children who had had property bestowed upon them.[111]

Principles on which the court would exercise its discretion: the paramountcy of the child's welfare

Much of the late nineteenth century legislation was influenced by the movement for achieving legal equality for women,[112] particularly in relation to property and, although the child custody legislation gave the court a wide discretion, it did not give any specific guidance in respect of the *principles* upon which this discretion should be exercised. In practice, the courts seem often to have regarded the welfare of the child as identical to the father's wishes.

The Guardianship of Infants Act 1925[113] made its objectives clear in the preamble:

> '... whereas Parliament by the Sex Disqualification (Removal) Act 1919, and various other enactments, has sought to establish equality in law between the sexes, and it is expedient that this principle should obtain with respect to the guardianship of infants and the rights and responsibilities conferred thereby.'

The Act provided that where, in any proceedings before any court,[114] the custody or upbringing of an infant, or the administration of any property belonging to or held on trust for an infant, or the application of the income thereof, was in question, the court, in deciding that question, should regard the welfare of the infant as the first and paramount consideration, and should not take into consideration, whether from any other point of view the claim of the father, in respect of such custody, upbringing, administration or application was superior to that of the mother, or the claim of the mother was superior to that of the father.

There would seem to be little room for doubt that this legislation was designed to secure equality of rights *as between father and mother* in relation to their children, and to make the welfare of those children paramount in relation to the two, henceforth equal, interests of their parents.[115] The Act did not, in terms, apply to cases in which the dispute was between a parent and an outsider; and for many years it seems to have been thought that a parent –

---

[111] See Lord Thring *Hansard* 3rd series (1891) Vol 349, cols 1508–10.

[112] Culminating in the Married Women's Property Act 1882.

[113] For a detailed examination of the legislative history of the Act, see SM Cretney '"What Will the Women Want Next?": The Struggle for Power Within the Family 1925–1975' (1996) 112 LQR 110.

[114] The Act thus extended the principles applied by the Chancery Division of the High Court to the magistrates' court.

[115] *A v Liverpool City Council* [1982] AC 363 at 377, per Lord Roskill; see also *Richards v Richards* [1984] 1 AC 174 at 203, per Lord Hailsham of St Marylebone.

certainly an 'unimpeachable' parent – still had 'rights' in respect of a child's upbringing, which would prevail as against a stranger. For example, in *Re Thain*:[116]

> ... a father who on his wife's death had no means of looking after his eight month old daughter, accepted an offer by the child's uncle and aunt to look after her. Six years later he had re-married and was in a position to provide the child with a permanent and suitable home. He applied for and obtained an order that she be handed back to him. The trial judge said[117] that he could quite understand that the little girl would be 'greatly distressed and upset' at the parting from her foster parents, but 'at her tender age, one knows from experience how mercifully transient are the effects of partings and other sorrows, and how soon the novelty of fresh surroundings and new associations effaces the recollection of former days and kind friends' ...

It was only in the landmark case of *J v C*,[118] more than 40 years later, that the House of Lords unequivocally ruled that the principles of the 1925 legislation were applicable whether the dispute was between parents, or between parents and outsiders. In *J v C*:

> ... the question was whether a 10-year-old boy should be returned to his natural parents (Spanish nationals resident in Spain) or whether he should continue to be in the care of English foster parents who had looked after him for all save some 18 months of his life. The House of Lords upheld the decision of the trial judge and Court of Appeal that the boy should stay in the care of the foster parents in England. The consequences of returning a boy who scarcely knew his natural parents and had been brought up as an English boy with English ways to a foreign country might have been disastrous, the more so since the parents would have been unable to cope with the problems of adjustment and consequent maladjustment and suffering. The fact that the parents were 'unimpeachable' could not prevail. The legislation required the child's welfare to be treated as the paramount consideration.

In recent years, as we shall see, the higher courts have reaffirmed the application of the welfare principle in cases involving disputes between parents and others but have nonetheless conceded that parents have a special significance for the child. Thus, while unwilling to articulate or apply a legal presumption in favour of parents, the House of Lords held that the welfare principle accommodates the notion of the 'special contribution' of the natural parent and that 'a child should not be removed from the primary care of his or

---

[116] [1926] Ch 676.
[117] Eve J at 684.
[118] [1970] AC 668. For a modern re-evaluation of the significance of the decision see N Lowe '*J v C*: Placing the child's welfare centre stage' in S Gilmore, J Herring and R Probert (eds) *Landmark Cases in Family Law* (Hart Publishing, 2011), ch 3.

her biological parents without compelling reason'.[119] This approach was subsequently confirmed by the new Supreme Court in one of the first cases to be heard by it.[120]

Child still not entitled to access to courts

This clear acceptance of the paramountcy of the child's welfare establishes a principle which is comprehensible, however difficult it may be to apply it in practice.[121] But for many years it was an inflexible rule that a child could not, directly, bring or participate in legal proceedings in the superior civil courts, and that a guardian ad litem or next friend should be required to act on the child's behalf.[122] The child's father was, in principle, entitled to act in that capacity, and would only be removed if it could be shown that he was acting improperly. The difficulties to which this rule gave rise – as well as the difficulty of deciding what precisely is in a child's best interests, even in the context of legal and financial matters – was vividly demonstrated in *Re Taylor's Application*:[123]

> The defendants in actions brought on behalf of children claiming to have been damaged by the drug Thalidomide made an offer of settlement on terms that all the 365 plaintiffs accepted. The parents of five children refused to do so; and the defendants sought to remove the father from his position as next friend with a view to a person being appointed who would accept the proposed settlement. The court rejected the application: the only impropriety alleged against the father was that he was in a small minority in believing that the settlement was not in his child's best interests; but (as Lord Denning MR remarked) being in a minority is not itself evidence of unreasonableness.

The age of majority

A child is not entitled to full legal capacity[124] until he or she attains the age of majority. For many years, this was fixed at 21 years of age, but the Family Law Reform Act 1969 reduced the age of majority to 18 years.[125]

---

[119] Per Lord Nicholls of Birkenhead in *Re G (Children)* [2006] 2 FLR 629, 631.

[120] *Re B (A Child)* [2010] 1 FLR 551. For a critique of the decision see A Bainham 'Rowing back from *Re G*? Natural parents in the Supreme Court' [2010] Fam Law 394.

[121] See chapter 2 below.

[122] In certain circumstances, a child may now participate in family proceedings without it being necessary for a guardian or litigation friend to act: see chapter 14 below.

[123] [1972] 2 QB 369 (CA).

[124] Until the *Gillick* decision (*Gillick v West Norfolk and Wisbech Area Health Authority* [1986] 1 AC 112), it was widely assumed that a child was legally incapable for all purposes (except where capacity was specifically conferred on the child by statute) until he or she attained full age, but that case held that this view was erroneous: see, particularly, chapters 7 and 8 below.

[125] Following the *Report of the Committee on the Age of Majority* ('the Latey Report') (1967) (Cmnd 3342). The position is the same in Scotland but it should be noted that under the Age of Legal Capacity (Scotland) Act 1991 children over the age of 16 enjoy a large measure of active legal capacity to enter into civil transactions. See JM Thomson *Family Law in Scotland* (6th edn, Bloomsbury Professional, 2011) Part III, and see chapter 7 below. Most developed countries have 18 as the age of majority. Austria lowered its age of majority from 19 to 18 in

THE ROLE OF THE STATE

The Poor Law

Lord Scarman has said that the historic base from which Parliament advanced to meet the needs of the orphans, the deserted, and the abandoned child was the Poor Law;[126] and it is certainly true that, for centuries, the problems associated with poverty, and particularly the problems of fatherless children begging and vagrancy, have been a major concern of Government. The statute which established the Elizabethan Poor Law in 1601 put legal sanctions, for the first time, behind the observance of what had formerly been regarded as the ordinary obligations of kinship.[127] Parents, grandparents and children were statutorily obliged to support their relatives, and this general principle survived in the obligation imposed on 'liable relatives' for the purposes of means-tested social security benefits and in the provisions of the Child Support Act 1991 imposing maintenance obligations on non-resident parents. It should, however, be noted that the scope of the obligation was greatly narrowed after the days of the Poor Law (which was abolished by the National Assistance Act 1948).

The 'liable relative' rule has now been abolished by the Child Maintenance and Other Payments Act 2008.[128] The obligation on parents to support their children remains very much alive, though the principles of liability and mechanisms for enforcing the obligation have been greatly affected by the passage of that legislation and the establishment of the Child Maintenance and Enforcement Commission.[129] The emphasis is now on private ordering with the machinery of state enforcement being capable of being invoked by either parent in default of agreement between them. The obligation on parents to support their children is not, at least for the present, a reciprocal obligation placed on children to support their parents.[130]

The impact of the Poor Law was not confined to financial obligations; and two, often related, developments of practice in relation to the care of children can, in retrospect, be seen to have played a major part in the development of child care law and practice.

2001 to bring it in line with the other States in the Council of Europe. See B Verschraegen 'The New Austrian Child Law 2001' in A Bainham (ed) *The International Survey of Family Law (2002 Edition)* (Family Law, 2002), at pp 57 and 58.

[126] *Leeds City Council v West Yorkshire Metropolitan Police* [1983] 1 AC 29 at 41.

[127] *Report of the Finer Committee on One-Parent Families* (1974) (Cmnd 5629) Vol 2, Appendix 5, para 51.

[128] As to which see N Wikeley 'The strange death of the liable relative rule' (2008) 30 (2) JSWFL 330.

[129] See chapter 9.

[130] In some jurisdictions adult children may be liable to support their parents in a range of specified circumstances. For North American perspectives see C Bracci 'Ties that bind: Ontario's filial responsibility law' (2000) 17 *Canadian Journal of Family Law* 455 and J Blair 'Honour thy father and thy mother – but for how long? Adult children's duty to care for and protect elderly parents' (1996) 35 *Journal of Family Law* 765.

Boarding-out: assumption of parental rights

In the latter part of the nineteenth century, it increasingly became the practice for pauper children to be 'boarded out' under the authority of the Poor Law Board with foster parents;[131] and the Poor Law Act 1889 empowered the Poor Law guardians to assume all the powers and rights in respect of a child deserted by his parents and maintained by the Poor Law guardians.[132] The Poor Law Act 1889 extended the grounds on which such action could be taken – it sufficed if the parent (for example) was thought to be unfit to have control of the child 'by reason of mental deficiency, or of vicious habits or mode of life'.[133] These procedures were seen to provide a means of caring for poor children without institutionalising them in a workhouse or other Poor Law institution, and a further stimulus to the practice of boarding-out was provided by the Poor Law Institutions Order of 1913, which made it illegal to retain a healthy child over the age of three years in a workhouse for more than six weeks.

Local authorities' responsibilities for child care

In some ways, the most significant step in the evolution of modern child care practice[134] came in 1929, when the responsibilities of the Poor Law guardians were taken over by local authorities.[135] The Second World War impeded any comprehensive reforms, but also provided a stimulus for further reform. A growing sense of dissatisfaction[136] led to the appointment of a committee 'to enquire into existing methods of providing for children who, from loss of parent or from any cause whatever, are deprived of a normal home life with their own parents or relatives; and to consider what further measures should be taken to ensure that these children are brought up under conditions best calculated to compensate them for parental care'.

---

[131] See I Pinchbeck and M Hewitt *Children in English Society* (Routledge, 1973) Vol 2, at p 522. For further discussion of the powers of the Poor Law authorities in the context of the social and legal background to the introduction of legal, as opposed to informal, adoption in 1926, see S Cretney 'From Status to Contract?' in FD Rose (ed) *Consensus Ad Idem: Essays in the Law of Contract in honour of Guenther Treitel* (Sweet & Maxwell, 1996) pp 251 et seq, especially at pp 252–255.

[132] Poor Law Act 1889, s 1(1).

[133] Ibid, s 1. The Poor Law Act 1889 is commonly described as the Poor Law Adoption Act; and informal adoption was statutorily recognised by the Poor Law Act 1899, s 3, which dealt with the case where a child had been adopted notwithstanding the fact that at the time there was no legal machinery for adoption.

[134] See the Literature Surveys by RA Parker in 'Residential Care, The Research Reviewed', commissioned by the *Independent Review of Residential Care Chaired by Gillian Wagner OBE PhD* (I Sinclair, ed) (HMSO, 1988).

[135] Local authorities could also be appointed as 'fit persons' to whom the care of children removed from their parents under the child protection legislation could be committed.

[136] For an account of practice, see *Report of the Care of Children Committee* ('the Curtis Report') (1946) (Cmnd 6922).

The Curtis Report

In 1946, the Committee (under the chairmanship of Miss Myra Curtis) published its report[137] which led directly[138] to the enactment of the Children Act 1948. That Act sought to give effect to a policy that, so far as possible, all children deprived of a normal home life should have the advantages of which they had been deprived, and to that end the Act required local authorities to provide care for extended categories of children. The Act remained the cornerstone of the structure of children's social services for more than 40 years; and marked a significant step away from the traditional reliance on voluntary organisations, family doctors, the clergy and neighbours for dealing with welfare problems, and towards reliance on paid, trained, professional social workers employed by local authorities.

Caring involves paying

Although the Children Act 1948 imposed a duty on local authorities to provide care for children deprived of a normal home life, it soon came to be recognised that prevention was better than cure, and children's departments tried to forestall the need for children to come into care by working, in co-operation with the other community services, to keep the family in being whenever this was in the best interests of the children. But the legal basis on which such help could be given was often obscure; and in 1960 the Ingleby Committee[139] pointed out that authorities had no power to give help in cash or kind to the families of children in care or of children who might have to be received into care because of their home circumstances. The Children and Young Persons Act 1963 sought to deal with this problem by imposing on local authorities a duty 'to make available such advice, guidance and assistance as may promote the welfare of children by diminishing the need to receive children into or keep them in care' or to bring children before a juvenile court under the provisions then in force.

The range of services which could be provided under the Act was wide: authorities would provide general social work support, and also specific facilities such as the relief of overburdened mothers by admitting young children to day care and older children to after-school play schemes, and assistance with housekeeping and budgeting; while there was power for a local

---

[137] *Report of the Care of Children Committee* (above). See, generally, J Packman *The Child's Generation* (2nd edn, Blackwell, 1981). For a brief account of the background, see the speech of the Lord Chancellor moving the second reading *Hansard* (HL) Vol 153, cols 913–925.

[138] The death of two children while in the care of foster parents and the subsequent inquiry by Sir Walter Monckton, *Report on the circumstances which led to the boarding out of Dennis and Terence O'Neill …* ('the Monckton Report') (1945) (Cmnd 6636), highlighted some of the issues and may have contributed to the creation of a climate of opinion favouring change; but it seems that the Monckton Report did not directly influence the legislation: R Parker in Bean and MacPherson *Approaches to Welfare* (Routledge, 1983). For a more detailed examination of the legislative history and influences which contributed to the enactment of the Children Act 1948, see S Cretney 'The Children Act 1948 – lessons for today?' [1997] CFLQ 359 and 'The State as a Parent: The Children Act 1948 in Retrospect' (1998) 114 LQR 419.

[139] *Committee on Children and Young Persons* (1960) (Cmnd 1191).

authority to provide housing for a family if the children would otherwise stand in peril of being received into care.[140] The Act[141] also empowered local authorities to make provision 'in kind or, in exceptional circumstances, in cash', and this power enabled local authorities to pay off rent arrears in order to keep a roof over the family's head, and to give help with fuel debts.

Child care: a subject for specialists?

The Children Act 1948 accepted the need for specialisation in the provision of the child care service. Each local authority had to have a children's committee, and each local authority was obliged to appoint a specialist children's officer and adequate staff. However, the Local Authority Social Services Act 1970 gave effect to the view that family needs were best integrated with all other relevant social services; and Directors of Social Services were thenceforth to manage integrated social services departments. The Children Act 1989 (as will be seen)[142] gave further impetus to the concept that services for families and children in need should be developed on the basis of a collaborative and inter-disciplinary approach, and this was given yet further emphasis in the Children Act 2004 which brought about a major reorganisation of children's services at the local level.

The voluntary principle and its erosion

The emphasis of the Children Act 1948 was on the need to return children to their parents; and the main purpose of so-called voluntary care was to cater for short-term difficulties without overriding the rights and duties of a parent and without recourse to the courts.[143] The legislation imposed a duty on local authorities to receive children into their care in certain circumstances; it did not give the local authorities any right to compel a parent to place a child in care. Parents needed to be confident that, in using the child care service, they would not run any greater risk of losing their child than if they had made private fostering arrangements; and the 1948 Act provided that a local authority was not to keep a child in its care if any parent or guardian desired to take over the care of the child. It also imposed a duty on local authorities, in all cases where it appeared to them consistent with the welfare of the child so to do, to endeavour to secure that the care of the child would be taken over by a parent or guardian or by a relative or friend. It is true that local authorities could, in

---

[140]   See *Attorney-General, ex rel Tilley v Wandsworth London Borough Council* [1981] 1 WLR 854 (CA).

[141]   Child Care Act 1980 (a consolidating measure), s 1(1).

[142]   See particularly chapter 10 below.

[143]   See, per Lord Scarman, *Lewisham London Borough Council v Lewisham Juvenile Court Justices* [1980] AC 273 at 306 (HL): 'No court proceedings are required for action under these subsections. The Act provides for social casework to relieve a child's distress and anger: it is not concerned to vindicate rights or to set a scene for litigation. The rescue of a lost or abandoned child, advice and help to a parent in difficulty are the objectives of the legislation. An emergency must be met, and the child protected. This is the world of social administration, not a legal battlefield. The purpose of the Act is to help in an emergency which will at best be only temporary but may be prolonged'.

certain conditions – mostly involving parental culpability[144] – pass a resolution vesting the parental rights and duties in the local authority, but this could only be done[145] if the child was already in care. Moreover, the decision could be tested in the courts. The principle was thus clearly established that a child was not to be 'removed from his home or family against the will of his parent save by the order of the court, where the parent will have the opportunity to be heard before the order is made'.[146]

However, it came to be thought that the voluntary principle sometimes led to the long-term future of children who were in voluntary care being neglected, since it was difficult to make plans for them. The Children Act 1975 was much influenced by the perceived dangers of allowing children to 'drift' in care; and that Act, accordingly, contained provisions which may be thought significantly to have undermined the parents' rights over a child who had been received into voluntary care. First, once a child had been in care for a period of six months, a parent or guardian would be guilty of a criminal offence if he removed the child from the accommodation provided for him by the authority unless the parent or guardian had given the authority not less than 28 days' notice in writing of his intention or had the authority's consent; and, if a parent did give such a notice, the local authority would no doubt consider whether to take other action – for example, making the child a ward of court[147] – to enable it to protect the child's interests. Secondly, it was provided that the foster parents of a child who had been boarded out with them for three years were to be entitled to seek a custodianship order[148] giving them legal custody of the child. Finally, the fact that a child had been in the care of a local authority for three years was made a ground on which the authority could pass a parental rights resolution assuming the parental rights and duties over a child in their care. Taking these three provisions of the Children Act 1975 together, it was clear that the rights of parents whose children had been in care for any length of time had been significantly eroded: consideration of the parents' rights should no longer be allowed to inhibit proper long-term planning for the welfare of children.

The Children Act 1989 marked a decisive swing away from the philosophy of the 1975 Act, whilst still seeking to protect children from the dangers of drift. As we shall see, the voluntary principle is now underscored by the European Convention for the Protection of Human Rights and Fundamental Freedoms (ECHR). The opportunities for parents to challenge in the courts the various actions which local authorities take in relation to their children have increased significantly now that the Human Rights Act 1998 has been implemented.[149] On the other hand, more recent legislation may be thought to display some

---

[144] See *O'D v South Glamorgan County Council* (1980) LGR 522 at 526, per Sir J Arnold P.

[145] A court could, in certain circumstances, make a care order in favour of a local authority: see Children and Young Persons Act 1969, s 1; see also chapter 12 below.

[146] See *Lewisham London Borough Council v Lewisham Juvenile Court Justices* [1980] AC 273 at 307, per Lord Scarman.

[147] See chapter 12 below.

[148] See chapter 12 below.

[149] For a good introduction to the issues see R Tolson QC *Care Plans and the Human Rights Act* (Family Law, 2002), a special bulletin on the House of Lords decision in *Re S (Minors) (Care*

continuing ambivalence about the importance of the voluntary principle. The Adoption and Children Act 2002, for example, amended the Children Act 1989 to make it easier for local authority foster parents to seek various court orders by reducing the qualification period of caring for the child from three years to one year.[150] This might be viewed as an erosion of the voluntary principle. Rather in contrast to this, the Children and Young Persons Act 2008 emphasises the importance of 'kinship care' and establishes a clear statutory priority that children looked after by local authorities should be placed with their parents or, if this is not consistent with the child's welfare, their relatives, friends or other persons connected with them, rather than with unrelated foster carers or in institutional care.[151]

Adoption

Background

It has already been mentioned that the Poor Law Act 1889 empowered poor law guardians to assume parental rights in respect of children who had been deserted, and legislation[152] sometimes referred to this procedure as 'adoption'. In fact – in marked contrast to other systems of law, which had long accepted the possibility of transferring a child from one family unit to another – English law made no provision for legal adoption until 1926, but it appears that the practice of informal adoption grew considerably in the first part of the twentieth century.[153] There were a number of reasons for this.[154] First, World War One led to an increase in the numbers of orphans who were available for adoption. In addition, it may have led to an increase in the number of those who were unable or unwilling to look after their own children. Secondly, growing knowledge of child psychology led to a preference in informed circles for bringing up children as a member of a family in a normal home surrounding rather than in an institution. Thirdly, there was an increasing tendency on the part of those who had no children of their own, or desired another child, to value a child's life and to desire association with and companionship with children. Finally, societies formed to encourage adoption gave publicity to the practice.

Order: Implementation of Care Plan); Re W (Minors) (Care Order: Adequacy of Care Plan) [2002] 1 FLR 815. See also S Choudhry and J Herring, *European Human Rights and Family Law* (Hart Publishing, 2010) at 218–223.

150   See chapter 9 below.
151   See chapter 10 below.
152   For example, the Poor Law Act 1899.
153   On the history of legal adoption in England, see S Cretney 'From Status to Contract?' in FD Rose (ed) *Consensus Ad Idem: Essays in the Law of Contract in honour of Guenther Treitel* (Sweet & Maxwell, 1996), at pp 251–268, S Cretney *Family Law in the Twentieth Century: A History* (Oxford University Press, 2003), ch 17, N Lowe 'English Adoption Law: Past, Present, and Future' in S Katz, J Eekelaar and M Maclean (eds) *Cross Currents* (Oxford University Press, 2000) and, on its more recent history, J Lewis 'Adoption: The Nature of Policy Shifts in England and Wales, 1972–2002' (2004) 18 IJLPF 235.
154   See *Report of the Committee on Child Adoption* (1921) (Cmnd 1254) and *Report of the Child Adoption Committee* (1925) (Cmnd 2401).

Not surprisingly, there was considerable dissatisfaction about the lack of any legal framework to regulate the practice of adoption. This dissatisfaction came from two main sources. First, there were those who were primarily concerned to provide security for the adopters: the law forbade a parent to bargain away his parental rights, and a parent might at any time seek to reclaim his child from the 'adopters'; conversely, a parent who had placed her child with adopters might then, at any time, be forced to take the child back. Secondly, there were those who were primarily concerned with the evils of child trafficking. Under the law as it stood before 1926, children could be handed from one person to another, with or without payment, or sent out of the country without any record being kept; intermediaries could accept children for adoption, and dispose of them as and when they chose; and 'homes' and institutions for the reception of children existed which were not subject to any system of inspection or control. A particularly obtrusive feature was the use of newspaper advertisements, often inserted by professional agents who would charge, both the natural parent and the adopters, large fees. For example, one individual was found to have inserted advertisements in these terms:

'Good refined home required for an army officer's twin boy and girl, fortnight old.'

'Adoption – beautiful blue-eyed boy wishes to be adopted where he would give love in return for parents and home.'

Pressure led to the appointment of the Hopkinson Committee on Adoption, in 1921. This Committee was favourably disposed to the introduction of legislation legalising adoption; and it considered that adoption was the next best thing to a stable home with natural parents. It thought that it was a proper object of the law to satisfy the natural desire of the childless to have the care and upbringing of a child, and it considered that this was often, in itself, the best guarantee of an adopted child's welfare. The Committee recognised that legal adoption would never be more than one link in the chain and proposed measures to prevent abuse of long-term child care arrangements.

There was still a reluctance, however, to legislate. Ultimately, the Government appointed a second Committee under the chairmanship of Mr Justice Tomlin. That Committee was unenthusiastic about the validity of the arguments for legal adoption, but concluded that a case had been made for giving some legal recognition to the link between the adopter and the adopted child, and for creating a procedure for the transfer of parental rights and duties. The Adoption of Children Act 1926, which laid the foundation for the modern law, followed.

The changing nature of adoption

The picture so far presented of adoption corresponds with its popular image; it is a legal procedure enabling those who are unable to have children to adopt a baby whom the adopters will thenceforth treat in all respects as if the child had been born to them. But, in fact, adoption increasingly came to be seen as an appropriate legal technique to be employed by local authorities concerned to provide a secure home for children in their care – often older children (who might have been in care for some years) and disabled children. The nature and purposes of adoption and adoption law were the subject of an extensive review culminating in the Adoption and Children Act 2002, largely implemented at the end of 2005. One of the prime objectives of this legislation was to make increased use of adoption as a permanent solution for children in long-term care.[155] But, as will become apparent, there are tensions between this policy direction and the demands of human rights conventions which require that action to protect children be limited to that which is necessary and proportionate. Every effort should be made by the State to reunify children with their birth families and state care is viewed primarily as a temporary expedient.[156]

Since 2011, adoption has once again been on the political agenda. Following a campaign by *the Times* for radical reforms to the adoption system, Martin Narey, a former chief executive of Barnado's and former head of the prison service was commissioned by that newspaper to produce a report. The report[157] made a raft of recommendations designed to show preference for adoption as a long-term solution for children where the view is taken in public law proceedings that their parents are no longer able to care for them. It is predicated on the assumption that 'no-one disputes that adoption offers the most stable and secure environment for a child who can no longer live with his or her own parents' and that 'far too few are being given this chance'.[158] This is, as commentators were quick to point out, a questionable assumption. Sonia Harris-Short has pointed out that, while outcomes for babies relinquished by their mothers at birth (a very small group today) are generally very good, outcomes for children adopted out of public care are 'much less convincing, with significant disruption rates'.[159]

Among the more significant proposals in the Narey Report are that adoption ought not to be delayed by repeated assessments of the child's family and friends where there is clear evidence of their unsuitability[160] encouragement of concurrent planning;[161] greater prominence to be given to adoption in social work training so that social workers' role is seen as unequivocally that of

---

[155] In fact statistics gleaned from the Adopted Children Register reveal that in 2008 there were just 3,200 public law adoptions, down 5 per cent on the 2007 figures and 16 per cent fewer than in 2004.

[156] The leading decision of the ECtHR being *Johansen v Norway* (1996) 23 EHRR 33.

[157] *The Narey Report on Adoption: Our Blueprint for Britain's Lost Children*, The Times, July 5 2011.

[158] Ibid, at p 2.

[159] S Harris-Short 'Holding onto the past? Adoption, birth parents and the law in the twenty-first century' in R Probert and C Barton (eds) *Fifty Years in Family Law: Essays for Stephen Cretney* (Intersentia, 2012) 147, 150.

[160] Report, at p 7.

[161] 'A practice whereby a child is placed as soon as possible with foster carers who, in the event of adoption becoming necessary, will adopt the child'. Ibid, at p 10.

protector of the child rather than friend of the family;[162] and the provision of comparative information from local authorities with rolling totals and times taken to complete adoptions, with the prospect of a national adoption agency being set up unless there is an across the board increase in the number of public law adoptions.[163] There are frequent references in the Report to what is seen as the evil of delay and, in this respect, Narey shared the central concern of the Family Justice Review 2011 in so far as it relates to the public law.[164] Narey was subsequently appointed ministerial adviser on adoption and, just as Tony Blair before him had taken a personal interest in adoption reform, so it appears is the current Prime Minister, David Cameron.

Part I of the Children and Families Bill 2013 will, if enacted, implement a number of changes to adoption law the central purpose of which is to reduce delays and speed up the adoption process in relation to children looked after by local authorities.[165] These changes include requiring local authorities to consider 'concurrent planning' whereby they should consider placing children for whom adoption is an option in a 'fostering for adoption' placement where one is available;[166] to remove the current duty to have regard to the child's ethnicity;[167] to enable local authorities to prepare personal budgets for adoption support services[168] and to provide a range of information about such services;[169] to enable children who are being considered for adoption to be included in the Adoption and Children Act register before a decision to place for adoption has been taken;[170] to make it clear that local authorities' statutory duty to allow reasonable contact between children in the care of local authorities and parents and others is subject to their statutory duty to safeguard and promote the welfare of looked after children;[171] and to provide for the making of post-adoption orders or the prohibition of contact at the adoption order stage rather than s 8 contact orders.[172] These expected reforms must be seen alongside the reforms to the public law of which adoption is today increasingly an integral part.

Child protection legislation

What part does the criminal law have to play in promoting the welfare of children?[173] One technique which has been increasingly used is to prohibit

---

[162] Ibid, at pp 14–15.
[163] Ibid, at p 8.
[164] See below.
[165] Following Department of Education, *An Action Plan for Adoption: Tackling Delay* (2012) and *Further Action on Adoption* (2013).
[166] Clause 1.
[167] Clause 2.
[168] Clause 4.
[169] Clause 5.
[170] Clause 6 and Sch 1.
[171] Clause 7.
[172] Clause 8.
[173] As we shall see, there has been a longstanding debate about the tension between welfare and justice in the juvenile justice system where young people offend. For a recent assessment of the

activities, such as caring for children for reward, unless certain formalities, for example registration, are met. In recent decades there has been heightened concern about the fitness of those working with children, reflected particularly in the Protection of Children Act 1999 and the Care Standards Act 2000. The first example of such legislation is the Infant Life Protection Act 1872,[174] which was concerned to eradicate the worst evils of baby farming – then, often described as adoption. It seems that a pregnant unmarried woman would arrange for her child to be delivered in a private lying-in house, and pay the owner a lump sum (perhaps as little as £5) in exchange for the owner agreeing to arrange the baby's adoption. The baby was soon removed to the 'worst class of baby farming house', where children were 'so culpably neglected, so ill-treated, and so badly nurtured' (for example on a diet consisting of a mixture of laudanum, lime, corn flour, water, milk and washing powder) 'that with rare exceptions they all of them die within a very short time'. In response to a number of notorious cases, the Infant Life Protection Act 1872 required registration of persons who, for payment, took charge of two or more infants under one year of age for more than 24 hours. As will be seen,[175] legislation now requires registration and supervision of a wide range of activities, including the provision of private fostering, day care, residential care, and so on.

Punishment for ill-treatment of children

The Prevention of Cruelty to and Protection of Children Act 1889 was the first of many statutes seeking by the imposition of criminal penalties to deter mistreatment of children. Thus, it is an offence for a person over the age of 16 to assault, ill-treat, neglect or abandon any child for whom he has responsibility.[176] Over the years, criminal offences have often been created in the wake of particular well-publicised scandals – for example, it was made an offence to allow a child to be in a room containing an unguarded heating appliance if this resulted in serious injury to the child, and it was made an offence to cause the death of a child under the age of three by overlaying it in bed if the defendant was under the influence of drink when the defendant went to bed.[177] Legislation also criminalises conduct which is thought to expose children to danger – it is, for example, an offence under the Crossbows Act 1987 to sell or hire a crossbow to a person under the age of 17; the Children and Young Persons (Protection from Tobacco) Act 1991 created offences intended to prevent children having access to that drug; while the Tattooing of Minors Act 1969 made it an offence to tattoo a person under the age of 18 except for medical reasons. It is not always clear that such legislation serves any long-term need.

---

place of the child's welfare in juvenile justice see R Arthur 'Demise of welfare considerations in the youth justice system: The Criminal Justice and Immigration Act 2008' [2008] Fam Law 1117. And see further chapter 15 below.

[174] Following the *Report of the Select Committee on Protection of Infant Life* (1871).

[175] See chapter 10 below.

[176] The legislation is now embodied in the Children and Young Persons Act 1933, s 1, as amended.

[177] Children and Young Persons Act 1933, s 1(2)(b).

Preventing the economic exploitation of children

The Act to regulate the labour of children and young persons in the mills and factories of the UK enacted in 1883 was the first of many legislative attempts to prevent the economic exploitation of children, and the statute book contains general rules (for example, that no child be employed so long as he is under 14, or before 7 am and after 7 pm)[178] as well as specific prohibitions or regulations in respect of certain kinds of activity – such as acrobatics.[179]

Compulsory child care measures

As discussed earlier, the Poor Law allowed the Poor Law guardians to assume parental rights in respect of pauper children in some circumstances and, latterly, juvenile courts were allowed to commit children who were found to be in danger to the care of a local authority. The juvenile courts were primarily concerned with children who were accused of criminal offences, but in the 1960s it was asked increasingly whether the social control of harmful behaviour by the young on the one hand, and social measures designed to protect and help the young on the other, should remain distinct and separate processes. The view that the aim of protecting society from juvenile delinquency and the aim of helping children in trouble to grow up into mature and law-abiding persons were essentially complementary[180] became increasingly accepted, and with it came a reluctance to classify children in need into two distinct groups – the deprived and the depraved.

The Children and Young Persons Act 1969 was influenced by these views. The court was given power to make orders – including a care order committing a child to the care of a specified local authority – if any one of a number of primary conditions was proved, but the court was only to make an order if the so-called 'care and control' test was satisfied – that is to say, if the court considered that the child was in need of care and control which he was unlikely to receive unless the court made an order.[181] The primary conditions included[182] the condition that the child was guilty of an offence,[183] and it is fundamental to an understanding of the 1969 legislation that a primary focus of its concern was the delinquent child and that it was intended that care proceedings under the Act should routinely be used instead of prosecution in cases of delinquency.

---

[178] Ibid, s 18(1), as amended.

[179] Ibid, ss 23, 30; and see chapter 16 below.

[180] *Children in Trouble* (1968) (Cmnd 3601), at para 7.

[181] Children and Young Persons Act 1969, s 1(2). On the evolution of policy, see generally JM Eekelaar, R Dingwall and T Murray 'Victims or Threats? Children in Care Proceedings' (1982) JSWL 67.

[182] Children and Young Persons Act 1969, s 1(2)(f).

[183] Excluding homicide: ibid, s 1(2)(f). Homicides continued to be dealt with under the provisions of the Children and Young Persons Act 1933, s 53 and are now governed by s 90 of the Powers of Criminal Courts (Sentencing) Act 2000. See chapter 15.

This policy was always controversial; and it was abandoned by a Conservative government. Although the 'offence' condition remained in force, it was rarely used: the great majority of delinquent children against whom legal proceedings were taken continued to be prosecuted. Care proceedings were, in practice, taken by local authorities who considered that a child was being ill-treated or that his health or development was being avoidably impaired or neglected.[184] But the legislation was drafted to deal with both the delinquent and the needy, and this duality of function led to considerable ambivalence about the nature of the proceedings. For example, it seemed reasonable that the child accused of delinquency should be protected by strict rules of evidence, and that a high standard of proof be required if a finding of guilt was to be made. However, it increasingly came to be seen that these considerations sometimes prevented appropriate action being taken to protect a child who was suffering neglect. This ambivalence was only resolved by the provisions of the Children Act 1989 which impose a strict division between the prosecution of child offenders – henceforth to be dealt with in special youth courts[185] – and taking measures for the care and protection of children at risk of significant harm,[186] a matter handled in the first instance by the family proceedings court, also a magistrates' court but quite distinct from the youth court.

SPECIAL PROTECTION FOR CHILDREN ON PARENTAL DIVORCE

Background

After judicial divorce become available in the UK in 1858, there was a substantial upward trend in the divorce rate, though in recent years there has been a steady decline.[187] In 1858 there were only 244 divorce petitions. In 1914, for the first time, the number exceeded 1,000, and in 1942 the number of petitions rose above 10,000.[188] These figures may seem small by comparison with the 150,000 or so divorces which were the annual average in the last decade of the twentieth century, but there was grave concern about the impact of divorce on children, and there was also widespread agreement that the divorce process should do everything possible to mitigate any adverse effects. In the 1950s, divorce was not necessarily available to all who sought it: a matrimonial

---

[184]   Children and Young Persons Act 1969, s 1(2)(a).

[185]   See the Criminal Justice Act 1991; and see chapter 15 below.

[186]   See chapter 12 below.

[187]   Figures for 2007 released by the Office for National Statistics reveal that for the whole of the UK there was a fall in the number of divorces of 2.6 per cent from the 2006 figure to 144, 220, the lowest number since 1977 and 20 percent lower than the peak of divorce in 1993 when there were 180,018 divorces. In fact the figure for 2009 had dropped to 113, 900. See *Social Trends* 41 (2011), at p 1. In part this must reflect the decline in the number of marriages and is not necessarily an indication of their greater stability. The figures for 2010 (119, 589) and 2011 (117, 558) suggest a levelling out of the number of divorces per year at somewhere between 115,000 and 120,000. ONS, *Statistical Bulletin, Divorce in England and Wales*, 2011, December 20, 2012.

[188]   See the *Royal Commission on Marriage and Divorce* (1956) (Cmnd 9678), Appendix 2, Table 1.

offence had to be proved, amongst other conditions,[189] and there were those who thought that the interests of the children might be regarded as being of secondary importance. In particular, if the divorce was not opposed and there was no dispute about the custody of the children, the court would have no way of knowing whether the parties had done what was really best for the children, or whether (perhaps) one party had only agreed to the divorce in return for an assurance that he or she would be allowed custody. The traditional adversarial procedures of the courts – albeit, theoretically, not governing the practice of the divorce courts – did not enable the court to look behind the evidence which the parties chose to put before it, or to make orders which neither party had sought. There was, thus, a significant risk that the interests of the children would not be adequately safeguarded on divorce and, indeed, in 1947 the Denning Committee[190] expressed the view that, in divorce proceedings, the welfare of children was wrongly subordinated to the interest of the divorcing parents.

This concern weighed heavily with the Royal Commission on Marriage and Divorce in 1956 and the Commission concluded[191] that a procedure was needed to ensure that parents themselves had given full consideration to the question of their children's future welfare, and that the court had an effective control over the children's welfare.

Legislation

The scheme which was adopted was to enact that a decree nisi of divorce should not normally be made absolute unless, and until, the court had satisfied itself that the arrangements proposed for the care and upbringing of children were the best that could be devised in the circumstances. Legislation to give effect to this proposal was first enacted in 1958,[192] and was re-enacted with modifications in 1970.[193]

When this legislation was enacted, it was assumed that the divorce court would always hold a hearing but, in 1977, the 'special procedure' – under which undefended divorces are granted without the parties' attendance – was extended to cases involving children.[194] It was evidently thought important to ensure that the extension of the special procedure did not jeopardise the protection of children, and the Lord Chancellor said that he 'attached

---

[189] On the evolution of English divorce law see J Masson, R Bailey-Harris and R Probert *Cretney's Principles of Family Law* (8th edn, Thomson, Sweet and Maxwell, 2008), at pp 281–286. On the history of marital breakdown and divorce in England see L Stone, *Road to Divorce: England 1530–1987* (Oxford University Press, 1990).

[190] *Final Report of the Committee on Procedure and Matrimonial Causes* (Cmnd 7024), at para 31.

[191] Ibid, para 372.

[192] Matrimonial Proceedings (Children) Act 1958, s 2.

[193] The legislation was consolidated in the Matrimonial Causes Act 1973, s 41.

[194] In 1973 (when it was first introduced) the special procedure had been confined to undefended cases, based on living apart for two years, in which there were no children of the family: Matrimonial Causes Rules 1977 (SI 1977/334), rr 33(3), 48.

considerable importance' to the duty of the judges to protect children involved in divorce, and to the judges' ability to discuss the proposed arrangements with petitioners.[195] It was, accordingly, provided that if children were involved in divorce, a judge would hold a special children's appointment and would look into the arrangements to be made for the children's upbringing.

It was hoped that this procedure would be more effective than that available under the old system for the trial of undefended divorces in open court (which usually involved no more than the making of a formal enquiry to the petitioner as to whether there was anything to be added to the details already given in the papers). It was said that the greater informality of the children's appointment procedure would make for easier communication between parents and judge; and this would, in turn, help to uncover problems, as well as enabling judges to offer parents advice and encouragement. However, a major research project[196] demonstrated many imperfections in the system and, influenced by these considerations, Parliament amended the relevant statutory provisions. As explained below,[197] the parties now have to give extended details about the arrangements which are proposed for their children, but these are considered privately by a district judge sitting in his or her chambers. There is no necessity for a hearing or for any further investigation unless the district judge believes that there is ground for concern or further enquiry, and the circumstances in which a decree of divorce can be held up have been greatly restricted.[198]

The Family Law Act 1996 was intended to reform radically the law of divorce.[199] However, in early 2001 the Government announced that it intended to repeal Part II of the Act, which dealt with divorce and which had never been implemented.[200] The divorce aspects of the legislation as they affect children are considered further in chapter 4. From an historical perspective there are perhaps two features of the now defunct Part II[201] which ought to be highlighted. The first is that, by generally requiring a statutory period for 'reflection and consideration' to be extended by six months in cases where there were minor children,[202] the Act would have been a departure from the

---

[195]   *Hansard* Vol 371, col 1218.
[196]   E Elston, J Fuller and M Murch 'Judicial Hearings of Undefended Divorce Petitions' (1975) 38 MLR 609.
[197]   See chapter 5.
[198]   Ibid.
[199]   On the Act generally, see M Freeman *The Family Law Act 1996* (Sweet & Maxwell, 1996), and on the divorce aspects specifically, see R Bird and S Cretney *Divorce: The New Law* (Family Law, 1996). A more academic analysis is to be found in JM Masson, R Bailey-Harris and R Probert *Cretney's Principles of Family Law* (8th edn, Thomson, Sweet & Maxwell, 2008), at p 308 et seq. See also Dame Brenda Hale 'The Family Law Act 1996 – the death of marriage?' in C Bridge (ed) *Family Law Towards the Millennium: Essays for PM Bromley* (Butterworths, 1997) and the collection of materials in B Hale, D Pearl, E Cooke and D Monk *The Family, Law and Society* (6th edn, Oxford University Press, 2009), ch 4.
[200]   The reasons for this volte-face are a matter of considerable speculation. For the author's views on why it may have happened, see A Bainham 'Exciting Times in England – Human Rights, Children and Divorce' [2001] IFL 71, at pp 74–76 and, generally, chapter 4 below.
[201]   Finally to be repealed by Clause 18 of the Children and Families Bill 2013.
[202]   Section 7(11) and (13).

philosophy hitherto accepted by law reform bodies that divorce ought not to be made more difficult where there are children than where there are none.[203] Secondly, and most unusually for English legislation,[204] the Act sets out a list of 'general principles' in Part I, which has been brought into force and which are to be given effect by the court and 'any person, in exercising functions under or in consequence' of those parts of the legislation which deal with divorce and mediation. These principles refer, inter alia, to the need when bringing a marriage to an end to do so in a way which minimises distress or the risk of violence to children and which promotes 'as good a continuing relationship between the parties and any children affected as is possible in the circumstances'.[205] These statutory principles may have been viewed by some as a bold attempt to adjust the existing balance by giving greater emphasis to the interests of children, as opposed to those of adults, on divorce. Whether divorce practice has matched this rhetoric and how indeed the law *should* seek to balance the interests of children and parents on divorce are issues considered further below.[206]

Finally, in what may be seen by some as a striking change of philosophy by government, it was proposed by the Family Justice Review 2011,[207] accepted by the government[208] and now implemented by the Children and Families Bill 2013[209] that the courts should lose their role in overseeing the arrangements for children in uncontested divorces. The existing legal requirement would be swept away by this measure in the process of reforming undefended divorce procedure. Henceforth this is intended to be handled administratively by 'appropriately qualified persons' rather than by a judge. Divorcing parents should be required to utilise 'dispute resolution services' and, only if these are unsuccessful in resolving their differences, would they be able to bring their disputes before the courts.

THE HISTORY OF THE CHILDREN ACT 1989

The Children Act was not the product of one single influence. It rather emerged in its final form as a result of the happy coincidence of two independent reviews, and a general climate of opinion in which there was impatience to rectify what were seen as intolerable deficiencies in existing law and practice.

---

[203] A principle accepted by the Law Commission in its report of 1990. See Law Com No 192 *Family Law: The Ground for Divorce* (1990), at para 5.28.

[204] But not for Continental civil codes, as to which see MA Glendon *The Transformation of Family Law* (University of Chicago Press, 1987), ch 3.

[205] Section 1(c) and (d). See also s 11(3)(c).

[206] Chapter 4.

[207] Recommendation 130.

[208] Government Response, at para 82.

[209] Clause 17 which repeals Matrimonial Causes Act 1973, s 41 and Civil Partnership Act 2004, s 63.

The public law review

In 1982, the House of Commons Social Services Select Committee began an inquiry into aspects of the practice relating to children in care. Its report ('the *Short Report*') produced in 1984, concluded that a thorough-going review of the whole body of child care law was overdue. The Department of Health and Social Security (as it then was) set up an interdepartmental working party comprising civil servants from relevant government departments and representatives from the Law Commission. This Committee produced a lengthy consultation paper in October 1985, entitled the *Review of Child Care Law* ('the *Review*'). Most, but not all, of the recommendations were accepted by the Government in its White Paper entitled *The Law on Child Care and Family Services*[210] ('the White Paper') published in January 1987. It is important to appreciate that the bulk of the reforms to the public law now embodied in the Children Act derive from these two sources. The former document is the more significant since it sets out, in some considerable detail, the reasoning behind the reforms. The White Paper needs to be taken together with the *Review*, not least because it rejected certain of the *Review*'s recommendations, including the original proposal to retain the concept of 'voluntary care' and to sub-divide it into 'respite' care and 'shared' care.[211] In the event, the very idea of voluntary care was abandoned in favour of a new concept of 'looking after' or 'accommodating' children on a voluntary basis.[212]

It had been a popular misconception that the legislation in general, and the reforms to care procedures in particular, were a reaction to the crisis concerning the investigation of child sexual abuse which occurred in Cleveland in June 1987 and was the subject of a subsequent report by Lady Justice Butler-Sloss.[213] It is quite evident that this was not the case since, chronologically, the *Review* and the White Paper pre-date even the first murmurings of the crisis. Yet it is probably fair to say that, more than any other single influence, what happened in Cleveland contributed to the gathering impetus for early reform.

Just as Cleveland had alerted public opinion to the dangers of 'over-reaction' to the problems of child abuse, so a succession of public inquiries into the domestic homicide of individual children exposed the opposite danger of 'under-reaction'. Among these, the more influential were probably those relating to Jasmine Beckford, Tyra Henry and Kimberley Carlile.[214] Other

---

[210] Cmnd 62.

[211] The *Review*, chs 6 and 7. Cf the White Paper, at para 26.

[212] See chapter 10 below.

[213] *Report of the Inquiry into Child Abuse in Cleveland 1987* (1988) (Cmnd 412). See also chapter 12 below.

[214] *A Child in Trust: The Report of the Panel of Inquiry into the Circumstances surrounding the death of Jasmine Beckford* (London Borough of Brent, 1985); *Whose Child? The Report of the Public Inquiry into the death of Tyra Henry* (London Borough of Lambeth, 1987); *A Child in Mind: Protection of Children in a Responsible Society: Report of the Commission of Inquiry into the Circumstances surrounding the death of Kimberley Carlile* (London Borough of Greenwich, 1987); and more recently see Lord Laming *The Victoria Climbié Report* (London: The

major influences on the legislation were several decisions of the European Court of Human Rights[215] (which found aspects of English child care procedures incompatible with the ECHR) and the House of Lords decision in the *Gillick* case[216] (which highlighted children's claims to have their views heard as an aspect of children's rights).[217] Other provisions in the Children Act are the result of the many amendments to the Children Bill during its passage through Parliament, of which the most significant was probably the introduction of the 'child assessment order'.[218] This was not mentioned in the *Review* or the White Paper, was rejected by the Butler-Sloss report and only emerged at the eleventh hour following lengthy debate in Parliament.

The private law review

Contemporaneously with the review of child care law, the Law Commission had been conducting its own review of child law which was concerned with the 'private' law of custody, guardianship and wardship. Between 1985 and 1987 it produced four working papers on, respectively, *Guardianship*,[219] *Custody*,[220] *Care, Supervision and Interim Orders in Custody Proceedings*[221] and *Wards of Court*.[222] After consultation, the Commission unveiled its final report on *Guardianship and Custody*[223] in July 1988. It is this report which is the foundation for the private law reforms and the central principles which appear in Parts I and II of the Children Act. The content of the first three working papers was largely subsumed in the 1988 report but the fourth, on wardship, remains an important source of reference in its own right. This is because the Commission, after consultation, decided not to make final recommendations on the future of the wardship jurisdiction. Despite this, the Children Act (to the surprise of many) imposed drastic restrictions on the hitherto liberal use of

---

Stationery Office, 2003). For academic assessments of the role of public inquiries in children cases, see R Dingwall 'The Jasmine Beckford Affair' (1986) 49 MLR 489 and N Parton and N Martin 'Public Inquiries, legalism and child care in England and Wales' (1989) 3 IJLF 21. More recently, see B Corby, A Doig and V Roberts 'Inquiries into Child Abuse' (1998) 20 JSWFL 377 and B Corby 'Towards a new means of inquiry into child abuse cases' (2003) 25 JSWFL 229.

[215] Particularly *R v UK, O v UK, W v UK* [1988] 2 FLR 445, ECtHR.

[216] *Gillick v West Norfolk and Wisbech Area Health Authority* [1986] 1 AC 112. See chapter 8 below. For two later reappraisals of *Gillick* see M Freeman 'Rethinking Gillick' (2005) 13 *International Journal of Children's Rights* 201 and J Fortin 'The Gillick Decision: Not just a high water mark' in S Gilmore, J Herring and R Probert (eds), *Landmark Cases in Family Law* (Hart Publishing, 2011), ch 11.

[217] For discussion of the provisions in the Children Act which reflect this aspect of children's rights see A Bainham 'The Children Act 1989: Adolescence and Children's Rights' [1990] Fam Law 311.

[218] Section 43. See chapter 11 below.

[219] Law Com Working Paper No 91 *Review of Child Law: Guardianship* (1985).

[220] Law Com Working Paper No 96 *Review of Child Law: Custody* (1986). See also Law Com Supplement to Working Paper No 96 *Custody Law in Practice in the Divorce and Domestic Courts* (1986).

[221] Law Com Working Paper No 100 *Review of Child Law: Care, Supervision and Interim Orders in Custody Proceedings* (1987).

[222] Law Com Working Paper No 101 *Review of Child Law: Wards of Court* (1987).

[223] Law Com Report No 172 *Review of Child Law: Guardianship and Custody* (1988).

wardship and the inherent jurisdiction by local authorities. In future, the procedure would be largely confined to the private sphere, and there was some speculation on whether it could, or should, survive at all the radical remodelling of legal procedures effected by the Children Act.[224]

The position in 1988, when the Law Commission reported, was that the Government had already announced its proposals for the reform of child care law. This convenient conclusion of the two reviews presented, as the former Lord Chancellor, Lord Mackay, put it, 'an historic opportunity to reform the English Law into a single rationalised system as it applies to the care and upbringing of children'.[225] The draft Bill, which the Commission annexed to its report, reflected and incorporated the results of both reviews. This not only enabled all the public and private law to be gathered together in one place, it also presented the Commission with a unique chance to formulate common principles and establish common remedies which would apply, as far as possible, in both the public and private spheres.[226] Therefore, while the private law and public law remain distinct in certain important respects, the Children Act brought about a partial fusion of what were previously seen as two substantially distinctive codes.

THE FAMILY JUSTICE REVIEW 2011, THE GOVERNMENT RESPONSE AND THE CHILDREN AND FAMILIES BILL 2013

In the next chapter we consider the fundamental principles and underlying thinking in the Children Act. However, this historical account would not be complete without some reference to the radical changes to the operation of private and public law which we are likely to witness in the coming years consequential upon the recent Family Justice Review and the Government Response to it now largely embodied in the Children and Families Bill 2013.[227]

---

[224] See, for example, N Lowe 'Caring for Children' (1989) 139 NLJ 87 and A Bainham 'The Children Act 1989: The Future of Wardship' [1990] Fam Law 270. Cf J Eekelaar and R Dingwall 'The Role of the Courts under the Children Bill' (1989) 139 NLJ 217.

[225] Child and Co Lecture, April 1988.

[226] For a succinct explanation of the general aims of the legislation, see B Hoggett 'The Children Bill: The Aim' [1989] Fam Law 217. For a recent reappraisal of the relationship between the private and public law see A Bainham 'Private and public children law: an under-explored relationship' [2013] 25 CFLQ 138.

[227] *Family Justice Review, Final Report* (2011), chaired by David Norgrove. *The Government Response to the Family Justice Review: a system with children and families at its heart* (Ministry of Justice and Department for Education, 2012). See also *Dear David: A Memo to the Norgrove Committee from the Dartington Conference 2011* (Thorpe LJ and W Tyzack (eds) (Jordans, 2011). Some useful critiques are contained in the *Journal of Social Welfare and Family Law*, (2011) No 4 of which see in particular M Maclean 'Family law in hard times'; J Eekelaar '"Not of the Highest Importance": Family justice under threat'; and J Masson 'Public child law – a service priority?'.

The essential structure of the Children Act has remained in place over the last two decades or so, notwithstanding substantial amendments. These amendments have taken into account particularly the increased recognition of social parenting[228] including same-sex parenting,[229] the increased importance attached to kinship care in the public law;[230] responsibilities of local authorties towards children leaving care[231] and the introduction of independent reviewing officers in relation to children looked after by them;[232] the creation of the new status of special guardianship;[233] and attempts to promote the facilitation of contact and better enforcement of contact orders where these have proved necessary.[234] This framework will largely remain in place. But the thrust of the Family Justice Review and Government Response (which very substantially accepted its recommendations) is an emphasis on alternative dispute resolution, now to be rebranded as 'dispute resolution services', and diversion from the courts;[235] the establishment of a Family Justice Service;[236] and the creation of a single family court with a single point of entry to replace the current three tiers of courts.[237]

The private law

The key recommendations relating to the private law were as follows.[238]

Parents share an equal status in relation to their children. They should first go to an 'information hub' to be educated about this. They should be encouraged to reach parenting agreements to regulate their shared parenting role following separation. There should be an expectation that they attend 'parenting information programmes' and an expansion in the existing programmes available. Where parents require further support they should attend a 'mediation information and assessment meeting' (MIAM). If they do not reach agreement by this stage, they should attend a dispute resolution service such as mediation. Only if all this fails should they then have access to the courts.[239]

---

[228] See, for example, s 4A enabling the easier acquisition of parental responsibility by step-parents and s 10(5A) relaxing the residential requirements applying to local authority foster parents wishing to apply for a residence order in relation to a child for whom they have been caring.

[229] See, for example, s 4ZA which facilitates the acquisition of parental responsibility by the so-called 'second female parent' and s 4A which does the same in relation to civil partners. The current state of the law on same-sex parenting is described in A Hayden QC, M Allman, S Greenan, E Latvio and HHJ Penna *Children and Same Sex Families* (Family Law, 2012).

[230] See s 22C introduced by the Children and Young Persons Act 2008.

[231] Sections 23A–23E introduced by the Children (Leaving Care) Act 2000.

[232] Sections 25A–25C introduced by s 118 Adoption and Children Act 2002.

[233] Sections 14A–14G introduced by s 115 Adoption and Children Act 2002.

[234] The Act provides for the making of 'contact activity directions', 'contact activity conditions' and 'enforcement orders' in s 11A–11P and Sch A1.Under Clause 12 and Sch 2 of the Children and Families Bill 2013 they are to be renamed 'activity directions' and 'activity conditions' to indicate that they may be used for purposes other than just promoting contact.

[235] See FJR, at paras 4.13–4.14. and Government Response, at paras 69–72.

[236] See FJR recommendations 6–11 and Government Response, Annex 1, at p 37.

[237] FJR recommendations 29–33 and Government Response, Annex 1, at p 44.

[238] FJR, ch 4; *Government Response* Section F, at pp 18–24.

[239] FJR, at paras 4.11–4.14.

These proposals, which have been substantially carried forward in Part 2 of the Children and Families Bill 2013, must also be seen in the context of a substantial withdrawal of legal aid for private law cases, subject to exceptions, brought about by the Legal Aid, Sentencing and Punishment of Offenders Act 2012.[240]

Where private law cases do continue to come before the courts, the Review proposed and the Government accepted that the principal private law orders for residence and contact should be replaced by a new 'child arrangements order'.[241] The intention is to move away from what is thought to have become loaded terminology and to focus on the practical day-to-day care of the child.

The one major difference of view between the Family Justice Review and the Government related to whether or not there should be a legislative statement to the effect that it is normally in a child's best interests to have a 'meaningful relationship' with both parents post-separation. The FJR and the Government were at one in identifying the concern that legislation should not create or risk creating the perception that there is a parental right to substantially shared or equal time for separated parents with the child. There should therefore clearly be no 'time-sharing presumption'. But the FJR departed from its interim view that there *should* be a legislative statement to reinforce the importance to the child of continuing to have a meaningful relationship with both parents, albeit alongside the need to protect the child from the risk of harm. In its final report the FJR, relying on evidence of the practical workings of a similar provision in Australia, resiled from its support for such a principle.[242] The Government disagreed on the basis that 'many people continue to have concerns about the proper recognition of the role of both parents by the courts'.[243] The Government, although mindful of the need to avoid the problems which surfaced in Australia,[244] proposed to introduce a legislative statement of the importance of children having an ongoing relationship with both of their parents after family separation, where it is safe and in the child's best interests.[245] It is stressed that this reform was not about the rights of parents but about contributing to the advancement of the welfare principle which should remain the key principle in the private law.[246] The Government then issued a Consultation on the best form of words for any legislative amendment to encourage shared parenting.[247]

---

[240] The Act received the Royal Assent on 1 May 2012 and the changes to legal aid took effect in April 2013.

[241] FJR, at para 4.15.

[242] At para 4.40 it is concluded that 'the core principle of the paramountcy of the welfare of the child is sufficient and that to insert any additional statements brings with it unnecessary risk for little gain'.

[243] *Government Response*, at para 60.

[244] Which centre on the welfare of children being compromised by exposure to domestic violence following the legislative statement being interpreted by some courts as promoting shared care of the child. As to which see the evidence of Helen Rhoades to the FJR contained in Annex G.

[245] *Government Response*, at para 61.

[246] Ibid, at paras 62–64.

[247] Department for Education and Ministry of Justice, *Consultation: Co-operative Parenting*

As will be seen,[248] a legislative statement is now included in clause 11 of the Children and Families Bill 2013. This effectively creates a presumption that the ongoing involvement of both parents in the child's life is in the child's best interests post-separation.

The public law

The key mischief in the public law identified by the Family Justice Review is the problem of delay.[249] It will be appreciated that the issue of delay in children cases is not a new one and that the Act itself embodies a general principle that delay is generally likely to be harmful to children.[250] More than one signficant attempt has been made to address the problem of delay in the public law by detailed practice guidance.[251] Nonetheless, the FJR noted that, based on statistics for the first half of 2011, care and supervision cases were taking on average 61 weeks in the county court and 48 weeks in the family proceedings court.[252]

The FJR made a number of radical suggestions to combat the problem of delay more effectively which have been accepted by the Government. The most radical is that there should be a maximum time limit of six months for the conclusion of care proceedings, subject to the judge's discretion to extend it in exceptional cases.[253] It was also proposed that there should be a reduction in the court's reliance on multiple expert assessments especially where the information is already available to the court.[254] A further recommendation was that the court's role in scrutinising the details of the care plan should be reduced and it should instead confine its scrutiny to the core elements of the plan; namely whether the child is to be returned to the parents, members of the wider family, or placed in long-term substitute care outside the family.[255] In

---

Following Family Separation: Proposed Legislation on the Involvement of Both Parents in a Child's Life (June, 2012). Four alternative draft clauses were presented, at para 9.1 which ranged from including a 'presumption', 'principle' or 'starting point' that 'a child's welfare is likely to be furthered through involvement with both parents' or an 'additional factor' to be added to the statutory checklist to the effect that the court 'shall have regard in particular to enabling the child concerned to have the best relationship possible with each parent of the child'.

[248] Chapter 5.

[249] FJR, ch 3.

[250] Section 1(2).

[251] *Protocol on Judicial Case Management in Public Law Children Act Cases* (Lord Chancellor's Department, 2003) superseded by the *Public Law Outline* (Ministry of Justice, 2008). On what is seen as the failure of these attempts see J Masson 'A failed revolution: judicial case management of care proceedings' in R Probert and C Barton (eds) *Fifty Years in Family Law: Essays for Stephen Cretney* (Intersentia, 2012) 277.

[252] FJR, at para 3.2.

[253] Ibid, at paras 3.64–3.77.

[254] Ibid, at paras 3.120–3.143.

[255] Ibid, at para 3.12 et seq.

public law adoption cases it was proposed that the requirement that a plan for adoption be approved by the local authority's adoption panel before it could proceed be abolished.[256]

These proposals have been substantially incorporated in Part 2 of the Children and Families Bill 2013. Regarding the private law proposals, a concern will be whether unreasonable people can be turned into reasonable people simply by diversion from the courts and the withdrawal of legal aid. It may also be doubted whether the proposed change in the terminology of the orders will greatly affect the issue. It has been tried before and arguably failed to do so on that occasion.[257] Perhaps more significantly, the key battleground in the private law is the issue of how much time the child should spend with each parent and it is this which generates by far the greatest number of contested disputes. It may be doubted how far a change in legal labelling will affect the numbers remaining in dispute; but it does at least focus attention on what is the real issue.

So far as the public law is concerned, the greatest concern will be that the 'no delay' principle, juxtaposed in the Children Act with the 'welfare principle', will become an obsession which in reality will threaten to hijack the welfare of the child as the court's paramount consideration. There is concern too that this might lead to an insufficiently rigorous examination of the public law threshold by the court. There is substantial doubt among those who practise in the field that the six month limit is at all realistic or feasible. There is widespread suspicion that its imposition is driven by cost-saving for the state which is clearly the dominant feature of the withdrawal of legal aid from the private law sphere.[258] Whether such a limit would be compliant with the human rights obligation on the state to make sustained efforts to reunify parent and child may also be seriously doubted. This is likely to be tested in the courts should this proposal be enacted. The proposed reduction in reliance on expert assessments, which follows the capping of experts' fees, may be similarly criticised; even if it is acknowledged that some cases have certainly suffered from what might be termed 'expertitis' with an unwarranted multiplication of assessments.

---

[256] Ibid, at para 3.92 et seq.

[257] It will be recalled that the Children Act brought about a largely, though not exclusively, terminological change from 'custody' and 'access' to 'residence' and 'contact' orders respectively. It was Lady Hale's view, as expressed to the FJR, that: 'Over the years, "residence" and "contact" have taken on too much of the flavour of the old "custody" and "access" orders. These proposals [for the child arrangements order] would restore the original vision underlying the 1989 Act'. See FJR para 4.65.

[258] And, arguably, of the current enthusiasm for adoption exemplified in the Narey report.

THE INTERNATIONALISATION OF FAMILY LAW: CHILDREN IN THE INTERNATIONAL COMMUNITY

In this concluding section we look at the attempts which have been made historically to establish international standards[259] and co-operation between States to uphold the rights of children, whether as persons possessing human rights which apply to everyone,[260] or specifically as children.

The most significant international convention asserting the rights of children is undoubtedly the United Nations Convention on the Rights of the Child. Since this is now widely regarded as a fundamental source of children law, it will be discussed in chapter 2 alongside the Children Act 1989 – the principal source of domestic children law. The reader should therefore read this section in conjunction with chapter 2. In chapter 7 we will look at the European Convention on Human Rights and Fundamental Freedoms as it applies to children, together with the extensive and ever-growing jurisprudence of the European Court of Human Rights. In recent years the European Union has also taken an increasing interest in the promotion of children's rights.[261]

THE INTERNATIONAL CHILDREN'S RIGHTS MOVEMENT

There are really two aspects to the protection of children's rights at the international level. The first is the extension to children of those human rights which everyone possesses as a human being. The second is the development of special safeguards for children 'beyond those granted as human rights to adults because of their physical and mental immaturity and consequent dependence and vulnerability'.[262] International law has frequently singled out particular groups and their need for special protection, two of the more obvious examples

---

[259] An early, but still informative, evaluation of the significance of international law generally in the development of domestic family law (including many areas affecting children) is to be found in G Douglas 'The significance on international law for the development of family law in England and Wales' in C Bridge (ed) *Family Law Towards the Millennium: Essays for P M Bromley* (Butterworths, 1997), ch 3. *The International Survey of Family Law* (Jordans, published annually) contains an 'Annual Review of International Family Law'. Many useful articles are to be found in the journal *International Family Law*.

[260] Specifically on the application of the ECHR to children see chapter 7. A very helpful introduction to that subject is S Choudhry and J Herring *European Human Rights and Family Law* (Hart Publishing, 2012) especially chs 5–8. Useful papers on children and human rights may also be found in P Lodrup and E Modvar (eds) *Family Life and Human Rights* (Gyldendal Akademisk, 2004).

[261] See now H Stalford *Children and the European Union* (Hart Publishing, 2012). For shorter treatments of the subject see H Stalford, N Thomas and E Drywood 'The European Union and Children's Rights' (2011) 19 *International Journal of Children's Rights* 375 and H Stalford and M Schuurman 'Are we there yet?: the impact of the Lisbon Treaty on the EU children's rights agenda' (2011) 19 *International Journal of Children's Rights* 381.

[262] These two strands of protection are brought out particularly well in the seminal article, D Hodgson 'The Historical Development and "Internationalisation" of the Children's Rights Movement' (1992) 6 *Australian Journal of Family Law* 252. We draw heavily on this excellent

being civilians in time of war, and refugees. The case of warfare neatly illustrates both the generalised protection of children, along with adults, and also their special protection.[263] While the Geneva Conventions of 1949 generally protect the civilian population (of which children are a part) and individual civilians (which children undoubtedly are), they also contain certain specific Articles which prioritise the needs of children. Thus, for example, the fourth Geneva Convention of 1949 provides, inter alia, that:[264]

'Children shall be the object of special respect and shall be protected against any form of indecent assault. The parties to the conflict shall take all feasible measures in order that children who have not attained the age of fifteen years do not take a direct part in hostilities and, in particular, they shall refrain from recruiting them into their armed forces ...'

The primary focus here will be on this special recognition of children in international law but we must also refer to the debate about whether the more humanitarian aspects of international law apply in their entirety *by implication* to children. Here, reference will be made, in passing, to the jurisprudence of the US Supreme Court and the ECtHR – both of which lend support to the notion that, in general, fundamental rights enjoyed by adults also extend to children.

The Declaration of Geneva 1924

International recognition of the claims of children dates back to the early part of the twentieth century and the work of such organisations as the International Committee of the Red Cross, the League of Nations and the International Labour Organization.[265] In 1924 the Fifth Assembly of the League of Nations adopted the First Declaration of the Rights of the Child which became known as the Declaration of Geneva. The Declaration went beyond the earlier, more specific, concerns about the working conditions of children and the problem of slavery. It constituted a more general charter of child welfare dealing with such matters as material and spiritual development, shelter, food, medical aid, relief from distress and protection against

---

article which should be compulsory reading for anyone with an interest in the position of children under international law. See also G Van Bueren *The International Law on the Rights of the Child* (Kluwer, 1998), chs 1 and 2.

[263] See 'Children and the Laws of War' (1989) *Childright*, at p 19. See also G Van Bueren (above), ch 12. For a more detailed examination of the way in which international humanitarian law has been said to have failed to provide effective protection of children in the sphere of armed conflict, see G Goodwin-Gill and I Cohn *Child Soldiers: The Role of Children in Armed Conflicts* (Clarendon, 1994).

[264] Article 77, Protocol 1. And see now Art 38 of the UNCRC. Article 38 requires States, inter alia, to respect international humanitarian law; to take all feasible measures to ensure that persons who have not attained the age of 15 years do not take a direct part in hostilities; to refrain from recruiting children under that age and, where recruiting those between the ages of 15 and 18, to give priority to the eldest; and to take all feasible measures to ensure protection and care of children who are affected by armed conflict.

[265] D Hodgson 'The Historical Development and "Internationalisation" of the Children's Rights Movement' (1992) 6 Aust J Fam Law 252 at 259 et seq.

exploitation.[266] Yet the Declaration was limited, both in its concentration on welfare needs and in its lack of binding effect. It has been described as an essentially aspirational document, not requiring, but inviting States which were members of the League of Nations to be guided by its principles in the work of child welfare.[267] It was left to individual States to determine whether, and if so how, to implement its ideals.

Post-war developments

In the period immediately following World War II, several important international humanitarian Conventions and Declarations were adopted. These were, for the most part, aimed at improving international standards of treatment for *all* human beings and not just children. The two most significant were the drawing up of the Charter of the United Nations in 1945,[268] and the unanimous adoption by the General Assembly of the Universal Declaration of Human Rights in 1948.[269] This is now generally accepted as the most authoritative statement of the main human rights and fundamental freedoms flowing from the UN Charter. The Declaration explicitly recognises, inter alia, the right to education. Another Article provides:[270]

'Motherhood and childhood are entitled to special care and assistance. All children, whether born in or out of wedlock, shall enjoy the same social protection.'

Beyond this, the Declaration did not expressly mention children, and it is a matter of interpretation how far its other provisions apply to adults and children alike.

The Declaration of the Rights of the Child 1959

There was, at this time, a gathering feeling that the special claims of children required wider, more comprehensive, recognition. This came about in 1959 with the Second Declaration of the Rights of the Child ('the 1959 Declaration').[271] While the First Declaration (the Geneva Declaration) had focused rather narrowly on the material needs of children following World War I, the second looked more broadly at the claims and entitlements of children across a range of areas including housing, education, recreation, nutrition, medical services and social security. Hodgson's assessment of the place of the 1959 Declaration in the internationalisation of children's rights is that it 'reaffirmed and

---

[266] Earlier Conventions dealing with these specific concerns were the Minimum Age (Industry) Convention 1919 and the International Convention for the Suppression of Traffic in Women and Children 1921.

[267] D Hodgson (above) at 261. Indeed, the Declaration itself boldly proclaimed that 'Mankind owes to the child the best that it has to give ...'.

[268] The Charter does not specifically mention children at any point.

[269] Resolution 217A (III), 10 December 1948.

[270] Article 25(2).

[271] Resolution 1386 (XIV) adopted 20 November 1959. See D Hodgson (above).

expanded the provisions of the Declaration of Geneva, and applied generally
to children in a more specific way the provisions of the Universal Declaration
of Human Rights. Unlike the Universal Declaration, however, the 1959
Declaration [was] devoted almost exclusively to economic, social and cultural
rights, omitting such important civil rights as life and liberty, criminal due
process, and freedom from cruel, inhuman or degrading treatment or
punishment'.[272] The 1959 Declaration, therefore, while much wider in its scope
than what had gone before it, fell short of being comprehensive and,
furthermore, did not create binding legal obligations on States which were
parties to it.[273] This had to wait 30 years for the adoption of the UNCRC in
1989.[274] The true value of the 1959 Declaration was to establish many of the
generally accepted international norms of treatment for children which could
then be translated into binding legal obligations on States in the 1989
Convention.

The debate about general application

Between 1959 and 1989 the focus of debate was on whether the general human
rights instruments emanating from the United Nations and elsewhere[275] could
be applied to children. Those provisions which directly referred to children
clearly did apply to children, but the notion gathered ground that most of those
which did not specifically refer to children also applied to them as human
beings.[276]

Meanwhile in the USA, the Supreme Court from the 1960s had begun to accept
that the fundamental rights enshrined in the Bill of Rights, as constituted by
the various amendments to the US Constitution, were, in principle, available
also to children, although their application might be qualified in some cases.[277]
The breakthrough came in 1967 when, in *Re Gault*, the court said that 'neither
the Fourteenth Amendment nor the Bill of Rights is for adults alone'.[278] This
ruling was followed by a plethora of decisions extending to children protections
enjoyed by adults under the US Constitution.[279] In Europe also, the European
Commission and Court of Human Rights made a number of significant

---

272   D Hodgson (above) at 266.
273   Unless, that is, it could be said to have acquired the status of customary international law.
274   See chapter 2 below.
275   Debate focused particularly on the so-called 'twin' covenants of 1966 – the International
        Covenant on Civil and Political Rights and the International Covenant on Economic, Social
        and Cultural Rights. See D Hodgson (above) at 269 et seq.
276   But international lawyers were not in complete agreement on this. See D Hodgson (above) at
        271 et seq.
277   For an excellent collection of materials on the early constitutional breakthroughs for children
        in the USA, see W Wadlington, CH Whitebread and SM Davis *Children in the Legal System*
        (Foundation Press, 1983), ch II.
278   387 US 1, 13 (1967).
279   Such as freedom of speech in *Tinker v Des Moines Independent Community School District*
        393 US 503 (1969) and the right to a hearing in school discipline cases where suspension was at
        stake in *Goss v Lopez* 419 US 565 (1975).

decisions protecting the fundamental rights of children under Articles of the ECHR which did not mention children as such.[280]

The immediate background to the UNCRC was that the General Assembly designated 1979 as the 'International Year of the Child'.[281] As one of its contributions to this, the Polish Government produced a draft text for a UN Convention, the purpose of which was to translate the principles of the 1959 Declaration into international law. The intention was to create internationally binding legal obligations, and also to extend the coverage of international protections beyond social welfare needs to the more extensive human rights guaranteed to adults. The original Polish draft, which mirrored the 1959 Declaration, was rejected, but in its place, the General Assembly adopted a more wide-ranging document which had been 10 years in the making and which followed extensive consultation. Its adoption on 20 November 1989 was timed to coincide with the thirtieth anniversary of the 1959 Declaration.

We discuss the substance of the UNCRC, and highlight its more important Articles, in the following chapter.

---

[280] We discuss the ECHR in chapter 7 below.
[281] See D Hodgson (above) at 275 et seq.

Chapter 2

FUNDAMENTAL PRINCIPLES: THE CHILDREN ACT 1989 AND THE UNITED NATIONS CONVENTION ON THE RIGHTS OF THE CHILD

Coincidentally, the United Nations Convention on the Rights of the Child (UNCRC) was adopted by the General Assembly in November 1989 – the same month that the Children Act 1989 reached the statute book in England. Together, these two basic sources of children law represented a fresh beginning for children, and are the most important general sources of domestic and international law relating to children.[1] For this reason, we begin our examination of the law by considering the fundamental principles of children law as derived from these sources. The aim of this chapter is to provide an overview of the Children Act 1989 as a foundation for more detailed discussion in subsequent chapters, and also to enable the reader to situate discussion of domestic law with reference to the internationally recognised children's rights in the UNCRC. Providing an outline of the Children Act 1989 also allows us to explain at the outset the various changes which the legislation made to the previous law, and to highlight various developments since its enactment.

The chapter begins by examining the scope of the Children Act 1989. This is followed by examination of the central decision making principles within s 1 of the Act and an account of the structure of the Act. This seeks to explain the central organising concept within the Act – 'parental responsibility' – and how it can be regulated by various court orders. Examination of the Children Act closes with an exploration of the various philosophies and ideologies associated with it. The second part of the chapter focuses on the UNCRC, exploring its general aims and then more specifically some of its more important provisions, and concludes with a brief evaluation of the Convention's importance and impact.

---

[1]   Since that time, of course the Human Rights Act 1998 was implemented (on 2 October 2000), which introduced more directly into English law the rights and freedoms guaranteed by the European Convention for the Protection of Human Rights and Fundamental Freedoms (ECHR) and conferred on children so-called 'Convention rights' in Sch 1 to the 1998 Act. The effect that the ECHR has had on children law is discussed in more detail in chapter 7.

THE CHILDREN ACT 1989

The scope of the legislation

General

The Children Act 1989 (the Children Act) is now, undoubtedly, the most important single source of children law.[2] It was described by the then Lord Chancellor as 'the most comprehensive and far-reaching reform of child law which has come before Parliament in living memory'.[3] It constituted a completely new statutory code governing the 'public' and 'private' law[4] affecting children and drew those two branches much closer together.[5] It removed, in one fell swoop, much of the complex and technical statutory law which had grown up in characteristically English, piecemeal fashion over several decades. It was, in every sense, a fresh start. As if to emphasise this break with the past, the legislation was brought into force in its entirety on 14 October 1991, thereby avoiding the delay and disjointed implementation which had previously bedevilled this area of law.[6]

---

[2] The Children Act 1989 was the subject of extensive commentary and generated an unprecedented number of books within a short time of Royal Assent. These include: A Bainham *Children: The New Law* (Jordans, 1990); R White, P Carr and N Lowe *A Guide to the Children Act 1989* (4th edn, Butterworths, 2008); J Eekelaar and R Dingwall *The Reform of Child Care Law* (Routledge, 1990); J Masson *The Children Act 1989, Current Law Statutes Annotated* (Sweet & Maxwell, 1990); N Allen *Making Sense of the Children Act 1989* (Longman, 1990); J Bridge, S Bridge and S Luke *Blackstone's Guide to the Children Act 1989* (Blackstone Press, 1990); L Feldman and B Mitchels *The Children Act 1989: A Practical Guide* (Longman, 1990); and S Bell MP *Shaw's Annotated Acts: Children Act 1989* (Shaw & Sons, 1990). The Department of Health also issued its official guidance on the 1989 Act under the title *An Introduction to the Children Act 1989* (HMSO). Other commentaries on the legislation, which take account of the regulations and rules of court made under it, are: MDA Freeman *Children, Their Families and the Law* (Macmillan, 1992); and J Masson and M Morris *Children Act Manual* (Sweet & Maxwell, 1992). For more recent commentaries which take account of the extensive case-law under the Act, see JM Masson, R Bailey-Harris and RJ Probert *Cretney's Principles of Family Law* (8th edn, Sweet & Maxwell, 2008) Part V; S Gilmore and L Glennon *Hayes and Williams' Family Law* (3rd edn, Oxford University Press, 2012) chs 6–11; K Standley *Family Law* (8th edn, Palgrave Macmillan, 2013) Part V; and J Herring *Family Law* (6th edn, Pearson, 2013) chs 6 – 11. For a very succinct, yet scholarly, commentary, see R Probert *Cretney and Probert's Family Law* (8th edn, Sweet & Maxwell, 2012), Part 3. See also G Douglas *An Introduction to Family Law* (2nd edn, Clarendon, 2004) especially ch 5, and M Freeman 'The Next Children Act?' [1998] Fam Law 341.

[3] *Hansard* (HL) Vol 502, col 488.

[4] The expressions 'public' and 'private' law are used extensively throughout this book to indicate, respectively: the law governing care and related proceedings; and family proceedings involving disputes between private individuals such as divorce, guardianship or wardship.

[5] See for discussion of overlap of the public and the private, A Bainham 'Private and public children law: an under-explored relationship' [2013] CFLQ 138.

[6] The staggered implementation of the Children Act 1975 was a notorious example of this. While that Act, inter alia, introduced the concept of custodianship, it was a decade before this was eventually brought into force. See Part II of the 1975 Act; and the Children Act 1975 and the Domestic Proceedings and Magistrates' Courts Act 1978 (Commencement) Order 1985 (SI 1985/779).

The Children Act established parenthood as the primary legal status in relation to children and reformed the law of guardianship to reflect this. It introduced 'parental responsibility' as the central organising concept in children law and reasserted the significance of children's welfare as the paramount consideration in disputes concerning their upbringing. It gave to the courts wide-ranging and flexible powers to regulate the exercise of parental responsibility and introduced sweeping procedural and jurisdictional changes. In the public law, the legislation made fundamental adjustments to the powers and duties of local authorities regarding the family and to the relationship between local authorities and the courts in fulfilling their complementary child care functions. It established a wholly new basis for compulsory care or supervision and, while leaving intact the ancient wardship jurisdiction, imposed severe limitations on its use. New procedures for protecting children in emergencies were introduced and major changes made to the legal regulation of substitute care arrangements. Much of the detail of the reformed law is contained in the Act's many Schedules as amended, including the code now governing the courts' powers to make financial provision for children,[7] the specific duties of local authorities to children looked after by them[8] and, more controversially, the radically reformulated supervisory role of the divorce court. A vast amount of practical detail is consigned to the many regulations, rules of court and guidances issued under the Children Act's enabling provisions.[9]

The legislation substantially replaced all the existing private law governing the custody and upbringing of children, and the public law applying to social services for families, voluntary and compulsory care and supervision. This was no small feat. It entailed the repeal of eight post-war statutes, namely, the Nurseries and Child Minders Regulation Act 1948, the Guardianship of Minors Act 1971, the Guardianship Act 1973, the Children Act 1975, the Child Care Act 1980, the Foster Children Act 1980, the Children's Homes Act 1982 and the Children and Young Persons (Amendment) Act 1986. The Children and Young Persons Act 1969 and the Domestic Proceedings and Magistrates' Courts Act 1978 were significantly amended.

It is now over two decades since implementation of the legislation, and over time the Children Act has been amended to accommodate social change, and to align it with developments in other legislation, including the requirements of the Human Rights Act 1998.[10] Most notably, the Adoption and Children Act 2002 introduced the concept of special guardianship (ss 14A–14F of the Children Act),[11] and amended the law on parental responsibility to allow

---

[7] The legislation largely consolidated the existing law on this, although major changes, which have severely restricted the jurisdiction of the courts, were subsequently introduced by the Child Support Act 1991, as to which see chapter 9 below.

[8] Schedule 2.

[9] The principal enabling provisions are contained in ss 92 and 93 and Sch 11.

[10] See eg, Children Act 1989, s 31A and amendments to s 26 of the Act, in light of the House of Lords decision in *Re S (Minors) (Care Order: Implementation of Care Plan)* [2002] 1 FLR 815, and chapter 12 below.

[11] Discussed in chapter 13 below.

fathers to acquire parental responsibility through birth registration,[12] and to introduce new mechanisms by which step-parents could acquire it.[13] The law on parental responsibility was further developed in relation to same-sex parents by the Civil Partnership Act 2004[14] and the Human Fertilisation and Embryology Act 2008.[15] In addition, a raft of provisions concerned with facilitation and enforcement of contact between children and non-resident parents was introduced by Part I of the Children and Adoption Act 2006 (ss 11A–11P of the Children Act). The Act has been the subject of minor amendments by several other pieces of legislation,[16] but perhaps most notably the public and private law was the subject of various amendments by the Children and Young Persons Act 2008.

Children issues in adult litigation: beyond the Children Act 1989

Despite this extensive coverage, the Children Act still represents only one source of children law. The interests of children are affected, directly or indirectly, by a mass of statutory provisions and common law rules, many of which were left quite untouched by the Act. While, for example, the Children Act brought about some minor changes to adoption law, adoption continues to be governed by an essentially separate code.[17]

It is clear that the student will need to look well beyond the Children Act for a proper understanding of the many and varied legal issues which concern children and young people. Thus, there are many matters which are conceptualised as 'adult issues' because it is thought that they relate *predominantly* to the competing interests of two or more adults. The interests of any children are not considered the central concern. This is evidently so in the case of divorce. The general principles set out in s 1 of the Family Law Act 1996, as noted above, do attempt to give greater prominence to children's interests on divorce[18] but do not go so far as to allow the interests or wishes of children to influence the essential basis or 'grounds' for divorce.[19] The welfare principle in s 1 of the Children Act, which makes the welfare of children paramount, has no application to this question. Adult interests are also deemed to be relevant in varying degrees on other questions which clearly affect children. The interests of minor children are the 'first' but not paramount consideration where a court is considering what financial and housing

---

12   Adoption and Children Act 2002, s 111, inserting s 4(1)(a) into the Children Act 1989.
13   Adoption and Children Act 2002, s 112, inserting s 4A into the Children Act 1989.
14   Which, for example, extended the concept of step-parent to include the civil partner of a parent: see Civil Partnership Act 2004, s 75(2), amending s 4A of the Children Act 1989.
15   See, for example, Children Act 1989, s 4ZA.
16   For example, the Children Act 2004, the Childcare Act 2006, the Criminal Justice and Immigration Act 2008, the Welfare Reform Act 2009, the Policing and Crime Act 2009, the Welfare Reform Act 2012, the Legal Aid, Sentencing and Punishment of Offenders Act 2012.
17   The Adoption and Children Act 2002, and formerly (at the time of enactment of the Children Act), the Adoption Act 1976. See chapter 13 below.
18   See chapter 1.
19   For a full discussion of the ground for divorce, see Law Com Report No 192 *The Ground for Divorce* (1990).

provision to make for a parent and dependent children on divorce.[20] Since the decisions of the House of Lords in *White v White*[21] and *Miller v Miller; McFarlane v McFarlane*[22] it seems that considerations of equality and fairness as between the adult parties should be the court's principal focus, although how precisely this will relate to the duty of the court to give first consideration to the interests of minor children is not entirely clear.[23] The issue does not directly relate to the upbringing of the child, so this is a question which falls outside the provisions of the Children Act and continues to be governed by the Matrimonial Causes Act 1973.

Likewise, where the issue is whether an order should be made excluding a spouse/civil partner or partner from the family home, the interests of children (while relevant) are neither the 'first' nor the 'paramount' consideration. In this context the Family Law Act 1996 does attempt in some circumstances to give some weight to the interests of children on applications for occupation orders since, in the case of 'entitled applicants' and former spouses/civil partners, there is in effect a *presumption* that an order be made where 'the applicant or any relevant child is likely to suffer significant harm attributable to conduct of the respondent' unless at least as much, or more, harm is likely to be suffered if the order is made.[24] The position is complex, however, in that no such presumption applies in the case of 'non-entitled' cohabitants or former cohabitants, although the court must still have regard to the 'balance of harm' criterion.[25]

In all these instances, the welfare of children is bound to be affected by the various outcomes and, to the uninitiated, the way in which the law ascribes more or less relevance to this may appear somewhat arbitrary. Yet this may simply be a reflection of the relative importance which society is prepared to attach to the often competing claims of children and adults. It is not really surprising that this should vary depending on the question which is being asked or that a different answer to the same question may be given at different times. It must, moreover, be acknowledged that, notwithstanding the current trend to deny the existence of independent 'rights' for parents, the reality is that the law does not always give precedence to children's interests. Increasingly also there will be difficult questions about how to balance the 'Convention rights' of

---

[20] Matrimonial Causes Act 1973, s 25(1), and see for the distinction between 'first' and 'paramount' in this context: *Suter v Suter and Another* [1987] 2 FLR 232. For a case in which the interests of a child had a significant influence on the outcome, see *C v C (Financial Relief: Short Marriage)* [1997] 2 FLR 26.

[21] [2000] 2 FLR 981.

[22] [2006] UKHL 24, [2006] 1 FLR 1186.

[23] There is also a tension with the objective in s 25A of the Matrimonial Causes Act 1973 to seek to achieve a clean break between the parties to the marriage; and with the courts' more recent emphasis on respecting the autonomy of adults who have made ante-nuptial agreements: see *Granatino (formerly Radmacher) v Granatino* [2010] UKSC 42, [2010] 2 FLR 1900.

[24] Compare the position under the previous legislation, the Matrimonial Homes Act 1983, s 1(3) (now repealed), which specified as a factor the needs of the children alongside the conduct of the adult parties and their needs and resources.

[25] See Family Law Act 1996, ss 33(6) and (7), 35(6)–(8) and 38(4) and (5).

parents and children under the ECHR. This difficult question of balancing the claims of children with those of parents and other adults is considered below.[26]

Impact of the Children Act 1989 on other legislation

Broadly, the Children Act incorporates those jurisdictions and those issues which can conveniently be termed 'children jurisdictions' and 'children issues'. 'Adult jurisdictions' and 'adult issues' are governed by separate pieces of legislation. At the same time, proceedings under certain other enactments are 'family proceedings' for the purposes of the Children Act.[27] Where this is so, and a 'children issue' arises in family proceedings, that issue will fall to be determined by applying the welfare principle and the other principles in the Children Act which apply to all family proceedings. To that extent the Children Act has a direct impact on other legislation.

Take the example of an application for an occupation order, a matter involving the criteria in Part IV of the Family Law Act 1996. The ouster issue itself must be determined by the criteria in that legislation. But the proceedings are 'family proceedings' and the question of the residential arrangements for any children is, clearly, highly relevant. This latter issue relates to the upbringing of children, falling directly within s 1 of the Children Act, and is governed by the welfare principle. The child's welfare is only one of several factors relevant to the occupation issue but is the sole consideration on the residence issue. The beauty of the Children Act was that it enabled the court, for the first time, to hear these obviously related issues together in the same proceedings. This can, of course, give rise to further difficulties concerning the proper balance to be struck between the interests of children and adults in this context.

The Law Commission considered whether it might be possible to collect, in a single statute, all the courts' powers over upbringing and financial provision for children. But it concluded that it was 'convenient for the statutes dealing principally with the affairs of adults to contain those of the provisions relating to children which cannot readily be separated from those relating to adults'. Where these powers related exclusively to children, the Law Commission felt that they could be conveniently collected in one place, and the Children Act gave effect to this.[28]

Other children issues

The Children Act does not provide the answer to certain other fundamental questions regarding the legal position of children. The very nature of the legal relationship between parents and children still largely falls to be determined at common law. The Children Act did little more than repeat the open-ended and imprecise definition of 'parental rights and duties' in its definition of 'parental

---

26   See chapter 7 below.
27   Section 8(3) and (4).
28   Law Com Report No 172 *Review of Child Law: Guardianship and Custody* (1988), at para 1.8.

responsibility'.[29] Certain aspects of upbringing, notably education, are substantially regulated by separate statutory regimes.[30] The principles of child support are now substantially contained in the Child Support Acts 1991 and 1995, as amended by the Child Support, Pensions and Social Security Act 2000, the Child Maintenance and Other Payments Act 2008, and the Welfare Reform Act 2012, and cannot be properly understood without some knowledge of social security legislation.[31] In fact, a host of issues concerning the position of children in society, and their involvement with individuals and institutions outside the family, are governed by a mixture of common law and statutory rules.[32] This is true of employment, contractual capacity, tortious liability and criminal responsibility. There is also a plethora of ad hoc statutory provisions reflecting society's concern to protect children from harmful activities and influences which arise from time to time.[33] Increasingly, also, it is necessary to take account of the international dimension. There is, in particular, a burgeoning growth in domestic and international law dealing with the problem of child abduction;[34] and there is now strong international recognition of the 'rights' of children as an aspect of human rights, most obviously reflected in the UNCRC and the ECHR, and, increasingly, under other Conventions.[35]

The student of children in the modern law must therefore be prepared to search well beyond the confines of the Children Act, but it would be idle to deny the key significance of the Act. A good part of this book is thus concerned with the application of the Children Act in particular contexts. This can only be properly understood in the light of the central principles which are expressly enunciated by the Children Act and some of the underlying philosophies which those principles may be thought to encapsulate.

CENTRAL PRINCIPLES

Part I of the Children Act contains a number of fundamental principles which apply throughout the legislation and are common to the public and private law. It also introduces and defines the key concept of 'parental responsibility' which, again, has application in both the public and private spheres. In the following pages, the principles themselves as they appear in the Children Act are considered, after which the philosophies and ideologies which may be reflected in those principles are explored.

---

[29] Children Act 1975, s 85(1) and Children Act 1989, s 3(1).
[30] The various Education Acts are discussed in chapter 17 below.
[31] See chapter 9 below.
[32] Part IV of this book is largely concerned with the law affecting the position of children in wider society.
[33] Examples are the Tattooing of Minors Act 1969 and the Protection of Children Act 1978.
[34] See chapter 6.
[35] See, generally, G Van Bueren *The International Law on the Rights of the Child* (Martinus Nijhoff, 1998).

The welfare principle

Paramount or sole consideration

Section 1(1) of the Children Act re-enacted, in slightly modified form, what is the cardinal principle in children law. It provides:

'When a court determines any question with respect to:

(a)   the upbringing of a child, or
(b)   the administration of a child's property or the application of any income arising from it,

the child's welfare shall be the court's paramount consideration.'

The former provision in the Guardianship of Minors Act 1971 made the welfare of the child the 'first and paramount' consideration, but, in 1970, the House of Lords in *J v C*[36] interpreted similar wording in the Guardianship of Infants Act 1925 to mean that the child's welfare should be the court's *sole* concern. All other considerations were to be excluded, except insofar as they had a bearing on the determination of the child's best interests. The principle, as Lord MacDermott put it, means:[37]

'... more than that the child's welfare is to be treated as the top item in a list of items relevant to the matter in question. [The words] connote a process whereby, when all the relevant facts, relationships, claims and wishes of parents, risks, choices and other circumstances are taken into account and weighed, the course to be followed will be that which is most in the interests of the child's welfare as that term is now to be understood. That is the first consideration because it is of first importance and the paramount consideration because it rules upon or determines the course to be followed.'

Since, according to this interpretation, welfare is the *only* consideration, the Law Commission took the view that to describe it also as the 'first' consideration would be otiose.[38] Hence, this is the preferred formulation, but it should be noted that no change of substance was intended, and Lord MacDermott's settled interpretation applies as much today as it did in 1970. Indeed the House of Lords has confirmed this interpretation on several occasions. In *Re B (A Minor) (Wardship: Sterilisation)*[39] the House of Lords made clear that the sole focus in a case applying the paramountcy principle is the child's welfare and there is no scope for other arguments. In that case the House had to decide whether to sanction the sterilisation of a 17 year-old

---

[36]   [1970] AC 668. See N Lowe '*J v C*: Placing The Child's Welfare Centre Stage' in S Gilmore, J Herring, and R Probert (eds) *Landmark Cases in Family Law* (Oxford, Hart, 2011), ch 3.

[37]   Ibid at 710–711.

[38]   Law Com Report No 172 *Review of Child Law: Guardianship and Custody* (1988), at paras 3.12–3.16. In fact the Commission proposed that the welfare of the child should be the court's 'only concern' and this form of wording appeared in its draft Bill. In the event, the word 'first' was dropped while the 'paramount consideration' formula was retained.

[39]   [1988] 1 AC 199.

young woman who had the mental capacity of a six year-old. The House explained that the case was 'not about sterilisation for social purposes ... not about eugenics ... not about the convenience of those whose task it is to care for the ward or the anxieties of her family; and it involves no general principle of public policy'. It will be recalled from chapter 1 that *J v C* involved a dispute between the parents and foster parents of a child and that the decision confirmed that the paramountcy principle applied even in disputes between parents and a third parties. The House of Lords made clear that there is no presumption in favour of a parent in such a dispute, although it was acknowledged that the rights and wishes of parents 'can be capable of ministering to the total welfare of the child in a special way, and must therefore preponderate in many cases'.[40] In *Re G (Children) (Residence: Same-Sex Partner)*[41] the House of Lords endorsed Lord MacDermott's interpretation in *J v C*, and clarified that there 'is no question of a parental right'.[42] The House observed that the welfare principle 'is well able to encompass any special contribution which natural parents can make to the emotional needs of their child'[43] adding, however, that none of this means that the fact of parentage is irrelevant.[44] Rather, it is an important and significant factor in considering which proposals better advance the welfare of the child, although it does not establish a presumption or generate a preferential position in favour of a parent.[45] It seems therefore that the courts are now required to tread a careful line between recognising the special way in which parenthood can minister to the child's welfare, while not generating a preferential position in favour of the natural parent. *Re G* concerned a dispute about the residence of children conceived through assisted conception to the children's mother and her former female co-parent. The lower courts had ordered that the co-parent rather than the mother have the greater care of the children within a shared residence arrangement. The House of Lords held that the Court of Appeal had failed to explore the important factor that the mother was in every sense – genetic, gestational, and psychological – a parent of the children. Lord Scott commented that 'mothers are special',[46] and Lord Nicholls added that a child should not be removed from a parent without compelling reason; and he decried any attempt to diminish the general approach that 'in the ordinary way the rearing of a child by his or her biological parent can be expected to be in the child's best interests'.[47]

---

[40] *J v C* [1970] AC 668, at 715.
[41] [2006] UKHL 43, [2006] 4 All ER 241. For discussion of this case, see D Monk '*Re G (Children) (Residence: Same-Sex Partner)*' in R Hunter, C MacGlynn and E Rackley (eds) *Feminist Judgments: From Theory to Practice* (Oxford, Hart Publishing 2010), at pp 96–101; and K Everett and L Yeatman 'Are some parents more natural than others?' [2010] CFLQ 290.
[42] [2006] UKHL 43, at [31].
[43] Endorsing the Law Commission's view in its Working Paper No 96.
[44] [2006] UKHL 43, [2006] 4 All ER 241, at [31].
[45] Adopting the view expressed in Australia in *Hodak v Newman* (1993) 16 Fam LR 1, approved by the Full Court of the Family Court of Australia in *Rice v Miller* (1993) 16 Fam LR 970 and *Re Evelyn* [1998] FamCA 55.
[46] [2006] UKHL 43, [2006] 4 All ER 241, at [3].
[47] Ibid, at [2].

In *Re B (A Child)*[48] the Supreme Court, in another case involving a residence dispute, clarified that in *Re G* Lord Nicholls did not propound any general rule to the effect that a child should not be removed from the primary care of biological parents.[49] He 'was doing no more than reflecting common experience that, in general, children tend to thrive when brought up by parents to whom they have been born'. The Supreme Court added, however, that 'many disputes about residence and contact do not follow the ordinary way' and therefore 'one must not be slow to recognise those cases where that common experience does not provide a reliable guide'.[50]

It is striking that in neither *Re G* nor *Re B* was there any discussion of the possible impact of the Human Rights Act 1998 on interpretation of the paramountcy principle. Perhaps our highest court was simply reassured by the view, expressed as early as 1988, in *Re KD (A Minor) (Ward: Termination of Access)*[51] that there was nothing in the jurisprudence of the European Court of Human Rights to cast doubt on the interpretation of paramountcy in *J v C*. However, the welfare principle has been subjected to a good deal of academic analysis[52] and there has been much speculation about whether it can survive the incorporation of the ECHR into English law by the HRA 1998.[53]

Can paramountcy survive the Human Rights Act 1998?

Is Lord MacDermott's classic interpretation of the principle compatible with the balancing exercise which the courts are required to perform under the ECHR where children's interests may clash with the rights of adults? The problem, in a nutshell, is this: if the welfare of the individual child is the *sole* consideration for the court, does this not mean, as Lord MacDermott seemed clearly to say, that any adult rights in issue would simply be subsumed in the process of investigation of the child's best interests? On that basis adult rights as such would be regarded as *irrelevant* except in so far as they shed light on the central question of the child's best interests. This has been the understanding in English law for the last 30 years or so, although it must be said that in reality

---

48 [2009] UKSC 5, [2010] 1 FLR 551. For a critique of the decision see A Bainham 'Rowing back from *Re G*? Natural parents in the Supreme Court' [2010] Fam Law 394.

49 See ibid, at [34].

50 Ibid, at [35].

51 [1988] AC 806.

52 See especially J Eekelaar 'Beyond the Welfare Principle' [2002] CFLQ 237; H Reece 'The Paramountcy Principle – Consensus or Construct?' (1996) 49 *Current Legal Problems* 267; and N Lowe 'The House of Lords and the Welfare Principle' in C Bridge (ed) *Family Law Towards the Millennium: Essays for PM Bromley* (Butterworths, 1997).

53 See J Herring 'The Human Rights Act and the Welfare Principle in Family Law – Conflicting or Complementary?' [1999] CFLQ 223; J Herring 'The Welfare Principle and the Rights of Parents' in A Bainham, S Day Sclater and M Richards *What is a Parent? A Socio-Legal Analysis* (Hart Publishing, 1999); J Fortin 'The HRA's impact on litigation involving children and their families' [1999] CFLQ 237; A Bainham 'Can we Protect Children and Protect their Rights?' [2002] Fam Law 279; S Choudhry and H Fenwick 'Taking the Rights of Parents and Children Seriously: Confronting the Welfare Principle under the Human Rights Act' (2005) 25(3) *Oxford Journal of Legal Studies* 453–492; J Fortin 'Accommodating Children's Rights in a Post Human Rights Act Era' (2006) 69(3) *Modern Law Review* 299–326.

there has always been an awareness that children disputes are clearly about adult interests too.[54] But can this approach continue to be taken, particularly under Art 8 of the ECHR which seems to require something quite different?[55] Adult rights to respect for private and family life *must* be respected and must not be interfered with unless the specific justifications envisaged by Art 8(2)[56] exist and only then when they are *necessary* and *proportionate* to a legitimate State aim. This is prima facie very much more prescriptive than merely leaving it to a court to decide at large what course of action is in the best interests of a child.

So what is the answer? There has been no shortage of suggestions. It could be said that the welfare of the child acts as a qualification or limitation on the adult rights in Art 8. These rights must be respected and upheld except where to do this would be contrary to the best interests of the child. An objection to this approach put forward by Eekelaar is that it 'may place the interests of children too low. The sequence is: have regard first to the rights of adults and apply these, *unless* it can be shown that it is necessary in a democratic society to depart from them on account of the welfare of the child'.[57] Eekelaar has himself tentatively suggested a new approach which might involve abandonment of the welfare principle as we know it. Under this approach the concept of welfare would be replaced by the concept of 'well-being' since welfare is an expression which 'can be too easily used to cover anything someone else thinks is good for you'. The concept of 'well-being' would offer a more 'nuanced approach' and would be 'indicated by the degree of success achieved in realising the person's significant goals in life'.[58] He goes on to suggest a formulaic approach under which the well-being of all concerned, children and adults, is measured and favours the course of action which 'avoids inflicting the most damage on the well-being of any interested individual'.[59] He prefers this to a 'crude utilitarian attempt at maximising the well-being of the greatest number ... since this would pay insufficient regard to the extreme adverse effects of certain outcomes, on the well-being of particular individuals'. It is impossible to do justice to Eekelaar's complex thesis here but it repays closer attention because it does represent one attempt to accommodate the interests of *both* children and adults in an era of human rights which surely requires this.[60]

---

[54]   See, for example, A Bainham 'Children Law at the Millennium' in S Cretney (ed) *Family Law: Essays for the New Millennium* (Family Law, 2000) and M Freeman 'Disputing Children' in S Katz, J Eekelaar and M Maclean *Cross Currents* (Oxford University Press, 2000).

[55]   See further chapter 7 below.

[56]   Article 8(2) provides: 'There shall be no interference by a public authority with the exercise of this right except such as is in accordance with the law and is necessary in a democratic society, in the interests of public safety, for the protection of public order, health or morals, or for the protection of the rights and freedoms of others'.

[57]   J Eekelaar 'Beyond the Welfare Principle' [2002] CFLQ 237, at p 240.

[58]   Ibid, at p 243.

[59]   See for a similar approach, J Elster 'Solomonic Judgments: Against the Best Interest of the Child' (1987) 54(1) *University of Chicago Law Review* 1–45.

[60]   See further A Bainham 'Non-Intervention and Judicial Paternalism' in P Birks (ed) *The Frontiers of Liability* (Oxford University Press, 1994).

Of course a focus merely on the child's welfare leaves out of account a further dimension, that the child also has 'Convention rights' as do adults. The child has as much right to respect for family life under Art 8, for example, as does a parent. Therefore, one answer to Eekelaar's objection that to put rights before welfare would be to attach too great an importance to adult interests and too low a priority to children's, is that this need not be the position even under what he calls the 'Convention approach'. This is because the court would be having regard from the outset not merely to the child's welfare as perceived by the court but to that child's *Convention rights*.[61]

Take, for example, the facts of *Payne v Payne*[62] which is considered in greater depth in chapter 5. A mother wishes to relocate with her child on the other side of the world, leaving behind in England the father and the paternal family who have regular contact and a good relationship with the child. This could be presented as a straightforward clash between the rights of the father and his family to respect for family life with the child and the best interests of the child which might be thought to be associated with the mother's happiness as primary carer. This indeed has been largely how the case has been perceived. But it might be presented rather differently by focusing more closely on the child's own *Convention rights*. The starting point then would be that the child would have a right to respect for family life with *both* mother and father, and any interference with this should be justified as proportionate and necessary to a legitimate aim. It is more than likely that the result would be the same, except perhaps that greater attention might have been paid by the court to the need to safeguard in the longer term the contact between the child and the paternal family. But such an approach would take into account the interests of all concerned and would perhaps also meet Eekelaar's objection that the rights of adults are being given precedence over the interests of the child. The answer, it is submitted, is to make sure that children's *own* Convention rights are ranked and considered alongside the Convention rights of adults. The difficulty of course is that this involves further complex questions about how the child's Convention rights are to be defined.[63]

It is clear, however, that the *paramountcy principle* as currently interpreted by our highest court does not sit easily alongside respect for children's and adults' rights and that a more sophisticated approach which explicitly takes account of the *rights* is necessary. There appears to have been in recent case law, if not a shift of approach, at least some recognition of the difficulty of squaring the use of the words 'paramount' or 'sole' with the requirements of the ECHR to

---

[61] See further A Bainham 'Can We Protect Children and Protect their Rights?' [2002] Fam Law 279. For a case in which the content of a child's Convention rights was explored judicially, see *Re Roddy (A Child) (Identification: Restriction on Publication)* [2004] 2 FLR 949. See also the discussion in J Fortin 'Accommodating Children's Rights in a Post Human Rights Act Era' (2006) 69(3) *Modern Law Review* 299–326.

[62] [2001] 1 FLR 1052.

[63] See for criticism of the court's application of the paramountcy principle in the context of relocation disputes: J Herring and R Taylor 'Relocating Relocation' [2006] *Child and Family Law Quarterly* 517.

balance the interests of individuals. In *Re C (Direct Contact: Suspension)*,[64] a case concerning a dispute between parents about contact with a child, Munby LJ commented that our 'domestic jurisprudence, if somewhat differently expressed, is to the same effect'[65] as that required by the ECHR and he arguably sought to shift the use of language subtly to one in which the different expressions of the law might be more easily reconciled. He commented that the child's welfare is paramount in the sense that 'the child's interest must have precedence over any other consideration'.[66] Such an approach is of course reflected in the fact that the ECtHR has shown a willingness on many occasions to uphold the decisions of domestic courts which have in the final analysis been substantially grounded in the best interests of the child.[67] Attaching *priority* to the best interests of the child seems not to be a problem as long as adult interests are not ignored in the process. The welfare of the child plays a *preponderant* role but cannot be regarded as *paramount* in the sense of being the *sole* matter under consideration.

In addition to the criticisms of 'paramountcy' highlighted above, welfare decision making has been criticised for its indeterminacy. As Robert Mnookin has pointed out, making a rational decision in this context is predictive and future-oriented. It may involve identifying and choosing between possible, and probable, outcomes for the child, all of which requires considerable information and the adoption of particular values to inform choice.[68] The matter is further complicated by the fact that there are competing theories of child well-being,[69] and that how welfare is understood is capable of altering over time. It might be said, therefore, the outcome could depend upon when, and by whom, it is being addressed. The point is illustrated by Lord MacDermott's reference, in his now famous dictum, to welfare 'as that term is now to be understood'. Of course, it also highlights a positive aspect of

---

[64] [2011] EWCA Civ 521, [2011] 2 FLR 912.

[65] Ibid, at para [43].

[66] Ibid, at para [47].

[67] For one such example of many, see the ECtHR's decision in *Söderbäck v Sweden* [1999] 1 FLR 250.

[68] RH Mnookin 'Child Custody Adjudication: Judicial Functions in the Face of Indeterminacy' (1975) 39 *Law and Contemporary Problems* 226; see also S Parker 'The Best Interests of the Child – Principles and Problems' in P Alston (ed) *The Best Interests of the Child: Reconciling Culture and Human Rights* (Oxford, Clarendon Press, 1994). For an excellent critique of the paramountcy principle in English law, which also draws together earlier academic criticisms, see H Reece 'The Paramountcy Principle – Consensus or Construct?' (1996) 49 *Current Legal Problems* 267.

[69] For example, there are those who have asserted that the psychological well-being of children following divorce is best protected by 'exclusive' custodial arrangements which provide them with the security of one 'psychological parent'J Goldstein, A Freud and AJ Solnit *Beyond the Best Interests of the Child* (The Free Press, New York, 1973), while others have who have taken the very different position that children fare best where contact with *both* divorcing parents is maximised and maintained: see, for example, J Wallerstein and JB Kelly *Surviving the Breakup* (Grant McIntyre, 1980).

the welfare principle, that it is capable of adapting to changes over time, and can be applied flexibly to different (sometimes novel) situations.[70]

Welfare 'checklist' introduced

It is, perhaps, inevitable that individual value judgments must intrude to some extent into the determination of a child's best interests. However, in an effort to structure judicial discretion, the Children Act broke new ground and incorporated a statutory 'checklist' of factors for courts applying the welfare principle, although such an approach was not entirely revolutionary. Similar devices had operated for some years to structure judicial discretion in relation to property and financial adjustments on divorce and ouster orders, now replaced by 'occupation' orders under Part IV of the Family Law Act 1996.[71] The Adoption and Children Act 2002 has also introduced, for the first time in adoption law, a list of factors similar to that in the Children Act, with additional factors relevant only to the particular context of adoption.[72]

Under s 1(3) of the Children Act the court must have regard in particular to:

'(a) the ascertainable wishes and feelings of the child concerned (considered in the light of his age and understanding);

(b) his physical, emotional and educational needs;

(c) the likely effect on him of any change in his circumstances;

(d) his age, sex, background and any characteristics of his which the court considers relevant;

(e) any harm which he has suffered or is at risk of suffering;

(f) how capable each of his parents, and any other person in relation to whom the court considers the question to be relevant, is of meeting his needs;

(g) the range of powers available to the court under this Act in the proceedings in question.'

As Baroness Hale explained in *Re G (Children)*, 'in any difficult or finely balanced case ... it is a great help to address each of the factors in the list, along with any others which may be relevant, so as to ensure that no particular feature of the case is given more weight than it should properly bear'.[73] The application of these factors in individual cases is discussed below.[74] At this

---

[70]   For this and other arguments defending the welfare principle, see J Herring 'Farewell Welfare?' (2005) 27(2) *Journal of Social Welfare and Family Law* 159–171.

[71]   Matrimonial Causes Act 1973, s 25(1); Matrimonial Homes Act 1983, s 1(3); and Family Law Act 1996, ss 33(6) and (7), 35(6)–(8) and 38(4) and (5).

[72]   See chapter 13.

[73]   [2006] UKHL 43, [2006] 2 FLR 629, at [40].

[74]   See chapter 5.

stage, it is sufficient to note that the checklist applies whenever a court is dealing with an application for a special guardianship order and in *contested* private proceedings. It also applies in all public proceedings under Part IV of the Act whether or not they are opposed.[75] The absence of a duty to apply the checklist in unopposed private proceedings is consistent with what some may see as an essentially 'non-interventionist' role for the courts.[76] The implication appears to be that where all parties are in agreement about what should happen to children, the court's role may be limited to sanctioning officially that agreement. It has been suggested that the presence in the checklist of the final factor might also 'be taken as a tacit warning that too much should not be expected of court intervention'.[77]

No premium is attached to any of the factors in the list. They are all apparently to be accorded prima facie equal weight, along with any others which the court may think relevant,[78] and the weight actually accorded to particular factors will depend on the circumstances of the particular case. A considerable amount of discretion must, accordingly, remain vested in individual judges. There would appear to be nothing to prevent one judge from attaching greater importance to a child's wishes (factor (a)) than to considerations of the relative capabilities of the two parents (factor (f)). Another judge might, equally legitimately, place greater emphasis on the latter. While such differences might be put down to the distinctive features of individual cases, they might also be explained by divergent judicial attitudes on the value of children's views. Moreover, while checklists or statutory criteria may serve the function of trying to ensure that all relevant factors are taken into account[79] they cannot affect the fundamentally indeterminate nature of concepts like 'welfare', 'best interests', 'significant harm',[80] 'children in need',[81] and so on.

---

[75] Section 1(4).

[76] Although it has been said that, even where the application of the checklist is not mandatory, it may act as a useful aide-memoire of possibly relevant factors: see *Re B (Change of Surname)* [1996] 1 FLR 791, at 793A–793B.

[77] SM Cretney 'Defining the Limits of State Intervention' in D Freestone (ed) *Children and the Law* (Hull University Press, 1990), at p 65.

[78] Unlike other statutory checklists, this one does not contain a 'sweeping-up clause' but the clear implication, since the court must have regard to the specified factors 'in particular', is that the court may consider all other relevant circumstances not enumerated in the list.

[79] Failure to take one of the statutory criteria into account, such as a failure to explore the child's own views, ought to be a ground of appeal. See, for example, the pre-Children Act decision in *M v M (Minor: Custody Appeal)* [1987] 1 WLR 404. But in *H v H (Residence Order: Leave to Remove)* [1995] 1 FLR 529 at 532, Staughton LJ said that the checklist was not 'like the list of checks which an airline pilot has to make with his co-pilot, aloud one to the other before he takes off'. It is sufficient if the judge takes all the statutory factors into account.

[80] This is the key concept in care and emergency proceedings. See particularly ss 31, 43 and 44, and chapters 11 and 12 below.

[81] This is now the principal concept in preventive work and family support. See Part III of the Children Act, and chapter 10 below.

Application of the welfare principle: public and private law

Notwithstanding the practical limitations of the welfare principle, there is widespread agreement that the welfare of children should be an important priority in any civilised society. It may also be argued that the extent to which a legal system can offer effective protection of the rights of its most vulnerable members is a reasonable litmus test of the efficacy of that system. However, the welfare principle in the Children Act applies only in certain well-defined and restricted circumstances as set out in s 1(1), namely only when a *court* is considering a matter with respect to the child's upbringing or the administration of the child's property. It has already been noted that the welfare principle does not apply in relation to issues deemed to be 'adult issues', even where children's interests are liable to be affected. The principle also applies in quite different ways in public and private proceedings. In public law proceedings there is no question of care or supervision orders being made on the sole basis of a broad welfare criterion and, indeed, this was specifically rejected as a ground for State intervention in both the *Review* and the White Paper[82] which preceded the Act. The welfare principle only comes into play if the minimum 'threshold' condition relating to 'significant harm' has been established to the court's satisfaction so that there is, in effect, a 'threshold stage' and a 'welfare stage'.[83] It would, therefore, be fundamentally misleading to imply that the welfare principle has *equal* application in public and private law. This is not to deny that its application in care proceedings is a significant feature in the court's final determination at the 'welfare stage' when the court has to decide what, if any, orders to make. The significance of the child's welfare in the context of adoption proceedings has long been a matter of controversy. Traditionally, the welfare principle has not applied in adoption proceedings but the Adoption and Children Act 2002 controversially extended it to adoption law. It now governs not only the decision on whether adoption is the best option for the child but also whether a court should dispense with the consent of a parent opposed to adoption. Whether this new approach is compatible with parents' rights under the ECHR is discussed later.[84]

What is the situation where no court is involved at all? Local authorities are not bound by the welfare principle in performing their statutory functions; rather they have a general legal duty 'to safeguard and promote the welfare of children within their area who are in need'.[85] They are not obliged to regard the welfare of those children as their paramount or sole consideration. Indeed, their former statutory duty to give 'first consideration' to their welfare was removed by the Children Act.[86] Clearly, local authorities must have regard to

---

[82] The *Review*, at para 15.10, and the White Paper, at paras 59 and 60. The welfare principle will apply, however, where a local authority succeeds in obtaining leave to invoke the inherent jurisdiction of the High Court but the principle does not itself govern the question of whether leave should be granted. See ss 8(4) and 100(3).

[83] Section 31(2).

[84] See chapter 13.

[85] For example, s 17(1)(a).

[86] Formerly contained in the Child Care Act 1980, s 18(1), which was repealed by the Children Act.

factors other than the welfare of individual children when discharging their statutory obligations of which one (expressly mentioned in the legislation) is the need to protect members of the public from serious injury.[87] The Court of Appeal has also held that the issue of the use of secure accommodation in relation to children in care is governed by the criteria in s 25 of the Act and *not* by the welfare principle. The court went on to say that the welfare principle, significantly, did not apply to *any* of the decisions taken by local authorities under Part III of the Act.[88]

What if there is more than one child?

The courts have also had to grapple with the problem of conflicting interests between two or more children. The answer they originally gave was that it was the child who was the subject of the application whose interests were paramount. Thus, where care proceedings relate to the child of a mother who is herself a minor, it is the baby's and not the minor mother's interests which are paramount. This applies both to the question of contact with the child who has been taken into care[89] and on the initial application for the care order.[90] The same logic has been applied where the interests of siblings are thought to conflict.[91] Whether the interests of one child *should* as a matter of policy be preferred over the interests of another merely because the first child was technically the subject of the application and the other was not was doubted by some commentators.[92] A better approach, as the Law Commission had suggested,[93] might have been for the court to have regard in an even-handed way 'to the welfare of any child likely to be affected'.

In *Re A (Conjoined Twins: Medical Treatment)*,[94] however, the Court of Appeal was faced with a situation in which it could not resolve a conflict of interest between two children on the convenient basis that only one of them was the subject of the application. The majority of the court felt that they were faced with an irreconcilable conflict of interest between conjoined twins since the inevitable result of surgical separation with a view to saving the life of the stronger twin would be the almost immediate death of the weaker twin. The case is discussed in depth in chapter 8. We are only concerned for the moment with the court's approach to the application of the welfare principle in the event

---

[87] Section 22(6).

[88] *Re M (Secure Accommodation Order)* [1995] 1 FLR 418. See also *R (W) v Lambeth Borough Council* [2002] 2 FLR 327.

[89] *Birmingham City Council v H (No 3)* [1994] 1 FLR 224. For comment, see G Douglas 'In Whose Best Interests?' (1994) LQR 379; R Thornton 'Children and Children's Children: Whose Welfare is Paramount?' [1994] *Cambridge Law Journal* 41.

[90] *F v Leeds City Council* [1994] 2 FLR 60.

[91] *Re F (Contact: Child in Care)* [1995] 1 FLR 510 and *Re T and E (Proceedings: Conflicting Interests)* [1995] 1 FLR 581.

[92] For a critique of these decisions, see A Bainham 'The Nuances of Welfare' [1995] CLJ 512.

[93] Law Com Report No 172 *Review of Child Law: Guardianship and Custody* (1988), at para 3.13 and cl 1(2) of the draft Bill appended to that Report; and Working Paper No 96 *Custody* (1986), at para 6.16.

[94] [2001] 1 FLR 1.

of a conflict of interest between two children *both* of whom were the subject of the application. The court ultimately resolved this issue by applying a test of the 'least detrimental alternative'. This, in its view, was to authorise surgery, since it would offer the chance of life to one child in circumstances where the death of the other was inevitable.[95] This approach, which involves balancing the welfare of one child against the other, with the scales starting even, is not very far removed from the view of the Law Commission noted above. Another way of expressing it might be, taking both children's interests into account, to follow the course which maximises the total welfare of all concerned and, indeed, this is an approach which might be adopted where the interests of children conflict with those of adults.[96]

Are parents and others bound by the welfare principle?

It can hardly be argued that parents, in taking family decisions affecting a child, are bound to ignore completely their own interests, the interests of other members of the family and, possibly, outsiders. This would be a wholly undesirable, as well as unrealistic, objective. Again, it is sometimes said that third parties dealing with children and young people are legally obliged to act consistently with their best interests.[97] There is more than a suggestion of this in Lord Fraser's speech in *Gillick*[98] where he stated that a doctor should not provide contraceptive advice or treatment to a girl under 16 unless, inter alia, he regarded it as in her best interests to do so. But he did not say that this was to be the doctor's *sole* concern. In fact, he made it clear that he was obliged also to have regard to the interests of the girl's parents (by seeking to persuade the girl to involve them), and to her own *views* (as opposed to interests), judged in the light of her maturity and understanding. Lord Fraser clearly had in mind the application of a different kind of welfare test than that applied by the courts under Lord MacDermott's formulation. It is submitted that it would be a distortion to say that outsiders dealing with children are legally bound by the welfare principle.

Those who imply that the welfare principle has this much wider application are really expressing the hope that society in general, and individual adults, will, in their decisions, feel it appropriate to act in the best interests of children, as they see them. This hope appears to be behind many of the provisions in the Children Act as they affect parents. The Act reposes a great deal of trust in parents that they will know what is best for their children and act accordingly.

---

95   See for comment, A Bainham 'Resolving the Unresolvable: The Case of the Conjoined Twins' [2001] CLJ 49, and further discussion in chapter 8.
96   Such an approach would involve a complex calculus. See J Eekelaar 'Beyond the welfare principle' [2002] CFLQ 237.
97   See e g S Sedley 'Child's welfare limits parents' rights to punish or restrain' (1986) 26 *Childright* 18, who suggests that parents and others who deal with children are legally bound by the welfare principle.
98   *Gillick v West Norfolk and Wisbech AHA* [1986] 1 AC 112.

Whether this level of trust is justified by the historical record is something which at least one commentator was quick to question.[99]

The no order principle

The welfare principle must be read in conjunction with another fundamental principle which has come to be widely known as the 'no order' or 'non-intervention' principle. This states:[100]

> 'Where a court is considering whether or not to make one or more orders under this Act with respect to a child, it shall not make the order or any of the orders unless it considers that doing so would be better for the child than making no order at all.'

It should be noted therefore that this principle applies only when the court is making an order under the Children Act. The principle does not, however, govern applications for financial provision under Sch 1 to the Act.[101] The express purpose of this provision is to emphasise that there should be a demonstrable benefit to the child in any order which the court is contemplating. The Law Commission was concerned, specifically in the context of divorce, that orders for custody and access (as they were then known) were routinely made, notwithstanding that a very high percentage were uncontested. They had, in reality, become 'part of the package' of divorce. The Commission's position was that the law should not intrude unnecessarily into the divorce process. Where divorcing parents were able to reach amicable and workable arrangements concerning children it was not desirable for these to be embodied in court orders. It was concerned also to avert the danger of polarising parents who were already co-operating with each other.[102] This view of the role of court orders also accorded with the notion of parenthood as a continuing responsibility. Thus, the responsibility of *both* parents should survive the process of divorce, and court orders should be reserved for those cases in which there was a clear need to regulate the exercise of that responsibility. Most, if not all, of those instances, it was thought, would be situations in which the parties themselves failed to reach agreement

The principle again applies equally to public orders. Before making a care or supervision order the court should be satisfied not only that this would be in the child's best interests but also that the order can achieve something which is unlikely to be achieved without it. This requires consideration of the other ways, falling short of compulsory action, in which social services might assist a family in difficulty.[103] Such an approach is congruent with the jurisprudence of the ECtHR, which has emphasised that taking children into care is, for

---

[99] J Eekelaar 'Parental Responsibility: State of Nature or Nature of the State?' (1991) JSWFL 37.

[100] Children Act 1989, s 1(5).

[101] *K v H (Child Maintenance)* [1993] 2 FLR 61.

[102] Law Com Report No 172 *Review of Child Law: Guardianship and Custody* (1988), at paras 3.2 et seq.

[103] These services are discussed in chapter 10 below.

example, to be regarded as a temporary measure and that the ultimate aim should be that of reuniting parent and child.[104]

The no order principle may, on one view, be seen as complementary to the welfare principle, since it cannot be in the best interests of children to be the subject of unnecessary court orders. If it is not better for a child that an order should be made, than that it should not, then the welfare of the child is ex hypothesi not furthered by the order. Looked at in this way, the principle might almost be regarded as superfluous, since it appears to add little to the welfare principle itself. Yet the intention is clear enough. It is to emphasise the need for courts to apply their minds specifically to the various options open to them, and not to assume that any order is better than none. The onus is on the applicant, whether a private individual or institution, to convince the court of the alleged benefits of the order sought. While it can be argued that this was always the case under the former law there was an undoubted shift of emphasis which led to suggestions that there is now a *presumption* against court orders.[105] However, whether the principle may accurately be described as 'the non-intervention principle' or properly thought to embody a wider 'noninterventionist philosophy' about the relationship between the State and the family, as many commentators have been inclined to assert, is highly questionable.[106] The Law Commission's Report which is the source of the principle did not presume court orders to be unnecessary either[107] and the subsection merely says that orders ought not to be made *if they are unnecessary*.[108]

Indeed, the Court of Appeal in *Re G (Children)*[109] has clarified that there is no presumption against making an order even where parties reach agreement (indeed no presumption either way). Rather, the words of the subsection provide the appropriate direction to the court, and each case will depend on its facts.[110] Thus, in a particular case, the court may need to pay respect to the parties' views that an order may be beneficial in their management of the children despite their agreement, with regard to factors such as that the order might provide stability and dissipate mistrust and bitterness between the parties.[111]

---

[104] See eg *Johansen v Norway* (1996) 23 EHRR 33 and chapter 12 below.

[105] For evidence of a 'no order principle' in the sense of 'non-intervention', in practice, see R Bailey-Harris, J Barron and J Pearce 'Settlement culture and the use of the 'no order' principle under the Children Act 1989' [1999] CFLQ 55, and see S Phillimore and A Drane 'No More of the "No Order" Principle' [1999] Fam Law 40.

[106] See A Bainham 'Changing Families and Changing Concepts: Reforming the Language of Family Law' [1998] CFLQ 1, at pp 2–4.

[107] Law Com Report No 172, at para 3.2.

[108] See per Munby J in *Re X and Y* [2001] 2 FCR 398; and A Bainham 'Changing Families and Changing Concepts' (1998) *Child and Family Law Quarterly* 1.

[109] [2005] EWCA Civ 1283, [2006] 1 FLR 771.

[110] Ibid, at 774.

[111] As per the facts of *Re G (Children)* [2005] EWCA Civ 1283, [2006] 1 FLR 771.

Delay is prejudicial

Section 1(2) of the Children Act enshrines another central and innovative principle applying equally in public and private proceedings. It states:

> 'In any proceedings in which any question with respect to the upbringing of a child arises, the court shall have regard to the general principle that any delay in determining the question is likely to prejudice the welfare of the child.'

It has been known for a long time that delays in residence and related proceedings can have an adverse effect on children as well as prejudice the legitimate interests of the adult parties. Delay engenders uncertainty in the lives of children, and can prejudice the party who is not living with the children. Delay reinforces the status quo and makes it more difficult to argue effectively for a change of residential arrangements. This so-called 'status quo principle' is indirectly acknowledged in the statutory checklist which refers to 'the likely effect on [the child] of any change in his circumstances'.[112] Section 1(2) seeks to address the principled objection to delay. As can be seen, it merely embodies a principle that delay is likely to be prejudicial and the wording appears to concede that there may be some instances (perhaps many) in which *some* delay is readily justifiable. Indeed, the Law Commission identified occasions when delay might be beneficial, for example, the benefit to be derived from a full welfare report could outweigh the delay of having to wait for it.[113] Clearly, much will turn on the extent of the delay in such cases.

The Children Act underscores s 1(2) by giving the courts new powers and duties to ensure the expeditious disposal of cases. Thus, in both public[114] and private[115] cases the court is required to draw up a timetable with a view to determining the questions before it without delay and to give appropriate directions to ensure, as far as possible, that the timetable is followed.[116] The Family Procedure Rules 2010 spell out in greater detail the procedural requirements which may be imposed.

Despite the reforms in the Children Act, and no shortage of good intentions, delays in children cases regrettably often occurred and have long been the

---

[112] Section 1(3)(c).

[113] Law Com Report No 172 *Review of Child Law: Guardianship and Custody* (1988), at para 4.57. For some early empirical findings on the operation of these provisions, see I Butler et al 'The Children Act and the Issue of Delay' [1993] Fam Law 412. *The Children Act Advisory Committee Final Report June 1997* (Lord Chancellor's Department, 1997) Appendix 2, Table 5 contained statistics on the time taken for the disposal of care and supervision cases. These revealed a considerable regional variation, but showed that on average it took almost a year (48.3 weeks) from the date of application to the final hearing in the High Court; and 43.7 weeks in the county court. The time-lag, as might be expected, was significantly shorter in the magistrates' (family proceedings) courts, being in the region of 30 weeks.

[114] Section 32.

[115] Section 11.

[116] These provisions thus inject an inquisitorial feature, since they envisage that the court, and not the parties, should dictate the pace of children proceedings.

subject of judicial censure.[117] There have been several reports seeking to identify the principal causes of delay which have indicated that the problem lies with the system rather than with the Children Act itself.[118] The problem has been identified as particularly acute in public law proceedings, and it has even been said in that context that there are 'cases where children have clearly suffered significant harm as a result of the court process itself'.[119] Indeed, the Family Justice Review identified delay in public law children proceedings as particularly worrying and recommended legislation to set a time limit on care proceedings of 26 weeks, with extensions of time only very exceptionally.[120] The recommendation is being taken forward in the Children and Families Bill 2013.

Several initiatives have already been put in place to seek to improve the system. The Family Justice Council, chaired by the President of the Family Division, was established on 1 July 2004.[121] The Council's remit is to facilitate the delivery of better and quicker outcomes for families and children who use the family justice system. In public law proceedings there is now a Public Law Outline,[122] which is appended to Practice Direction 12A – *Public Law Proceedings Guide to Case Management*, which sets out appropriate time-frames for dealing with cases.[123] Similarly, for private law proceedings there is a Revised Private Law Programme in Practice Direction 12B which seeks to deal with such cases expeditiously and fairly.

THE STATUTORY SCHEME

This section describes the essential framework established by the Children Act. Before considering the application of the Children Act in distinctive contexts it

---

117 See, for example, Ewbank J in *Stockport Metropolitan Borough Council v B; Stockport Metropolitan Borough Council v L* [1986] 2 FLR 80. See also *Re S (Contact: Grandparents)* [1996] 1 FLR 158, in which there had been 17 hearings between 1992 and the end of 1994, and in which the Court of Appeal said that there had been an inappropriate use of the 'no order principle' in s 1(5); and the report by Dame Margaret Booth *Avoiding Delay in Children Act Cases* (Lord Chancellor's Department, 1996).

118 Such as availability of experts and judges, and judicial case management: see Dame Margaret Booth *Avoiding Delay in Children Act Cases* (Lord Chancellor's Department, 1996); Scoping Study on Delay in Children Act Cases: Findings and Action Taken (Lord Chancellor's Department, March 2002), at para 52; and see the various intitiatives examined by J Masson 'Reforming care proceedings – time for a review' [2007] CFLQ 411 together with her later evaluation in J Masson 'A failed revolution: judicial case management of care proceedings' in R Probert and C Barton (eds) *Fifty Years in Family Law: Essays for Stephen Cretney* (Intersentia, 2012) 277.

119 A McFarlane QC 'Delay: A Cause of Significant Harm' [2003] Fam Law 453.

120 The Family Justice Review's statistics showed that care cases take on average 61 weeks in care centres and 48 weeks in Family Proceedings Courts. See Final Report, at para 3.2.

121 See for the background the Consultation Paper, *Promoting inter-agency working in the family justice system* (Lord Chancellor's Department, 2002).

122 See Piers Pressdee, John Vater, Frances Judd QC, Jonathan Baker QC *The Public Law Outline: The Court Companion* (Family Law, 2008).

123 See Sir James Munby 'View from the President's Chambers: the Process of Reform' [2013] Fam Law 548, and [2013] Fam Law 816 for more on the new Public Law Outline.

is necessary to have an initial grasp of the function of parental responsibility, the way in which court orders relate to it, and the jurisdictional arrangements under which these orders are made.

One important effect of the legislation was to render less important the distinctions previously drawn between parents and non-parents and different categories of non-parent. Under the old law, the kind of proceedings and the kind of orders available to interested individuals varied considerably and were largely governed by technical rules on standing.[124] Thus, for example, it could make a difference whether a step-parent had married a divorced parent, a previously unmarried parent or a widowed parent.[125] The fact that access to the courts should depend on such technicalities reflected no credit on the legal system, and most have been swept away to be replaced by a new 'open-door' policy. In general, *anyone* with a genuine interest in a child's well-being may apply to the court (albeit that in some cases they may need leave) in family proceedings although some important distinctions, especially between parents and non-parents, remain.[126]

Another salient feature of the statutory scheme is its flexibility and the attempt to achieve a degree of uniformity in the orders available in different kinds of proceedings. 'Family proceedings' are defined expansively, with the result that, subject to certain qualifications, the same orders are available to the court whatever the nature of the particular proceedings. This has the added advantage of making available common remedies in public and private proceedings in accordance with the common principles discussed earlier.

The function of parental responsibility

Parental responsibility[127] is now the central legal concept which establishes the link between a child and the person or persons who have authority to care for him, or take decisions concerning his upbringing. It replaces the former concept of 'parental rights and duties' which performed a similar function. The change in terminology is intended to reflect changes in the way that the relationship between parents and children is perceived. The objective was to move away from the proprietorial connotations of 'rights' towards a more enlightened view which emphasises that children are persons rather than

---

[124] The general position can best be appreciated by referring to the relevant chapters of leading family law texts published before the Children Act, such as SM Cretney *Principles of Family Law* (4th edn, Sweet & Maxwell, 1984) Part IV, particularly chs 13–18, or PM Bromley and NV Lowe *Bromley's Family Law* (7th edn, Butterworths, 1987), particularly ch 9.

[125] The step-parent who married a divorced parent had the advantage of recourse to the matrimonial and divorce jurisdictions under the Domestic Proceedings and Magistrates' Courts Act 1978 and the Matrimonial Causes Act 1973. These jurisdictions were not open to other step-parents.

[126] See chapter 5.

[127] See generally, R Probert, S Gilmore and J Herring (eds) *Responsible Parents and Parental Responsibility* (Hart Publishing, 2009).

possessions.[128] According to this, parental powers and authority exist only to enable parents to discharge their responsibilities. In fact, the Children Act defines parental responsibility to include, inter alia, 'rights', and the new definition was remarkably similar to the old definition of parental rights and duties.[129] Thus, the unitary concept of parental responsibility includes within it 'all the rights, duties, powers, responsibilities and authority which by law a parent of a child has in relation to the child and his property'.[130]

As a legal concept, parental responsibility performs two distinct but inter-related functions.[131] First, it encapsulates all the legal duties and powers concerning upbringing which exist to enable a parent to care for a child and to act on his behalf. These duties and powers relate to all the obvious concerns such as the child's material needs and health care, the manner of his education and religious upbringing, legal representation, and administration of his property. There are many difficult questions about the extent of these powers and duties and how they relate to the capacities and responsibilities of children themselves.

Secondly, the concept of parental responsibility exists not only to determine the way in which the law expects a parent to behave towards his child, but also to determine that *someone* (usually, but not necessarily, a parent) is entitled to bring up a child without interference from others who do not have parental responsibility. It has been said that the focus here is *not* on the nature of the duties owed to a child 'but rather upon the distance between the parent and others in making provision for the child; indeed, on the degree of *freedom* given to parents in bringing up their children'.[132] The acquisition of parental responsibility thus becomes crucial in determining which individuals or institutions have decision-making authority concerning a child.[133] It is this legal status which is all-important, however close or distant the de facto relationship with the child may be. A grandparent physically caring for a child may have less

---

[128] On the view of children as property, see MDA Freeman *The Rights and Wrongs of Children* (Frances Pinter, 1983), at pp 13–18, and J Montgomery 'Children as Property?' (1988) 51 MLR 323; and for a contrary view, see H Reece 'The Degradation of Parental Responsibility' in R Probert, S Gilmore and J Herring (eds) *Responsible Parents and Parental Responsibility* (Hart Publishing, 2009), at p 87.

[129] Children Act 1975, s 85(1), which provided that the expression 'the parental rights and duties' meant 'all the rights and duties which by law the mother and father have in relation to a legitimate child and his property'.

[130] Section 3(1).

[131] These two senses in which the term 'parental responsibility' is used are brought out very helpfully by J Eekelaar in 'Parental Responsibility: State of Nature or Nature of the State?' (1991) JSWFL 37, at pp 38–39.

[132] J Eekelaar 'Parental Responsibility: State of Nature or Nature of the State?' (1991) JSWFL 37, at p 39.

[133] For the view that there may be little difference between being a parent and being a parent with parental responsibility because parents have powers to act in relation to a child which are correlative to duties imposed by law on parents, see J Eekelaar 'Rethinking Parental Responsibility' [2001] Fam Law 426. For counter-arguments, see S Gilmore, J Herring and R Probert 'Introduction: Parental Responsibility – Law, Issues and Themes' in R Probert, S Gilmore and J Herring (eds) *Responsible Parents and Parental Responsibility* (Hart Publishing, 2009), at pp 10–11.

power and authority in law than an absent parent who scarcely ever sees the child. And it is for this reason, amongst others, that court orders are available, to regulate the acquisition and exercise of parental responsibility.[134] The blanket statement that parental responsibility confers a legal status which others do not have to act in relation to a child requires qualification. First, it should always be remembered that parental responsibility may be vested in more than one person.[135] But, even where it is, the 'sharers' each have a status in relation to the child which distinguishes them from everyone else who does not have parental responsibility for that child. Secondly, it can be important to distinguish between the rights which parental responsibility confers, and the *enforcement* of the rights. For, while parental responsibility clearly implies freedom from external interference, it is by no means clear what legal action (if any) may be taken to prevent this interference.[136]

The effect of court orders on parental responsibility

The general thinking in the legislation has already been noted: that the primary responsibility of parents for raising children should not be unnecessarily disrupted by court orders. Accordingly, the intention is that court orders should be confined to those instances in which it is necessary to resolve specific disputes about upbringing or to pre-empt such disputes by regulating in advance possible areas of disagreement. The courts were therefore given flexible powers modelled on those which were traditionally available in wardship. These included a new range of orders in s 8 of the Act and a general power to attach conditions and give directions.[137] These orders comprise the residence order, the contact order, the prohibited steps order, and the specific issue order.[138] The effect of a residence order, for example, is simply to regulate the child's residence.[139] In practical terms, this means that the 'non-residential' parent is simply precluded from exercising that aspect of parental responsibility which relates to the question of with whom the child is to live. This is because parental responsibility must not be exercised in a way which is incompatible

---

[134] Thus, in this example, the grandparent could seek a residence order or one of the other 's 8 orders' in order to prevent the parent from trying to exercise parental responsibility against the child's best interests as she (the grandparent) sees them. The parent, although retaining parental responsibility, would then be precluded from exercising it in a way which was incompatible with the court order: s 2(8).

[135] Section 2(5) and (7). A special guardianship order under s 14A of the Children Act confers parental responsibility which may be exercised exclusively by the holder, but a special guardianship order could also be made in favour of more than one person, such as a couple looking after a child. See further, chapter 13.

[136] See A Bainham 'Interfering with parental responsibility: a new challenge for the law of torts?' (1990) 3 JCL 3, commenting on *F v Wirral MBC* [1991] 2 WLR 1132.

[137] These powers are largely contained in ss 10 and 11.

[138] These orders are not exhaustive of the 'private' orders which can be made. The Children Act also introduced a new 'family assistance order' (s 16) and there are various orders by which parental responsibility can be obtained: see ss 4, s 4ZA and s 4A.

[139] Section 8(1) provides quite simply that a residence order 'means an order settling the arrangements to be made as to the person with whom a child is to live'.

with a court order.[140] But parental responsibility itself remains intact, unaffected by the order,[141] and may be exercised to the full extent that is compatible with the order. Exactly the same reasoning applies to the other s 8 orders. Again, these orders simply regulate contact or other specific matters, such as religious upbringing or medical treatment, but do not otherwise affect parental responsibility or its exercise.

The main 'public' orders dealing with child care and protection are the care order and the supervision order[142] and, remarkably, similar principles apply to such orders. Hence, even where a child has been compulsorily removed from home on account of some parental failing, the parental responsibility of the parent concerned is preserved and is shared with the local authority which acquires it by virtue of the care order.[143] The Children Act was a considerable departure from the effect of orders under the old law, which was to *transfer* the bulk of parental rights exclusively to the local authority under a care order,[144] and in private proceedings to transfer to the custodial parent exclusively most of the major decision-making powers over the child by way of a custody order.[145] Now the theory in all of these instances is that court orders are strictly limited in their effect to the specific issues they purport to govern on their face.[146]

Although s 8 orders will usually be made in private law proceedings, they are available in any 'family proceedings' as discussed in the next section. Thus, s 8 orders may be made in care proceedings as an alternative option to a care or

---

[140] Section 2(8).

[141] A residence order *does* vest parental responsibility in the person in whose favour it is made, assuming he or she does not already have it (s 12(2)), but it does not transfer it *from* anyone else. Parental responsibility can only be removed by way of an adoption order under the Adoption and Children Act 2002, or a parental order under s 54 of the Human Fertilisation and Embryology Act 2008, or, if acquired under s 4 of the Children Act, by application to remove parental responsibility under s 4(3).

[142] Section 31(1). Again, these are not exhaustive of 'public' orders. Others include the 'education supervision order' (s 36 and Part III, Sch 3), the 'child assessment order' (s 43), the 'emergency protection order' (s 44) and the various orders relating to the regulation of substitute care arrangements for children (see chapters 11 and 12 below). Part IV of the Family Law Act 1996 also amended the Children Act to enable the courts in specified circumstances to include 'exclusion requirements' in interim care orders and emergency protection orders (Children Act 1989, ss 38A, 44A; and see chapters 11 and 12 below).

[143] Sections 2(5) and (6) and 33(3). For an extreme example, see *Re M (Care Order: Threshold Conditions)* [1994] 2 AC 424, where the father retained parental responsibility despite serving a life sentence for killing the mother in the presence of the children. The local authority has the power 'to determine the extent to which a parent or guardian of the child may meet his parental responsibility for him': s 33(3)(b). See further, chapter 12.

[144] Section 10(2) of the Child Care Act 1980. For an analysis of the legal effect of the various routes into care under the old law, see S Maidment 'The Fragmentation of Parental Rights and Children in Care' [1981] JSWL 21.

[145] Despite some contrary dicta in the Court of Appeal: *Dipper v Dipper* [1981] Fam 31; and, on the confusion surrounding the term 'custody', see M Parry 'The Custody Conundrum' [1981] Fam Law 213.

[146] For some criticism of judicial developments which go against the intention of the statute, see PG Harris and RH George 'Parental responsibility and shared residence orders: parliamentary intentions and judicial interpretations' [2010] CFLQ 151.

supervision order. Likewise, a local authority may intervene in private proceedings and seek a care or supervision order. There is much more interchangeability and flexibility than existed under the old law where there was a more rigid demarcation between public and private proceedings.[147]

Jurisdictional arrangements

The Children Act created a concurrent jurisdiction in 'family proceedings' to be exercised by magistrates' 'family proceedings courts', county courts and the High Court.[148] The definition of 'family proceedings' is drawn sufficiently wide to cover virtually all proceedings, public and private, in which issues affecting a child's upbringing might be raised. Thus, the definition[149] includes:

(i) proceedings under the inherent jurisdiction of the High Court (these include, but are not synonymous with, wardship); and

(ii) proceedings under:

(a) Parts I, II and IV of the Children Act;
(b) the Matrimonial Causes Act 1973;
(c) ...
(d) the Adoption and Children Act 2002;
(e) the Domestic Proceedings and Magistrates' Courts Act 1978;
(ea) Schedule 6 to the Civil Partnership Act 2004;
(f) ...
(g) Part III of the Matrimonial and Family Proceedings Act 1984;
(h) the Family Law Act 1996; and
(i) ss 11 and 12 of the Crime and Disorder Act 1998.

Although expansive, the definition is not quite all-embracing. In particular, it does not include proceedings under Part V of the Children Act which are concerned with the short-term protection of children, often emergency protection. There is, in effect, a special code governing these cases and it would have been inappropriate to make available the whole range of orders under the Children Act in that context. Also, it hardly needs saying that many proceedings which can affect the interests of children in some way are not in the nature of family proceedings and consequently fall outside the definition. The obvious examples are criminal proceedings and ordinary civil actions such as contractual or tortious claims.[150]

The broad objective of creating a concurrent jurisdiction is to achieve, as far as possible, uniformity of orders, flexibility and consistency in the procedure and remedies applying in different levels of court. This end is also promoted by regulations allocating cases between the different courts and facilitating the

---

[147] See for discussion, A Bainham 'Private and public children law: an under-explored relationship' [2013] CFLQ 138.
[148] Section 92(7).
[149] In s 8(3) and (4), as amended.
[150] See chapter 16.

transfer of cases either vertically between the various levels or horizontally within tiers.[151] Thus, cases may be transferred sideways from one magistrates' court to another; upwards from the magistrates' court to the county court or from the county court to the High Court; or downwards from the High Court to the county court or from the county court to the magistrates' court. While, in principle, concurrent jurisdiction means that a case could be heard at any of the three levels, in practice, cases are directed to the most appropriate court, depending on such factors as the complexity or gravity of the issues, the need to consolidate proceedings and the degree of urgency.[152]

It has already been observed that the Children Act attempts to incorporate the more valuable features of the wardship jurisdiction. An aspect of this is the procedural changes designed to emphasise the non-adversarial nature of family proceedings. It has long been regarded as a distinguishing feature of wardship that the proceedings are essentially inquisitorial rather than adversarial.[153] The legislation seeks to emulate this (and thereby reduce the need to resort to wardship) by promoting a non-adversarial style of proceedings. The increased role for the court was noted in controlling the progress of cases. In addition, the rules require all family proceedings to be commenced by application (rather than complaint or summons), to have preliminary hearings, and to require advance disclosure of the nature of the case, the orders sought and proposed plans for the child's future. Full rights of appeal are conferred on all parties to care proceedings, and appeals now lie to the High Court rather than the Crown Court to emphasise the civil nature of the proceedings.[154] The appointment of children's guardians (formerly guardians ad litem) to represent the independent interests of children in public proceedings has become the normal course, and further adds to the inquisitorial flavour of public family proceedings.[155] These fundamental procedural reforms are consistent with the general aim of encouraging a thorough investigation of a child's welfare, untrammelled by technicalities, which may be thought not only desirable but essential if the paramountcy of children's welfare is to be more than rhetoric.[156]

---

[151] Allocation and Transfer of Proceedings Order 2008 (SI 2008/2836), and see also Practice Direction 3 November 2008, [2009] 1 FLR 365.

[152] *The Children Act Advisory Committee Final Report June 1997* (Lord Chancellor's Department, 1997) contained statistics on upward transfers of public law cases from the magistrates' court which revealed that gravity of the case was the most important reason for such transfers (accounting for approximately 70 per cent): see Appendix 2, Table IB.

[153] See NV Lowe and RAH White *Wards of Court* (2nd edn, Barry Rose/Kluwer, 1986). Whether other children cases could really be described as 'adversarial' is debatable since the judges were often reluctant to insist on such matters as adherence to the strict rules of evidence.

[154] Section 94(1). Under the old law, only the child had a right of appeal and this was to the Crown Court, an unlikely situation which arose from the 'criminal' model of care proceedings established by the Children and Young Persons Act 1969.

[155] Section 41. It should be noted that the Family Law Act 1996, s 64 empowers the Lord Chancellor to make regulations providing for the separate representation of children in certain classes of 'private' proceedings under that Act and other legislation. The appointment of guardians in private law proceedings is now governed by r 16.4 of the Family Procedure Rules 2010. Such guardians were formerly known as 'rule 9.5 guardians' under the previous rules of court.

[156] Whether or not the courts were fully equipped to respond to the new challenges posed by this

Although there have been many calls for the establishment of a 'family court' in England,[157] the Children Act did not create a family court, in the sense in which that expression is normally used, but it was the Government's view that the new jurisdictional arrangements brought about by the reforms constituted a substantial move in that direction.[158] The Government felt that the substantive law affecting children should be rationalised before fundamental reforms to the court system were introduced. At the same time, it hoped that the jurisdictional and procedural reforms could incorporate some of the more desirable features associated with the concept of a family court.[159]

More recently, however, following recommendations of the Family Justice Review,[160] s 17 of the Crime and Courts Act 2013[161] inserts a new Part 4A and s 31A into the Matrimonial and Family Proceedings Act 1984, establishing a new family court for England and Wales. Schedules 10 and 11 to the Crime and Courts Act 2013 make further provision with respect to the new court concerning, inter alia, composition, distribution of business, and consequential amendments to other legislation. The legislation is expected to come into force in April 2014 and planning is in process for implementation. It seems there will be a designated family centre for each geographical location, each with a single point of entry to the system.[162] The family court will be staffed by a range of judges at different levels, and will deal with all family cases with the exception of (a) cases invoking the inherent jurisdiction of the High Court, whether in relation to children (wardship) or incapacitated or vulnerable adults; and (b) international cases under either the Hague Convention or Brussels IIR. Those exceptional categories will be reserved to the High Court Family Division. High Court judges will, however, also hear cases of an appropriate level/complexity in the Family Court.[163]

---

radical change of approach has been questioned. While informal or participatory justice has an undoubted appeal, it has been said that 'the danger of adjudicators who have the responsibility of deploying the coercive power of the State appearing to "descend into the arena" is a real one': SM Cretney 'Defining the Limits of State Intervention' in D Freestone (ed) *Children and the Law*, at p 74.

[157] See, particularly, B Hoggett 'Family Courts or Family Law Reform – which should come first?' (1986) 6 *Legal Studies* 1. Family courts have been operating in Australia since the mid-1970s. For a full evaluation of the Australian model, see A Dickey *Family Law* (2nd edn, The Law Book Co, 1990), ch 4, and S Parker, P Parkinson and J Behrens *Australian Family Law in Context* (The Law Book Co, 1994), ch 7.

[158] This at least was the view expressed by the Solicitor General: *Hansard* (HC) Vol 158, col 547.

[159] It should not be thought, however, that the concept of family court, or informal justice in family matters, commands universal support. The Australian experience revealed remarkable public hostility, initially, to such matters as the derobing of the judiciary. See A Dickey (above).

[160] MoJ, *Family Justice Review – Final Report* November 2011 (TSO, 2011); MoJ and DfE, *The Government Response to the Family Justice Review: A system with children and families at its heart* Cm 8273 (2012).

[161] The Act received the Royal Assent on 25 April 2013.

[162] The Single Family Court in London A Joint Statement by the President of the Family Division and HMCTS London Region [2013] Fam Law 740. For concerns about judicial independence, see J Doughty and M Murch 'Judicial independence and the restructuring of family courts and their support services' [2012] CFLQ 333.

[163] The Single Family Court A Joint Statement by the President of the Family Division and the HMCTS Family Business Authority [2013] Fam Law 600.

PHILOSOPHIES AND IDEOLOGIES

It would be surprising if a statute which was the product of such disparate influences (as outlined in chapter 1) embodied a single philosophy throughout. What exactly the values are which inform the legislation must, of necessity, be a matter of opinion. Different commentators have read different things into the Act[164] and it should be borne in mind that what follows is only one view of the Act. One commonly held view is that the Children Act attempted to bring about a substantial shift in the relationship between the State and the family. By emphasising that the *primary* responsibility for raising children rests with parents, the law might be thought to be 'in retreat from the private realm of family life'.[165] This change of direction was thought by some to be consistent with, if not positively inspired by, the neo-conservative political ideology of the 1980s, which in Britain has often been referred to as 'Thatcherism'.[166] An analogy has been drawn with the privatisation programme of the Thatcher administration, such that the Children Act might be seen as a move (perhaps a substantial move) towards 'privatising' the family. Others have noted the same phenomenon but prefer the term 'de-regulation'.[167] The issue is a complex one, not least because there is no unitary concept of the 'the State'. It is not clear how precisely the interaction between the State and the family is to be measured. Should we, for example, concentrate on the policies of central government as they affect families and, if so, should an attempt be made to evaluate their specific impact on children and young people?

---

[164] These include LM Fox Harding 'The Children Act 1989 in Context: Four Perspectives in Child Care Law and Policy' (1991) JSWFL 179 and 285; SM Cretney 'Defining the Limits of State Intervention' in D Freestone (ed) *Children and the Law* (Hull University Press, 1990), at p 58; SM Cretney 'Privatising the Family: The Reform of Child Law' (1988) *Denning Law Journal* 15; A Bainham 'The Privatisation of the Public Interest in Children' (1990) 53 MLR 206; G Douglas 'Family Law under the Thatcher Government' (1990) 17 *Journal of Law and Society* 411; J Eekelaar 'Parental Responsibility: State of Nature or Nature of the State?' (1991) JSWFL 37; M Ryan 'The Children Bill 1988 – The Philosophy and the Reality' (1989) 1 JCL 102; and M Freeman 'In the Child's Best Interests? Reading the Children Act Critically' in *The Moral Status of Children* (Martinus Nijhoff, 1997). For a re-evaluation of the Act's ideologies in the light of the experience since it came into force, see M Freeman 'The Next Children's Act?' [1998] Fam Law 341. For discussion of how judicial interpretation of the private law may have veered from parliamentary intentions, see PG Harris and RH George 'Parental responsibility and shared residence orders: parliamentary intentions and judicial interpretations' [2010] CFLQ 151.

[165] An expression originating in the decision of the US Supreme Court in *Prince v Massachussetts* 321 US 158 (1944) and borrowed by SM Cretney in 'Defining the Limits of State Intervention' (above).

[166] SM Cretney 'Defining the Limits of State Intervention' (above), at pp 67–68. For a discussion of the influence of neo-conservative philosophies on family law developments in North America, see B Dickens 'The Modern Function and Limits of Parental Rights' (1981) 97 LQR 462.

[167] See, for example, G Douglas (above), and K O'Donovan *Sexual Divisions in Law* (Weidenfeld & Nicolson, 1985), ch 1.

The advent of the Children's Commissioners

The need to consider the impact of national policies on children led to calls for the creation of a Children Rights Commissioner such as had existed in certain other countries, notably in Scandinavia.[168] Following devolution, Britain's first Children's Commissioner was established in Wales by the National Assembly for Wales under the Care Standards Act 2000.[169] A major influence was the publication of the Waterhouse Report[170] on the abuse of children in institutional care in Wales. The UN Committee on the Rights of the Child recommended that a Commissioner for England be established too, and this was achieved by Part I of, and Sch 1 to, the Children Act 2004.[171] There are also Commissioners for Northern Ireland and Scotland. The establishment of four Commissioners within the UK has obvious implications for coordination of implementation of the UNCRC in the UK,[172] although also might be seen positively as 'legislative experimentalism' within jurisdictions, which will allow comparison of outcomes and future improvement.[173]

The Children's Commissioner has the general function of promoting awareness of the views and interests of children[174] in England[175] and other parts of the UK insofar as the functions are not in the remit of the Commissioners for Wales,[176] Scotland[177] and Northern Ireland.[178] The general function is to be concerned particularly with the following five aspects of children's well-being:

---

[168] See M Rosenbaum and P Newell *Taking Children Seriously – A Proposal for a Children's Rights Commissioner* (Gulbenkian Foundation, 1991) and critique by A Bainham [1992] JSWFL 552. Children's 'ombudsmen' existed in certain other countries, notably in Scandinavia and New Zealand, and it was argued that the ratification of the UNCRC highlighted the need for a similar office to be established in the UK.

[169] See also the Children's Commissioner for Wales Regulations 2001 (SI 2001/2787). For discussions of the Commissioner's work, see O Rees 'Beyond the Hype – A Year in the life of the Children's Commissioner for Wales' [2002] Fam Law 748, J Williams 'The Children's Commissioner for Wales' (2001) 1 *Wales Law Journal* 203, and K Hollingsworth and G Douglas 'Creating a Children's Champion for Wales? The Care Standards Act 2000 (Part V) and the Children's Commissioner for Wales Act 2001' (2002) 65 MLR 58. For a critique of the Commissioner's powers, see O Rees *Recommendations for strengthening the powers and functions of the Children's Commissioner for Wales* (Children's Commissioner for Wales, 2007), and O Rees 'Devolution and Development of Family Law in Wales' [2008] CFLQ 45.

[170] *Lost in Care – Report of the Tribunal of Inquiry into the Abuse of Children in the Former County Council Areas of Gwynedd and Clwyd since 1974* (HMSO, 2000).

[171] This followed a Green Paper *Every Child Matters* (2003) (Cm 5860) and a White Paper *Every Child Matters: Next Steps* (2004).

[172] See for criticism, J Williams 'Effective government structures for children?: The UK's four Children's Commissioners' [2005] CFLQ 37.

[173] O Rees 'Devolution and Development of Family Law in Wales' [2008] CFLQ 45, at 58.

[174] Child has an extended meaning to include certain care leavers and young persons with learning disabilities who are over 18 years: see Children Act 2004, s 9.

[175] Children Act 2004, s 2(1).

[176] The Commissioner is not responsible for matters within the remit of the Children's Commissioner for Wales (ie, under s 72B, 73 or 74 of the Care Standards Act 2000).

[177] The Commissioner is responsible only with respect to reserved matters within the meaning of the Scotland Act 1998.

[178] The Commissioner is responsible only with respect to excepted matters within the meaning of the Northern Ireland Act 1998.

(a) physical and mental health and emotional well-being; (b) protection from harm and neglect; (c) education, training and recreation; (d) the contribution made by them to society; and (e) social and economic well-being.[179] The Commissioner is required to take reasonable steps to involve children themselves in the discharge of his functions[180] and, in considering the interests of children, must have regard to the principles of the UNCRC.[181] The Commissioner is not generally permitted to conduct investigations into the cases of individual children, but where the Children's Commissioner considers that the case of an individual child in England raises issues of public policy of relevance to other children, he may hold an inquiry into that case for the purpose of investigating and making recommendations about those issues,[182] provided the inquiry will not duplicate work which is the function of another.[183] Commissioners are required to produce an Annual Report covering the way in which they have discharged their function, what has been found during the exercise of that function and the matters they intend to consider or research during the next financial year.[184]

In 2010 an independent review of the office, role and functions of the Children's Commissioner for England was undertaken by Dr John Dunford,[185] who recommended, inter alia, a strengthening of the remit, powers and independence of the Commissioner. The creation of a new Office, merging the Children's Commissioner with the Office of the Children's Rights Director in Ofsted, was suggested, together with a new function: to promote and protect the rights of children as set out in the UNCRC. The new office would report directly to Parliament, advise Government on new policies, and undertake assessment of the impact of new policies on children's rights. The Government accepted the recommendations in principle,[186] and draft legislation underwent pre-legislative scrutiny by the Joint Committee on Human Rights during July to November 2012.[187] The Committee recommended, inter alia, tightening up the definition of children's rights within the proposed legislation but commented very positively that 'the proposed reforms constitute a very significant development with the potential to transform the Office of Children's Commissioner into a national human rights institution capable of becoming an international example of best practice if sufficiently well-resourced'. At the

---

[179] Children Act 2004, s 2(3).
[180] Ibid, s 2(4). There is a power to enter premises (except a private dwelling) at a reasonable time, to interview children accommodated there: s 2(8).
[181] Ibid, s 2(11) and (12).
[182] Ibid, s 3(1). The Secretary of State can also direct the Commissioner to hold an inquiry: see s 4.
[183] Ibid, s 3(2).
[184] Children Act 2004, s 8. The Office of the Commissioner for England has a website on which are displayed its various intitiatives, and the annual reports can be found: http://www. childrenscommissioner.gov.uk.
[185] J Dunford *Review of the Office of Children's Commissioner (England)* (Department for Education, December 2010) CM 7981.
[186] Sarah Teather, 6 December 2010, Minister of State for Children and Families Written Ministerial Statement to Parliament.
[187] Human Rights Joint Committee – Sixth Report Reform of the Office of the Children's Commissioner: draft legislation, 7 December 2012.

time of writing amendments to effect the necessary changes to the Children Act 2004 are before Parliament in the Children and Families Bill 2013.

Instead of looking at policies emerging from central government, another approach to interrogating the relationship between the State and families might be to look more closely at adjustments to the powers and duties of local authorities in view of their primary functions regarding family support and child protection. Another focus of attention might be on examining the (changing) role of the courts (as an organ of state) in upholding the interests of parents, children and others, vis-à-vis each other and defending them against unwarranted action by other public agencies. Any meaningful attempt to evaluate the effect of the Children Act 1989 on the balance between the State and the family would need to consider such matters. The legislation also affected the balance of other relationships. It redrew the division of responsibility for child welfare between the courts and local authorities; it altered the relative legal positions of men and women (in their respective roles as fathers and mothers); and it redefined the relationship in law between children and adults. Below, some views are offered on how the legislation may have impacted on these various relations.

Partnership

One arguably consistent theme throughout the legislation is that of 'partnership'.[188] The concept of a 'voluntary partnership' between parents and the State was crucial to the thinking behind the public law reforms. This implies public support for parents in discharging their primary responsibilities, social work assistance where families experience difficulty, and continuing co-operation with parents in the more extreme circumstances where it has proved necessary to remove a child from the family.

This was the classic use of the partnership notion in the debates leading up to the reforms, but it is by no means the only sense in which the legislation underscores the essential nature of partnerships. The persistence of parental responsibility means that, increasingly, it will be shared between two (or conceivably more) individuals. It has been seen that divorced parents will, in law, each retain parental responsibility. If this is to be taken at all seriously it must imply that the law expects a degree of co-operation between them. Similarly, where a foster parent obtains parental responsibility through a residence order, this will be shared with the current holder or holders of parental responsibility (usually parents). This must surely give rise to a similar

---

[188] The White Paper, at para 5. It should be said that this idea of partnership between parents and the State is not a new one. Sir William Beveridge, in producing his report which laid the foundations for the post-war Welfare State, clearly proceeded on the assumption that the financial responsibility for the cost of raising children should be shared between parents and the wider community through a system of family allowances. See *Report of the Committee on Social Insurance and Allied Services* (1942) (Cmnd 6404). See for discussion of the Children Act 1989, F Kaganas, M King, C Piper *Legislating for Harmony: Partnership Under the Children Act 1989* (Jessica Kingsley, 1995).

implication of co-operation between all those who now hold parental responsibility. It is equally clear that courts and local authorities are expected to work together to secure the welfare of children. Thus, for example, the court in family proceedings may direct an authority to investigate the circumstances of a child.[189] The same may also be said of the various statutory and voluntary agencies having particular responsibilities which may affect children. The urgent need to improve inter-agency co-operation was a significant feature of various public inquiry reports,[190] and the legislation sought to give effect to this in a number of ways. Local education, housing and health authorities were thus placed under new statutory duties to assist social services departments where a request for help is made.[191] And the increased importance which the legislation attaches to children's views means that parents, social workers, judges and others now have to bring them into deliberations about their future more than has traditionally been the case. Indeed, following enactment of the HRA 1998, even where a child has been compulsorily taken into care, a local authority may need to take care to consult parents on important matters so as to avoid a breach of the parents' rights under the ECHR.[192]

The general thrust of all these developments may be seen as consistent with the partnership ideal. People and institutions having the care of children or dealings with them are apparently expected to work together to promote their welfare. In so doing they are expected to take account of what children want for themselves. This must surely mean that there is bound to be much more of what used to be described as the 'fragmentation' of parental rights.[193] This conveys the idea that the legal powers and responsibilities for children are not centralised in one carer but shared or allocated between two or more individuals or institutions.

The impact of the Children Act on these various 'partnerships' will now be addressed briefly.

---

[189] Section 37(1).

[190] See, particularly, *A Child in Trust: The Report of the Panel of Inquiry into the Circumstances surrounding the death of Jasmine Beckford* (London Borough of Brent, 1985). As noted in chapter 1, concerns about inter-agency cooperation in the context of child protection continued post-Children Act 1989, as highlighted by Lord Laming's inquiry into the death of Victoria Climbie, which led to some restructuring of services in the Children Act 2004 and new guidance.

[191] Section 27. It should be noted that the duty of local education authorities referred to is now repealed. Local Education Authorities and Children's Services Authorities (Integration of Functions) Order 2010 (SI 2010/1158), art 5(1), Sch 2, Pt 2, para 37, with effect from 5 May 2010.

[192] See eg *Re G (Care: Challenge to Local Authority's Decision)* [2003] EWHC 551 (Fam), [2003] 2 FLR 42.

[193] An expression originally coined by J Eekelaar in 'What are Parental Rights?' (1973) 89 LQR 210, at p 229 and taken up by S Maidment in 'The Fragmentation of Parental Rights' [1981] CLJ 135. See also for more recent discussion in the context of the concept of parental responsibility under the Children Act 1989, H Reece 'The Degradation of Parental Responsibility' in R Probert, S Gilmore and J Herring *Responsible Parents and Parental Responsibility* (Hart Publishing, 2009), at pp 85–102.

The State and the family

Strengthening of the parental position

Most commentators agreed that the Children Act strengthened considerably the legal standing of parents (and others with parental responsibility) vis-à-vis local authorities.[194] Foremost among those changes was the abolition of the 'parental rights resolution', an administrative mechanism for retaining compulsory control of a child originally placed voluntarily in the care of social services.[195] Although susceptible to a subsequent judicial challenge, the resolution procedure failed to extend to parents the minimum participatory rights mandated by the ECHR.[196] In the same vein, the Children Act placed important restrictions on the length of time for which a child might be kept away from home without an opportunity for challenge under emergency procedures.[197]

Other provisions which marked a distinct shift of power away from local authorities have been criticised as emanating from an ideological stance which takes insufficient account of the practicalities involved. These include the abolition of the requirement of notice where parents wish to resume the care of a child voluntarily 'accommodated' by a local authority.[198] Here, there was an obvious unwillingness to allow any period of notice, however short, to detract (even in theory) from the apparently strict demarcation of voluntary services and compulsory care which the Children Act establishes.[199] Other provisions which involve a distinct loss of control by local authorities are those which were designed to ensure that parents are allowed to participate fully in decision-making.[200] These 'participatory' rights can be viewed merely as the

---

[194] See SM Cretney 'Defining the Limits of State Intervention' in D Freestone (ed) *Children and the Law* (Hull University Press, 1990), at p 68; J Eekelaar 'Parental Responsibility: State of Nature or Nature of the State?' (1991) JSWFL 37; and A Bainham 'The Children Act 1989: The State and the Family' [1990] Fam Law 231. For a chapter looking back on the deficiencies of the previous public law, see M Hayes 'Removing Children From Their Families – Law and Policy Before the Children Act 1989' in G Douglas and N Lowe *The Continuing Evolution of Family Law* (Family Law, 2009), ch 4.

[195] For a critique of the resolution procedure, see M Adcock, R White and O Rowlands *The Administrative Parent* (BAAF, 1983) and LM Harding 'The Hundred Year Resolution' (1989) 2 JCL 12.

[196] See *R v UK, O v UK, W v UK* [1988] 2 FLR 445, ECtHR.

[197] Section 45, and see chapter 11 below.

[198] Formerly parents were required to give 28 days' notice. Failure to do so constituted a criminal offence under s 13 of the Child Care Act 1980.

[199] There was great concern that voluntary arrangements should not be allowed to slip into compulsion, as had frequently happened under the existing law, since this was thought to discourage some families in difficulty from seeking voluntary assistance. See the discussion of the 'voluntary principle' in BM Hoggett *Parents and Children: The Law of Parental Responsibility* (3rd edn, Sweet & Maxwell, 1987), at pp 130 et seq. See, however, the research by J Masson, which indicates that in practice the boundary between compulsory and 'voluntary' engagements with local authorities may be more blurred: J Masson 'Emergency Intervention to Protect Children: Using and Avoiding Legal Controls' [2005] CFLQ 75.

[200] These participatory rights are, to some extent, implicit in the very notion of continuing parental responsibility, but the Children Act also confers on parents specific rights to be consulted. See particularly s 22, and chapter 10 below.

logical accompaniments of the statutory commitment to reuniting children with their families.[201] But, equally, some may see in them the potential for inhibiting local authorities in the discharge of their statutory functions, for no better reason than an ideological commitment to the primacy of parenthood.[202]

Despite these apparent shifts of power away from local authorities, it should be said that in several important respects the Children Act strengthened their powers to take protective action. These include the re-casting of the grounds for care and supervision orders to embrace prospective harm,[203] and the introduction of child assessment orders alongside emergency protection orders, thereby increasing the short-term options for compulsory assessment and protective action.[204]

Restriction of court intervention in divorce

In the private sphere, there is an equally strong affirmation of the parental role and the need to restrict public intervention through the courts. Nowhere is this thinking more strikingly obvious than in the reforms to the court's supervisory role on divorce. These changes are considered in chapter 5.

Agents of the State: the courts and local authorities

Former use of wardship by and against local authorities

Courts and local authorities may be seen as partners in upholding the public interest in child welfare.[205] While local authorities are given primary responsibility for the protection of children, they may take compulsory action only with the sanction of the courts.[206] More importantly, perhaps, the courts have long performed an independent role in safeguarding the welfare of children in a variety of family proceedings. The archetypal protective jurisdiction has been wardship, where the courts have traditionally exercised wide and flexible powers to deal with any serious issues affecting individual children.[207] The existence of this potentially unlimited jurisdiction alongside the statutory powers and duties of local authorities gave rise to much litigation

---

[201] See s 23(6) and Sch 2, para 15, discussed by M Ryan 'The Children Bill 1988 – The Philosophy and the Reality' (1989) 1 JCL 102, at p 104.

[202] See the views of J Eekelaar 'Parental Responsibility: State of Nature or Nature of the State?' (1991) JSWFL 37, at pp 48 et seq.

[203] Section 31(2) overcoming the technical difficulties exposed in *D (A Minor) v Berkshire County Council* [1987] 1 All ER 33, discussed in chapter 12 below.

[204] Sections 43 and 44. See chapter 11 below.

[205] See A Bainham *Children, Parents and the State* (Sweet & Maxwell, 1988), at p 103.

[206] See *R (G) Nottingham City Council* [2008] EWHC 152 (Admin), [2008] 1 FLR 1660, at para [17].

[207] On the nature of the wardship jurisdiction, see particularly NV Lowe and RAH White *Wards of Court* (2nd edn, Barry Rose/Kluwer, 1986), ch 1; and Cross 'Wards of Court' (1967) 83 LQR 200.

in the decade or so preceding the 1989 legislation.[208] The result which had appeared to emerge was that, whereas local authorities were at liberty to seek the 'supplementary assistance' of the courts in discharging their child care functions, it was not open to parents and others to invoke wardship to question the merits of decisions taken by social services.[209] A clear disparity had therefore grown up in the treatment of local authorities and other applicants.

The Children Act addressed this disparity in dramatic fashion by curtailing drastically the circumstances in which local authorities might have access to the inherent jurisdiction of the High Court.[210] The broad effect is that neither social services, nor anyone else, may act outside the statutory regime. The authority must prove the statutory ground for care and supervision orders if it wishes to take compulsory action, and it cannot resort to wardship or the inherent jurisdiction as an extra-statutory alternative. Similarly, any judicial challenges to the actions of the authority must be based on an alleged failure to satisfy the criteria in the legislation. By way of exception, where impropriety or ultra vires action is alleged against the authority this may be challenged through the judicial review procedure but no longer in wardship proceedings. There is now also the possibility of challenges under the HRA 1998.

Parliament and the courts

The restriction on the use of wardship, outlined above, proved controversial from the start and the arguments will be discussed later. The main concern here is to explore the essential thinking in the legislation about the proper relationship between the different organs of the State. The first point concerns Parliament and the courts, and here the reasoning is patently clear. Where Parliament has through legislation defined with particularity the basis for State intervention in the family, it is not for the courts to gainsay this by allowing a 'back-door' entry into care. Authorities must operate within the statutory framework either by proving the grounds for compulsory action, or by securing the voluntary co-operation of the family concerned. By the same token, it is improper for the courts to countenance extra-statutory challenges to the legitimate exercise of statutory discretion. To allow them to do so on the strength of some broad or open-ended welfare criterion would make a complete nonsense of that which Parliament has ordained.[211] As a matter of

---

[208] The leading cases were *A v Liverpool City Council* [1982] AC 363 and *Re W (A Minor) (Wardship: Jurisdiction)* [1985] AC 791.

[209] An example of the former type of case was *Re CB* [1981] 1 All ER 16, where the local authority had insufficient grounds for passing a parental rights resolution.

[210] Section 100. On the distinction between wardship and the other uses of the inherent jurisdiction of the High Court, see R White, P Carr and N Lowe *A Guide to the Children Act 1989* (4th edn, Butterworths, 2008), at paras 12.1–12.3. See also, for an assessment of the role of wardship post-Children Act 1989, N Lowe 'Inherently Disposed to Protect Children – The Continuing Role of Wardship' in R Probert and C Barton (eds) *Fifty Years in Family Law: Essays for Stephen Cretney* (Cambridge, Intersentia, 2012), at pp 161–173.

[211] It is also the case that to allow a wider, welfare-based criterion for compulsory intervention could be an unjustifiable violation of both parents' and children's rights to respect for family life under Art 8 of the ECHR.

pure logic this is impeccable, despite the practical ramifications of removing from local authorities what some regarded at the time as the crucially important safety net of wardship.[212] If it is illegitimate for the courts to ignore Parliament's scheme at the behest of parents and relatives then, logically, it must be improper for them to do so at the behest of local authorities.

Relationship between local authorities and the courts

It is more difficult to discern a consistent philosophical position regarding the appropriate relationship between local authorities and the courts.[213] The limitations imposed on wardship are characteristic of a number of provisions which assert the primary responsibility of local authorities (rather than the courts) for children falling within their statutory functions. It is for the authority to determine what level of social work involvement is appropriate to safeguard the well-being of children in families experiencing difficulties. It is not for the courts to act unilaterally of their own volition. Thus, it is no longer possible for a court, in family proceedings, to direct that a child be taken into care or put under supervision, unless the authority itself seeks such an order in those proceedings. All the court may do, where it is concerned about the welfare of a child before it, is to direct the authority to investigate his circumstances with a view to determining what level of intervention (if any) is necessary.[214]

This represented a significant re-casting of the respective roles of the courts and social services. Before the reforms, the court might, of its own motion in wardship and certain other family proceedings, commit a child to care.[215] It could, thereafter, give directions to the authority about aspects of upbringing and, in wardship, it preserved for itself an ongoing supervisory role.[216] The reasoning under the Children Act was that the courts were not equipped to perform this kind of 'managerial' role and that the local authority should be firmly in control of case management provided only that it does not exceed its statutory powers.[217] This reasoning is apparent in the decision to improve the review procedures within authorities and the requirement that every authority establish an internal procedure to deal with representations or complaints.[218] Here, again, it was thought inappropriate that the detailed matters concerning

---

[212]   N Lowe 'Caring for Children' (1989) 139 NLJ 87.

[213]   See SM Cretney 'Defining the Limits of State Intervention' in D Freestone (ed) *Children and the Law* (Hull University Press, 1990), at pp 71–74; J Dewar 'The Courts and Local Authority Autonomy' (1995) 7 JCL 15; and M Hayes 'The proper role of the courts in child care cases' [1996] CFLQ 201. And see R Tolson QC *Care Plans and the Human Rights Act* (Family Law, 2002) for a discussion of the human rights issues involved in this question.

[214]   Section 37.

[215]   Under, for example, Guardianship Act 1973, s 2(2)(b) or Matrimonial Causes Act 1973, s 43(1).

[216]   For a good example of the implications of this ongoing role, see *Re E (SA) (A Minor) (Wardship)* [1984] 1 All ER 289.

[217]   Where it does exceed its statutory powers the appropriate procedure is now judicial review rather than wardship. See *Re DM (A Minor) (Wardship: Jurisdiction)* [1986] 2 FLR 122.

[218]   Section 26.

the treatment of children 'looked after' by social services should be subject to external review by the ordinary courts. Instead, the concentration should be on trying to ensure good practice through a better system of internal reviews.[219]

The courts' role: adjudicative or managerial?

These developments suggest strongly that the courts' role in children cases is conceptualised as an adjudicative rather than managerial one. Yet it has been observed that the legislation may not be entirely consistent on this since, in certain respects, the courts are now required to involve themselves much more with the substance of case management.[220] Nowhere is this more obvious than in relation to the vexed issue of contact (formerly access) with children in care.[221] Local authorities are now required to justify to the courts, to a greater extent than ever before, decisions to terminate or restrict contact between the child and prescribed individuals.[222] The impact of this greater level of scrutiny should not be underestimated given the crucial significance of the issue for the prospects of the child returning to the family and longer-term management of the child's case. It is also, without doubt, the single issue which generated the greatest number of wardship applications by parents and others.[223] Alongside this, the more inquisitorial role expected of the courts has been noted, with regard to the progress of proceedings. The House of Lords held in effect that the courts remain in control of the interim stage of care proceedings, namely after making an interim care order but before the final hearing.[224]

It may, therefore, be that there is some ambiguity in the way that the role of the courts is perceived. But it is fair to say that, in general, while the courts exercise significant control over entry into, and discharge from, care, most issues concerned with the treatment of children once in care (with the exception of the sensitive questions concerning contact, the use of secure accommodation and issues arising at the interim stage) were, following the Act, seen as internal matters for the local authority. Whether this is the appropriate distribution of functions is, naturally, debatable.

The whole issue was reopened by the implementation of the HRA 1998 and by the necessity for compatibility with the ECHR. Article 6 of the ECHR in

---

[219] See the White Paper, at para 31.

[220] See SM Cretney 'Defining the Limits of State Intervention' in D Freestone (ed) *Children and the Law* (Hull University Press, 1990), at p 68.

[221] This is governed by a modified statutory code contained in s 34 and the regulations made under that section.

[222] Under the former law, the courts had jurisdiction over decisions to 'refuse' or 'terminate' access but not over decisions regulating the amount or frequency of access; see the Child Care Act 1980, ss 12A–12G. It has been emphasised that the courts now have the final say on the whole question of contact. See, particularly, the remarks of Hale J in *Berkshire County Council v B* [1997] 1 FLR 171.

[223] The leading wardship case of *A v Liverpool City Council* [1982] AC 363 was such a case in which a mother's access had been curtailed by the local authority to one hour per month under supervision at a day nursery.

[224] See *Re C (Interim Care Order: Assessment)* [1997] 1 FLR 1 discussed in chapter 12 below.

particular requires that parents and children have effective access to the courts to determine disputes in relation to major issues affecting the life of the child following the making of a care order. In *Re S (Minors); Re W (Minors)*[225] the House of Lords did not go so far as to find the public law regime of the Children Act incompatible with the Convention but found that there was a 'lacuna' in the legislation in that there was no mechanism for monitoring on behalf of a young (incompetent) child the implementation of a local authority's care plan. Accordingly, s 26 of the the Children Act was amended, and regulations were introduced, to ensure that independent reviewing officers are charged with that task and can refer any problematic case to CAFCASS.[226]

Children and adult society

The Children Act, more than any legislation before it, gave recognition to the views of children and young people. As such, it can be argued that it marked a distinct movement away from the perception of children as recipients of welfare and towards the view that they are juristic persons with distinctive rights.

In several different instances, the legislation requires the wishes of children to be taken into account, to an extent appropriate to the individual child's age and understanding. This is a requirement which binds courts,[227] local authorities, voluntary organisations and private children's homes[228] and, arguably (following *Gillick*), school authorities, medical personnel and other outsiders.[229] Curiously, there is no corresponding legal duty placed on parents and others with parental responsibility, but the Scottish Law Commission proposed that such an obligation should be introduced into Scots law.[230] This was achieved by s 6(1) of the Children (Scotland) Act 1995, under which the parent, when reaching any major decision in fulfilling parental responsibilities or exercising parental rights, must have regard so far as practicable to the views of the child if he or she wishes to express them. The Children Act also gives greater autonomy to young people aged over 16 by providing that court orders should not generally be made or extended beyond that age,[231] that they should be able

---

[225] [2002] 1 FLR 815.
[226] Discussed further in chapter 12.
[227] Section 1(3)(a).
[228] Sections 22(4) and (5), 61(2) and (3) and 64(2) and (3).
[229] Since *Gillick* decides, at least in the context of children wishing to access medical treatment, that it is lawful for outsiders to have direct dealings with mature adolescents this might arguably imply an obligation to consult with them on major matters rather than to deal exclusively with their parents or other carers. See chapters 7 and 8 below.
[230] Scottish Law Com Discussion Paper No 88 *Parental Responsibilities and Rights: Guardianship and the Administration of Children's Property* (1990), at paras 2.41–2.42, and Law Com Report No 135 *Report on Family Law* (1992), at paras 2.64–2.65.
[231] Sections 9(6) and (7) and 91(10).

to seek a 'self-referral' into 'care'[232] and that those leaving substitute care should be given more assistance in making the transition to independent living in the community.[233]

The Children Act does not go so far as to confer complete independence on adolescents. It should be appreciated that parental responsibility continues right up to the age of majority, but the degree of control exercised by parents gradually diminishes as the child grows older.[234] There is, however, a more radical view that parental powers (responsibility if this is preferred) should terminate completely when a child has sufficient level of competence to be able to make his own decisions.[235] There is little in the Children Act to support this theory except, perhaps, the mature child's right to refuse a medical or psychiatric examination or other assessment.[236] Instead, the Children Act generally supports the notion of participatory decision-making which gives to young people a degree of self-determination. This general principle to have regard to children's views[237] marked an important adjustment in the balance of power between children and adult society.

Fathers and mothers

It is not difficult to discover in the Children Act provisions which adjust the relative positions of men and women in their role as parents. The Act does not openly differentiate between men and women but perpetuates distinctions between parents inside and outside marriage or civil partnership, although these have been reduced by the Adoption and Children Act 2002. The courts, too, have abandoned in theory their former practice of applying presumptions to the effect that young children should be with their mothers or that older boys should be with their fathers. Nonetheless, the House of Lords has (in a case from Scotland) reasserted the value of mothers to young children in a way

---

[232] 'Care' is used here in the non-technical sense since, by definition, a child who asks voluntarily to be accommodated is not in 'care' in the technical sense in which that term is now used in the legislation. See s 20, and chapter 10 below.

[233] Sections 23A–24C. The duties of local authorities towards such children have been significantly increased by the Children (Leaving Care) Act 2000, as amended and supplemented by the Children and Young Persons Act 2008.

[234] This was the classic view of the relationship between parents and adolescents expressed by Lord Denning MR in *Hewer v Bryant* [1970] 1 QB 357 at 369 and apparently accepted by the House of Lords in *Gillick*. For a perspective on Lord Denning's contribution in *Hewer v Bryant* itself see A Bainham 'Lord Denning as a Champion of Children's Rights: The Legacy of *Hewer v Bryant*' (1999) *Denning Law Journal* 81.

[235] J Eekelaar 'The Eclipse of Parental Rights' (1986) 102 LQR 4. For direct criticism of this radical interpretation of *Gillick*, see S Gilmore 'The Limits of Parental Reponsibility' in R Probert, S Gilmore and J Herring (eds) *Responsible Parents and Parental Responsibility* (Hart Publishing, 2009), ch 4.

[236] Sections 38(6), 43(8), 44(7) and Sch 3, para 4(4). The courts, however, have controversially taken the view that a child's objections, even under these provisions, may be overridden where his or her best interests require it by invoking the jurisdiction of the High Court. See, particularly, *South Glamorgan County Council v W and B* [1993] 1 FLR 574.

[237] See, particularly, ss 1(3)(a) and 22(4) and (5).

which some may think goes close to applying a presumption. In *Brixey v Lynas* Lord Jauncey of Tullichettle (who gave the only speech) said:[238]

> '... the advantage to a very young child of being with its mother is a consideration which must be taken into account in deciding where lie its best interests in custody proceedings in which the mother is involved. It is neither a presumption nor a principle but rather recognition of a widely held belief based on practical experience and the workings of nature ...'

He went on:

> 'Where a very young child has been with its mother since birth and there is no criticism of her ability to care for the child only the strongest competing advantages are likely to prevail.'

The abolition of parental guardianship, primarily to distinguish parenthood from guardianship, removed the anachronistic rule that the married father was the sole guardian of his child. When the Guardianship Act 1973 gave to the married mother equal parental rights and authority, it left untouched the sole guardianship of the father.[239] The Children Act thus completed the process of conferring on married parents equal status (by giving to each of them parental responsibility).[240] More significantly, the Children Act adjusted the legal position of unmarried parents and strengthened, in a number of respects, the legal position of the father. While the unmarried mother remained exclusively entitled to automatic parental responsibility,[241] the Children Act widened the mechanisms whereby the father might acquire it by agreement with the mother or by court order.[242] The Children Act did not confer on the unmarried man automatic parental responsibility, although it did bring him within the definition of 'parent' for most other purposes.[243] Thus, although the Act attached greater significance to unmarried fatherhood, especially in the context of stable cohabitation, it still preserved the essential inequality of motherhood and fatherhood outside marriage while supporting equality within marriage.[244] These differences have been greatly reduced, though far from eliminated, by the amendment introduced by the Adoption and Children Act 2002, the effect of which is to confer parental responsibility on the great majority of unmarried fathers who are registered as such at the time of the child's birth.

Where parental responsibility is shared between father and mother, either in marriage or where an unmarried father has acquired it by legal process, the law

---

[238] [1996] 2 FLR 499 at 505. See also *Re S (Children)* (unreported, 17 April 2002) CA in which the court referred to 'the very different role and functions of men and women'.

[239] See Law Com Working Paper No 91 *Review of Child Law: Guardianship* (1985), at paras 2.7–2.8.

[240] Section 2(1), and see chapter 4.

[241] Section 2(2).

[242] Section 4, discussed in detail in chapter 4.

[243] This arises by virtue of the incorporation of s 1 of the Family Law Reform Act 1987 by s 2(3) of the Children Act.

[244] These issues are discussed further in chapter 4 below.

takes a gender-neutral view of parenthood, at least in theory. The father or mother may exercise parental responsibility independently and each has an equal say in upbringing.[245] There has, nonetheless, been some speculation concerning the possible effect of the legislation on the respective child-rearing roles of men and women. One viewpoint is that the statutory framework was grounded in the notion of 'time-sharing' and a legal presumption of co-parenting which disguises and perpetuates substantial inequalities of power and responsibilities between men and women.[246] Some feminists have long argued that the concept of joint custody enabled 'absent' men to exercise control over their ex-wives without shouldering the responsibility of child care.[247] The idea of continuing parental responsibility could be viewed as a variant on this theme.

Against this, it has been argued that the legislation, if anything, further strengthened the relative position of women by placing so much weight on parental agreements.[248] There is overwhelming evidence that a very high percentage of these agreements result in women obtaining the primary, if not exclusive, child care role.[249] As will be discussed in chapter 5, the legislation and its judicial interpretation has to date resisted addressing this through the use of presumptions in matters of parental responsibility, contact and shared residence,[250] although the Children and Families Bill 2013 proposes to introduce a presumption in parental applications for contact and parental responsibility that a parent should have an involvement in the life of the child unless such involvement would put the child at risk of suffering harm.

It is unclear whether the Children Act has had any significant impact on the way in which society perceives the parenting responsibilities of men and women. But in asserting parenthood as a primary and gender-neutral status and in making it so difficult for either parent to divest himself or herself of parental responsibility, the Children Act has given tacit encouragement to the notion of equal co-parenting.

---

[245] Section 2(7).

[246] See, particularly, J Brophy 'Custody Law, Child Care, and Inequality in Britain' in C Smart and S Sevenhuijsen (eds) *Child Custody and the Politics of Gender* (Routledge, 1989), at p 217.

[247] See, for example, A Bottomley 'Resolving Family Disputes: a critical view' in MDA Freeman (ed) *The State, the Law and the Family* (Tavistock, 1984), at p 293. For a collection of essays offering feminist perspectives on the law affecting children see J Bridgeman and D Monk *Feminist Perspectives on Child Law* (Cavendish, 2000).

[248] A Bainham 'The Privatisation of the Public Interest in Children' (1990) 53 MLR 206, at pp 216–219.

[249] The empirical evidence of the Law Commission testified to this. See Priest and Whybrow, Law Com Supplement to Working Paper No 96 *Custody Law in Practice in the Divorce and Domestic Courts* (1986). There are approximately 10 times as many lone parent households headed by women as there are by men. See chapter 1.

[250] As in certain other jurisdictions. See chapter 4 below.

THE UNITED NATIONS CONVENTION ON THE RIGHTS OF THE CHILD

The United Nations Convention on the Rights of the Child (UNCRC) now constitutes the most authoritative and comprehensive statement of the fundamental rights of children covering civil and political, social, economic, cultural, recreational and humanitarian rights.[251] The expression 'rights' must be treated with some caution, since many of the aspirations for children set out in the UNCRC could arguably never be enforced directly as *legal* rights by *individual* children in the courts.[252] They are of a progressive and programmatic nature and, thus, dependent on political will and the availability and commitment of resources in individual countries. Others are more specific, and many of these were arguably already implemented in English law before the advent of the UNCRC.

The legal effect of the UN Convention

The UK ratified the UNCRC on 16 December 1991, but this does not mean that its substantive provisions directly form part of English domestic law.[253] In broad terms, the UK Government is legally bound to follow policies which are in conformity with the general and specific obligations set forth in the UNCRC. There have been tentative steps in recent years to give the UNCRC greater emphasis domestically. In Wales, ministers are now required to have regard to the UNCRC when deciding on provisions in enactments, formulating policy, or

---

[251] See, generally: D McGoldrick 'The United Nations Convention on the Rights of the Child' (1991) 5 IJLF 132; B Walsh 'The United Nations Convention on the Rights of the Child: A British View' (1991) 5 IJLF 170; and see also (1992) 6 IJLF at Part I which issue is devoted entirely to a re-evaluation of the concept of children's rights in the light of the UNCRC. It is also published as a separate volume: see P Alston, S Parker and J Seymour *Children, Rights and the Law* (Oxford University Press, 1992). For more detailed treatment, see R Hodgkin and P Newell *Implementation Handbook for the Convention on the Rights of the Child* (Unicef, 3rd edn, 2007); LJ LeBlanc *The Convention on the Rights of the Child* (University of Nebraska Press, 1995), and G Van Bueren *The International Law on the Rights of the Child* (Martinus Nijhoff, 1995). For further assessments of the contribution of the Convention to the cause of children's rights see J Fortin *Children's Rights and the Developing Law* (Cambridge University Press, 2009), ch 2; M Freeman *The Moral Status of Children* (Martinus Nijhoff, 1997) ch 6; M Freeman 'The End of the Century of the Child?' (2000) 53 *Current Legal Problems* 505, CM Lyon 'Children and the Law – towards 2000 and beyond' in C Bridge (ed) *Family Law Towards the Millennium: Essays for PM Bromley* (Butterworths, 1997). For a volume of essays evaluating the first decade of the Convention's operation see D Fottrell (ed) *Revisiting Children's Rights: 10 Years of the UN Convention on the Rights of the Child* (Kluwer, 2000), and for a more recent appraisal see U Kilkelly 'The CRC at 21: Assessing the Legal Impact' (2011) 62 *Northern Ireland Legal Quarterly* 143.

[252] Nonetheless, it can be persuasively argued that it is important to ascribe 'rights' to children even if some are unenforceable. See J Eekelaar 'The Importance of Thinking that Children have Rights' (1992) 6 IJLF 221, and M Freeman (above), especially ch 2.

[253] For a general discussion of the enforceability of the UNCRC, see G Van Bueren 'The United Nations Convention on the Rights of the Child: The Necessity of Incorporation into United Kingdom Law' [1992] Fam Law 373.

reviewing/changing existing policy.[254] From May 2014 the duty to pay regard to the obligations of the UNCRC will extend to the exercise by Welsh ministers of all of their functions.[255] Welsh ministers must set out and publish a scheme setting out the arrangements for compliance with these new duties,[256] and in due course report on compliance.[257] There is also a duty to promote knowledge of the UNCRC.[258] As we have seen above, it is also proposed to alter the role of the Children's Commissioner to provide for a greater focus on promoting and protecting the rights of children as set out in the UNCRC. However, the UNCRC is otherwise not incorporated into domestic law in England and Wales and it is not, therefore, open to individual children to bring proceedings before the national courts, based solely on alleged violations of the UNCRC which affect them.[259] In this respect its effect is quite different from that of the ECHR since implementation of the HRA 1998. Some countries, for example the Netherlands and Spain, have a tradition of incorporating human rights treaties such as this directly into national law, but this is not the case in the UK.[260]

This means that the accountability of the Government is likely to be achieved more through political than legal means. Quite apart from legal redress, however, Van Bueren has noted that human rights treaties may be utilised as educational instruments and as evidence of the need for reform of national laws. So far as education is concerned, there is a specific obligation on States, under Art 42, to make the UNCRC's provisions and principles, by appropriate and active means, widely known to adults and children. Political accountability leading to reform of national laws and practices is perhaps the key to enforcement of the UNCRC at the national level. In this respect, the Committee on the Rights of the Child, established under Art 43, has a vital role.[261] This Committee consists of 'ten experts of high moral standing and

---

[254] The Rights of Children and Young Persons (Wales) Measure 2011, s 1(2) and (3).

[255] Ibid, s 1(1).

[256] Ibid, ss 2 and 3.

[257] Ibid, s 4.

[258] Ibid, s 5.

[259] It is not, however, improbable that the spirit if not the letter of the UNCRC will increasingly be used in legal arguments in future. For a good example, see Ward LJ's judgment in *Re H (Paternity: Blood Test)* [1996] 2 FLR 65 which was clearly influenced by Art 7 of the Convention. See also *Re H and A (Paternity: Blood Tests)* [2002] 1 FLR 1145; and see further chapter 3 below. The principles of the UN Declaration of the Rights of the Child 1959 are, however, now likely to be of less assistance, especially where they may be thought to conflict with, or at least be superseded by, the 1989 UNCRC. Thus, in *Re A (Children: 1959 UN Declaration)* [1998] 1 FLR 354, the Court of Appeal held that the judge had erred in granting residence to the mother in relation to a toddler and rejecting the welfare officer's recommendations for a residence order to be made in favour of the father. The mother had relied in part on Principle 6 of the 1959 Declaration to the effect that a child of tender years should not, save in exceptional circumstances, be separated from its mother. The court said that the relevance and value of the 1959 Declaration, then 40 years old, was most doubtful. Moreover, the UNCRC of 1989 was gender-neutral. See also *Brixey v Lynas* [1996] 2 FLR 499.

[260] See Van Bueren (above) for further discussion. In English law domestic legislation is required for this purpose, as in the case of the HRA 1998.

[261] But for criticism of the effectiveness of the Committee and the reporting system under the UNCRC, see L Woll 'Reporting to the UN Committee on the Rights of the Child: A catalyst

recognised competence in the field covered by [the] Convention',[262] elected by the States parties. The main function of the Committee is to produce periodic reports on the operation of the UNCRC under Arts 44 and 45.[263] States have undertaken to report on the 'measures they have adopted which give effect to the rights recognised ... and on the progress made on the enjoyment of those rights'.[264] These 'reports' must indicate factors and difficulties affecting the degree of fulfilment of the obligations in individual countries.[265] The Reports are to be made public, and the Committee must report biennially to the General Assembly through the Economic and Social Council.[266] More significantly, the Committee may make suggestions and general recommendations on the strength of the information which it receives under Arts 44 and 45. These are then transmitted to the General Assembly and the State concerned, together with any comments made by that State.[267]

A poor track record of implementation by individual States may, through these procedures, become a matter of public record and accountability within the international community. It is conceivable that this may have a potentially greater impact than recourse to an international tribunal might have done. The UK's first report was submitted in 1994, followed by a second report in 1999 which was updated in 2002. Combined third and fourth UK reports were sent to the Committee in July 2007.[268] The Committee's first report on the UK was less than glowing about the Government's record under the Convention. Among the matters it criticised were the extent of child poverty, the law permitting corporal punishment of children, the low age of criminal responsibility and the lack of children's rights in the educational sphere.[269] These criticisms were substantially repeated in the Committee's second report on the UK.[270] The Committee's concluding observations on the third and

---

for domestic debate and policy change?' (2000) *International Journal of Children's Rights* 71; and M Freeman 'The End of the Century of the Child?' (2000) 53 *Current Legal Problems* 505 at 509–510.

262 UNCRC, Art 43(2).

263 For discussion of the Committee's role, see C Hamilton 'Children's Rights and the role of the UN Committee on the Rights of the Child: Underlying Structures for States in Implementing the Convention on the Rights of the Child' [2010] *International Family Law* 31.

264 Ibid, Art 44(1).

265 Ibid, Art 44(2); and see Committee on the Rights of the Child 'Treaty-specific Guidelines regarding the Form and Content of Periodic Reports to be Submitted by States Parties under article 44, paragraph 1 (b), of the Convention on the Rights of the Child' (CRC/C/58/Rev.2, 2010).

266 Ibid, Art 44(5).

267 Ibid, Art 45.

268 See also the UK Children's Commissioners' Report to UN Committee on the Rights of the Child (June 2008).

269 See United Nations *Concluding Observations of the Committee on the Rights of the Child: United Kingdom of Great Britain and Northern Ireland* CRC/C/15Add34 (1995), and see U Kilkelly 'The UN Committee on the Rights of the Child – an evaluation in the light of recent UK experience' [1996] CFLQ 105.

270 See United Nations Committee on the Rights of the Child, Thirty-First Session *Concluding Observations: United Kingdom of Great Britain and Northern Ireland* (2002).

fourth UK reports in 2008[271] pursued similar themes, and demonstrated that the UK was falling short in implementing the UNCRC at a general level and across a range of specific areas. The Committee was particularly concerned at the 'general climate of intolerance and negative public attitudes towards children, particularly adolescents ... including in the media' which 'may be often the underlying cause of further infringements of their rights', and called for urgent action to address this. Specific areas of concern included children's civil liberties, in particular rights of protest and protection of children's privacy from media intrusion, children's health and welfare, measures to improve protection from violence and bullying, and to address the UK's high teenage pregnancy rates. The UK's fifth periodic report is expected by 14 January 2014.

General aims and general obligations

The general aims of the UNCRC have been referred to as the '4 Ps' – *prevention, protection, provision*, and *participation*.[272] As to *prevention*, there are Articles relating to preventive health care,[273] preventing child abduction[274] and prohibiting discrimination against children.[275] As to *protection*, the UNCRC seeks to protect children from all forms of torture, cruel, inhuman and degrading treatment and punishment, abuse and exploitation.[276] As to *provision*, there are Articles creating rights of recipience in education[277] and social security,[278] the right to rest and leisure,[279] as well as the more general right to an adequate standard of living.[280] Rights of *participation* are recognised in Articles which provide for access to information,[281] freedom of expression[282] and the right of the child to express his views.[283]

The UNCRC applies to 'every human being below the age of eighteen years unless, under the law applicable to the child, majority is attained earlier'.[284] Parties to the Convention are required to 'respect and ensure' that the rights in the UNCRC are extended to all children within their jurisdiction 'without discrimination of any kind, irrespective of the child's or his or her parents' or

---

[271] United Nations *Concluding Observations of the Committee on the Rights of the Child: United Kingdom of Great Britain and Northern Ireland* CRC/C/GBR/CO/4, 3 October 2008, 49th session.
[272] See the discussion in G Van Bueren 'The UN Convention on the Rights of the Child' (1991) 3 JCL 63.
[273] UNCRC Art 24.
[274] Ibid, Art 11.
[275] Ibid, Art 2.
[276] Ibid, Art 37.
[277] Ibid, Art 28.
[278] Ibid, Art 29.
[279] Ibid, Art 31.
[280] Ibid, Art 27.
[281] Ibid, Art 17.
[282] Ibid, Art 13.
[283] Ibid, Art 12.
[284] Ibid, Art 1.

legal guardian's race, colour, sex, language, religion, political or other opinion, national, ethnic or social origin, property, disability, birth or other status'.[285]

Article 3 arguably contains the most important principle in the UNCRC, since it is the general standard which must be applied throughout the Convention to the more specific rights guaranteed by it. The Declaration of Geneva 1924 and the Declaration of the Rights of the Child 1959 had both embodied the general principle that 'mankind owes the child the best it has to give'. The UNCRC provides:[286]

> 'In all actions concerning children, whether undertaken by public or private social welfare institutions, courts of law, administrative authorities or legislative bodies, the best interests of the child shall be a primary consideration.'

Family lawyers will immediately detect echoes of the 'welfare principle' in English law but will also be struck by the difference in wording between the two provisions. First, the best interests of the child are expressed to be *primary*, but not paramount, and secondly, they are only *a* primary consideration and not *the* primary consideration. As argued above, it may be that a reformulation of the welfare principle in the Children Act, making children's welfare the primary but not paramount consideration, might be more realistic in the light of human rights obligations towards adult parties. On the other hand, the domestic welfare principle applies only to courts and only in those instances in which the upbringing of the child is the central issue. The UN principle, in contrast, applies to a much wider range of public and private institutions, courts, authorities and bodies.[287] Quite apart from all the difficulties of interpretation of 'welfare',[288] it is plain that States may, under the UNCRC, have regard to other factors in discharging their obligations and may, conceivably, find that these outweigh the interests of the children in issue. Article 3[289] goes on to provide:

> 'States parties undertake to ensure the child such protection and care as is necessary for his or her well-being, taking into account the rights and duties of his or her parents, legal guardians, or other individuals legally responsible for him or her, and, to this end, shall take all appropriate legislative and administrative measures.'

Reading this with the preamble, which talks of taking due account of 'the importance of the traditions and cultural values of each people for the protection and harmonious development of the child', Eekelaar has commented that, prima facie, 'the way seems open for almost unrestricted welfarism by the injection of adult values into a conception of what constitutes the "best interests" of the child', but he notes that this must be read 'in the

---

[285] Ibid, Art 2(1).
[286] Ibid, Art 3(1).
[287] See Part I of this chapter for a discussion of the nuances of the welfare principle.
[288] Ibid.
[289] UNCRC, Art 3(2).

context of the series of explicit rights which the Convention protects'.[290] Thus, the apparently open-ended discretion which States have in promoting the best interests of children is circumscribed by a whole range of specific duties. This is not unlike the position of parents themselves, exercising parental responsibility.[291] Difficult questions can undoubtedly arise concerning the application of the best interests doctrine in very different cultural contexts.[292]

The obligations of States to children are also in a sense qualified by specific duties owed to parents and other carers. The UNCRC assumes that many of the child's welfare needs will be met by his primary carers[293] but also requires States to respect the rights and duties of these adults. Article 5 provides:[294]

> 'State parties shall respect the responsibilities, rights and duties of parents or, where applicable, the members of the extended family or community as provided for by the local custom, legal guardians or other persons legally responsible for the child, to provide, in a manner consistent with the evolving capacities of the child, appropriate direction and guidance in the exercise by the child of the rights recognised in the present Convention.'

One way of looking at this provision is to regard it as merely reflecting the realities of life. Children do not exist in a vacuum and 'the Convention is not simply an exercise in abstraction'.[295] The rights of children must inevitably be secured in large measure by the actions of adults, usually those with their primary care, but in exercising these adult rights and duties in relation to children, the UNCRC requires those concerned to provide direction and guidance which is *consistent* with the rights set out in the Convention and not inconsistently with them.[296] Another way of viewing the Article is that it imports into the international arena all the uncertainties and difficulties which surround the interaction of children's rights and parental rights and responsibilities in domestic law.[297] The fact is that there may be a conflict between adults' and children's rights, and the UNCRC acknowledges this.[298] As McGoldrick has astutely observed, 'those charged with providing "appropriate direction and guidance" to the child on the exercise of its rights may well have an interest, personal or institutional, in ensuring that the child does not exercise

---

[290] J Eekelaar 'The Importance of Thinking that Children have Rights' (1992) 6 IJLF 221, at p 231.

[291] See chapter 4 below.

[292] This question is explored in depth in P Alston (ed) *The Best Interests of the Child* (Clarendon, 1994).

[293] UNCRC, Art 3(2).

[294] See also Art 14(2) which similarly recognises the parental role in the context of the child's right to 'freedom of thought, conscience and religion'.

[295] J Eekelaar (above), at p 233.

[296] J Eekelaar (above), at p 233.

[297] As to which, see particularly chapter 7 below.

[298] For further discussion see A Bainham 'Children Law at the Millennium' in S Cretney (ed) *Family Law: Essays for the New Millennium* (Family Law, 2000) especially, at pp 113–114.

its rights'.[299] The practical application of the concept of evolving capacities of the child may, therefore, be no less fraught than it is in English domestic law.

Specific rights

It is not possible here to provide a comprehensive analysis of each and every Article of the UNCRC, or of what the various rights may mean for children in English law. Instead, an attempt will be made to identify some of the more significant Articles commenting, where appropriate, on the current state of English law. It should also be noted that Optional Protocols to the Convention governing, respectively (i) the sale of children, child prostitution and child pornography, and (ii) the involvement of children in armed conflicts, came into force early in 2002.[300] In December 2011, a third optional protocol was approved on a Communications Procedure, which will allow individual children to submit complaints regarding specific violations of their rights under the Convention. The Protocol opened for signature in 2012.

The right to life and development

Article 6 requires States to recognise that every child has the inherent right to life and to ensure, to the maximum extent possible, the survival and development of the child. This provision clearly has implications for medical decision-making but, as discussed later, the right to life and survival may have to be qualified in those instances in which a minimal quality of life is not sustainable.[301]

The right to an identity

Two Articles are concerned with this. Article 7(1) requires that the child 'shall be registered immediately after birth and shall have the right from birth to a name, the right to acquire a nationality, and, as far as possible, the right to know and be cared for by his or her parents'.[302] This is fast becoming one of the most significant and frequently cited provisions in the Convention since it is closely associated with recent claims that children have a right to knowledge of their biological origins.[303] It will be noted here that the UNCRC does not distinguish between married and unmarried parents and also that Art 2, the

---

[299] D McGoldrick 'The United Nations Convention on the Rights of the Child' (1991) 5 IJLF 132, at pp 138–139.

[300] See U Kilkelly 'Annual Review of International Family Law' in A Bainham (ed) *The International Survey of Family Law (2004 Edition)* (Family Law, 2004) p 1, at pp 17–18.

[301] The right to life is also enshrined in Art 2 of the ECHR. Neither of these Articles, it must be said, greatly influenced the Court of Appeal in *Re A (Conjoined Twins: Medical Treatment)* [2001] 1 FLR 1, a case in which the right to life was surely at issue. See further chapter 8 below.

[302] See K O'Donovan 'Interpretations of Children's Identity Rights' in D Fottrell (ed) *Revisiting Children's Rights* (Kluwer, 2000); and S Besson 'Enforcing the Child's Right to know her Origins: Contrasting Approaches under the Convention on the Rights of the Child and the European Convention on Human Rights' (2007) 21(2) *International Journal of Law, Policy and the Family* 137.

[303] This is an issue in many different contexts such as where there is a dispute over paternity (see

anti-discrimination provision, prohibits discrimination on the basis of status. The implications for English law, and for the laws of many other countries, may be that procedures for establishing paternity and giving recognition to the parental responsibility of unmarried fathers need to be improved.[304]

Under Art 8, States undertake to 'respect the right of the child to *preserve* his or her identity, including nationality, name and family relations as recognised by law without unlawful interference'. This Article was an Argentinian initiative inspired by the 'disappearance' of an estimated 150–170 children in Argentina between 1975 and 1983.[305]

The English reforms providing for the continuity of parental responsibility, especially post-divorce, may be viewed as an aspect of preserving the child's identity, as may the shift towards more open adoption;[306] and preserving family relations clearly has implications for rights of ongoing contact between parent and child.[307]

Separation from parents

Article 9 requires States to 'ensure that a child shall not be separated from his or her parents against their will, except when competent authorities subject to judicial review determine, in accordance with applicable law and procedures, that such separation is necessary for the best interests of the child'.[308] Where the child *is* separated, the State must respect the right of the child 'to maintain personal relations and direct contact with both parents on a regular basis, except if it is contrary to the child's best interests'.[309]

The right of the child to express views

Article 12(1) is another of the Convention's most important Articles. It requires States to 'assure to the child who is capable of forming his or her own views the right to express those views freely in all matters affecting the child, the views of the child being given due weight in accordance with the age and maturity of the child'.[310]

This is close to the formulation which appears in several places in the Children Act[311] but its ambit extends well beyond those specific instances. Rather more

---

chapter 3), where the child has been conceived with the use of donated gametes (see chapter 3) and following the adoption of a child (see chapter 13).

[304] See chapters 3 and 4 below.
[305] See Van Bueren (above), at pp 118–120.
[306] See chapters 4 and 13 below.
[307] See chapter 5.
[308] UNCRC, Art 9(1).
[309] Ibid, Art 9(3).
[310] Many useful articles, case reports and other materials relating to the general issue of the representation of children in legal proceedings are to be found in the journal *Representing Children* published by the National Youth Advocacy Service.
[311] Especially that in s 1(3)(a).

troubling from an English perspective is Art 12(2), which states that 'the child shall in particular be provided the opportunity to be heard in any judicial and administrative proceedings affecting the child, either directly, or through a representative or an appropriate body, in a manner consistent with the procedural rules of national law'. Although it has been doubted that this necessarily entails separate representation of the child[312] it is the case that representation in England is patchy, and there must also be doubt about whether the lack of independent representation of children's views in the educational sphere conforms with the spirit, if not the letter, of this Article. Article 12(2) should now be considered alongside the European Convention on the Exercise of Children's Rights 1996, which has as its essential aim to grant *procedural* rights to children in family proceedings and to improve their rights of participation in such proceedings.

Civil rights

Articles 13–17 deal with some of the classic civil liberties recognised by liberal democracies and expressly apply these to children. Thus, subject to certain qualifications, Art 13 recognises the child's right to 'freedom of expression'. Article 14 requires States to respect the right of the child to 'freedom of thought, conscience and religion' but this is qualified by the rights and duties of parents to give direction to the child. Article 15 upholds the right of the child to 'freedom of association and to freedom of peaceful assembly'. Article 16 protects the child against interference with 'his or her privacy, family, home or correspondence', while Art 17 requires States to ensure that the child has 'access to information' on a range of material, especially that aimed at the promotion of his or her social, spiritual and moral well-being and physical and mental health.

Parental responsibilities

Under Art 18(1), States must 'use their best efforts to ensure recognition of the principle that both parents have common responsibilities for the upbringing and development of the child'. They must also recognise that parents or guardians 'have the primary responsibility for the upbringing and development of the child'.

This would, again, appear to have implications for the law applying to unmarried fathers. The Scottish Law Commission was clearly of the view that it required *automatic* rights for parents whether they were married or not and proposed changes to Scots law to give effect to this. These proposals were not accepted by the Westminster Parliament and did not find their way into the Children (Scotland) Act 1995. The reference to the *primary* responsibility of parents implies a *secondary* responsibility in the State. This is borne out by Art 18(2) which requires States to 'render appropriate assistance to parents and

---

[312] D McGoldrick 'The United Nations Convention on the Rights of the Child' (1991) 5 IJLF 132, at p 141.

legal guardians in the performance of their child-rearing responsibilities and [to] ensure the development of institutions, facilities and services for the care of children'. Article 18(3) also requires them to 'take all appropriate measures to ensure that children of working parents have the right to benefit from child-care services and facilities for which they are eligible'.

Child protection

Articles 19–24 can all be said to relate to aspects of the protection of children, either generally, or specifically, to such groups of children as refugees[313] or disabled children.[314] Article 19 requires States to 'take all appropriate legislative, administrative, social and educational measures to protect the child from all forms of physical or mental violence, injury or abuse, neglect or negligent treatment, maltreatment or exploitation, including sexual abuse, while in the care of parent(s), legal guardian(s) or any other person who has the care of the child'. Article 20 provides that a child 'temporarily or permanently deprived of his or her family environment … shall be entitled to special protection and assistance provided by the State'. It also states that, when considering solutions, 'due regard shall be paid to the desirability of continuity in a child's upbringing and to the child's ethnic, religious, cultural and linguistic background'. As discussed later,[315] these considerations are now incorporated in the Children Act, and the adequacy of Part IV, regulating care and supervision, should be evaluated in the light of the above Articles.

Article 21 regulates various aspects of adoption. Of particular interest is the requirement that States which 'recognise and/or permit the system of adoption shall ensure that the best interests of the child shall be the paramount consideration'. This is now the position under the Adoption and Children 2002, whereas under the Adoption Act 1976 the child's welfare was the 'first' but not 'paramount' consideration.[316] This controversial change is discussed in chapter 13. Article 24 deals with protection of the child's health, and requires States to 'recognise the right of the child to the enjoyment of the highest attainable standard of health and to facilities for the treatment of illness and rehabilitation of health'.[317] This and several other Articles have major resource implications and the State's obligations must be viewed as programmatic or progressive.

---

[313] UNCRC, Art 22.

[314] Ibid, Art 23. English law has responded to some extent to the concerns of this Article in the Carers and Disabled Children Act 2000. For an account of state support of care, see J Herring *Caring and the Law* (Oxford: Hart Publishing, 2013), esp ch 4 and B Sloan *Informal Carers and Private Law* (Hart, 2012).

[315] See chapters 10–12 below.

[316] For discussion in this context, see B Sloan 'Conflicting rights: English adoption law and the implementation of the UN Convention on the Rights of the Child' [2013] CFLQ 40.

[317] UNCRC, Art 24(2) also importantly requires States to take appropriate measures in relation to various forms of preventive medicine.

Recipience of social welfare

Articles 26–31 are a cluster of Articles dealing with the right of the child to receive various forms of social welfare. Article 26 protects the child's right to social security while taking into account in particular 'the resources and the circumstances of the child and persons having responsibility for the maintenance of the child'.

Article 27(1) requires States to recognise 'the right of every child to a standard of living adequate for the child's physical, mental, spiritual, moral and social development'. However, this is then qualified by references to the 'abilities and financial capacities' of the child's carers[318] and the national conditions and means of States.[319] Subject to this, States are required to assist carers to implement the child's right by providing material assistance and support programmes directed, in particular, towards nutrition, clothing and housing. Article 27(4) is an interesting provision from the English perspective since it would seem to provide some justification for the controversial principles of the child support legislation.[320] It requires States to 'take all appropriate measures to secure the recovery of maintenance for the child from the parents or other persons having financial responsibility for the child ...'. While the motivation behind this provision is undoubtedly to benefit the child rather than the Exchequer (as contrasted with that of the English Child Support Acts), this must be seen in the light of the principle that the *primary* responsibility for the child's financial support under the UNCRC is the *parent's*, and the State's responsibility, through social security, is *secondary*.

Articles 28 and 29 relate to education which is considered later.[321] Article 30 deals with rights of minority groups and provides that, in those States 'in which ethnic, religious and linguistic minorities or persons of indigenous origin exist, a child belonging to such a minority or who is indigenous shall not be denied the right, in community with other members of his or her group, to enjoy his or her own culture, to profess and practise his or her own religion, or to use his or her own language'.[322] Article 31(1) upholds the child's recreational rights. It requires States to recognise 'the right of the child to rest and leisure, to engage in play and recreational activities appropriate to the age of the child and to participate freely in cultural life and the arts'.

---

[318] UNCRC, Art 27(2).

[319] Ibid, Art 27(3).

[320] See chapter 9.

[321] See chapter 17.

[322] For an excellent discussion of children's rights and cultural issues, which addresses the rival philosophical positions of monism, cultural relativism and cultural pluralism, see M Freeman *The Moral Status of Children* (Martinus Nijhoff, 1997) ch 7. See also M Freeman 'Children and Cultural Diversity' in D Fottrell (ed) *Revisiting Children's Rights* (Kluwer, 2000), and J Eekelaar 'Children Between Cultures' (2004) 18(2) *International Journal of Law, Policy and the Family* 178 – 194. Also useful, especially in the context of medical procedures, is C Bridge 'Religion, Culture and the Body of the Child' in A Bainham, S Day Sclater and M Richards (eds) *Body Lore and Laws* (Hart Publishing, 2002).

Protection against exploitation

Articles 32–35 recognise the child's right to protection from various forms of exploitation, including economic exploitation,[323] protection against narcotics,[324] sexual exploitation and sexual abuse,[325] and trafficking in children.[326] Other Articles: protect the child against torture or other cruel, inhuman or degrading treatment or punishment;[327] require States to abide by the rules of international humanitarian law regarding children and armed conflicts;[328] place States under rehabilitative duties towards child victims of the kinds of harm contemplated by the UNCRC;[329] and regulate the treatment of children under the criminal law.[330]

Evaluation of the UNCRC

Critics of international law often question its value and whether it is truly law at all, in view of the difficulties of enforcement. Yet, while it is fair to say that there is much in the UNCRC which can only be achieved with political will and a massive commitment of resources, the UNCRC, like domestic law, should not be evaluated solely on the basis of its lack of direct legal enforceability. The educative and symbolic effect of internationally agreed norms (against which domestic standards may be measured)[331] is also important. In this respect the Convention is extremely successful. McGoldrick has pointed out that the UNCRC is evidence that the international community has adopted a broad consensus on what rights children have, and on what the obligations of the family, society and the international community should be.[332] The Convention has been ratified by almost all States, a high number of which have engaged in law reform since ratification. Of 52 States studied in research by UNICEF in 2007,[333] two thirds had incorporated the Convention directly into national law and one third had made provision for children's rights in constitutional documents. The Convention has also had an impact on international law, influencing the development of other Conventions.[334] The UNCRC is

---

[323] UNCRC, Art 32.

[324] Ibid, Art 33.

[325] Ibid, Art 34.

[326] Ibid, Art 35. See J Jones 'Human trafficking in the UK: a focus on children' [2012] CFLQ 77.

[327] Ibid, Art 37.

[328] Ibid, Art 38.

[329] Ibid, Art 39.

[330] Ibid, Art 40.

[331] See U Kilkelly and L Lundy 'Children's Rights in Action: Using the UN Convention on the Rights of the Child as an Auditing Tool' [2006] CFLQ 331.

[332] D McGoldrick 'The United Nations Convention on the Rights of the Child' (1991) IJLF 132, at p 158.

[333] See UNICEF Innocenti Research Centre *Law Reform and Implementation the CRC* (Florence, 2007) and see the discussion in U Kilkelly 'The CRC at 21: Assessing the Legal Impact' (2011) 62 *Northern Ireland Legal Quarterly* 143, at pp 146–148.

[334] For example the European Convention on the Exercise of Children's Rights. See Kilkelly (above) for other examples and further discussion.

increasingly cited in case law of both national and supra-national courts.[335] The Convention is thus playing an important role in applying or extending to children many of the human rights incontestably possessed by adults, and in enabling a more child-orientated or child-centred jurisprudence of human rights to develop.

A possible criticism is that it fails to go far enough in the direction of empowerment rights and is over-concerned with protection. It is certainly true that the majority of its Articles are protectionist in nature. One commentator's view is that it is a decidedly conservative instrument, built on compromise and concession, which is largely confined to reiterating existing human rights norms in their application to children.[336]

The UNCRC gives explicit expression to the primary duties of parents while also reaffirming the secondary role of the State, but goes beyond a recognition of adults' duties, to underline the importance of recognising children as persons capable of possessing rights. It is the possession of these rights which has the potential for transforming, not simply childhood, but adulthood as well. The point has been eloquently made by Eekelaar:[337]

'The strength of the rights formulation is its recognition of humans as individuals worthy of development and fulfilment. This is not an appeal to narrow self-interest. On the contrary it recognises the insight that people can contribute positively to others only when they are respected and fulfilled. And to recognise people as having rights from the moment of their birth continuously into adulthood could turn out, politically, to be the most radical step of all. If all *young people* are secured all the physical, social and economic rights proclaimed in the Convention, the lives of millions of adults of the next generation would be transformed. It would be a grievous mistake to see the Convention applying to childhood alone. Childhood is not an end in itself, but part of the process of forming the adults of the next generation. The Convention is for all *people*. It could influence their entire lives. If its aims can be realised, the Convention can truly be said to be laying the foundations for a better world.'

---

[335] See the examples of citation in the US Supreme Court and the ECHR given by Kilkelly (above), at pp 151–152.

[336] LJ LeBlanc (above). See also M Freeman (above), especially ch 4.

[337] J Eekelaar 'The Importance of Thinking that Children have Rights' (1992) 6 IJLF 221, at p 234.

Part II

CHILDREN AND FAMILIES

The chapters in Part II are all concerned primarily with legal questions which relate to children's relationships with their families or carers. Chapter 3 examines how the law attributes legal parentage/parenthood for a child. This is followed, in chapter 4, with an account of the concept of parental responsibility in the Children Act 1989, how it is allocated or acquired, and some general principles as to its nature and scope. Chapter 5 then considers how the courts address issues or disputes concerning children in the private law. One issue between parents, which is addressed in chapter 5 and which is increasingly exercising the courts, is a parent's wish to relocate from the jurisdiction with a child. Chapter 6 builds on that discussion by examining the issue of international child abduction and the various remedies available to secure a swift return to the jurisdiction when a child is unlawfully removed. Having explained the law on parenthood and parental responsibility and how disputes concerning the exercise of parental responsibility are resolved by the courts, chapter 7 reflects more generally on the legal relationship between children and parents, examining the concepts of children's and parents' rights and responsibilities, and their interaction.

The remaining two chapters in Part II deal with two of the most significant spheres of parental responsibility which have, particularly in recent years, been fertile areas of dispute. Chapter 8 considers medical decision-making which has often been the site of the most difficult questions concerning the interrelationship of children's rights and parents' rights and responsibilities. Chapter 9 discusses the principles which govern the ownership and management of children's property and responsibility for their financial support.

Chapter 3

PARENTAGE

INTRODUCTION

Distinction between parentage or parenthood and parental responsibility

Who in law are a child's parents? English law draws a distinction between *being a legal parent* ('parentage', sometimes also referred to as 'parenthood') on the one hand and *having parental responsibility* ('parenting' or raising a child) on the other.[1] Distinctive legal incidents attach to each and it may therefore be important in relation to a child to know whether a person is his parent or has parental responsibility for him, has both, or neither.

It should also be noted that the common understanding of the term 'parentage' may well not coincide with the legal concept of 'being a parent'. It has been pointed out[2] that issues about 'parentage' are generally associated with questions about the *biological* position. If we say that someone's parentage is unknown or in doubt this usually means that it is unclear who his biological father (much less commonly, his mother) is. We are not usually concerned here with the question of who is looking after a child or has the legal right to do so, perhaps more associated with the notion of 'parenthood'. A meaningful distinction might therefore be drawn between these two ideas with 'parentage' being a term confined to describing the child's relationship with his or her two biological parents, irrespective of whether they are also the legal parents. The term 'parenthood' might then be used to describe the latter. If that were to happen clearly the two would coincide the majority of the time, but there would also be instances in which they would not. In those cases 'parentage' could be seen as a useful concept for encapsulating the child's interest in having a connection with the biological parents. It should be emphasised, however, that this distinction is not drawn in legislation or in judicial decisions. While therefore this debate should be borne in mind, the primary focus of this chapter is on how the law determines the *legal parents* of the child.

---

[1]   On the definition of parenthood generally see A Bainham, S Day Sclater and M Richards (eds) *What is a Parent?* (Hart Publishing, 1999), ch 2. For a recent succinct exploration of the debates around parenthood see J Herring, R Probert and S Gilmore *Great Debates: Family Law* (Palgrave Macmillan, 2012), ch 2. For an exploration of issues surrounding parental responsibility see R Probert, S Gilmore and J Herring (eds) *Responsible Parents and Parental Responsibility* (Hart Publishing, 2009).

[2]   A Bainham, ibid.

The great majority of biological[3] parents have the status of legal parent *and* parental responsibility for the child. That is as might be expected in a society which imposes on biological parents the primary duties to care for the child from birth. The biological parent's legal position will usually therefore be the aggregate of having parentage and parental responsibility. It is still the case however that a small minority of fathers do not possess parental responsibility.[4] It is therefore possible to be a parent without parental responsibility. Of much greater statistical significance is the converse situation. Many of those who look after children, but who are not biological parents, can now acquire parental responsibility by a variety of mechanisms. Such carers are not legal parents; they do not generally have legal parentage but do possess parental responsibility and have an important legal status deriving from this. A key question therefore is whether the law, in seeking to give greater recognition to those who act as parents to children, should go so far as to make them the legal parents or should stop at allowing them to acquire parental responsibility.[5] While a respectable argument can be made for the latter approach, the trend in recent legislation is perhaps towards the former.[6]

So what in essence is the distinction between the legal concepts of parentage and parental responsibility?

Parentage is principally about formal kinship and family membership. The parent's own parents will, for example, in law be the child's grandparents and their brothers and sisters will be the child's uncles and aunts. While it may not matter a great deal of the time whether a child is formally related to someone or not, it clearly will in some contexts of which inheritance is perhaps the most obvious example.[7] The legal connection of parent and child matters for child support liability[8] and for automatic access to the courts in the event of disputes

---

3   In this chapter we use the term 'biological' parents where other terms, such as 'natural', 'birth' or 'genetic' parents might be and often are alternatively used. This is for consistency rather than for any other reason. Clearly 'genetic' may not always be easily equated with 'biological' as where, for example, a woman donates eggs and another woman undertakes the pregnancy and birth. The first woman is undoubtedly the 'genetic' mother but few would regard her, rather than the surrogate, as the 'biological' mother. It might also be argued that the man whose sole connection with a child is a single, fleeting act of sexual intercourse with the mother is better described as the 'genetic' rather than 'biological' father. In law nothing much turns on these terminological differences.

4   This can now only arise where the father is not registered, or where having acquired parental responsibility it is later removed by court order. See below.

5   For the argument that legal policy should be to confer parental responsibility but not parentage see A Bainham 'Arguments about Parentage' (2008) 67 *Cambridge Law Journal* 322 and T Callus 'First "designer babies", now à la carte parents' [2008] Fam Law 143. See also B Almond *The Fragmenting Family* (Oxford University Press, 2006).

6   Legal parentage for same-sex parents has, for example, been conferred in the context of adoption by the Adoption and Children Act 2002 and following assisted reproduction by the Human Fertilisation and Embryology Act 2008 discussed below.

7   Where the deceased left no will, succession is determined on intestacy in accordance with a ranked list of relatives under s 46 Administration of Estates Act 1925. These relationships derive from establishing parentage of an individual in the first instance and from there his or her wider family relationships.

8   See chapter 9.

arising about the child's upbringing.[9] A parent's consent is required, or must be dispensed with, before a child may be adopted which is not true of those who merely possess parental responsibility.[10] Perhaps most importantly, it is parents who on birth (in the case of unmarried fathers, birth registration) are given parental responsibility *automatically* for the child, with all the powers and duties which go with it. It is this which, more than anything else, distinguishes the parent's position from that of others who may be raising the child but are not his or her legal parents.

Parental responsibility is, in contrast, a very practical concept which encapsulates in law the powers and duties which are involved in caring for the child. It is defined in the Children Act 1989[11] as:

> 'all the rights, duties, powers, responsibilities and authority which by law a parent of a child has in relation to the child and his property.'

This so-called definition has been thought by some to be unhelpful in that it tells us nothing of the legal content of the parent-child relationship.[12] But in fact the general idea is clear enough. It is about the legal authority or power which someone raising a child needs to have in order to deal properly with third parties such as schools and hospitals, and generally to take the important decisions which may arise in the course of childhood. It can be seen to create a form of intermediate status between that of being the legal parent and merely someone looking after a child on an informal basis.[13] It creates a legal superiority for the holder. If, for example, a dispute arises between someone with and someone without parental responsibility, the decision will legally rest with the former.

A good illustration of the distinction between parentage and parental responsibility is provided by the decision of Moylan J in *T v B (Parental Responsibility: Financial Responsibility)*.[14] A lesbian couple had a child together with the aid of donor sperm under the licensed system under the then Human Fertilisation and Embryology Act 1990. The relationship broke down but the mother's former partner succeeded in obtaining a shared residence order which, importantly, gave her parental responsibility along with the mother. In due course the mother sought financial relief from her former

---

9   A parent of a child, whether or not possessing parental responsibility, may apply under s 10(4) Children Act 1989 for s 8 orders without leave.

10   Section 47(2) of the Adoption and Children Act 2002. It should be noted however that parental responsibility must also be possessed by the parent. The consent of a father who does not have it is not required. 'Parent' is defined by s 52(6) to mean a 'parent having parental responsibility'.

11   Section 3(1).

12   We consider this further in chapter 4.

13   Informal carers of children, of whom there are very many, have limited legal status. Under s 3(5) Children Act 1989 a person who does not have parental responsibility, but has care of a child, may 'do what is reasonable in the circumstances of the case for the purpose of safeguarding or promoting the child's welfare'.

14   [2010] 2 FLR 1966.

partner under Sch 1 of the Children Act 1989 on the basis that she was a 'parent' of the child. Moylan J rejected this construction of the legislation. 'Parent', he held, meant biological parent except where its meaning was expressly extended by statute. Legal parentage did not encompass social or psychological parents unless they were expressly given that status by statute. Obtaining parental responsibility did not make someone a parent. The point should be made that the facts of this case would now be unlikely to recur as, under the HFEA 2008, the partner of a mother is now likely to be the second legal parent where the child was the result of a joint enterprise by them.[15]

This chapter is concerned with *parentage*, or the question of how a child's legal parents are identified. The following chapter is concerned with *parental responsibility*, how it is acquired and what its significance is.

WHO ARE THE PARENTS?

It should be noted at the outset that we are not concerned here with *social* parenthood. Our task, for the moment, is to examine how a child's *legal* parents are identified. The great majority of the time we are talking about the processes whereby the child's two biological parents, his mother and father, are established and formally recorded, and with the legal procedures which exist for resolving disputes over parentage. It would be convenient for the student if the inquiry were unproblematically one of ascertaining the child's 'mother' and 'father'. However, a difficulty needs to be borne in mind in this respect.

Profound changes to law and society in recent decades have increasingly led to speculation about whether it is any longer the correct approach to take a gender-specific view of parentage. Developments in relation to same-sex parenting have especially raised this question. It is striking that, in both the modern adoption legislation[16] and the new legislation governing assisted reproduction,[17] Parliament has shrunk from recognising formally that a child may have two 'mothers' or two 'fathers', preferring in each case the gender-neutral language of the second 'parent'. Such an approach not only questions whether a child should be limited, as has historically been the case, to *one* mother and *one* father but also whether a child might be capable of having *more than two* legal parents.[18] For the present, English law does limit the child to two parents. This is another of the key distinctions between parentage and

---

[15] See below.

[16] Section 68(3) of the Adoption and Children Act 2002: 'A reference (however expressed) to the adoptive mother and father of a child adopted by: (a) a couple of the same sex, or (b) a partner of the child's parent, where the couple are of the same sex, is to be read as a reference to the child's adoptive *parents*' (authors' emphasis).

[17] Where the couple concerned is heterosexual, the 'agreed *fatherhood* conditions' must be satisfied under s 37. But when it comes to a same-sex female couple, we find that it is not the agreed motherhood conditions but the 'agreed female *parenthood* conditions' which must be met under s 44 (emphasis added).

[18] For further discussion see E Jackson 'What is a Parent?' in A Diduck and K O'Donovan, *Feminist Perspectives on Family Law* (Routledge-Cavendish, 2006), ch 4.

parental responsibility, since there may be more than two holders of parental responsibility and this is not infrequently the case.[19]

A key battleground between conservative traditionalists and modern liberals on this issue was the parliamentary struggle over the former provision in the Human Fertilisation and Embryology Act 1990 which required clinics as a condition of their licences to have regard in providing treatment services not only to the welfare of any intended child but also, specifically, to 'the need of that child for a father'.[20] The Joint Parliamentary Committee which considered the question,[21] had regard to evidence concerning the importance of the involvement of fathers in the well-being of children. In the end the Committee preferred the research evidence which appears to support the view that what is more important to the outcomes for children than relations with fathers as such is the presence of a *second parent*, of whatever gender, in their lives.[22] Accordingly the 2008 Act amends the provision still in the 1990 legislation to require clinics to have regard to the need of any intended child for 'supportive parenting'.

A related question is whether a child should always have, *at least potentially*[23] two parents, a mother and a father. There has long been a debate about whether women should be able to elect to have children without the inconvenience, as they might see it, of the involvement of a man except to the extent that sperm is required for conception. Does the autonomy and independence of women require that they be permitted to elect, from the very outset, to be single mothers by choice?[24] What are the implications of such an approach for the interests or rights of the child and the man in question?[25]

A final matter relevant to the question of gender and parentage is the position of transsexual or transgendered parents. The first rule to note is that only a man may be registered as the father of a child and only a woman as the mother.[26] In *X, Y and Z v The United Kingdom*[27] a female-to-male transsexual

---

[19] As where, for example, a step-father acquires it but the divorced father still retains and shares it, or where a child enters the care of the local authority which may involve a tripartite sharing of parental responsibility with the mother and father.

[20] HFEA 1990, s 13(5).

[21] *Joint Committee on the Human Tissue and Embryos (Draft) Bill, Volume I, Report*, HL Paper 169-I, HC Paper 630-I (2007).

[22] For the evidence the committee received on this question see paras 224–243.

[23] Potentially only because of the difficulties of establishing paternity in some cases.

[24] It is important to distinguish between single mothers by choice and single mothers/single parents more generally because the incidence of the latter is, of course, quite high following the breakdown of relationships.

[25] This is an issue which has recently been explored in F Kelly 'Autonomous from the start: single mothers by choice in the Canadian legal system' [2012] CFLQ 257.

[26] It should be noted however that under s 53(2) Human Fertilsation and Embryology Act 2008 'any reference (however expressed) to the father of a child who has a parent by virtue of s 42 or 43 is to be read as a reference to the woman who is a parent of the child by virtue of that section'. See the discussion of the 2008 Act below.

[27] (1997) 24 EHRR 143 and for commentary see A Bainham 'Sex, gender and fatherhood: does biology really matter?' (1997) CLJ 512.

unsuccessfully sought to be registered as the father of a child conceived through artificial insemination by donor. The Registrar-General refused to register him on the basis that only a biological male could be so registered. English law at the time did not recognise gender change and such a case would now be decided differently, provided that a full gender recognition certificate is obtained by the individual in question in accordance with the procedures established by the Gender Recognition Act 2004. Under this legislation, the effect of the full certificate is that 'the person's gender becomes for all purposes the acquired gender (so that, if the acquired gender is the male gender, the person's sex becomes that of a man and, if it is the female gender, the person's sex becomes that of a woman)'.[28]

The above position must, however, be carefully distinguished from the situation where a man is *already* a father, or a woman is *already* a mother, of a child before a change of gender takes place. In these circumstances they *remain*, respectively, the father or mother of the child. The 2004 Act[29] expressly preserves the existing position by providing that a full certificate does 'not affect the status of the person as the father or mother of the child'. It is possible that this could lead to the apparently bizarre situation in which the same individual is the mother to one child and the father to a subsequent child following a change of gender. The courts have also had to grapple already with the appropriate welfare response to a situation in which a parent has changed gender.[30]

In summary, it should be borne in mind in reading the following sections that legislation does not usually refer directly to 'mothers' or 'fathers'.[31] Most of the time the gender-neutral concept of the 'parent' is used though, exceptionally, provisions do refer specifically to 'mothers' or 'fathers'. The same may be said of international conventions.[32] It is nonetheless the case that, leaving aside the small minority of exceptional cases involving same-sex parents, the law usually does have to determine who is the child's mother and who is the father.

WHO IS THE MOTHER?

The Latin maxim *mater est quam gestio demonstrat* encapsulates the truth that, in the vast majority of cases, it will be obvious who is the mother of the child through the very act of childbirth. This will usually conclusively demonstrate who is the biological, and hence legal, mother from the moment of birth. This

---

[28]   Gender Recognition Act 2004, s 9(1).

[29]   Section 12.

[30]   See the Court of Appeal decision in *Re C (Contact: Moratorium: Change of Gender)* [2007] 1 FLR 1642.

[31]   There are noteworthy exceptions of which the most obvious are perhaps ss 2 and 4 Children Act 1989 which distinguish between mothers and fathers for the purposes of the acquisition of parental responsibility.

[32]   The UNCRC, for example, refers to parents throughout; it does so even in those articles such as Art 7 and Art 18 where its concern is clearly for the child's rights in relation to both father and mother. Rather than saying so as such, the references are to *both parents*.

presupposes, of course, that the birth was witnessed and then accurately recorded. This is a very unsafe assumption to make in many parts of the world in which there is an inadequate system of birth registration, or in which birth registration details are known to have been deliberately falsified for ulterior purposes.[33] But in England there is a direct connection between the National Health Service and the registration of births which means that the registrar will be automatically alerted when a child is born.[34] This will trigger statutory duties on the mother (and, where she is married, the father) to register the birth.

Even in English law there have been historical and contemporary examples of situations in which uncertainty has surrounded maternity; as where one woman tried to pass off another woman's child as her own[35] or, more recently, where a child has come to England from another country and there is uncertainty about whether the woman presenting as the mother is in fact so.[36] English law, unlike French law, does not permit a woman to give birth anonymously.[37] Every mother is under a legal obligation to register the child's birth within 42 days of its occurrence.[38] Where the mother is married this legal duty rests on both parents.[39] Where she is unmarried it is hers alone, though, as noted below, provisions in the Welfare Reform Act 2009 when implemented are intended to establish a norm of joint registration of birth by mother and father outside marriage just as within it.

Mothers and family life

Mention should also be made at this point of the ECHR and the important question of when 'family life' arises between a child and his mother. This can be

---

[33] For a good discussion of the lack of proper birth registration worldwide see L Huawen 'The child's right to birth registration' in P Lødrup and E Modvar (eds) *Family Life and Human Rights* (Gyldendal Akademisk, 2004), at p 441.

[34] See the discussion in A Bainham 'What is the point of birth registration?' (2008) 20 CFLQ 449, especially at 452.

[35] *Slingsby v Attorney-General* (1916) 33 TLR 120.

[36] *Re P (Identity of Mother)* [2012] 1 FLR 351 where the Court of Appeal in care proceedings held that it was manifestly unacceptable for an issue as important as a child's maternity to be left up in the air. If there was a refusal to take a sample for DNA testing, appropriate adverse inferences could be drawn under s 23 Family Law Reform Act 1969.

[37] As to which see *Odièvre v France* [2003] 1 FCR 621 and *Kearns v France* [2008] 1 FLR 888. For commentary on *Odièvre* see E Steiner 'Desperately seeking mother – anonymous births in the European Court of Human Rights' [2003] 15 CFLQ 425. Whether or not a woman should have this right is controversial as is the question whether she should be able to relinquish her child for adoption without informing the biological father or the maternal or paternal family. For a recent exploration of some of these issues see J Marshall 'Concealed births, adoption and human rights law: being wary of seeking to open windows into people's souls' (2012) 71 *Cambridge Law Journal* 325. For a Canadian perspective on these issues see L Chambers 'Newborn adoption: birth mothers, genetic fathers and reproductive autonomy' (2010) 26 *Canadian J of Family Law* 339. And generally see chapter 13 below.

[38] Section 2 of the Births and Deaths Registration Act 1953. And on birth registration generally see A Bainham, n 24 above.

[39] Ibid.

of critical importance since any parent wishing to invoke the concept of respect for family life under Art 8 must first establish that it in fact existed with the child. In the case of mothers this is straightforward, as the European Court of Human Rights ruled over thirty years ago in the *Marckx* case[40] that family life between mother and child arises at the moment of birth and is not dependent on the Mother undertaking any formal process of voluntary recognition of the child. In requiring Paula Marckx to do so, the Belgian state had violated both her convention rights and those of her child under Art 8 taken in conjunction with Art 14, which prohibits discrimination in relation to the enjoyment of convention rights. As we shall see, the position is very different in relation to the child's relationship with the father.

Adoption and assisted reproduction

The discussion so far has been concerned with biological mothers but English law now treats quite openly certain women as legal mothers who are *not* the biological mothers of the children concerned. Historically, this has been possible ever since the legal institution of adoption was introduced in England. Where a woman adopts a child, legally she is the mother.[41] More recently, radical changes to the law of parentage introduced by the Human Fertilisation and Embryology Act 2008 enable certain women to become legal parents (effectively legal mothers, though that terminology is not used) following licensed treatment involving them and their female partners. Before looking at these provisions it should be noted that, very unlike adoption, where the statutory procedures are followed, legal parentage is conferred more or less automatically, and certainly without any judicial scrutiny. The point is important because legal parentage through adoption and assisted reproduction are often viewed together as two mechanisms which separate legal and biological parentage. But in fact the two situations are quite different for a number of reasons.[42]

The 2008 Act governs the acquisition of legal parentage following use of techniques of assisted reproduction. In the case of women, the following rules apply. First, the woman who carries and gives birth to the child (the 'gestational' mother) is in law the child's mother whether or not she is also the child's genetic mother.[43] Secondly, it is expressly provided that a woman is not to be regarded as the legal parent by reason only of egg donation and being the genetic mother.[44] Thirdly, the civil partner of a legal mother will now become

---

[40]   *Marckx v Belgium* (1979–80) 2 EHRR 14 described by Pintens and Scherpe as not merely a landmark case but a 'meta-landmark' case because of the scale of its influence. See J Scherpe and W Pintens 'The Marckx Case: A Whole Code of Family Law?' in S Gilmore, J Herring and R Probert (eds) *Landmark Cases in Family Law* (Hart Publishing, 2011), at p 155.

[41]   Section 67 of the Adoption and Children Act 2002.

[42]   See below.

[43]   Section 33(1) provides: 'The woman who is carrying a child as a result of the placing in her of an embryo or of sperm and eggs, and no other woman, is to be treated as the mother of the child'.

[44]   Section 47.

the child's other legal parent unless, at the time of the mother's treatment, it is shown that she did not consent to it.[45] Fourthly, another woman (usually, but not necessarily, the female partner of a legal mother) may become the child's other legal parent if the so-called 'female parenthood conditions' are satisfied.[46] These conditions[47] in essence require that where a woman, W, has received licensed treatment, a second woman, P, will be treated as the second legal parent if both women have given formal notice to the responsible person (the clinic concerned) that they each consent to P being treated as the parent of any resulting child;[48] neither has withdrawn consent; W has not given a subsequent notice to the responsible person that she consents to another woman being treated as the parent of the child or a man being treated as the father; and W and P are not within the prohibited degrees of relationship to each other.

The final condition is of wider interest in that it involves extending the role of the prohibited degrees, which have traditionally controlled access into *marriage*. They now also control, at least in this context, access into *parentage*. In practice it means that, for example, a woman cannot nominate her sister or mother as the second legal parent.

It is finally provided that where either the mother's civil partner, or another woman, acquires parental status under these provisions, that no man is to be treated as the father of the child.[49] This rule preserves the position in English law that there cannot be three legal parents of a child, however much it might be arguable that there would be no social objection to a child having three such parents. If three people are involved in parenting, there is at least an argument that all three, whether two women and one man or two men and one woman, could be appropriately designated as legal parents. But that takes us back to the argument alluded to at the start of this chapter about whether parental responsibility, as opposed to parentage, might be the better vehicle for achieving this.

It is worth reflecting on how far we have come as a society in recognising the desires of adults, and their claims to equality in the treatment of their

---

[45] Section 42(1). This mirrors the rule relating the husband of a married mother and is one of many provisions both here and in the Civil Partnership Act 2004 designed to produce substantial equality between spouses and civil partners. The rule will apply even where the mother and her civil partner choose to engage the assistance of a known donor outside the licensed system. See *Re G; Re Z (Children: Sperm Donors: Leave to Apply for Children Act Orders)* [2013] EWHC 134 (Fam), [2013] 1 FLR 1334.

[46] Section 43.

[47] Section 44. The conditions are *not*, as noted above, referred to as the 'agreed motherhood conditions', perhaps reflecting the law's reluctance to accept that a child can have two legal mothers.

[48] If the status of legal parent is to be achieved there must be strict adherence to the formal requirements laid down in the legislation. In particular a properly informed consent must be given to the fertility clinic before treatment commences. See *AB v CD and the Z Fertility Clinic* [2013] EWHC 1418 (Fam), [2013] Fam Law 962.

[49] Section 45(1). Section 45(3) provides that this does not affect any presumption that a child is the legitimate child of the parties to a marriage.

relationships. It would be possible (though perhaps unlikely) for a woman during the course of treatment/pregnancy to have several relationships, with women or men. She is legally able to change her nomination of parentage, albeit with the consent of those involved, several times before a birth ultimately takes place. The question which perhaps needs to be asked is whether this is consistent with the emphasis which the law places elsewhere on the best interests, and increasingly the rights, of children. As indicated above, the adoption analogy is not a fair one because adoption occurs only after there has been some 'failure', in an entirely non-pejorative sense, in the birth family. It cannot take place without extensive social work and later judicial scrutiny. This is a far cry from the more or less automatic processes of the HFEA.

Surrogacy

In practice it might be said that there are many more instances of surrogate fatherhood than there are of surrogate motherhood in the sense that donation of sperm is common place. In contrast, the number of occasions on which a woman is prepared to carry and give birth to a child to be handed by agreement over to others is for obvious reasons much smaller. It is an arrangement which nonetheless raises profound questions with which the law must grapple.

Surrogate mothers

Surrogacy is an arrangement whereby a woman agrees to bear a child for someone else and to hand over that child, on birth, to another person or persons (the 'commissioning parents') with a view to relinquishing parental responsibility in their favour.[50] Contrary to popular belief, the idea of surrogacy is not revolutionary or new but has ancient antecedents. Pinhas Shifman has described how the practice was not unusual in biblical times as a means of compliance with the religious duty to procreate.[51] Such births were achieved through sexual intercourse with a concubine or, as Shifman puts it, 'surrogate wife'.[52] Nowadays, while this may still be the method in a small

---

[50] On surrogacy generally, see: D Morgan 'Making Motherhood Male: Surrogacy and the Moral Economy of Women' (1985) 12 *Journal of Law and Society* 219; D Morgan 'Who to be or not to be: The Surrogacy Story' (1986) 49 MLR 358; L Nielsen 'The Right to a Child versus the Rights of a Child'; and M Field 'Surrogate Motherhood' in J Eekelaar and P Sarcevic (eds) *Parenthood in Modern Society* (Martinus Nijhoff, 1993), chs 13 and 14 respectively. See also E Jackson *Regulating Reproduction: Law, Technology and Autonomy* (Hart Publishing, 2001), ch 6; RG Lee and D Morgan *Human Fertilisation and Embryology: Regulating the Reproductive Revolution* (Blackstone Press, 2001); D Morgan 'Enigma Variations: Surrogacy, Rights and Procreative Tourism' in R Cook, S Day Sclater and F Kaganas *Surrogate Motherhood* (Hart Publishing, 2003); M Brazier 'Can You Buy Children?' [1999] CFLQ 345; and M Hibbs 'Surrogacy: Who will be left holding the baby?' [2000] Fam Law 736.

[51] P Shifman 'A Perspective on Surrogate Motherhood in Jewish and Israeli Law' in A Bainham, DS Pearl and R Pickford (eds) *Frontiers of Family Law* (2nd edn, John Wiley & Sons, 1995), at pp 65–66.

[52] The classic examples being the transaction between Abraham, his wife Sarah, and Hagar the

minority of cases, the focus is on assisted reproduction in its various forms.[53] The carrying mother may have been inseminated artificially with the sperm of the commissioning 'father' or she may be genetically unrelated to the child where donated gametes from the commissioning parents or others may be used to create an embryo which is then carried to term by her. Either way, the carrying mother is deemed, in law, to be the mother of the child.[54]

Surrogacy arrangements, perhaps more than any other kind of familial arrangement, focus our attention on what is meant by being a parent. They might be thought to exemplify the case of the *intentional* parent having claims derived from intending to perform the social role of a parent.[55] Who could be more of an intentional parent than a man and woman, or two same-sex partners, who go to the extraordinary length of commissioning a woman to bear a child for them? Yet, paradoxically, surrogacy will often be inspired by what is thought to be the value of *biological* parenthood. More often than not, surrogacy will be triggered by a *man's* desire to have his own biological child where his wife or partner is unable to conceive or bear a child. We shall see that in order to obtain a 'parental order' at least *one* of the commissioning parents must be genetically related to the child. In surrogacy we can perhaps observe the deep ambivalence in society, reflected in the law, about the true nature of parenthood.

The effectiveness of surrogacy arrangements

The position in English law could be described as an official policy of discouraging surrogacy arrangements whilst providing some 'back-door' mechanisms for indirectly giving effect to them.[56] The matter was considered in depth by the Warnock Committee.[57] The Committee did not recommend either the recognition or the outright prohibition of surrogacy but did propose a ban on commercial arrangements. This recommendation was implemented by the

---

Egyptian, which resulted in the birth of Ishmael (Genesis 16:1–3) and that between Jacob, his wife Rachel, and Bilhah her maid, which led to the births of Dan and Naphtali (Genesis 30: 1, 3).

[53] For a readable and succinct description of the principal available methods of assisted conception, see B Dickens 'Reproductive Technology and the "new family"' in E Sutherland and A McCall Smith (eds) *Family Rights* (Edinburgh University Press, 1990), at p 21. For a more recent description of the various techniques, see E Jackson (above), ch 5.

[54] Section 33(1) HFEA 2008.

[55] On the doctrine of intention as it applies to parenthood, see C Barton and G Douglas *Law and Parenthood* (Butterworths, 1995), especially, at pp 50–52. See also *Johnson v Calvert* 5 Cal 4th 84 (1993) the leading authority on surrogacy in California. Here the genetic commissioning mother in a surrogacy arrangement was held to be the legal mother largely on the basis of her intention to act as such. The position contrasts starkly with the attribution of parentage under English law.

[56] A succinct summary of the then English law and policy relating to surrogacy arrangements may be gleaned from the judgment of Hale LJ in *Briody v St Helen's and Knowsley Area Health Authority* [2001] 2 FLR 1094 at 1098–1102.

[57] *Report of the Committee of Inquiry into Human Fertilisation and Embryology* (1984) (Cmnd 9314).

Surrogacy Arrangements Act 1985[58] which makes it an offence to be involved in prescribed ways with assisting, on a commercial basis, the making of surrogacy arrangements. The commissioning parents and surrogate mother are, however, specifically exempted from liability.[59] Following the Surrogacy Arrangements Act 1985, there was uncertainty, and a good deal of speculation, about the enforceability (as opposed to legality) of surrogacy arrangements. The majority view was that they were not enforceable and this was later confirmed by the Human Fertilisation and Embryology Act 1990.[60]

Further amendments to the 1985 Act have been introduced by the Human Fertilisation and Embryology Act 2008. Their purpose is to make it plain that *non-profit making* bodies who facilitate surrogacy arrangements in the ways which are proscribed by the Act[61] do not thereby contravene it.[62] Beyond this, the recommendations of the Review conducted by Brazier, Campbell and Golombok[63] for greater regulation of surrogacy agencies have not been implemented. On occasions the judges have been overtly critical of the current lack of regulation.[64] This can lead to inadequate advice by agencies on the legal complications which can arise, especially where (as is often the case) the arrangement involves a foreign element and consideration of the parentage laws of more than one jurisdiction and the immigration laws of the United Kingdom. On the other hand, explicit regulation might be thought by some to give legitimacy to a practice which it is public policy to discourage, or at least not encourage.

Although a criminal offence may conceivably have been committed, and although an agreement may be unenforceable, there remains the question of the destiny of a child born into such an arrangement. Here, the courts and the legislature have shown some ingenuity in dealing pragmatically with the situation.

First, it has been the case since before the Surrogacy Arrangements Act that the courts have exercised jurisdiction to determine, in accordance with the welfare principle, who should have the care of the child.[65] This can lead to a decision in favour of the commissioning parents, thereby achieving indirectly the intended result of the agreement.

---

58   Surrogacy Arrangements Act 1985, s 2(1).

59   Ibid, s 2(2).

60   Ibid, s 1A and HFEA 1990, s 36(1).

61   These are initiating or taking part in any negotiations, offering or agreeing to negotiate or compiling any information with a view to its use in making, or negotiating the making, of surrogacy arrangements.

62   Section 2(2A)–(2C) Surrogacy Arrangements Act 1985 as introduced by s 59 HFEA 2008.

63   M Brazier, A Campbell and S Golombok, *Surrogacy – Review for the UK Health Ministers of Current Arrangements for Payments and Regulation. Report of the Review Team* (1998) Cm 4068.

64   See particularly McFarlane J in *Re G (Surrogacy: Foreign Domicile)* [2008] 1 FLR 1047.

65   The first such case came before the courts as early as 1978 but was not reported until 1985. See *A v C* [1985] FLR 445. See also *Re C (A Minor) (Wardship: Surrogacy)* [1985] FLR 846 (the 'Baby Cotton' case).

Two comparatively recent decisions demonstrate the arguments which can arise between the surrogate mother and the commissioning parents after a child is born following a surrogacy arrangement. The obvious scenario is where the birth mother changes her mind and wants to keep the baby. This may well be accompanied by deterioration in the relationship between the parties. In *Re TT (Surrogacy)*[66] the court reached perhaps the more likely outcome. It favoured the child remaining with the surrogate/birth mother under a residence order, in the face of a demand for the child to be handed over to the commissioning parents, but with interim contact (to be reviewed) for the commissioning couple. In this case Baker J was influenced by the lack of insight of the commissioning couple with regard to the importance of the child's relationship with the birth mother. He distinguished the earlier case of *Re P (Surrogacy: Residence)*[67] in which there was a high degree of deception on the part of the surrogate mother and her husband. Here a residence order was made by Coleridge J in favour of the commissioning biological father and his wife, with good contact to the surrogate mother and her husband. The governing principle is of course the welfare principle. The test adopted in both these cases was to ask, in relation to the two competing parental regimes, in which home was the child most likely to mature into a happy and balanced adult and to achieve his fullest potential as a human being. Issues of which potential parents are likely to be the more 'inclusive' in their approach to the other party or parties are likely to influence the outcome.[68]

Secondly, the same result might be brought about by allowing the commissioning parents to adopt the child, perhaps turning a blind eye to violation of the rules prohibiting payment for adoption by retrospectively authorising the payments.[69] *Re MW (Adoption: Surrogacy)*[70] is an illustration of the use of adoption where a surrogacy arrangement has gone wrong and the parties are at loggerheads. Here, the initial agreement between the commissioning parents and the surrogate mother was that the former would apply to adopt the child following the birth. The handover took place and for a time there was continued contact between the baby and the surrogate mother. Relations then deteriorated, contact ceased and the mother began a media campaign to draw attention to her situation. She withheld her consent to the adoption and, alternatively, sought post-adoption contact with the child. The court applied the test of whether the advantages of adoption for the welfare of the child were sufficiently strong to justify overriding the views and interests of the objecting mother. It also took into account the fact that the mother had been independently advised and had previously given her consent to adoption. In these circumstances, the court dispensed with her consent and denied her contact with the child during the child's minority. Adoption is now much less

---

[66] [2011] 2 FLR 392.
[67] [2008] 1 FLR 177.
[68] As they did in *Re TT* (above).
[69] *Re Adoption Application (Payment for Adoption)* [1987] Fam 81 and *Re An Adoption Application* [1992] 1 FLR 341.
[70] [1995] 2 FLR 759.

likely to be the solution given the procedure for parental orders discussed below; but it could still be useful where the conditions for the making of a parental order are not met.

Thirdly and most significantly the Human Fertilisation and Embryology Act 2008, as did the 1990 Act before it, provides a means of avoiding the need to resort to adoption or the unbridled discretion of the courts. It is provided[71] that a so-called 'parental order' may be made 'providing for a child to be treated in law as the child of the applicants',[72] provided certain conditions are met. The major change brought about by the 2008 Act is the widening of the categories of those eligible to apply. Now such an application may be brought by married couples, civil partners, and 'two persons who are living as partners in an enduring family relationship and are not within the prohibited degrees of relationship in relation to each other'.[73] It will be readily appreciated that these rules of eligibility mirror those which now govern eligibility to adopt.[74] But beyond that there are special conditions which also apply to parental orders.

The conditions which must be satisfied are as follows. At least one of the applicants must be genetically related to the child in that his or her gametes must have been used; the child must be resident with them; the application must be brought within 6 months of the birth; either or both of the applicants must be domiciled in the UK;[75] both applicants must have attained the age of 18; and both the surrogate mother and anyone else who is legal parent of the child (effectively the biological father of the child) must have agreed unconditionally to the making of the order.[76] The agreement of a person who cannot be found or is incapable of giving agreement is not required.[77]

---

[71] HFEA 2008, s 54 and see the helpful discussion of the earlier provision in s 30 HFEA 1990 in *Bromley's Family Law* (9th edn, Butterworths, 1998), at pp 267–269 and in RG Lee and D Morgan (above), at pp 219–221. See also *Re W (Minors) (Surrogacy)* [1991] 1 FLR 385, the case which inspired the introduction of 'parental orders'. Here, twins born under a surrogacy arrangement were allowed, in wardship proceedings, to remain under the care of the genetic (commissioning) parents on their undertaking to make an application for a parental order, within 28 days of the implementation of s 30 of the HFEA 1990.

[72] The order may be made only on the application of 'two people' and is hence unavailable to single applicants. However, in *A v P (Surrogacy: Parental Order: Death of Applicant)* [2012] 2 FLR 145 a joint application was made by a married couple but the husband died of liver cancer before the hearing. Theis J held that to make a parental order in these circumstances did not offend against the policy of the Act and in particular it would not pave the way for applications by single commissioning parents. The Court noted that, but for the husband's death, the child would have remained in the couple's joint care.

[73] HFEA 2008, s 54(2).

[74] See chapter 9 below.

[75] A condition which has caused considerable difficulty in practice given the prevalence of oversees arrangements. See, for example, *Re G (Surrogacy: Foreign Domicile)* [2008] 1 FLR 1047, *Z and B v C (Parental Order: Domicile)* [2012] 2 FLR 797 and *Re A and B (Parental Order: Domicile)* [2013] EWHC 426 (Fam), [2013] Fam Law 675.

[76] Section 54(1)–(6).

[77] Section 54(7) as to which see *Re D and L (Surrogacy)* [2012] EWHC 2631 (Fam), [2013] 2 FLR 275.

A final condition, which has caused a good deal of difficulty in practice, is that there must be no unauthorised payment or other benefit involved.[78] The Act permits 'reasonable expenses' but, quite apart from definitional problems, it is abundantly clear that in a number cases the money which has changed hands goes well beyond anything which could be so described. The courts are then called upon to decide whether they should give retrospective authorisation to these payments and sanction the making of the parental order despite these contraventions. In a string of reported decisions they have done so.[79] The decisive factor which has influenced this approach is the need to safeguard the welfare of the child which is seen to be achieved by the making of the order more often than not. The Regulations made under the 2008 Act[80] have applied s 1 Adoption and Children Act 2002 to parental order applications, thus making the welfare of the child concerned the court's paramount consideration. Accordingly, it has been held that where the payments concerned, although in excess of reasonable expenses, were not disproportionate, it can be in the welfare interests of the child that a parental order be made.[81]

There has been a recent judicial decision on the question of revocation of parental orders. In *G v G (Parental Order: Revocation)*[82] a commissioning father (who was also the biological father) applied to set aside a parental order on the basis that the procedural requirements relating to the making of the order had not been properly observed.[83] After the order had been made and the child placed with the commissioning couple, he had separated from the commissioning mother. The child remained in her primary care. He also asserted that concealment by his wife of her intention to separate and live as a sole parent with the child also should have resulted in no order being made. Hedley J, dismissing the application, applied by analogy the principles applicable to the setting aside of adoption orders and especially the leading

---

[78] Section 54(8) provides: 'The Court must be satisfied that no money or other benefit (other than for expenses reasonably incurred) has been given or received by either of the applicants for or in consideration of –
   (a) the making of the order,
   (b) any agreement required by subsection (6),
   (c) the handing over of the child to the applicants, or
   (d) the making of arrangements with a view to the making of the order,
   unless authorised by the court'.

[79] See for example, *Re IJ (Foreign Surrogacy Agreement: Parental Order)* [2011] 2 FLR 646 and *Re L (Commercial Surrogacy)* [2011] 1 FLR 1423. For such a case under the previous s 30 HFEA 1990 see *Re C (Application by Mr and Mrs X under s 30 of the Human Fertilisation and Embryology Act 1990)* [2002] 1 FLR 909. Most recently see *J v G (Parental Order)* [2013] EWHC 1432 (Fam), [2013] Fam Law 972.

[80] The Human Fertilisation and Embryology (Parental Orders) Regulations 2010 (SI 2010/985).

[81] *Re X and Y (Parental Order: Retrospective Authorisation of Payments)* [2012] 1 FLR 1347. See also *Re S (Parental Order)* [2010] 1 FLR 1156 and *Re A and B (Parental Order) (Domicile)* [2013] EWHC 426 (Fam), [2013] Fam Law 675.

[82] [2012] EWHC 1979 (Fam), [2013] 1 FLR 286.

[83] There had been no parental report from CAFCASS, the court relied on the natural mother's acknowledgment of service as consent, there had been no analysis of s 58(4) though £10,000 had changed hands and no consideration had been given by the judge to welfare issues.

authority of *Re M (Minors) (Adoption)*.[84] He held that parental orders, like adoption orders, created a status and that there needed to be clarity and certainty as far as possible. The circumstances here were not exceptional, it would not be consistent with the child's welfare to set aside the order and, even had the requirements of the legislation been properly observed, it would have made no difference to the decision to make the order. The integrity of the system and welfare considerations militated against setting the order aside.

Hedley J did indicate however that he would be disposed to grant permission to appeal if asked because the whole area of surrogacy, which to date is governed entirely by first instance decisions, was one which would benefit from appellate consideration.

Some policy considerations

Surrogacy cases continue to attract media attention both when there is a successful outcome and when they go drastically wrong. There have been periodic calls for the review of surrogacy legislation and suggestions for a more regulated system.[85] In 1997, as noted above, a Review team was set up by Health Ministers and asked to report on certain aspects of surrogacy arrangements. The terms of reference included whether payments, including expenses, should continue to be paid to surrogate mothers, whether surrogacy arrangements should be regulated by a recognised body and whether legislative change was required to either the 1985 or the 1990 Act.

The Review team reported in 1998.[86] It found that the failure to implement all the recommendations of the Warnock Committee had created a policy vacuum in which surrogacy had developed in a haphazard fashion. It examined the conflicting considerations involved in balancing the welfare of children with procreative liberty and concluded that the risks of harm, primarily to children but also to adults involved in surrogacy arrangements, justified a degree of regulation. It expressed concern about payments being made to surrogate mothers which exceeded genuine expenses because of the implications regarding the consent of surrogate mothers, the commodification of children and the social norms of British society that, just as bodily parts could not be sold, nor should it be possible to sell such intimate services.

The central recommendations of the Review were that payments to surrogate mothers should be expressly limited to actual expenses occasioned by the pregnancy and that those expenses should be defined in the legislation; that agencies involved in surrogacy arrangements, such as COTS,[87] should continue

---

84   [1991] 1 FLR 458.

85   See M Hibbs 'Surrogacy Legislation – Time for Change?' [1997] Fam Law 564.

86   The Review was chaired by Professor Margaret Brazier. See M Brazier, A Campbell and S Golombok *Surrogacy: Review for Health Ministers of Current Arrangements for Payments and Regulation* (1998) (Cm 4068).

87   'Childlessness Overcome Through Surrogacy', the leading agency which has been involved in several of the reported cases in the UK such as the 'Baby Cotton' case (above).

to operate on a non-profit-making basis but should also have to register with the Department of Health; that such agencies should be required to operate within a code of practice setting out minimum standards for surrogacy arrangements; and that contravention of the reasonable expenses restriction on payments should result in ineligibility for a parental order. The Review went on to recommend that these changes should be effected by new surrogacy legislation.

Parliament has not acted on these recommendations. However, there is perhaps an ongoing drift towards the acceptance of the phenomenon of surrogacy and a gathering view that regulation, rather than prohibition, is the way forward. Lee and Morgan,[88] writing a decade or so ago, went so far as to describe this shift as a 'metamorphosis'. In particular it was their view that the underlying assumption of the Review was that 'public concern had moved on from Warnock, from regarding surrogacy as being an almost offensive offering on the reproductive menu to being a legislative service after all other courses have been sampled and found wanting'.[89]

English law is ambivalent about surrogacy. On the one hand it is seeking to discourage the making of agreements, whilst on the other it is providing mechanisms for giving effect to a proportion of them. This ambivalence can be explained as follows.

Whilst the initial agreement is not considered to be in the best interests of the *intended* child, when the *actual* child is born it may be, at that point, that it is in his best interests (perhaps as the lesser of two unsatisfactory alternatives) to be with the commissioning parents rather than the surrogate mother. The solutions adopted at this stage are not very different to other substitute care arrangements which the courts can sanction where the natural or 'normal' family 'fails'. Douglas and Lowe, in drawing attention to the debate about whether assisted reproduction is more akin to 'normal' reproduction or adoption, refer to the view of Warnock, rejecting the adoption analogy.[90] According to Warnock:[91]

> 'It is plausible to talk about the good of the child when the child exists and there are alternative futures before it, between which someone must choose. To choose whether or not a baby should be born in the first place is a different kind of choice altogether. The whole undertaking is *in fact* for the sake of the infertile would-be parents. It is *they* who want the baby.'

Herein lies the initial objection to surrogacy. It sits awkwardly with the law's general commitment to the welfare of children since it is predicated on the priority being attached to adult interests. It is difficult to see how it could be

---

[88] RG Lee and D Morgan *Human Fertilisation and Embryology: Regulating the Reproductive Revolution* (Blackstone, 2001) ch 8, especially, at pp 201–211.

[89] Ibid, at p 206.

[90] G Douglas and NV Lowe 'Becoming a Parent in English Law' (1992) 108 LQR 414, at p 416.

[91] M Warnock 'The Good of the Child' (1987) 1 *Bioethics* 141, at p 144.

argued that surrogacy is designed *primarily* for the benefit of the intended child. But there are unresolved difficulties with this view. The fact is that many 'normal' births in 'normal' families are also the result of decisions by adults who *want* to have a child. These adults are distinguishable from commissioning parents only because their wants can be satisfied in the context of what society currently accepts as 'normal' while this is not so with surrogacy. The distinction can only be sustained if we think of the child having an interest in or, perhaps, a right to a 'normal' start to life. Yet, given the variety of social parenting arrangements examined in this chapter and elsewhere in this book,[92] it may be no easy matter to define what 'normality' is, if indeed it exists at all.

Biological mothers and surrogate fathers

The legal rules which determine paternity generally and specifically in the context of assisted reproduction are considered below. But one phenomenon which is perhaps more appropriately considered at this stage, is the situation of the surrogate 'known' father. This usually occurs where a lesbian couple advertises for a man to donate sperm or have sexual intercourse with one of them, or where such involvement takes place with someone known to one or other of the women. In any event, when the child is born there is no doubt at that time of the identity of the father. In several reported cases, the courts have been asked to rule in effect on whether the father, who is undoubtedly a legal parent in these cases, is to be treated as the parent or as performing some subordinate role to the two women who themselves are to be regarded as the child's two parents. The known father will be the legal parent, albeit lacking parental responsibility, because he is the biological father. The mother's female partner will *not* be the legal parent. The basic legal rule or default position, as we shall see, is that where a child is conceived outside the licensed system, the man who is genetically related to the child, whether through sperm donation or conception achieved in intercourse, is the legal father of the child,[93] albeit lacking parental responsibility other than where he is registered as the father.

In *R v E and F (Female Parents: Known Father)*[94] two same-sex couples, one female and one male, embarked on a joint enterprise to have a child. At the time of the proceedings the boy was seven years of age. The mother's civil partner had parental responsibility for him by agreement with the mother. The biological father was registered on the child's birth certificate but did not have parental responsibility as it did not flow automatically from birth registration when the child was born. For a time a co-operative, transatlantic relationship existed between the two couples; the women were resident in England and the men were resident in the United States but able to travel to England for contact with the child. Following a fall out, the father sought parental responsibility, shared residence and staying contact with the child. A child and adolescent

---

[92]   See also chapter 5 below.
[93]   A useful illustration of this default position is *Re B (Parentage)* [1996] 2 FLR 15. An exception arises where two women are civil partners, in which case they are the legal parents to the exclusion of the man concerned. See *Re G; Re Z* (above) discussed further below.
[94]   [2010] EWHC 417 (Fam), [2010] 2 FLR 383.

psychologist gave evidence that the child saw the mother and her partner as his parents, but was also aware of and loved his father. Bennett J made a joint residence order in favour of the mother and her partner, dismissed the father's application for parental responsibility and shared residence and ordered contact between him and the child for up to 50 days per year. In his view, the female partners had been exercising the parental responsibilities. The father had not acted as a co-parent and was not regarded by the child as a parent. He rejected the father's assertion that the four adults constituted one family; the reality was that the child's family was the nuclear family comprising the female partners and the child.[95]

A rather different result was reached by the Court of Appeal in *T v T (Shared and Joint Residence Orders)*,[96] another case involving an arrangement between male and female couples. Here the Court of Appeal made a three-way shared residence order in favour of the female partners and the biological father. The judge, it was held, had properly regarded all three adults as 'parents' and the order reflected how the two children, a boy aged 10 and a girl aged 7 at the time of the proceedings, probably saw things.

A recent decision of the Court of Appeal emphasises that there are no hard and fast rules relating to these cases which are fact-specific. In *A v B and C (Lesbian Co-Parents: Role of Father)*,[97] the donor was a male friend of a lesbian couple. All had expected him to play a 'secondary' role after the birth of the intended child now aged three at the time of the appeal. Relations deteriorated between the women and the man and, as in other cases, the issue was the extent of the role it was appropriate for him to have. An unusual feature was that one of the women had gone through a ceremony of marriage with the man (for cultural and religious reasons) before birth. thus conferring on him automatic parental responsibility. The father asserted that his role was to be analogous to that of a divorced father who could generally look forward

---

[95] A similar conclusion was reached by Hedley J in *Re B (Role of Biological Father)* [2008] 1 FLR 1015. Here the sperm donor was the brother of the mother's civil partner. The female partners claimed that his agreed role was a 'distant avuncular one'. The father claimed that his role was intended to include contact and participation in major decisions affecting the child. Refusing to grant parental responsibility, but allowing direct contact four times a year, it was held that contact would benefit the child in knowing that the uncle figure was in fact his father, but it should not be exercised so as to assert a full parental status which could leave the female partners feeling assailed and undermined. See also *MA v RS (Contact: Parenting Roles)* [2012] 1 FLR 1056, another dual couple case in which there was disagreement over the extent of involvement of the father. Here Hedley J, making contact orders in favour of the applicant male partners, held that it might be more helpful to think in terms of *principal* and *secondary* parenting. The father's position was not the equivalent of a separated parent post-divorce and there had been a clear agreement that the women would do the principal parenting of the two children. The secondary role of the men was however important to the children's identity interests. And for a further decision of Hedley J in similar vein see *Re P and L (Contact)* [2012] 1 FLR 1068. This was another 'two couple' case in which the male couple's application for a residence order was struck out, thereby recognising the primary parenting role of the female couple and limiting that of the male couple to defined contact.

[96] [2011] Fam Law 240.

[97] [2012] EWCA Civ 285, [2012] 2 FLR 607. For commentary see A Zanghellini 'A, B and C – Heteronormativity, poly-parenting, and the homo-nuclear family' [2012] 24 CFLQ 475.

to visiting contact and overnight stays with the child. The women asserted that they had never intended the child to be born into a broken home, that it had always been intended that they would be the 'parents' providing stability and taking all the decisions on upbringing. They visualised a 'secondary' role for the father, albeit that they recognised his 'special' relationship with the child.

The judge had granted the father 5 or 6 hours contact alternately per fortnight and granted a joint residence order to the women. No restriction was placed on the exercise of the father's parental responsibility. Allowing the father's appeal and remitting the case to the High Court, the Court of Appeal held that the judge had erred in applying a general rule which supposedly governed these cases. All were fact-specific and governed only by the welfare principle. The concept of 'primary' and 'secondary' parenting rules was in danger of demeaning the known donor who in some cases might have an important role. The women here were clearly the primary carers but the Father was only on the threshold of secondary care. Whether or not it was likely to be crossed was a question to be determined by a judge in the near future. He was certainly not to be characterised as a secondary parent. The purpose of contact was to promote the welfare of the child. The extent of contact should be determined in the light of the accumulating evidence. There were too many unforeseeable factors in this case for the judge to have decided this question as definitively as he did.

A final recent decision concerns the position of female civil partners where a known donor provides sperm. In *Re G; Re Z (Children: Sperm Donors: Leave to Apply for Children Act Orders)*[98] two male civil partners successively provided sperm outside the licensed system to two female partner couples, successfully resulting in children.[99] In accordance with the new provisions of the 2008 Act, the women were the legal parents to the exclusion of the donors/fathers. There was then the familiar dispute over the extent of involvement intended for the men and no agreement attempting to regulate this. The issue was whether those men should be given leave to apply for s 8 orders under the Children Act to regulate their relationships with the respective children.

Baker J held that they should have leave to seek contact orders but no other s 8 orders, specifically not residence orders. The application by one of the men for a residence order was considered disproportionate. On the other hand, following *Anayo v Germany*[100] the social relationships which the women had allowed the men to develop with the children arguably amounted to 'family life' for the purposes of the ECHR or alternatively 'private life'. Thus, to refuse them at least permission to apply for s 8 orders would amount to a breach of their rights under Art 6 and Art 8 of the Convention.

---

[98] [2013] EWHC 134 (Fam), [2013] 1 FLR 1334.
[99] A third, earlier child had born by these means but before the implementation of the Human Fertilisation and Embryology Act 2008. Accordingly, the known father was also the legal father in relation to that child and hence did not require leave to seek Children Act orders.
[100] (Application No 0578/07) [2011] 1 FLR 1883.

An interesting feature of the new law, apparent from this case, is the continued significance attached by English family law to formalised relationships, in this case civil partnership. While this mirrors the significance also attached to marriage in the assignment of parentage, it does so in a context in which there can be no pretence that the mother's partner, unlike a woman's husband, is the biological parent of the child.

In general the decided cases, while concerned in part with the correct terminology,[101] can be said to support the primary parenting role of the birth mother and her partner which is clearly more easily achievable if the licensed system is used. Although the role of the father (and in some cases his male partner) is often seen as subsidiary, these known fathers cannot however be ignored with the same impunity as the licensed sperm donor. Decisions, as we now know, are fact-specific and to be welfare driven. It may therefore be that no consistent pattern of approved legal arrangement will emerge in these cases and that further litigation may be expected.

WHO IS THE FATHER?

While the process of childbirth clearly demonstrates who is the mother of a child, self-evidently it cannot establish the identity of the father. Whether the mother is married, cohabiting or single, and whether or not the birth is attended by any partner she may have, the identity of the father has to be legally determined by means other than observation of the birth. The law therefore has to take refuge in presumptions though, in doing so, it should be borne in mind that such presumptions are capable of being rebutted in the light of biological evidence to the contrary. As it was once famously put in an American case presumptions are:[102]

> 'the bats of the law, flitting in the twilight, but disappearing in the sunshine of actual facts.'

We therefore concentrate in this section first on the legal presumptions which apply and how they may be rebutted. We then look at the determination of paternity in cases of assisted reproduction.

The pater est presumption

The starting point for the law relates to birth to a married mother. The law presumes her husband to be the father of the child in accordance with the Latin maxim *pater est quem nuptiae demonstrant*. In English law this is known as the

---

[101] Though in *T v T* (above) the Court of Appeal expressed its profound disappointment that even when the practicalities of how the child's time should be split are worked out, the parties can continue to fight over the label which is to be put on them. Shared or joint residence orders have in particular proved problematic in this respect where, instead of being used for children's benefit they could simply serve as a further battlefield.

[102] *Macowik v Kansas City St J & CBR. Co* (1906) 94 SW 256, 262.

presumption of *legitimacy* though, as we discuss below, it is a matter of debate how far the concept of legitimacy is, or should be, part of the modern law.[103]

The presumption applies where a man was married to the mother either at the time of the conception or the birth. It may be rebutted by evidence which establishes, on the balance of probabilities, that the mother's husband is not the father.[104] This is a less exacting requirement than used to be imposed at common law where it was necessary to establish the matter beyond reasonable doubt. The courts had not been wholly consistent in their attitude to the amount of evidence required[105] but the reality today is that DNA testing can now, in contrast to conventional blood testing, establish the true position virtually conclusively. Scientific tests may be directed in any civil proceedings in which the parentage of any person falls to be determined.[106] The question is rather whether there is any good reason why such tests ought *not* to be directed.[107] It should however be appreciated that, whatever may be the true biological position, where the mother's husband does not deny paternity and no other man asserts that *he* is the father, the husband will remain the legal father with all the legal consequences which flow from this. It should also be noted that it is not the *fact of marriage* which results in presumed paternity. If that were the case, every step-father would be the legal father. It is rather the presumption of biological fatherhood which arises from marriage to the mother at the relevant time.

Many countries have resolutely defended the presumption and put up formidable legal obstacles to its rebuttal, no doubt in the belief that the institution of marriage should be supported and the child's stability within it. We consider below the resolution of paternity disputes in England.[108] But it should be noted that the European Court of Human Rights, in a raft of decisions, has found violations of the ECHR where a number of countries had created legal hurdles preventing the opportunity of challenging paternity within marriage except in very restricted circumstances.[109]

---

[103] It has been suggested that the concentration should now be on removing the concept of legitimacy rather than on its concomitant illegitimacy. See A Bainham 'Is legitimacy legitimate?' (2009) *Fam Law* 673 and see p 153 below.

[104] Section 26 Family Law Reform Act 1969.

[105] *S v S; W v Official Solicitor* [1972] AC 24. Cf *Serio v Serio* (1983) 4 FLR 756, *W v K (Proof of Paternity)* [1988] 1 FLR 86 and *F v Child Support Agency* [1999] 2 FLR 244.

[106] Section 20(1) FLRA 1969.

[107] See below.

[108] See pp 139 et seq.

[109] See especially *Shofman v Russia* [2006] 1 FLR 680; *Mizzi v Malta* [2006] 1 FLR 1048, *Paulik v Slovakia* [2007] 1 FLR 1090 and *Tavli v Turkey* [2007] 1 FLR 1136. For commentary see A Bainham ' "Truth will out": Paternity in Europe' [2007] CLJ 278. Cf *Kautzor v Germany* [2012] 2 FLR 396 in which the ECtHR found no violation of the applicant ex-husband's Art 8 rights where the mother, after divorcing him within a year of marriage, gave birth to a child 5 months after the divorce and consented to the acknowledgment of the child's paternity by the man who was her partner at the time of the child's birth. The decision of the German courts not to allow genetic testing was held to be within the state's margin of appreciation.

What happens where a married woman, while pregnant, divorces? At common law, it appears that the courts will continue to apply the *pater est* presumption, provided that the child is born within the normal period of gestation. Some jurisdictions specify precisely the number of days within which the child must be born following divorce for the presumption to continue to apply. In Chile, for example, the period is 300 days.[110] In Estonia it is 10 months.[111] The English courts have also applied the presumption where the mother has remarried before the birth of the child.[112] In this situation, there may be a *clash* of presumptions. The child would be presumed the child of the first husband (H1), but birth after the second marriage would also trigger a presumption of paternity of the second husband (H2). It seems likely that if the mother and H2 jointly register the birth with H2 named as the father, and if H1 does not dispute this, then the presumption arising from registration of the birth will prevail. If H1 should dispute the paternity of H2, the matter would nowadays be likely to be settled by a direction for DNA testing.[113]

Birth registration

The principal means by which the law determines the paternity of a child born to an *unmarried* mother is through the process of birth registration.[114] But before coming to the rules which govern registration in this context, we should briefly note the position on registration where the child is born to a *married* mother.

Births to married mothers

It is a popular misunderstanding that a married mother has a legal right to register her husband as the father of the child and cause his name to be placed on the child's birth certificate, whether or not he is in fact the biological father. The legal position is however more subtle than this. It depends on whether the mother knows or suspects that her husband may not be the father. There is no difficulty in her registering him if she either knows or believes him to be the father, or perhaps also where she suspects he may not be. But where she knows that he is not, or perhaps thinks it more likely than not that he is not, she will

---

[110] See I Pardo de Carvallo 'Identifying Parentage and the Methods of Proof in the New Chilean Law' in A Bainham (ed) *The International Survey of Family Law (2000 Edition)* (Family Law, 2000), at p 83.

[111] K Kullerkupp 'Family Law in Estonia' in A Bainham (ed) (above), at p 95.

[112] *Re Overbury (deceased)* [1954] Ch 122. It should be noted, however, that this remarkable case arose from a birth which took place in 1869 and which occurred some eight months after the death of H1 and just two months after the mother's second marriage to H2. The case for allowing the first presumption to apply in such circumstances was a strong one, especially in the social conditions which prevailed in the mid-nineteenth century. Whether the preference for the first presumption would be appropriate in the very changed social circumstances of the early twenty-first century and in the context of divorce is questionable.

[113] But for the European Court of Human Rights' approach to this situation see *Kautzor v Germany* [2012] 2 FLR 396 (above) in which the decision of the German courts not to allow genetic testing was held not to violate the Convention.

[114] See generally A Bainham 'What is the point of birth registration?' [2008] 20 CFLQ 449.

commit perjury if she acts dishonestly in registering him.[115] It might be thought that there are good policy arguments for giving the married woman a completely free hand to register her husband as the father and perhaps keep secret her knowledge of extra-marital affairs, but this has to be set against the growing claim that a child has a right to knowledge of biological origins.[116]

Births to unmarried mothers

Where the mother is *unmarried*, English law does not apply any presumption that a particular man is the father, even in the case of long-term cohabitation by her or the supportive involvement of any man during the pregnancy or at the birth. Instead, the matter turns very largely on birth registration. The law provides that registration of a man as the father in the birth register gives rise to a rebuttable presumption of paternity.[117] Since 1 December 2003 it has also given rise to the important legal consequence that the registered father automatically acquires parental responsibility.[118] The circumstances under which registration is permitted or required are therefore of the utmost importance. These will change significantly if and when the relevant provisions of the Welfare Reform Act 2009 are implemented.[119]

As the law currently stands, the mother has the *sole* duty and right to register the child's birth.[120] The father is neither under a duty, nor does he have an independent right, to register his paternity. In *AAA v Ash, Registrar-General for England and Wales*[121] the parents had gone through an Islamic marriage ceremony but they knew the marriage was invalid in English law. The father of the child then went to register the birth alone. He had no right to do so as he was not in fact married. He thus did not acquire parental responsibility or 'rights of custody' for the purposes of the Hague Convention governing international child abduction.

The circumstances under which the father's name might be registered were significantly extended by the Family Law Reform Act 1987 and the Children Act 1989.[122] In essence, registration of the father's name normally requires the co-operation and joint attendance by both the mother and father. Independent registration of the father by either the mother or the father will be allowed only on production of a relevant court order or declaration of parentage which entails the determination of parentage together with a declaration that the order has not been terminated by a court. Such orders include parental

---

115   Section 4 Perjury Act 1911.
116   See below.
117   Section 34(2) Births and Deaths Registration Act 1953.
118   Section 4(1)(a) Children Act 1989 and see chapter 4 below.
119   Section 56 and Sch 6. See below.
120   Section 10(1) Births and Deaths Registration Act 1953.
121   [2010] 1 FLR 1.
122   Births and Deaths Registration Act 1953, s 10(1), as amended.

responsibility orders under s 4 of the Children Act 1989 and an order that the father make financial provision for the child under the residual jurisdiction of the courts.[123]

Where none of the above circumstances apply, the father's name will be left blank on the child's birth certificate but may subsequently be added to the register by re-registration, subject to the same conditions set out above,[124] or where the parents have married following the birth.[125] We noted in chapter 1 that a high percentage of births outside marriage are registered jointly by the personal attendance of the mother and father together.[126] It is clearly the case that some men registered as fathers under these procedures will not in fact be the genetic fathers. As with the *pater est* presumption at common law, registration of paternity provides a means of *attributing* legal parentage, which may or may not coincide with the biological reality. It is usually only in the event of a dispute that there will be an occasion to look behind the attribution of parentage arising from the fact of registration, and we look at how these disputes are resolved below.

These provisions governing registration of births to unmarried women have now been radically amended by the as yet unimplemented provisions of the Welfare Reform Act 2009. The reforms followed a White Paper on the joint registration of births outside marriage[127] and are intended to create a norm of joint registration, subject to exemptions.[128] They were inspired by evidence of an association between social exclusion and sole birth registration and the disproportionate representation of very young, disadvantaged mothers in the statistics.[129]

The new scheme establishes that both parents are qualified informants to give information regarding the birth.[130] Where the mother registers the birth alone, she will be required to provide information about the father to the registrar subject to certain specified exemptions. These include[131] where the father has

---

[123] See further chapter 9 below.

[124] Births and Deaths Registration Act 1953, s 10A(1).

[125] Ibid, s 14.

[126] See p 12 above.

[127] Department for Work and Pensions and Department for Children, Schools and Families, *Joint birth registration: recording responsibility*, Cm 7293 (TSO, 2008) preceded by the Green Paper, *Joint birth registration: promoting parental responsibility* (DWP, 2007).

[128] For commentaries on these reforms see A Bainham, above n 94 especially, at pp 457–461; C Barton 'Joint birth registration: "recording responsibility" responsibly' [2008] Fam Law 789; J Wallbank ' "Bodies in the shadows": joint birth registration, parental responsibility and social class' [2009] CFLQ 267; and L Smith 'Clashing symbols? Reconciling support for fathers and fatherless families after the HFEA 2008' [2010] CFLQ 46.

[129] The research which influenced the government was J Graham, C Creegan, M Barnard, A Mowlam, S McKay, *Sole and joint birth registration: exploring the circumstances, choices and motivations of unmarried parents* (Department for Work and Pensions Research Report No 463, 2007).

[130] 1953 Act, s 1(2) as amended. Section 1(2) (aa) (ii) now extends qualified informants to certain unmarried fathers and second female parents.

[131] The full list of exemptions is contained in s 2B (4) Births and Deaths Registration Act 1953.

died, his identity or whereabouts are unknown to the mother and, perhaps most significantly, where 'the mother has reason to fear for her safety or that of the child if the father is contacted in relation to the registration of the birth'. Where the mother has given information about the alleged father, the Act now provides for the making of regulations which will enable him to be registered as the father if he accepts that he is the father following a notice sent to him by the registrar.[132] A procedure is also to be established which will, for the first time in English law,[133] allow a man to initiate his registration as father, albeit subject to the mother's subsequent confirmation.[134] It is envisaged that this may be done by the man concerned giving information to the registrar *before* the mother has registered the birth. Finally, there is to be provision for scientific tests to be taken with the consent of the mother and the alleged father and their agreement that if the test is positive that man will be registered as the father.[135]

The reforms are grounded in the right of the child to knowledge of biological origins[136] and the official view that this should not be dependent on the nature of the relationship between the two parents.[137] The aim is to create a culture in which 'people are clear that fatherhood as well as motherhood always comes with rights as well as responsibilities'.[138] Yet these objectives are qualified by concerns about the vulnerability of women and children where it is thought disclosure of the name of the father may undermine their security or place them in danger.[139] In many ways these fears are not unlike those which have led to resistance to conferring automatic parental responsibility on all fathers.[140] In fact the connection is all too obvious because where the father is registered he will also thereby acquire parental responsibility. The real issue is whether it is the proper role of the birth registration system to act as a protective mechanism or whether such protection, where necessary, should be provided by other means. It can, moreover, be argued that birth registration is fundamentally a matter of the child's right to an accurate record of the birth and the birth parents, and is not a process which should be concerned with welfare considerations at all. Certainly, it has not been historically, and the reforms also raise questions about the proper functions of registrars.[141]

---

[132] Section 2C.
[133] Cf the position in civil law jurisdictions which in contrast to English law have long permitted a man claiming to be the father to undertake a formal process of 'recognition' of the child. For an informative discussion see M-T Meulders 'The position of the father in European legislation' (1990) 4 *International Journal of Law and the Family* 131.
[134] Section 2D.
[135] Section 2E.
[136] As to which see pp 150 et seq below.
[137] White Paper, at para 6.
[138] Ibid.
[139] For a critique of this position see Bainham, n 94 above, at pp 459–461.
[140] See chapter 4 below.
[141] In their responses to the Green Paper, *Joint birth registration: promoting parental responsibility* (DWP, 2007), which preceded the White Paper, registrars expressed their concern about a possible extension of their role to one of 'interrogator, investigator or counsellor'. See White Paper, Annex A, para 17.

Paternity and assisted reproduction

Where a child is born after the use of donated gametes following licensed treatment, the HFEA 2008 contains rules for the determination of the legal father. Again, the law treats quite openly some men as legal fathers who are clearly not biological fathers and excludes from legal paternity some who are. It should however be remembered before coming to these rules, that the first rule and default position where the HFEA does not expressly provide otherwise, is that legal paternity follows the biological link.[142] Hence, known fathers who have donated sperm outside the licensed system, as we saw above, will be the legal fathers of the children concerned by virtue of the biological connection except where the mother is in a civil partnership with another woman.[143]

The first rule relates to *married* mothers and provides that where a married woman gives birth following licensed treatment,[144] her husband is to be treated as the father of the child unless it is shown that he did not consent to it.[145] The second rule relates to *unmarried* mothers and provides that a man (who will usually but not necessarily be her partner) will be treated as the father of the child if the 'agreed fatherhood conditions' are satisfied.[146] In each case these rules apply where the creation of the embryo was not brought about with the husband or partner's sperm; if it had been he would be the legal father by virtue of the genetic connection. The agreed fatherhood conditions[147] mirror the agreed female parenthood conditions considered above. In essence the mother and the man concerned must each give notice in writing to the responsible person that they consent to him acquiring legal paternity, neither has given notice of withdrawal of their consent and the mother has not given a further notice consenting to another man or woman becoming the legal parent of the child. They must not be within the prohibited degrees in relation to each other. Finally, there are provisions dealing with the situation where there has been the use of donated sperm, or the transfer of an embryo, after the death of the man providing sperm.[148] Essentially, the deceased may be treated as the father of the child for the limited purpose of enabling him to be registered as the child's father, where he consented to the use of his sperm after his death and where the mother has elected in writing within the 42-day registration period for him to be so registered.[149]

---

[142] *Re B (Parentage)* [1996] 2 FLR 15.

[143] See the discussion above.

[144] The placing in her of an embryo, sperm or eggs or of her artificial insemination.

[145] Section 35(1).

[146] Section 36.

[147] Section 37.

[148] Issues brought to public attention particularly by the Diane Blood case where the particular difficulty was the absence of the late Mr. Blood's consent to the use of his sperm to inseminate his wife after his death. See *R v Human Fertilisation and Embryology Authority ex parte Blood* [1997] 2 All ER 687 [1997] 2 All ER 687.

[149] Section 39. Under s 46 a similar rule applies to the transfer of an embryo after the death of a civil partner or intended female parent.

The 'agreed fatherhood conditions', which place formal consent to legal parentage centre stage, have replaced the previous unsatisfactory test in the HFEA 1990 which attributed fatherhood where a woman received infertility treatment 'in the course of treatment services provided for her and man together'.[150] It should be borne in mind that the former test in the 1990 Act continues to govern the attribution of fatherhood in the case of births prior to 6 April 2009 when the parentage provisions of the 2008 Act were largely implemented.[151]

The final issue to address is the acquisition of parentage in a same-sex *male* partnership. As we have seen in the case of female partners, it has been the case since December 2005 that a male couple, whether or not civil partners, have been eligible to adopt a child together and acquire legal parentage in that way.[152] The 2008 Act however similarly extends the procedure for obtaining parental orders, hitherto confined to married couples, to same-sex couples of each gender and also to unmarried heterosexual couples.[153] The procedure is unlikely to be of significant practical use to same-sex female couples for the obvious reason that their preference is likely to be in, the great majority of cases, to produce a child who is born to one of them with donated sperm. The 2008 Act as we have seen provides a fast track to parentage for the female partner in these circumstances. But there will be some cases in which, for whatever reason, neither female partner is able or willing to carry a child. In those circumstances, the procedure may be invoked.

It is self-evident that the legal position of female and male partners cannot be identical because of the central need for a woman to undergo pregnancy and carry the child. At least in the current state of medical advance, a woman's participation in pregnancy and child birth is universally required. We are therefore talking about a surrogacy arrangement whereby a woman carries a child for two male partners. We discussed the legal position on surrogacy above. What is worthy of note here is that whereas two female partners can acquire parentage with a minimum of scrutiny and without the necessity of bringing the matter before the courts, male partners are required to do so even where

---

[150]   Section 28(3). For a full discussion of the provision, the problems it caused in practice and the cases which it generated, see the 3rd edition of this work, at pp 93–97. The leading cases were *Re Q (Parental Order)* [1996] 1 FLR 369; *U v W (Attorney-General Intervening)* [1997] 2 FLR 282; *Re R (IVF: Paternity of Child)* [2005] 2 FLR 843; and *Leeds Teaching Hospitals NHS Trust v A and B* [2003] 1 FLR 412.

[151]   By the Human Fertilisation and Embryology Act 2008 (Commencement No 1 and Transitional Provisions) Order 2009. Note also that s 54, governing parental orders, was not implemented until one year later and is effective from 6 April 2010. See Human Fertilisation and Embryology Act 2008 (Commencement No 3) Order 2010.

[152]   Section 50 Adoption and Children Act 2002 contains the basic rule that an adoption order may be made on the application of a 'couple' where both of them have attained the age of 21 years. The radical change permitting same-sex adoption is buried away in s 144(4) which defines 'couple' to include not only a married couple but also civil partners and 'two people (whether of different sexes or the same sex) living as partners in an enduring family relationship'.

[153]   Section 54.

one of them is the biological father of the child, as will often be the case. The position reflects the law's commitment to the centrality of the biological mother's position.

Disputed paternity

How many cuckoos are there in other men's nests? While it is clearly known that a proportion of husbands and partners are not in fact the biological fathers of children they are ostensibly raising as such with the mothers, for rather obvious reasons reliable statistics are likely to remain elusive.[154]

Whether we are talking about a husband or partner, the man registered in the register of births and on the child's certificate as the father, will remain the legal father unless and until the registered paternity is successfully challenged by someone else. The question for all legal systems is the extent to which they will allow such challenges to take place. Increasingly, the law has had to bow to scientific advance in that, if it can be established relatively easily by DNA testing what the true biological position is, the case for maintaining a fiction in the light of this evidence is not a strong one. Moreover, if the courts do not themselves direct testing, those affected may resort surreptitiously or openly to 'DIY' methods. The issue can also be important in public law children cases. The father with parental responsibility is automatically a party to such proceedings and his consent would have to be dispensed with if a placement order is sought at the conclusion of those proceedings. If another man (as is often the case) may be the biological father it will be important for this issue to be determined during the currency of the proceedings.

The most effective way of proving paternity in legal proceedings is through the use of tests, although at least historically other evidence was also valuable.[155] Whilst tests will usually be court directed, there is no reason why they should not be undertaken voluntarily.

Traditionally, the best available evidence was the conventional blood test. This entailed a comparison of the blood of the mother, the child and the alleged father. Since blood has certain inherited characteristics it is possible to identify those which have been derived from the father. Such a test, however, could not identify conclusively who was the father, since the blood of more than one man may exhibit the relevant characteristics. Yet where these characteristics were absent, it was possible to *exclude* conclusively the man in question. Where the alleged father was not excluded by the test, his blood group characteristics were examined as a percentage of the general population. If the incidence of men in

---

[154] For discussion of the law's attitude to 'adulterine' children or perhaps, more neutrally, the children of affairs see A Bainham '*S v S; W v Official Solicitor*: Welfare, truth and justice: the children of extra-marital liaisons' in S Gilmore, J Herring and R Probert (eds) *Landmark Cases in Family Law* (Hart Publishing, 2011), at p 113.

[155] Such as evidence of the mother's sexual relationships during the relevant period or the physical absence of her husband.

the group was small, this was strong evidence that he was the father, especially if supported by other evidence concerning, for example, the mother's sexual relationships at the relevant time.

The Family Law Reform Act 1987[156] extended the court's powers to order 'scientific tests' based on samples of genetic material other than blood. This power was finally implemented on 1 April 2001.[157] The DNA profiling technique now enables paternity to be established virtually conclusively, thus overcoming the limitations of the conventional blood test. The technique entails the analysis of genetic samples such as blood specimens, semen, saliva or hair roots. It examines the deoxyribonucleic acid in chromosomes which contains an individual's unique genetic pattern of characteristics transmitted by that individual's parents.[158]

The court has a general power to direct such tests,[159] but may not order a party to undergo them without that party's consent.[160] The consent of a person with care and control of a child under 16 years of age was initially also required.[161]

The question arose in two reported decisions as to whether the court had the power to *order* a parent to produce a child for testing where that parent objected. In *Re R (Blood Test: Constraint)*[162] Hale J held that there was such a power deriving from the parent's own right to compel a child to submit to a test. The court, she said, had power under its inherent jurisdiction to authorise the use of physical constraints against a child if satisfied that this was the right course of action. In this case the child, aged 22 months, was ordered to be delivered into the care and control of the Official Solicitor for the purposes of compliance with the court's direction. But in *Re O and J (Paternity: Ordering Blood Tests)*[163] Wall J reluctantly reached the conclusion that he lacked jurisdiction to oblige a mother to produce her child for testing. Amendments to the legislation introduced in 2000 now make it plain that a 'bodily sample' may be taken from a person under the age of 16 years, either if the person who has care or control of him consents or 'if the court considers that it would be in his best interests for the sample to be taken'.[164]

While it is the case now that the 'best interests' principle governs the question whether a sample should be taken from a child without parental consent, it does not govern the question whether testing should be directed in the first

---

[156] Family Law Reform Act 1987, s 23(1).
[157] Family Law Reform Act 1987 (Commencement No 3) Order 2001 (SI 2001/777).
[158] See, particularly, R White and J Greenwood 'DNA Fingerprinting and the Law' (1988) 51 MLR 145, and K Kelly, J Rankin and R Wink 'Method and Applications of DNA Fingerprinting: A Guide for the Non-Scientist' [1987] Crim LR 105.
[159] Family Law Reform Act 1969, s 20(1), as amended.
[160] Ibid, s 21(1).
[161] Ibid, s 21(3).
[162] [1998] 1 FLR 745.
[163] [2000] 1 FLR 418.
[164] Section 21(3) of the Family Law Reform Act 1969, as amended by s 82 of the Child Support, Pensions and Social Security Act 2000.

place. It was held forty years ago by the House of Lords in *S v S; W v Official Solicitor*[165] that the issue was not governed by the welfare principle but that the correct principle is whether the direction of the test would be *against* the best interests of the child. The 'best evidence principle' and considerations of justice militate towards the directing of tests unless it can be positively shown that they would be deleterious to the child's best interests. The test was applied and reaffirmed by the Court of Appeal comparatively recently in *Re L (A Child)*.[166]

In contrast to the testing of a child, where an adult refuses to comply with a direction, the court may not compel him or her to submit to the test but may draw adverse inferences from a refusal.[167] This will often result in a finding of paternity against an alleged father and the very fact of refusal may amount to corroboration of the mother's evidence.[168] Refusal by a certain man to undergo a test may result in an adverse inference that he is the father.[169] Conversely, where a man believes he is the father and does not want to put his paternity to the test, he may have an adverse inference drawn against him that he is *not* the father.[170] The court has a discretion to direct tests and, as noted above, is not bound by the welfare principle in exercising this, since the child's welfare is not directly in issue.[171] It is clear that the court should have regard to the interests of the child in arriving at its decision, although (at least historically) it might not always be easy to determine where those lay. Undoubtedly, there is a case for saying that the child himself (in addition to the other parties) has an interest in discovering the truth about his identity.[172] One of our greatest judges, Lord Denning, clearly believed in such right when over forty years ago he said:[173]

---

[165] [1972] AC 24. For detailed commentary on the case and its significance see A Bainham, above n 141.

[166] [2009] EWCA Civ 1239, [2010] 2 FLR 188. Whether this divergence in the statutory tests under s 20(1) and s 21(3) can be justified is arguable.

[167] Family Law Reform Act 1969, s 23(1).

[168] *McVeigh v Beattie* [1988] Fam 69.

[169] See *Re A (A Minor) (Paternity: Refusal of Blood Test)* [1994] 2 FLR 463, in which it was held that since a DNA test could have conclusively established who the father was, a man could put the issue beyond doubt by submitting to the test. See also *F v Child Support Agency* [1999] 2 FLR 244.

[170] *Re G (Parentage: Blood Sample)* [1997] 1 FLR 360.

[171] *S v S; W v Official Solicitor* [1972] AC 24. Such a test should not be directed where the court is satisfied that it would be *against* the best interests of the child concerned, but a direction can be made despite the opposition of a parent if it is consistent with the child's welfare. See *Re H (Paternity: Blood Test)* [1996] 2 FLR 65.

[172] Discussed in K O'Donovan 'A Right to Know One's Parentage?' (1988) 2 IJLF 27; E Haimes '"Secrecy": What Can Artificial Reproduction Learn from Adoption?' (1988) 2 IJLF 46; S Maclean and M Maclean 'Keeping secrets in assisted reproduction – the tension between donor anonymity and the need of the child for information' [1996] CFLQ 243; and K O'Donovan 'Interpretations of Children's Identity Rights' in D Fottrell (ed) *Revisiting Children's Rights: 10 years of the UN Convention on the Rights of the Child* (Kluwer, 2000) p 73.

[173] *W v W* [1970] 1 All ER 1157 at 1159.

'Whenever there is a question mark as to the parenthood of a child, the one thing a child will want to know as he grows up is: who is my father? He will be torn apart unless he knows. It is better for him, as for everyone else, that the truth should out.'

Any such right may however have to be weighed against a possible risk to the disruption of existing relationships. Several decisions illustrate the dilemmas with which the courts have had to wrestle in these cases. They also reveal how the courts have wavered in the weight which they have attached to ascertaining the biological truth as opposed to considerations of family stability.

Re F (A Minor: Paternity Test)[174] shows the traditional preference of the courts for leaving the status quo undisturbed and refusing to direct tests where the child is being raised in an ongoing marriage. Here, the mother had had sexual relations with her husband and another man claiming to be the father at around the time of conception. This man's relationship with the mother had ceased but he nonetheless applied for a parental responsibility order and contact order in relation to the child. The Court of Appeal upheld the judge's refusal to direct blood tests. It was held that the child's welfare depended primarily for the foreseeable future on her relationship with her mother and the stability of the family unit and that this need was not outweighed by any advantage to the child which could accrue from knowledge of the biological truth.

A very different view was taken in *Re H (Paternity: Blood Test)*,[175] but here there was a crucial distinguishing feature in that the mother's husband had had a vasectomy well before the birth of the child. Again the child was being raised as a child of the marriage – the mother having become reconciled to her husband following an affair. Her former lover sought contact with the child and a parental responsibility order. Here, the Court of Appeal upheld the judge's decision to direct tests notwithstanding the mother's opposition to tests on her child. Ward LJ said that it was in the child's best interests to be told 'the truth' unless the child's welfare justified a 'cover up'. The mother ought not to be 'living a lie' but ought to be following the maxim which she should be teaching her children 'at her knee' that 'honesty is the best policy'. Moreover, the sooner the child was told the truth, the better. Importantly, the court did not see any necessary inconsistency between upholding the *social* fatherhood of the husband while possibly establishing the *biological* parentage of the former lover.

In *Re T (Paternity: Ordering Blood Tests)*[176] a married couple had been unable to conceive a child together. They agreed that the mother would have sex with someone else for this purpose and she tried unsuccessfully to produce a child

---

[174] [1993] 1 FLR 598.
[175] [1996] 2 FLR 65. For comments, see A Bainham 'Vasectomies, Lovers and Disputed Offspring: Honesty is the Best Policy (Sometimes)' (1996) CLJ 444, and B Gilbert 'Paternity, truth and the interests of the child' [1996] CFLQ 361.
[176] [2001] 2 FLR 1190.

with the applicant, who was a friend of the family. Ten years later she tried again, this time with four men including the applicant. She gave birth in due course to a child who was raised by her and her husband as a child of the marriage. Initially the applicant saw the child regularly but the mother eventually found the visits too demanding and ended them. This led in due course to speculation in the wider family and local community about the child's paternity. The applicant applied for a parental responsibility order and a contact order. Having failed with his application he made another some six years later relying on his rights under the ECHR.

Bodey J directed blood tests under the newly amended s 21(3) of the Family Law Act 1969[177] and considered the balance to be struck between the various interests under domestic law and under the ECHR. In most cases, he said, it was likely to be in the child's best interests to know the truth. In this case this was so because of the doubts which were already in the public domain and bearing in mind that the marriage was stable notwithstanding these doubts. Further, the result of the tests, depending on what it was, might well determine the applications for contact and parental responsibility. So far as the ECHR was concerned, it was a matter of balancing Convention rights. The child had a right to know his true identity and to have the possibility of contact with each of his parents, but this had to be set against the child's competing right to have the current stability of his family life protected. Likewise the mother, her husband and the applicant had conflicting rights under Art 8. These rights pulled in different directions but the child's rights and best interests fell particularly to be considered. The child's right to know here emerged as the weightiest. In his view the interference with other rights was *proportionate* to the legitimate aim of providing the child with the possibility of certainty of his real paternity.

Re H (Contact with Biological Father)[178] is a recent case in which the mother's husband had a vasectomy and, hence, they were unable to conceive a child together. They enlisted the help of a friend who had been intended to be a sperm donor but who, in the event, had sexual intercourse with the mother and achieved conception that way. DNA testing confirmed his paternity, a declaration of parentage was made under s 55A Family Law Act 1986 and the child's birth certificate was amended to record him as the father; a consequence of which was to confer parental responsibility on him. The issue was the appropriate level of contact which he should have with the child. The Court of Appeal held, inter alia, that the judge at first instance, who had dismissed the application for contact, had placed disproportionate emphasis on the potential for instability in the mother's marriage which could be occasioned by the father having contact. Where the child, as here, was the product of a full relationship between the parents, the starting point was that it normally benefited children to have a full and meaningful relationship with both parents. The judge should

---

[177] See p 140 above.
[178] [2012] 2 FLR 627.

have given that factor priority and then balanced it against the other issues in the case. A new judge should determine the issue of what level of contact was appropriate.

A fascinating feature of this decision is the Court's apparent view that the *manner of conception* of the child, viz via a sexual relationship rather than sperm donation, was significant and might have a bearing on the appropriate level of contact allowed. It is not immediately obvious why participation in sexual involvement, as opposed to the provision of sperm, by an obliging friend should really make a difference in terms of the relationship with the resulting child. It should however be said that on the facts of this case there was an affair of significant duration between the mother and the man concerned.

Re H and A (Paternity: Blood Tests)[179] is now the leading authority. The mother gave birth to twins following an extra-marital affair. She told the man concerned that he was the father and allowed him some contact with the children. When they fell out he brought a paternity suit which the mother successfully concealed from her husband for almost a year. She refused to consent to blood tests, and the husband's evidence was that he was likely to leave the family home if the tests established that he was not the father. The judge refused to direct tests on the basis that this would risk the stability of the children's family life. The Court of Appeal, remitting the case for rehearing, disagreed taking the view that the judge had given insufficient weight to the benefits of certainty in a situation in which there had been much speculation and gossip. The judge had also concluded too readily that the children's family would be destroyed since he had based this on the assumption, not necessarily borne out by the evidence, that the marriage was sound. The court said that the paternity of a child was now to be established by science and not by legal presumption or inference. Most significantly, perhaps, the court gave a clear indication that there would be few cases where the best interests of children would be served by the suppression of truth.

There may be some cases in which the question of *when* the child should be told the truth arises. In *Re D (Paternity)*[180] Hedley J took the view that it would not be in the best interests of the child (described as an 'angry young man' aged 10 at the relevant time) to be tested immediately but that it would be in his best interests to know the truth of paternity in the longer term. Accordingly, he directed samples to be taken from the man claiming to be the father to be stored and from the child but stayed that part of the order for the time being to be restored on application later. The case is one example of the more general temporal question of when children or young people should be told the truth of their biological origins assuming that it is their right to know it.

---

179 [2002] 1 FLR 1145.
180 [2007] 2 FLR 26

Finally there are circumstances in which there is no dispute over paternity and in which it is *known* who the father is, but where there may again be an issue as to whether the child should be told the truth. This has arisen in a number of reported cases.

Re K (Specific Issue Order)[181] concerned a child aged 12. His father was a well-known disc jockey from King's Lynn. The mother had told the child when he was aged 5 that his father was dead and had persisted with this story thereafter because of the father's adverse behaviour towards her. The child had originally been jointly registered and given the father's name but the mother later changed this to her own and resisted all forms of contact between the father and the child. The father applied for a specific issue order requiring the mother to inform the child of his paternity arguing that it was fundamental that he be told the truth and that, since it was inevitable that sooner or later the child would find out the true position when he looked at his birth certificate, it was better that he be told as soon as possible. Judge Hyam disagreed. Although generally a child had a right to be told the truth about his father's identity, his welfare was paramount. Here there was, he thought, a cogent reason for denying the right to know. The mother's hatred of the father was such that informing the child about him would cause emotional disruption to the child's life which would be seriously detrimental to his welfare.

As where there is a dispute over paternity, there can be a question here too of when the child should be told the truth. In *Re J (Paternity: Welfare of Child)*[182] the court upheld the mother's view that a child ought not to be told the truth of paternity until he attained 16. The court thought that the benefits of revealing the truth there and then were outweighed by the impact this would be likely to have on her reconstituted family in which the child regarded her partner as his father. Where the court does determine, however, that the truth should be revealed to the child, if the mother is unwilling to tell the child, the court has jurisdiction to direct that the truth be conveyed to the child by other means, most likely to be by an officer of CAFCASS.[183]

It may be that increasingly in the future it will not be assumed that a choice necessarily has to be made between stability and truth or between potential fathers. With the very high incidence of social parenting and a growing emphasis on the child's right to knowledge of biological origins, the way forward may be to acknowledge the child's interests in *both* potential fathers albeit performing different roles. Certainly, the courts do not regard the genetic link as crucial to the contact question and have openly recognised in this context the importance to the child of the social father.[184] Part of the problem may be thought to arise from the legal position that there can only be *two*

---

[181] [1999] 2 FLR 280.
[182] [2007] 1 FLR 1064.
[183] *Re F (Paternity Jurisdiction)* [2008] 1 FLR 225.
[184] See, for example, *O v L (Blood Tests)* [1995] 2 FLR 930.

parents which in turn can create a mindset that the child can have only two significant adults in his life. This is a view which is likely to be increasingly questioned.

At the same time, it is clear that biological truth remains most important to some people, not least *some* 'fathers' whose interest in children can rapidly wane when it is discovered that they are not in fact the biological fathers. One extreme manifestation of this attitude is the emergence of civil actions in several jurisdictions, including England, seeking damages for paternity fraud. The classic situation is one in which the mother is aware that she had a long-running affair around the time of conception and that her lover is likely to be the father. She nonetheless deliberately induces her husband or partner to believe that he is the biological father and accept responsibility, social and financial, for the child. In these circumstances the English courts have recognised that this behaviour is actionable in the tort of deceit.[185] In *A v B*[186] the mother's cohabitant was deceived by her into believing that he had fathered her second child. He was awarded a sum of £7,500 general damages for the 'substantial and continuing degree of distress and deep sense of loss suffered'.[187] This approach is not however universal. It has not been followed in Australia where the High Court of Australia in *Magill v Magill*[188] rejected such an action, partly on the basis that to allow it would be inconsistent with the no-fault ethos of the reformed Australian divorce law and family justice system.

Fathers and 'family life'

Here, as in relation to establishing paternity, the position is far from straightforward. What is certain is that the *mere fact* of genetic parentage will not per se establish family life between a man and a child. This is clear from the jurisprudence of the ECtHR. The uncertainty surrounds how much more is required. This is something which has exercised not just the ECtHR but also the English courts in a string of cases concerning the right of a genetic father to participate in adoption proceedings.[189]

If family life were to be established by the genetic connection alone, it would arise between, inter alia, a sperm donor and the resulting child. In *G v The Netherlands*[190] the European Commission was unwilling to accept that it did.

---

[185] *P v B (Damages for Deceit)* [2001] 1 FLR 1041.

[186] [2007] 2 FLR 1051.

[187] Cf *Webb v Chapman* [2009] EWCA Civ 55 where an ex-husband failed to obtain damages for deceit against his ex-wife and unsuccessfully sought permission to appeal to the Court of Appeal.

[188] (2006) 231 ALR 277 and for commentary see N Wikeley and L Young 'Secrets and lies: no deceit down under for paternity fraud' [2008] CFLQ 81.

[189] See further A Bainham 'Can we Protect Children and Protect their Rights?' [2002] Fam Law 279, at pp 280–284 and the cases cited at p 200 of the 3rd edition of this work. See also chapter 9 below.

[190] (1990) 16 EHRR CD 38.

What is required then beyond this? The answer which the Court gave in *Söderback v Sweden*[191] was that 'certain ties' must exist between father and child. However, we also know from this case that cohabitation between the mother and father is not an essential prerequisite to the establishment of family life – although doubtless where it has existed this will be a factor tending towards a finding that family life exists. In *Söderback* the natural father was attempting to prevent adoption of a child by the step-father. The Court found that certain ties did exist between the biological father and the child but that the interference with the father's family life with the child could be justified on the basis of the child's best interests. The ties here appear to have been the father's commitment to contact with the child, although little had in fact taken place. In *Kroon v The Netherlands*[192] family life was established on the basis that there was a relationship of 'sufficient constancy' to create de facto family ties. The mother and father had had a relationship of considerable duration and had produced no less than four children together, but they had never cohabited.

Two further cases from the Netherlands have also been concerned with this question of when family life begins between a father and a child. In *Haas v The Netherlands*[193] the applicant was born out of wedlock and was seeking to establish that he was the son of the deceased and therefore entitled to the deceased's estate as against a nephew of the deceased. The deceased had never 'recognised' him as his son, but he had made payments for his care and upbringing, visited him and occasionally gone on day trips with the boy and his mother. The applicant argued that he had family life with the deceased and that Dutch laws which discriminated against the illegitimate and 'unrecognised' child violated Art 14 of the ECHR. Having failed in the Dutch courts, the applicant took his case to Strasbourg. The ECtHR held unanimously that there was no violation of the ECHR. In the Court's view, it was not truly faced with an issue of 'family life' or 'private life' within the meaning of Art 8 but with a question of evidence going to the issue of whether family ties between the applicant and the deceased should be recognised. It was held that the evidence was insufficient to establish this link and that the applicant could not derive from Art 8 a right to be recognised as heir of the deceased for inheritance purposes.

On the other hand, in *Yousef v The Netherlands*[194] 'family life' was found to have existed even though the mother (as she was entitled to do under Dutch law) had refused to permit the father to 'recognise' his child. Here there was no dispute as to biological paternity, and the mother and father had cohabited for a certain period. Further, after the mother's death, the father had some contact with the child. In these circumstances family life did exist between the father and the child.[195] The Court went on to hold, however, that there was no

---

[191] [1999] 1 FLR 250.
[192] (1994) 19 EHRR 263.
[193] [2004] 1 FLR 673.
[194] [2003] 1 FLR 210.
[195] See also *Lebbink v The Netherlands* [2004] 2 FLR 463, where family life was also found to exist between the father and child even though the mother and father had never cohabited. The

violation of the father's rights under Art 8 when engaging in the balancing exercise required by Art 8(2). The denial under Dutch law of the father's right to recognise his child was in accordance with the law and pursued a legitimate aim which was necessary in a democratic society in that it was considered to be in the child's best interests. The Court also held that, where it was necessary to balance the *rights* of parents and the *rights* of children, the child's rights must be the paramount consideration and, in any balancing of *interests*, the interests of the child must prevail.

The significance of finding that family life did exist between the father and the child is demonstrated by *Görgülü v Germany*.[196] In this case a child was collected from hospital when four days old and placed for adoption. The biological father did not learn of the birth for three months but, when he did, he got fully involved and was even granted custody of the child at one point. Nonetheless, the decision of the German authorities to plough on with adoption was upheld by the Appeal Court. Finding a violation of Art 8 in relation to the refusal of custody and access rights to the father, the European Court emphasised that there was an obligation on the state to aim at reuniting a natural parent with his or her child, and that future relations between them could not be legitimately determined by the mere passage of time. The decision of the German courts to suspend the father's access rights had rendered any form of family reunion and the establishment of further family life impossible.

Article 8 is concerned not simply with respect for 'family life' but also respect for 'private life'. The European Court of Human Rights in *Mikulić v Croatia*[197] found the facts surrounding disputed paternity to fall within the latter rather than the former. The father had no more than a casual relationship with the mother, but the child's right to knowledge of biological origins, and the state's duty to provide procedures to facilitate this, was recognised by the Court as an aspect of the right to respect for private life.

Finally, we must turn to the very significant decision of the European Court in *Anayo v Germany*.[198] Here the Nigerian biological father of twins born to a married woman was shut out of all contact with them by the mother and her husband. In this they were supported by the German courts which gave priority to the family unit over a father who had never met the children. They refused to allow him to contest the legal paternity of the husband. In a landmark decision, the European Court held that *intended* family life might exceptionally fall within the ambit of family life where the fact that family life had not been

---

ECtHR reiterated the principle that mere biological kinship, without further legal or factual elements indicating the existence of close personal ties, could not be enough to establish family life. Here, such ties were found to exist based on the fact that the father had been the child's 'auxiliary guardian' under Dutch law, had been present at the birth, had visited the mother, had changed the baby's nappy a few times and baby-sat once or twice, and had had contact with the mother concerning the child's impaired hearing.

[196] [2004] 1 FLR 894.

[197] [2002] 1 FCR 20.

[198] [2011] 1 FLR 1883. For commentary see B Sloan 'Unmarried fathers and the frustration of family life' [2011] CLJ 314.

established was not attributable to the applicant. The Court did not rule out the possibility that the concept of family life *could* extend to a *potential* relationship between a child and a biological father. Close relationships which fell short of family life would generally fall within the scope of *private* life. In the present case, the biological father's two year relationship with the mother and intended relationship *might* give rise to family life with the children but certainly fell within the notion of private life. The Court's refusal to allow him contact had been an unjustifiable interference with his Art 8 rights, balancing the competing rights and in particular by reference to the best interests of the children. The decision is potentially of considerable importance to any man who is effectively prevented from early involvement with a child by the mother who, following the termination of their relationship, wants nothing further to do with him.

A final matter is whether the mother's husband automatically has family life with the child. It seems clear that this would be the case where the marriage is intact at the time of the birth. But the European Court of Human Rights has recently given the perhaps surprising answer that this is not necessarily so if the child was conceived during marriage but born after divorce where the mother has allowed another man to acknowledge paternity and act as the social father to the child. In *Kautzor v Germany*[199] the Court held that, although the child had been conceived during marriage, it had not been established that the mother's then husband was the biological father. He had never seen the child and there had never been a close personal relationship between him and the child which could amount to established family life. Family life could be established by de facto family ties, and it was not unreasonable for a state to base the original assignment of paternity on the assumption that the man who acknowledged paternity with the Mother's consent was indeed the father. This decision clearly attaches priority to social rather than biological parentage, perhaps in contrast to the thrust of the Court's earlier decisions.

The Court has, however, taken a similar view of the importance of social relationships in the assignment of parentage in *Ahrens v Germany*.[200] The case concerned a mother who had two relationships respectively with M1 and M2. After apparently terminating her relationship with M1 she formed a stable relationship with M2. However, during the course of this second relationship, a further 'fling' with M1 resulted in the birth of a child. Notwithstanding that M1 was clearly established by testing to be the biological father, the German Appeal Court's refusal to allow M1 to challenge the legal acknowledgment of paternity by M2 (supported by the mother) was found by the European Court not to violate his Convention rights. The resumed relationship between the mother and M1 was said to be of a purely sexual nature and there had been no intention to found a family. Accordingly, 'family life' had not been established between M1 and the child.

---

[199] [2012] 2 FLR 396.
[200] [2012] 2 FLR 483.

From an English perspective the decision is striking in recognising a state's decision to uphold a legal filiation which corresponds with social reality rather than biology as within that state's margin of appreciation. In England such a filiation is not currently recognised outside the limited context of assisted reproduction or adoption.

DECLARATIONS OF PARENTAGE AND THE RIGHT TO KNOWLEDGE OF BIOLOGICAL ORIGINS

As we have seen above, the issue of parentage may arise in a range of different legal proceedings. This may be an integral issue in those proceedings as where, for example, a man seeks contact with a child and it is necessary to determine whether he is in fact the father before a decision can be made on contact or, to take another example, where rights of succession depend on establishing that a particular relationship existed. In some cases, however, the sole question may be parentage as where someone is merely interested in establishing the truth or in having the truth, as perceived by him or her, recorded. In these circumstances a declaration of parentage may be sought.

There were formerly two separate procedures for obtaining a declaration of parentage.

Under the Family Law Act 1986,[201] s 56 it was possible for any person to obtain a declaration:

(a)   that a named person is or was his parent, or

(b)   that he was legitimate, or

(c)   that he had or had not become a legitimated person.

This was a procedure in essence only open to someone wishing to establish that he or she was a *child* of a particular person. In most cases the applicant would of course be an adult and would be seeking a declaration for purposes such as the right to amend a birth certificate, to establish a right to inherit property, or to acquire nationality or citizenship. Such a declaration, if obtained, was binding for *all* purposes but it should be noted that the procedure was limited in two significant ways. First, it was available only to someone seeking to establish that he or she was a *child* and to no one else. It was not, for example, open to someone to seek a declaration that he or she was a *parent* of a person. Secondly, it was not possible to obtain a declaration that a named person was *not* the applicant's parent or a declaration of illegitimacy.

---

[201]   The 1986 Act followed Law Com Report No 132 *Declarations in Family Matters* (1984).

Alongside this procedure was a quite separate procedure for obtaining a declaration of parentage under the Child Support Act 1991, s 27.[202] This procedure was open to either the Secretary of State or the person with care of the child where a maintenance assessment was under consideration and there was a denial of paternity. But such declarations were limited to the single purpose of establishing whether or not there was liability for child support and could not be relied upon for other purposes. In particular, they could not be relied upon for the purposes of birth registration or for applying for contact with the child. One especially adverse consequence of this was that the process of s 27 declarations actually impeded the registration of some fathers since the obtaining of a court order for maintenance (one of the forms of evidence which allowed a man to register himself as father of a child) had been largely superseded by child support maintenance assessments which did not have this effect.[203]

Accordingly, there was a need for a simplified and unified procedure for obtaining declarations of parentage. This was achieved by inserting a new s 55A into the Family Law Act 1986.[204] Alongside this there were amendments to s 27 of the Child Support Act 1991.[205] The effect of those amendments was to widen the availability of the procedure. Now *any person* may apply for a declaration of status, and the application need not relate to the applicant's own position. The procedure now extends to a declaration as to whether *or not* a named person is or was the *parent* of another person named in the application. Any person seeking a declaration that *he or she* is the *parent* of a named person may bring the application as of right.[206] Beyond this the court has a discretion whether or not to hear the application and may refuse to do so 'unless it considers that the applicant has a sufficient personal interest in the determination of the application'.[207]

These reforms reflect in part the greater emphasis which is now being given throughout the law to establishing the biological truth of parentage, although they also recognise that there may be circumstances in which this might not be desirable especially where to do so might be considered to be against a child's best interests.[208]

Where the court grants a declaration of parentage, the prescribed officer of the court must notify the Registrar-General of the making of the declaration

---

[202] Law Com Report No 132 (above), at paras 20–25.

[203] Ibid, at para 29.

[204] By s 83 of the Child Support, Pensions and Social Security Act 2000. For a helpful analysis of the reform see N Wikeley 'Child Support, Paternity and Parentage' [2001] Fam Law 125, especially at pp 127–128.

[205] By virtue of the Child Support, Pensions and Social Security Act 2000, Sch 8, para 13.

[206] Family Law Act 1986, s 55A(4).

[207] Ibid, s 55A(3).

[208] Ibid, s 55A(5). See also *L v P (Paternity Test: Child's Objections)* [2013] 1 FLR 578 where Hedley J refused to override the objections of a 15-year-old girl to DNA testing. The applicant was seeking a declaration of parentage that he was *not* her father and thereby resist enforcement proceedings brought by the CSA in relation to arrears of child support.

within a prescribed period, currently 21 days.[209] The court has no jurisdiction
to direct the Registrar to rectify the birth register which is a matter for the
discretion of the Registrar-General on receipt of notification by the court.[210]

In *M v W (Declaration of Parentage)*[211] the court granted a declaration of
parentage to a middle-aged man. He was adopted but was aware of who his
biological father was. The latter had lived in Australia but was deceased, leaving
behind a widow and other children. The applicant wanted a declaration of
parentage because he felt stigmatised by the description 'Father Unknown' on
his birth certificate. The declaration was not opposed either by the deceased's
Australian family or by the applicant's adoptive parents. Granting the
declaration, Hogg J said that it was 'of great value for everyone who is adopted
to know about their background'.[212]

The broad question which is raised by these various instances of doubtful
parentage, is how far there may be said to be a right to knowledge of biological
origins on the part of the child. Prima facie, there is support for such a right in
the United Nations Convention on the Rights of the Child. Article 7 upholds
the right of the child, admittedly only as far as possible, to knowledge of *both*
parents, *from birth,* and the right thereafter to be cared for by them. It can be
argued that this implies an obligation on the part of the state to take positive
action to establish both maternity and paternity in *every* case of the birth of a
child.[213] The impending reforms to birth registration under the Welfare Reform
Act 2009 are certainly a move in this direction, though it may be questioned
whether the exemptions from the obligation to give particulars of the father
may detract unduly from the rights of the child.

The rights of adopted persons to information concerning their birth family are
now well-established and it is good adoption practice for adopted persons to be
told that this is the case.[214] The position contrasts with that of the
donor-conceived who have no such rights, following regulations which have
removed the former right of sperm donors to anonymity.[215] Those who know
they that were donor-conceived will therefore be able to access identifying

---

[209] Section 55A(7) and r 8.22 of the Family Procedure Rules 2010 (SI 2010/2955).

[210] Section 14A Births and Deaths Registration Act 1953. And see *Re F (Paternity: Registration)*
[2011] EWCA Civ 1765, [2012] Fam Law 522 in which the Court of Appeal made it clear that
there is a distinction between the issue of when a child should be informed about the true
position on parentage and the formal processes of birth registration. The latter was a matter of
public record and it was in the public interest that records were maintained effectively and
swiftly reflected the decisions of the courts.

[211] [2007] 2 FLR 270.

[212] Ibid, at 273.

[213] This certainly seems to be the Nordic approach. On the traditional role of the state in
establishing paternity in the Scandinavian countries see A Eriksson and Å Saldeen
'Parenthood and science: establishing and contesting parentage' in J Eekelaar and P Sarcevic
(eds), *Parenthood in Modern Society: Legal and Social Issues for the Twenty-First Century*
(Martinus Nijhoff, 1993) 75, especially at 82–83.

[214] See chapter 9.

[215] Anonymity was removed for donors from April 2005 by the Human Fertilisation and
Embryology Authority (Disclosure of Donor Information) Regulations 2004 (SI 2004/1511).

information about those donors on attaining 18 but this apparent right will clearly turn out to be illusory unless they are aware (and most are not) that they were conceived in this way.[216] This has lead to speculation on how the birth registration system might be adapted to provide information at the time of registration concerning the facts of donation.[217]

What can be said at the present time is that although the child's interest or right in knowledge of biological origins has been recognised many times, both domestically and internationally, we are still a long way from accepting that this is an absolute right. It is subject to many qualifications. Some of these are natural limitations arising from the fact that, even in the new world of DNA sampling, there are going to be a significant number of instances in which it is just impossible to establish where the truth lies. In other cases, the truth could be discovered and imparted to the child but a paternalistic view is taken that it is not in the best interests of the child for this to happen. The real question then is how this is weighed against the child's autonomy interest; the child's ability to determine for himself whether his birth parents matter to him or not and what steps, if any, he wishes to take to establish a relationship. If the facts of birth are not clearly established and accessibly recorded, then this autonomy interest is stifled.

LEGITIMACY AND ILLEGITIMACY
Illegitimacy before 1987

The history of the gradual reform of illegitimacy and its legal consequences in England is the story of an attempt to equalise the positions of children born in and out of wedlock by removing the disadvantages suffered by the latter, but to do so in a way which did not unnecessarily weaken the institution of marriage. This was a piecemeal and incremental process over many years, culminating in the Family Law Reform Act 1987 which at least came close to removing the concept of illegitimacy.[218] It nonetheless lingers on alongside its more openly recognised concomitant, legitimacy.[219]

In practice this means, since the information can be accessed at 18, that the first donor-conceived persons able to seek identifying information about the donors will be able to do so in 2023.

[216] The matter is further discussed in A Bainham, above n 94, at pp 462–467.

[217] For the various mechanisms as to how this might be done see E Blyth, C Jones, L Frith and J Speirs 'The role of birth certificates in relation to access to biographical and genetic history in donor conception' (2009) 17 *International Journal of Children's Rights* 207 and see also E Blyth and L Frith 'Donor-conceived people's access to genetic and biographical history' (2009) 23 *International Journal of Law, Policy and the Family* 174.

[218] The Family Law Reform Act 1987 removed most of the remaining legal disadvantages suffered by children born out of wedlock and it became a matter of some doubt whether the distinctions which remained were enough to add up to a discriminatory status.

[219] In particular the Legitimacy Act 1976 remains on the statute book.

The 'illegitimate' child suffered significant legal disadvantages and a considerable social stigma. The disadvantages at common law were principally the absence of succession rights, rights of financial support and the lack of a legal nexus with the father. These legal distinctions were slowly whittled away by widening the categories of those children who were regarded as legitimate[220] and by removing some of the specific disadvantages attaching to illegitimacy more directly by legislation.[221] When, at the end of the 1970s, the Law Commission came to examine the whole question of illegitimacy, a fundamental issue had to be addressed. This was whether the removal of the residual legal discrimination could be achieved simply by sweeping away the few legal distinctions which were left, or whether the status of illegitimacy itself would have to be removed. The Law Commission provisionally preferred the more radical alternative[222] but later resiled from this position.[223] It concluded that the advantages of removing the status of illegitimacy were outweighed by the disadvantages which would flow from conferring automatic parental rights on unmarried fathers.[224]

Meanwhile, the Scottish Law Commission was also considering this issue. It, too, concluded that it would be undesirable to give automatic parental rights to unmarried fathers but that all remaining legal distinctions between *children* could, nonetheless, be removed. Insofar as it was necessary to distinguish between fathers, this could be done by reference to the marital status of the parents and not by attaching labels to the children.[225] The Scots preferred to avoid any labelling of children at all in contrast to the English Commission's initial proposal to replace 'illegitimate' with the more morally-neutral 'non-marital'.[226] The Scottish reasoning was that any new labels would rapidly take on old connotations. The English Commission subsequently produced a second report which substantially adopted the Scottish solution.[227] Consequently, s 1 of the Family Law Reform Act 1987 embodies a general rule of construction which applies to all legislation and instruments made after 4 April 1988. This is that:

> 'references (however expressed) to any relationship between two persons shall, unless the contrary intention appears, be construed without regard to whether or not the father and mother of either of them, or the father and mother of any person through whom the relationship is deduced, have or had been married to each other at any time.'

---

[220] Particularly through the process of legitimation under the Legitimacy Acts of 1926, 1959 and 1976. It should however be noted that while legitimation by subsequent marriage of the parents was possible from 1926 it was extended to adulterine children only in 1959.

[221] Thus, under the Family Law Reform Act 1969, ss 14 and 16, an illegitimate child could claim under his father's intestacy or under his will.

[222] Law Com Working Paper No 74 *Illegitimacy* (1979).

[223] Law Com Report No 118 *Illegitimacy* (1982).

[224] Ibid, particularly at paras 4.29–4.36. The Commission considered, but rejected, the suggestion that the law might be able to distinguish between meritorious and unmeritorious fathers. Ibid, at paras 4.29–4.42.

[225] Scot Law Com No 82 *Illegitimacy* (1984).

[226] English report para 4.51.

[227] Law Com Report No 157 *Illegitimacy* (Second Report) (1986).

The position after 1987

The position, following the 1987 legislation, was that all but a few legal distinctions between children born in and out of wedlock had been removed, along with an attempt to remove the stigmatising language and terminology of illegitimacy. The only remaining differences (apart from the relationship with the father) related to titles of honour[228] and citizenship.[229] The latter distinction was removed from 1 July 2006.[230] In the light of this, it is an unresolved question whether it is still accurate to talk of a status of legitimacy and illegitimacy.[231]

In 1992 the Scottish Law Commission recommended the complete abolition of the concepts of legitimacy, illegitimacy and legitimation in Scotland. The Commission's view was that a separate status could only be justified where the person possessing it was in a significantly different legal position from other people. Since this would no longer be so if the Commission's proposals were accepted, these concepts would be unnecessary, anachronistic and regarded by some as offensive. Thus, the Commission recommended that they all ought to be removed from Scots law, subject to certain savings relating to hereditary titles and existing deeds and enactments. As the Commission put it, 'In the new Scottish Family Law children should just be children, and people should just be people, whether their parents were married to each other or not'.[232] These proposals were not, however, accepted by the Westminster Parliament, and Scots law thus continues to distinguish between married and unmarried fathers.[233]

What, then, is the current position in English law? There is no doubt that legal distinctions of substance do remain between children born in and out of wedlock and that the concept of legitimacy remains on the statute book, albeit in pre-1987 legislation not repealed by the 1987 Act. It is moreover the case that this concept has been extended in recent years into the context of same-sex

---

[228] See *Re Moynihan* [2000] 1 FLR 113.

[229] See *R (Montana) v Secretary of State for the Home Department* [2001] 1 FLR 449 in which the Court of Appeal rejected the argument that the refusal to register the citizenship of a child born abroad to unmarried parents, where only the father was British (the mother being Norwegian), amounted to a violation of either the father's or the child's right to respect for family life under Art 8 of the ECHR.

[230] When the Nationality, Immigration and Asylum Act 2002 was implemented. See S Sheldon 'Unmarried fathers and British Citizenship: the Nationality, Immigration and Asylum Act 2002 and British Nationality (Proof of Paternity) Regulations 2006 [2007] 19 CFLQ 1.

[231] The Scottish Law Commission concluded in 1992 that, at least in Scotland, the equivalent legislation (the Law Reform (Parent and Child) (Scotland) Act 1986) had *not* removed the status of legitimacy or illegitimacy: Scot Law Com No 135 *Report on Family Law* (1992), at para 17.3.

[232] Scot Law Com No 135 (above), at para 17.4.

[233] For a critique, see E Sutherland 'Scotland: Child Law Reform – At Last!' in A Bainham (ed) *The International Survey of Family Law 1995* (Martinus Nijhoff, 1997) p 435, at pp 438–439 and E Sutherland 'How Children are Faring in the "New Scotland" ' in A Bainham (ed) *The International Survey of Family Law (2001 Edition)* (Family Law, 2001) p 363, especially at pp 368–369.

relationships both by the adoption legislation and the Human Fertilisation and Embryology Act 2008, albeit by amending pre-1987 legislation. On the other hand, it is equally clear that it was an express purpose of the Family Law Reform Act 1987 to remove the discriminatory labelling of children and in this way to lessen any social stigma there might be attaching to birth outside marriage. As long ago as 1979 the English Law Commission recognised the force of the language used by the law. It said:[234]

> 'We believe that the law can help to lessen social prejudices by setting an example clearly based upon the principle that the parents' marital relationship is irrelevant to the child's legal position. Changes in the law cannot give the illegitimate child the benefits of a secure, caring, family background. They cannot even ensure that he does not suffer financially ... But they can at least remove the *additional* hardship of attaching an opprobrious description to him.'

Hence the policy of the 1987 legislation was to distinguish only between *parents* and not between children where it was still thought necessary to perpetuate legal distinctions. A reasonable question, therefore, if 'illegitimacy' is considered to have survived the 1987 reforms, is whether we should be talking about *illegitimate parents* rather than *illegitimate children*.[235] Rightly or wrongly, the evidence is that the media, judges, academics and society in general continue to use the language of illegitimacy in some cases apparently oblivious of the policy of the law over the last decade. Many illustrations could be given from post-1987 case-law,[236] but one is the Court of Appeal decision in *Dawson v Wearmouth*[237] where the judgment (given by Hirst and Thorpe LJJ) is peppered with references to 'an illegitimate child'.

Another is the single judgment in the Court of Appeal in *R (Montana) v Secretary of State for the Home Department*.[238] In contrast, Hale J in *Re R (Surname: Using Both Parents')*[239] was outspoken in her view that law reporters should avoid using the language of illegitimacy. What she said bears extended citation:

> 'It is a matter of huge regret that the Incorporated Council of Law Reporting chose to entitle that case *In Re W (A Child) (Illegitimate Child: Change of Surname)*.[240] It is now more than 14 years since the Family Law Reform Act 1987 sought to remove such language from our law, and in particular that no opprobrious adjectives should be attached to the child. If there is to be any opprobrium stemming from the birth of a child to parents who are not married to one another (and for my part I would not necessarily say that there was to be any

---

[234] Law Com Working Paper No 74 *Illegitimacy* (HMSO, 1979), at para 3.15.

[235] See B Hale, D Pearl, E Cooke and P Bates *The Family, Law and Society* (5th edn, Butterworths, 2002) where there is a section headed 'Illegitimate children or illegitimate parents?'.

[236] For illustrations of the use of the language of illegitimacy post-1987 in the press, by judges and by academics, see A Bainham 'Changing families and changing concepts: reforming the language of family law' [1998] CFLQ 1, at pp 8–11.

[237] [1997] 2 FLR 629.

[238] [2001] 1 FLR 449.

[239] [2001] 2 FLR 1358 at 1362.

[240] [2000] 2 WLR 258.

such opprobrium), it should be attached to the parents, whose choice it was, and not to the child, whose choice it definitely was not. I very much hope that the Incorporated Council will pay attention to these observations, should the problem arise in the future.'

Is this use of language perhaps justifiable? If there are still distinctions of substance, and if the concepts of legitimacy and illegitimacy remain on the statute book, perhaps differentiating language is still required. It could be argued that to refrain from using the language of legitimacy/illegitimacy in relation to children is to prefer 'political correctness' to accuracy.[241] An opposing view is that the spirit, if not the letter, of the 1987 legislation together with international obligations require that the language of illegitimacy be expunged from the law[242] even if certain substantive legal distinctions survive. The essence of this argument is that in the real world the question of status is going to be bound up to a large extent with the use of language. If those most involved with applying and interpreting the law continue to use the language of illegitimacy, it is not really surprising that it remains in common usage in society.[243]

Perhaps of greatest significance is the continued differentiation between married and unmarried fathers in terms of the acquisition of parental responsibility, though the distinctions have been greatly reduced by the use of birth registration as the principal means of conferring parental responsibility on the father outside marriage. There is a respectable view that the notions of legitimacy and illegitimacy can never be completely expunged unless there is a total equalisation of the legal position of fathers in terms of acquiring parental responsibility and with it what might be seen as a full parental relationship with the child. We consider these arguments in the next chapter.[244]

---

[241] This was certainly Cretney's view. See SM Cretney *Family Law* (4th edn, Sweet & Maxwell, 2000), at p 218.

[242] Mary Ann Glendon, writing in 1989, clearly thought that the Family Law Reform Act 1987 had succeeded in expunging the terminology of illegitimacy from English law. See MA Glendon *The Transformation of Family Law* (University of Chicago Press, 1989), at p 269.

[243] A Bainham 'Changing families and changing concepts: reforming the language of family law' [1998] CFLQ 1, at p 11.

[244] And for the views of one of the authors on these questions see A Bainham 'Is legitimacy legitimate?' (2009) *Fam Law* 673 and 'The illegitimacy saga' in *Fifty Years in Family Law: Essays for Stephen Cretney* (Intersentia, 2012) 83.

Chapter 4

PARENTAL RESPONSIBILITY

In the previous chapter, we saw that English and Welsh law distinguishes between the concepts of parentage/parenthood and parental responsibility. While legal parenthood carries with it certain legal incidents, s 3 of the Children Act 1989 provides that the full range of 'rights, duties, powers, responsibilities and authority which by law a parent of a child has in relation to the child and his property' is comprised in the concept of 'parental responsibility'. As discussed in chapter 2, parental responsibility is a central organising concept within the Children Act, which allows the law to regulate who has responsibility for the upbringing of children, whether it be parent or other person (or persons). This chapter examines how parental responsibility is allocated as a matter of law, how it may be acquired, and the various general rules on its exercise set out in s 2 of the Children Act. As we shall see, the law on allocation/acquisition of parental responsibility is controversial in the distinctions it makes between certain parents.

ALLOCATION OF PARENTAL RESPONSIBILITY

English and Welsh law distinguishes in the allocation of parental responsibility between children whose parents are in the formal relationship of marriage or civil partnership and those whose parents are not. Section 2(1) of the Children Act 1989 provides that, where a child's father and mother were married to each other at the time of the child's birth, each has parental responsibility for the child. Where a child's parents are not married to each other, parental responsibility is held automatically by operation of law only by the mother.[1] As we shall see, however, there are various methods by which parental responsibility can be acquired by a parent, and indeed by a non-parent.

Being married to each other at the time of the birth is given an extended meaning for the purpose of s 2(1), in accordance with the Family Law Reform Act 1987.[2] The broad effect of that legislation is that certain children will be *regarded* as being born to married parents. These include some children of void marriages, legitimated and adopted children, and children who are treated as legitimate.[3] Section 2(1) now also applies in the case of a mother and her civil partner, where the civil partner is a parent of the child pursuant to either s 42

---

[1]   Children Act 1989, s 2(2).
[2]   Section 2(3), incorporating, by reference, s 1 of the Family Law Reform Act 1987.
[3]   For a brief account of the landmarks in the law of legitimacy, see A Bainham 'Is Legitimacy Legitimate?' [2009] Fam Law 673, 674.

or 43 of the Human Fertilisation and Embryology Act 2008.[4] Thus for these purposes, the meaning of 'marriage' within s 2(1) is extended to include civil partnership. A child of the mother and the parent under s 42 is the legitimate child of the couple, whereas a child of the mother and a parent under s 43 is illegitimate unless legitimated by a subsequent civil partnership between the mother and parent. This legislation is not easy to reconcile with the position in adoption law, in that if a same-sex couple who are not civil partners choose to adopt a child, the child will be their legitimate child.[5] More fundamentally, it has been questioned 'whether an outmoded concept like legitimacy should simply be transported into the modern, liberal context of same-sex relationships'.[6] While a number of other jurisdictions have removed any distinctions between children based on their parents' marital status,[7] by contrast English law has, through the 2008 Act, extended the remit of the anachronistic and offensive concepts of legitimacy and illegitimacy. It seems clear that in seeking to secure equality for same-sex couples, the same priority has not been given to securing equality between children.[8]

THE LEGAL POSITION OF A PARENT WITHOUT PARENTAL RESPONSIBILITY

As can be seen, English law treats some parents less favourably than others in the allocation of parental responsibility. The distinctions operated by the law are twofold. Mothers are favoured over other legal parents; and parents who are in the formal relationships of marriage or civil partnership with the mother are favoured over those who are not. Later in the chapter we shall explore some of the debates surrounding these positions, which may strike some readers as unjustifiably discriminatory. In order to assess the law, however, it is necessary first to have some understanding of its impact. The effect of the law on allocation of parental responsibility is to leave some parents (at least initially) without parental responsibility. What is the legal position of such parents, and how does it differ from parents who have parental responsibility?

Certain legal consequences flow automatically from the legal status of *being a parent* and are not dependent on the possession of parental responsibility. Indeed, s 3(4) of the Children Act 1989 provides that the 'fact that a person has, or does not have, parental responsibility for a child shall not affect (a) any obligation which he may have in relation to the child (such as a statutory duty to maintain the child); or (b) any rights which, in the event of the child's death, he (or any other person) may have in relation to the child's property'. The parent without parental responsibility is thus in the same position as all other parents for the purposes of succession. He or she may succeed to the child's estate, or the child may succeed to the parent's estate, in the event of either of

---

4   Amended by HFEA 2008, Sch 6, paras 16 and 17.
5   A Bainham 'Is Legitimacy Legitimate?' [2009] Fam Law 673, 677.
6   Ibid, 676.
7   For example, Australia did so as long ago as the 1970s.
8   A Bainham 'Is Legitimacy Legitimate?' [2009] Fam Law 673, 679.

them dying intestate.[9] The parent has an obligation to maintain the child financially.[10] There is a presumption of reasonable contact in favour of a parent where the child is in care and the parent has a right to be consulted by a local authority about decisions taken in relation to the child, where the authority is accommodating the child.[11] A parent may apply without leave for any s 8 order.[12]

It has been suggested by John Eekelaar that in some aspects of a child's upbringing the difference between being a parent and being a parent with parental responsibility may be rather limited. Eekelaar argues that a parent has a duty to ensure that a child receives an education and to ensure that a child in his or her care is not neglected, and it must follow that a parent must have correlative rights to fulfill those duties, such as a right to obtain medical treatment for the child and to consent to such treatment.[13]

However, the law does distinguish between the rights of those who have parental responsibility and those who do not. As against a parent with parental responsibility, a parent who does not have parental responsibility has no right to look after the child physically and no right to take or participate in decisions regarding upbringing.[14] Third parties have no duty to deal with him or to take his views into account. For these purposes, it must be appreciated that no distinction is made between the parent who is in stable cohabitation with the mother and the parent who is living separately from the mother, except that the former is very likely now to acquire parental responsibility through birth registration. There will, of course, be practical distinctions since the cohabitant, unlike the non-cohabitant, is likely to be performing the role of social parent. Indeed, it is the case that at least some unmarried mothers have been unaware of their partner's lack of legal responsibility for the child.[15] While they are living together amicably it is unlikely that much will turn on the strict legal

---

9   Family Law Reform Act 1987, s 18, as amended by Human Fertilisation and Embryology Act 2008, s 56, Sch 6, para 25.

10 Child Support Act 1991, ss 1(1) and 54. This obligation applies notwithstanding that the father has not acquired parental responsibility. See the Children Act 1989, s 3(4).

11 Children Act 1989, ss 34(1) and 22(4) respectively.

12 Ibid, s 10(4).

13 J Eekelaar 'Rethinking Parental Responsibility' [2001] Family Law 426. For criticism of Eekelaar's arguments, see S Gilmore, J Herring, and R Probert 'Parental Responsibility – Law, Issues and Themes' in R Probert, S Gilmore, and J Herring *Responsible Parents and Parental Responsibility* (Oxford: Hart, 2009), ch 1.

14 A good example is *Dawson v Wearmouth* [1997] 2 FLR 629, where an unmarried father tried unsuccessfully to persuade the courts that the child should be known by his surname rather than the surname of the mother's ex-husband which she had chosen. The initial choice of name is the mother's alone (as the person with sole parental responsibility) and the father's claims are limited to a possible change of name based on the child's best interests.

15 This was certainly what Pickford found in her study involving unmarried fathers. See R Pickford *Fathers, Marriage and the Law* (Family Policy Studies Centre/Joseph Rowntree Foundation, 1999). See also R Pickford 'Unmarried Fathers and the Law' in A Bainham, S Day Sclater and M Richards (eds) *What is A Parent? – A Socio-Legal Analysis* (Hart Publishing, 1999).

position between the parents and, of course, the parent will, in any event, have the powers and responsibilities which are held by any de facto carer.[16]

Lack of parental responsibility not only affects the parent's relationship vis-à-vis the mother, but also, significantly, standing in relation to the State.[17] A parent who does not have parental responsibility has no right to object to a voluntary arrangement between the mother and the local authority for the authority to look after the child.[18] Although a parent has standing to apply for a residence or contact order in these circumstances, the reality is that this may prove a difficult hurdle where the child has, in the meantime, been placed in substitute care. It is certainly not as effective, from the parent's point of view, as an initial right of objection would be.

Neither does a parent without parental responsibility have the right to appoint a guardian.[19] All of these limitations on parental status will, however, be overcome if the parent succeeds in obtaining parental responsibility. In the next section we examine how the current legal position on allocation and acquisition of parental responsibility developed in policy debate and the various ways in which the parent who is not allocated parental responsibility can now acquire it.

POLICY DEBATE AND DEVELOPMENT OF THE LAW

The current law on allocation and acquisition of parental responsibility has been the subject of debate and of reports by the English[20] and Scottish Law Commissions,[21] and the Lord Chancellor's Department,[22] for over 30 years, focusing on the question of the circumstances under which the unmarried *father*[23] should acquire parental responsibility. Much attention has been focused on the different circumstances in which children may be conceived and on ways of distinguishing between so-called 'meritorious' and 'unmeritorious' men.[24] The English Law Commission, after provisionally favouring the view that parental responsibility should automatically flow from the determination

---

16   Section 3(5) of the Children Act 1989.
17   For a particularly good example of this under the old law, see the House of Lords decision in *Re M and H (Minors) (Local Authority: Parental Rights)* [1988] 3 All ER 5.
18   The right of objection extends only to those with parental responsibility, as does the subsequent right of removal of the child. See s 20(7) and (8) of the Children Act 1989.
19   The right extends only to parents with parental responsibility and guardians. See s 5(3) and (4) of the Children Act 1989.
20   Law Com Working Paper No 74 *Illegitimacy* (1979); Law Com Report No 118 *Illegitimacy* (1982); and Law Com Report No 157 *Illegitimacy (Second Report)* (1986).
21   Scot Law Com Report No 82 *Illegitimacy* (1984) and Scot Law Com No 135 *Report on Family Law* (1992).
22   Lord Chancellor's Department, *1. Court Procedures for the Determination of Paternity, 2. The Law on Parental Responsibility for Unmarried Fathers* (March 1998).
23   By which we mean the father who is not married to the child's mother.
24   Alongside this view there has been another to the effect that parental responsibility should flow automatically from the determination of legal paternity – a position adopted in almost all the States of Eastern Europe in the period after World War II and by Australia in 1975.

of paternity, came out against it in 1982,[25] largely because of the perceived threats to the security of unmarried mothers raising children on their own. By contrast the Scottish Law Commission, a decade later, had come around to the view that all fathers should have parental responsibility irrespective of marital status, and that it would have the additional advantage of being able to abolish illegitimacy conclusively.[26] The English solution, however, was to retain a distinction between married and unmarried fathers, but to allow the 'unmarried father' to apply to a court for a 'parental rights and duties order', which was subsequently enacted in s 4 of the Family Law Reform Act 1987. The Family Law Reform Act 1987 stopped short of allowing unmarried parents to share parental responsibility by agreement without the necessity of going to court. The Law Commission originally rejected that idea on the basis that it had the potential for eroding the institution of marriage by 'blurring the legal distinction between marriage and other relationships'.[27] This view was criticised by some commentators who felt that to recognise private agreements could be a means of allowing 'meritorious' fathers in stable relationships to acquire full parental status while excluding 'unmeritorious' men from parental participation.[28] The Law Commission was, in due course, persuaded of this view,[29] and s 4 of the Children Act 1989 gave effect to its recommendation, allowing the mother to agree to the father's acquisition of parental responsibility through the making of a formal 'parental responsibility agreement'. The Children Act 1989 brought with it a change in terminology, from 'rights and duties' to the concept of 'parental responsibility', and the parental rights and duties order in the 1987 Act was effectively re-enacted in s 4 of the 1989 Act as a 'parental responsibility order'.

In the late 1990s the Lord Chancellor's Department consulted on several options for reform of the law on parental responsibility and unmarried fathers, expressing the view that discrimination was increasingly seen as unacceptable, in view of the large numbers of children born to unmarried parents, many of whom were in stable relationships.[30] Following consultation, the Government decided that parental responsibility should be conferred on a father through joint registration with the mother of the father's name on the child's birth certificate,[31] and s 4 of the Children Act 1989 was subsequently amended by the Adoption and Children Act 2002 to achieve this.[32] While generally welcomed,

---

[25] Law Com Report No 118 *Illegitimacy* (1982).
[26] Scot Law Com No 135 *Report on Family Law* (1992). For a detailed account of the reasoning of the Scottish Law Commission see the second edition of this work, at pp 172–173.
[27] Law Com Report No 118 (above), at para 4.8.
[28] See, in particular, J Eekelaar 'Second Thoughts on Illegitimacy Reform' [1985] Fam Law 261.
[29] Law Com Report No 172 *Guardianship and Custody* (1988), at para 2.18.
[30] Lord Chancellor's Department, 1. Court Procedures for the Determination of Paternity, 2. The Law on Parental Responsibility for Unmarried Fathers (March 1998), at para 51.
[31] For a discussion of the consultation and responses, see S Sheldon 'Unmarried Fathers And Parental Responsibility: A Case For Reform?' (2001) 9 *Feminist Legal Studies* 93.
[32] Adoption and Children Act 2002, s 111. See D Sharp 'Parental Responsibility – Where Next?' [2001] Fam Law 606; J Masson 'The Impact of the Adoption and Childen Act 2002 Part I – Parental Responsibility' [2003] Fam Law 581; P Booth 'Parental Responsibility – What Changes' [2004] Fam Law 353.

some commentators objected to this provision, expressing the view that it would do nothing to promote and enhance the relationship between children and fathers but would represent a considerable incursion into the control that women, as primary carers, have in relation to their children.[33]

ACQUISITION OF PARENTAL RESPONSIBILITY BY 'UNMARRIED FATHERS'

There are now therefore three methods in s 4 of the Children Act 1989 by which an unmarried father can acquire parental responsibility. Section 4 provides:

(1) Where a child's father and mother were not married to each other at the time of his birth, the father shall acquire parental responsibility for the child if –

(a) he becomes registered as the child's father under any of the enactments specified in subsection (1A);[34]

(b) he and the child's mother make an agreement (a "parental responsibility agreement") providing for him to have parental responsibility for the child; or

(c) the court, on his application, orders that he shall have parental responsibility for the child.

Parental responsibility through birth registration: s 4(1)(a)

Those men who are *registered* on the child's birth certificate as the father on or after 1 December 2003 will acquire parental responsibility under s 4(1)(a) of the Children Act 1989 by virtue of that registration. As we have seen,[35] in the case of an unmarried father, registration requires the co-operation of both father and mother. A registration which fails to comply with the Births and Deaths Registration Act 1953, for example by reason of a father's erroneous attendance alone to register, will not confer parental responsibility upon him.[36] There will be a number of fathers who, even if registered as the child's father, may not have parental responsibility if registration took place prior to 1 December 2003, as s 4(1)(a) is not retrospective in effect.[37] However, on the basis of what is known about patterns of birth registration, now about four-fifths of all fathers who are not married to the mother acquire parental responsibility more or less immediately after the birth of the child when the process of birth registration is completed. This still leaves about one-fifth of

---

33 J Wallbank 'Clause 106 of the Adoption and Children Bill: Legislation for the "good" father?' (2002) 22 *Legal Studies* 276.

34 The enactments as they relate to England and Wales are paras (a), (b) and (c) of s 10(1) and of s 10A(1) of the Births and Deaths Registration Act 1953. Once provisions of Sch 6 to the Welfare Reform Act 2009 are implemented, they will also include regulations under s 2C, 2D, 2E, 10B or 10C of the Births and Deaths Registration Act 1953.

35 See chapter 3.

36 See *AAA v ASH, Registrar General for England and Wales and the Secretary for Justice* [2009] EWHC 636 (Fam), [2010] 1 FLR 1.

37 Adoption and Children Act 2002, s 111(7).

unmarried fathers who will not acquire parental responsibility swiftly in this way, and will be 'parents without parental responsibility', unless they acquire it in some other way. The failure to register the father can arise for several reasons: because fathers themselves are unwilling to acknowledge their paternity through the process of registration, perhaps because of indifference or perhaps because they deny it. But this may also be because the mother, for whatever reason, wants no further contact with the man concerned or, at any rate, does not wish him to have formal legal standing in relation to the child. As mentioned in chapters 1 and 3, Sch 6 to the Welfare Reform Act 2009, once implemented, will seek to ensure that more fathers are acknowledged on the child's birth certificate. This amends, and inserts new provisions into the Births and Deaths Registration Act 1953, which *inter alia* impose upon the child's mother a (qualified) duty to disclose information about her child's father.[38] This is likely to increase further the number of fathers acquiring parental responsibility through birth registration.[39] Overall, the effect of s 4(1)(a) of the Children Act 1989 is that a very substantial *majority* of unmarried fathers have parental responsibility, and over time the proportion of fathers having parental responsibility is likely to increase. The Welfare Reform Act 2009 will also insert a new (1C) into s 4 which will provide as follows:

> The father of a child does not acquire parental responsibility by virtue of subsection (1)(a) if, before he became registered as the child's father under the enactment in question –
>
> (a)   the court considered an application by him for an order under subsection (1)(c) in relation to the child but did not make such an order, or
> (b)   in a case where he had previously acquired parental responsibility for the child, the court ordered that he was to cease to have that responsibility.

This seeks to ensure that prior decisions of the courts on parental responsibility are not superseded by the grant of parental responsibility through birth registration.

Parental responsibility agreement: s 4(1)(b)

Section 4(1)(b) provides that 'the father and mother may by agreement … provide for the father to have parental responsibility for the child'. The agreement must be made in prescribed form and recorded in the Principal Registry of the Family Division.[40] The purpose of these formalities is to warn parents that the agreement will seriously affect their legal position, to advise them to seek legal advice and to inform them about the ways in which the

---

[38]   Inserting new ss 2A and 2B into the Births and Deaths Registration Act 1953.

[39]   See for discussion of the changes, S Sheldon 'From "Absent Objects of Blame" to "Fathers Who Want to Take Responsibility": Reforming Birth Registration Law (2009) 31 (4) *Journal of Social Welfare and Family Law* 373–389; and A Bainham 'What is the Point of Birth Registration?' [2008] CFLQ 449.

[40]   Section 4(2), and the Parental Responsibility Agreement Regulations 1991 (SI 1991/1478), as amended by the the Parental Responsibility Agreement (Amendment) Regulations 2009 (SI 2009/2026).

agreement can be brought to an end. This is a purely administrative matter and there is no power to question the desirability of the agreement for the welfare of the child. The agreement is, however, revocable by the court on the application of anyone with parental responsibility, or on the application of the child himself where the court has given the child leave on being satisfied that he has sufficient understanding to make the application.[41] It has been held that the making of a parental responsibility agreement is not itself an exercise of parental responsibility, and thus a local authority cannot prevent the parents of a child making a parental responsibility agreement with respect to a child in its care by using the local authority's powers under a care order to determine the extent to which the parent may meet his parental responsibility.[42]

The parental responsibility agreement was primarily designed for unmarried couples in stable relationships who wished to bring the legal situation into line with the factual position in which they were effectively raising a child together. It was also the case that at least some agreements were made to head off applications to the courts for parental responsibility orders. Given the apparently liberal attitude of the courts to the making of such orders (discussed below), in many instances the mother should be advised to share parental responsibility voluntarily rather than go to court. In fact, in most instances, cohabiting couples will now share parental responsibility through joint registration of the birth and it may be that these agreements will become largely redundant. Under the old law, this sharing of parental status was not possible, even by court order.[43] Yet it was questionable from the outset how far these agreements would be used in practice.[44] Parents living together amicably might see no advantage in formalising their arrangements, especially since some people choose to cohabit precisely because of their dislike of the formalities which attach to marriage. They might also be unaware of the disparity in their respective legal positions or of the provision for agreements.[45] The father may not feel comfortable about broaching the issue for fear of upsetting his

---

[41] Section 4(3) and (4).

[42] *Re X (Parental Responsibility Agreement: Children in Care)* [2000] 1 FLR 517.

[43] It was possible for a legal custody order to be obtained by the father but this was unenforceable where he was cohabiting with the mother and lapsed after three months' cohabitation. See the Guardianship of Minors Act 1971, s 9(3). In effect, an order for joint legal custody was not possible.

[44] The statistics for the registration of parental responsibility agreements shortly after implementation reveal that these misgivings were warranted. After an initial surge of interest which led to the registration of over 5,000 agreements in 1994, by 1996 there were only around 3,000 such agreements. There was little evidence of greater use of parental responsibility agreements in Scotland than in England. In 1998, there were just 230 agreements set against a figure of 22,319 children born to unmarried parents in Scotland that year. In 1999 there were 335 such agreements. See E Sutherland 'How Children are Faring in the "New Scotland" in A Bainham (ed) *The International Survey of Family Law (2001 Edition)* (Family Law, 2001) p 363, at pp 368–369. The Scottish Law Commission thought that these agreements were only a 'second best solution' and that an automatic status was preferable. See Scot Law Com Report No 135 *Report on Family Law* (1992), at para 2.51.

[45] This is certainly borne out by Pickford's research: see R Pickford *Fathers, Marriage and the Law* (above).

relationship with the mother.[46] There is yet a further possibility that the mother may not be sufficiently confident about the relationship, or the father's parenting role, that she would wish to dilute her own legal control by sharing parental responsibility. Indeed, one of the fears expressed concerning the acquisition of parental responsibility by registration of the father is that this may result in a minority of mothers being unwilling to name the father on registering the child's birth because of the consequential sharing of parental responsibility. Some mothers may see this as undermining their central parental role.

Parental responsibility order: s 4(1)(c)

If the mother is unwilling to register the father or to share responsibility voluntarily, the father may apply to the court for a parental responsibility order (PRO).[47] Clearly, this will most commonly arise where the father and mother are living apart and do not have an on-going relationship.

The order, if granted, has the same effect as the parental responsibility agreement and may be similarly terminated only by the court.[48] Its effect is to give the father an equal say in all matters of upbringing but it will not give him any superior claim vis-à-vis the mother to look after the child. If the father wishes to have the child in his care, he will need to apply for a residence order, which will also confer parental responsibility by way of a PRO.[49]

The making of a PRO is a matter with respect to a child's upbringing[50] and therefore the child's welfare is the paramount consideration upon the application.[51] Very early in the 'life' of the parental rights and duties order, the Court of Appeal established that the degree of commitment the father had shown to the child, the degree of attachment existing between father and child, and the father's reasons for applying, were material (albeit not exhaustive) factors in considering whether to make the order.[52] If fulfilled, those factors would establish prima facie that an order would be for the child's welfare.[53]

It was also quickly established that the primary purpose of the former 'parental rights order' was to confer on the father the full status of legal parent and that the order was appropriately used even where it was not contemplated that the man in question would be actively involved in the child's upbringing. Thus, the

---

[46] Pickford, ibid.

[47] For a detailed account of the case law, see S Gilmore 'Parental responsibility and the unmarried father – a new dimension to the debate' [2003] CFLQ 21.

[48] Section 4(2A).

[49] Section 12(1).

[50] *In the Matter of Z (Children)* [2008] EWCA Civ 1556, at para [13]. See contra, S Gilmore 'Parental responsibility and the unmarried father – a new dimension to the debate' [2003] CFLQ 21, especially at pp 31–34.

[51] See eg, *Re H (Parental Responsibility)* [1998] 1 FLR 855 (CA).

[52] *Re H (Minors) (Local Authority: Parental Rights (No 3)* [1991] Fam 151 (CA).

[53] *Re G (A Minor) (Parental Responsibility Order)* [1994] 1 FLR 504; and *Re E (Parental Responsibility: Blood Tests)* [1995] 1 FLR 392.

order could be of value even where the child was in the care of the local authority since it could give him the standing to challenge the authority's plans for the child[54] or to resist a proposed adoption of the child.[55] It was not therefore fatal to an application that the father would not in practice be in a position to exercise parental rights or responsibilities.[56]

These principles were carried forward and reinforced by the jurisprudence of the courts dealing with applications for PROs,[57] which has further emphasised that the PRO is designed to confer status upon a father. The leading authority is *Re S (Parental Responsibility)*.[58] Here, the unmarried parents had intended to marry. The birth of their daughter was jointly registered and the child took her father's surname. The relationship between the parents broke down when the father was convicted of possessing obscene literature. The mother suspected that he might be involved in paedophiliac activities and became reluctant to allow him contact with the girl. The father applied for contact (which ceased to be an issue) but also for a PRO which was refused by the judge. Allowing the father's appeal, the Court of Appeal set out the principles applicable to the use of these orders. The court emphasised that the purpose of the order was to give the father the full status 'for which nature had already ordained that he must bear responsibility'. The order would not, however, entitle the father to interfere in matters concerned with the management of the child's life.[59] Any abuse of the order or any interference with upbringing which was inconsistent with the child's welfare could be controlled by the court through s 8 orders. The court went on to say that expert psychological evidence regarded it as important that a child should grow up with good self-esteem and have a 'favourable positive image' of the 'absent' parent. Ward LJ emphasised that, wherever possible, the law should confer the stamp of its approval on a committed father lest the child should grow up with a belief that the father was in some way disqualified from fulfilling his parental role. Butler-Sloss LJ emphasised the significance of the conceptual and linguistic change from the notion of parental 'rights' to that of 'responsibility':[60]

> 'It is important for parents to remember the emphasis placed by Parliament on the order which is applied for. It is that of duties and responsibilities as well as rights and powers. Indeed the order itself is entitled "parental responsibility". A father who has shown real commitment to the child concerned and to whom there is a

---

54   *D v Hereford and Worcester County Council* [1991] 1 FLR 205.

55   *Re H (Illegitimate Child: Father: Parental Rights) (No 2)* [1991] 1 FLR 214.

56   *Re C (Minors) (Parental Rights)* [1992] 1 FLR 1. However, this is no authority for the converse proposition, that an order must be made in such circumstances: see *W v Ealing London Borough Council* [1993] 2 FLR 788, at 796.

57   See, for example, *Re H (A Minor)* [1993] 1 FLR 484; *Re CB (A Minor) (Parental Responsibility Order)* [1993] 1 FLR 920, [1994] 1 FLR 504; and *Re E (Parental Responsibility: Blood Tests)* [1995] 1 FLR 392.

58   [1995] 2 FLR 648. See also for similar reasoning *Re C and V (Contact and Parental Responsibility)* [1998] 1 FLR 392.

59   This interpretation of the Children Act 1989 is open to question since, unless a s 8 order has been made, all holders of parental responsibility at least in theory have an equal and independent say in the child's upbringing.

60   [1995] 2 FLR 648, at 659.

positive attachment ... ought ... to assume the weight of those duties and cement that commitment and attachment by sharing the responsibilities for the child with the mother.'

The reported cases and judicial statistics[61] do indicate a readiness on the part of the courts to make PROs.[62] It should not, however, be assumed that such orders will be routinely granted simply because fathers ask for them. The court will want to make an evaluation of the individual father's potential contribution to the child's life. For example, in *M v M (Parental Responsibility)*[63] the father, who had suffered a head injury in a motorcycle accident, had a low IQ and was prone to violent outbursts. Wilson J held that granting parental responsibility presupposes that a father is sufficiently capable of reasoning, and concluded that the father's injury meant that he was unable to exercise parental responsibility appropriately. The court will also wish to consider the father's motives for wanting parental responsibility. Where his motives are improper, parental responsibility may be denied. In *Re P (Parental Responsibility)*[64] the Court of Appeal upheld the judge's decision not to make a PRO on the basis that the father would use it inappropriately to interfere with and undermine the mother's care for the child. The father had been highly critical of the mother's care of the children and had made several groundless reports to the local authority about the children's care.[65]

Inappropriate conduct may also lead to an order being refused. In *Re T (A Minor) (Parental Responsibility: Contact)*[66] the father was violent to the mother and refused to return the child for nine days after a contact session. Upholding the judge's denial of parental responsibility as 'clearly the right decision', the Court of Appeal commented that the father had acted with no thought for the child's welfare. In *Re P (Parental Responsibility)*[67] a judge refused to grant parental responsibility where the father was serving a long prison sentence for several offences of robbery. Upholding the decision, the Court of Appeal held that the judge had properly taken into account the fact that the father had incurred a further long prison sentence for committing a robbery while on home leave from prison, and the effect of his incarceration as a restriction on his ability to exercise parental responsibility. In *Re H (Parental*

---

[61] For example, in 2010, 5,520 orders were made out of 5,980 disposals: *Judicial and Court Statistics 2010*, Table 2.4.

[62] Not even a failure to pay maintenance for the benefit of the child should by itself be enough to deprive a father of the order if he is otherwise devoted to the children. It was held in *Re H (Parental Responsibility: Maintenance)* [1996] 1 FLR 867 that withholding the order should not be used as a weapon to extract money from the applicant father even where the court was critical of his failure to contribute financially.

[63] [1999] 2 FLR 737.

[64] [1998] 2 FLR 96.

[65] See also *Re M (Contact: Parental Responsibility)* [2001] 2 FLR 342 (FD) (likely misuse by father in context of tensions between mother's and father's respective families because of father's allegations that mother's new partner constituted a risk of sexual abuse to the child), and *W v Ealing London Borough Council* [1993] 2 FLR 788 (CA) (father wanting parental responsibility to thwart adoption).

[66] [1993] 2 FLR 450 (CA).

[67] [1997] 2 FLR 722.

Responsibility) [68] the judge had found that the father had injured the child and had displayed cruel behaviour with an element of sadism. The Court of Appeal held that the judge had been entitled to conclude that the father posed a future risk to his son and that his previous behaviour rendered him unfit to have parental responsibility. In *Re L (Contact: Genuine Fear)* [69] the mother was intensely fearful, indeed phobic, of the father, who had a violent past. Consequently the father only had indirect contact and neither knew the child's home address nor school. The judge made no order as to parental responsibility. While recognising that parental responsibility had sometimes been seen as a status carrying rights in waiting, he nevertheless concluded that in these circumstances any chance of the father playing a meaningful role in the child's life was wholly imaginary; parental responsibility would confer a bare status on the father and would cause distress to the mother and child.

As we saw in chapter 3, in recent years the courts have increasingly been asked to adjudicate upon parenting roles in cases in which a man assists a woman to have a child where the intention is that the child is to be brought up by the mother and her lesbian partner. [70] In several such cases, an issue before the court has been whether the father of the child should be granted a parental responsibility order. The issue arose in *Re D (Contact and parental responsibility: lesbian mothers and known father)*. [71] In that case a child, D, was born to Ms A, who was in a lesbian relationship with Ms C. The child was fathered by Mr B. The couple's view was that Mr B would be acknowledged as D's father, but that his role would be a minimal one, perhaps seeing the child every few weeks. However, Mr B envisaged a greater role and sought parental responsibility. The application was opposed by A and C because of concern that Mr B would interfere in their upbringing of the child. They cited in support various instances of his interference, in particular on matters of the child's education and medical treatment.

Black J was not convinced that it was appropriate simply to apply to the novel facts of this case the existing principles with their heavy concentration on commitment, attachment and motivation. Expert evidence was sought from a child psychiatrist, who advised that parental responsibility should lie with the nuclear family, but that Mr B should also be officially recognised in some way. Black J was concerned to afford Mr B some status, but was concerned about his potential to interfere. This dilemma was eased, however, by Mr B's offer to be bound by conditions which would prevent him from being intrusive in the areas of D's schooling and health care. [72] By way of this conditional PRO, the respective statuses of the parties could properly be recognised. [73]

---

[68] [1998] 1 FLR 855.
[69] [2002] 1 FLR 621 (FD).
[70] See S Blain and A Worwood 'Alternative Families and Changing Perceptions of Parenthood' [2011] Fam Law 289.
[71] [2006] 1 FCR 556 (FD) (Black J).
[72] Ibid, at para [91].
[73] Ibid, at para [93].

Both the expert and Black J highlighted the difficulty of finding appropriate language to describe the roles of the adults concerned. In a subsequent case, *ML v RW*,[74] Hedley J had resort to the terms principal and secondary parents to describe the respective roles of the parties. However, as noted in chapter 3, in *A v B and another (Contact: Alternative Families)*[75] the Court of Appeal cautioned against the use of such categories,[76] and emphasised that each case is fact-specific.[77]

In *Re B (Role of Biological Father)*,[78] Hedley J, addressing a similar scenario to that in *Re D*, likewise observed that while it has become 'a somewhat hallowed process for the court to consider questions of commitment, attachment and motivation' it was particularly important where a case is outside the ordinary run of parental dispute on separation to remember that applications remain subject to the overriding provision of s 1(1) of the Children Act 1989.[79] On the facts of that case, however, Hedley J could see no benefit of a restricted grant of parental responsibility. He was concerned that forceful exercise of parental responsibility by the father would undermine the parental status of the lesbian couple by whom the child was being raised. His Lordship thus granted the father contact four times a year so as to allow the child to picture the father as someone significant in her life, but denied the father parental responsibility so as to preserve the autonomy of the nuclear family.

Faced with a similar case in *R v E and F (Female Parents: Known Father)*[80] Bennett J respectfully agreed with Hedley J's observations in *Re B (Role of Biological Father)*, and commented that 'dicta from well-known decisions in what might be called "conventional" or "usual" parental responsibility applications do not readily transfer to cases such as the instant one'.[81] He noted, however, that in similar cases the courts had continued to be mindful of the authorities which stress the status aspects of parental responsibility, and indicated that he emphatically did not ignore the well-known decisions.[82] In *R v E and F (Female Parents: Known Father)* the child lived with his mother and her civil partner, with whom she shared parental responsibility. The child's father was also in a same-sex relationship. Initially the relationship between the respective couples had been very good but deteriorated significantly following a dispute about how the child should be disciplined. Bennett J found that the father was erroneously equating his situation with a post-divorce father and was failing to recognise the reality that the child's nuclear family consisted of

---

74 [2011] EWHC 2455 (Fam).
75 [2012] EWCA Civ 285, [2012] 2 FLR 607. For comment, see A Zanghellini '*A v B and C* [2012] EWCA Civ 285 – heteronormativity, poly-parenting, and the homo-nuclear family' [2012] CFLQ 475.
76 [2012] EWCA Civ 285, [2012] 2 FLR 607, at [30].
77 Ibid, at [48] and [49].
78 [2007] EWHC 1952 (Fam), [2008] 1 FLR 1015.
79 At para [26], citing *Re H (Parental Responsibility)* [1998] 1 FLR 855 (CA).
80 [2010] EWHC 417 (Fam) [2010] 2 FLR 383 [2010] 2 FLR 383.
81 Ibid, at para [85].
82 Ibid.

the child and his female parents. He concluded that in these circumstances the grant of parental responsibility to the father would create conflict and not benefit the child.

In an insightful analysis of *Re D (Contact and parental responsibility: lesbian mothers and known father)*[83] and other cases which stress the status aspect of parental responsibility, Helen Reece has argued that there has been a degradation of the concept of parental responsibility in recent years from the notion of 'parental authority' to 'nothing more than official approval'.[84] However, as many of the cases denying fathers parental responsibility reveal, the courts do recognise the powers that the status of parental responsibility confers, and the impact its conferral can have for the welfare of the child concerned. The courts have emphasised that the making of a PRO is in the nature of the grant of a status so as to ensure that undue emphasis is not given to the potential exercise of parental responsibility in the process of deciding whether or not to grant parental responsibility, and to ensure that in deserving cases the making of an order cannot be vitiated solely by the applicant's inability to exercise parental responsibility (for example because of the father's temporary illness, or the mother's attitude to his active involvement in his child's life).

ACQUISITION OF PARENTAL RESPONSIBILITY BY FEMALE OTHER LEGAL PARENT

Section 4ZA of the Children Act 1989 provides that where a child has a parent by virtue of s 43 of the Human Fertilisation and Embryology Act 2008 and is not a person to whom s 1(3) of the Family Law Reform Act 1987 applies, that parent shall acquire parental responsibility in similar ways to the unmarried father, as discussed above: through birth registration, a formal parental responsibility agreement, or parental responsibility order. It remains to be seen whether the fact that the female parent will necessarily have embarked upon a formal process to acquire legal parenthood will lead the courts to adopt an approach different from that adopted in relation to 'unmarried fathers'.

DEBATES SURROUNDING ALLOCATION OF PARENTAL RESPONSIBILITY TO PARENTS

As we have seen, the parent who has never married, or never been in a civil partnership with, the child's mother will not have parental responsibility

---

83   [2006] 1 FCR 556 (FD) (Black J).
84   H Reece 'The Degradation of Parental Responsibility' in R Probert, S Gilmore and J Herring (eds) *Responsible Parents and Parental Responsibility* (Oxford, Hart Publishing, 2009), at p 102.

automatically. These distinctions, between mothers and other parents, and between parents who are in formal relationships and those who are not, have attracted considerable debate.[85]

More than once it has been argued that for the law to differentiate between parents in this way and between the children of those parents is contrary to the ECHR.[86] The arguments have been explored with respect to fathers and their children because the law has only very recently extended legal parenthood to the mother's partner in a same sex relationship. The ECtHR has thus far rejected the arguments of unmarried fathers. In *B v United Kingdom*[87] an unmarried father applied for a PRO and contact but, shortly afterwards, the mother took the child to Italy. The English courts dismissed his claim that this amounted to child abduction since, following *Re B (Abduction) (Rights of Custody)*,[88] he lacked 'formal rights of custody' which in this context largely hinged on his lack of parental responsibility.[89] He complained unsuccessfully of a breach of his rights under Art 8 of the ECHR taken in conjunction with Art 14. The essence of the argument was that unmarried fathers were discriminated against in the protection given to their relationships with their children when compared with that given to married fathers. The ECtHR, however, found the complaint inadmissible in that there was an objective and reasonable justification for the difference in treatment between married and unmarried fathers regarding the range of possible relationships between fathers and children. Specifically, fathers who had children in their care to any degree had different responsibilities from those who simply had contact. This, the Court held, justified the difference in treatment between those fathers with

---

[85] For a detailed account of the debates, see S Gilmore and L Glennon *Hayes and Williams' Family Law* (3rd edn, Oxford University Press, 2012), at pp 393–400; and see also J Herring, R Probert and S Gilmore *Great Debates in Family Law* (Palgrave MacMillan, 2012), ch 2, esp pp 38–45. For journal articles and chapters addressing the issue see: A Bainham 'When Is A Parent Not A Parent? Reflections On The Unmarried Father And His Child In English Law' (1989) 3 *International Journal of Law, Policy and the Family* 208; R Deech 'The unmarried father and human rights' (1992) 4 *Journal of Child Law* 3; H Conway 'Parental responsibility and the unmarried father' (1996) 146 NLJ 782; C Barton 'Equal responsibility for all fathers?' (1998) 142 (17) *Solicitors Journal* 401; P Townsend and A Baker 'Unmarried fathers – are we ending discrimination at last?' (1998) 162(13) JP 236; S Sheldon 'Unmarried Fathers And Parental Responsibility: A Case For Reform?' (2001) 9 *Feminist Legal Studies* 93; J Eekelaar 'Rethinking Parental Responsibility' [2001] Fam Law 426; S Gilmore 'Parental responsibility and the unmarried father – a new dimension to the debate' [2003] CFLQ 21; JM Scherpe 'Establishing and Ending Parental Responsibility: A Comparative View' in R Probert, S Gilmore and J Herring (eds) *Responsible Parents and Parental Responsibility* (Oxford, Hart Publishing, 2009).

[86] See especially *McMichael v United Kingdom* (1995) 20 EHRR 205, and see G Branchflower 'Parental Responsibility and Human Rights' [1999] Family Law 34.

[87] [2000] 1 FLR 1.

[88] [1997] 2 FLR 594.

[89] The concept of 'rights of custody' under the Hague Convention on the Civil Aspects of International Child Abduction 1980 does not precisely translate into the possession of parental responsibility under English law since there are circumstances, where, for example, a father has the primary care of the child, in which he may be held to have rights of custody for the purposes of the Convention despite lacking formal parental responsibility. See chapter 6 below.

parental responsibility and those without it.[90] In light of that decision, the Court of Appeal in *Re Z (Children)*[91] indicated that it would be inappropriate to develop an argument that the current law on allocation of parental responsibility is discriminatory.

However, the jurisprudence of the ECtHR and the position taken by the English legislation both appear to be at odds with the requirements of the UNCRC. The key points are that the UNCRC, as we saw in chapter 2, upholds the right of the child, admittedly only as far as possible, to knowledge of *both* parents, viz the mother and the father, *from birth* and the right thereafter to be cared for by them.[92] Further, it is explicit about States using their best endeavours 'to ensure recognition of the principle that both parents have common responsibilities for the upbringing and development of the child'.[93] Even allowing for the fact that these are not absolute, unqualified obligations there is an incongruity between what the UNCRC requires and what the ECtHR has held is required by the ECHR. There is an incongruity too between the UNCRC's requirements and English legislation, even after the recent reform.

The UNCRC has as its starting point the position that, once a child's parents are identified, the child has a right to knowledge of them and a relationship with them if this is possible to achieve. Specifically, in the case of the father these requirements would appear to be satisfied automatically once paternity is established. Of course, the child's rights cannot come into being in a concrete sense until paternity is established, but even that is not the end of the matter since it is more than plausible to argue that the UNCRC requires States to take positive action to try to establish both maternity and paternity whenever a child is born.

In contrast the ECtHR, as we have seen, has been unwilling thus far to accept that the determination of paternity per se gives rise to 'family life' between the child and the father. It is difficult to see how this can be reconciled with Art 7 of the UNCRC, and this then raises a further question about how to resolve a possible conflict between the two Conventions. In similar vein, English legislation has never conferred parental responsibility, and hence the full legal status of parent, on proof of paternity alone.

Automatic legal effects of parenthood per se are limited to such matters as financial obligations and succession rights. Yet there is an ongoing debate about whether the parent's moral and legal obligations ought to be only financial, or whether they should be the more wide-ranging obligations which

---

[90] It is important to appreciate that this decision is confined to the question of automatic parental responsibility. The Court has held that discrimination under German law between married and unmarried fathers in relation to the question of the right of access (contact) *did* breach the Convention: see *Sahin and Others v Germany* [2002] 1 FLR 119.

[91] [2008] EWCA Civ 1556.

[92] Article 7(1).

[93] Article 18(1).

the law imposes on parents with parental responsibility. The conceptual shift from parental 'rights' to parental 'responsibility' has led some to question why it is that every parent is not encouraged or required to accept more responsibility. In this sense, the law's discrimination may properly be seen as against mothers, who are compelled to have parental responsibility while other parents are not.

A major difficulty with the current law is that, as the Scottish Law Commission pointed out in 1992,[94] it is impossible to remove entirely the discriminatory status of illegitimacy and its concomitant legitimacy unless all distinctions between married and unmarried fathers vis-à-vis their children are removed. The question which needs to be asked is whether the continuation *at all* of the legal status of illegitimacy can be reconciled with a commitment to children's rights.

The second difficulty is also concerned with the theme of rights. It is that the granting of automatic parental responsibility to registered fathers, most of whom are living with the mother, will not address most of the serious human rights issues which have been surfacing in the reported cases. The reason for this is that it is not likely to be the father who has a sound, co-operative relationship with the mother who is before the court. It is much more likely to be the man who is *not* living with the mother and who may *not* have been registered as the father, or even told of the pregnancy or birth in some cases. This sort of case will not be affected by what is, it is argued, only a partial rectification of deficiencies in the law.

It is now *women* who substantially control the conception, birth and upbringing of children.[95] In England, as we have seen, it is still impossible for the unmarried man to make a voluntary acknowledgement of paternity without either the mother's co-operation or a relevant court order. Acquisition of full parental responsibility where the father is not registered is, likewise, dependent on the father persuading either the mother or the court that he is deserving of this level of involvement.

The fundamental issue is the extent to which the father's involvement, if any, with the child should continue in effect to be controlled by the mother.[96] The question of the mother's attitude is now especially significant in the light of the provision in s 4 of the Children Act conferring parental responsibility on birth registration. The traditional view of English law has been that, except where she is in receipt of social security benefits and the State thus has a financial

---

[94]   Scot Law Com Report No 135 *Report on Family Law* (1992) (above).

[95]   In a seminal article considering the position of fathers (married and unmarried) in the legislation of Western European States, Marie-Thérèse Meulders-Klein observed that scientific and cultural developments had reversed the historical dominance of men in relation to children: see M-T Meulders-Klein 'The Position of the Father in European Legislation' (1990) 4 IJLF 131.

[96]   For discussion, see JM Scherpe 'Establishing and Ending Parental Responsibility: A Comparative View' in R Probert, S Gilmore and J Herring (eds) *Responsible Parents and Parental Responsibility* (Oxford, Hart Publishing, 2009).

interest, it is largely a matter for the mother whether or not she wishes to identify the father and, thereafter, her attitude to his continuing involvement with the child is likely to have a significant bearing on the outcome of any application he might make for contact or parental responsibility. The central question which this poses is whether it is compatible with the notion of Convention rights for fathers and children, vis-à-vis each other, for access to those rights to be contingent on the view of another person, that is the mother.

To some extent the difficulties will be addressed in relation to birth registration upon full implementation of Sch 6 to the Welfare Reform Act 2009, which will impose a qualified legal duty on the mother to co-operate in disclosing the identity of the man believed by her to be the father. This is to be welcomed since social policy, it is submitted, should be concerned not simply with the financial liability of parents but also with the wider aspects of parental responsibility.[97]

ACQUISITION OF PARENTAL RESPONSIBILITY BY A STEP-PARENT

There are several options open to a step-parent for acquiring parental responsibility. One approach would be to apply for a residence order which grants parental responsibility to the holder of the order (discussed below), or to apply to adopt the child. The Adoption and Children Act 2002 provides that an adoption order may now be made on the *sole* application of a step-parent who is married to, or the civil partner of, the parent of a child.[98] This is considered further in chapter 13. The Adoption and Children Act 2002 also provided a new mechanism by which a step-parent (defined to include the civil partner of a child's parent) can acquire parental responsibility by inserting a new s 4A into the Children Act 1989. This responded to the views of several commentators who had argued for greater recognition of the step-parent relationship,[99] mooting various options, such as an automatic legal status by giving parental responsibility to all step-parents,[100] allowing private arrangements for sharing it,[101] or continuing to require an application to the court. Section 4A was consistent with several other provisions in the 2002 Act which sought to offer

---

[97] For a very different view of the position of fathers in relation to human rights, which denies that they should have rights to family life except where they are cohabiting with the mother, see R Deech 'The Unmarried Father and Human Rights' (1992) 4 JCHL 3. Cf A Bainham 'When is Parent not a Parent? Reflections on the Unmarried Father and his Child in English Law' (1989) 3 IJLF 208. See further the second edition of this work, at pp 170–172.

[98] Adoption and Children Act 2002, s 51(2).

[99] See, for example, J Masson, D Norbury and SG Chatterton *Mine, Yours or Ours? A Study of Step-Parent Adoption* (HMSO, 1983); J Masson 'Old Families into New: A Status for Step-Parents' in MDA Freeman (ed) *State, Law and Family* (Tavistock, 1984), ch 14.

[100] See eg, J Masson 'Old Families into New: A Status for Step-Parents' (above), at p 237.

[101] As advocated, eg, by G Douglas and NV Lowe 'Becoming a Parent in English Law' (1992) 108 LQR 414, at p 431, and recommended in the *Review of Adoption Law* and which found its way into the Draft Adoption Bill 1996: see the White Paper, *Adoption: The Future* (1993) (Cm 2288), at para 5.21.

alternatives to adoption, and s 4A was presumably enacted in the hope that an alternative means of acquiring parental responsibility would satisfy some step-parents who might otherwise be inclined to apply to adopt the child. Section 4A of the Children Act 1989 provides:

'(1) Where a child's parent ("parent A") who has parental responsibility for the child is married to a person who is not the child's parent ("the step-parent") –

(a)   parent A or, if the other parent of the child also has parental responsibility for the child, both parents may by agreement with the step-parent provide for the step-parent to have parental responsibility for the child; or

(b)   the court may, on the application of the step-parent, order that the step-parent shall have parental responsibility for the child.'

The provisions relating to the formalities for parental responsibility agreements and their termination are similar to those which apply to parental responsibility agreements and parental responsibility orders (PROs) in the context of unmarried fathers.[102]

Yet the analogy between the step-parent and the unmarried father, though strong, is less than perfect. First, in relation to agreements, it should be noted that in the most common situation of remarriage following divorce, it will be necessary to obtain the consent not only of the spousal parent but also of the non-resident parent. The agreement, unlike the bilateral one involving two unmarried parents, will involve a tripartite sharing of responsibility. It is only likely to be in those post-divorce situations in which there is a high degree of co-operation and understanding between all parties that such an agreement will be made. It is possible therefore to speculate that there may be a greater need for step-parents to apply for PROs than has been the case with unmarried fathers living with the mothers. They have not had to face the opposition of a third party. The second way in which the analogy with unmarried fathers breaks down is in the importance attached to marital or civil partnership status which these new provisions reflect. In the case of applications by unmarried fathers it is the very lack of marital status which is the raison d'être for agreements and PROs. However, in the case of the step-parent provisions, marriage or civil partnership is centre stage in two respects. First, neither the agreement nor the order may be made in favour of the mere cohabitant of a parent, however stable that cohabitation may be. Secondly, the consent of an unmarried father who has not acquired parental responsibility is not required for a parental responsibility agreement. Although, in most cases, the unmarried father will now have parental responsibility by registration, marriage is still significant to the extent that some unmarried fathers will continue not to have it. Whether a private sharing of parental responsibility without the consultation or consent of fathers in this position is consistent with evolving human rights obligations is open to doubt.

---

[102]   Compare s 4(2) (unmarried fathers) and s 4A(2).

A third difference is that upon the breakdown of the relationship between the child's parent and step-parent, there may not be the same expectation of future exercise of parental responsibility on the part of a step-parent as there is in the case of parents who are separated. In *Re R (Parental Responsibility)*[103] the mother and step-father of a three-year-old child were divorcing, the step-father having erroneously believed for most of the child's life that he was the natural father. The step-father sought a parental responsibility order under s 4A(1)(b). Peter Jackson J noted that the power to make an order would not exist if the couple were already divorced. He declined to grant the order, holding that 'in normal circumstances the beneficiary of such an order will be a person who might be described as an incoming step-parent who wishes to bring up a child together with the parent with parental responsibility and will be centrally participating in the upbringing of the child in future', and that 'the other situations in which an order might be made are likely to be limited.'

Do the reforms effected by s 4A reflect a sound policy? A distinction should perhaps be made between the different circumstances of step-parenthood. For, while the spouse of a widowed or formerly unmarried parent would be likely to share parental responsibility *only* with that parent, this is manifestly not the case where the marriage is with a divorced parent. The case for allowing automatic or informal sharing may be stronger where there is no third parental figure on the scene, since this would not entail a tripartite power-sharing arrangement.

There is room for argument about how consistent this sort of arrangement is with the philosophy of the Children Act. On the one hand, this undoubtedly favours an 'inclusive' model of child-rearing which might appear to support the regularisation of the step-parent's position. On the other hand, the principle of continuing parental responsibility might appear to militate against anything which would weaken or detract from the position of the non-resident father who remains, in all respects, a parent. The view expressed in one leading textbook that it is 'unclear why this parent's agreement is thought necessary' and that 'granting parental responsibility to a person does not involve the reduction of the power of others holding it'[104] is questionable. On the contrary, the policy of the Children Act was very clear. The essential philosophy of the Children Act is that parents remain parents and continue to exercise parental responsibility regardless of divorce. It would thus be quite improper to allow a voluntary sharing of parental responsibility by one parent without the other's concurrence or a court order. Moreover, to share decision-making for a child between three rather than two adults is equally clearly a weakening of the position of the parent who is not in the household.

The problem with an enhanced status for step-parents may therefore be that it could be seen as shutting out, or at least diluting, the parental contribution of the non-resident parent, contrary to the spirit of the legislation. There is plenty

---

[103] [2011] EWHC 1535 (Fam), [2011] 2 FLR 1132.
[104] See J Masson, R Bailey-Harris and RJ Probert *Cretney's Principles of Family Law* (8th edn, Sweet & Maxwell, 2008), at p 569.

of evidence that this is precisely what *some* step-families have tried to do by attempting to change the child's surname and/or adopt the child.[105] While a triangular sharing of parental responsibility may work well where all parties have an interest in the child and wish to enter into a co-operative arrangement, it could be a recipe for conflict where this is not the case. It is also questionable whether the proliferation of parental responsibility which could occur where children are caught up in serial marriages would be in their best interests, or workable at all, on a practical level. There is, therefore, an argument for saying that, contrary to these reforms, any acquisition of parental responsibility by a step-parent should continue to be subject to judicial scrutiny. As Brenda Hale once observed, the step-relation is not the same as the 'normal' family constituted within marriage and 'perhaps we should not pretend that it is'.[106]

FURTHER METHODS OF ACQUIRING PARENTAL RESPONSIBILITY

There are various other ways in which parental responsibility can be acquired, which are available also to a wider class of persons than parents and step-parents.

Parental responsibility conferred by a residence order

A residence order, defined in s 8 of the Children Act 1989,[107] allows a court to settle the arrangements as to the person or persons with whom a child lives. While the residence order is in force it confers parental responsibility on the person in whose favour the order is made.[108] Parental responsibility conferred in this way upon a non-parent does not carry the right to agree, or refuse to agree, to the making of an adoption order or an order under s 84 of the Adoption and Children Act 2002, nor the right to appoint a guardian for the child.[109] If a residence order is made in favour of a child's parent who does not already have parental responsibility, the court is obliged also to make a parental responsibility order in favour of the parent,[110] and this must not be terminated while the residence order is in force.[111] Parental responsibility is retained by the parent through the parental responsibility order even if the residence order is brought to an end.

---

[105] This is part of the rationale for the former restrictions on step-parent adoptions.

[106] BM Hoggett *Parents and Children: The Law of Parental Responsibility* (3rd edn, Sweet & Maxwell, 1987), at p 126. This view does not appear to have been repeated in the fourth edition of the book.

[107] Discussed in more detail in chapter 5.

[108] Children Act 1989, s 12(2).

[109] Children Act 1989, s 12(3).

[110] Under Children Act 1989, s 12(1) (in relation to father) or s 12(1A) (in relation to a woman who is a parent by virtue of the Human Fertilisation and Embryology Act 2008, s 43).

[111] Children Act 1989, s 12(4).

Parental responsibility conferred by orders in child protection proceedings

Some of the court orders which can be obtained in child care and protection proceedings, for example an emergency protection order or a care order, confer parental responsibility upon the applicant.[112] These are discussed in detail in chapters 11 and 12.

Parental responsibility conferred by an adoption order

When an adoption order is made under the Adoption and Children Act 2002, parental responsibility is acquired by the adoptive parent or parents.[113] Adoption is considered in detail in chapter 13.

Parental responsibility conferred by special guardianship order

Special guardianship is a legal status introduced by the Adoption and Children Act 2002[114] with a view to providing greater legal security for long-term carers of children without removing legal parenthood and parental responsibility of parents as adoption does. A special guardianship order confers upon the applicant an exclusive power to exercise parental responsibility. Special guardianship is considered alongside adoption in chapter 13.

GUARDIANSHIP

Guardianship is now the means by which parental responsibility can be conferred upon individuals in the event of the death of a holder or holders of parental responsibility. The law is now set out in ss 5 and 6 of the Children Act. Before examining those provisions it is helpful briefly to set the notion of guardianship in historical context. Historically, at common law a man was the 'natural guardian' of his legitimate children,[115] exercising all parental rights, to the exclusion of the mother. Even when the mother was eventually given equal rights and authority by the Guardianship Act 1973, the father remained, in theory, the sole guardian, through which he apparently retained certain residual rights.[116] Alongside this natural or parental guardianship there was another kind of guardianship which arose where someone other than a parent took

---

112   See ibid, ss 44(5) and 33.
113   Adoption and Children Act 2002, ss 46 and 67.
114   Inserting Children Act 1989, ss 14A–14F.
115   Guardianship has a long history.The best account of this is probably to be found in Law Com Working Paper No 91 *Guardianship* (1985), especially Part II.
116   For example, the concept of natural guardianship was invoked by the courts as the basis for the father's right to object to a unilateral change of the child's surname by the mother, following divorce. The leading authority was *W v A* [1981] Fam 14.

over legal responsibility for a child on the death of a parent.[117] The Children Act 1989 abolished the notion of parental guardianship and replaced it with the concepts of parenthood and parental responsibility.[118] Henceforth, parents would just be parents. The concept of 'guardianship' was retained, however, to describe those non-parents who step into the shoes of deceased parents. Recognising that guardians in practice take on all the responsibilities of parents and are, accordingly, in an analogous position, the Children Act 1989 sought to assimilate the legal position of parents and guardians by conferring parental responsibility on guardians as a matter of status.[119]

Guardianship differs significantly from all other forms of social parenthood. It is by far the least regulated, the appointment of guardians being largely a private matter not subject to public scrutiny, judicial or otherwise. It is also the most far-reaching in its legal effects since it carries some of the incidents which are normally associated with legal parenthood, but which do not arise merely by possessing parental responsibility. Yet the status of guardianship, although closely resembling parenthood, is not identical. For example, guardians are not liable for child support as parents are.[120] More importantly, they may voluntarily disclaim their appointment, whereas the obligations of parenthood are imposed by operation of law and may not be voluntarily relinquished or transferred. The status of guardianship may also be revoked by court order, whereas parenthood survives all court orders except an adoption order[121] or parental order.[122]

The view has been expressed that:[123]

> 'Given the gamut of safeguards, or controls ... existing to ensure that a transfer of parental responsibility to a non-parent is consistent with the child's welfare, their absence in the case of guardianship is striking.'

This emphasis on private ordering may be accounted for partly by the principle of testamentary freedom. Just as testators enjoy a wide measure of independence from legal controls in disposing of their material wealth[124] on death, so also should they be able to plan appropriate arrangements for the care of their minor children should death be untimely. It is also, to some extent, consistent with the lack of legal controls on the acquisition of parenthood in

---

[117] Guardianship was previously largely governed by the Guardianship of Minors Act 1971, and formerly by the Guardianship of Infants Act 1925.

[118] This had the incidental advantage of finally equalising the legal position of the married mother and father.

[119] This removed the anachronistic distinctions which the old law made between guardianship of the person and guardianship of the estate. For an explanation of these distinct offices, see Law Com Working Paper No 91 (above), at paras 2.21–2.25.

[120] See chapter 9.

[121] Adoption and Children Act 2002, s 46.

[122] Human Fertilisation and Embryology Act 2008, s 54.

[123] G Douglas and NV Lowe 'Becoming a Parent in English Law' (1992) 108 LQR 414 at 428.

[124] But less so since the Inheritance (Provision for Family and Dependants) Act 1975.

the majority of cases.[125] The Law Commission did consult on the question whether there ought to be restrictions on private appointments or the disqualification of certain individuals analogous to those applying to become private foster parent,s but rejected the idea.[126] Indeed, the Law Commission thought guardianship was such a desirable institution that it wanted to encourage more private appointments by relaxing the formalities governing appointment; and the Children Act gives effect to this policy.

The appointment of guardians

The Children Act preserved the two ways in which guardians might be appointed before it, ie by private appointment or by appointment by the court.[127]

Private appointments

Private appointments of guardians may be made by parents with parental responsibility or by guardians and special guardians,[128] but not by anyone else, even where they hold parental responsibility. The unmarried father may not appoint a guardian unless he has acquired parental responsibility. One of the effects of conferring parental responsibility automatically on fathers who are registered at the time of the child's birth will therefore be to allow many more, indeed the vast majority of, unmarried fathers to appoint a guardian if they so wish – although in practice the incidence of appointment of guardians is likely to remain insignificant in numerical terms. The extension of the power of private appointment to guardians reflects the general legislative policy of assimilating their position to parenthood. Under the old law, appointments were valid only if made by will or deed, but the Children Act allows a simple appointment by any written document which is dated and signed.[129] The hope is that this will encourage more people, especially younger adults who may have a natural disinclination to contemplate death, to appoint guardians. Having said that, the more formal method of appointment by will is likely to remain the norm. A most common situation is that of joint appointments by parents who are fearful of sudden death together, most obviously in an accident. In many cases, they are likely to discuss together and agree upon a suitable individual or individuals. The Children Act confirms that such appointments may be made jointly by two or more persons.[130]

Court appointments

The court may appoint a guardian where there is no parent with parental responsibility, where a deceased parent or special guardian had a residence

---

[125] See chapter 3.
[126] Law Com Working Paper No 91 (above), at paras 3.27–3.29.
[127] Sections 5 and 6 constitute the new statutory framework for guardianship.
[128] Section 5(3) and (4).
[129] Section 5(5).
[130] Section 5(10).

order in his or her favour at the time of death or where the child's only or surviving special guardian dies.[131] The appointment may be made on the application of the intended guardian or by the court of its own motion, during the course of family proceedings.[132]

The first situation could arise where both parents have died, having failed to appoint guardians. The court's intervention might be necessary, for example, to avoid a family wrangle, where more than one relative is asserting the right to look after the children. It could also arise where an unmarried father survives an unmarried mother. The appointment of an unmarried father by either the mother or the court is the only remaining way in which a parent may also become a guardian, and this would also have the effect of conferring parental responsibility on him where he did not otherwise have it.

The second situation most obviously includes the case where a divorced parent with a residence order is survived by the non-residential parent. The implication of this power is that it is not automatically desirable that the latter should be entitled to take over the care of the children which he has not had during the subsistence of the residence order. There must be cases in which a former spouse would be the very last person the deceased parent would have wished to look after the child. Where the court makes an appointment in these circumstances, the guardian will share parental responsibility with the survivor. It may become apparent that the level of actual or potential disagreement between them is such that the court will need to back up the appointment with a s 8 order.[133]

The legal effects of guardianship

Guardianship can only take effect on the death of a parent. Its express purpose is to provide a complete replacement for a deceased parent. Where it is thought in the best interests of a child that a living parent be replaced, this can be achieved through adoption, by special guardianship, or by a residence order. The Law Commission did float the idea of inter vivos guardianship, but it did not attract much support and was not pursued.[134] Subsequently, the interdepartmental *Review of Adoption Law* took up the idea and proposed that it ought to be possible to make the social parent holding parental responsibility under a residence order the guardian of the child. This would enable parental responsibility to be extended to the child's majority, viz up to the child's eighteenth birthday.[135] This could be thought desirable since court orders in relation to children generally cease at 16.[136] The Draft Adoption Bill presented in 1996 did not incorporate this proposal as such but did make provision for the

---

[131] Section 5(1).
[132] Section 5(2).
[133] A residence order might, for example, be required to resolve the question of the child's home.
[134] Law Com Working Paper No 91 *Guardianship* (1985), at paras 4.4 et seq.
[135] Department of Health and Welsh Office *Review of Adoption Law* (HMSO, 1992), at para 6.5, and the White Paper *Adoption: The Future* (1993) (Cm 2288), at para 5.24.
[136] Section 9(6).

extension of residence orders to the child's majority.[137] That amendment to the Children Act was eventually enacted by the Children and Young Persons Act 2008.[138] Under amendments to the Children Act 1989 introduced by the Adoption and Children Act 2002, the notion of inter vivos guardianship was resurrected in the slightly different guise of special guardianship (mentioned above, and discussed in detail in chapter 13).

Before the Children Act 1989, the appointment of a guardian always took effect immediately on the death of the appointing parent. The effect was that the guardian would share parental 'rights', if there was a surviving parent, with that parent. This was a peculiarly English phenomenon. No comparable rule existed in any member country of the Council of Europe. The Law Commission considered that the rule had the potential for creating unnecessary conflict between the guardian and surviving parent, and that a surviving parent should normally be protected from unwelcome interference by an outsider. The Law Commission thought that the general aim of guardianship law should be 'to balance the claims of the surviving parent and the wishes of the deceased in the way which will be best for the child'.[139] To this end, the Children Act established the general rule that a guardian should only take office on the death of the surviving parent.[140] But this rule is displaced where the deceased parent had a residence order at the date of death. Here, the guardianship takes effect immediately.[141] This exception will not apply where *both* parents had residence orders, ie where a shared residence order has been made.[142]

The thinking behind these provisions can be called into question. The implication is that, while a surviving parent who was living with the deceased in a united household can be trusted to assume the sole care of the children without assistance, the divorced survivor cannot. The primary rule is understandable enough. Few would disagree with the notion that the surviving parent, in what was a united family, should receive help only if this is requested informally and should not have it thrust upon him or her by unwelcome interference from inside or outside the family. The issue is why a non-resident parent should not be similarly protected. The thinking seems to be that the deceased parent should be able, through guardianship, to preserve the 'advantage' of the residence order after his death. It is questionable how far this can be squared with the central principle of continuing parental responsibility of both parents.

Apart from the residence issue, the non-resident parent is as much a parent as was the deceased resident parent.[143] To make him share parental responsibility

---

137   Clause 86.
138   Section 37(1), amending Children Act 1989 s 9(6).
139   Law Com Report No 172 *Guardianship and Custody* (1988), at para 2.27.
140   Section 5(8).
141   Section 5(7).
142   Section 5(9).
143   It should also be recalled that there will be many instances of so-called 'non-resident' parents who survive the parent looking after the child but, because of the no order principle, no

with a guardian may seem inappropriate where he has continued, in fact, to be actively connected with the child. It would arguably have been more consistent with the general aims of the legislation to have placed the onus on the guardian to seek immediate appointment where it could be demonstrated that this was in the child's best interests.[144] On the other hand, the view has been expressed that where one person had responsibility for a child under a residence order, it is reasonable that he or she should be able to control the arrangements made for the child immediately following his or her death.[145]

Another difficulty is that the rule appears to create uncertainty about who is entitled to take over the physical care of a child. Both the guardian and the surviving parent have parental responsibility and, with it, an equal claim to look after the child. An initial dispute over where the child is to live would, therefore, appear to require a residence order to resolve it. This could have been avoided if the survivor held sole parental responsibility unless and until challenged by the guardian. The rather unsatisfactory outcome is that the onus to commence proceedings will be on 'the person wishing to change the existing arrangements'.[146]

Assuming the appointment is operative, what are the essential legal effects of guardianship? The most immediate and significant effect is that the guardian acquires parental responsibility.[147] But, as noted above, the incidents of guardianship extend beyond this. In fact, the guardian occupies a position somewhere between legal parents and social parents who merely have parental responsibility. Like a parent, the guardian (or special guardian) is entitled to object to adoption and to appoint a guardian,[148] but unlike a parent (and in common with other social parents with parental responsibility), the guardian is not a liable relative for the purposes of public[149] or private[150] financial responsibility for children. No succession rights arise on the death intestate of either the guardian or the child (although they may, of course, arise expressly by will) and the child cannot derive citizenship from his guardian.

---

residence order will have been made. These 'non-resident' parents will in these cases have *sole* parental responsibility, and the onus will be on the appointed guardian to challenge this position.

[144] See A Bainham 'The Children Act 1989: Parenthood and Guardianship' [1990] Fam Law 192, at pp 194–195.

[145] R Probert *Cretney and Probert's Family Law* (8th edn, Sweet & Maxwell, 2012), at p 298.

[146] Law Com Report No 172 *Guardianship and Custody* (1988), at para 2.28. This rather resembles the law of the jungle since it turns on whether the guardian or the survivor has managed to get to the child first. For other practical difficulties which may arise under the regime, see R Oswald 'The Appointment of Testamentary Guardians and the Children Act 1989' [1992] Fam Law 519.

[147] Section 5(6).

[148] Adoption and Children Act 2002, s 47, and s 5(4) of the Children Act respectively.

[149] Social Security Administration Act 1992, s 78.

[150] Section 15 of and Sch 1 to the Children Act.

Children – The Modern Law

Revocation, disclaimer and termination of guardianship

An appointed guardian may never take office because the appointment is revoked. He may disclaim his appointment or may be removed by order of the court.

Revocation

An appointment may be revoked in a number of ways.[151] This may be achieved expressly by a written and dated instrument, made by the appointing parent or guardian,[152] or impliedly by the destruction of the written document,[153] by the later appointment of a guardian unless there was a clear intention to appoint an additional guardian,[154] or by subsequent revocation of a will or codicil in which the appointment was made.[155] Following a later amendment, the appointment of a spouse as guardian will be automatically revoked by a subsequent divorce.[156]

Disclaimer

The Children Act allowed, for the first time, a guardian to disclaim his appointment in writing within a reasonable time.[157] It is perhaps a surprising feature of the law relating to guardians that the consent of the intended guardian is not required before appointment. There is not even a requirement of notification. Common sense dictates that the appointing parent ought to approach the person concerned and discuss the matter before making the appointment. The right of disclaimer ought to cover the minority of cases in which this sensible approach has not been taken or where, perhaps, a change of circumstances has caused the guardian to change his mind about accepting responsibility.

---

[151] Section 6.

[152] Section 6(2). The document must be signed by him, or at his direction, in his presence and in the presence of two witnesses who attest the signature.

[153] Section 6(3). It has to be shown that the intention was to revoke the appointment but this may be implied from the destruction.

[154] Section 6(1). The intention to appoint an additional guardian might be express or by necessary implication.

[155] Section 6(4).

[156] Section 6(3A), added by the Law Reform (Succession) Act 1995.

[157] Section 6(5). There is provision for the Lord Chancellor to prescribe the manner in which disclaimers are to be recorded. This is analogous to the similar provision for recording parental responsibility agreements. The objective in each case is to resolve any doubt about who has parental responsibility for a child at a given time. At the time of writing, no such regulations had been made.

Termination

Guardianship will automatically terminate on the death of the child[158] or the guardian, or on attainment of majority of the child.[159] It may also be brought to an end by court order.[160] The court may act on the application of anyone with parental responsibility (including the guardian himself), the child (with the leave of the court), or of the court's own motion in family proceedings. In all cases, the court must apply the welfare principle. A termination is likely to be ordered where the guardian himself wishes to be released (and the allowable time for disclaimer has elapsed) or where the guardian's continued involvement with the child is considered undesirable for whatever reason. One example would be where there is suspicion of abuse. A more likely scenario would be where a guardian and surviving parent are at loggerheads, although such disputes could also be resolved in some cases by a lesser order such as a s 8 order, perhaps with directions or conditions attached. Where the court does remove a guardian, it may need to consider whether to appoint another guardian, especially where a sole guardian is involved, since there might otherwise be a hiatus in parental responsibility for the child.

It has been observed that, apart from the legal framework outlined above, little is known about the operation of private guardianship appointments in practice, despite their encouragement in the Children Act.[161] It has been suggested that research could usefully be carried out into the incidence of such appointments and disclaimers and to ascertain whether there is any evidence of abuse by guardians.

THE TERMINATION OF PARENTAL RESPONSIBILITY

Parental responsibility, within the meaning of the Children Act, terminates on the child's achieving majority. Until that time, parental responsibility which is allocated by operation of law under s 2(1) of the Children Act through motherhood or marriage/civil partnership, cannot be terminated except by way of an adoption order or parental order. Parental responsibility orders and agreements terminate automatically when the child attains the age of 18,[162] or in the case of parental responsibility conferred under ss 4, 4A or 4ZA, by

---

[158] Although it has been argued that a guardian would remain under a duty to bury or cremate the deceased child, unlike a local authority where the child was in care. See *R v Gwynedd County Council ex parte B* [1991] 2 FLR 365, and the evaluation of the decision in *Bromley's Family Law* (10th edn, Oxford University Press, 2007), at p 400 and 447.

[159] Section 91(7) and (8). Cf parenthood which can, in effect, continue beyond majority for limited purposes such as succession and financial support, where the child is in further education or undergoing training for a trade, profession or vocation.

[160] Section 6(7).

[161] *Bromley's Family Law* (10th edn, Oxford University Press, 2007), ch 5, at p 449. This is arguably the best academic treatment of guardianship, and the whole of chapter 12 repays attention. See also G Douglas and NV Lowe 'Becoming a Parent in English Law' (1992) 108 LQR 414, at pp 427–430.

[162] Children Act 1989, s 91(7) and (8).

earlier order of the court upon application.[163] Although a PRO cannot be terminated while a residence order is in force, the converse is not true. Thus, when a residence order is terminated, the father will continue to have parental responsibility unless the court specifically decides to terminate it, which it may do where it considers that the welfare of the child requires it.[164] Applications to remove parental responsibility are most likely to arise where, following an agreement, the relationship between the parents breaks down. In *Re P (Terminating Parental Responsibility)*,[165] the child had suffered very severe non-accidental injuries when nine weeks old which were later attributed to the father. The father was convicted and sent to prison but sought contact with the girl, who by this time was in the care of foster parents. The mother, unaware of the father's guilt, had previously entered into a parental responsibility agreement with him. She succeeded in having this revoked and in obtaining an order under s 91(14) preventing further applications by the father without the leave of the court. Singer J emphasised that, once obtained, parental responsibility ought not to be terminated except on solid grounds and there was a strong presumption in favour of its continuance. However, the paramountcy principle applied to an application to revoke parental responsibility in the same way that it would apply to an application for parental responsibility. It was relevant to consider whether in the circumstances now obtaining the court would have made a PRO which required evidence of attachment and commitment to the child. These requirements were clearly not met in the circumstances of this case.

In *Re M (Minors)*[166] the Court of Appeal endorsed Singer J's approach in *Re P* as 'exactly the appropriate way in which a judge should approach an application of this nature'.[167] The Court in *Re M* dismissed a father's appeal against revocation of parental responsibility where he had done everything to undermine the mother and make her life a misery. The principles in Singer J's judgment in *Re P* were also followed in *CW v SG*[168] in revoking the parental responsibility of a father who had been convicted of sexual offences against the mother's eldest two children. Jonathan Baker J rejected counsel's argument that the facts of the case could be distinguished from *Re P* and also rejected an argument that s 4(2A) of the Children Act is incompatible with Arts 8 and 14 in that a married father in these circumstances could not have his parental

---

[163]   Ibid, s 4(2A), s 4ZA(5), and s 4A(3).

[164]   This is in contrast to the position in marriage where the parental responsibility of a married or divorced parent cannot be terminated through any legal mechanism short of adoption. For a particularly striking example, see *Re M (A Minor) (Care Order: Threshold Conditions)* [1994] 2 AC 424, where the father retained parental responsibility despite murdering the mother in the presence of the children. Ironically, he was one of several fathers of the mother's children but the only one who happened to be married to her. It might be argued that there *should* be power to terminate parental responsibility in such cases. The case is discussed further in chapter 12.

[165]   [1995] 1 FLR 1048, endorsed by the Court of Appeal in *Re M (Minors)*, 11 October 1995 (unreported), Hale J and Pill LJ.

[166]   Court of Appeal, 11 October 1995 (unreported) (Hale J and Pill LJ).

[167]   However, the court's task might more relevantly be put as evaluating 'how he has gone about meeting that responsibility since the order was made and what benefit the children have derived from it or may be expected to derive from it in the future' (per Hale J).

[168]   [2013] EWHC 854 (Fam) (Jonathan Baker J).

responsibility revoked in this way. *Re M (Minors)*, a decision which does not appear to be widely known, was not cited to the court.

PRINCIPLES IN S 2 OF THE CHILDREN ACT CONCERNING THE NATURE AND EXERCISE OF PARENTAL RESPONSIBILITY

Parental responsibility may be shared

Section 2 of the Children Act 1989 confirms that parental responsibility may be held contemporaneously by more than one person[169] and that parental responsibility is not lost because someone else acquires it.[170] As we have seen, therefore, the potential for a multiplicity of sharing arrangements is considerable, for example: between parents; in a triangular relationship, as where a mother and step-father have parental responsibility and a divorced father retains his own parental responsibility; and shared between parents and non-parents, such as grandparents, foster parents or guardians. The precise legal effect of sharing parental responsibility is, therefore, a matter of some theoretical and practical importance.

The Children Act provides that where parental responsibility is shared between two or more people 'each of them may act alone and without the other (or others) in meeting that responsibility'.[171] There are just two statutory limitations on this right of independent action. The first is where statute requires the consent of more than one person.[172] The second is that parental responsibility may never be exercised in a way which is incompatible with a court order.[173] The best example of the first limitation is adoption, which requires the consent of all parents or guardians.[174] Statute also imposes certain automatic restraints on changing a child's surname unilaterally or taking him out of the country. In both of these instances, the consent of all those with parental responsibility is normally required, unless the court orders otherwise.[175]

The right of independent action represents something of a change from the position before the Children Act. Under the old law it was provided that parents might exercise parental rights alone but this was thought to be qualified by a separate provision which restricted unilateral action where another joint holder of parental rights had signified prior disapproval of the proposed

---

[169] Section 2(5).

[170] Section 2(6).

[171] Section 2(7).

[172] Ibid.

[173] Section 2(8).

[174] Adoption and Children Act 2002, s 47(2). This is subject to the court's power to dispense with consent on specified grounds. See chapter 13 below.

[175] Section 13; Child Abduction Act 1984, s 1, discussed in chapter 6.

action.[176] There was some doubt whether this encompassed the situation of married parents or was confined to non-parental holders of parental rights. What is clear is that there was never any statutory duty of consultation between parents. The Law Commission was concerned with the practicalities of daily living and thought it would be unworkable to require parents to consult with each other.[177] There is evidently force in this argument with respect to the myriad of trivial actions parents perform on a daily basis, but its wisdom may be doubted where major or irreversible decisions are concerned. It is also questionable whether the scheme can work where parental responsibility is shared by two or more persons who do not live in the same household.[178] No doubt aware of these difficulties, the courts have interpreted s 2(7), apparently contrary to its clear wording and the background to the provision, to mean that there is still a 'right to be consulted on schooling, serious medical problems and other important occurrences in the child's life'.[179]

The effect of independent exercises of parental responsibility on third parties is an important practical matter. Since a single holder of parental responsibility may act alone, it follows that outsiders such as schools, hospitals or churches may safely deal with him or her alone without risking any legal liability. It would seem that this applies even where the third party is aware of a disagreement between those with parental responsibility, although the prudence of going ahead with a course of action in these circumstances is questionable.[180] But, in principle, the third party is free to choose between two equally valid yet discordant views and is, indeed, *obliged* to choose between them even if this involves inactivity. An added complication in the case of an older child is that the child may be '*Gillick* competent' so that a third party could lawfully choose to comply with the wishes of a competent child rather than those of one or both parents.[181]

---

[176] Guardianship Act 1973, s 1(1); and the Children Act 1975, s 85(3).

[177] Law Com Report No 172 *Guardianship and Custody* (1988), at para 2.10.

[178] Such as, for example, a surviving parent and an appointed guardian, a natural parent and a foster parent, or two divorced parents.

[179] *Re H (Parental Responsibility)* [1998] 1 FLR 855 at 859A per Butler-Sloss LJ. For specific examples of exceptions to s 2(7), see *Re G (Parental Responsibility: Education)* [1994] 2 FLR 964; *Re PC (Change of Surname)* [1997] 2 FLR 730; *Re J (Specific Issue Orders: Child's Religious Upbringing and Circumcision)* [2000] 1 FLR 571. For criticism, see J Eekelaar 'Do Parents have a Duty to Consult?' (1998) 114 LQR 337; J Eekelaar 'Rethinking Parental Responsibility' [2001] Family Law 426; and S Maidment 'Parental Responsibility – Is there a Duty to Consult?' [2001] Family Law 518.

[180] Technically, for example, a doctor would be acting lawfully in performing an abortion on a minor which was supported by one parent but opposed by the other; but the more sensible course in this situation would be to seek the authority of the court. For further discussion, see J Herring 'Children's Abortion Rights' (1997) 5 *Medical Law Review* 257.

[181] Although see in relation to the child's refusal of treatment, *Re R (A Minor) (Wardship: Consent to Treatment)* [1992] Fam 11 and *Re W (A Minor) (Medical Treatment: Court's Jurisdiction)* [1993] Fam 64, discussed in chapter 8.

Parental responsibility cannot be transferred

An aspect of the lifelong nature of parenthood is that the legal status of parent and the parental responsibility which goes with it is 'non-transferable'.[182] While parents may delegate the exercise of parental responsibility, they may not surrender or transfer it.[183] Thus, they may arrange for someone to take temporary care of their children, or meet some aspect of parental responsibility, but this does not result in the temporary carer acquiring parental responsibility or in the parent losing it. Such an arrangement may be made with someone who already has parental responsibility as well as with someone who does not.[184] The former situation could cover married parents who might agree that one of them should take all the decisions on some aspect of upbringing, for example, education. It might be particularly appropriate to come to some definite arrangement where, for example, one parent is frequently absent from the home, perhaps for employment reasons. In all cases, however, the parent retains parental responsibility and may be held liable for 'any failure to meet any part of his parental responsibility for the child concerned'.[185] The natural parent could thus be civilly or criminally liable for any harm caused to the child arising from his failure to ensure satisfactory care.[186]

THE POSITION OF PERSONS WITHOUT PARENTAL RESPONSIBILITY

The common law would protect anyone who acted to protect a child from even a threat of injury.[187] Furthermore, s 3(5) of the Children Act provides that any person who does not have parental responsibility but has the care of a child may 'do what is reasonable in all the circumstances of the case for the purpose of safeguarding or promoting the child's welfare'.[188] While there is some doubt about the scope of this provision, it seems that it does not empower the carer to take 'major', as opposed to 'minor' or day-to-day, decisions, except perhaps

---

[182] This is subject only to the right of a parent to consent to the ultimate step of adoption of the child or to a parental order under s 54 of the Human Fertilisation and Embryology Act 2008, as to which see chapters 13 and 3 respectively.

[183] Children Act 1989, s 2(9). This was also the case at common law. See *Vansittart v Vansittart* (1858) 2 De G&J 249. The unmarried mother may, however, agree to share parental responsibility with the father (who does not otherwise have it through the process of birth registration), and a parent may agree to share it with a step-parent under an amendment to s 4 of the Children Act 1989 introduced by the Adoption and Children Act 2002. See further chapter 6 below.

[184] Ibid, s 2(9) and (10).

[185] Section 2(11).

[186] This issue is explored from a comparative perspective in C McIvor 'Expelling the Myth of the Parental Duty to Rescue' [2000] CFLQ 229, and see further chapters 15 and 16 below.

[187] See *R (G) v Nottingham City Council* [2008] EWHC 152 (Admin), [2008] 1 FLR 1660 (QBD), at para [21]: any person may intervene to prevent an actual or threatened criminal assault taking place, and a 'threat of immediate significant violence is enough, particularly if it involves a young child'.

[188] Children Act 1989, s 3(5), and see chapter 2 above.

where there is some urgency. It does not give any legal right to retain the care of a child. These greater responsibilities and rights, as before the Children Act, can only be acquired by court order.

CONCLUDING COMMENTS

We have now completed our examination of the rules on allocation and acquisition of parental responsibility and the general principles of law regarding its exercise. By way of conclusion, two features of the law might be highlighted. First, English law still discriminates in the allocation of parental responsibility against parents who are not mothers, or who are not in a formal relationship of marriage or civil partnership with the mother. Rather than eradicating this discrimination, the law has preferred to increase the mechanisms by which parents may acquire parental responsibility. In extending such provisions to same-sex parents, English law has also extended the outmoded and offensive concept of illegitimacy when most other jurisdictions have long ago removed it or are retreating from it. Moreover, the incremental changes in the law on acquisition of parental responsibility may, in practice, represent a barrier for further wholesale change of the law. As the mechanisms by which parental responsibility can be acquired increase, and with them the number of parents who have parental responsibility, the political impetus for wholesale change of the law may well be diminishing. There is certainly no indication in recent case law, nor in political debate that there is much appetite for change. It will be important for this debate therefore that there is continued critical examination and on-going evaluation of the arguments, and that gradual developments do not obscure the bigger picture.

Another feature of recent developments in the law of parental responsibility is the wider range of individuals who can acquire it, and this has led some commentators to talk of a degradation in the meaning of *parental* responsibility. In practice, this means that there is a wider range of individuals with scope to argue about matters of parental responsibility. In the next chapter, we examine how the courts deal with such private law issues and disputes concerning children.

Chapter 5

PRIVATE DISPUTES AND ISSUES IN CHILDREN CASES

As explained in chapter 4, parental responsibility may be held by more than one person contemporaneously and there is scope, therefore, for disagreements to arise on matters of children's upbringing. Where agreement cannot be reached, ultimately it may be necessary for a court to adjudicate, and in this chapter we examine how the courts deal with such private disputes and issues in children cases. The most likely context in which the courts will be called upon to adjudicate is upon parental separation when the circumstances surrounding a break-up may make agreement difficult. In such cases there are likely to be both practical and emotional upheavals, perhaps especially for any children of the relationship whose usual family life and relationship with both parents is disrupted. With these features of private law disputes in mind, the chapter begins with a brief discussion of the possible impact of parental separation upon children as disclosed by research findings and the major policy conclusions which have been drawn from the research. We then turn to consider in more detail the various orders at the courts' disposal in family proceedings in relation to private law matters which were outlined in chapter 2. It will be recalled that s 8 of the Children Act contains four orders which are capable of dealing with practical matters concerning a child's upbringing; namely a residence order, contact order, prohibited steps order and specific issue order. The chapter examines who is entitled to apply for these orders and the circumstances in which the orders can (and cannot) be made. Each order is then considered in turn, examining the contexts in which it has been used and its attendant case law.

CHILDREN AND PARENTAL SEPARATION: RESEARCH EVIDENCE AND POLICY

There is now clear evidence from a large number of research projects that there are negative associations between parental separation or divorce and the development of children and young adults.[1] No summary can do justice to this extensive body of research, but Martin Richards has described these associations as follows:

---

[1] The published research is extensive and includes PR Amato and B Keith 'Parental divorce and adult well being: a meta-analysis' (1991) 53 *Journal of Marriage and the Family* 26 and its update in PR Amato 'Children of divorce in the 1990s: An update of the Amato and Keith (1991) meta-analysis' (2001) 15(3) *Journal of Family Psychology* 355–370; PR Amato and B

'Compared with those of similar social backgrounds whose parents remain married, children whose parents divorce show consistent, but small differences in their behaviour throughout childhood and adolescence and somewhat different life courses as they move into adulthood. More specifically, the research indicates on average lower levels of academic achievement and self-esteem and a higher incidence of conduct and other problems of psychological adjustment during childhood. Also during childhood a somewhat earlier social maturity has been recorded. A number of transitions to adulthood are typically reached at earlier ages; these include leaving home, beginning heterosexual relationships and entering cohabitation, marriage and child bearing. In young adulthood there is a tendency toward more changes of job, lower socio-economic status, a greater propensity to divorce and there are some indications of a higher frequency of depression and lower measures of psychological well-being. The relationships (in adulthood) with parents and other kin relationships may be more distant.'[2]

This all sounds rather drastic and might be thought to justify the mantra that divorce or parental separation 'is bad for children'. It is clear, however, that these findings must be treated with very great caution and are subject to significant qualifications.

The first and most important point is that there has frequently been a tendency on the part of the public, the media and, it must be said, governments of all complexion, to make the rather naïve assumption that *association* is to be equated with *cause*. It does not follow in the least that because an *association* can be established between the fact of divorce or parental separation and certain developmental disadvantages for children and young people, that the divorce or separation was actually the *cause* of those disadvantages. As Richards puts it:[3]

> '... while it is relatively easy to establish associations, it is a great deal more difficult to unravel the processes that may produce them ... Simple cause and effect models of divorce are not very helpful.'

Keith 'Parental divorce and the well being of children: a meta-analysis' (1991) 110 *Psychological Bulletin* 16; PR Amato 'Children's adjustment to divorce: theories, hypotheses and empirical support' (1993) 55 *Journal of Marriage and the Family* 23; KE Kiernan 'The impact of family disruption in childhood on transition in young adulthood' 46 *Population Studies* 213; and BJ Elliott and MPM Richards 'Children and Divorce: educational performance and behaviour, before and after parental separation' (1991) 5 IJLF 258. For an evaluation of the evidence from a comparative perspective relating to the experience of children in the context of divorce and reconstituted families see J Pryor and B Rodgers *Children in Changing Families: Life After Parental Separation* (Blackwell, 2001). This book aims especially to offer insights into why some children survive change in families better than others. See also B Rodgers and J Pryor *Divorce and Separation: the Outcomes for Children* (Joseph Rowntree Foundation, 1998).

2   M Richards 'The Interests of Children at Divorce' in M-T Meulders-Klein (ed) *Familles et Justice* (Bruylant, Bruxelles, 1997), at p 543.

3   Ibid, at p 545.

Other factors which may have a bearing on outcomes for children are economic factors, 'welfare provision, housing policies, availability of child care, minimum wage legislation, as well as attitudes to divorce and marriage'.[4]

The second qualification is that there is a great deal of variation in outcomes for individual children and between children of different social class or gender. The research findings are based on *averages* between groups of children whose parents stay together and those whose parents divorce. But this disguises the fact that 'some children whose parents divorce will do very well at school with excellent psychological well-being while others whose parents remain together will have unhappy or traumatic childhoods and do poorly at school'.[5] Allied to this is the third qualification that, in a sense, to compare the position of children whose parents divorce with those whose parents stay together is almost bound to be a flawed operation from a policy perspective since it is making the wrong comparison. What policy-makers might wish to know is whether there is evidence to show that the children of *unhappy* marriages do better if the parents stay together rather than separate, but the research does not, and probably cannot, isolate happy from unhappy marriages in the samples of parents who stay together. In other words, there is a qualitative element which is missing and which would be difficult, if not impossible, to pin down. What *is* beginning to be realised is that 'some (but not all) of the attributes in children which have been associated with divorce can be seen *before* a couple separate', but 'pre-divorce effects cannot account for all the differences which have been described after divorce'.[6] This again suggests that there should be greater emphasis placed on the *quality* of relationships between parents and children both pre- and post-separation.

In recent years the very conceptualisation of children as 'victims' of the divorce process has been challenged by a number of writers.[7] Smart, Wade and Neale criticise 'the prevailing discursive framework in which the couplet "children and divorce" is set as one in which children are unmistakably objects of concern'.[8] According to this 'it is clear that in popular imagery and narrative, children are inevitably hailed as the victims of divorce and harm to children is virtually unavoidable'. And they go on:[9]

> 'It is almost impossible to find a counter-balance to this vivid imagery – even if the research on which it is based is far more equivocal than the popular image would suggest. On the one hand the image is employed by the anti-divorce lobby as a means to try to reform the divorce laws, on the other it is employed by those who

---

4   Ibid, at p 544.

5   Ibid.

6   Ibid, at p 545, and Elliott and Richards 'Children and Divorce: Educational Performance and Behaviour, Before and After Parental Separation' (above).

7   See C Smart, A Wade and B Neale 'Objects of Concern? – Children and Divorce' [1999] CFLQ 365. See also S Day Sclater and C Piper (eds) *Undercurrents of Divorce* (Ashgate, 1999), and S Day Sclater and C Piper 'Social Exclusion and the Welfare of the Child' (2001) 28 *Journal of Law and Society* 409.

8   C Smart, A Wade and B Neale (above), at p 366.

9   Ibid.

wish to remoralise the family and to curb delinquency and school failure. So, although there is genuine concern about children intermingled with the rhetoric, there is very little room left in the public debate in which to refashion the child of divorced parents as a person rather than merely an object of concern.'

These writers argue for the development of mechanisms which would allow children themselves to participate more meaningfully in the divorce process,[10] and some writers have already identified an image of the responsible, autonomous child emerging in this context.[11]

In the light of available research, two policy conclusions seem to have been drawn. The first is that exposure to parental *conflict* is bad for children, and the legal system should do what it can to minimise this.[12] The second is that children are likely to do better if they can preserve a good ongoing relationship with *both* parents following divorce.[13] The first of these is relatively uncontroversial but the second represents a considerable shift in thinking over the last few decades and continues to provoke some disagreement. For some years, the dominant philosophy favoured sole custodial arrangements and a central role for the so-called 'psychological parent'.[14] This was, in part, reflected in England and Wales by the overwhelming number of sole custody orders in favour of mothers and an apparent preference for maternal care and control even where 'joint custody' orders were made.[15]

This view was, in the 1980s and 1990s, largely supplanted by empirical evidence suggesting that the childen who suffer least from the breakdown of parental relationships tend to be those who are able to maintain good ongoing relationships with *both* parents. Conversely, those who suffer most are those whose parents carry on the conflict which was apparent during the marriage and at divorce.[16] This thinking originally manifested itself in the growth of 'joint custody', especially in the USA, but also in England,[17] and was taken forward in the Children Act 1989 in the notion of joint parental responsibility

---

[10]   There has been an increase in empirical work with children focusing on their own experiences of the divorce process. See, for example, C Smart, B Neale and A Wade *The Changing Experience of Childhood: Families and Divorce* (Polity Press, 2001).

[11]   F Kaganas and A Diduck 'Incomplete Citizens: Changing Images of Post-Separation Children' (2004) 67(6) MLR 959–981

[12]   This can be seen in the general principles for dealing with cases of divorce, set out in the Family Law Act 1996 which are discussed below.

[13]   The most influential research was probably JS Wallerstein and JB Kelly *Surviving the Breakup* (Grant McIntyre, 1980) and JS Wallerstein and S Blakeslee *Second Chances* (Bantam, 1989).

[14]   J Goldstein, A Freud and AJ Solnit *Beyond the Best Interests of the Child* (The Free Press, New York, 1980) was the classic exposition of this view.

[15]   Research conducted for the Law Commission, based on the statistical returns of 174 divorce registries, found, for example, that in 1985 sole custody orders were made in 86 per cent of cases, 77.4 per cent being in favour of the mother and 9.2 per cent in favour of the father. See JF Priest and JC Whybrow *Custody Law in Practice in the Divorce and Domestic Courts*, Supplement to Law Com Working Paper No 96 (1986), at para 4.21.

[16]   See Wallerstein and Kelly, fn 13 above.

[17]   JA Priest and JC Whybrow (above), at paras 5.2–5.6, found that joint custody orders were made in 12.9 per cent of cases in 1985 but there were marked regional variations.

and the possibility to make shared residence orders.[18] In recent years debate has centred on seeking to find expression to a legal norm which seeks to ensure that the courts do not overlook the possibilities for maximising on-going relationships between parents and children[19] when parents separate, while also ensuring that such a norm does not obscure any possible dangers in particular cases. Increasingly, especially since enactment of the Human Rights Act 1998, the debates have also become infused with the notion of human rights. Both parent and child are viewed as possessing a right to respect for family life under Art 8 of the ECHR, a fundamental element of which is a continued relationship with one another. The rights-based discourse has, however, been challenged by some feminist writers who argue that there has been too great an emphasis placed on the 'ethic of justice' (as reflected in fathers' rights' claims) and not enough on the 'ethic of care' (often reflecting the existing day-to-day relationships between mothers and their children). The debates are discussed in more detail below. First, however, we need to build upon our outline in chapter 2, by explaining in more detail the various orders available to regulate parental responsibility, and the circumstances in which they can be made.

ORDERS IN FAMILY PROCEEDINGS: PART II OF THE CHILDREN ACT 1989

Section 8 orders

As outlined in chapter 2, s 8 of the Children Act 1989 sets out and defines four orders, known as 's 8 orders': a contact order, a prohibited steps order, a residence order, and a specific issue order. These practical orders regulate the *exercise* of particular aspects of parental responsibility, whilst leaving parental responsibility itself intact. The 'residence order' and 'contact order' allow the courts to address two commonly arising issues, respectively questions concerning the person or persons with whom the child shall live or have contact. A 'prohibited steps order' allows the court to prohibit the exercise of certain aspects of parental responsibility, for example to prohibit a parent from relocating from the jurisdiction. A 'specific issue order' allows the court to determine a specific question, for example which school the child shall attend, or whether the child should have particular medical treatment. The orders are more precisely defined in s 8 as follows:

> "a contact order" means an order requiring the person with whom a child lives, or is to live, to allow the child to visit or stay with the person named in the order, or for that person and the child otherwise to have contact with each other;

---

[18] Children Act 1989, s 11(4) discussed in detail below.

[19] See, arguing for this, A Bainham 'Contact as a Right and Obligation' in A Bainham, B Lindley, M Richards and L Trinder (eds) *Children and their Families* (above), at p 61 (by way of a presumption); cf S Gilmore 'Disputing Contact: Challenging Some Assumptions' [2008] CFLQ 285 (arguing against the use of a presumption but in favour of judges considering the whole range of possible post-separation parenting arrangments when applying s 1(1) of the Children Act 1989).

"a prohibited steps order" means an order that no step which could be taken by a parent in meeting his parental responsibility for a child, and which is of a kind specified in the order, shall be taken by any person without the consent of the court;

"a residence order" means an order settling the arrangements to be made as to the person with whom a child is to live; and

"a specific issue order" means an order giving directions for the purpose of determining a specific question which has arisen, or which may arise, in connection with any aspect of parental responsibility for a child.

The courts have a power in s 11(7) of the Children Act 1989 when making a s 8 order to give directions about how it is to be carried into effect or impose conditions on certain persons,[20] which must be complied with. Section 8 orders may be limited to a specific period and individual provisions in the orders may be subject to time-limits.[21] The court can also 'make such incidental, supplemental or consequential provision as the court thinks fit'.[22] It has been said that s 11(7) provides 'a wide and comprehensive power to make orders which will be effective',[23] although the powers are limited to matters incidental to the making of the s 8 order. It has been said, for example, that s 11(7) cannot be used to impose injunctions in the nature of non-molestation orders which are more properly made under Part IV of the Family Law Act 1996,[24] nor to regulate occupation of a person's home.[25] This means that the court cannot impose a regime of what is known as 'bird's nest contact' (ie, where contact with both parents is facilitated by the parents occupying the former family home at different times), even if the court is of the opinion that such a regime would be most in the child's welfare.[26] The width and flexibility of the powers in s 11(7) should, however, enable the court in an appropriate case to tailor its orders to the individual circumstances of the case. No doubt the courts will be mindful that to attempt to regulate a child's future upbringing too closely might actually generate opportunities for dispute, and an extensive use of detailed orders could run counter to the ethos of continuing parental responsibility. The use of s 11(7) is discussed further below at appropriate points in the text in relation to particular s 8 orders.

---

[20] The categories are: a person (i) in whose favour the order is made; (ii) who is a parent of the child concerned; (iii) who is not a parent of his but who has parental responsibility for him; or (iv) with whom the child is living; (v) to whom the conditions are expressed to apply; and see *Re M (Judge's Discretion)* [2001] EWCA Civ 1428, [2002] 1 FLR 730, at para [17] (no power to impose obligations or conditions upon persons not listed in s 11(7)(b) of the Children Act 1989).

[21] Thus abolishing the former general distinction between interim and final orders.

[22] Children Act 1989, s 11(7).

[23] *Re O (Contact: Imposition of Conditions)* [1995] 2 FLR 124 (CA), at 128.

[24] *D v N (Contact Order: Conditions)* [1997] 2 FLR 797.

[25] See *Re D (Prohibited Steps Order)* [1996] 2 FLR 273 and *Re K (Contact: Condition Ousting Parent from Family Home)* [2011] EWCA Civ 1075.

[26] See Ward LJ's criticism in *Re K (Contact: Condition Ousting Parent from Family Home)* [2011] EWCA Civ 1075 of his own earlier decision in *Re D (Prohibited Steps Order)* [1996] 2 FLR 273.

When can s 8 orders be made?

The making of s 8 orders is subject to some restrictions set out in s 9 of the Children Act 1989. No court can make a residence order or a contact order in favour of a local authority, and indeed such applications are not permitted.[27] This reflects the policy of the Children Act 1989 that a local authority should only be allowed to intervene in family life via various public law orders in Parts IV and V of the Children Act 1989, which set out proper thresholds for state intervention. Once a child is in the care of a local authority, however, no court can make any s 8 order, other than a residence order, with respect to the child.[28] This provision reflects the policy that when a child is in such care decisions are to be taken by the local authority which should not be susceptible to interference by individuals making applications to the courts. By exception, an application for a residence order is permitted because the making of a residence order will discharge a care order, and thus goes to the very decision-making power of the local authority.

Section 8 orders will not normally be made after the child has attained 16 years of age but may be made, in exceptional circumstances, such as those of a mentally disabled young person.[29]

Subject to these restrictions, s 10 of the Children Act 1989 empowers the court to make a s 8 order 'in any family proceedings in which a question arises with respect to the welfare of any child', either upon an application[30] or of the court's 'own motion'.[31] As noted in chapter 2, 'family proceedings', for the purpose of the Children Act 1989, means any proceedings 'under the inherent jurisdiction of the High Court in relation to children'[32] or under any of the enactments listed in s 8(4).[33] It is also possible to make a freestanding application[34] for a s 8 order, which would be necessary when there are no relevant existing family proceedings, and such freestanding applications under Part II of the Children Act 1989 are themselves designated in s 8(4) as family proceedings. It is unlikely that serious disagreements over children between partners who are married or in a civil partnership will lead to freestanding

---

[27] Children Act 1989, s 9(2).
[28] Children Act 1989, s 9(1).
[29] Section 9(7). For the reasoning behind the change in the law (the age limit under the old law generally being 18), see Law Com Report No 172 (above), at para 3.25.
[30] Children Act 1989, s 10(1)(a).
[31] Ibid, s 10(1)(b).
[32] Children Act 1989, s 8(3).
[33] See chapter 2 for further discussion. They are repeated here for convenience: Parts I, II, and IV of the Children Act 1989; the Matrimonial Causes Act 1973; Sch 5 to the Civil Partnership Act 2004; the Adoption and Children Act 2002; the Domestic Proceedings and Magistrates' Courts Act 1978; Sch 6 to the Civil Partnership Act 2004; Part III of the Matrimonial and Family Proceedings Act 1984; the Family Law Act 1996; and ss 11 and 12 of the Crime and Disorder Act 1998.
[34] Children Act 1989, s 10(2).

litigation about the children,[35] although a specific issue order might be sought by parents who agree on a particular exercise of parental responsibility but wish to have the court's approval on the matter.[36] Where disputes over children between a married couple or between civil partners reach the point of litigation, it is a virtual certainty that the parents will be seeking divorce or dissolution as the case may be, or some other more limited relief, or a more comprehensive order relating to the care of the children.

Section 1 of the Family Law Act 1996 sets out some general principles which Parliament considered should guide the courts when dealing with the breakdown of a marriage, some of which are particularly concerned with the welfare of any children concerned. Although s 1 is in force, it applied only when 'exercising functions under or in consequence of Parts II and III' of the 1996 Act. Those provisions were never implemented and are repealed, and thus s 1 is not directly implicated in the current legal process of divorce or dissolution of civil partnership. The principles are still, however, an indication of what Parliament would see as good practice. So far as material to the children of a marriage, s 1 provides that a marriage should be brought to an end 'with minimum distress to the children affected';[37] 'with questions dealt with in a manner designed to promote as good a continuing relationship between the parties and any children affected as is possible in the circumstances';[38] and 'that any risk ... to any children, of violence from the other party should, so far as reasonably practicable, be removed or diminished'.[39]

Scrutiny of the arrangements for children on divorce or dissolution of civil partnership

Upon parents' divorce or dissolution of civil partnership, the court must consider whether there are any relevant 'children of the family'[40] and, if so, 'whether (in the light of the arrangements which have been, or are proposed to be, made for their upbringing and welfare) it should exercise any of its powers under the Children Act 1989 with respect to any of them'.[41] This duty, a more

---

35   The former provision in the Guardianship Act 1973, s 1(3), which enabled a parent to bring such disagreements before the courts, was seldom, if ever, utilised.
36   For example, whether their child should be sterilised: see, for example, *Re HG (Specific Issue Order: Sterilisation)* [1993] 1 FLR 587.
37   Family Law Act 1996, s 1(c)(i).
38   Family Law Act 1996, s 1(c)(ii).
39   Family Law Act 1996, s 1(d).
40   By Children Act 1989, s 105 'child of the family' means in relation to the parties to a marriage:
      '(a) a child of both of those parties;
      (b) any other child, not being a child who is placed with those parties as foster parents by a local authority or voluntary organisation, who has been treated by both of those parties as a child of their family'.
      The most important category of children (who are not the children of both parties) to be included in the expression are step-children. Other children, however, may also be regarded as children of the family, for example the grandchild in *Re A (Child of the Family)* [1998] 1 FLR 347.
41   MCA 1973, s 41(1) or Civil Partnership Act 2004, s 63(1) as the case may be. See, generally, G

limited one than under the previous law (which formerly had required the court to declare itself satisfied with the arrangements proposed for the children), was introduced by an amendment made by the Children Act 1989.[42] Parents are, however, required to file a more detailed statement of arrangements[43] in the hope that this may alert the court to problem cases and facilitate reference to mediation services.[44]

The court's duty is exercised by the district judge on the strength of the written statements about the arrangements for children filed with the court.[45] The court has power in 'exceptional circumstances which make it desirable in the interests of the child that the court should give a direction' to direct that the decree of divorce or nullity is not to be made absolute or the decree of judicial separation not granted until the court orders otherwise.[46] This provision is not much used, but there are a significant number of cases in which the district judge exercises his power to call for further evidence or for the attendance of the parties at a hearing in chambers, or to direct welfare reports in cases where it may be necessary to exercise the court's powers – usually, but not invariably, because the parties are not in agreement. Where a hearing is held, it is usual for a children and family reporter to be present and to attempt 'in-court conciliation' between the parties. But there is thought to be no reason why the decree itself should be delayed where the court made appropriate directions regarding the resolution of the children issues.[47] There is, thus, no requirement of judicial approval or, indeed, scrutiny in any real sense of the existing and proposed arrangements. The reality is that what parents agree about the children will initially be followed, and the cases in which the court seeks to intervene in any way are likely to be only a small minority of the total.

While most s 8 orders are likely to be made in the context of divorce or dissolution, it should be noted that the court has jurisdiction to regulate any aspect of a child's upbringing during a marriage or civil partnership. As noted

---

Douglas, M Murch, L Scanlon and A Perry 'Safeguarding Children's Welfare in Non-contentious Divorce: Towards a New Conception of the Legal Process?' (2000) 63 MLR 177. Under the law prior to enactment of the Children Act 1989, the court was required to declare itself satisfied with the arrangements proposed for the children.

[42] Schedule 12, para 31. The former rule that a decree absolute which was made without the necessary declaration was void was also abolished.

[43] FPR 2010, r 7.8 and Practice Direction 5A.

[44] Law Com No 172 *Guardianship and Custody* (1988), at para 3.10, and *The Children Act 1989 Guidance and Regulations Vol 1 Court Orders* (HMSO, 1991), at paras 2.54 et seq.

[45] The Family Law Act 1996 s 11(3) and (4) would have introduced the important modification that the court have particular regard to a checklist of factors in deciding whether it needed to exercise its powers, but the provisions were never implemented.

[46] Ibid, s 41(2)(c). Section 41(2) of the Matrimonial Causes Act 1973, provides: 'Where ... it appears to the court that (a) the circumstances of the case require it, or are likely to require it, to exercise any of its powers under the Act ... with respect to any such child; (b) it is not in a position to exercise that power (or as the case may be those powers) without giving further consideration to the case; and (c) there are exceptional circumstances which make it desirable in the interests of the child that the court should give a direction under this section, it may direct that the decree of divorce or nullity is not to be made absolute, or that the decree of judicial separation is not to be granted, until the court orders otherwise'.

[47] The court has a duty to set a timetable in this respect under Children Act 1989, s 11.

above, it could do so, for example, on a freestanding application for such an order, in proceedings for financial relief under the Domestic Proceedings and Magistrates' Courts Act 1978, or in wardship proceedings, all of which are 'family proceedings'. In the case of children whose parents are not married or not civil partners there is of course no process regulating the legal dissolution of the parents' relationship, and therefore no (automatic) formal process by which the arrangements for any children of the relationship are scrutinised.[48]

Applications for s 8 orders

Subject to limited qualifications, *anyone* may, in principle, apply for a s 8 order. The Children Act divides applicants into two categories – those who are entitled to apply for orders as of right, and those who require the leave of the court.[49] Those entitled to apply for *any* s 8 order are: any parent,[50] guardian or special guardian of the child; any person who by virtue of s 4A of the Children Act 1989 has parental responsibility for the child; or any person in whose favour a residence order is in force with respect to the child.[51] These are people whose interest in the child is self-evident since they already possess parental responsibility. The legislation then prescribes a further category of persons whose presumed closeness to the child entitles them to apply for residence or contact orders, but not for other orders, without leave.[52] The reasoning for this distinction is not obvious, but it probably reflects the view that prohibited steps and specific issue orders are sufficiently unusual and intrusive that a preliminary filter is appropriate to weed out unmeritorious applications. The reason why these orders might be thought intrusive is that their effect is to interfere with and curtail the normal exercise of parental responsibility by a person who has it. Those persons who are entitled to apply for residence or contact orders without leave include parties to a marriage[53] or civil partnership[54] (whether or not subsisting) in relation to whom the child is a 'child of the family',[55] persons with whom the child has lived for at least three

---

[48] The question of whether there should be is a fascinating one: see G Douglas, M Murch, L Scanlon and A Perry 'Safeguarding Children's Welfare in Non-contentious Divorce: Towards a New Conception of the Legal Process?' (2000) 63 MLR 177, at 195. The issues is also touched upon briefly in J Eekelaar *Regulating Divorce* (Clarendon Press, 1991), and in M Richards 'Private Worlds and Public Intentions – The Role of the State at Divorce' in A Bainham, DS Pearl and R Pickford (eds) *Frontiers of Family Law* (2nd edn, John Wiley & Sons, 1995).

[49] Section 10.

[50] For this purpose parent does not include a former natural parent after the child has been adopted: see *Re C (A Minor) (Adopted Child: Contact)* [1995] 2 FLR 483.

[51] Children Act 1989, s 10(4).

[52] Children Act 1989, s 10(5).

[53] Children Act 1989, s 10(5)(a).

[54] Children Act 1989, s 10(5)(aa).

[55] Defined in s 105(1) as:
(a) a child of both of those parties;
(b) any other child, not being a child who is placed with those parties as foster parents by a local authority or voluntary organisation, who has been treated by both of those parties as a child of their family'.

years,[56] and persons who have obtained relevant consent(s) to make the application. The relevant consent in particular cases is specified. In any case in which a residence order is in force with respect to the child, the consent required is that of each of the persons in whose favour the residence order was made. If the child is in the care of a local authority, the authority's consent is needed. In any other case, the consent which must be obtained is that of each of those (if any) who have parental responsibility for the child.[57] A local authority foster parent or a relative[58] of the child is entitled to apply for a residence order with respect to a child if the child has lived with the foster parent or relative for a period of at least one year immediately preceding the application.[59] The thinking behind these provisions is that, in all the above cases, the genuineness of the concern for the child would be so palpable that in most cases a requirement of leave would be an empty ritual.

Rules of court may extend the categories of those entitled to apply without leave, of which grandparents were thought, by some, to be prime contenders, given that under the old law some grandparents did have an automatic right to intervene in certain proceedings. This was a rare example of the Children Act tightening, rather than relaxing, the rules on standing.[60]

Applications with leave of the court

Where interested persons are unable to bring themselves within any of the above categories they may, nonetheless, make applications with the leave of the court,[61] provided a leave application is permitted. There is, for example, a (partial) statutory restriction in s 9(3) of the Children Act 1989 in the case of applicants who are local authority foster parents. A person who is, or was at any time within the last six months, a local authority foster parent of a child may not apply for leave to apply for a s 8 order with respect to the child unless he or she has the consent of the authority, is a relative of the child, or the child

---

[56] Children Act 1989, s 10(5)(b). It is provided by s 10(10) that the period of three years need not be continuous but must not have begun more than five years before, or ended more than three months before, the making of the application.

[57] The categories in s 10(5)(b) and (c) are those who would have qualified to apply for an order under the former custodianship procedure under the Children Act 1975, s 33, but not implemented until 1985. The most comprehensive treatment of the subject is to be found in MDA Freeman *The Law and Practice of Custodianship* (1986).

[58] 'Relative', in relation to a child, means a grandparent, brother, sister, uncle, or aunt (whether of the full blood or half blood or by marriage or civil partnership) or step-parent: see Children Act 1989, s 105.

[59] Section 10(5A) and (5B).

[60] Section 10(7). No such rules have been made at the time of writing.

[61] Section 10(2)(b). In an urgent case, an application for leave may be made without notice. In *Re O (Minors) (Leave to Seek Residence Order)* [1994] 1 FLR 172, such an application for leave to apply for a residence order was granted to a paternal cousin who had been looking after two boys while the mother was in hospital. The mother was demanding their immediate return and was proposing to return to her alcoholic husband. Leave was granted together with an interim residence order, although the length of the latter was reduced on appeal.

has lived with the foster parent for at least one year preceding the application.[62] This is to allow parents and local authorities confidence that short-term foster placement with persons other than a child's relative does not risk more significant interference in the child's upbringing through applications to court.

In the majority of cases in which applications for leave are permitted, the purpose is to provide a 'filter to protect the child and his family against unwarranted interference in their comfort and security'.[63] The statutory scheme is designed to be flexible enough to obviate the need to resort to the wardship jurisdiction. The leave requirement should thus be relatively easily satisfied, except where the motives of the applicant are improper or where there is a sound reason for regarding the application as inappropriate.[64] The Children Act prescribes a checklist of factors for the court considering leave applications,[65] including the nature of the proposed application, the applicant's connection with the child,[66] any risk there might be of that proposed application[67] disrupting the child's life to such an extent that he would be harmed[68] by it and, where the child is being looked after by a local authority, the authority's plans for the child's future[69] and the wishes and feelings of the child's parents.

---

[62]   Contrast this one year requirement with that for entitlement to apply for a residence order in s 10(5A), discussed above, which requires a one year period immediately preceding the application.

[63]   Law Com Report No 172 *Guardianship and Custody* (1988), at para 4.41.

[64]   But it should be noted that this is, in some ways, more restrictive than the more traditional wardship proceedings in which there was never a leave requirement as such. The wardship could, of course, have been discontinued at the court's discretion. See also SM Cretney 'Litigation May Seriously Endanger Your Welfare: Locus Standi and the Family' (1993) 109 LQR 177.

[65]   Section 10(9). These guidelines are equally applicable where the applicant is seeking to be joined as a party to existing proceedings with a view to seeking a s 8 order; see *Re B (Paternal Grandmother: Joinder as Party)* [2012] EWCA Civ 737, [2012] 2 FLR 1358 (CA). In *Re A (A Minor) (Residence Order: Leave to Apply)* [1993] 1 FLR 425, Hollings J held that the factors in the checklist were not exhaustive and did not exclude consideration of the ascertainable wishes and feelings of the child concerned.

[66]   For examples of cases considering this criterion, see *G v F (Contact and Shared Residence)* [1998] 2 FLR 799 (application by mother's lesbian partner who had co-parented child); *Re H (Leave to Apply for Residence Order)* [2008] 2 FLR 848 (application by adoptive parents of child's half-sibling); *Re G; Re Z* [2013] EWHC 134 (Fam) (potential importance of genetic and psychological parenthood not automatically extinguished by the the fact that a sperm donor was not a legal parent).

[67]   As Wall LJ pointed out in *Re R (Adoption: Contact)* [2005] EWCA Civ 1128, [2006] 1 FLR 373, at para [55], s 10(9)(c) 'refers to the risk of disruption posed by the application, not by the outcome of the application'; also stressed by Thorpe LJ in *Re H (Children)* [2003] EWCA Civ 369, [2003] All ER (D) 290 (Feb).

[68]   Harm as defined by the Children Act 1989, so it must be sufficiently severe as to impair health or development.

[69]   The assumption is likely to be that the authority's plans are designed to advance the welfare of the child since the local authority is under a statutory duty to promote and safeguard the child's welfare; see *Re A and others (Minors) (Residence Orders: Leave to Apply)* [1992] Fam 182.

The Court of Appeal has held that the initial application for leave is not governed by the welfare principle. In *Re A and W (Minors) (Residence Order: Leave to Apply)*,[70] the mother had had a colourful personal life in which she had accumulated three husbands (two she divorced and one committed suicide), a cohabitant and six children. The application for leave to apply for a residence order was by the foster mother of the four younger children. The judge granted her leave on the basis that the children's welfare was paramount. The local authority (supported by the mother) appealed. Allowing the appeal, the Court of Appeal held that the leave application was governed by the particular statutory checklist in s 10(9), which included such matters as the local authority's plans for the children, the mother's wishes and feelings, any risk of disruption to the children's life, etc. The upbringing of the children was *not*, however, directly in issue. That would arise for determination on the substantive application if leave were granted. On the facts, the children were of an age where they could express a view, it was unlikely in the circumstances that a residence order would be made and leave should therefore be refused.

For several years the leading authority on the criteria for determining applications for leave to apply for a s 8 order was *Re M (Care: Contact: Grandmother's Application for Leave)*.[71] That was a case which in fact did not involve an application for leave to apply for a s 8 order, but rather an application for leave to apply under s 34(3) of the Children Act 1989 for contact with a child who was in the care of a local authority. No leave criteria are specified in the Children Act for the purpose of leave applications under s 34 and the Court of Appeal felt that it would be anomalous not to adopt the criteria in s 10(9) of the Children Act 1989 to that similar situation. The Court of Appeal added that if the application is frivolous or vexatious or otherwise an abuse of the process of the court, or fails to disclose any eventual real prospect of success, it must be dismissed. The court also specified that the applicant must satisfy the court that there is a serious issue to try and must present a good arguable case. In *Re J (Leave to Issue Application for Residence Order)*,[72] a case directly on s 10(9), Thorpe LJ expressed the Court of Appeal's concern that *Re M* had resulted in 'the development of a practice that seems to substitute the test, "has the applicant satisfied the court that he or she has a good arguable case" for the test that Parliament applied in s 10(9)'. The Court held that the checklist in s 10(9) must be given its proper weight. Thorpe LJ explained in a later case[73] that the purpose of the decision in *Re J* was to seek to ensure that trial judges adopt a careful review of the s 10(9) criteria and do not replace those tests simply with a broad evaluation of the applicant's future

---

[70] [1992] Fam 182. For commentaries, see J Masson 'Leave, Local Authorities and Welfare' [1992] Fam Law 443, and R White 'Liverpool Revisited? *Re A and W (Minors)*' (1992) 4 JCL 190.
[71] [1995] 2 FLR 86 (CA).
[72] [2002] EWCA Civ 1364, [2003] 1 FLR 114 (CA). For comment, see G Douglas 'Case Commentary – *Re J (Leave To Issue Application For Residence Order)* – Recognising Grandparents' Concern or Controlling Their Interference?' [2003] *Child and Family Law Quarterly* 103.
[73] *Re H (Children)* [2003] EWCA Civ 369, [2003] All ER (D) 290 (Feb).

prospects of success. In *Re R (Adoption: Contact)*[74] Wall LJ clarified further that what is prohibited 'is the determination of the application on the "no reasonable prospects of success" criterion',[75] not 'a broad assessment of the merits of a particular application'.[76]

The family assistance order

In seeking to deal with particularly difficult cases, the court also has the possibility of making a family assistance order (FAO) under s 16 of the Children Act.[77] It is, in essence, a form of short-term voluntary assistance to the parties, usually in the immediate transitional period following breakdown of their relationship.[78] The FAO may be made, in principle, whenever family proceedings take place, and the court has power to make it whether or not it makes any other order. Its effect is to require either a CAFCASS officer or an officer of the local authority to be made available 'to advise, assist and (where appropriate) befriend anyone named in the order'.[79] This could be a parent, guardian, special guardian, any person with whom the child is living or in whose favour a contact order has been made, or the child himself.[80]

The order requires the consent of every person named in it other than the child.[81] The consent requirement underlines the voluntary nature of the order but it is noticeable that there is no obligation to obtain the child's consent or, it would appear, to ascertain or take into account his wishes.[82] Those persons named in the order must keep the specified officer informed of their addresses and must permit visits by that officer. The order will last for a maximum of

---

[74]   [2005] EWCA Civ 1128, [2006] 1 FLR 373.

[75]   [2005] EWCA Civ 1128, [2006] 1 FLR 373, at [46].

[76]   Ibid, at [46]. See also Wall LJ in *Re H (Leave to Apply for Residence Order)* [2008] 2 FLR 848, at [14] and Wilson LJ, at [33]. Where a child is applying under s 10(9) for a s 8 order in respect of another child, the applicant child's level of understanding will also be a specific consideration: see *Re S (Contact Application by Sibling)* [1998] 2 FLR 897.

[77]   This was an innovation of the Children Act; see Law Com Report No 172 *Guardianship and Custody* (1988), at paras 5.19–5.20. Prior to the Children Act, the court could make a supervision or care order on the basis that there were 'exceptional circumstances making it desirable that the child should be under the supervision of an independent person'. The FAO was the product of the Law Commission's wish to achieve a clear distinction between those cases in which the court simply wished to assist with difficulties which might occur following relationship breakdown and those in which it was concerned to protect the child from possible harm. Discussed in Law Com Report No 172, at paras 5.10 et seq.

[78]   For a discussion of the use of the order, see J Seden 'Family Assistance Orders and the Children Act 1989: Ambivalence about Intervention or a Means of Safeguarding and Promoting Children's Welfare?' (2001) IJLPF 226; and R Little 'Family Assistance Orders: Rising to the Challenge' [2009] Fam Law 435.

[79]   Section 16(1).

[80]   Section 16(2). In *Leeds City Council v C* [1993] 1 FLR 269, Booth J held that the FAO was the correct order to achieve local authority supervision of contact between a mother and her three children. The court should not try to achieve this result by making directions under s 11(7).

[81]   Section 16(3).

[82]   The statutory checklist, which applies to s 8 orders and care and supervision orders, does not apply to family assistance orders. Nonetheless, it is suggested that, as a matter of good practice, the wishes of the child concerned should be explored.

twelve months or such shorter period as the court specifies,[83] although it can be renewed. If a s 8 order is also made, the court may direct the officer concerned to report on matters relating to a s 8 order including the question of whether it should be varied or discharged.[84] Following an amendment made by the Children and Adoption Act 2006 as part of a package of measures to increase the courts' powers to facilitate contact between children and non-resident parents, the section now specifically provides that a family assistance order may direct the officer concerned to give advice and assistance as regards establishing, improving, and maintaining contact to such of the persons named in the order as may be specified.[85]

Re C (Family Assistance Order)[86] shows the potential limitations of the order in some cases in practice. In this case, a boy of 10, who had left home to live with his uncle and aunt, succeeded, with leave, in obtaining a residence order in their favour. The court also made a family assistance order directed to the local authority with a view to repairing the damaged relationship between the boy and his mother. The local authority complained that it lacked the resources to carry out the order and Johnson J, noting the limited options for enforcement of the order, felt that it was not in the child's best interests to attempt to force the authority to carry it out.

Section 37 directions

Prior to the Children Act, the courts had powers in a variety of family proceedings to take the initiative and make a supervision order or, in cases of more serious concern, to commit a child to care.[87] While the local authority might itself have been intervening in the proceedings and seeking an order, there was nothing to preclude the court from, in effect, over-ruling the authority and imposing an order on it. A major objective of the reforms in the public sphere was to spell out and standardise the basis upon which a child might be placed compulsorily under supervision or committed to care. There was concern that the courts in private proceedings, particularly but not exclusively wardship, could reserve to themselves a wider power of compulsory intervention based not on the criteria laid down by Parliament but on some more open-ended criterion such as 'best interests' or 'exceptional circumstances'.[88] The Children Act removed this power to act independently,

---

[83] Section 16(4) and (5).

[84] Section 16(6).

[85] Section 16(4A). For use of the order in this context, see e g *Re M (Contact: Family Assistance: McKenzie Friend)* [1999] 1 FLR 75; and *Re E (Family Assistance Order)* [1999] 2 FLR 512 in which the order was used against a local authority which was reluctant to provide facilities for supervised contact between a mother and her child.

[86] [1996] 1 FLR 424. See also *S v P (Contact Application: Family Assistance Order)* [1997] 2 FLR 277, in which the court refused to make the order, the effect of which would have been to provide an 'escort service' for the children to visit their father in prison.

[87] Law Com Report No 172 (above), at paras 5.2–5.9.

[88] See the DHSS *Review of Child Care Law* (1985), at paras 8.20–8.23 and 15.35–15.38, and the White Paper *The Law on Child Care and Family Services* (1987) (Cmnd 62), at para 36.

except the power to make interim care orders.[89] The new principle is that the local authority, which has primary statutory responsibility for child protection, must seek care or supervision orders which must only be made where the statutory threshold is crossed.[90]

The court is, however, given a more limited power of independent action. It may, in any family proceedings, direct an authority to investigate a child's circumstances.[91] In this way, the court can still take the lead in the sense of triggering action by the authority. The power to make the direction exists wherever 'a question arises with respect to the welfare of any child' and 'it appears to the court that it may be appropriate for a care or supervision order to be made with respect to him'. This power is additional to the authority's right to intervene in family proceedings to seek such orders.[92] Where a direction is made, the authority must investigate and consider whether any action is required and, if so, what this should be.[93] It must then report back to the court within eight weeks but, significantly, where it decides to take no action, the court may not overrule it by imposing a care or supervision order. This is one area in which the Children Act effected a clear shift in the balance of power for child protection away from the courts and towards local authorities although, as we shall see, the requirements of the ECHR and the HRA 1998 may well shift the balance back in the direction of the courts.[94]

The remarkable case of *Re H (A Minor) (Section 37 Direction)* illustrates the use of the s 37 direction.[95] Here, a child was born to a couple who already had one child and did not want a second. They agreed to hand the baby over to a lesbian couple (A and B) who lived nearby and wanted to bring up the child as their own. In fact, the birth had taken place at their home. A and B wished to adopt or foster the child but were not permitted to do so. Scott Baker J made an interim residence order in A and B's favour, coupled with an interim supervision order and a s 37 direction to the local authority. While he made no criticism of the care offered by A and B, he thought that there were long-term concerns which justified investigation by the local authority.

In *Re L (Section 37 Direction)*[96] the Court of Appeal held that there had been an inappropriate use of the direction. In this case the child, a girl aged six, had been looked after with devotion by her maternal grandmother but the parents, though not wishing to challenge her as primary carer, were unhappy with the extent and detail of contact which they had with the child. The judge had, inter alia, made a s 37 direction on the basis that some evidence related to the mother might *eventually* justify a care or supervision order. The Court of

---

[89]　Section 38(3).
[90]　Section 31(2), and see chapter 12 below.
[91]　Section 37(1).
[92]　Thus, under s 31(4) an application for a care or supervision order may be made 'on its own or in any other family proceedings'.
[93]　Section 37(2).
[94]　See chapter 12 below.
[95]　[1993] 2 FLR 541. For another illustration, see *Re CE (Section 37 Direction)* [1995] 1 FLR 26.
[96]　[1999] 1 FLR 984.

Appeal thought this too speculative. The case came nowhere near the public law threshold and, in purely private law proceedings, matters requiring investigation, it was held, should be conducted by other means. Perhaps this was a case in which an FAO would have been more appropriate. In contrast, in *Re M (Intractable Contact Dispute: Interim Care Order)*[97] the s 37 procedure was invoked by Wall J to address an intractable contact dispute where the children were found to be suffering significant harm by being denied all contact with the non-resident parent in breach of the court's orders. Although the consequences of making the direction should be seriously thought through, it could be used as a means of removing children who were being obstructed from having contact with a parent because of the primary carer's false and distorted beliefs about the non-resident parent.

DECIDING WHETHER TO MAKE A S 8 ORDER

As noted in chapter 2, in deciding a matter with respect to a child's upbringing a court must apply s 1(1) of the Children Act 1989 (the welfare principle), thus treating the child's welfare as its paramount consideration. This principle will apply, therefore, where the court is considering whether to make a s 8 order with respect to the child's upbringing.[98] The court must also apply the 'no order' principle in s 1(5), that is, the court shall not make an order unless it is better for the child than making no order at all. In contested private proceedings the court must also have regard to a checklist of factors in s 1(3) (the so-called welfare checklist). While it is not required to do so in uncontested private cases, the court is still likely to see the factors in the checklist as a useful guide for decision making.[99] The factors in the checklist represent, for the most part, those which were habitually taken into account by the courts under the old law.[100]

Under the law prior to the Children Act 1989, the court had a largely unfettered discretion and, beyond the general principles represented in the checklist, other principles emerged from appellate decisions to guide the courts on particular issues. Although the Children Act ushered in a completely new set of principles and orders, well-established principles are, to an extent, still applied under the Children Act. Such guideline judgments make it possible to discern the kind of factors which the courts take into account and the sort of

---

[97] [2003] 2 FLR 636.

[98] The courts are not always explicit about whether the s 8 order is dealing with a matter with respect to a child's upbringing. For example, it might be asked whether the question of which surname a child should have is such a matter. In specific issue order cases concerning children's surnames, however, the courts have assumed that the welfare principle applies.

[99] See for example *Re B (Change of Surname)* [1996] 1 FLR 791, at 793A–B.

[100] The reasoning behind the introduction of a statutory checklist is to be found in Law Com Report No 172 *Guardianship and Custody* (1988), at paras 3.17–3.21. For a useful historical perspective on the resolution of children disputes over the period of the second half of the twentieth century, see M Freeman 'Disputing Children' in SN Katz, J Eekelaar and M Maclean *Cross Currents* (Oxford University Press, 2000).

reasoning which forms the basis of their decisions[101] but they should not be seen as creating hard precedents in view of the infinite number of variables which have to be taken into account and the court's overriding duty to treat the *individual* child's welfare as the paramount consideration.[102] A s 8 order application is decided by the judge by applying to the facts of the particular case the relevant statutory principles, overlaid where appropriate with judicial guidance. It is important that the application of the welfare principle by the judge, who sees and hears the witnesses, should not be too readily interfered with by an appellate court (which does not have those advantages), and the House of Lords has made clear that the Court of Appeal should not interfere with the order of the judge unless satisfied that his decision was wrong.[103]

We shall now consider briefly some of the principles which emerged from previous decisions of the higher courts and which are likely to carry weight when applying the statutory checklist in s 1(3).[104] Again it must be emphasised that in view of the infinite number of variables which are inevitably present in individual cases, these should be treated with caution – the more so in relation to decisions prior to the Children Act 1989, since the scheme introduced by the 1989 Act has no precise equivalence with what existed before.[105]

Applying the welfare checklist (s 1(3) Children Act 1989)

The factors in the checklist are not exhaustive since the court is merely required to have regard 'in particular' to them. At the same time the Court of Appeal has held[106] that the checklist represents an extremely useful and important discipline in ensuring that all relevant factors are considered and balanced. Where the factors are finely balanced it is, moreover, important for the judge to give reasons for his decision. As Baroness Hale explained in *Re G (Children) (Residence: Same-Sex Partner)*, 'in any difficult or finely balanced case ... it is a great help to address each of the factors in the list, along with any others which may be relevant, so as to ensure that no particular feature of the case is given more weight than it should properly bear'.[107]

---

[101] On assumptions made within the family justice system about children's best interests, see C Piper 'Assumptions about Children's Best Interests' (2000) 22 JSWFL 261.

[102] See the discussion in S Gilmore 'The *Payne* Saga: Precedent and Family Law Cases' [2011] Fam Law 970.

[103] *G v G (Minors) (Custody Appeal)* [1985] 1 WLR 647, and *Re B* [2013] UKSC 33. See further on *Re B*, chapter 12.

[104] For a concise trawl through the checklist, see R Probert *Cretney and Probert's Family Law* (8th edn, Sweet & Maxwell, 2012), at pp 249–259.

[105] While there may, for example, be similarities between custody and residence orders or between access and contact orders, there are also important differences.

[106] *B v B (Residence Order: Reasons for Decision)* [1997] 2 FLR 602.

[107] [2006] UKHL 43, [2006] 4 All ER 241, at [40].

The ascertainable wishes and feelings of the child concerned (considered in the light of his age and understanding)

The increased importance attached to the views of children in the legislation has already been noted.[108] We have also noted that the importance of listening to children is underlined by Art 12 of the UNCRC.[109] As can be seen, however, the Children Act merely requires the court to *consider* the ascertainable wishes and feelings of the child in the light of the child's age and understanding. The court's overriding duty is to do what is dictated by the child's welfare and that may not always coincide with what the child wishes or feels.[110] The message of the modern law, however, is that, the ascertainable wishes and feelings of children of all ages on matters affecting them must not be underestimated but must be taken seriously.[111] How the child's wishes and feelings are ascertained will depend to some extent on the child's age. In the case of very young children, their feelings might be ascertained through observation of their behaviour (eg interactions with, or reactions to, a person). Older children will be more able to use language to express their views. How a child's views are conveyed to the court will also depend on the proceedings in question and the child's age. In private proceedings, children will usually be unrepresented.[112] The judge may (rarely) decide to interview older children in private[113] or may

---

[108] See chapter 2 above. See generally P Parkinson and J Cashmore *The Voice of a Child in Family Law Disputes* (Oxford University Press, 2008). On the practical problems involved in ascertaining and conveying the views of children in family proceedings, see C Piper 'Ascertaining the Wishes and Feelings of the Child' [1997] Fam Law 796. For a thorough examination of the question of children's participation in the different kinds of proceedings in which their interests may arise, see N Lowe and M Murch 'Children's Participation in the Family System – Translating Principles into Practice' [2001] CFLQ 137.

[109] See chapter 2 above.

[110] In *Re P (Minors) (Wardship: Care and Control)* [1992] 2 FCR 681. Butler-Sloss LJ emphasised that the court was not *bound* by the wishes of the children, in this case brothers aged 13 and 11 years respectively, and should depart from them when their future welfare required it. For a striking example of the court's refusal to follow children's wishes, see *Re B (Change of Surname)* [1996] 1 FLR 791. For a case in which the child's views proved decisive, see *Re P (A Minor) (Education)* [1992] 1 FLR 316. In *Re S (Contact: Children's Views)* [2002] 1 FLR 1156 the court was highly critical of the father's failure to accord sufficient respect to the views of his young adolescent children in relation to contact. Judge Tyrer said that children of that age were entitled to have their views respected and that they should have been allowed to make decisions without the pressure of being asked to select between one parent or another.

[111] By contrast, the Children Act makes no express provision for the court to take into account the wishes of parents or other interested adults in private proceedings, although the court will, of necessity, be presented with these views and it is implicit in the legislation that it should take them into account.

[112] By contrast, in public proceedings the child will usually be represented by a children's guardian (formerly known as a guardian ad litem) whose duties include conveying the child's views to the court: see s 41. The difference in approach as between private law and public law proceedings can be questioned: see, for example, M Richards 'But what about the children? Some reflections on the Divorce White Paper' [1995] CFLQ 223. However, there would be massive resource implications in any proposal for the routine representation of children in, for example, divorce proceedings and it can certainly be argued that this degree of intervention would be contrary to the philosophy of the legislation.

[113] See, for example, *H v H (Child: Judicial Interview)* [1974] 1 WLR 595. It seems, however, that in this jurisdiction the idea of judicial interviewing of children is not widely admired: see for discussion and comparison with New Zealand, J Caldwell 'Common law judges and judicial

rely on the report of a children and family reporter (formerly known as a court welfare officer). In wardship, the Official Solicitor has traditionally acted as the child's representative. Having ascertained and considered the child's wishes and feelings, how much weight a court may give to them will depend on the circumstances of the case, but it seems that a failure to accord proper weight in the circumstances would constitute a good ground of appeal.[114]

The physical, emotional and educational needs of the child

The court's task is to take a broad and wide-ranging view of the various needs of the child. Needs other than those specifically mentioned may be taken into account. It is well-established that the court will not allow itself to be unduly swayed by considerations of the child's material needs.[115] The court would clearly wish to satisfy itself that a parent had the practical resources to ensure that the child's material needs were adequately looked after,[116] but the fact that one parent can offer a higher standard of living than the other should not weigh heavily unless the standard of living which one of the parents is able to provide is wholly inadequate. The court is much more likely to be influenced by the quality of the relationship which the child has with each parent.[117]

Educational needs ought not often to be decisive in determining who has the care of a child, since they can usually be met by attaching conditions to the court's principal orders or by accepting undertakings from the primary carer, for example to preserve the existing religious education of the child.[118] Whilst

---

interviewing' [2011] CFLQ 41. The idea that by interviewing children's wishes will thereby automatically be better heard has been questioned: see R Hunter 'Close encounters of a judicial kind: "hearing" children's "voices" in family law proceedings' [2007] CFLQ 283: 'the conditions of production of children's wishes and feelings and the frameworks of interpretation applied need to be attended to and critically scrutinised'; F Raitt 'Hearing children in family law proceedings: can judges make a difference?' [2007] CFLQ 204.

[114] For example, even before the Children Act, in *M v M (Transfer of Custody: Appeal)* [1987] 2 FLR 146 the Court of Appeal had held that failure to accord proper weight to the strongly held views of a 12-year-old girl was a good ground of appeal.

[115] As Griffiths LJ put it in *Re P (Adoption: Parental Agreement)* [1985] FLR 635 at 637: 'Anyone with experience of life knows that affluence and happiness are not necessarily synonymous'. In *Richards v Richards* [1984] AC 174 at 205, Lord Hailsham said that 'the court ought not to confine itself to a consideration of purely material requirements or immediate comforts'.

[116] See *D v M (Minor) (Custody Appeal)* [1983] Fam 33.

[117] The spirit of the court's approach to ascertaining welfare is captured particularly well in the following passage from the judgment of Hardie Boys J, in the New Zealand case of *Walker v Walker and Harrison* noted in [1981] *NZ Recent Law* 257:
'"Welfare" is an all-encompassing word. It includes material welfare, both in the sense of an adequacy of resources to provide a pleasant home and a comfortable standard of living and in the sense of an adequacy of care to ensure that good health and due personal pride are maintained. However, while material considerations have their place, they are secondary matters. More important are the stability and the security, the loving and understanding care and guidance, the warm and compassionate relationships, that are essential for the full development of the child's own character, personality and talents'.

[118] For a case which did apparently turn on the relative capacities of the parents to provide educational stimulus and discipline, especially in the periods immediately before and after the school day, see *May v May* [1986] 1 FLR 325.

the assessment of needs is supposed to be wholly objective, the intrusion of value judgments is perhaps an inevitable hazard with indeterminate welfare tests.[119]

The likely effect on the child of any change in his circumstances

This provision draws attention to the effect of change upon the child, and indirectly to the value to the child of the status quo in the sense that change might disrupt the child's current familiar environment, for example connections with school, friends, nearby relatives and locality. It implies that existing arrangements for the child's care should not be unnecessarily disturbed. However, Ormrod LJ once sagely observed:[120]

> 'the status quo argument depends for its strength wholly and entirely on whether the status quo is satisfactory or not. The more satisfactory the status quo, the stronger the argument for not interfering. The less satisfactory the status quo, the less one requires before deciding to change.'

The child's age, sex, background and any characteristics of his which the court considers relevant

The child's age and sex will be relevant to the child's needs and possibly the relative abilities of the parents to meet the child's needs. However, as we shall see below in more detailed discussion of the courts' approach to disputes between parents about a child's residence, there are no hard and fast rules as to how these factors are to be treated. The reference in the checklist to the background and characteristics of the child should ensure that matters such as religious,[121] racial and linguistic factors are considered by the court.[122]

Any harm which the child has suffered or is at risk of suffering

Harm is defined as 'ill-treatment or the impairment of health or development' including, for example, impairment suffered from seeing or hearing the ill-treatment of another, and ill-treatment includes sexual abuse and forms of

---

[119] Indeed, the view has been put forward that 'the heavily subjective nature of the power granted to the judge means that, so long as he does not claim to be applying it as a conclusive rule of law, a judge can consider almost any factor which could possibly have a bearing on the child's welfare and assign to it whatever weight he or she chooses'. See J Eekelaar *Regulating Divorce* (Clarendon Press, 1991), at p 125. An example is, perhaps, *B v B (Custody of Children)* [1985] FLR 166 where the judge's decision to deny custody to the father had been influenced by his alleged moral duty to find work and not to take advantage of welfare benefits.

[120] *S v W* (1981) Fam Law 81 at 82.

[121] *Re P (Section 91(14) Guidelines) (Residence and Religious Heritage)* [1999] 2 FLR 573.

[122] See particularly the Court of Appeal decision in *Re M (Child's Upbringing)* [1996] 2 FLR 441, in which the court ordered that a Zulu boy should return to his natural parent in South Africa despite his being cared for in England for some years by a white Afrikaner woman. Cf *Re B (Residence Order: Leave to Appeal)* [1998] 1 FLR 520.

ill-treatment which are not physical.[123] A conclusion that a child is at risk of suffering harm must be founded on facts proved on the balance of probabilities.[124]

Where the court considers the child to have suffered or be at risk of suffering harm, it may wish to direct the local authority under s 37 of the Children Act 1989 to investigate that child's circumstances and consider whether it should apply for a care order or supervision order. Whether or not the court makes such a direction may be a question of degree, since only 'significant' harm is sufficient to found a care or supervision order. In other cases, the court might wish to give consideration to short-term protective remedies under the legislation governing domestic violence and occupation of the family home.[125] Where the court's concern is of a lesser degree, a family assistance order may be appropriate.

How capable each of the child's parents (and any other person in relation to whom the court considers the question to be relevant) is of meeting the child's needs

The most obvious 'other person' contemplated in the legislation will be any step-parent or partner of a parent. Where a parent has remarried, the court may see advantages, especially material advantages, to the child living in a two-parent household rather than a one-parent household.[126] Much is likely to turn, in individual cases, on the perceived value of the existing relationship between the child and the parent who does not have primary care.[127] Where a parent is in full-time employment, his or her capacity to undertake the day-to-day care of the child will be limited and the court will want to be satisfied that adequate arrangements for day care have been proposed. This may be a problem for fathers more than for mothers, given prevailing employment patterns.[128]

The range of powers available to the court under the Children Act in the proceedings in question[129]

The court is not confined to making those orders specifically sought by the parties. It has power to make orders of its own volition.[130] A rather obvious example is that it might, in making a residence order in favour of a mother, wish to couple this with a contact order in favour of the father – even if the

---

[123] Children Act 1989 s 31(9) and 105(1).

[124] *Re M and R (Child Abuse: Evidence* [1996] 2 FLR 195.

[125] Part IV of the Family Law Act 1996.

[126] As in *Re DW (A Minor) (Custody)* [1984] Fam Law 17.

[127] The abolition of the former statutory directives is discussed in A Bainham 'The Privatisation of the Public Interest in Children' (1990) 53 MLR 206, at pp 214–216.

[128] The fact that a father may have to give up employment or remain unemployed will not necessarily prevent an order in his favour. See *B v B (Custody of Children)* [1985] FLR 166.

[129] This provision was discussed in chapter 2 above.

[130] Section 10(1)(b).

latter were not specifically sought. The critical question will be which order, if any, from the range of orders at the court's disposal, would best advance the welfare of the child.

Recommendations in welfare reports

In contested cases the court will pay particular regard to any recommendations in welfare reports[131] and, indeed, must give reasons where it decides not to follow them.[132] The court's power to order a welfare report in family proceedings is a general one whenever it is considering a question with respect to a child under the Children Act.[133] The report may be requested from a child and family reporter (formerly court welfare officer). Although the court may direct that the report should deal with specific matters relevant to the welfare of the child, it may be more wide-ranging.[134] The Law Commission resisted the suggestion that the court should be obliged to order a report in every case, partly because it was mindful of the need to target limited resources, and partly because of the delays which might otherwise be engendered.[135]

The welfare report may be oral or in writing.[136] Where it is in writing, rules of court require its disclosure to the parties in advance of the hearing.[137] The court is entitled to have regard to any statement in the report, or any evidence in it insofar as the court thinks it is relevant to what it is considering.[138] There can, thus, in children cases, be a relaxation in the normal rules of evidence and, in particular, hearsay evidence may be permitted. Evidential issues involving children are discussed in greater depth later.

Residence orders

A residence order is 'an order settling the arrangements to be made as to the person with whom a child is to live'. It thus defines *the person(s) with whom the child shall live* as opposed to *where* the child shall live in the sense of the location of the child's home, although the two matters are of course not

---

[131] For the argument that the legal system could usefully allow a greater role for primary prevention before children become embroiled in contested cases, see A Buchanan and V Bream 'Do some separated parents who cannot agree arrangements for their children need a more therapeutic rather than forensic service?' [2001] CFLQ 353.

[132] *Stephenson v Stephenson* [1985] FLR 1140. Failure to do so may be a ground of appeal: see *W v W (A Minor: Custody Appeal)* [1988] 2 FLR 505; *Re CB (Access: Attendance of Court Welfare Officer)* [1995] 1 FLR 622; and *Re W (Residence)* [1999] 2 FLR 390.

[133] Section 7(1). The court is not confined to ordering one report if it thinks a second report would be useful. See *Re W (Welfare Reports)* [1995] 2 FLR 142.

[134] Section 7(2).

[135] Law Com Report No 172 *Guardianship and Custody* (1988), at para 6.15.

[136] Section 7(3).

[137] In *Re C (A Minor: Irregularity of Practice)* [1991] 2 FLR 438, the Court of Appeal held that while it was permissible for a judge to see a court welfare officer privately in his chambers during the course of a trial he should only do so in exceptional circumstances, which did not exist in this case.

[138] Section 7(4).

unconnected to the decision whether the order should be granted.[139] Only in exceptional cases will a condition be attached to a residence order restricting residence to a particular geographical location.[140] It seems that 'no case will be an exceptional case unless the absence of such a condition would be incompatible with the welfare of the child'.[141]

Most residence order applications concern parental disputes about the care of children upon the breakdown of the parents' relationship. In such cases, there is a rebuttable presumption of fact that a baby's best interests are served by being with its mother,[142] although in relation to children who are not babies, there is no presumption that one parent should be preferred to another parent for the purpose of looking after a child at a particular age.[143] However, it is still recognised as 'a consideration but not a presumption' that it is natural for young children to be with their mothers,[144] and it has been observed that 'the unbroken relationship of the mother and child is one which it would be very difficult to displace, unless the mother was unsuitable to care for the child'.[145] In *Brixey v Lynas*,[146] the House of Lords drew on the English Court of Appeal authorities in setting out the legal position in Scotland and the judgment can therefore probably be taken also to reflect the House's view of the law of England and Wales. Lord Jauncey explained:[147]

'the advantage to a very young child of being with its mother is a consideration which must be taken into account in deciding where lie its best interests in custody proceedings in which the mother is involved. It is neither a presumption nor a principle but rather recognition of a widely held belief based on practical

---

[139] The 'correct approach is to look at the issue of where the children will live as one of the relevant factors': *Re E (Residence: Imposition of Conditions)* [1997] 2 FLR 638 (CA).

[140] An 'exceptional case means truly exceptional and there will be few of them': see *Re S (A Child) (Residence Order: Condition) (No 2)* [2002] EWCA Civ 1795, [2002] 1 FCR 138, at [23]. See also in *Re S (A Child) (Residence Order: Condition)* [2001] EWCA Civ 847, [2001] 3 FCR 154, at [35] per Clarke LJ: 'should only be imposed in genuinely exceptional cases'. The same approach applies in cases of shared residence: see *Re L (Shared Residence Order)* [2009] EWCA Civ 20, [2009] 1 FLR 1157. See R George '*Re L (Internal Relocation: Shared Residence Order)* [2009] EWCA Civ 20, [2009] 1 FLR 1157' [2010] *Journal of Social Welfare and Family Law* 71.

[141] *Re S (A Child) (Residence Order: Condition)* [2001] EWCA Civ 847, [2001] 3 FCR 154, at [37]. For examples of exceptional cases, see: *Re H (Children: Residence Order: Condition)* [2001] EWCA Civ 1338, [2001] 2 FLR 1277 (impact of father's relocation on mother's potential recovery from alcoholism); *Re S (A Child) (Residence Order: Condition) (No 2)* [2002] EWCA Civ 1795, [2002] 1 FCR 138 (difficulty of relocation for child with Down's Syndrome); *B v B (Residence: Condition Limiting Geographic Area)* [2004] 2 FLR 979 (impact of mother's relocation on father's contact); compare *Re E (Residence: Imposition of Conditions)* [1997] 2 FLR 638 (CA) (inappropriate imposition of condition by judge).

[142] *Re W (A Minor) (Residence Order)* [1992] 2 FLR 332.

[143] *Re S (A Minor) (Custody)* [1991] 2 FLR 388 (judge erred in presuming that two year-old child should be with mother).

[144] Ibid, at 390. See also *Re A (A Minor) (Custody)* [1991] 2 FLR 394 at 400: 'There is no presumption which requires the mother, as mother, to be considered as the primary caretaker in preference to the father'.

[145] *Re A (A Minor) (Custody)* [1991] 2 FLR 394, at 400.

[146] [1996] 2 FLR 499.

[147] *Brixey v Lynas* [1996] 2 FLR 499, at 505.

experience and the workings of nature. Its importance will vary according to the age of the child and to the other circumstances of each individual case such as whether the child has been living with or apart from the mother and whether she is or is not capable of providing proper care. Circumstances may be such that it has no importance at all. Furthermore it will always yield to other competing advantages which more effectively promote the welfare of the child. However, where a very young child has been with its mother since birth and there is no criticism of her ability to care for the child only the strongest competing advantages are likely to prevail.'

There is also a well-established principle that siblings should be kept together where possible,[148] a rationale for this being that they will be able to support each other and provide some continuity, especially following family breakup. Again this is only a consideration for the court, and the argument for keeping siblings together may be less powerful in some cases, for example where there is a large age difference between the children.[149]

Disputes about residence have sometimes involved concerns by one parent about another's religious beliefs or practices. In *Hoffmann v Austria*[150] the European Court of Human Rights held that to draw a distinction between parents in a custody dispute simply on the basis of one parent's religion would violate the parent's rights under Arts 8 and 14 of the ECHR taken together. It would be permissible, however, to base a court's decision on the impact of religious practices.[151] The domestic courts have similarly held that, while it is not for the court to pass any judgment on the beliefs of the parents where they are socially acceptable and consistent with a decent and respectable life,[152] the impact of religious practices (such as indoctrination[153] or isolation[154]) may be material. The child's religious heritage, while an important matter, may need in some cases to defer to other welfare considerations.[155]

Residence disputes have also sometimes raised the issue of a parent's sexual orientation. The European Court of Human Rights has made clear that to make a parent's sexual orientation a decisive factor in a residence dispute would constitute a breach of Arts 8 and 14 of the ECHR.[156] Clearly the parent's

---

[148] See, for example, *C v C (Minors: Custody)* [1988] 2 FLR 291.

[149] See, for example, *B v B (Minors) (Custody, Care and Control)* [1991] 1 FLR 402 (FD) and *B v B (Residence Order: Restricting Applications)* [1997] 1 FLR 139 (CA).

[150] *Hoffmann v Austria* (Application No 12875/87) [1993] ECHR 25, (1994) 17 EHRR 293, [1994] 1 FCR 193, ECtHR.

[151] See for example *Ismailova v Russia* [2008] 1 FLR 533, at para [62] (children frightened by what they heard in religious meetings at home, together with other reasons).

[152] See, for example, *Re T (Minors) (Custody: Religious Upbringing)* (1981) 2 FLR 239 (decided in 1975). The most striking example of judicial disapproval of a religious sect and the effect of this on custody arrangements is probably the Court of Appeal's diatribe against Scientology in *Re B and G (Minors) (Custody)* [1985] FLR 493.

[153] See, for example, *Wright v Wright* (1981) 2 FLR 276.

[154] See, for example, *Re R (Residence: Religion)* [1993] 2 FLR 163.

[155] See *Re P (Section 91(14) Guidelines) (Residence and Religious Heritage)* [1999] 2 FLR 573 (CA).

[156] *Salgueiro da Silva Mouta v Portugal* (Application No 33290/96) [1999] ECHR, [2001] 1 FCR 653, ECtHR. To the extent that the view expressed by the Court of Appeal in *C v C (A Minor)*

relationships will be relevant in so far as they impact upon the child's welfare, but the parent's sexual orientation is not relevant per se.

The 'status quo principle', alluded to earlier, is likely to be important in the context of residence disputes. The courts are likely to wish to avoid unnecessary disruption to children and, depending on the circumstances, the status quo may be a powerful factor outweighing competing considerations.[157] For example, in *Re B (Residence Order: Status Quo)*[158] major difficulties with the child's contact to a non-resident parent did not justify upsetting a longstanding status quo as to the child's residence.[159]

However, while the value of the status quo should not be overlooked, the Children Act 1989 appears to provide at least tacit encouragement for the exploration of a range of possible caring arrangements and it does not support any kind of presumption that existing arrangements should be preserved. The impression of 'winners and losers' which the labels of a sole residence order to one parent and a contact order to the other may carry was recognised by the Family Justice Review, which recommended replacing residence and contact orders with a single 'child arrangements order'. This is being taken forward in the Children and Families Bill 2013, clause 12 of the which proposes to amend s 8 of the Children Act to replace the definitions of contact and residence orders with the new order which is defined as 'an order regulating arrangements relating to any of the following:

(a)   with whom a child is to live, spend time or otherwise have contact, and

(b)   when a child is to live, spend time or otherwise have contact with any person.

More fundamentally, however, as we shall see in the next section, the courts in recent years have been increasingly receptive to the idea of making shared residence orders instead.

(Custody: Appeal) [1991] 1 FLR 223 that all other things being equal the norm is heterosexual parenting may not be consistent with *Salgueiro da Silva Mouta v Portugal*, it must be viewed with considerable caution. Compare *G v F (Contact and Shared Residence)* [1998] 2 FLR 799.

[157] There is a wealth of empirical evidence that courts in the past made orders which preserved the existing child care arrangements predominantly involving sole care by mothers: see the discussion in SM Cretney, JM Masson and R Bailey-Harris *Principles of Family Law* (7th edn, Sweet & Maxwell, 2002), at p 646 and the studies cited there. However, it has been said that this was much more a reflection of what parents agreed themselves than any conscious maternal preference on the part of the judges; J Eekelaar *Family Law and Social Policy* (2nd edn, Weidenfeld & Nicolson, 1984), at pp 79–80.

[158] [1998] 1 FLR 368. For an illustration of the status quo principle in the context of human rights see *Hokkanen v Finland* [1996] 1 FLR 289.

[159] Note, however, that a parent's approach to contact is highly relevant to the determination of whether the child should live with him or her: see *Re A (A Minor) (Custody)* [1991] 2 FLR 394, at 400, per Butler-Sloss LJ.

Shared residence orders[160]

The Children Act enables an order to be made 'in favour of two or more persons who do not themselves all live together' and it 'may specify the periods during which the child is to live in the different households concerned'.[161] This marked a shift away from the attitude previously expressed judicially which was antagonistic to the idea of joint custody orders which included joint physical care and control on the basis that a child needed a settled home and such arrangements could be disruptive.[162] The Law Commission considered that such an order, now known as a shared residence order, would be more realistic than a sole residence order coupled with a contact order where it is proposed that the child should spend substantial periods in the care of each parent. In *Re K (Shared Residence Order)*[163] the Court of Appeal emphasised that equal division of time is not a requirement for making a shared residence order. The correct approach is 'to rule first upon the optimum division of the child's time in his interests and then, in the light of that ruling, to proceed to consider whether the favoured division should be expressed as terms of a shared residence order or of a contact order'.[164] In this way a variety of different types of arrangement might be properly reflected in a shared residence order, provided the situation can be characterised as the child having two homes rather than one.[165] The principal purpose of a shared residence order is to provide legal confirmation of the factual reality of a child's life.[166]

An order might be made, for example, where a child spends school holidays with one parent and term-time with the other. In *Re F (Shared Residence Order)*[167] the Court of Appeal held that the use of a shared residence order was not confined to the situation where children alternated between two homes evenly. Where the two parents lived a considerable distance apart there was the possibility that the children's year could be divided up between their homes in such a way as to validate the making of a shared residence order. If the home offered by each parent was of equal status and importance to the child a shared residence order could be valuable. A shared residence order may also be appropriate where the parties continue to reside geographically close to one

---

[160] For discussion of the use of the shared residence order, see S Gilmore 'Shared Residence: A Summary of the Courts' Guidance' [2010] Fam Law 285, PG Harris and RH George 'Parental Responsibility and Shared Residence Orders: Parliamentary Intentions and Judicial Interpretations' [2010] *Child and Family Law Quarterly* 151; S Gilmore 'Court Decision-Making in Shared Residence Order Cases: A Critical Examination' (2006) 18(4) *Child and Family Law Quarterly* 478; C Bridge 'Shared residence in England and New Zealand – a comparative analysis' [1996] CFLQ 12; and A Baker and P Townsend 'Post divorce parenting – rethinking shared residence' [1996] CFLQ 217.

[161] Section 11(4).

[162] *Riley v Riley* [1986] 2 FLR 429.

[163] [2008] 2 FLR 380 (CA).

[164] Ibid, [6].

[165] In *Re H (Children)* [2009] EWCA Civ 902, Ward LJ explained that his practical test is 'to postulate the question, ask the children, where do you live?'.

[166] *Re A (Joint Residence: Parental Responsibility)* [2008] EWCA Civ 867, [2008] 2 FLR 1593, at para [66].

[167] [2003] 2 FLR 397. See also *A v A (Shared Residence)* [2004] 1 FLR 1195.

another and to the child's school,[168] thereby increasing the practicability of the arrangement and minimising the risk that the child will be 'shunted about', or where it is necessary to accommodate to the parents' working patterns.[169]

The leading case on shared residence is the House of Lords' decision in *Holmes-Moorhouse v Richmond-Upon-Thames LBC*[170] where the issue of shared residence arose in the unusual context of examining a local authority's housing duties rather than a dispute between parents. The father of four children had been rendered homeless by a judge's order that he leave the rented family home, but the judge also made a shared residence order that the children reside with the father on alternate weeks. The father claimed that by reason of the shared residence order he was a priority housing need within s 189(1) of the Housing Act 1996, being 'a person with whom dependent children ... might reasonably be expected to reside'. The House of Lords concluded that the authority was not bound to provide accommodation simply by reason of the judge's shared residence order, which in any event should never have been made. The House explained that shared residence orders are practical, not aspirational, orders which should only be made where it appears reasonably likely that both parties will have accommodation in which the children can reside.[171] The House of Lords recognised that while shared residence orders 'are not nowadays unusual'[172] they are also 'not always or even usually practicable'.[173] The House emphasised that s 1(1) of the Children Act 1989 means that the court 'must choose from the available options the future which will be best for the children, not the future which will be best for the adults'[174] and emphasised that the children's wishes and feelings ought to be particularly important in shared residence cases, because it is the children who will have to divide their time between two homes and it is all too easy for the parents' wishes and feelings to predominate.[175]

The House of Lords' reference to shared residence orders nowadays not being unusual reflects a gradual relaxing of the Court of Appeal's approach to the making of such orders. Early case law, reflecting the pre-Children Act approach in *Riley v Riley,*[176] suggested obiter that such orders were confined to

---

[168] See eg, *Re C (A Child)* [2006] EWCA Civ 235.

[169] *G v G (Joint Residence Order)* [1993] Fam Law 570.

[170] [2009] UKHL 7, [2009] 1 FLR 904.

[171] Ibid, at paras [8] and [38].

[172] Ibid, at [7]; and see the similar statement by Sir Mark Potter P in *Re A (Joint Residence: Parental Responsibility)* [2008] EWCA Civ 867, [2008] 2 FLR 1593 (CA), at [66].

[173] *Holmes-Moorhouse*, at [38]. And note that it is *not* the case that a shared residence order 'is nowadays the rule rather than the exception': see *T v T (Shared Residence)* [2010] EWCA Civ 1366 (CA).

[174] Ibid, at [30].

[175] Ibid, at [36]. See also *Re R (Residence: Shared Care: Children's Views)* [2005] EWCA Civ 542, [2006] 1 FLR 491. And see for some research supporting the point made by the House of Lords, K Skørten and R Barlindhaug 'The Involvement of Children in Decisions about Shared Residence' (2007) 21 *International Journal of Law, Policy and the Family* 373–385.

[176] [1986] 2 FLR 429.

exceptional circumstances,[177] although soon thereafter in *A v A (Minors) (Shared Residence Orders)*[178] the Court of Appeal clarified that the new statutory framework required a more flexible approach. Nevertheless, the court was still quite cautious, observing that it would be confusing for many children to have two homes, sole residence orders would be more usual and it would need to be shown that there was some positive benefit to the child in making the unconventional order. Shared residence orders were thus still seen as unusual orders to be made in unusual circumstances. Butler-Sloss LJ warned that such an order would be inappropriate where there were still concrete issues which required resolution, such as a dispute concerning the amount of contact. This view that the shared residence order ought not to be confined to exceptional circumstances was reiterated by the Court of Appeal in *D v D (Shared Residence Order)*[179] where the court clarified that there was no onus on the person seeking the order to demonstrate that it would be of positive benefit to the child. It was sufficient that it was in the best interests of the child as required by the welfare principle. The Court of Appeal subsequently commented that the effect of *D v D* was to remove any restrictive judicial gloss on the making of shared residence orders.[180]

D v D also marked a greater recognition that existing arrangements might properly be reflected in an order. Hale LJ stated that if 'it is either planned or has turned out that the children are spending substantial amounts of their time with each of their parents then ... it may be an entirely appropriate order to make'.[181] Subsequent case law has given further emphasis to this point. In *Re P (Children) (Shared Residence Order)*[182] Wall LJ commented that 'where children divide their time between their parents in proportions approaching equality', a shared residence order 'is most apt to describe what is actually happening on the ground; and ... good reasons are required if a shared residence order is not to be made'.[183]

To what extent is the quality of the parents' relationship relevant to the making of a shared residence order? It has been said that an application for a shared residence order may rightly be refused where 'the motivation seems to be to strike at the other parent's role in the management of the child's life.[184] Equally, however, deliberate and sustained marginalisation of one parent by the other

---

[177] *Re H (A Minor) (Shared Residence)* [1994] 1 FLR 717: 'it must be an order which would rarely be made and would depend upon exceptional circumstances'.

[178] [1994] 1 FLR 669.

[179] [2001] 1 FLR 495.

[180] See *Re W (Shared Residence Order)* [2009] EWCA Civ 370, [2009] 2 FLR 436, at [13], although see S Gilmore 'Court Decision-Making in Shared Residence Order Cases: A Critical Examination' [2006] CFLQ 478 for the doctrinal complexity.

[181] *D v D* [2001] 1 FLR 495, at para [32].

[182] [2005] EWCA Civ 1639, [2006] 1 FCR 309.

[183] Ibid, at [22]. See also *Re A (Children) (Shared Residence)* [2002] EWCA Civ 1343, [2003] 3 FCR 656, at [10]: the judge 'should have given the greatest weight to ensuring that the order duly reflected the realities, unless there were some counterbalancing welfare consideration that prevented that sensible outcome'.

[184] *Re K (Shared Residence Order)* [2008] 2 FLR 380 (CA), at [21] per Wilson LJ. See e g *Re M (Children) (Residence Order)* [2004] EWCA Civ 1413 (order made unworkable by the father's

may mean that a shared residence is appropriate to make clear expectations as to parental time with the child concerned.[185] The courts have been willing to make shared residence orders in cases in which the parents' relationship is quite poor[186] and have not tended to place much emphasis on this factor in the case-law. The Court of Appeal has indicated that the inability to work in harmony is of itself neither a reason for declining to make an order,[187] nor a reason for making a shared residence order.[188] The courts' approach has been criticised in light of some research which suggests that shared residence may be an independent risk factor for negative impacts on child well-being in cases in which parents are highly conflicted. Children can get particularly caught up in their parents' conflict in such arrangements when they are spending considerable time periods with each.[189] It has been suggested that the courts' current approach, with its focus on reflecting in orders what is happening in practice, may run the risk that shared care arrangements will be too readily and uncritically reflected in court orders, in particular without a careful assessment of the nature and intensity of any parental conflict and the children's abilities to cope with it.[190]

Shared residence and parental responsibility

As explained in chapter 4, one effect of a residence order is to confer parental responsibility, and another independent basis for the making of a shared residence order is as a means to confer parental responsibility on an individual who would otherwise not be able to apply for a free-standing parental responsibility order.[191] In *Re A (Joint Residence: Parental Responsibility)*,[192] for example, the Court of Appeal upheld the making of a shared residence order to confer parental responsibility on the mother's former cohabitant who was not the child's father but who had been, and continued to be, the only father-figure in the child's life. Another early example is *Re H (Shared*

---

domestic violence, rigidity, and failure to co-operate over arrangements for the children, and manipulation of the children by involving them in inappropriate discussions).

185   *Re W (Shared Residence Order)* [2009] EWCA Civ 370, [2009] 2 FLR 436, and see eg *Re G (Residence: Same-Sex Partner)* [2006] UKHL 43, [2006] 2 FLR 629 (HL).

186   See eg, *Puxty v Moore* [2005] EWCA Civ 1386, [2006] 1 FCR 28.

187   *Re W (Shared Residence Order)* [2009] EWCA Civ 370, [2009] 2 FLR 436.

188   Ibid, at [15], explaining Wall J's decision in *A v A (Shared Residence)* [2004] EWHC 142 (Fam), [2004] 1 FLR 1195, at [124].

189   See eg, J McIntosh and R Chisholm 'Cautionary Notes on the Shared Care of Children in Conflicted Parental Separation' (2008) 14(1) *Journal of Family Studies* 37–52; J McIntosh and R Chisholm 'Shared Care and Children's Best Interests in Conflicted Separation – A Cautionary Tale from Current Research' (2008) 20(1) *Australian Family Lawyer* 1; CM Buchanan, EE Maccoby and SM Dornbusch 'Caught Between Parents: Adolescents' Experience in Divorced Homes' (1991) 62(5) *Child Development* 1008; CM Buchanan, EE Maccoby and SM Dornbusch *Adolescents After Divorce* (Cambridge, MA, Harvard University Press, 1996).

190   S Gilmore 'Court Decision-Making in Shared Residence Order Cases: A Critical Examination' [2006] CFLQ 478, at 496–497. Harmful arrangements should not be endorsed simply because they exist.

191   *Re A (Joint Residence: Parental Responsibility)* [2008] EWCA Civ 867, [2008] 2 FLR 1593, at [70], drawing on *Re H (Shared Residence: Parental Responsibility)* [1995] 2 FLR 883.

192   [2008] EWCA Civ 867, [2008] 2 FLR 1593.

Residence: Parental   Responsibility).[193]   Although   the   case   involved   an
application by a step-parent which now would be dealt with under s 4A of the
Children Act 1989, it illustrates a situation in which conferring parental
responsibility through a residence order was seen as valuable by the court. The
mother's husband was the father of her younger child and the step-father of her
elder child, but he accepted both children as his own. After separation there
had been a shared residence order by consent and both children continued to
see a lot of the father with the mother's full co-operation. The mother sought
to vary the order to a sole residence order but the court upheld the original
order on the basis that it had value in giving the father parental responsibility
in relation to the elder boy. The Court of Appeal acknowledged that, from the
child's perspective, a shared residence order 'has a different psychological
impact'[194] from a contact order; the making of a shared residence order in this
case was of important practical importance to alleviate the children's confusion
and to provide comfort and security through their knowledge that the law had
given its stamp of approval to the factual position that both children were
treated by the man as his own.

Can a shared residence order be made for the psychological benefit of a parent?

In *Re A   (Joint   Residence: Parental   Responsibility)*[195]   the Court of Appeal
suggested that there is a further independent basis upon which a shared
residence order could be made: 'where, in a case where one party has the
primary care of a child, it may be psychologically beneficial to the parents in
emphasising the equality of their position and responsibilities'.[196] It may be
doubted whether this is an accurate statement of the law.[197] It is not consistent
with the parliamentary intention behind residence orders,[198] and several earlier
authorities have emphasised that apart from the exceptional case of conferring
parental responsibility (as discussed in the preceding section) a shared residence
order 'is not intended to deal with issues of parental status'.[199] In *Re P (Shared
Residence   Order)*[200]   the Court of Appeal noted that an order may have
additional benefits, for example emphasising the fact that both parents are
equal in the eyes of the law and conveying a message that neither is in
control.[201] However, to identify psychological benefit to the child's parents as
an independent, separate basis for making an order is rather different and is at

---

[193]   [1995] 2 FLR 883. See also *Re AB (Adoption: Joint Residence)* [1996] 1 FLR 27.
[194]   [1995] 2 FLR 883, 889.
[195]   [2008] EWCA Civ 867, [2008] 2 FLR 1593.
[196]   Ibid, at [66].
[197]   For criticism, see S Gilmore 'Shared Residence: A Summary of the Courts' Guidance' [2010]
       Fam Law 285.
[198]   See P G Harris and R H George 'Parental Responsibility and Shared Residence Orders:
       Parliamentary Intentions and Judicial Interpretations' [2010] CFLQ 151.
[199]   *Re H (Children)* [2009] EWCA Civ 902. See also *Re F (Children)* [2003] EWCA Civ 592,
       at [21].
[200]   [2005] EWCA Civ 1639, [2006] 2 FLR 347, at [22].
[201]   Ibid, at [22], repeated in *Re K (Shared Residence Order)* [2008] 2 FLR 380 (CA), Buxton LJ
       agreeing. See also *T v T (Shared Residence)* [2010] EWCA Civ 1366 where a factor in making

odds with the child focus required by s 1(1) of the Children Act 1989 as emphasised by the House of Lords in *Holmes-Moorhouse v Richmond-Upon-Thames LBC* (discussed above). The Court of Appeal in *Re A* preceded its conclusion that orders can be made for the psychological benefit of parents with a reference to the case of *Re H (Shared Residence: Parental Responsibility)*[202] which was mentioned in the previous section. It will be recalled that in *Re H* the court was concerned with the psychological benefit of the order to the children, not the parents, and it may be that the Court of Appeal's conclusion in *Re A* is a misreading of the earlier decision.[203]

Debate surrounding the promotion of shared residence

The extent to which, if at all, the legal system should positively promote shared residence, for example by the creation of a rebuttable presumption for 50: 50 time sharing, has been the subject of considerable debate in England and Wales and in other jurisdictions.[204] Fathers' rights organisations, in particular, have campaigned for a norm of shared parenting post-separation to counter the existing usual common approach of sole residence to the child's mother and periods of contact to the father.[205] Research evidence, however, would suggest caution in assuming that shared residence will be appropriate or beneficial in any particular case.[206] Shared residence can work well for some children, usually when parents are not unco-operative and inflexible, and when such arrangements are practicable. Sometimes, however, children can find the arrangements burdensome.[207] Outcomes for children tend to depend more on the personalities and behaviours of those involved than on the particular residence arrangement adopted, although there is some evidence that shared residence may be an independent risk factor for the well-being of children under four years old[208] and, as noted above, for those who become caught between parents in high conflict. Concern has been expressed by some

---

the mother's partner a party to a shared residence order was the mother's partner's equality with the father in the event of the mother's untimely death.

[202] [1995] 2 FLR 883.

[203] See S Gilmore 'Shared Residence: A Summary of the Courts' Guidance' [2010] Fam Law 285.

[204] See, for example, F Kaganas and C Piper 'Shared Parenting – a 70% solution?' [2001] CFLQ 365.

[205] R Collier and S Sheldon (eds), *Fathers' Rights Activism and Law Reform in Comparative Perspective* (Hart Publishing, 2006). As Harris-Short points out, however, there has been less focus on gender equality in intact families: S Harris-Short 'Resisting the March Towards 50/50 Shared Residence: Rights, Welfare and Equality in Post-Separation Families' (2010) 32(3) *Journal of Social Welfare and Family Law* 257–274.

[206] See B Fehlberg, B Smyth, M Maclean, and C Roberts 'Legislating for Shared Time Parenting After Separation: A Research Review' (2011) 25(3) *International Journal of Law, Policy and the Family* 318 at 321; L Trinder 'Shared Residence: A Review of Recent Research Evidence' [2010] CFLQ 475; S Gilmore 'Contact/Shared Residence and Child Well-Being – Research Evidence and its Implications for Legal Decision Making' (2006) 20 *International Journal of Law, Policy and the Family* 344–365.

[207] See C Smart 'From Children's Shoes to Children's Voices' (2002) 40(3) *Family Court Review* 307–319, and C. Smart, B Neale, and A Wade *The Changing Experience of Childhood: Families and Divorce* (Cambridge: Polity Press, 2001); and see B Neale, J Flowerdew and C Smart 'Drifting Towards Shared Residence?' [2003] Fam Law 904.

[208] See J McIntosh, B Smyth, M Kelaher, Y Wells, and C Long *Post-Separation Parenting*

commentators, drawing on recent experience in Australia of legislating to encourage shared parenting, that to introduce a presumption of shared residence would lead to an increase in court-ordered shared residence in just such risky, high conflict cases.[209] The Family Justice Review,[210] having examined the evidence and the Australian experience, recommended no change to the current law. However, contrary to that advice, the Government intends to legislate in the Children and Families Bill 2013 with a form of words which will give emphasis to the idea that both parents should have a continuing involvement with a child upon parental relationship breakdown. The proposed legislation is discussed further below under the topic of 'contact'.

The contact order[211]

The most common form of post-separation parenting arrangement is residence to one parent with contact to a so-called non-resident parent. Where contact cannot be agreed, the court can make a contact order, which is 'an order requiring the person with whom a child lives, or is to live, to allow the child to visit or stay with the person named in the order, or for that person and the child otherwise to have contact with each other'.[212] The order, which replaced the former access order, is 'child-centred' in form, providing for *the child* to visit or stay with a named individual. This is a deliberate change of emphasis from the old law, under which access orders were 'adult-centred' and allowed a named adult to visit the child. Note that an order for direct contact places an obligation upon the resident parent to allow contact;[213] the order is 'not directed at the child to submit to, still less to be forced into, visits or staying with the absent parent',[214] nor is any duty placed upon the person named in the order. In *Re LW (Children) (Enforcement and Committal: Contact); CPL v CH-W and others*[215] the word 'allow' within the definition of a contact order was considered in the context of an application to commit a father for breach of an order. The order stated that the father was to 'allow' contact and to make the child available. He had presented the child for the mother on the doorstep of his home but did no more to encourage contact, and contact did not take

---

Arrangements and Developmental Outcomes for Infants and Children (Victoria: Family Transitions for the Australian Government Attorney-General's Department, 2010), at 9.

[209] See Fehlberg et al above, and Trinder above, at fn 206.

[210] Family Justice Review Final Report (Ministry of Justice, November 2011), and see Ministry of Justice and Department for Education *The Government Response to the Family Justice Review: A System with Children and Families at its Heart* (Cm 8273, February 2012), at paras 59–64.

[211] We are concerned here with contact in private law proceedings. The public law governing contact is constituted by a separate code in Part IV of the Children Act 1989, creating inter alia, a *presumption* of reasonable contact in favour of parents and certain other individuals, and local authorities are placed under a statutory duty to promote contact between the child, his relatives and friends: Children Act 1989, s 34 and Sch 2, para 15.

[212] Section 8(1).

[213] It follows that, in the case of direct contact, one 'cannot have a contact order without having first determined who the person is with whom a child lives': see *Re B (A Child: Contact)* [2001] EWCA Civ 1968 at [9]. See also *In the matter of S (A Child)* [2010] EWCA Civ 705: court only has power to make an order in the terms of the definition of a contact order.

[214] *Re M (Minors)* (CA) (26 January 2000).

[215] [2010] EWCA Civ 1253, [2011] 1 FCR 78.

place because the child refused to go. Munby LJ said that 'to "allow" is to concede or to permit; to "make available" is to put at one's disposal or within one's reach. That was the father's obligation; no more and no less'.[216] As can be seen from its definition, a contact order can also require contact in ways other than face to face contact, and it may also in particular cases be necessary for contact to be supervised, or supported in some way.[217] In *Re O (Contact: Imposition of Conditions)*[218] the Court of Appeal indicated that s 11(7) of the Children Act 1989 can be used to impose positive obligations on a parent to facilitate contact. It upheld an order for indirect contact between a father and a two year-old child, which provided that the mother was to: send to the father photographs of the child every three months; send the father copies of all reports pertaining to the child's progress at nursery or play group; inform the father and supply to him medical reports in the event of the child suffering a significant illness; and accept delivery of all cards and presents for the child via the postal system and read and show such deliveries to the child. The contrast between the passive and active nature of orders in *Re LW* and *Re O* respectively is striking, and it remains unclear quite how far positive obligations can be imposed to facilitate direct contact.

Orders for 'reasonable contact', which leave the parties to work out the precise arrangements, are likely where a residence order is made. Indeed, without a contact order, the non-resident parent's right to see the child would be in doubt, notwithstanding his retention of parental responsibility, since to take physical control of the child for however short a period would arguably contravene the terms of the residence order.[219] Where, on the other hand, there is no residence order, parents will each have rights of contact as an aspect of parental responsibility and, provided they can work out an arrangement which is acceptable to both of them, a contact order will not be necessary.[220] A parent, while exercising contact, will also exercise parental responsibility to the full, but this arises quite independently of any order.

The courts' approach to deciding contact disputes

Providing an account of the current law on contact is complicated by the fact that it must accommodate the human rights expressed in the United Nations Convention on the Rights of the Child[221] (UNCRC) and the ECHR (as scheduled to the Human Rights Act 1998), and the domestic statutory criterion in s 1(1) of the Children Act 1989 that the child's welfare is the court's paramount consideration. As we have seen, the latter, with its focus on the

---

216 Ibid, at [76].
217 See for an indication of the relative frequency of types of interim and final orders, A Perry and B Rainey 'Supervised, Supported and Indirect Contact Orders: Research Findings' (2007) 21 *International Journal of Law, Policy and the Family* 21.
218 [1995] 2 FLR 124 (CA).
219 Although this is a contentious issue.
220 This follows automatically from the no order principle in s 1(5).
221 Adopted 20 November 1989, entered into force 2 September 1990, 1577 UNTS 3.

child's welfare as effectively the sole consideration, is not easy to reconcile with independent recognition of others' rights.

Article 9(3) of the UNCRC provides that:[222]

> States Parties shall respect the right of the child who is separated from one or both parents to maintain personal relations and direct contact with both parents on a regular basis, except if it is contrary to the child's best interests.

The relationship between parent and child is also protected by the right to respect for family life within Art 8 of the ECHR, and the ECtHR has stated that:[223]

> 'the mutual enjoyment by parent and child of each other's company constitutes a fundamental element of family life, even if the relationship between the parents has broken down, and domestic measures hindering such enjoyment amount to an interference with the right protected by Art 8 of the Convention.'

Any interference must be in accordance with the law, necessary in a democratic society, and pursue legitimate aims as set out in Art 8(2). Where the parent/child relationship has broken down there is a positive obligation on national authorities to take measure to reunite parent and child,[224] although it is not an absolute obligation.[225] The duty is to take 'all necessary steps to facilitate contact as can reasonably be demanded in the special circumstances of each case'.[226] It is clear, however, that a parent cannot have 'such measures taken as would harm the child's health and development'.[227]

The ECtHR has explained that:[228]

> 'the interests as well as the rights and freedoms of all concerned must be taken into account, and more particularly the best interests of the child and his or her rights under Art 8 of the Convention. Where contact with the parent might appear

---

[222] See also United Nations Convention on the Rights of the Child, Arts 7, 8, and 18(1), which are usefully identified and discussed in A Bainham 'Contact as a Right and Obligation' in A Bainham, B Lindley, M Richards and L Trinder (eds) *Children and Their Families: Contact, Rights and Welfare* (Oxford, Hart Publishing, 2003), at p 62.

[223] *Johansen v Norway* (Application No 17383/90) (1996) 23 EHRR 33, at para 52; *Bronda v Italy* (Application No 22430/93) (2001) 33 EHRR 4, at para 51; *Elsholz v Germany* (Application No 25735/94) (2002) 34 EHRR 58, at para 43; *Kosmopoulou v Greece* (Application No 60457/00) [2004] 1 FLR 800, at [47]; *Gnahoré v France* (Application No 40031/98) (2002) 34 EHRR 38, at para 50.

[224] *Kosmopoulou v Greece* (Application No 60457/00) [2004] 1 FLR 800, at para 44.

[225] *Glaser v United Kingdom* (Case No 32346/96) (2001) 33 EHRR 1, [2001] 1 FLR 153, at para 65.

[226] Ibid, at para 66.

[227] Eg, *Scozzari and Giunta v Italy* (Application Nos 39221/98 and 41963/98) (2002) 35 EHRR 12, sub nom *S and G v Italy* (Case Nos 39221/98 and 41963/98) [2000] 2 FLR 771, ECHR, at para 169.

[228] *Glaser v United Kingdom* (Case No 32346/96) (2001) 33 EHRR 1, [2001] 1 FLR 153, at para 65. There is strict scrutiny of the state's margin of appreciation in this context: see *C v Finland* (Application No 18249/02) (2008) 46 EHRR 485, [2006] 2 FLR 597, at para 60, and see *Re C (Direct Contact: Suspension)* [2011] EWCA Civ 521 [2011] 2 FLR 912, at para [41].

to threaten those interests or interfere with those rights, it is for the national authorities to strike a fair balance between them.'

It is clear therefore from the jurisprudence of the ECtHR that the parent/child relationship is to some extent protected by the *Convention rights* of both parent and child.[229] This arises as an aspect of respect for their mutual family life under Art 8. Of course, this right to respect for family life is not absolute, and caution should be exercised in calling it a 'right of contact'.[230] However, a court examining the issue of parent/child contact will start from the position that the parent/child relationship is protected as an aspect of the right to respect for family life, and liable to be displaced only by the justifications for interfering with the right to respect for family life under Art 8(2). It is important to emphasise that it is *only* those justifications expressly contemplated by the Convention which will provide a lawful basis for disrupting the mutual relationship between parent and child. This has important implications for the obligations of the State in this supposedly private area of law. A failure on the part of the State to take reasonable steps to enforce contact may lead to breach of the ECHR with all the consequences that entails. In this way, there is a very real *public* aspect to what is normally conceived as an issue of private law and what might be seen as a blurring of the public and private.[231]

In contrast with the requirements of Art 8 of the ECHR, s 1 of the Children Act 1989 enjoins a court deciding a contact dispute to treat the welfare of the child concerned as *paramount*, and identifies a (different) checklist of factors for particular consideration. The domestic courts have rather side-stepped the tensions between s 1 and Art 8 in the context of contact disputes, merely observing that our 'domestic jurisprudence, if somewhat differently expressed, is to the same effect'.[232] Accordingly, it is rare to find references to, let alone detailed analyses of, the Art 8 interests of the parties in the case law on contact orders. The courts instead apply s 1 of the Children Act 1989 to the particular facts of the case, with reference to the domestic case law. In *Re M (Contact: Welfare Test)*,[233] Wilson J (sitting in the Court of Appeal) indicated that it is helpful to cast the issues in a contact case into the framework of the checklist of considerations set out in s 1(3) of the Children Act 1989 and to ask:[234]

'whether the fundamental emotional need of every child to have an enduring relationship with both his parents (s 1(3)(b)) is outweighed by the depth of harm

---

[229] See A Bainham 'Contact as a Right and Obligation' in A Bainham, B Lindley, M Richards and L Trinder (eds) *Children and Their Families: Contact, Rights and Welfare* (Oxford, Hart Publishing, 2003).

[230] S Gilmore 'Disputing Contact: Challenging Some Assumptions' [2008] CFLQ 285.

[231] On which, see generally, A Bainham 'Private and public children law: an under-explored relationship' [2013] CFLQ 138.

[232] *Re C (Direct Contact: Suspension)* [2011] EWCA Civ 521, [2011] 2 FLR 912, at para [43].

[233] [1995] 1 FLR 274 (CA), a comparatively unusual case in that it involved denial of contact to a *mother*, discussed alongside the ECtHR decision in *Hokkanen v Finland*, in A Bainham 'Contact as a Fundamental Right' [1995] CLJ 255.

[234] [1995] 1 FLR 274 (CA), at 278.

which, in the light, inter alia, of his wishes and feelings (s 1(3)(a)), this child would be at risk of suffering (s 1(3)(e)) by virtue of a contact order.'

Following enactment of the Human Rights Act 1998, the Court of Appeal in *Re H (Contact Order (No 2))*[235] reassured judges that:

'a proper application of the checklist in s 1(3) of the Children Act 1989 is equivalent to the balancing exercise required in the application of Art 8, which is then a useful cross-check to ensure that the order proposed is in accordance with the law, necessary for the protection of the rights and freedoms of others and proportionate.'

The leading decisions providing guidelines as to the general approach for judges applying the welfare principle in contact disputes are *Re O (Contact: Imposition of Conditions)*,[236] *Re L (A Child) (Contact: Domestic Violence); Re V (A Child); Re M (A Child); Re H (Children)*[237] (hereafter *Re LVMH*) and *Re C (Direct Contact: Suspension)*.[238]

In *Re O (Contact: Imposition of Conditions)*[239] Sir Thomas Bingham MR explained that:[240]

'Where parents of a child are separated and the child is in the day-to-day care of one of them, it is almost always in the interests of the child that he or she should have contact with the other parent. The reason for this scarcely needs spelling out. It is, of course, that the separation of parents involves a loss to the child, and it is desirable that that loss should so far as possible be made good by contact with the non-custodial parent, that is the parent in whose day-to-day care the child is not.'

His Lordship added that 'in cases in which, for whatever reason, direct contact cannot for the time being be ordered, it is ordinarily highly desirable that there should be indirect contact'. The Master of the Rolls was also clear that 'the court has power to enforce orders for contact, which it should not hesitate to exercise where it judges that it will overall promote the welfare of the child to do so'. Subsequently, the Court of Appeal has pointed out that there may be a limit beyond which the court should not strive to promote contact[241] but has also said that all available options must be explored,[242] and it is most important

---

[235] [2002] 1 FLR 22.

[236] [1995] 2 FLR 124, at 128–130. For comment, see S Jolly 'Implacable Hostility, Contact, and the Limits of Law' (1995) 7 CFLQ 228.

[237] [2001] Fam 260 (CA).

[238] [2011] EWCA Civ 521, [2011] 2 FLR 912.

[239] [1995] 2 FLR 124, at 128–130.

[240] Ibid, at 128, drawing upon Balcombe LJ's judgment in *Re H (Minors) (Access)* [1992] 1 FLR 148 (CA) at 152 and Latey J's judgment in *M v M (Child: Access)* [1973] 2 All ER 81 (DC). *Re H (Minors) (Access)* [1992] 1 FLR 148 and earlier authorities indicated that cogent reasons were required for denying contact. See eg, *Re C (Minors) (Access)* [1985] FLR 804, *Williams v Williams* [1985] FLR 509 *and Wright v Wright* (1981) 2 FLR 276.

[241] *Re S (Contact: Promoting Relationship with Absent Parent)* [2004] EWCA Civ 18, [2004] 1 FLR 1279, at [28]; and see, eg, *Re O (Contact: Withdrawal of Application)* [2003] EWHC 3031 (Fam), [2004] 1 FLR 1258.

[242] *Re P (Children)* [2008] EWCA Civ 1431, [2009] 1 FLR 1056, at para [38].

that the attempt to promote contact should not be abandoned until it was clear that the child would not benefit from continuing the attempt.[243]

The policy is thus that contact should be ordered whenever practicable.[244] The Court of Appeal in *Re LVMH*[245] agreed with Sir Thomas Bingham MR's summary of the law in *Re O (Contact: Imposition of Conditions)*.[246] However, the court in *Re LVMH* recognised that different terminology had been employed in the case law at different times to express that general approach. The courts have sometimes referred to 'contact' as a parental right[247] or have talked of a presumption[248] of contact with a parent, or have seen contact as the child's right.[249] In *Re LVMH* Thorpe LJ (with whom Waller LJ expressly agreed) saw difficulty with the language of rights in this context,[250] since the making of a contact order is dictated not by recognition of a claim-right, but by application of the welfare principle. Thorpe LJ also apparently disapproved of the use of the term presumption, being wary that a presumption will 'inhibit or distort the rigorous search for the welfare solution' or 'be used as an aid to determination when the individual advocate or judge feels either undecided or overwhelmed'.[251] Instead therefore he preferred to talk of an 'assumption that contact is beneficial' or an 'assumption in favour of contact', commenting that the term assumption:[252]

> 'perhaps more accurately reflects the base of knowledge and experience from which the court embarks upon its application of the welfare principle in each disputed contact application.'

---

[243] *Re S (Contact: Promoting Relationship with Absent Parent)* [2004] EWCA Civ 18, [2004] 1 FLR 1279.

[244] *Re B (Contact: Stepfather's Opposition)* [1997] 2 FLR 579.

[245] [2001] Fam 260 (CA).

[246] [1995] 2 FLR 124, at 128–130.

[247] See eg *S v S* [1962] 1 WLR 445 at 448 per Willmer LJ. A particularly helpful discussion on the nature of the right to the 'society' of parents and child is to be found in A McCall Smith 'Is Anything Left of Parental Rights?' in McCall Smith and Sutherland (eds) *Family Rights* (Edinburgh University Press, 1990), at p 10. For a more recent similar assessment, see A Bainham ' Is Anything Now Left of Parental Rights?' ch 2 in R Probert, S. Gilmore and J. Herring (eds) *Responsible Parents & Parental Responsibility* (Oxford: Hart Publishing, 2009), 23–42.

[248] See S Gilmore 'Disputing Contact: Challenging Some Assumptions' [2008] CFLQ 285 for an account of judicial use of the term 'presumption' in the context of contact applications.

[249] It was first described judicially as a right of the child by Wrangham J in *M v M (Child: Access)* [1973] 2 All ER 81 at 85. See also *A v L (Contact)* [1998] 1 FLR 361 at 365, Holman J describing contact as 'a fundamental right of a child'. For the view that it is *both* the child's and the parent's interest, see A Bainham 'Changing Families and Changing Concepts: Reforming the Language of Family Law' [1998] CFLQ 1 at 5–8. The Scottish approach is to accept that parents have both responsibilities and rights and that contact falls into both categories. The view in Scotland must therefore be that contact is a right of *both* parent and child.

[250] Drawing on observations of Ormrod LJ in *A v C* [1985] FLR 445 at 455, and Lord Oliver of Aylmerton in *Re KD (A Minor) (Ward: Termination of Access)* [1988] AC 806.

[251] *Re LVMH* [2001] Fam 260 (CA), at 295.

[252] Ibid, at 295.

However, the idea that the courts should assume the benefits of contact in any particular case or in all cases is controversial, and not supported by social science research evidence, including the view of the author of the general expert psychiatric report upon which the court relied.[253]

Thorpe LJ added that he doubted 'that sufficient distinction had been made in the authorities between cases in which contact is sought in order to maintain an existing relationship, to revive a dormant relationship or to create a non-existent relationship', and commented:[254]

> 'The judicial assumption that to order contact would be to promote welfare should surely wane across that spectrum. I would not assume the benefit with unquestioning confidence where a child has developed over its early years without any knowledge of its father, particularly if over those crucially formative years a psychological attachment to an alternative father has been achieved.'

Drawing on the ECtHR jurisprudence and the leading domestic authorities, the Court of Appeal in *Re C (Direct Contact: Suspension)*[255] helpfully summarised the overall position in a series of bullet points as follows:

'•   Contact between parent and child is a fundamental element of family life and is almost always in the interests of the child.[256]
•   Contact between parent and child is to be terminated only in exceptional circumstances, where there are cogent reasons for doing so[257] and when there is no alternative. Contact is to be terminated only if it will be detrimental to the child's welfare.

---

[253] See Dr C Sturge's correspondence with one of the authors, as discussed in S Gilmore 'Disputing Contact: Challenging Some Assumptions' [2008] CFLQ 285. The research evidence reveals a complex range of factors impacting on child well-being in relation to post-separation parenting arrangements which does not suggest reliance on generalisations: see for recent research, J Fortin, J Hunt and L Scanlan, *Taking a longer view of contact: The perspectives of young adults who experienced parental separation in their youth* (Nuffield Foundation, Sussex Law School, 2012); and for reviews of research, see S Gilmore 'Contact/Shared Residence and Child Well-Being: Research Evidence and its Implications for Legal Decision-Making' (2006) 20 *International Journal of Law, Policy and the Family* 344, at 358; J Dunn 'Annotation: Children's Relationships with their Nonresident Fathers' (2004) 45(4) *Journal of Child Psychology and Psychiatry* 659; J Hunt, *Researching Contact* (London: National Council for One Parent Families, 2003). J Hunt with C Roberts *Child Contact with Non-Resident Parents*, Family Policy Briefing 3 (Oxford: University of Oxford, 2004).

[254] *Re LVMH* [2001] Fam 260, at 294–295.

[255] [2011] EWCA Civ 521, [2011] 2 FLR 912.

[256] See, eg, *Re O (Contact: Imposition of Conditions)* [1995] 2 FLR 124 at 128, drawing upon Balcombe LJ's judgment in *Re H (Minors) (Access)* [1992] 1 FLR 148 (CA), at 152, and Latey J's judgment in *M v M (Child: Access)* [1973] 2 All ER 81(DC); *Re S (Contact: Promoting Relationship with Absent Parent)* [2004] EWCA Civ 18, [2004] 1 FLR 1279, per Dame Elizabeth Butler-Sloss P, at para [19]; *Re T (A Minor) (Parental Responsibility: Contact)* [1993] 2 FLR 450 at 459; and *Görgülü v Germany* (Application No 74969/01) [2004] ECHR 89, [2004] 1 FLR 894, at para 48: 'it is in a child's interest for its family ties to be maintained, as severing such ties means cutting a child off from its roots, which can only be justified in very exceptional circumstances'.

[257] *Re M (Contact: Supervision)* [1998] 1 FLR 727, at 730; *Re O (Contact: Withdrawal of Application)* [2003] EWHC 3031 (Fam), [2004] 1 FLR 1258, at para [6].

- There is a positive obligation on the State, and therefore on the judge, to take measures to maintain and to reconstitute the relationship between parent and child, in short, to maintain or restore contact. The judge has a positive duty to attempt to promote contact. The judge must grapple with all the available alternatives before abandoning hope of achieving some contact.[258] He must be careful not to come to a premature decision, for contact is to be stopped only as a last resort and only once it has become clear that the child will not benefit from continuing the attempt.[259]

- The court should take both a medium-term and long-term view and not accord excessive weight to what appear likely to be short-term or transient problems.[260]

- The key question, which requires 'stricter scrutiny', is whether the judge has taken all necessary steps to facilitate contact as can reasonably be demanded in the circumstances of the particular case.

- All that said, at the end of the day the welfare of the child is paramount; 'the child's interest must have precedence over any other consideration'.[261]

The use in this last sentence of the phrase 'precedence over any other consideration' may evidence a very subtle attempt to shift the courts' understanding of the paramountcy principle (or at least the language used in respect of it) to a position more consistent with the workings of the ECHR.

It will be apparent from the courts' general approach to contact disputes that the power to deprive a parent and child of contact is not one which will be exercised lightly, and the courts will require a sound justification for doing so.[262] We provide below a brief account of examples from case law of circumstances in which contact may be refused.

Sometimes contact may be denied where a child expresses a wish not to have contact with a parent, perhaps because the child finds contact, or the circumstances surrounding it, distressing. For example in *Re F (Minors) (Denial of Contact)*[263] direct contact was not ordered where children found their father's transsexualism distressing and did not wish to see him in his new gender.[264] By contrast, in cases in which a child is merely ambivalent about contact, for example because it is not stimulating or a parent's behaviour is bizarre or baffling to the child, a court may still order contact, taking the view that the child should know and accept the parent as he or she is.[265]

---

[258] *Re P (Children)* [2008] EWCA Civ 1431, [2009] 1 FLR 1056, at para [38].

[259] *Re S (Contact: Promoting Relationship with Absent Parent)* [2004] EWCA Civ 18, [2004] 1 FLR 1279, at para [32].

[260] *Re O (Contact: Imposition of Conditions)* [1995] 2 FLR 124, at 129.

[261] *Re C (Direct Contact: Suspension)* [2011] EWCA Civ 521, [2011] 2 FLR 912, at paras [37]–[47].

[262] For a recent case in which the Court of Appeal found that a judge had erroneously denied direct contact, see *Re W (Direct Contact)* [2012] EWCA Civ 999, [2013] 1 FLR 494, which is discussed further below on the matter of facilitation of contact.

[263] [1993] 2 FLR 677 (CA).

[264] cf *Re L (Contact: Transsexual Applicant)* [1995] 2 FLR 438 (Fam). See also *Re C (Contact: No Order for Contact)* [2000] 2 FLR 723 (Fam) (all contact, including indirect contact ordered to cease because of child's distress at contact in context of allegation of sexual abuse by father's new stepson).

[265] See, for example, *Re B (Minors: Access)* [1992] 1 FLR 140 (CA).

It is important for the court to be clear that the child's desire not to have contact represents the child's true wishes and feelings,[266] and is not the product of any alienation of the child from one parent by the other. There is disagreement as to whether such behaviour is properly characterised as a syndrome[267] and the English courts to date have been cautious of such a conclusion,[268] preferring to see it merely as an element of implacable hostility to contact.[269]

In *Re D (A Minor) (Contact: Mother's Hostility)*[270] the Court of Appeal recognised that it is now 'well settled'[271] that contact may be denied where a parent is implacably opposed to contact, and where to compel the parent to accept contact will 'have adverse effects on the child and injure it'.[272] A step-parent's opposition to contact has also constituted a reason for denying the child's contact with a parent. In *Re B (Contact: Stepfather's Opposition)*[273] the step-father of a 9-year-old girl opposed the girl's contact with her natural father, with whom she had virtually had no contact since birth. For cultural reasons the stepfather genuinely could not contemplate another man's involvement in his household, and contact would risk upsetting the mother's marriage and destabilising the child's current family unit. While the Court of Appeal made plain that the mere fact of a step-father's opposition to contact between the child and the natural father would not prevent the court making a contact order if the best interests of the child required it, on the facts of this case the child's interests required that no order for contact be made.[274]

The term 'implacable hostility' is only properly applied to cases where there is hostility and also no good reason can be discerned either for the hostility or for the opposition to contact.[275] It is not appropriate to use the term where a parent's reason for the hostility are genuine and rationally held.[276]

---

[266] If necessary, the matter should be investigated: see *Re T (A Child: Contact)* [2002] EWCA Civ 1736, [2003] 1 FLR 531 (cause of child's sudden and adamant refusal to stay with the father not adequately investigated).

[267] T Hobbs 'Parental Alienation Syndrome and UK Family Courts' [2002] Fam Law 182; C Bruch 'Parental Alienation Syndrome and Alienated Children – getting it wrong in child custody cases' [2001] CFLQ 381.

[268] See, for example, *Re O (Contact: Withdrawal of Application)* [1995] 2 FLR 124 (CA), at [92]; *Re C (Prohibition on Further Applications)* [2002] 1 FLR 1136 and *Re S (Contact: Children's Views)* [2002] 1 FLR 1156.

[269] For this view, see also C Sturge and D Glaser 'Contact and Domestic Violence – The Experts' Court Report' [2000] Fam Law 615, at 622.

[270] [1993] 2 FLR 1 (CA).

[271] Ibid, at 7.

[272] *Re B (A Minor) (Access)* [1984] FLR 648, at 649. See also *Re BC (A Minor) (Access)* [1985] FLR 639 (CA). See also for examples of implacable hostility, *Re J (A Minor) (Contact)* [1994] 1 FLR 729, *Re S (Unco-operative Mother)* [2004] 2 FLR 710, and *V v V (Contact: Implacable Hostility)* [2004] 2 FLR 851. See J Parker and D Eaton 'Opposing Contact' [1994] Fam Law 636; S Jolly 'Implacable Hostility, Contact and the Limits of Law' [1995] CFLQ 228; and H Conway 'Implacable Hostility – Seeking a Breakthrough' [1997] Fam Law 109.

[273] [1997] 2 FLR 579.

[274] See also *Re H (A Minor) (Parental Responsibility)* [1993] 1 FLR 484 (CA).

[275] *Re D (Contact: Reasons for Refusal)* [1997] 2 FLR 48 (CA).

[276] Ibid. For criticism of the courts' earlier approach, see J Wallbank 'Castigating Mothers: The

In *Re D (A Minor) (Contact: Mother's Hostility)*[277] the court concluded on the facts that the mother's attitude placed the child 'at serious risk of major emotional harm if she were to be compelled to accept a degree of contact to the natural father against her will'.[278] In *Re O (Contact: Imposition of Conditions)* Sir Thomas Bingham MR drew attention to this use of the words 'serious risk of major emotional harm' and added that:[279]

> 'The court should not at all readily accept that the child's welfare will be injured by direct contact. Judging that question the court should take a medium-term and long-term view of the child's development and not accord excessive weight to what appear likely to be short-term or transient problems.'

Reviewing the authorities, the Court of Appeal in *Re D (Contact: Reasons for Refusal)*[280] concluded that in a case of implacable hostility:[281]

> 'the court will be very slow indeed to reach the conclusion that contact will be harmful to the child. It may eventually have to reach that conclusion but it will want to be satisfied that there is indeed a serious risk of major emotional harm before doing so.'

In contrast to cases of so-called implacable hostility are those in which it is transparently plain that a parent has a sound justification for refusing contact, such as anxiety that the other parent will abduct the child or a fear of a former partner's involvement based on past violent behaviour[282] or other anxiety such as possible abduction,[283] or previous abuse, of the child. The courts have been clear, however, that the fact that a parent has abused a child is not a blanket reason for denying contact, although clearly it is also an important factor to be taken into consideration.[284] The Children Act 1989 defines harm so as to include impairment of health or development 'suffered from seeing or hearing

---

Judicial Response to "Wilful" Women in Disputes Over Paternal Contact in English Law' (1998) 20(4) *Journal of Social Welfare and Family Law* 357; C Smart and B Neale 'Arguments Against Virtue – Must Contact Be Enforced?' (1997) 27 Fam Law 332; and for articles charting a shift in the courts' approach, see R Bailey-Harris 'Contact – Challenging Conventional Wisdom?' (2001) 13(4) CFLQ 361; F Kaganas and S Day Sclater 'Contact and Domestic Violence – The Winds of Change' [2000] Fam Law 630.

277   [1993] 2 FLR 1 (CA).
278   Ibid.
279   [1995] 2 FLR 124 (CA).
280   [1997] 2 FLR 48 (CA).
281   Ibid, 53. See also *Re P (Contact: Discretion)* [1998] 2 FLR 696 (Fam).
282   *Re L (Contact: Genuine Fear)* [2002] 1 FLR 621 and *Re D (Contact: Reasons for Refusal)* [1997] 2 FLR 48. Sadly, there is no shortage of reported cases where contact has been refused in the context of domestic violence. See also *Re H (Contact: Domestic Violence)* [1998] 2 FLR 42; *Re M (Contact: Violent Parent)* [1999] 2 FLR 321; *Re S (Violent Parent: Indirect Contact)* [2000] 1 FLR 481; and *Re L (Contact: Genuine Fear)* [2002] 1 FLR 621.
283   *Re K (Contact: Mother's Anxiety)* [1999] 2 FLR 703.
284   *H v H (Child Abuse: Access)* [1989] 1 FLR 212 (CA); *L v L (Child Abuse: Access)* [1989] 2 FLR 16 (CA); *Re E-L (A Child) (Contact)* [2003] EWCA Civ 1947 at [8]: 'There is simply no principle or practice that would justify an inevitable conclusion for the termination of direct contact from the bare finding of past inappropriate sexual conduct'. For other examples of the courts' approach, see *Re R (A Minor) (Child Abuse: Access)* [1988] 1 FLR 206 (CA), *S v S (Child Abuse: Access)* [1988] 1 FLR 213 (CA).

the ill-treatment of another',[285] and the courts have adopted a similar approach with regard to domestic violence. In *Re LVMH*[286] the Court of Appeal held that there is no presumption against making an order for direct contact in cases of domestic violence, which is:[287]

'not to be elevated to some special category; it is one highly material factor amongst many which may offset the assumption in favour of contact when the difficult balancing exercise is carried out by the judge applying the welfare principle and the welfare checklist, s 1(1) and (3) of the Children Act 1989.'

The court's decision not to adopt a presumption against contact in cases of proved domestic violence was taken against the recommendation of a general psychiatric report on contact and domestic violence which was before the court, and which was endorsed by the Royal College of Psychiatrists.[288] The court's rejection of a presumption was in part based on the observation that domestic violence comes in a spectrum of many forms, which makes it difficult to adopt a presumptive universal approach.[289] However, this reasoning does not sit easily with the court's general conclusion (discussed earlier) that there should be an assumption in all cases that contact is beneficial.[290]

The Court of Appeal also had the benefit of a, then recent, report to the Lord Chancellor,[291] which recognised that there needed to be a heightened awareness of the impact of domestic violence in the context of contact disputes.[292] The court took the opportunity to reinforce this point and to

---

[285] Children Act 1989, s 31 as amended by s 120 of the Adoption and Children Act 2002.

[286] [2001] Fam 260, [2000] 2 FLR 334. On the general question of contact in the context of domestic violence, see C Humphreys and C Harrison 'Squaring the Circle – Contact and Domestic Violence' [2003] Fam Law 419. See also F Kaganas 'Contact and domestic violence' [2000] CFLQ 311.

[287] [2001] Fam 260, at 301.

[288] C Sturge and D Glaser 'Contact and Domestic Violence – The Experts' Court Report' [2000] Fam Law 615. For discussion of the impact of domestic violence, see e g O Mills 'Effects of Domestic Violence on Children' [2008] Fam Law 165; C Humphreys and RK Thiara 'Neither Justice Nor Protection: Women's Experiences of Post-separation Violence' (2003) 25(3) *Journal of Social Welfare and Family Law* 195; M Hester, C Pearson, and N Harwin *Making an Impact: Children and Domestic Violence* (London, Jessica Kingsley, 2000); C McGee, *Childhood Experiences of Domestic Violence* (London, Jessica Kingsley, 2000); L Bowker, M Arbitell, and J McFerron 'On the Relationship Between Wife Beating and Child Abuse' in K Yllo and M Bograd (eds) *Feminist Perspectives on Wife Abuse* (London: Sage, 1989); The Rt Hon Lord Justice Wall 'Domestic Violence and Access: The Impact on Families and Enforcement Problems' [2009] *International Family Law* 22.

[289] For criticism, see J Herring 'Connecting Contact: Contact in a Private Law Context' in A Bainham, B Lindley, M Richards, and L Trinder (eds), *Children and Their Families: Contact, Rights and Welfare* (Oxford, Hart Publishing, 2003), at p 105. See also, calling for a presumption: M Kaye 'Domestic Violence, Residence and Contact' (1996) 8 CFLQ 285; M Fineman 'Domestic Violence, Custody and Visitation' (2002) 36 *Family Law Quarterly* 211.

[290] For criticism of the court's reasoning, see S Gilmore 'The Assumption that Contact is Beneficial: Challenging the Secure Foundation' [2008] Fam Law 1126.

[291] Advisory Board on Family Law Children Act Sub-Committee, *A Report to the Lord Chancellor on the Question of Parental Contact in Cases Where There Is Domestic Violence* (Lord Chancellor's Department, 2000).

[292] The fact that domestic violence issues were downplayed by the courts was demonstrated by

incorporate into its judgment some of the guidance in the Report. The court made clear that allegations of domestic violence must be properly investigated and findings of fact made. Where the allegations are proved, the court must engage in a balancing exercise, weighing the risk against the positive benefits of contact. The willingness of a party to recognise past conduct and to make genuine efforts to change would be an important factor in this assessment. The process of dealing with residence and contact disputes involving domestic violence is now guided by a Practice Direction supplementing Part 12 of the Family Procedure Rules.[293] This provides that in a case in which domestic violence has been found, the court 'should only make an order for contact if it can be satisfied that the physical and emotional safety of the child and the parent with whom the child is living can, as far as possible, be secured before during and after contact.'

The impact on a parent's health of ordering contact may also be a crucial factor. In *Re H (Contact Order) (No 2)*,[294] the father suffered from Huntington's disease which could bring adverse effects on mood and personality. There had been an incident in which the father had attempted to take his own life and those of his children too, but from which the children were saved by a member of the public. The mother thereafter opposed direct contact. Wall J reached the conclusion that direct contact could not be risked in these circumstances since the mother was at genuine risk of having a nervous breakdown if contact were ordered. It was particularly important that the mother remained well given the father's degenerative illness. Wall J expressed the confidence that the mother would promote indirect contact through letters and telephone calls.

Facilitation and enforcement

The jurisprudence of the ECtHR makes it plain that there is a *positive* obligation on the State, acting through the courts and social welfare agencies, to make all reasonable efforts to facilitate contact between parent and child and to reunite them where they have become separated. Thus, in *Hokkanen v Finland*[295] the Court found that the State of Finland had breached Mr Hokkanen's right to respect for family life by the failure of the Finnish authorities over many years to enforce his right of access to his daughter who was in the care of her maternal grandparents following the death of her mother.[296] It is clear, however, that the duty to reunite is not an absolute one

---

research: see eg, R Bailey-Harris, J Barron, and J Pearce 'From Utility to Rights? The Presumption of Contact in Practice' (1999) 13 *International Journal of Law, Policy and the Family* 111.

[293] FPR PD 12J – Residence and Contact Orders: Domestic Violence and Harm.

[294] [2002] 1 FLR 22.

[295] [1996] 1 FLR 289.

[296] See also *Ciliz v The Netherlands* [2000] 2 FLR 469 in which the deportation of the father and refusal to extend his residence permit by the Dutch authorities was held to breach his right to respect for private and family life. The father had separated from the mother and had only had intermittent contact with the child. Nevertheless, the ECtHR found that it was enough to amount to family life between them. The interference with this right, though in pursuance of

and, in contrast, in *Glaser v United Kingdom*[297] the father unsuccessfully argued that the UK authorities in England and Scotland had breached his Convention rights in their failure to enforce adequately English contact orders in relation to his three children. The mother had managed to disappear to Scotland with the child and dodged compliance with the court orders. Although the orders of the English court were registered in Scotland, they proved very difficult to enforce because of the mother's determination to be obstructive. The ECtHR concluded that the UK authorities had done all that could reasonably be expected of them. Domestic case law has recognised that there is a limit beyond which the court should not strive to promote contact if to do so would not be in the child's best interests,[298] although it has also been emphasised that the attempt to promote contact should not be abandoned prematurely when contact is in the child's long-term best interests. As the Court of Appeal commented in *Re M (Contact: Long-Term Best Interests)*[299] where 'the court has the picture that a parent is seeking, without good reason, to eliminate the other parent from the child's, or children's lives, the court should not stand by and take no positive action. Justice to the children and the deprived parent ... require the court to leave no stone unturned that might resolve the situation and prevent long-term harm to the children.'

The question of how best to facilitate contact gained some momentum in policy debate in England and Wales when it was the subject of a report to the Lord Chancellor by the Children Act Sub-Committee of the Advisory Board on Family Law.[300] This was prompted largely by the concerns of non-resident fathers (taken up politically by fathers' rights organisations)[301] that court orders were too easily flouted and not properly enforced.[302] The Board recommended a greater emphasis on resolving contact disputes by negotiation, conciliation and mediation, based on 'a widespread feeling that an application

---

the legitimate aim of preserving the economic well-being of the country, was not *necessary* in a democratic society since it prejudged the decision on the father's pending application for access (contact) and it interfered with his ability to develop family ties with the child. See also *Elsholz v Germany* [2000] 2 FLR 486.

[297] [2001] 1 FLR 153.

[298] *Re S (Contact: Promoting Relationship with Absent Parent)* [2004] EWCA Civ 18, [2004] 1 FLR 1279, at [28]. See eg, *Re O (Contact: Withdrawal of Application)* [2003] EWHC 3031 (Fam), [2004] 1 FLR 1258.

[299] [2006] 1 FLR 627 (CA).

[300] *Making Contact Work* (Lord Chancellor's Department, 2002). Among its recommendations were: the provision of better information about the principles of contact to be provided to separating and divorcing parents and to children themselves; that judges and magistrates should have the power to refer parties to mediation; that there should be better funding for contact centres; and that there should be funding for additional facilities for resolving disputes through negotiation, conciliation and mediation.

[301] See R Collier and S Sheldon (eds) *Fathers' Rights Activism and Law Reform in Comparative Perspective* (Oxford, Hart Publishing, 2006), especially ch 3.

[302] The judiciary acknowledged the problems in some cases: see eg, *Re D (Intractable Contact Dispute: Publicity)* [2004] 1 FLR 1226 in which there was a staggering 43 court hearings before 16 different judges and numerous adjournments. The mother, who had sabotaged contact with the father by various means over a five-year period, had flouted court orders, which had resulted in penal notices, suspended prison sentences and eventually imprisonment itself. Munby J said that in this case at least the father was fully entitled to blame the system. Cf *Re*

to the court should be the last resort'.[303] It was also suggested that the courts be given much wider powers to ensure that their orders are obeyed and otherwise to facilitate their implementation.[304] A subsequent survey of non-resident parental contact noted that only 10 per cent of separating couples resorted to the courts while the overwhelming majority already reached agreement without this.[305] In light of this finding and other research evidence,[306] the Government concluded that more should be done to facilitate contact by agreement in this minority of cases, while also augmenting the courts' powers to deal with intractable disputes. The Advisory Board's recommendations were taken forward by the then Government,[307] and led to Part I of the Children and Adoption Act 2006. This amended s 16 of the Children Act 1989 to provide that a family assistance order may direct the officer concerned to give advice and assistance as regards establishing, improving, and maintaining contact to such of the persons named in the order as may be specified in the order.[308] The 2006 Act also inserted into the Children Act 1989 ss 11A–11P, which introduced further measures for facilitating and enforcing contact. When considering whether to make a contact order, the court has power to require 'an individual who is a party to the proceedings to take part in an activity that promotes contact with the child concerned'.[309] When the court actually makes

---

O (Contact: Withdrawal of Application) [2004] 1 FLR 1258, in which Wall J held that it was not enough for a father to blame the system where he himself bore a substantial share of the blame for contact breaking down.

[303] This premise might be challenged by some commentators who have warned of the dangers involved in over-reliance on the settlement approach.

[304] For comment on the Children and Adoption Bill 2005, 2005–06 HL-96 54/1, see J Masson and C Humphreys 'Facilitating and Enforcing Contact: the Bill and the Ten Per Cent' [2005] Fam Law 548. See House of Commons and House of Lords Joint Committee on the Draft Children (Contact) and Adoption Bill 'Draft Children (Contact) and Adoption Bill Volume 1: Report' (2004–05) HC 400-I, HL 100-I.

[305] A Blackwell and F Dawe *Non-Resident Parental Contact with Children* (Department of Constitutional Affairs, 2003). The report also revealed some differences in perception as between resident and non-resident parents about frequency of contact. While 14 per cent of non-resident parents reported that they never saw their children, twice as many resident parents, 28 per cent, said that the non-resident parent never saw the child. While 77 per cent of non-resident parents said that they saw their children either every day, at least once a week or at least once a month, the figure was only 60 per cent among resident parents who reported this. Even greater discrepancies in these perceptions were observed in relation to indirect contact. There is a tendency for contact to break down with the passage of time: see J Bradshaw and J Millar *Lone Parent Families in the UK* (HMSO, 1991). For evidence from research in Australia, see P Parkinson and B Smyth 'Satisfaction and dissatisfaction with father–child contact arrangements in Australia' [2004] CFLQ 289.

[306] See C Smart, V May, A Wade, and C Furniss, *Residence and Contact Disputes in Court Volume 1*, Research Series 6/03 (London: Department for Constitutional Affairs, 2003), esp ch 6. The Government also had regard to existing research: see HM Government, *Children's Needs, Parents' Responsibilities: Supporting Evidence for Consultation Paper*.

[307] Government's Response to the Report of the Children Act Sub-Committee of the Lord Chancellor's Advisory Board on Family Law 'Making Contact Work' (2002); Department for Constitutional Affairs and Department for Education and Skills, The Government's Response to the Children Act Sub-Committee (CASC) Report: 'Making Contact Work' (2004); HM Government, *Parental Separation: Children's Needs and Parents' Responsibilities* (Cm 6273, 2004).

[308] Section 16(4A).

[309] Section 11A(3). The activities include, in particular: '(a) programmes, classes and counselling

a contact order it can impose a similar requirement, known as a contact activity condition,[310] upon a wider range of persons.[311] The child's welfare is the paramount consideration when deciding whether to impose an activity. The activity cannot require a person to undergo medical or psychiatric examination, assessment, or treatment or to take part in mediation[312] and the court must consider the suitability of the activity and its possible conflict with a person's religious beliefs or work schedule.[313] Both contact activities and contact itself can be the subject of monitoring by a CAFCASS or Welsh family proceedings officer and of report back to the court,[314] although monitoring cannot exceed a period of 12 months.[315] Whenever a court makes a contact order it must attach a notice warning of the consequences of failing to comply with the contact order.[316] All of these provisions are aimed at trying to ensure that contact takes place.

In recent case law judges have sought to emphasise that facilitating contact is one of the duties comprised in parental responsibility. In a postscript to McFarlane LJ's judgment in *Re W (Direct Contact)*,[317] the Court of Appeal emphasised that where 'there are significant difficulties in the way of establishing safe and beneficial contact, the parents share the primary responsibility of addressing those difficulties'[318] and therefore 'the courts are entitled to look to each parent to use their best endeavours to deliver what their child needs, hard or burdensome or downright tough though that may be'.[319]

Where, however, a parent remains obdurate in refusing to comply with an order, there are various methods by which attempts[320] to enforce contact can be made. One possibility is to commit the resident parent to prison for contempt of court in failing to comply with the court's order. This is, however, not an easy option for the court since in many cases it is likely to inflict distress on the child by depriving the child of his or her primary carer. At one time the Court of Appeal took the view that such an approach was damaging and futile,

---

or guidance sessions of a kind that (i) may assist a person as regards establishing, maintaining or improving contact with a child; (ii) may, by addressing a person's violent behaviour, enable or facilitate contact with a child; (b) sessions in which information or advice is given as regards making or operating arrangements for contact with a child, including making arrangements by means of mediation'.

[310] Section 11C.

[311] See s 11C(3): the person with whom the child concerned lives or is to live; (b) the person whose contact with the child concerned is provided for in that order; or (c) a person upon whom that order imposes a condition under s 11(7)(b).

[312] Ibid, s 11A(6).

[313] Section 11E.

[314] See ss 11G and 11H.

[315] Section 11H(6).

[316] Section 11I, and see S Evans 'To Warn or Not To Warn: Contact Enforcement' [2009] Fam Law 530.

[317] [2012] EWCA Civ 999, [2013] 1 FLR 494 (Tomlinson and Rix LJJ agreeing).

[318] Ibid, at para [77].

[319] Ibid, at para [76].

[320] The issue of enforcement is a difficult one. Children, especially older children, cannot be forced to see parents, 'absent' parents cannot be forced to be actively involved in parenting and resident parents cannot be forced to be welcoming and co-operative towards an ex-partner.

Ormrod LJ stating that the 'court is only concerned with the welfare of the children and ought not to trouble itself too much about its own dignity'.[321] Against this view, however, it can be argued that the *attempt* to enforce needs to be made not least for ideological reasons. Unless the courts are seen to be taking the contact issue seriously, the message of the law that contact is an important right of the child may be lost.[322] Moreover, as we have seen, the ECHR *requires* the State to take action to enforce orders for contact. The Court of Appeal is now more robust in its approach, having observed in *A v N (Committal: Refusal of Contact)*[323] that 'against the wisdom of the observations of Ormrod LJ is to be balanced the consideration that orders of the court are made to be obeyed'. In that case an order was eventually made committing a mother to prison for contempt where she refused to comply with the court's orders for contact for over a year and continued to dispute the father's paternity despite clear DNA evidence to the contrary.[324] Subsequent case law has echoed the sentiments in *A v N*,[325] and it has been said that:[326]

> 'The days are long gone when mothers can assume that their role as carers of children protects them from being sentenced to immediate terms of imprisonment for clear, repeated and deliberate breaches of contact orders.'

Committal to prison ought to be seen as a last resort, but it has been said that a court need not wait unduly before resorting to it, and that a willingness to grasp the nettle by threat, or implementation, 'of a very short period of imprisonment – just a day or two – may at an earlier stage of the proceedings achieve more than the threat of a longer sentence at a much later stage in the process'.[327]

Another method is for the judge to order a change of residence, and the courts have been willing to order an immediate transfer of residence in some cases. For example, in *Re C (Residence Order)*[328] transfer was ordered where the mother had a new baby and committal to prison was not appropriate.[329] As the Master of the Rolls commented in *Re O (Contact: Imposition of*

---

[321] [1984] FLR 635, at 638. See also *I v D (Access Order: Enforcement)* [1988] 2 FLR 286.

[322] And it has been said that caution needs to be exercised in equating too readily the interests of women (usually the so-called 'primary carers') and children in this matter: see A Bainham 'Changing Families and Changing Concepts: Reforming the Language of Family Law' [1998] CFLQ 1 at 7. Compare, however, the view of Smart and Neale 'Arguments against virtue – must contact be enforced?' [1997] Fam Law 332, that 'the public and judicial treatment of contact has taken on an increasingly rigid and dogmatic form, which is becoming a harmful trend in family law'.

[323] [1997] 1 FLR 533.

[324] For another case of committal to prison, against which the mother successfully appealed, see *Re K (Contact: Committal Order)* [2003] 1 FLR 277.

[325] See eg [2004] EWCA Civ 1790, [2005] 1 FLR 812, at [14].

[326] *B v S* [2009] EWCA Civ 548, at para [16].

[327] *Re L-W (Enforcement and Committal: Contact); CPL v CH-W and Others* [2010] EWCA Civ 1253, [2011] 1 FLR 1095, at para [108].

[328] [2007] EWCA Civ 866, [2008] 1 FLR 211.

[329] See also, eg, *Re S (Transfer of Residence)* [2010] EWHC 192 (Fam), [2010] 1 FLR 1785.But compare *Re B (Residence Order: Status Quo)* [1998] 1 FLR 368 (inappropriate change in the child's residential arrangements precipitated by contact difficulties).

Conditions),[330] 'no residence order is to be regarded as irrevocable'.[331] The courts have also put in place a threat to change residence by way of a suspended residence order, suspended on condition of compliance with contact arrangements.[332]

In a case in which the judge forms the view that a child may be suffering significant harm as a result of parental behavior surrounding contact, it should be recalled that the judge has power under s 37 of the Children Act 1989 to direct the relevant local authority to investigate the child's situation with a view to deciding whether they should apply for a care order or supervision order under s 31 of the Act. Such cases are likely to be relatively rare, but this approach was adopted in *Re M (Intractable Contact Dispute: Interim Care Orders)*[333] in which one parent was alienating the other from the children by instilling in the children a false belief that they had been sexually abused. Wall J made a direction in this case which ultimately led to an interim care order under which the children resumed contact with their father. Wall J made clear that the use of a s 37 direction must be seen as 'a well-focused tool, to be used only when the case fits its criteria'.[334]

Section 11J of the Children Act 1989 (inserted by the Children and Adoption Act 2006) provides a further statutory mechanism for enforcing contact, known as an 'enforcement order'. This allows the court to impose on a person an unpaid work requirement if the court is satisfied beyond reasonable doubt that the person has failed to comply with the contact order.[335] There is a defence of reasonable excuse.[336] The order can only be made upon application[337] and not of the court's own motion. A court can also order a person to pay compensation to another who has suffered financial loss by reason of that person's failure to comply with a contact order.[338]

Recent developments: ensuring continuing involvement between parents and children

The policy debate which led to the changes effected by the Children and Adoption Act 2006 was still firmly committed to the paramountcy principle as the appropriate criterion for deciding contact or residence disputes. The Government was not convinced by the perception of some fathers' groups that the courts are biased against them[339] and rejected the view that there was a need for a change in the law or to the core principles in the Children Act. While it

---

[330] [1995] 2 FLR 124 (CA).

[331] Ibid, at 130.

[332] *Re A (Suspended Residence Order)* [2009] EWHC 1576 (Fam), [2010] 1 FLR 1679.

[333] [2003] EWHC 1024 (Fam), [2003] 2 FLR 636.

[334] [2003] EWHC 1024 (Fam), [2003] 2 FLR 636, at [8].

[335] Section 11J(2).

[336] Section 11J(3).

[337] See s 11J(5) for the categories of applicant.

[338] Children Act 1989, s 110(2). In this case proof of breach need only be to the civil standard of the balance of probabilities.

[339] For a vehemently expressed opinion that they are so biased, see Bob Geldof 'The Real Love

was accepted that 'in the event of parental separation, a child's welfare is best promoted by a continuing relationship with both parents as long as it is safe to do so',[340] the Government rejected the notion that there should be a statutory 'presumption of contact' or an automatic 50: 50 division of the child's time between the two parents.[341] It was acknowledged, albeit rather cursorily, that 'rights' have a part to play in that the ECHR requires respect for private and family life and that 'this includes respect for the rights of both parents who enjoy family life with their children to have contact with those children, provided this is consistent with the welfare of the children, and also the rights of children to have beneficial relationships with their parents'.[342] However, there was no real engagement with how such rights fit, if at all, with the paramountcy principle.

More recently the Family Justice Review revisited this issue and likewise recommended no change to the substantive law.[343] The Government acknowledged that, in light of experiences of legislating in Australia,[344] the law should avoid giving any impression that there is a presumption of equal division of a child's time between parents.[345] However, contrary to the overall advice of the Review, the Government concluded that 'there should be a legislative statement of the importance of children having an ongoing relationship with both parents after family separation, where that is safe, and in the child's best interests'.[346] Following consultation[347] the Government has taken its proposal forward in clause 11 the Children and Families Bill 2013, which will insert new provisions into s 1 of the Children Act 1989. The provision is complex and it is convenient to set out the relevant provisions in full. Clause 11 of the Children and Families Bill provides:

---

that Dare Not Speak its Name' in A Bainham, B Lindley, M Richards and L Trinder (eds) *Children and their Families: Contact, Rights and Welfare* (Hart Publishing, 2003), at p 171.

[340] *Parental Separation: Children's Needs and Parents' Responsibilities* (2004) (Cm 6273), at para 4.

[341] Ibid, at para 42. The various critiques against introduction of a presumption of shared residence, especially one of 50:50 time-sharing, are discussed above under the heading of shared residence.

[342] Ibid, at para 45.

[343] Family Justice Review Final Report (Ministry of Justice, November 2011), and see Ministry of Justice and Department for Education, *The Government Response to the Family Justice Review: A System with Children and Families at its Heart* (Cm 8273, February 2012), at paras 59–64.

[344] For discussion of the Australian experience, see H Rhoades 'Legislating to promote children's welfare and the quest for certainty' [2012] CFLQ 158; B Fehlberg 'Legislating for shared parenting: how the Family Justice Review got it right' [2012] Fam Law 709; B Fehlberg, B Smyth, M Maclean, and C Roberts 'Legislating for Shared Time Parenting After Separation: A Research Review' (2011) 25(3) *International Journal of Law, Policy and the Family* 318.

[345] Ministry of Justice and Department for Education, *The Government Response to the Family Justice Review: A System with Children and Families at its Heart* (Cm 8273, February 2012), at para 62.

[346] Ibid, at para 61.

[347] Department for Education and Ministry of Justice, *Co-operative Parenting Following Family Separation: Proposed Legislation on the Involvement of Both Parents in a Child's Life* (13 June 2012).

'(2A) A court, in the circumstances mentioned in subsection (4)(a)[348] or (7), is as respects each parent within subsection (6)(a) to presume, unless the contrary is shown, that involvement of that parent in the life of the child concerned will further the child's welfare ...

(6) In subsection (2A) "parent" means parent of the child concerned; and, for the purposes of that subsection, a parent of the child concerned –

(a)   s within this paragraph if that parent can be involved in the child's life in a way that does not put the child at risk of suffering harm; and

(b)   s to be treated as being within paragraph (a) unless there is some evidence before the court in the particular proceedings to suggest that involvement of that parent in the child's life would put the child at risk of suffering harm whatever the form of the involvement.

(7) The circumstances referred to are that the court is considering whether to make an order under section 4(1)(c) or (2A) or 4ZA(1)(c) or (5) (parental responsibility of parent other than mother).'

This provision means that, generally, in proceedings for the making or revocation of a parental responsibility order in favour of a parent, or for the making, variation or discharge of a s 8 order which is contested, there will be a presumption that the parent's involvement in the child's life will further the child's welfare. The only circumstance in which the presumption will not apply is where no matter the form of parental involvement the child would be put at risk. There are likely to be very few such cases, so the presumption is likely to apply almost universally. The provision, which will be welcomed by some, is controversial. Its detractors will no doubt point to the fact that it is not needed, given the courts' current approach to contact orders and parental responsibility orders; that its introduction goes against judicial opinion that it would be incompatible with the welfare principle and would be likely to distort the rigorous search for the welfare solution; that it is not supported by research findings; and that it fails to give sufficient emphasis to circumstances in which particular parental involvements should not be presumed. For example, a parent's domestic violence may be such that involvement by indirect contact would not put the child at risk and hence the presumption of involvement would apply. However, it may also be in such a case that a parent's involvement in the sense of direct contact should not be ordered, and yet in the circumstances just outlined the general presumption in favour of parental involvement will apply. It remains to be seen, however, whether the provision will make any difference in practice.

Prohibited steps and specific issue orders

These orders are designed to resolve what might be described as 'single issues' affecting children and are modelled on the powers of the court in wardship. It

---

[348]   That is when 'the court is considering whether to make, vary or discharge a s 8 order, and the making, variation or discharge of the order is opposed by any party to the proceedings'.

was an aim of the Children Act to emulate and incorporate the better features of the wardship jurisdiction.[349] Both orders may be made in conjunction with other s 8 orders or on freestanding applications. They are intended to be subsidiary to residence and contact orders (which are the principal orders governing the exercise of parental responsibility) and they must not therefore be made with a view to achieving a result which could be achieved by the main orders[350] or in a way which is denied to the High Court in the exercise of its inherent jurisdiction.[351] The court in wardship exercises a degree of continuing control over a child's situation and retains parental responsibility (formerly 'custody') in the wider sense of the decision-making powers. The statutory powers are narrower (at least conceptually) than this all-embracing 'custodial' control. In wardship, every major issue affecting the ward must be referred back to the court for its determination.[352] The statutory orders do not vest parental responsibility in the court but do enable it to exercise control over particular areas of difficulty.

A prohibited steps order is an order 'that no step which could be taken by a parent in meeting his parental responsibility for a child, and which is of a kind specified in the order, shall be taken by any person without the consent of the court'.[353] The order can be directed against any person, provided what is sought to be prohibited is a matter of parental responsibility for a child.[354] The order is entirely prohibitive or negative in substance as its name suggests. The kinds of involvements with children which might be prohibited are infinitely various but, most obviously, a child's unlawful removal from the jurisdiction, or contact between the child and an 'undesirable adult', could be restrained.[355] The last example highlights some of the limitations of the order. First, in view of the reference to the exercise of parental responsibility, it seems that the order cannot be used to prohibit a mature child herself from having such contact. It may be that this is one instance in which the wardship jurisdiction will continue to have a special usefulness, especially in view of the Court of Appeal's ruling that the court in wardship or under the inherent jurisdiction has power to

---

[349] Law Com Report No 172 *Guardianship and Custody* (1988), Part IV.

[350] Section 9(5)(a). See *Nottinghamshire County Council v P* [1994] Fam 18; cf *Re H (Prohibited Steps Order)* [1995] 1 FLR 638.

[351] Section 9(5)(b), and Law Com Report No 172 (above), at paras 4.18–4.20.

[352] There were several good examples under the old law of a failure to refer issues back to the court. See, particularly, *Re GU (A Minor) (Wardship)* [1984] FLR 811 where a local authority was criticised by the High Court for arranging an abortion for an adolescent girl in its care, who was also a ward of court, without first referring the issue to the High Court. The ongoing control exercised by the court in wardship is best illustrated by the House of Lords decision in *Re E (SA) (A Minor) (Wardship)* [1984] 1 All ER 289.

[353] Section 8(1).

[354] See *Croydon London Borough Council v A* [1992] Fam 169 (CA) (order could not be used to prohibit contact between parents, since this was not a matter of meeting parental responsibility). There are limits to the order's use in principle; for example it cannot be used to interfere with a parent's right to occupy his or her home: see *Re D (Prohibited Steps Order)* [1996] 2 FLR 273.

[355] The so-called 'teenage wardship' cases would fall within this category – as to which, see NV Lowe and RAH White *Wards of Court* (2nd edn, Barry Rose/Kluwer, 1986), ch 12.

override the wishes of a mature minor.[356] Secondly, because a contact order (which, it will be recalled, directs the resident parent to allow contact) is also defined to include a 'no contact order',[357] it is not possible to use a prohibited steps order to prohibit a resident parent from allowing a child contact with another named person. This should rather be achieved by the making of a 'no contact order'. To make a prohibited steps order in such circumstances would fall foul of s 9(5) of the Children Act 1989, which provides that a prohibited steps order cannot be used to achieve a result which could be achieved by the making of a contact order (or residence order).[358]

An interesting use of the prohibited steps order occurred in *Re Z (A Minor) (Freedom of Publication)*[359] which concerned a child of famous parents who was receiving treatment at a special unit for her special educational needs. The courts had previously granted an injunction under the inherent jurisdiction restraining the media from publishing information which could lead to revelation of the child's identity. The mother then wished her daughter to take part in a television programme about the unit. It was held by the Court of Appeal that the child had a right of confidentiality concerning her attendance at the unit. The mother could, prima facie, waive this right of confidentiality on the child's behalf but to do so would amount to an exercise of parental responsibility. A prohibited steps order could therefore be made to control the exercise of this aspect of parental responsibility. Here, the child's welfare prevailed over the freedom of publication and the order should be made.

A specific issue order[360] is an order giving directions for the purpose of determining a specific question which has arisen, or which may arise, in connection with any aspect of parental responsibility for a child. The order may thus be pre-emptive or reactive in nature, but it must address an aspect of parental responsibility. In *Re HG (Specific Issue Order: Sterilisation)*,[361] the parents of a severely epileptic young woman with a chromosomal deficiency sought on her behalf and were granted a specific issue order to authorise her sterilisation. The court held that the making of a specific issue order did not require there to be any dispute between the parties, provided there was an issue for the court to decide. Although sterilisation of a child requires court sanction, the issue in this case was still seen as a matter in connection with an aspect of parental responsibility, in the sense that it was the parent's duty to bring the

---

[356] *Re R (A Minor) (Wardship: Medical Treatment)* [1992] 1 FLR 190, discussed in chapter 8 below.

[357] *Nottinghamshire County Council v P* [1993] 2 FLR 134.

[358] *Re H (Prohibited Steps Orders)* [1995] 1 FLR 638, and see for comment M Roberts 'Ousting Abusers – Children Act 1989 or Inherent Jurisdiction? *Re H (Prohibited Steps Orders)*' (1995) 7 CFLQ 243.

[359] [1996] 1 FLR 191. For an analysis of the decision in the wider context of protecting children's privacy, see J Moriarty 'Children, Privacy and the Press' [1997] CFLQ 217, especially at pp 226 et seq.

[360] For an account of this order, see S Gilmore 'The Nature, Scope and Use of the Specific Issue Order' [2004] CFLQ 367.

[361] [1993] 1 FLR 587. On sterilisation generally, see further chapter 8 below. On the capacity of children to seek court orders, see chapter 14 below.

matter before the court. Similarly, in *Re F (Specific Issue: Child Interview)*,[362] interviewing children involved an aspect of parental responsibility which could be controlled through s 8 orders. In that case the father of two boys was due to stand trial for assaulting the mother. The father's defence lawyers succeeded in obtaining a specific issue order to authorise them to interview the boys in order to prepare the father's defence. In contrast, in *Re J (Specific Issue Order: Leave to Apply)*,[363] it was held by Wall J that the determination of whether a child came within the meaning of 'children in need' for the purposes of Part III of the Children Act was not intended by Parliament to be susceptible to adjudication by the courts through s 8 orders. Accordingly, a 17-year-old boy failed in his attempt to obtain leave to apply for a specific issue order requiring the local authority to deem him to be a child in need.

A specific issue order may be especially useful where a sole residence order is *not* made. Where the court makes a shared residence order, or no order at all, both parents will exercise full responsibility. However, it is possible that there may be an area of disagreement which could jeopardise the whole arrangement if it is not resolved. Where it appears to the court, on making a residence or contact order, that there is likely to be a potential area of dispute, for example over education, it may wish to address the difficulty in advance. On the other hand, such difficulties may only manifest themselves some time later, at which point it will be open to a parent to return to court for those difficulties to be resolved. Where the court is seised of a dispute over a matter of upbringing it must be prepared to adjudicate. In *Re P (Parental Dispute: Judicial Determination)*[364] the divorced parents disagreed over the private school the children should attend. The judge, favouring the mother's choice of school, made an order that 'in respect of both M and O, future questions which may arise about either child's schooling ... shall be finally determined by the child's mother following consultation with their father'. The Court of Appeal held that this amounted to the plainest failure to adjudicate, that the parent had a right to judicial determination and that the court should not abdicate from its primary obligation to decide.

The case law illustrates the wide range of questions that might be addressed by a specific issue order, although use of the order tends to cluster around certain categories of case. The order is quite often used in the context of children's medical treatment, and case law has addressed such questions as whether a child should be immunised[365] tested for the presence of HIV,[366] have a blood transfusion to treat leukaemia in the face of parent's religious objection,[367] be

---

[362] [1995] 1 FLR 819.

[363] [1995] 1 FLR 669.

[364] [2003] 1 FLR 286.

[365] *Re C (Welfare of Child: Immunisation)* [2003] EWHC 1376 (Fam), [2003] 2 FLR 1054, affirmed by the Court of Appeal in *Re B (A Child) (Immunisation)* [2003] EWCA Civ 1148, [2003] 2 FLR 1095.

[366] *Re C (HIV Test)* [1999] 2 FLR 1004, upholding Wilson J's decision in *Re C (A Child) (HIV Testing)* [2000] Fam 48.

[367] *Re R (A Minor) (Blood Transfusion)* [1993] 2 FLR 757 (Booth J).

circumcised for religious reasons,[368] or (as we have seen) be sterilised. Several cases have also concerned disputes surrounding children's education.[369] In *Re A (Specific Issue Order: Parental Dispute)*,[370] for example, a French father succeeded in obtaining a specific issue order, as against the mother who had primary care, that the two children attend a French-speaking school, the Lycée Français in London. The court was influenced by the need to preserve the children's bi-cultural identity and by bilingual considerations, although the court was clear that there is no principle that such children should receive a bicultural education. Another use of the order has been in relation to issues of disclosure of information. For example in *Re K (Specific Issue Order)*[371] a father failed (controversially) to obtain an order requiring the mother to inform the child, aged 12 at the time of the proceedings, of his paternity and his existence.

Change of surname

An area that has attracted considerable case law is the issue of change of a child's surname.[372] The issue can be contentious, since it may be, as Gillian Douglas has observed, that 'disputes over surnames are really concerned with determining the child's "affiliation" with a particular parent' and it is thus no surprise 'that parents may hold very strong, conflicting views on the child's surname where their own relationship has ended and they are no longer seen to constitute an "intact" family group'.[373] In addition, there has long been an *automatic* restraint on unilateral change of a child's surname, deriving originally from the concept of the residual rights of the natural guardian, and which the courts have consistently upheld.[374] Following enactment of the Children Act 1989, it was suggested that this restraint in relation to change of surname had not survived by reason of the so-called right of independent action in s 2(7) of the Act. However, the argument was scotched by Holman J in *Re PC (Change of Surname)*,[375] who held that where two or more persons have parental responsibility for a child, one of them may lawfully effect a change of surname only if everyone with parental responsibility consents. The restriction in relation change of surname is underlined by s 13 of the Children

---

[368] *Re J (Specific Issue Order: Child's Religious Upbringing and Circumcision)* [2000] 1 FLR 571. For a detailed commentary on *Re J* and for an assessment of the place of religion and culture in decisions affecting children, see C Bridge 'Religion, Culture and the Body of the Child' in A Bainham, S Day Sclater and M Richards (eds) *Body Lore and Laws* (Hart Publishing, 2002).

[369] *Re A (Specific Issue Order: Parental Dispute)* [2001] 1 FLR 121; *Re Z (A Child) (Specific Issue Order: Religious Education)* [2002] EWCA Civ 501.

[370] [2001] 1 FLR 121.

[371] [1999] 2 FLR 280 and see also *Re F (Specific Issue: Child Interview)* [1995] 1 FLR 819, discussed above.

[372] For a good discussion of the issue, see J Herring 'The Shaming of Naming: Parental Rights and Responsibilities in the Naming of Children' in R Probert, S Gilmore, and J Herring (eds) *Responsible Parents and Parental Responsibility* (Oxford, Hart Publishing, 2009).

[373] G Douglas *An Introduction to Family Law* (2nd edn, Oxford University Press, 2004), at p 88.

[374] The leading authority before the Children Act was *W v A (Child: Surname)* [1981] Fam 114.

[375] [1997] 2 FLR 730. See J Eekelaar 'Do Parents Have a Duty to Consult?' (1998) 114 LQR 337; A Bond 'Reconstructing families – changing children's surnames' [1998] CFLQ 17, and M Ogle 'What's in a Name?' [1998] Fam Law 80.

Act 1989 which provides that in any case in which there is a residence order in force with respect to a child no person may change the child's surname or remove the child from the United Kingdom for more than a month, without either the written consent of every person who has parental responsibility for the child or the leave of the court. While a general right of independent action might be supported by the wording of s 2(7) and comments of the Law Commission paper which informed it,[376] the suggestion that this included a unilateral right to change a child's surname was in one sense bizarre, since, if correct, it would have meant that the mother without a residence order in her favour would have been in a stronger legal position in this respect than the mother who had one! Holman J's conclusion has been endorsed by the Court of Appeal[377] which appears to have gone further, to suggest that consultation with the father is required whether or not he has parental responsibility.[378]

The leading decision on change of surname is *Dawson v Wearmouth*.[379] In that case, the mother's relationship with the child's father, Mr Mark Dawson, broke down shortly after the child's birth and the mother registered the child with the surname of her former husband, Tony Wearmouth. Mr Dawson strongly objected to this and sought a specific issue order that the child's surname be changed to his. The judge decided the matter as if the registration had never taken place and changed the child's surname to Dawson. That decision was overturned by the Court of Appeal, and a further appeal to the House of Lords was dismissed. The House of Lords held that the fact of registration is an important (although not conclusive) factor and the correct approach is to apply s 1(1)[380] and (5) of the Children Act 1989, 'and not make an order for the change of name unless there is some evidence that this would lead to an improvement from the point of view of the welfare of the child'.[381] While not dissenting, two of the Law Lords clearly felt the significance of the name as a means of linking a child to the biological father. As Lord Jauncey put it, 'the surname is ... a biological label which tells the world at large that the blood of the name flows in its veins' and, in this case, the child had 'not a drop of

---

376 See J Eekelaar 'Do Parents Have a Duty to Consult?' (1998) 114 LQR 337.

377 See, for example, *Re T (Change of Surname)* [1998] 2 FLR 620.

378 However, it should be noted that where the child's father (parent) does not have parental responsibility, the mother alone is entitled to choose and register the name of the child: see *Dawson v Wearmouth* [1997] 2 FLR 629.

379 *Dawson v Wearmouth* [1997] 2 FLR 629. See for comment, M. Hayes '*Dawson v Wearmouth*: What's in a Name? A Child by Any Other Name is Surely Just as Sweet?' [1999] CFLQ 423, and A Bainham 'In the Name of the Father?' [1999] CLJ 492. The issue is discussed here in the context of a private law dispute. In the context of a child in care, see the Children Act 1989, s 33(7) and *Re S (Change of Surname)* [1999] 1 FLR 672; and in the context of special guardianship, see *Re L (Special Guardianship: Surname)* [2007] EWCA Civ 196, [2007] 2 FLR 50.

380 See also Ward LJ in *Re C (Change of Surname)* 1998] 2 FLR 656 at 660 to the effect that change of a child's surname is a matter with respect to a child's upbringing.

381 [1999] 2 AC 308 at 320–321. Lord Hobhouse of Woodborough said that the applicant 'has to make out a positive case in accordance with s 1 of the Act that it is in the interests of the child that the order should be made. If he fails to make out that positive case, his application will fail' (at 326).

Wearmouth blood in his veins'.[382] Neither has the significance of a child's name been lost on the international community: the question of the name is closely bound up with the child's right to an identity and to preservation of identity and family relations under the UNCRC.[383]

At the same time, the courts have occasionally found it necessary to warn that too much importance should not be attached to the single issue of the child's name. In *Re R (Surname: Using Both Parents')*[384] Hale LJ offered the view that it was a matter of great sadness that it was so often assumed that fathers needed the outward and visible link of a shared surname in order to retain their relationship with and commitment to their child. For her, the crucial point was rather that it was important for there to be transparency about a child's parentage and for it to be acknowledged that a child always had two parents.

In *Re W (A Child) (Illegitimate Child: Change of Surname); Re A (A Child); Re B (Children)*,[385] the Court of Appeal, having reviewed their Lordships' opinions in *Dawson v Wearmouth*, provided a useful non-exhaustive summary of matters that might impact on a court's decision in relation to change of surname, as follows:[386]

> 'Among the factors to which the court should have regard is the registered surname of the child and the reasons for the registration, for instance recognition of the biological link with the child's father.[387] Registration is always a relevant and an important consideration but it is not in itself decisive.[388] The weight to be given to it by the court will depend upon the other relevant factors or valid countervailing reasons which may tip the balance the other way[389] ... The relevant considerations should include factors which may arise in the future as well as the present situation ... Reasons given for changing or seeking to change a child's name based on the fact that the child's name is or is not the same as the parent making the application do not generally carry much weight.[390] The reasons for an earlier unilateral decision to change a child's name may be relevant ... Any changes of circumstances of the child since the original registration may be

---

[382] See A Bainham 'In the Name of the Father?' [1999] CLJ 492.

[383] Articles 7 and 8; and see chapter 2 above.

[384] [2001] 2 FLR 1358.

[385] [2001] Fam 1, [1999] 2 FLR 930.

[386] See [2001] Fam 1, at p 7G, explanatory footnotes in the quotation added.

[387] See *Dawson v Wearmouth* at 323B and 324E–G, per Lord Jauncey of Tullichettle.

[388] See *Dawson v Wearmouth* at 328C–D, per Lord Hobhouse of Woodborough.

[389] For example, the impact on the child of the father's criminal notoriety, or his involvement in sexual abuse: see *Re W (A Child) (Illegitimate Child: Change of Surname); Re A (A Child); Re B (Children)* [2001] Fam 1, [1999] 2 FLR 930. See also in a public law context, *Re M, T, P, K and B (Care: Change of Name)* [2000] 2 FLR 645 (where the children were frightened their family would locate them).

[390] For example, embarrassment. See *Note: Re F (Child: Surname)* [1993] 2 FLR 837, at 838E; see also *Re B (Change of Surname)* [1996] 1 FLR 791 (no opprobrium nowadays upon a child who carries a surname different from that of the adults in his home); and *Re C (Change of Surname)* [1998] 2 FLR 656. Convenience of medical and school records is also likely to be of limited weight: see *Re T (Change of Surname)* [1998] 2 FLR 620, at 624A. In *Re R (Surname: Using Both Parents')* [2001] EWCA Civ 1344, [2001] 2 FLR 1358, Hale LJ explained that the case-law was not to be read as meaning 'that considerations of confusion, anxiety and

relevant ... In the case of a child whose parents were married to each other, the fact of the marriage is important[391] and I would suggest that there would have to be strong reasons to change the name from the father's surname if the child was so registered ... Where the child's parents were not married to each other, the mother has control over registration. Consequently on an application to change the surname of the child, the degree of commitment of the father to the child, the quality of contact, if it occurs, between father and child, the existence or absence of parental responsibility are all relevant factors to take into account.'

To these factors can be added the following relevant matters: the lawfulness of any change of name, and the length of time for which the change has endured;[392] the security of the foundation of any name;[393] a parent's change of name;[394] and children's wishes. The courts have, however, shown some reluctance to be influenced by children's wishes.[395] In *Re B (Change of Surname)*[396] Wilson J refused to order the change of surname of children aged 16, 14, and 12 who wished to expunge their father from their lives. He commented that to do so 'would have sent out a wholly inappropriate message to the children, namely that the court agreed with them that their father was of the past, not of the present'.[397] The decision does not sit easily with Lord Scarman's opinion in *Gillick v West Norfolk and Wisbech Area Health Authority and Department of Health and Social Security*[398] and it may be argued that this is precisely the type of area to which the principle in *Gillick*– of respect for the mature minor's views – ought to apply.[399]

Sometimes a change of surname may be warranted by the need to protect the child or promote the child's welfare. In *Re A (A Child)*,[400] for example, a change of surname to the mother's maiden name was ordered where the child would be at risk in his new locality by reason of his association with the name of his father, who was a notorious criminal. Another example is provided by *Re*

---

embarrassment for the child were of little account: it is more that the problem for the parent is of little account. It all depends upon the facts and circumstances of the particular case' (at para [16]).

[391] Although compare *Re C (Change of Surname)* [1998] 2 FLR 656, at 660C–660D: 'The judge's reference to finding more merit in the father's case had he not declined to marry the mother is an irrelevant consideration'.

[392] *Re T (Change of Surname)* above: 'the fact that the unlawful state had endured for a period of approximately 7 months to the date of commencement of the trial could not possibly justify denying the applicant relief' (at 624G–624H). See also *A v Y (Child's Surname)* [1999] 2 FLR 5 for the relevance of delay in applying for a specific issue order.

[393] *Re R (Surname: Using Both Parents')* [2001] EWCA Civ 1344, [2001] 2 FLR 1358, at para [8].

[394] *Re C (Change of Surname)* [1998] 1 FLR 549.

[395] See *Re B (Change of Surname)*, n 86 above, at 794G–H and 796A–B.

[396] [1996] 1 FLR 791 (CA).

[397] Ibid, at 795–796.

[398] [1986] AC 112, [1986] 1 FLR 224.

[399] See M Hayes '*Dawson v Wearmouth*: What's in a Name? A Child by Any Other Name is Surely Just as Sweet?' [1999] CFLQ 423.

[400] One of the three cases reported at [2001] Fam 1.

S (Change of Names: Cultural Factors),[401] which concerned a child born to a Muslim mother and a Sikh father. The child had been given Sikh names but, following divorce, the mother wished to change his name to a Muslim name, arguing that socially and culturally the Muslim community would never accept a child with Sikh names. Wilson J held that in order to be accepted into the Muslim community it was necessary that the child be known on a day-to-day basis by Muslim names. Accordingly, he should be registered with Muslim names at schools and a health practice. However, nothing more than this should be formally done by deed poll since it was important to preserve the reality of his parentage and Sikh heritage.

This distinction between the formal and informal use of names surfaced again in *Re H (Child's Name: First Name)*,[402] the first reported case to consider a dispute over the child's first names, as opposed to surname. Here the married parents separated when the mother was six weeks pregnant. The father then reappeared at the birth and, following a discussion with the mother in hospital about names, registered the child without her approval with the names of his choice. The mother then tried to register her own choice of name but the Registrar took the position that the first registration only was effective and that the mother's should be cancelled. The issue was whether the mother could use her own choice of names with educational and other authorities. Allowing her appeal, the Court of Appeal held that there was nothing to prevent the mother from using her choice of names in this way provided that it was recognised that the child had an immutable series of names by statutory registration. The court went on to say that, unlike surnames, which denoted the family to which the child belonged, a number of given names might legitimately be used over the course of a child's life.

RELOCATION FROM THE JURISDICTION

Another issue which has attracted considerable case law is a parent's desire to relocate from the jurisdiction with a child (with inevitable consequences for the child's contact with the non-resident, left-behind, parent). There are several reasons why this issue arises frequently. Under s 1 of the Child Abduction Act 1984 it is an offence for anyone 'connected with a child' to take or send a child under the age of 16 years out of the UK without the appropriate consent.[403] This is the consent of each person who is the child's mother, father

---

[401] [2001] 2 FLR 1005. See S Jivraj and D Herman 'It is Difficult for a White Judge to Understand: Orientalism, Racialisation, and Christianity in English Child Welfare Cases' [2009] CFLQ 283.

[402] [2002] 1 FLR 973.

[403] It is also an offence under the Child Abduction Act 1984, s 2 for anyone who does *not* have parental responsibility or 'custody' of the child to remove a child aged under 16, or keep him, out of the lawful control of the person entitled to lawful control. It is a defence to show that the person concerned acted with lawful authority or had a reasonable excuse, and there is a special defence which can be relied on by the unmarried father or by someone who believes that he is the child's father. This chapter is concerned only with international abductions and the detailed provisions of s 2 are beyond the scope of the present discussion. For a

(assuming in the case of the unmarried father that he has acquired parental responsibility), guardian, or anyone with a residence order or the leave of the court. There are limited defences available.[404] Section 13(2) of the Children Act 1989 provides that an exception applies where a residence order is in force – anyone with such an order may unilaterally remove a child for a period of up to one month. Thus, apart from this provision, in the usual case where there is no court order in existence, it is a criminal offence for *one* parent to take a child out of the country without the consent of the other.[405] In the case of unmarried parents (assuming the father has not taken steps to acquire parental responsibility),[406] the mother has authority to act alone. A parent may also commit the common law offence of kidnapping,[407] or false imprisonment[408] in removing the child without the appropriate consent, although these charges should not be brought where the facts upon which they are grounded would constitute the statutory offence.[409] In the light of these criminal offences and the fact that relocation is likely to be a contentious issue between parents, lawful removal is likely to require a court's authorisation, and there is thus a tendency for the issue to come before the courts. Relocation disputes appear to be a growing phenomenon, possibly owing to increased international mobility, and changes in dating behaviour (such as meeting via the internet).[410]

---

comparatively rare report of a prosecution under s 2, see *O v Governor of Holloway Prison and Government of USA* [2000] 1 FLR 147 in which the Divisional Court held that the section requires proof of mens rea and does not create an offence, as the justices had thought, of strict liability.

[404] Child Abduction Act 1984, s 1(5).

[405] It is not entirely clear whether a positive consent is required or whether an absence of objection on the part of the other parent would suffice. The latter seems more practicable, especially in view of the defences in s 1(5) of the Child Abduction Act 1984.

[406] See chapter 4 above, where we noted that many more such men will now acquire parental responsibility through the process of birth registration.

[407] *R v D* [1984] AC 778.

[408] *R v Rahman* (1985) 81 Cr App R 349.

[409] *R v C (Kidnapping: Abduction)* [1991] 2 FLR 252.

[410] P Parkinson, J Cashmore, and J Single 'The Need for Reality Testing in Relocation Cases' (2010) 44(1) *Family Law Quarterly* 1–34 at 2–3. There is a burgeoning literature on the well-being of children affected by such arrangements. See N Taylor, M Gollop, and M Henaghan, *Relocation Following Parental Separation: The Welfare and Best Interests of Children Research Report* (Centre for Research on Children and Families and Faculty of Law, University of Otago, Dunedin, June 2010) ch 3 for an excellent account of the existing empirical research on relocation following parental separation, and an extensive bibliography of relevant literature; see also the review of research by N Taylor and M Freeman 'International Research Evidence on Relocation: Past, Present and Future' (2010) 44(3) *Family Law Quarterly* 317–339 and B Horsfall and R Kaspiew 'Relocation in Separated and Non-Separated Families: Equivocal Evidence from the Social Science Literature' (2010) 24 *Australian Journal of Family Law* 34; W Austin 'Relocation, Research, and Forensic Evaluation, Part I: Effects of Residential Mobility on Children of Divorce' (2008) 46 *Family Court Review* 137; J Kelly and M Lamb 'Developmental Issues in Relocation Cases Involving Young Children: When, Whether, and How?' (2003) 17 *Journal of Family Psychology* 193.

LEAVE TO TAKE CHILDREN OUT OF THE JURISDICTION

Where a parent who is the child's primary carer (usually, but not invariably, the mother) wishes to emigrate from the UK, or at least leave for an extended period of time, with the child, the appropriate course of action will be to apply to the court for permission to take the child out of the jurisdiction,[411] either by obtaining leave under s 13 of the Children Act 1989 where a residence order is in force with respect to the child, or by an application for a specific issue order.[412] In such cases the courts have to grapple with a conflict of interest between the mother who wishes to make a new life abroad, with or without a new partner, and the father who wishes to maintain a realistic relationship with the child.

The leading decision on how the courts should approach their task of applying the welfare principle in this context is *Payne v Payne*.[413] In that case the Court of Appeal held that the enactment of the Human Rights Act 1998 did not necessitate a change in the courts' approach to relocation applications which, since *Poel v Poel*[414] some three decades earlier, have:

'been consistently decided upon the application of the following two propositions: (a) the welfare of the child is the paramount consideration;[415] and (b) refusing the primary carer's reasonable proposals for the relocation of her family life is likely to

---

[411] For a discussion of the 'relocation' issue in law, policy and practice, see R George *Relocation Disputes: Law and Practice in England and New Zealand* (Oxford, Hart Publishing, 2014). For a practical guide to the law, see R George, F Judd QC, D Garrido and A Worwood *Relocation A Practical Guide* (Jordan Publishing Ltd, 2013). See also C Bruch and J Bowermaster 'The Relocation of Children and Custodial Parents: Public Policy, Past and Present' (1995) 30 *Family Law Quarterly* 245; C Bruch 'Sound Research or Wishful Thinking in Child Custody Cases? Lessons from Relocation Law' (2006) 40 *Family Law Quarterly* 281; P Stahl and L Drozd (eds) *Relocation Issues in Child Custody Cases* (Binghamton, NY: Haworth Press, 2006); SB Boyd 'Relocation, indeterminacy, and burden of proof: lessons from Canada' [2011] CFLQ 155; L Young 'Resolving relocation disputes: the "interventionist" approach in Australia' [2011] CFLQ 203; R George 'Practitioners' views on children's welfare in relocation disputes: comparing approaches in England and New Zealand' [2011] CFLQ 178; M Henaghan 'Relocation cases – the rhetoric and the reality of a child's best interests – a view from the bottom of the world' [2011] CFLQ 226.

[412] For discussion of the courts' dicta on the appropriate route, see S Gilmore 'The Nature, Scope and Use of the Specific Issue Order' [2004] CFLQ 367 and R George 'Changing Names, Changing Places: Reconsidering Section 13 of the Children Act 1989' [2008] Fam Law 1121.

[413] [2001] Fam 473. For commentary, see A Perry 'Case Commentary: Leave to Remove Children from the Jurisdiction: *Payne v Payne*' [2001] CFLQ 455; A Bainham 'Taking Children Abroad: Human Rights, Welfare and the Courts' [2001] CLJ 489.

[414] [1970] 1 WLR 1469. For a detailed assessment, see R Taylor 'Poels Apart: Fixed Principles and Shifting Values in Relocation Law' in S Gilmore, J Herring, and A Probert *Landmark Cases in Family Law* (Oxford, Hart Publishing, 2011). *Poel v Poel* was developed in *Nash v Nash* [1973] 2 All ER 704; *Chamberlain v De La Mare* (1983) 4 FLR 434; *Lonslow v Hennig* [1986] 2 FLR 378; *Belton v Belton* [1987] 2 FLR 343; *Re F (A Ward) (Leave to Remove Ward Out of the Jurisdiction)* [1988] 2 FLR 116.

[415] The court is concerned with the impact of the removal on the welfare of the child primarily as a minor, not in the future as an adult: see *Re A (Leave to Remove: Cultural and Religious Considerations)* [2006] EWHC 421 (Fam), [2006] 2 FLR 572.

impact detrimentally on the welfare of her dependent children. Therefore her application to relocate will be granted unless the court concludes that it is incompatible with the welfare of the children.'[416]

The father, Mr Payne, argued that the Convention enshrined a right of contact between parent and child, as an aspect of the right to respect for family life under Art 8, and that the Children Act also required much greater significance to be attached to the preservation of such contact. He went on to argue that the effect of the case-law was to create an unwarranted legal presumption in favour of leave which was in breach of his right of contact. The court made clear that there is no presumption in favour of relocation, and at para [40] of the court's judgment suggested the following approach:

(a) Pose the question: is the mother's application genuine in the sense that it is not motivated by some selfish desire to exclude the father from the child's life? Then ask is the mother's application realistic, by which I mean founded on practical proposals both well researched and investigated?[417] If the application fails either of these tests refusal will inevitably follow.

(b) If however the application passes these tests then there must be a careful appraisal of the father's opposition: is it motivated by genuine concern for the future of the child's welfare or is it driven by some ulterior motive? What would be the extent of the detriment to him and his future relationship with the child were the application granted?[418] To what extent would that be offset by extension of the child's relationships with the maternal family and homeland?

(c) What would be the impact on the mother, either as the single parent or as a new wife, of a refusal of her realistic proposal? (d) The outcome of the second and third appraisals must then be brought into an overriding review of the child's welfare as the paramount consideration, directed by the statutory checklist insofar as appropriate.

---

[416] [2001] Fam 473, at [26].

[417] The bar may not be high where a relocating parent is familiar with the relocation jurisdiction: see eg, *Re F and H (Children: Relocation)* [2007] EWCA Civ 692, [2008] 2 FLR 1667. Nor, it seems, will the court wish to descend into the valley of detail on the relocating parent's plans: see eg, *Re G (Removal from Jurisdiction)* (detailed business plan not required) and also *Re M-K (A Child) (Relocation Outside the Jurisdiction)* [2006] EWCA Civ 1013, [2007] 1 FLR 432. For examples of cases in which the practicalities were not properly thought through, see: *K v K (A Minor) (Removal from Jurisdiction)* [1992] 2 FLR 98 (mother's plan to pursue post-graduate education in the USA considered to be ill-thought out); and *M v A (Wardship: Removal from Jurisdiction)* [1993] 2 FLR 715.

[418] In *J v S (Leave to Remove)* [2010] EWHC 2098 (Fam), [2011] 1 FLR 1694, Eleanor King J highlighted the significance of the child's existing attachments, commenting that it 'is important that no court dealing with these cases shrinks from examining what the children involved will lose if the application is granted' (at para [99]). See also for examples of cases in which leave was refused, *Re C (Leave to Remove from Jurisdiction)* [2000] 2 FLR 457; *Re B (Leave to Remove)* [2008] EWCA Civ 1034, [2008] 2 FLR 2059; *Re AR (A Child: Relocation)* [2010] EWHC 1346 (Fam), [2010] 2 FLR 1577; and *Re S (Relocation: Interests of Siblings)* [2011] EWCA Civ 454, [2011] 2 FLR 678.

At para [41][419] Thorpe LJ added:

> 'In suggesting such a discipline I would not wish to be thought to have diminished the importance that this court has consistently attached to the emotional and psychological wellbeing of the primary carer.[420] In any evaluation of the welfare of the child as the paramount consideration great weight must be given to this factor.'

Agreeing, Dame Elizabeth Butler-Sloss P set out a useful summary, as follows:[421]

> '(a) The welfare of the child is always paramount.
>
> (b) There is no presumption created by section 13(1)(b) in favour of the applicant parent.
>
> (c) The reasonable proposals of the parent with a residence order wishing to live abroad carry great weight.
>
> (d) Consequently the proposals have to be scrutinised with care and the court needs to be satisfied that there is a genuine motivation for the move and not the intention to bring contact between the child and the other parent to an end.
>
> (e) The effect upon the applicant parent and the new family of the child of a refusal of leave is very important.
>
> (f) The effect upon the child of the denial of contact with the other parent and in some cases his family is very important.
>
> (g) The opportunity for continuing contact between the child and the parent left behind may be very significant.'

In *Re B (Children) (Removal from Jurisdiction); Re S (A Child) (Removal from Jurisdiction)*[422] the Court of Appeal added to this discipline by emphasising the importance of the interests of the reconstituted family where the need for relocation was brought about primarily because of the employment or nationality of the step-parent or new partner. In the first case the mother wanted to relocate to South Africa having formed a relationship with a South African businessman, while in the second case the mother had repartnered with a citizen of the Philippines who had a right of residence in Western Australia and wished to move to Perth. Both were granted leave subject to agreed contact for the respective fathers. The Court of Appeal held

---

[419] Which is as much a part of the discipline as para 40: see *Re B (Leave to Remove: Impact of Refusal)* [2004] EWCA Civ 956, [2005] 2 FLR 239, at [14].

[420] Note, however, that evidence of the impact of refusal on the parent who proposes to relocate is not essential for an application to succeed: see eg, *Re W (A Child) (Removal from Jurisdiction)* [2005] EWCA Civ 1614, [2006] 1 FCR 346.

[421] At para 85.

[422] [2003] EWCA Civ 1149, [2003] 2 FLR 1043. See also on the significance of re-marriage, *Re H (Application to Remove from the Jurisdiction)* [1998] 1 FLR 848.

that a mother's attachment to a man whose employment required him to live abroad could be a decisive factor. Secondly, the court had to consider the impact of refusal of permission on the new family and on the step-father, which applied with greater force where he was a foreign national. In such circumstances, to frustrate relocation could jeopardise the new family's survival and potential for fulfilment and happiness. This would be manifestly contrary to the child's welfare.[423]

The case law following *Payne v Payne* has been criticised by academics as putting in place such a strong emphasis on the primary caretaker's welfare that it has led to trial judges' careful application of the welfare checklist being frequently overturned on appeal.[424] Some judges have acknowledged that there is a respectable argument that *Payne* 'places too great an emphasis on the wishes and feelings of the relocating parent'.[425] It has also been said that the focus on the paramountcy principle fails to engage properly with the various interests of the child and the parties as required by Art 8 of the ECHR.[426] To allow one parent permanently to leave the jurisdiction with the child is potentially an unjustified invasion of the rights of the other parent and the child to respect for family life under Art 8. The balancing exercise under Art 8(2) is complicated by the fact that the parent seeking leave also has the right under Art 8 to respect for his or her *private life*, a notion which embraces such personal decisions as the desire to emigrate.[427]

---

[423] See also the decision of the Court of Appeal in *Re H (Application to Remove from Jurisdiction)* [1998] 1 FLR 848 in which a father who had been very involved with the care of the child nevertheless failed to prevent the mother from obtaining leave to take the child to Alabama. The mother had by this time married an American, and the court held that there had to be some compelling reason to justify a court preventing the primary carer from taking a reasonable decision to live outside the jurisdiction. Another example is *L v L (Leave to Remove from Jurisdiction: Effect on Children)* [2003] 1 FLR 900: the mother's proposed relocation to the USA with the children was opposed on the basis that the elder child had moderate learning difficulties and special educational needs. The risk to disruption of the child's education was recognised but nonetheless the mother's plan was based on perfectly conventional career advancement. She was an exceptionally committed mother, and Johnson J took the view that to allow her reasonable expectations and those of her husband to be frustrated would seriously impair her emotional security and that of the children.

[424] M Hayes 'Relocation Cases: Is the Court of Appeal Applying the Correct Principles?' [2006] CFLQ 351; RH George 'Reassessing Relocation: A Comparative Analysis of Legal Approaches to Disputes Over Family Migration After Parental Separation in England and New Zealand', DPhil Thesis, University of Oxford (2010), at p 100 observes that of 23 international relocation judgments from the Court of Appeal since 1999, only four ended with relocation being refused; by contrast, 13 of the 23 cases were refused by the trial judges. See also for critical discussion: P Pressdee 'Relocation, Relocation, Relocation: Rigorous Scrutiny Revisited' [2008] Fam Law 220; C Geekie 'Relocation and Shared Residence: One Route or Two?' [2008] Fam Law 446; R George 'The Shifting Law: Relocation Disputes in New Zealand and England' (2009) 12 *Otago Law Review* 107; M Freeman, *Relocation: The Reunite Research* (London: Reunite, 2009); F Judd and R George 'International Relocation: Do We Stand Alone?' [2010] Fam Law 63.

[425] *Re D (Leave to Remove: Appeal)* [2010] EWCA Civ 50, [2010] 2 FLR 1605, at para [33], per Wall LJ; and see also the criticisms of Mostyn J in *Re AR (A Child: Relocation)* [2010] EWHC 1346 (Fam), [2010] 2 FLR 1577.

[426] J Herring and R Taylor 'Relocating Relocation' [2006] CFLQ 517.

[427] For an illustration of the balancing exercise, see *Re G-A (A Child) (Removal from Jurisdiction:*

The courts have addressed mounting criticism of *Payne* by pointing out that one must beware of criticising a parody of the decision represented by paras [40] and [41] of the judgment. As Eleanor King J pointed out in *J v S (Leave to Remove)*,[428] the leading judgments in *Payne* must be read together and paras [40] and [41] must not confine the court in a straitjacket. 'Care must be taken to ensure that the question of the impact of refusal of the mother is but one component of an assessment of the best interests of the [children] and not the only feature'.[429] In addition, recent cases have emphasised that the guidance in *Payne* must be heeded, but that it also admits of some flexibility. In *Re W (Relocation: Removal Outside Jurisdiction)*[430] the Court of Appeal made clear that *Payne* is binding,[431] 'to the extent at least that guiding principles can be said to bind a court'.[432] In *K v K (Relocation: Shared Care Arrangement)*[433] Moore-Bick LJ added that *Payne* is binding in the true sense only for its ratio decidendi'[434] and that 'the only principle of law enunciated in *Payne v Payne* is that the welfare of the child is paramount; all the rest is guidance'.[435] However, judges 'must pay heed to that guidance and depart from it only after careful deliberation and when it is clear that the particular circumstances of the case require them to do so in order to give effect to fundamental principles.[436] As Black LJ put it, the guidance must be heeded 'not as rigid principle or so as to dictate a particular outcome in a sphere of law where the facts of individual cases are so infinitely variable'.[437]

It is clear that paras [40] and [41] of *Payne* apply to all types of case in which a *primary carer* applies to relocate.[438] Whether *Payne* does, and should, apply more widely beyond such cases has attracted more debate. Recent case law has now clarified, however, that, so far as relevant and helpful, the guidance in *Payne* may be considered in other types of case too. In *K v K (Relocation: Shared Care Arrangement)*[439] the question arose whether *Payne* applied in a case in which the child's residence is shared. Thorpe LJ held that *Payne* did not

---

Human Rights) [2001] 1 FCR 43 where the court balanced the mother's right to decide to take up employment in New York against the father's right to respect for family life, coming down in favour of the mother.

[428] [2010] EWHC 2098 (Fam), [2011] 1 FLR 1694.

[429] Ibid, at [81].

[430] [2011] EWCA Civ 345, [2011] 2 FLR 409.

[431] Ibid, at [13]. R George 'The International Relocation Debate' [2012] *Journal of Social Welfare and Family Law* 141.

[432] [2011] EWCA Civ 345, at para [156], per Elias LJ.

[433] [2011] EWCA Civ 793, [2012] 2 FLR 880.

[434] Ibid, at [86]. See for discussion of the difference between *ratio* and guidance, see S Gilmore 'The *Payne* Saga: Precedent and Family Law Cases' [2011] Fam Law 970.

[435] [2011] EWCA Civ 793, [2012] 2 FLR 880, at para [86], and see also, at para [141] per Black LJ.

[436] Ibid, at [86].

[437] Ibid, at [142].

[438] *Re B (Leave to Remove: Impact of Refusal)* [2004] EWCA Civ 956, [2005] 2 FLR 239, at [14]. For an example of an exceptional case to which it did not apply, see: *Re J (Leave to Remove: Urgent Case)* [2006] EWCA Civ 1897, [2007] 1 FLR 2033 (CA) (in effect not a relocation dispute; judge required to decide between a mother's proposal for a residence order to be implemented in this jurisdiction and a father's residence order application to be implemented in another state – see para [27]).

[439] [2011] EWCA Civ 793, [2012] 2 FLR 880, at para [35]. For commentary, see R George

apply in such a case because the guidance in *Payne* was premised upon the fact that the relocating parent is the child's primary carer. Endorsing Hedley J's approach in *Re Y (Leave to Remove From Jurisdiction)*,[440] his Lordship opined that in a shared residence case the correct approach is simply to apply the welfare checklist in s 1(3) of the Children Act 1989.[441] However, Black LJ did not see '*Re Y* as representative of a different line of authority from *Payne*', but rather 'as a decision within the framework of which *Payne* is part', exemplifying 'how the weight attached to the relevant factors alters depending upon the facts of the case'.[442] Her Ladyship was concerned that having different categories of case might lead to cases getting 'bogged down with preliminary skirmishes over the label to be applied to a child's arrangements'. Moore-Bick LJ agreed with Thorpe LJ that the judge had failed to give sufficient consideration to authority subsequent to *Payne*[443] but also added:[444]

> 'Guidance of the kind provided in *Payne v Payne* is, of course, very valuable both in ensuring that judges identify what are likely to be the most important factors to be taken into account and the weight that should generally be attached to them. It also plays a valuable role in promoting consistency in decision-making. However, the circumstances in which these difficult decisions have to be made vary infinitely and the judge in each case must be free to weigh up the individual factors and make whatever decision he or she considers to be in the best interests of the child.'

In *Re F (Child: International Relocation)*[445] the Court of Appeal, in a judgment delivered by Munby LJ, held that the above passage from Moore-Bicke LJ's judgment evidenced Moore-Bick LJ's agreement with Black LJ, which represented the correct majority view. The court emphatically endorsed Black LJ's concerns, commenting that: 'The last thing that this very difficult area of family law requires is satellite jurisprudence generating an ever-more detailed classification of supposedly different types of relocation case'.[446] *Re F* was a case in which the child's mother wished the child to relocate to live in Spain with her, yet the father was the child's primary carer. It was not therefore a case like *Payne* of a primary carer wishing to relocate, nor was it a shared residence case. Nevertheless the Court of Appeal held that the judge had

---

'Reviewing Relocation? *Re W (Relocation: Removal Outside Jurisdiction)* [2011] EWCA Civ 345 and *K v K (Relocation: Shared Care Arrangement)* [2011] EWCA Civ 793' [2012] CFLQ 110.

[440] [2004] 2 FLR 330, at paras [14]–[16]. In that case the American mother was refused leave to take the child from Wales to the USA. There were, however, special factors in the case which distinguished it from the ordinary run of applications for leave. The child was bilingual, with Welsh as the preferred language, and care was shared more or less equally between the mother and the father. In these circumstances, it was held that, weighing the gains and losses to the child, the least detrimental course would be for the child to remain in Wales.

[441] *K v K* [2011] EWCA Civ 793, at para [57].

[442] Ibid, at para [144].

[443] Ibid, at para [87].

[444] At para [86].

[445] [2012] EWCA Civ 1364, [2013] 1 FLR 645. For criticism, see R George 'International relocation, care arrangements and case taxonomy' [2012] Fam Law 1478.

[446] [2012] EWCA Civ 1364, [2013] 1 FLR 645, at para [60].

not erred in referring to *Payne v Payne* in so far as anything in that case might be material. The Court underlined again, however, that:[447]

> 'The focus from beginning to end must be on the child's best interests. The child's welfare is paramount. Every case must be determined having regard to the 'welfare checklist', though of course also having regard, where relevant and helpful, to such guidance as may have been given by this court.'

Re F is likely henceforth to represent the courts' approach in practice, although as a matter of doctrine the position is complicated by the fact that in neither *K v K* nor *Re F* was the Court of Appeal's judgment in *Re C and M (Children)*[448] cited. That case, which was arguably a binding authority,[449] held that the approach in *Poel v Poel* (as endorsed in *Payne*) does not apply to shared residence cases. Furthermore, while the point about avoiding satellite litigation is a strong one, and there may therefore be some value in a set of guidelines which apply universally to all types of cases,[450] it might, however, be questioned whether the decision in *Payne* provides the right guidelines to apply universally, especially since Thorpe LJ himself does not believe they should be applied to a shared residence case.[451]

In some cases a parent may remove a child without seeking parental permission or the court's leave, or may remove the child despite a parental or court refusal to grant leave. In the next chapter we examine the various legal mechanisms for seeking to return a child promptly to the jurisdiction when a child is unlawfully removed.

---

[447] At para [61].

[448] [1999] EWCA Civ 2039. Thorpe LJ delivered the leading judgment but either his Lordship did not recall the case or chose not to cite it in *K v K*.

[449] R George 'Reviewing Relocation? *Re W (Relocation: Removal Outside Jurisdiction)* [2011] EWCA Civ 345 and *K v K (Relocation: Shared Care Arrangement)* [2011] EWCA Civ 793' [2012] CFLQ 110.

[450] For this argument and a suggested set of flexible guidelines, see R George *Relocation Disputes Law and Practice in England and New Zealand* (Hart Publishing, 2014).

[451] The point is made by R George 'International relocation, care arrangements and case taxonomy' [2012] Fam Law 1478, at p 1482.

Chapter 6

CHILD ABDUCTION

Better transport communications across the world have contributed to the growing problem of international child abduction,[1] and the English law reports are now replete with such cases .[2] About 70 per cent of abductions are carried out by the child's mother who is usually also the primary carer of the children. Thus the majority are not cases of 'non-custodial' parents snatching their children, as might be supposed.[3]

Child abduction can occur for a variety of reasons, such as ignorance of the legal requirements regarding permission to relocate, fleeing a partner's violent or abusive behaviour, or result from more malign behaviour, such as a wish for

---

[1] Two books on the subject are P Beaumont and P McEleavy *The Hague Convention on International Child Abduction* (1999) and A-M Hutchinson and H Setright *International Parental Child Abduction* (2nd edn, Jordans, 2003). See also L Silberman 'The Hague Children's Conventions: The Internationalization of Child Law' in SN Katz, J Eekelaar and M Maclean (eds) *Cross Currents* (Oxford University Press, 2000), at pp 590–596. For an evaluation of the principles of the Convention set against the principles in the UNCRC, see R Schuz 'The Hague Child Abduction Convention and the United Nations Convention on the Rights of the Child' in P Lodrup and E Modvar (eds) *Family Life and Human Rights* (Gyldendal Akademisk, 2004), at p 721. See also D Harris 'Is the Strength of the Hague Convention on Child Abduction being Diluted by the Courts? – the English Perspective' [1999] IFL 35; and G Van Bueren *The Best Interests of the Child: International Cooperation on Child Abduction* (Queen Mary and Westfield College, London, 1993). The Reunite website in England (www.reunite.org) contains much useful information. See also D McClean and K Beevers 'International Child Abduction – back to common law principles' [1995] CFLQ 128. Specifically on English practice under the Convention, see N Lowe and A Perry 'International Child Abduction – the English Experience' (1999) 48 ICLQ 127.

[2] For evidence of increasing numbers of applications to courts for return of children, see NV Lowe, *A Statistical Analysis of Applications Made in 2008 Under the Hague Convention of 25 October 1980 on the Civil Aspects of International Child Abduction* (Hague Conference on Private International Law, 2011). Comparing data of 2003 and 2008 surveys there has been a 44 per cent increase in the total number of applications made under the Convention with a 45 per cent increase in return applications and a 40 per cent increase in access applications (at para 25). There was a maximum of 2,460 applications in 2008 comprising 2,080 return and 380 access applications. In 2003 there were an estimated 1,610 applications. In 2008 England and Wales had 466 applications (para 30). In 2011 Reunite, the international child abduction centre, handled 512 new abduction cases: 479 children abducted out of the UK, 189 children abducted into the UK, 16 children abducted between UK jurisdictions, and 56 children abducted between non-UK jurisdictions.

[3] See NV Lowe, *A Statistical Analysis of Applications Made in 2008 Under the Hague Convention of 25 October 1980 on the Civil Aspects of International Child Abduction* (Hague Conference on Private International Law, 2011). See comments by Baroness Hale on the shift in types of cases since the 1980s, in *Re E (Children) (Abduction: Custody Appeal)* [2011] UKSC 27, [2011] 2 FLR 758, at para [6]. See also D McClean 'International child abduction – some recent trends' [1997] CFLQ 387.

control, or to punish the child's other parent. In some cases there can be lasting negative effects on the well-being of the children concerned.[4] We consider here the legal mechanisms for attempting to prevent the unlawful removal of children from England and Wales, and the law and procedures which govern attempts to recover abducted children. We also look at the jurisprudence of the English courts when considering requests for the return of children abducted to England. This provides some insight into what might be expected of a foreign court in the converse situation of a child taken *from* England.[5] Two international Conventions of 1980, the Hague Convention on the Civil Aspects of International Child Abduction (the Hague Convention) and the European Convention on Recognition and Enforcement of Decisions concerning Custody of Children and Restoration of Custody of Children ('the European Convention'), regulate the return of children from those States which are parties to the respective Conventions. Both Conventions were implemented in the UK by the Child Abduction and Custody Act 1985. The European Convention has in practice largely been superseded by Council Regulation (EC) No 2201/2003 of 27 November 2003 Concerning Jurisdiction and the Recognition and Enforcement of Judgments in Matrimonial Matters and in Matters of Parental Responsibility,[6] Brussels II bis.

The Brussels II Regulation lays down exclusive rules of jurisdiction to determine the competency of the court of a Member State to rule on status and matters relating to parental responsibility. The central governing concept is that of 'habitual residence'. The aim, wherever possible, is to avoid parallel proceedings taking place in Member States. Member States are under a general obligation to recognise judgments given in other Member States without any special procedure being required.[7] In limited circumstances, any interested party may apply for a decision for non-recognition of such a judgment[8] which includes situations where recognition would be manifestly contrary to public policy, for procedural defects relating to the judgment or because the judgment was irreconcilable with an earlier judgment given in another Member State or a non-Member State or, importantly, where taking into account the best interests of the child, it was given (except in the case of urgency) without the child being given an opportunity of being heard, contrary to the fundamental principles of procedure in the Member State in question.[9] An enforceable judgment on the exercise of parental responsibility made in one Member State can be declared enforceable in another Member State on the application of an interested party. The regulation also contains provisions which, in relation to the issue of

---

[4]   See M Freeman, *International Child Abduction – The Effects* (Reunite, 2006).
[5]   For a discussion of the workings of the Hague Convention in the English courts, see CS Bruch 'Child Abduction and the English Courts' in A Bainham, DS Pearl and R Pickford (eds) *Frontiers of Family Law* (2nd edn, John Wiley & Sons, 1995), at p 52; and see also CS Bruch 'International Child Abduction Cases: Experience Under the 1980 Hague Convention' in J Eekelaar and P Sarcevic (eds) *Parenthood in Modern Society: Legal and Social Issues for the Twenty-First Century* (Martinus Nijhoff, 1993).
[6]   Repealing Regulation (EC) No 1347/2000 (Brussels II Revised) (2003) OJ L 338/1.
[7]   Article 14(1).
[8]   Article 14(3).
[9]   Article 15(1).

contact with children, enable an order in one Member State to be directly enforceable in another Member State. Clearly there will be overlap here with the principles of the Council of Europe's Contact Convention, always remembering that membership of the European Union is not identical with that of the Council of Europe.

The Brussels Regulation explicitly governs cases of child abduction. Article 11 of the regulation modifies the Hague Convention in a way which takes precedence over the Hague Convention in cases between Member States of the European Union (apart from Denmark).[10] We shall draw attention to the modifications made to the Hague Convention by the regulation in the text below at appropriate points.

In what follows we examine the provisions of the Conventions. We also examine the situation of those children taken to or from countries which are not party to either Convention. We also look briefly at abduction *within* the different parts of the UK, a matter regulated by the Family Law Act 1986.

PREVENTING ABDUCTION

It is axiomatic that prevention is better than cure. Where a child is successfully removed from England, it may be difficult even to establish his whereabouts and more difficult still to secure his return. All available means should therefore be utilised to prevent removal in the first place. The matter is complicated by the fact that the Hague Convention can operate only where there has been a *wrongful taking* and, especially since the Children Act 1989, there may be some ambiguity about whether one parent is acting wrongfully in taking a child abroad. Nevertheless, the general principles and procedures of the criminal and civil law can be stated with some confidence.

The criminal law

Under s 1 of the Child Abduction Act 1984 it is an offence for anyone 'connected with a child' to take or send a child under the age of 16 years out of the UK without the appropriate consent.[11] This is the consent of each person

---

[10] Most materially, Art 11 provides: 2. When applying Articles 12 and 13 of the 1980 Hague Convention, it shall be ensured that the child is given the opportunity to be heard during the proceedings unless this appears inappropriate having regard to his or her age or degree of maturity. 3. A court to which an application for return of a child is made as mentioned in paragraph 1 shall act expeditiously in proceedings on the application, using the most expeditious procedures available in national law. Without prejudice to the first subparagraph, the court shall, except where exceptional circumstances make this impossible, issue its judgment no later than six weeks after the application is lodged. 4. A court cannot refuse to return a child on the basis of Art 13b of the 1980 Hague Convention if it is established that adequate arrangements have been made to secure the protection of the child after his or her return.

[11] It is also an offence under the Child Abduction Act 1984, s 2 for anyone who does *not* have

who is the child's mother, father (assuming in the case of the unmarried father that he has acquired parental responsibility), guardian, or anyone with a residence order or the leave of the court. There are limited defences available.[12] An exception applies where a residence order is in force – anyone with such an order may unilaterally remove a child for a period of up to one month.[13] Thus, apart from this provision, in the usual case where there is no court order in existence, it can be a criminal offence for *one* parent to take a child out of the country without the consent of the other.[14] In the case of unmarried parents (assuming the father has not taken steps to acquire parental responsibility),[15] the mother has authority to act alone.

Since child abduction is a criminal offence, the assistance of the police may be sought to prevent its commission. In an emergency, when an imminent removal is suspected, informing the police is the best short-term action to take. The police have power to arrest anyone they reasonably suspect of attempting to take a child out of the UK. More importantly, they can effect a 'port stop' through their computerised 'All Ports Warning System'. The effect of a port stop is that immigration officers at all ports and airports will hold the name of the child at risk on an index and will thereafter seek to assist the police in preventing the child's removal. Under a Practice Direction,[16] the police will not automatically institute a port alert. They must be convinced that the risk of removal is real and imminent, ie within 48 hours. In order to enable them to act, the police should be given full particulars about the child, the alleged abductor and travel plans where these are known. The child's name will remain on the stop list for four weeks. After this, a renewed complaint will become necessary if continuing protection is sought. Where the 'child' is aged 16 years or over, the Child Abduction Act 1984 does not apply and a court order is required. But in view of the increased legal autonomy of this age group, it is doubtful how often it will be appropriate to intervene in what may be a joint decision by parent and child to leave the country.

---

parental responsibility or 'custody' of the child to remove a child aged under 16, or keep him, out of the lawful control of the person entitled to lawful control. It is a defence to show that the person concerned acted with lawful authority or had a reasonable excuse, and there is a special defence which can be relied on by the unmarried father or by someone who believes that he is the child's father. This chapter is concerned only with international abductions and the detailed provisions of s 2 are beyond the scope of the present discussion. For a comparatively rare report of a prosecution under s 2, see *O v Governor of Holloway Prison and Government of USA* [2000] 1 FLR 147 in which the Divisional Court held that the section requires proof of mens rea and does not create an offence, as the justices had thought, of strict liability.

[12] Child Abduction Act 1984, s 1(5).

[13] Children Act 1989, s 13(2).

[14] It is not entirely clear whether a positive consent is required or whether an absence of objection on the part of the other parent would suffice. The latter seems more practicable, especially in view of the defences in s 1(5) of the Child Abduction Act 1984.

[15] See chapter 3 above, where we noted that many more such men will now acquire parental responsibility through the process of birth registration.

[16] *Practice Direction (Child: Removal from Jurisdiction)* [1986] 1 All ER 983, [1986] 2 FLR 89 and Home Office Circular 21/1986.

The civil law

Passport control

Until 1998 it was possible for children to be added to their parent's passport, but since October of that year this has no longer been possible. The change in the rules was designed to combat the problem of abduction. If the court has made an order prohibiting the removal of the child from the jurisdiction, the Passport Agency may be requested by a concerned person not to issue a passport to the child. The court itself may order the surrender of an existing passport in these circumstances. Under its inherent jurisdiction the court may order the deposit of a foreign passport with solicitors. Thus in *Re A-K (Foreign Passport: Jurisdiction)*[17] the Court of Appeal upheld the order of the judge for the surrender of the father's Iranian passport to his solicitors. The judge had expressly stated that this course would give him easier access to his passport. If a request were unreasonably refused by the mother, the father could make an application to the court and the mother's conduct could be reviewed.

Private court orders

A number of options exist for obtaining orders in the civil courts which have the effect of restraining a child's removal from the jurisdiction. One is to ward the child, since wardship has, as one of its immediate effects, an automatic prohibition on removing the ward from the jurisdiction.[18] A cheaper alternative since the Children Act may be to seek a s 8 order. A residence order will regulate where the child is to live and it will be incompatible with its terms for the *non-resident* parent to take the child abroad even when exercising contact or otherwise discharging parental responsibility.[19] In *Re K (Residence Order: Securing Contact)*[20] the father was (unusually) given a residence order in relation to a two-year-old boy, largely because of the judge's assessment that the mother was untrustworthy, might spirit the child away to India and thereafter deny the father contact. A residence order will also empower the *resident* parent to take the child abroad for up to one month without the non-resident parent's knowledge or consent. Thus, the court should be wary of granting a residence order to a parent if there is the slightest suspicion that that parent might use the apparently innocuous 'holiday provision' as a cloak for a permanent abduction.[21] However, the residence order is more likely to be invoked as a device *against* abduction rather than a vehicle for it, and it is established that a short-term residence order may be granted in exceptional

---

[17] [1997] 2 FLR 569.

[18] Although this is now qualified by the Family Law Act 1986, s 38 as regards removal to another part of the UK.

[19] Section 2(8) of the Children Act precludes the exercise of parental responsibility in a way which is incompatible with a court order.

[20] [1999] 1 FLR 583.

[21] The danger of the provision being used for a disguised abduction was acknowledged during the debates on the Children Bill, but it was the view of Sir Nicholas Lyell (the then Solicitor-General) that the law should reflect 'normal and reasonable' behaviour. In other words, such cases would be vastly outnumbered by those of parents taking bona fide holidays, and the law should reflect this.

cases without notice.[22] Residence orders should always be sought 'if there have been threats of abduction, or if the parents come from different countries or either has strong foreign connections (such as lengthy vacations, a second residence, extended family or employment opportunities abroad)'.[23] The more appropriate order directly to prohibit abduction will be the prohibited steps order (discussed in chapter 5), the specific purpose of which can be to restrain removal.[24] As a practical matter, it would still be necessary to instigate a port alert to enforce s 8 orders, but the existence of the orders should certainly secure the ready co-operation of the police.

There are several reasons why civil procedures may be additionally advantageous:[25] they may act as a deterrent to abduction; they may secure official assistance in tracing the child; breach of the order will constitute contempt of court and may be punished as such; and passport control, as we have seen, will be facilitated.

RECOVERY OF CHILDREN

Action under the Hague Convention[26]

The Hague Convention has been widely ratified by countries in various regions of the world.[27] It may be invoked in relation to any child[28] under the age of 16 years, habitually resident in one contracting State, who has been wrongfully removed to or retained in another contracting State.[29] The aim of the Convention is 'to secure the prompt return of children wrongfully removed to or retained in any Contracting State',[30] so that any dispute as to their care is determined in the place with which the child has currently most connection, and that the alleged abductor is denied any tactical advantage from the abduction.[31] In this way, it is also hoped to deter other such removals. As a general proposition, there will be a heavy presumption in favour of returning the child, and only to a limited extent will the court be able or prepared to

---

22 *Re B (A Minor) (Residence Order: Ex Parte)* [1992] 2 FLR 1.
23 CS Bruch 'Child Abduction and the English Courts' in A Bainham, DS Pearl and R Pickford (eds) *Frontiers of Family Law* (2nd edn, John Wiley & Sons, 1995), at p 55.
24 As in *Re D (A Minor) (Child: Removal from Jurisdiction)* [1992] 1 All ER 892.
25 See the discussion in an earlier edition of *Bromley's Family Law* (9th edn, Butterworths, 1998), at pp 481–483.
26 For an explanation of the workings of the Convention, see Elisa Pérez-Vera, *Explanatory Report on the 1980 Hague Child Abduction Convention* (HCCH, 1982).
27 The list of countries which have ratified or acceded to the Convention can be found on the Hague Conference website at www.hcch.net. To date there are 89 States party to it.
28 It is not possible to abduct a foetus: see *Re F (Abduction: Unborn Child)* [2006] EWHC 2199 (Fam), [2007] 1 FLR 627.
29 Article 4. As to the meaning of the child's habitual residence, see P Stone 'The habitual residence of a child' (1992) 4 JCL 170.
30 Article 1.
31 See Baroness Hale in *Re M (Abduction:Zimbabwe)* [2007] UKHL 55, [2008] 1 FLR 251: the message should go out to abductors that there are no safe havens amongst the contracting States.

investigate the merits of disputes over residence or upbringing. Otherwise, the very purpose of the Convention would be frustrated, but in exceptional cases return of the child may be successfully resisted. There is thus a tension between the dual objectives of securing the welfare of the child while upholding the integrity of the system, and it must be the case that the best interests of individual children are occasionally sacrificed in the more general interests of the wider class of children in the international community.

Procedural matters – how is the Hague Convention invoked?

Each contracting state is required to set up a Central Authority responsible for discharging the obligations under the Convention,[32] and thus undertaking responsibility for the administration and handling of child abduction cases. The Central Authority for England and Wales is the Lord Chancellor who delegates those duties to the International Child Abduction and Contact Unit (ICACU). The ICACU is based within the office of the Official Solicitor and Public Trustee. The applicant seeking return of a child will usually begin by applying to the 'Central Authority' for the country of the child's habitual residence. It is the task of the Central Authority to receive applications, collect all relevant information and institute the necessary action, perhaps including judicial proceedings, for recovery of the child.[33] In practice, the Department will instruct a solicitor to act for the applicant who will then file an application in the High Court, which has exclusive jurisdiction in these cases.[34] As an alternative, the applicant could decide to approach the foreign Central Authority direct, or even institute proceedings in that country. However, at least as far as removals *from* England are concerned, there are distinct advantages in going through the ICACU given the expert assistance there available. Interim directions can be given by the court before any application is determined for the purposes of securing the welfare of the child concerned or of preventing changes in the circumstances relevant to the determination of the application.[35] The court will then decide, in summary proceedings, whether to order the child's immediate return to his place of habitual residence, if it finds that the child's removal or retention violated the custody rights of the applicant.[36]

---

[32] Article 6. The measures required to be taken are set out in Art 7.

[33] A Special Commission at The Hague, which met in 2002, has produced a Guide to Good Practice for Central Authorities which also deals with implementation measures: see *Guide to Good Practice under the Hague Convention of 25 October 1980 on the Civil Aspects of International Child Abduction, Part I: Central Authority Practice* and *Part II: Implementing Measures* (Hague Conference on Private International Law/Jordans, 2003). See also D Carter 'Child Abduction: The Role of the Central Authorities and Reunite' [2000] *International Family Law* 102.

[34] Child Abduction and Custody Act 1985, s 4.

[35] Child Abduction and Custody Act 1985, s 5. See, for example, a direction against a local authority for provision of accommodation for the child and mother: *Re A (Abduction: Interim Directions: Accommodation by Local Authority)* [2010] EWCA Civ 586, [2011] 1 FLR 1.

[36] In *Re N (Child Abduction) (Habitual Residence)* [1993] 2 FLR 124, the Court of Appeal said that proceedings under the Hague Convention are neither adversarial nor inquisitorial but sui generis. The court has a statutory duty to apply the Convention if the necessary facts are present and, in so doing, it is concerned not only with the interests of the child but also with those of abducted children more generally.

It must be emphasised that the circumstances in which the court will refuse to order the return of the child are narrowly defined, and generally restrictively interpreted, since it is an aim of the Hague Convention to prevent the domestic courts of the 'receiving' State from entering into the merits of the matter. Article 11 of the Hague Convention provides that 'judicial or administrative authorities of Contracting States shall act expeditiously in proceedings for the return of children'.[37] This is important because, notwithstanding the illegality of the removal, the child may become settled in the new state, which can affect the ultimate decision whether or not to return the child. If the judicial or administrative authority concerned has not reached a decision within six weeks from the date of commencement of the proceedings,[38] the applicant or the Central Authority of the requesting State has the right to request a statement of the reasons for the delay. Cases in England are summary proceedings, heard and decided on the basis of written evidence, and the use of oral evidence should only rarely be permitted.[39]

Wrongful removal or retention

The Hague Convention can only be activated where the removal or retention was 'wrongful'. This is defined in Art 3. It must be shown that, according to the law of the child's habitual residence, the actions were in breach of rights of custody attributed to a person, an institution or any other body *and* that, at the time of the removal or retention, those rights were actually exercised jointly or alone, or would have been but for the removal or retention.[40] The rights of custody may arise in particular by operation of law or by reason of a judicial or administrative decision, or by reason of an agreement having legal effect under the law of that State. It is thus *not* necessary for the applicant to hold a court order, although clearly the existence of a court order in the applicant's favour, especially a residence order, will help.[41]

Habitual residence

A crucial question will be what the child's habitual residence was *immediately before* the alleged wrongful removal or retention.[42] The question of the child's habitual residence may cause difficulties where the family has lived in more

---

[37] In England the time to conclude abduction cases in 2011 still fell far short of the six week target of the 1980 Convention (now an obligation for applications under the Brussels II Regulation) with only 33 per cent of applications under the Regulation being disposed of by the court in this time, and 26 per cent of applications overall. (Study by Victoria Stephens and Nigel Law, Nuffield Foundation).

[38] In cases to which the Brussels II Revised Regulation applies, this six week period is an obligation. See discussion below.

[39] See *Re K (Abduction: Case Management)* [2010] EWCA Civ 1546, [2011] 1 FLR 1268 and *Re E (Children) (Abduction: Custody Appeal)* [2011] UKSC 27, [2011] 2 FLR 758.

[40] Article 3.

[41] Because of the ambiguities surrounding the concept of wrongfulness as it applies to parental responsibility.

[42] *Re S (A Minor) (Abduction)* [1991] 2 FLR 1.

than one jurisdiction in the recent past.[43] Habitual residence[44] is 'primarily a question of fact to be determined by reference to all the relevant circumstances' and 'not to be treated as a term of art nor is it a legal concept in the sense of a set of pre-determined rules designed to produce a particular legal result in given circumstances.'[45] A child 'does not automatically take the habitual residence of its parents or custodial parent and there is no mandatory coincidence between them'.[46] It is not necessary for a person to remain continuously present in a particular country in order for a person to retain habitual residence there.[47] The question whether habitual residence in any country requires the person in question to have been at some time physically present there, was considered by the Supreme Court in *Re A (Children)*.[48] In that case a mother took her three children to Pakistan on holiday to see the father. When she disclosed that she was pregnant she was held there by the father against her will and gave birth to her fourth child in Pakistan. She managed to escape, albeit without the children, and obtained orders of the High Court in England for the return of all four children. On appeal, the Court of Appeal held that the order in respect of the youngest child had been made without jurisdiction, since he had never been habitually resident in the UK. By a majority,[49] the Court of Appeal ruled that the acquisition of habitual residence in a country requires the child to be physically present there. The mother appealed to the Supreme Court where an alternative basis for jurisdiction, namely the child's British nationality, was also raised.

The Supreme Court[50] held that the orders made by the High Court for the return of the children were orders relating to parental responsibility to which the Brussels II Revised Regulation[51] applied. Under Art 8 of the Regulation, jurisdiction on matters of parental responsibility are founded upon habitual residence. The Supreme Court in this case was thus examining the notion of habitual residence as understood by the Court of Justice of the European Union (CJEU), and the Supreme Court noted that the concept of habitual

---

[43] See the review of cases under the Hague Convention by P Stone 'The Habitual Residence of a Child' (1992) 4 JCL 170, especially at pp 171–172, and the House of Lords decisions in *Re J (A Minor) (Abduction: Custody Rights)* [1990] 2 AC 562 and *Re S (A Minor) (Custody: Habitual Residence)* [1997] 4 All ER 251. See also R Schuz 'Habitual Residence of Children under the Hague Child Abduction Convention: Theory and Practice' [2001] CFLQ 1, who discusses two models for determining a child's habitual residence – the 'parental rights model' and the 'child-centred or objective model', preferring the latter, while acknowledging that it is the former that has held sway in English practice.

[44] See the useful summaries of the principles that apply, in *ZA and PA v NA (Abduction: Habitual Residence)* [2012] EWCA Civ 1396, [2013] 1 FLR 1041, at para [47], and *Re P-J (Abduction: Habitual Residence: Consent)* [2009] EWCA Civ 588, [2009] 2 FLR 1051, at paras [24] et seq.

[45] See *Re J (A Minor) (Abduction: Custody Rights)* [1990] 2 AC 562, [1990] 3 WLR 492, sub nom *C v S (A Minor) (Abduction)* [1990] 2 FLR 442.

[46] Ibid, citing *Re M (Abduction: Habitual Residence)* [1996] 1 FLR 887 (CA), at 891.

[47] *Re M (Abduction: Habitual Residence)* [1996] 1 FLR 887 (CA), at 895.

[48] [2013] UKSC 60, on appeal from *ZA and PA v NA (Abduction: Habitual Residence)* [2012] EWCA Civ 1369, [2013] 1 FLR 1041.

[49] Rimer and Patten LJJ, Thorpe LJ dissenting.

[50] Lady Hale delivered the leading judgment with which Lords Wilson, Reed and Toulson agreed. Lord Hughes expressed a minority view.

[51] (Council Regulation (EC) No 2201/2003).

residence as developed by the English courts for the purpose of the Hague Child Abduction Convention may be different from the concept of habitual residence as interpreted by the CJEU.[52] However, the Supreme Court stated obiter that 'it is highly desirable that the same test be adopted and that, if there is any difference, it is that adopted by the Court of Justice'.[53] In *Proceedings brought by A* the CJEU had held that habitual residence:[54]

> 'must be interpreted as meaning that it corresponds to the place which reflects some degree of integration by the child in a social and family environment. To that end, in particular the duration, regularity, conditions and reasons for the stay on the territory of a member state and the family's move to that state, the child's nationality, the place and conditions of attendance at school, linguistic knowledge and the family and social relationships of the child in that state must be taken into consideration. It is for the national court to establish the habitual residence of the child, taking account of all the circumstances specific to each individual case.'

In *Mercredi v Chaffe*[55] the CJEU added that:

> 'where the situation concerned is that of an infant who has been staying with her mother only a few days in a member state – other than that of her habitual residence – to which she has been removed, the factors which must be taken into consideration include, first, the duration, regularity, conditions and reasons for the stay in the territory of that member state and for the mother's move to that state and second, with particular reference to the child's age, the mother's geographic and family origins and the family and social connections which the mother and child have with that member state.'

The CJEU also stated that:[56]

> 'in order to determine where a child is habitually resident, *in addition to the physical presence of the child* in a member state, other factors must also make it clear that that presence is not in any way temporary or intermittent.'

The Supreme Court expressed the view that the test adopted by the CJEU is preferable to that previously adopted by the English courts, the former being focussed on the situation of the child.[57] Applying the CJEU test, the majority of the Supreme Court[58] concluded that an approach which holds that presence in a country is a necessary pre-cursor to habitual residence accords most closely with the child's situation, rather than an approach which focusses on the relationship between the child and the primary carer. The Court explained:[59]

---

52   [2013] UKSC 60, at para [34].
53   Ibid, at para [35].
54   (Case C-523/07) [2010] Fam 42.
55   Case C-497/10 PPU, [2012] Fam 22.
56   Ibid, at para 49.
57   [2013] UKSC 60, at para [54].
58   Lord Hughes dissenting.
59   Ibid, at para [55].

'It is one thing to say that a child's integration in the place where he is at present depends upon the degree of integration of his primary carer. It is another thing to say that he can be integrated in a place to which his primary carer has never taken him. It is one thing to say that a person can remain habitually resident in a country from which he is temporarily absent. It is another thing to say that a person can acquire a habitual residence without ever setting foot in a country. It is one thing to say that a child is integrated in the family environment of his primary carer and siblings. It is another thing to say that he is also integrated into the social environment of a country where he has never been.'

However, the Court concluded that the position was not entirely clear for the purpose of EU law, and that it would not be able to dispose of the case on this basis without making a reference to the CJEU.[60] The Court also concluded, however, that it was not necessary at present to seek a reference, since the case could be dealt with on another basis of jurisdiction. The Supreme Court held that the inherent jurisdiction could be exercised on the basis that the child was a British national,[61] albeit also noting that in recent cases this basis of the jurisdiction had only been exercised exceptionally.[62] The Court therefore allowed the appeal, remitting the case back to the High Court for determination of whether on the facts the inherent jurisdiction should be exercised. If the High Court concluded on the facts that the inherent jurisdiction should not be exercised then the parties had liberty to apply to the Supreme Court for a reference to be made to the CJEU for clarification of the meaning of habitual residence on the facts of this case.

Lord Hughes disagreed with the Court of Appeal's and the Supreme Court's conclusion on habitual residence, seeing no occasion for a rule preventing a person from being habitually resident in a place where he has not yet set foot.[63] He observed:[64]

'If current physical presence is not essential, then so also can habitual residence exist without any physical presence yet having occurred, at least if it has only been prevented by some kind of unexpected force majeure.'

In contrast to the majority, Lord Hughes concluded that the youngest child, like his siblings, is 'a member of a family unit which is firmly based in England and when born into it he was like the rest of its members habitually resident there'.[65]

---

[60]   Ibid, at para [58].
[61]   Ibid, at para [60]. The jurisdiction exists in so far as it has not been taken away by provisions of the Family Law Act 1986.
[62]   See for example in the context of forced marriage, *Re B; RB v FB and MA (Forced Marriage: Wardship: Jurisdiction)* [2008] 2 FLR 1624 (Hogg J). See the comments of Thorpe LJ in *Al Habtoor v Fotheringham* [2001] 1 FLR 951, at para [42], and of McFarlane LJ in *Re N (Abduction: Appeal)* [2013] 1 FLR 457, at para [29].
[63]   [2013] UKSC 60, at para [90].
[64]   Ibid, at para [92].
[65]   Ibid, at para [93].

There is some force in the reasoning of Lord Hughes, and given the Supreme Court's inability to decide the issue without the future assistance of the CJEU, the issue must surely come before the Supreme Court again at some point in the future for clarification.

Temporary absence on holiday, or for educational purposes, will not bring to an end habitual residence. Thus in *Re P-J (Abduction: Habitual Residence: Consent)*[66] the children's habitual residence in Spain was not altered by the fact that they were spending a year in Wales while the family home was being renovated, in order to allow them some experience of English education. While temporary change will not alter habitual residence, equally however the question is not whether the family has settled in the sense of putting down substantial roots. Habitual residence 'may be acquired despite the fact that the purpose of the move was intended to be fulfilled within a comparatively short duration' or 'the move was only on a trial basis'.[67] It seems, however, that physical presence in a new jurisdiction will not be capable of changing a person's habitual residence if the presence in the new jurisdiction is enforced.[68] Where both parents have joint parental responsibility, neither of them can unilaterally change the habitual residence of the child by removing the child wrongfully and in breach of the other party's rights.[69]

The action must be in breach of 'custody' rights,[70] defined in Art 5(a) as including 'rights relating to the care of the person of the child and, in particular, the right to determine the child's place of residence'.

Under Art 15 the court can seek a determination from the authorities of the State of the child's habitual residence as to whether or not the removal or retention of the child was in breach of rights of custody under the law of that country. Indeed the foreign court is asked to rule on whether the removal is wrongful in Convention terms. In *Re D (Abduction: Rights of Custody)*[71] the House of Lords observed that the Hague Convention terms have an autonomous meaning, and therefore a foreign court's characterisation of the effect of its domestic law in Hague Convention terms could be mistaken. However, the House of Lords also indicated that the 'foreign court is much better placed than the English court to understand the true meaning and effect

---

[66]   [2009] EWCA Civ 588, [2009] 2 FLR 1051.
[67]   *Al Habtoor v Fotheringham* [2001] EWCA Civ 186, [2001] 1 FLR 951, at paras [37] and [38].
[68]   See *DT v LBT (Abduction: Domestic Abuse)* [2010] EWHC 3177 (Fam), [2011] 1 FLR 1215 (although not so finding on the facts of the case. The mother had suffered sustained emotional, sexual and physical abuse at the hands of the husband, who, she claimed, bullied her into moving to Italy with the children. It was held on the facts that the mother's will had not been overborne and the children's habitual residence was Italy).
[69]   *Re J* above, at 572 and 449 respectively per Lord Donaldson MR and *Re N (Abduction: Habitual Residence)* [2000] 2 FLR 899. Breach of a shared care arrangement can be a wrongful retention of the child: see *K v L (Child Abduction: Declaration)* [2012] EWHC 1234 (Fam), [2013] 1 FLR 998.
[70]   For a case in which grandparents were found to have joint custodial rights, see *Re O (Child Abduction: Custody Rights)* [1997] 2 FLR 702.
[71]   [2006] UKHL 51 [2007] 1 FLR 961.

of its own laws in Convention terms', and the court in the requested state should decline to follow it only 'if its characterisation of the parent's rights is clearly out of line with the international understanding of the Convention's terms'.[72] Courts 'must attach considerable weight to the authoritative decision of the requesting state on both issues' since 'we still have something to learn from the requesting state's characterisation of the position'.[73] Lord Brown of Eaton-under-Heywood was clear that 'on the rare occasions on which such determinations may be expected to be sought, they should, to my mind, be treated almost invariably as conclusive on both limbs of the issue to which they are ultimately directed'.[74]

Article 5(a), with its reference to the right to determine the child's place of residence, invites the question whether a veto on change of residence constitutes 'rights of custody'. In *Re H (A Minor) (Abduction: Rights of Custody)* the House of Lords held that a court's right of veto will constitute 'rights of custody'.[75] Here the unmarried father had obtained an interim order for access with the child in the Irish courts. His application for guardianship and access was adjourned. At this point the mother removed the child from Ireland to England, and the father sought summary return of the child under the Convention. The House of Lords upheld the decision of the Court of Appeal, which had found that at the relevant time the Irish court had 'rights of custody'. It interpreted the expression 'other body' in Art 8 to include a court. The definition of 'rights of custody' was also wide enough to include the right to determine the child's place of residence, which the court had. The court's rights of custody arose on the date on which the court's jurisdiction was invoked which, at the latest, was the date on which proceedings were served and jurisdiction would continuously be invoked until disposal of the application. It was recognised that jurisdiction could arise before service of the proceedings in special circumstances.[76]

By analogy with the decision in *Re H*, in *Re D (Abduction: Rights of Custody)*[77] the House of Lords held that an individual's right of veto amounts to 'rights of custody' within the meaning of Art 5(a). The mere right to go to court to seek an order which would provide a veto does not itself amount to rights of custody within the meaning of Art 5(a) since that would be to remove

---

[72] As may have been the case in *Hunter v Murrow (Abduction: Rights of Custody)* [2005] EWCA Civ 976, [2005] 2 FLR 1119.

[73] [2006] UKHL 51 [2007] 1 FLR 961, at para [45].

[74] Ibid, at para [83].

[75] [2000] 2 AC 291, [2000] 1 FLR 374. See, for example, *X County Council v B (Abduction: Rights of Custody in the Court)* [2009] EWHC 2635 (Fam) (court seised of application in care proceedings when parents absconded to Ireland – held that removal was in breach of court's custody rights).

[76] In *Re C (Child Abduction) (Unmarried Father: Rights of Custody)* [2003] 1 FLR 252 the court held that the mere issue of proceedings which had not yet been served did not suffice and that there were no special circumstances justifying the vesting of rights of custody in the court.

[77] [2006] UKHL 51 [2007] 1 FLR 961 [2007] 1 FLR 961, at para [37].

the distinction between 'rights of custody' and 'rights of access' altogether.[78] Nor can a subsequent order grant a veto by way of right of custody if by then the child's habitual residence has been changed.

The issue of what is wrongful will often be straightforward, but can be difficult in some cases, and the Children Act may have produced some added complications.[79] Parental responsibility may, because of its durability, be held by more than one person or institution jointly, each of which may prima facie be acting lawfully in taking independent action in relation to the child.[80] The matter is complicated further in that in some cases the courts have found a breach of 'custody' rights where the left-behind parent or carer does *not* possess parental responsibility. We need to distinguish those cases in which there is a court order from those where there is none.

Where there is a court order

Where a court order is in existence, the position ought to be clear, since the order will usually make plain where the child is to live and what degree of contact or involvement parents or others are to have with the child. Thus, if the mother has a residence order in her favour, it will be incompatible with that order for the father to take the child abroad.[81] This would be a clear breach of the mother's 'custody' rights, despite the fact that, for many purposes other than residence, parental responsibility continues to be shared by *both* parents. But what if the mother, having obtained a residence order, herself takes the child out of the country? She is entitled under the order to do so, unilaterally, for up to one month, but what is the position if she then *retains* the child abroad for an extended period, perhaps indefinitely? The question is whether that retention is unlawful, given that the initial removal was lawful. The better view, advanced by Bruch,[82] is that it is unlawful, since the mother's right to remove the child was a temporary one. The habitual residence of the child would thus remain in England and, according to English law, the retention beyond one month would be wrongful. However, the matter is not wholly free from doubt.[83] Bruch points out that the way around this problem is for the

---

78   Ibid, at para [38], and as held in *Re J (A Minor) (Abduction: Custody Rights)* [1990] 2 AC 562 sub nom *C v S (A Minor) (Abduction)* [1990] 2 FLR 442.

79   CS Bruch 'Child Abduction and the English Courts' in A Bainham, DS Pearl and R Pickford (eds) *Frontiers of Family Law* (2nd edn, John Wiley & Sons, 1995), at p 55.

80   In particular, there is generally no duty to consult the other parent before taking action.

81   Section 2(8) of the Children Act.

82   See CS Bruch (above), at pp 54 et seq.

83   This is because the House of Lords decision in *Re J (A Minor) (Abduction: Custody Rights)* [1990] 2 AC 562 might suggest that the removal of a child by a parent who is entitled to remove him and who has no intention to return brings about a change in the child's habitual residence. On the other hand, the loss of one habitual residence does not necessarily mean that a new one has been acquired. It is thus possible for a child to have no habitual residence at some point in time. See *Re M (Minors) (Residence Order: Jurisdiction)* [1993] 1 FLR 495. For another case in which wrongfulness was not established because the child could not be said to be habitually resident in the State (Canada) from which the removal took place, see *Re R (Wardship: Child Abduction) (No 2)* [1993] 1 FLR 249.

residence order itself to deal expressly with the question of trips abroad, if this appears to be in issue. The point is that the one-month rule will be subject to any express conditions inserted in the court's order. Thus, a s 8 order might prohibit the child's removal by either parent, unless specific consent requirements, court approval or other conditions are satisfied.[84] Even where a 'shared residence order' is granted,[85] Bruch argues that 'wrongfulness can be established, inter alia, by acts that are inconsistent with the periods in which the order provides that the child is to live in the respective households'.[86]

Where there is no court order

The position may be less clear where there is no court order. It cannot be emphasised strongly enough that this will be so in the overwhelming majority of cases and, in accordance with the 'no order' principle in the Children Act,[87] it will also be the usual position following divorce. The 'custody' rights which arise by operation of law are, therefore, crucial. The position of *unmarried* parents will usually be straightforward. Assuming that the father has not acquired parental responsibility by agreement or court order, or more likely registration on the child's birth certificate, the mother will be solely entitled to it. She may, therefore, take the child abroad unilaterally for as long as she wishes.[88] As noted above, the father will generally have no 'custody' rights capable of being breached, as held in the case of *Re J (A Minor) (Abduction: Custody Rights)*.[89] The matter was, however, complicated by the decision of the Court of Appeal in *Re B (A Minor) (Abduction)*[90] in which the father, together with the maternal grandmother, had de facto care of the child before the child was abducted. The majority (Peter Gibson LJ dissenting) drew a distinction between strict legal rights and de facto or 'inchoate' rights and held that the factual care of the child could give rise to 'rights of custody' within the meaning of the Convention. This was, however, an unusual case in which the mother's behaviour was particularly reprehensible and it is clear that mere

---

[84] The court has a general power to attach conditions to s 8 orders under s 11(7) of the Children Act. For a case illustrating these principles in the 'holiday' context, see *Re D (A Minor) (Child: Removal from Jurisdiction)* [1992] 1 WLR 315.

[85] Section 11(4) of the Children Act.

[86] CS Bruch (above), at p 55.

[87] Section 1(5).

[88] Removal by the mother of a child who is habitually resident in England or Wales will be wrongful under the Hague Convention where: (a) the father has parental responsibility either by agreement or court order; or (b) there is a court order in force prohibiting removal; or (c) there are relevant proceedings pending in a court in England and Wales; or (d) the father is currently the primary carer for the child, at least if the mother has delegated such care to him. See *Re W; Re B (Child Abduction: Unmarried Father)* [1998] 2 FLR 146, and also *Practice Note (Hague Convention: Applications by Fathers Without Parental Responsibility)* [1998] 1 FLR 491.

[89] [1990] 2 AC 562. A case, in fact, decided under Western Australian law, but the principles would be the same under English law.

[90] [1994] 2 FLR 249.

contact, however extensive, is not sufficient to establish 'rights of custody'.[91] In the vast majority of cases outside marriage, the mother will be the primary carer. Where the father *has* acquired parental responsibility, the position will be identical to that relating to married parents.[92]

There have been several cases exploring exactly when an unmarried father can be said to have 'rights of custody' for the purposes of the Convention. These cases explore the limitations on the acquisition of 'rights of custody' where parental responsibility has not been acquired. Thus, in *Re C (Child Abduction) (Unmarried Father: Rights of Custody)*[93] the father had *shared* the care of the child with the mother for four months before she left, taking the child to Ireland. Munby J held, inter alia, that sharing the care of a child with the mother as joint primary carer was not enough to generate rights of custody, nor was the mere fact of having contact with the child.[94] The case was distinguishable from those in which the mother was no longer the primary carer as was the case in *Re F (Abduction: Unmarried Father: Sole Carer)*.[95] Here there was a dispute as to the paternity of the youngest child of four children, but no dispute that the mother's former partner had effectively had sole care of all the children for a number of years. In these circumstances Dame Elizabeth Butler-Sloss P held that there were circumstances in which a person who was not related by blood to a child, but who had a 'quasi-parental role' and exclusive care of the child, might be found to have inchoate rights of custody for the purposes of the Convention. Such rights were those which were capable of being affected by court applications in which there was a reasonable prospect of success. The father here, even if proved not to be the natural father, had reasonable prospects of obtaining a residence order and thus had inchoate rights capable of being perfected.

What then amounts to a wrongful taking by a parent who has joint parental responsibility but there has been no court order? Again, wrongfulness must be determined by the statutes and case-law[96] in the country of the child's habitual residence, which in England means the Children Act 1989 and the Child Abduction Act 1984. Section 1 of the Child Abduction Act 1984 makes it a criminal offence for one parent to remove a child without the consent of the

---

[91] See, particularly, the decision of the Court of Appeal in *Re B (Abduction) (Rights of Custody)* [1997] 2 FLR 594 and *Re D (Abduction: Rights of Custody)* [2006] UKHL 51, [2007] 1 FLR 961, discussed above.

[92] The father may also have 'custody rights' where he has interim care and control of the child in wardship proceedings. See *Re S (Abduction: Hague and European Conventions)* [1997] 1 FLR 958. It has been held that imprisonment does not suspend custody rights where the father has parental responsibility. See *Re A (Abduction: Rights of Custody: Imprisonment)* [2004] 1 FLR 1, a case from Australia under which jurisdiction unmarried fathers automatically acquire parental responsibility on the birth of the child.

[93] [2003] 1 FLR 252. See also *Re G (A Child) (Custody Rights: Unmarried Father)* [2002] EWHC 2219 (Fam) where the mother was the primary carer.

[94] See also on this point *S v H (Abduction: Access Rights)* [1997] 1 FLR 971.

[95] [2003] 1 FLR 839.

[96] Central Authorities are authorised under the Hague Convention to provide the court with information on the custody law of the child's habitual residence.

other but, perhaps significantly for present purposes, there are a number of defences available. Under s 1(5), no offence is committed where the child is removed:

(1) in the belief that the other person (parent for the present purposes) has consented or would have done had he been aware of all the relevant circumstances; or

(2) after taking all reasonable steps to communicate with the other person, the accused had been unable to do so; or

(3) the other person has unreasonably refused to consent.

While a former Lord Chancellor[97] and certain commentators[98] appeared to think that the regime of the Children Act would not make it more difficult to establish a wrongful taking or retention, others were more doubtful.[99] It is, to say the least, unfortunate that the question of wrongfulness under the civil law would appear to turn on what may be implied from the existence of a criminal offence, itself qualified by defences which are grounded in the nebulous notion of reasonableness. Also, it may not be very easy at all to establish a wrongful *retention* if the initial removal was reasonable under s 1(5) of the Child Abduction Act 1984.[100] Again, the answer would appear to be to obtain a residence or prohibited steps order in advance, but there are practical difficulties with this. First, child abductors are not in the habit of giving notice of their intention to snatch a child, and applying for an order really depends on being forewarned. Secondly, s 1(5) of the Children Act militates against the granting of orders unless it can be positively demonstrated that they are necessary. Thus, unless there is clear evidence of the risk, the court may simply refuse to make an order. This is one instance in which the courts, notwithstanding the general thinking in the Children Act, should, perhaps, be more ready to make orders.

Wrongfulness may also be established where the taking contravened the defendant's own rights (in the sense that he exceeded them),[101] or those of an institution (such as a local authority where the child is in care, or the court where a child is a ward of court).[102] Ignorance of the wrongfulness of the removal has been held to be no defence.[103] Finally, one of the objects of the Hague Convention is 'to ensure that ... rights of access under the law of one

---

[97] See the reference in CS Bruch (above), at p 59, to the Lord Chancellor's speech on 12 October 1991.

[98] M Everall 'Child Abduction after the Hague Convention' [1990] Fam Law 169.

[99] CS Bruch (above).

[100] On the distinction between removal and retention, see the House of Lords decision in *Re H (Minors) (Abduction: Custody Rights); Re S (Minors) (Abduction: Custody Rights)* [1991] 2 AC 476.

[101] *Re H (A Minor) (Abduction)* [1990] 2 FLR 439.

[102] *Re J (A Minor: Abduction: Ward of Court)* [1989] Fam 85. See also *B v B (Abduction)* [1993] 1 FLR 238 and see the discussion above as to when a court may possess 'rights of custody'.

[103] *C v C (Minors) (Child Abduction)* [1992] 1 FLR 163.

Contracting State are effectively respected in the other Contracting States',[104] and Central Authorities are required 'to make arrangements for organising or securing the effective exercise of rights of access'.[105] In the English context this, of course, now means contact. However, the Court of Appeal has held that the duties of the Central Authority under Art 21 are of an *executive* rather than judicial nature, creating no rights in private law which a parent can directly enforce.[106]

The Hague Convention has proved to be rather ineffectual in the enforcement of rights of access largely because a mere right of access does not amount to 'custody rights' within the meaning of the Convention.[107] Thus, removal of a child is not a wrongful taking merely because it frustrates the access rights of the aggrieved parent.[108] It may be that this is one area in which the Hague Protection of Children Convention 1996 may have a role to play,[109] although, for those countries within the Council of Europe, the Convention on Contact concerning Children is likely in future to be a significant international instrument governing contact issues.

WHEN SHOULD THE CHILD'S RETURN BE ORDERED?

As has been seen, the court is generally precluded under the Hague Convention from becoming embroiled in the merits of rights to custody.[110] The general rule under Art 12 is that, provided the application is brought within 12 months of the removal, the court must order return of the child. This is subject to a number of limited exceptions under Art 13, although, even where one of these is established, the court retains its discretion to order a return under Art 18.

---

[104] Article 1.
[105] Article 7(f).
[106] *Re G (A Minor) (Hague Convention: Access)* [1993] 1 FLR 669 and *Practice Note (Child Abduction Unit – Lord Chancellor's Department)* [1993] 1 FLR 804. This makes it plain that Art 21 confers no jurisdiction to determine matters relating to access, or to recognise or enforce foreign access orders. It merely provides for executive co-operation in the enforcement of such recognition as national law allows. Thus, the Central Authority should discharge its duty by providing the applicant with solicitors who may act on his behalf instituting proceedings in the High Court under s 8 of the Children Act.
[107] See generally N Lowe 'Problems Relating to Access Disputes under the Hague Convention on International Child Abduction' (1994) 8 IJLF 374.
[108] See *S v H (Abduction: Access Rights)* [1997] 1 FLR 971.
[109] The Convention came into force on 1 November 2012. See for commentary, NV Lowe and M Nicholls *The 1996 Hague Convention on the Protection of Children* (Family Law, 2012). See also A-M Hutchinson and MH Bennett in 'The Hague Child Protection Convention 1996' [1998] Fam Law 35, and NV Lowe 'Problems relating to access disputes under the Hague Convention on International Child Abduction' (1994) 8 IJLF 374.
[110] Article 16.

Consent or acquiescence

Under Art 13(a) the court may refuse to return a child where 'the person, institution or other body having care of the person of a child was not actually exercising the custody rights at the time of removal or retention, or had consented to or subsequently acquiesced in the removal or retention'.

Most of the reported cases on Art 13(a) have been concerned with the concept of acquiescence which we discuss below. So far as the notion of consent is concerned, it has been held that consent may be oral and need not be in writing but must be positive and unequivocal.[111] Consent, like acquiescence, may be passive rather than active and inferred from the conduct of the parties.[112] It is not necessary that the party consenting be 'happy' about the move as long as consent may clearly be inferred from what took place. Thus in *Re M (Abduction) (Consent: Acquiescence)*[113] it was possible to establish consent on the part of the Greek father where, according to the mother's evidence, she had made her preparations for leaving Greece openly, had given notice to the nursery and sold her belongings. The father had not at any stage objected to her leaving. In *Re L (Abduction: Future Consent)*[114] Bodey J saw 'no reason in principle why a consent should not be valid if tied to some future event even of uncertain timing, provided that the happening of the event is of reasonable ascertainability'[115] and whether such consent subsisted would be a matter of common sense in the circumstances. In *Re P-J (Abduction: Habitual Residence: Consent)*[116] Ward LJ listed the principles to be deduced from the authorities.

'(1) Consent to the removal of the child must be clear and unequivocal.

(2) Consent can be given to the removal at some future but unspecified time or upon the happening of some future event.

(3) Such advance consent must, however, still be operative and in force at the time of the actual removal.

(4) The happening of the future event must be reasonably capable of ascertainment. The condition must not have been expressed in terms which are too vague or uncertain for both parties to know whether the condition will be fulfilled. Fulfilment of the condition must not depend on the subjective determination of

---

[111] *Re K (Abduction: Consent)* [1997] 2 FLR 212. See also *Re B (Abduction: Article 13 Defence)* [1997] 2 FLR 573.

[112] See *Re R (Abduction: Consent)* [1999] 1 FLR 828. On the relationship between the defence of consent under Art 13 and the notion of wrongful removal, see the Court of Appeal's decision in *Re P (Abduction: Consent)* [2004] 2 FLR 1057.

[113] [1999] 1 FLR 171.

[114] [2007] EWHC 2181 (Fam), [2008] 1 FLR 914, at para [29].

[115] That is, not too vague, too uncertain or too subjective: e g 'If my job application succeeds ...' or 'when the child comes out of hospital'. See also *BT v JRT (Abduction:Conditional Acquiescence and Consent)* [2008] 2 FLR 972.

[116] [2009] EWCA Civ 588, [2009] 2 FLR 1051 (consent can be conditional or for a limited time).

one party, for example, "Whatever you may think, I have concluded that the marriage has broken down and so I am free to leave with the child". The event must be objectively verifiable.

(5) Consent, or the lack of it, must be viewed in the context of the realities of family life, or more precisely, in the context of the realities of the disintegration of family life. It is not to be viewed in the context of nor governed by the law of contract.

(6) Consequently consent can be withdrawn at any time before actual removal. If it is, the proper course is for any dispute about removal to be resolved by the courts of the country of habitual residence before the child is removed.

(7) The burden of proving the consent rests on him or her who asserts it.

(8) The inquiry is inevitably fact specific and the facts and circumstances will vary infinitely from case to case.

(9) The ultimate question is a simple one even if a multitude of facts bear upon the answer. It is simply this: had the other parent clearly and unequivocally consented to the removal?'

Wilson LJ[117] added that 'the most obvious (albeit not always decisive) indication of whether in reality an advance consent subsisted at the time of removal is whether the removal was clandestine', and ' a clandestine removal will usually be indicative of the absence *in reality* of subsistence of the consent'.[118]

The notion of acquiescence has caused considerable difficulty.[119] It can be active, where some step is taken by the aggrieved parent which is thought to be inconsistent with insistence on summary return of the child, or it may be passive, as where the aggrieved parent allows time to pass by without any words or actions indicating such insistence.

The leading authority is the decision of the House of Lords in *Re H (Minors) (Abduction: Acquiescence)*,[120] where the parties were Orthodox Jews living in Israel. The mother brought the children to England without the father's consent and, initially, he sought relief through the Rabbinical courts in Israel in accordance with his religion. Only when the mother did not comply with a summons issued by the Beth Din did the father, with the approval of the court, take action under the Hague Convention. The Court of Appeal, which had

---

[117] Ibid, at para [57].

[118] See, for example, *P v P (Abduction: Acquiescence)* [1998] 2 FLR 835 at 836H–837A.

[119] See, for example, *Re A and Another (Minors: Abduction)* [1991] 2 FLR 241; *Re F (A Minor) (Child Abduction)* [1992] 1 FLR 548; *Re AZ (A Minor) (Abduction: Acquiescence)* [1993] 1 FLR 682; *Re S (Minors) (Abduction: Acquiescence)* [1994] 1 FLR 819; and *Re R (Child Abduction: Acquiescence)* [1995] 1 FLR 716. See also *P v P (Abduction: Acquiescence)* [1998] 2 FLR 835, *Re D (Abduction: Acquiescence)* [1998] 2 FLR 335 and *Re S (Abduction: Acquiescence)* [1998] 2 FLR 115.

[120] [1997] 1 FLR 872.

found for the mother, attempted to draw a distinction between the nature of the test to be applied where the alleged acquiescence was passive and that where it was active. It held that only in the case of passive acquiescence could account be taken of the subjective attitude of the aggrieved parent.

The House of Lords rejected any such distinction, holding that under the Hague Convention the concept of acquiescence was always concerned with the subjective state of mind of the wronged parent, whether or not any positive action had been taken by that parent. Since acquiescence was a question of fact, this subjective intention could be inferred from the outward and visible acts of the wronged parent. The burden of proof was on the abducting parent to show acquiescence. In this case, there was nothing inconsistent in the father pursuing remedies in the courts of his habitual residence, whether religious or civil, and having subsequent recourse to the Hague Convention.

In *Re B (Abduction: Acquiescence)*[121] an American father was held to have acquiesced in the child's removal[122] from the USA to England, by virtue of his failure to demand the immediate return of the child and his decision to attempt to settle in England and seek contact orders through the English courts. This was so despite the failure on the part of his legal advisers to inform him earlier about his rights under the Hague Convention. In *Re I (Abduction: Acquiescence)*[123] an Australian father was held *not* to have acquiesced in the children's remaining in England (where they had been taken by their mother on holiday) by his willingness to enter into negotiations over their future. It was clear that in writing to the mother's solicitor the father, while wishing the children to return to Australia, was prepared to consider other arrangements in the interests of the family. Hogg J ordered the return of the children in the circumstances. Similarly in *Re W (Abduction: Acquiescence: Children's Objections)*[124] a father who came to England to attempt a reconciliation with the mother did not by that fact acquiesce in the abduction of his children to this jurisdiction.

Grave risk of harm or intolerable situation

The court may also refuse to order the child's return where 'there is a grave risk that his or her return would expose the child to physical or psychological harm or otherwise place the child in an intolerable situation'.[125] In *Re E (Children) (Abduction: Custody Appeal)*[126] the Supreme Court made clear that there is no need for Art 13 to be 'narrowly construed' since by its very terms, it is of restricted application. The words 'are quite plain and need no further

---

[121] [1999] 2 FLR 818.

[122] See also *Re H and L (Abduction: Acquiescence)* [2010] EWHC 652, [2010] 2 FLR 1277.

[123] [1999] 1 FLR 778.

[124] [2010] EWHC 332 (Fam), [2010] 2 FLR 1150.

[125] Article 13(b). For discussion of the scope of Art 13, see J Caldwell 'Child welfare defences in child abduction cases – some recent developments' [2001] CFLQ 121.

[126] [2011] UKSC 27, [2011] 2 FLR 758.

elaboration or "gloss".[127] The burden lies on the 'person, institution or other body' which opposes the child's return.[128] The risk to the child must be grave rather than the harm, but the Supreme Court observed that:[129]

> ' there is in ordinary language a link between the two. Thus a relatively low risk of death or really serious injury might properly be qualified as 'grave' while a higher level of risk might be required for other less serious forms of harm.'

The Court added that:[130]

> 'the words "physical or psychological harm" are not qualified. However, they do gain colour from the alternative "or *otherwise*" placed "in an intolerable situation" [emphasis supplied] ... "Intolerable" is a strong word, but when applied to a child must mean "a situation which this particular child in these particular circumstances should not be expected to tolerate"'.

Such situations include physical or psychological abuse or neglect of the child, and exposure to the harmful effects of seeing and hearing the physical or psychological abuse of the parent. The court also explained that Art 13(b) looks to the future, and 'the situation which the child will face on return depends crucially on the protective measures which can be put in place to secure that the child will not face an intolerable situation.[131] In a case to which the Brussels Regulation applies, a court cannot refuse to return a child on the basis of Art 13(b) of the 1980 Hague Convention if it is established that adequate arrangements have been made to secure the protection of the child after his or her return. Thus where 'there are disputed allegations which can neither be tried nor objectively verified, the focus of the inquiry is bound to be on the sufficiency of any protective measures which can be put in place to reduce the risk. The clearer the need for protection, the more effective the measures will have to be'.[132]

Importantly, the Supreme Court in *Re E* indicated[133] that, if there is such a risk, the source of it is irrelevant. So, for example, the requirements of the Article could be fulfilled where a mother's subjective perception of events leads

---

[127]   Ibid, at para [31].
[128]   Ibid, at para [32].
[129]   Ibid, at para [33].
[130]   Ibid, at para [34].
[131]   Ibid, at para [35].
[132]   Ibid, at para [52]. For a case in which adequate arrangements to prevent grave risk of harm were put in place, see *Re K (Abduction: Case Management)* [2010] EWCA Civ 1546, [2011] 1 FLR 1268. For example, undertakings may be required of the aggrieved parent as a condition of the child's return. See particularly *C v C (Minor: Abduction: Rights of Custody Abroad)* [1989] 1 WLR 654. See also *Re O (Child Abduction: Undertakings)* [1994] 2 FLR 349 and *Re M (Abduction: Undertakings)* [1995] 1 FLR 1021. For a critique of the practice of accepting undertakings, see D McClean 'International child abduction – some recent trends' [1997] CFLQ 387, at pp 392–395. The practice of accepting undertakings where there has been a context of domestic violence has been criticised. See M Kaye 'The Hague Convention and the Flight from Domestic Violence: How women and children are being returned by coach and four' [1999] IJLPF 191.
[133]   By way of acknowledging counsel's concession on the point.

to a mental illness which could have intolerable consequences for the child. The courts have made it plain that it is the psychological harm to *the child* which is in issue and that a parent may not rely on her own psychological problems in resisting return of the child.[134] The subjective approach was reaffirmed by the Supreme Court in *Re S (A Child) (Abduction: Rights of Custody)*,[135] a case in which the Court of Appeal appeared to have difficulty accepting that approach.[136] Clearly whether grave risk of harm is established will depend on the particular facts of each case. The defence has succeeded where there has been a history of abuse or violence giving rise to a wholly understandable fear of returning on the part of the children and/or the parent[137] and in one case where there was a dislike and fear of the maternal grandmother who was seeking the child's return.[138] In other cases grave risk has not been made out.[139] The court will refuse to listen to the argument of the parent who has effected the removal that it would place the child in danger to allow him to return *unaccompanied*. This would be to allow that parent to profit from his wrongdoing. Instead, the court will accept that a degree of discomfort to the child is bound to be involved in a return, and will leave it to the parent to decide whether he wishes to return with the child. In practice, parents often do return with children, perhaps with the financial support of the parent left behind.[140]

In *Re E (Children) (Abduction: Custody Appeal)*[141] the Supreme Court took the opportunity to explain certain dicta of the European Court of Human Rights in *Neulinger and Shuruk v Switzerland*[142] which had caused some

---

[134] Thus in *Re S (Abduction: Custody Rights)* [2002] 2 FLR 815 a mother could not rely on the argument that her panic and agoraphobia would be exacerbated if she returned to Israel because of the security situation there, since the court was not satisfied that the child was at risk from a breakdown in the mother's health. See also *Re S (Abduction: Intolerable Situation: Beth Din)* [2000] 1 FLR 454 in which an Orthodox Jewish mother failed to establish an intolerable situation based on the alleged lack of impartiality of the Israeli Beth Din and the existence of discrimination against Orthodox Jewish women.

[135] [2012] UKSC 10, [2012] 2 FLR 442, at para [34].

[136] Ibid, at para [32].

[137] See *DT v LBT (Abduction: Domestic Abuse)* [2010] EWHC 3177 (Fam), [2011] 1 FLR 1215 (grave risk was established on the facts in the context of substantial domestic abuse); *Re D (Article 13b: Non-Return)* [2006] EWCA Civ 146, [2006] 2 FLR 305 (mother had been shot by hired gunman, return refused); *Klentzeris v Klentzeris* [2007] EWCA Civ 533 [2007] 2 FLR 996 (child had panic attack when recounting events in country of habitual residence – return refused). See also as examples, *Re F (Child Abduction: Risk if Returned)* [1995] 2 FLR 31 and *Re G (Abduction: Psychological Harm)* [1995] 1 FLR 64. See also *Re M (Abduction: Psychological Harm)* [1997] 2 FLR 690.

[138] *The Ontario Court v M and M (Abduction: Children's Objections)* [1997] 1 FLR 475.

[139] See, for example, *C v B (Abduction: Grave Risk)* [2005] EWHC 2988 (Fam) (despite risk that mother's psychological state might deteriorate there would be no serious impairment of her ability to care for the child); *Re S (Abduction: Custody Rights)* [2002] EWCA Civ 908 (terrorist threat in Israel not sufficient); *Re W (Abduction: Domestic Violence)* [2004] EWHC 1247 (Fam), [2004] 2 FLR 499 (alleged abuse of child not sufficient).

[140] CS Bruch (above), at p 62 notes that this is common where the abducting parent has alleged abuse or other difficult home circumstances, and the petitioner is prepared to offer undertakings to alleviate the court's concern. See, for example, *Re O (Child Abduction: Undertakings)* [1994] 2 FLR 349.

[141] [2011] UKSC 27, [2011] 2 FLR 758.

[142] (Application No 41615/07) [2011] 1 FLR 122, ECtHR.

consternation. In holding that there had been a violation of Art 8 of the ECHR in an abduction case, the ECtHR had stated that:[143]

> 'the court must ascertain whether the domestic courts conducted an in-depth examination of the entire family situation and of a whole series of factors, in particular of a factual, emotional, psychological, material and medical nature, and made a balanced and reasonable assessment of the respective interests of each person, with a constant concern for determining what the best solution would be for the abducted child in the context of an application for his return to his country of origin.'

The Supreme Court explained that the President of the Strasbourg Court had subsequently acknowledged extra-judicially[144] that *Neulinger* 'does not therefore signal a change of direction' and that the case needed to be seen in the context of its facts. In *Neulinger* there had been considerable delay, and so whether the child was to be returned engaged an in-depth consideration of the Art 8 interests involved. As the Supreme Court pointed out, in those circumstances the Art 8 violation in *Neulinger* arose, not from the proper application of the Hague Convention, but from the effects of subsequent delay. The court concluded:

> 'The best interests, not only of children generally, but also of any individual child involved are a primary concern in the Hague Convention process.[145] We agree with the Strasbourg court that in this connection their best interests have two aspects: to be reunited with their parents as soon as possible, so that one does not gain an unfair advantage over the other through the passage of time; and to be brought up in a 'sound environment', in which they are not at risk of harm. The Hague Convention is designed to strike a fair balance between those two interests. If it is correctly applied it is most unlikely that there will be any breach of Art 8 or other European Convention rights unless other factors supervene. *Neulinger* does not require a departure from the normal summary process, provided that the decision is not arbitrary or mechanical'.[146]

In *Re S (A Child) (Abduction: Rights of Custody)*,[147] the Supreme Court was concerned that the view in *Neulinger* had been repeated by the ECtHR in *X v Latvia*,[148] and commented:[149]

> 'With the utmost respect to our colleagues in Strasbourg, we reiterate our conviction, as Reunite requests us to do, that neither the Hague Convention nor, surely, Art 8 of the European Convention requires the court which determines an

---

143 Ibid, at para 139.
144 In a paper given at the Franco-British-Irish colloquium on family law on 14 May 2011.
145 See R Schuz, *The Hague Child Abduction Convention and Children's Rights* (2002) 12 *Transnational Law and Contemporary Problems* 393 for an account of how the focus on children's interests could be improved.
146 [2011] UKSC 27, [2011] 2 FLR 758, at para [52].
147 [2012] UKSC 10, [2012] 2 FLR 442, at para [34].
148 (Application No 27853/09) [2012] 1 FLR 860.
149 [2012] UKSC 10, [2012] 2 FLR 442, at para [34].

application under the former to conduct an in-depth examination of the sort described. Indeed it would be entirely inappropriate.'

The child's wishes

Article 13 of the Hague Convention also provides that the child's return may be refused where the court 'finds that the child objects to being returned and has attained an age and degree of maturity at which it is appropriate to take account of its views'.[150]

In *Re D (Abduction: Rights of Custody)*[151] the child concerned was adamantly opposed to returning to Romania, yet no defence based on the child's objections was raised. He was over 7 years old when the trial took place. Baroness Hale suggested that it could not be taken for granted that the child's wishes should not be heard and appropriate means of ascertaining them should have been put in place. She commented:[152]

'Especially in Hague Convention cases, the relevance of the child's views to the issues in the case may be limited. But there is now a growing understanding of the importance of listening to the children involved in children's cases. It is the child, more than anyone else, who will have to live with what the court decides.'

As Baroness Hale pointed out, Brussels II Revised recognises this by reversing the burden in relation to hearing the child. Article 11.2 provides:

'When applying articles 12 and 13 of the 1980 Hague Convention, it shall be ensured that the child is given the opportunity to be heard during the proceedings unless this appears inappropriate having regard to his or her age or degree of maturity.'

However, Baroness Hale went on to say that while strictly this only applies to cases within the European Union, the principle is:[153]

'of universal application and consistent with our international obligations under Art 12 of the United Nations Convention on the Rights of the Child 1989. It applies, not only when a 'defence' under art 13 has been raised, but also in any case in which the court is being asked to apply Art 12 and direct the summary return of the child – in effect in every Hague Convention case. It erects a presumption that the child will be heard unless this appears inappropriate.'

This can be achieved through full scale legal representation of the child, through the report of an independent CAFCASS officer or a face-to-face interview with the judge. Baroness Hale explained that in most cases an interview with a CAFCASS officer will suffice, 'but where the child has asked

---

[150] See for an assessment, P McEleavy 'Evaluating the views of abducted children: trends in appellate case–law'[2008] CFLQ 230.
[151] [2006] UKHL 51, [2007] 1 FLR 961.
[152] Ibid, at para [57].
[153] Ibid, at para [58].

to see the judge, it may also be necessary for the judge to hear the child. Only in a few cases will full scale legal representation be necessary'.[154] The obligation to hear a child must not override the obligation in Art 11 to conclude proceedings within 6 weeks.[155]

In *Re J (Abduction: Children's Objections)*[156] the Court of Appeal commented that the flow of authority pointed towards the desirability of a face-to-face meeting between judge and children in appropriate cases.[157] In *Re G (Abduction: Children's Objections)*[158] a 13 year-old girl, E, wrote a letter to the judge expressing her objection to return to Canada. The judge made no mention of it in his judgment. Allowing an appeal against a return order the Court of Appeal said that judges needed to be alive to the difficulties of a return order which involved 'an articulate, naturally determined and courageous adolescent', and 'given the fact that E was seeking to communicate her views to the decision-maker, it is perhaps with hindsight a pity that [the judge] did not have the opportunity of meeting her and hearing from her own lips'.[159]

In *Re M (Abduction: Child's Objections)*[160] the Court of Appeal explained that where a child's objections are raised by way of defence, there are three stages in the court's consideration:

'The first question to be considered is whether or not the objections to return are made out. The second is whether the age and maturity of the child are such that it is appropriate for the court to take account of those objections (unless that is so, the defence cannot be established). Assuming a positive finding in that respect, the court moves to the third question, whether or not it should exercise its discretion in favour of retention or return.'

The requirement to 'take into account' the child's views 'represents a fairly low threshold requirement. In particular, it does not follow that the court should "take account" of a child's objections only if they are so solidly based that they are likely to be determinative'.[161] However, the child's objections are likely to need a proper foundation if they are to be acted on by the judge. In *Re D*

---

[154] Ibid, at para [60]. See also *Re M (Abduction: Zimbabwe)* [2007] UKHL 55, [2008] 1 FLR 251.
[155] *Re F (Abduction: Child's Wishes)* [2007] EWCA Civ 468, [2007] 2 FLR 697, at para [28].
[156] [2011] EWCA Civ 1448, [2012] 1 FLR 457, at para [33].
[157] See for examples *JPC v SLW and SMW (Abduction)* [2007] EWHC 1349 (Fam), [2007] 2 FLR 900; and *Re L v H* [2009] EWHC 3074 (Fam), [2010] 1 FLR 1229; and *Re G (Abduction: Children's Objections)* [2010] EWCA Civ 1232 [2011] 1 FLR 1645, at para [15].
[158] [2010] EWCA Civ 1232 [2011] 1 FLR 1645.
[159] Ibid, at para [15]. A child could change his or her mind, which may result in a return order being set aside and the case remitted again to the court: see *Re C (Abduction: Setting Aside Return Order: Permission)* [2012] EWCA Civ 1144, [2013] 1 FLR 403.
[160] [2007] EWCA Civ 260, [2007] 2 FLR 72, at para [60].
[161] *Re W (Abduction: Child's Objections)* [2010] EWCA Civ 520, [2010] 2 FLR 1165, at para [22] (taking into account the views of a six year-old child). A child with learning difficulties may still articulate objections sufficiently rationally and intelligently: see *B v B (Abduction: Child with Learning Difficulties)* [2011] EWHC 2300 (Fam) (14 year-old child with Asperger's Syndrome).

(Abduction: Child's Objections)[162] the child objected to return to France on the basis that he had been racially abused at school. This had occurred but the child had moved to another school in which he was well adjusted before the abduction.

The discretion must be exercised in the context of the approach of the Convention[163] In *Zaffino v Zaffino (Abduction: Children's Views)*[164] the Court of Appeal said that in the exercise of the discretion under Art 13, 'the court must balance the nature and strength of the child's objections against both the Convention considerations (obviously including comity and respect for the judicial processes in the requesting state) and also general welfare considerations'.[165] A judge will be correct to consider each child separately in deciding whether or not that child objected to being returned and had attained an age and degree of maturity at which it was appropriate to take account of his or her views. However, in *Zaffino v Zaffino* Wall LJ expressed the view that the exercise of discretion cannot 'properly be made by treating each child in isolation. The child's place within the family, and the consequences of the exercise of discretion on that child, must be considered'. Thus the judge should first 'consider whether or not the gateway to discretion was open in relation to each child' and only if it is, then go on to exercise his discretion appropriately.[166]

It is plain that the views, even of a *Gillick*-competent child, will be accorded less weight than in domestic proceedings,[167] again on the principle that to do otherwise would frustrate the principal aim of the Hague Convention – to secure that the substantive issues are determined in the place of the child's habitual residence.[168] Despite this, there is evidence from several reported cases that the courts are prepared to listen to a child's objections, in appropriate circumstances,[169] but will not allow the child's wishes to determine the matter.[170] It is clear that something more than just a preference on the part of the child will be required to forestall an order for his return: a mere assertion

---

[162] [2011] EWCA Civ 1294.

[163] See *Re A (Abduction: Custody Rights)* [1992] Fam 106 sub nom *Re A (Minors) (Abduction: Acquiescence)* [1992] 2 FLR 14, at p 28 per Lord Donaldson of Lymington MR, and *Re S (a Minor) (Abduction: Custody Rights)* [1993] Fam 242, sub nom *S v S (Child Abduction) (Child's Views)* [1992] 2 FLR 492, per Balcombe LJ at 251–252 and 501 respectively.

[164] [2005] EWCA Civ 1012, [2006] 1 FLR 410, at para [19], per Thorpe LJ.

[165] Ibid, at para [19], per Thorpe LJ. See also, per Wall LJ, at paras [30]–[31].

[166] Ibid, at para [34].

[167] Where they must be taken into account as the first item in the statutory checklist. See s 1(3)(a) of the Children Act, and chapter 5 above.

[168] The court may, thus, not be prepared to adjourn proceedings for the purpose of ascertaining the views of the child. See *P v P (Minors) (Child Abduction)* [1992] 1 FLR 155.

[169] For a review of some of the earlier cases, see T Sachs 'The Views of the Child in Abduction Cases: *Re R* and *S v S*' (1993) 5 JCL 43.

[170] *Re S (Minors) (Abduction: Custody Rights)* [1994] 1 FLR 819. See also *Re M (A Minor) (Abduction: Child's Objections)* [1994] 2 FLR 126, where the child's party status and separate representation were upheld by the Court of Appeal in a case where the dispute was really between the boy and his mother and not between the parents.

will not suffice.[171] However, where the child's views accord with the court's own view of his best interests, the court may be prepared to attach greater significance to them.[172] It has been held that, where the court, taking into account the views of two children aged nine and seven respectively, decided not to return them, this may also justify failing to return a younger sibling, too young to express his own views.[173]

Absence for more than a year

It has been noted that the principle of the child's return is mandatory (but for the exceptions) where the application is brought within a year of the removal. Where the absence of the child has lasted in excess of a year, the Hague Convention still requires the child's return 'unless it is demonstrated that the child is now settled in its new environment'.[174] The strength of the status quo principle in domestic proceedings has been commented upon.[175] This is displaced in the case of wrongful takings, but there comes a point when the possible harm and disruption to the child of a further move must be taken into account, whatever the rights and wrongs of the original behaviour. Even here, however, the delay may be attributable to the child having been secreted by the abducting parent or may be the result of inadequate or incorrect legal advice being given to the applicant.[176]

The leading case on this is the House of Lords decision in *Re M (Abduction: Zimbabwe).*[177] The case concerned two girls from Zimbabwe, aged 13 and 10 at the time the House of Lords heard the case, who were brought to this country in 2005 without their father's knowledge, by their mother who claimed asylum. The English central authority did not receive notification of the abduction until 2007. The family remained in the UK because of a moratorium on the return of failed asylum-seekers to Zimbabwe and the children were settled. The judge found that there was no grave risk in returning to Zimbabwe and rejected the girls' objections as not sufficiently strong to be determinative. He found that there was settlement, but that he still had a discretion to return the children,

---

171 See *P v P* (above). See also *Re HB (Abduction: Children's Objections)* [1997] 1 FLR 392 and *Re K (Abduction: Child's Objections)* [1995] 1 FLR 977. For cases in which the courts upheld the objections of the children, see *Re B (Abduction: Children's Objections)* [1998] 1 FLR 667; *The Ontario Court v M and M (Abduction: Children's Objections)* (above); and *Re L (Abduction: Child's Objections to Return* [2002] 2 FLR 1042.

172 As in *Re R (A Minor) (Abduction)* [1992] 1 FLR 105 and *S v S (Child Abduction: Child's View)* [1992] 2 FLR 492.

173 *B v K (Child Abduction)* [1993] 1 FCR 382. See also *Re T (Abduction: Child's Objection to Return)* [2000] 2 FLR 192 where the Court of Appeal, having attached significance to the clearly expressed fears of an 11-year-old girl in not wishing to return to her alcoholic mother in Spain, also refused the return of her six-year-old brother on the basis that it would be intolerable if he were to be returned to Spain alone.

174 Article 12. The applicant must, however, act expeditiously in the proceedings, which may otherwise be struck out. See *Re G (Abduction: Striking Out Application)* [1995] 2 FLR 410.

175 See chapter 5 above.

176 Examples given by CS Bruch (above), at p 63.

177 [2007] UKHL 55, [2008] 1 FLR 251.

which he exercised. The Court of Appeal dismissed the mother's appeal, but the House of Lords allowed a further appeal. The House of Lords held that Art 12 'does envisage that a settled child might nevertheless be returned within the Convention procedures'.[178] The House was clear, however, that it 'is wrong to import any test of exceptionality into the exercise of discretion under the Hague Convention. The circumstances in which return may be refused are themselves exceptions to the general rule. That in itself is sufficient exceptionality. It is neither necessary nor desirable to import an additional gloss into the Convention'.[179] The House of Lords pointed out that the object of the Convention, of securing a swift return to the country of origin, cannot be met in a settlement case, so the policy of the Convention would not necessarily point towards a return in such cases.[180] There were powerful considerations on the facts of this case pointing to the merits of the case being determined in England rather than Zimbabwe.[181]

Violation of human rights and fundamental freedoms

A final defence is that the child's return would be contrary to the fundamental principles of the requested State regarding protection of human rights and fundamental freedoms. As yet, little or no use appears to have been made of the provision. Bruch attributes this, possibly, to the democratic reforms in Eastern Europe and the absence of cases yet raising issues of gender-based or religiously based custody laws.[182]

Action under the European Convention

When may the European Convention be invoked?

The European Convention (also known as the 'Luxembourg' Convention or the 'Custody' Convention) is utilised less than the Hague Convention, since it applies only as between certain European countries, and then only if the applicant has a court order in his favour. It is rarely used now given that the Brussels II Regulation and the Council of Europe Contact Convention together cover much of the same ground. The European Convention[183] applies only to 'improper removals', which are defined as those which involve removal across international boundaries in breach of decisions relating to custody. These are defined widely enough to embrace orders for residence or contact.[184] The European Convention is really, therefore, about the reciprocal enforcement

---

[178] Ibid, at para [31]. For criticism, see R Shuz 'In Search of a Settled Interpretation of Article 12(2) of the Hague Child Abduction Convention' [2008] CFLQ 64.

[179] Ibid, at para [40].

[180] Ibid, at para [47].

[181] See for a case in which the judge failed to apply *Zimbabwe*: *Re O (Abduction: Settlement)* [2011] EWCA Civ 128, and compare with the *Zimbabwe* case *Re F (Abduction: Removal Outside Jurisdiction)* [2008] EWCA Civ 842 (children not settled where mother was a failed asylum seeker who was to be deported).

[182] Bruch (above), at p 63.

[183] Article 1.

[184] Article 1(c).

of court orders in contracting States and, to that extent, it is similar in nature to the Family Law Act 1986 which does the same in relation to orders in different parts of the UK.[185] The Central Authorities perform similar functions under this Convention. The Convention[186]requires the Central Authority in the country of the child's original residence, on receiving a proper application, to act without delay to secure the recognition and enforcement of the custody order. The order must be registered in a court of the contracting State to which the child has been removed. Thereupon, *that* court will have the same powers of enforcement as if it had made the original order,[187] and this will enable it to order return of the child.

Can registration be refused?

In limited circumstances, a court may refuse to register an order. The court cannot reopen the merits of the original order, but it may refuse to register or enforce the order if the proceedings were defective, if the order is incompatible with another order which has already been recognised or if the child or defendant has insufficient connection with the State in which it was made.[188] These are matters principally relating to procedural impropriety. Of greater substance is Art 10, which allows a refusal to register 'where it is found by reason of a change of circumstances including the passage of time but not including a mere change in the residence of the child after an improper removal, the effects of the original decision are manifestly no longer in accordance with the welfare of the child'. This, in essence, means that the decision is no longer consistent with the welfare principle.[189] The effect would seem to be to allow the courts to consider the merits of cases more readily than they can under the Hague Convention. Thus, for example, in *Re L (Abduction: European Convention: Access)*[190] Bennett J refused registration and enforcement of a French order for contact between two children and their grandparents. At the time of the order all the parties were in France but the parents had subsequently relocated in England with the children. In these circumstances it was thought to be neither practicable nor in the best interests of the children that they should have to travel twice a month from England to France. Article 8 provides for the virtual mandatory registration of orders, where the application is made within six months of the child's removal, but a number of countries, including the UK, have entered a reservation to this

---

[185]   See p 293 below.
[186]   Article 5.
[187]   Child Abduction and Custody Act 1985, s 18.
[188]   Articles 9 and 10, and see *Re M (Child Abduction) (European Convention)* [1994] 1 FLR 551.
[189]   See, for example, *F v F (Minors) (Custody: Foreign Order)* [1989] Fam 1; *Re G (A Minor) (Child Abduction: Enforcement)* [1990] 2 FLR 325; and *Re R (Abduction: Hague and European Conventions)* [1997] 1 FLR 663.
[190]   [1999] 2 FLR 1089. And see A-M Hutchinson 'Enforcement of Contact Orders and the Luxembourg Convention' [2000] *International Family Law* 106.

Art.[191] Where registration is refused, other applications can, nonetheless, be made which will be heard on their merits.[192]

In view of the greater scope and success of the Hague Convention there will be only limited circumstances in which the European Convention can be invoked where the Hague Convention does not have application. Nonetheless, there will occasionally be such instances, as illustrated by *T v R (Abduction: Forum Conveniens)*.[193] Here the Hague Convention did not apply because the Swedish mother had *sole* custody of the child under a Swedish court order at the time she removed her to England. As such there was no 'wrongful taking or retention' for the purposes of the Hague Convention. However, the father was later awarded sole custody, which he sought to register and enforce in the English courts under the European Convention. Again, however, this was refused by Charles J on the basis of the change of circumstances arising from the mother's now being settled in England. The immediate enforcement of the Swedish order and return of the child to Sweden were not thought to be in the child's best interests.

Despite the more restricted operation of the European Convention, Bromley and Lowe have instanced two situations in which an applicant, having a choice between the two Conventions, might invoke it. The first is where the removal took place *before* implementation of the European Convention by one of the contracting States involved. This is because the European Convention has been held to have retrospective operation, whereas the Hague Convention has not.[194] The second is where the child is taken to a contracting State which has implemented Art 8. Here, an order for the return of the child is a virtual certainty if the application is made within six months of the removal. In practice, they note that there is likely to be little difference, since an order for return under the Hague Convention is also very likely in the circumstances. In any event, where an application is brought under both Conventions, the Hague Convention has precedence.

Non-Convention countries

Although the Hague Convention has been widely ratified, there are still many countries which fall outside it. In these cases, the prospects for recovery of abducted children may be bleak.[195] Where the English courts become seised of the matter they are liable to order the return of the child on principles similar to those which are applied under the Conventions, as in *Re F (Minor:*

---

[191] The effect is that registration may be refused even where the application is made within six months of the child's removal under the terms of Art 10.
[192] Child Abduction and Custody Act 1985, s 20(1).
[193] [2002] 2 FLR 544.
[194] *Bromley's Family Law* (8th edn, Butterworths, 1992), at p 494.
[195] *Re H (Minors) (Abduction: Custody Rights); Re S (Minors) (Abduction: Custody Rights)* [1991] 2 AC 476. Cf *Re L (Child Abduction: European Convention)* [1992] 2 FLR 178. For a general discussion, see H Setright 'Removals to and from Non-Convention Countries – The Perspective of Courts in England in England and Wales' [2000] *International Family Law* 125.

Abduction: Jurisdiction).[196] As a general proposition there is a presumption that, in the absence of good reasons to the contrary, it is in the best interests of the child for questions about his or her future to be determined by the court in the child's country of habitual residence.[197] However, in *C v C (Abduction: Jurisdiction)*[198] Cazalet J applied the principles of the Hague Convention in *refusing* the return of a three-year-old child to Brazil. The decision was based primarily on the delay which would be occasioned (over a year) if the case were to be heard in the Brazilian courts. Although the courts will try to act in accordance with the spirit of the Convention, the Court of Appeal has emphasised that the issue of the return of the child in non-Convention cases is governed by the welfare principle. Thus, in *Re P (A Minor) (Child Abduction: Non-Convention Country)*[199] the court refused to order the return of the child to India on the basis that the mother would suffer psychological harm which would affect her ability to care for the child if ordered to return there. Likewise in *Re JA (Child Abduction: Non-Convention Country)*[200] the Court of Appeal held that it would be an abdication of responsibility for the High Court to surrender the determination of its ward's future to a foreign court (in this case the United Arab Emirates) whose regime might be inimical to the child's welfare. The applicant must, however, be given an opportunity to counter allegations made.[201]

Notwithstanding these decisions, the courts will endeavour to be sensitive as to the child's cultural, religious and ethnic background, although it is fair to say that decisions in the case of non-Convention countries may not appear wholly consistent. There is no principle that return of the child will be refused merely because the country in question applies a different conception of the welfare of the child. Thus, in *Re E (Abduction: Non-Convention Country)*[202] the Court of Appeal held that the welfare principle was the paramount consideration in non-Convention countries, but that what constituted the welfare of the child in an individual case was subject to the cultural background and expectations of the State of habitual residence, in this case, the Sudan. Under Islamic law which applied there, the mother, who had remarried, was disqualified from obtaining custody of the children which passed to the grandparents. Nonetheless, upholding the judge's order for return of the children, the court emphasised that it was not permissible to criticise other family justice systems other than in exceptional circumstances, such as cases of persecution or ethnic, sex or other discrimination. In this case the application of Muslim law to a Muslim family was appropriate and acceptable, and a solution in accordance with local law was capable of being in the best interests of these children. Similarly, in *B v*

---

[196] [1991] Fam 25.
[197] See, for example, *Re Z (Abduction: Non-Convention Country)* [1999] 1 FLR 1270 where the child was returned to Malta.
[198] [1994] 1 FCR 6.
[199] [1997] 1 FLR 780.
[200] [1998] 1 FLR 231.
[201] See, for example, *Re H (Abduction: Dominica: Corporal Punishment)* [2006] EWCA Civ, [2007] 1 FLR 72 (father given no opportunity to counter allegations of corporal punishment and that children were afraid of violence).
[202] [1999] 2 FLR 642.

El-B (Abduction: Sharia Law: Welfare of Child)[203] the father of two children succeeded in securing their return from England to Lebanon where their fate would also be determined in accordance with Muslim sharia law.

The picture world-wide can only be improved by the process of further ratifications of the Hague Convention. The options for a parent of a child abducted to a non-Convention country are very limited. They boil down to trying to secure the extradition of the abductor, if an extradition treaty exists between the two countries concerned, or trying to pursue civil proceedings in the country to which the child has been taken. In the case of children taken *to* England, an application must be brought in the High Court in wardship or under the inherent jurisdiction.[204] Some parents, in desperation, have, in the past, resorted to extra-legal means, such as attempting to snatch the child back, with or without the assistance of private investigators.

Abductions between different parts of the UK

This section is concerned with abductions *within* the UK from one of its constituent jurisdictions to another, ie between England and Wales, Scotland and Northern Ireland.[205] Under the Family Law Act 1986, 'Part I orders' made in one of these jurisdictions are recognised and enforceable in both of the others as if made there.[206] This is with a view to avoiding conflicts of jurisdiction between courts in different parts of the UK.[207] The Family Law Act 1986 applies to orders relating to children under 16 years of age but, since the Children Act, there will, in any event, be few English orders relating to children over this age.

The procedure is that the holder of the order applies to the court in the jurisdiction to which the child has been taken. In England and Wales and Northern Ireland this is the High Court, and in Scotland it is the Court of Session.[208] Registration is achieved by sending to the appropriate court a certified copy of the order. Once the order has been registered, the registering

---

[203] [2003] 1 FLR 811.

[204] The court will only have jurisdiction if the child is habitually resident in England. See *Al Habtoor v Fotheringham* [2001] 1 FLR 951.

[205] See Law Com Report No 138 *Custody of Children – Jurisdiction and Enforcement within the United Kingdom* (1984) upon which the legislation was based.

[206] Family Law Act 1986, s 25.

[207] For an example of a conflict of jurisdiction, see *T v T (Custody: Jurisdiction)* [1992] 1 FLR 43. Courts in one jurisdiction will consider themselves bound by the principle of comity and will not, in effect, purport to act as a Court of Appeal where, for example, an interim order has been made in another jurisdiction. For a post-Children Act decision involving conflicts of jurisdiction between England and Wales and Scotland, turning on the correct habitual residence of the child, see *Re M (Minors) (Residence Order: Jurisdiction)* [1993] 1 FLR 495 and the commentary by G Douglas at [1993] Fam Law 285. See also *S v S (Custody: Jurisdiction)* [1995] 1 FLR 155; *M v M (Abduction: England and Scotland)* [1997] 2 FLR 263; *A v A (Forum Conveniens)* [1999] 1 FLR 1; and *Re B (Court's Jurisdiction)* [2004] 2 FLR 741.

[208] Family Law Act 1986, s 32(1).

court can enforce it.[209] An interested party may intervene in enforcement proceedings and ask that the application be stayed or dismissed. The grounds for doing so are limited to such cases as where the original court lacked jurisdiction to make the order, or the circumstances have changed such that a variation of the order is justified.[210] The Family Law Act 1986 confers important ancillary powers on the courts which include ordering disclosure of a child's whereabouts, recovery of the child, restricting removal of a child from the jurisdiction and ordering the surrender of passports.[211]

The Family Law Act 1986 applies only to moves *between* different parts of the UK and not to moves *within* one of its constituent parts. Thus, it could not be invoked where, for example, a child is moved from London to Swansea, Inverness to Glasgow or Coleraine to Belfast. In such cases, there will be no potential conflict of jurisdiction and, with regard to moves within England and Wales, an application would need to be made for a s 8 order to be granted and enforced. Since parental responsibility is shared between married parents, and it may be exercised independently, moves like this are not unlawful, however distressing they may be to the parent who is left behind. The answer will be to obtain a residence order and enforce it.

---

209 Ibid, s 29.
210 Ibid, ss 30 and 31.
211 Ibid, ss 33–37.

Chapter 7

CHILDREN AND PARENTS: THE CENTRAL ISSUES

Do children have 'rights'? Do parents have 'rights' or only 'responsibilities'? Can it be said that parents have independent interests which the law does or should recognise; or must we conceive of a legal position in which everything which parents do is subject to an overriding obligation to act in the best interests of their children? According to this view, nothing which they do and which involves their children can legitimately be done for their *own* benefit. This is an area in which rhetoric and the use of language can perhaps obscure the realities of ordinary life. In coming to these theoretical debates, it is as well to keep in mind that the law must try to keep in touch with reality. If it does not, it will quickly fall into disrespect or be disregarded.

We turn first to a general discussion of the concept of children's rights, drawing on some influential theories by British family lawyers and philosophers. This is followed by a brief account of the views of two rights sceptics who do not believe that it is at all helpful to conceive of children's position in terms of rights. After pausing to consider whether children have any duties, we then look briefly at the notion of children's *human* rights as a distinct dimension to the wider question of children's rights. We note briefly the increasing interest of the European Union but concentrate on the notion of children's 'convention rights' under the European Convention on Human Rights and Fundamental Freedoms. We then focus more specifically on the nature of parents' position, revisting the question whether they have rights or independent interests and the nature and limits of parental responsibility. We consider the basis on which the law tries to resolve conflicts of interest between parents and children. We conclude with a brief discussion of the relevance of 'justice' in children cases.

THE CONCEPT OF CHILDREN'S RIGHTS

'Welfare' versus 'rights'

An obvious question is whether there is any difference of substance between protecting the 'welfare' of children and protecting their 'rights'. English law has a strong theoretical commitment to the welfare or best interests of children, but is this the same as upholding their rights?

Some liberationist writers have been inclined to draw a sharp distinction between the two ideas, expressed most graphically by Farson, who differentiated between protecting children and protecting their rights.[1] For Farson, the critical birthright which children possess is self-determination and this overrides all other rights. The extreme liberationist school represented by Farson and others would treat children as adults and extend to them all the liberties normally associated with adulthood. A child of any age would, in principle, have contractual freedom, sexual freedom, the right to work, the right to vote and so on. These 'kiddie libbers', as Mnookin has called them, stand in stark contrast to the 'child savers'.[2] The latter stress the vulnerability of children and the need to protect them from others and indeed from themselves.[3] According to this position, restrictions on contractual capacity, the prohibition of certain forms of sexual activity with minors, restrictions on child labour, and the disenfranchisement of children may all be justified. The very status of minority, with its attendant disabilities, has, as its raison d'être, children's assumed inability to act in their own best interests. Child protectionism is thus a highly paternalistic notion[4] for it supports the right of adults to take decisions for children and not the right of children to act for themselves.[5]

There can be no doubt that the English law affecting children, although historically dominated by such influences as the devolution of property and preservation of the social order rather than the protection of children for their own sake,[6] has had a strongly protectionist orientation.[7] It is certainly arguable that it was the concentration on safeguarding the welfare of children which obscured the issue of their rights and which explains, at least until the closing decades of the twentieth century, the absence of serious debate about the concept of children's rights.

Emergence of children's rights in the USA

Meanwhile, in the USA, the issue of rights had to be directly confronted because of the written constitution and bill of rights enshrined within it.[8] In the

---

[1]   R Farson *Birthrights* (Harmondsworth, 1978). See also J Holt *Escape from Childhood* (Penguin, 1975).

[2]   RH Mnookin 'Thinking About Children's Rights – Beyond Kiddie Libbers and Child Savers' (1981) *Stanford Lawyer* 24.

[3]   These protectionist concerns can clearly justify interferences with the civil liberties of children which would be unacceptable if imposed on adults. In the United States, certain forms of intervention, such as the prohibition of the sale of obscene materials to minors, may be constitutional as they apply to children, but would be unconstitutional if imposed on adults. See *Ginsberg v New York* 390 US 629 (1968).

[4]   On the philosophical justifications of paternalism in the writings of Hobbes, Locke and Mill, see MDA Freeman *The Rights and Wrongs of Children* (Frances Pinter, 1983), at pp 52–54.

[5]   This is why it is argued that the choice of decision-maker is crucial. See RH Mnookin (above).

[6]   See, particularly, JM Eekelaar and T Murray 'Childhood as a Social Problem: A Survey of the History of Legal Regulation' (1984) *Journal of Law and Society* 207 and J Eekelaar, R Dingwall and T Murray 'Victims or Threats? Children in Care Proceedings' (1982) JSWL 68.

[7]   Perhaps epitomised by the all-embracing wardship jurisdiction in which a 'ring of protection' is thrown around a ward of court.

[8]   The earlier developments of the constitutional guidelines affecting children's rights are discussed and extracted in W Wadlington, CH Whitebread and SM Davis *Children in the Legal*

1960s, the Supreme Court firmly grasped the nettle by holding that children were persons under the constitution and thus capable of possessing fundamental rights.[9] This did not mean that all those rights enjoyed by adults would automatically be extended to children,[10] but it did mean that apparent infringements of those rights in the case of children would have to be justified by some other legitimate interest protected by the constitution.[11] Children's rights accordingly have a strong theoretical foundation in the USA since there is, in effect, a presumption that they are entitled to all the normal civil liberties possessed by adults. The onus is firmly on those who would withhold them to find a legal justification for doing so. Parents are also self-evidently persons under the Constitution, and have rights both as individuals and in their capacity as parents.[12] This can give rise to a clash of constitutional rights between parents and children which the courts have occasionally had to resolve.[13] These conflicts of interest have been confronted less openly and more subtly in England;[14] though, as noted below, there is now a more transparent balancing of children's and parents' rights under the European Convention on Human Rights. In some ways, making due allowance for the different constitutional and societal contexts, the process of balancing the rights and interests of parents and children under the US constitution and ECHR is not dissimilar.

Development of children's rights in England

Despite the absence of a written constitution or bill of rights in England, the rights of children have been firmly on the agenda since the early 1980s. The cause received major boosts from the *Gillick* decision in 1985 and the Children Act 1989.[15] The debate has tended to focus on the autonomy claims of adolescents and there has been a strong inclination to associate, if not to equate, the concept of children's rights with the claim to self-determination.[16]

System (Foundation Press, 1983), ch II. There were also calls there for a Bill of Rights for children. See Foster and Freed 'A Bill of Rights for Children' (1972) 6 Fam LQ 343. For commentary on the development of children's rights in the USA, see BB Woodhouse 'The Status of Children: A story of emerging rights' in SN Katz, J Eekelaar and M Maclean *Cross Currents* (Oxford University Press, 2000).

[9]   *Re Gault* 387 US 1 (1967).

[10]   See RH Mnookin (above).

[11]   In the case of children, the standard is a 'significant state interest' – a somewhat lower standard than the 'compelling state interest' required in the case of adults.

[12]   See, for example, *Prince v Massachusetts* 321 US 158 (1944).

[13]   See H Wingo and SN Freytag 'Decisions Within the Family: A Clash of Constitutional Rights' 67 (1982) Iowa Law Rev 401.

[14]   In chapter 2 above we discussed the different weightings given to children's welfare which may be seen as one manifestation of this.

[15]   Other significant developments were the International Year of the Child in 1979 and the establishment of the Children's Legal Centre in London. Children's rights received a further boost with the recognition of their 'convention rights' when the ECHR was incorporated into English law by the Human Rights Act 1998 though its impact has been more substantial in some spheres than in others. See below p 324.

[16]   This might well have been a reaction to what has been seen as the over-paternalistic attitude of English law before the *Gillick* ruling.

Yet, in reality, the notion of children's rights is a multi-faceted idea, not a one-dimensional one. At the very least, all serious theories must acknowledge and admit elements of both protection and self-determination, and most do.

The concept of children's rights, although distinct from commitment to their welfare, therefore includes within it concerns about welfare and protection. We should also question the assumption, sometimes made, that the protection of children as an idea is antithetical to their self-determination. It can be persuasively argued that the welfare of children dictates that they be allowed a degree of self-determination or qualified autonomy. Ronald Dworkin brings this out rather well in his philosophical analysis of distributional equality.[17] Dworkin discusses the various theories of welfare, one species of which is the 'success theories' which suppose that 'a person's welfare is a matter of his success in fulfilling his preferences, goals and ambitions'.[18] Although Dworkin is talking specifically about the distribution of resources, the welfare of children can be similarly viewed as a matter of individual self-fulfilment which must, by its nature, imply an element of independence from adult control. It was also noted that, under the statutory checklist governing the application of the welfare principle, the wishes of children must, in principle, be taken into account.[19] It is submitted that the converse is also true. As we shall see, the jurisprudence of the ECtHR makes it very plain that it will uphold, as consistent with the notion of children's Convention rights, determinations of domestic courts which in the final analsyis are based on the court's assessment of the child's best interests.[20]

In one respect, the concept of rights performs a valuable function for which the concept of welfare is ill-adapted. It draws attention to the universality of children's claims. Welfare or best interests, as interpreted in English case-law, is a highly individualistic notion which may not be an appropriate means of expressing the many legal and moral claims which children may be thought to have as a matter of social justice. The concentration is wholly on doing what is best for an individual child in an individual set of circumstances and it is often said that each case must turn on its own facts. Rights, on the other hand, although clearly capable of assertion in individual cases, are designed to safeguard the interests of all children as a class. Indeed, it has been said that 'a necessary feature of children's rights is that they be genuinely universal, appropriate for children everywhere'.[21]

---

17   R Dworkin 'What is Equality Part I: Equality of Welfare' (1981) 10 *Philosophy and Public Affairs* 185.

18   Ibid, at p 191.

19   Children Act 1989, s 1(3)(a).

20   See below.

21   V Worsfold 'A Philosophical Justification for Children's Rights' (1974) 44 *Harvard Educational Review* 142, at p 149.

The significance of language and terminology

We have alluded above to the dangers of attaching too much significance to the use of particular language.[22] Does it really matter whether the law's protection of children's interests is analysed in terms of 'rights' or 'welfare'? Would disputes be resolved any differently, or better results achieved, with the adoption of different terminology?

There is some truth in the assertion that playing with conceptual labels will not necessarily have any effect on the substance of family relations.[23] Perhaps, too, there ought to be some healthy scepticism about the limits of what the law can achieve for children.[24] There are dangers in indulging in 'rights-talk' too loosely since it has been said that this can be a reductionist device for lawyers, reducing the complexity of human relationships (with which the law is ill-equipped to deal) to manageable concepts.[25] Against this, it can be argued that the use of certain expressions can have an influence on society. If this is correct, the modernisation of terminology *is* an important issue because it may have a symbolic or educative effect on social attitudes. Indeed, one of the most striking features of the reform of family law has been the reformulation of concepts and the shift in values which this represents.[26] Seen in this light, it may become important to assert and defend the notion of rights for children, but it should be acknowledged that the *substance* of the relationships between children and the adult world are, in the final analysis, of greater significance than any theoretical description applied to them.

SOME THEORIES OF CHILDREN'S RIGHTS

Before attempting to explore the substantive rights which children may have, the initial question of what is a 'right' arises and this is a matter of considerable controversy.[27] Yet it is of crucial significance since someone who denies, for

---

22 A concern shared by the judiciary and by the *Family Justice Review* in the context of parental litigation over shared residence and other legal terms describing what in reality are time-sharing arrangements. See chapter 5 above and the remarks of the Court of Appeal in *T v T (Shared and Joint Residence Orders)* [2010] EWCA Civ 1366, [2011] Fam Law 240 discussed at p 129 above. The Children and Families Bill 2013 seeks to overcome these difficulties by the replacement of residence and contact orders with a new 'child arrangements order' which focuses on the practicalities of child care arrangements rather than the status of the parents. See chapters 1 and 4.

23 See A Bainham *Children, Parents and the State* (Sweet & Maxwell, 1988), at pp 57–61.

24 See M King 'Playing the Symbols – Custody and the Law Commission' [1987] Fam Law 186. See also M King, *A Better World for Children?* (Routledge, 1997) for a wide-ranging critique of decision-making, policy formulation and moral campaigns designed to improve the lot of children from the perspective of autopoietic theory – a social theory of self-regulation systems in 'society' of which law is said to be one.

25 M King and C Piper, *How the Law Thinks about Children* (Gower, 1990) particularly, at pp 68–70.

26 See A Bainham 'Changing Families and Changing Concepts: Reforming the Language of Family Law' [1998] CFLQ 1.

27 For a discussion of the problem of children's rights in the context of the general dispute about

example, that children have a right to 'love and affection' may be saying one of two things. Either he may be saying that children have no claim or interest of any kind, whether legal or moral, in receiving love and affection or, alternatively, he may be saying that any such claim or interest is not properly classified as a 'right'. The second is the more likely interpretation, since almost everyone would recognise the moral claims of children in this respect while there may be substantial doubt about whether they could ever be elevated to the status of legal rights, far less enforceable ones.

This general difficulty should always be kept in mind since there are many statements, particularly in international instruments,[28] which assert rights for children which go well beyond what is normally understood by lawyers to constitute rights. It may be that much of this can be accounted for by distinguishing between legal rights and moral claims. The issue of children's rights is further complicated by the uncertainties surrounding the content of individual substantive claims. While it may be possible to conclude that children have rights to adequate food, medical care and education, the content of these rights may be uncertain. Thus, it may be fairly obvious what is adequate care and nourishment for a newborn baby, but far less clear what is an adequate education for an older child. How far the child's basic right to an education extends may well be something on which there is no consensus. To take just two rather obvious examples, do all children have a right to sex education or religious education?[29]

With these initial difficulties in mind, a brief account will now be given of some of the more influential British theories of children's rights, put forward by MacCormick, Eekelaar and Freeman respectively. This is followed by a short section summarising the views of two children's rights sceptics. Onora O'Neill's distinctive contribution to the debate is to argue that a concentration on children's rights is misplaced and that the emphasis should rather be on the duties or responsibilities of adults towards children. Martin Guggenheim argues that children's rights have often been advocated by adults as a mechanism for advancing their own interests and do not therefore serve children well. Finally, before leaving the subject of children's rights, we pause to ask the often neglected question whether children themselves have, or ought to have, any duties.

---

rights, see WNR Lucy 'Controversy about Children's Rights' in D Freestone (ed) *Children and the Law* (Hull University Press, 1990), at p 213. For a succinct review of the literature on the concept of rights and the principal theories of rights more generally see NE Simmonds *Central Issues in Jurisprudence: Justice, Law and Rights* (3nd edn, Sweet & Maxwell, 2008), Part III and B Bix *Jurisprudence: Theory and Context* (6th edn, Sweet and Maxwell, 2012), Part C. For the most detailed treatment of children's legal rights in English law see J Fortin *Children's Rights and the Developing Law* (3rd edn, Cambridge University Press, 2009), especially Part One. For a recent succinct summary of the debates abut children's rights see J Herring, R Probert and S Gilmore, *Great Debates: Family Law* (Palgrave Macmillan, 2012), ch 3.

[28] See, particularly, the United Nations Declaration of the Rights of the Child 1959 and the United Nations Convention on the Rights of the Child 1989.

[29] See chapter 17 below.

MacCormick's test case

In an article first published in 1976,[30] Neil MacCormick used the claim that children have rights as a test case for theories of rights in general. MacCormick pointed out that before substantive theories of particular rights of children could be constructed it was necessary to address the fundamental issue of whether they have rights at all.

The 'will theory' and the 'interest theory'

There are broadly two competing theories of the nature of rights – the 'will theory' and the 'interest theory'. MacCormick sought to demonstrate that the former could not accommodate the rights of children and was accordingly suspect as a general theory. However, in his view, it was possible to make sense of the claim that children have rights by formulating a variant of the interest theory. The will theory is based on the notion that to have a legal or moral right is to be able to exercise individual choice over the enforcement or waiver of duties imposed on someone else. The essence of the theory is the pre-eminence of the right-holder's will over the will of others with respect to the subject-matter of the right. The interest theory concentrates on the protection of an individual's interests by the imposition of duties on others – what MacCormick refers to as 'the imposition of (legal or moral) normative constraints on the acts and activities of other people with respect to the object of one's interests'. Therefore, an important element in both theories is the existence of duties in others, correlative to the rights asserted.[31] The critical difference is that the will theory regards as crucial the capacity for individual autonomy, ie the ability to waive or enforce the duty in question, whereas under the interest theory it is sufficient for the existence of a right that there is an identifiable interest and a corresponding duty.

The will theory

MacCormick drew attention to the difficulty (in his view impossibility) of accommodating the concept of children's rights within the will theory. He took as an example the right of a baby to care, nurture and love.[32] The will theory is inept as a foundation for this, essentially for two reasons. First, a baby clearly lacks the physical and mental capacity to exercise any will or choice about whether to relieve his parents from their duty to provide him with these things. Secondly, and more importantly, it was MacCormick's contention that neither the baby, nor anyone acting on the baby's behalf, should be allowed to waive the parents' duty or acquiesce in its non-performance. For MacCormick it is the fundamental interest and moral claim of the infant to care and nurture

---

[30] N MacCormick 'Children's Rights: A Test-Case for Theories of Right' (1976) 62 *Archiv für Rechts und Sozialphilosophie* 305; also published as ch 8 in *Legal Right and Social Democracy* (1982).

[31] Correlativity was crucial to Hohfeld – see *Fundamental Legal Conceptions* (Yale University Press, 1919).

[32] N MacCormick 'Children's Rights: A Test-Case for Theories of Right' (above).

which justifies the imposition of the duty on the parent. The duty is not constitutive of the right but rather a means of securing that right. When outside agencies, such as social services, intervene where parents have failed to provide adequate care, this does not remove the duty placed on parents. Rather, such action constitutes substituted performance of the duty as opposed to a waiver or release for parents. MacCormick concludes that to see such powers as constitutive of the child's right is to confuse the substantive right with ancillary remedial provisions.

The interest theory

MacCormick, instead, saw the rights of children as being located somewhere in the interest theory and grounded in the basic jural precept of respect for persons. Thus, to argue:[33]

'... that each and every child is a being whose needs and capacities command our respect, so that denial to any child of the wherewithal to meet his or her needs and to develop his or her capacities would be wrong in itself (at least in so far as it is physically possible to provide the wherewithal) and would be wrong regardless of the ulterior disadvantages or advantages to anyone else – so to argue, would be to put a case which is intelligible as a justification of the opinion that children have such rights.'

Although MacCormick conceded that rights require the imposition of duties, for him the existence of a right preceded the imposition of a duty. It is because children have a right to care and nurture that parents have a duty to care for them.[34]

If this is correct, it means that it may be possible to recognise that children have rights even where there is uncertainty about who is to bear the corresponding duty. MacCormick gave the example of education. While there may be a wide measure of agreement that children have a right to be educated to the limits of their abilities, it is far less clear who has the duty or power to provide it as between parents, local authorities, central government, a church or the children themselves.[35] MacCormick attempted to fit this reasoning into a general interest theory. His thesis was that to ascribe to all members of a class C (for present purposes, children) a right to treatment T (in the above examples, care and nurture or education) is to presuppose that T is, in all normal circumstances, a good for every member of C and that T is a good which it would be wrong to withhold from any member of C.

It should be noted that MacCormick's theory, as applied to children (especially young children) incorporates a measure of paternalism. Whereas in a liberal democracy it is generally accepted that a right-holder should be allowed the liberty to determine when to enforce his rights, this is not so, according to

---

[33] Ibid, at pp 310 et seq.
[34] Ibid, at p 313.
[35] N MacCormick 'Children's Rights: A Test-Case for Theories of Right' (above).

MacCormick, in the case of children – an exception acknowledged by the exponents of classical liberalism including JS Mill.[36] This is based on a contentious argument which will be discussed later: 'Children are not always or even usually the best judges of what is good for them'.

The emergence of children's rights according to Eekelaar

In a seminal article, published in 1986,[37] John Eekelaar assessed the then status of the concept of children's rights in English law in the context of an historical overview and two (then) recent decisions of the House of Lords.[38] Like MacCormick, Eekelaar relied on the interest theory of rights, especially that version propounded by Joseph Raz that 'a law creates a right if it is based on and expresses the view that someone has an interest which is sufficient ground for holding another to be subject to a duty'.[39]

Historical background

Eekelaar was at pains to demonstrate that, historically, the earliest legal duties towards children emerged not to protect the interests of children themselves but to further other interests, usually the interests of fathers or the wider community. Thus, the legal enforcement of parental support obligations in the sixteenth century arose primarily from the threat to social stability posed by the growth of mass unemployment and labour mobility. Insofar as this advanced the interests of children it did so only incidentally and was not its aim or purpose.[40] The same, he argued, might be said of the limited incursions into the father's right to custody of his legitimate children during the nineteenth century. Although, apparently, conceived as protective of the child's independent interests, the reality was that the father's interests were seen as paramount unless his behaviour posed a severe threat to the child's well-being. But the courts would only hold this to be so where it consisted of such matters as 'immorality, profligacy, impiety and radical social views, all of which might undermine the child's commitment to the dominant social values'.[41] For Eekelaar these judicial interventions had the effect of equating the welfare of children with the transmission of conventional social norms. In other words, their thrust was to uphold the prevailing community interest rather than the independent interests of children.

Isolation of interests

The key precondition for rights in Eekelaar's theory is the social perception that an individual or class of individuals has certain interests. Crucial to this is that

---

[36]   JS Mill *Essay on Liberty* (1859).
[37]   J Eekelaar 'The Emergence of Children's Rights' (1986) 6 *Oxford Journal of Legal Studies* 161.
[38]   *Richards v Richards* [1984] AC 174 and the *Gillick* case.
[39]   J Raz 'Legal Rights' (1984) 4 *Oxford Journal of Legal Studies* 1, at p 13.
[40]   J Eekelaar 'The Emergence of Children's Rights' (above), at pp 166–169.
[41]   See, for example, *Shelley v Westbrooke* (1817) Jac 266 and *Symington v Symington* (1875) LR 2 SC and Div 415.

the interests in question must be capable of isolation from the interests of others. Thus, to assert the existence of a particular right for children is to identify an independent interest which they have in the subject-matter or, as Eekelaar puts it, 'those benefits which the subject himself or herself might plausibly claim in themselves'. He gives the example of a parent's power to take decisions concerning his daughter's medical welfare. Although the parent might claim that this power is in the child's interests, the parental interest is not identical with the child's interest. Her interest or right is that only the best medical decisions are taken for her. Accordingly, it cannot per se be enough to see the child's interests as synonymous with those of the parent, despite the force of parental autonomy claims. Eekelaar's thesis is that no child would plausibly claim parental independence as an end in itself. If it is claimed at all it must be because it is perceived to advance other ends such as material or emotional stability.[42] He acknowledged, however, that children might lack the information or ability to evaluate their own best interests and, accordingly, the construction of a theory of children's rights involves 'some kind of imaginative leap and guess what a child might retrospectively have wanted once it reaches a position of maturity'.

Eekelaar identified three separate kinds of interest which might form the foundation of these retrospective claims. These he described as 'the basic interests', 'the developmental interests' and 'the autonomy interests'.

Basic interests

The 'basic interests' relate to what might be described as the essentials of healthy living, including physical, emotional and intellectual care.[43] The duty to secure these interests is placed initially on the child's parents but, where this is abused or neglected, the State may intervene in care proceedings.[44] These interests are 'basic' because they require compliance with minimally acceptable standards of upbringing. The parents' duty is 'to refrain from the actual prevention or neglect of proper development or natural health rather than the maximum promotion of these qualities'.

Developmental interests

The 'developmental interests' are wider and may be asserted not just against parents but against the wider community. They are more nebulous than the basic interests and, hence, more difficult to categorise as legal rights. The developmental interest, according to Eekelaar, is that, subject to the socio-economic constraints in a particular society, 'all children should have an equal opportunity to maximise the resources available to them during their childhood (including their own inherent abilities) so as to minimise the degree to which they enter adult life affected by avoidable prejudices incurred during childhood'. Eekelaar doubted that these interests, while the subject of moral

---

42   J Eekelaar 'The Emergence of Children's Rights' (above), at p 170.
43   Ibid, at pp 171–172.
44   Under s 31(2) of the Children Act 1989, discussed in chapter 12 below.

claims, could legitimately be classified as legal rights since, beyond education, the law imposes no duty on parents to fulfil children's developmental interests, which depend rather on 'the natural workings of the economies of families which are themselves dependent on the wider social and economic mechanisms of the community'.[45]

Autonomy interest

The 'autonomy interest', which a child might retrospectively claim, is 'the freedom to choose his own lifestyle and to enter social relations according to his own inclinations uncontrolled by the authority of the adult world, whether parents or institutions'. This is, of course, the classic claim of the child liberationists which was alluded to above. Eekelaar argued that this could be interpreted as a version of the developmental interest, no doubt on the basis that healthy development implies a measure of self-determination or autonomy. The justification for adopting a separate categorisation is that the autonomy interest has the potential for conflicting with the developmental interest or the basic interest. It is, for example, likely that the removal of age restrictions on drinking or driving would further the autonomy interest but would also result in more deaths or injury among children from road accidents, thereby infringing their developmental and basic interests. Eekelaar, agreeing with Freeman,[46] would rank the autonomy interest as subordinate to the other two interests, since it is likely that the majority of adults would not give their retrospective approval to exercises of autonomy while children which damaged their life chances in adulthood when compared with other children.

The value of Eekelaar's thesis is that it alerts us to potential conflicts both between the distinctive interests or rights which children may claim and between those interests and rights and the competing claims of the adult world, especially those of parents. Eekelaar has subsequently attempted to build on his earlier theory by suggesting a way in which furthering the best interests of children might be reconciled with treating them as possessors of rights. His theory, which is based on the concept of 'dynamic self-determinism', relies on the argument that the welfare principle, or best interests principle, should be properly understood to accommodate an opportunity for the child to determine what those best interests are.[47] He proposes, subject to two limitations, that a competent child's decision should determine the outcome of the issue in question. These are 'compatibility with the general law and the interests of others' and, more controversially, situations in which a child might take a decision which is 'contrary to his or her self-interest ... narrowly defined

---

[45] J Eekelaar (above), at p 173.

[46] MDA Freeman *The Rights and Wrongs of Children* (Frances Pinter, 1983).

[47] J Eekelaar 'The Interests of the Child and the Child's Wishes: The Role of Dynamic Self-Determinism' in P Alston (ed) *The Best Interests of the Child* (Clarendon, 1994), at p 42. Also published at (1994) 8 IJLF 42. See further J Eekelaar 'Beyond the Welfare Principle' [2002] CFLQ 237.

in terms of physical or mental well-being and integrity'.[48] This, of course, raises again the central question of precisely what are the acceptable limits of paternalism.

Freeman's liberal paternalism

The most extensive theoretical study of children's rights in England is still *The Rights and Wrongs of Children* by Michael Freeman.[49] This was augmented by his collection of essays, *The Moral Status of Children*,[50] which in some respects was intended by Freeman to serve as a second edition to his earlier work. The principal change in his position was a shift of emphasis. He was later inclined to believe that he had underestimated the importance of giving children participatory rights in *The Rights and Wrongs of Children*. Freeman stressed the importance of rights for children as against benevolence towards them, or other morally significant values such as love, friendship or compassion. Rights enable, at least in theory, the right-holder to stand with dignity and demand or insist on certain treatment without embarrassment or shame. They represent entitlements and avoid the need to grovel, beg or show gratitude for favours. At the same time, Freeman was quick to warn that the enactment of legal rights could become merely an abstract affirmation of principle if the will was lacking to put it into practice. He pointed to examples from juvenile justice in which well-intentioned measures, designed to enhance the rights of children, back-fired and had the opposite effect of eroding them.[51]

Freeman's distinctive contribution to the children's rights debate has been to demonstrate the extremely diverse nature of the substantive rights which children might claim and to fit a categorisation of these rights into an over-arching theory of liberal paternalism. His theory adapts Rawls' influential theory of justice[52] to apply to children. Freeman produced a fourfold classification of children's rights, comprising rights to welfare, rights of protection, rights to be treated like adults and rights against parents.[53]

---

[48]   J Eekelaar (above).

[49]   (Frances Pinter, 1983). See also J Fortin *Children's Rights and the Developing Law* (3rd edn, Cambridge University Press, 2009) which is a very detailed and wide-ranging treatment of the law affecting children from a children's rights perspective. For a recent, shorter, theoretical discussion see L Ferguson 'Not merely rights for children but children's rights: the theory gap and the assumption of the importance of children's rights' (2013) 21 *International Journal of Children's Rights* pp 1–32.

[50]   (Martinus Nijhoff, 1997). See also M Freeman 'The End of the Century of the Child?' (2003) 53 *Current Legal Problems* 505 for a more succinct distillation of the author's views on the successes and failures of the twentieth century from a children's rights perspective.

[51]   *The Rights and Wrongs of Children* (above), at pp 32–34. Freeman's attacks were levelled particularly at the system of juvenile justice and the juvenile court where well-intentioned measures designed to decriminalise juvenile misbehaviour, particularly those embodied in the Children and Young Persons Act 1969, had the unintended effect of establishing, inter alia, a 'criminal model' in care proceedings. See chapter 15 below.

[52]   J Rawls *A Theory of Justice* (Harvard University Press, 1972). A similar adaptation of the theory to children was put forward by V Worsfold in 'A Philosophical Justification for Children's Rights' (1974) 44 *Harvard Educational Review* 142.

[53]   MDA Freeman *The Rights and Wrongs of Children* (above), at pp 40–54.

Rights to welfare

Freeman's first category, welfare rights, was located in the more general notion of human rights and he drew freely on the statements of children's rights in the United Nations Declaration of the Rights of the Child.[54] Freeman regarded this as politically important because, by expressing children's rights as human rights, 'the United Nations was not saying that children ought to have these rights but, since children are undoubtedly human beings ... they already have them'.[55]

The rights in question are wide-ranging and include: entitlement to a name and nationality; freedom from discrimination based on, for example, race, colour or religion; social security extending to adequate nutrition, housing, recreation and medical care; entitlement to free education and equal opportunities; protection from all forms of cruelty, neglect and exploitation; and special treatment for the disabled. These rights are not, as Freeman acknowledged, easily formulated against anyone in particular. They are, in essence, 'manifestos' of the rights which children ought to have against everyone. Typically, these types of 'rights against the world' are vague, perhaps deliberately so, to reflect cultural and economic differences between societies. Some, such as the provision of adequate nutrition and medical care, are clearly fundamental since they relate to survival and fall within what Eekelaar termed the 'basic interests'. The rights listed are essentially protectionist rather than liberationist and, to that extent, there is an overlap with Freeman's second category, rights of protection. But 'welfare rights' is a wide enough idea to include within it rights of recipience, ie rights to receive positive welfare benefits such as education, social security or (perhaps more controversially in rights analysis) love, understanding and affection.

Rights of protection

Freeman's second category, protective rights, was more overtly concerned with protection from negative behaviour and activities[56] such as inadequate care, abuse or neglect by parents, exploitation by employers or environmental dangers. Whereas welfare rights are pitched at a high level and are grounded in the assumption that society owes children the best it has to offer, protective rights are concerned that minimally acceptable standards of treatment are observed and, as such, are largely, although not exclusively, the province of the criminal law.[57]

---

[54] Adopted by the General Assembly on 20 November 1959. See also the United Nations Convention on the Rights of the Child, adopted on the thirtieth anniversary of the Declaration.

[55] A point which can be made with even greater force now that children have 'Convention rights' under the ECHR.

[56] MDA Freeman *The Rights and Wrongs of Children* (above), at pp 43–45.

[57] As to which see chapter 15 below. Care proceedings are also, of course, concerned directly with protection.

The first two categories of rights have a common paternalistic approach. They are rights which the adult world would deem to be appropriate for children whether or not they would be claimed by children for themselves. They contrast sharply with Freeman's third and fourth categories, both of which belong more to the liberationist school.

The right to be treated like adults

Freeman's third category was the right of children to be treated like adults. This right is grounded in social justice and egalitarianism. It is essentially that the rights and liberties extended to adults should also be extended to children as fellow human beings, unless there is a good reason for differentiating between them. Comment has already been made on this in the context of the USA. The point should also be made that children, prima facie, enjoy the same fundamental civil liberties as adults, while making due allowance for the concern to protext them adequately and the role of parents, under both the UNCRC and the ECHR.[58]

Although the UK has not had a bill of rights, there is, nonetheless, a strong tradition of respect for civil liberties and this must pose the question of how far the civil liberties enjoyed by adults are, or should be, extended to children and young people. Freeman regarded the claim that children should be treated as adults with some scepticism. While distinctions between children and adults are social and legal constructs which may appear arbitrary, Freeman's view was that respect for children as persons requires that society provides 'a childhood for every child'[59] and not an adulthood for every child. Yet Freeman also questioned the double standard involved in the differential treatment of children and adults.[60] He pointed out that the basis for this was the supposed incapacity or lack of maturity which would prevent children from taking sound decisions on their own behalf. He nonetheless rejected the removal of all age-related disabilities since to do so would ignore the evidence about the cognitive abilities of children provided by developmental psychology. But he argued that children's rights at least required that age-related restrictions be kept under review in the light of this evidence. His own preference was for legal capacity to be determined on a case-by-case basis, by assessing the *actual* capacity for particular activities of individual children. This, he argued, could be achieved by employing an objective test of rationality determined in accordance with a neutral theory of what is 'good' for children.

---

[58]   These include the rights to freedom of expression, conscience and religion, freedom of association and the right to privacy (see Arts 13–16 of the UNCRC and Arts 8–11 of the ECHR).

[59]   MDA Freeman *The Rights and Wrongs of Children* (above), at p 3. Freeman borrowed the quotation from M Gerzon *A Childhood for Every Child – Politics of Parenthood* (Outerbridge and Lazard, New York, 1973).

[60]   The legal capacities and liabilities of children and young people under the civil law are considered in chapter 16 below.

Rights against parents

Freeman's fourth category was rights against parents.[61] This is also concerned primarily with self-determination or autonomy but, whereas the third category is concerned with the justification of civil liberties and the child's position under the general law, this fourth category is concerned with the claim for independence from parental control.[62] Claims in this category range from the trivial (eg length of hair, choice of clothes, bedtimes, etc) to serious matters (eg consent to abortion or provision of contraceptives). Freeman noted two variants of this claim. The first is the claim that the child should be able to act entirely independently. The second is the claim that the child should be able to act independently but with the sanction of an outside agency, usually a court.[63] Freeman's general position on parent–child conflicts was to view the parental role as a representative one. Where parents' and children's views accord with one another there is no problem. Where they do not, Freeman would uphold parental decisions insofar as they are consistent with an objective evaluation of what Rawls called 'primary social goods'. These include liberty, health and opportunity and are, in short, the things which any rational person would want to pursue. Where parents purport to take decisions not in accordance with this objective, Freeman would hold that parental representation ceases at that point and that the intervention of an outside agency is justified, his own preference being a court.

Rawls' fundamentals of justice

It is clear from this analysis that Freeman favoured a degree of paternalism as a feature of children's rights.[64] The critical requirement of respect for persons was, he thought, that the potential capacity of children for taking responsibility as free and rational agents should be recognised. But, since in the case of children we are often talking about potential rather than actual capacity, a limited amount of intervention could be justified to protect them against irrational actions. The obvious question is, what kind of actions are to be considered irrational for these purposes? What test of rationality can be employed? Here, Freeman found that it was Rawls' idea of equality at the stage of a hypothetical social contract which best captured the idea of treating people as equals with regard to their capacity for autonomy.

Rawls was concerned with the principles which individuals would hypothetically choose in a just society in order to secure fair treatment for everyone.[65] Everyone in society would participate in choosing these principles in a hypothetical state ('the original position') and in ignorance of their own

---

[61] MDA Freeman (above), at pp 48–52.

[62] See below for discussion of resolving conflicts between parents and children.

[63] An approach favoured in the United States where the 'judicial by-pass' has been utilised to avoid parental notification requirements in relation to abortions performed on minors, as to which see chapter 8 below.

[64] His theory of liberal paternalism is set out, at pp 54–60 of his book.

[65] See the explanation of Rawls' theory by V Worsfold in 'A Philosophical Justification for Children's Rights' (1974) 44 *Harvard Educational Review* 142, at pp 151 et seq.

specific interest and circumstances (behind 'the veil of ignorance'). Since they would be hypothetically unaware of what would be to their own advantage or disadvantage, all individuals would choose principles of justice impartially and with a view to equality. According to Rawls, individuals in this state of ignorance, but acting in self-interest, would choose two fundamental principles of justice. These were, first, that each person should have as much personal liberty as was compatible with similar liberty for everyone else and, secondly, that social and economic inequalities should be tolerated only to the extent that they were to the greatest benefit of the least advantaged and attached to offices and positions open to everyone under conditions of fair equality of opportunity.

Rawls included children in the initial social contract when they reached the 'age of reason'. Freeman interpreted this as meaning participation to the extent that they were capable. Justice required, therefore, that children be brought to a capacity whereby they were able to take responsibility as free and rational agents. In order to achieve this, Freeman argued that they required two types of right. The first was equal opportunity extending to such matters as good parenting and good teaching. The second was liberal paternalism. This would allow intervention to protect the child's potential for development. The test propounded by Freeman is 'what sorts of action or conduct would we wish, as children, to be shielded against on the assumption that we would want to mature to a rationally autonomous adulthood and be capable of deciding our own system of ends as free and rational beings'?[66] Within this framework, protection from death or injury and compulsory education could be readily justified. While there was no guarantee that every individual would consent to these principles, Freeman's thesis was that they were the ones which were most consistent with a neutral theory of the good and which would appeal to those in the 'original position'.

Common ground between the theories

This analysis has touched briefly on just three of the many theories of children's rights which have been advanced.[67] There is much common ground between the three theories discussed above which, at the risk of over-simplification, might be summarised in the following propositions:

---

[66]   MDA Freeman *The Rights and Wrongs of Children* (above), at p 57.
[67]   Many of the earlier theories, particularly those put forward in North America, are cited by Freeman. For a Scottish perspective on children's rights, see R Adler *Taking Juvenile Justice Seriously* (Scottish Academic Press, 1985); and the review by J Eekelaar at (1986) 6 *Oxford Journal of Legal Studies* 439. For significant collections of essays on the general subject of children's rights, see M Freeman and P Veerman (eds) *The Ideologies of Children's Rights* (Martinus Nijhoff, 1992) and P Alston, S Parker and J Seymour (eds) *Children, Rights and the Law* (Clarendon, 1992). See also J Eekelaar, *Family Law and Personal Life* (Oxford University Press, 2006), Ch 6, especially at pp 155–162; D Archard *Children, Rights and Childhood* (Routledge, 2004); T Campbell 'The Rights of the Minor' in P Alston et al (above) and C Smith 'Children's Rights: Judicial Ambivalence and Social Resistance' (1997) 11 IJLPF 103.

(1)   Children have rights which arise from the fundamental moral requirement of respect for persons which underlies all human rights.

(2)   The particular rights which children have are grounded in the interests which society recognises they possess and which justify the imposition of duties on others.

(3)   'Children's rights' is not a unitary concept but a catch-all expression for a range of legal and moral claims.

(4)   The imposition of a duty on *someone* (perhaps unspecified) is a necessary concomitant of any right asserted for children. Where this is imposed on an identifiable entity, especially a parent, it may be possible to recognise the existence of a legal right *stricto sensu* – a 'claim right' in the Hohfeldian sense.[68] Where, conversely, the right is asserted against the world, it is less clear that it can be regarded as a legal right but may have the status of a moral right. The existence of such a moral claim may itself justify the creation of a legal right and, but for potential difficulties of enforcement, many such claims probably would be.

(5)   Children's rights must embrace elements of both qualified self-determination and limited paternalism.

(6)   Rights, although asserted by individual children, must have a general or universal character such that they can be applied to all children as a class.

Perhaps the most controversial issue arising from these theories is the basis upon which paternalistic interventions are justified. Broadly, there would appear to be two schools of thought on this. The first, accepted by Eekelaar and Freeman, entails a hypothetical enquiry by adult decision-makers into what children would ideally want for themselves. The judgment of adult society is effectively substituted for that of the child who is (as yet) unable to exercise it for himself. This can only be made on the basis of a projection of what rational persons would have wished for themselves as children. The second, adopted by Ruth Adler in her study of juvenile justice in Scotland,[69] is that adult decision-making reflects the value judgments of the decision-maker about what is good for children and not the decision-maker's projection of what children would want for themselves. Adler would, accordingly, allow a form of modified protectionism based on external assessments of what is good or necessary for children. Whatever may be the theoretical merits of the former school of thought, it is likely that the latter is a more realistic reflection of what actually happens in practice. We will return to this issue in the context of medical decision-making, where the 'substituted judgment test' has a certain following, especially in North America.[70]

---

[68]   Hohfeld regarded these 'claim rights' as the only true legal rights: see Hohfeld *Fundamental Legal Conceptions* (Yale University Press, 1919).

[69]   R Adler *Taking Juvenile Justice Seriously* (above).

[70]   See chapter 8 below.

RIGHTS SCEPTICS

Onora O'Neill: children's rights or adults' duties?

Onora O'Neill has made a distinctive contribution to the children's rights debate by questioning whether 'children's positive rights are best grounded by appeals to fundamental (moral, natural, human) rights'. Instead, she argues they are 'best grounded by embedding them in a wider account of fundamental obligations'.[71] In essence, her thesis is that regarding 'rights as fundamental in ethical deliberation about children has neither theoretical nor political advantages'. Instead, she thinks that the best way to achieve rights for children is to shift the concentration on to the fundamental obligations of adult society.

O'Neill does not deny the force of the rhetoric of rights in the claims of those who lack power but she is concerned that such rhetoric can lead to claims of 'spurious rights even when no corresponding obligations can be justified'. She warns that:[72]

> 'many of the rights promulgated in international documents are not perhaps spurious, but they are patently no more than "manifesto" rights ... that cannot be claimed unless or until practices and institutions are established that determine against whom claims on behalf of a particular child may be lodged. Mere insistence that certain ideals or goals are rights cannot make them into rights ...'

Thus, the rhetoric of rights cannot, according to O'Neill, establish positive rights for children. She goes on to consider whether the use of the language of children's rights might have a political usefulness contributing to the 'realisation of fundamental imperfect obligations'. Here, she rejects the analogy between children and other (formerly) oppressed groups such as colonial peoples, the working classes, religious or racial minorities and women, all of which 'have sought recognition and respect for capacities for rational and independent life and action that are demonstrably there and thwarted by the denial of rights'.[73] For O'Neill, the 'crucial difference between (early) childhood dependence and the dependence of oppressed social groups is that childhood is a stage of life, from which children normally emerge and are helped and urged to emerge from by those who have most power over them'. She concludes:[74]

> 'Those who urge respect for children's rights must address not children but those whose action may affect children; they have reason to prefer the rhetoric of obligations to that of rights, both because its scope is wider and because it addresses the relevant audience more directly.'

---

71   O O'Neill 'Children's Rights and Children's Lives' (1988) 98 *Ethics* 445, also reproduced in Alston, Parker and Seymour *Children, Rights and the Law* (Clarendon, 1992), at p 24.
72   Ibid, at p 37.
73   Ibid.
74   O O'Neill (above), at p 39.

O'Neill's thesis has provoked considerable disagreement, as it was bound to do.[75] Its value is to remind us that where any 'right' is being asserted for children we ought to pause to consider on whom there is, or might be, a correlative obligation and whether such obligation is enforceable.

Martin Guggenheim: children's rights as a screen for the pursuit of adult interests?

In *What's Wrong with Children's Rights* published in 2005,[76] Guggenheim, writing from an American perspective, presents the case for saying that the call for the advancement of children's rights has been largely about promoting the interests of adults who have more to gain from it than children themselves. Guggenheim does concede the importance and value of the children's rights movement in the context of protecting children against the unwarranted exercise of state power against them; but he is far less confident that they need 'rights' in the family context, or that to speak in terms of rights is even good for them.[77]

Like O'Neill, Guggenheim is suspicious of rhetoric and is particularly scathing about what he calls the shibboleth of 'child-centredness'; an 'attractive phrase' which 'tells us nothing about how to use it or what are its sensible limits'.[78] In his view, adults claim to be arguing for children's rights in a whole range of disputes primarily affecting those adults because it pays them to present themselves as caring about children. He attempts to demonstrate this by analysing disputes before the American courts involving, inter alia, biological and social parents, adoptive parents and unmarried fathers, grandparents and parents, divorcing parents and child welfare agencies and parents. In all these contexts the notion of children's rights, he argues:[79]

> 'serves as a useful subterfuge for the adult's actual motives. It can be an effective diverter of attention, shifting the focus to a more sympathetic party than the adult. Other times, it is used to assuage guilt for the adult's bad behaviour or intentions. Children's rights can be useful for masking selfishness by invoking the language of altruism. It can also provide a legal basis to achieve a result that would be difficult to achieve otherwise. Time and again we will see the frequency with which the concept of children's rights is used by adults to try to gain some advantage in their struggles with other adults.'

Guggenheim's conclusion is that the greatest goal for the advancement of children's rights is perhaps to 'return to a time when we treated children like children' and he too favours a stronger focus on adult obligations. He sees the

---

[75] For a particularly readable critique, see M Freeman *The Moral Status of Children* (Martinus Nijhoff, 1997), at pp 25–29.

[76] M Guggenheim, *What's Wrong with Children's Rights* (Harvard University Press, 2005). Note that there is no question mark in the title.

[77] Ibid, Preface, at p xi.

[78] Ibid, at p xii.

[79] Ibid, at pp xii-xiii.

reliance on children's rights as being of little value to children unless it is accompanied by real commitment to their needs and interests.[80]

Does Guggenheim's thesis have any resonance in England? An obvious point to make is that there appears to be (even allowing for the incorporation of the ECHR into English law) much less appeal to the notion of children's rights in the English than in the American courts. The English courts are still very largely preoccupied with applying the welfare principle and with resisting attempts to water it down in any way.[81] So the question, perhaps, is whether adults use the welfare principle to advance their own interests in the way that American parties might be resorting to the concept of children's rights.

There is surely little doubt that they do. The rhetoric of the best interests of the child will undoubtedly be useful, to take just one example, to a father seeking contact with his child, or a mother who is seeking to resist it. They will both claim to be doing what the child wants and what is in the child's best interests. But anyone who has ever set foot in the family courts will immediately appreciate that these are adult disputes between adult parties. Except in a small minority of cases, there will be no child in sight; and judges have not infrequenty chastised parents directly where they have brought children to court. This is the picture in the private law. In the public law it could be said that the separate representation of children by a children's guardian[82] makes it much less easy for adults to use proceedings to advance their own interests. But, even here, the reality is that governmental failure to fund the system properly means that children's interests are often not adequately represented.[83]

Perhaps a criticism of Guggenheim's position is that it may under-estimate the ability of judges, assisted by welfare professionals and professional experts, to see through the attempts by adults to hijack either the children's rights argument or the welfare argument and to get at the truth of where the child's best interests or rights really lie.

Guggenheim also powerfully highlights an issue to which we must return below. This is that it may be impossible to isolate completely the rights (or interests) of children from those of adult society. He sees a problem with 'child-centredness' in that it implies that it is possible to examine matters affecting children exclusively from the child's perspective. He sees this as unrealistic because it is fundmentally not the way in which society functions. As he puts it: '... there are other perspectives apart from a child's that we rightly take into account even

---

[80]   Ibid, at p 266.

[81]   See chapter 2.

[82]   Note, however, that guardians are also appointed to represent children in a small minority of *private law* proceedings under r 16.4 of the Family Procedure Rules 2010. See further chapter 14 below.

[83]   As to which see particularly the unsuccessful appeal in *R and Others v CAFCASS* [2012] EWCA Civ 853, [2012] 2 FLR 1432 in which the Official Solicitor sought a declaration that CAFCASS had acted unlawfully by failing to allocate children's guardians sooner than it did.

when we talk about children's rights and needs. Children are, to be sure, a precious part of our world, but they are only a part'.[84]

It might be responded that the fact that it may not be possible exclusively to focus on the child's rights or interests does not prevent a *primary* focus on these which historically may have been lacking. But Guggenheim's general point is a valuable one. In particular it may not be either possible or appropriate for the law to deny that parents have rights or, at least, independent interests which the law should openly recognise and uphold. We turn to this question below.

Do children have duties?

The whole children's rights debate raises one other important question. This is whether children themselves have any duties or responsibilities. Those rights which aim to protect children or secure positive welfare benefits for them largely entail, as perhaps O'Neill's thesis reminds us, the exercise of responsibility by others. But those rights which are autonomy based and would extend to children greater liberties, by treating them like adults or by giving them freedom from parental control, do invite consideration of how much responsibility children have for their own actions. It is noticeable how rarely the advocates of children's rights even mention, let alone deal with, this issue.

The short answer is that, whereas many jurisdictions do explicitly recognise the existence of certain obligations upon children and set them out in civil codes or legislation, English law is largely silent on the question.[85] Historically, the common law did enable a parent to sue for the loss of his child's services but this was only actionable where the child in fact performed some service for the parent – even if it was only making the tea![86] The action fell into disuse and was eventually abolished in 1982.[87] A more modern approach to the general obligation which children might be thought to have is a duty of respect for parents and this is acknowledged expressly in a number of jurisdictions.[88] Certain jurisdictions provide expressly for the financial obligations of children (for these purposes including 'adult children') towards parents who are unable to support themselves.[89]

---

[84]   Op cit, n 76, at p xii.

[85]   For a general discussion, see A Bainham '"Honour Thy Father and Thy Mother": Children's Rights and Children's Duties' in G Douglas and L Sebba (eds) *Children's Rights and Traditional Values* (Dartmouth, 1998).

[86]   So where a two-year-old was run down by the defendant's carriage no action would lie. See *Hall v Hollander* (1825) 4 B&C 660, and for a more detailed discussion, PM Bromley *Bromley's Family Law* (6th edn, Butterworths, 1981), at pp 329–332.

[87]   Administration of Justice Act 1982, s 2(b).

[88]   Perhaps not surprisingly in Israel, given its traditions, but less obviously in Indonesia and the new family code of Croatia. See further Bainham (above) and the sources cited at fn 28 to that article.

[89]   This is so in Indonesia. See Wila Chandrawila Supriadi 'Indonesia: Indonesian Marriage Law' in A Bainham (ed) *The International Survey of Family Law 1995* (Martinus Nijhoff, 1997). More strikingly, Singapore passed the Maintenance of Parents Act 1995 which gives to parents, in specified circumstances, the right to obtain maintenance from their children. See P

In English law such legal obligations as children have really arisen, if at all, by implication. These include criminal responsibility from the age of 10 and limited tortious liability.[90] There is no direct statutory obligation on the child to attend school, although this arguably arises by implication from the parental duty to ensure the child receives a proper education and from the very existence of the compulsory education system.[91] It can be argued that the express imposition of certain duties on children would be desirable, or is even a necessary concomitant, of the acquisition of limited autonomy. The younger the child the less actual and legal capacity that child will possess and the less justification there is for imposing duties or responsibilities on that child. As the child gets older and gradually acquires greater actual and legal independence so the case gets stronger for requiring increased actual and legal responsibility on the part of the child or, perhaps more accurately, young person. This might appear to justify, inter alia, a specific duty on the child to attend school or a duty to remain in contact with parents – albeit one which would be qualified by the operation of the welfare principle.[92] Finally, it is noteworthy that the UNCRC gives all manner of rights to children but nowhere addresses this question of responsibility.

CHILDREN AND HUMAN RIGHTS

At the European level there is an added dimension to the children's rights debate. This is the question of what human rights children may have under the various European treaties and conventions applicable to the family. Our concern here will be to introduce some of the key provisions of the European Convention on Human Rights and Fundamental Freedoms which have relevance to children and parents. First, however, a brief note concerning the growing interest of the European Union in children is warranted.[93]

The European Union and children

The European Union has not historically been much concerned with families except in the context of free movement of persons. Its power to legislate in ways which affect children is limited to its restricted areas of competence, covering

---

de Cruz 'Singapore: Maintenance, Marital Property and Legislative Innovation' in A Bainham (ed) *The International Survey of Family Law 1996* (Martinus Nijhoff, 1998). On the position in North America see J Blair '" Honour thy father and thy mother" – but for how long? Adult children's duty to care for and protect elderly parents' (1996) 35 *Journal of Family Law* 765.

90 See chapters 15 and 16.

91 See chapter 17.

92 See chapter 5. In its decision in *Hansen v Turkey* [2004] 1 FLR 142, the ECtHR held, inter alia, that although measures against children obliging them to reunite with one or other parent were not desirable in the sensitive area of contact, such action could not be ruled out in the event of non-compliance or unlawful behaviour by the parent with whom the children lived. It could be argued that this is implicit recognition that children may have an obligation to see a parent.

93 For recent detailed treatment of the subject see H Stalford *Children and the European Union: Rights, Welfare and Accountability* (Hart Publishing, 2012).

such issues as the international movement of children, immigration and child labour issues, including the evils of trafficking and sexual exploitation.

In more recent years, however, a number of developments, including the declaration of the European Charter of Fundamental Rights in 2000 and the constitutional changes effected by the Treaty of Lisbon in 2007, have put the issue of children's rights more firmly on the EU's agenda.[94]

So far as the former is concerned, Art 24 of the Charter is of particular note in enacting the welfare principle and also recognising children's rights of participation.[95] The Treaty of Lisbon also acknowledges children's rights directly by incorporating them in the EU's core objectives. Article 3 of the Treaty on the European Union as amended includes within these core objectives 'protection of the rights of the child' and, further, 'protection of human rights, in particular the rights of the child'. Stalford and Schuurman, commenting on the Treaty of Lisbon, attach greater significance to 'the highly effective non-legislative EU activities which are undoubtedly driven by a primary desire to offer better protection and provision for children'.[96] They also speculate on the potential of the new 'Citizens' Initiative'.[97] This provides a democratic mechanism whereby one million EU citizens from at least one quarter of the Member States may formally invite the Commission to legislate on any issue falling within its powers. Children themselves are excluded from participation but it is suggested that the mechanism could prove useful if a sufficient number of adult children's rights advocates could be mobilised to lobby the EU on a certain issue.[98] Their conclusion however is that legislation is rarely the most effective EU response to children's rights issues and that 'broader campaigns to encompass policy, budgetary, research, educative and knowledge exchange initiatives are equally, if not more crucial to achieving adequate responses to the diverse and distinct range of needs that children have'.[99]

---

[94] For a succinct introduction to developents in the EU relevant to the campaign for children's rights see H Stalford and M Schuurman 'Are we there yet?: the Impact of the Lisbon Treaty on the EU Children's Rights Agenda'(2011) 19 *International Journal of Children's Rights* 381.

[95] Article 24 (2) provides: 'In all actions relating to children, whether taken by public authorities or private institutions, the child's best interests must be a primary consideration'. Article 24 (1) provides: 'Children ... may express their views freely. Such views shall be taken into consideration on matters which concern them in accordance with their age and maturity'. Stalford and Schuurman (above, at p 396) point out that this is a somewhat weaker formulation than appears in Art 12 UNCRC which provides that children have *the right* to express their views.

[96] Ibid, at p 399.

[97] Article 11 (4) Treaty on the European Union and Art 24 Treaty on the Functioning of the European Union.

[98] Above, at p 391.

[99] Ibid, at p 402.

THE ECHR AND HUMAN RIGHTS ACT 1998

The combined effect of the ECHR and the HRA 1998[100] is that the rights under the ECHR and the jurisprudence of the ECtHR interpreting those rights form an integral part of English law. It is therefore necessary to take account of the Convention principles as they affect every aspect of the law concerning children, and reference will be made to the implications of the ECHR throughout this book. At this stage it is necessary merely to set out the fundamental principles of the HRA 1998, to look briefly at the main Articles which are likely to affect children and families and to offer some comments on the impact of the convention in children cases. We focus specifically on the concept of children's convention rights. At this stage we only touch upon the issue of how the rights of children and parents are balanced under the Convention as this is something which arises in many different contexts which are covered elsewhere in the book.

The HRA 1998 was implemented on 2 October 2000 and from that date the ECHR became part of English law.[101] Before that time the ECHR was occasionally invoked in English family cases and there was ultimately a right of individual petition to the European Commission and, if declared admissible, from there to the ECtHR. This was a lengthy process which could take many years but there were nonetheless some significant successes, especially in relation to the eradication of corporal punishment in schools[102] and the improvement of procedural rights for parents in care proceedings.[103]

---

[100] On the Convention generally, see M Janis, R Kay and A Bradley *European Human Rights Law* (3nd edn, Oxford University Press, 2008) and R White and C Ovey *The European Convention on Human Rights* (3rd edn, Oxford University Press, 2010). The most comprehensive treatment of the ECHR and HRA 1998 from the perspective of family law is S Choudhry and J Herring *European Human Rights and Family Law* (Hart Publishing, 2010). For an earlier treatment of the subject see H Swindells, A Neaves, M Kushner and R Skilbeck *Family Law and the Human Rights Act 1998* (Family Law, 1999). For a major collection of papers on human rights and the family see P Lodrup and E Modvar (eds) *Family Life and Human Rights* (Gyldendal Akademisk, 2004). U Kilkelly *The Child and the European Convention on Human Rights* (Ashgate, 1999) is essential reading for a perspective on the ECHR as it applies to children. Relevant articles are J Fortin 'Rights brought home for children' (1999) 62 MLR 350; A Bainham 'Family Rights in the Next Millennium' (2000) 53 *Current Legal Problems* 471; H Swindells '"Crossing the Rubicon" – Family Law post the Human Rights Act 1998' in S Cretney (ed) *Family Law: Essays for the New Millennium* (Family Law, 2000), U Kilkelly 'The impact of the Convention on the case-law of the European Court of Human Rights' in D Fottrell (ed) *Revisiting Children's Rights* (Kluwer, 2000). And more recently, see J Fortin 'Accommodating children's rights in a post-Human Rights era' (2006) 69 MLR 299 and especially J Fortin 'A decade of the HRA and its impact on children's rights' (2011) Fam Law 176.

[101] For a useful article looking at the effect of implementation from a family law perspective, see G Kingscote 'Incorporation of the European Convention on Human Rights' [1998] Fam Law 195. See also J Fortin *Children's Rights and the Developing Law* (3nd edn, Cambridge University Press, 2009), at pp 53–72. The Act followed the Government's White Paper *Rights Brought Home: The Human Rights Bill* (Home Office) (Cm 3782).

[102] See especially *Tyrer v UK* (1978) 2 EHRR 1; *Campbell and Cosans v UK* (1982) 4 EHRR 293 and *Costello-Roberts v UK* (1995) 19 EHRR 112.

[103] *W, O, H and B v UK* (1988) 10 EHRR 29.

The broad effect of the HRA 1998 is that 'Convention rights' are now directly enforceable in the English courts.[104] It is now possible for a person who claims that a 'public authority' (which includes a court or tribunal)[105] has acted in a way which is incompatible with his Convention rights to bring proceedings against that authority directly in the English courts.[106] It is also the case that domestic courts and tribunals, in arriving at their decisions, are required to take into account the judgments, decisions and opinions of the European Court and Commission 'so far as, in the opinion of the court or tribunal, it is relevant to the proceedings in which the question has arisen'.[107] English courts are therefore required to apply the existing and evolving jurisprudence of the ECtHR. Moreover, the effect of applying the Convention directly is that a substantial domestic jurisprudence has been generated which takes account of human rights arguments. A significant proportion of children cases which reach the higher courts will involve arguments under the ECHR.[108] While it may well be that the outcome would not have been greatly different if they had been decided before 2000[109] the process of reasoning, which involves a careful balancing of rights, has had to change.

So far as it is possible, primary and subordinate legislation must be read and given effect in a way which is compatible with Convention rights.[110] The higher courts are empowered to make declarations of incompatibility where this is not the case.[111] Legislation affecting children may therefore be scrutinised to examine its compatibility with the ECHR,[112] and the domestic judicial precedents are also liable to be attacked on the basis that they no longer conform with the requirements of the Convention.[113]

The ECHR: key Articles for children and families

While any part of the ECHR can potentially be invoked in cases involving children and families, it is plain that some Articles are of key importance. What follows is no more than an attempt to introduce the more important Articles.

---

[104] 'Convention rights' under s 1 of the HRA 1998 are essentially the 'rights and fundamental freedoms' set out in the Convention and the Protocols to it.

[105] HRA 1998, s 6.

[106] Ibid, s 7.

[107] Ibid, s 2.

[108] This has been true, for example, of a succession of cases considering the procedural rights of unmarried fathers in adoption proceedings. For an assessment of these cases and the general attitude of the English courts to children's Convention rights, see A Bainham 'Children's Rights and Human Rights' (2002) *Human Rights* 142.

[109] The strong adherence of the judges to the application of the welfare principle is a major factor here.

[110] HRA 1998, s 3.

[111] Ibid, s 4.

[112] A good example being the House of Lords decision in *Re S; Re W (Minors)* [2002] 1 FLR 815.

[113] A good example here is the practice of the courts relating to the granting of leave to take children out of the jurisdiction which came under attack (unsuccessfully) from a human rights perspective in *Payne v Payne* [2001] 1 FLR 1052.

Article 8

The most important Article in the ECHR for families is undoubtedly Art 8.[114]
This provides:

'1. Everyone has the right to respect for his private and family life, his home and
    his correspondence.
2. There shall be no interference by a public authority with the exercise of this
    right except such as is in accordance with the law and is necessary in a
    democratic society in the interests of national security, public safety or the
    economic well-being of the country, for the prevention of disorder or crime,
    for the protection of health or morals, or for the protection of the rights and
    freedoms of others.'

The Article guarantees to children and parents and, to a lesser extent, wider
members of the family the right to respect for their family life with one another.
The rights which family members enjoy under this article are qualified and not
absolute. Interferences with them by the state may be justified by reference to
the criteria in Art 8(2). Frequently this will involve balancing rights so that, for
example, a father's prima facie right to contact with his child may be curtailed if
it is necessary for protection of the mother and child.

The right to respect extends to private life, family life, home and
correspondence which are separate rights. In most cases involving children it
will be the concept of respect for 'family life' which will arise; but there are
cases in which, although 'family life' has not been established between a child
and a parent, issues of respect for that parent's 'private life' nonetheless arise.[115]
It is an important feature of the established jurisprudence under Art 8 that the
notion of 'respect' is not confined to negative obligations on the part of the
state, not to interfere unjustifiably in the family, but also with *positive*
obligations, in particular to foster family life once it has been established
between a child and a parent.[116]

The notion of respect for family life implies, in the private law,[117] mutual rights
of contact between parent and child and, in the public law, that the emphasis
should be on reuniting parent and child where it has been necessary for the
child to spend time in substitute care.[118] 'Family life' for these purposes is not
confined to marriage but difficult questions have arisen concerning when family

---

[114] For the most important case-law generated under Art 8, see M Janis et al (above), ch 6 and
    Swindells et al (above), at pp 119 et seq.
[115] See chapter 3 below.
[116] See chapter 3. Good examples of cases raising the question of positive obligations are *Johnston
    v Ireland* (1986) 8 EHRR 203 and, more recently, *Görgülü v Germany* [2004] 1 FLR 894.
[117] See chapter 5.
[118] See chapter 12.

life comes into being between a genetic, unmarried father and a child.[119] The Article has implications for when the adoption of a child should, or should not, be allowed.[120]

Article 6

Article 6 has significant implications for the procedural rights of family members, including children,[121] in the many kinds of legal proceedings in which their interests may arise,[122] though it should be noted that such rights can also fall within the ambit of Art 8.[123] It is not uncommon therefore for both articles to be relied upon together. Article 6 provides:

> 'In the determination of his civil rights and obligations or of any criminal charge against him, everyone is entitled to a fair and public hearing within a reasonable time by an independent and impartial tribunal established by law.'

Article 6 has been interpreted to require effective access to the courts.[124] The key distinction between Art 6 and Art 8 appears to be that Art 6 is largely confined to fairness in the trial process,[125] and issues surrounding court proceedings,[126] whereas Art 8 has a wider reach and is concerned with procedural fairness to parents at all stages of involvement by the state.[127] It would include, for example, the decision-making processes leading up to a

---

[119] See chapter 3.

[120] See chapter 9.

[121] The Court of Appeal has recently held in *Re P-S (Children: Child as Witness)* [2013] EWCA Civ 223, [2013] Fam Law 792 that Art 6 (and Art 12 of the UNCRC) confer on the child a right *to be heard* in care proceedings. This did *not* however necessarily entail a right to *give evidence*. Article 6 requires a fair and public hearing and judges must be very cautious when they see children (in this case a 15-year-old who had been separately represented) in the absence of other parties. They should not use such a meeting to take evidence from the child. The other parties could legitimately claim that their right to a fair trial under Art 6 had been invaded in such circumstances.

[122] For discussion of jurisprudence under Art 6 see Janis et al (above) ch 8 and Swindells et al (above), at pp 23–38 and ch 8.

[123] *McMichael v United Kingdom* (1995) 20 EHRR 205.

[124] See particularly *Airey v Ireland* (1979) 2 EHRR 305 in which it was held by the ECtHR that, in certain circumstances, this could imply an obligation to provide legal aid. On the question of publicly funded legal representation see also *P, C and S v United Kingdom* [2002] 2 FLR 631.

[125] A good recent illustration being *AM v RM (Children: Judge's Visit to Private Homes)* [2012] EWHC 3629, [2013] Fam Law 529 where the judge took it upon herself to 'play detective' and to enter the private homes of the mother and maternal grandparents. The parties were given little time for proper consideration of the suggestion or to object to it. Baron J held that the entire procedure had been wholly unacceptable. It was in effect litigation by ambush and a prima facie breach of the mother's Art 6 rights to a fair trial.

[126] In *MD and Others v Malta* (Application No 64791/10) [2013] Fam Law 29 the European Court of Human Rights held, inter alia, that it was a breach Art 6 where the applicants had not had access to court to challenge a care order which was, in Maltese law, a matter for the discretion of the Social Policy Minister. The Court held that the issue was a matter of family law and not public law as the government had asserted.

[127] In *MD and Others v Malta* (above) the European Court of Human Rights held that Art 6 affords a procedural safeguard, namely the right to access to a court whereas Art 8 serves the wider purpose of ensuring respect for family life. The different circumstances could justify the examination of the same set of facts under both articles.

decision to issue care proceedings, such as parental involvement in child protection conferences and also those which arise after a child has entered care. On the other hand it has been pointed out that, as the protection of Art 6 rights are absolute and not qualifed in the way that Art 8 rights are, it may be preferable to rely on Art 6 where it is applicable.[128]

Section 91(14) of the Children Act 1989 permits a court to restrict applications to it without first obtaining leave of the Court. This apparent restriction on access to the courts clearly raised issues under the Convention. But in *Re P (Section 91 (14) Guidelines)*[129] the Court of Appeal held that Art 6 was not breached by this provision. Access to the Court was not, it was held, denied by a partial restriction which only prevented the applicant from having access to an immediate inter partes hearing.

Article 14

Article 14 constitutes a general prohibition on discrimination in the delivery of Convention rights. It is not a freestanding provision and may only be taken in conjunction with other Articles. It provides:

> 'The enjoyment of the rights and freedoms set forth in this Convention shall be secured without discrimination on any ground such as sex, race, colour, language, religion, political or other opinion, national or social origin, association with a national minority, property, birth or other status.'

Although the prohibition on discrimination is unqualified in the article itself, discrimination will only violate the convention if it is unjustified. The European Court will ask whether the differential treatment has a reasonable and objective justification and is proportionate to the pursuit of a legitimate aim.[130] Specifically in relation to children, this Article invites consideration of whether the differential treatment of children and adults by the State can be justified and, if so, to what extent. It will be recalled that Art 14, inter alia, prohibits discrimination on the basis of 'birth or other status'. Could 'childhood' or 'minority' be regarded as falling within the term 'other status'? If so, the onus would be on the State to justify the different application of its laws to children and adults. The legal disabilities which attach to minority[131] would, for example, need to be kept under review and it is not difficult to imagine challenges under the ECHR to the kinds of paternalistic interventions in relation to adolescents which we have seen.[132] It may well be that greater State paternalism or protectionism is justified towards children than towards adults, but the starting point in future may have to be that children are persons with fundamental rights and the burden will be squarely on those who seek to interfere with these rights. If the jurisprudence of the ECHR does develop

---

[128] Choudhry and Herring (above), at p 312.
[129] [1999] 2 FLR 573.
[130] See, for example, *Fretté v France* [2003] 2 FLR 9.
[131] See chapter 16.
[132] See chapters 7 and 8.

along these lines it will reflect what the United States Supreme Court has been doing under the United States Constitution for decades.[133]

Other Articles

These are perhaps the three most important Articles affecting children. Other Articles can come into play on certain children issues. Article 12 enshrines the right to marry and found a family, but is clearly of greater relevance to adult family members than to children. More important for children, perhaps, are Art 2, which protects the right to life and which has an obvious relevance to serious medical decisions affecting them,[134] and Art 3, which prohibits torture or inhuman and degrading treatment and which has had an important impact on the evolution of English law governing corporal punishment in schools[135] and latterly on the parental right to discipline the child.[136]

Children's Convention rights

The whole idea of children's Convention rights is still a comparatively new one for the English courts which have been much more accustomed to thinking in terms of interests and applying the welfare principle, largely unfettered by other considerations. Since the HRA 1998 came into force there is plenty of evidence that, while the family judges have embraced and applied the idea of adult Convention rights, they have followed an approach which ultimately involves deciding disputes as hitherto, in accordance with the welfare principle.[137] It should also be borne in mind that the vast majority of applications to the domestic courts and petitions to Strasbourg are brought by adults seeking to vindicate their interests and that, in so far as children's convention rights are recognised, this will often be as a by-product of finding violations of parents' rights.

Accordingly, the notion of children's Convention rights itself, to say nothing of how it might relate to adult Convention rights, remains at the time of writing

---

[133] See particularly *Re Gault* 387 US 1 in which the Supreme Court acknowledged that 'neither the Fourteenth Amendment nor the Bill of Rights is for adults alone'. See also *Tinker v Des Moines Independent Community School District* 393 US 503 (1969), which was concerned with children's rights to freedom of speech, and *Goss v Lopez* 419 US 565 (1975), which was concerned with the right to a hearing in school discipline cases. Perhaps the case which best illustrates the issue of the differential treatment of children and adults is *Ginsberg v New York* 390 US 629 (1968), where it was held that prohibitions on the sale of obscene materials to minors could be constitutional but that they might be unconstitutional if imposed on adults.

[134] Although this Article did not greatly influence the Court of Appeal decision in *Re A (Conjoined Twins: Medical Treatment)* [2001] 1 FLR 1 where it certainly might have done. See chapter 8.

[135] See cases cited at chapters 12 and 17.

[136] See particularly *A v UK (Human Rights: Punishment of Child)* [1998] 2 FLR 959 and *R v H (Assault of Child: Reasonable Chastisement)* [2001] 2 FLR 431. See also the Government's consultation document *Protecting Children, Supporting Parents* (2000) and the restrictions on corporal punishment consequentially imposed by s 58 Children Act 2004.

[137] See Bainham 'Children's Rights and Human Rights' (above).

largely under-developed. The reaction of the English courts is, however, thought to be somewhat fragmented in that they have been more receptive to convention arguments in some areas of the law than in others. This was certainly the view of Jane Fortin commenting on the impact of the Convention on children's rights in the first decade following the implementation of the Human Rights Act.[138]

Fortin's view is that the record of the courts is 'patchy'. In areas such as educational litigation,[139] medical law,[140] juvenile justice[141] and freedom of the press[142] there has been a much greater willingness to acknowledge children's convention rights than in what we might describe as 'mainstream family law'. One possible explanation for this is that the areas in which rights have been principally acknowledged often involve the child's relationships outside the family where the institutions of the state are more directly concerned, whether educational, health or prison authorities or the media. This might also explain the somewhat larger impact of the ECHR in the context of public law, as opposed to private law,[143] children cases. Again, the involvement of the state is more direct in the former in the shape of the local authority.[144] Commentators have questioned whether the child's own, separate convention rights have been sufficiently well-identified in public law cases or whether the tendency has been to equate them rather too readily with those of their parents.[145] In such cases, the rights of parents and children can be seen to be united against unwarranted state intervention in the family, but it has been questioned whether the courts have given sufficient consideration to the child's *separate* claim to be protected.

There are some noteworthy examples of the explicit recognition of children's convention rights by the English courts.

---

[138] J Fortin 'A decade of the HRA and its impact on children's rights' (2011) Fam Law 176.

[139] See chapter 17 and particularly the House of Lords decision in *R (Begum) v Governors of Denbigh High School* [2006] UKHL 15, a particularly useful case in that it considers not only the convention rights of the applicant child but also the collective rights of the other children at the school in question on the matter of religious dress at school.

[140] See particularly *R (Axon) v Secretary of State for Health and Family Planning Association* [2006] 2 FLR 206 discussed further below.

[141] Chapter 15.

[142] For example, *Re Roddy (A Child) (Identification: Restriction on Publication)* [2004] 2 FLR 949. See also *Murray v Big Pictures (UK) Ltd* [2008] 2 FLR 599 concerning the privacy of the son of J K Rowling, author of the Harry Potter books.

[143] Fortin draws attention to major private law cases such as the House of Lords decision in *Re G (Children)* [2006] 2 FLR 629 which have wholly ignored the question of children's convention rights. The same may be said of the subsequent Supreme Court decision in *Re B (A Child)* [2009] UKSC 5. For commentary see A Bainham 'Rowing back from *Re G*? Natural parents in the Supreme Court' (2010) Fam Law 394.

[144] Though it should be noted that local authorites can be, and frequently are, involved in *private law* proceedings in which they may, inter alia, be directed to provide s 7 or s 37 reports. See further chapter 5 below.

[145] Fortin, n 133 above and J Masson, D McGovern, K Pick and M Winn Oakley, *Protecting Powers: Emergency Intervention for Children's Protection* (John Wiley and Sons Ltd, 2007).

In *Mabon v Mabon*[146] the Court of Appeal, ordering the separate representation of three teenage boys in private law proceedings, made wide-ranging remarks about the need to recognise the growing autonomy of children in the light of international obligations. Their right to freedom of expression was said to outweigh the paternalistic judgment of welfare. *Re Roddy*,[147] was concerned with a teenage girl's right to sell her story to the *Mail on Sunday*. She became pregnant at the age of 12 but was persuaded by the Roman Catholic Church to give birth and place the baby for adoption. Munby J upheld her right to freedom of expression under Art 10 ECHR and her right to waive her right of privacy arising from repect for her private life under Art 8. The case is a good illustration of the balancing exercise required in relation to competing rights under the Convention, in this case involving the rights of the baby, the father of the child, freedom of the press and the public interest as well as those of the young mother.

It should not be thought that the recognition of children's convention rights has been confined to the autonomy interests of adolescents. In *B v S (Contempt: Imprisonment of Mother)*[148] the mother of a 3-year-old was committed to prison for failing to comply with court orders as to contact and her attendance at court. She also had a baby and the prison authorities were not appropriately notified of this fact. Imprisonment would therefore have necessitated separation of the mother and her baby. The Court of Appeal held that the baby's right to respect for family life under Art 8 had been inadvertently breached by the judge who had not considered whether separation of mother and baby was proportionate and justified. Strikingly, Wilson LJ referred to the baby's 'very potent rights' under Art 8.

The definition of children's Convention rights can be expected to continue to evolve. The ECHR was drawn up with adults and not with children in mind. Indeed children are scarcely mentioned in the Convention and its Protocols.[149] Children are the holders of rights under the ECHR, not because they are children but because they are persons and all persons enjoy the rights and freedoms guaranteed by the Convention except to the extent that the Convention itself permits interferences with them.

How then might the courts determine the substance of children's Convention rights? One answer to this is given by Ursula Kilkelly.[150] She argues that the content of children's Convention rights should be influenced by the comprehensive rights set out for children in the UNCRC. She takes the position that the much better enforcement mechanisms under the ECHR (and in the context of the UK under the HRA 1998) could combine with the much clearer articulation of the substance of rights in the UNCRC to become a potent force

---

[146] [2005] 2 FLR 1011.
[147] Above n 137.
[148] [2009] 2 FLR 1005.
[149] For the exceptional instances in which the Convention and its Protocols make express reference to 'children', 'minors' or 'juveniles', see Kilkelly in Fottrell (ed) (above), at pp 89–90.
[150] See the two works cited above.

for the advancement of children's rights. She goes on to give examples of ECHR case-law, which has often been informed by the provisions of the UNCRC and indeed those of other international Conventions.

PARENTS AND CHILDREN: BALANCING RIGHTS AND INTERESTS

Increasingly, it may be necessary to admit the co-existence of independent rights and interests for children and parents whilst emphasising the primacy of the rights and interests of children.[151] This has led to the suggestion that the welfare principle should itself be reformulated as a principle 'giving priority to children's rights over those of parents (or others) in cases where they cannot be reconciled'.[152] In the final analysis this would probably represent a more realistic and theoretically accurate approach than that which attempts to subsume everything within the notion of parental responsibility and the welfare role of the courts. It would moreover chime better with the formulation of the welfare commitment in the UNCRC[153] and with the notion of balancing rights under the ECHR. Yet, here too, there is a lack of clarity in the European Court about exactly how the balance is to be struck between the competing rights and interests of children and parents. In *Yousef v the Netherlands*[154] the Court took the position that where parents' convention rights clashed with the rights or interests of the child, it was the latter which must prevail. The child's rights were said to be the 'paramount' consideration though the Court was clearly not using this term in the English sense of 'sole' consideration. On the other hand, the more traditional approach of the Court is exemplified in *Johansen v Norway*[155] and many other cases which followed it. Here the Court said that a 'fair balance must be struck between the rights and interests of the child and the rights and interests of the parent'.

This latter approach does not make the assumption that children's interests should always be given precedence over adult interests. It is certainly open to question whether children's interests should always be given priority. An alternative approach might be to devise criteria for determining specific instances in which the interests of children or parents (or other adults) should be preferred.[156] The conclusion would not be automatic that children's interests come first and others' second, or vice versa. Instead, there would be an exploration of which interest should be regarded as the more significant or

---

[151] But see the Court of Appeal decisions in *Re R (A Minor)* [1992] Fam 11 and *Re W* [1992] 3 WLR 758 discussed in chapter 8 below which are rather against this trend.

[152] J Eekelaar 'The wardship jurisdiction, children's welfare and parental rights' (1991) 107 LQR 368, at 389.

[153] Article 3 expresses the child's welfare to be 'a *primary* consideration' (authors' emphasis).

[154] [2003] 1 FLR 210.

[155] (1996) 23 EHRR 33.

[156] See generally A Bainham 'Non-Intervention and Judicial Paternalism' in P Birks (ed) *The Frontiers of Liability*, Vol 1 (Oxford University Press, 1994), at pp 161, 173–174. And see John Eekelaar's analysis of what might happen if we were to abandon the welfare principle as we know it, in J Eekelaar 'Beyond the Welfare Principle' [2002] CFLQ 237.

serious. That interest might then be designated as the primary interest and given priority.[157] Matters can become yet further complicated when the wider family interest is thrown into the balance since children and parents are not merely individuals with independent interests but members of a family unit. It may be that the family as a whole has a collective interest which in some cases should outweigh the interests of its individual constituent members.[158]

PARENTS: RIGHTS, RESPONSIBILITIES AND DISCRETIONS

Do parents have rights?

The change in terminology from 'parental rights' to 'parental responsibility' has already been noted, and the function performed by these two concepts described. But did this reformulation of the parent's position represent any real change in the substance of the legal relationship between parents and children? During the late 1980s and the 1990s there was a marked reluctance to accept that parents have 'rights'. John Eekelaar more or less coupled the 'eclipse of parental rights' with the 'emergence of children's rights'.[159] It was stressed frequently that any rights which parents had existed only to enable them to discharge their duties to their children.[160] The law was apparently seeking to express parenthood in a different way which played up the responsibility of parents and played down any rights which they might have.[161]

The best restatement of the parental position was perhaps that of the Law Commission. In its first report on illegitimacy in 1982, taken up in its working paper on custody in 1986 in which it put it thus:[162]

> 'Parenthood would entail a primary claim and a primary responsibility to bring up the child. It would not, however, entail parental "rights" as such. The House of Lords in *Gillick v West Norfolk and Wisbech Area Health Authority* has held that the powers which parents have to control or make decisions for their children are simply the necessary concomitant of their parental duties. This confirms our view

---

[157] Ibid.

[158] Discussed further in A Bainham in '"Honour Thy Father and Thy Mother": Children's Rights and Children's Duties' in G Douglas and L Sebba (eds) *Children's Rights and Traditional Values* (Dartmouth, 1998).

[159] J Eekelaar 'The Eclipse of Parental Rights' (1986) 102 LQR 4 and 'The Emergence of Children's Rights' (1986) 6 *Oxford Journal of Legal Studies* 161.

[160] For a post-*Gillick* restatement of this position, see the views of the Scottish Law Commission, in its Discussion Paper No 88 *Parental Responsibilities and Rights*, at paras 2.1 et seq.

[161] On the general question whether it is accurate to talk at all in terms of parental 'rights' see A McCall Smith 'Is anything left of parental rights?' in E Sutherland and A McCall Smith (eds), *Family Rights: Family Law and Medical Advance* (Edinburgh University Press, 1990) and for a reappraisal of the same question two decades later, A Bainham 'Is anything now left of parental rights?' in R Probert, S Gilmore and J Herring (eds) *Responsible Parents and Parental Responsibility* (Hart Publishing, 2009) 23.

[162] Law Com Working Paper No 96 *Custody* (1986), at para 7.16 and Law Com Report No 118 *Illegitimacy* (1982), at para 4.18.

that "to talk of parental 'rights' " is not only inaccurate as a matter of juristic analysis but also a misleading use of ordinary language.'

This view of parenthood as embracing powers in order to discharge responsibilities accords with what has been termed the 'exchange view'.[163] Parents have rights because they have responsibilities and they have responsibilities because they have rights.[164] On this view, the correct way of looking at parenthood is one which implies reciprocity.

Do parents have independent interests?

The emphasis on parental responsibility raises a fundamental issue. Whether or not it is jurisprudentially accurate to say that parents have 'rights', can it at least be said that they have independent interests which can be asserted in law? After a period in which it was fashionable to deny that they do, judicial decisions[165] and academic commentaries[166] began to acknowledge that they did.

There are two separate questions here. First, is it possible to identify independent interests which parents have in relation to their children? Second, if so, should the law recognise and accommodate these?

As to the first question, leading philosophers have had little difficulty in concluding that there is an independent parental interest in raising children which is not merely a matter of promoting those children's own interests. It is something personal to the parent. David Archard puts it this way:[167]

> 'Being a parent is extremely important to a person. Even if a child is not to be thought of as the property or even an extension of the parent, the shared life of a parent and child involves an adult's purposes and aims at the deepest level ... parents have an interest in parenting – that is, in sharing a life with, and directing the development of, their child. It is not enough to discount the interests of a parent in a moral theory of parenthood. What must merit full and proper consideration is the interest of someone in being a parent.'

If the first question is relatively easy to answer, the second is undoubtedly more difficult. Just because parents might wish to act in relation to their children in a

---

163   On the similar trend in North America, see KT Bartlett 'Re-Expressing Parenthood' (1988) 98 *Yale Law Journal* 293.

164   See KT Bartlett (above), at pp 297 et seq.

165   See, for example, *Re K (A Minor) (Custody)* [1990] 2 FLR 64; and *Re K (A Minor) (Wardship; Adoption)* [1991] 1 FLR 57, discussed in J Eekelaar 'The Wardship Jurisdiction, Children's Welfare and Parents' Rights' (1991) 107 LQR 386. See also the decision of the ECtHR in *Hokkanen v Finland* (1995) 19 EHRR 139 which can surely only be explained on the basis that a parent has a right to and an independent interest in contact with his child. See further chapter 5 below.

166   J Eekelaar (above), and A Bainham 'Growing Up in Britain: Adolescence in the post-*Gillick* Era' (1992) *Juridical Review* 155.

167   D Archard *Children, Family and the State* (Ashgate, 2003), at p 94. See also C Macleod 'Conceptions of parental autonomy' (1997) 25 *Politics and Society* 117, especially at 119.

way which advances their own, rather than their children's interests, it is not obvious that the law should support them in doing so, especially given the central commitment to the welfare of children.

Let us accept for the moment what has been called the 'minimum provision thesis'.[168] There is widespread, if not universal, agreement that parents are under a moral (and indeed legal) obligation to provide their children with the basic necessities of life such as food, clothing and shelter, medical attention and education. They are not permitted, by commission or (more likely) omission, to fail in the performance of these duties and the state may intervene if they do. Put another way parents may not pursue their own selfish interests if, in so doing, they fail to discharge their fundamental responsibilities. All of this can be readily agreed. The argument is about the nature of the parents' position once these basic responsibilities have been discharged.

A close examination of the law reveals that, for all the rhetoric suggesting that parents are obliged always to act in their children's best interests and that only their children's interests count, the reality is that the law does allow parents a good deal of latitude within which they are perfectly free to pursue their own interests and aims.[169]

Let us take an example which may appear to trivialise the issue, but which illustrates the kind of decisions parents take day in and day out. A family is on holiday and the parents decide to visit Cheltenham. Mum and Dad dutifully make enquiries and discover that there is a children's adventure playground in which their seven- and four-year-olds may spend a happy hour or two. After this, they decide that they, the parents, would like to see the Regency architecture along the Promenade and in Imperial Square. The children are bored with Regency architecture and protest. Nonetheless, they are dragged along to see it, the parents deciding to prioritise their own interests at that point. Can it be seriously suggested by anyone that the law does not, or should not, support them in this?

There are at least two good reasons why the law should recognise the position that parents are free to satisfy their own interests.[170] First on the birth of a child, once parentage is established, very wide-ranging and extensive burdens are placed by the law on those identified as parents – financial, emotional and practical.[171] Moreover, these responsibilites last for 18 years and a good deal longer than that if more than one child is involved. Neither should the major sacrifices involved in pregnancy and childbirth be discounted. Secondly, the law

---

[168] Macleod (above) at 120.

[169] The nature of parental discretion is examined in depth by Bernard Dickens in his seminal article 'The Modern Function and Limits of Parental Rights' (1981) 97 LQR 462. Dickens analysis is considered in detail in the 3rd edition of this work, at pp 119–122.

[170] Amplified in Bainham, n 156 (above) at 30–33.

[171] See the discussion of parental responsibility in chapter 4. McCall Smith calls the responsibility of parents 'status responsibility' in that it comes as a package of obligations which cannot be negotiated away. McCall Smith (above) at 7.

needs to reflect the reality of everyday life. The honest position is that parents do not, and are not required, to act at all times with their children's interests paramount in their minds. It would be far better for this to be transparently and openly acknowledged rather than to act out a pretence that only children's interests count.

The legal incidents of parenthood

It has never been possible to state with complete confidence the legal incidents of parenthood. This is because they have never been set out in statutory form. The statutory definitions of 'parental rights and duties' and now 'parental responsibility' simply refer back to the general law. Therefore, in order to appreciate the full legal implications of the parent–child relationship, it has been necessary to piece this together by taking into account the legal effects recognised at common law and under various statutory provisions. A number of commentators attempted to do this[172] before the Children Act 1989, although the Law Commission eschewed the opportunity to do so in its report on *Guardianship and Custody* which preceded the Children Act. The Commission argued that, although it would be superficially attractive to provide a list, this would be a practical impossibility given the need for change periodically to meet different needs and circumstances.[173] It is nonetheless possible to collate with some accuracy the major incidents of parenthood. The following list is taken from *Bromley's Family Law*:[174]

(a) bringing up the child;

(b) having contact with the child;

(c) protecting and maintaining the child;

(d) disciplining the child;

(e) determining and providing for the child's education;

(f) determining the child's religion;

(g) consenting to the child's medical treatment;

(h) consenting to the child's marriage;

(i) consenting to the child's adoption;

---

[172] See, for example, J Eekelaar 'What are Parental Rights?' (1973) 89 LQR 210 and S Maidment 'The Fragmentation of Parental Rights' (1981) CLJ 135.

[173] Law Com Report No 172 *Review of Child Law: Guardianship and Custody* (1988), at para 2.6.

[174] PM Bromley and NV Lowe *Bromley's Family Law* (10th edn, Oxford University Press, 2007), at p 377.

(j)   vetoing the issue of a child's passport;

(j)   taking the child outside the United Kingdom and consenting to the child's emigration;

(k)   administering the child's property;

(l)   naming the child;

(n)   representing the child in legal proceedings;

(o)   disposing of the child's corpse;

(p)   appointing a guardian for the child.

One could possibly add to this list, sharing responsibility for criminal offences committed by the child given the liability of parents to pay the child's fines or have parenting orders made against them.[175] Each of the listed matters requires qualification and there is considerable debate about their content and extent, but they do at least convey, in general terms, the areas of control which fall within parenthood. There is little cause for surprise since they relate to all the most important matters which can affect a child's upbringing and it would be expected that parents would exercise primary control over them.

The approach in Scotland

The Scottish Law Commission took a slightly different view of the nature of the parental position in law from that of the English Commission.[176] It agreed that it was correct to emphasise the responsibility of parents but recommended that parental rights should also be expressly recognised in legislation accepting that such rights would be subordinate to the child's best interests. The Commission also felt that it was helpful to set out the principal responsibilities and rights of parents in legislation, and the Scottish legislation does just that.[177] Section 1 of the Children (Scotland) Act 1995 sets out the following responsibilities of parents:

(a)   to safeguard and promote the child's health, development and welfare;

(b)   to provide, in a manner appropriate to the stage of development of the child

---

[175]   See further chapter 15.
[176]   See Scot Law Com No 135 *Report on Family Law* (Edinburgh HMSO, 1992) especially, at paras 2.1–2.35.
[177]   See E Sutherland 'Scotland: Child Law Reform – At Last!' in A Bainham (ed) *The International Survey of Family Law 1995* (Martinus Nijhoff, 1997). For a subsequent evaluation see E Sutherland 'How Children are Faring in the New Scotland' in A Bainham (ed) *The International Survey of Family Law (2001 Edition)* (Family Law, 2001), at p 363.

(i) direction;

(ii) guidance;

to the child;

(c) if the child is not living with the parent, to maintain personal relations and direct contact with the child on a regular basis; and

(d) to act as the child's legal representative.

These responsibilities, together with the rights set out below (which replace common-law, but not specific statutory, duties) must be exercised to the extent that it is 'practicable and in the interests of the child' to do so.

Section 2 of the Act sets out a corresponding list of parental rights which a parent has in order to fulfil these responsibilities. They are:

(a) to have the child living with him or her or otherwise to regulate the child's residence;

(b) to control, direct or guide, in a manner appropriate to the stage of development of the child, the child's upbringing;

(c) if the child is not living with him, to maintain personal relations and direct contact with the child on a regular basis; and

(d) to act as the child's legal representative.

It will be noted that there is a close correspondence, almost direct correlation, between the above responsibilities and rights, emphasising the reciprocal nature of rights and responsibilities which essentially conforms with the 'exchange view' of parenthood discussed earlier.

Parent–child conflicts

It is now clear, both at common law and under a variety of statutory provisions, that children have the capacity to perform certain acts and take certain decisions.[178] Sometimes this is dependent upon them having attained a certain age and sometimes it falls to be determined by the test of maturity propounded by the House of Lords in the *Gillick* case. That case will be discussed in depth later when medical issues are considered.[179] The present concern is to explore the interaction between children's capacity for decision-making and parental discretion.[180]

---

[178] See chapter 8 below for a further discussion.

[179] In chapter 8 below.

[180] For these purposes it is assumed that the ratio of *Gillick* is sufficiently wide to govern a range of issues other than contraception or medical issues, an interpretation certainly adopted by Silber J in the *Axon* case (above) and widely favoured by academic commentators.

The critical question is whether the child's acquisition of capacity, whether through age or maturity, *terminates* any parental claim to involvement, or whether the child's capacity and parental discretion *co-exist* in some form until the child reaches maturity. The traditional view was that parental rights 'dwindle' as the child approaches majority but at least survive until then. The older the child, the less likely it has been that a court would enforce parental control against his wishes.[181] But, although it was not always enforceable, it was thought that parental control continued to exist even where it amounted, in the case of older teenagers, to no more than a right to give guidance or advice.[182]

A radical interpretation of *Gillick* would suggest that any right of parental control is completely eclipsed by the child's ability to act for himself.[183] Such a view relies heavily on the speech of Lord Scarman in which he said that 'the parental right yields to the child's right to make his own decisions when he reaches a sufficient understanding and intelligence to be capable of making up his own mind on the matter requiring decision'.[184] This radical interpretation appears to have been adopted, at least in the context of human rights,[185] by Silber J in the subsequent *Axon* case[186] where he held that any parental right to respect for family life under Art 8 would not survive the child's acquisition of capacity to take medical decisions on her own behalf.

Lord Scarman himself in *Gillick*, however, appeared to acknowledge that parental rights would survive until majority and he was in general agreement with Lord Fraser. Lord Fraser adopted a noticeably more cautious approach to the inter-relationship of adolescent capabilities and parental control. He evidently took the view that maturity alone should not be enough to justify the provision of contraceptives to 'under-age' girls without parental knowledge or consent.[187] Lord Fraser was especially concerned that, in every case, the medical professionals should attempt to persuade the girl to allow parental involvement in the decision, although it has been suggested that failure to do so might be merely a breach of professional ethics rather than unlawful.[188] Taken as a whole, the majority opinion in *Gillick* did appear to recognise the potential value of parents' participation in adolescent decision-making but accorded priority to the views of a competent adolescent. On this interpretation, the decision could be viewed as supportive of a form of participatory or inclusive decision-making which involves parents, children and third parties (in the

---

[181] See *Krishnan v Sutton London Borough Council* [1970] Ch 181 and the views of Lord Denning MR in *Hewer v Bryant* [1970] 1 QB 357 at 369.

[182] It could be argued that the adolescent child has a right of recipience to this parental guidance and advice. See A Bainham 'Growing Up in Britain: Adolescence in the post-*Gillick* Era' (1992) *Juridical Review* 155.

[183] See J Eekelaar 'The Eclipse of Parental Rights' (1986) 102 LQR 4.

[184] [1986] 1 AC 112 at 186.

[185] See below.

[186] *R (Axon) v Secretary of State for Health and Family Planning Association* [2006] 2 FLR 206. For commentary on the case see A Hall 'Children's rights, parents' wishes and the state: the medical treatment of children' (2006) Fam Law 317. See further chapter 8 below.

[187] In all, he laid down five preconditions. See chapter 8 below.

[188] J Eekelaar (above).

Gillick case, the medical profession). Further, it might be concluded that the final decision rests with neither parents nor children but with the third party with whom they are dealing and that they each have only consultative rights.[189] This might provide a way of reconciling the continuing responsibilities and discretions of parents, particularly to provide advice and guidance, with the gradual legal emancipation of children, although later Court of Appeal decisions represent something of a retreat from *Gillick* in that they appear to support the right of outsiders to act on parental authority in the face of objection by the competent child.[190]

JUSTICE

The relevance of justice

It must be obvious, surely, that the 'family justice system' is concerned with 'justice'. Children cases are part of this system and therefore it might be thought that justice is an important consideration in the resolution of children disputes. In fact no such assumption can be safely made. The reason will be immediately apparent. The legal system as it affects children is dominated by welfare considerations. This generates substantial doubts not merely about how far the claims of justice are relevant in these disputes, but whether they are relevant at all. Over forty years ago the House of Lords twice confronted this issue[191] in a short space of time and reached differing conclusions in the two separate contexts in which the question arose.

In *J v C* the House famously reinterpreted the welfare principle and in particular the meaning of 'paramount' in such a way that, in a dispute concerning the upbringing of a child, the child's best interests were to be the court's sole consideration, ruling upon the course to be followed.[192] The corollary of this proposition was that adult interests, especially parents' interests, were not only to be subordinated to those of the child but were relevant only to the extent that they fed into the process of ascertaining where the child's best interests lay. It did not take the courts very long to take the

---

189 A Bainham (above), at pp 172 et seq.
190 See *Re R (A Minor) (Wardship: Consent to Treatment)* [1992] Fam 11, *Re W (A Minor) (Medical Treatment: Court's Jurisdiction)* [1993] Fam 64, and chapter 8 below. For re-evaluations of Gillick see M Freeman 'Gillick revisited' (2005) 13 IJLPF 201 and J Fortin 'The Gillick decision – not just a high water mark' in S Gilmore, J Herring and R Probert (eds), *Landmark Cases in Family Law* (Hart Publishing, 2011), at p 199.
191 *J v C* [1970] AC 668; *S v S; W v Official Solicitor* [1972] AC 24. For a recent reappraisal of the significance of the former decision see N Lowe, *J v C*: Placing the child's welfare centre stage' in S Gilmore, J Herring and R Probert (eds) *Landmark Cases in Family Law* (Hart Publishing, 2011) 27 and of the latter decision A Bainham 'Welfare, truth and justice: the children of extra-marital relations' in the same volume at 113.
192 See further chapter 2 where we discuss the welfare principle in greater depth.

position that 'misconduct' as between the parents was irrelevant in the determination of welfare, though many might think this 'unjust' to the 'wronged' parent.[193]

Then in *S v S; W v Official Solicitor*, the House of Lords ruled that the welfare principle did not govern the direction of blood tests in paternity disputes.[194] The formulation adopted in that case, that a test should be directed unless it was shown to be *against* the best interests of the child concerned, had the effect of allowing considerations of justice to enter into the equation. The House was particularly concerned that the court should have the best available evidence before it. The most striking statement of this approach is that of Lord Denning in the Court of Appeal where he said:[195]

> 'Finally, I must say that, over and above all the interests of the child, there is one overriding interest which must be considered. It is the interests of justice. Should it come to the crunch, *then the interests of justice must take first place.*'

Lord Denning then was clearly of the view that the interests of justice, at least in this context, took priority even over the interests of the child. It is noteworthy, however, that the House of Lords did not see any conflict in this case between the dual considerations of welfare and justice, holding that the direction of testing was consistent with both.

This perhaps raises another fundamental issue. Perhaps it can be legitimately argued that for the courts to reach decisions on the basis of what they see as the best interests of children, is in fact justice. On this view, to impose a welfare-based solution is also to produce a just solution. It is the one which is likely to command the greatest respect. The difficulty with this argument, seductive though it is, is that it may work better for children than it does for adults.

There is no better illustration of this problem than the Court of Appeal decision in *Webster v Norfolk County Council and the Children (By Their Children's Guardian)*.[196] Three children were removed from their parents, made the subject of final care orders and in due course adopted on the basis that the parents had physically abused one of them. When the authority brought care proceedings in relation to the parents' fourth child, they produced fresh expert evidence which strongly suggested that the older child's fractures had been caused by scurvy or iron deficiency and were inconsistent with abuse. Care proceedings were then discontinued in relation to the youngest child but the parents sought permission to appeal the adoption orders in relation to the

---

[193] See especially *Re K (Minors) (Children: Care and Control)* [1977] Fam 179 where the issue was the adultery of the mother, the father being an Anglican clergyman. On the relevance of conduct in family disputes generally, including children disputes, see A Bainham 'Men and women behaving badly: is fault dead in English family law?' (2001) 21 *Oxford Journal of Legal Studies* 219.

[194] See further chapter 3 above.

[195] *S v McC* [1970] 1 All ER 1162, 1165. Authors' emphasis.

[196] [2009] 1 FLR 1378.

other three children out of time and to adduce fresh evidence. The Court of Appeal dismissed their appeal. Even if the parents had suffered a serious injustice (something which has never been determined) public policy considerations and the relevant authorites on adoption, made it impossible to set aside adoption orders which had been made some three years previously.

While a strong argument can be presented for saying that this decision was more or less inevitable on welfare grounds, its claim to be a just decision is much more open to doubt. The instinctive reaction of most fair-minded people will probably be that what happened to the parents here was monstrously unjust; and that, at the very least, justice required a proper examination of the whole available evidence as to whether the older child was physically abused or not. But in the circumstances there is no doubt the current welfare of the children trumped any considerations of justice to the parents. It is an interesting question whether it was a just decision from the children's point of view. This is a matter upon which they themselves may well reflect when, on attaining majority, it will be for them to decide the extent to which they wish to pursue a relationship with their biological parents, if at all.

It seems clear that in addressing the relevance of justice in children cases, the context needs to be kept carefully in mind. Notwithstanding the unusually difficult circumstances of Webster, more generally it could be said that justice to parents is a feature of the child protection system. Unlike the private law, it is not governed solely by the welfare principle. A statutory threshold exists,[197] ostensibly to ensure that the state does not interfere with those parents who are capable of 'good enough' parenting. It will often be very clear that someone else could provide a higher standard of care. But is it not perhaps a distortion to say that considerations of justice to both parents and children require that the birth parents, whatever their deficiencies, be given a fair opportunity of raising them.[198]

Despite their unwavering commitment to the welfare principle, the family courts are also conscious of the requirements of justice, especially procedural fairness. One example of this is their greater willingness to accept that justice may require that children themselves be permitted to give evidence.[199] In *Re W (Child Abuse: Oral Evidence)*[200] the House of Lords abandoned the former presumption against a child giving evidence in family proceedings on the basis that the court needs the best evidence before it. It was accepted that the

---

[197] Section 31(2) Children Act 1989 as to which see the recent re-evaluation of the threshold in C Cobley and N Lowe 'The statutory "threshold" under section 31 of the Children Act 1989 – time to take stock' (2011) 127 LQR 396.

[198] But not everyone agrees with this. There have been calls for many years by those who feel that parents should in effect be 'licensed' by attempting to screen out potentially neglectful and abusive parents and remove the child from them at birth. For one manifestation of this argument see J Dwyer, *The Relationship Rights of Children* (Cambridge University Press, 2006) especially, at pp 254–262.

[199] See chapter 14 below on the position of children in court proceedings generally.

[200] [2010] UKSC 12.

interests of justice would need to be balanced against other considerations, especially the welfare considerations affecting the child concerned.

Access to Justice

Another aspect of the justice issue is the question of access to the courts in children cases.[201] George has recently addressed this question as part of a wider analysis of family justice.[202] He replies to the charge commonly made that the courts are unsuitable for the resolution of family disputes. Drawing on the writings of legal philosophers on the meaning of 'justice',[203] he concludes that the principal reason why the courts do need to remain involved is that we are dealing, even in what is often seen as the private sphere of the family, with people's legal rights. Law has a particularly important role to play in protecting the weak against the strong and in rectifying power imbalances within the family.

A moment's thought confirms that this must be the case as far as children are concerned; the younger the child the more obvious is the point. It may also be rather more obvious in the context of the public law than the private law. Only a court, surely, should be empowered to take a decision which involves removing a child from the family into substitute care. But in the private law too, who other than a judge has the authority to require a recalcitrant parent to allow the other parent some contact with the child in the face of a stubborn refusal to do so? And who, other than a judge, can impose the necessary sanctions where required?

An important aspect of the role of the courts in children cases, as indeed in other family cases, relates to negotiation at the door of the court. It is unhelpful to conceptualise the determination of family disputes as confined to a dual classification of those which are resolved by agreement and negotiation without involving the courts and those which are the subject of judicial determination. This does not encapsulate well enough what happens in a great many cases which, although the subject of applications to the court, do not involve a judicial determination in any real sense.[204] Many are brought to a negotiated conclusion outside court and the solutions adopted by the parties are then endorsed by the judge in consent orders. Only a relatively small minority of cases, certainly in the private law, can be expected to go to final, fully-contested hearings.

---

[201] The issue of the place of justice in the family justice system has undergone something of a renaissance in recent years. A recent treatment of the subject is J Eekelaar and M Maclean, *Family Justice: The Work of Family Judges in Uncertain Times* (Hart Publishing, 2013) which in part considers the nature and role of the family justice system.

[202] R George *Ideas and Debates in Family Law* (Hart Publishing, 2012) especially, at pp 16–22 and 142–146.

[203] Especially those of Rawls. See J Rawls, *Justice as Fairness: A Restatement* (Harvard University Press, 2001).

[204] On the negotiating role of barristers in family proceedings, including children proceedings, see J Eekelaar and M Maclean *Family Law Advocacy* (Hart Publishing, 2009).

What needs to be understood in many of these cases is that it is the *environment* of the court which has produced agreements. They would not have been achieved outside it, especially not in mediation. The reason for this is the authority of the judge. Unreasonable people[205] can often turn into reasonable people at the door of the court. This metamorphosis occurs only because of the awareness that there is someone sitting on the other side of the door who can impose solutions on them if they do not negotiate sensibly. It is common therefore for the time spent outside court greatly to exceed the time spent in it. We can call this process one of 'coerced negotiation' (if looked at from outside court) or 'negotiated coercion' (if seen from inside the court when the order is made). Its importance should not be under-estimated in any evaluation of the contribution of law and justice to the determination of children disputes.

There are grave concerns, highlighted by George and others,[206] that the government may be under-valuing the importance of the courts in the resolution of family disputes and moving too strongly in the direction of diverting people away from them.[207] The substantial withdrawal of legal aid from private law children disputes is perhaps the clearest example of the retreat from justice in family matters.[208] This needs to be seen alongside the abject failure over a number of years to fund properly the system of children's guardians provided by CAFCASS, let alone make adequate provision for the use of such guardians where necessitated in the private law.[209] As in so many areas of life, actions speak much louder than words.[210] No government which allows such things to happen can be taken seriously when it claims to be giving priority to children.

---

[205] Unreasonableness is not gendered. Men and women are capable of being, and very frequently are, unreasonable in equal measure.

[206] See particularly M Maclean and J Eekelaar 'Family Justice' (2011) Fam Law 3 and J Eekelaar '"Not of the highest importance": family justice under threat' [2011] *Journal of Social Welfare and Family Law* 311.

[207] The government's position is set out in Ministry of Justice, *Proposals for the Reform of Legal Aid in England and Wales: Consultation Paper* (HMSO, 2010).

[208] By the Legal Aid, Sentencing and Punishment of Offenders Act 2012.

[209] Such private law guardians were previously known as 'Rule 9.5 guardians' under the then Family Proceedings Rules 1991. Their appointment is now governed by r 16.4 Family Procedure Rules 2010.

[210] On the general issue of the failure of government to match its child protection rhetoric with the commitment of resources see A MacDonald 'The caustic dichotomy – political vision and resourcing in the care system' [2009] 21 CFLQ 30.

Chapter 8

CHILDREN AND MEDICAL DECISIONS

INTRODUCTION

The principles which now govern the relationship between the legal capacities of children, the responsibilities of parents and the limits of State intervention have, to a considerable extent, been fashioned in the context of medical decision-making. This is not really surprising since the health of children is self-evidently the most basic and essential consideration in protecting their welfare. In this chapter we take a close look at some of the more important decisions of the courts which have determined whether medical procedures should, or should not, be carried out on individual children.[1] These decisions,

---

[1]   There are now several established texts on medical law including: JK Mason and GT Laurie *Mason & McCall Smith's Law and Medical Ethics* (9th edn, Oxford University Press, 2013); E Jackson *Medical Law Text, Cases, and Materials* (3rd edn, Oxford University Press, 2013); J Herring *Medical Law and Ethics* (4th ed) (Oxford University Press 2012); A Grubb, J Laing, and J McHale (eds) *Principles of Medical Law* (3rd edn, Oxford University Press, 2010; J McHale and M Fox *Health Care Law: Text and Materials* (2nd edn, Sweet & Maxwell, 2006); J Montgomery *Health Care Law* (2nd edn, Oxford University Press, 2002); I Kennedy and A Grubb *Medical Law* (3rd edn, Butterworths, 2000); For discussion in the context of family law and parental responsibility, see J Bridgeman *Parental Responsibility, Young Children and Healthcare Law* (Cambridge University Press, 2007) and E Sutherland and A McCall Smith *Family Rights: Family Law and Medical Advance* (Edinburgh University Press, 1990). A very readable account and critique of the relationship between doctors, children and parents is provided in M Brazier and E Cave *Medicine, Patients and the Law* (5th edn, Penguin Books, 2011), ch 14. For an introduction to the central issues involving medical decisions and children, see MDA Freeman *The Rights and Wrongs of Children* (Frances Pinter, 1983), ch 7; and see also R Huxtable *Law, Ethics and Compromise at the Limits of Life: To Treat or Not to Treat?* (Routledge Cavendish, 2012). Also of use is M Freeman *The Moral Status of Children* (Martinus Nijhoff, 1997), especially ch 15 (which deals with adolescents' rights to take their own decisions) and ch 16 (which deals with sterilisation of the mentally handicapped). Many useful articles may now be found in the *Medical Law Review* published by Oxford University Press. Among the more recent commentaries are A Morris 'Selective treatment of irreversibly impaired infants: decision-making at the threshold' (2009) 17(3) *Medical Law Review* 347; R Heywood 'Parents and medical professsionals: conflict, cooperation and best interests' (2012) 20(1) *Medical Law Review* 29; S Gilmore and J Herring ' "No" is the Hardest Word: Consent and Children's Autonomy' [2011] CFLQ 3; E Cave and J Wallbank 'Minors' Capacity to Refuse Treatment: A Reply to Gilmore and Herring' (2012) 20 *Medical Law Review* 423; S Gilmore and J Herring 'Children's Refusal of Treatment: The Debate Continues' [2012] Fam Law 973. Among earlier commentaries are: P Lewis 'The Medical Treatment of Children' in J Fionda (ed) *Legal Concepts of Childhood* (Hart Publishing, 2001) and C Bridge 'Religion, Culture and the Body of the Child' in A Bainham, S Day Sclater and M Richards (eds) *Body Lore and Laws* (Hart Publishing, 2002), at p 265. A useful guide published by the British Medical Association is *Consent, Rights and Choices in Health Care for Children and Young People* (BMJ Books, 2001). See also Department of Health *Seeking Consent: Working with Children* (DoH, 2001).

important in their own right, have a significance which goes beyond this, since they are probably the best practical applications of the theoretical perspectives discussed in chapter 7. They present acute dilemmas concerning the limits of parents' powers and duties, the extent of children's rights (whether to be protected or to exercise autonomy) and the acceptable limits of State paternalism over children exercised through the courts. It is for this reason that we go into the facts and reasoning of decisions in greater depth than we do elsewhere in the book.

The Children Act 1989 defines a child as a person below the age of 18 years, but of course within that spectrum there is a world of difference between the sort of medical questions which can arise in relation to babies or young children on the one hand and adolescents on the other. The latter have a capacity for self-help in seeking medical assistance, whilst the former are wholly dependent on the support of interested adults. The general question relating to young children, given that there must be a proxy decision-maker, is when precisely an outside party or agency should be able to challenge parental authority. The general issue regarding adolescents, on the assumption that they themselves have legal capacity, relates to the circumstances in which they may act in conjunction with medical advice and by-pass parental involvement or go ahead with a medical procedure in the face of parental opposition.

In this chapter we discuss the legal framework within which medical decisions are taken, and examine the operation of these principles in two key areas which illustrate the particular problems affecting infants and young children and also the special considerations applying to adolescents. We begin, however, by highlighting two central questions which apply to the numerous medical issues affecting children.

CENTRAL QUESTIONS

Medical issues affecting children may perhaps be reduced to two central questions:

(1) who decides what medical procedures or treatment are appropriate for a child; and

(2) on what criteria ought such decisions to be based?

Who decides?

As to the first question, there are any number of possibilities. It would be possible to give parents (or others exercising parental responsibility) an unfettered discretion, although there might need to be a mechanism for resolving disagreements between parents.[2] Equally, decisions could be handed over entirely to children themselves, at least where they have acquired a certain age or level of understanding.

Another alternative might be to allow an outside agency, such as a court, to take the final decision. In that case, the circumstances under which the courts would become involved would need to be addressed. There could, for example, be a mandatory judicial procedure for certain operations.[3] Yet another possibility is that decisions could be left to the medical profession subject to a requirement that they be taken in accordance with accepted medical practice.[4]

However, the English case-law alerts us to the danger of assuming that there must necessarily be a single decision-maker. Whilst it is incontrovertibly true that *someone* has to have the final say, it is equally clear, in the family context, that the law has had to accommodate forms of participatory or inclusive decision-making which take at least some account of *all* the legitimate views involved. The crucial question in any given situation therefore becomes one of determining precisely how this balance should be struck. It is only in the event of serious disagreement that the matter is likely to be brought before the courts.

On what criteria?

As to the second question, there is an argument for saying that, since the facts of no two cases are ever identical, all medical decisions affecting individual children should be taken on an individualistic basis applying the welfare principle. Indeed, this largely represents current practice in England. Even the minority of cases which have reached the higher courts have, on the whole, failed to establish general criteria to determine with any precision such matters as when life-saving treatment should be given or withheld or when the

---

[2] For a review of the place that parental opinion has held in the reported decisions on medical treatment for children, see J Loughrey 'Medical Treatment – the Status of Parental Opinion' [1998] Fam Law 146.

[3] Such procedures, especially for abortions on minors without parental consent, have been adopted in the USA, but English law has so far stopped short of this, while accepting that for sterilisation of mentally incompetent minors judicial authorisation is required in virtually all cases. See *Practice Note (Official Solicitor: Declaratory Proceedings: Medical and Welfare Decisions for Adults who Lack Capacity)* [2001] 2 FLR 158.

[4] This would be in line with the general requirement imposed by the law of tort that doctors act in accordance with the practice accepted by a responsible body of medical men skilled in that particular art. See *Bolam v Friern Hospital Management Committee* [1957] 2 All ER 118. This duty has been the subject of a decision of the House of Lords in *Bolitho v City and Hackney Health Authority* [1997] 3 WLR 1151, a case in which a two-year-old child with acute respiratory difficulties died after a doctor negligently failed to attend him in hospital. Here, the House refined the *Bolam* test by holding that there could be *rare* cases in which it might be demonstrated that professional medical opinion was incapable of withstanding logical analysis. In these rare cases, a judge might be entitled to hold that the body of opinion concerned was not reasonable or responsible. On the facts, however, this was not such a case, since there was good reason to accept the defendant's expert opinion, and it had therefore not been proved that the doctor's failure to attend the child had caused the injuries which had led to his death. For commentary, see J Keown 'Reining in the Bolam test' [1998] CLJ 248.

sterilisation of mentally incapacitated young women should be authorised or prohibited. Occasionally, the courts have appeared to go out of their way to deny that general principles of public policy are involved in such cases.[5] Moreover, they will often defer to the expertise of the medical profession on what are seen as clinical matters, preferring to confine themselves to giving broadly defined directions.[6] Indeed, it has been put more strongly by Montgomery (specifically in the context of selective treatment of the newborn) whose assessment is that it has become 'clear that the courts will respect the clinical freedom of doctors and refuse to force them to act against their clinical judgment'.[7]

Serious difficulties can arise, of course, where parents fundamentally disagree with the clinical judgment of the medical team and with the regime of treatment proposed for a child. This can result in a complete loss of confidence in the health professionals involved and it may be necessary for the courts to intervene. The courts have set out the principles which should govern such situations.[8] They have emphasised in particular the importance of *consultation* between the doctors and the parents, and the desirability of them reaching agreement wherever possible. Where, however, this is not possible, the specific problems should be brought before the court. The point here is not that the court is likely to order the medical team to act against their clinical judgment but rather that the involvement of the court will *reinforce* those judgments. It may also bring the parents to accept what is proposed even where their natural inclination is to attempt to prolong the life of their child at all cost.[9] As Caroline Bridge has put it, in these situations, 'the court often assumes the role of a compassionate authority, empathising with the parents but leading them to accept what doctors say is best for the child'.[10]

Thus, in *R v Portsmouth Hospitals NHS Trust ex parte Glass*[11] there had been a complete breakdown of trust between the hospital team and the family of a severely disabled boy aged 12 with a limited lifespan. The hospital wished to administer palliative care only but the mother wished him to receive whatever

---

[5]   A particularly striking example is the speech of Lord Hailsham in *Re B (A Minor) (Wardship: Sterilisation)* [1988] AC 199, in which he offered the view that no general issues of public policy were raised by the proposed sterilisation of a mentally incompetent teenager. See for a recent example, *An NHS Trust v MB (A Child Represented by Cafcass as Guardian Ad Litem)* [2006] EWHC 507 (Fam), [2006] 2 FLR 319, at para [107], per Holman J.

[6]   See, for example, *Re C (A Minor) (Wardship: Medical Treatment)* [1989] 2 All ER 782.

[7]   J Montgomery *Health Care Law* (2nd edn, Oxford University Press, 2002), at p 440.

[8]   See particularly *R v Portsmouth Hospitals NHS Trust ex parte Glass* [1999] 2 FLR 905 and *Wyatt v Portsmouth NHS Trust* [2005] EWCA Civ 1181, [2006] 1 FLR 554.

[9]   This may be because of parents' strongly held religious beliefs. For a study of such cases at Great Ormond Street Hospital, see J Brierley, J Linthicum, A Petros 'Should religious beliefs be allowed to stonewall a secular approach to withdrawing and withholding treatment in children?' (2012) *Journal of Medical Ethics* (published online 30 March 2012) (http://jme.bmj. com/content/early/2012/08/24medeithics-2011–100104.abstract). See the discussion by D Ranton 'Parental religious beliefs when making decisions for terminally ill children' [2013] Fam Law 684.

[10] C Bridge (above), at p 274.

[11] [1999] 2 FLR 905.

medical treatment would prolong his life. She applied for judicial review and sought an anticipatory declaration regarding the course to be taken if the boy were to be admitted for emergency treatment and a disagreement arose. The Court of Appeal upheld the judge's refusal to grant it. It was inappropriate to dictate in advance to the medical team what treatment should or should not be given in circumstances which had not yet arisen. In the event of an irreconcilable conflict, the court would rule in the actual circumstances if and when they arose, on the basis of the child's best interests. However, the case was subsequently taken by the boy's mother to Strasbourg.[12] In an important ruling, the ECtHR held that a decision to impose treatment in defiance of a parent's objections gave rise to an interference with the child's right to respect for his private life, in particular his right to physical integrity, under Art 8 of the ECHR. The interference could not be justified as 'necessary' under Art 8(2) since the earlier disputes between the parent and the hospital team in the event of an emergency highlighted their disagreement and placed a clear onus on the hospital to bring the matter before the court for resolution. Accordingly, there was a violation of Art 8. The key point of this decision is therefore that the obligation is on the medical authorities and not on the parent to bring serious disagreements before the courts (although of course it is also open to the parent to take the initiative and do so).

In some cases, even where doctors and parents do not initially agree, it may be possible, as in *Re MM (Medical Treatment)*,[13] to reach agreement in the course of proceedings. In that case the medical team and the parents, who were Russian, disagreed about the specific treatment regime for a child who suffered from immunodeficiency which had been treated in Russia with a programme of immunostimulant therapy. The parents wanted a continuation of this treatment while the local authority, supported by the Official Solicitor, wanted instead a course of replacement immunoglobin administered intravenously and designed to continue through the child's life. Ultimately it was agreed that the doctors were to determine what course of treatment was appropriate, following consultation with the parents at all stages as far as reasonably practicable, and that there should be consideration of alternative forms of management suggested by the parents. Black J, approving the agreed course, did however indicate that, although the parents' objection to the recommended treatment had been a rational objection, she would have overridden it if necessary since the evidence that it was in the child's best interests was overwhelming.

In cases in which agreement cannot be reached, however, it may be necessary for a court to decide whether treatment would be lawful in the face of parental objection. In deciding such cases the courts' approach is to seek to identify the best interests of the child concerned, broadly construed, and as we shall see below the courts have sought to provide some guidance to judges in that task. Many of the disputes between parents and doctors have arisen in the context of the treatment of severely disabled babies and young children and the principles

---

12   *Glass v United Kingdom* [2004] 1 FLR 1019.
13   [2000] 1 FLR 224.

which are applied have developed over a series of decisions. The leading cases are discussed in detail later in this chapter. For the moment, however, we might note that the practical value of the actual decisions in such cases (even those of the House of Lords or Supreme Court) as precedents must inevitably be limited since they are fact-specific. Moreover, while the courts have sought to provide some guidance, the question might be posed whether a more concerted attempt should be made to formulate, through legislation, legal standards for decision-making.[14] The difficulty with this is that any such attempt would be bound to raise awkward moral questions about the value and quality of life which are, in the end, dependent on individual beliefs and on which there is never likely to be a societal consensus. Yet the consequence of failing to establish reasonably clear criteria is that this can lead to widespread variations in the treatment or non-treatment of children with broadly similar medical conditions and this may be thought to offend principles of formal equality.[15]

GENERAL PRINCIPLES

The parental consent principle

The consent requirement

As a general proposition it is accepted that the consent of the patient is required for any medical examination or procedure. The principle is rooted in the idea of self-determination. The patient should be left alone to decide what is or is not done to his body.[16] Prima facie, any unauthorised 'touching', which for these purposes includes medical procedures, would constitute an assault or, more accurately, a battery. But provided that the patient has an essential understanding of what is proposed and consents to it, no assault will have been committed. It is possible that a doctor may be liable in negligence where the patient's consent was induced by his failure to disclose information which any

---

[14]   Such attempts were made in relation to the treatment or non-treatment of severely disabled infants in the USA, as to which see RH Mnookin and DK Weisberg *Child, Family and State* (5th edn, Aspen Publishers, 2005), at pp 398 et seq.

[15]   The principle entails treating like cases alike. A good theoretical discussion of what is involved in equal treatment is to be found in B Williams 'On Equality' in *Problems of the Self* (Cambridge University Press, 1976).

[16]   The consent issue is discussed generally in JK Mason and GT Laurie *Mason and McCall Smith's Law and Medical Ethics* (9th edn, Oxford Univeristy Press, 2013), ch 4; E Jackson *Medical Law Text, Cases, and Materials* (3rd edn, Oxford University Press, 2013), ch 4 and ch 5; J Montgomery *Health Care Law* (2nd edn, Oxford University Press, 2002), ch 10; J McHale and M Fox *Health Care Law: Text and Materials* (Sweet & Maxwell, 2006) deal with the consent issue in ch 6 and devote ch 7 specifically to issues involving children; I Kennedy and A Grubb *Medical Law* (3rd edn, Butterworths, 2000), ch 6. For a view from the Official Solicitor's office, dealing particularly with the problems of incapacity, see M Nicholls 'Consent to Medical Treatment' [1993] Fam Law 30. See also J Montgomery 'Consent to Health Care for Children' (1993) 5 JCL 117 and for children's views, P Alderson *Children's Consent to Surgery* (Open University Press, 1993). For the view of the British Medical Association, see *Consent, Rights and Choices in Health Care for Children and Young People* (BMJ Books, 2001) ch 2 (English law) and ch 3 (Scots law).

prudent medical practitioner would have disclosed.[17] But beyond this there is no requirement in English law that the patient give an 'informed consent'.[18] The consent requirement throws up an immediate problem in the case of children. The very status of minority has, as its raison d'être, the assumed incapacity of children to act on their own behalf. Thus, as a general rule, the law allows parents (and others in loco parentis) to provide a proxy consent for medical treatment and procedures performed on children.

Who can give consent?

This power, recognised at common law, is now included in the concept of parental responsibility within s 3 of the Children Act 1989.[19] As we shall see below, the fact that parental responsibility may be conferred on a parent who is a minor can lead to the anomaly that the minor parents may have more control over their child's medical treatment than their own.[20]

The Act, as already discussed, allows anyone with de facto care of a child, for however short a time, to 'do what is reasonable in all the circumstances of the case for the purpose of safeguarding or promoting the child's welfare'.[21] The Law Commission specifically instanced the operation of this provision in relation to medical care. It offered the view that it would enable a temporary carer to arrange medical assistance following an accident to the child but would not allow a temporary carer to consent to major elective surgery for the child.[22] While there could be some difficult line-drawing, the essence of the distinction would appear to be that emergency or routine medical care would be covered, but procedures with long-term or irreversible implications would require the consent of a person with parental responsibility. It should also be said that anyone looking after a child might be criminally liable or liable in negligence for failing to secure essential medical aid for a child,[23] although there is no wider legal, as opposed to moral, duty on members of the public at large to come to the aid of a distressed child.[24]

---

[17] See Lord Bridge in *Sidaway v Board of Governors of the Bethlem Royal Hospital and Maudsley Hospital* [1985] 1 All ER 643, at 663.

[18] But we discuss below the apparently high level of understanding required of minors wishing to provide their own consent to medical matters.

[19] The general principles concerning acquisition of parental responsibility are discussed in chapter 4 above.

[20] See for discussion of this issue, S Fovargue 'Doctrinal incoherence or practical problem? Minor parents consenting to their offspring's medical treatment and involvement in research in England and Wales' [2013] CFLQ 1. See also J Bridgeman 'Old Enough to Know Best?' (1993) 13 *Legal Studies* 69, at p 80.

[21] Section 3(5).

[22] Law Com Report No 172 *Guardianship and Custody* (1988), at para 2.16.

[23] Criminal liability arises primarily under the Children and Young Persons Act 1933, s 1. On the basis of the duty imposed by this provision, John Eekelaar has argued that a parent with care of a child who does not have parental responsibility must have a duty to seek out medical treatment where necessary and must have a right to consent on the child's behalf to the treatment offered: see J Eekelaar 'Rethinking parental responsibility' [2001] Fam Law 426.

[24] Thus, no criminal offence is committed where an unconnected bystander watches a child drown in a shallow pool, however morally reprehensible this inactivity might be. For a

So far the discussion has assumed that both parents (or all those with parental responsibility) are in agreement. But what is the position where there is a dispute between parents concerning a medical procedure for the child? This is very unlikely to arise in the context of a united family but could easily occur between divorced or separated parents. This is what happened in *Re C (Welfare of Child: Immunisation).*[25] Two unmarried fathers who had obtained parental responsibility orders sought specific issue orders that their respective children be vaccinated with the MMR triple vaccine. In each case the mother, who was the primary carer, was vehemently opposed to immunisation. The Court of Appeal upheld the decision of Sumner J authorising immunisation. The court rejected the contention of the mothers that the judge had applied the wrong test. They had argued that he had adopted a two-stage test, asking first what was in the children's best *medical* interests and then asking whether there were sufficient *non-medical* reasons for refusing to order immunisation. In the court's view the judge could not be criticised for making an assessment on the basis of the expert evidence first and he had reached a proper conclusion in accordance with the single welfare test. The court went on to emphasise that a decision concerning immunisation against infectious disease was not one which either parent had the right to take independently. It belonged to a small group of decisions which, despite the provisions of s 2(7) of the Children Act 1989, required the ruling of the court based on the child's best interests in the event of disagreement. Nonetheless, this decision may perhaps be criticised for failing to clarify the significance of best medical interests as opposed to other factors in cases like this.

Another more recent case of parental disagreement which attracted considerable media attention was the case of *An NHS Trust v SR (Radiotherapy and Chemotherapy),*[26] in which the parental disagreement over a child's medical treatment was brought to court by the NHS Trust concerned rather than a parent. In addition, the remedy sought was not a specific issue order but a declaration. A boy aged 7 had had surgery for a malignant brain tumour. The child's mother objected to the boy having post-operative radiotherapy and chemotherapy because she was concerned that the side-effects of such treatment would be some intellectual and cognitive impairment. The boy's father, however, agreed with the doctors, who considered the post-operative treatments as standard, routine procedures complementary to the surgery in order to prevent microscopic cancerous cells remaining and therefore to reduce the possibility of relapse. The evidence was that such treatment significantly increased the prospects of overall success. The mother went missing with the boy for several days and was eventually located with the

---

discussion of these principles, see D Ormerod *Smith and Hogan's Criminal Law* (13th edn, Oxford University Press, 2011), at para 4.4.2.1. In similar vein, there is no mandatory reporting law in England which would require anyone to inform the relevant authorities of child abuse or neglect.

[25] [2003] 2 FLR 1054 (Sumner J) and 1095 (CA). For commentary on the case, see H Baker 'MMR: Medicine, Mothers and Rights' [2004] CLJ 49, and K O'Donnell 'Room to Refuse? Immunisation, welfare and the role of parental decision-making' [2004] CFLQ 213. See also *F v F* [2013] EWHC 2683 (Fam), Theis J.

[26] [2012] EWHC 3842 (Fam), [2013] 1 FLR 1297.

help of the press. Bodey J acceded to the NHS Trust's application for a declaration that treatment in the face of the mother's refusal would nevertheless be lawful, explaining:[27]

> 'The balance of advantage and disadvantage tilts well in favour of radiotherapy and chemotherapy, notwithstanding the detrimental side effects. One cannot enjoy even a diminished quality of life if one is not alive.'

In light of the mother's earlier absconding behaviour, a residence order was made in favour of the child's father.

Wilful neglect

The position of parents as proxies gives rise to both a duty and a discretion, and the primary difficulty is to determine when duty ends and discretion begins. Anyone over the age of 16 years, with 'responsibility' for a child, who 'wilfully assaults, ill-treats, neglects, abandons, or exposes him ... in a manner likely to cause him unnecessary suffering or injury to health' commits a criminal offence.[28] The offence specifically includes failure to provide adequate medical aid or failure to take steps to secure it to be provided. This offence of 'wilful neglect' imposes certain minimum standards of medical care on anyone, most obviously a parent, who has the physical care of a child. It has been held that the test of 'wilfulness' is a subjective one, requiring actual appreciation of the risk to the child's health. Consequently, it can be a defence to show that parents of low intelligence did not have this appreciation at the relevant time.[29] On the other hand, the offence may be committed where there is failure to summon medical aid even though *in fact* there was no help which a doctor could have given.[30]

When can a parent withhold medical care?

In addition to this special offence, parents and others are, of course, subject to the ordinary criminal law and may, for example, be liable for the death of the child where death was caused by their unwillingness to summon essential aid. Such refusals are sometimes influenced by religious considerations, but while parents may lawfully make martyrs of themselves, they may not make martyrs of their children.[31]

---

[27] Ibid, at para [23].

[28] Children and Young Persons Act 1933, s 1(1). The statute makes it explicit that the suffering or injury to health is widely defined and includes 'injury to or loss of sight, or hearing, or limb, or organ of the body, and any mental derangement'.

[29] *R v Sheppard* [1981] AC 394. Failure to satisfy an objective test of reasonableness might, however, give rise to tortious liability.

[30] *R v S and M* [1995] Crim LR 486.

[31] *People (ex rel Wallace) v Labrenz* 104 NE 2d 769 (Ill, 1952). The principle has been illustrated by cases in which the courts have sanctioned blood transfusions for children in the face of religious objections by their parents. See *Re S (A Minor) (Medical Treatment)* [1993] 1 FLR 376 and *Re O (A Minor) (Medical Treatment)* [1993] 2 FLR 149. Moreover, the courts may be prepared to override the *combined* objections of the parents and an adolescent, as in *Re E (A*

Thus, in *R v Senior*,[32] a parent's conviction for manslaughter by gross negligence was upheld where for religious reasons he failed to summon medical aid for his dangerously ill child who then died of diarrhoea and pneumonia.[33] It is clear then that parental rights or responsibility 'do not clothe parents with life and death authority over their children'.[34] However, it cannot be concluded from this that in no circumstances is it proper for parents, acting in conjunction with the medical profession, to withhold life-saving treatment from certain children.[35] A fortiori, the extent of the parent's duty to secure medical treatment in *non*-life-threatening situations requires careful examination in individual cases.

Therapeutic versus non-therapeutic treatment

Where parents are not under a positive duty to secure medical treatment they nevertheless, as a general principle, have a discretion to consent to or veto it.[36] Although the courts have been loathe to draw rigid distinctions between therapeutic and non-therapeutic procedures, it is generally accepted that parents have power to consent to treatment of a therapeutic nature, but their capacity to authorise non-therapeutic treatment is more doubtful.[37] It is thought that they *do* have power to consent to non-therapeutic procedures

---

       Minor) (Wardship: Medical Treatment) [1993] 1 FLR 386. In this case, Ward J, while giving full weight to the religious principles accepted by the patient (a boy aged 15) and his parents (all of whom were devout Jehovah's Witnesses), held that the welfare of the patient, objectively judged, led to the inevitable conclusion that blood transfusions should be authorised. The principle was reasserted in *Re A (Conjoined Twins: Medical Treatment)* [2001] 1 FLR 1, where there was an extensive examination of the degree of respect to be accorded to parental views. We consider the case in depth below.

[32]   [1899] 1 QB 283.

[33]   The accused belonged to a sect known as the 'Peculiar People' who objected to the use of doctors because of their interpretation of verses 14 and 15 of the Epistle of St James – 'Is there any sick among you? Let him call for the elders of the church and let them pray over him, anointing him with oil in the name of the Lord; and the prayer of faith shall save the sick, and the Lord shall raise him up; and if he have committed sins, they shall be forgiven him'. Accepting evidence that proper medical aid could have prolonged and probably saved the child's life, the judge had pointed out that Christ himself had, according to biblical text, said: 'They that are whole need not a physician but they that are sick'.

[34]   *Custody of a Minor* 379 NE 2d 1053 (1978).

[35]   See particularly now *Re T (Wardship: Medical Treatment)* [1997] 1 FLR 502, discussed below. For an examination of the whole issue of parents' powers in relation to the medical treatment of children, see C Bridge 'Parental powers and the medical treatment of children' in C Bridge (ed) *Family Law Towards the Millennium: Essays for PM Bromley* (Butterworths, 1997), ch 9.

[36]   It should be noted, however, that a parent's objection to a scientific test on a child for the purposes of establishing paternity may be overridden by the court if the court considers this to be in the child's best interests: see Family Law Reform Act 1969, s 21(3), as amended, and see further chapter 3 above. On the question of consent to genetic screening and tests associated with this, see J McHale 'Genetic screening and testing the child patient' [1997] CFLQ 33.

[37]   An illustration of this principle is *Re E (A Minor) (Medical Treatment)* [1991] 2 FLR 585 where it was held that, contrary to normal requirements regarding the sterilisation of mentally incompetent minors, parents might provide a valid consent to a *therapeutic* hysterectomy without obtaining a judicial declaration.

insofar as they are for the benefit of the child.[38] Thus, they may consent to scientific tests on the child for the purposes of establishing paternity, since it is usually thought to be in the child's best interests for this question to be determined.[39] The Court of Appeal has confirmed that such a direction should not be given where the court is satisfied that it would be *against* the child's interests.[40]

Particularly difficult questions can arise where the benefits to the child are less obvious, as where it is proposed that a child should participate in non-therapeutic research[41] or become an organ donor.[42] Such research may be justified on the altruistic basis that it benefits *other* children but may be of no direct benefit to the child undergoing the procedure, which might be hazardous and uncomfortable.[43] Here, the difficult legal issue is whether parents and others are bound by a legal duty to act *only* in the best interests of the child in question.[44] The point is uncertain but it appears to be accepted medical practice that, in *some* circumstances, research on individual children which is intended to benefit other children, may be justifiable. This is subject to significant qualifications concerning the older child's right to object and the need to obtain the consent of the parent or guardian. It is also accepted that parental consent per se should not justify participation in research.

---

[38] It is non-medical benefits which are referred to here, since medical benefits to the child would render the procedure therapeutic in nature.

[39] *S v S; W v Official Solicitor* [1972] AC 24.

[40] *Re H (Paternity: Blood Test)* [1996] 2 FLR 65. And for a yet more recent confirmation of the test see *Re L (A Child)* [2009] EWCA Civ 1239 which contrasts this test with the more straightforward welfare test in the Family Law Reform Act 1969, s 21(3) as amended.

[41] For a related discussion, see J Driscoll 'Children's rights and participation in social research: balancing young people's autonomy rights and their protection' [2012] CFLQ 452.

[42] The issue is discussed in JK Mason and GT Laurie *Mason and McCall Smith's Law and Medical Ethics* (9th edn, Oxford University Press, 2013), at pp 594 et seq, I Kennedy and A Grubb *Medical Law* (3rd edn, Butterworths, 2000), ch 14, and J Montgomery *Health Care Law* (2nd edn, Oxford University Press, 2002) ch 14, especially at pp 363–366. See also British Medical Association *Consent, Rights and Choices in Health Care for Children and Young People* (BMJ Books, 2001) ch 9. See also *Re Y (Mental Incapacity: Bone Marrow Transplant)* [1996] 2 FLR 787. This case concerned organ donation between two adult sisters but there is no reason why the principles should not be extrapolated to children. Connell J held that the test to be applied was the best interests of the prospective donor. Here, there was a closely knit family and it was possible to conclude that it was in the best interests of a severely mentally and physically disabled woman (who was unable to provide a valid consent) that she should donate bone marrow to her elder sister who suffered from leukaemia. For assessments of the decision, see D Feenan 'A good harvest?' [1997] CFLQ 305 and SE Mumford 'Bone marrow donation – the law in context' [1998] CFLQ 135.

[43] JK Mason and GT Laurie (above) cite the example of a French project involving lumbar punctures on newborn infants. See also the discussion in J Montgomery *Health Care Law* (2nd edn, Oxford University Press, 2002), at pp 363–366.

[44] This may be the implication of the welfare principle but it has already been noted that the application of this principle to parents is problematic.

Parents may not validly consent to a procedure which is to the obvious *detriment* of the child and, more generally, it is considered ethically unsound to proceed except where the risks to the child concerned are minimal.[45]

Consequences of proceeding without parental consent

We discuss below the circumstances in which parental consent may not be required, but there is a preliminary question. On the assumption that the consent of a parent *is* necessary, what course of action is open to that parent if the doctor or other medical personnel go ahead without his or her consent? Here, it has been established by the Court of Appeal in *F v Wirral Metropolitan Borough Council*[46] that no civil action will lie for interference with parental 'rights' and this principle must surely apply equally to the concept of 'parental responsibility'. Any tortious action a parent has must, therefore, be based on trespass to the *child's* person. The function of parental consent is thus to prevent a tort being committed against the *child* and not to protect any independent parental claim.[47] Where a 'touching' is involved (which would be the case with most medical examinations and procedures), it ought not to be difficult to establish the tort of battery. But the position is much less clear if all that is involved is the giving of advice or the prescription of medication since here there is no obvious physical contact. It is doubtful whether the doctor would be acting unlawfully in those situations although a parent, forewarned of these dealings, might seek to prevent them in wardship, by invoking the inherent jurisdiction or by seeking a prohibited steps order.[48]

Exceptions to the parental consent requirement

There are several well-established qualifications to the general rule that the consent of a parent is both a necessary and sufficient consent to treatment for a child. First, the State may, in certain circumstances, restrict the area of parental discretion, either directly through legislation or indirectly through the protective agency of local authorities or the courts. Secondly, the child's own view may prevail over that of a parent in some instances in which they are in

---

[45]   The attitude of various medical professional bodies to the issue is discussed by JK Mason and
       GT Laurie (above), at ch 20.

[46]   [1991] 2 FLR 114.

[47]   The dangers of the medical profession proceeding with an operation on a child without
       obtaining parental consent were graphically illustrated in the tragic case of six-year-old Debbie
       Jenkins which received a great deal of media attention in March 1998. Dr James Taylor, a
       senior consultant heart surgeon at Great Ormond Street Hospital, was found guilty of
       professional misconduct by the General Medical Council. The child had died following
       irreparable brain damage which she sustained when Dr Taylor performed a procedure which
       involved using a balloon catheter to try to enlarge a narrowed artery. He was fully aware of the
       lack of the parents' consent to this procedure and had evidently informed them that he would
       not use it. He was found to have had insufficient medical grounds to undertake the procedure
       without parental consent. It was also reported that the parents were considering a civil action
       against the hospital following the ruling of the GMC. (See (1998) *The Times*, March 21.)

[48]   Section 8(1) of the Children Act 1989. This issue is relevant to other professionals such as
       teachers.

conflict. Thirdly, there will be instances in which the medical profession may proceed lawfully without a parent's consent. Some of these instances will arise where no consent is either available or required, while in other cases it may be lawful for a doctor, in effect, to choose between the conflicting views of parents and children.

The State as decision-maker

As has been seen, the State may, through the criminal law, cut down the area of parental discretion by imposing duties to ensure certain minimum standards of health for children.[49] An alternative mechanism, used extensively in the USA, is to require compliance with a variety of screening procedures designed to detect particular diseases in children or to require certain immunisations against, for example, diphtheria, whooping cough, tetanus, measles and polio, as a condition of school admission. In the USA, some State legislation has made provision for parents' objections to these procedures, in some cases only on religious grounds, but there has been no consistent pattern.[50] In England, the courts have occasionally exercised their powers to direct that children be tested for HIV infection, although the basis for exercising this jurisdiction is not wholly clear. Such tests should only be directed by the High Court.[51] Interventions like these represent restrictions on parental discretion grounded in the public interest in the prevention of disease.

The State may intervene through the local authority or the court (on the initiative of some interested party) to protect the health of *individual* children. Traditionally, this was achieved in wardship proceedings. While the inherent jurisdiction may remain the appropriate one in sensitive or complex cases, the alternative of applying in family proceedings for a prohibited steps or specific issue order might now be used.[52] A genuine applicant for a s 8 order should not experience difficulty in obtaining leave where a serious medical issue has arisen. Where there is more general concern about the ability of parents or other carers to safeguard the health of a child on an ongoing basis, this will usually be a matter for action by social services. Social services may also, with leave, invoke the court's inherent jurisdiction, where the child is not in care, to resolve a single medical issue of concern.[53]

Sterilisation: an illustration of the court's protective role

The court's protective role in relation to children is seen most obviously in life-saving cases. Yet the courts can also be involved other than in life-saving

---

49   Children and Young Persons Act 1933, s 1.
50   RH Mnookin and D Weisberg *Child, Family and State* (6th edn, Wolters and Kluwer, 2009), ch 4.
51   See, particularly, *Note: Re HIV Tests* [1994] 2 FLR 116, *Re O (Minors) (Medical Examination)* [1993] 1 FLR 860 and *Re C (HIV Test)* [1999] 2 FLR 1004.
52   As in *Re HG (Specific Issue Order: Sterilisation* [1993] 1 FLR 587.
53   See chapter 12 below.

situations, of which the best example is arguably the sterilisation of the
mentally incapacitated. In this section we concentrate on this controversial
issue.[54]

The issue first came to the fore in *Re D (A Minor) (Wardship: Sterilisation)*[55]
where an educational psychologist invoked wardship in an attempt to prevent
the sterilisation of an 11-year-old girl who suffered from an uncommon
disorder known as 'Sotos syndrome'. While the principles governing
sterilisation have been much refined in later cases, *Re D* arguably remains one
of the classic examples of judicial intervention in the medical sphere and repays
close attention. The symptoms of the disease in this case included accelerated
growth during infancy, epilepsy, generalised clumsiness, emotional instability,
aggressive tendencies and the impairment of mental function. The girl's
widowed mother, fearful that the girl might become pregnant and give birth to
an abnormal child, proposed that she be sterilised. The mother had the support
of a paediatrician and a gynaecologist who was prepared to perform the
operation. Heilbron J held that it was an appropriate case for wardship and
that the procedure should be prohibited. It was not in the girl's best interests,
since it involved an irreversible procedure of a non-therapeutic nature, which
would entail the deprivation of a 'basic human right to reproduce'. The girl's
future role in society and subsequent development could not be accurately
predicted but there was medical evidence that her condition was improving and
that she might, at some future time, acquire the capacity to make an informed
choice about the procedure. Thus, it was not a matter which fell within a
doctor's sole, clinical judgment, and the court should intervene.

The decision in this case was no more than a straightforward application of the
welfare principle, ie that it was not in this particular girl's best interests to
undergo a sterilisation. This is the characteristic approach of the English
courts, and later cases have revealed a marked reluctance to lay down any
general guidelines or standards.[56] Hence, it was not possible to extract from this
decision any general principle against sterilisation of mentally incapacitated
minors. It is clear, both from evidence in the case itself, and from later reported
cases,[57] that sterilisation operations will often be sanctioned where the level of

---

[54] For a scathing attack on the compulsory sterilisation of the mentally incapacitated, see M
      Freeman 'Sterilising the Mentally Handicapped' in *The Moral Status of Children* (Martinus
      Nijhoff, 1997) ch 16. See also M Beaupré 'Decision-making and the sterilisation of
      incompetent children' in A Grubb (ed) *Decision-Making and Problems of Incompetence* (John
      Wiley & Sons, 1994), at p 89.

[55] [1976] Fam 185.

[56] Thus in *Re B (A Minor) (Wardship: Sterilisation)* [1988] AC 199 the House of Lords rejected
      any distinction between therapeutic and non-therapeutic sterilisation on the basis that it would
      detract from the application of the welfare test.

[57] See, particularly: *Re M (A Minor) (Wardship: Sterilisation)* [1988] 2 FLR 497; *Re P (A
      Minor) (Wardship: Sterilisation)* [1989] 1 FLR 182; *T v T* [1988] Fam 52; *Re F (Mental
      Patient: Sterilisation)* [1990] 2 AC 1; and *Re W (Mental Patient: Sterilisation)* [1993] 1 FLR
      381 (young woman aged 20 suffering from severe epilepsy and minor degree of cerebral palsy).
      In *Re HG (Specific Issue Order: Sterilisation)* [1993] 1 FLR 587, Peter Singer QC (sitting as a
      deputy High Court judge) held that, in principle, it was possible for an issue such as
      sterilisation to be the subject of an application for a specific issue order under the Children

disability is greater than that which was suffered by the girl in *Re D*. Nevertheless, there was, in *Re D*, more than a suggestion that Heilbron J was influenced by what the girl's own view might be on attaining adulthood and making the discovery of what had happened to her whilst a child. This has a flavour of 'substituted judgment' about it, but this was only one element in the judge's thinking.[58] The decision was, in the final analysis for the court, based on what it thought best for the child and this is conceptually distinct from a judicial process which attempts to project what a child would have wanted if she was not suffering from incapacity. The case was significant also from a procedural angle. It revealed that child protection can be dependent on the chance intervention of an interested third party. It thus paved the way for consideration in later cases of the need for a mandatory judicial procedure designed to ensure some consistency in the practice of sterilisation.[59]

In *Re B (A Minor) (Wardship: Sterilisation)*[60] (popularly known as '*Jeanette's case*') the more serious case of mental incapacity, visualised in *Re D*, materialised.

Jeanette was 17 years of age and approaching majority. She had a mental age of five or six years. The evidence was that she was unable to appreciate the causal connection between sexual intercourse and childbirth and would be incapable of consenting to marriage. If she should carry a child to term it was predicted that she would need to be delivered by Caesarean section and that she would thereafter be likely to pick at the operational wound. It was also found that she had no maternal instincts and lacked the ability to care for a child. There was, however, evidence that she was becoming sexually aware and that there was a realistic danger of pregnancy resulting from casual sexual activity. Other methods of contraception were found not to be feasible, apart from an oral contraceptive, progesterone. She would be required to take this for the

---

Act. But he was of the view that such proceedings ought always to be commenced in a district registry of the High Court and that the Official Solicitor should always be involved. For a case in which leave to perform a sterilisation on a severely disabled 21-year-old was *refused*, the arguments being fairly evenly balanced, see *Re LC (Medical Treatment: Sterilisation)* [1997] 2 FLR 258. See also *Re S (Medical Treatment: Adult Sterilisation)* [1998] 1 FLR 944, where sterilisation of a 22-year-old mentally incompetent young woman, with no understanding of sexuality, was emphatically refused by Johnson J. Here, the risk of sexual exploitation was found to be speculative and not identifiable. Sterilisation was also refused by the Court of Appeal in *Re S (Sterilisation: Patient's Best Interests)* [2000] 2 FLR 389 in which it was held that it would be a disproportionate response to the problems of an attractive woman aged 29 with a severe learning disability. The court thought that the insertion of an intra-uterine device called Mirena would be less intrusive, reduce S's periods and offer adequate contraceptive protection. Cf *Re ZM and OS (Sterilisation: Patient's Best Interests)* [2000] 1 FLR 523 in which Bennett J sanctioned a laparoscopic subtotal hysterectomy on a 19-year-old young woman with Down's syndrome on the basis that Mirena would not end her heavy and distressing periods nor wholly remove the risk of pregnancy, both of which were in her best interests.

[58] Heilbron J clearly attached significance to the evidence that in later years the girl would be able to make her own choice and that 'the frustration and resentment of realising (as she would one day) what had happened, could be devastating'.

[59] Discussed below.

[60] [1988] AC 199.

remainder of her reproductive life, the success rate was only 40 per cent, and the long-term side effects were speculative. Sunderland Borough Council, in whose care Jeanette had been since 1973, decided, with the support of her mother, that sterilisation was the best course.

The House of Lords upheld the decision of the judge in wardship proceedings and the Court of Appeal that the operation be sanctioned. The reasoning was again based on the single consideration that the procedure was in her best interests. The House of Lords rejected all other criteria which were considered extraneous to the welfare test. Lord Hailsham stressed that the case involved no general issue of public policy and, in particular, had nothing to do with eugenics. Lord Oliver said that the operation was not sought for social purposes, the convenience of those taking care of Jeanette or to allay family anxieties. The House of Lords specifically rejected as unhelpful a Canadian distinction between therapeutic and non-therapeutic purposes, with only the former being regarded as a legitimate reason for sterilisation in Canada.[61] Lord Hailsham thought that any reference to a 'basic human right to reproduce' was meaningless where an individual lacked the mental capacity to make an informed choice in matters of pregnancy and childbirth. Lord Templeman alone expressed the view that sterilisation, as a procedure of last resort, should only be carried out with the leave of a High Court judge. The House was unanimous that the operation was the only way of averting the 'unmitigated disaster' of pregnancy. Since there was some doubt about whether the court would have jurisdiction once Jeanette reached 18 years of age, it sanctioned performance of the operation without delay.[62]

This case rejected the notion that there is any absolute right to reproduce. It showed that, in cases of severe mental incapacity, the court's intervention might be required to protect the child's right *not* to reproduce. It was open to the court to determine that it was in the best interests of a minor not to be denied medical care which would be available to a competent person and which could guarantee a better lifestyle.[63] At the same time, it is questionable whether the objection to sterilisation for contraceptive or social purposes, as opposed to medical purposes, is sustainable in the light of subsequent decisions.[64] The distinction between therapeutic and non-therapeutic sterilisation, rejected by

---

[61]   *Re Eve* (1987) 31 DLR (4th) I; and see CAP Finch-Noyes 'Sterilisation of the Mentally Retarded Minor: The *Re K* Case' (1986) 5 Can J of FL 277. The matter has also exercised the higher courts in Australia a good deal, as to which see F Bates 'In the Shadow of Change – Australian Family Law in 1995' in A Bainham (ed) *The International Survey of Family Law 1995* (Martinus Nijhoff, 1997), at pp 29 et seq, and F Bates '"Disputes Do Not Always End Where They Begin": Australian Family Law in 1996' in A Bainham (ed) *The International Survey of Family Law 1996* (Martinus Nijhoff, 1998), at pp 33 et seq.

[62]   It has since been decided that the courts *do* have jurisdiction to grant declarations as to the lawfulness of sterilisations performed on mentally incompetent adults. See *Re F (Mental Patient: Sterilisation)* [1990] 2 AC 1.

[63]   This was a matter emphasised by Lord Jauncey at 83. It has more than a suggestion of a right to be sterilised which can conveniently be contrasted with Heilbron J's view of the alleged human right to reproduce in *Re D (A Minor) (Wardship: Sterilisation)* [1976] Fam 185.

[64]   See fn 57, at p 352 above.

the House of Lords, was specifically utilised in *Re E (A Minor) (Medical Treatment)*[65] where it was held that parents could consent (without the necessity of going to court) to a therapeutic sterilisation occasioned by the need for a hysterectomy.

The courts are likely to take a restrictive approach to applications for male sterilisation by vasectomy. The matter arose in *Re A (Male Sterilisation)*[66] which concerned a man aged 28 with Down's syndrome. His elderly mother was anxious that she would be unable to supervise him and that he might make a woman pregnant. The evidence was that A was sexually aware and active but that he had a high degree of care and supervision which minimised the risk of sexual intercourse. The Court of Appeal upheld the judge's refusal to grant a declaration that sterilisation was in A's best interests. In doing so the court took a somewhat gender-specific approach to the issue. In relation to sterilisation the court's view was that the best interests of a man were not equivalent to the best interests of a woman because of the obvious biological differences. The only direct consequence of sexual intercourse for a man, it was said, was the risk of sexually transmitted diseases. The other consequences which arose from fathering a child would only be psychological, as where his activity might attract disapproval and criticism. In this case the court was not convinced that this would be a major factor because of his mental incapacity and left open the question whether third party interests ought properly to be considered in an assessment of a patient's best interests.

There has remained some doubt about the criteria which should be used in assessing when a sterilisation is justified in individual cases. These concerns were to some extent met by a number of Practice Notes.[67] It is now clear that sterilisation, whether of a minor or of a mentally incompetent adult, requires 'in virtually all cases' the prior sanction of a High Court judge. Applications may be either under the inherent jurisdiction of the High Court or for a specific issue order. The purpose of the proceedings must be to establish whether or not the proposed sterilisation is in the best interests of the patient. The court, accordingly, must be satisfied 'that the patient lacks capacity and that the operation will promote the best interests of the patient rather than the interests or convenience of the claimant, carers or public'. The note goes on to advise that in sterilisation cases there are three particular components to the 'best interests' test. First, the risk of pregnancy arising from the likelihood of sexual activity must be identifiable and not purely speculative. Secondly, there must be clear evidence of potentially damaging consequences deriving from conception and/or menstruation. Thirdly, the court will require a detailed analysis of all

---

[65] [1991] 2 FLR 585.

[66] [2000] 1 FLR 549.

[67] See *J v C (Note)* [1990] 3 All ER 735; *Practice Note: Official Solicitor: Sterilisation* [1993] 2 FLR 222; and *Practice Note: Official Solicitor: Sterilisation* [1996] 2 FLR 111; *Practice Note (Official Solicitor: Declaratory Proceedings: Medical and Welfare Decisions for Adults who Lack Capacity)* [2001] 2 FLR 158. This was superseded by *Practice Note (Official Solicitor: Declaratory Proceedings: Medical and Welfare Decisions for Adults who Lack Capacity)* [2006] 2 FLR 373, which applied pending the coming into force of the Mental Capacity Act 2005.

available and relevant methods of dealing with the patient's problems. There should be expert evidence explaining each relevant method and listing its advantages and disadvantages for the individual patient, taking into account any relevant aspects of her physical and psychological health.

The statutory role of the local authority

Where it has come to the attention of social services that a child's health may be jeopardised by potential parental abuse or neglect, or because of a parent's inability to cope, there will be a number of options.[68] As a starting point, the local authority will probably wish to explore the possibility of some form of voluntary social work assistance which could include the temporary accommodation of the child away from home. In *F v Wirral Metropolitan Borough Council*,[69] for example, the children had been born with phenylketonuria (PKU), a metabolic disease which can lead to severe mental retardation and which calls for skilled dietary management. The parents were persuaded to allow the children to be cared for by social services and to be boarded out with foster parents.

Where parents are unwilling to co-operate, the local authority may need to take compulsory action for a care or supervision order.[70] Where the authority is merely concerned to secure authorisation for a medical procedure (rather than to assume the overall care of a child), it may apply for leave to invoke the inherent jurisdiction of the High Court. There have been a number of controversial uses of this jurisdiction, which we discuss in chapter 12. An alternative for the authority will be to apply for a specific issue order under the Children Act.

In *Re C (HIV Test)*[71] the authority obtained a specific issue order that a baby be tested for the HIV virus. Both parents were opposed to conventional medicine and the mother intended to continue breastfeeding the child until the age of two. The judge found that there was a 20–25 per cent chance that the baby was infected and that breastfeeding increased the risk. The Court of Appeal refused the parents permission to appeal. Although the parents' views on treatment were important they were liable to be overridden in the best interests of the child. In this case it was not in the child's best interests that either the parents or the health professionals should remain ignorant of the child's state of health. The test would provide a comparatively unintrusive way of establishing the child's medical status. All concerned with her future welfare would thereby be better informed of the appropriate avenues of treatment in the event of her illness. The court emphasised that it was only concerned at this stage with testing for information purposes. The issues about the appropriate

---

[68] Public intervention is discussed in greater depth in chapters 10–12 below.
[69] [1991] 2 FLR 114.
[70] Under s 31 of the Children Act, discussed in chapter 12 below.
[71] [1999] 2 FLR 1004. For comment, see A Downie '*Re C (HIV Test)* The limits of parental autonomy' [2000] CFLQ 197.

treatment if the child tested positive, or the risks associated with breastfeeding if the child tested positive, had not yet arisen.

It is important to appreciate the limitations of this decision. While it can be seen as support for the proposition that parental discretion in relation to treatment is limited by the welfare principle this would be an over-simplification. First, it should be borne in mind that this will only be so if someone decides to bring the matter before the court.[72] If the medical authorities or children's services do not intervene, then parental discretion is likely to rule even if what might be seen as the optimum medical decision for the child is not taken by the parents. The law does not, for example, *require* that parents consent to the immunisation of their children.[73] Secondly, this was a case in which the intrusion was very minor when compared with the major benefits which would be derived from the test. Where matters are more evenly balanced it is less likely that parental views will be overridden even if a *marginal* benefit to the child might arise by doing so.

Where the local authority is refused access to a child whose health is suspected to be at risk, the local authority may apply for a child assessment order or emergency protection order and may obtain a direction that the child be produced for medical or psychiatric examination.[74] The grounds for these orders are considered later. Suffice it to note here that the definition of 'significant harm' includes within it the impairment of the child's health and, for these purposes, health includes physical or mental health.[75] It has been said that this is wide enough to include such matters as poor nutrition, low standards of hygiene, poor emotional care, and failure to seek treatment for an illness or condition.[76] The 'significant harm' test requires a comparison of the state of health of the particular child with that of a hypothetical child with similar attributes.[77] A disabled child, for example, requires a higher standard of care than a normal child. It is not clear how far cultural expectations would be taken into account in applying the test.[78]

---

[72] Subsequent to this decision, the President of the Family Division issued a Direction indicating that the need to make application to the court for a child to be tested for HIV was likely to arise only rarely. It is *not* necessary where all those with parental responsibility agree to the testing. It *is* necessary where a child of sufficient understanding to make an informed decision opposes the testing. See *President's Direction: HIV Testing of Children* [2003] 1 FLR 1299.

[73] See the discussion of *Re C (Welfare of Child: Immunisation)* [2003] 2 FLR 1054 (above).

[74] Sections 43 and 44 of the Children Act, discussed in chapter 11 below. For a general discussion of the medical examination of children under the scheme of the Children Act, see G Brasse 'Examination of the Child' [1993] Fam Law 12.

[75] Section 31(9) of the Children Act.

[76] J Masson *The Children Act 1989 Current Law Statutes Annotated* (Sweet & Maxwell, 1990).

[77] Section 31(10) of the Children Act, which provides: 'where the question of whether harm suffered by a child is significant turns on the child's health or development, his health or development shall be compared with that which could reasonably be expected of a similar child'.

[78] See *In re B* [2013] UKSC 33 for the Supreme Court's most recent pronouncements on the interpretation of significant harm, which is discussed further in chapter 12. Cultural considerations gave rise to difficulty under the old law, as to which see particularly *Alhaji Mohammed v Knott* [1969] 1 QB 1. For a thorough examination of cultural and religious issues

There was considerable uncertainty before the Children Act concerning the power of local authorities to assume compulsory control of new-born babies whose health was considered to be at risk if left under the control of inadequate or irresponsible parents. The House of Lords had held in *D (A Minor) v Berkshire County Council*[79] that a child requiring intensive care, having been born with drug-withdrawal symptoms, could legitimately be the subject of a care order based, in part, on the mother's abuse of her own body while pregnant. Despite some academic commentary to the contrary,[80] it is now reasonably clear that a care order may be made, if necessary, exclusively on the strength of an apprehended risk to the child's health, even where present harm cannot be established. This is because the Act applies where the child is not merely suffering significant harm but is *likely* to suffer significant harm.[81] It is subject to the limitation that the local authority cannot make a pre-emptive strike *before* the birth of the child since 'foetus' does not fall within the definition of 'child' in the legislation, although it is possible to obtain an advance declaration as to the lawfulness of removal of the child at birth,[82] where appropriate even without informing the parents.[83] The local authority cannot insist on supervision and management of the later stages of pregnancy and the birth itself, however concerned it may be about the mother's situation.[84] As soon as the child is born, protective action may be instigated. In *A Metropolitan Borough Council v DB*,[85] for example, an emergency protection order was obtained at birth in relation to the child of a 17-year-old crack cocaine addict. The mother herself had undergone a Caesarean birth following an application to the High Court and was later detained in the maternity ward under judicial authorisation.[86]

---

affecting medical procedures on children, see C Bridge 'Religion, Culture and the Body of the Child' in A Bainham, S Day Sclater and M Richards (eds) *Body Lore and Laws* (Hart Publishing, 2002).

79 [1987] 1 All ER 20.

80 MDA Freeman 'Care After 1991' in D Freestone (ed) *Children and the Law* (Hull University Press, 1990), ch 6. Cf A Bainham 'Care After 1991 – a Reply' (1991) 3 JCL 99.

81 There will, however, be important human rights requirements to observe where compulsory action is taken in relation to a child at birth. See *P, C and S v United Kingdom* [2002] 2 FLR 631, discussed in chapter 11 below.

82 See eg *Re D (Unborn Baby)* [2009] EWHC 446 (Fam), [2009] 2 FLR 313 (serious risk that disturbed mother who was in prison would lash out at her child immediately it was born).

83 The test is a stringent one (see ibid, at para [11], per Munby J: 'Is the step which the local authority is proposing to take, that is, the step of not involving the parents in its planning and not communicating to the parents its plan for immediate removal at birth, something which is justified by "the overriding necessity of the interests of the child" or something which is "essential to secure [the child's] safety"?'

84 Neither may the unborn child be made a ward of court nor, presumably, otherwise the subject of the inherent jurisdiction of the High Court. See *Re F (In Utero) (Wardship)* [1988] 2 FLR 307.

85 [1997] 1 FLR 767.

86 For discussion of this case in the context of the inherent jurisdiction, see chapter 12 below. On the issues surrounding compulsory Caesarean sections generally, see J Weaver 'Court-ordered Caesarean Sections' in A Bainham, S Day Sclater and M Richards (eds) (above).

The child as decision-maker

Another approach to the whole question of medical decision-making would be to allow older children complete independence of action. The obvious incapacity of young children for rational decision-making precludes this option in their case, but wholly different considerations apply to adolescents. Their factual capacity for self-help prompts the question of how far this should be legally recognised. If the law does recognise the ability of some children to provide or refuse a valid consent to medical treatment, how precisely should this relate to the powers of parents? Should parental consent be viewed simply as a *substitute* consent to be made available only where the child lacks capacity, or should it be viewed as an *alternative* consent remaining available *despite* the child's capacity? If so, we then have *concurrent* capacities and this raises the further issue of priority, in the event of a conflict of opinion. Should the law prioritise the view of the child or that of the parent, or should the medical profession be allowed to determine its own ranking order of consents?

These questions may become yet more complicated by ethical considerations of medical confidentiality.[87] Even if the requirement of parental consent is by-passed, it does not necessarily follow that a parent is not entitled to participate at all in the decision-making process. The issues of parental consent and notification have tended to be conflated in England,[88] but have been treated as distinct, especially with respect to abortion, in the USA. Certain decisions of the US Supreme Court are thus of considerable interest, provided that due allowance is made for the constitutional setting within which they were made. So far as English law is concerned, Silber J in *R (Axon) v Secretary of State for Health (Family Planning Association intervening)*[89] confirmed what had been implied by the House of Lords in *Gillick v West Norfolk and Wisbech Area Health Authority*,[90] that a competent child is entitled to medical confidentiality, even as against his or her parents. Academic opinion is divided on the position of the *immature* or *incompetent* minor.[91] The better view is that

---

[87] The confidentiality issue is treated at length in JK Mason and GT Laurie *Mason and McCall Smith's Law and Medical Ethics* (9th edn, Oxford University Press, 2013), ch 6, especially in relation to confidentiality within the family, at pp 203–208. See also J Montgomery *Health Care Law* (2nd edn, Oxford University Press, 2002) ch 11 and, specifically in relation to children, at pp 308–311; and British Medical Association *Consent, Rights and Choices in Health Care for Children and Young People* (BMJ Books, 2001), ch 4.

[88] This was so in *Gillick v West Norfolk and Wisbech Area Health Authority* [1986] 1 AC 112 where the issue was whether a doctor might lawfully provide contraceptives to an under-age girl without parental knowledge or consent. There was no direct discussion in the case about whether the issues of knowledge and consent could be separated, although Lord Fraser's requirement that the doctor should always seek to persuade the girl to allow him to involve her parents is perhaps some indication of what his thinking was.

[89] [2006] EWHC 37 (Admin), [2006] QB 539.

[90] [1986] 1 AC 112.

[91] The arguments either way are rehearsed in J Montgomery *Health Care Law* (2nd edn, Oxford University Press, 2002), at pp 308–311. Montgomery's discussion also takes account of the obligations under the Data Protection Act 1998. For a throrough examination of the issues concerning confidentiality of medical information in relation to children see J Loughrey 'Can you keep a secret? Children, human rights, and the law of medical confidentiality' [2008] CFLQ 312 and J Loughrey 'Medical Information, Confidentiality and a Child's Right to

'children are entitled to expect confidentiality, quite independently of their consent to treatment'.[92] This is also the position taken by the British Medical Association although there remain some uncertainties.[93] Given the inherent uncertainties surrounding the evaluation of individual competence, this would seem to be a more practical solution than attempting to differentiate between children for the purposes of confidentiality. A final complication is the power of the State, through the courts, to override the wishes of a mature minor. These issues are considered further below in relation to the medical treatment of adolescents.

Medical paternalism – the doctor as decision-maker

Under certain circumstances, the decisive say may be left to the medical professionals concerned; where a doctor declines to carry out a medical procedure which either a parent or child is requesting, this may be stating the obvious. The mere fact that a parent or a young woman wishes, for example, that an abortion or sterilisation be performed does not lead to the automatic conclusion that a doctor is obliged to perform it. Any doctor would be acting lawfully in refusing to do so unless it would be negligent not to proceed.[94]

These principles were graphically illustrated in *R v Cambridge District Health Authority ex parte B*.[95] Here a 10-year-old girl had received extensive treatment for acute myeloid leukaemia including two courses of chemotherapy, total body irradiation and a bone marrow transplant. Sadly, she suffered a further relapse, and the doctors who had treated her and other experts concluded that she had a very short time to live and that no further treatment could usefully be administered. Her father, unwilling to accept this, secured a further medical opinion which gave his daughter a 10–20 per cent chance of life if further chemotherapy were carried out and successful, and a second transplant were

---

Privacy' (2003) 23 *Legal Studies* 510. For other general accounts, see R Gilbar 'Medical Confidentiality in the Family: The doctor's duty reconsidered' (2004) 18(2) *International Journal of Law, Policy and the Family* 195; R Gilbar 'Medical confidentiality and communication with the patient's family: legal and practical perspectives' [2012] CFLQ 199.

[92] Montgomery (above), at p 311.

[93] See *Consent, Rights and Choices in Health Care for Children* (BMJ Books, 2001) ch 4. At p 80 it is stated: 'Children who lack the competence to give consent to treatment are also entitled to confidentiality. These patients should be encouraged to allow their parents to be involved but if they cannot be persuaded, doctors must judge whether disclosure to parents is necessary in the child's medical interests'. The BMA also notes the concern, revealed by research, that 'worries about confidentiality dissuade young people from approaching their doctor about health matters'.

[94] There is more than a suggestion in *Re F (Mental Patient: Sterilisation)* [1990] 2 AC 1, however, that a doctor could be under a duty arising from the principle of necessity to perform a sterilisation on a mentally incompetent young woman in certain circumstances. Thus, Lord Brandon said that 'it will not only be lawful for doctors on the grounds of necessity to operate on or give other medical treatment to adult patients disabled from giving their consent: it will also be their common law duty to do so'. This was a view with which Lord Goff specifically concurred. On this point, there would seem to be no good reason for distinguishing between the incompetent adult and the incompetent minor.

[95] [1995] 1 FLR 1055.

then successfully performed. The initial cost was projected at £15,000, with the cost of the second transplant being £60,000.

The health authority refused to go ahead on the basis: (i) that the proposed treatment would cause considerable suffering and was not in the child's best interests; and (ii) that the substantial expenditure on treatment with such a small prospect of success and being of an experimental nature would not be an effective use of limited resources bearing in mind the present and future needs of other patients. The child applied, through her father as litigation friend, for this decision to be quashed in judicial review proceedings.

At first instance she succeeded. Laws J attached considerable importance to her right to life as a fundamental right. He held that the authority had not put forward a sufficiently substantial objective justification on public interest grounds for its decision which infringed this right. However, on appeal, the Court of Appeal emphasised that, in judicial review proceedings, the court's role was only to rule on the *lawfulness* of the authority's decision and not to substitute its own view of the merits. It could not be said here that the authority had exceeded its powers or acted unreasonably in the legal sense. It had been aware of the family's strongly held views but the treatment proposed was at the frontier of medical science and appropriately described as experimental. The authority was entitled also to have regard to the competing claims on its resources.

Much more difficult legal questions arise where the doctor wishes to go ahead and either no one is available to give the consent normally required or someone, be it the child or parent, objects.

The doctrine of necessity

Perhaps the easiest principle to state (although not the easiest to apply) is that, in limited circumstances, the doctrine of necessity will allow the doctor to proceed without any consent at all. The obvious example is an accident. The law allows not only the doctor, but *anyone*, to render first aid to the child, subject only to the requirement that what is done to the child must not exceed what is required by the exigencies of the situation. It is arguable that a doctor would have a legal duty to assist, as would anyone having the care of the child. The case of accidents is a relatively simple one yet, even here, it might become complicated where a conscious child, or a parent on the scene, is refusing emergency aid.[96] The doctrine is difficult to apply in those cases in which there is time to consult parents and, if necessary, obtain judicial authorisation. A difficult case is that of the opposition of parents to blood transfusions on religious grounds. In a succession of cases,[97] the courts have been prepared to

---

[96] The better view is, however, that the doctor ought to be empowered to take all essential emergency action on the principle of necessity, whatever the parents' view.

[97] *Re E (A Minor) (Wardship: Medical Treatment)* [1993] 1 FLR 386, *Re S (A Minor) (Medical Treatment)* [1993] 1 FLR 376, and *Re O (A Minor) (Medical Treatment)* [1993] 2 FLR 149. And see *Re P (Medical Treatment: Best Interests)* [2004] 2 All ER 1117, although in this case

override the objections of Jehovah's Witnesses, both parents and children, to life-saving blood transfusions. But would the hospitals concerned have been covered by the doctrine of necessity if they had decided to go ahead *without* judicial authorisation and in the face of parental opposition? Given the uncertain application of the doctrine, the better view would seem to be that life-saving procedures should be carried out without parental approval only in cases of real emergency in which there is no time to bring the matter to court.

The extent of a doctor's power to act

What, then, is the extent of a doctor's power to act where what is proposed is *not* urgent or necessary but is considered by the doctor to be desirable, and in the best medical interests of the child? In *Re F (Mental Patient: Sterilisation)*,[98] the House of Lords held that beneficial medical treatment might be performed on a mentally incompetent *adult* where to do so would save her life or ensure the improvement of, or prevent deterioration in, her mental or physical health. Provided that individual decisions and treatment conformed with medical practice which would be accepted by a responsible body of medical opinion skilled in the particular field, they would be lawful.[99] In earlier cases, it had been suggested that all 'touchings' by the medical profession which conformed to this standard could be lawful on the basis of a general principle that they were not 'hostile' (and therefore non-tortious) if they were 'acceptable in the ordinary conduct of everyday life'.[100] However, in *T v T*,[101] Wood J rejected the view that all actions taken in accordance with good medical practice were non-tortious. In his opinion, medical procedures performed without consent were prima facie unlawful unless a justification could be found for them. This position was accepted by the House of Lords in *Re F*. A justification for sterilisation was nevertheless found in the twin concepts of necessity and the best interests of the patient, which appear to have been used interchangeably in this case.[102]

---

there was a hint by Johnson J that there could be a case in which it might be appropriate for the court to follow the wishes of a child. On the facts of the present case, however, the best interests of the patient (a 16-year-old boy) in the widest sense, including medical, religious and social interests, required that leave be granted to the medical authorities to administer blood or blood products if his situation became immediately life-threatening 'unless no other form of treatment [was] available'.

[98] [1990] 2 AC 1.

[99] The *Bolam* test: see *Bolam v Friern Hospital Management Committee* [1957] 2 All ER 118 but see now *Bolitho v City and Hackney Health Authority* [1997] 3 WLR 1151 (fn 4, at p 341 above).

[100] *Wilson v Pringle* [1987] QB 237 and *Collins v Wilcock* [1984] 3 All ER 374.

[101] [1988] Fam 52.

[102] Take, for example, the following passage from the speech of Lord Brandon:
'In my opinion the solution to the problem which the common law provides is that a doctor can lawfully operate on, or give other treatment to, adult patients who are incapable, for one reason or another, of consenting to his doing so, provided that the operation or other treatment concerned is in the *best interests* of such patients. The operation or other treatment will be in their best interests if, but only if, it is carried out in order to save their lives or to ensure improvement or prevent deterioration in their physical or mental health ... the principle is that when persons lack the capacity for whatever reason to take decisions about the

Procedures performed on children without consent

It is not certain how far these principles could be used to justify procedures performed on children without parental consent.[103] It is clear from the *Gillick* case that the medical profession may act in cases of parental abandonment or abuse.[104] It is equally clear that they may obtain the court's authority to act against parents' wishes either under the inherent jurisdiction or by seeking a specific issue order. But it has been pointed out by Lavery that a key objection to this process of obtaining judicial approval is that 'it should not be necessary to invoke the court's authority for medical treatment which is clearly in the child's best interests'.[105] Following *Gillick*, a doctor may be able to act against parental wishes where he has the agreement of the child who is herself competent to produce a valid consent. Even though, following *Re R*[106] and *Re W*,[107] the parent retains a concurrent right to consent, the doctor would appear to be acting lawfully in electing to give priority to the child's view.[108] But what of the immature child who would fail the test of *Gillick* competence? Here, the obvious implication of *Gillick* was that the parent's right to give or withhold consent would remain intact, and this has been confirmed by the later Court of Appeal decisions. Are there, then, any circumstances under which a doctor may act against parental wishes, in non-urgent cases, because he judges it to be in the child's best interests to do so?

---

performance of operations on them, or the giving of other medical treatment to them, it is necessary that some other person or persons, with the appropriate qualifications, should take such decisions for them'. [Emphasis added.]

It should, however, be noted that this justification can only be used, at least in the case of adult patients, where they are incompetent to take the particular decision involved. Thus, in *Re C (Refusal of Medical Treatment)* [1994] 1 FLR 31, the court held that it had not been established that a paranoid schizophrenic in Broadmoor lacked the competence to decide whether or not to have his gangrenous leg amputated. An order was therefore made prohibiting the operation without his consent. See also *Re JT (Adult: Refusal of Medical Treatment)* [1998] 1 FLR 48 in which a woman of 25, despite suffering from mental disability involving learning difficulties and extremely severe behavioural disturbances, was found to have the capacity to refuse dialysis for renal failure. As such, Wall J held that it would have been a criminal and tortious assault to perform physically invasive treatment without her consent. The Court of Appeal has now made it very plain in *St George's Health Care NHS Trust v S; R v Collins and Others ex parte S* [1998] 2 FLR 728 that a competent adult patient has an absolute right to refuse treatment even if the consequence may be the death of the patient.

[103] For an excellent analysis of the implications of *Re F* for the non-emergency treatment of children, see R Lavery 'Routine Medical Treatment of Children' [1990] JSWL 375. An article focusing on non-urgent treatment specifically in the context of dental treatment for children is P Booth and S Proud 'Embracing Children – Non-urgent Treatment, Dental Legal Issues and Children' [2002] Fam Law 917.

[104] *Gillick v West Norfolk and Wisbech Area Health Authority* [1986] 1 AC 112, although this situation is not entirely unproblematic in practice: see Lavery (above), at pp 378–379.

[105] Ibid, at p 377.

[106] [1992] Fam 11.

[107] [1993] Fam 64.

[108] Discussed further in A Bainham 'Non-Intervention and Judicial Paternalism' in P Birks (ed) *The Frontiers of Liability*, Vol 1 (Oxford University Press, 1994), especially at pp 162–166.

It must be said that, as the law stands, this would be a precarious course of action for the medical profession. Much may turn on how far the courts would be prepared to extend the concept of necessity or apply the reasoning in *Re F*, outside the rather special case of sterilisation. Alternatively, some support for such independent action might be found in those cases which have determined that parental responsibility must be exercised *reasonably* and that where parents exceed the bounds of reasonableness they themselves act unlawfully and may, indeed, commit a criminal offence.[109] The difficulty with relying on these principles is that, in the medical context at least, parents do appear to have been allowed considerable latitude in non-life-saving situations. Thus, a refusal to agree to treatment, even if adjudged undesirable, might still be regarded as falling within a band of reasonable decisions and within the scope of parental discretion.

Dispensing with parental consent

Ruth Lavery has argued convincingly that the concept of necessity should be redefined in its application to immature children. She has advocated the adoption of a principle which would enable a doctor to dispense with parental consent where there is a clear consensus within the medical profession that treatment is for a child's benefit in a given set of circumstances. This would ensure that particular children would not be denied the benefit of treatment, which is clearly in their best interests, because of parental prejudice, phobia or carelessness. On the other hand, the parent's right to consent, she argues, ought to be preserved where there is a difference of medical opinion as to what is in a child's best interests or where the decision is not a purely medical one but has other social, moral or long-term implications.[110]

Lavery saw her proposal as a 'fairly modest inroad' into the parental right to consent. Once a procedure ranges beyond the routine, the prudent course for the doctor would be to seek the sanction of the court. Even where the doctor is dealing with an adolescent, the interaction of the child's competence and parental responsibility is now so uncertain that the doctor could not be confident about whose view should prevail in law, in the event of a clash – although it is perhaps debatable how far the courts would want to question retrospectively the clinical judgment of the medical profession. These doubts must arise, a fortiori, where the child himself is thought to be possibly incapable of providing a valid consent. The courts may have an increasingly important role in resolving these uncertainties.

---

[109] See, particularly, *R v D* [1984] AC 778 and *R v Rahman* (1985) 81 Cr App R 349.
[110] See R Lavery 'Routine Medical Treatment of Children' [1990] JSWL 375, at pp 383–384.

THE PROBLEM OF INFANTS AND YOUNG CHILDREN: THE SELECTIVE TREATMENT OF THE NEWBORN

The issue of treating, or not treating, newly-born infants with serious medical conditions, illustrates the operation of these principles in an extreme context, where life itself is at stake.[111] The reported cases in England have largely been concerned with neonates but there is no good reason why the principles which have emerged from these decisions should not also be applied to young children.[112] The giving or withholding of life-saving treatment for babies or young children, who are self-evidently incapable of expressing any view, gives rise to a multitude of legal and ethical issues.[113] Where, as in the case of the conjoined twins,[114] the best medical interests of the child may appear to conflict with those of another, the issues may seem almost incapable of resolution.

When may a parent and/or a doctor be liable under the criminal or civil law *for refusal* to authorise or carry out life-saving treatment or be liable *for performing* such surgery? Can the law realistically distinguish for these purposes between acts and omissions? Is, for example, the decision to withhold life-saving surgery or food to be equated with the positive act of administering a drug which has the effect of hastening death? And, in the case of the latter, does it matter that the primary purpose was to relieve pain and suffering and that the acceleration of death was an unavoidable effect of this? Is the duty of the medical profession towards chronically disabled newborns the same as it is to 'normal' babies and, if it is not, what are the implications of this for the treatment of disabled adolescents or adults?

Leaving aside the question of criminal liability, the civil law issues are no less complex. What is the extent of parental discretion in this area? How big a part should parents' views play in medical decisions – are doctors bound by them and, if not, how much value ought to be attached to them? When might the State intervene, through the local authority or the court, to impose its own view, and on what basis should it do so? If such intervention does occur, whose responsibility does the child become? Do children have an absolute right to life or ought the quality of life to be taken into account – and who decides, and on which criteria, what *is* a worthwhile life? Ought we, for example, to differentiate between those infants who are terminally ill, those who have reasonable prospects of an appreciable life-span and those where the prognosis is

---

[111] See JK Mason, RA McCall Smith and GT Lawrie *Mason and McCall Smith's Law and Medical Ethics* (6th edn, Oxford University Press, 2013), ch 15, and J Montgomery *Health Care Law* (2nd edn, Oxford University Press, 2002), ch 18.

[112] In fact, two of the leading Canadian cases did involve young children rather than neonates and repay examination for this reason. See *Re Superintendent of Family and Child Service and Dawson* (1983) 145 DLR (3rd) 610 and *Couture-Jacquet v Montreal Children's Hospital* (1986) 28 DLR (4th) 22.

[113] These issues were particularly well identified in M Mulholland 'Neo-Natal Care and Treatment – The Doctor's Dilemma' (1989) 5 *Professional Negligence* 109.

[114] *Re A (Conjoined Twins: Surgical Separation)* [2001] 1 FLR 1.

uncertain? Finally, and perhaps most importantly, what is the correct allocation of decision-making responsibility where neither the court nor the local authority is involved? Are the prevailing standards and practices of the medical profession conclusive or are there moral and philosophical questions which ought to be outside the exclusive control of the profession?

English law has given a definite response to some of these questions while others remain shrouded in uncertainty. In order to illustrate the way in which English law approaches these issues, we will now look closely at some of the leading cases. We do this, not only because the cases sometimes raise different issues, but also because the law as set out in the latest authorities has built upon the gradual development of the law in the earlier cases. A full understanding of the current position is best achieved, therefore, through a thorough understanding of how it was reached. We begin with a much publicised decision of the Court of Appeal over 30 years ago which authorised life-saving surgery on a baby who suffered from Down's syndrome and conclude with the similarly controversial case of Charlotte Wyatt in which the Court of Appeal set out the correct approach to deciding whether doctors may be permitted lawfully not to provide life-sustaining treatment to a child. We conclude our journey through the case law with the even more publicised case of the conjoined twins which confronted that court with horrendously complex legal and moral issues.

The baby Alexandra case

In *Re B*,[115] a baby was born in July 1981 with the double disadvantage of Down's syndrome[116] and duodenal atresia, an intestinal blockage. The latter condition is not uncommon in Down's syndrome infants but, if not operated upon, death by starvation results. The baby's parents, acting with what was accepted to be the best of motives, thought it kinder to let her die in view of her condition. The doctors concerned contacted the local authority which made her a ward of court. Ewbank J gave care and control to the authority and initially authorised the surgery. But when the baby was transferred to another hospital, surgeons there declined to operate in the face of parental objection. The authority then returned to court but, after hearing the parents' views, Ewbank J refused to consent to the operation. The Court of Appeal heard evidence that other surgeons were available who were prepared to operate. There was a good prognosis for success of the surgery which was thought to give the child a life expectancy of 20 to 30 years – the normal life span of someone with the disorder.

---

[115] *Re B (A Minor) (Wardship: Medical Treatment)* (1982) 3 FLR 117. This decision should now be compared closely with *Re T (Wardship: Medical Treatment)* [1997] 1 FLR 502 – see p 380 below – and the reasoning in the conjoined twins case.

[116] Down's syndrome is a chromosomal aberration occurring in an estimated 1 in 700 live births. It produces mental retardation and is often accompanied by other congenital abnormalities of which the most common are gastro-intestinal blockages and congenital heart defects. Corrective surgery is usually required in the first year of life.

The Court of Appeal, applying the welfare principle, authorised the surgery. Templeman LJ thought that the judge had attached too much weight to parental wishes and was wrong to conclude, in this case, that those wishes should be respected. The issue was what was in the best interests of the child, and the test which ought to be applied was whether her life was demonstrably going to be so awful that she should be condemned to die, or whether it was so imponderable that she should be allowed to live. The evidence here was that the operation would give the child the normal life expectancy of a Down's syndrome child with the disabilities associated with Down's syndrome. He concluded that it was not for the court (on whom the decision devolved) to say that a life of that description ought to be extinguished. He did, however, visualise more serious cases where 'severe proved damage where the future is so certain and where the life of the child is so bound to be full of pain and suffering that the court might be driven to a different conclusion'.

Already in this case, several important principles had emerged. First, it confirmed that, in English law, there was no absolute principle that parents' wishes should be respected in life and death cases. The court in wardship had jurisdiction to override them in appropriate cases. Secondly, it was equally clear that the court rejected any absolute right to life of the child. The court had to make a qualitative assessment of the sort of life the child might lead and balance this with the risks involved in the operation. In this case, where the operation was considered to be relatively routine and where the prognosis was good, the balance was in favour of intervening unless the court was prepared to conclude (which it was not) that a life afflicted by Down's syndrome was not worth living. Thirdly, it was accepted that the responsibility for, and cost of, substitute care for the child should fall on the local authority if the child should ultimately be rejected by the parents following corrective surgery. In this case, adoptive parents were available if necessary.[117] The case left open the question of what the *automatic* legal position might have been had the court not become involved. Since the court here decided that intervention was required by the child's welfare, does this mean that the parents and medical profession, acting in conjunction, would have behaved unlawfully if they had agreed to allow nature to take its course? That no such simple deduction can be made is implicit from the result in the next case.

The trial of Dr Arthur[118]

John Pearson was also born with Down's syndrome, but without any additional complication. He died within three days of birth, and Dr Arthur, a highly respected consultant paediatrician, was charged with his murder – a charge

---

[117] It is understood that, in the event, adoptive parents were not required since the natural parents accepted the child.

[118] The case never appeared in the official law reports but was reported in (1981) *The Times*, November 6, and at (1981) 12 BMLR 1. Passages from the judge's direction to the jury are extracted in I Kennedy and A Grubb *Medical Law* (3rd edn, Butterworths, 2000), at pp 2164–2165 and there is a penetrating analysis of the case in MJ Gunn and JC Smith 'Arthur's Case and the Right to Life of a Down's Syndrome Child' [1985] Crim LR 705.

reduced to attempted murder during the course of his trial at Leicester Crown Court.[119] The baby was discovered at birth to have Down's syndrome and was immediately rejected by the mother. After discussion with both parents, Dr Arthur wrote in the casenotes: 'Parents do not wish the baby to survive. Nursing care only'. On the treatment chart, he prescribed the drug dihydrocodeine (DF 118) to be given 'as required' at doses of 5mg every four hours by the nurse in charge. The baby died 57.25 hours after birth. The cause of death was stated to be broncho-pneumonia resulting from Down's syndrome. A member of the 'Life' organisation alleged that the baby had been drugged and starved to death. The pathologist's evidence was that the cause of death was lung stasis produced by DF 118 poisoning. The prosecution case was that this was the result of the defendant's decision to cause the death of the child. The jury acquitted Dr Arthur.

Academic opinion is divided on whether the case of Dr Arthur can be said to have established any principles at all. Since it did not reach the higher courts, what is left is a jury decision which can scarcely have value as a legal precedent. Nevertheless, it has been argued that inferential guidance on the principles of the criminal law, within which these decisions must be taken, can be drawn from the directions which Farquharson J gave to the jury.[120] In particular, the judge regarded the distinction between acts and omissions as crucial. He directed the jury to consider whether 'there was an act properly so-called on the part of Dr Arthur, as distinct from simply allowing the child to die'. The judge contrasted the administration of a deliberately lethal dose of a drug (a positive act) with a decision to decline to operate on an intestinal blockage (an omission). No one, he said, could regard the latter as an act of murder. At the same time, he directed that no one, doctors included, had the right to kill a disabled child any more than they had a right to kill anyone else.

In a powerful critique of this reasoning, Gunn and Smith point out that the criminal law *does* impose liability for omissions where there is a duty to act. Such a duty arises in principle where *anyone*, including a doctor, has physical care of a child. It would include an obligation to provide proper sustenance and medical aid to a 'normal' child.[121] They conclude that the implication of the case is that the duty to an abnormal child must be different from, and lower than, that owed to a normal child. The duty appears to be limited to doing what is reasonable in all the circumstances, something acknowledged by

---

[119] The child was found to have been suffering from certain inherent defects at birth so that the precise cause of death was uncertain. Nonetheless, the prosecution was relying in the murder charge on an intention to kill so that the reduction of the charge was of no relevance to the alleged mental state of the doctor. See *R v Whybrow* (1951) 35 Cr App R 141.

[120] See an earlier edition of JK Mason and GT Laurie *Law and Medical Ethics* (6th edn, Butterworths, 2002), at pp 477–478.

[121] 'Arthur's Case and the Right to Life of a Down's Syndrome Child' [1985] Crim LR 705, at pp 709–711.

Dunn LJ in the baby Alexandra case, where the parents' decision to allow the child to die was viewed as 'entirely responsible' and could not properly be regarded as an intention to kill.[122]

It is difficult to regard the baby Alexandra case and the case of Dr Arthur as reconcilable. What is clear is that, simply because a court might have exercised *its* discretion in favour of life, it does not mean that parents and doctors exercising *their* discretion in favour of death would automatically commit an offence.[123] The issue of the limits of decision-making powers under the civil law is a quite separate question from that of criminal liability for homicide. But this leads to the unsatisfactory conclusion that neither case could truly be said to have established standards capable of determining, with any precision, the extent of legal duties owed to disabled infants. And there is a stark incongruity between the life-saving decision for baby Alexandra and the decision to terminate the life of the Pearson baby, who had a comparatively less complicated condition. It is difficult to resist the conclusion that the decisive factor was that the parents and doctors were in agreement in one case but not in the other.

The case of the hydrocephalic baby: *Re C*[124]

Re C (A Minor) concerned the situation of a terminally ill infant. The local authority had decided, before the child's birth, and without knowledge of her medical abnormality, that the parents would be unable to cope. When the child was born, she was found to be hydrocephalic – a condition involving a blockage of cerebral spinal fluid within the brain. In addition, her brain structure was poorly formed.[125] The issue was whether medical staff should seek to prolong her life and whether they should provide treatment appropriate to a child with her condition or appropriate for a child without this disability. The Official Solicitor, acting as guardian ad litem, obtained a report from a foremost paediatrician which stated that the aim of treatment should be to ease suffering rather than achieve a short prolongation of life.

In wardship proceedings, Ward J gave leave to the hospital authorities 'to treat the ward to die; to die with the greatest dignity and the least of pain, suffering and distress'. He also gave specific directions that they should not be required

---

[122] A similar view was expressed by Ward LJ in the case of the conjoined twins (see below) in which he said that if the hospital had bowed to the weight of the parental opposition to surgical intervention 'there could not have been the slightest criticism of them for letting nature take its course in accordance with the parents' wishes': see *Re A (Conjoined Twins: Medical Treatment)* [2001] 1 FLR 1 at 27.

[123] Gunn and Smith (above).

[124] *Re C (A Minor) (Wardship: Medical Treatment)* [1989] 2 All ER 782. See J Stone '*Re C* – Any Nearer a Solution to the Problem of Severely Handicapped Newborns?' (1989) 1 JCL 1, and D Morgan 'Severely Handicapped Babies and the Courts' (1989) 139 NLJ 723.

[125] The most extreme form of brain malformation occurs in anencephalic infants and this entails the absence of all or most of the higher brain. For an illuminating discussion of this condition, see the materials extracted in I Kennedy and A Grubb *Medical Law* (3rd edn, Butterworths, 2000), at pp 2225–2233.

to treat any serious infection or set up an intravenous feeding system. On the Official Solicitor's appeal against these directions, the Court of Appeal held that it was appropriate to authorise treatment for the purpose of alleviating suffering, but it would accept the opinions of medical staff if they decided that the aim of nursing care should be limited to this and not to achieve a short prolongation of life. But it was not appropriate for the judge's directions to be worded in that way or to be that specific. The directions concerning infections and feeding were therefore removed and the general direction was amended to authorise the hospital authorities 'to treat the minor to allow her life to come to an end peacefully and with dignity'.

The facts of this case were clearly distinguishable from those in the baby Alexandra case. The child in this case was already dying and no treatment could enable her to have a significant future life. Moreover, the existing 'quality' of her life was far removed from that of the Down's syndrome child. Her brain was incapable of even the most limited intellectual function and she suffered major physical disabilities which *would* render her life demonstrably awful and intolerable. These included a mixture of severe mental incapacity, blindness, probably deafness and spastic cerebral palsy of all four limbs. She was already not absorbing food properly or growing. In these circumstances there was a prognosis of an extremely short life and any treatment could be no more than a temporary palliative.

This decision confirmed that there was no absolute right to life and it provided the classic illustration of the more serious case of disability envisaged in the baby Alexandra case. There were, at the same time, strong echoes of the Dr Arthur case and the refusal of the law to countenance anything which smacks of positive killing.

Hence, the judge's direction required amendment in form if not in substance. While it remains the case that the courts are the final arbiters of what kind of treatment is warranted for a child, the decision in *Re C* revealed that they will usually wish to confine themselves to giving broad directions about the general nature of treatment or non-treatment and will prefer to leave the detailed management of the case to the medical professionals. Beyond this, the case went no further than the baby Alexandra case in articulating, other than indirectly, the scope of parental and medical authority or the standards which should govern these cases.

What then of the child who is *not* terminally ill but whose medical condition is arguably far worse than that of the uncomplicated Down's syndrome child?

The case of the premature baby: *Re J*[126]

Re J concerned a baby born very prematurely at 27 weeks' gestation. At birth, J weighed 1.1 kg. He was not breathing and was placed on a ventilator and given

---

[126] *Re J (A Minor) (Wardship: Medical Treatment)* [1990] 3 All ER 930.

antibiotics on a drip to avoid infection. His pulse rate remained low for the next 10 days and it was touch and go whether he would survive. At three to four months old, he was taken off the ventilator but thereafter suffered repetitive fits and cessations of breathing requiring resuscitation by ventilation. The prognosis was severe brain damage arising from prematurity. The most optimistic neonatalogist thought that there would be serious spastic quadriplegia. It was likely that J would never be able to sit up or hold his head upright, he would probably be blind and deaf and would be most unlikely to develop even the most limited intellectual abilities. On the other hand, since pain was a very basic response, there was evidence that he would be able to feel pain to the same extent as a normal baby. Life expectancy at its highest was late teens and would probably be considerably shorter.

The issue concerned what should be done in the event of J suffering a further collapse which could occur at any time but was not inevitable. Scott Baker J, at first instance, directed that there should be no further ventilation. The Court of Appeal held that the court could, acting in a child's best interests, approve a medical course of action which failed to prevent death. There was *no* absolute rule that life-prolonging treatment should never be withheld except in the case of a terminally ill child. Nor was the 'demonstrably so awful' test propounded in the baby Alexandra case to be treated as a quasi-statutory yardstick. While there was a strong presumption in favour of life, the court had to have regard to the quality of life, and to any additional suffering which might be caused by the life-saving treatment itself. In assessing the quality of life if treatment were given, the correct approach was to assess whether such a life *judged from the child's viewpoint* would be intolerable to him. In this case, the court authorised treatment within the parameters of a medical report which advised that, in the event of J requiring further resuscitation, it would not be in his best interests for this to be done unless this seemed appropriate to the doctors caring for him in the prevailing clinical situation. Again, the court was at pains to emphasise that what was at issue was not the right to impose death, but rather the right to choose a course of action which would fail to avert it. Where a patient had full capacity, this choice fell to him, but where, as an infant, he lacked capacity, the choice had to be a co-operative effort between the parents and the doctors or, where a court was involved, between the court and the medical profession, taking into account the views of the parents. In the end, the conclusion might be legitimately reached that it would not be in the *best* interests of a child to subject him to treatment which would cause increased suffering and no commensurate benefit, while giving full weight to the child's desire to survive.

This case was significant for its apparent application of the 'substituted judgment' test. The court emphasised the need for assessments of the quality of life to be made from the *assumed view of the child patient* and not from that of the adult decision-maker. Thus, severely disabled people might subjectively find a quality of life rewarding which to normal people would appear intolerable. The doctrine does not sit well with the traditional English approach which, applying the welfare principle, requires the decision-maker to arrive at his own view of what is best for the child.[127] The court here did, of course, have to apply this principle, but it did so in a way which appeared to equate the best interests of the child with a hypothetical projection of what that child would have wished if fully competent. This approach is, arguably, not merely contrary to the usual application of the welfare principle (which, as has been seen, does not require the actual wishes of competent children to be followed)[128] it also involves the use of a legal fiction. Disabled babies have never possessed the capacity to express a rational view on anything and there is, therefore, no basis upon which their supposed wishes can be predicted, except that of the individual judgment of the decision-maker. In reality, it is necessary to fall back on what the court itself thinks would be best for a particular child. The decision confirmed that the court must engage in a balancing exercise in determining the quality of life, if prolonged, against the pain and suffering involved in the treatment itself. It was also a further illustration of the court's preference for deferring to the medical profession's clinical judgment within broadly based guidelines. Subsequent decisions have applied this approach,[129] and it has been further refined and clarified by the Court of Appeal in *Wyatt v Portsmouth NHS Trust*.[130]

The Charlotte Wyatt case and subsequent decisions

The leading decision now, which has built on some of the earlier judgments, is *Wyatt v Portsmouth NHS Trust*.[131] The case concerned a little girl, Charlotte Wyatt, who was born at just 26 weeks' gestation weighing only 458 grammes, and who since birth had been cared for in hospital by Portsmouth NHS Trust.

---

[127] Although it fits better with some theories of children's rights which involve retrospective inquiries about what adults would have wished for themselves while children. See chapter 7.

[128] For a critique of the use of the substituted judgment test in cases like this, see Wells, Alldridge and Morgan 'An Unsuitable Case for Treatment' (1990) 140 NLJ 1544.

[129] See *Re J (A Minor) (Medical Treatment)* [1992] 2 FLR 165 (not to be confused with the earlier case under discussion). In this later case, the Court of Appeal held that it would be an abuse of judicial power for the court, in the exercise of its inherent jurisdiction, to require a medical practitioner to treat a minor in a manner contrary to his fundamental duty to exercise his best clinical judgment. In this case, the child aged 16 months suffered from severe cerebral palsy, epilepsy and cortical blindness following a fall. He required 24-hour attention and medical opinion was unanimous that his life expectancy was short. The Court of Appeal refused, in these circumstances, to order the health authority to continue with artificial ventilation and other life-saving measures. See also *Re C (A Baby)* [1996] 2 FLR 43, in which Sir Stephen Brown P said that the courts were ready to assist the medical profession with taking responsibility in cases of grave anxiety. In this case, the baby suffered severe brain damage after developing meningitis. She could not survive without continuing artificial ventilation. This would involve her in increasing pain and distress, and the prognosis was hopeless. The medical experts were agreed that further artificial ventilation was not in her best interests and the court in wardship proceedings granted leave to discontinue it. It has been held, again by Sir Stephen Brown P, that the court may authorise the withdrawal of ventilation for a terminally ill baby where this is advised by the medical team but opposed by the parents. See *Re C (Medical Treatment)* [1998] 1 FLR 384, in which the parents were orthodox Jews and did not believe that their religion permitted them to contemplate a course of action which would indirectly shorten life.

[130] [2005] EWCA Civ 1181, [2006] 1 FLR 554.

[131] [2005] EWCA Civ 1181, [2006] 1 FLR 554.

Charlotte had brain damage, was blind and deaf, unable to move or respond voluntarily, but was capable of experiencing pain and distress. She also suffered from chronic respiratory and kidney problems. The case first came before Hedley J[132] when a disagreement arose between Charlotte's parents (Mr and Mrs Wyatt) and the doctors who were treating her. Charlotte was then nearly a year old and required high levels of oxygen to survive, which in themselves damaged her lungs, and her kidney function was deteriorating. The medical opinion was that Charlotte would likely succumb to a respiratory infection over the winter and her prognosis for survival for 12 months was put optimistically at a 25 per cent chance and realistically at a 5 per cent chance. It was the unanimous medical opinion that in those circumstances artificial ventilation, if and when required, would not be in Charlotte's best interests. The parents disagreed, seeing it as their duty to maintain Charlotte's life, and hoping for a divine miracle. Against this background, Hedley J considered the existing law and the correct approach to applying the test of the child's 'best interests'. Hedley J saw the case as evoking 'some of the fundamental principles that undergird our humanity', such as the sanctity of life and respect for the dignity of the individual, which are to be found 'the deep recesses of the common psyche' whether 'they be attributed to humanity being created in the image of God or whether it be simply a self-defining ethic of a generally acknowledged humanism'.[133] Hedley J emphasised that the general principles are not always compatible with each other and whilst the sanctity of Charlotte's life and her right to dignity were to be respected, the court had to choose on the basis of what was in her best interests.[134] Hedley J held that bests interests 'must be given a generous interpretation', citing the view of Dame Elizabeth Butler-Sloss P in *Re A (Male Sterilisation)* that 'best interests encompasses medical, emotional and all other welfare issues'[135] and the view of Thorpe LJ in *Re S (Adult Patient: Sterilisation)*[136] that 'it would be undesirable and probably impossible to set bounds to what is relevant to a welfare determination'.[137] Hedley J cited a passage from *Re J (A Minor) (Wardship: Medical Treatment)*[138] in which Lord Donaldson had concluded that:[139]

'there will be cases in which the answer must be that it is not in the interests of the child to subject it to treatment which will cause increased suffering and produce no commensurate benefit, giving the fullest possible weight to the child's, and mankind's, desire to survive.'

He also cited Taylor LJ's view that the 'correct approach is for the court to judge the quality of life the child would have to endure if given the treatment

---

[132] *Portsmouth NHS Trust v Wyatt and Wyatt, Southampton NHS Trust Intervening* [2004] EWHC 2247 (Fam), [2005] 1 FLR 21.
[133] Ibid, at para [21], citing Hoffman LJ in the Court of Appeal in *Airedale NHS Trust v Bland* [1993] AC 789, at p 826.
[134] Ibid, at paras [21] and [22].
[135] [2000] 1 FLR 549, at 555.
[136] [2001] Fam 15, [2000] 2 FLR 389.
[137] Ibid, at 403.
[138] [1991] Fam 33, [1991] 1 FLR 366.
[139] Ibid, at 46–47 and 375 respectively.

and decide whether in all the circumstances such a life would be so afflicted as to be intolerable to that child'. However, Hedley J cautioned:[140]

'Helpful though these passages are, it is, in my view, essential that the concept of 'intolerable to that child' should not be seen as a gloss on, much less a supplementary test to, best interests. It is a valuable guide in the search for best interests in this kind of case.'

Hedley J added that the suggestion made by Thorpe LJ in *Re A (Male Sterilisation)*[141] that 'the first instance judge with the responsibility to make an evaluation of the best interests of a claimant lacking capacity should draw up a balance sheet' could, 'with necessary variations (not the least of which is the weight to be given to the views of the parents)', be usefully 'applied to children as well'.[142]

Applying this approach to the law, Hedley J considered Charlotte's prospects of survival, the quality of her life viewed as far as possible from her perspective, the quality of Charlotte's sensory faculties, and Charlotte's parents' views. He also identified as a consideration in the case of a person at risk of imminent death, the securing of a 'good' death. He concluded that further aggressive treatment, even if necessary to prolong life, was not in Charlotte's best interests.[143] He added:[144]

'Although I believe and find that further invasive and aggressive treatment would be intolerable to Charlotte, I prefer to determine her best interests on the basis of finding what is the best that can be done for her.'

Thus Hedley J granted declaratory relief which was permissive in nature, authorising the hospital, in the event of disagreement between the parents and themselves, not to send the child for artificial ventilation or similar aggressive treatment.[145]

Charlotte Wyatt defied all the odds and survived the winter,[146] and the case came back before Hedley J[147] when she was 18 months old, by which time her oxygen dependency had reduced by 50 per cent and she was now able to make some response to human stimulation and contact, responding to a loud noise and tracking movement of a large object.[148] Mr and Mrs Wyatt sought

---

[140] *Portsmouth NHS Trust v Wyatt and Wyatt, Southampton NHS Trust Intervening* [2004] EWHC 2247 (Fam), [2005] 1 FLR 21, at para [24].

[141] [2000] 1 FLR 549, at 560.

[142] *Portsmouth NHS Trust v Wyatt and Wyatt, Southampton NHS Trust Intervening* [2004] EWHC 2247 (Fam), [2005] 1 FLR 21, at para [26].

[143] Ibid, at para [38].

[144] Ibid.

[145] Ibid, at para [41].

[146] See the report in *Wyatt v Portsmouth NHS Trust and Wyatt (By Her Guardian) (No 3)* [2005] EWHC 693 (Fam), [2005] 2 FLR 480, at para [3].

[147] [1990] 3 All ER 930. See *Wyatt v Portsmouth NHS Trust and Wyatt (By Her Guardian) (No 3)* [2005] EWHC 693 (Fam), [2005] 2 FLR 480

[148] Ibid, at para [4].

discharge of the declarations. Hedley J dismissed the application, applying the same approach to best interests as previously, an approach which had since been endorsed in the judgment of Dame Elizabeth Butler Sloss P in *Re L (Medical Treatment: Benefit)*.[149]

Hedley J concluded that, despite the improvement, Charlotte was still terminally ill and, although her life was now not intolerable, it would still not be in Charlotte's best interests in the event of respiratory collapse to attempt aggressive invasive treatment by way of intubation and ventilation. He concluded that the decision should be taken now and not await a crisis. In reaching that conclusion he considered with care the judgment of Lord Woolf MR in *R (Glass) v Portsmouth Hospitals NHS Trust*,[150] in which it was made clear that the general rule is that declarations should be sought and considered in the light of circumstances as they are and not as they may be. However, Hedley J was content to continue the declaration since this was 'a fairly precisely anticipated medical emergency', albeit subject to two qualifications. First 'the judgment whether to rely upon the declarations must be taken by Portsmouth in the light of all the circumstances pertaining at the time of crisis on the basis of Charlotte's best interests and in close consultation with the parents'[151] and it was agreed that the declaration would not be open-ended, but subject to review.[152]

Mr and Mrs Wyatt applied to the Court of Appeal for permission to appeal on the best interests question, which was refused, and appealed (with permission) on the timing of the declarations.[153] Although on the best interests question the court was only dealing with an application for permission to appeal the court took the view that the point was one of importance and that the case offered a convenient opportunity to address it.[154] The Court examined the earlier decisions in *Re B (A Minor) (Wardship: Medical Treatment)*[155] and *Re J (A Minor) (Wardship: Medical Treatment)*[156] and concluded that a best interests test based on the intolerability of the child's quality of life had its origins in extempore dicta in *Re B* which were not approved by Lord Donaldson or Balcombe LJ in *Re J*. These judges had deprecated any attempt to lay down an all-embracing test other than best interests. Only in Taylor LJ's judgment was

---

[149] [2004] EWHC 2713 (Fam), [2005] 1 FLR 491, at para [12]. In that case Butler-Sloss P considered the best interests of a 9 month-old boy who suffered from an incurable genetic disorder with multiple medical problems, which meant he would be unlikely to survive beyond a year. She concluded that he should not be mechanically ventilated since there was a high risk of permanent dependency on the ventilator. Looking at the child's 'best interests, seen in the broadest possible way, taking into account his emotional need to continue his relationship with his mother', ventilation would deprive him of any closeness with this mother (see para [26]).

[150] [1999] 2 FLR 905.

[151] *Wyatt v Portsmouth NHS Trust and Wyatt (By Her Guardian) (No 3)* [2005] EWHC 693 (Fam), [2005] 2 FLR 480, at para [22].

[152] Ibid.

[153] *Wyatt v Portsmouth NHS Trust* [2005] EWCA Civ 1181, [2006] 1 FLR 554.

[154] Ibid, at para [63].

[155] [1981] 1 WLR 1421, (1982) 3 FLR 117.

[156] *Wyatt v Portsmouth NHS Trust* [2005] EWCA Civ 1181, [2006] 1 FLR 554, at para [75].

there an attempt to find a 'correct approach' by reference to the notion of 'intolerability'. The Court of the Appeal in the *Wyatt* case thus concluded that:[157]

> 'Hedley J was right to observe that the concept of 'intolerable to the child' should not be seen as a gloss on, much less a supplementary test to, best interests. It is, as the judge observed, a valuable guide in the search for best interests in this kind of case.'

The court endorsed Hedley J's formulation of the best interests test, including the balance sheet approach, and the various dicta on which he had relied to reach it,[158] explaining:[159]

> 'In our judgment, the intellectual milestones for the judge in a case such as the present are, therefore, simple, although the ultimate decision will frequently be extremely difficult. The judge must decide what is in the child's best interests. In making that decision, the welfare of the child is paramount, and the judge must look at the question from the assumed point of view of the patient (*Re J*). There is a strong presumption in favour of a course of action which will prolong life, but that presumption is not irrebuttable (*Re J*). The term 'best interests' encompasses medical, emotional, and all other welfare issues (*Re A*). The court must conduct a balancing exercise in which all the relevant factors are weighed (*Re J*) and a helpful way of undertaking this exercise is to draw up a balance sheet (*Re A*).'

The court stressed that each case will be 'highly fact specific'[160] but this is not 'to say that the judge has *carte blanche* to do what he or she likes. The judge must in each case perform the balancing exercise identified by the Master of the Rolls in *Re J*, helpfully amplified by the "balance sheet" approach advocated by Thorpe LJ in *Re A*'.[161]

With regard to the timing of the declaration, the court detected 'a tension between the concept of a declaration, which is designed to state what is lawful in given circumstances, and a situation which is sufficiently fluid to render it likely that the circumstances may change, with the consequence that the lawfulness of the conduct identified in the declaration may be called in question'.[162] The court concluded that whether a declaration is lawful or not was fact and case specific, and each case had to be decided on its particular facts.[163] While the Court of Appeal counselled caution in making open-ended

---

[157] Ibid, at para [76]. Thus it is not dismissed as a factor altogether (see para [91]) but it is clear that the court preferred Hedley J's view over that of Munby J in *R (Burke) v General Medical Council* [2004] EWHC 1879 (Admin), [2005] QB 424, [2004] 2 FLR 1121, at para [111], who had said that the 'touchstone of best interests in this context is intolerability' which the court said was, at best, obiter (see *Wyatt*, at para [90]).

[158] *Wyatt v Portsmouth NHS Trust* [2005] EWCA Civ 1181, [2006] 1 FLR 554, at paras [62] and [79].

[159] *Wyatt v Portsmouth NHS Trust* [2005] EWCA Civ 1181, [2006] 1 FLR 554, at para [87].

[160] Ibid, at para [88].

[161] Ibid, at para [89].

[162] Ibid, at para [111].

[163] Ibid, at para [114].

declarations in cases involving seriously damaged or gravely ill children, and observed that it is not the function of the court to oversee the treatment plan for a gravely ill child,[164] it concluded that on the facts of this case Hedley J had been entitled to make and renew the declarations.[165]

There had been a delay in hearing the Court of Appeal case by which time Charlotte was two years old and had continued to make some limited progress. The Court of Appeal saw this new information as not going to the merits of the appeal but to the need for a more urgent review, and the court remitted the case to the judge accordingly.

The balance sheet approach endorsed by the Court of Appeal in the *Wyatt* case was applied by Holman J in *An NHS Trust v MB (A Child Represented by Cafcass As Guardian ad Litem)*.[166] The case concerned an 18-month-old boy who suffered from the congenital condition, spinal muscular atrophy. This degenerative, progressive condition meant that he could hardly move at all, nor breathe unaided. He was kept alive through artificial ventilation. The medical team treating him considered that his quality of life was so low and the burdens of living so great that it was unethical to continue artificially to keep him alive, although the boy was conscious and it was assumed that he was able to process sights and sounds like any other child.[167] Holman J usefully summarised (and filled out) the intellectual milestones to which the Court of Appeal referred in the *Wyatt* case:[168]

'(i) As a dispute has arisen between the treating doctors and the parents, and one, and now both, parties have asked the court to make a decision, it is the role and duty of the court to do so and to exercise its own independent and objective judgment.

(ii) The right and power of the court to do so only arises because the patient, in this case because he is a child, lacks the capacity to make a decision for himself.

(iii) I am *not* deciding what decision I might make for myself if I were, hypothetically, in the situation of the patient; nor for a child of my own if in that situation; nor whether the respective decisions of the doctors on the one hand or the parents on the other are reasonable decisions.

(iv) The matter must be decided by the application of an objective approach or test.

(v) That test is the best interests of the patient. Best interests are used in the widest sense and include every kind of consideration capable of impacting on the

---

[164] Ibid, at para [117].
[165] Ibid, at para [118].
[166] [2006] EWHC 507 (Fam), [2006] 2 FLR 319.
[167] Ibid, at para [10].
[168] See *Re B (Medical Treatment)* [2008] EWHC 1996 (Fam), [2009] 1 FLR 1264, at para [15], per Coleridge J, describing Holman J's judgment as a 'very useful summation of the position'. See also *Re KH (Medical Treatment: Advanced Care Plan)* [2013] 1 FLR 1471, at para [17], per Peter Jackson J: 'a helpful summary'.

decision. These include, non-exhaustively, medical, emotional, sensory (pleasure, pain and suffering) and instinctive (the human instinct to survive) considerations.

(vi) It is impossible to weigh such considerations mathematically, but the court must do the best it can to balance all the conflicting considerations in a particular case and see where the final balance of the best interests lies.

(vii) Considerable weight (Lord Donaldson of Lymington MR referred to 'a very strong presumption': see (viii) below) must be attached to the prolongation of life because the individual human instinct and desire to survive is strong and must be presumed to be strong in the patient. But it is not absolute, nor necessarily decisive; and may be outweighed if the pleasures and the quality of life are sufficiently small and the pain and suffering or other burdens of living are sufficiently great.

(viii) These considerations remain well expressed in the words as relatively long ago now as 1991 of Lord Donaldson of Lymington MR in *Re J (A Minor) (Wardship: Medical Treatment)* [1991] Fam 33, [1991] 1 FLR 366, at 46 and 375 respectively ... [quotation omitted]

(ix) All these cases are very fact specific, ie they depend entirely on the facts of the individual case.

(x) The views and opinions of both the doctors *and* the parents must be carefully considered. Where, as in this case, the parents spend a great deal of time with their child, their views may have particular value because they know the patient and how he reacts so well; although the court needs to be mindful that the views of any parents may, very understandably, be coloured by their own emotion or sentiment. It is important to stress that the reference is to the views and opinions of the parents. Their own wishes, however understandable in human terms, are wholly irrelevant to consideration of the objective best interests of the child save to the extent in any given case that they may illuminate the quality and value *to the child* of the child/parent relationship.'

Holman J avoided reference to the concept of 'intolerability'[169] as he clearly found the guidance given by the Court of Appeal in *Wyatt* in this respect difficult to apply. He doubted his own intellectual capacity to exclude intolerability 'even as a "gloss on", much less a supplementary test to, best interests: and yet on the other hand treat it as a "valuable guide"'.[170]

Drawing on *Airedale NHS Trust v Bland*[171] Holman J concluded that there was no legal distinction between withholding or withdrawing life support and that the best interests test applies equally to both situations. He examined the various 'benefits' and 'burdens' associated with ventilator support continuing,[172] and, stressing that this was a very fact specific decision,[173]

---

[169] Ibid, at para [17].
[170] Ibid.
[171] [1993] AC 789, [1993] 1 FLR 1026.
[172] See [2006] EWHC 507 (Fam), [2006] 2 FLR 319, at para [60], the balance sheet prepared by the guardian in the case.

concluded that it was not currently in the child's best interests to discontinue ventilation with the inevitable result that he would immediately die.[174] In reaching his conclusion the judge was influenced by the fact that the child had age appropriate cognition, continued to have a valuable relationship with his family, and also gained pleasures from touch, sight and sound.[175]

A case which can be contrasted with *An NHS Trust v MB* is *Re K (Medical Treatment: Declaration)*.[176] The question was similarly whether life-sustaining treatment (in this case artificial intravenous feeding) could lawfully be withdrawn from a girl aged six months who suffered from an inherited disorder of chronic muscle weakness and learning difficulties, which meant she would likely die within her first year. In granting the declaration sought by the child's medical team (which was unopposed), Sir Mark Potter P contrasted K's case with that of *MB* above, commenting that there was 'no realistic sense in which one can assign to her the simple pleasure of being alive or having other than a life dominated by regular pain, distress and discomfort'.[177] Similarly, in *NHS Trust v Baby X*[178] Hedley J declared that it was lawful to withdraw life-sustaining treatment in the case of a one-year-old baby who had suffered a catastrophic brain injury which meant that he was unaware of self and others and with no realistic hope of improvement.[179]

In *Re B (Medical Treatment)*[180] Coleridge J made an advance declaration authorising doctors to withhold intensive resuscitation of a 22-month-old child with profound mental and physical disabilities in the event of a steep downward gradient in a child's condition. The judge attached a short joint experts' report to the declaration to assist doctors caring for the child in the exercise of what might in future be a very difficult, sensitive and finely balanced clinical judgment. The case is also interesting because the child was in the care of a local authority, which raised the question of the scope of the local authority's powers to consent to the contents of the declaration. The local authority took the view that the care order did not invest them with such power and invited the NHS trust to apply to court. Coleridge J did not decide this 'nice point' but said that he thought the local authority were probably right and even if they did have sufficient authority they were entirely right and sensible to take the course they had.[181]

---

[173] Ibid, at paras [106] and [107].
[174] Ibid, at para [89].
[175] Ibid, at para [101].
[176] [2006] EWHC 1007 (Fam), [2006] 2 FLR 883.
[177] Ibid, at para [57].
[178] [2012] EWHC 2188 (Fam), [2013] 1 FLR 225.
[179] Ibid, at para [28].
[180] [2008] EWHC 1996 (Fam), [2009] 1 FLR 1264.
[181] Ibid, at para [7].

Re KH (Medical Treatment: Advanced Care Plan)[182] also concerned a severely disabled child,[183] KH, who was in the care of a local authority (looked after by a foster parent) and in respect of whom an NHS Trust was seeking a declaration as to the lawfulness of a care plan which involved the withholding of life-sustaining treatment if there was a serious deterioration in the child's condition. Peter Jackson J made the declaration in advance, being satisfied that the child's condition was well understood, that there was almost no chance of improvement, and the prospect and manner of deterioration were inevitable;[184] and aggressive treatment in such circumstances would not be in KH's best interests.

KH's parents had problems of their own and lacked capacity to take decisions about KH's medical treatment and to conduct proceedings on their own. They were represented by the Official Solicitor. The mother disagreed with some aspects of the NHS Trust's plan and counsel for KH's guardian submitted that the irrelevance of the wishes of others, save to the extent that they cast light on the objective best interests of the child, must apply more forcefully to the views or wishes of parents without capacity who are not themselves looking after the child in question. On this point, Peter Jackson J commented:[185]

> 'I readily accept that an involved and capacitous parent may be better placed to express views that assist in assessing best interests than one who is less involved or capacitous, but that is a matter of evidence and not one of principle. Parents who lack capacity may still make telling points about welfare and it would be wrong to discount the weight to be attached to their views simply because of incapacity. It is the validity of the views that matter, not the capacity of the person that holds them. In the present case, I have not discounted the views of the mother on the ground that she is represented by a litigation friend (the Official Solicitor) who does not oppose the declarations sought by the Trust, but have tried to approach her views on their merits.'

The resurgence of parental rights: *Re T*

A case which illustrates that the wishes and feelings of parents can be a powerful factor in decision making in some cases is *Re T (Wardship: Medical Treatment)*.[186] The decision came close to reasserting the concept of parental 'rights' in the medical context and was the subject of much critical academic comment.[187] The baby, C, suffered from a life-threatening liver defect known as biliary artresia. There was a unanimous medical prognosis that without a liver transplant C could not live beyond the age of two-and-a-half years, but the prospects of success were thought to be good if a donor liver became available.

---

[182] [2013] 1 FLR 1471 (FD).
[183] At 5 weeks old the child had suffered viral encephalitis resulting in widespread brain destruction.
[184] [2013] 1 FLR 1471, at paras [42] and [43].
[185] Ibid, at para [19].
[186] [1997] 1 FLR 502.
[187] See particularly M Fox and J McHale 'In Whose Best Interests?' (1997) MLR 700, and A Bainham 'Do Babies Have Rights?' [1997] CLJ 48.

All the medical experts thought it was in C's best interests to undergo such an operation but the parents (who were unmarried)[188] were opposed to it. The case undoubtedly had special features. Both parents were health care professionals with experience of caring for sick children; C had previously undergone unsuccessful surgery which had caused him much pain and distress; and the parents had, albeit against medical advice, gone to a 'distant Commonwealth country'. The issue was whether the mother should be ordered to return to the jurisdiction with C and present him to hospital for liver transplantation assessment.

At first instance, Connell J held that she should, but he appeared to ground his decision on an assessment that the mother's opinion was unreasonable, rather than on a straightforward application of the welfare principle. Allowing the mother's appeal, the Court of Appeal emphasised that the matter was governed by the welfare principle. While there was a strong presumption in favour of life, prolonging life was not the court's sole objective. The judge, it was held, had failed to give adequate weight to certain factors which ought to have been fed into the welfare test. According to Butler-Sloss LJ, he had given insufficient emphasis to 'the enormous significance of the close attachment between the mother and baby' and 'whether it [was] in the best interests of C for [the court] in effect to direct the mother to take on this total commitment where she [did] not agree with the course proposed'. Roch LJ thought that there was a clinical aspect to the bond between mother and child 'because in the absence of parental belief that a transplant [was] the right procedure for the child, the prospects of a successful outcome [were] diminished'.

As we have seen, there is nothing unusual or unprincipled about a court refusing life-saving surgery to a child in an appropriate case. What makes the decision in *Re T* so controversial is the close association which the Court of Appeal was prepared to make between the interests of the mother and the child, and this gave the case a significance which exceeded the fate of the individual child. Here, the focus of the court's attention went beyond the child's best *medical* interests which had, it is submitted, been the decisive factor in the earlier cases. It was prepared to attach significance to the issues surrounding the care of the child in the event of a successful operation – yet nowhere was there the suggestion, as there was in the baby Alexandra case (above), that if necessary the State should be prepared to provide a substitute home. It was sufficient for Butler-Sloss LJ that C's future treatment 'should be left in the hands of his devoted parents'. Waite LJ thought it unhelpful to indulge in 'rights-talk'. This was 'not an occasion – even in an age preoccupied with "rights" – to talk of the rights of the child, or the rights of a parent, or the rights of the court'.[189] Whether or not it is jurisprudentially accurate to assert 'rights' for children or parents, the real criticism of this ruling is that it failed to differentiate sufficiently between the *interests* of the mother and the child which were assumed to coincide but which, it might be argued, were in conflict. In

---

[188] The significance of their being unmarried was that sole parental responsibility was with the mother although it was clear, in any event, that the father agreed with her.

[189] On children's rights as a concept, see chapter 7.

Waite LJ's opinion, 'in the last analysis the best interest of every child incudes an expectation that difficult decisions affecting the length and quality of its life will be taken for it by the parent to whom its care has been entrusted by nature'. Yet to take this literally would be to turn the clock back to the nineteenth century and ignore the advances made for children as persons over the last hundred years.

The dilemma of the conjoined twins: *Re A*

In September 2000, ironically perhaps immediately before the implementation of the HRA 1998, the Court of Appeal in *Re A (Children) (Conjoined Twins: Surgical Separation)*[190] was called upon to resolve what many saw as a clash between the fundamental rights and interests of two children. Jodie and Mary were ischiopagus conjoined twins (joined at the pelvis). The medical prognosis should they remain joined was hopeless. The twins shared a common aorta. Mary's heart and lungs were severely deficient and her life was sustained only by this common artery. She was therefore entirely dependent on Jodie for life. It was also known that the death of *both* twins would be inevitable within a few months since Jodie's heart would be unable to cope with the strain. Surgical separation would give Jodie, the stronger twin, a reasonable prospect of a worthwhile life but would be bound to cause the almost immediate death of Mary. The parents were devout Roman Catholics from Malta. They were unwilling to agree to surgery since they took the view that in God's eyes the twins were equal and that morally one could not be sacrificed to save the other.

What was the court to do in a situation like this? The Court of Appeal,[191] with much agonising, reached the conclusion that it should uphold the decision of Johnson J who had granted a declaration that the operation might lawfully be performed. This subsequently took place in St. Mary's Hospital, Manchester. Mary, as expected, died during the course of the operation while Jodie survived and was later understood to be progressing remarkably well. The issues in the case were immensely complicated but they can be conveniently grouped together as the family law issues and the criminal law issues. There was also an important issue under the ECHR, although this received surprisingly cursory examination by the court.

Taking first the family law issues, what was the correct principle to apply when the interests of two children conflict and what was the proper weight to be attached to the genuinely and firmly held opinions of the parents? As to the conflict of interest between the twins, it should first be acknowledged that there was a division of opinion about whether there was indeed a conflict at all. Johnson J at first instance and Robert Walker LJ in the Court of Appeal both

---

[190] [2001] 1 FLR 1.
[191] For the views of one of the authors on the decision see A Bainham 'Resolving the Unresolvable: The Case of the Conjoined Twins' [2001] CLJ 49. See also M Freeman 'Whose Life is it Anyway?' (2001) 9 *Medical Law Review* 259. For a commentary attacking the decision see S Michalowski 'Sanctity of Life – are some lives more sacred than others?' (2002) *Legal Studies* 377.

thought that there was not since, as the latter put it, 'continued life, whether long or short, would hold nothing for Mary, except possible pain or discomfort, if indeed she can feel anything at all'.[192] The majority in the Court of Appeal (Ward LJ and Brooke LJ), however, took the view that an invasive procedure which would bring about the sudden death of Mary could not properly be said to be in her best interests and there was therefore a clash of interests between the twins. The court's obligation in cases like this, as we have seen, is to determine the matter in accordance with the welfare principle. But in a case in which the best interests of two children pull in opposite directions and in which both were the subject of the proceedings the court could not give effect to the paramountcy principle in relation to both children simultaneously. Faced with this impossibility, the majority decided that they could not abdicate from the responsibility of deciding, since to do nothing would in itself be to take a position. They reached the conclusion that they should balance the interests of the two children and choose the least detrimental alternative. This was to sanction the operation since it would offer Jodie the chance of a relatively normal life while not fundamentally affecting the sad condition of Mary whom Ward LJ (controversially) described as 'designated for death'. The court therefore followed what might be seen as a utilitarian approach which maximised the welfare of those whose interests were at stake when taken collectively. There is clearly a tension between such an approach and one which emphasises individual rights. Yet it may well prove less controversial in less emotive contexts in which the issue is not one of life and death. Indeed it is the approach essentially taken by the Law Commission in its Report which preceded the Children Act 1989.[193]

The other family law issue was how much weight to attach to the religiously inspired views of the parents. Here the court reiterated the principle that the parental view is not sovereign and that the court's role was not confined to reviewing the reasonableness of a parental decision. The approach in *Re T (Wardship: Medical Treatment)*,[194] which many commentators had criticised, was therefore firmly rejected. The court did not in the final analysis attach decisive importance to considerations of respecting the parents' religious views[195] when to do so would jeopardise the life of one child and in this respect the decision reaffirms a long-standing principle.[196]

These issues of family law arose within a context in which there was a substantial argument that to authorise the operation would be to bring about the unlawful killing, indeed murder, of Mary. Much of the judgments, especially that of Brooke LJ, are therefore devoted to a close examination of

---

[192] [2001] 1 FLR 1, at 119.

[193] Report No 172, at paras 3.13 and 3.14, and clause 1(2) of the Draft Bill appended to that Report.

[194] [1997] 1 WLR 242, discussed above.

[195] It should be recalled that religious freedom is a fundamental right protected by the ECHR, Art 9 of which upholds the right, inter alia, to 'freedom of thought, conscience and religion ... and freedom ... to manifest ... religion or belief, in worship, teaching, practice and observance'.

[196] See chapter 2 above.

the law of homicide which is beyond the scope of the present discussion. But the essential point is that the criminal law draws a fundamental distinction between *omissions*, such as the withdrawal of life-sustaining treatment, and *positive acts* of killing. While the former will not generally be unlawful, it has long been accepted that the latter will, prima facie, amount to homicide. What was proposed here was a surgical intervention which would directly bring about the almost immediate death of a child. It was inevitable too that the doctors who performed it would foresee this death as a virtual certainty and hence the inference would be inescapable that they *intended* that death.[197] The altruistic motives of the medical team, to save another life, would not normally exculpate them since the law of homicide, at least in theory, takes no account of motive. The sanctity of life generally means that one life cannot be valued less than another.[198]

The issue was therefore whether there could be a defence to what would otherwise be murder. The court found, in the unique circumstances, that the doctrine of necessity applied and, in the case of Ward LJ, that this was a situation of 'quasi self-defence'. So far as necessity was concerned, the court found that the three essential prerequisites were satisfied – the action was needed to avoid inevitable and irreparable evil, no more was proposed than was reasonably necessary for this purpose and the evil inflicted would not be disproportionate to the evil avoided. As to the novel notion of quasi self-defence, Ward LJ relied heavily on the consideration that just as to operate would be to kill Mary, not to operate would kill Jodie. The reality, therefore, 'harsh as it is to state it, and unnatural as it is that it should be happening', was that Mary was effectively killing Jodie. He could 'see no difference between ... resort to legitimate self-defence and removing the threat of fatal harm to her presented by Mary's draining her life blood'. While this formulation has attracted severe criticism, it is one which had the support of the late JC Smith, perhaps the leading criminal lawyer of his generation, who found it unremarkable on the basis that private defence has always been an answer to a charge of murder.[199]

A final matter is the question of what human rights, if any, were engaged by the case. Surely this, of all cases, brought sharply into focus the fundamental rights of children. This was not the way in which it was viewed by the Court of Appeal, which decided the matter almost entirely on the traditional basis of applying the welfare principle. The primary focus was therefore on the *best interests* of the twins and not on their *rights*. There were some arguments presented under the ECHR but these were given short shrift by the court. The court's view was that there was nothing in the ECHR or in Strasbourg jurisprudence which would lead to a different conclusion than the one it reached. The arguments, such as they were, revolved around Art 2 of the

---

[197] Murder requires an intention to kill or cause grievous bodily harm and the House of Lords in *R v Woollin* [1998] 3 WLR 382 has confirmed that a finding of intention might be made by a jury in these circumstances.

[198] A principle with a long history. See especially *R v Dudley and Stephens* (1884) 14 QBD 273.

[199] JC Smith *Smith and Hogan: Criminal Law* (10th edn, Butterworths, 2002), at p 282.

ECHR which provides that 'everyone's right to life shall be protected by law' and that 'no one shall be deprived of his life intentionally'. Thus, the State is under a *positive* obligation to protect life and a *negative* obligation not to deprive someone of life intentionally. The court quickly rejected the argument for Mary that the negative obligation – not to deprive Mary of life intentionally – was a stronger obligation than the positive obligation to act to save Jodie's life. It took the position that the negative obligation was discharged by the State insofar as it put in place a law against unlawful killing, which was clearly the case in English law. As we have seen, the court's view was that in the very peculiar circumstances of the case the operation would not fall foul of the law of homicide.

Is it really the case that human rights are largely irrelevant in a case such as this? It is submitted that there could have been some benefit to Jodie in a closer concentration on the rights which she might legitimately have asserted in this situation. In order to make out this case it is necessary to speculate on what the position would have been if, contrary to the facts, the hospital had agreed, or at least acquiesced in, the parents' wish to allow nature to take its course. Ward LJ was quite definite about this. It would, he said, 'have been a perfectly acceptable response for the hospital to bow to the weight of the parental wish however fundamentally the medical team disagreed with it. Had St Mary's done so, there could not have been the slightest criticism of them for letting nature take its course in accordance with the parents' wishes'. Yet rather contradictorily, elsewhere in his judgment, he emphasises the duty on both the hospital and the parents to act and even speculates that the parents might have been criminally liable for not doing so.[200]

A failure to conceptualise the issue in terms of Jodie's *rights* might lead us in the direction of the conclusion that there was no duty to intervene. Yet it is worth considering what would have happened to the human rights of Jodie in that event. Alternatively, if her position were viewed from the perspective of rights, it might have focused attention more clearly on the scope of the duty to intervene, whether the duty of the parents, the hospital or the court.

The case of the conjoined twins provokes considerable disagreement. It is one rather stark demonstration of the lack of a shared morality about these life and death decisions. For the Roman Catholic parents it was morally wrong to kill Mary. For others it was morally wrong not to bring about her death since there was a moral duty to save Jodie.

Quality of life over sanctity of life

The reported decisions focus on the quality of the child's life and establish, beyond question, that there is no absolute duty to save life, either on the part of parents, or the medical profession, and they generally draw a theoretical distinction between acts of positive killing and omissions which do not prevent

---

[200] See the discussion of wilful neglect, at pp 347 et seq above.

natural death occurring. The case of the conjoined twins, as indicated above, is to be regarded as wholly exceptional and confined to its own peculiar facts. It is, of course, true that the medical profession has a certain duty to act in the interests of the patient so that the distinction between acts and omissions can be somewhat artificial in this context. It is also true that positive acts, such as the administration of drugs which are designed to alleviate pain and suffering, can have the 'double effect' of also hastening death. The most difficult question is the *extent* of the doctor's duty to act and it seems that this now turns on the notoriously vague notion of 'reasonableness'. The effect of the House of Lords decision in *Airedale NHS Trust v Bland*[201] is that a doctor would be acting lawfully in allowing a patient to die if a responsible body of medical opinion would support that course of action in the circumstances as being in the patient's best interests. This is effectively an application in life-saving cases of the *Bolam* test for medical negligence.[202] A principle of proportionality appears to have emerged whereby a qualitative assessment of the life of the child must be made and this must be balanced with an evaluation of the treatment required to sustain that quality of life.

Yet these principles are themselves problematic and there remain many unanswered questions. It is not obvious that a sensible distinction can really be drawn between acts and omissions. It is even less clear that, if such a distinction can indeed be made, there is a valid moral distinction between failing to keep a child alive and actively helping to hasten death. It may be that a more justifiable moral distinction can be drawn between different kinds of acts and different kinds of omissions. Refusing surgical intervention is arguably of a quite different moral order than withholding food. But the greatest area of concern must be the absence of accepted standards or guidelines to regulate the decisions taken by parents, in conjunction with the medical profession, in the large number of cases which never reach the courts. There is substantial evidence that the decision about whether to treat or not to treat a child is significantly influenced by parental attitudes. A decision to withhold life-saving treatment is much more likely to be taken where parents desire it. It might be argued that children's rights demand like treatment for like cases, making due allowance for the fact that no two cases are wholly identical.

Children's rights to equality of treatment

The concern to try to ensure a measure of equality of treatment led to successive attempts in the USA, at both the federal and State levels, to formulate legal standards to govern the circumstances under which non-treatment is allowable.[203] What kind of standards then could be evolved?

---

[201] [1993] 2 WLR 316. For later applications of the *Bland* decision in relation to adults, see *Re D (Medical Treatment)* [1998] 1 FLR 411, *Re D (Medical Treatment: Mentally Disabled Patient)* [1998] 2 FLR 22, and *Re H (A Patient)* [1998] 2 FLR 36.

[202] But see now the refinement of the test in *Bolitho v City and Hackney Health Authority* [1997] 3 WLR 1151 (above).

[203] These were triggered by the *Baby Doe* case; as to which see J Dunsay Silver 'Baby Doe: The Incomplete Federal Response' (1986) 20 Fam LQ 173.

One possibility is that a relatively plain distinction could be drawn between purely *mental* defects and severe *physical* defects. Selective non-treatment of the latter could be justified, in certain circumstances, since the state of the physical disorder might mean that the child in question would die anyway and that nature should, therefore, take its course. On the other hand, children with purely mental disorders will not die unless encouraged and guided towards death by some positive act and, for these purposes, an instruction to withhold food can be viewed as such. A distinction like this may mean that the non-treatment of an uncomplicated Down's syndrome child could *never* be justified, whereas clearly it could be justified in the case of a hydrocephalic or anencephalic child. Between these extremes there would, undoubtedly, be difficult judgments to be made. What view, for example, ought to be taken of spina bifida and how can the line be drawn between different levels of severity of particular disorders? The formulation and application of statutory standards would inevitably be contentious but would at least address the inescapable problem that, in numerical terms at least, what happens in the cases which do not reach court is of much greater practical significance than what happens in the few which do.

THE PROBLEM OF OLDER CHILDREN: MEDICAL ISSUES ARISING IN RESPECT OF ADOLESCENTS

Section 8(1) of the Family Law Reform Act 1969 provides that:

> '... the consent of a minor who has attained the age of sixteen years to any surgical, medical or dental treatment ... shall be as effective as it would be if he were of full age; and where a minor has by virtue of this section given an effective consent to any treatment it shall not be necessary to obtain any consent for it from his parent or guardian.'

This provision clarified the position regarding young people of 16 and 17 years of age, by conferring on them legal capacity to provide a valid consent to treatment, and dispensing with the normal requirement of parental consent. The Family Law Reform Act 1969 did not deal directly with the question of a clash between the views of a 16-year-old and his parents, but the implication appeared to be that, at least where the minor was consenting, this could be effective to override any parental objection. The position was somewhat less clear in the converse situation, where the minor was *objecting* and the parent was purporting to consent. On one view the effect of the provision was to confer complete independence in medical decision-making on the 16-year-old – in effect to equate his position with that of an adult. On this interpretation, the objection of the minor would be conclusive. However, the better view, as evidenced by the pre-Parliamentary history of this provision, is that s 8 intended to supplement existing parental powers of consent.[204] This

---

[204] See the detailed analysis in S Gilmore and J Herring '"No" is the hardest word: consent and children's autonomy' [2011] CFLQ 3, at pp 17–19.

interpretation of s 8 has now been confirmed as a matter of law in the Court of Appeal decisions in *Re R* and *Re W*,[205] although quite how parents' and children's powers of consent are to interact is a matter of considerable debate.[206]

Uncertainty surrounded the position of those under 16 years of age where perhaps four major issues are involved:

(1) Can the child under 16 years of age ever have legal capacity to take independent medical decisions?

(2) What are the limits of parental authority?[207]

(3) What is the effect of the child's competence on the legal responsibility of parents? Does the child's view prevail and are parents entitled to be involved at all in the decision-making process?

(4) When may the courts intervene to override the wishes of parents and/or the views of a competent child?

The answer to these questions must be gleaned from three leading cases – the *Gillick* case, *Re R* and *Re W*.[208] *Gillick* was concerned only with the first three questions, while *Re R* and *Re W* were directly concerned with the fourth but reopened the debate about the other issues.

The *Gillick* case

Background

In 1980, the then Department of Health and Social Security issued a notice[209] to the effect that, although it would be 'most unusual', a doctor could, in exceptional circumstances, lawfully give contraceptive advice or treatment to a girl under 16 years of age without prior parental consultation or consent. In so doing, he would be required to act in good faith to protect her against the harmful effects of sexual intercourse. Victoria Gillick, a Roman Catholic mother, with five daughters then under 16 years of age, objected to this advice and sought assurances from her area health authority that no minor daughter of hers would receive such advice or treatment without her permission. When

---

[205] [1992] Fam 11 and [1992] 3 WLR 758, respectively.

[206] Put briefly, the issue is how the idea of concurrent consents in parent and child is to be reconciled with the view expressed by Lord Scarman in *Gillick v West Norfolk and Wisbech Area Health Authority* [1986] 1 AC 112 that the parental right yields to the competent child's right to make his or her own decision. The issue is discussed in the text below.

[207] See generally, S Gilmore 'The Limits of Parental Responsibility' in R Probert, S Gilmore and J Herring (eds) *Responsible Parents and Parental Responsibility* (Hart Publishing, 2009), ch 4.

[208] *Gillick v West Norfolk and Wisbech Area Health Authority* [1986] 1 AC 112, *Re R (A Minor) (Wardship: Consent to Treatment)* [1992] Fam 11 and *Re W (A Minor) (Medical Treatment: Court's Jurisdiction)* [1992] 3 WLR 758, respectively.

[209] HN (80) 46.

she failed to receive a response acceptable to her, she applied for a declaration that the advice in the Circular was unlawful.

In what was arguably to become the most significant twentieth-century decision on the legal relationship between parents and children, Victoria Gillick lost at first instance, won unanimously in the Court of Appeal and eventually lost to a 3:2 majority in the House of Lords. Such was the measure of judicial disagreement at the time, and the analysis of the two principal majority speeches of Lord Scarman and Lord Fraser continues to provide a fertile source of argument both academic and judicial.[210]

Doctor as secondary party to offence of unlawful sexual intercourse

Victoria Gillick advanced several arguments in support of her claim. The first of these is noted only briefly here, since it concerned the scope of the criminal law and is peripheral to the present discussion.[211] The argument that a doctor who provided contraceptives to a girl under 16 years of age would be a secondary party to the then offence of unlawful sexual intercourse[212] was rejected by four of the five Law Lords, following the reasoning of Woolf J at first instance. This was, in essence, that, while the doctor who provided contraceptives *with the intention* of encouraging the commission of the offence would be liable, the doctor who acted in compliance with the DHSS advice would not necessarily commit the offence. His motives were much more likely to be to protect the girl from the possible adverse consequences of sexual intercourse, including unwanted pregnancy and/or abortion, and not to encourage the offence.[213]

---

[210] For recent discussions of academic interpretations of the case and its impact, see J Fortin 'The *Gillick* Decision – Not Just A High-water Mark' in S Gilmore, J Herring and R Probert (eds) *Landmark Cases in Family Law* (Hart Publishing, 2011) ch 11 and S Gilmore 'The Limits of Parental Responsibility' in R Probert, S Gilmore and J Herring (eds) *Responsible Parents and Parental Responsibility* (Hart Publishing, 2009), ch 4. For the leading commentaries at the time of the decision, see J Eekelaar 'The Eclipse of Parental Rights' (1986) 102 LQR 4 which can usefully be compared with A Bainham 'The Balance of Power in Family Decisions' (1986) CLJ 262; G Williams 'The Gillick Saga' (1985) 135 NLJ 1156 and 1169; and SM Cretney 'Gillick and the Concept of Legal Capacity' (1989) 105 LQR 356. Judicial disagreement is perhaps best illustrated by the apparent reluctance of Farquharson and Staughton LJJ to associate themselves with the more wide-ranging remarks of Lord Donaldson MR in *Re R* [1992] Fam 11.

[211] Chapter 15 below considers the protective function of the criminal law in relation to children.

[212] Offences Against the Person Act 1861, s 6. The girl herself does not commit an offence on the basis that the criminal law exists for her own protection: *R v Tyrell* [1894] 1 QB 710. This offence has now been abolished and replaced by other sexual offences relating to children in the Sexual Offences Act 2003. See chapter 15 below.

[213] While this may have been a sound decision on policy grounds, it is rather more difficult to justify as a correct application of legal principle since the criminal law distinguishes between motive and intention, concerning itself only with the latter.

Issue 1: capacity of child under 16 years to provide valid consent

The first issue was whether a girl under 16 years old could ever provide a valid consent and thus prevent the commission of the tort of battery by the doctor.[214] The Family Law Reform Act 1969 did not address the position of those under 16 years of age, but it did provide in s 8(3) that 'nothing in this section shall be construed as making ineffective any consent which would have been effective if this section had not been enacted'. The majority held that the cumulative effect of this provision and s 8(1) was simply to avoid doubt in relation to those *over* 16 years old. The child *under* 16 years did not lack capacity by virtue of age alone, but acquired it, according to Lord Scarman, when 'he reaches a sufficient understanding and intelligence to be capable of making up his own mind on the matter requiring decision'. The test propounded by Lord Scarman involves an individualistic assessment of a particular child's level of maturity and intellectual ability. The clear implication is that, if a child fails the test of competence, the doctor will need to look to a person with parental responsibility for a proxy consent and that to go ahead without this will be to risk committing a tort on the child. Further, to make an incorrect assessment of competence will likewise be to run the risk of committing a tort if the matter should subsequently be taken to court. *Gillick* was concerned with the child's capacity to *give* consent and not expressly with the child's capacity to *refuse* it, but many commentators at the time thought that the two must stand or fall together.[215]

A key question is what precisely must be understood by the child in order to achieve '*Gillick* competence'? Lord Scarman envisaged that a high level of understanding would be required, extending beyond the purely medical issues. Dealing specifically with contraception, he said:

> 'It is not enough that she should understand the nature of the advice which she is being given: she must have sufficient maturity to understand what is involved. There are moral and family questions especially her relationship with her parents, long-term problems associated with the emotional impact of pregnancy and its termination and there are risks to health of sexual intercourse at her age, risks which contraception may diminish but cannot eliminate. It follows that a doctor will have to satisfy himself before he can safely proceed on the basis that she has at law capacity to consent to contraceptive treatment.'

It will be seen, following *Re R* and *Re W*, that a similarly high level of competence is evidently demanded where a child is *objecting* to a medical procedure.

---

[214] It should be said that while a medical examination involving 'touching' would clearly be tortious without an appropriate consent it is difficult to see how the giving of advice about contraception or the prescription of contraceptive pills could have this tortious character.

[215] This has now been exploded by Lord Donaldson's remarks in *Re R* [1992] Fam 11 and by the decision in *Re W (A Minor) (Medical Treatment: Court's Jurisdiction)* [1992] 3 WLR 758, which drew a distinction between *consent* and *refusal*.

Issue 2: the limits of parental authority

The second issue relates to the legal limits on parental authority and, here, the majority in the House of Lords was quite clear that parental power was not absolute. According to Lord Scarman 'parental rights are derived from parental duty and exist only so long as they are needed for the protection of the person or property of the child'. Lord Fraser emphasised that such rights existed for the benefit of the *child* and not for the benefit of the parent.

Issue 3: the clash of views – whose view prevails?

The third issue was the effect of a child achieving competence on the parental 'right' to give or withhold consent. Whose view should be decisive in the event of disagreement? Both Lord Scarman and Lord Fraser were of the opinion that a doctor could, in certain circumstances, proceed on the competent child's consent alone, but Lord Scarman appeared to take a more radical view than Lord Fraser of the effect of the child acquiring capacity.[216] According to Lord Scarman 'the parental right yields to the child's right to make his own decisions when he reaches a sufficient understanding and intelligence to be capable of making up his own mind on the matter requiring decision'.[217] This was interpreted by one commentator quite literally to mean that the attainment of competence by the child would *terminate* parental responsibility over the matter in question and would give to the child an *exclusive* right to decide.[218] Lord Fraser, on the other hand, adopted a more guarded approach. In his view, the mere acquisition of capacity would not, per se, enable a doctor to proceed without parental notification or consent. Lord Fraser laid down five further conditions which would have to be satisfied in order that the doctor could proceed without parental notification or consent:[219]

'(1) that the girl will understand his advice;

(2) that he cannot persuade her to inform her parents or allow him to do so;

(3) that she is very likely to begin or to continue having sexual intercourse with or without contraceptive treatment;

(4) that unless she receives advice or treatment her physical or mental health or both are likely to suffer; and

(5) that her best interests require him to act without consent.'

---

[216] Lord Bridge, unhelpfully for present purposes, simply agreed with both of them.

[217] [1986] 1 AC 112 at 186.

[218] J Eekelaar 'The Eclipse of Parental Rights' (1986) 102 LQR 4. For direct criticism of Eekelaar's interpretation, see S Gilmore 'The Limits of Parental Responsibility' in R Probert, S Gilmore and J Herring (eds) *Responsible Parents and Parental Responsibility* (Hart Publishing, 2009), ch 4; and see also counter-arguments in J Fortin 'The *Gillick* Decision – Not Just A High-water Mark' in S Gilmore, J Herring and R Probert (eds) *Landmark Cases in Family Law* (Hart Publishing, 2011), ch 11.

[219] [1986] 1 AC 112 at 174.

These extra requirements might have been explained away on the basis that they are not strict legal requirements but rather matters which pertain only to good professional practice.[220] But, equally, Lord Fraser's formulation might have been interpreted as one which supports a *participatory* decision-making process in which neither the parents nor the child would have the sole right to decide. The final decision would rather rest with the doctor who would take into account the girl's own capacity and wishes and, if possible, the views of the parents, and would then make an evaluation of her best medical and other interests before deciding whether to proceed. Such an interpretation would be in keeping with the tradition of medical paternalism in England.[221] Certainly, Lord Fraser did not appear to think that a competent girl was entitled to contraceptives on demand.

The Axon Case

In 2006, in *R (Axon) v Secretary of State for Health (Family Planning Association intervening)*[222] another mother, Sue Axon, challenged the approach of the House of Lords in *Gillick*. This time the challenge was in relation to abortion advice and treatment contained in an updated version of the relevant Guidance.[223] Basing her claim in part upon her Art 8 right to respect for private and family life, Ms Axon sought, in judicial review proceedings, a declaration that medical professionals are under no obligation to maintain confidentiality in relation to abortion advice and treatment unless disclosure might prejudice the child's physical or mental health. Ms Axon's claims were rejected by Silber J who held that the approach in *Gillick* 'was and is of general application to all forms of medical advice and treatment'. He clarified that Lord Fraser's guidelines in *Gillick* are legal pre-conditions and to be strictly observed. Silber J also held that the requirement that a child understands the doctor's advice, was to be read in light of Lord Scarman's stringent test for capacity, and explained that 'all relevant matters' were included within the meaning of 'understanding'.

Silber J held that 'any right to family life on the part of a parent dwindles as their child gets older and is able to understand the consequence of different choices and then to make decisions relating to them' and that 'this autonomy must undermine any Art 8 rights of a parent to family life'. Thus parents do not have Art 8 rights to be notified of any advice of a medical professional after the young person is able to look after himself or herself and make his or

---

220 J Eekelaar (above).

221 This is the position taken by A Bainham in 'Growing Up in Britain: Adolescence in the post-*Gillick* Era' (1992) *Juridical Review* 155 and which, it is submitted, is reflected in the later Court of Appeal decisions in *Re R* and *Re W*.

222 [2006] EWHC 37 (Admin), [2006] QB 539. For comment, see J Bridgeman 'Case Comment: Young People and Sexual Health: Whose Rights? Whose Responsibilities?' [2006] *Medical Law Review* 418; R Taylor 'Reversing the Retreat from *Gillick*? *R (Axon) v Secretary of State for Health*' [2007] CFLQ 81.

223 Guidance for Doctors and other Health Professionals on the Provision of Advice and Treatment to Young People under 16 on Contraception, Sexual and Reproductive Heath (29 July 2004), gateway reference No 3382. Relevant parts of the Guidance are set out at [2006] EWHC 37 (Admin), [2006] QB 539, at [22]–[24].

her own decisions. He observed that 'the right of young people to make decisions about their own lives by themselves at the expense of the views of their parents has now become an increasingly important and accepted feature of family life'. He concluded that there was nothing in the Guidance which interferes with a parent's Art 8 rights since the medical professional must act in the child's best interests. Alternatively, any infringement could be justified under Art 8(2): the legislative objective (of reducing unwanted pregnancies and addressing sexually transmitted diseases) justified limiting parents' Art 8 rights; and Lord Fraser's guidelines were rationally connected to that objective and impaired freedom no more than necessary to achieve it.

Post-Gillick case law: children's refusal to consent

As noted above, the precise inter-relationship of adolescent capacities and parental responsibility was the subject of considerable speculation following the *Gillick* case, and this has been accentuated by obiter remarks of Lord Donaldson in the Court of Appeal in *Re R (A Minor) (Wardship: Consent to Treatment)*[224] and by the later decision in *Re W (A Minor) (Medical Treatment: Court's Jurisdiction)*.[225] The *Gillick* case was not directly concerned with the extent of the courts' jurisdiction over adolescents. It has fallen to the Court of Appeal to define the limits of their powers in *Re R* and *Re W*. While *Re R* was concerned with a young person *under* the age of 16, crucially *Re W* involved a young person *over* 16. This gave the court the opportunity of ruling upon the relationship between s 8 of the Family Law Reform Act 1969 and the courts' powers under the inherent jurisdiction. In addition, unlike *Gillick* in which the issue was consent to treatment, *Re R* and *Re W* concerned children who were *refusing* consent.

Re R

Background

Re R[226] was not concerned with issues of adolescent sexuality but with the competence of an adolescent to refuse the forcible administration of sedative drugs. The principles can nevertheless be applied to questions such as contraception, abortion or sterilisation.

R was a young woman aged 15 years and 10 months at the time of the hearing. Following a history of mental disturbances and a deterioration in her mental health, she entered the care of the local authority and was, in due course,

---

[224] [1992] Fam 11.

[225] [1993] Fam 64.

[226] *Re R (A Minor) (Wardship: Consent to Treatment)* [1992] Fam 11. For comment, see A Bainham 'The Judge and the Competent Minor' (1992) 108 LQR 194; G Douglas 'The Retreat from *Gillick*' (1992) 55 *Modern Law Review* 569; P Fennell 'Informal Compulsion: The Psychiatric Treatment of Juveniles under Common Law' [1992] *Journal of Social Welfare and Family Law* 311; J Montgomery 'Parents and Children in Dispute: Who Has the Final Word?' (1992) 4 *Journal of Child Law* 85; R Thornton 'Multiple Keyholders – Wardship and Consent to Medical Treatment' [1992] *Cambridge Law Journal* 34.

placed in an adolescent psychiatric unit. She had a mental condition which fluctuated between periods of lucidity and rationality, and times when she displayed 'florid psychotic symptoms'. In these latter periods, she was considered a serious suicide risk and 'sectionable' under the Mental Health Act 1983. As part of its regime, the unit used sedative drugs as a last resort. It indicated to the local authority (which had parental responsibility for R) that it was not prepared to retain her unless its whole regime, including medication where appropriate, was accepted by it. Initially, the local authority acceded to this, but later withdrew its consent following a long telephone conversation between R and one of its social workers. R indicated, during this conversation, that the unit were trying to give her drugs which she neither wanted nor needed. The social worker was of the opinion that R was lucid and rational during the conversation, and this view of her mental state was subsequently confirmed by a consultant child psychiatrist. The authority made R a ward of court to resolve the disagreement.

Gillick competence – can it be overridden?

In the proceedings, the unit sought leave to administer such medication as was medically necessary, including anti-psychotic drugs, without R's consent. The Official Solicitor, acting as guardian ad litem, opposed this. His principal argument was that, where a child had capacity to withhold consent to treatment (based on sufficient understanding and intelligence to comprehend fully what was proposed) any parental right to give or withhold consent terminated. He argued further that, since, in wardship, the court steps into the shoes of a parent, the court could have no greater power to give or withhold consent. The two main issues were, therefore, whether R was '*Gillick*-competent' and, if so, whether the court would have power to override her wishes. These were the only issues directly raised, but Lord Donaldson MR felt it necessary to reopen the whole question of the relationship between the capacity of a competent minor and a parent's right to consent on a minor's behalf.

Competence as a developmental concept

The Court of Appeal upheld the decision of Waite J, that R failed the test of competence and that it was in her best interests for the treatment to be authorised. The court rejected the idea that competence could fluctuate from day to day or week to week. Competence was seen as a developmental concept, although it was acknowledged that a child could be competent for some purposes but not for others. But the *extent* of competence regarding any particular matter (in this case, medication) could not be variable. Farquharson LJ even doubted that *Gillick* could sensibly be applied at all to 'on/off' situations where the impact of a mental illness had to be taken into account. In his view, mental state and capacity could not be isolated from the medical history and background. Lord Donaldson emphasised, as Lord Scarman had in *Gillick*, that the acquisition of capacity was no easy matter. It required not only the ability to understand the procedure of compulsory medication but also 'a full understanding and appreciation of the consequences both of the treatment in terms of the intended and possible side effects and, equally important, the anticipated consequences of a failure to treat'.[227] She would particularly need to be aware of the risk that she might lapse into her former psychotic state, and of the possible harmful consequences of this to herself.

Determination and consent

Despite the court's decision that R was not *Gillick*-competent, Lord Donaldson alone made controversial obiter remarks about what the position would have been had she been adjudged competent. He used the metaphor of keys and locks to illustrate what he took to be the position. Consent was a key which could unlock a door. Both the competent child and the parent were keyholders but neither had a master key. Thus, *either* the child's key *or* the parent's key could unlock the door and open it for the doctor to proceed. He thus drew a distinction between *determination* and *consent*. The former, he said, was a wider concept than the latter since it implied a right of veto. He interpreted Lord Scarman's speech in *Gillick* to mean that it was this right of *determination* which terminated where the child achieved a state of competence. In other words, the parent would, at that point, lose the *exclusive* right to consent. But this did not mean that the parent's independent right to consent would be lost. The parent and child in these circumstances would enjoy *concurrent* rights to consent and it would be open to a doctor to act on either consent.[228] Otherwise, said Lord Donaldson, a doctor would be faced with the 'intolerable dilemma' of having to choose between two potentially valid, but also potentially invalid, consents. An incorrect assessment of maturity might then expose the doctor to criminal or tortious liability. He was also of the opinion that the same principles applied to a young person over 16 years, notwithstanding s 8(1) of the Family Law Reform Act 1969. He adopted a literal interpretation of this provision to the effect that, whilst it was unnecessary for a doctor to secure parental consent in relation to a young person of 16 years of age, there was nothing to preclude him from acting on a parent's consent alone.

Power of the court to override objections

The most significant issue in this case, since it had not been addressed in *Gillick*, was whether the court, exercising its protective jurisdiction was empowered to override the wishes of a competent minor.[229] Here, the court held that such a power existed, since the *Gillick* reasoning had no application in

---

[227] [1992] Fam 11.

[228] Lord Donaldson's concurrent consents approach cannot overcome the essential reality that, where a doctor is aware of a disagreement between parent and child, he must, of necessity, choose between the two opposing views. If he elects to comply with what the parent wants, then he effectively gives to that parent a veto over the child's wishes, and this would appear to conflict directly with the decision in *Gillick*.

[229] The court's decision on this point was, strictly speaking, obiter, since R was adjudged *incompetent*. Nevertheless, it was the principal point of law in the case and one which was unanimously answered by all three judges.

wardship proceedings.[230] The court's powers, it was said, were not derived from parents but from the Crown's duties of protection.[231] The court had wider powers than those enjoyed by natural parents including, for example, the power to restrain the publication of information about a child or the power to grant injunctions restraining contact between the child and others. It was also beyond doubt that the court could override the wishes of parents in exercising its powers of protection.[232] By analogy, there was no reason why it should not override the wishes of a competent minor if this was thought to be in her best interests. In wardship, this was the court's sole objective and it was perfectly possible that the application of the welfare test and the *Gillick* test could lead to different results. Whilst the issue had not been directly raised before, there was ample previous authority which had assumed that the court was not obliged to follow the wishes of a mature child.[233]

The court's powers to override the objection of a minor have subsequently been dramatically illustrated in the case of *Re M (Medical Treatment: Consent)*.[234] Here a 15-year-old girl required a heart transplant to save her life but she refused to consent. Her reasons were that she did not want to have someone else's heart and did not wish to take medication for the rest of her life. The judge, Johnson J, was faced with an unenviable dilemma given the strength of her feelings and the recognition that she was an intelligent young woman who had thought seriously about the matter. The essence of this dilemma is captured in the notes of the solicitor who acted as agent for the Official Solicitor and interviewed M in hospital. According to these, M said:

> 'Death is final – I know I can't change my mind. I don't want to die, but I would rather die than have the transplant and have someone else's heart, I would rather die with 15 years of my own heart. If I had someone else's heart, I would be different from anybody else – being dead would not make me different from anybody else. I would feel different with someone else's heart, that's a good enough reason not to have a heart transplant, even if it saved my life ...'

Johnson J acknowledged the gravity of the decision to override M's wishes. There were, of course, risks which attached to the operation itself and there were continuing risks thereafter, both in terms of the bodily rejection of the heart and M's own rejection of continuing medical treatment. There was the further risk that she might carry resentment of the court's intervention for the rest of her life. Notwithstanding all this, the risks had to be measured against

---

[230] Although the court was specifically only concerned with wardship, there is no reason why the logic cannot be applied to other jurisdictions.

[231] In fact, the analogy between natural and judicial parenthood was always a rather crude and imperfect one. See A Bainham 'Handicapped Girls and Judicial Parents' (1987) 103 LQR 334.

[232] Many examples of this power might be cited, but one in the medical arena is *Re B (Wardship: Abortion)* [1991] 2 FLR 426 where the wish of a 12-year-old girl to have an abortion, supported by a grandparent, was upheld by the court in the face of objection by her mother. The court took the view that the operation was in her best medical interests.

[233] See, particularly, the abortion cases of *Re P (A Minor)* [1986] 1 FLR 272 and *Re G-U (A Minor) (Wardship)* [1984] FLR 811.

[234] [1999] 2 FLR 1097. For commentary, see R Huxtable '*Re M (Medical Treatment: Consent)* Time to remove the "flak jacket"?' [2000] CFLQ 83.

the certainty of death. M's severe condition of heart failure had developed only very recently and she had been overwhelmed by the decision which she had to make within the time span of a few days. He accordingly authorised the operation as being in her best interests.

The decision is perhaps the best illustration we are ever likely to get of the virtually limitless powers of the courts over children. There was no express finding of competence or incompetence in the case but the court, which had to act quickly, proceeded on the assumption that it could if necessary override the wishes of a competent child. The contrast between the court's powers over children and the much more limited powers over adults is plain to see. Had M been aged 18 and competent, rather than 15, it would have been entirely her decision and there would have been no legal basis for intervention by the court.[235] We have already considered[236] the arguments concerning the legitimate extent of paternalistic interventions from a children's rights perspective and this decision should be evaluated in the light of that discussion.

Re W

The principles governing the role of the courts in relation to adolescents and medical decision-making were further considered in the important decision of the Court of Appeal in *Re W (A Minor) (Medical Treatment: Court's Jurisdiction)*.[237] The decision proved no less controversial than that in *Re R*.[238]

In this case, it was held that the High Court could properly exercise its inherent jurisdiction over children[239] to order a 16-year-old girl, suffering from anorexia nervosa, to be transferred, against her wishes, to a London unit specialising in the treatment of eating disorders. The court extended the reasoning in *Re R* to 'children' over 16 years having prima facie capacity to consent under s 8 of the Family Law Reform Act 1969. It held unanimously that that section had not been designed to confer absolute autonomy on 16-year-olds in medical matters but rather to enable them to provide a consent upon which the medical profession could safely act without incurring legal liability. The court's jurisdiction had not been excluded by the Act and, owing to the serious deterioration in W's health, this was a case in which the court should act. Lord Donaldson (now joined by Balcombe LJ) also reiterated his view in *Re R*

---

[235] *St George's Healthcare NHS Trust v S; R v Collins, ex parte S* [1998] 3 All ER 673.

[236] See chapter 7 above.

[237] [1992] 3 WLR 758.

[238] It was the subject of extensive critical comment. See, for example, J Eekelaar 'White Coats or Flak Jackets? Doctors, Children and the Courts – Again' (1993) 109 LQR 182, and J Masson '*Re W*: Appealing from the Golden Cage' (1993) 5 JCL 37. The decisions of *Re R* and *Re W* were applied by Thorpe J in *Re K, W and H (Minors) (Medical Treatment)* [1993] 1 FLR 854 who held that if parents were willing to consent to treatment no application to the court was necessary, and by Douglas Brown J in *South Glamorgan County Council v W and B* [1993] 1 FLR 574, who held that the statutory power of a competent child to refuse assessment under s 38(6) of the Children Act 1989 could be overridden in the exercise of the inherent jurisdiction of the High Court.

[239] On the distinction between the inherent jurisdiction and wardship, see chapter 12 below.

that a parent might provide a *concurrent* consent in the case of a '*Gillick*-competent child', although he cast off the metaphor of the 'keyholder' which he had employed in *Re R*, for that of the legal 'flak jacket'. According to this, consent is a flak jacket which protects the doctor from legal actions. He can acquire it from a child over 16 years (under s 8), *or* a *Gillick*-competent child under 16 years, *or* someone with parental responsibility – but he only needs one consent. The decision is in much the same vein as *Re R*, and together the two cases compound the uncertainties about the inter-relationship of adolescent capacities and parental responsibility. The issue must surely return at some point to the Supreme Court.

The decisions in *Re R* and *Re W* should now also be read with other decisions of the higher courts evincing a greater willingness to make paternalistic interventions in the case of *adults*.[240] If the courts are willing to intervene in the case of adults, the objection to doing so in the case of children (at least if based on the unwarranted differential treatment of children and adults) rather falls apart. The issue of the proper limits of State paternalism in either case, of course, remains.[241]

The decision of the Court of Appeal in *St George's Healthcare National Health Service Trust v S*[242] perhaps heralded a new era in which the courts may be less willing to intervene paternalistically in the case of adults. Here, the court held that a pregnant woman could not be forced to undergo a Caesarean section even where her objections were bizarre and irrational and contrary to the views of the overwhelming majority of the community at large. This was so even where her own life depended on receiving medical interventions and where failure to consent would result in the death of her unborn child. The court further held that a person detained under the Mental Health Act 1983 for

---

[240] See, for example, *Re T (An Adult) (Consent to Medical Treatment)* [1992] 2 FLR 458 in which the Court of Appeal sanctioned a blood transfusion where the patient (who had been raised by her mother as a Jehovah's Witness) had apparently refused consent. In this case the decision was, however, based in part on the view that the patient's purported refusal may have been the product of external influence and thus not a genuine refusal. Nonetheless, the decision is perhaps evidence of a greater willingness to intervene in emergency situations in which the concept of necessity may apply. Intervention in the case of adults now, however, requires a judgment that the adult in question lacks competence, as where they are in a permanent vegetative state, and the court is asked to declare that the withdrawal of life-sustaining treatment would be lawful as being in the best interests of the patient. See, for example, *An NHS Trust v M; An NHS Trust v H* [2001] 2 FLR 367 where such declarations were granted by Dame Elizabeth Butler-Sloss P. Cf *Re SS (Medical Treatment: Late Termination)* [2002] 1 FLR 445, where Wall J refused a declaration that it would be in the best interests of a 34-year-old schizophrenic woman to undergo a termination of pregnancy at 23 weeks. In fact the case did not reach the court until the day before expiry of the 24-week statutory limit for terminations.

[241] For further discussion, see A Bainham 'Children, Parents and the Law: Non-Intervention and Judicial Paternalisation' in P Birks (ed) *The Frontiers of Liability* (Oxford University Press, 1993).

[242] [1998] 2 FLR 728.

mental disorder could not be forced into medical procedures unconnected with her mental condition unless her capacity to consent to such treatment was diminished.[243]

Authorisation for intervention can now be sought from the Court of Protection where a patient lacks capacity, pursuant to the Mental Capacity Act 2005. The Court has power to take a decision in the best interests of the patient or appoint a person to do so. For the purposes of the Act, it is provided in s 2 that 'a person lacks capacity in relation to a matter if at the material time he is unable to make a decision for himself in relation to the matter because of an impairment of, or a disturbance in the functioning of, the mind or brain'. A person is 'assumed to have capacity unless it is established that he lacks capacity'[244] and lack of capacity cannot be established merely by reference to a person's age or appearance.[245] A 'person is not to be treated as unable to make a decision merely because he makes an unwise decision'.[246] A person is unable to make a decision for himself if he is unable to understand, retain, use or weigh, information and communicate a decision.[247] However, the Act applies only in a limited way to children. No power which a person could exercise under the Act is exercisable in relation to a person under the age of 16.[248] Powers are exercisable in relation to 16- and 17-year-olds,[249] so that if a 16- or 17-year-old lacked capacity as defined in s 2 of the Mental Capacity 2005, then his or her parents could provide consent to act in the child's best interests.[250] It is important to note, however, that the Act is only concerned with incapacity because of 'an impairment of, or a disturbance in the functioning of, the mind or brain' and only for the purposes of the Act. Thus the Act would not apply,

---

[243] See also *Re AK (Medical Treatment: Consent)* [2001] 1 FLR 129 in which Hughes J granted a declaration that it would be lawful to discontinue life-sustaining treatment in the case of a 19-year-old patient suffering from motor neuron disease, a progressive, incurable and fatal condition. The patient was only able to communicate through the movement of one eyelid by which he could indicate 'yes' or 'no' to questions. He indicated that he wished his ventilator to be removed and the court held that the refusal to consent to treatment by an adult of full capacity must be observed in law. In *Re B (Consent to Treatment: Capacity)* [2002] 1 FLR 1090 Dame Elizabeth Butler-Sloss P granted a declaration that a hospital had been treating a patient unlawfully and awarded nominal damages against it. The patient, who could not survive without artificial ventilation, was found to have demonstrated a high standard of mental competence, intelligence and ability. A patient with such competence had the right to refuse medical treatment even where this would lead to his or her death.

[244] Ibid, s 1(2).

[245] Ibid, s 2(3).

[246] Ibid, s 1(4).

[247] Ibid, s 3. Reflecting the common law test in *Re MB (Medical Treatment)* [1997] 2 FLR 426, at 436G–437H: 'the patient is unable to comprehend and retain the information which is material to the decision, especially as to the likely consequences of having or not having the treatment in question'.

[248] Mental Capacity Act 2005, s 2(5). Subject to exceptions in the Mental Capacity Act 2005, s 18(3): see s 2(6).

[249] However, only a person aged 18 can make a Lasting Power of Attorney or an advance decision to refuse medical treatment, and the Court of Protection can only make a statutory will for a person aged 18 or over: see Department of Constitutional Affairs, *Mental Capacity Act Code of Practice* (TSO, 2007), ch 12.

[250] Or apply to the Court of Protection for a ruling as to what is in the child's best interests: see Mental Capacity Act 2005, s 50(1)(b).

for example, to a child who is incapable of consenting because he or she is overwhelmed by the implications of the decision,[251] or through lack of maturity not connected to impairment or disturbance of functioning of the mind or brain. It is unclear how far the principles in the Act apply beyond the Act and, in particular, to children.

Cumulative effect of the leading cases

What then is the cumulative effect of *Gillick, Re R* and *Re W*? The only principle which can be stated with any confidence is that the court has jurisdiction to overrule the parents, the child, the medical profession or, indeed, all of them in performing its protective functions and, even here, there are arguments about whether it should do so. The distribution of decision-making power which arises by operation of law is now a matter of considerable uncertainty and it is extremely difficult to state the law with any precision. Perhaps this is an inevitable hazard of an appellate system, in which multiple opinions are delivered. Thus, in *Gillick* only three Law Lords were in the majority, two of whom said materially different things and the third of whom simply agreed with the other two. In *Re R*, the then Master of the Rolls gave an opinion which incorporated a controversial interpretation of the majority decision in *Gillick* which some commentators have not found easy to understand, while the other two Lords Justices of Appeal appeared almost anxious to distance themselves from his views.[252] On the other hand, the decision in *Re R* has now been reinforced by that in *Re W* and must be taken to be the law in the absence of a further ruling by the Supreme Court.

We will now attempt an evaluation of the present position.

Acquiring legal capacity

It seems reasonably uncontentious that the 16-year-old acquires capacity, is presumed to have capacity for consenting to medical decisions on attaining that age, and that there is no question of having to engage in an evaluation of individual maturity or intelligence. The sole exception to this will be where the young person is mentally incapacitated and therefore lacks the ability to give a real consent, where the presumption of capacity will be rebutted. Those under 16 years of age must pass the *Gillick* test and, in theory at least, the leading cases require a high level of understanding, extending beyond the mechanics of the medical procedure involved, to the wider medical, moral and family considerations surrounding what is proposed.[253]

---

[251] See Department of Constitutional Affairs, *Mental Capacity Act Code of Practice* (TSO, 2007), ch 12, at para 12.13.

[252] Staughton and Farquharson LJJ confined themselves to the questions of the girl's competence and the power of the court in wardship.

[253] The British Medical Association has provided detailed and useful guidance on what is involved in assessing competence in practice. See *Consent, Rights and Choices in Health Care for Children and Young People* (BMJ Books, 2001) ch 5.

The issues surrounding capacity were illustrated in a life-and-death situation in *Re L (Medical Treatment: Gillick Competency)*.[254] Here a 14-year-old girl had sustained very serious burns from scalding having fallen into a bath. Her condition was life-threatening and she required treatment which would involve blood transfusions. She was, however, a Jehovah's Witness holding sincere religious objections to this. The surgeon responsible made it clear that the transfusion was necessary to save her life and that, without it, she would suffer a horrible death. Gangrene would set in and this would be followed by a very distressing period for both the girl and all those attending her.

In these circumstances Sir Stephen Brown P ordered that the hospital be allowed to go ahead with treatment without the girl's consent. He accepted that her views were sincerely held and derived from strongly held religious beliefs, but he held that there was a distinction between a view of that kind and the constructive formulation of an opinion which occurred with adult experience. It should not be overlooked, he said, that she was still a child or that she had led a sheltered life largely influenced by the Jehovah's Witness congregation. Neither had she been made aware of the painful death she would suffer if gangrene supervened, because the doctors felt that it would be too distressing for her to know and therefore not in her best interests to be told. Accordingly, Sir Stephen Brown P found that the girl was not *Gillick*-competent and it was vital that the court should intervene in her best interests to ensure that she receive the treatment despite her lack of consent. He went on to say that *even if she were Gillick-competent* he would still have authorised treatment without her consent because this was an extreme case and she was in a grave situation.

There are, however, several features of this approach to capacity which may be considered unsatisfactory. First, on the basis of the girl's best interests she was prevented from access to the relevant information about her situation, which she would need to take an informed decision. Secondly, the more that is required of the individual child, the greater is the opportunity for manipulation by adult decision-makers. Someone, whether it be a doctor or the court, has to determine whether an individual child is competent, and there is an obvious danger that the child will be deemed incompetent because his views happen to diverge from the adult assessment of his best interests[255] or that the child's views will simply be overridden under the inherent jurisdiction. Thirdly, it is not obvious that the medical profession should be allowed to pass judgment on non-medical matters such as moral and family issues. A young woman's decision to have an abortion may, for example, be seen essentially as a *moral* choice and there may be no decisive medical reason pointing to termination or continuation of the pregnancy.[256] Fourthly, it is arguable that the law is

---

[254] [1998] 2 FLR 810. For an assessment of the decision, see C Bridge 'Religious Belief and Teenage Refusal of Medical Treatment' (1999) 62 MLR 585.

[255] A point forcefully presented in J Eekelaar 'Parents' Rights to Punish – Further Limits after *Gillick*' (1986) 28 *Childright* 9.

[256] A similar view of the decision whether or not to make contraceptives available was expressed in the US Supreme Court by Brennan J in *Carey v Population Services International* 431 US 678, 699 (1977). The British Medical Association, however, appears to view competence as the

demanding *more* of adolescents in the way of emotional or intellectual maturity than it requires of adults (or, in the case of medical treatment, those over 16 years of age).[257] Adults, many of whom are not noted for their prudent and cautious approach to sexual involvements, are *not* required to demonstrate (but are rather assumed to have) the necessary maturity to make this all-round judgment of their interests. Many of them make mistakes and this must at least prompt the question, from a civil libertarian and children's rights standpoint, whether those under 16 years should not also have the right to make mistakes.

Finally, the extent of what has to be understood under the *Gillick* formulation has led to some speculation that, in the case of minors, the doctrine of informed consent has been admitted through the back door. This might prompt further speculation about the extent of a doctor's duty of disclosure in the case of young people.[258]

Reconciling adolescent capacity, parental responsibility and medical paternalism

There is now considerable uncertainty about when a doctor ought to proceed on either a parent's or a child's consent alone.[259] *Gillick* had ostensibly supported the view that the wishes of a competent child should have priority over those of a parent, at least after suitable attempts had been made to persuade the child to involve her parents. It was apparent from the terms of the original departmental Circular, and from the majority speeches, that it would be seen as unusual for a doctor to deal with a child without parental participation. There was evidently concern that any positive contribution which parents might make in the context of the particular family situation should be explored.[260] It is, however, beyond doubt that both Lord Scarman and Lord Fraser took the position that a doctor would be acting lawfully in dealing

---

capacity to make a choice and not whether it is a wise choice. See British Medical Association *Consent, Rights and Choices in Health Care for Children and Young People* (BMJ Books, 2001), at p 93. Montgomery also offers the view that 'in principle it is clear that competence should not be assessed by reference to the outcome of the decision, but the ability to engage in the process of weighing options against each other': *Health Care Law* (2nd edn, Oxford University Press, 2002), at pp 292–293.

[257] It may be argued that the purpose of the test of understanding in both *Gillick* and *Re R* is simply to ensure that minors measure up to adult levels of understanding. Against this it may be argued that the reality is that they are being required to demonstrate more than is demanded of adults: see D Archard and M Skivenes 'Balancing a Child's Best Interests and a Child's Views' (2009) 17 *International Journal of Children's Rights* 1, at p 10.

[258] The point is raised in B Hoggett 'Parents, Children and Medical Treatment: The Legal Issues' in P Byrne (ed) *Rights and Wrongs in Medicine* (1986) 165, at p 173.

[259] Although J Montgomery *Health Care Law* (2nd edn, Oxford University Press, 2002), at pp 299–300 draws attention to an important consideration, relying on the decision of the Court of Appeal in *Northampton Health Authority v The Official Solicitor and the Governors of St Andrews Hospital* [1994] 1 FLR 162. This is that a health authority may find costs awarded against it if it takes a case to court when presented with a child's refusal to consent but where parental consent is forthcoming. In fact, in this case, on appeal, the hospital rather than the health authority was ordered to pay half the Official Solicitor's costs.

[260] In *Re R* itself it was the possible contribution of the local authority, which had parental

exclusively with the child in appropriately defined circumstances. There was no suggestion that a parent's view should be allowed to trump the view of a competent minor.

The view expressed in *Re R* and *Re W* that a doctor would be acting lawfully in reliance on parental consent to a child's treatment in the face of a child's objection was expressed in very general terms, and certainly casts some doubt on the above analysis of what *Gillick* achieved.[261] However, Gilmore and Herring[262] have sought to show that Lord Donaldson's view that there can be 'concurrent consents' is not necessarily always incompatible with the above analysis of *Gillick*. They argue that it is important to distinguish the following two ways of saying 'no' to treatment: (1) refusing to consent to proposed treatment (that is, declining to accept treatment offered) and (2) refusing treatment in the sense of consciously deciding to incur all the consequences of a total failure to treat.[263] Gilmore and Herring argue that these are two very different decisions on the part of the child, which are also likely to require different capacities. They go on to argue that:[264]

'it does not necessarily follow from the fact that a child has capacity to consent (and/or capacity to decline consent) to certain specific treatment, X, that he or she will have capacity to refuse all treatment ... the child considering whether or not to consent will not necessarily have addressed the 'refusal of treatment' question (not least because he or she may only have been told by the doctor about the proposed treatment). In a case in which the child has capacity to consent to X but does not fully understand the consequences of a total failure to treat, parental responsibility to consent is not fully extinguished by the child's capacity and it is necessary for a parent to have the power to consent to treatment, including, if necessary, treatment X.'

Thus in some cases Lord Donaldson's concurrent consents approach is entirely justifiable. Indeed it was justifiable in *Re R* and *Re W*, at least as far as the facts presented to the Court of Appeal, since the expert evidence in those cases showed only that the children concerned were capable of consenting to

---

responsibility for the girl, which was at issue. But the principles would appear to be the same whether parental responsibility is held by a parent or by someone else.

[261] Compare, however, N Lowe and S Juss 'Medical Treatment – Pragmatism and the Search for Principle' (1993) 56 *Modern Law Review* 865 who see the decisions operating consistently in favour of protecting children's welfare.

[262] S Gilmore and J Herring '"No" is the Hardest Word: Consent and Children's Autonomy' [2011] CFLQ 3; and see also S Gilmore and J Herring 'Children's Refusal of Medical Treatment: Could *Re W* be Distinguished?' [2011] Family Law 715.

[263] For criticism of Gilmore and Herring's focus on consent to particular treatment, see E Cave and J Wallbank 'Minors' Capacity to Refuse Treatment: A Reply to Gilmore and Herring' [2012] *Medical Law Review* (from 'a clinician's point of view, competence cannot always be judged in relation to specific treatment, but instead must relate to the decision'). For a response, see S Gilmore and J Herring 'Children's Refusal of Treatment: The Debate Continues' [2012] Fam Law 973.

[264] S Gilmore and J Herring 'Children's Refusal of Medical Treatment: Could *Re W* be Distinguished?' [2011] Family Law 715, at 716. They go on to argue that *Re W* might be distinguished in a future case of a fully competent child on the basis that the girl in *Re W* was only shown to have capacity to consent and not to refuse all treatment.

treatment; it did not show that they had full capacity to take a decision to refuse all treatment with the consequences that that might entail. It is submitted, however, that the precedent status of *Re R* and *Re W* should be confined to such cases, and in a case in which a child has full capacity to refuse treatment, a parent should not be permitted override the child's decision. If, as *Gillick* held, the competent child's right to consent prevails over a parent's right to object, the converse should be true provided the child is competent fully to refuse. This is especially so since a doctor's decision to examine or treat a child against that child's wishes is a potential assault, whereas a doctor's refusal to do so cannot be. The case is, if anything, stronger for giving precedence to the child's views in this situation.

Yet if it is accepted that the competent child ought to have the decisive say in the event of a conflict, this does not necessarily mean that parents should be completely excluded from the process. Can it be said that, although deprived of decision-making capacity, parents yet have a right to be *notified* of dealings between their children and the medical profession? This immediately runs into the problem of medical confidentiality.[265] Of all the matters a young person might want to keep from her parents, those arising from sexual activity are the most likely and, of these, abortion is the one which has generated the greatest amount of litigation in the USA.[266] There, it has been held that States may not constitutionally give to parents an absolute and arbitrary right of veto over abortion.[267] But, in some circumstances, it can be constitutional for a State to require notification of an abortion to parents.[268] States may also act constitutionally in requiring either parental notification or, alternatively, the consent of a judge.[269] The effect of *Gillick* on this would seem to be to preserve the right of the competent child to confidentiality where the doctor is unable to persuade her to inform her parents and, as noted earlier, this was confirmed by Silber J in the *Axon* case. The position is less certain in relation to a child who is adjudged incompetent.[270] The question did not arise in *Re R* and *Re W*, and in *Gillick* it was conflated with the consent issue. It may be that this will be an area in which attempts may be made to find a middle course between giving absolute control to either parent or child over a decision which may affect the

---

[265] See fn 91, at p 359 above.

[266] The leading US Supreme Court decisions on the constitutional framework for abortions on minors are *Planned Parenthood of Central Missouri v Danforth* 428 US 52 (1976); *Bellotti v Baird* 428 US 662 (1979); *Bellotti II* 443 US 662 (1979); *HL v Matheson* 450 US 398 (1981); *Ohio v Akron Center for Reproductive Health* 110 S Ct 2972 (1990); and *Hodgson v Minnesota* 110 S Ct 2926 (1990). A good discussion of the leading cases and the issues raised by them is to be found in RH Mnookin and DK Weisberg *Child, Family and State* (6th edn, Wolters and Kluwer, 2009) ch 4. For an exploration of the issues surrounding abortions on minors, see J Herring 'Children's Abortion Rights' (1997) 5 *Medical Law Review* 257.

[267] *Danforth* and *Bellotti* (above).

[268] *HL v Matheson* (above).

[269] *Ohio* and *Minnesota* cases (above).

[270] See the discussion above and also J Montgomery 'Confidentiality and the Immature Minor' [1987] Fam Law 101.

functioning of the whole family. On balance, the argument for preserving medical confidentiality is probably the stronger.[271]

The role of the court

Should the courts have power to override the wishes of a competent child? Staughton LJ warned, in *Re R*, that 'good reason must be shown before the State exercises any power to control the decisions of a competent person whether adult or minor, which only concern his own well-being'. It has, moreover, been argued that, whatever may be the letter of the law, the *spirit* of *Gillick* requires that the courts should not arrogate to themselves a right to intervene in the lives of children which is denied to natural parents.[272] It should also be said that there must be a danger that a parent might invoke the court's jurisdiction in an attempt, for example, to force an abortion against the wishes of a competent child. This has the potential for driving a coach and horses through the *Gillick* decision. The view which is ultimately taken of these interventions must depend on a judgment as to the appropriate level of paternalism in promoting children's rights. Is this only justified to enable children to become rationally autonomous adults or should the courts continue to exercise a protective jurisdiction in the face of evidence that this rationality has, in fact, been achieved before majority?[273]

The Children Act 1989 gives conflicting messages in this respect. While many of its provisions reject the notion that children's views ought to be decisive,[274] it supports the right of a child (in the context of certain proceedings) who 'has sufficient understanding to make an informed decision' to refuse to submit to medical or psychiatric examination or treatment, even where a court is otherwise minded to direct it.[275] The decisions in *Re R* and *Re W* are difficult to reconcile with these provisions, since their underlying principle seems to be that the competent child should have a *conclusive* right of objection.

Yet it is possible to take a more positive view of the role of the courts in these decision-making processes. It can be argued that, since many of these medical decisions are irreversible and of long-term significance to the young people concerned, an objective view is, if not strictly necessary, nevertheless desirable. Given the uncertainty about who in law does have the right to take the final decision, the use of the court is a way of resolving this. In England, there is no mandatory judicial procedure except that judicial authority is considered a necessary precaution before a sterilisation is performed on an incompetent

---

[271] A convincing defence of confidentiality in all minor cases is to be found in the judgment of Marshall J in *Matheson* (above) at 438–440.

[272] J Eekelaar 'The Eclipse of Parental Rights' (1986) 102 LQR 4, at pp 7–8.

[273] Chapter 7 above discussed this question. See also A Bainham 'Children, Parents and the Law: Non-Intervention and Judicial Paternalism' in P Birks (ed) *The Frontiers of Liability* (Oxford University Press, 1993). The issue arises particularly in relation to the exercise of the inherent jurisdiction, as to which see chapter 12 below.

[274] See chapter 2 above.

[275] See ss 38(6), 43(8), 44(7) of, and Sch 3, para 4(4) to, the Children Act and the discussion in chapters 11 and 12 below.

minor. In the USA, greater use is made of judicial procedures for these purposes. A number of States have enacted 'judicial by-pass' procedures which attempt to accommodate the interests of both parents and adolescents. Typically, the legislation will require notification of an abortion decision to one or possibly both parents and will allow a short time, perhaps 48 hours, to elapse after notification and before the operation is performed. But the notice requirement may be waived, on application to the court, where the court is satisfied that a specified ground is established. The grounds usually include a finding that parents have been guilty of abuse or neglect, that the child is mature and competent to take her own decision, or that the court, for other reasons, finds it to be in her best interest that the abortion should go ahead without parental notification.[276] While parental consent statutes[277] and parental notification statutes without by-pass procedures[278] have been struck down as unconstitutional,[279] appropriately drafted notification statutes incorporating adequate by-pass procedures have been held to be constitutional.[280]

In England, as in the USA, the challenge is to find a middle course which allows for a degree of autonomy in decision-making for adolescents but which does not exclude the opportunity for potentially beneficial parental involvement.[281] Whether a judicial by-pass could provide the answer depends on the unanswerable question of whether judges are better qualified than others to take what may be seen ultimately as value judgments about the desirability of medical interventions.[282]

Guidance[283] issued by the Department of Health recognises the need to involve children and parents fully in the decision-making process. In particular, it states the expectation that children's views should be properly taken into account even where they lack formal legal capacity to decide. In short it supports participatory or shared decision-making in all matters relating to the health of children.

---

[276] A particularly good example is the Minnesota legislation reviewed in *Hodgson v Minnesota* 110 S Ct 2926 (1990).

[277] As in *Planned Parenthood of Central Missouri v Danforth* 428 US 52 (1976).

[278] As in *Bellotti v Baird* 428 US 662 (1979).

[279] Except, as in *HL v Matheson* 450 US 398 (1981), where they relate to notification in the case of an immature and unemancipated minor.

[280] As in *Ohio v Akron Center for Reproductive Health* 110 S Ct 2972 (1990) and *Minnesota* (above).

[281] The arguments for regarding parental involvement as potentially beneficial, rather than negative, are rehearsed in the *Minnesota* decision (above).

[282] There may also be seen to be a need for clear principles to govern the activities of the medical profession to avoid the necessity of seeking judicial authorisation in every case.

[283] *Seeking Consent: Working with Children* (DoH, 2001).

Chapter 9

CHILDREN, MONEY AND PROPERTY

INTRODUCTION

Historically, children's financial interests have not been well served by the law: there was, in theory, a common law duty on a father to maintain his legitimate children, but no procedure was available to enforce that right,[1] while children were not entitled as of right to any share in a deceased parent's property.[2] This chapter first summarises the rules governing children's rights in relation to property, and the evolution of the obligation to provide financial support for children is also summarised. It then seeks to summarise the child support legislation, and the residual role of the courts in making financial orders for children. The text then outlines some of the most significant features of the welfare benefits system as it affects young people. The chapter concludes with some observations on the policy considerations relating to financial responsibility for children.

CHILDREN AND PROPERTY[3]

Children's capacity to own property

Most of the distinctive rules relating to children's interests in property stem from the common law notion that a child has no legal capacity. Although (as has already been seen)[4] the *Gillick* decision[5] means that this denial of legal capacity is no longer absolute, the rules governing children's ownership of

---

[1] A father was not even obliged to reimburse a person who supplied his child with necessary goods or services: *Mortimer v Wright* (1840) 6 M&W 482. However, someone who supplied a wife with goods necessary for a child might be able to recover from the husband under the doctrine of agency of necessity: *Bazeley v Forder* (1868) LR 3 QB 559.

[2] The feudal lord became entitled to the profits of land during an heir's minority. The right was abolished by the Tenures Abolition Act 1660.

[3] For an extremely helpful article which looks at the various angles of children's interests in property and which incorporates discussion of the Trusts of Land and Appointment of Trustees Act 1996, see E Cooke 'Children and Real Property – Trusts, Interests and Considerations' [1998] Fam Law 349. There is also a useful discussion in D Cowan and N Dearden 'The Minor as (a) Subject: the Case of Housing Law' in J Fionda (ed) *Legal Concepts of Childhood* (Hart Publishing, 2001) and in E Cooke 'Don't Spend It All at Once!: Parental Responsibility and Parents' Responsibilities in Respect of Children's Contracts and Property' in R Probert, S Gilmore and J Herring (eds) *Responsible Parents and Parental Responsibility* (Hart Publishing, 2009), ch 11.

[4] See chapters 7 and 8.

[5] *Gillick v West Norfolk and Wisbech Area Health Authority* [1986] 1 AC 112.

property are in general[6] founded on express statutory provisions unaffected by the *Gillick* approach to legal capacity. For example, statute provides that an infant cannot hold a legal estate in land, nor be registered as the registered proprietor of registered land.[7] Statute denies an infant the right to make a will[8] (unless he[9] is a soldier in actual military service or a mariner or seaman at sea),[10] and a child cannot be appointed a trustee,[11] nor act as an administrator.[12]

Management of children's property

The rules debarring a child from holding a legal estate are probably of little practical significance. This is because – as a result of legislation[13] and professional practice – most property to which a child is entitled is held by trustees on the child's behalf; and the Trustee Act 1925 contains provisions[14] which facilitate the making of maintenance payments from property which is held in trust for a child.[15]

It should also be noted that – in addition to the court's general jurisdiction in respect of the administration of a child's property in wardship[16] – statute[17] specifically empowers the court to approve trust variations on behalf of infants and others incapable of themselves consenting, provided the scheme is beneficial to the persons concerned.

---

6   But not always. See, for example, the rule that a child cannot give a valid receipt for a legacy paid to him: *Philip v Paget* (1740) 2 Atk 80; *Re Somech; Westminster Bank Ltd v Phillips* [1957] Ch 165. It appears that, as a result of provisions defining parental responsibility contained in the Children Act 1989, s 3(2), any person with parental responsibility may now give such a receipt on the child's behalf. For a discussion of the position before the enactment of the Children Act, see Law Com Working Paper No 91 *Guardianship* (1985), at paras 2.32–2.35.

7   Law of Property Act 1925, ss 1(6) and 205(1)(v), and see now Sch 1, para 1(1)(a) to the Trusts of Land and Appointment of Trustees Act 1996. However, this does not mean that a child may not hold an equitable interest in land. There is no prohibition on a child disposing of property, but any deed executed by a child is voidable and can be repudiated during minority or within a reasonable time after attainment of full age.

8   Wills Act 1837, s 7.

9   *In the estate of Stanley* [1916] P 192; *In the estate of Rowson* [1944] 2 All ER 36.

10   Wills Act 1837, s 11, as amended by the Wills (Soldiers and Sailors) Act 1918.

11   Senior Courts Act 1981, s 118.

12   *Re Manuel* (1849) 13 Jur 664.

13   See, for example, Sch 1, para 1(1) to the Trusts of Land and Appointment of Trustees Act 1996 (repealing the Law of Property Act 1925, s 19): conveyance of legal estate to a minor takes effect as a declaration of trust; legal estate conveyed to a child jointly with one or more other persons of full age vests in those of full age on trust for the minor.

14   Trustee Act 1925, s 31.

15   This provision will apply where a child is entitled under the statutory trusts arising on an intestacy: see p oo below. For a consideration of the trustees' broad discretion under the Trustee Act 1925, see *J v J (C Intervening)* [1989] 1 FLR 453.

16   See chapter 1.

17   Variation of Trusts Act 1958, s 1(1)(a).

Guardians have parental responsibility for the child, and consequently they have the power to administer a child's property. In certain specified circumstances,[18] the Official Solicitor may be appointed to be guardian of a child's estate.

Inheritance rights

English law – in contrast to the law of Scotland and many other legal systems[19] – does not give members of the family any legal right to share in a deceased relative's estate, and, to that extent, English law still embodies the traditional common law principle of freedom of testation. It is true that children do have rights to succeed on the intestacy of a parent, but, in practice, those rights are often not of any real significance. This is because English law treats a surviving spouse generously and treats the deceased's children correspondingly ungenerously. In outline, the rule is that a spouse is entitled to a statutory legacy (currently amounting to £250,000)[20] and to a life interest in one-half of any balance of the estate. Hence, it is only in cases where the deceased had significant means that the children's rights to succeed are likely to prove valuable. The extent of this preference for the surviving spouse may be questioned in an era of high divorce and remarriage. It might be argued that proportionately greater weight should be given to the claims of the deceased's biological children from a former marriage vis-à-vis the claims of the surviving spouse than is so under the existing law.[21] However, the Law Commission recently considered the issue of family provision on death and recommended in its Report[22] that where a person dies intestate and is survived by a spouse and children or other descendants, the surviving spouse should receive, in addition to the deceased's personal chattels and a statutory legacy, half of any balance of the estate.[23] Clause 1(2) of the draft Inheritance and Trustees' Powers Bill, appended to the Report puts this recommendation into effect by amending the table at s 46(1) of the Administration of Estates Act 1925. Where the value of the estate exceeds the statutory legacy, the children and other descendants of the deceased would therefore share the half of the balance that the spouse did

---

18 See s 5(11) of the Children Act; RSC Ord 80, r 13 (as inserted by the Rules of the Supreme Court (Amendment No 4) 1991). Such appointments are made, for example, for the purpose of administering an award to the child under the Criminal Injuries Compensation Scheme where it would be unsuitable for the parents to be involved – for example if they had caused the injuries: see Law Com Working Paper No 91 *Guardianship* (1985), at p 51, note 95.

19 For example, the law of Germany: see *MT v MT (Financial Provision: Lump Sum)* [1992] 1 FLR 362.

20 Family Provision (Intestate Succession) Order 1993 (SI 1993/2906).

21 For a comparative discussion of the policy underlying the inheritance laws of England, the USA, France and Germany, see MA Glendon *The Transformation of Family Law* (University of Chicago Press, 1989), at pp 238–251. For a critique of the attempts to reform the English law of intestacy, see SM Cretney 'Reform of Intestacy: The Best We Can Do?' (1995) 111 LQR 99.

22 The Law Commission *Intestacy and Family Provision Claims on Death* (Law Com No 331) 13 December 2011 HC 1674.

23 Ibid, at para 2.62.

not take.[24] On 21 March 2013 the Government announced acceptance of this and other recommendations of the Commission. So, while there has been some suggested change to the law, the principle that a spouse will usually inherit the majority of the deceased's spouse's estate will continue.

Currently, subject to the interest of the surviving spouse, the deceased's estate is held 'on the statutory trusts' for the deceased's issue.[25] Under the statutory trusts,[26] the intestate's children may receive maintenance out of income until they are 18, and any income not applied for their maintenance is accumulated for the children's benefit. On reaching 18 years of age, a child becomes entitled to the appropriate share of the capital. If any of the intestate's children predeceases the intestate (or dies subsequently, but before attaining the age of 18 years) leaving issue, the issue take the child's presumptive share.

Failure to provide for children

There are two situations in which a child may be left without adequate financial provision on the death of a relative. First, the child may be disinherited by a will which makes no provision for him or her and, secondly, the rules of intestacy may (in consequence of the preference they embody for a surviving spouse) leave a child without any provision. For example, in *Re Sivyer*,[27] the intestate left a widow, and a 13-year-old daughter by a previous marriage. The widow was entitled, under the rules of intestacy, to the whole of his estate; the child was entitled to nothing.

Even more strikingly, in *Re Collins, dec'd*,[28] Mrs Collins had obtained a decree nisi of divorce before her death, but the decree had not been made absolute. In the result, her husband was, at law, entitled on her intestacy to the whole of her estate, and her children – a son of Mr and Mrs Collins and a daughter of hers – were not entitled, under the rules of intestacy, to anything.

Court's power to order that reasonable financial provision be made

The Inheritance (Provision for Family and Dependants) Act 1975 permits certain defined categories of 'dependant' to apply to the court for reasonable financial provision to be made for them out of the deceased's estate. If the court considers that the will or intestacy does not make such provision, it may make appropriate orders (for example, for periodical income payments, or for payment of a lump sum). The categories of dependant include a child of the deceased, and also:

---

24 Ibid, at para 2.64.
25 The term issue now extends equally to those born in wedlock and to those born outside marriage: Family Law Reform Act 1987, s 18(1).
26 See *J v J (C Intervening)* [1989] 1 FLR 453.
27 [1967] 1 WLR 1482.
28 [1990] Fam 56.

'any person (not being a child of the deceased) who in the case of any marriage to which the deceased was at any time a party, was treated by the deceased as a child of the family in relation to that marriage.'

The term 'child' extends to illegitimate, adopted and posthumous children of the deceased, and there is no restriction of age or marital status so that an adult child is entitled to apply. This is an interesting illustration of the way in which, at least for some purposes, the relationship of parent and child and wider kinship links endure for life and do not end on the child attaining majority.[29]

The category of 'children of the family' is similar to, but not identical with, that in the legislation governing financial provision on divorce:[30] under the divorce legislation, the child must have been treated as a child of the family by *both* parties to the marriage, but under the inheritance legislation, the criterion is treatment *by the deceased* in relation *to the deceased's marriage*. Thus, in *Re Leach*,[31] the deceased was the applicant's step-mother who had married the applicant's father at a time when she was aged 32. The applicant had a good relationship with her step-mother and became particularly close to her after her father's death. The judge rejected an argument that the 'treatment' which was required was treatment at or about the time of the marriage; and he did not regard it as directly relevant that most of the treatment in this case had occurred after the end of the marriage.

Exercise of the court's discretion

In deciding whether 'reasonable financial provision' has been made, and if not, what order it should make, the court is given certain guidance. In all cases of applications by children, the court is required to have regard to the following matters:[32]

'(a) the financial resources and financial needs which the applicant has or is likely to have in the foreseeable future;

(b) the financial resources and financial needs which any other applicant for an order made under the Act has or is likely to have in the foreseeable future;

(c) the financial resources and financial needs which any beneficiary of the estate of the deceased has or is likely to have in the foreseeable future;

(d) any obligations and responsibilities which the deceased had towards any applicant for an order or towards any beneficiary of the estate of the deceased;

(e) the size and nature of the net estate of the deceased;

---

[29] It has also been recognised by the courts and legislature that benefits to a child of being adopted may endure into adulthood and that this may justify the making of an adoption order, even where the child is close to attaining majority. See, for example, *Re D (A Minor) (Adoption Order: Validity)* [1991] 2 FLR 66. The Adoption and Children Act 2002 recognises the benefits of adoption during adulthood in several provisions. See, for example, ss 1(4)(c), 47(9) and 49(4) and (5) and the discussion in chapter 13.

[30] See p 440 below, where the scope of the definition is discussed.

[31] [1986] Ch 226.

[32] Inheritance (Provision for Family and Dependants) Act 1975, s 3(1).

> (f)   any physical or mental disability of any applicant for an order under the Act or any beneficiary of the estate of the deceased;
>
> (g)   any other matter, including the conduct of the applicant or any other person, which in the circumstances of the case the court may consider relevant',

and the court is also to have regard to the manner in which the applicant was being or in which he might expect to be educated or trained.[33]

Where the applicant is someone who makes a claim as a 'child of the family' in relation to the deceased, the court is also required to have regard to the following matters:

> '(a)   whether the deceased had assumed any responsibility for the applicant's maintenance and, if so, to the extent to which and the basis upon which the deceased assumed that responsibility and to the length of time for which the deceased discharged that responsibility;
>
> (b)   whether in assuming and discharging that responsibility the deceased did so knowing that the applicant was not his own child;
>
> (c)   the liability of any other person to maintain the applicant.'

These provisions obviously give the court a wide discretion. In respect of applications by children, it has been held that children born outside marriage are to be treated on the same basis as those born within it.[34] In *Re C (Deceased)*,[35] for example, the eight-year-old daughter of the deceased was granted permission to make an application for provision out of time through her mother as next friend. The deceased was wealthy whereas the applicant child and her mother lived in humble circumstances. The court held that the fault for delay in making the application lay with the mother and that this should not bar the child, the merits of whose claim were clear – the more so since the estate had not yet been distributed.

What is the position of the 'child' now an adult? On the one hand, it has been held that claims by adults are not exceptional, but it has to be remembered that the policy of the Inheritance (Provision for Family and Dependants) Act 1975 is not to decide how the deceased's assets should be fairly divided. Instead, it is concerned with making reasonable provision for *dependants* and, accordingly, it is not surprising that the courts have adopted the view that claims for maintenance by able-bodied and comparatively young people who are in employment and able to maintain themselves, will be rare and are to be approached with a degree of circumspection.[36] This does not mean that a claim by an adult son or daughter is viewed with disfavour; rather it means that, faced with a claim by a person who is physically able to earn his own living, the

---

[33]   Inheritance (Provision for Family and Dependants) Act 1975, s 3(3).

[34]   *In the estate of McC* (1978) Fam Law 26.

[35]   *Re C (Deceased) (Leave to Apply for Provision)* [1995] 2 FLR 24.

[36]   *Re Coventry, dec'd* [1980] Ch 461, at 495.

court will be inclined to ask 'why should anybody else make provision for you if you are capable of maintaining yourself?'[37]

The leading case is *Re Jennings (Deceased)*.[38] The deceased and his wife had separated as long ago as 1945 when the applicant, their son, was aged two. The applicant had thereafter been raised by his mother and step-father. The deceased left the bulk of his estate to charities and remote relatives. The applicant was married with two children and successfully acquired two companies which provided his family with a comfortable standard of living. He applied for financial provision out of the estate and succeeded at first instance largely on the basis that the deceased had failed to discharge his moral and financial obligations to the applicant during his minority. The Court of Appeal, however, held that the Act could not be construed to include obligations and responsibilities in the distant past but, as a general rule, should be confined to those which the deceased had immediately before his death. The relationship of father and son could not, as such, impose on the deceased a continuing financial obligation up to the time of death. Neither had it been demonstrated that financial provision was reasonably required for the applicant's maintenance since no further provision was necessary to enable the applicant to discharge the cost of his daily living at a standard appropriate to him. The case is an interesting illustration of the way in which the mere presence of a genetic link is not enough, at least under this legislation, to trigger moral and legal financial responsibilities. The position should be contrasted with that under the child support legislation (discussed below), where entirely the opposite is true, albeit in relation to minor, not adult, children. Nevertheless, where such moral obligations to provide do exist at the time of death and where the adult child is in straitened financial circumstances, an order may be appropriate. This was the situation in *Re Goodchild (Deceased) and Another*[39] where the Court of Appeal, although unwilling to find that a father and mother had made effective mutual wills in favour of their son, did find that the father owed a moral obligation to provide for his son out of that part of the estate which he had inherited from his deceased wife. Similarly in *Re Pearce (Deceased)*[40] moral obligations again appeared to weigh heavily in the decision, in this case deriving from the adult son's unpaid work on his father's farm throughout much of his childhood and early adulthood, and his father's (broken) promise to him that he would leave the farm to him on his death. In these circumstances the Court of Appeal upheld an award of £85,000 free of inheritance tax.

At the same time it has been held that a moral obligation on the part of the deceased is not a prerequisite of an order. In *Re Hancock (Deceased)*[41] the Court of Appeal held that an adult son or daughter did not necessarily have to show that the deceased owed him or her a moral obligation or that there were other special circumstances, but that a claim by an adult with an established

---

37   *Re Dennis, dec'd* [1981] 2 All ER 140 at 145.
38   [1994] 1 FLR 536.
39   [1997] 2 FLR 644.
40   [1998] 2 FLR 705.
41   [1998] 2 FLR 346.

earning capacity might very well fail in the absence of such factors. In this case there was found to be no moral obligation, but an order for £3,000 per annum was made largely on the basis of the poor financial situation in which the 58-year-old daughter now found herself.

Several reported decisions have concerned adult daughters. An example, involving an adopted daughter, is provided by *Williams v Johns*,[42] where the applicant (who was 43, unemployed, impecunious and divorced with no capital beyond the houseboat in which she lived) had had a stormy childhood after being adopted as a baby by the deceased. She was a delinquent, and this caused emotional distress and suffering to her adoptive parents who, nevertheless, continued to assist her financially and morally whenever possible. She had not done anything to help the deceased, and indeed it was suggested that the deceased was afraid of her. The deceased made no provision in her will for the adopted daughter, and left a written statement that she felt no obligation towards her. The court held that, in these circumstances, it was not unreasonable for the deceased to have made no financial provision for the applicant.

In contrast, in *Re Debenham (Deceased)*,[43] the applicant was an unwanted child brought up by her grandparents abroad. When she discovered the facts about her parentage she tried to establish a link with her mother, but these attempts were unsuccessful and the deceased continued to remain aloof, distant and indeed cruel to her daughter. It was held that a legacy of £200 out of an estate of £172,000 was not, in all the circumstances, reasonable provision for the daughter. In particular, the daughter was an epileptic and any mother might have felt some obligation to help her in those circumstances. The court ordered payment of a small capital sum to meet the claimant's immediate needs, and a payment of £4,500 per annum by way of income payments.

In *Espinosa v Burke*[44] the spotlight was turned on the supposedly adverse conduct of the adult daughter and the effect that this should or should not have on her application.[45] The judge had refused her claim largely on the basis of her behaviour towards the deceased in the final years of his life. She had been married five times and regularly brought male partners into her elderly father's home. In the last year of his life she spent most of her time in Spain with the Spanish fisherman she later married. Meanwhile the deceased was left to be looked after by his grandson and a cleaner. Nonetheless, the Court of Appeal allowed her appeal taking the view that the judge had attached too much significance to the failure of the daughter to discharge her moral obligation to her father and too little to her needs and the promises made to her by the deceased.

---

[42] [1988] 2 FLR 475.
[43] [1986] 1 FLR 404.
[44] [1999] 1 FLR 747.
[45] For a discussion of the relevance of fault in family law generally, see A Bainham 'Men and Women Behaving Badly: Is Fault Dead in English Family Law?' (2001) 21 *Oxford Journal of Legal Studies* 219.

Finally, in *Robinson v Bird*[46] Blackburne J refused the claim of an adult daughter for what amounted to a larger share in her late mother's estate. The deceased had by will left the residue of her estate equally to her grandson, the only child of her late son and the claimant. The claimant argued that 80 per cent of the residuary estate to her would better reflect the deceased's wishes at the time of her death. It was held that the fact the claimant's reasonable maintenance requirements could not be satisfied from her own resources did not lead to the conclusion that it was unreasonable that the will did not make greater provision for her. Notwithstanding the closeness of her relationship with the deceased, and the deceased's apparent wish to treat her more favourably than the grandson, there was no sufficient basis for disturbing the equal division of the residuary estate.

Re Abram (Deceased)[47] is an example of a successful claim by an adult son against his mother's estate. Here, the mother had owned a prosperous warehouse business and substantial family home. The applicant was her only son who had, since the age of 17, worked long hours in the business for a minimal wage. He eventually married and broke clear of the home in the face of strong opposition by his mother. The deceased had made a will leaving the whole of her estate to her son but later revoked this, disinheriting him. She never changed this will, although there was evidence that she had intended to do so. Matters were complicated following the death of the deceased in that her company had failed and the sole asset was the family home. The applicant had also hit on hard times. His own business had failed and he had entered into an individual voluntary arrangement with creditors under the Insolvency Act 1986.

The court held that these were special circumstances and that the deceased had been under a moral obligation to provide for her son. In view of the arrangement under the Insolvency Act (under which any capital paid to the applicant would have to go to his creditors), the court ordered a settlement under which, inter alia, the income from 50 per cent of the estate would be paid to him for life.

EVOLUTION OF THE OBLIGATIONS TO PROVIDE FINANCIAL SUPPORT FOR CHILDREN[48]

The enforcement of the obligation to maintain is governed entirely by statute, and a brief account of the historical development of the law will help put the modern law in context.

The Matrimonial Causes Act 1857 first gave English courts power to dissolve marriages, and it provided that the court granting a decree could make such

---

[46] [2003] All ER (D) 190.
[47] [1996] 2 FLR 379.
[48] See generally N Wikeley *Child Support Law and Policy* (Hart Publishing, 2006).

order as it deemed just and proper with respect to the 'custody, maintenance and education' of children, the marriage of whose parents was in issue.[49] The court's powers to make financial orders in divorce and other matrimonial causes were greatly extended[50] over the years, and courts were given power to make orders for the children in other proceedings.

In 1878, magistrates were given power[51] to make what were, in effect, separation orders where a wife had been the victim of assault by her husband, and they were empowered to give custody of any children under the age of 10 to the wife, and to make financial orders. Magistrates also had power to make financial orders against the father of an illegitimate child in affiliation proceedings.[52] In 1886, the Guardianship of Infants Act[53] empowered the court to make a custody or access order on the application of a child's mother, and legislation[54] subsequently provided that the court could order a father to pay the mother weekly or other periodical sums by way of maintenance.

The Children Act 1989 reformed and assimilated the private law provisions governing financial provision and property adjustment for children, extended the court's powers, and achieved a substantial measure of simplification, rationalisation and harmonisation. The magistrates' court retained its power to make maintenance orders[55] in matrimonial proceedings, and the divorce court retained its extensive powers to make orders over capital or income for the benefit of children of the family.[56] The Children Act itself[57] provided for a wide range of financial orders to be made in respect of children, on the application of a parent, a guardian, a person who had a child residing with him under a court order, and (in certain circumstances) a child of 18 years or over.[58] The scheme of the legislation was that financial support for a child could be sought as an incident in matrimonial proceedings between the child's parents, and that in other cases – for example, where the unmarried mother of a child wanted an order for financial support for the child – similar relief would be available under the Children Act. Although the provisions of the matrimonial legislation

---

[49]   Matrimonial Causes Act 1857, s 35.

[50]   Both in respect of the types of order which could be made and in respect of the class of children eligible to benefit: the Matrimonial Proceedings (Children) Act 1958 gave the divorce court power to make orders for a child of one spouse who had been 'accepted' by the other; and the Matrimonial Proceedings and Property Act 1970 gave the court its present wide powers to make both capital and income payments to, or for the benefit of, any 'child of the family'.

[51]   Matrimonial Causes Act 1878, s 4.

[52]   This jurisdiction dates back to the Poor Law Amendment Act 1844: the history of the obligation to maintain is traced in the *Report of the Committee on One-Parent Families* ('the Finer Report') (1974) (Cmnd 5629).

[53]   Guardianship of Infants Act 1886, s 5.

[54]   Ibid, s 3.

[55]   And orders for the payment of small lump sums under the Domestic Proceedings and Magistrates' Courts Act 1978.

[56]   See pp 438 et seq below.

[57]   Schedule 1.

[58]   The applicants now also include a special guardian, as noted later in the chapter.

and of the Children Act remain on the statute book and in force, their practical importance was greatly reduced when the Child Support Act 1991 (CSA 1991)[59] was enacted.

Background to the Child Support Act 1991[60]

The introduction of the Child Support Act 1991 was driven by the view of the then Prime Minister, Margaret Thatcher,[61] that the system of discretionary, court-ordered child maintenance upon parental relationship breakdown was ineffective in many cases in securing appropriate maintenance for children, and was placing too great a financial burden on the State rather than on individual parents. Even where the courts were involved, there was a tendency for some lawyers to seek court orders which would have the effect of maximising the availability of welfare benefits. In July 1990, Thatcher announced that responsibility for assessing claims for child maintenance was largely to be removed from the courts, and that the Government intended to set up a Child Support Agency,[62] which would have access to information to trace absent parents and assess, collect and enforce maintenance payments. A White Paper,[63] *Children Come First*, diagnosed the problem as follows:

> 'The present system of maintenance is unnecessarily fragmented, uncertain in its results, slow and ineffective. It is based largely on discretion. The system is operated through the High and county courts, the Magistrates' Courts ... and the offices of the Department of Social Security. The cumulative effect is uncertainty and inconsistent decisions about how much maintenance should be paid. In a great many instances, the maintenance award is not paid or the payments fall into arrears and then take weeks to re-establish. Only 30% of lone mothers and 3% of lone fathers receive regular maintenance for their children. More than 750,000 lone parents depend on income support. Many lone mothers want to go to work but do not feel able to do so.'

Maintenance assessments would be calculated by reference to a non-discretionary formula intended to produce a level of maintenance reflecting both the day-to-day living costs of raising a child, and the essential living expenses of the person caring for a child and the absent parent. The proposed introduction of an administrative approach was in part influenced by such

---

[59] As amended by the Child Support Act 1995, the Child Support, Pensions and Social Security Act 2000, the Child Maintenance and Other Payments Act 2008, and the Welfare Reform Act 2012.

[60] See generally, M Maclean and J Eekelaar 'Child Support: The British Solution' (1993) 7 *International Journal of Law and the Family* 205; M Maclean 'The Making of the Child Support Act: Policy Making at the Intersection of Law and Social Policy' (1994) 21(4) *Journal of Law and Society* 505.

[61] See the detailed discussion of Thatcher's influence in 'Prime Ministerial Intervention: The Child Support Act 1991', in M Maclean with J Kurczewski *Making Family Law* (Oxford, Hart Publishing, 2011).

[62] For a penetrating analysis of the work of the Child Support Agency based on empirical research involving privileged access to the Agency's staff, see G Davis, N Wikeley and R Young, with J Barron and J Bedward *Child Support in Action* (Hart Publishing, 1998).

[63] (1990) (Cmnd 1263).

schemes in other jurisdictions.[64] The passage of the 1991 Act through Parliament was controversial – although, perhaps surprisingly, the official opposition did not question the basic principles underlying the new law – but few amendments were made and the Act was brought fully into force on 5 April 1993.[65] While the Act's passage through Parliament was relatively smooth, the administration of the scheme has provoked widespread and sustained criticism, and the Act has been amended on several occasions in order to seek to address concerns.[66]

The first problem encountered related to the calculation of child support. Unlike some other jurisdictions, the Child Support Act 1991 initially adopted a complex social security style formula for calculating child support,[67] which proved too rigid and inflexible and led, in some cases, to disproportionately

---

[64]   See Maclean and Eekelaar, n 60 above. For comparison of developments in Australia and the UK since the late 1980s, see B Fehlberg and M Maclean 'Child Support Policy in Australia and the United Kingdom: Changing Priorities But A Similar Tough Deal for Children?' (2009) 23(1) *International Journal of Law, Policy and the Family* 1–24. See also K Cook and Kristin Natalier 'The Gendered Framing of Australia's Child Support Reforms' (2013) 27(1) *International Journal of Law, Policy and the Family* 28–50. For earlier discussions of other jurisdictions: M Harrison 'Child Maintenance in Australia: the New Era' in Weitzman and Maclean (eds) *The Economic Consequences of Divorce* (1991); 'Child Support in Australia: Children's Rights or Public Interest' (1991) 5 *International Journal of Law and the Family* 24. On experience in the USA, see I Garfinkel *Assuring Child Support* (New York, 1992). On the scheme in New Zealand, see N Richardson 'The New Zealand Child Support Act' [1995] CFLQ 40. See also JT Oldham 'Lessons from the New English and Australian Child Support Systems' (1996) 29 *Vanderbilt J Transnat'l L* 691. For an academic assessment of the issues surrounding child support in the USA, with some comparative material, see JT Oldham and MS Melli *Child Support: The Next Frontier* (University of Michigan Press, 2000). See also S Altman 'A Theory of Child Support' (2003) 17 *International Journal of Law, Policy and the Family* 173.

[65]   The effect of the transitional provisions was complex: see the Child Support Act 1991 (Commencement No 3 and Transitional Provisions) (Amendment) Order 1993 (SI 1993/966). All new cases – ie all cases in which there was no previous court order or maintenance agreement – were taken on by the Child Support Agency with effect from 5 April 1993. Between that date and April 1996, existing cases in which a claimant was on income support or family credit were taken over by the Agency, and by 1997 the Agency had assumed responsibility for all child support cases.

[66]   For discussion of some of the difficulties encountered in implementing the child support scheme, see e g R Collier 'The Campaign Against the Child Support Act, Errant Fathers and Family Men' [1994] Fam Law 384; C Glendinning, K Clarke, and G Craig 'Implementing the Child Support Act'(1996) 18(3) *Journal of Social Welfare and Family Law* 273–289; D Abbott 'The Child Support Act 1991: The Lives of Parents With Care Living in Liverpool' (1996) 18(1) *Journal of Social Welfare and Family Law* 21; G Gillespie 'Child Support – The Hand that Rocks the Cradle' [1996] Fam Law 162.

[67]   See the second edition of this work at pp 302 et seq for the detail. Briefly, the formulae involved first calculating a 'maintenance requirement' for the children, a process which was linked to the income support rates payable for the children and the parent with care but deducting the child benefit which was payable to the family. Stage two involved the calculation of the 'maintenance assessment' which required the 'assessable income' of the 'absent parent' less any so-called 'exempt income' to be ascertained. This was then added to the income of the parent with care, and the aggregate was divided by two. The 'assessable income' was then computed by making allowances for the personal expenditure of the 'absent parent' and adding this to the income support rates for any children living with him plus allowable housing costs. There was also provision for an additional element where the total assessable income

high calculations.[68] The Child Support Act 1995 was thus enacted in an attempt to meet some of these criticisms, by introducing the possibility, in exceptional cases, of discretionary 'departures' (now known as variations) from the formula.[69] These are discussed in more detail below, but they include inter alia such cases as costs incurred by an 'absent parent' in maintaining contact with his children; costs attributable to long-term illness or disability; pre-existing debts and financial commitments; and costs incurred in supporting a child of the family who was not the applicant's own child. The discretion is exercised on the basis that it is 'just and equitable' to do so, taking into account the financial circumstances of the parties and the welfare of any child likely to be affected by the decision. The 1995 Act also addressed some criticisms of terminology used in the 1991 Act, replacing the term 'absent parent', which was perceived as carrying pejorative connotations, with 'non-resident parent'.[70]

The administration of the child support scheme continued to provoke widespread criticism, indeed hostility, in practice and the subsequent Labour Government published, first, a Green Paper entitled *Children First: A New Approach to Child Support*[71] and then a White Paper, *A New Contract for Welfare: Children's Rights and Parents' Responsibilities*.[72] In its White Paper the Government identified what it saw as the major problems with the operation of the scheme. Many parents were not meeting their responsibilities, with only around 40 per cent of non-resident parents paying in full. Moreover, the system was riddled with complexity. It was estimated that it could take more than 100 pieces of information to enable a calculation of child support maintenance to be made, since the formula embraced not only the resources of the non-resident parent, but also the needs and resources of the parent with care. This resulted in a slow and cumbersome system which was prone to errors, frequent changes of circumstances, and open to abuse by unco-operative parents.

The Government's proposed changes to the Child Support Act 1991, to which the the Child Support, Pensions and Social Security Act 2000 gave effect, were

---

exceeded the maintenance requirement, and there was provision for a 'protected income' which was designed to secure that the absent parent's disposable income did not fall below a certain minimum level.

[68] For example, the formula made no allowances for property transfers made before the child support scheme came into effect in April 1993, the effect of which had been to reduce the amount of periodical payments which would otherwise have been payable in relation to a child. See *Crozier v Crozier* [1994] 1 FLR 26. The transfer of part of a beneficial interest qualified for these purposes. See *Secretary of State for Social Security v Henderson* [1999] 1 FLR 496.

[69] For commentary on the changes made by the 1995 Act, see M Horton 'Improving Child Support – A Missed Opportunity' [1995] CFLQ 26. See also the second edition of this work at pp 304–306.

[70] See for discussion J Wallbank 'The Campaign for Change of the Child Support Act 1991: Reconstructing the "Absent Father"' (1997) 6 *Social and Legal Studies* 191.

[71] (Cm 3992) (The Stationery Office, 1998). For comment, see C Barton 'Third Time Lucky for Child Support? – The 1998 Green Paper' [1998] Fam Law 668 and N Mostyn 'The Green Paper on Child Support' [1999] Fam Law 95.

[72] (Cm 4349) (The Stationery Office, 1999). For comment, see C Barton 'Child Support – Tony's Turn' [1999] Fam Law 704, and J Pirrie 'The Child Support, Pensions and Social Security Bill' [1999] Fam Law 199.

designed to enable the system to work more fairly and expeditiously. The Act introduced a much more straightforward formula, based solely on a simple slice of the non-resident parent's net income with reference to the number of children concerned. The income of the 'person with care' is ignored, thus removing at a stroke much of the complication of the original formula. A simpler minimum flat rate of payment for those with low incomes or on benefit, and a sliding scale for those with incomes just above the minimum was also introduced.[73] In addition, the Act brought tougher sanctions for recalcitrant parents who refuse to cooperate or fail unreasonably to pay, such as the threat to withdraw a driving licence.

Despite these efforts to improve the system, by 2006 public confidence in the Child Support Agency reached such a low that Sir David Henshaw was asked by the government to undertake a complete review. He concluded[74] that perceptions of the Child Support Agency were so tarnished that it should be replaced by a new body called the Child Maintenance and Enforcement Commission (C-MEC), a non-departmental public body, with a role similar to the CSA. This recommendation, and others to amend the CSA 1991,[75] were enacted in the Child Maintenance and Other Payments Act 2008.[76] The 2008 Act builds on the 2000 Act's approach by seeking to simplify even further the formula for calculating child support maintenance by making the calculation by reference to gross income. Further mechanisms for enforcing child support are also introduced. The most significant change, however, is that parents on welfare benefits are no longer compelled to pursue child maintenance through the C-MEC. This change was driven by an overload of cases being dealt with by the child support agency. The fact that some parents were prevented from making private arrangements meant that there was a large group of clients who were forced to use the service who did not wish to and might otherwise have made private agreements. Removing this barrier would, it was said, allow the state to focus on the more difficult cases where effective enforcement was needed. The number of cases being dealt with the by the Child Support Agency came at a cost; while it was the purpose of the Child Support Agency to save the taxpayer money, at the time of the Henshaw report the Agency was running at a net cost to the taxpayer of around £200 million a year.

This is one aspect of a significant policy shift towards encouraging private ordering of child maintenance. The CSA 1991 was recently further amended by the Welfare Reform Act 2012 to provide that the C-MEC 'may take such steps as it considers appropriate to encourage the making and keeping of maintenance agreements' and, before accepting an application to it, may 'invite

---

73 Replacing the concept in the old formula of a 'protected income' below which a non-resident parent's income should not fall.

74 Sir David Henshaw's Report to the Secretary of State for Work and Pensions, *Recovering Child Support: Routes to Responsibility* (Cm 6894, July 2006).

75 Accepted by the government: see Department for Work and Pensions, *A New System of Child Maintenance* (Cm 6979, December 2006).

76 For useful summaries of the changes effected by the 2008 Act, see N Wikeley 'Child Support: the Brave New World' [2008] Fam Law 1024 and 'Child Support: Carrots and Sticks' [2008] Fam Law 1102.

the applicant to consider with the Commission whether it is possible to make such an agreement'.[77] A new s 9A[78] of the CSA 1991 will allow C-MEC to give an indication of what the child support maintenance calculated under the 2008 Act would be, as a basis for parents privately agreeing an appropriate amount.

In October 2011 the Department for Work and Pensions (DWP) intiated a public consultation on its proposal to abolish, and transfer, the functions of C-MEC to DWP.[79] The aim was to bring the functions more directly under the control and accountability of the Secretary of State, and the change was achieved by the Public Bodies (Child Maintenance and Enforcement Commission: Abolition and Transfer of Functions) Order 2012, made pursuant to the Public Bodies Act 2011. The Order came into effect on 1 August 2012. The name of the new service (replacing C-MEC) is the Child Maintenance Service which operates in parallel now with the Child Support Agency, both under the control of DWP.

As will be apparent from the above discussion, there may be three different schemes for calculating child support maintenance in operation, depending upon when an application was made to the CSA or to the Child Maintenance Service (as the case may be) – the original scheme, as refined by the 1995 Act; the 2000 Act scheme; and the most recent 2008 Act scheme, as also developed by the Welfare Reform Act 2012. The Government's aim is eventually to move all cases to the 2008 scheme, and it is proposed in what follows to explain the detailed workings of the CSA 1991 by reference to the latest scheme.

The Child Support Act's impact on the private law governing financial provision for children

As will be clear from the foregoing account of the background to the CSA 1991, a principal aim of the Act was to shift assessment of child support maintenance from the courts to an administrative system. This is achieved in the Act by s 8(1) and (3), which provide that in any case where there would be jurisdiction to make a maintenance calculation under the CSA 1991 with respect to a qualifying child, on an application duly made by a person entitled to apply for such a calculation with respect to that child, no court shall exercise any power which it would otherwise have, to make, vary or revive any maintenance order (ie an order to make periodical payments), in relation to the child and non-resident parent concerned. In other words, when the CMS has jurisdiction, the general rule is that the courts' powers to make orders for child

---

[77] Welfare Reform Act 2012, s 136, inserting s 9(2A) of the CSA 1991. For the background, see DWP, *Strengthening Families, Promoting Parental Responsibility: The Future of Child Maintenance* (Cm 7990, 2011); DWP, *Government's Response to the Consultation on Strengthening Families, Promoting Parental Responsibility* (Cm 8130, 2011); Work and Pensions Select Committee, *The Government's Proposed Child Maintenance Reforms* (2011).

[78] As inserted by the Welfare Reform Act 2012, s 138.

[79] DWP *Government response to the consultation on the abolition of the Child Maintenance and Enforcement Commission and the transfer of its functions to the Secretary of State for Work and Pensions* (March 2012).

maintenance are paralysed. The relevant statutory provisions still exist but in general they cannot be exercised. In *R (Kehoe) v Secretary of State for Work and Pensions*[80] there was an unsuccessful challenge under the HRA 1998 to the child support scheme's limits to the use of the courts. A mother sought to argue that the legislation was incompatible with her Convention rights under Art 6 of the ECHR. She argued that the effect of the scheme was to deny a parent access to the courts in connection with disputes as to whether the non-resident parent had paid or ought to pay the sums due under a maintenance calculation or as to the manner in which maintenance assessment should be enforced. The House of Lords held that a deliberate feature of the child support legislation was that it was for the Secretary of State to assess and enforce the maintenance obligation to be owed by a non-resident parent to a child. The mother, as parent with care, did have the right to require the Secretary of State to make an assessment and to request him to take steps to enforce the obligation to pay. However, she had no legal right as against the non-resident parent to a child maintenance payment and, therefore, her civil rights under Art 6 were not engaged. Mrs Kehoe was also unsuccessful in her claim when she took the matter to the European Court of Human Rights.[81]

As we shall see later in the chapter, there are some exceptions to the general rule precluding the courts' jurisdiction. But the general rule means that the first question to be asked, in any case in which an issue relating to the provision of financial support for a child arises, must be whether the provisions of the CSA 1991 debar the court from proceeding because there would be jurisdiction to make a maintenance calculation if an application were made under the CSA 1991.

General principles of the child support legislation

Support for parents, not payments to children

The law governing child support has traditionally been concerned with applications by parents and other adults for financial support in respect of a child's maintenance. Only in exceptional circumstances[82] could a child or young person seek financial support by way of court order. The CSA 1991 follows this traditional policy. It makes no provision for a child to seek support but is concerned to define the liability of each parent of a qualifying child to support that child, to assess the amount of periodical payments of maintenance which will be treated as sufficient to discharge the non-resident parent's responsibility for maintaining children, and to provide machinery for enforcing that responsibility. In this context, it is interesting to note that in Scotland a

---

[80] [2005] UKHL 48. For commentary, see N Wikeley 'A Duty but Not a Right: Child Support after *R (Kehoe) v Secretary of State for Work and Pensions*' [2006] *Child and Family Law Quarterly* 287; and S Gilmore (2006) 28(2) *Journal of Social Welfare and Family Law* 180.

[81] *Kehoe v UK* [2008] ECHR 528, [2008] 2 FLR 1014.

[82] See p 445 below.

qualifying child who has attained the age of 12 years may apply for a maintenance assessment in his or her own right.[83]

Child Support Act 1991 concerned only with parent–child obligations

As already noted, the legislation dealing with financial orders relating to children had gradually extended the basis upon which a person was to be treated as having an obligation to support a child, and liability could usually be imposed on anyone who had treated a child as a child of his or her family,[84] with the result that a step-parent would, for example, be liable to maintain a step-child. The CSA 1991, however, is concerned only with the obligations of a parent, and this word is defined to mean any person who is, in law, the mother, father, or otherwise a legal parent of the child.[85] The CSA 1991 is therefore not directly concerned with the liability of step-parents, or others who may have treated children as children of their family.[86] Since around two-fifths of all marriages are now remarriages for at least one of the partners,[87] it is inevitable that there are many cases in which the CSA 1991 has an uneasy relationship with the private law.

Child Support Act 1991 concerned only with income payments

The CSA 1991 is not concerned with capital: it contains no power to require a parent to make capital payments to a child, and it also largely ignores the fact that capital provision – for example, the transfer of a tenancy or other interest in the family home for the benefit of child – may have been made in satisfaction of the child's claims for support.[88] In this respect, the relationship between the new child support system and the older law has become a source of tension.

Two decisions illustrate this concentration on income, and the failure of the CSA 1991 to treat income and capital resources as inter-related.

In *Crozier v Crozier*[89] the divorcing parties had agreed to an all too typical consent order under which the husband was to transfer his interest in the former matrimonial home to the wife in return for being released from any

---

[83]   CSA 1991, s 7(1).
[84]   See p 440 below.
[85]   CSA 1991, s 54.
[86]   Although the presence of step-children or other children in the non-resident parent's household will, under amendments to the calculation, have a significant bearing on the extent of liability. See below.
[87]   For marriages in 2010, 44 per cent of marriages involved at least one partner who was remarrying (Source ONS Table showing previous marital status, released 26 June 2013).
[88]   See *K v K (Minors: Property Transfer)* [1992] 2 FLR 220 (CA).
[89]   [1994] 1 FLR 26. For other cases exploring the relationship between the clean break and child support, see *Mawson v Mawson* [1994] 2 FLR 985 and *Smith v McInerney* [1994] 2 FLR 1077. Specifically on the relationship between lump sum orders and liability for child support, see *AMS v Child Support Officer* [1998] 1 FLR 955. See also *V v V (Child Maintenance)* [2001] 2 FLR 799.

maintenance obligations towards the wife and paying only nominal maintenance for the five-year-old child. The wife had always been in receipt of income support and the Secretary of State for Social Security was content with a contribution of £4 per week in respect of the child from the husband. When the husband subsequently received the documentation from the Child Support Agency it was anticipated that his liability under the CSA 1991 would amount to £29 per week for the child. In these worsened circumstances he applied to have the consent order set aside or varied. Both parties by this time had new partners and, indeed, both had a child of their new relationships.

Booth J refused leave to appeal out of time against the order. The 'clean break' approach which applied in the divorce jurisdiction had no application to *public* obligations to support children arising under the child support legislation. This public liability to maintain children remained on both parents irrespective of their intentions. Although the wife was prepared to assume sole legal liability to maintain the child she could not in fact do so without public assistance. The State was not bound by any agreement between the parties designed to trade off capital provision against liability for child support.

Crozier illustrated the inflexible nature of an income-based scheme which fails to take proper account of capital transfers which in reality might be viewed as a form of capitalised maintenance. This was only partially ameliorated by the reforms introduced by the Child Support Act 1995 regarding 'departure directions' and by provision for 'variations' following the 2000 reforms. *Crozier* was a case in which the father found himself the worse off for having parted with his capital. *Phillips v Peace,*[90] a case decided prior to the introduction of 'departure directions', illustrates the opposite problem – the way in which the child support scheme can be artificially generous to a man who has substantial capital but little or no income. Here, the father successfully owned and operated a company which dealt in shares. He lived in a house worth £2.6 million but, applying the child support formula, it was found that he had no actual income. Hence, a child support assessment could not be made against him. Johnson J said it was absurd that the legislation resulted in the father's liability to support the child being assessed at zero. It was, however, open to the court to order a lump sum for the benefit of the child, exercising its jurisdiction under the Children Act 1989, s 15 and Sch 1. It should not, however, do so in a way designed to provide income, and thereby circumvent the policy of the child support legislation. A lump sum ought only to be ordered to meet the need of the child in respect of a particular item of capital expenditure. A sum of £90,000 was ordered to enable the mother to buy a house plus £24,307.51 for furniture and birth and other expenses.

Child support and the welfare of the child

We noted in chapter 2 that the 'welfare principle' applies in only a limited number of legal contexts and that the weight to be attached to children's

---

90 [1996] 2 FLR 230.

welfare varies depending on the kind of proceedings in question. So far as the child support scheme is concerned, there was a good deal of Government rhetoric about how this was intended to give priority to the interests of children but in fact the statutory commitment on a closer examination is really rather weak. It is provided:[91]

'Where, in any case which falls to be dealt with under this Act, the Secretary of State or any child support officer is considering the exercise of any discretionary power conferred by this Act, he shall have regard to the welfare of any child likely to be affected by his decision.'

Hence, welfare is not the 'first' consideration, let alone the 'paramount' consideration, and it is only in cases where there is any *discretion* that the welfare of the child will be relevant at all. As will be seen, there is little discretion in the child support system, which rather involves the mandatory application of rigid rules, albeit somewhat tempered by the possibility of a 'variation'. Thus the welfare of the child is, in practice, unlikely to play much of a part in the calculation and enforcement of child support. Any redress on the basis that the Child Support Agency or Child Maintenance Service has failed to give any or proper weight to the welfare of the child will be restricted to the limited possibility of a challenge by way of judicial review.[92]

Scheme of the Child Support Act 1991

The underlying principle of the CSA 1991 was said to be that parents have a clear moral duty to maintain their children until they are old enough to look after themselves. Events may change the relationship between the parents but they cannot change their responsibilities towards their children.[93] The CSA 1991 seeks to give effect to this philosophy in several ways: first by providing formulae whereby the liability of parents in respect of their children's maintenance is to be met; secondly by prescribing a nil rate, flat rate and reduced rate where the non-resident parent's income falls below certain prescribed levels; thirdly by conferring wide powers to obtain information on the officials charged with the administration of the CSA 1991; and fourthly by giving wide powers of enforcement and collection in respect of maintenance calculations.

Administration of child support

The Government initially established the Child Support Agency with the responsibility of administering the provisions of the CSA 1991, although the Act itself makes no mention of the Agency. Subsequently, the role of administering child support maintenance was placed in the hands of the non-departmental body called C-MEC, whose remit, as we have seen, has now

---

[91] CSA 1991, s 2.
[92] See *R v Secretary of State for Social Security ex parte Lloyd* [1995] 1 FLR 856 and *R v Secretary of State for Social Security ex parte Biggin* [1995] 1 FLR 851.
[93] *Children Come First* (1990) (Cmnd 1263).

been transferred to the Secretary of State for the Department for Work and Pensions and named the Child Maintenance Service. The CSA 1991 imposes responsibilities and confers powers on the Secretary of State and provides that he shall appoint persons to be known as 'child support officers' for the purposes of the legislation.[94] The responsibility for the administration of the Act therefore remains with a Minister responsible to Parliament.

Liability to maintain: non-resident parents

The underlying principle of the CSA 1991 is that each parent of a 'qualifying child' is responsible for maintaining that child,[95] but a child is only a 'qualifying child' if one or both of his parents is, in relation to him, a "non-resident parent'.[96] This provision underscores the fact that the CSA 1991 is concerned with the situation in which child and parent are living apart. The Act is not concerned to define the level of support appropriate to a child living under the same roof with the parents.

Who is a parent?

The fact that the CSA 1991 is solely concerned to impose obligations on 'parents' has already been mentioned, and the Act states that the term 'parent', in relation to any child, means any person who is, in law, the mother or father of the child[97] (ie including, an adoptive parent, or a person treated as a child's parent under the Human Fertilisation and Embryology Acts 1990 or 2008, as applicable).[98]

---

94   CSA 1991, s 13(1). The Act, under s 15, also empowered the Secretary of State to appoint persons to act as inspectors who have powers of entry, questioning, etc. There is a Chief Child Support Officer who must make an annual report which must be published: CSA 1991, s 13(3)–(5).

95   Ibid, s 1(1).

96   Ibid, s 3(1). The language of the Act was amended by the 2000 legislation to replace the term 'absent parent', which was thought to have pejorative connotations, with the more neutral 'non-resident parent'. The parent of any child is a non-resident parent in relation to him if that parent is not living in the same household with the child, and the child has his home with a person who is, in relation to him, a 'person with care': ibid, s 3(2). A person with care is defined as a person with whom the child has his home and who usually provides day-to-day care for the child, whether exclusively or in conjunction with any other person, and who does not fall within a prescribed category of person: ibid, s 3(3). There can be difficult questions of fact concerning which parent is the 'person with care' where the child is at boarding school, as to which see *C v Secretary of State for Work and Pensions and B* [2003] 1 FLR 829.

97   CSA 1991, s 54.

98   See *Re M (Child Support Act: Parentage)* [1997] 2 FLR 90. In this case, children who were conceived by AID were born in 1981 and 1986 respectively. The Secretary of State sought a declaration of parentage under s 27 of the 1991 Act in relation to the mother's husband on the basis that he had consented to the procedure. The husband denied that he had consented and argued that he was not therefore the 'parent' of the child. Bracewell J found the issue of consent to be immaterial since the status provisions of the 1990 Act did not have retrospective operation and it was clear that the husband was not the genetic father. If these facts were to recur today the matter *would* turn on whether or not the husband consented or objected to the procedure.

The key to liability is therefore having the status of legal parent,[99] and it is to be noted that treating the child as a 'child of the family' for the purposes of the Matrimonial Causes Act 1973 is not sufficient.

Disputes about parentage

We considered in chapter 3 the general principles governing the resolution of disputes as to parentage. There will seldom be any doubt about the identity of the mother but the question of who is the natural father has often been disputed. In chapter 3 we noted the growing phenomenon of men wishing to establish paternity with a view to having contact with their children and perhaps playing a parental role. In the context of support for children, a significant number of men have always sought to evade liability by denying paternity.

The resolution of these disputes is governed by s 26 of the CSA 1991. This was extensively amended by the Child Support, Pensions and Social Security Act 2000.[100] The Act provides that no maintenance calculation may be made where parentage is denied unless the circumstances fall within a number of specified cases.[101] Where, however, the case *does* fall within the specified categories, a calculation may be made notwithstanding the denial of parentage. The prescribed cases are as follows:[102]

(i) where the alleged parent was married to the child's mother at some time between conception and birth;

(ii) where he has been registered as the child's father on the child's birth certificate;[103]

(iii) where a scientific test reveals that there is no reasonable doubt that he is the father or where he refuses to take such a test;

(iv) where the alleged parent has adopted the child;

(v) where he is the legal parent of the child by virtue of an order under s 30 of the Human Fertilisation and Embroyology Act 1990 or s 54 of the Human Fertilisation and Embryology Act 2008;[104]

(vi) where the Secretary of State is satisfied that the alleged parent is the parent of the child under the 'status provisions' in ss 27 and 28 of the

---

[99] See chapter 3 above.
[100] For the detail see N Wikeley 'Child Support, Paternity and Parentage' [2001] Fam Law 125.
[101] Section 26(1).
[102] Section 26(2).
[103] As we noted in chapter 4, this will now also have the consequence that he will acquire parental responsibility, beyond just financial responsibility, for the child. See Children Act 1989, s 4, as amended by the Adoption and Children Act 2002.
[104] See chapter 3 above.

Human Fertilisation and Embryology Act 1990 or any of the ss 33–46 of the Human Fertilisation and Embryology Act 2008;[105]

(vii) where there has been a declaration of parentage under s 55A or 56 of the Family Law Act 1986;[106]

(viii) where the child is in Scotland and one of the presumptions under s 5(1) of the Law Reform (Parent and Child) (Scotland) Act 1986 applies; and

(ix) where the alleged parent has been found or adjudged to be the father of the child in prevous legal proceedings.[107]

Where the case does *not* fall within those enumerated above, s 27 of the CSA 1991 provides that the Secretary of State or the person with care may apply to the court for a declaration of parentage under s 55A of the Family Law Act 1986 to establish whether or not the alleged parent is the parent. The court may direct scientific tests and may draw adverse inferences from failure to submit to them.[108]

The obligation

The CSA 1991 provides that a non-resident parent is, for the purposes of the Act, to be taken to have met his responsibility to maintain any qualifying child of his by making periodical payments of maintenance with respect to the child, in accordance with the provisions of the Act,[109] and it imposes a duty to make such payments on a non-resident parent where a maintenance calculation has been made requiring him to make periodical payments.[110]

The maintenance calculation

Part I of Sch 1 to the CSA 1991 as amended contains the general rule that the weekly rate of child support maintenance is to be the 'basic rate' unless a 'reduced rate', a 'flat rate' or the 'nil rate' applies.[111]

---

[105] See chapter 3 above.
[106] See chapter 3 above.
[107] See *R v Secretary of State for Social Security ex parte West* [1999] 1 FLR 1233 and *R v Secretary of State for Social Security ex parte W* [1999] 2 FLR 604.
[108] For further discussion of the principles applying to the direction of tests, see chapter 3 above. And for an example of such an adverse inference being drawn, see *Secretary of State for Work and Pensions v Jones* [2004] 1 FLR 282. Here it was held by Dame Elizabeth Butler-Sloss P that the justices had erred in concluding that the presumption that the child was the legitimate child of the mother's husband had not been rebutted. Although the mother had become reconciled with her husband, she had also had a relationship with another man and had applied for a maintenance assessment under the Child Support Agency against him. The man had refused to comply with a direction for DNA testing and refused to attend court on any occasion. An extension of the time-limit to appeal against the magistrates' determination was granted.
[109] CSA 1991, s 1(2).
[110] Ibid, s 1(3).
[111] Schedule 1, para 1(1).

The basic rate

The basic rate is expressed as a percentage of the non-resident parent's gross weekly income.[112] For income of £200 or over up to a ceiling of £800, the percentages are 12 per cent for one qualifying child, 16 per cent for two qualifying children and 19 per cent where there are three or more qualifying children. For weekly income over £800 up to £3,000, the respective percentages are 9, 12 and 15. Any income above £3,000 is to be ignored.[113] The courts, however, retain their jurisdiction to make 'top up' orders in cases involving wealthy parents, where appropriate.[114] Secondly, the Act now makes substantial allowance for 'relevant other children' living with the non-resident parent. It was a widespread criticism of the original formulae that they were insufficiently sensitive to the new obligations which the non-resident parent might have acquired in a reconstituted family in which his new partner had children. The amended scheme takes into account responsibilities for step-children and the children of cohabitants and, in so doing, mirrors the percentages applicable to the non-resident parent's own children.[115] Thus, where there are other relevant children, the appropriate percentages will instead be applied to gross weekly income *less* 12 per cent for one relevant other child, 16 per cent for two and 19 per cent where there are three or more relevant other children. In this way the Act attempts to provide some sort of parity in the obligations of natural and social parenthood and some sort of equality of treatment for the various children concerned, although it still results in a relative preference for the natural family. This is perhaps in contrast to the original clearly stated policy which was to the effect that the obligations to the 'first family' and to natural children should receive priority.

The reduced rate

A reduced rate is payable where the non-resident parent's weekly income is less than £200 but more than £100, and neither the nil rate nor the flat rate applies. The rate is on a sliding scale and is calculated by adding to the flat rate of £7, the non-resident parent's weekly income and then applying a percentage to the resulting figure which takes into account both the number of qualifying children and other relevant children.[116]

The flat rate

The flat rate[117] of £7 applies where the non-resident parent's weekly income is £100 or less and the non-resident parent is receiving prescribed benefits or has a partner who is, provided that the nil rate does not apply.

---

[112] Child Maintenance and Other Payments Act 2008, Sch 4, para 2.
[113] CSA 1991, Sch 1, para 10(3).
[114] CSA 1991, s 8(6).
[115] Schedule 1, para 2(2).
[116] Child Support Maintenance Calculation Regulations 2012 (SI 2012/2677), reg 43, as amended by the Child Support and Claims and Payments (Miscellaneous Amendments and Change to the Minimum Amount of Liability) Regulations 2013 (SI 2013/1654).
[117] Paragraph 4 of Sch 4, and para 1(28) of Sch 7, to the Child Maintenance and Other Payments

The nil rate

The nil rate[118] applies to certain prescribed categories of non-resident parents, viz students, children under 16, prisoners, 16- and 17-year-olds where they or their partners are in receipt of certain welfare benefits (discussed below), patients in hospital, and those in residential care homes or nursing homes who are in receipt of certain benefits. In each case the gross weekly income must be less than £7.

The effect of shared care on the rates

The scheme also makes allowance for responsibilities, especially financial responsibilities, arising from the non-resident parent's own children spending substantial periods of time with him. Some allowance for this was made under the old scheme[119] but the new formula takes greater account of shared care.[120] The threshold for the decrease in liability is now 52 nights and the amount of the decrease depends on the number of nights the qualifying child spends with the non-resident parent. The basic or reduced rate is decreased by the following fractions: 52–103 nights, one-seventh; 104–155 nights, two-sevenths; 156–174 nights, three-sevenths and 175 nights or more, one-half.

These decreases go some way to recognising the expense incurred by the non-resident parent while the children are with him and that the parent with care is relieved of some of the financial burden of raising children while they are not with her. It is only possible to speculate on whether the change will result in greater enthusiasm for exercising contact with children. In any event, it is arguable that the new scheme does give official recognition to the association between contact with and financial responsibility for children.[121] This connection has often been denied, although there is at least some empirical evidence from the USA to suggest that it does exist in fact.[122]

Act 2008, and see also the Child Support and Claims and Payments (Miscellaneous Amendments and Change to the Minimum Amount of Liability) Regulations 2013 (SI 2013/1654).

[118]   Schedule 1, para 5.

[119]   Maintenance liability was apportioned where each parent cared for the child in excess of 104 nights per annum.

[120]   CSA 1991, Sch 1, paras 7, 8 and 9.

[121]   Although the Court of Appeal has held that the effect upon child support liability of the quantum of contact should not be taken into account when deciding on contact arrangements: see *Re B (Contact: Child Support)* [2006] EWCA Civ 1574, [2007] 1 FLR 1949. For criticism of the case and discussion of the connection between contact and child support, see S Gilmore 'Re B (Contact: Child Support) – Horses and Carts: Contact and Child Support' [2007] CFLQ 357.

[122]   See J Seltzer 'Child Support and Child Access' in JT Oldham and MS Melli *Child Support: the Next Frontier* (University of Michigan Press, 2000), at p 69.

Variations

The objective of the child support scheme from the start has been to produce a mathematically fair system for determining individual financial liability for children. At the same time it has been recognised that there would be a small number of exceptional or unusual cases in which justice requires some adjustments of an otherwise rigid formula.

The original scheme had made provision for so-called 'special cases', but where these arose they involved applying another fixed formula. As we have seen, the Child Support Act 1995 introduced 'departure directions'[123] which have been renamed 'variations' under the new scheme.[124] The specified cases under which a variation may be made follow closely the pattern of the former departure directions but are not identical and are somewhat more tightly drafted.

Under s 28F the Secretary of State may agree a variation if he is satisfied that the case falls within those specified and 'it is his opinion that, in all the circumstances of the case, it would be just and equitable to agree to a variation'.[125] In reaching this decision the Secretary of State 'must have regard, in particular, to the welfare of any child likely to be affected if he did agree to a variation' and *must* or *must not* take certain prescribed factors into account.[126] The factors which must not be taken into account are set out in the regulations[127] and are fascinating as an illustration of the underlying philosophy of the whole scheme. Thus, for example, the Secretary of State must not take into account, in determining what is just and equitable, that the conception of the qualifying child was not planned by one or both of the parents; whether either parent was responsible for the breakdown of the relationship between them; the fact that either of them had formed a new relationship with another person; the existence of particular arrangements for contact with the qualifying child and whether they are being adhered to, and so on. One way of looking at these factors would be to see them as an attempt by the State to be 'morally neutral' as regards the making and breaking of relationships and the circumstances surrounding pregnancy. We return to the question of the fundamental basis of liability for child support below.[128]

The detail of the specified cases where variations are permitted is beyond the scope of the present work. But in essence they fall into two groups: those which will tend towards a reduction in liability; and those which will tend towards an

---

[123] For the then Conservative Government's reasoning, see *Improving Child Support* (1995) (Cm 2745).
[124] The details of the new system of variations are to be found in Sch 4B to the CSA 1991, and the Child Support Maintenance Calculation Regulations 2012 (SI 2012/2677).
[125] CSA 1991, s 28F(1).
[126] Ibid, s 28F(2).
[127] Child Support Maintenance Calculation Regulations 2012 (SI 2012/2677), reg 60.
[128] See p 457.

increased liability. The first category includes so-called 'special expenses'[129] and relates to such things as costs associated with maintaining contact with a child; expenses incurred in relation to another relevant child who has long-term illness or disability; prior debts; boarding school expenses; and mortgage payments in relation to the former family home. It also includes 'property or capital transfers'[130] which took place before the CSA 1991 came into effect on 5 April 1993 and will therefore apply to a decreasing number of cases in future. These are transfers which were made on the understanding that they would relieve a parent of liability to make maintenance payments for the children. The second category, known as 'additional cases',[131] includes where the non-resident parent has assets which exceed a prescribed value; a person's lifestyle is inconsistent with his income; a person has income which is not taken into account in the calculation of child maintenance; and a person has unreasonably reduced the income which is taken into account in the calculation.

Revisions

The legislation contains provisions to enable decisions, once made, to be revised periodically and also to be revised if there is a change of circumstances.[132]

Assessment will be made only on application

If (but only if) a maintenance calculation has been made, the non-resident parent is required to make payments. An application for a maintenance calculation can be made pursuant to s 4 of the CSA 1991. However, it is important to understand that there is no general obligation on a person who has care of children to apply for a maintenance calculation against a non-resident parent:[133] the CSA 1991 does not prevent parents from settling their financial affairs by agreement.[134] Indeed, as noted earlier, the policy now is to encourage parents to make private arrangements.

---

[129] See Sch 4B, para 2, and the Child Support Maintenance Calculation Regulations 2012 (SI 201/2677), regs 63–68 and 72.

[130] Schedule 4B, para 3.

[131] Schedule 4B, paras 4 and 5, and the Child Support Maintenance Calculation Regulations 2012 (SI 2012/2677), regs 69–71 and 73.

[132] CSA 1991, ss 16 and 17, as amended.

[133] The obligation to make payments is found in the provisions of the CSA 1991 which state that where a maintenance calculation made under the Act requires the making of periodical payments it is the duty of the non-resident parent to make those payments (s 1(3)), and payments of child support maintenance under the calculation are to be made in accordance with regulations made by the Secretary of State (s 29(2)).

[134] Section 9(2) of the CSA 1991 provides that nothing in the Act should be taken to prevent any person from entering into a maintenance agreement.

Agreements and the Agency's jurisdiction

Although there is no reason why a couple should not agree on the financial arrangements to be made for their children, it is expressly provided that the existence of a maintenance agreement[135] shall not prevent any party to the agreement (or any other person) from applying for a maintenance calculation with respect to any child to whom or for whose benefit periodical payments are to be made or secured under the agreement. Any provision in an agreement which purports to exclude the right to apply for a maintenance calculaton is void.[136] In practice, therefore, every parent must assume that he or she may be made to support the children by way of periodical income payments up to the amount of any maintenance calculation which could be made under the CSA 1991. There are some exceptions to this general rule. No application can be made where there is in force: a written maintenance agreement made before 5 April 1993 (ie, before the CSA 1991 was first implemented);[137] or a maintenance order made before 3 March 2003;[138] or if a maintenance order made on or after the date 3 March 2003 is in force but has been so for less than the period of one year beginning with the date on which it was made.[139]

Information

The Secretary of State has extensive powers[140] to require a non-resident parent and a person with care to give information on a wide range of matters to enable the absent parent to be identified, and the maintenance calculation computed. There are also powers to require employers, local authorities and others to give information. Inspectors may be appointed[141] who have power to enter at all reasonable times any specified premises (other than premises used solely as a dwelling house) and any other premises used by a specified person for the purpose of carrying on any trade, profession, vocation or business, and to make such examination and enquiry there as the inspector considers appropriate. Any person who is, or has been, an occupier of the premises in question, or an employee, is required to furnish the inspector with all such information and documents as the inspector may reasonably require, and it is a criminal offence intentionally to delay or obstruct any inspector exercising those powers, or (without reasonable excuse) to refuse or neglect to answer any question or furnish any information or produce any document which is required under the provisions of the CSA 1991. These powers enable the Child Support Agency or

---

[135] Defined as any agreement for making or for securing the making of periodical payments by way of maintenance to or for the benefit of any child: s 9(1) of the CSA 1991.

[136] Ibid, s 9(4).

[137] Ibid, s 4(10)(a).

[138] Child Support (Applications: Prescribed Date) Regulations 2003 (SI 2003/194), reg 10(1)(a).

[139] CSA 1991, s 4(10)(aa).

[140] CSA 1991, s 14. Failure to provide required information, or providing false information is an offence: see s 14A.

[141] CSA 1991, s 15(1).

the Child Maintenance Service to trace non-resident parents, investigate their means, and exercise the powers[142] of collection and enforcement given to the authorities by the CSA 1991.

Information held by the Agency or Service is confidential and not to be disclosed without lawful authority.[143] It has been held that the courts have no power under the Act to give leave to, or direct, the Secretary of State to disclose information to a child as to his father's whereabouts. A court may, however, *request* the Secretary of State to disclose it in the context of an application for a s 8 order.[144]

Collection and enforcement

The CSA 1991 contains exceptionally wide powers of collection and enforcement.[145] Among the methods of enforcement, there is power to require a person, from whom payments are due under a maintenance calculation, to make them by way of direct debit or standing order,[146] and the Secretary of State may – without having to obtain any court order – require an employer to make deductions from earnings in order to satisfy a maintenance calculation.[147] However, there is a protected earnings rate, below which the employer must not reduce the payments made to the employee. There is also power to order a deposit taker (such as a bank or building society) to deduct regular payments from, for example, a bank account,[148] or to order deduction of a lump sum from the same.[149]

If there is a failure by a liable person to make a payment of child support and it appears to be 'inappropriate' to make a deduction of earnings order – for example because the person concerned is not in employment, or because such an order has proved ineffective[150] – the Secretary of State may apply to the magistrates for a liability order.[151] The magistrates' court is required to make

---

[142] See below.

[143] CSA 1991, s 50.

[144] *Re C (A Minor) (Child Support Agency: Disclosure)* [1995] 1 FLR 201.

[145] Sections 29–41E of the CSA 1991; and the Child Support (Collection and Enforcement) Regulations 1992 (SI 1992/1989), as amended by the Child Support (Collection and Enforcement and Miscellaneous Amendments) Regulations 2000 (SI 2001/162), and Child Support Collection and Enforcement (Deduction Orders) Amendment Regulations 2009 (SI 2009/1815). See generally N Wikeley 'Compliance, Enforcement and Child Support' [2000] Fam Law 888.

[146] Child Support (Collection and Enforcement) Regulations 1992 (SI 1992/1989), Part II.

[147] Sections 31–32 of the 1991 Act. It has been held that disputes relating to quantification or validity of a maintenance calculation, in which it is alleged that a deduction of earnings order was defective, are to be dealt with through the review and appeal structure under the child support legislation and are outside the jurisdiction of the magistrates' court. See *Secretary of State for Social Security v Shotton and Others* [1996] 2 FLR 241.

[148] CSA 1991, s 32A.

[149] Ibid, ss 32E and 32F.

[150] Ibid, s 33.

[151] Such an order was found to be necessary and proportionate for the purposes of the ECHR in *R (Denson) v Child Support Agency* [2002] EWHC 154 (Admin), [2002] 1 FLR 938.

such an order if the court is satisfied that the payments in question have become payable and have not been paid. Apparently, following the precedent of the community charge legislation, the making of a liability order confers on the authorities a wide range of enforcement powers. In particular, distress may be levied,[152] and it appears to be the intention to use distress in preference to other procedures.[153] If distress (or other enforcement procedure) fails, the Secretary of State may apply to the magistrates' court for an order committing the liable person to prison, and the court may commit the defaulter to prison if, but only if, it is of the opinion that he has been guilty of wilful refusal or culpable neglect.[154] Alternatively, in such circumstances the court can order disqualification from holding or obtaining a driving licence for a period up to two years.[155]

In addition, the Act provides[156] for 'penalty payments' to be made where arrears have accumulated but these must not exceed 25 per cent of the amount of child support payable for the week in question. The potential disqualification from driving is a Draconian measure which has been tried in other jurisdictions. Indeed, some have gone further. The city of Buenos Aires, for example, adopted a policy of 'naming and shaming' recalcitrant parents in a public register (the *Registro de Deudores Morosos*).[157] Consequences of being so named include restrictions on the ability of the debtor to open bank accounts or obtain credit cards. There are undoubtedly civil libertarian objections to such measures, but they do illustrate how far the State might be able to go if it attached a high enough priority to enforcement of child support liability.

The residual role of the court in relation to financial provision for children

As noted above, the general rule is that where the Secretary of State would have jurisdiction to make a maintenance calculation, the court is debarred from exercising any power which it would otherwise have[158] to make, vary or revive

---

[152] CSA 1991, s 35; Child Support (Collection and Enforcement) Regulations 1992 (SI 1992/1989), regs 30–32.

[153] A garnishee or charging order may be sought in the county court: CSA 1991, s 36.

[154] CSA 1991, s 40(3). The maximum period of imprisonment is six weeks: ibid, s 40(7).

[155] CSA 1991, ss 39A and 40B.

[156] Ibid, s 41A.

[157] See C Grosman and DB Inigo 'Non-Payment of a Maintenance Obligation: New Rules, Judicial Decisions and Initiatives in Argentina' in A Bainham (ed) *The International Survey of Family Law (2001 Edition)* (Family Law, 2001).

[158] See *R (Kehoe) v Secretary of State for Work and Pensions* [2005] UKHL 489 (discussed earlier), and *Department of Social Security v Butler* [1996] 1 FLR 65, in which the Court of Appeal said that the Child Support Act provided a complete code for assessing and enforcing the financial responsibility of absent parents. This was a comprehensive legislative scheme which left no lacuna to be filled by the High Court's jurisdiction, in this case to grant a *Mareva* injunction. For a brief discussion of the relationship between the courts' powers to award child maintenance and the statutory child support scheme, see J Pirrie 'The Courts and Child Maintenance' [2003] Fam Law 431. For the argument in favour of a judicial system of child

any maintenance order, ie an order for *periodical* payments[159] in relation to the child and non-resident parent concerned.[160] The court may, however, revoke a maintenance order,[161] and there are certain circumstances in which the court may still have a role. First, the court has power to make an order if the maximum child maintenance calculation is in force,[162] provided that the court is satisfied that the circumstances of the case make it appropriate for the non-resident parent to make, or secure the making of, periodical payments in addition to those under the assessment. Secondly, the court may exercise its powers to make an order in cases where the child is, will be or (if the order were to be made) would be receiving instruction or training requiring provision of some or all of the expenses incurred in connection with the provision of the instruction or training.[163] Thirdly, in cases where a child is disabled, orders may be made to meet some or all of the expenses attributable to the child's disability.[164] Fourthly, the court may exercise its powers to make orders in the case of 17- and 18-year-olds who are not in full-time education;[165] and the Bar on making periodical payments orders does not apply if, for any reason, the Secretary of State has no jurisdiction to make a maintenance calculation – perhaps, for example, because the non-resident parent is not habitually resident in this country. The court may also make periodical payment orders against the

---

support, see H Xanthaki 'The judiciary-based system of child support in Germany, France and Greece – an effective suggestion?' (2000) JSWFL 295.

[159] Orders for lump sum payments or other capital transfers are not within this definition.

[160] Section 8(1) and (3) of the 1991 Act. 'Maintenance order' is defined in s 8(11) of the 1991 Act to mean an order which requires the making or securing of periodical payments under: Part II of the Matrimonial Causes Act 1973; the Domestic Proceedings and Magistrates' Courts Act 1978; Part III of the Matrimonial and Family Proceedings Act 1984; Sch 1 to the Children Act 1989; or any other prescribed enactment.

[161] CSA 1991, s 8(4).

[162] Ibid, s 8(6). See S Mahmood and C Hallam 'Schedule 1 and the CSA: Getting into the Top-up Zone' [2011] Fam Law 266.

[163] Ibid, s 8(7).

[164] Ibid, s 8(8), (9). See *C v F (Disabled Child: Maintenance Orders)* [1998] 1 FLR 151 in which Sir Stephen Brown P upheld a magistrates' order that the father pay £190 per month to the mother for the benefit of the seriously disabled child. This represented the difference between the mother's total monthly expenditure attributable to the child's disability (£820) and what she actually received by way of disability benefit (£630). He held that the magistrates had been right to conclude that jurisdiction to make the order derived from the CSA 1991, although the application itself was made under Sch 1 to the Children Act. Accordingly, he held that the order could not extend beyond the child's nineteenth birthday by virtue of s 55 of the 1991 Act. However, the Court of Appeal, at [1998] 2 FLR 1, allowed the mother's appeal both as to the duration of the order and as to the calculation of the appropriate amount. It held that s 8(8) did not restrict the court to making a 'top-up' order but allowed it to make a freestanding order under the Children Act. The age restriction of 19 which applied under the CSA 1991 did not apply to such Children Act maintenance orders and therefore the order could extend beyond the child's nineteenth birthday. In calculating the appropriate maintenance, the magistrates had taken too narrow a view. They should have taken the broadest view of expenses, including costs associated with, for example, additional help, feeding those providing such additional help, a larger house, heating, clothing, running a car and respite care. The case was remitted to the family proceedings court for reconsideration on this basis.

[165] Such persons are not within the CSA 1991 definition of 'child': see s 55(1).

parent with care; and the court also has power[166] to make an order giving effect to a written agreement between the parties. It is, therefore, still open to a couple to make an overall financial settlement to be embodied in a consent order, and as we have seen there are only limited circumstances in which such an order or agreement can prevent a parent with care subsequently applying for child support maintenance.[167] The court also retains jurisdiction to vary a maintenance order where application for a maintenance calculation is not possible.[168]

As noted earlier, it is no longer possible to prevent an application for a maintenance calculation by the Child Support Agency to be made, because of a court order for maintenance, for more than the period of one year.[169] Private settlements will need to be negotiated in future in the knowledge that there may well be a subsequent application to the Child Maintenance Service and that child support liability will normally be imposed at the basic rate. This may effectively remove much of the existing latitude to reach private agreements and to determine the level of child support in private cases as part of an overall post-divorce package.

The hiving off of one important component in such settlements in this way has been criticised by Wilson J in *V v V (Child Maintenance)*[170] where he referred to the 'unsatisfactory interface between the jurisdictions' of the Child Support Agency and the courts. The key point is that the level of child support influences the content of other parts of the settlement and that there was an absurdity in the court, which has its 'hard-won' possession of all relevant material, having to leave out of account one vital element in this – namely child support. At least the new simplified rates should mean that the courts will be able to predict child support liability with rather greater certainty, and settlements will need to reflect this.

The court's powers in respect of lump sums and property adjustment

The CSA 1991 does not affect the court's power to make orders for lump sums, or transfers or settlements of property.

---

[166] CSA 1991, s 8(5); the Child Maintenance (Written Agreements) Order 1993 (SI 1993/620).
[167] See p 433 above.
[168] See CSA 1991, s 8(3A).
[169] CSA 1991, s 4(10)(aa).
[170] [2001] 2 FLR 799.

THE COURTS' POWERS TO MAKE FINANCIAL ORDERS FOR THE BENEFIT OF CHILDREN

Although the scope for the exercise of the courts' powers to make financial orders in respect of children is now greatly restricted, the powers themselves still exist and may, on occasion, be exercised. A brief account must therefore be given here.

The Children Act 1989 introduced a considerable measure of simplification and rationalisation into the law governing the circumstances in which the court may, in the exercise of its discretion, make financial orders intended to benefit children, but the situation is still somewhat complex. It is most easily understood on the basis that the law draws a distinction between divorce and other matrimonial proceedings, on the one hand, and applications by one partner against the other under the provisions of the Children Act, on the other.

Powers exercisable in matrimonial proceedings

Most orders about children were,[171] as the Law Commission pointed out,[172] made in the course of divorce or other matrimonial proceedings. Since the provisions relating to children could not readily be separated from those relating to adults, the statutory provisions enabling the court to make financial orders for children in divorce and other matrimonial proceedings are still contained in the relevant statutes dealing with the matrimonial proceedings.

Divorce is far and away the most important of these proceedings,[173] but it should also be mentioned that either party to a marriage may apply to the court for an order, on the ground that the other spouse has failed to provide or make a proper contribution towards reasonable maintenance for any child of the family.[174] If that ground is made out, the court has power to order either periodical payments (secured or unsecured) or payment of a lump sum. Furthermore, either party to a marriage may apply to the family proceedings court for an order – for periodical payments or a lump sum (not exceeding £1,000) – under the Domestic Proceedings and Magistrates' Courts Act 1978. The grounds are that the respondent: (a) has failed to provide reasonable maintenance for the applicant; or (b) has failed to provide, or make a proper contribution towards, reasonable maintenance for any child of the family; or (c) has behaved in such a way that the applicant cannot reasonably be expected to live with the other party; or (d) has deserted the applicant. It was intended that the last two grounds, which are redolent of the old matrimonial offence doctrine, would be repealed by the Family Law Act 1996. But the divorce aspects of that legislation were never brought into force and are expected to be

---

[171] Ie prior to the coming into force of the CSA 1991.
[172] Law Com No 172 *Guardianship and Custody* (1988), at para 1.8.
[173] See below.
[174] Matrimonial Causes Act 1973, s 27.

finally repealed by the Children and Families Bill 2013. Matrimonial offences therefore remain a basis for obtaining a decree of divorce and also for financial orders in the magistrates' court. These provisions are, however, rarely relevant after the coming into force of the CSA 1991.[175]

Powers of the divorce court: provision for parents and children

Provision for children may be either direct or indirect. The court has extensive powers to make orders in favour of the parties, and for the benefit of the children. The Matrimonial Causes Act 1973 provides that, in the exercise of these financial powers,[176] it is the duty of the court, in deciding to exercise its powers and, if so, in what manner, 'to have regard to all the circumstances of the case ... first consideration being given to the welfare while a minor of any child of the family who has not attained the age of 18'.[177] This statutory directive recognises that the financial position of children and their parents is inter-related. It has been said, for example, that it is not in the children's interest that their mother be in straitened circumstances[178] and it may, accordingly, be thought appropriate to make an order for periodical payments in favour of a wife so as to enable her the better to care for the children.[179] Again, the court may consider that this provision requires it to ensure that the children's housing needs are protected, and this may often best be done by making an order for the transfer of the house to the parent with whom the child is to live, or for settlement of the house on terms that it is not sold during the parent's lifetime, or the children's dependency.[180]

The fact that orders in favour of parents may indirectly benefit their children assumed a new significance following the coming into force of the CSA 1991. The divorce court is still required, in exercising its financial powers, to give first consideration to the welfare of children of the family who have not attained the age of 18 years, and the CSA 1991 imposes no restriction on the exercise of powers to make orders against parents.

---

[175] For fuller consideration, see JM Masson and R Bailey-Harris and RJ Probert *Cretney's Principles of Family Law* (8th edn, Sweet & Maxwell, 2008), at p 99, para 3–014 et seq.

[176] Ie the power to make financial provision orders (divorce, nullity and judicial separation): s 23; property adjustment orders: s 24; the power to order sale of the property: s 24A; and pension-sharing orders (divorce and nullity only): s 24B.

[177] Matrimonial Causes Act 1973, s 25(1), as substituted by the Matrimonial and Family Proceedings Act 1984, s 3.

[178] See *E v E (Financial Provision)* [1990] 2 FLR 233, at 249.

[179] See *Waterman v Waterman* [1989] 1 FLR 380 (CA).

[180] The so-called *Mesher* and *Martin* orders. Such orders will not, however, be appropriate where it is doubted that the parent with care of the children (usually the mother) will be able to raise sufficient capital to rehouse herself at the end of the period or 'trigger' prescribed by the order for sale of the home. For an example, see *B v B (Mesher Order)* [2003] 2 FLR 285.

Meaning of 'child of the family'

The court's powers and duties in divorce proceedings[181] arise in respect of any child of the family, and this term is defined,[182] in relation to the parties to a marriage, to mean a child of both those parties, and any other child (not being a child who has been placed with those parties as foster parents by a local authority or voluntary organisation) who has been treated by both of those parties as a child of their family.

This definition therefore brings within the category of children of the family all children who have been 'treated' as a child of the family – apart from those placed as foster children[183] – and makes the existence of a biological[184] (or even a formal legal relationship such as adoption) between the child and the parties irrelevant. A step-child living with a married couple is the classic example of a child of the family who is not the child of both spouses. Of course, such a step-child also remains a 'child of the family' in respect of his birth parents, and the broad definition thus accurately reflects the erosion of traditional kinship patterns incidental to increasing divorce and remarriage: a child may have biological and/or factual links with several different marriages and may move in and out of several households.[185]

The one limitation which has been placed on the scope of the definition is that it has been held to be impossible to treat an unborn child as a child of the family: if a man marries a woman who is pregnant by someone else, the baby will be a child of their family if the husband treats it as such after birth – even if only for a very short time and even if the wife has deceived him into thinking that he is the father – but if the relationship breaks down before the birth, the child will be outside the definition, whatever the husband may have said about his intentions to treat the baby as his own.[186]

Orders the court may make

The court is given wide (but not limitless) powers. It can, subject to the restrictions imposed by the CSA 1991, make periodical payment orders.

Those orders may be either in favour of the other party to the marriage[187] or they may direct payments to the child or to someone else on his behalf for the

---

[181] And in most of the other proceedings mentioned in this chapter.

[182] Matrimonial Causes Act 1973, s 52.

[183] The implication is that the local authority or voluntary organisation will be responsible for the provision of financial support for the child.

[184] Or a relationship created by law by operation of the provisions of the Human Fertilisation and Embryology Acts 1990 or 2008 (as the case may be).

[185] For an illuminating study of the nature of the parental obligation as children move between households during the course of their minority, see M Maclean and J Eekelaar *The Parental Obligation* (Hart Publishing, 1997).

[186] *A v A (Family: Unborn Child)* [1974] Fam 6.

[187] Matrimonial Causes Act 1973, s 23(1)(a) and (b).

benefit of a child of the family[188] – and they may be either secured or unsecured.[189] The court may also order the payment of a lump sum or sums by one spouse to the other[190] or a payment for the benefit of a child of the family to the child or to someone else on his behalf.[191]

The court may also order the transfer of specified property to the other party, or to a child, or to a third party on a child's behalf.[192] It may order the settlement of such property for the benefit of the other party and/or of the children of the family[193] and it may make an order varying any 'ante-nuptial or post-nuptial' settlement made on the parties to the marriage for the benefit of the parties to the marriage and/or of the children of the family.[194]

If the court makes a secured periodical payments order, a lump sum, or a property adjustment order, it may also order the sale of any property in which one or both of the parties has a beneficial interest.[195]

Factors influencing the exercise of the court's discretion

As has already been seen, the court is required, in the exercise of all these powers, to give first consideration to the welfare, while a minor, of any child of the family who has not attained the age of 18 years. However, notwithstanding this requirement, there was some evidence that, in the past, the courts have underestimated the cost of maintaining children. It seems that orders for conventional sums (rarely exceeding £20 weekly in respect of each child) were often made. In an attempt to remedy this situation, the courts were given details of the income support scale rates for children's requirements, produced by the National Foster Care Association (which were designed to show the actual cost of bringing up a child) and the rates actually paid by local authorities to foster parents.[196] In practice, however, there will now be little need to refer to such scales since the rates of child support as a proportion of the non-resident

---

[188] Ibid, s 23(1)(d) and (e).

[189] Ibid, s 23(1)(b) and (e).

[190] Ibid, s 23(1)(c).

[191] Ibid, s 23(1)(f). It is specifically provided that an order for payment of a lump sum to the other spouse may be made for the purpose of enabling that other party to meet any liabilities or expenses reasonably incurred in maintaining any child of the family before making an application for an order, or for meeting any liabilities or expenses reasonably incurred by or for the benefit of the child of the family: ibid, s 23(3)(a) and (b).

[192] Ibid, s 24(1)(a).

[193] Ibid, s 24(1)(b).

[194] Ibid, s 24(1)(c). The court may also make an order extinguishing or reducing the interest of either of the parties to the marriage under any such settlement, s 24(1)(d).

[195] Ibid, s 24A.

[196] Information about these scales should have been of real value to the court because, as Simon Brown J put it in *Cresswell v Eaton* [1991] 1 All ER 484 at 489, 'although not insubstantial, [the payments] are paid entirely by way of reimbursement of the expense incurred in maintaining children: food, clothing, heating, travel and so forth. The underlying philosophy of the fostering scheme is that it should not be undertaken for gain. There is thus no profit to be made from such payments, no reward for a personal care involved in fostering children'.

parent's income under the amended child support scheme should provide the baseline for any consideration of a child's needs.

Limited focus on child welfare

The legislation does not make the welfare of the children the 'paramount' consideration. It has been said that the court must simply consider all the circumstances, always bearing the children's welfare in mind, and then try to make a financial settlement which is *just* as between husband and wife.[197]

For example, in *Suter v Suter and Jones*,[198] an order had been made on the basis that the husband should pay the whole of the wife's mortgage outgoings. This was done because preservation of the home was considered necessary to ensure the welfare of the children. The Court of Appeal held that the court should have taken account of the fact that the wife had a cohabitant who could have been expected to make a contribution, and that the court had been wrong to attach overriding importance to the child's welfare.

Since the House of Lords decision in *White v White*[199] it has been the overall objective of the courts in exercising their discretion to achieve 'fairness' and a result which avoids discrimination between husband and wife. Nonetheless, the courts must still apply the statutory criteria which include giving first consideration to the welfare of any minor children and factors relating to children might still influence the question of fairness. For example, in *Cordle v Cordle*[200] the Court of Appeal found that the circuit judge had erred in failing to recognise the husband's continuing liability to maintain the children.

Circumstances to be considered

It is now provided that, as regards the exercise of its powers to make periodical payment orders, transfer of property orders or orders for the sale of property and pension-sharing orders in relation to a child of the family, the court should have regard to all the circumstances of the case and, in particular, to a list of specific matters which (it has been said) cover almost every conceivable factor.[201] These specified matters are as follows:[202]

'(a) the financial needs of the child;
(b) the income, earning capacity (if any), property and other financial resources of the child;
(c) any physical or mental disability of the child;
(d) the manner in which he was being and in which the parties to the marriage expected him to be educated or trained;

---

[197] *Suter v Suter and Jones* [1987] 2 FLR 232.
[198] [1987] 2 FLR 232.
[199] [2001] 1 AC 596.
[200] [2002] 1 FLR 207.
[201] *Mortimer v Mortimer-Griffin* [1986] 2 FLR 315, at 318 per Sir John Donaldson MR.
[202] Matrimonial Causes Act 1973, s 25(3).

(e)   the considerations mentioned in relation to the parties to the marriage in paragraphs (a), (b), (c) and (e) of section 25(2) of the Matrimonial Causes Act 1973 [ie their financial resources, financial needs, the standard of living enjoyed by the family before the breakdown and any disability of either party to the marriage].'

Orders against step-parents and others

As pointed out above,[203] financial orders may be made against a spouse in respect of any child of the family, and this term is very broadly defined. The legislation seeks to structure the court's discretion by providing that, with regard to the exercise of its financial powers against the party to a marriage in favour of a child of the family who is not the child of that party, the court is also to have regard to the following specified matters:[204]

'(a)   to whether that party assumed any responsibility for the child's maintenance, and, if so, to the extent to which, and the basis upon which, that party assumed such responsibility and to the length of time for which that party discharged such responsibility;

(b)   to whether in assuming and discharging such responsibility that party did so knowing that the child was not his or her own;

(c)   to the liability of any other person to maintain the child.'

Applications by a child in parents' divorce proceedings

The divorce legislation is primarily concerned with applications by one spouse for an order against the other, but it has been held that a child of the family who has attained the age of 18 years may make an application for financial relief by intervening in the parents' matrimonial proceedings – notwithstanding the fact that the decree may perhaps have been granted many years ago.[205] Such a child may also intervene to seek a variation of an existing order.[206]

Duration of orders and age limits

The general rule in the divorce legislation as to duration of orders (which is subject to some exceptions) is as follows.

(1)   Financial provision orders and transfer of property orders cannot be made in respect of a child who has attained the age of 18.[207]

---

[203]   See p 440.

[204]   Matrimonial Causes Act 1973, s 25(4).

[205]   *Downing v Downing (Downing Intervening)* [1976] Fam 288. However, the court can make orders continuing after a child's eighteenth birthday only if the child is receiving education or training or there are special circumstances: see below.

[206]   Matrimonial Causes Act 1973, s 31.

[207]   Ibid, s 29(1). A child attains a particular age at the commencement of the relevant anniversary of his birth: Family Law Reform Act 1969, s 9.

(2) Periodical financial provision (whether secured or unsecured, and whether in nullity, divorce, judicial separation or failure to maintain proceedings) will not, in the first instance, be ordered beyond the child's attaining the upper limit of compulsory school age.[208] However, the court may extend the obligation to make the payments to a later date (but not beyond the age of 18 years) if it considers that, in the circumstances of the case, the welfare of the child so requires.[209]

(3) Periodical orders must terminate when the child attains the age of 18.[210]

However, these three restrictions do not apply if: (a) the 'child is, or will be or [if provision extending beyond 18 years of age were made] would be, receiving instruction at an educational establishment, or undergoing training for a trade, profession or vocation, whether or not he is also or will also be in gainful employment'; or (b) there are 'special circumstances which justify' the making of a different order.[211]

These restrictions do not apply to the court's powers to order a settlement of property or to vary a nuptial settlement. However, it has been held[212] that a court should not normally exercise the power to order a settlement of property so as to order life-long provision for a child who is under no disability and whose education is secured.

The basic principle of the legislation is thus that special justification must be shown if an order is to be made or continued in respect of an adult child. This justification will often relate to the child's education (which is specifically referred to) but there may be other 'special circumstances', such as disability or ill health, or the fact that a parent had given a child to understand that support would continue until the child had completed a course of professional training.

Finally, it should be noted that periodical payments orders[213] in favour of a child terminate on the death of the payer, whether or not the order so provides.[214]

---

[208] Matrimonial Causes Act 1973, s 29(2).

[209] Ibid, s 29(2)(a).

[210] Ibid, s 29(1), (2)(b).

[211] Ibid, s 29(3). See *B v B (Adult Student: Liability to Support)* [1998] 1 FLR 373 in which a father unsuccessfully argued that his daughter's full maintenance grant while at university and any supplementary income she might make during those substantial parts of the year when she was not required to be in residence should absolve him of any continuing financial liability for her. For a useful round-up of the circumstances under which parents may be liable to provide support for their adult children, see the comment on this decision by S Cretney at [1998] Fam Law 131.

[212] *Lilford (Lord) v Glynn* [1979] 1 WLR 78; *Chamberlain v Chamberlain* [1973] 1 WLR 1557.

[213] But not a *secured* periodical payments order.

[214] Matrimonial Causes Act 1973, s 29(4).

Financial orders for children under the Children Act 1989[215]

Before the coming into force of the Children Act there were a number of ill-related procedures for getting financial provision orders for children outside matrimonial proceedings. Of these, the most commonly invoked was the procedure whereby an affiliation order could be sought against the putative father of an illegitimate child. There were also powers to make orders in guardianship proceedings and in proceedings in which parents simply sought orders about the upbringing of their children and did not seek any order about their own marriage. The Children Act reformed and assimilated the various private law provisions relating to the courts' powers to order financial provisions in proceedings which are not connected with the marriage of a child's parents. The Act adopted the divorce legislation as a model and, to a large extent, generalises for all children the benefit of principles which have already been established in the context of particular proceedings.[216]

Qualified applicants

The following persons may apply for a financial order in respect of a child.[217]

(1) *A parent*: this expression extends to adoptive parents and to parents who are not married to each other. The ordinary meaning of the word is extended so as to 'include any party to a marriage (whether or not subsisting) in relation to whom the child ... is a child of the family'.[218] Hence, it will be possible for a child's biological parent to initiate proceedings claiming support for the child against the child's step-parent[219] or for the step-parent to seek an order against the biological parent. In *T v B (Parental Responsibility: Financial Provision)*[220] the child had been conceived through anonymous sperm donation at a clinic, and had been brought up by the mother and her female partner, until their relationship broke down. The partner was not a legal parent, but had obtained parental responsibility by way of a shared residence order. The mother then sought orders under Sch 1 to the Children Act 1989 against her former partner, and the question arose as to the meaning of 'parent' within Sch 1. Moylan J held that the word 'parent' for the purpose of Sch 1 means legal parent;[221] and the 'the mere obtaining of parental

---

[215] See generally, J Bazley QC et al (One Garden Court Chambers), *Applications under Schedule 1 to the Children Act 1989* (Bristol: Family Law, 2010).

[216] Law Com No 172 *Guardianship and Custody* (1988), at para 4.63, and Children Act, s 15 and Sch 1.

[217] Children Act, Sch 1, paras 1 and 2.

[218] Ibid, Sch 1, para 16(2).

[219] But a parent's cohabitant is not within this definition, irrespective of the length of time for which he has been in loco parentis to the child: *J v J (A Minor) (Property Transfer)* [1993] 2 FLR 56.

[220] [2010] EWHC 1444 (Fam), [2010] 2 FLR 1966.

[221] Ibid, at [67]. See also *J v J (A Minor: Property Transfer)* [1993] 2 FLR 56 at 59.

responsibility is clearly not intended to make someone a legal parent when they would not otherwise be such'.[222]

(2)   *A guardian or special guardian.*

(3)   *Any person in whose favour a residence order is in force with respect to a child*: a residence order settles the arrangements to be made about where a child is to live; and accordingly anyone who has been given the right to care for a child by court order can now seek a financial order for the child's support.

(4)   *An adult student or trainee or person who can show special circumstances*: anyone from this category may make an application for an order. However, in this case, there are two restrictions on the court's powers. First, no order may be made if the parents are living together in the same household,[223] so that it is still impossible for a child to compel parents who are living in a conventional relationship to provide support. Secondly, the court's powers on such an application are limited to making periodical payment or lump sum orders and the power to make periodical payment orders is now severely restricted by the CSA 1991.[224]

In addition, there are certain circumstances in which the court may make a financial order even though no application for such an order has been made. It is provided that the court may make a financial order whenever it makes, varies or discharges a residence order[225] – and a residence order may be made in any family proceedings, whether or not applied for, if the court considers that the order should be made. The court can also make financial orders if the child is a ward of court, whether or not any application has been made for such an order.[226]

Orders which may be made

The range of orders available is now very wide, on the pattern of the range of orders available for children in divorce proceedings. On an application under the Children Act, the court may order the child's parent or parents:[227]

(1)   to make periodical payments, secured or unsecured;

---

222   [2010] EWHC 1444 (Fam), at [63].
223   Children Act, Sch 1, para 2(4).
224   Ibid, Sch 1, para 2(2).
225   Ibid, Sch 1, para 1(6).
226   Ibid, Sch 1, para 1(7).
227   Defined to include step-parents, etc: see above.

(2) to pay a lump sum (and it is expressly provided[228] that such an order may be made to enable expenses in connection with the birth or maintenance of the child which were reasonably incurred before the making of the order to be met);[229]

(3) to make a transfer or settlement of specified property to which the parent is entitled either in possession or reversion. This power gives the court greater flexibility in dealing with the home in which an unmarried couple have lived. It has been held that there is power to order the transfer of a secure tenancy to the other parent for the child's benefit,[230] and it is possible for the court to order a settlement of such property on trust for the child – perhaps until the child ceases full-time education.[231] Where the issue relates to the competing considerations of sale of a family home jointly owned by unmarried parents as against deferment of the sale during the children's minority, applications may be made under both Sch 1 to the Children Act and s 14 of the Trusts of Land and Appointment of Trustees Act 1996. It has been held that, where this is so, the exercise of the court's powers under both statutes should normally be considered by the same county court at the same time under conjoined applications.[232]

Interim orders and variation of orders

The court has wide powers[233] to make interim orders, and to vary periodical payment orders.

---

[228] Children Act, Sch 1, para 5(1).

[229] In *CF v KM (Financial Provision for Child: Costs of Legal Proceedings)* [2010] EWHC 1754 (Fam), [2011] 1 FLR 208, Charles J held that an interim lump sum could be awarded for the benefit of the child in respect of the legal fees of Sch 1 proceedings. Compare Bennett J in *W v J (Child: Variation of Financial Provision)* [2004] 2 FLR 300, who held that such an order to cover legal costs would be for the benefit of the *parent* and not for the child.

[230] *K v K (Minors: Property Transfer)* [1992] 2 FLR 220; but it seems that a cautious approach will be taken to the exercise of this power: *J v J (A Minor) (Property Transfer)* [1993] 2 FLR 56. It should be noted, however, that much wider powers to transfer certain tenancies are now given to the courts under Part IV of the Family Law Act 1996 where an unmarried cohabitation breaks down. These powers may well be exercised in future to provide a continuing home for the children. See Family Law Act 1996, s 53 and Sch 7, and S Bridge 'Transferring Tenancies of the Family Home' [1998] Fam Law 26.

[231] Children Act, Sch 1, para 1(1)(d). For examples of the settlement of capital sums to provide homes for children, see *H v P (Illegitimate Child: Capital Provision)* [1993] Fam Law 515 and *Phillips v Peace* [1996] 2 FLR 230.

[232] *W v W (Joinder of Trusts of Land Act and Children Act Applications)* [2004] 2 FLR 321.

[233] The powers of a (magistrates') family proceedings court in relation to financial orders are limited: such a court cannot make orders for transfer or settlement of property, or for secured periodical payments, and its power to order a lump sum is restricted to a maximum payment of £1,000: Children Act, Sch 1, paras 6 and 7 (variation) and 9 (interim orders).

The exercise of the discretion

The Children Act[234] lays down guidelines for the exercise of the court's powers which largely follow the precedent of matrimonial law.[235] It is provided[236] that, in deciding whether to exercise its powers and if so in what manner, the court shall have regard to all the circumstances including:

(a) the income, earning capacity, property and other financial resources which the applicant, parents[237] and the person in whose favour the order would be made has or is likely to have in the foreseeable future;

(b) the financial needs, obligations and responsibilities which each of those persons has or is likely to have in the foreseeable future;

(c) the financial needs of the child;

(d) the income, earning capacity (if any), property and other financial resources of the child;

(e) any physical or mental disability of the child;

(f) the manner in which the child was being, or was expected to be, educated or trained.[238]

The legislation also contains a provision similar to that in the matrimonial legislation dealing with the factors to be taken into account where the 'parent' against whom the order is sought is not the child's mother or father.[239]

The scheme of the CSA 1991 has made these provisions somewhat academic, in the vast majority of cases, in relation to the power to order periodical payments. It is only when the question of a payment in excess of the level provided for by the CSA 1991 is a possibility – for example to pay school fees for independent education – that the court will be likely to be asked to exercise its powers to make periodical payments – and, indeed, it is only in such unusual circumstances that it will have jurisdiction to do so.[240]

---

[234] Children Act, Sch 1, para 4(1).

[235] Law Com No 172 *Guardianship and Custody* (1988), at para 4.64.

[236] Children Act, Sch 1, para 4(1).

[237] This states the general effect of Sch 1, para 4(1)(b) to the Children Act; but not the distinction drawn in the Act between applications for orders for persons over 18 and others.

[238] There are minor differences between the guidelines for the exercise of the discretion in proceedings instituted under the Children Act and those laid down in relation to divorce and other matrimonial proceedings. The divorce legislation does not require the court (in relation to orders sought for children) to have regard to the contributions which each of the parties has made or is likely, in the foreseeable future, to make to the welfare of the family. In proceedings under the Children Act there is no reference to the standard of living enjoyed by the family before the breakdown of the marriage, and there is no reference to the age of each party to the marriage and the duration of the marriage.

[239] Schedule 1, para 4(2) to the Children Act.

[240] See p 435 above.

The CSA 1991 does not, however, affect the exercise of the court's powers to make lump sum or property adjustment orders, and it may be that there will be more applications for such orders than in the past – not least because, where a couple are not married, the court has only limited powers to make orders as between the adults concerned in respect of their family home. Accordingly, any such order must usually be sought in proceedings under the Children Act. However, in the past, the courts have been reluctant to make capital provision orders in respect of children.[241] In *A v A (A Minor: Financial Provision)*[242] Ward J held that property adjustment orders should not ordinarily be used to make an outright transfer to a child. They should normally only be made to provide for the child's maintenance during minority or until the child completes education. In this case, the property was settled on trust for the 10-year-old child for a term expiring six months after she attained 18 or completed full-time education (including tertiary education). This approach in the Children Act jurisdiction followed the longstanding approach of the courts when exercising the jurisdiction to make provision for children under the Matrimonial Causes Act 1973. For example, in *Kiely v Kiely*,[243] the Court of Appeal pointed out that lump sum orders in favour of chidren and, in particular, of children whose parents were of limited means, were rare[244] and stated that the statutory scheme of the divorce legislation was to enable the court to make proper financial provision for children as children or dependants.[245]

An example is provided by *J v C (Child: Financial Provision)*,[246] which also made other important statements of principle. The parents were unmarried and their relationship broke down while the mother was still pregnant. After the birth of the child, the father won £1.4 million on the national lottery and the mother applied for financial relief for the child. The father argued that the child was not wanted, a fact disputed by the mother. Hale J held that this was not crucial since there was nothing in the private or public law which distinguished between wanted and unwanted children. An irresponsible or uncaring attitude should not be allowed to prejudice a child. Although the welfare principle did not govern the matter, the child's welfare was a relevant consideration. On the facts, the child was entitled to be brought up in circumstances which bore some relationship to the father's current resources and standard of living. She therefore made an order requiring the father to purchase a four-bedroomed house for the child to live in together with her mother and two half-sisters, to revert to the father on the child attaining 21 or completing full-time education.

---

[241] In *A v A (A Minor: Financial Provision)* [1994] 1 FLR 657, Ward J held that property adjustment orders should not ordinarily be used to make an outright transfer to a child. They should normally only be made to provide for the child's maintenance during minority or until the child completes education. In this case, the property was settled on trust for the 10-year-old child for a term expiring six months after she attained 18 or completed full-time education (including tertiary education).

[242] [1994] 1 FLR 657.

[243] [1988] 1 FLR 248 (CA). Cf *J v J (C Intervening)* [1989] 1 FLR 453. See also *Lilford (Lord) v Glynn* [1979] 1 WLR 78.

[244] Ibid, at 251 per Booth J.

[245] Ibid, at 252.

[246] [1999] 1 FLR 152.

She further ordered capital provision to provide a reasonable family car, to cover the mother's past expenditure and provide adequate furnishings for the new property. In *F v G (Child: Financial Provision)* Singer J added that the nature of the parents' relationship, particularly if they have lived together, might be relevant to 'the extent to which the unit of primary carer and child have become accustomed to a particular level of lifestyle can impact legitimately on an evaluation of the child's needs, reasonably to be viewed against his or her history'.[247]

The decisions in *A v A (A Minor: Financial Provision)* and in *J v C (Child: Financial Provision)* were endorsed by the Court of Appeal in *Re P (Child: Financial Provision)*.[248] Here the father of a very young child was a fabulously wealthy international businessman who conceded that he had the resources to pay a lump sum of £10 million if ordered to do so. At first instance the mother was awarded £450,000 for the child's housing needs, £30,000 for furnishing and annual periodical payments of £35,360 reducing to £9,333 on the child's seventh birthday, together with backdated maintenance of £7,500. On appeal these sums were greatly increased to £1 million to settle a property for the benefit of the child, £100,000 for internal decoration, annual periodical payments of £70,000 (less State benefits) and backdated maintenance of £40,000. Building on what was said in *J v C*, the court said that the child's welfare should be a constant influence on the court's exercise of discretion. The Court of Appeal included within the periodical payments order a generous allowance for the mother as carer of the child. The court, it was said, should recognise the responsibility, and often the sacrifice, of the unmarried parent who acted as carer. She should have control of a budget which reflected her position and that of the father, both social and financial.[249] The court also confirmed that the usual method of providing housing for a child will be settlement of a property during the child's minority with the reversion to the settlor.[250]

In *Re S (Unmarried Parents: Financial Provisions)*[251] the judge used *Re P* as a benchmark for assessing the sum to be provided for housing the child, and made a lower award on the basis that the father in the case before him was less wealthy than the father in *Re P*. The Court of Appeal held that the judge had erroneously fettered the wide exercise of discretion required under Sch 1 to the Children Act 1989.[252] The judge's award was also influenced by his perception that the mother was fulfilling her own needs by wishing to remain in a fashionable area of London. The Court of Appeal held that the judge had

---

247 [2004] EWHC 1848 (Fam), [2005] 1 FLR 261, at para [35].
248 [2003] 2 FLR 865.
249 R Bailey-Harris, commenting on the case at [2003] Fam Law 717, 718, notes, however, that 'it remains necessary for the court to guard against unreasonable claims made on behalf of the child but with a disguised element of providing for the mother's independent benefit'.
250 However, this statement in *Re P* does not preclude the possibility of making housing provision for the child by way of a rented property: see *Re C (Financial Provision)* [2007] 2 FLR 13, at para [45].
251 [2006] EWCA Civ 479, [2006] 2 FLR 950.
252 Ibid, at [14].

thereby erred in failing to focus on the child's distinct interests in maintaining the security of her familiar environment.[253] This, said the court, was 'a neat illustration of the advantages of ensuring separate representation for the child in some cases' brought under Sch 1.[254]

We have now completed our examination of how financial support for children is assessed under the CSA 1991 and under the residual jurisdictions left to the courts. However, no examination of the issue of child support would be complete without some reference to state provision for children by way of welfare benefits, to which we now turn.

WELFARE BENEFITS AND THEIR IMPACT

The Finer Report:[255] welfare benefits as the third system of family law

As long ago as 1974, the Finer Committee on One-Parent Families produced the Finer Report, which made a telling analysis of the inadequacy of the procedures then available to provide financial support for children. The Committee pointed out that there were, in effect, three systems of law governing financial support: the system administered by the divorce court; the system administered by the magistrates' courts in domestic proceedings; and what it described as the 'third system of family law' embodied in the system of welfare benefits, administered by an administrative agency. The Finer Report drew attention to the defects caused by this division of function, and to the hardship thereby caused to one-parent families, and made far-reaching proposals under which many issues relating to the quantification and enforcement of financial support obligations would be dealt with by an administrative agency by reference to clear guidelines rather than by the courts in the exercise of a loosely structured discretion. The Finer Report also proposed the creation of a so-called 'guaranteed maintenance allowance' which was intended to provide an income for single-parent families which was significantly higher than what was then available to them by way of welfare benefits.

Although the Finer Report had a profound impact on opinion, nothing was done to give effect to the Committee's proposals. The law continued to develop in separate compartments.

Changing approaches to the State's role

The State has, ever since the enactment of the Elizabethan Poor Law, assumed some obligation to provide for those persons who would otherwise be

---

[253] Ibid, at [15].
[254] Ibid, at [17].
[255] *Report of the Committee on One-Parent Families* (1974) (Cmnd 5629).

completely destitute, but a dramatic change in the philosophy underlying the principles on which provision for the poor should be made took place with the creation of the Welfare State in the period immediately following the end of the Second World War.[256] This change was first manifested in the context of the provision of support for the family in the system of family allowances introduced in 1945. That benefit was replaced in 1975 by child benefit,[257] which does not depend on the making of contributions, and is payable to certain persons who are responsible for a child under 16 years old (or under 19 years old if certain prescribed conditions are met).[258] The benefit is universal and not means-tested. However, now when a taxpayer parent or their partner receives child benefit, and either of them has taxable income over £50,000 per annum, a 1 per cent tax charge is imposed for every £100 taxable income over £50,000. Where the parent's income is over £60,000 the tax charge effectively wipes out any entitlement to the benefit. Put simply, the sum actually received will depend on the extent to which one of the persons in the child's household is earning over £50,000, if at all. There is, however, an anomaly in the system, in that the tax liability is imposed on individuals not households, so child benefit would still be paid in full to a household in which each parent earns just under the £50,000 threshold. Thus a household bringing in, say, £55,000 from one parent will receive less in child benefit than a household bringing in, say, £98,000 from two parents with £49,000 salaries. Child benefit is payable to the mother in the first instance and it has been held that it may not be split in a situation where care of the child is shared.[259] The current rate of child benefit is £20.30 per week for the eldest child and £13.40 per week for other children.

In 2004 Parliament legislated to provide a new universal benefit for children. Under the Child Trust Funds Act 2004, payments will be made by the Government to children which may only be invested in child trust fund accounts, which will be long-term savings and investment accounts. No withdrawals will be allowed until the child attains the age of 18, at which point he or she will be entitled to withdraw the money. This benefit has now been stopped and applies only to children born between 1 September 2002 and 2 January 2011.

---

[256] These changes followed the publication in 1942 of the Beveridge Report (the *Report on Social Insurance and Allied Services* (1942) (Cmnd 6404)). For a concise account of the evolution of social security and social policy in Britain, see Wikeley, Ogus and Barendt *The Law of Social Security* (5th edn, Butterworths, 2002), ch 1.

[257] The former lone parent benefit payable for the first or only child of a lone parent was abolished from 6 July 1998.

[258] For a full description of the current principles and regulations governing child benefit, see Child Poverty Action Group *Welfare Benefits and Tax Credits Handbook* (2013–2014), April 2013, ch 26.

[259] *R (Barber) v Secretary of State for Work and Pensions* [2002] 2 FLR 1181.

Means-tested benefits for the poor: supplementary benefit and family income supplement

The most important change in policy governing welfare benefits was achieved by the abolition of the Poor Law in 1948 and the creation of the supplementary benefit system under which every person in Great Britain of or over the age of 16 years, whose resources (as defined) were insufficient to meet his requirements (defined, at a modest level, in statute), became entitled to receive a supplementary allowance. At that time, it was the policy of the law to eradicate the stigma attached to the Poor Law, and to insist that supplementary benefits were 'the subject of rights and entitlement and that no shame attached to the receipt of them'.[260]

Reducing the burden of welfare benefit provision

Over the years, the supplementary benefit system became increasingly burdensome to the taxpayer. Part of this increase was attributable to the costs apparently caused by family breakdown: the number of lone-parent families in Great Britain rose to over one million in 1986, and such families now constitute about 30 per cent of all families with dependent children.[261] It should be noted in passing that adult children are no longer legally liable to support their parents,[262] but this is not so in every jurisdiction. Singapore, for example, enacted the Maintenance of Parents Act in 1995 which enables parents who are unable to support themselves adequately to apply to the court for maintenance from any or all of their children.[263] In England, such obligations (including obligations to support wider kin) existed under the Poor Law but were finally abolished with the advent of the post-war Welfare State.[264] But with changing attitudes it increasingly came to be said that the law failed, in practice, to give effect to the 'clear moral duty' which all parents have to maintain their children until the children are old enough to look after themselves.[265]

---

[260] *Reiterbund v Reiterbund* [1974] 1 WLR 788 at 797, per Finer J.

[261] See *Social Trends* 2011 No 41 *Households and families*, Table 1.

[262] However, in *Bouette v Rose* [2000] 1 FLR 363 an ingenious argument succeeded in the Court of Appeal that a deceased child aged 14 had, at the time of her death, effectively been maintaining her mother for the purposes of s 1(1)(e) and (3) of the Inheritance (Provision for Family and Dependants) Act 1975. The mother succeeded in obtaining leave to apply for financial provision out of her deceased daughter's estate. The daughter had been awarded compensation after suffering severe physical and mental disabilities due to negligence at birth. The Court of Protection had used some of this to pay out capital and regular income to the mother to enable her to buy a house and care for the daughter. The court felt able to characterise this as a situation in which the mother was being maintained by the child.

[263] See P de Cruz 'Singapore: Maintenance, Marital Property and Legislative Innovation' in A Bainham (ed) *The International Survey of Family Law 1996* (Martinus Nijhoff, 1998), at p 401.

[264] For a concise discussion, see M Maclean and J Eekelaar *The Parental Obligation* (Hart Publishing, 1997), especially at pp 41–44. For discussion of the issue, see J Herring 'Together forever? The rights and responsibilities of adult children and their parents' in J Bridgeman, H Keating and C Lind (eds), *Responsibility, Law and the Family* (Ashgate, 2008).

[265] Per Lord Mackay of Clashfern *Hansard* Vol 526, col 775 (25 February 1991).

In response to these pressures, the supplementary benefit system was replaced by 'income support',[266] and legislation was introduced[267] to reinforce the obligations of parents and others. The CSA 1991, as we have seen, is an ambitious system intended to ensure that non-resident parents meet their fair share of the cost of supporting their children. Spouses remain liable in public law to maintain *each other* (as well as their children) while separated but this public liability ceases on divorce. In 1996 unemployment benefit was replaced by jobseeker's allowance,[268] which is divided into income-based and contributory varieties. The contributory jobseeker's allowance is based on national insurance contributions made, while the income-based version is means-tested and has to a large extent replaced income support. It must be claimed, rather than income support, by those who are unemployed, or employed for less than 16 hours per week, and are required actively to seek work. Income support, however, continues to apply to those who are not actively required to seek work. From around the turn of the millennium and until recently, however, the policy was to shift financial support for children by the State away from the benefits system and in the direction of tax credits administered by the Inland Revenue.[269] This policy was part of a general philosophy that it is better to encourage work than dependency and was reflected particularly by the introduction of a 'working families tax credit' in 1999. Accordingly, those elements in some of the major welfare benefits which reflected the cost of raising children were received instead through a new system of tax credits.[270] The former working families tax credit was split into two separate tax credits: the 'child tax credit' and the 'working tax credit'. The former is a means-tested, income-based credit for families with children, in or out of employment, who have responsibility for children who are under 16 or under 19 and in full-time, non-advanced education. The latter is a means-tested, income-based credit for working adults who work for more than 16 hours per week and satisfy certain other conditions, one of which is having responsibility for a child.

Income support and income-based jobseeker's allowance, together with child tax credits and the working tax credit are to be replaced by a new benefit called universal credit, which was enacted by the Welfare Reform Act 2012. The national roll-out of this scheme will commence in October 2013 and by 2014 it is intended that all new claimants will come under the system. By the end of 2017 it is intended that all claimants for means-tested benefits will be transferred to universal credit. The universal credit system is outlined below since an important category for present purposes of those seeking this benefit will be those with dependent children, of whom lone mothers are a significant

---

[266] Social Security Act 1986.

[267] Social Security Administration Act 1992, s 106; Income Support (Liable Relative) Regulations 1990 (SI 1990/1777).

[268] Jobseekers Act 1995.

[269] See generally the Tax Credits Act 2002 and regulations made thereunder.

[270] For the details, see Child Poverty Action Group *Welfare Benefits and Tax Credits Handbook* (2013/14), ch 9 and 10.

category. Universal credit is available not only to those who do not work but to those who do, and whose income may need to be supplemented by the State.

The Universal Credit Scheme

Universal credit is means tested, and calculated over a monthly assessment period.[271] It is not payable to a person or persons whose capital is more than £16,000. There are a series of allowances for a claimant or claimants, currently £246.81 for single claimant and £489.06 for joint claimants.[272] There is also a child element per monthly assessment period of £272.08 for the first child and £226.67 for any subsequent child. There is also a 'limited capability for work allowance' of £123.62 and a childcare costs element for those who are working (70 per cent of child care costs up to a maximum of £532.29 per month for one child and £912.50 a month for two or more children), and a housing costs element. These elements of universal credit are added up as they apply to the family concerned. For those who are working, the next step is to calculate earned income. There are then 'work allowances' which are amounts used to calculate how much universal credit can be retained. The work allowances vary according to a claimant or claimants' circumstances, and there are higher and lower amounts. The lower work allowance applies where a claimant has housing costs which are included in the universal credit. The higher work allowance applies when there are no housing costs. The work allowances for a single person responsible for one or more child are £734 and £263 respectively, and for a couple, £536 and £222 respectively. There is then a calculation of the amount by which income exceeds the work allowance. Sixty-five per cent of the excess is calculated. Whatever figure is reached is taken into account when calculating payment of universal credit. Any further income, for example from capital, is also added in. Universal credit paid is then calculated by deducting the total income to be taken into account from the maximum universal credit initially calculated. Usually the claimant for universal credit must be at least 18 years old.

Eligibility of 16 and 17 year-olds[273]

There are some circumstances in which children aged 16 and 17 may be eligible for benefits. First it should be noted that such children will not usually[274] be eligible if they were formerly looked after by a local authority.[275] This is because the relevant local authority will have duties in repect of such children. In order for a child aged 16 or 17 to qualify for universal credit, he or she must

---

[271] For the relevant calculations, see Child Poverty Action Group *Welfare Benefits and Tax Credits Handbook* (2013–2014), April 2013, ch 3 and 19.

[272] These figures are for persons over 25 years old; there are slightly lower allowances for persons under 25 years old.

[273] See generally Child Poverty Action Group *Welfare Benefits and Tax Credits Handbook* (2013 – 2014), April 2013, ch 45 and 46.

[274] There are some exceptions, for example, where a child is a lone parent.

[275] See e g the Universal Credit Regulations 2013 (SI 2013/376), reg 8(4).

have limited capability for work, or be unfit for work, have substantial caring responsibilities, be responsible for a child, or be without parental support (ie, orphaned or estranged from parents for good reasons, or parents are unable to support, for example by reason of being in prison). A 16 or 17 year-old may also qualify for contribution-based jobseeker's allowance if he or she fulfils the contribution conditions. Such a person cannot claim jobseeker's allowance if in full-time non-advanced education.

Maximising welfare benefits following family breakdown: welfare benefit planning

As noted earlier in the chapter, lawyers soon began to appreciate that welfare benefits could be a significant resource for families after divorce, and (in particular) could be used to make practicable the 'clean break' philosophy embodied in the divorce legislation after the Matrimonial and Family Proceedings Act 1984. Three features of the welfare benefit legislation were particularly relevant. First, income support made allowance for a claimant's 'housing costs' and, subject to certain restrictions, income support payments would cover the interest paid on a mortgage taken out to buy the house or to buy out the interest of a divorced partner. Secondly, although the social security legislation[276] imposed an obligation to maintain the spouse and children, there was no such obligation to maintain a former spouse. Moreover, although the obligation to maintain children continued notwithstanding divorce and was not affected by the terms of any order made by the divorce court,[277] it seemed that, in practice, the DSS did not attach a high priority to seeking to recover income support from parents and others.[278] Thirdly, the courts increasingly began to take account of the availability of State benefits in deciding how to exercise their powers to make financial orders on divorce. In particular, it began to be questioned whether a man should be made to go on paying maintenance out of his own small income when the payments would be of no benefit for the former wife but would merely reduce the amount of income support for which she was eligible. This point of view was put eloquently by Waite J:[279]

> 'no humane society could tolerate – even in the interest of saving its public purse – the prospect of a divorced couple of acutely limited means remaining manacled to each other indefinitely by the necessity to return at regular intervals to court for no other purpose than to thrash out at public expense the precise figure which the one should pay the other – not for any benefit to either of them, but solely for the relief of the tax-paying section of the community to which neither of them has sufficient means to belong.'

---

[276] The relevant provisions are now consolidated in the Social Security Administration Act 1992, ss 78(6) and 105(3).

[277] *Hulley v Thompson* [1981] WLR 159.

[278] National Audit Office Report *Support for Lone Parent Families* (1990) HC 328.

[279] *Ashley v Blackman* [1988] 2 FLR 278, at 284–285.

The welfare benefit 'clean break'

An appreciation of these factors increasingly led to financial orders being made under which the family home would be transferred to the wife outright. She would give up any claim to periodical maintenance and a small – perhaps even nominal – periodical payment order would be made for the children. In some cases, the wife would increase the mortgage on the house so that she could make a lump sum payment to the husband, sufficient to enable him to pay a deposit on a house for himself and his new family. The outcome would be as follows: the wife would remain eligible for income support, and the costs of meeting interest payments on the mortgage would be added to her basic entitlement. The DSS would have no right to pursue the former husband in respect of income support payments made to the wife; and, although the DSS would be entitled to recover income support paid in respect of the children, it may be that this right would not be vigorously exercised. The husband would have lost his interest in the former matrimonial home but he would have no on-going maintenance liability, and he would be in a position to buy another house on mortgage, and would be eligible for tax relief on the interest.

It seems probable that such planning became common. Certainly a large number of so-called clean break orders were made[280] and, by 1989, less than one-quarter of families on income support were receiving periodical maintenance from the absent parent (whereas one half of such families had received maintenance 10 years earlier).[281] These developments were not welcome to those responsible for the administration of the social security budget. Not only was the financial cost high, it was also thought that these developments played a part in eroding personal responsibility for the family. It was this context which drove Mrs Thatcher's strong desire to reform the child support system.

FINANCIAL RESPONSIBILITY FOR CHILDREN: SOME CONCLUDING POLICY CONSIDERATIONS

Ultimately, the question of financial support for children is about the appropriate apportionment of responsibility between the two parents concerned (or, perhaps more accurately, the two households concerned) and the wider community. The child support legislation shifted the emphasis decisively towards the notion that the *primary* responsibility rests with parents and any obligation on the part of the State is *secondary*. Yet, even if this is accepted, the respective *levels* of responsibility remain a contentious issue as does the view that these obligations of parenthood should fall very largely on biological parents[282] to the exclusion of the legal and moral obligations of social

---

[280] See *Judicial Statistics Annual Report 1991* at Table 5.5.
[281] *Children Come First* (1990) (Cmnd 1263), at para 1.5.
[282] But not entirely, since social parents are regarded as legal parents in the case of adoption and

parenthood.[283] It is fair to say, however, that the greater allowance now made for the presence of children in the non-resident parent's household, in calculating his income, does represent a significant shift towards the view that there should be something approaching parity in the obligations towards biological children and those children for whom the non-resident parent has a social, if not legal, responsibility. The fact that almost everyone would agree with the principle that parents have *some* continuing financial responsibility for their children even where they no longer live with them does not mean that there is anything like a consensus about precisely what this responsibility should be. As one policy publication of the Child Poverty Action Group put it: 'the superficial simplicity of support for this principle hides a complex and shifting array of attitudes about family obligations. Public agreement with the general principle does not necessarily mean that people think it should be unconditional or overriding'.[284] The amended scheme certainly reflects in part a widely held perception that some non-resident parents had been required to pay too much and the new rates will result in a lower liability in many cases.

Another angle to this issue is the inconsistency in the legal treatment of the financial obligations of parents in ongoing, intact households as compared with those in separate households. The child support regime applies only where a parent is 'non-resident' and has left the household in which the children are present. The law does not concern itself directly with the management of family finances while the family remains intact.[285] This can lead to the ironic situation in which a 'non-resident' father is legally required to pay more, perhaps much more, for children than he would ever have done had the family remained a going concern. The irony is heightened in those cases in which the man concerned was never in the household at all and whose only link with the child is genetic. As Harry Krause once put it: 'it does not seem at all obvious that the same (or a greater) level of parental responsibility that makes sense in the ongoing family should be grafted (1) onto consanguinity based on what is understood as permissible recreational sex or (2) onto the essentially terminated post-divorce relationship between the typical father and his child' and he urges a search 'for a level of responsibility that is commensurate with the social reality of the situation'.[286] As we have seen, the child support scheme is blind to the circumstances of conception, but there is at least an argument

---

some instances of assisted reproduction under the status provisions of the Human Fertilisation and Embryology Act 1990. See chapter 3 above.

[283] Social parents may have legal, as well as moral, obligations towards children who are treated as 'children of the family'. See p 440 above. It should also be remembered that the presence of a working social father in a household would, under the aggregation rules which apply to social security entitlements, often preclude a mother from making an independent claim for herself and her children for means-tested income support and other benefits. In this sense, there is an assumed indirect legal responsibility on the man concerned to support his 'second' family. For discussion of the aggregation rule, see Wikeley, Ogus and Barendt's *Law of Social Security* (5th edn, Butterworths, 2002), at pp 291 et seq.

[284] F Bennett *Child Support: Issues for the Future* (CPAG Ltd, 1997), at p 23.

[285] For a concise and useful discussion, see M Maclean and J Eekelaar *The Parental Obligation* (Hart Publishing, 1997), at pp 37–44.

[286] HD Krause 'Child Support Reassessed: Limits of Private Responsibility and the Public

that the responsibility which is voluntarily *assumed* for a child in the context of an ongoing relationship is of a different kind to that which is *imposed* merely because a pregnancy, and in due course a child, results from what may be an isolated act of sexual intercourse. The basis of liability in this case appears to be negligence in relation to the use of contraception.[287]

Another issue needs to be confronted when considering whether parenthood and its obligations are principally a matter of genetics or of assumed social responsibility. Whichever it is, there remains something of an inconsistency at the heart of English law, although one which is undoubtedly diluted by the reforms in the Adoption and Children Act 2002. This is that, while genetics is apparently all-important for *financial responsibility*, it is not so regarded for the wider aspects of *parental responsibility*, at least not outside marriage. Neither is it so regarded in applying the test of whether 'family life' comes into being for the purposes of the ECHR.[288] It is difficult to resist the conclusion that the law would command more respect if it made what may appear to some to be necessary connection between the financial and non-financial aspects of parental responsibility.

One way of doing this might have been to remove the financial responsibility of the non-resident parent and to emphasise instead the responsibility of the social parent. The other approach is to recognise, along with financial responsibility, the wider parental responsibility of the non-resident, genetic parent. It is this second course which has been pursued by the Government and, to a degree, has been implemented by the Adoption and Children Act 2002.[289] The Lord Chancellor's Department's Consultation paper which preceded the legislation recognised that it was 'a particular source of grievance for some unmarried fathers that they have been forced to support their children financially, whether or not they have acquired parental responsibility under the Children Act'.[290] The great majority of fathers are likely to acquire parental responsibility through registration as the father of the child on the child's birth certificate. But there will remain a substantial minority who are not so registered. These men will continue to be automatically liable for child support, on proof of paternity, but will not thereby acquire parental responsibility. There will therefore remain some discordance in the law's treatment of these men for the purposes of the financial and non-financial aspects of being adjudged a legal parent.

A final question relates to the State's obligations towards the costs of raising children. This is a question which relates not just to children whose parents

---

Interest' in Kay and Sugarman (eds) *Divorce Reform at the Crossroads* (Yale University Press, 1990), at p 181. Cf S Sheldon 'Unwilling Fathers and Abortion: Terminating Men's Child Support Obligations' (2003) 66 MLR 175.

[287] The point is developed further in A Bainham 'Men and Women Behaving Badly: Is Fault Dead in English Family Law?' (2001) *Oxford Journal of Legal Studies* 219, at 229–231.

[288] See chapters 3 and 4.

[289] A Bainham (above).

[290] See Consultation Paper *Court Procedures for the Determination of Paternity: the Law on Parental Responsibility for Unmarried Fathers* (Lord Chancellor's Department, March 1998).

have separated, but also to intact families with children. It has long been accepted, and certainly since the Second World War, that the cost of raising children is something to be met by parents and the State acting in partnership. The public subsidies which the State provides are wide-ranging, the more obvious benefits relating to health and education and, within the social security system, the universal child benefit.[291] But it was the burden of social security in a period of widespread family breakdown and a high incidence of lone parenthood which foreshadowed the introduction of the child support legislation in 1991. In recent decades the policy orientation has been to act in pursuit of a 'welfare to work' philosophy. The principal objective is for the State to support families by a package of measures designed to assist people in moving away from welfare dependency and into work.

Nonetheless, beyond the intricacy of the child support scheme, social security system and fiscal policy, there remain fundamental and largely unanswered questions about why it is that liability for the casualties of family breakdown is seen primarily as a matter of *private* rather than *public* responsibility. This is an issue which has not always been well addressed in England, where the tendency has been to assume rather uncritically that the financial support of children and their carers is primarily a private, individual responsibility, rather than a public, collective one. As we have seen, in England there has been a distinct shift recently also towards encouraging parents to make private arrangements rather than involving the state in the assessment of child support. The view that child support is a private matter, has been challenged in the USA by Martha Fineman,[292] who sees the child support question as 'merely one component of a complex series of issues surrounding the question of who should bear the economic and social costs of caring for dependent members of society'[293] and who takes the view that there is 'a fundamental obligation in a just society for the collective to provide for its weaker members'.[294] Within this context, Fineman argues that 'in continuing to allocate dependency automatically to the private sphere, society forgoes the opportunity to develop a theory of collective responsibility for children and other dependents'.[295]

When the child support legislation was introduced in 1991, no one doubts that there was a fundamental change of emphasis away from *public* and towards *private* responsibility. This was not debated as well as it might have been then, but the successive changes to the detail and administration of the child support scheme have not wholly managed to disguise the underlying uncertainty about the essential theoretical basis of liability; and that is one thing which is unlikely to change.

---

[291] See p 451 above.
[292] M Fineman 'Child Support is not the Answer: The Nature of Welfare Reform' in JT Oldham and MS Melli (eds) *Child Support: The Next Frontier* (The University of Michigan Press, 2000), at p 209.
[293] Ibid.
[294] M Fineman (above), at p 211.
[295] Ibid, at p 212.

PART III

CHILDREN AND LOCAL AUTHORITIES

Part III, 'Children and Local Authorities', is deliberately not called 'Children and the State'. The concept of the State, broadly defined, impinges on children and families in many different ways – through social security and fiscal policy, education and employment, the criminal law, and in a host of other ways. Yet the relationship between local authorities and families is crucial, since it is local authorities which have the primary statutory responsibility for supporting families and for protecting children who are thought to be at risk of abuse or neglect. The historical development of these responsibilities was discussed in chapter 1.

Chapter 10 analyses the *supportive* functions of local authorities towards children in need and their families. It also deals briefly with the regulation of substitute care arrangements by way of children's homes, fostering services, and child-minding/childcare services. The focus in chapters 11 and 12 is on *protection* rather than support. Chapter 11 considers the critical question of short-term protection for children. Here, the emphasis is on immediate legal remedies for dealing with emergencies. Chapter 12 then discusses the statutory regime for compulsory (longer-term) action whether through care or supervision. Part III ends with a discussion, in chapter 13, of various ways in which permanent placements for children can be achieved, in particular by way of adoption or special guardianship.

In theory, a sharp distinction can be drawn between *voluntary* assistance governed by Part III of the Children Act 1989 (see chapter 10) and the *compulsory* measures under Parts IV and V of the Act (see chapters 11 and 12). Yet, for various reasons, it is not a true reflection of what goes on in practice to postulate so rigid a demarcation. It is important to get some sense of the relationship between voluntary services and more coercive action and this should be constantly kept in mind when reading Part III.

Chapter 10

LOCAL AUTHORITY SUPPORT FOR CHILDREN AND FAMILIES

INTRODUCTION

Part III of the Children Act 1989 regulates support services for families and the powers and duties of local authorities towards children looked after by them.[1] In this chapter, we sketch the legal framework of Part III. It is inevitable that the legal boundaries for *compulsory* State intervention in the family should be the subject of close critical evaluation. But to see these compulsory powers as relatively more important, and voluntary services as relatively less important, would be an unbalanced and distorted way of looking at things. In a nutshell, one of the primary purposes of the support services under Part III is to prevent, wherever possible, the circumstances under which it becomes necessary for compulsory action to be taken. Court orders for care and supervision are, in this sense, very much the ambulance at the bottom of the cliff while the support services are the (however inadequate) fence at the top.

This emphasis on voluntary assistance to families in difficulty, or those who would be in difficulty but for that assistance, is consistent with the general thinking behind the Children Act which was identified in earlier chapters.[2] Essentially, it is that first responsibility for children rests with the family. Public support should be viewed as positive, designed to underscore the primary role of parents and not to emphasise their failure. Thus, the local authority's powers should be exercised in *partnership* with parents, implying full participation in decisions, even where the child is looked after by the local authority.[3] Court

---

[1] The genesis of the reforms in Part III is the Second Report of the House of Commons Social Services Committee 1983–4, *Children in Care* HC 360 (the 'Short Report'). This was followed by the DHSS *Review of Child Care Law* (1985) Part II and the White Paper *The Law on Child Care and Family Services* (1987) (Cm 62), ch 2. See generally S Gore *The Children Act 1989 Local Authority Support for Children and Families* (Family Law, 2011). See also R White, P Carr and N Lowe *The Children Act in Practice* (4th edn, Butterworths, 2008) ch 6. Many useful materials are extracted in B Hale, D Pearl, E Cooke and D Monk *The Family, Law and Society* (6th edn, Oxford University Press, 2009) ch 11, especially p 530 et seq. See also J Thoburn 'The Children Act 1989: Balancing Child Welfare with the Concept of Partnership with Parents' [1991] JSWFL 331. For a longer perspective taking in the post-war period, see N Parton *Governing the Family* (Macmillan, 1991), ch 2.

[2] See particularly chapter 2 above.

[3] Department of Health *The Challenge of Partnership in Child Protection: Practice Guide* (London: HMSO, 1995); F Kaganas, M King, and C Piper (eds) *Legislating for Harmony – Partnerships under the Children Act 1989* (London, Jessica Kingsley, 1996).

orders should only be made where they are strictly necessary.[4] Promotion of upbringing within the family[5] and of contact with relatives and friends[6] should be an important objective. There is also a strong presumption that arrangements should be made for a child looked after by a local authority to live with his parents, family or friends.[7] The local authority should be accountable for its actions through an adequate system of internal reviews, there should be procedures for accommodating representations and complaints and access to the courts for aggrieved parents in accordance with the requirements of the ECHR.

These principles, evident in the Children Act itself, are greatly reinforced by the ECHR and the HRA 1998.[8] We will look at the Convention principles as they apply to emergency and compulsory action in chapters 11 and 12 respectively. In those contexts the issue will often be whether the local authority has resorted to a higher level of intervention than is necessary to protect the child, as where it is seeking to justify the making of a care order and it is argued that a supervision order would be sufficient.[9] We also consider in chapter 12 the human rights issues surrounding care plans and contact with children in care, two related and fertile areas of dispute which now require engagement with human rights considerations. Why these human rights issues are relevant to the scheme under Part III is precisely because voluntary assistance may be the appropriate level of intervention if the action taken by the authority is to comply with the requirements of the ECHR. If it could be demonstrated that it resorted to coercive measures where sufficient protection of the child's welfare could have been achieved by agreement with the parents, this would constitute, prima facie, a violation of Art 8 Convention rights since it would be disproportionate and unnecessary action.

Yet, there is another side to Convention obligations which should also be borne in mind. This is that the ECHR imposes not merely *negative* obligations not to interfere unjustifiably with family life, but also *positive* obligations to support it. This is an area in which the higher courts and the ECtHR have been very active, and we consider some of the jurisprudence in this chapter. The essential point is that a *failure* on the part of the State to make sufficient efforts to protect a child will, if that child should subsequently suffer abuse or neglect, leave the local authority exposed to the possibility of a civil action for negligence and the State may be held responsible for violation of the child's Convention rights. The balance between upholding parental autonomy and

---

4 Ibid.
5 See, particularly, Children Act 1989, s 17(1)(b).
6 Schedule 2, para 15.
7 Section 23(6).
8 For an account of the implications of the HRA 1998 for child protection law, see S Choudhry and J Herring *European Human Rights and Family Law* (Hart, 2010), ch 8. See also H Swindells, A Neaves, M Kushner and R Skilbeck *Family Law and the Human Rights Act 1998* (Family Law, 1999), especially ch 6. Chapter 10 of the same work looks more directly at the duties of local authorities and considers the implications of the *positive* obligations imposed on the State by the ECHR.
9 As, for example, in *Re C and B (Care Order: Future Harm)* [2001] 1 FLR 611.

family integrity while offering sufficient protection to children is a notoriously difficult one for local authorities to strike but suffice it to say that there may be, quite apart from public criticism, legal liability if the authority intervenes too much or too little.

Relationship between voluntary and compulsory action

The legislation differentiates between children who are formally 'in care' as a result of a court having made a care order, and those who are cared for without such an order. In the latter, non-compulsory case, the child is described as 'accommodated' by the local authority. In either case, the child will be being 'looked after' by the local authority, and 'looked after' is the generic term used in the Children Act for both children 'in care' and those in local authority accommodation under voluntary arrangements. Where it is necessary to distinguish the two groups it is preferable to describe the 'voluntary' children as 'accommodated'.[10] The Act and its terminology aim to clarify the difference between seeking voluntary help from social services and the circumstances in which compulsion can be justified. It removes from the seeking of voluntary help any pejorative connotation of failure or inadequacy. Any features of the former law which could be interpreted as inconsistent with this ideal were removed.[11] Yet it has been questioned how far this is really a true reflection of what occurs in practice. Judith Masson has argued that the provision of services for children in need can be characterised, not so much as voluntary assistance, but as a form of 'diversion' from the more coercive forms of intervention.[12] She argues that the Children Act 'contains separate but interlinked frameworks for managing risk with and without court orders'. On this analysis, the primary preoccupation of children's services will be with those children who are thought to be at risk. As she puts it:[13]

'The fact that there is no order should not be taken as indicating that the relationship between the family and the local authority is entirely voluntary. The local authority has duties to provide services and to protect children; the family accepts services against the coercive backdrop of the authority's powers to take proceedings.'

The Children Act Advisory Committee in its final report[14] commented adversely on the inappropriate use of voluntary accommodation of children under Part III as an alternative to an application for a care or supervision order. Yet, local authority resources are finite and there is evidence that the decisive factor influencing authorities in some cases is the cost involved in

---

[10] Children must be accommodated for a continuous period of more than 24 hours to fall within the definition of 'looked after' children (s 22(2)).

[11] See chapter 2 above and the discussion below.

[12] JM Masson 'Managing Risk Under the Children Act 1989: Diversion in Child Care?' (1992) 1 *Child Abuse Review* 103. The concept of 'diversion' is familiar in the context of juvenile justice.

[13] Ibid, at p 119. For further research confirming this view, see J Masson 'Emergency intervention to protect children: using and avoiding legal controls' [2005] CFLQ 75, especially at p 80 et seq.

[14] *The Children Act Advisory Committee Final Report June 1997* (Lord Chancellor's Department, 1997), at pp 29–30. See below.

taking a child into care.[15] The potential influence of this factor has certainly not diminished in recent years since the cost of initiating care proceedings has increased significantly.[16] That said, it should be noted that a countervailing factor which has resulted in a signficant increase in care proeedings in recent years has been the scandal surrounding the death of Baby P.[17] It may well be that the alleged philosophy of 'non-intervention' which is said to permeate the legislation and the 'no order' principle in s 1(5) of the Act have also had some influence in persuading social services to go down the voluntary route where there is doubt that the basis for a care order would be established. And, as discussed above, human rights requirements dictate that the least coercive form of intervention which is consistent with protecting the child's welfare should be the course which is followed. In these ways, the apparently clear distinction between *voluntary* 'services' and *compulsory* 'care' may be less sharp in practice than in theory.

These concerns about the blurring of the distinction between what is voluntary and what is compulsory do seem to be borne out by research studies.[18] What these reveal is that *short-term* or respite accommodation of children has been successfully used as a family service.[19] Such placements are usually with the same carer, should not exceed four weeks in duration, and the total duration of such placements should not exceed 90 days. On the other hand, *full-time* accommodation tended to be used in the context of a negotiated partnership between the local authority and the parents. The parents were presented with the choice of either agreeing to the provision of accommodation or going to court, an arrangement which 'tests the balance between compulsion and voluntariness'.[20] In such cases any supposed partnership between parents and the local authority may be more illusory than real.

Children in need: eligibility for services

The concept of 'children in need' is central to the operation of Part III of the Children Act.[21] It constitutes an all-important threshold, since it creates an

---

[15] See, for example, *Nottinghamshire County Council v P* [1994] Fam 18. See also the discussion, in chapter 12 below, of the House of Lords decision in *Re C (Interim Care Order: Residential Assessment)* [1997] 1 FLR 1, where financial considerations loomed large at the interim stage of care proceedings.

[16] Court fees were significantly increased to £4,825 in May 2008. A review subsequently recommended that the fees be abolished: see R Plowden *Review of Court Fees in Child Care Proceedings* (Ministry of Justice, 2009), at para 1.20. On 15 March 2010, Jack Straw, the former Secretary of State for Justice, announced that the court fees would be abolished from April 2011, but following a change of government, it was announced in October 2010 that the fees were to be retained.

[17] Haringey Local Safeguarding Children Board, Serious Case Review: Baby Peter (February 2009).

[18] See *Children Act Now: Messages from Research* (2001), at pp 49–52 and the research studies cited there. See also J Masson, above, [2005] CFLQ 75.

[19] *Messages from Research* (2001) above, at p 49.

[20] Ibid, at p 51.

[21] Defined in s 17(10) and discussed below.

eligibility for a wide range of statutory services. The local authority *must* provide these services to children once it has been determined that a child is in need. The claims of such children are described as an 'eligibility' rather than a 'right' or 'entitlement'. This is because local authorities have very wide discretions in determining how precisely to discharge their many statutory duties. While, therefore, a blanket refusal to provide *any* services to such children could render an authority's decision susceptible to judicial review,[22] it will frequently be difficult, perhaps impossible, to argue that the children have a legal right to any *particular* service. The legislation does not give children in need unlimited rights of recipience, and the enforcement of the local authority's duties is highly problematic.[23]

This leads us to the 'universality versus selectivity' debate which has so dominated policy-making in the field of social security provision.[24] In the present context, the question is whether publicly provided benefits for children ought to be regarded as available to *all* children on a universal basis or only to *some* children by applying selective criteria. Children are major beneficiaries of State provision of health, education, social security, housing and other welfare needs of the public.[25] In broad terms, it might be said that all children are in need of adequate provision in these areas and that, accordingly, they might have a *right* to claim, and society a *duty* to make available, the best possible provision. Universalist claims like these permeate international commitments to children, most obviously in the UNCRC.[26] The concept of 'children in need' in the Children Act is not used in this sense. It has a much narrower and technical definition, the purpose of which is to mark out those families who need the help of specialist services offered by local authorities, in short to target them. Thus, during the parliamentary debates on the Children Bill, the Government rejected the argument that, since nursery education is generally acknowledged to be beneficial to young children, *all* children in the relevant age group could be said to be 'in need' of it, since they could all profit from it.[27] Such an interpretation would have necessitated comprehensive nursery provision which the then Government wanted to resist. The debate highlights the chief dilemma in this area. This is that, however well-intentioned the legislation, and however laudable the efforts of local authorities to implement

---

[22] For a good discussion of judicial review in this context, see N Lowe and G Douglas *Bromley's Family Law* (10th edn, Oxford University Press, 2007), at pp 805–810.

[23] The possibilities are discussed at pp 510 et seq below.

[24] As to which, see Wikeley, Ogus and Barendt's *The Law of Social Security* (6th edn, Butterworths, 2002), ch 1.

[25] Indeed, many of these benefits are specifically geared to children or, at least, to families with children. Obvious examples are child benefit and the 'priority need' which arises where a homeless person has dependent children.

[26] Take, for example, Art 27(1) which requires States to 'recognise the right of every child to a standard of living adequate for the child's physical, mental, spiritual, moral and social development'.

[27] The debate on this provision took an entire session at the Committee Stage of the Children Bill. See *Hansard*, 16 May 1989 (afternoon).

it, its effectiveness is largely determined by the level of resources committed to it.[28] This has prompted one commentator to conclude thus:[29]

'Government policies to improve services but to control local authority spending are in direct conflict. Despite a common legal framework, there are huge differences in provision of children's services nationally which relate to many things including variations in resources. Implementation of legislation relating to children's services involves changes in attitude, reformulation of local policies, and the development of new services ... Without new services, provision will continue to be resource rather than needs-led ... There is now a wide recognition amongst local authorities that without an adequate level of resources there will be no development of services for children in need.'

A particularly difficult issue is the balance to be struck between providing family support services under Part III and services focused on families where a child is thought to be *at risk*. There is substantial evidence that local authorities have, in the overall context of inadequate funding, prioritised the latter to the detriment of the former.[30] This is, arguably, to put the cart before the horse but, in fairness to those who have to administer these scarce resources, a counter-pressure ought to be identified. This is that there is now more potential for legal liability in negligence or under the HRA 1998 where an authority fails to take appropriate or sufficient action to protect a child at risk who is then subsequently abused or neglected. We consider these developments below. For the moment it is sufficient to comment that local authorities are caught in something of a 'catch-22' situation. They need to divert resources into family support and 'preventative' work, but equally there are dangers in doing so if that means that services to protect children at risk will be left under-resourced.

The Department of Health[31] took the position that these are not, in any event, two entirely separate spheres of activity. It acknowledged that 'early intervention is essential to support children and families before problems, either from within the family or as a result of external factors, which have an impact on parenting capacity and family life escalate into crisis or abuse'.[32] But it recognised also that 'safeguarding children should not be seen as a separate

---

[28] See, for example, *R v Royal Borough of Kingston upon Thames, ex p T* [1994] 1 FLR 798. On resources for the Children Act generally, see the informative article by JM Masson 'Implementing Change for Children: Action at the Centre and Local Reaction' (1992) 19 *Journal of Law and Society* 320. See also JM Masson R Bailey-Harris and RJ Probert *Cretney's Principles of Family Law* (8th edn, Sweet & Maxwell, 2008), at pp 721–723 and the sources cited there. And for a scathing attack on the mismatch between government rhetoric and adequate resourcing of the child protection system see A MacDonald 'The caustic dichotomy-political vision and resourcing in the care system' [2009] 21 CFLQ 30.

[29] JM Masson above (1992) 19 *Journal of Law and Society* 320, at pp 335–336.

[30] See *Children Act Now: Messages from Research* (2001) p 22 at which it is noted that research studies have concluded that there is on the part of local authorities 'a continuing emphasis on linking interpretations of "in need" with eligibility criteria based on risk'. See also the succinct and helpful commentary in JM Masson, R Bailey-Harris and RJ Probert *Cretney's Principles of Family Law* (8th edn, Sweet & Maxwell, 2002), at pp 721–723.

[31] *Framework for the Assessment of Children in Need and Their Families* (Department of Health, 2000).

[32] Ibid, at p xi.

activity from providing for their welfare. They are two sides of the same coin'.[33] It should also be said that the level of state intervention can fluctuate in individual cases. Children may be thought to be at risk and subject to child protection plans only for these plans to be scaled down later to children in need plans where the level of risk subsides. Conversely, a children in need plan can be scaled up to a child protection plan where the level of risk is thought to be more immediate or to have intensified.

The Department of Health issued a framework for the assessment of children in need. This sets out, inter alia, a set of principles which should guide inter-agency, inter-disciplinary work with children in need[34] and it identifies three 'domains' of assessment, namely the child's developmental needs, the parents' or caregivers' capacities to respond appropriately and the wider family and environmental factors. It goes on to advise that the 'interaction between these three domains and the way they influence each other must be carefully analysed in order to gain a complete picture of a child's unmet needs and how to identify the best response to them'.[35] Failure to carry out proper assessments in accordance with the framework may now be a basis for judicial review. In *R (AB and SB) v Nottingham City Council*[36] the authority had without good reason failed to identify the child's needs, produce a care plan or provide identified services.

Central and local government: division of functions

Finally by way of introduction, something should be said about the division of functions between central and local government and the important principle of inter-agency co-operation at the local level. This was very much a theme of the reforms and finds expression in several places in the Children Act.[37] Central government responsibility for child care resided in the Department of Health, which took over from the former Department of Health and Social Security in 1989, until 2003. Its brief included the formulation of policy, preparation of legislation and the issuing of guidance.[38] In 2003 responsibility for children's services and child care was transferred from the Department of Health to the Department for Education and Skills under the direction of the First Minister of State for Children. There is a Social Services Inspectorate which has

---

[33] Ibid, at para 1.17.
[34] Ibid, at para 1.23.
[35] Ibid, at paras 1.40 and 1.42. On the role of assessment in different contexts and on the development of a 'common assessment framework', see C Piper 'Assessing Assessment' [2004] Fam Law 736.
[36] [2001] 3 FCR 350.
[37] Particularly in s 27.
[38] The point was forcefully made that there was no single government department responsible for policies affecting children and that this was one reason why an office of Children's Commissioner was required. See M Rosenbaum and P Newell *Taking Children Seriously* (Gulbenkian Foundation, 1991) (revised edn, 2000) and critique by A Bainham (1992) JSWFL 552.

responsibility for inspecting social services departments.[39] The responsibility for day-care, family support and protection of children is delegated by central government to local authorities. The legislation defines a local authority as a county council, metropolitan district or London Borough[40] or common council of the City of London. These councils are obliged to establish social services departments under the overall control of a Director of Social Services.[41] They replaced the former children departments with a much wider remit including responsibility for other potentially vulnerable groups such as the mentally ill and the elderly. It should also be noted, however, that many of the duties previously performed by local authorities in relation to the inspection and regulation of children's social care services including children's homes are now performed by The Office for Standards in Education, Children's Services and Skills (Ofsted).[42]

The lack of co-ordination in local services, especially between different departments within individual authorities, was a frequently-voiced criticism prior to the Children Act.[43] The Act attempted to address these deficiencies, in part, by creating new duties of inter-departmental co-operation. Hence, the local authority's statutory responsibilities are imposed not simply on its social services department (although clearly this will bear primary responsibility), but also on related departments and authorities, especially those responsible for housing and health.[44] These authorities are, subject to limited qualifications, required to co-operate with social services, and social services departments in different authorities are similarly required to co-operate with each other.[45] In 2003, Lord Laming's report following his inquiry into the death of Victoria

---

[39] For further discussion of the relationship between central and local government in this field, see JM Masson (above).

[40] Section 105(1).

[41] Local Authority Social Services Act 1970.

[42] The Education and Inspections Act 2006, transferring the powers from the Care Standards Commission which had been set up under the Care Standards Act 2000. Inspections are carried out taking account of the requirements of the 2000 Act, the Children's Homes Regulations 2001, the *Children's homes: national minimum standards* (DfE, 2011), and *Children Act 1989 guidance and regulations volume 5: children's homes* (DfE, 2011).

[43] Not least in public inquiries into the deaths of children in care – as to which see chapter 12 below. The importance of inter-agency co-operation was promoted in *Working Together Under the Children Act 1989* (HMSO, 1991), which has subsequently been updated. For discussion of earlier versions, see B Lindley and M Richards 'Working Together 2000 – how will parents fare under the new child protection process?' [2000] CFLQ 213. See also R Smith 'The Wrong End of the Telescope: Child protection or child safety?' (2002) 24 JSWFL 247.

[44] Education Authorities were formerly included, but were removed by the Local Education Authorities and Children's Services Authorities (Integration of Functions) Order 2010 (SI 2010/1158), art 5(1), Sch 2, Pt 2, para 37, with effect from 5 May 2010.

[45] The House of Lords decision in *R v Northavon DC, ex parte Smith* [1994] 2 AC 402 illustrates the limitations of the legal duty on authorities to co-operate with one another. The housing authority refused to rehouse an 'intentionally homeless' family despite being requested to do so by the social services department. The House of Lords held that it was entitled to refuse given the legal framework of the housing legislation and that the burden fell instead on social services to offer the family assistance, financial or otherwise, under Part III. See G Holgate 'Intentional Homelessness, Dependent Children and their Statutory Rights of Accommodation' [1994] Fam Law 264, which comments on the Court of Appeal decision. See also D Cowan and J Fionda 'Housing Homeless Families – An Update' [1995] CFLQ 66 for comment

Climbié[46] showed the system failing to protect a child who had been known to several social services departments, two police child protection teams, and had been admitted to two hospitals because of suspected deliberate harm. The Report recommended structural change and, following Green and White Papers,[47] led to the Children Act 2004.

Children's Services and the Children Act 2004

Following the Children Act 2004, children's services authorities,[48] headed by a Director of Children's Services, have duties aimed at safeguarding and promoting children's welfare,[49] and various other bodies (such as health services and the police) are required to ensure that their services and functions are discharged with regard to the need to safeguard and promote the welfare of children.[50] Similar duties are imposed by other statutes on those carrying out education functions,[51] on the Children and Family Court Advisory and Support Service (CAFCASS),[52] and on the UK Border Agency.[53]

Section 10 of the Children Act 2004 imposes a duty on local authorities to promote cooperation between the authority and its relevant partners[54] regarding children's well-being in their area,[55] and relevant partners have a duty to cooperate with the local authority.[56] Each children's services authority is required to establish a Local Safeguarding Children Board[57] (replacing Area Child Protection Committees) to coordinate and ensure the effectiveness of the work of various organisations on the Board for the purposes of safeguarding and promoting the welfare of children in the relevant local authority's area.[58]

---

on the House of Lords decision. Detailed consideration of the housing responsibilities of local authorities is beyond the scope of the present discussion.

[46] Lord Laming, *The Victoria Climbié Inquiry: Report of an Inquiry by Lord Laming* (Cm 5730, January 2003). See H Conway 'The Laming Inquiry – Victoria Climbié's Legacy' [2003] Fam Law 513.

[47] *Every Child Matters* and *Every Child Matters: Next Steps*, respectively.

[48] A metropolitan district council; district councils where there is no county council, a London Borough Council, the Common Council of the City of London, the Council of the Isles of Scilly.

[49] Children Act 2004, s 18.

[50] Children Act 2004, s 11.

[51] See Education Act 2002, ss 175 and 157 and regulations; Children Act 1989, s 87 (accommodation at independent schools); Childcare Act 2006, s 40 (duty in respect of Early Years Foundation Stage).

[52] Criminal Justice and Court Services Act 2000.

[53] Borders, Citizenship and Immigration Act 2009, s 55.

[54] These include health, education, police, and probation services amongst others. The full list of relevant partners is set out in s 10(4).

[55] The focus of the arrangements referred to is children's physical and mental health and emotional, social, and economic well-being; protection from harm and neglect; and education, training, and recreation.

[56] Children Act 2004, s 10(5).

[57] See Children Act 2004, ss 13–16 and the Local Safeguarding Children Boards Regulations 2006 (SI 2006/90) (made under s 13(2)); Local Safeguarding Children Boards (Amendment) Regulations 2010 (SI 2010/622) (made under s 13(4)).

[58] See Children Act 2004, s 14.

The legislation is supplemented by updated guidance on inter-agency cooperation, *Working Together to Safeguard Children*.[59]

SERVICES FOR CHILDREN AND FAMILIES

Before the Children Act, local authorities owed a duty to *all* children 'to make available such advice, guidance and assistance' as might promote their welfare 'by diminishing the need to receive children into or keep them in care ... or to bring children before a juvenile court'.[60] More specific powers and duties arose under other statutes relating to particular groups of children, including the mentally and the physically disabled.[61] There was a good deal of regional variation in the quality and extent of services provided to these different groups. The *Review* and the White Paper[62] accepted that it would be in the interests of all the children concerned to unify the relevant parts of child care law and health and welfare legislation, in particular to extend the protection of child care law to disabled children. Part III, accordingly, constitutes a single code governing the voluntary services offered by local authorities to children and families, regardless of the particular reason why these services are needed.[63]

Reformulation of the general duty

The general duty of local authorities to provide services is now contained in s 17(1) of the Children Act which states:

> 'It shall be the general duty of every local authority (in addition to the other duties imposed on them by this Part) –
>
> (a)   to safeguard and promote the welfare of children within their area who are in need; and
>
> (b)   so far as is consistent with that duty, to promote the upbringing of such children by their families, by providing a range and level of services appropriate to those children's needs.'

It is crucial to appreciate that this general duty to safeguard and promote welfare is not the same as being bound by the 'welfare principle' articulated in

---

59   See HM Government, *Working Together to Safeguard Children: A Guide to Inter-Agency Working to Safeguard and Promote the Welfare of Children* (London: DfE, April 2013), issued pursuant to the Local Authority Social Services Act 1970, s 7, and with which local authorities must therefore comply in carrying out their social services functions.

60   Child Care Act 1980, s 1.

61   The main statutes were the National Health Service Act 1977, the National Assistance Act 1948 and the Chronically Sick and Disabled Persons Act 1970.

62   DHSS *Review of Child Care Law* (1985) ('the *Review*') and *The Law on Child Care and Family Services* (1987) (Cmnd 62) ('the White Paper').

63   For a comment on how Part III of the Children Act has been affected by the Adoption and Children Act 2002, see J Masson 'The Impact of the Adoption and Children Act: Part 2 – The Provision of Services for Children and Families' [2003] Fam Law 644.

s 1 of the Act.[64] The Court of Appeal has made this clear in *Re M (Secure Accommodation Order)*.[65] Here, the question was whether the use of secure accommodation under s 25 of the Act was a matter to be governed by the welfare principle. The court held that, although the child's welfare was a relevant factor, the Act prescribed the circumstances under which secure accommodation might be used, including where the child was likely to cause injury to others, and accordingly there might be circumstances in which the exercise of the power would not be consistent with the idea that the child's welfare was paramount. But the court did not stop there. It went on to say that the welfare principle in s 1 did not apply to *any* of the powers and duties arising under Part III of the Act. Thus, while the individual child's welfare is a factor, indeed an important factor, in the exercise of the authority's obligations under Part III, it may be outweighed by other factors and policy considerations which the authority needs to take into account.

The legal duties towards children in need are imposed on the local authority in relation to those children who are 'within their area'.[66] We have also seen that there is a duty on different authorities to co-operate with one another. Authorities have a statutory obligation to comply with a request for help from another authority 'if it is compatible with their own statutory or other duties and obligations and does not unduly prejudice the discharge of any of their functions'.[67] This has led to some difficult questions concerning the proper boundaries between the statutory obligations of different authorities and especially between social services and housing authorities.

The matter came before the House of Lords in *R v Northavon District Council ex parte Smith*[68] and returned there in *R (G) v Barnet London Borough Council*.[69] In the latter case the principal issue was whether a local authority might, in discharging its statutory duties, accommodate a child *alone* without his or her family. One of the local authorities in the case had adopted a policy of dealing with the accommodation needs of homeless children by making accommodation available to them but not to their parents. The reasoning was that, although the provision of accommodation for the entire family would be

---

[64] For the welfare principle generally, see chapter 2. It has been held that, while the court may direct a local authority to reconsider the question of the services it should provide for a child, it may not direct it what to decide or direct it to make any *specific* provision for the child. See *Re T (Judicial Review: Local Authority Decisions Concerning Child in Need)* [2004] 1 FLR 601.

[65] [1995] 1 FLR 418.

[66] The child's *physical presence* in the area of the authority is required and is sufficient. See *R (S) v London Borough of Wandsworth, London Borough of Hammersmith and Fulham, London Borough of Lambeth* [2002] 1 FLR 469 in which there was something of a 'turf war' between the three authorities.

[67] Children Act 1989, s 27(2).

[68] [1994] 2 AC 402.

[69] *R (G) v Barnet London Borough Council; R (W) v Lambeth London Borough Council; R (A) v Lambeth London Borough Council* [2004] 1 FLR 454. For commentary, see D Cowan 'On Need and Gatekeeping' [2004] CFLQ 331. On the interaction of local authorities' powers to accommodate children under the Children Act with the Nationality, Immigration and Asylum Act 2002, see *M v London Borough of Islington and Secretary of State for the Home Department* [2004] 2 FLR 867.

at no greater cost to the authority, its experience was that a suggestion that a child might be removed and accommodated separately might lead parents to find family accommodation themselves at no cost to the authority. The House of Lords held by a slim majority that local authorities' duties under s 17 were of a *general* character and the duty to assess the child's needs under s 17 did not crystallise into a specific duty owed to the child as an individual. The services provided might include the provision of accommodation for a child, but the provision of residential accommodation to rehouse a child to enable him to live with his family was not the principal or primary purpose of the legislation. Housing was the function of the local housing authority. Thus, an authority providing a child with accommodation was not under a duty to accommodate the child's family as well. Dissenting, Lord Nicholls of Birkenhead and Lord Steyn took the view that, while it might be reasonable in the case of an older child to accommodate the child but not the parent, where the child was not old enough to understand what was going on and would be likely to be significantly upset at being separated from the parent, the authority could not fulfil its duty to meet the needs of the child by accommodating the child alone.

The duty in s 17 is a substantial recasting of the local authority's preventative role. Before the Children Act, the duty was to endeavour to avert not only compulsory care proceedings but also the need to receive children into voluntary care. The concept of voluntary care was abolished by the Children Act and replaced with the notion of children 'accommodated' or 'looked after' by local authorities. This voluntary provision of accommodation is now viewed as just one kind of service offered to children and families in difficulty and it was considered important that this should be seen as *positive* assistance and not as a negative or stigmatising procedure. Accordingly, local authorities are no longer required to diminish the need to accommodate children but it remains the case that they must attempt to prevent more coercive measures being required. This other aspect of the local authority's duty has to be ferreted out of Sch 2 to the Children Act, which lists a range of more specific duties. Here, there is a duty to take reasonable steps to reduce the need to bring proceedings for care or supervision orders, criminal proceedings against children, family proceedings which could result in them being placed in a local authority's care, or proceedings under the inherent jurisdiction of the High Court; to encourage children not to commit criminal offences; and to avoid the need to use secure accommodation.[70] The common characteristic of all these actions is that they are compulsory in nature and stand in contrast to voluntary family support. It is generally agreed that voluntary assistance, where possible, is preferable.

The other respect in which the duty was refashioned was by the addition of the word 'general'. The view of most commentators was that the effect of this was

---

[70]   Schedule 2, para 7.

to reverse a decision under the old law that the former preventive duty applied to individual children,[71] and this interpretation has been confirmed by the courts.[72]

Children in need

The statutory definition of 'children in need' is crucial. While it is true that some of the local authority's more specific duties and powers do extend to *all* children, even these are directed at a more restricted group since they exist 'for the purpose principally of facilitating the discharge of their general duty'.[73] Thus, specific duties like the duty to take reasonable steps to prevent the ill-treatment or neglect of children,[74] or the duty to provide 'family centres',[75] are intended to prevent children from *becoming* children in need.

The importance of the classification of 'child in need' is that it operates as a threshold condition or 'passport' to the services offered by the local authority, and these are not simply those services offered by the children's services department. The general duty binds all departments within the local authority and it has already been mentioned that they are under an obligation to co-operate with each other. An assessment that a child is, or is not, in need, may therefore have important repercussions, not simply for family support by social services, but in the determination of housing, health and educational priorities. In short, the legislation appears to authorise positive discrimination in favour of childen in need. The negative side of this is that the label 'child in need' can acquire a stigma akin to that which has often been thought to attach to means-tested social security benefits – some of which also have the 'passport' effect of securing entitlement to a range of other benefits. This might become a real danger if local authorities too readily equate 'child in need' with 'child at risk'. It seems that scarce resources and competing claims on those resources may mean that local authorities will resort to some form of rationing device. We discussed above what can be a blurring of the distinction between voluntary and compulsory action, of which this is perhaps another aspect.

The Children Act defines a child as being in need if:[76]

> '(a) he is unlikely to achieve or maintain, or to have the opportunity of achieving or maintaining, a reasonable standard of health or development without the provision for him of services by a local authority under this part;
> (b) his health or development is likely to be significantly impaired, or further impaired, without the provision for him of such services; or
> (c) he is disabled.'

---

[71] *A-G (ex rel Tilley) v London Borough of Wandsworth* [1981] 1 All ER 1162.
[72] The *Barnet* case discussed above, and see also *R v London Borough of Barnet ex parte B* [1994] 1 FLR 592.
[73] Section 17(2).
[74] Schedule 2, para 4(1).
[75] Schedule 2, para 9.
[76] Section 17(10).

This definition is rather broad and indeterminate, except insofar as it is clear that we are dealing with a restricted category of children. The Childen Act does, however, go on to define various components in the definition with greater particularity, if not precision. It is evident from the definition itself, that the local authority must concern itself not only with those children who are already in need (in the sense that they already have a low standard of health or development) but also with those who are likely to find themselves in that position unless services are provided. The inclusion of the prospective element emphasises prevention rather than cure and mirrors the reformulated ground for compulsory action.[77] 'Development' for these purposes is expressed to include 'physical, intellectual, emotional, social or behavioural development' and 'health' includes 'physical or mental health'. 'Disabled' means a child who is 'blind, deaf or dumb or suffers from mental disorder of any kind or is substantially and permanently handicapped by illness, injury or congenital deformity or such other disability as may be prescribed'.[78] The use of terminology like this was criticised as unduly stigmatic during the parliamentary debates and it has been said that it is inappropriate today.[79] The reasoning appears to be that Parliament wanted to ensure the specific inclusion of all those categories of children for whom it was intended that the local authority's duty should apply. Direct payments may now be made[80] to a person with parental responsibility for a disabled child of 16 or 17 years of age. The purpose is to enable them to purchase a service which would otherwise have been provided by the authority itself.

It has been held that the local authority's determination that a child is, or is not, in need is not susceptible to challenge except through the judicial review procedure. In *Re J (Specific Issue Order: Leave to Apply)*,[81] a 17-year-old boy was refused leave to seek a specific issue order deeming him to be a child 'in need' and requiring the local authority to make appropriate provision for him. Wall J held that Parliament could not have envisaged that the exercise of the duties imposed on local authorities under Part III of the Act should be exposed to judicial intervention except where the statute expressly provided for this, for example in relation to secure accommodation. The courts had not been given any power under the legislation to regulate the selection of children in need or to enforce the statutory duty to accommodate such children.

If it is decided that a child is in need, then before determining what (if any) services to provide for a particular child in need, a local authority shall, so far as is reasonably practicable and consistent with the child's welfare: (a) ascertain the child's wishes and feelings regarding the provision of those services; and (b) give due consideration (having regard to his age and understanding) to such wishes and feelings of the child as they have been able to ascertain.

---

[77]   Section 31(2), and see chapter 12 below.
[78]   Section 17(11).
[79]   MDA Freeman *Children, Their Families and the Law* (Macmillan, 1992), at p 57.
[80]   Children Act 1989, s 17A, inserted by the Carers and Disabled Children Act 2000, s 7(1).
[81]   [1995] 1 FLR 669.

Available services

If the definition of children in need is full of indeterminate concepts, so also is the statutory basis upon which a number of particular services are offered by local authorities. There are duties to 'take reasonable steps' or to make such provision 'as is appropriate'. The combined effect of such provisions (including the definition of 'children in need') is to give local authorities an almost unassailable controlling discretion and to make legal challenges very difficult. However, such a challenge succeeded in *R v Hammersmith and Fulham London Borough Council ex parte D*.[82] Here a Swedish mother had arrived in England with her two sons, having left a situation of domestic violence in Sweden. The local authority accepted that the children were in need, inter alia, by reason of their homelessness. Initially they provided bed and breakfast accommodation and a subsistence allowance but thereafter they wanted to discharge their statutory functions by financial assistance to enable the mother and her children to return to Sweden. They declared that they would terminate the provision of accommodation and financial support in the event that the mother declined this offer. The mother successfully challenged this decision in judicial review. Kay J held that in limiting the use of its statutory powers in this way the authority was in breach of its duties under Part III of the Children Act. It was quite in order for the authority to offer financial assistance to enable the family to return to another country if it thought that the needs of the child would be best met in that way. But it was wrong for it to withdraw further assistance, or threaten to withdraw it, if the offer was declined. In the present case there was no immediate prospect, realistically, that the mother would be able to return to Sweden, and the authority was therefore obliged to continue to provide accommodation and financial support while the mother had no funds to cater for their needs.[83]

Services may not only be made directly available to children but also to members of their family. A major aim of the legislation is to promote the upbringing of children within their own families and it is the duty of the local authority to try to give effect to this aim.[84] One aspect of this is that services may be offered to any member of the family of a child in need, provided that this is with a view to safeguarding the welfare of that child.[85] Suppose, for example, that the presence of a severely disabled child within a family is affecting the health or development of other children of the family and putting everyone under strain. The statutory provision would enable extra support to be provided for that child with a view to alleviating the overall family situation. 'Family' for these purposes has an extended meaning and includes 'any person who has parental responsibility for the child and any other person with whom he has been living'.[86] The local authority is therefore able to concentrate on

---

[82] [1999] 1 FLR 642.
[83] The mother was not yet eligible for income support because she had not yet become habitually resident in the UK.
[84] Section 17(1)(b).
[85] Section 17(3).
[86] Section 17(10).

those who have the actual care of a child, without having to concern itself with technical questions about who has parental responsibility.

As under the old law, services may include giving assistance in kind or in cash.[87] Prima facie, it might appear more attractive for local authorities to spend a relatively small amount of money on improving the home conditions of a family in which there are children who might otherwise need to be accommodated by it. There is no question that the cost of accommodating the child would far exceed any cash assistance given under this provision. But the issue is politically sensitive, since to make widespread use of these payments could be seen as usurping the role of the social security system which, however inadequately, caters for the material needs of families. Moreover, in keeping with the social security reforms of the 1980s, the local authority may, in some circumstances, require repayment of its assistance or its value.[88] It must, however, have regard to the means of parents and there is an automatic exemption from liability for those in receipt of the principal means-tested benefits.[89]

The principle of inter-agency co-operation has been noted. Another facet of this is that local authorities are required to facilitate the provision by others of services which they themselves lack the power to provide, and to make arrangements for others to act on their behalf in the provision of any service.[90] This underlines the need for co-operation between the public, private and voluntary sectors. The specific services which local authorities are required or empowered to provide are largely contained in Sch 2 to the Children Act.

Specific powers and duties

It is not appropriate in a work of this nature to analyse every detail of Sch 2 to the Children Act. But it is necessary to gain a general sense of what local authorities are required to provide beyond their broad umbrella power, and to highlight some of the more significant services. Freeman has helpfully identified the general character of the services in question:[91]

> 'Local authorities cannot be expected to meet every individual need, but they are
> to take "reasonable steps" to identify the extent of need in their area and then to
> use their discretion reasonably and sensibly to make decisions about service
> provision in the light of the information they receive and their statutory

---

[87] Section 17(6). This used to be referred to under the old law as 'section 1 money'.

[88] Section 17(7). The obvious analogy is with the abolition of 'single payments' in 1988 and their replacement with loans under the newly constituted 'Social Fund'. For a discussion of these reforms under the Social Security Act 1986 (implemented in April 1988), see Wikeley, Ogus and Barendt's *The Law of Social Security* (6th edn, Butterworths, 2002), ch 13.

[89] Section 17(8) and (9). The principal means-tested benefits are now income support (formerly supplementary benefit), working families tax credit (introduced in 1999 to replace family credit which itself replaced family income supplement), disabled person's tax credit and income-based jobseeker's allowance, to be replaced by Universal Credit. See chapter 9.

[90] Section 17(5)(a) and (b).

[91] MDA Freeman *Children, Their Families and the Law* (Macmillan, 1992), at p 53.

obligations. They must ensure that a range of services is available to meet the need they identify. What is required will vary from area to area but is likely to include day care, foster care, some provision of residential care. They will need to offer a range of placements to reflect the racial, cultural, religious and linguistic needs of the children of their area (s 22(5)(c)). They will also have to have a range of short-term and longer term accommodation as well as permanent placements.'

We noted above some of the local authority's specific duties. Further duties and powers are listed below, followed by a closer examination of those duties relating to day-care and other services offered to children who are living with their families.

Among the local authority's duties are:

(1)   a duty to publicise the services provided by it[92] and by others (particularly voluntary organisations) and to take such steps as are reasonably practicable to ensure that the information is received by those who might benefit from the services;[93]

(2)   a duty to open and maintain a register of disabled children;[94]

(3)   a duty to minimise the effects of disability suffered by disabled children;[95]

(4)   a duty to take reasonable steps to prevent the ill-treatment or neglect of children by the provision of services;[96]

(5)   a power to assist someone (possibly through cash) with removal expenses and the costs of obtaining alternative accommodation where that person is living with a child and the child is suffering, or is likely to suffer, ill-treatment at the hands of the person in question;[97]

(6)   a duty to provide family centres at which a child, his parents and others may receive advice, guidance and counselling or take part in various activities of an occupational, social, cultural or recreational nature;[98]

---

[92]   Services provided under ss 17, 18, 20, 23B to 23D, 24A and 24B.
[93]   Schedule 2, para 1(2).
[94]   Schedule 2, para 2(1).
[95]   Schedule 2, para 6. The best discussion of the application of the Children Act to disabled children is Freeman (above) especially, ch 11.
[96]   Schedule 2, para 4.
[97]   Schedule 2, para 5. This provision should now be taken alongside the provision enabling local authorities to ask for 'exclusion requirements' to be inserted into emergency protection orders and interim care orders under Part IV of the Family Law Act 1996. This followed the recommendations of the Law Commission in (1992) Law Com Report No 207 *Domestic Violence and Occupation of the Family Home.* We discuss this regime in chapter 11.
[98]   Schedule 2, para 9.

(7)   a duty, where a child in need is living apart from his family, to take
      reasonable steps to enable him to live with them or to promote contact
      with them if, in the authority's opinion, it is necessary to do so to
      safeguard or promote his welfare;[99]

(8)   in making arrangements for the provision of day-care or arrangements
      designed to encourage persons to act as local authority foster parents, a
      duty to have regard to the different racial groups to which children in need
      within its area belong.[100]

Day-care and pre-school provision

Section 18 sets out the duties and powers of authorities regarding day-care for
pre-school children and supervision of school-age children outside school.[101]
Local authorities *must* provide day-care for children in need 'as is
appropriate'.[102] In Wales there is also power to provide day-care for children in
their area who are *not* in need.[103] This reserves a wide discretion to individual
local authorities. They are also empowered to provide back-up support for
those people who are directly involved in providing day-care facilities.[104] In
addition, they have corresponding duties to older children in need, who are
attending school, to provide for such care or supervised activities as is
appropriate outside school hours or during school holidays. Again, in Wales
this provision extends to children who are not in need.[105] This is intended to
assist working parents, after school hours but before the end of the working
day, and during school holidays. It is for individual local authorities to decide
how precisely to discharge these responsibilities, but the most obvious examples
are day nurseries, playgroups, child-minding, out-of-school clubs, holiday
schemes and parent and toddler groups.[106]

Assistance for children living with their families

Schedule 2, para 8 to the Children Act requires local authorities to make 'such
provision as they consider appropriate' for specified services to be made
available for children in need while they are living with their families. The
services in question are:

(1)   advice, guidance and counselling;

(2)   occupational, social, cultural or recreational activities;

---

[99]   Schedule 2, para 10.
[100] Schedule 2, para 11.
[101] For a more detailed discussion, see Freeman (above), at pp 85–88.
[102] Section 18(1). Section 18(4) provides that 'day care' means 'any form of care or supervised
       activity provided for children during the day (whether or not it is provided on a regular basis)'.
[103] Section 18(2).
[104] Section 18(3).
[105] Section 18(5) and (6).
[106] Other examples are given in *The Children Act 1989 Guidance and Regulations Vol 2* (above), at
       paras 3.8–3.17.

(3)   home help (including laundry facilities);

(4)   travel facilities or assistance with travelling to and from home for the purpose of taking advantage of services;

(5)   assistance to enable the child and the family to have a holiday.

This, then, is another duty which encapsulates the ethos of family support. As far as possible, every effort should be made to keep functioning families together. In some cases, for whatever reason, this may not be possible, and it may prove necessary for the local authority to look after a child itself. We now turn to the important duty to provide accommodation.

Similar duties are owed under Sch 2, para 8A to children who are accommodated by the local authority. Paragraph 8A provides that the services shall be provided with a view to promoting contact between each accommodated child and that child's family, and may, in particular, include:

(1)   advice, guidance and counselling;

(2)   services necessary to enable the child to visit, or to be visited by, members of the family;[107]

(3)   assistance to enable the child and members of the family to have a holiday together.

We turn now to consider in detail the provision of accommodation.

THE PROVISION OF ACCOMMODATION

Prior to the Children Act, children who were accommodated by local authorities with the consent of parents were 'in care' albeit 'voluntary care'. Yet, although the initial arrangement was voluntary, this could slip into compulsion with the passage of time. 'Voluntary care' began to acquire a negative, even 'threatening',[108] image as local authorities were empowered to pass administrative resolutions assuming parental rights.[109] Parents were required to give 28 days' notice before resuming the care of a child who had been in voluntary care for at least six months. Moreover, it was held that the local authority was not obliged to return the child immediately on demand, even where that child had been in care for less than six months, and that the child remained in care despite the notice having been given.[110] This, it was said,

---

[107]   It is specifically provided that nothing in para 8A is to prejudice Sch 2, para 10.
[108]   The description of J Eekelaar and R Dingwall *The Reform of Child Care Law* (Routledge, 1990), at p 74.
[109]   Under the Child Care Act 1980, s 3.
[110]   *London Borough of Lewisham v Lewisham Juvenile Court Justices* [1980] AC 273.

gave the local authority a 'breathing space' to take further action to protect the welfare of the child, usually by passing a resolution to assume parental rights.

All of this was inconsistent with the objectives of the Children Act, in particular the voluntary partnership which is supposed to exist between parents and the local authority. Eekelaar and Dingwall have identified the problem confronted in the *Review of Child Care Law* that preceded the 1989 Act as the 'increasingly sharp distinction between being in and out of care'.[111] If this was the most significant distinction under the old law, the crucial legal distinction following the Children Act is between the children who are formally 'in care' under a court order and those who are not, either because they are at home or because they are voluntarily accommodated. Yet, as Eekelaar and Dingwall go on to point out, it was not the intention of the *Review* to create such an obvious demarcation.[112] The *Review* sought to establish 'finer gradations' of voluntary accommodation which would have embraced 'respite care' and 'shared care'. *Respite care* (a concept previously utilised in connection with disabled children) would have been a short-term arrangement of up to one month. Parents would not have been required to give any notice of removal, the local authority would have been wholly dependent on parental delegation, and parental responsibility would not have passed to the local authority.[113] *Shared care* would, in contrast, have involved a transfer of parental responsibility to the authority by agreement.[114] The 28 days' notice would have been preserved and, since it envisaged 'shared' control, the local authority would have been obliged to allow parents to participate in decision-making and plans for the child.

In the event, the Government rejected the distinction between respite care and shared care as unworkable.[115] Hence, *all* children who are not 'in care' under a court order are now not in care at all. Parental responsibility for them does not pass to the local authority, and parents may remove them without notice. There is no longer any power to assume parental rights without a court order. These issues are now governed by formal agreements between authorities and parents, and the law is in retreat from these voluntary arrangements. We now turn to the legal framework under which these agreements operate.

Before doing so however it is important for the reader to be aware that s 20 agreements are frequently an *integral aspect* of care proceedings and not merely a precursor or alternative to them. A common scenario at the first hearing in public law proceedings will be for a s 20 agreement to be concluded with the parents whereby the children are accommodated with relatives or foster carers while the proceedings take their course. This is an important example of how the 'voluntary' and the 'compulsory' can become blurred, even perhaps inexorably connected in practice.

---

[111] J Eekelaar and R Dingwall (above), at pp 74–75. See DHSS *Review of Child Care Law* (1985).
[112] J Eekelaar and R Dingwall (above), at pp 74–75.
[113] See DHSS *Review of Child Care Law* (1985), chs 6 and 7.
[114] Ibid, at ch 7.
[115] *The Law on Child Care and Family Services* (1987) (Cmnd 62) ('the White Paper'), at para 26.

The duty to accommodate

Section 20(1) of the Children Act sets out the circumstances under which local authorities must accommodate children in need.[116] It states:

> 'Every local authority shall provide accommodation for any child in need within their area who appears to them to require accommodation as a result of:
>
> (a)   there being no person who has parental responsibility for him;
> (b)   his being lost or having been abandoned; or
> (c)   the person who has been caring for him being prevented (whether or not permanently, and for whatever reason) from providing him with suitable accommodation or care.'

In simple terms, the duty under s 20 arises in relation to orphaned or abandoned children[117] and children whose parents or carers are prevented by temporary or long-term illness, disability or other reason from properly looking after them. The duty in s 20 applies to individual children and 'involves an evaluative judgment on some matters but not a discretion'.[118] The section poses a series of questions which must be considered, and satisfactorily answered, if s 20 is to apply.[119] Section 20 applies to a child, and in cases of doubt concerning a person's age this must be determined objectively as a matter of fact.[120] Whether a child is a 'child in need' is a matter for the judgment of the local authority and cannot be interfered with unless no authority could

---

[116] It should be noted that under s 21 of the Children Act the local authority has other duties to accommodate children in specified circumstances. These are:
(i) where the child is removed or kept away from home under the short-term protective measures in Part V;
(ii) where the child is in police protection;
(iii) where the authority is requested to receive the child under s 38(6) of the Police and Criminal Evidence Act 1984 (which generally requires arrested juveniles to be moved to local authority accommodation);
(iv) where the child is the subject of a supervision order imposing a local authority residence requirement under Sch 5, para 6 to the Powers of Criminal Courts (Sentencing) Act 2000 or under paragraph 21 of Sch 2 to the Criminal Justice and Immigration Act 2008 (breach of youth rehabilitation orders); or
(v) where the child is the subject of a youth rehabilitation order with a local authority residence requirement.

[117] It should be noted that, since the accommodation of children under s 20 does not confer parental responsibility on the local authority, it may be desirable in the case of an orphan for the authority to seek a care order to enable it to plan for the child's long-term welfare. See, for example, *Re SH (Care Order: Orphan)* [1995] 1 FLR 746, and chapter 12 below.

[118] *R (G) v Southwark London Borough Council* [2009] UKHL 26, [2009] 2 FLR 380, at para [31]. For a helpful analysis of cases interpreting s 20, see S Gore *The Children Act 1989 Local Authority Support for Children and Families* (Family Law, 2011), ch 5.

[119] *R (G) v Southwark London Borough Council* [2009] UKHL 26, [2009] 2 FLR 380, at para [28], per Baroness Hale of Richmond, drawing on Ward LJ's judgment *in R (A) v Croydon London Borough Council; R (M) v Lambeth London Borough Council* [2008] EWCA Civ 1445, [2009] 1 FLR 1324, at [75].

[120] *R (A) v Croydon London Borough Council; R (M) v Lambeth London Borough Council* [2009] UKSC 8, [2009] 3 FCR 607. The problem arises, for example, where persons who are perhaps seeking asylum arrive in this jurisdiction without a birth certificate.

rationally have reached the same view. The child must be within the local authority's area and appear to require accommodation for the reasons set out in paras (a) to (c) of s 20(1). It seems clear from the wording of s 20(1)(c) that a child can require accommodation even if already housed if present conditions do not provide suitable care. Indeed, it has been said that the words 'for whatever reason' in s 20(1)(c) indicate that the widest possible scope should be given to the provision.[121] It would seem to apply, therefore, even where a parent has made himself intentionally homeless.[122] Before providing accommodation under this section, a local authority shall, so far as is reasonably practicable and consistent with the child's welfare (a) ascertain the child's wishes and feelings regarding the provision of accommodation; and (b) give due consideration (having regard to his age and understanding) to such wishes and feelings of the child as they have been able to ascertain. The local authority would also need to consider any relevant objection of a person or persons with parental responsibility who is willing and able to provide accommodation, and indeed the wishes of any competent child[123] (both of which are discussed in more detail below).

The most obvious practical implication of accommodating the child is the provision of a home and care for the child. However, once accommodated by the local authority the child becomes a 'looked after' child within the meaning of the Children Act 1989. This status, which is discussed in more detail later in this chapter, imposes a number of duties upon the local authority in respect of the child, which in some cases can extend long-term into the accommodated person's adulthood. Thus accommodation may bring to the child a range of services beyond just a roof over the child's head, and has considerable resource implications for the local authority. In *R (G) v Southwark London Borough Council*.[124] the House of Lords made clear, however, that when the duty to accommodate applies, the child must be accorded that status, and the local authority are 'not entitled to "side-step" it by giving the accommodation a different label'.[125] In that case a 17-year-old had been excluded from home by his mother and was sleeping on friends' sofas. On advice, he approached his local children's services department requesting accommodation under s 20(1) of the Children Act 1989. After a detailed assessment the local authority

---

[121] *R (G) v Barnet London Borough Council; R (W) v Lambeth London Borough Council; R (A) v Lambeth London Borough Council* [2003] UKHL 57, [2004] 2 AC 208, [2003] 3 WLR 1194, [2004] 1 FLR 454, at [100] per Lord Hope of Craighead.

[122] *R (G) v Barnet London Borough Council; R (W) v Lambeth London Borough Council; R (A) v Lambeth London Borough Council* [2003] UKHL 57, [2004] 1 FLR 454, at [24]; see also *Attorney-General ex rel Tilley v Wandsworth London Borough Council* [1981] 1 WLR 854, *sub nom Attorney-General ex rel Tilley v London Borough of Wandsworth* (1981) 2 FLR 377.

[123] As supported by Children Act 1989, s 20(11), and see *R (G) v Southwark London Borough Council* [2009] UKHL 26, [2009] 2 FLR 380, at para [28](6) and *R(M) v Hammersmith and Fulham London Borough Council* [2008] UKHL 14, [2008] 1 FLR 1384, at para [43].

[124] [2009] UKHL 26, [2009] 2 FLR 380.

[125] Ibid, at [28]. See also *H, Barhanu and B v Wandsworth Hackney and Islington LBC* [2007] EWHC 1082 (Admin), [2007] 2 FLR 822; *R (L) v Nottinghamshire County Council* [2007] EWHC 2364 (Admin), [2007] All ER (D) 158 (Sept); *London Borough of Southwark v D sub nom R (D) v A Local Authority* [2007] EWCA Civ 182, [2007] 1 FLR 2181, [2007] Fam Law 701; *R (S) v Sutton London Borough Council* [2007] EWCA Civ 790, (2007) 10 CCLR 625.

concluded that s 20 was 'not appropriate' and that his needs could be provided merely through provision of housing and other support. In judicial review proceedings the House of Lords ultimately held that the young man's circumstances had fallen within s 20(1), that duty had arisen, and he was accommodated by the local authority,[126] with all the attendant local authority responsibilities.[127]

The Children Act Advisory Committee in its *Final Report* commented on what were appropriate and inappropriate uses of the power to accommodate children.[128] The Committee said that accommodation was properly used by the local authorities to work in partnership with parents in a variety of circumstances of need, such as hospital admission of a parent, bereavement, housing difficulties and respite care. But it went on to say that it was crucial that accommodation should not be regarded as an alternative to an application for a care order or supervision order since, if used inappropriately, drift and damaging delay could occur to the detriment of the child. There was evidence in some cases that parents were agreeing to accommodation as an alternative to court proceedings, in return for generous contact with the child. This could lead to delay in decision-making and planning, a failure to address fundamental problems and failure to plan properly for the future. There was also evidence that some parents used accommodation too frequently as a means of crisis resolution, especially in the context of changes of school, resulting in harm to the child from instability.

The relevance of objections

It is the very essence of these arrangements that they are voluntary. This means that they cannot be effected in the face of opposition by parents, although this blanket statement requires some qualification in the case of divorced or unmarried parents. There is no requirement of positive consent since it is obvious that this will be unobtainable in the case of orphaned or abandoned[129] children. Instead, what is required is an absence of *relevant* opposition. Where the arrangement is opposed by someone with the right to oppose it, the local authority will have to resort to compulsory measures if it wishes to take over the care of the child. Where the child is accommodated under s 20 during care

---

[126] See also *Re T (Accommodation by Local Authority)* [1995] 1 FLR 159. Compare *R (M) v Hammersmith and Fulham London Borough Council* [2008] UKHL 14, [2008] 1 FLR 1384 in which the House of Lords held that no duty had arisen because the child presented to the Housing Department and her situation had not therefore been drawn to the attention of the children's services of the local authority. For criticism, see J Driscoll and K Hollingsworth 'Accommodating Children in Need: *R (M) v Hammersmith and Fulham London Borough Council* [2008] CFLQ 522.

[127] He thus became an eligible child within the meaning of para 19B(2) of Sch 2 to the Act, and, upon reaching 18, a 'former relevant child' within the meaning of s 23C(1).

[128] *Children Act Advisory Committee Final Report June 1997* (Lord Chancellor's Department, 1997), at pp 29–30.

[129] The concept of abandonment was examined in the context of adoption legislation as long ago as 1955. In *Watson v Nikolaisen* [1955] 2 QB 286 the court defined it to mean 'leaving the child to its fate'.

proceedings a parent may threaten to withdraw his or her consent if dissatisfied with the authority's decisions or management of the case, for example in relation to contact. However, to do so carries the serious risk that the authority will retaliate by restoring the matter to court and immediately seeking an interim care order. Here again what might appear at first sight to be a voluntary arrangement is most definitely one which operates in a coercive environment.

Right of objection if suitable alternative accommodation offered

The primary rule is that no child may be accommodated where a person with parental responsibility (most obviously a parent) objects.[130] In *R v Tameside Metropolitan Borough Council ex parte J*[131] it was held that this right of objection extended to the *kind* of accommodation offered to the child. Here a child with severe disabilities was accommodated in a residential home for disabled children under a voluntary arrangement with the local authority. The council later wished to move her to a foster home believing this to be in her best interests. The parents objected and, when their objections were overruled, applied for judicial review of the decision. Scott Baker J granted a declaration that the authority had no power to place the child with foster parents without her parents' consent, since they retained parental responsibility and with it the right to decide where the child lived. Neither party to a voluntary arrangement had the right to dictate to the other where the child should live. It was a matter for co-operation between the parents and the authority. The authority under a voluntary arrangement, possessed only day-to-day powers of management. If it wished to secure compulsory control over a child it would need to obtain a care order. Under a voluntary arrangement the only alternative open to the authority, if agreement could not be reached, would be to give parents the choice of accepting its solution or caring for the child themselves. This right of objection is qualified in that it must be shown that the objector is himself willing and able to provide accommodation for the child. It appears that this was inspired by concern that an estranged or 'absent' parent might seek to frustrate an arrangement between the caring parent and the local authority, with no intention of proposing a more suitable alternative. The second, and complementary, rule is that anyone with parental responsibility 'may at any time remove the child from accommodation provided by or on behalf of the local authority'.[132] Both rules are displaced where a residence order is in force and where the person or persons in whose favour it is made has agreed to the arrangement. The same applies where, instead of a residence order, there is an

---

[130] Section 20(7). There can be no compulsory removal from parental care without a court order: see *R (G) Nottingham City Council*. [2008] EWHC 152 (Admin), [2008] 1 FLR 1660, discussed in chapter 11.

[131] [2000] 1 FLR 942.

[132] Section 20(8). It is, of course, implicit in this that the person with parental responsibility can object to the continuation of an arrangement previously made with his approval.

order under the inherent jurisdiction of the High Court.[133] In either case, where more than one person holds a residence order, each of them must agree to the child being accommodated.[134]

Operation of provisions in different family situations

Where each of the child's parents has parental responsibility, an objection by *either* parent will preclude the arrangement, and either parent may remove a child accommodated originally with the agreement of the other. In practice, it is unlikely that parents will disagree over so fundamental an issue, but it is not impossible, especially where their relationship is breaking down or they have already separated. The normal rule which allows parental responsibility to be independently exercised, even were parents disagree with each other, is clearly superseded by the statutory right of objection.

In some cases, the mother alone may have parental responsibility, because the other parent did not obtain parental responsibility by operation of law[135] and has not acquired it.[136] She may thus enter in an arrangement with the local authority, and the other parent has no right of objection or removal unless he or she has previously acquired parental responsibility. It has been pointed out that this puts the small minority of unmarried fathers who have actual care of their children but do not have parental responsibility in a peculiarly vulnerable position vis-à-vis children's services.[137] It would, of course, be open to a parent to seek a parental responsibility order and/or a residence order, the effect of which would be to authorise removal of the child from the local authority. But where the child is by this time settled, perhaps in a foster home, the court may be reluctant to upset the status quo by making an order.

Where the marriage or civil partnership of parents has been dissolved, a parent, although physically absent, retains equal parental responsibility. This will be the situation in the majority of cases because of the 'no order' principle. In the minority of cases in which a residence order is made, its effect is to displace the primary rule and to 'trump' the non-resident parent's right of objection.[138] How far this is consistent with the notion of continuing parental responsibility has been questioned.[139]

---

[133] Section 20(9).

[134] Section 20(10).

[135] For example, through marriage or civil partnership to the mother, a parental order pursuant to s 54 of the Human Fertilisation and Embryology Act 2008, or an adoption order pursuant to the Adoption and Children Act 2002.

[136] Under s 4 or s 4ZA of the Children Act 1989. The law on parental responsibility is discussed in detail in chapter 4.

[137] A Bainham *Children: The New Law* (Family Law, 1990), at para 4.25, citing the case of *Re L (A Minor)* (1984) *The Times*, June 21.

[138] This is not, of course, a situation confined to divorce or dissolution, but divorce is easily the most significant context numerically.

[139] A Bainham (above), at para 4.26.

Abolition of statutory notice requirement

The abolition of the statutory notice requirement has caused concern. The fear is, as Freeman has put it, that local authorities may become 'dumping grounds'. Children might come in and out of local authority accommodation 'at a parent's whim, with no opportunity for planning, and little attention to the needs of the child for security and stability'.[140] The hope is that this sort of capricious behaviour on the part of parents will be avoided by carefully negotiated agreements which deal specifically with the issue of the child returning home. The possibility of an attempt by parents to remove their child suddenly from local authority care, cannot, however, be discounted, and this had led to widespread speculation about what action the local authority could legally take to forestall such an occurrence.[141] The local authority's general duty to safeguard the child's welfare, and the allied power which de facto carers have to do what is reasonable in the circumstances, ought to be sufficient to resist a summary removal and to fill what might otherwise be a legal vacuum.[142] But if the authority wished to continue to hold the child, it would need to seek a care order, probably preceded by an emergency protection order.[143] Police protection could be invoked, or a foster parent might conceivably seek a residence order or care and control in wardship proceedings. Probably the most unsatisfactory aspect of not requiring at least a short period of notice is that this may hinder the legitimate plans of local authorities in trying to ensure a smooth transition back to the family, possibly by means of a phased return. In some cases, the reluctance of children's services to hand a child over on demand may simply reflect its wish to be satisfied that the home circumstances have improved sufficiently for the child to return. It would be extremely unfortunate if this wholly reasonable concern were to force the local authority into coercive action. An amendment in the House of Lords which would have required a mere 24 hours' notice was rejected as inconsistent with the voluntary partnership principle.[144] While it is likely that in most cases parents will stick to the agreements they make with children's services, and will not try to remove children in inappropriate circumstances, it is still arguable that a statutory requirement would have been desirable.

---

[140] MDA Freeman *Children, Their Families and the Law* (Macmillan, 1992), at p 65.

[141] The options are extensively canvassed by Freeman (above), at pp 66–69, and by J Eekelaar and R Dingwall *The Reform of Child Care Law* (Routledge, 1990), at p 77.

[142] See ss 17(1) and 3(5). The right to remove appears to be supported by an unreported decision of Ward J (as he then was) in *Nottinghamshire County Council v J* (26 November 1993). For the position under the old law, see *Krishnan v Sutton London Borough Council* [1970] Ch 181. It has been pointed out that the right to remove may be illusory, since in practice the local authority would, if concerned, respond with some form of emergency protection: see JM Masson, R Bailey-Harris and RJ Probert *Cretney's Principles of Family Law* (8th edn, Sweet & Maxwell, 2008), at p 727.

[143] As to which, see chapters 11 and 12 below.

[144] House of Lords, Official Report, 20 December 1988, col 1335.

The child's point of view

How far should children themselves be able to decide whether or not they wish to be admitted to local authority accommodation or, once there, to remain there or leave? The legislation distinguishes between those over 16 years of age and those under that age.

Provision for children over 16 years of age

The position of those over the age of 16 is clear. The Children Act provides that neither the parental right of objection nor the parental right of removal applies where a child of 16 years of age agrees to being provided with accommodation.[145] The authority *must* accommodate any child of 16 years 'in need', whose welfare it considers 'is likely to be seriously prejudiced if they do not provide him with accommodation',[146] and it *may* provide accommodation for any child in its area if it considers that to do so 'would safeguard or promote the child's welfare'.[147] The purpose of these provisions is to cater for teenagers who have a seriously dysfunctional relationship with their parents. The local authority's duty is a very restricted one, although it retains a wider *discretion*. The reason why the local authority's duty is so restricted is not entirely clear, but it may serve as a controlling mechanism for those local authorities which might otherwise be swamped by demands for accommodation from homeless young people in this age group. Again, the relationship between this provision, social security provision and the statutory responsibilities of housing authorities is a politically sensitive one.[148] The legislation does not deal expressly with the issue of a child leaving accommodation but, since the local authority will have no statutory basis on which to retain a 16- or 17-year-old child against his wishes,[149] the implication is that the child can discharge himself. The local authority will then have statutory duties to advise and assist that child.

Provision for children under 16 years of age

The position is less clear where the child is under 16 years of age, since, here, difficult questions arise surrounding the relationship between the wishes of 'competent' minors, parental responsibility and dealings with third parties (in this case children's services) which have caused such consternation in other areas.[150] It could be argued that a '*Gillick*-competent' child should have the decisive say. Eekelaar and Dingwall have speculated that parents might lose the

---

[145] Section 20(11).

[146] Section 20(3).

[147] Section 20(4). This applies even though a person with parental responsibility for the child is able to provide him with accommodation.

[148] But note that housing authorities are required to co-operate with social services under s 27.

[149] Neither may the authority make the young person a ward of court for this purpose, s 100(2) effectively reversing the decision in *Re SW (Wardship: Jurisdiction)* [1986] 1 FLR 24.

[150] Most particularly in relation to medical issues. See chapter 8 above.

legal power to direct where the competent child is to live.[151] This argument probably takes insufficient account of the effect of relevant statutory provisions. It should be remembered that the '*Gillick* principle' must always be subject to express statutory provisions. As already noted, s 20(6) states that the local authority, before providing accommodation, shall:

'so far as is reasonably practicable and consistent with the child's welfare –

(a)   ascertain the child's wishes and feelings regarding the provision of accommodation; and

(b)   give due consideration (having regard to his age and understanding) to such wishes and feelings of the child as they have been able to ascertain.'

This would appear to fall short of giving the competent child the exclusive right to decide,[152] and it also has to be set against the more concrete parental right of objection. The result seems to be that, where a parent is objecting to the proposed arrangement, the child's wishes cannot prevail, and the local authority would need a court order to 'look after' the child. Most obviously, this could be sought where the child is alleging physical or sexual abuse. There is a precedent, under the old law, which suggests that the local authority might not be obliged to return an objecting teenager.[153] Freeman discusses whether this might be a case in which the local authority could apply for leave to invoke the inherent jurisdiction of the High Court[154] or, alternatively, to seek a care order on the basis that the child is beyond parental control.[155] The parent's statutory right of removal would seem to prevail, short of compulsory action like this, but the argument for giving greater weight to the child's view is perhaps stronger where the child is already out of the family home than where he is still there. The teenager in local authority accommodation already has a kind of semi-independence.

As for the converse position, in *R (G) v Southwark London Borough Council*[156] Baroness Hale of Richmond stated that 'there is nothing in s 20 which allows the local authority to force their services upon older and competent children who do not want them;'[157] and in *R(M) v Hammersmith and Fulham London Borough Council*[158] that: 'It is most unlikely that s 20 was intended to operate

---

[151]   J Eekelaar and R Dingwall *The Reform of Child Care Law* (Routledge, 1990), at p 78.

[152]   See *R(M) v Hammersmith and Fulham London Borough Council* [2008] UKHL 14, [2008] 1 FLR 1384, at para [17] (child's voice not decisive). A full assessment of the child's needs cannot be overlooked simply on the basis of following the child's wishes: see *R (Liverpool City Council) v Hillingdon London Borough Council* [2009] EWCA Civ 43, [2009] 1 FLR 1536.

[153]   *Krishnan v Sutton London Borough Council* [1969] 3 All ER 1367, where the court refused to order the return of a 17-year-old girl, against her wishes, to her father. There would seem to be no reason in principle why, with the current state of the law, this principle could not be applied to significantly younger children.

[154]   Under s 100(3).

[155]   Under s 31(2). See MDA Freeman *Children, Their Families and the Law* (Macmillan, 1992), at pp 68–69.

[156]   [2009] UKHL 26, [2009] 2 FLR 380, at [28](6).

[157]   As supported by s 20(11) discussed later.

[158]   [2008] UKHL 14, [2008] 1 FLR 1384.

compulsorily against a child who is competent to decide for herself. The whole object of the 1989 Act was to draw a clear distinction between voluntary and compulsory powers and to require that compulsion could only be used after due process of law'.[159]

The use of secure accommodation

In certain circumstances the local authority may wish to make use of secure accommodation in relation to children in its care. Always controversial, the practice must now comply not only with the procedural safeguards of the Children Act 1989 but also with human rights requirements.[160]

'Secure accommodation' is defined under the Children Act to mean 'accommodation provided for the purpose of restricting liberty'.[161] The legislation provides that 'a child who is being looked after by a local authority may not be placed and, if placed, may not be kept' in such accommodation:

'unless it appears –

    (a)   that –
        (i)   he has a history of absconding and is likely to abscond from any other description of accommodation and;
        (ii) if he absconds, he is likely to suffer significant harm; or
    (b)   that if he is kept in any other description of accommodation, he is likely to injure himself or other persons.'

Regulations[162] prescribe a maximum period beyond which a child may not be kept in secure accommodation without the authorisation of a court. These provide that detention for up to 72 hours in a period of 28 days does not require court approval but anything in excess of this does. The court has power under the regulations[163] to authorise the use of such accommodation for up to three months initially, with extensions of up to six months on a renewal

---

[159] Ibid, at [43].
[160] The regime under the Children Act is described in depth in R White, P Carr and N Lowe *The Children Act in Practice* (4th edn, LexisNexis, 2008) ch 9. The legal principles and practice issues are set out in chapters 7 and 8 respectively of S Gore *The Children Act 1989 Local Authority Support for Children and Families* (Family Law, 2011). See also C Smith 'Secure Accommodation' [1995] Fam Law 369; P Bates 'Secure Accommodation – In Whose Interests?' [1995] CFLQ 70; and J Butler and S Hardy 'Secure Accommodation and Welfare' [1997] Fam Law 425; A Perry 'Approaches to the Human Rights Act 1998 in Family Law Cases' (2001) *Wales Law Journal* 161, especially at pp 162–166, which considers the human rights implications; M Parry 'Secure Accommodation – the Cinderella of Family Law' [2000] CFLQ 101, and J Fortin 'Children's Rights and Physical Force' [2001] CFLQ 243. Among the earlier reported cases under the Children Act regime, see *Re W (A Minor) (Secure Accommodation Order)* [1993] 1 FLR 692, *Re M (Secure Accommodation Order)* [1995] 1 FLR 418 and *Re D (Secure Accommodation Order) (No 1)* [1997] 1 FLR 197.
[161] Section 25(1).
[162] Principally the Children (Secure Accommodation) Regulations 1991 (SI 1991/1505), as amended under s 25(2).
[163] Regulations 11 and 12.

application. Any use of secure accommodation must be necessary and proportionate to a legitimate aim if it is to comply with the ECHR.

In *Re K (Secure Accommodation: Right to Liberty)*[164] an attempt was made to argue that the Children Act regime was incompatible with Art 5 of the ECHR. This provides that everyone has the right to liberty and security of the person. No one may be deprived of this except in the cases specified in the Article and in accordance with a procedure prescribed by law. The fourth of these prescribed cases is in relation to 'the detention of a minor by lawful order for the purpose of educational supervision or his lawful detention for the purpose of bringing him before the competent legal authority'.[165]

In *Re K* the child in question had a long history of destructive, aggressive and sexualised behaviour involving fire-setting and sexual assaults. At the age of 11 he was diagnosed as having hyperkinetic conduct disorder and was described as presenting a serious risk to himself and others. He was placed in a secure unit and remained there under a series of secure accommodation orders.

The Court of Appeal rejected the incompatibility argument. The use of secure accommodation did amount to a deprivation of liberty but was justified as detention by lawful order for the purpose of educational supervision within the meaning of the above exception. The court held that 'educational supervision' for the purposes of the ECHR was not to be equated rigidly with the notion of classroom teaching but, especially in the care context, should embrace many aspects of the exercise by the local authority of parental rights for the benefit and protection of the child concerned. It would be a breach of the Convention for the authority to use such an order without providing any educational supervision, but s 25 was not incompatible with the Convention merely because it did not itself mention educational supervision. Thorpe LJ dissented, holding that the use of secure accommodation orders could not be justified on welfare grounds on the basis that the deprivation of liberty was a necessary consequence of an exercise of parental responsibility for the protection and promotion of the boy's welfare. In any event, the clear ruling of the whole court was that the statutory regime was compatible with Convention rights.

Involving as it does the deprivation of liberty, a secure accommodation order is a Draconian order. An application for such an order does not involve a criminal charge within the meaning of Art 6(2) and (3) of the ECHR but, in view of the gravity of the application, it has been held by the Court of Appeal[166] that the child should be afforded the five minimum procedural rights in Art 6(3) which are given to those facing criminal charges. These rights are:

(a) to be informed promptly, in a language which he understands and in detail, of the nature and cause of the accusation against him;

---

[164] [2001] 1 FLR 526.
[165] Article 5(1)(d).
[166] *Re C (Secure Accommodation Order: Representation)* [2001] 2 FLR 169.

(b) to have adequate time and facilities for the preparation of his defence;

(c) to defend himself in person or through legal assistance of his own choosing or, if he has not sufficient means to pay for legal assistance, to be given it free when the interests of justice so require;

(d) to examine or have examined witnesses against him and to obtain the attendance and examination of witnesses on his behalf under the same conditions as witnesses against him;

(e) to have free assistance of an interpreter if he cannot understand or speak the language used in court.

These rights were found not to have been violated in *Re C*, despite the fact that C's new solicitor was informed of the application for a secure accommodation order only on arrival at court. The Court of Appeal took the view that there was an imperative need to protect C, a 15-year-old girl, from herself. She was a heroin and crack cocaine user, and medical problems had resulted from her use of dirty needles. In the circumstances a secure accommodation order was the only management realistically open to the court and the local authority, although with hindsight it was regrettable that there had not been an adjournment for a few days to give C a full opportunity to respond to the application.

Section 25 proceedings are also 'specified proceedings' within the meaning of s 41 of the Children Act 1989 and, as such, it will invariably be necessary to appoint a children's guardian in order to safeguard the child's interests.

POWERS AND DUTIES OF LOCAL AUTHORITIES TO CHILDREN LOOKED AFTER BY THEM

The powers and duties which local authorities exercise over children 'looked after' are set out in the Children Act 1989 and in the Care Planning, Placement and Case Review (England) Regulations 2010.[167] The expression 'looked after' includes children who are 'in care' and also those 'accommodated' under voluntary arrangements,[168] provided that the accommodation is for more than 24 hours.[169] Yet there is a crucial legal distinction between these two groups. Whereas the local authority acquires parental responsibility (albeit shared with

---

[167] SI 2010/959. These are both new and consolidating provisions. See also HM Government, *The Children Act 1989 Guidance and Regulations Volume 2: Care Planning, Placement and Case Review* (2010).

[168] Section 22(1) is in fact somewhat wider than this since it embraces all children 'provided with accommodation by the authority in the exercise of any functions ... which stand referred to their social services committee under the Local Authority Social Services Act 1970' apart from functions under Children Act 1989, ss 17, 23B and 24B.

[169] Section 22(2).

parents) over children in care,[170] it does not acquire it where the children are merely 'accommodated'. Where the child is in care, the local authority is *not* dependent on parental delegation of responsibility since it has parental responsibility under the care order. Yet the statutory duties owed to each category of children are broadly similar, as they were under previous legislation.[171]

Statutory duties

The general duty

The general duty which local authorities owed to children in their care used to be contained in s 18(1) of the Child Care Act 1980.[172] This was substantially recast in the Children Act which provides:[173]

'It shall be the duty of a local authority looking after any child –

(a)   to safeguard and promote his welfare; and
(b)   to make such use of services available for children cared for by their own parents as appears to the authority reasonable in his case.'

The former duty under the Child Care Act 1980 expressed the child's welfare to be the 'first consideration' for the local authority. The effect of this formula was thought to be that, although the interests of the child were not the local authority's sole or paramount consideration, they were to receive priority over other competing interests. Under the old law, this was relied on successfully in a number of judicial challenges to the closure of children's homes where the relevant local authorities had failed to give first consideration to the welfare of the individual children affected.[174] While the point is not free from doubt, it would seem that the former duty has been diluted and that similar challenges might fail under the new law.[175]

It is not clear how far the local authority's general duty to safeguard and promote the child's welfare is qualified by other considerations, particularly those of administrative convenience. The local authority may have to balance the interests of particular children against those of other children or other potential clients, especially given the pressure of finite resources. One way in

---

[170]   Section 33(3)(a), discussed in chapter 12 below.
[171]   Child Care Act 1980.
[172]   This provided that: 'In reaching any decision relating to a child in their care, a local authority shall give first consideration to the need to safeguard and promote the welfare of the child throughout his childhood ...'.
[173]   Section 22(3). The duty to promote the child's welfare includes the duty to promote educational achievement; see s 22(3A).
[174]   See, for example, *Liddle v Sunderland Borough Council* (1983) Fam Law 250; *R v Solihull Metropolitan Borough Council ex parte C* [1984] FLR 363; and *R v Avon County Council ex parte K* [1986] 1 FLR 443.
[175]   Freeman takes the view that the argument, once accepted in *AG v Hammersmith and Fulham London Borough Council* (1979) *The Times*, December 18, that the authority is entitled to consider a child's welfare *after* it has taken a decision to close a home, may again be tenable.

which the general duty is certainly limited is that the local authority is permitted to act inconsistently with it where it thinks it is necessary 'for the purposes of protecting members of the public from serious injury'.[176] The Secretary of State may also direct the local authority to act inconsistently and the local authority must comply.[177] It might be necessary, in such a case, to contemplate the use of secure accommodation.[178] Along with the issue of contact with children in care, the use of secure accommodation is unusual in being one type of decision by local authorities which is subject to judicial scrutiny on its merits.[179]

Specific duties

Many specific duties are imposed by the legislation. Some are contained in the body of the Children Act, while others are set out in Part II of Sch 2. We discuss below some of the more important specific duties.

The duty to consult

The Children Act made much wider provision for consultation than was the case before it. It states:[180]

> 'Before making any decision with respect to a child whom they are looking after, or proposing to look after, a local authority shall, so far as is reasonably practicable, ascertain the wishes and feelings of –
>
> (a) the child;
> (b) his parents;
> (c) any person who is not a parent of his but who has parental responsibility for him; and
> (d) any other person whose wishes and feelings the authority consider to be relevant, regarding the matter to be decided.'

The nature of this duty of consultation came before the courts in *Re P (Children Act 1989, ss 22 and 26: Local Authority Compliance)*.[181] Here the father was in prison having been convicted of rape and buggery of the mother and indecent assault on a child. He continued to represent a significant risk to the children, and the issue arose as to whether the local authority was obliged to continue to consult the father about matters of upbringing and decision-making processes relating to the four children. The children were the subject of care orders and the mother had agreed to care plans which involved

---

[176] Section 22(6).

[177] Section 22(7) and (8).

[178] Discussed above.

[179] This kind of ordinary access to the courts should be contrasted with the more restricted mechanism of judicial review.

[180] Section 22(4). It was established in *R v North Yorkshire County Council ex parte M* [1989] 1 All ER 143 that where the child has a guardian ad litem (now children's guardian) he should be consulted.

[181] [2000] 2 FLR 910.

their long-term placement outside the family. The father had participated in those care proceedings, but the authority now wished to cut him out of the future decision-making process except to the limited extent of providing him with a basic annual report on the children's general well-being and telling him of any emergencies.

Charles J held that the authority was entitled to follow this course. Its duties of consultation were *directory* rather than mandatory, in the sense that any failure to consult as required would be treated as an irregularity rather than rendering its decisions void. In complying with its duties the authority was entitled to have regard to s 33(3)(b) of the Children Act[182] which allowed it to determine the extent to which a parent could meet his responsibility and also to the case-law under s 91(14)[183] which involved excluding or limiting a parental right. In this case, because of the continuing risk which the father represented, restricted consultation was justified which would be backed up by an order under s 91(14).

This was an exceptional case and should not detract from the central requirement that, in the overwhelming majority of cases, the statutory scheme requires full and continuing consultation.

The local authority must then, after consulting, go on to give 'due consideration' to the views of those consulted, in the case of a child, commensurate with his age and understanding.[184] It must also, in making its decision, give due consideration to the child's 'religious persuasion, racial origin and cultural and linguistic background',[185] a recurrent theme in the legislation.[186] These considerations are probably of greatest relevance to the question of placement. They suggest that, all other things being equal, efforts should be directed to placing children in families of similar race, culture and linguistic background. But clearly this is only a guideline and there will be some instances in which this would be undesirable or impossible having regard to the overriding consideration of the child's welfare. If the only available foster parents of similar cultural background are considered inappropriate, it may be necessary to place the child elsewhere.[187] There is no indication in the legislation of the relative weight to be attached to individual views where these conflict, and this must be a matter for the local authority's discretion.

---

[182] See chapter 12 below.

[183] See chapter 5 above.

[184] Section 22(5)(a) and (b).

[185] Section 22(5)(c).

[186] There is a particularly useful discussion of these considerations in MDA Freeman (above), at pp 73–77 and, more generally, on cultural considerations in the context of children's rights, see M Freeman 'Children's Rights and Cultural Pluralism' in *The Moral Status of Children* (Martinus Nijhoff, 1997), ch 7.

[187] Note that a repeal of the duty to have regard to ethnicity in the Adoption and Children Act 2002 is pending in the Children and Families Bill 2013.

The duty to provide accommodation

The duties of the local authority with respect to providing accommodation for a child who is looked after by the authority are set out in the legislation.[188] Unless not consistent with the child's welfare or not reasonably practicable, the child should be placed with a parent, a person with parental responsibility, or in a case where the child is in the care of the local authority and there was a residence order in force with respect to the child immediately before the care order was made, the person in whose favour the residence order was made.[189] If the local authority are unable to make such arrangements then the child may be placed in the most appropriate placement as follows:[190]

(a) with an individual who is a relative, friend or other person connected with the child and who is also a local authority foster parent;

(b) with a local authority foster parent who does not fall within paragraph (a);

(c) in a children's home;[191] or

(d) otherwise in accordance with other arrangements which comply with regulations.

Preference is to be given to placement under paragraph (a) above.[192] So far as reasonably practicable, the local authority must ensure that the placement allows the child to live near home; does not disrupt education or training; enables the child to live with a sibling (if any); and is suitable for the child's needs arising from a disability (if any).[193] Unless not reasonably practicable, the accommodation must be within the local authority's area.[194] These provisions show that clearly an option is to allow the child to remain at home, possibly subject to supervision. The local authority's general rehabilitative objective militates towards this solution but there is always the counter-pressure of adequately protecting the child's welfare. Accordingly, placements are subject to regulations[195] which ensure that the child's welfare is sufficiently safeguarded in the placement.

Under the regulations the local authority must produce a plan for the child's care which must, so far as reasonably practicable, be agreed with any parent and person with parental responsibility for the child (or the child if over 16).[196] The plan must cover a range of issues such as the child's health, education,

---

[188] Sections 22A and 22C.
[189] Section 22C(3) and (4).
[190] Section 22C(5) and (6).
[191] Registered under Part 2 of the Care Standards Act 2000.
[192] Section 22C(7).
[193] Section 22C(8).
[194] Section 22C(9).
[195] Care Planning, Placement and Case Review (England) Regulations 2010 (SI 2010/959).
[196] Ibid, reg 4.

family and social relationships, emotional and behavioural development, identity, and self-care skills,[197] and the child's health must be assessed[198] A placement plan must also be prepared[199] and the placement must be notified to various persons connected to the child, such as a parent or persons with whom the child has contact, and the child's doctor and school.[200] There are special rules relating to particular types of placement, for example placements with parents,[201] or with local authority foster parents.[202] The child must be visited[203] by a representative of the local authority within the first week of placement, then at least every six weeks in the first year, and thereafter at intervals of not more than three months.[204] The child's case must be reviewed regularly, first within 20 days of becoming 'looked after', then not more than three months later, and thereafter at intervals not exceeding six months.[205] An independent reviewing officer is involved in the process of review of the case, who will speak to the child and ensure that the parents' wishes have been ascertained and taken into account.[206]

The duty to maintain

The local authority is required to maintain a child looked after by it[207] but may, in certain circumstances, recoup some of the cost by requiring a financial contribution to the child's maintenance or services provided for him from certain other persons.[208] The local authority must charge only what is reasonable, given the financial means of the recipients of the service, but those on the principal means-tested social security benefits are exempt.[209] Contributions towards maintenance are governed by a separate code.[210] These

---

[197] Ibid, reg 5.

[198] Ibid, reg 7.

[199] Ibid, reg 9. It must address detailed matters set out in Sch 2 to the regulations.

[200] Ibid, reg 14.

[201] Ibid, regs 15–20 and Sch 3. These provisions are the successors of the Children and Young Persons (Amendment) Act 1986, which legislation was inspired by public anxiety over the deaths of certain children at the hands of parents and others, most notably that of Jasmine Beckford. See *A Child in Trust: Report of the Panel of Inquiry Investigating the Circumstances Surrounding the Death of Jasmine Beckford* (London Borough of Brent, 1985).

[202] Ibid, regs 21–26.

[203] See Children Act 1989, s 23ZA.

[204] Care Planning, Placement and Case Review (England) Regulations 2010 (SI 2010/959), regs 28–30.

[205] Ibid, regs 32–38.

[206] Ibid, regs 33–36.

[207] Section 22B.

[208] Section 29. Those who may be liable are the child's parents, a child over 16 years of age himself, and, where the service is provided for a member of the child's family, that person (s 29(4)). For the correct approach in assessing a parent's contribution, see *Re C (A Minor) (Contribution Notice)* [1994] 1 FLR 111.

[209] Section 29(3) and (3A). This will be likely to be a high proportion, given the close association between poverty and care.

[210] Section 29(6) and Sch 2, Part III.

charges have always been controversial and the Children Act brought about a change of emphasis whereby local authorities are required to charge only where they consider it reasonable to do so.[211]

The duty to promote contact

Consistent with the primary emphasis on reunification in the legislation, local authorities are required to endeavour to promote contact, so far as is reasonably practicable and consistent with his welfare, between the child, his family, relatives, friends and others connected with him.[212] To this end, the local authority and persons with parental responsibility are obliged to stay in touch with each other. The local authority must take steps to keep them informed of the child's whereabouts and they must keep the local authority informed of their respective addresses.[213] Local authorities must also co-operate among themselves where a child moves into a different area.[214]

Other powers and duties

Other powers and duties are set out in Part II of Sch 2 to the Children Act. They include assistance with travelling expenses where visits are made to children in care, the appointment of independent visitors where visits by the family have become very infrequent, assistance in arrangements for the child to live outside England and Wales (subject to significant safeguards), and arrangements for the funeral of a child who dies while being looked after by the local authority.

Duties to children leaving accommodation and after-care

The Children Act substantially increased the duties of local authorities towards children ceasing to be looked after by them up to the age of 21 years.[215] The purpose was to assist these often vulnerable young people in making the difficult transition to independent living in the community. It was recognised that many of them would have no family on which to rely for support. These duties have been greatly increased by amendments to the Children Act 1989 brought about by the Children (Leaving Care) Act 2000. That Act followed a consultation document published in 1999[216] and reflects the view that far too little was still being done for young people leaving care. The amendments extend the duties of local authorities by requiring them to assess and meet the

---

[211] Schedule 2, para 21(2).
[212] Schedule 2, para 15, which should be read with ss 17(1) and 22C(3). Taken together they add up to a strong duty to endeavour to reunite the child with the family – something which, as we have seen, is required by the ECHR.
[213] Schedule 2, para 15(2).
[214] Section 20(2) and Sch 2, para 15(3) and (4).
[215] Following the recommendations in the DHSS *Review of Child Care Law* (1985), ch 10; and see generally L Jordan 'Accommodation and Aftercare: Provision for Young People' (1992) 4 JCL 162.
[216] *Me, Survive, Out There? – New Arrangements for Young People Living in and Leaving Care* (July 1999).

care and support needs of *eligible* and *relevant* children and young people and to assist *former relevant children*, in particular in relation to their employment, education and training.[217] The legislation is mainly concerned with those over the age of 16 and imposes obligations to support them up to the age of 21 at the level required for the different categories defined in the legislation.

Eligible children are those who are aged 16 or 17 and are currently being looked after by a local authority and have been so looked after for a period prescribed by regulations.[218] The intention is to exclude certain groups for whom the package of support envisaged by the legislation would be inappropriate, such as those who normally live at home with their families and have been looked after only for short periods of respite care to give their families a break.[219] The authority must for each eligible child carry out an assessment of his needs with a view to determining what advice, assistance and support it would be appropriate for it to provide:

(a)   while it is still looking after him, and

(b)   after it ceases to look after him.[220]

The authority must arrange for the child to have a personal adviser,[221] and prepare what is called a pathway plan[222] and keep it under regular review.[223] The Plan must be in writing and must set out:

(a)   the manner in which the responsible authority proposes to meet the needs of the child and

(b)   the date by which, and by whom, any action required to implement the Plan will be carried out.

In addition to assisting with the drawing up of the Pathway Plan, the personal adviser must stay in touch with the young person until he or she attains 21 and must ensure the implementation of the Pathway Plan as modified to meet the child's shifting needs.

---

[217]   Explanatory notes to the Children (Leaving Care) Act 2000. For judicial examination of these terms see the decision of Sullivan J in *R (Berhe) v Hillingdon London Borough Council* [2004] 1 FLR 439.

[218]   For a period of 13 weeks, or periods amounting in all to 13 weeks, which began after he reached the age of 14 and ended after he reached the age of 16: Children Act 1989, Sch 2, para 19B(2)(b) and Care Planning, Placement and Case Review (England) Regulations 2010 (SI 2010/959), reg 40. The rules are modified in the case of a series of short-term placements, see reg 48.

[219]   Explanatory notes to the Children (Leaving Care) Act 2000, para 20.

[220]   Children Act 1989, Sch 2, para 19B.

[221]   Schedule 2, para 19C.

[222]   Ibid, para 19B(4).

[223]   Ibid, para 19B(5).

Relevant children[224] are those aged 16 or 17 who meet the criteria for eligible children, but who leave local authority accommodation and cease to be looked after children. In such a case, as well as the duties already mentioned in relation to eligible children, the local authority must take reasonable steps to keep in touch with a 'relevant child'. The authority has a duty to safeguard and promote the child's welfare and, unless they are satisfied that his welfare does not require it, to support the child by maintaining him and providing suitable accommodation and support,[225] which may be in cash.[226]

Former relevant children[227] are those who, before reaching the age of 18, were either eligible or relevant children. Similarly, the local authority has a duty to take reasonable steps to keep in touch with a former relevant child,[228] to continue the appointment of his or her personal adviser, and to keep the pathway plan under review. There is also a duty to give assistance[229] as set out in the section, or other assistance, as the child's welfare and educational or training needs require it, up to the age of 21[230] or beyond if the former relevant child remains in education.[231] The local authority has a duty to pay an amount of money to such a person who is pursuing higher education.[232] Even where the duties have ceased, they can be resurrected provided he or she is under 25 and informs the authority that he or she is pursuing or wishes to pursue a programme of education.[233]

Young persons qualifying for advice and assistance

A wider category of young persons qualify to receive advice and assistance from local authorities. First, it should be noted that local authorities have a general duty to a child being looked after by them to 'advise, assist and befriend him with a view to promoting his welfare, when they have ceased to look after him'.[234] Secondly, the Children Act imposed additional duties towards young people who are under 21, but who were, while 16 or 17, looked after by a local authority, accommodated by a voluntary organisation or fostered. These duties are to be found in s 24, as amended by the Children (Leaving Care) Act 2000. The essential duty is to advise, befriend and assist such young people and help certain of them with education, employment and training.[235]

---

[224] Ibid, s 23A.
[225] Section 23B(8).
[226] Section 23B(9).
[227] Ibid, s 23C.
[228] Section 23C(2).
[229] Section 24B(1) and (2).
[230] Section 23C(6).
[231] Section 23C(7).
[232] Section 23C(5A).
[233] Section 23CA(1), inserted by Children and Young Persons Act 2008, s 22(2).
[234] Children Act 1989, Sch 2, para 19A.
[235] The details are beyond the scope of the present work, but are contained in ibid, ss 24, 24A, 24B and 24C.

Consistent with the growth of complaints procedures elsewhere in child care law, the local authority is obliged to establish a procedure for considering representations, including complaints, made by young persons in all the qualifying categories about the discharge of its functions under this part of the legislation.[236]

LEGAL REGULATION OF SUBSTITUTE CARE ARRANGEMENTS

The background

The Children Act 1989 contained a mass of detail on regulating the different kinds of substitute care for children, and a large amount of delegated legislation was introduced under its enabling powers.[237] Much of what was originally in the Children Act was a consolidation of previous law.[238] A lot of the framework in Parts VI to XI and some of Part XII still remains, but it has been heavily amended, and to some extent repealed, by the Care Standards Act 2000 and the regulations introduced by that legislation.[239] In general, this section is concerned with the many different kinds of arrangements for looking after children who are living away from home which include residential care, fostering arrangements, child-minding and day-care provision. The major change which occurred as a result of the Care Standards Act 2000 was a substantial shifting of responsibility for monitoring and supervising these arrangements from local authorities to a new National Care Standards Commission (NCSC) and, in the case of child-minding and day-care, to Her Majesty's Chief Inspector of Schools (HMCI) within the Office for Standards in Education, Children's Services and Skills (Ofsted). The NCSC was subsequently abolished[240] and the functions under Part 2 of the Care Standards Act 2000 as the registration authority responsible for standards in relation to children's homes, residential family centres, fostering services, and adoption agencies were transferred to HMCI by the Education and Inspections Act 2006.[241] That is the position in England. In Wales the transfer of responsibility is largely to a new arm of the National Assembly for Wales.

---

[236] Ibid, s 24D.

[237] For a detailed discussion of the scheme under the Children Act, see MDA Freeman *Children, Their Families and the Law* (Macmillan, 1992), ch 9.

[238] The law before the Children Act was extensively reviewed in MDA Freeman and C Lyon *The Law of Residential Homes and Day Care Establishments* (Sweet & Maxwell, 1984). On the law after the Children Act, see A Bainham *Children: The New Law* (Family Law, 1990), ch 7 and *The Children Act 1989 Guidance and Regulations Vol 4* (HMSO, 1991).

[239] Most importantly, perhaps, the Children's Homes Regulations 2001 (SI 2001/3967), which have since been amended by the Children's Homes (Amendment) Regulations 2011 (SI 2011/583). See also HMCI (Fees and Frequency of Inspections) (Children's Homes etc.) (Amendment) Regulations 2013 (SI 2013/523).

[240] Health and Social Care (Community Health and Standards) Act 2003, Sch 14, Part 2, para 1 and SI 2004/759, repealing Care Standards Act 2000, s 6.

[241] Section 148.

The Care Standards Act 2000

This Act,[242] which received the Royal Assent on 20 July 2000, has as its principal aim the reform of the regulatory system for care services in England and Wales. An attempt will be made to draw out its salient features as they affect children and the principal changes which the Act has made to the scheme under the Children Act.

The relevant registration authorities (now HMCI and the National Assembly for Wales, discussed above), are given power in Part II of the Act to issue *national minimum standards* applicable to all services and to which registration authorities and providers must have regard. These arrangements replaced the provisions in the Children Act which dealt with the registration of voluntary homes and registered children's homes and regulate community homes for the first time. Voluntary adoption societies fall within the Act, and local authority fostering and adoption services are subject to inspection. The welfare arrangements in all boarding schools and further education colleges which accommodate children are within the Act.[243] The Act's tentacles therefore stretch a long way, and one of its main purposes is to bring the regulation of a wide range of children's services under one regime and to seek to achieve some consistency in the minimum standards of these services.

Children's homes

The Children Act divides children's homes into three categories – community homes, voluntary homes and registered children's homes.

Community homes[244] are further sub-divided. There are 'maintained community homes' which are homes provided and financed by local authorities, 'controlled' and 'assisted' community homes. These are homes provided by voluntary organisations and differ only in the extent to which the local authority is directly involved in their management. Community homes under the Children Act were subject to inspection by the local authority but not to the registration requirements which applied to voluntary homes and registered children's homes.

Voluntary homes[245] were under the Children Act registered with the Secretary of State. They are established and managed by voluntary organisations and the Children Act spells out the general duties of voluntary organisations, to children looked after by them.[246]

---

[242] The Act itself and the most important primary and delegated legislation affecting care services are brought together in one place in HH Judge D Pearl *The Care Standards Legislation Handbook* (7th edn, Jordan Publishing, 2009). See also P Ridout (ed) *Care Standards: A Practical Guide* (2nd edn, Jordan Publishing, 2009).

[243] See the explanatory notes to the Care Standards Act 2000.

[244] Children Act 1989, Part VI and Sch 4.

[245] Ibid, s 60(1).

[246] Ibid, s 61.

Registered children's homes were required to register with the local authority.[247] They are now required to register with the Secretary of State. These homes are essentially private homes, set up by individuals and run for profit, and were largely unregulated before the Children Act.[248] The Children Act contains provisions regarding the conduct and management of registered homes and the duties of those persons carrying on or in charge of registered homes.[249] Small private children's homes which accommodate fewer then four children were not required to register and were not inspected. As an interim measure, s 40 of the Care Standards Act 2000 amended the Children Act to require such homes also to register with the local authority pending the establishment of the new regulatory regime under that Act.

The Care Standards Act 2000 seeks to introduce some uniformity in place of these fragmented regulatory mechanisms by establishing a broad definition of a 'children's home' as an establishment which 'provides care and accommodation wholly or mainly for children'.[250] This definition catches all the categories of home under the Children Act, as well as homes for disabled children. The Act excludes from the definition an establishment where 'a child is cared for and accommodated there by a parent or relative of his or by a foster parent'.[251] Also excluded from the definition are health service hospitals, independent hospitals and clinics, residential family centres and any other exceptions introduced by regulations.[252] On the other hand, it is made explicit that any school which provides accommodation for more than 295 days a year for any individual child must register as a children's home.[253]

All children's homes within this definition are now governed by the Children's Homes Regulations 2001,[254] as amended,[255] and must comply with the national minimum standards[256] produced under the Act and those regulations.[257] Registration with the new registration authorities is mandatory[258] and will be allowed only where that authority is satisfied that the applicant has complied with all relevant requirements in the legislation.[259] Registration may also be cancelled where there has been a failure to comply with the conditions of registration.[260] There is a right of appeal to the Care Standards Tribunal against the refusal to register or cancellation of registration.[261]

---

[247] Ibid, s 63(1).
[248] The Children's Homes Act 1982 did regulate these homes, but the legislation was never implemented.
[249] Children Act 1989, Sch 6, Part II.
[250] Care Standards Act 2000, s 1(2).
[251] Care Standards Act 2000, s 1(3).
[252] Ibid, s 1(4).
[253] Ibid, s 1(6).
[254] SI 2001/3967.
[255] Children's Homes (Amendment) Regulations 2011 (SI 2011/583).
[256] See DfE *Children's Homes: National Minimum Standards* (2011).
[257] Care Standards Act 2000, ss 22 and 23.
[258] Ibid, ss 11 and 12.
[259] Ibid, s 13.
[260] Ibid, s 14.
[261] Ibid, s 21.

The Children's Homes Regulations 2001 govern the conduct of children's homes and provide for such matters as the fitness of the registered provider and manager of the home; adequate staffing levels; the fitness of the premises used including suitable and proper equipment and furniture; dietary standards; provision of clothing and pocket money; and inappropriate disciplinary or control management. Where a child is not looked after by a local authority, the regulations require the registered person, before placing that child in a children's home, or as soon as is reasonably practicable thereafter, to cooperate with a voluntary organisation in agreeing a placement plan for the child, or in the case of a child placed other than by a voluntary organisation in a private children's home, to prepare a 'child placement plan', in accordance with the Arrangements for Placement of Children by Voluntary Organisations and Others (England) Regulations 2011.[262] This must set out in particular:

(a) how, on a day-to-day basis, the child will be cared for and his welfare safeguarded and promoted by the home;

(b) the arrangements made for his health and education; and

(c) any arrangements made for contact with his parents, relatives and friends.[263]

In the case of a child who is looked after by a local authority the placement plan must be agreed in accordance with the Care Planning, Placement and Case Review (England) Regulations 2010.[264]

Given the history of abuse in children's homes, highlighted particularly in the Waterhouse Report[265] which preceded the Care Standards Act and was a major influence on it, the regulations also require the registered person to prepare and implement a written policy which is intended to safeguard children accommodated in a children's home from abuse or neglect and which sets out the procedure to be followed in the event of any such allegation.[266]

In June 2013 the government issued a consultation seeking views on its proposal to further amend the Children's Homes Regulations 2001.[267] The consultation puts forward recommendations[268] which are aimed at strengthening children's homes safeguarding systems. This was prompted by the highly publicised convictions of a group of men in Rochdale for child sexual

---

[262] SI 2011/582, regs 4 and 5, as required by reg 12 of the Children's Homes Regulations 2001 (SI 2001/3967) (as amended).

[263] Children's Homes Regulations 2001, reg 12.

[264] Regulation 9, and see the the Children's Homes Regulations 2001, reg 12A.

[265] *Lost in Care – The Report of the Tribunal of Inquiry into the abuse of children in care in the former county council areas of Gwynedd and Clwyd since 1974* (2000).

[266] Children's Homes Regulations 2001, reg 16.

[267] *Reforming children's homes care: consultation on changes to The Children's Homes Regulations 2001 (as amended) and The Care Standards Act 2000 (Registration) (England) Regulations 2010* (25 June 2013). The consultation ended on 17 September 2013.

[268] Of the report of an Expert Group on Children's Homes Quality.

exploitation of vulnerable girls, a report on such risks to children by the Office of the Children's Commissioner[269] and the Joint All Party Parliamentary Group Inquiry on children who go missing from care.[270] Concerns were expressed about children placed in children's homes a long way from the authorities responsible for their care, who were vulnerable to going missing from their placements and could be targeted for exploitation. The proposals include requiring children's homes to complete risk assessments concerning the local area, and an amendment to mirror the requirements in the Care Planning Regulations so that children's homes must notify the authority where they are located, whenever a child is admitted or leaves the home.

Concern largely arising from the abuse of children in residential establishments has also resulted in legislation under which lists are kept of those thought to be unsuitable to work with children. The current framework is to be found in the Safeguarding Vulnerable Groups Act 2006.[271] This scheme is now administered by the Disclosure and Barring Service (DBS), which was set up under the Protection of Freedoms Act 2012, and which carries out functions that were previously undertaken by the Criminal Records Bureau (CRB) and the Independent Safeguarding Authority.[272] The DBS is responsible for carrying out criminal record checks, and is required under the Safeguarding Vulnerable Groups Act 2006 to maintain a list of persons who are included in a 'children's barred list'.[273] If included in the list, the person is barred from regulated activity[274] relating to children.[275] Providers of regulated activities must check whether a person is barred before allowing him or her to carry out such activity,[276] and also have a duty to refer to DBS concerns about a person employed in regulated activity.[277]

---

[269] Office of the Children's Commissioner, *Briefing for the Rt Hon Michael Gove MP, Secretary of State for Education, on the emerging findings of the Office of the Children's Commissioner's Inquiry into Child Sexual Exploitation in Gangs and Groups, with a special focus on children in care* (July 2012).

[270] The APPG for Runaway and Missing Children and Adults and the APPG for Looked After Children and Care Leavers *Report from the Joint Inquiry Into Children Who Go Missing From Care* (June 2012).

[271] Replacing the Protection of Children Act 1999.

[272] Protection of Freedoms Act 2012 (Disclosure and Barring Service Transfer of Functions) Order 2012 (SI 2012/3006).

[273] Section 2. The list is determined in accordance with Sch 3, Part 1.

[274] Section 5, and Sch 4. It sets out a range of activities, such as care, supervision, teaching, training, instruction of children and provision of advice and guidance.

[275] Section 3(2).

[276] Section 34ZA.

[277] See s 35, which sets out in some detail the circumstances in which the duty to inform will apply.

Fostering arrangements

Fostering agencies and local authority fostering services

The Fostering Services (England) Regulations 2011, as amended,[278] together with published national minimum standards,[279] form the detailed regulatory framework for fostering services, which are subject to inspection by HMCI. The regulations address both independent fostering agencies and local authority fostering services. Each 'fostering service provider', whether local authority or some other agency, is required to be registered under Part 2 of the Care Standards Act 2000 as carrying on a fostering service. The regulations set out provisions concerning the fitness of those providing and managing fostering services,[280] and the conduct of the service in so far as it is required to safeguard and promote the welfare of children.[281] The regulations require the service to establish a fostering panel, which in particular considers applications for approval of prospective foster parents. The regulations set out the information that is required and checks to be carried out on the foster parent and his or her household for the purpose of assessing suitability.[282] Regulation 26 specifically provides that a person is not suitable if he or she has been convicted or cautioned for an offence against a child or certain sexual offences against adults as listed in Part 1 of Sch 4.[283] The placement of the child is subject to regulations which require there to be a placement plan for the child, and set out minimum requirements for visits to the child and reviews of the child's case.[284] They also govern such matters as revocation of a placement where it ceases to be suitable, immediate placements in emergencies, registration of children in local authority foster care, and the maintenance of case records.

Fostering allowances are paid to all local authority foster parents by the authority. Although the amount paid varies between authorities, the National Foster Care Association annually recommends a minimum fostering allowance which depends on the age of the child and whether the child lives in London or elsewhere. The weekly rates for 2013/14 (for children outside London) were: for babies £116, children pre-primary school, £119; for those aged between 5 and 10, £132; for those aged between 11 and 15, £151; and for those aged 16 and over, £175.

---

[278] The Care Planning, Placement and Case Review and Fostering Services (Miscellaneous Amendments) Regulations 2013 (SI 2013/984).

[279] DfE Fostering Services: National Minimum Standards (2011).

[280] Fostering Services (England) Regulations 2011 (SI 2011/581), Part 3.

[281] Ibid, Part 4.

[282] Ibid, Part 5.

[283] Such as offences under ss 1 and 2 of the Sexual Offences Act 2003 (rape and assault by penetration), and various sexual offences against persons with a mental disorder.

[284] In the case of placement by a voluntary agency, see Arrangements for Placement of Children by Voluntary Organisations and Others (England) Regulations 2011 (SI 2011/582). Placements by the local authority are regulated by the Care Planning, Placement and Case Review (England) Regulations 2010 SI 2010/959).

The fostering services provider must take all reasonable steps to ensure that a fostered child is not subject to corporal punishment.[285] is expressly prohibited from administering corporal punishment[286] and must comply with the terms of the foster placement agreement.[287]

Private foster parents

The local authority would not, in the ordinary course of events, have any knowledge of privately arranged placements and this could be a cause for concern. Hence, the chief regulatory mechanism is *notification* rather than registration.[288] The statutory scheme is contained in Part IX of the Children Act together with the Children (Private Arrangements for Fostering) Regulations 2005.[289]

A prominent feature of the scheme is the requirement that the local authority should satisfy itself as to the welfare of children who are, or are proposed to be, privately fostered children in its area[290] and, where it is not so satisfied, take further specified action.[291] The notification requirements were tightened significantly by the Children Act. They now extend to parents, persons with parental responsibility and those involved directly or indirectly in making arrangements, as well as the foster parents themselves.[292] The other key element in the statutory scheme is the *disqualification* of unsuitable persons from private fostering.[293] Those persons who are disqualified include parents whose children have been in care, those convicted of criminal offences against children, and those on the barred children list under the Safeguarding Vulnerable Groups Act 2006.[294] The local authority may also prohibit the use

---

[285] Fostering Services (England) Regulations 2011, reg 13.

[286] Ibid, Sch 5, para 8.

[287] Ibid, Sch 5, para 10.

[288] See Children (Private Arrangements for Fostering) Regulations 2005 (SI 2005/1533), reg 3 for the duty to notify within six weeks of placement, or otherwise immediately.

[289] The Children Act provisions replaced the Foster Children Act 1980. The limits on the numbers of foster children who may be fostered are governed by Sch 7 to the Children Act and apply to children fostered by local authority foster parents and voluntary organisations as well as those privately fostered.

[290] Section 67(1). Under the Children (Private Arrangements for Fostering) Regulations 2005, Sch 2 the authority must satisfy itself in particular as to such matters as the intended purpose and duration of the arrangement, the child's development, financial arrangements, suitability of the accommodation, health, education, etc: in short, *all* matters relevant to the child's healthy development.

[291] Section 67(5). It must essentially secure that the child's accommodation is taken over by a parent, person with parental responsibility or relative or, where that is not reasonably practicable, it must consider whether to exercise its functions under the legislation.

[292] Children (Private Arrangements for Fostering) Regulations 2005, reg 3.

[293] Children Act 1989, s 68; Disqualification from Caring for Children (England) Regulations 2002 (SI 2002/635); and Disqualification from Caring for Children (Wales) Regulations 2004 (SI 2004/2695).

[294] Children Act 1989, s 68(3A).

of unsuitable premises for private fostering.[295] There is an appeals system, and the disqualification provisions are backed up by criminal offences.[296]

Child-minding and other childcare provision for children

The Childcare Act 2006 now regulates the provision of childcare in England and Wales[297] by way setting standards as to children's development requirements, and a system of registration and inspection. Her Majesty's Chief Inspector of Ofsted is required to maintain two registers.[298] These are an early years register which lists everyone who is required to be registered as an early years provider of childcare;[299] and a general childcare register, which deals with later years provision.[300] The general childcare register is split into two parts: a Part A which lists those who must register on the general list, namely those caring for children over 5 and under 8 years of age; and a Part B which lists all childcare providers who have been registered voluntarily. Provision for children is divided into childminding, provided on domestic premises by no more than three people, and other early years providers.[301] Sections 33 and 34 require early years providers to register on the early years register, and ss 52 and 53 respectively require later years childminders and other providers to be registered under Part A of the general register. The relevant provision without registration is prohibited. A person can be prosecuted if he or she continues to provide services without being registered.[302] Sections 35 and 36 deal with applications for registration in relation to childminding and other provision respectively, and ss 54 and 55 apply similarly for later years provision. The Chief Inspector is required to refuse an application if the applicant is disqualified as provided by the Act.[303] Successful applicants are placed on the register and issued with a certificate of registration.[304] The Secretary of State has a duty to specify, and implement, learning and development requirements

---

[295] Section 69(2)(b).

[296] Section 70 and Sch 8, para 8.

[297] Child-minding and day-care was formerly regulated by Part XA of and Sch 9A to the Children Act, as inserted by s 79 of the Care Standards Act 2000. The Children Act had replaced the previous system of registration under the Nurseries and Child-Minders Regulation Act 1948, which was widely thought to be ineffective.

[298] Childcare Act 2006, s 31.

[299] Childcare is defined in s 18(2) as any form of care for a child, and care includes (a) education for a child, and(b) any other supervised activity for a child, except education (or any other supervised activity) provided by a school during school hours.

[300] Early years and later years provision are defined respectively in s 96.

[301] In respect of other provision, the premises are registered. For a case under earlier legislation, see *Woodward v North Somerset District Council* [1998] 1 FLR 950. Mrs Woodward failed to be registered as a provider of nursery and other day-care services whereupon she forfeited the lease on the premises in which she had intended to run her business. Her appeal to the magistrates against refusal of registration failed on the preliminary ground that she had no premises in which such services could be provided and, thus, her personal fitness could not be assessed. Bracewell J held that this was the correct interpretation of the legislation, since it contemplated the registration of a person in respect of a particular set of premises.

[302] Childcare Act 2006, s 33(7) and 34(5).

[303] The relevant provisions are listed in s 75 and attendant regulations.

[304] Section 37 and 56. Conditions can be attached to registration: see ss 38 and 58.

for children in their 'early years foundation stage',[305] together with requirements for securing children's welfare.[306] The Chief Inspector has a duty to inspect childcare provision[307] and to make reports in writing thereon.[308] As noted above, there is also the possibility of voluntary registration[309] under Part B of the register by those who are not required to register, for example because they provide care only for children aged 8 and over.[310] The Chief Inspector is required to cancel any registration if a person becomes disqualified from caring for children or conditions of registration are not complied with.[311] Usually 14 days' notice must be given, an opportunity must be provided for the person to object if they wish,[312] and there is an appeal to the Care Standards Tribunal.[313] In an emergency, an application can be made without notice to a magistrate for an order cancelling registration, who may do so if it appears that a child for whom care is being provided is suffering or is likely to suffer significant harm.[314] There are various powers of entry onto premises, and to require disclosure of information, for the purpose of ensuring that the law on registered provision is not contravened.[315]

QUESTIONING LOCAL AUTHORITIES' DECISIONS UNDER PART III OF THE CHILDREN ACT 1989

What redress is available to someone who is aggrieved by a decision of the local authority affecting a child looked after by it? The potential remedies, in theory at least, apply equally to children in care and to accommodated children. The general policy of the Children Act 1989 is that when a child is 'looked after', managerial control is in the hands of the local authority, and it is not thought appropriate to expose most areas of decision-making to judicial scrutiny. By

---

[305] Sections 39–42.
[306] Sections 43–46.
[307] Sections 49–60.
[308] Section 50–61.
[309] See ss 63–66.
[310] Or are exempt for some other reason (eg under s 33(2) or 52(2)).
[311] Section 68. Registration may be suspended: see s 69.
[312] Section 73.
[313] Section 74. For a case under the earlier Children Act 1989 legislation, see *London Borough of Sutton v Davis* [1994] 1 FLR 737 in which a child-minder challenged a local authority's automatic determination of unfitness in relation to any applicant who refused to undertake not to smack a minded child. Anne Davis's position on corporal punishment was that she wished to have the authority to 'smack gently' in accordance with parental wishes. She refused to give the required undertaking whereupon the authority, although satisfied that she met its child-minding criteria in every other respect, refused her registration. The magistrates allowed her appeal against this refusal, and their decision was upheld by the High Court. Wilson J held that there was nothing in the legislation which required the authority to adopt so inflexible a policy that Anne Davis was, by reason of her views on corporal punishment, per se unfit to be a child-minder. The magistrates had been entitled to look at the applicant's fitness more generally and to reach the conclusion that they did.
[314] Section 72.
[315] Sections 77–85.

way of exception, the decision to commit a child to care[316] or discharge a child from care[317] is left in the hands of the courts, as is the emotive question of contact between children in care and their families.[318] We discuss these issues in chapter 12. When a care order is sought a local authority must present a care plan for the child concerned, and it is convenient to discuss in that chapter the various rules relating to such plans and their monitoring. We have already touched on the issue in this chapter when outlining some of the provisions of the Care Planning, Placement and Case Review (England) Regulations 2010.

Representations and complaints

Local authorities are required to establish procedures for considering representations including complaints.[319] Those entitled to use the procedures are any child being looked after by the local authority, a child in need, the child's parent, any other person who has parental responsibility for the child, any local authority foster parent, and 'such other person as the authority considers has a sufficient interest in the child's welfare to warrant his representations being considered by them'. The representations may relate to the discharge of any of the local authority's functions under Part III of the Children Act and are also available to persons using the local authority's adoption and special guardianship services.[320] The representations could relate to serious issues such as a change of placement or a medical operation, or to relatively trivial matters.[321]

Regulations set out the procedure for dealing with a representation,[322] which must be publicised,[323] and every local authority shall make arrangements for the provision of assistance to children who make or intend to make representations under s 26,[324] including assistance by way of representation.[325]

Usually representations must be made within a year of the ground for complaint arising.[326] The local authority will initially seek to resolve the matter

---

[316] Section 31(1).

[317] Section 39.

[318] Section 34. The use of secure accommodation is also subject to judicial control under s 25. See above.

[319] Children Act 1989, s 26(3). Section 24D of the Children Act 1989 also requires establishment of a similar representations procedure by a relevant child for the purposes of s 23A or a young person falling within s 23C, a person qualifying for advice and assistance, or a person falling within s 24B(2), about the discharge of functions in relation to him.

[320] Section 26(3B) and (3C).

[321] Section 26(3).

[322] Children Act 1989 Representations Procedure (England) Regulations 2006 (SI 2006/1738). For Wales the procedure is set out in SI 2005/3365. References hereafter are to the English regulations.

[323] Section 26(8). For interesting research about the variable nature of this publicity, see C Williams and H Jordan 'Factors Relating to Publicity Surrounding the Complaints Procedure under the Children Act 1989' (1996) 8 *Child and Family Law Quarterly* 337.

[324] Children Act 1989, s 26A(1).

[325] Ibid, s 26A(2).

[326] Ibid, reg 9(1). The local authority may still consider the representation if it would not be

locally[327] usually within ten working days. Where, however, the matter is not resolved, the complainant may request[328] that the representations be investigated by the local authority together with an independent person.[329] The response must be notified within 25 working days. If the matter is still not resolved, the matter can be further considered by a review panel[330] which will send its report to the complainant with its response and proposals, along with information about making a complaint to a Local Commissioner. Where the complaints procedure is fully pursued and where the panel make recommendations then normally the local authority must abide by those recommendations unless it has substantial reasons for not doing so. As Freeman has commented, the procedures are no substitute for good practice, but they may be an integral part of good practice, contributing to a cultural change which encourages clients to express views about services and for these comments to be used as opportunities to improve services, relationships and, ultimately, the image of children's services departments.[331]

Other potential remedies

The complaints procedure must first be exhausted before any proceedings for judicial review can be pursued. Since local authorities have a vast amount of discretion under the children legislation, it does not follow that, because some third party might disagree with the line a local authority has taken, that authority has acted beyond its powers or otherwise improperly. Public law remedies should not, therefore, be viewed as offering a great deal of hope to aggrieved individuals, except in the more obvious cases of abuse of power or failure to discharge public duties. We also look at the possibility of obtaining a private order under the Children Act and we conclude by considering the new and potentially important mechanisms for challenge under the HRA 1998.

Judicial review

Despite the restrictive nature of the remedy of judicial review, there has been a steady growth in applications for judicial review in recent years, perhaps initially reflecting the refusal of the courts to entertain wardship applications which were designed to challenge local authorities' decisions.[332] In order to

---

reasonable to expect the complainant to have made the representations within the time limit; and it is still possible to consider the representations effectively and fairly.

327 Regulation 14.

328 Personally or through his advocate if appointed.

329 Regulations 15(2) and reg 17.

330 Regulation 18.

331 MDA Freeman *Children, Their Families and the Law* (Macmillan, 1992), at p 145.

332 In several cases it was held specifically that judicial review, rather than wardship, was the appropriate remedy. See particularly *Re RM and LM (Minors)* [1986] 2 FLR 205, and *Re DM (A Minor) (Wardship: Jurisdiction)* [1986] 2 FLR 122. For a general discussion, see M Sunkin 'Judicial Review and Part III of the Children Act 1989' (1992) 4 JCL 109. But it has been held that the applicant must exhaust other remedies, particularly the statutory complaints procedure, before resorting to judicial review. See *R v Kingston upon Thames RBC ex parte T* [1994] 1 FLR 798 and *R v Birmingham City Council ex parte A* [1997] 2 FLR 841.

succeed, the applicant must show that the local authority has acted in a way in which no reasonable authority would have acted,[333] that it has acted *ultra vires*, ie exeeded its statutory powers,[334] or that there has been a breach of the rules of natural justice.[335] Permission is required before an application may be brought. Apart from the narrowness of the grounds, the powers of the Divisional Court[336] are limited. It may order the local authority to discharge its statutory duty properly through a mandatory order (formerly the order of mandamus) but, more likely, it will simply quash the local authority's decision through a quashing order (formerly the order of certiorari). It may issue a prohibiting order (formerly prohibition) to prevent a public body from acting unlawfully. It may also grant a declaration that something is unlawful or an injunction to restrain unlawful conduct. The court cannot go on to make orders which it considers to be in the best interests of the child as it can in wardship. The procedure contrasts sharply with the extremely flexible powers which the courts have under the Children Act, and its suitability in individual children cases must be doubted. Where it can prove useful is as a means of challenging *policy* decisions of local authorities. A formal decision, for example, to restrict services for children in need to those considered 'at risk' would clearly be susceptible to challenge. In recent years there have been a number of successful challenges to the policies of local authorities.

A good example is *R v Cornwall County Council ex parte LH*.[337] Here the authority, as a matter of policy, would not permit solicitors to attend child protection conferences except to the extent that they were allowed to read out a prepared statement. Neither would it permit a parent who had attended such a conference to be provided with a copy of the minutes except by order of the court. Scott Baker J granted a declaration that both policies were unlawful. As to the first, although the statutory guidance under the Children Act, *Working Together under the Children Act 1989*, warned of case conferences becoming confrontational and stated that legal representation as such was inappropriate, it nonetheless envisaged a parent being accompanied by a friend or a lawyer. Solicitors could make a useful contribution and should generally be allowed to attend and participate. As to the second policy, this was described by Scott Baker J as 'ludicrous' and a blatant contravention of the statutory guidelines. If an accurate record of the meeting had been taken, nothing in the minutes should be new to anyone who attended it, including the parent, and parents should be trusted to act responsibly with the paperwork.

---

[333] See, for example, *R v Lancashire County Council ex parte M* [1992] 1 FLR 109.

[334] Good examples of ultra vires action under the old law arose where there was a failure to follow the correct procedure for passing a parental rights resolution, as in *Re L (AC)* [1973] 3 All ER 743. This was a successful challenge in wardship but would now be a matter for judicial review.

[335] There have been several notable successes under this head. See, for example, *R v Bedfordshire County Council ex parte C* [1987] 1 FLR 239 and *R v Norfolk County Council ex parte M* [1989] QB 619.

[336] The Divisional Court of the Queen's Bench Division. Judges from the Family Division may, however, sit in children cases.

[337] [2000] 1 FLR 236.

An inflexible policy by the Prison Service which prohibited children remaining in mother and baby units after attaining the age of 18 months was found to be unlawful,[338] and there was a successful challenge in judicial review of the placement of a child on the child protection register where there was insufficient evidence of emotional abuse.[339] On the other hand, there have been a good many unsuccessful applications for judicial review in the child care sphere, some of which turn on the conclusion that the aggrieved applicant should have resorted to the statutory complaints procedures[340] of the local authority rather than the courts. An example is *R v East Sussex County Council ex parte W*[341] where a disabled 13-year-old boy, who had repeatedly run away, failed in a challenge to the local authority's decision not to seek a care order. Another is *Re S (Sexual Abuse Allegations: Local Authority Response)*[342] where the claimant, a consultant gynaecologist, failed to establish that the local authority had acted unreasonably, and therefore unlawfully, in its statutory duty to assess the risk of sexual abuse which he posed to unrelated children living with him in the same house.

Just as the complaints procedure may in some cases be a more appropriate alternative than an application for judicial review, so in future it is likely that, in a significant number of the more serious allegations against local authorities, the HRA 1998 may be invoked rather than judicial review. We consider these remedies below.

The Secretary of State's default powers

The Secretary of State has a number of functions in the child care sphere,[343] one of which is the so-called 'default power'. This enables him to intervene in limited circumstances where he is satisfied that a local authority has failed, without reasonable excuse, to comply with any of its duties under the legislation. He may then make an order, giving reasons and declaring the local authority to be in default with respect to the relevant duty. The order may include directions to comply with that duty within a specified period,[344] which may be enforced through judicial review and specifically by a mandatory order.[345]

It is extremely unlikely that this kind of intervention by central government would be of assistance in individual cases. Again, where it does occur, it is likely to be directed against a policy decision of the local authority with regard to a *class* of children.

---

[338] *R (P and Q and QB) v Secretary of State for the Home Department* [2001] 2 FLR 1122.

[339] *R v Hampshire County Council ex parte H* [1999] 2 FLR 359.

[340] Under s 26 discussed above.

[341] [1998] 2 FLR 1082.

[342] [2001] 2 FLR 776.

[343] For a general discussion, see A Bainham *Children: The New Law* (Family Law, 1990), at paras 7.71–7.78.

[344] Section 84(3).

[345] Section 84(4).

The Local Commissioner

It is possible to make a complaint to the Commissioner for Local Administration. This requires proof of 'maladministration', and the main disadvantage of the procedure is that it takes too long to be of immediate benefit to individual children, parents, or anyone else directly affected by an authority's decision.[346] Again, it may, if successful, be instrumental in securing the reversal of an ill-conceived policy. In Wales complaints may be made to the Children's Commissioner for Wales.[347]

Civil actions

In recent years there have been attempts by adults to obtain damages from local authorities in tort for injuries caused to them when children, allegedly resulting from the acts or omission of the authorities concerned.[348] The complaints have ranged from failure to act on reports of abuse made by doctors, teachers, neighbours and others;[349] the separation of a girl from her mother arising from the incorrect identification of an alleged abuser;[350] failure to prevent abuse by a foster father through inadequate monitoring and supervision of the placement;[351] and failure to act as a reasonable parent would towards a child in care, allegedly resulting in a series of personal catastrophies in adulthood.[352] At first these claims failed whether they were based on common law negligence or breach of statutory duty.

In *X (Minors) v Bedfordshire County Council*[353] the House of Lords, in a consolidated appeal, held that no cause of action arose either in negligence or for breach of statutory duty. The House was much exercised by policy considerations and by the consideration that the existence of a common law duty of care would interfere unduly with the performance of local authorities'

---

[346] A case in which a complaint was successful was *Re BA (Wardship and Adoption)* [1985] FLR 1008 where the local ombudsman found procedural irregularities in the passing of a parental rights resolution. As a result the local authority agreed to the continuation of wardship proceedings and a sub-committee of the authority recommended that the resolution be rescinded.

[347] Created by the Care Standards Act 2000 and the Children's Commissioner for Wales Act 2001. The functions of the Commissioner are further regulated by the Children's Commissioner for Wales Regulations 2001 (SI 2001/2783). For more detailed consideration of the Commissioner's role, see J Williams 'The Children's Commissioner for Wales' (2001) 1 *Wales Law Journal* 203 and K Hollingsworth and G Douglas 'Creating a Children's Champion for Wales' (2002) 65 MLR 58.

[348] For a thorough and informative critique of the various remedies against local authorities in relation to the discharge of their child care functions, see R Bailey-Harris and M Harris 'Local Authorities and Child Protection – the Mosaic of Accountability' [2002] CFLQ 117. See also C Brennan 'Third party liability for child abuse: unanswered questions' (2003) 25 JSWFL 23, and J Wright 'Local Authorities, the Duty of Care and the European Convention on Human Rights' (1998) 18 *Oxford Journal of Legal Studies* 1.

[349] *X (Minors) v Bedfordshire County Council* [1995] 2 AC 633.

[350] *M (A Minor) and Another v Newham London Borough Council v Others* [1995] 2 AC 663.

[351] *H v Norfolk County Council* [1997] 1 FLR 384.

[352] *Barrett v Enfield London Borough Council* [1999] 2 FLR 426.

[353] [1995] 2 AC 633.

statutory obligations to protect children at risk. It was concerned that potential liability might lead to a more cautious and defensive approach to the discharge of those duties and to a multiplicity of law suits.[354] The House of Lords did not close the door completely on civil actions for damages but drew a distinction between *policy* decisions and decisions which were not policy decisions. In the case of the latter, there could be liability if the authority had acted so unreasonably that its decisions went beyond the proper exercise of its statutory discretions.

Having failed in the House of Lords, the aggrieved 'children' and one mother took their cases to Strasbourg. In two landmark decisions in *Z v United Kingdom*[355] and *TP and KM v United Kingdom*[356] the ECtHR found that there had been violations of a number of Convention rights. In *Z v United Kingdom* the Court awarded damages of £32,000 to each child plus costs and expenses. It found that the welfare system had failed to protect the children from serious, long-term neglect and abuse in violation of Art 3 which prohibits torture, or inhuman or degrading treatment or punishment. This imposed on States an obligation to prevent ill-treatment of which the authorities had or ought to have had knowledge. It also found, by a substantial majority of 15:2, a violation of Art 13 which enshrines the right to an effective remedy, in that the children were unable to sue a local authority in negligence for compensation however foreseeable and severe the harm suffered and however unreasonable the conduct of the authority in failing to take steps to prevent the harm.[357] In *TP and KM v United Kingdom* the ECtHR also found a violation of Art 13 and, in this case, held that there had been a breach of the applicants' rights to respect for family life under Art 8 in that the authority had failed to disclose to the mother an interview video with the child or submit the question of the disclosure of the video to the court for its determination. This had deprived the mother of adequate involvement in the decision-making process concerning the care of her daughter and amounted to a failure to respect the family life of both of them. In each case the Court found no violation of Art 6, which guarantees the right to a fair hearing, since there had been no denial of access to the court.

These decisions opened up the possibility of actions under the HRA 1998 or for damages for negligence or breach of statutory duty. In any event, with the backdrop of the European proceedings, the House of Lords had itself already

---

[354] For a scathing attack on the decision, see M Freeman 'The End of the Century of the Child?' (2000) 53 *Current Legal Problems* 505, at 542. See also R Bailey-Harris and M Harris 'The immunity of local authorities in child protection functions – is the door now ajar?' [1998] CFLQ 227.

[355] [2001] 2 FLR 612.

[356] [2001] 2 FLR 549. For commentary, see J Miles 'Human Rights and Child Protection' [2001] CFLQ 431.

[357] See also *E and Others v United Kingdom* [2003] 1 FLR 348 in which the ECtHR similarly found violations of Arts 3 and 13 where the local authority should have been aware of the risk of sexual and physical abuse to the child posed by the step-father and failed to take steps which would have enabled it to discover the exact extent of the problem and, potentially, to prevent further abuse taking place.

begun to shift its stance dramatically. In *Barrett v Enfield London Borough Council*[358] the House allowed the appeal of a young man who had been continually in the care of the local authority from the age of 10 months through to adulthood. He brought an action for damages based on psychiatric injury allegedly caused by the authority's negligence and breach of statutory duty. He asserted that it had failed to place him in suitable foster homes or for adoption or to take sufficient steps to reintroduce him to his mother. As a consequence he claimed to have experienced alcohol problems, a tendency to self-harm, behavioural problems and a failed marriage. He argued that the local authority had a common law duty of care to provide him with the standard of care to be expected of a reasonable parent, which it had failed to do.

His claim was struck out by the judge and the Court of Appeal as disclosing no cause of action, but the House of Lords reinstated it holding that it was in principle possible for certain acts done pursuant to a statutory discretion, such as the treatment of a child in care, to give rise to a duty of care. The question would be whether or not they were justiciable actions. The initial decision about whether or not to apply to take a child into care was not justiciable unless it reached the level of being so unreasonable that it was not to be regarded as the proper exercise of a statutory discretion. On the other hand, the treatment of children once in care, the issue here, was one in which it was potentially possible to find a breach of duty. Such a decision did not clearly involve competing policy factors which rendered it non-justiciable. The House went on to hold that it was not necessarily unjust or unreasonable to impose a duty of care on a local authority in relation to a child in its care. While it would be inappropriate to permit a child to sue his parents, it was not necessarily wrong to allow a child to sue the authority whose duties and responsibilities were not identical to those of a parent.[359] The potential existence of the duty was, however, far from the same as establishing liability merely because something had gone wrong. Whether the duty existed and, if so, whether it had been broken depended on the statutory context and the nature of the tasks involved. The court should be careful to have regard to the delicate and difficult factors involved in much local authority work, particularly child welfare work. On the other hand, unless the court exercised its jurisdiction to address these questions, the interests of the child could not be sufficiently protected.

The House of Lords considered related issues in *W v Essex County Council.*[360] Foster parents made it known to the local authority that they were not prepared to foster any child who was known or suspected of being a child abuser. Despite this the authority placed a boy who was a known sexual abuser with their family without informing them of his history. The foster parents alleged that he had sexually abused their own children and that, as a consequence, both they and their children had suffered serious psychiatric injury. The Court of Appeal allowed the children's claims to proceed, holding

---

[358] [2001] 2 AC 550.

[359] For a critique of the view in this case that it is inappropriate for a child to sue a parent, see M Freeman (above), at pp 543–544.

[360] [2000] 1 FLR 657.

also that the authority could be vicariously liable for the acts of its social worker, but it struck out the parents' claim on the basis that the authority did not owe them a duty of care since they were not primary victims and did not qualify as secondary victims either. The House of Lords reinstated the parents' claim as at least arguable. Whether in the circumstances a duty of care would ultimately be found to have existed or to be breached would depend on an investigation of the full facts known to, and the factors influencing the decision of, the local authority. It was also impossible to say that the parents' psychiatric injury would necessarily fall outside the range of injury recognised by the law, since the concept of secondary victims was still being developed. These decisions then established *in principle* that a cause of action could lie in negligence and were followed by later decisions.[361]

In *D v East Berkshire Community Health NHS Trust and Others; MAK and Another v Dewsbury Healthcare NHS Trust and Another; RK and Another v Oldham NHS Trust and Another*[362] three cases in which parents were wrongly suspected of child abuse were heard together. In each case the suspicions arose through misdiagnosis by doctors or child care workers. In the first case, a five-year-old child had been placed on the 'at risk register' when his mother was misdiagnosed as suffering from Munchausen's syndrome by proxy and as mistreating her child, when in fact the child suffered from severe allergies. In the second case, it was alleged that a father had sexually abused his nine year-old daughter. Suspicion arose from discoloured patches on her skin but these were in fact caused by Schamberg's disease. In the third case a two month-old child suffered a spiral fracture of the femur, which was wrongly regarded by the doctor as non-accidental when in fact it resulted from brittle bone disease. This was diagnosed eight months later when the child was living with an aunt under an interim care order and suffered similar symptoms. The parents in each case alleged negligence and claimed damages for psychiatric injury. In the *Dewsbury* case the daughter also claimed damages. On a preliminary issue, the judge held that it would not be fair, just and reasonable to impose a duty of care in these circumstances.

The Court of Appeal allowed the child's appeal in the *Dewsbury* case, holding that the decision in *X (Minors) v Bedfordshire* could not survive the Human Rights Act 1998. A local authority was required to respect a child's European Convention rights, and since breach of a duty of care in negligence would frequently also amount to a violation of Art 3 or Art 8, the imposition of a duty of care would not have a significantly adverse effect on the manner in which they perform their duties. There could be no blanket rule therefore that

---

[361] *S v Gloucestershire County Council; Tower Hamlets London Borough Council and Havering London Borough Council* [2000] 1 FLR 825, and *C v Flintshire County Council* [2001] 2 FLR 33 See also *A and B v Essex County Council* [2003] 1 FLR 615 where a negligence action succeeded against the local authority for its failure properly to inform prospective adoptive parents of serious behavioural problems which one of two siblings exhibited. This led to attacks on both prospective adoptive parents and other children, and psychiatric injury to the prospective adoptive mother. On the question of quantum of damages in negligence cases involving child abuse, see *R v Bryn Alyn Community (Holdings) Ltd* [2003] 1 FLR 1203.

[362] [2005] UKHL 23, [2005] 2 AC 373, [2005] 2 FLR 284.

no common law duty of care was owed to a child in relation to the investigation of suspected child abuse and each case would need to be determined on its own particular facts.[363]

The parents' appeals, however, were dismissed by the Court of Appeal and they appealed to the House of Lords. The parents were also unsuccessful in the House of Lords. The House held that in such cases the doctor's patient is the child, in whose best interests the doctor is obliged to act. Where child abuse is suspected, the interests of the parents and the child do not coincide, and healthcare and other child care professionals need to be able to act single-mindedly in the interests of the child without being subject to conflicting duties to the parent. As Lord Brown of Eaton-under-Heywood acknowledged, the denial of a duty of care to the parents who had legitimate grievances is:[364]

> 'the price they pay in the interests of children generally. The well-being of innumerable children up and down the land depends crucially upon doctors and social workers concerned with their safety being subjected by the law to but a single duty: that of safeguarding the child's own welfare. It is that imperative which in my judgment must determine the outcome of these appeals.'

The *Dewsbury* case above was taken to the ECtHR in *MAK and RK v United Kingdom*[365] where breaches of the father's and child's rights to respect for family life under Art 8 of the ECHR were found arising from the fact that intimate photographs of the child were taken without the parents' consent, and delay in consulting a dermatologist had unduly extended the period during which the father was unable to see his daughter. The court also found a breach under Art 13 in the UK's failure, at the time, to provide the father with a remedy to pursue breach of this rights. That has since been rectified by implementation of the HRA 1998 and the possibility of making a claim pursuant to that Act.

---

[363] [2003] 2 FLR 1166, at paras [83] and [84]. The case renders social workers and healthcare professionals to fairly wide-ranging liability. The approach to local authority liability involves a two stage inquiry: first whether the issue is non-justiciable, as in the case of high policy decisions, or an operational matter. Question of professional judgement fall within the latter. In cases involving social work, this test will almost always be satisfied. The second stage involves application of the test of whether imposition of a duty is fair, just and reasonable: see *Carty v Croydon London Borough Council* [2005] EWCA Civ 19, [2005] 1 WLR 2312, at paras [20]–[37].

[364] Ibid, at para 138. See also *Lawence v Pembrokeshire CC* [2007] EWCA Civ 446, [2007] 2 FLR 705; and *L and B v Reading Borough Council and Others* [2007] EWCA Civ 1313, [2008] 1 FLR 797. See Elaine Palser 'Shutting the door on negligence liability: *Lawrence v Pembrokeshire County Council* and *L v Reading Borough Council*' [2009] CFLQ 384.

[365] (Application Nos 45901/05 and 40146/06) [2010] 2 FLR 451. For comment, see K Greasley 'A negligent blow to children at risk: *MAK and RK v United Kingdom* (2010) 73(6) MLR 1026–1035 (ECtHR).

ACTIONS UNDER THE HUMAN RIGHTS ACT 1998

Before the HRA 1998 was implemented it was possible for an individual to petition the European Commission and ECtHR alleging a breach by a local authority of the ECHR. Although this was a slow and cumbersome procedure usually taking many years, there were some significant successes notably in relation to contact with children in care,[366] parental access to the courts in the context of care procedures,[367] and access to case records.[368]

The effect of implementation of the HRA 1998, while not removing the 'long stop' remedy of recourse to Strasbourg, was to provide new remedies based on violation of Convention rights which are directly available in the English courts. The framework is contained in ss 6, 7 and 8 of the HRA 1998. The interaction of these provisions was helpfully described by Lord Nicholls of Birkenhead in the leading case of *Re S; Re W*[369] as follows:

'Sections 7 and 8 have conferred extended powers on the courts. Section 6 makes it unlawful for a public authority to act in a way that is incompatible with a Convention right. Section 7 enables victims of conduct made unlawful by section 6 to bring court proceedings against the public authority in question. Section 8 spells out in wide terms, the relief a court may grant in those proceedings. The court may grant such relief or remedy, or make such order, within its powers as it considers appropriate. Thus if a local authority conducts itself in a manner which infringes the Art 8 rights of a parent or child, the court may grant appropriate relief on the application of a victim of an unlawful act.'

It is important to appreciate that actions brought under the HRA 1998 can only be based on a breach of the ECHR and must be brought by the *victim*.[370] If the complaint relates to something which does not involve this, then these remedies will be unavailable and the appropriate course of action will be to use one of the other remedies discussed above, such as the complaints procedure, judicial review or a civil action based on negligence. In many cases, however, the alleged unlawful behaviour will *both* constitute a breach of Convention rights and be susceptible to judicial review or an action in negligence. In such cases, there will be a choice of remedy and it is more than likely that in some cases the aggrieved applicant will seek to invoke these remedies in the alternative. The effect of the HRA 1998 is to make available in English law the remedies visualised by Art 13 of the ECHR and which were found to be lacking in *Z v United Kingdom* and *TP and KM v United Kingdom*.

---

[366] *R v United Kingdom* [1988] 2 FLR 445.

[367] *W v United Kingdom* (1987) 10 EHRR 29.

[368] *The Gaskin case* [1990] 1 FLR 167. See also *McMichael v United Kingdom* [1995] 2 FCR 718, in which the ECtHR found Scottish child care procedures under the Social Work (Scotland) Act 1968 to be in breach of parents' rights under Art 8(1) in denying them access to reports concerning adoption.

[369] *Re S (Minors) (Care Order: Implementation of Care Plan); Re W (Minors) (Care Order: Adequacy of Care Plan)* [2002] 1 FLR 815, at para [45].

[370] This precludes an action by a secondary victim such as in *W v Essex County Council* [2000] 1 FLR 657 (discussed above).

Actions under the HRA 1998 either may be 'freestanding' in the sense that proceedings are specifically brought for the purpose[371] or may arise in the course of existing proceedings. Thus, someone may rely on a Convention right in the course of family proceedings.[372] In the case of freestanding proceedings, the application must be brought within one year of the alleged unlawful act[373] but the court may at its discretion allow an application within 'such longer period as the court or tribunal considers equitable having regard to all the circumstances'.[374] How this discretion is exercised may clearly have a significant bearing on the availability of these remedies as where, for example, an adult alleges breaches of Convention rights arising from abuse as a child, with which so many of the cases discussed above were concerned. The influence of the HRA 1998 is of course discussed throughout this book, where relevant.

Private orders

The final possibility is for the aggrieved individual to apply for a s 8 order. Where the child is 'accommodated' by the local authority, all s 8 orders are, in principle, available, subject to the leave requirement.[375] These orders are likely to be sought, if at all, by someone without parental responsibility, since those who have parental responsibility are able to terminate an accommodation arrangement.

Where the child is in care, the jurisdiction of the courts to make private orders is severely curtailed,[376] but it is possible to apply for a residence order. This would only be an appropriate course for those persons who are willing and able to offer a home to the child. This course would not be appropriate if the person's grievance related only to some aspect of the local authority's plan for the child. Where the dispute is about contact (as it often is), there is a statutory regime.[377] It was the case prior to the Children Act,[378] and it is the case after it,[379] that wardship may not be used as an extra-statutory device for challenging local authority decision-making.

CONCLUSION

The important work of local authorities in partnership with children and families to support children is underpinned by the general duty in s 17 of the Children Act 1989 to 'children in need' and more specific duties in Sch 2 to the Act, together with the duty to accommodate children in the circumstances set

---

[371] HRA 1998, s 7(1)(a).
[372] Ibid, s 7(1)(b).
[373] Ibid, s 7(5)(a).
[374] Ibid, s 7(5)(b).
[375] Reversing, in effect, the House of Lords decision in *M v H* [1988] 3 All ER 5.
[376] See chapter 5 below.
[377] Section 34, also discussed in chapter 12 below.
[378] *A v Liverpool City Council* [1982] AC 363 ('the *Liverpool* principle').
[379] Section 100(2)(c).

out in s 20(1). Children who are accommodated, or in the care of the local authority are 'looked after' children, to whom various duties under the Children Act 1989 are owed, in some cases even when the children cease to be 'looked after'. The substitute care of children in children's homes, by way of fostering, child-minding or other childcare services is regulated by a complex array of statutes and associated regulations. The overarching aims of such provisions, however, are to safeguard and promote the welfare of children. This is achieved through systems of approval (and where appropriate registration) of substitute carers and ongoing monitoring of the quality of care (for example, through inspection). There are also in the case of children's residential placements 'placement plans' to ensure that placements promote children's welfare, together with ongoing reviews of children's well-being within their placement.

Part III of the Children Act 1989 also provides a system for making representations about provision of services under that Part, and in relation to decisions concerning adoption and special guardianship. While it is difficult to challenge successfully the exercise of the local authority's statutory discretions, there is no doubt that there has been a substantial shift in recent decades in the direction of greater accountability and availability of remedies for aggrieved parents and others. For the less serious grievances, the internal procedures of the local authority, including informal negotiation with social workers, the review process and the complaints procedures, will remain the principal means of questioning the local authority's actions in relation to a particular child. At the same time there is now a keener awareness of the human rights requirements and the importance of procedural fairness in the decision-making process. There is no question that the development of potential liability for negligence has occurred within the context of a greater commitment to human rights.

Chapter 11

INVESTIGATION AND SHORT-TERM PROTECTION

INTRODUCTION

This chapter looks at the investigative duties of local authorities where children are suspected to be at risk, and the legal framework within which short-term or emergency protection is undertaken. The connection between investigation and protection is a necessary one since no court is likely to grant an order to protect a child unless there has been a prior investigation of the circumstances.[1] The focus of attention here is on short-term remedies for the purposes of assessment and dealing with emergencies, which are to be found in Part V of the Children Act 1989. The medium and long-term solutions of care and supervision[2] are considered in chapter 12.

Historical background

Emergency procedures prior to the Children Act 1989 were arguably criticised even more than other areas of child care law – understandably, since they regulate the initial stages of compulsory intervention in the family. They have, in the past, been associated with Draconian and unceremonious removals of children from their homes, of which the so-called 'dawn raids' in Orkney and Rochdale were glaring examples.[3] Place of safety orders were the chief mechanism for emergency action, but there was much evidence of their misuse. In many instances, orders appeared to be used, not in genuine emergencies, but as a means of gaining control of children for diagnostic or investigatory purposes. The orders were apparently routinely granted, often ex parte, by single magistrates from home.[4] They came to be seen by some social services

---

[1]   *The Children Act 1989 Guidance and Regulations Vol 1 Court Orders* (TSO, 2008), at para 4.73. On orders under Part V of the Children Act generally, see ch 4 of the *Guidance*.

[2]   For a particularly penetrating analysis of the issues in the use of 'apprehension' powers relating to children, which also looks at the human rights requirements, see J Masson 'Human Rights in Child Protection: Emergency Action and its Impact' in P Lodrup and E Modvar (eds) *Family Life and Human Rights* (Gyldendal Akademisk, 2004), at p 457.

[3]   See, particularly, *Re A (Minors) (Child Abuse) (Guidelines)* [1992] 1 All ER 153. Some of the case law, and similar cases, were referred to by Lord Hope in *In re J (Children)* [2013] UKSC 9.

[4]   'A Magistrate sitting at home in his pyjamas', in the graphic phrase of Stuart Bell MP (*Hansard*, 23 Oct 1989, col 594).

departments as stage one of a three-stage process leading to a care order.[5] The process lacked elementary procedural fairness, bearing in mind the seriousness of the intrusion. The grounds were based on the applicant's belief that one of the conditions for a care order might be satisfied;[6] the removal of children was authorised for as long as 28 days; and the effects of the order were vague, especially regarding the powers and obligations of the local authority.

The most damning criticism of emergency procedures was the way in which they could be used to ride roughshod over the rights of parents and children. Parents had little input into the process. They had no rights of prior notification, consultation or appeal, and only a limited right to an explanation of the reasons for the order once made. The absence of proper avenues of redress led to applications by parents for interim care orders, as a back-door mechanism for challenging place of safety orders.[7] Even this option was, in due course, removed.[8] It was the large-scale use of place of safety orders in dubious circumstances in Cleveland which was the 'last straw' and led to a clamour for immediate reform.[9] At the same time, there remained widespread anxiety about undetected child abuse in general, and sexual abuse in particular.[10]

The emergency protection order

The aim of Part V of the Children Act 1989 is therefore 'to ensure that effective protective action can be taken when this is necessary within a framework of proper safeguards and reasonable opportunities for parents (or others with parental responsibility for the child) to challenge such actions before a court'.[11] The legislation tried to achieve this by revamping the investigative duties of local authorities, by requiring other authorities to co-operate, and by replacing the discredited place of safety order with a new emergency protection order (EPO) with more stringent grounds, more clearly defined legal effects, and shorter time-limits for detaining children in emergencies.

---

5   The process would begin with a place of safety order which would be followed up by one or more (usually more) interim care orders and finally the full care order.

6   The test was part objective in the sense that it focused on the *reasonableness* of the applicant's belief, but partly subjective in that it was the *applicant's* belief, not the court's, which was crucial.

7   *R v Lincoln (Kesteven) County Justices, ex parte M* [1976] QB 957.

8   *Nottinghamshire County Council v Q* [1982] Fam 94.

9   The evidence in Cleveland was that between 1 January 1987 and 31 July 1987 there were 276 applications for place of safety orders. Of these, 174 were granted by a single justice from home. See *Report of the Inquiry into Child Abuse in Cleveland 1987* (HMSO, 1988) (Cmnd 412), at para 10.9.

10 Considerable media attention was devoted to this, most notably in the BBC television programme 'That's Life' which led to the establishment of 'Childline'.

11 See *The Children Act 1989 Guidance and Regulations Vol 1 Court Orders* (TSO, 2008), at para 4.6. For further discussion of the basis of the reforms in Part V of the Children Act, see the *Review of Child Care Law* (1985), chs 12 and 13, and the White Paper *The Law on Child Care and Family Services* (1987), ch 4.

The need for a 'half-way house': the child assessment order

While the Children Bill was progressing through Parliament, a major issue arose as to whether another type of order for assessment of children was required as an alternative to an EPO. The idea had its origins in the *Carlile Report*.[12] There was concern that there could be many cases in which there was suspicion of abuse, but insufficient evidence to justify emergency action. In such cases, the aim of social services is to make an assessment of the child's situation and, where suspicion of abuse persists, to obtain an accurate diagnosis. This, of course, may require medical and/or psychiatric examination of the child. But what if parents are refusing to co-operate either to let social services see the child at all or to allow the child to be examined? The dilemma for the social worker caught in this situation has been whether to take highly interventionist emergency action to remove the child, or to do nothing.

It was asserted in Parliament that a 'half-way house' was needed which would require a child to be produced and authorise an assessment but which would not necessarily lead to the removal of the child. There was considerable disagreement about whether the additional order was really required, not least between professional bodies such as the NSPCC and the Association of Directors of Social Services. The opponents of the order were worried about the possible confusion which might arise about when to seek each order and also the potential of the assessment order, as they saw it, for undermining attempts at voluntary cooperation with parents.[13] The proponents of the order stressed that this would not be so, especially since parental responsibility would not pass to the local authority. They argued that the 'lesser' order would allow action to be taken where there was serious, but not urgent, concern for the child's well-being.

It was this view which ultimately prevailed with the introduction of the innovative child assessment order (CAO). The features of the CAO, as it eventually emerged, when compared with those of the EPO, are evidence of the compromise which had to be struck.[14] The extremely short time-limit (seven days), for example, reflects the perceived need to make this shorter than the limit for EPOs (eight days). Both orders can be utilised in 'non-access' cases, and both make provision for medical and psychiatric examination. This is, at least in part, the result of grafting on to the statutory scheme, at the eleventh

---

[12]   *A Child in Mind: Protection of Children in a Responsible Society, Report of the Commission of Inquiry into the Circumstances surrounding the death of Kimberley Carlile* (1987).

[13]   Baroness Faithfull, for example, said in the House of Lords that a court-ordered medical examination would be likely to 'upset an enormous number of good parents who have a finger pointed at them' (House of Lords Official Report, 19 January 1989, col 429).

[14]   For a further informative discussion of the parliamentary background, see, generally, N Parton *Governing the Family* (Macmillan, 1991), ch 6. For critical commentary on child assessment orders and their operation in practice, see R Lavery 'The Child Assessment Order – a reassessment' [1996] CFLQ 41, and Dickens 'Assessment and Control of Social Work – analysis or reasons for the non-use of the child assessment order' (1993) JSWFL 88, and G Mitchell 'The Child Assessment Order – A Breach of Principle?' [1991] XIII(I) *Liverpool Law Review* 53.

hour, an alternative mechanism for dealing with some of the difficulties which had already been addressed when formulating the EPO.[15] Nevertheless, conceptually at least, the two orders are quite distinct and, as the *Guidance* says, the CAO is most relevant when the child concerned is not thought to be at immediate risk.[16]

Other reforms under the Children Act 1989

The legislation also redefined police powers to protect children and powers of entry and search. These powers should not be underestimated since, in the worst cases of severe violence against children, the police will need to be involved. Finally, the legislation reformed the law governing abduction of children from care, and addressed, for the first time, the legal position of those organisations which provide assistance to young 'runaways'.

INVESTIGATION[17]

Local authorities, it will be recalled, are required to use the voluntary services offered to families under Part III of the Children Act to 'take reasonable steps ... to prevent children within their area suffering ill-treatment or neglect'.[18] It is not necessary to mention again here the connection between voluntary and compulsory action or the primary focus on the former,[19] but what this means is that where children's services, because of the information available to them, believe a child may be at risk, they will first have to consider whether this risk can adequately be met through voluntary assistance to the family. A good example of this working is where an alleged abuser can be induced to move out of the home, perhaps with assistance from the local authority.[20]

Sources of initial information

How do local authorities get their initial information? There is no single source. Neighbours may hear suspicious noises, or fail to see a child for some time; children's services may have had previous dealings with the family and be aware of the problems; the child himself may be sufficiently resourceful to contact the local authority direct or, more likely, confide in a trusted adult; the family doctor or health visitor may become aware of what looks like a non-accidental

---

[15] A point made very well by MDA Freeman in *Children, Their Families and the Law* (Macmillan, 1992), at pp 173–175.

[16] The Children Act 1989 Guidance and Regulations Vol 1 Court Orders (TSO, 2008), at para 4.10.

[17] A particularly good account of the legislative framework governing the investigative stage of child protection is to be found in R White, P Carr and N Lowe *The Children Act in Practice* (4th edn, Butterworths, 2008).

[18] Schedule 2, para 4(1).

[19] See chapter 10 above.

[20] Under Sch 2, para 5. The issue of removing adults rather than chilolen is discussed below.

injury. Perhaps the most likely source of information in the case of older children is the school. Children spend almost as much time at school as they do at home, and teachers and welfare assistants are in direct contact with them for substantial periods of the day. As such, they are uniquely placed to observe behavioural aberrations (which could point to sexual abuse) or to notice signs of physical injury. Physical education classes and swimming activities provide opportunities for discreet observation. It should also be noted that every school has a designated child protection officer among its staff who will liaise with children's services where suspicions or concerns arise. Similarly, maternity wards have designated midwives who perform a similar role in relation to newborn babies. It must be stressed, again, that there is no mandatory reporting law in England,[21] but various authorities, including local education authorities (LEAs), are required to assist the local authority with their investigations, unless it would be unreasonable to expect them to do so in all the circumstances.[22]

Local authority's investigations

The local authority's investigative duties may arise by direction of the court in family proceedings,[23] and also in certain other circumstances specified in s 47 of the Children Act 1989. These circumstances are where the local authority is informed that a child living or found in its area:

(1)   is the subject of an EPO;

(2)   is in police protection; or

(3)   where the local authority has reasonable cause to suspect that the child is suffering, or is likely to suffer, significant harm.[24]

'Suspicion' as required for an investigation is a lower standard than that required by the tests for making EPOs or interim care orders or taking a child into police protection. It has been said by Hale LJ that the courts should be slow to hold that a local authority does not have reasonable grounds such as will justify it in making enquiries under s 47.[25]

---

[21]   This was not favoured in the DHSS *Review of Child Care Law* (1985), at para 12.4.
[22]   See below.
[23]   Under s 37(1).
[24]   Section 47(1) as amended. There was formerly another ground, namely that the child had contravened a ban imposed by a curfew notice within the meaning of Chapter 1 of Part I of the Crime and Disorder Act 1998 but it was repealed by the Policing and Crime Act 2009, Sch 8, Part 13 para 1 (January 12, 2010). For discussion of the earlier provison, see the third edition of this book.
[25]   See *Gogay v Hertfordshire County Council* [2001] 1 FLR 280 at 294. It has also been held by Scott Baker J that the authority is not required to make a finding on the balance of probabilities as to past conduct before assessing a risk and taking protective steps under s 47. See *Re S (Sexual Abuse Allegations: Local Authority Response)* [2001] 2 FLR 776.

If s 47 applies, the local authority must make, or cause to be made, 'such enquiries as they consider necessary to enable them to decide whether they should take any action to safeguard or promote the child's welfare'.[26] It is a broader and more positive obligation to conduct enquiries than the pre-Children Act duty. This was limited to making enquiries on receipt of any information which suggested that there were grounds for care proceedings, unless the local authority was satisfied that this was unnecessary.[27] The present duty is more directly focused on the child's welfare. Where the child is already subject to an EPO or in police protection, by definition that child is considered to be at risk and this is an automatic trigger for the local authority to investigate. Under the Children Act 1989 there is also a duty to obtain access to the child so far as is reasonably practicable.[28]

Possible courses of action following enquiries

The legislation requires the local authority to decide, following its enquiries, whether to make any application to the court. This will mean that the authority must consider whether to seek a CAO, an EPO, or a care or supervision order under Part IV, or to offer voluntary assistance under Part III.[29] Where a child who is subject to an EPO is not currently in local authority accommodation, the local authority must consider whether the child should be placed there for the duration of the EPO.[30] Where the child is in police protection, the local authority must determine whether it would be in the child's best interests to apply for an EPO.[31] The strongest duty arises where, in the course of the local authority's enquiries, an officer of the authority is refused access to the child or denied information as to his whereabouts. Here, the local authority *must* apply for an EPO, care order or supervision order unless satisfied that the child's welfare can otherwise be satisfactorily safeguarded.[32]

Following its investigations, the local authority may conclude that an order is not required. Where it takes the view that no order is necessary, it must still consider whether there should be a later review of the child's circumstances and, if so, it must fix a date for the review to begin.[33] Where it decides that it *should* act to safeguard or promote the child's welfare, it is obliged to take that action, insofar as it is within its power and reasonably practicable for it to do so.[34] Eekelaar has drawn attention to the local authority's 'peculiar position of being allowed to decide whether or not to put itself under additional duties'

---

26   Section 47(1). The authority must, so far as reasonably practicable and consistent with the child's welfare, ascertain the wishes and feelings of the child and give due consideration to them in the light of the child's age and understanding: see s 47(5A).
27   Children and Young Persons Act 1969, s 2(1).
28   Section 47(4).
29   Section 47(3).
30   Section 47(3)(b).
31   Sections 47(3)(c) and 46(7).
32   Section 47(6).
33   Section 47(7). It should be remembered that the authority may not have decided to do 'nothing', since it may well be offering voluntary assistance under Part III of the Children Act.
34   Section 47(8).

and has been critical of the absence of a 'clear and unambiguous duty to take action on the basis of the results of the inquiries where the child is likely to be harmed if no such action is taken'.[35] He speculates on whether it could be lawful for the local authority to decide to do no more, for example, because of pressure of resources. And he contrasts the position with the local authority's duty where there has been a s 37 direction to justify to the court a decision to take no action.[36] It is arguable that the local authority is not accountable enough for the proper discharge of these duties.

The value of co-operation

The importance of inter-agency co-operation is stressed again at this preliminary investigative stage. Local authorities must co-operate with each other in the investigation of child abuse.[37] Where, as a result of its enquiries, an authority decides that there is an educational issue which requires investigation it must consult the relevant LEA.[38] Housing authorities, health authorities and others specified by the Secretary of State must assist the local authority with its enquiries, if called upon to do so, by providing information and advice,[39] unless this would be unreasonable in all the circumstances of the case.[40] Freeman has questioned whether the police should have been left off this list, arguing that some police forces have been obstructive in the past.[41] The spirit of the Act certainly requires police co-operation and, in most cases, no doubt this will be forthcoming.

CHILD ASSESSMENT ORDERS

A CAO deals with the issues of examination or assessment of the child in the specific circumstances of non-co-operation by the parents and lack of evidence of the need for an order to protect the child. The hope is that the assessment ordered by the court will provide this evidence and enable the local authority to decide what action (if any) is required.

It cannot be emphasised strongly enough that the CAO is not suitable for emergencies, which must be the subject of applications for EPOs. Indeed, the court is precluded from making a CAO where it is satisfied that there are

---

[35] J Eekelaar 'Investigation Under the Children Act 1989' [1990] Fam Law 486 at 487.
[36] The relevant provision is s 37(3) which requires the authority to inform the court of the reasons for its decision, any service or assistance which it has provided, or intends to provide, for the child and his family and any other action which it has taken, or proposes to take, with respect to the child.
[37] Section 47(12) provides that, where a local authority is making enquiries with respect to a child who appears to it to be ordinarily resident within the area of another authority, it must consult the other authority, which may undertake the necessary enquiries in its place.
[38] Section 47(5) and 47(5ZA).
[39] Section 47(9) and (11).
[40] Section 47(10).
[41] MDA Freeman *Children, Their Families and the Law* (Macmillan, 1992), at p 178.

grounds for making an EPO and that it ought to make this order rather than the CAO.[42] It may then treat the application for the CAO as an application for an EPO.[43] The local authority must, in every case, decide whether the case is a genuine emergency or whether there is sufficient doubt about this to push it instead in the direction of a CAO.

Who may apply and on what grounds?

In contrast to the EPO (which, as we shall see, may be sought by anyone), the CAO may only be requested by a local authority or 'authorised person' (the NSPCC). The rationale for this distinction is that in *emergencies* anyone should be able to act decisively to protect a child but that, in non-urgent cases, the policy should be to leave action to the primary child protection agencies. The court is empowered to make a CAO where:[44]

'(a) the applicant has reasonable cause to suspect that the child is suffering, or is likely to suffer, significant harm;
(b) an assessment of the state of the child's health or development, or of the way in which he has been treated, is required to enable the applicant to determine whether or not the child is suffering, or is likely to suffer, significant harm; and
(c) it is unlikely that such an assessment will be made, or be satisfactory, in the absence of an order under this section.'

The order is thus designed to enable the local authority to satisfy themselves about the welfare of children where they have suspicions of abuse or neglect but lack hard evidence.

The grounds for CAOs (and for EPOs) involve the satisfaction of minimum threshold criteria, followed by the application of the general principles in Part I of the Children Act. Taking the threshold criteria first, the first element requires the court to be satisfied about the reasonableness of the *applicant's* belief regarding the risk of significant harm to the child. A more stringent test is required for EPOs where the *court itself* must be satisfied about the risk. This reflects the more intrusive nature of the order. The other two elements in the CAO criteria require the court to satisfy itself that an assessment is really needed and that it cannot be arranged voluntarily. No doubt the court will want to hear evidence of the attempts to persuade parents to co-operate.

If the threshold is fulfilled, some of the principles in s 1 of the Children Act 1989 come into play. Ultimately, the court must consider whether a CAO is the right course of action, applying the welfare principle and s 1(5). However, in this context there are two points of distinction. The first is that proceedings under Part V of the Children Act are outside the definition of 'family proceedings' so that the court may not make s 8 orders in lieu of a CAO. The

---

42   Section 43(4).
43   Section 43(3).
44   Section 43(1).

second is that the statutory checklist of factors in s 1(3) does not apply.[45] The reasoning is that Part V is an essentially separate code governing short-term remedies. It would be inappropriate for the court to be inhibited in its ability to act expeditiously, by having to plough through a range of factors in relation to which there may well, as yet, be insufficient information.

An important difference between the CAO and the EPO is that the application for a CAO must be brought before a full court on notice and involves an inter partes hearing.[46] By definition, this is not an emergency and, therefore, parents, those with parental responsibility, anyone with a contact order and the child himself must be given a proper opportunity to participate in the proceedings.

The *Guidance* suggests that the CAO 'will usually be most appropriate where the harm to the child is long-term and cumulative rather than sudden and severe'.[47] Examples given are of nagging concerns about a child apparently failing to thrive; parents ignorant of, or unwilling to face up to the child's condition; and where there is some evidence that the child may be subject to continuing or periodic wilful neglect or abuse, but not to such an extent as to place him at serious immediate risk.

What are the effects of the CAO?

Compulsory production of the child/authorisation of assessment

A CAO has two automatic effects. The first is to require production of the child by anyone able to do so to the person named in the order and thereafter to comply with any directions the court makes regarding assessment.[48] The second effect is to authorise the assessment itself.[49] Parental responsibility does not vest in the applicant. It is expected that the court will spell out with some particularity what the assessment is to involve and, in doing so, it should take advice from those presenting the case and from other professionals. The most obvious directions are likely to relate to medical and/or psychiatric examination, but the assessment may range wider than this to cover other aspects of the child's health and development. Again, a child of sufficient understanding to make an informed decision may refuse to submit to any examinations or form of assessment.[50]

The effect of this provision, together with similar provisions which apply to directions made where a court makes an EPO or interim care order,[51] is diluted by the power of the High Court to override the child's objections under its

---

45 Part V proceedings are not within those proceedings specified in s 1(4) as attracting the application of the checklist.
46 Section 43(11).
47 *The Children Act 1989 Guidance and Regulations Vol 1 Court Orders* (TSO, 2008), at para 4.12.
48 Section 43(6).
49 Section 43(7) authorises any person carrying out the assessment, or any part of the assessment, to do so in accordance with the terms of the order.
50 Section 43(8).
51 Sections 44(7) and 38(6) respectively.

inherent jurisdiction.[52] This exercise of the inherent jurisdiction is controversial since it appears to run contrary to the spirit, if not the letter, of the legislation. This appears to give to 'mature minors' a clear right to refuse to submit to such examinations and assessments. The issue is at the heart of the debate about the nature of children's rights.[53] Suppose, for example, there is suspicion that a teenage girl is being sexually abused by her father, and children's services succeed in obtaining either an EPO, a CAO or an interim care order. They need to have the girl medically examined in order to determine whether or not there is sufficient evidence of sexual abuse. The court orders the examination but the girl objects to it. Is it her right to do so or is it her right to be protected from the risk of sexual abuse on the assumption that it may have occurred? The answer to this question must ultimately turn on the view which is taken of children's rights and the balance which is struck between autonomy and protection.

Keeping the child away from home

The CAO, unlike the EPO, is not designed to remove the child from home. As a general proposition, therefore, the child should only be kept away from home where this is strictly necessary for the purposes of the assessment. Overnight stays can be authorised, but this requires a specific direction from the court, and the child may be kept away only for the period or periods specified in the order.[54] Assessment should be carried out with as little trauma to children and parents as possible, and the CAO should not be regarded as a variant of the EPO. Examples of when an overnight stay might be justifiable are where the child has eating difficulties, seriously disturbed sleeping patterns or other symptoms which might appear to require 24-hour observation and monitoring.

Where the child is kept away from home, the court must give directions about contact between the child and the parents or others.[55] Restrictions on contact can only be justified where contact would unduly interfere with the assessment process.

How long does the order last?

Somewhat controversially, the maximum duration of a CAO is seven days from the date specified in the order.[56] But, significantly, there is no power to extend this. A CAO is therefore strictly a 'one-off' order. No further application for a CAO may be made within six months of the disposal of the last, without the leave of the court.[57] Seven days is not a long time and it is imperative that the local authority should make the necessary arrangements for the assessment in

---

[52] *South Glamorgan County Council v W and B* [1993] 1 FLR 574. See also (in a rather different context but again involving the court's power to override mature minors) *Re K, W and H (Minors) (Medical Treatment)* [1993] 1 FLR 854.

[53] As to which, see chapters 7 amd 8.

[54] Section 43(9).

[55] Section 43(10).

[56] Section 43(5).

[57] Section 91(15).

advance of the commencement date. Some scepticism has been expressed about the adequacy of the seven day period, and about the adequacy of the eight-day limit for EPOs.[58] The argument is that a proper diagnosis of a child's condition may take several weeks and that the rigid time-limit for the CAO might force the local authority to seek an interim care order. This could be seen by everyone as 'a significant escalation in the interventive process'.

Finally, to put CAOs in perspective, it should be remembered that a formal order will often not be required, since even the suggestion of an application for this (a fortiori one for an EPO) may bring about voluntary co-operation by the parents.

EMERGENCY PROTECTION ORDERS[59]

The *Guidance* states that the purpose of the EPO is 'to enable the child in an emergency to be removed from where he is, or be kept where he is, if and only if this is what is necessary to provide immediate short-term protection'.[60] Drawing on the domestic authorities, which have sought to apply the approach of the ECtHR, the *Guidance* comments further:

> 'It should be remembered that an EPO, which has the effect of separating a child from his parents, is a "draconian" and "extremely harsh" measure, and one requiring "exceptional justification" and "extraordinarily compelling reasons". The courts have confirmed the findings of the European Court of Human Rights. The child must be in "imminent danger". The court must be satisfied that the EPO is both necessary and proportionate and that there is "no less radical form of order available". Local authorities should obtain and consider legal advice before making an application for an EPO.'

This guidance reflects two High Court decisions which have provided general guidance on how courts should approach an application for an EPO, *X Council v B (Emergency Protection Order)*[61] and *Re X (Emergency Protection Orders)*.[62]

In *X Council v B (Emergency Protection Order)*[63] Munby J considered the court's jurisdiction to make an EPO. The local authority became concerned at the mother's alleged failure to administer her children's medication, and to engage appropriately with medical services. The local authority obtained without notice EPOs, each lasting for eight days, and three children were taken into foster care. The case came before Munby J for leave to withdraw care proceedings, which was granted. However, Munby J was concerned by some

---

[58]   J Eekelaar 'Investigation Under the Children Act 1989' [1990] Fam Law 486 at 488.
[59]   See generally, J Masson, D McGovern, K Pick and M Winn Oakley, *Protecting Powers: Emergency Intervention for Children's Protection* (Chichester, Wiley, 2007).
[60]   *The Children Act 1989 Guidance and Regulations Vol 1 Court Orders* (TSO, 2008), at para 4.25.
[61]   [2004] EWHC 2015 (Fam), [2005] 1 FLR 341.
[62]   [2006] EWHC 510 (Fam), [2006] 2 FLR 701.
[63]   [2004] EWHC 2015 (Fam), [2005] 1 FLR 341.

aspects of the EPO. While he considered that the without notice application could be justified because of the possibility that the mother might administer medication and thus thwart the local authority's investigation into her failures, he was concerned that the order had been made to last for more than 24 or 48 hours, the time necessary to carry out tests, and that the children had been removed to foster care.

Munby J drew on case law of the European Court of Human Rights which has considered emergency removal with reference to removal of newborn babies, and by way of providing some context to Munby J's judgment it is convenient to illustrate the ECtHR's approach by reference to some of the authorities.

In *K and T v Finland*[64] the mother was schizophrenic and had been hospitalised many times. While she was pregnant her son, who had behavioural problems, was placed in a children's home for short-term support for the family. When the new baby was born she was immediately removed from the mother under an emergency care order. Both the baby and her elder brother were then placed in provisional public care. The mother and the baby's father were informed of this only after the care orders had been made and they were allowed only supervised access to the children. There followed a further period of treatment for the mother, including compulsory psychiatric care. During this period the father was said to have played an important part in looking after the baby, a fact acknowledged by the social welfare authorities. Nevertheless, both children were placed in public foster care together, and the parents' access was restricted. Both parents complained of violations of their Convention rights. They argued that the Finnish authorities had not given them a sufficient chance to try to overcome their problems with the assistance of relatives and other available support measures and that they had failed to attach sufficient importance to the aim of reunification of the family.

The Grand Chamber of the ECtHR (by majority) agreed with them about several, but not all, alleged violations of the Convention. The Court held that there had been no violation of Art 8 in relation to the emergency care order concerning the son in the light of his behavioural problems and the fact that he had already been separated from his family. Neither had there been a violation in relation to the normal care orders which had been based on relevant and sufficient reasons. However, Art 8 was violated, both in relation to the emergency care order removing the baby and as a result of the authorities' failure to take seriously the aim of reuniting the family. The Court said that 'extraordinarily compelling reasons' were needed to justify the physical removal of a baby from the care of her mother against her will, immediately after the birth. Here the reasons did not exist and the authorities had failed to consider whether some less intrusive interference would have sufficiently protected the baby. Even allowing for the wide margin of appreciation given to the State in such matters, the level of interference could not be regarded as necessary in a democratic society. As to the second violation, the Court found that there was a

---

[64]   [2001] 2 FLR 707.

positive duty on the authorities to take measures to facilitate family reunification as soon as reasonably feasible, but in this case there had been no serious or sustained effort to do so. Indeed, the striking feature in the case was the exceptionally firm negative attitude of the authorities.

The decision was reinforced by the later case of *P, C and S v United Kingdom*.[65] The facts are very complex and the ECtHR found violations of Art 6 in relation to several unacceptable procedural irregularities surrounding the obtaining of the various orders. In the present context we are only concerned with the issue of the removal of the baby from birth under an EPO.

The background was that the mother, an American citizen, had been convicted in California of an offence relating to the care of her first child and had been sentenced to three years' probation and three months in custody by a Californian court. This was based on the allegation that she had been administering laxatives to the child inappropriately. Now in the UK, she gave birth to a second child by her second husband, a qualified social worker with a doctorate the subject of which was women who were wrongly accused of being Münchausen's Syndrome by Proxy (MSBP) abusers. Rochdale Metropolitan Borough Council obtained an EPO at 10.30 am on the day of the birth and at about 4.30 pm social workers took the baby from hospital and placed her with foster parents. The parents complained, inter alia, that the removal of the baby was not necessary and was disproportionate, arguing that she could have remained with her mother at the hospital under supervision.

The ECtHR distinguished between the obtaining of the EPO and the removal of the child under it. The former was held not to violate Art 8 of the ECHR while the latter did amount to a violation in the circumstances. The Court recognised that social services were legitimately concerned, and had a duty under s 47 of the Children Act 1989 to investigate where it came to their attention that a mother who was about to have another baby had a conviction for harming one of her other children. The Court refused to accept that there had been a failure to involve the parents in the investigative process and it was apparent that they had been made aware that removal at birth was one of the options under consideration. It also found that there were relevant and sufficient reasons for seeking the EPO in that the mother had been convicted of harming her son and had been found by an expert to suffer from a syndrome which manifested itself in exaggerating and fabricating illness in a child with consequent significant physical and psychological damage to that child. The decision to seek the EPO might therefore be regarded as necessary in a democratic society to safeguard the health and rights of the baby. However, the Court reiterated that the removal of a baby at birth required exceptional justification. It was a traumatic step for the mother which put her own physical and mental health under strain. It deprived the newborn baby of close contact with her birth mother and of the advantages of breastfeeding. It also deprived the father of being close to his daughter after birth. The Court was not persuaded that it was impossible for the child to remain in hospital and spend at least some time with her mother under supervision. Even if the mother represented a risk to the child, her capacity and opportunity for causing harm immediately after the birth were limited and there was no suspicion of life-threatening conduct. Thus, the Draconian step of removing the child from her mother shortly after birth was not supported by relevant and sufficient reasons. It was not necessary to safeguard the child and there had been a breach of both parents' rights under Art 8.

What these decisions establish is that local authorities must be able to demonstrate that an emergency measure is really necessary and that no lesser form of intervention would have been sufficient to protect the child. In many cases it be possible to secure the 'voluntary' co-operation of the parents in agreeing to supervision by social services. The decisions also make it plain that even where an EPO may be warranted to give children's services the authority to intervene in an emergency, it should not be assumed that removal of the child from birth is necessarily justified.[66]

In *X Council v B (Emergency Protection Order)*[67] Munby J observed that (as we have seen) the European Court had stressed in the context of the removal of a newborn baby that emergency removal is a 'draconian' and 'extremely harsh' measure, requiring 'exceptional justification' and 'extraordinary compelling reasons'.[68] He said that these principles should equally apply to older children, who may find removal more frightening or distressing because they are conscious of what is happening to them. Munby J said that local authorities must approach EPO applications with ' a scrupulous regard for the European Convention rights of both the child and the parents'.[69] Intervention 'must be proportionate to the legitimate aim of protecting the welfare and interests of the child', particularly in the context of interim care orders or EPOs 'when there have as yet been no adverse findings against the parent(s)'.[70] Munby J held that the test is one of 'necessity' and there is a requirement that there be 'imminent danger',[71] and any order 'must provide for the least interventionist

---

66 In *Re M (Care Proceedings: Judicial Review)* [2003] 2 FLR 171, Munby J dealt in depth with the human rights requirements where a baby is removed from his mother. The least the local authority could do, he said, was to make generous arrangements for contact, including suitable arrangements for the mother who wished to breastfeed. In these cases, contact should be allowed most days of the week for lengthy periods. Nothing less, in his view, would satisfy the requirements of the ECHR. An application to remove a child at birth would moreover require that the court be provided with the fullest possible information and the evidence would need to be full, detailed, precise and compelling. Unparticularised generalities would not be sufficient.

67 [2004] EWHC 2015 (Fam), [2005] 1 FLR 341.

68 Citing *K and T v Finland* (2000) 31 EHRR 484, [2000] 2 FLR 79, [2001] 2 FLR 707, *P, C and S v UK* (2002) 35 EHRR 31, [2002] 2 FLR 631; *Venema v Netherlands* [2003] 1 FLR 552; *Covezzi and Morselli v Italy* (2003) 38 EHRR 28; and *Haase v Germany* [2004] 2 FLR 39.

69 [2004] EWHC 2015 (Fam), [2005] 1 FLR 341, at para [41].

70 Ibid, at para [44].

71 Ibid, at para [46], and citing *Haase v Germany*, above, at paras [90]–[95].

solution consistent with the preservation of the child's immediate safety.'[72] He added that the evidence in support of the application for an EPO must be full, detailed, precise, and compelling.[73]

In *Re X (Emergency Protection Orders)*[74] McFarlane J advised that Munby J's guidance should always be drawn to the attention of the justices hearing an EPO.[75] In that case, the local authority had concerns about emotional abuse of the child and the mother's personality. The application for an EPO arose from the mother's presentation with her child at a local hospital saying that the child was complaining of abdominal pain and insisting on seeing a doctor despite a triage nurse finding no problem. It was said in court that the mother had demanded investigations and treatment, and the court was also told that the mother was suffering from fabricated or induced illness syndrome, although this had never been professionally diagnosed. McFarlane J considered that the processes by which the EPO was obtained were badly flawed. There was no imminent danger of harm that justified X's removal, and the local authority testimony was misleading. McFarlane J observed that cases of emotional abuse, and cases of fabricated or induced illness where there is no medical evidence of immediate risk of direct physical harm to the child, will rarely, if ever, warrant an EPO, and similarly in cases of sexual abuse where there is no evidence of immediate risk. He said that in such cases the justices should actively consider refusing an EPO on the basis that the local authority should issue an application for an interim care order.

Who may apply and on what grounds?

Applications

Unlike CAOs, care orders or supervision orders, EPOs may be sought by *anyone* and not only by the local authority or NSPCC, except where 'non-access' is the basis of the application.[76] This may also be contrasted with the rules governing standing to apply for private orders. Whilst there is much more flexibility under the Children Act, the applications are, nevertheless, still restricted, either by the class of applicant, or by the requirement of leave. EPOs are the one example in the legislation of wholly unrestricted access to the courts. The reasoning is obvious. Where a child is thought to be in immediate danger, the policy is not to stand on ceremony but to allow any concerned individual to act post haste to protect the child. It is anticipated that this will, in the vast majority of cases, be the local authority or NSPCC but it could be a concerned relative, neighbour, teacher, doctor or other professional. The police might also wish to apply but are more likely to rely on their independent

---

[72] [2004] EWHC 2015 (Fam), [2005] 1 FLR 341, at para [57].
[73] Ibid.
[74] [2006] EWHC 510 (Fam), [2006] 2 FLR 701.
[75] Ibid, at para [65].
[76] Section 44(1) provides that 'any person' may be the applicant. This was the position regarding place of safety orders, and the DHSS *Review of Child Care Law* (1985) found no evidence of abuse (see para 13.7). If someone other than the local authority succeeds in obtaining an EPO, this will trigger the authority's investigative duties under s 47(1).

emergency powers in the legislation.[77] However, regulations provide that, where the applicant is not the local authority, the local authority may take over the order, and the power and responsibilities which go with it, where it considers that this would be in the child's best interests.[78] In deciding whether to do so, the local authority must consult the applicant and must have regard to a range of factors reminiscent of those in the statutory checklist in s 1(3).[79] It is not thought that these transfer powers will be exercised in relation to the NSPCC, since it is expected that there will be local dialogue and consultation between the NSPCC and the local authority.

Without notice applications

An important procedural distinction between the EPO and the CAO is that the EPO may be made without notice.[80] However, the *Guidance* provides that 'save in wholly exceptional circumstances the application must be made on notice' and if 'an EPO is obtained without notice then the parents must be given information about what happened at the hearing, whether or not they request it'.[81] Where the application is heard without notice the rules require the applicant to serve a copy of the application and the order within 48 hours on the parties to the proceedings, anyone with the care of the child and the local authority where it is not the applicant.[82] They emphasise the crucial need to inform parents of their rights and responsibilities under the order – something severely neglected in the past.

The application must usually be made in the family proceedings court unless there are pending proceedings and there is no provision for transfer to a higher court.[83] As was the case with place of safety orders, the application may be made to a single justice and in most cases this will be necessary – not least because emergencies arise when courts are not sitting.[84] Time will usually be of the essence. The rules provide that, wherever possible, the application should be

---

[77] Under s 46 which is discussed at p 556 below.

[78] Section 52(3), and the Emergency Protection Order (Transfer of Responsibilities) Regulations 1991 (SI 1991/1414).

[79] Emergency Protection Order (Transfer of Responsibilities) Regulations 1991, reg 3 provides that the authority must have regard to: the wishes and feelings of the child; his physical, emotional and educational needs; the likely effect of any change of circumstances on him; his age, sex and family background; the circumstances which gave rise to the application for the EPO; any court order or directions; the relationship of the applicant to the child; and any plans which the applicant may have for the child.

[80] Family Procedure Rules 2010, r 12.16.

[81] *The Children Act 1989 Guidance and Regulations Vol 1 Court Orders* (TSO, 2008), at para 4.40(c). This reflects the case law: see *X Council v B (Emergency Protection Order)* [2004] EWHC 2015 (Fam), [2005] 1 FLR 341, at para [57](8); and *Re X (Emergency Protection Orders)* [2006] EWHC 510 (Fam), [2006] 2 FLR 701 (hearing should be tape recorded or verbatim note taken).

[82] FPR 2010, r 12.16; PD12E.

[83] Allocation and Transfer of Proceedings Order 2008, arts 5, 14 and 15(2).

[84] Most obviously in the middle of the night or at weekends.

made to the court. This reflects concern that place of safety orders were too often requested of single justices where an application to a full court would have been possible.

Identification of the child in the order

Any child may be the subject of an EPO and, wherever practicable, the order should name the child. Where it does not do so, it should identify him as clearly as possible.[85] In some situations, the name of the child who is thought to be in danger will not be known to the applicant.

Grounds

There are three alternative grounds for obtaining an EPO set out in s 44(1), the first of which is open to any applicant. This may be relied on where the court is satisfied that:

> 'there is reasonable cause to believe that the child is likely to suffer significant harm if –
>
> (i) he is not removed to accommodation provided by or on behalf of the applicant or
> (ii) he does not remain in the place in which he is then being accommodated.'

Satisfying the court of significant future harm

The first point is that it is the *court* rather than the applicant which must be satisfied that the statutory criteria are met.[86] 'Significant harm' bears the same interpretation as elsewhere in the legislation.[87] The grounds for an EPO are *entirely* prospective in nature.[88] Past or present harm will not be sufficient to found an EPO and are relevant only to the extent that they indicate future risk. The court or magistrate must be satisfied of the likelihood of significant harm occurring or recurring (in the sense of having reasonable cause to believe the same).

How likely does 'likely' have to be?

It seems that, in applying this test, the court will need to relate the chance of harm occurring to the gravity of harm if it should occur. Where there is even an outside chance that the child could be exposed to someone convicted of offences against children, this may be seen as an unacceptable risk to run.

---

[85] Section 44(14).
[86] Cf the 'non-access' grounds, discussed below, in relation to which it is the *applicant's* belief which is crucial.
[87] Ie in relation to care, supervision and child assessment orders.
[88] Unlike in applications for a care or supervision order under s 31 of the Children Act 1989, where the court may also consider whether the child 'is suffering' significant harm. Section 31 is discussed in detail in chapter 12.

Equally, where the nature of the possible harm is less grave, it may be that the court should look for a higher risk of its occurrence.[89]

Removing or detaining the child

This ground covers two alternative situations. The first is where the intention is to *remove* a child from where he is currently living – most obviously where abuse or neglect is alleged against the parents. Here, it is not necessary for the applicant to prove that the need for the child's removal is *immediate*,[90] although, as noted above, case law now suggests that the child must be in imminent danger. However, the EPO is intended to be flexible enough to cover the situation where, on investigation, the applicant concludes that it is not necessary to remove the child immediately. An example would be where a suspected adult is prepared 'voluntarily' to leave the home and to undertake not to return to it. The EPO allows the local authority to adopt a 'wait and see' policy, albeit over a short period. The power to remove the child remains for the duration of the order. Thus, in the above example, if the alleged abuser agrees to leave immediately, but 24 hours later is still in the home, steps could then be taken to remove the child without having to go back to court.

The second alternative relates to the situation where the child is currently in a safe environment but there is a threat that he may shortly be removed to a potentially unsafe one, or where the removal itself (for example, from hospital) places the child at risk.

No other requirements

It should be noted that there is no need to show that the risk of harm is attributable to a likely lack of parental care or the child being beyond parental control (as is the case for the making of longer-term orders of care or supervision under s 31 of the Act). The thinking is that at the emergency stage it is not possible to conduct the kind of forensic inquiry which could determine this issue. Valuable time could be lost and the child might be exposed to unnecessary danger.

Frustrated access: alternative grounds for an EPO

Section 44(1) goes on to prescribe two further alternative grounds for an EPO. They apply to local authorities[91] and authorised persons (the NSPCC)[92] respectively and are designed to cater for emergencies arising from 'frustrated access'. In the case of a local authority an order may be made where:

(1)   the applicant is making enquiries under s 47; and

---

[89]   See in the context of care proceedings, *In re B (A Child)* [2013] UKSC 33.
[90]   See Lord Mackay LC, House of Lords, Official Report, 19 January 1989, col 426.
[91]   Section 44(1)(b).
[92]   Section 44(1)(c).

(2) those enquiries are being frustrated by access to the child being unreasonably refused to a person authorised to seek access, and the applicant has reasonable cause to believe that access to the child is required as a matter of urgency.

In the case of the NSPCC, the requirements are that the applicant has reasonable cause to suspect that the child is suffering, or is likely to suffer, significant harm, and enquiries into the child's welfare are similarly being frustrated (as set out in (2) above).

EPO or CAO?: degree of urgency

The obvious question is: when should an EPO be requested in non-access cases, given the existence of similar grounds for a CAO and given that the CAO was largely introduced to deal with these situations? The answer lies in the degree of urgency which is felt about the child's situation. Where the circumstances suggest that the child is in imminent danger, the EPO is appropriate. Where this is not the case, but an investigation and assessment of the child's circumstances is required, the CAO will be appropriate. It all depends on the circumstances surrounding the refusal and whether they add up to an emergency.[93] In this context, the test is whether the *applicant*, and not the court, has reasonable cause to suspect that access is required urgently.

Whichever ground is relied on, the principles of s 1 again apply, although the statutory checklist does not. What this means is that the court must ultimately exercise a discretion as to whether the order is really necessary and in the best interests of the child. It is not obliged to make the order. Having said that, unless there is voluntary co-operation to avert the emergency, it is difficult to visualise circumstances in which the court would not feel bound to act to protect a child exposed to imminent danger.

What are the effects of the EPO?

An EPO has three automatic legal effects under s 44(4) while it remains in force. It:

'(a) operates as a direction to any person who is in a position to do so to comply with any request to produce the child to the applicant;
(b) authorises –
  (i) the removal of the child at any time to accommodation provided by or on behalf of the applicant and his being kept there; or
  (ii) the prevention of the child's removal from any hospital, or other place, in which he was being accommodated immediately before the making of the order; and

---

[93] There is evidence, however, that powers which are conceived for emergencies may be used 'to allow intervention without the formalities that ordinary child protection proceedings require'. See J Masson 'Human Rights in Child Protection: Emergency Action and its Impact' in P Lodrup and E Modvar *Family Life and Human Rights* (Gyldendal Akademisk, 2004), at p 457.

(c)   gives the applicant parental responsibility for the child.'

Acquisition of parental responsibility by the applicant

This partly reflects the fact that, unlike the position under a CAO, the child will not be at home and will have to be looked after by arrangements made by the applicant.[94] But there are restrictions on the *exercise* of parental responsibility, which reflect the transient nature of the applicant's position. Hence, this may only be exercised 'as is reasonably required to safeguard or promote the welfare of the child (having regard in particular to the duration of the order)'.[95] The applicant must, therefore, ensure that the child is properly looked after while away from home, but should not take major or irreversible decisions which affect the longer-term interests of the child. In keeping with this, the child must not be kept away from home for longer than is strictly necessary. The legislation provides that the child must, accordingly, be allowed to return home or be removed (as the case may be) where it appears to the applicant safe to do so, even though the EPO remains in force.[96] Where this duty arises (which does not involve a return to court) the child must be returned to the care of the person from whom he was removed. Where this is not reasonably practicable, the child must be returned to his parent, a person with parental responsibility or someone else whom the applicant (with the approval of the court) thinks appropriate.[97] Importantly, however, the applicant retains the power, while the order remains in force, to remove the child again if this should prove necessary.[98]

Reasonable contact

An EPO gives rise to a presumption of reasonable contact in favour of prescribed individuals, rather like the situation which applies where the child is in care.[99] Subject to any directions by the court, the applicant must allow the child reasonable contact with his parents, persons with parental responsibility, persons with whom he was living before the EPO, those who have contact orders, and any person acting on their behalf.[100] The court may give specific directions about contact[101] when the order is made or while it remains in force,[102] and it may impose conditions.[103] What is 'reasonable' will depend on the circumstances, and in many cases it may be necessary to have supervised

---

[94]   Under s 21(1) the local authority is obliged to make provision for the reception and accommodation of children who are removed or kept away from home under Part V of the Children Act.
[95]   Section 44(5)(b).
[96]   Section 44(10).
[97]   Section 44(11).
[98]   Section 44(12).
[99]   Under s 34(1), discussed in chapter 12.
[100]   Section 44(13).
[101]   Section 44(6)(a).
[102]   Section 44(9)(a).
[103]   Section 44(8).

contact, in view of the nature of the allegations.[104] At the same time there are dangers, well illustrated in Cleveland, of depriving parents of contact, only to find that the allegations against them are unsubstantiated. In view of the short timescale, it is unlikely that the courts will seek to interfere unduly with this process. The drastic reduction in the allowable period of emergency detention, in itself, goes some way in removing grievances about contact.[105] In *X Council v B (Emergency Protection Order)*[106] Munby J indicated that arrangements for contact must be driven by the needs of the family, not stunted by lack of resources.[107]

Other directions which the court can make

These include the power to direct that medical and/or psychiatric examinations or assessments should, or should not, take place.[108] Again, the competent child has a right to refuse to co-operate.[109] It has been pointed out that the applicant, by virtue of having parental responsibility, could, in any event, probably provide a valid consent, and this may not be wholly dependent on the court's direction.[110] But it would be unwise not to seek this in so sensitive a matter – especially bearing in mind the uncertainties involved in establishing the child's level of understanding.[111] It is possible that the EPO may be used *primarily* with a view to securing an examination of some sort where parents are unwilling to co-operate. This can, of course, be achieved under a CAO where the matter is not urgent. The EPO has the advantage that, if the parents should fail to comply with the court's directions, the local authority will have an automatic right to remove the child.

The court may give other ancillary directions to assist with the enforcement of the EPO.[112] First, where it appears to the court that adequate information about the child's whereabouts is not available to the applicant, but is available to someone else, the court may order that person to disclose the information.[113] Secondly, the court may authorise the applicant to enter specified premises and search for the child.[114] This may extend to other childen, where the court is reasonably satisfied that there may be another child on the premises with respect to whom an EPO ought to be made.[115] Where a second child is then

---

[104] See the DHSS *Review of Child Law* (1985), at para 13.17.

[105] From 28 days to eight days.

[106] [2004] EWHC 2015 (Fam), [2005] 1 FLR 341.

[107] At para [57].

[108] Section 44(6)(b) and (8).

[109] Section 44(7), and see the discussion in chapter 8 above. But again, the competent child's refusal may be overridden by the High Court exercising its inherent jurisdiction. See above.

[110] N Lowe and G Douglas *Bromley's Family Law* (9th edn, Butterworths, 1998), at pp 593–594. This is not the case where a CAO is made, since parental responsibility does not pass to the applicant under this.

[111] And also the uncertain relationship between adolescent capacities and the exercise of parental responsibility explored in chapters 7 and 8 above.

[112] Section 48.

[113] Section 48(1).

[114] Section 48(3).

[115] Section 48(4).

found on the premises, the court's order may operate as an EPO and authorise removal of *that* child,[116] subject to a duty to notify the court.[117] Thirdly, where it appears that the use of force may be necessary, the court may grant a warrant authorising a police constable to assist in the exercise of powers under an EPO, using reasonable force if necessary.[118] When executing the warrant, the constable must allow the applicant to accompany him, unless the court directs otherwise,[119] and the court may also direct that the applicant be accompanied by a registered medical practitioner, registered nurse or registered midwife[120] (including Specialist Community Public Health Nurses)[121] if he so chooses. None of these directions is automatically part and parcel of an EPO. They must be specifically sought where the applicant, on the strength of information received or his knowledge of the family situation, thinks they may prove necessary.

How long does the EPO last?

One of the most important reforms was the major reduction in the length of time for which emergency orders can last, or remain unchallenged, and in the number of 'extensions' which can be made.

The legislation prescribes eight days, rather than 28 days as was the case for the place of safety order under the old legislation, as the initial maximum duration of an EPO.[122] No EPO should be made for any longer than is absolutely necessary to protect the child.[123] A limited extension for a further seven days may be granted where the applicant is the local authority or NSPCC, but not where the applicant is an individual.[124] Only one extension is allowed and the maximum period of emergency protection is therefore 15 days.[125] The expectation is that extensions will be uncommon since the initial eight-day

---

[116] Section 48(5).

[117] Section 48(6).

[118] Section 48(9). The court may grant a warrant where it appears to it that a person attempting to exercise power under an EPO has been prevented from doing so by being refused entry to premises or access to the child or that he is likely to be so prevented. These powers are complementary to the general power of the police to act in 'dire emergencies' under the Police and Criminal Evidence Act 1984, ss 17(1)(e) and 24 – as to which see *The Children Act 1989 Guidance and Regulations Vol 1 Court Orders* (TSO, 2008), at para 4.49.

[119] Section 48(10).

[120] Section 48(11).

[121] Section 48(11A).

[122] Section 45(1). Special provision is made for holidays (s 45(2)). Where the EPO follows police protection, the eight-day period runs from the first day on which the child was taken into police protection (s 45(3)).

[123] *X Council v B (Emergency Protection Order)* [2004] EWHC 2015 (Fam), [2005] 1 FLR 341, at para [57].

[124] Section 45(4).

[125] Section 45(6).

period is thought to give the applicant sufficient time in which to decide what further action (if any) to take, and particularly to decide whether to seek an interim care order.[126]

There is no appeal, as such, from the making of an EPO, but there is an opportunity for judicial challenge by an application to discharge the order. This may be brought by the child, the parents, persons with parental responsibility and any person with whom the child was living immediately before the order.[127] No discharge application may be made where the potential applicant was given notice of the original hearing and was present at it.[128] In the majority of cases, this will not be the case, since the order will have been made without notice. But, where it was made following an on notice hearing, an opportunity for challenge has already arisen. To allow a 'second bite at the cherry' would be unacceptably disruptive of protection procedures.

The local authority has no right of appeal against the refusal of justices to extend an EPO. *Re P (Emergency Protection Order)*[129] was a disturbing case which illustrates the problems which can arise where there is a refusal to extend the order. Here, a young baby nearly died from what was suspected to be an attempt by his mother to suffocate him. There was clear medical evidence by a paediatrician, later confirmed by a brain scan, that there was no medical cause for what had happened. The local authority did eventually obtain a care order but only after prolonged investigations by experienced paediatricians. Johnson J criticised the justices for their failure to extend the EPO in the face of firm medical evidence pointing to the risk of life-threatening abuse. He considered that there was a lacuna in the legislation and a need for some mechanism of review. Meanwhile, the only options open to a local authority in this situation are to apply immediately for a care order and seek an interim care order or to seek to have the matter transferred to the county court.

Can the alleged abuser be removed instead?

The background: before the Family Law Act 1996

Few people would argue with the general proposition that children are better off left in the family wherever possible. This is, of course, central to the philosophy of the legislation. Removal from home should be confined to those cases in which it is really necessary; something which is now required by the ECHR. One possible solution, and perhaps a better one for the child, may be to remove the alleged abuser from the home. This will be a more viable option where that person's partner or spouse is in agreement with the proposal. It will

---

[126] *The Children Act 1989 Guidance and Regulations Vol 11* (above), at para 4.66. See also the DHSS *Review of Child Care Law* (1985), at para 13.23.
[127] Section 45(8), (10). For a case in which practical difficulties occurred in applying these provisions, see *Essex County Council v F* [1993] 1 FLR 847.
[128] Section 45(11).
[129] [1996] 1 FLR 482.

be much more difficult where this co-operation is not forthcoming and, a fortiori, where there is collusion in the abuse.

As the law stood before 1996 there was no public law remedy which was available to evict an alleged abuser. The options were to try to persuade the abuser to leave voluntarily or to persuade his partner to pursue private law remedies which could at least authorise temporary exclusion. The *Guidance* advised that these options be explored.[130] It stated that the local authority would always want to canvass the possibility of providing voluntary services to the person concerned, perhaps also providing alternative housing or even cash assistance.[131] The same result might be achieved if the non-abusing parent was prepared to apply for an ouster order under the domestic violence legislation.[132] The *Guidance* suggested that this might be particularly appropriate where sexual abuse was alleged. In this instance, the non-abusing parent might have no wish to protect or shield the alleged abuser, but immediate removal of the child might well not be in the child's best interests.

Family law commentators, at least for the purposes of exposition, have been much inclined to put child abuse and domestic violence[133] into different compartments. Yet in reality this distinction has always been somewhat artificial. If a man is being violent towards children, or threatening them with violence, this can be viewed both as child abuse which might give rise to *public* care proceedings or domestic violence which could trigger the *private* remedies relating to non-molestation or ouster from the family home. In the years between the implementation of the Children Act 1989 and of Part IV of the Family Law Act 1996,[134] local authorities, not wishing to take the ultimate step of seeking a care order, began to explore whether they might exclude an alleged abuser by resorting to the private law orders under s 8 of the Children Act.

The matter came to a head in *Nottinghamshire County Council v P*[135] where the Court of Appeal found, partly for technical reasons arising under the provisions of s 9 of the Children Act and partly on broader policy grounds, that in general local authorities were precluded from invoking *private* s 8 orders, and, in fulfilling their statutory child protection role, ought instead to pursue the *public* remedies which Parliament had provided in the Children Act. Indeed, the court was very critical of Nottinghamshire's failure to do so. What had happened in this case was that there were allegations of sexual abuse

---

[130] *The Children Act 1989 Guidance and Regulations Vol 1 Court Orders* (HMSO, 1991), at para 4.31.

[131] Under Sch 2, para 5 to the Children Act.

[132] Ie under the previous legislation, the Domestic Violence and Matrimonial Proceedings Act 1976, s 1 (county court) or the Domestic Proceedings and Magistrates' Courts Act 1978, s 16 (magistrates' courts).

[133] In the context of housing legislation, the Supreme Court has held that domestic violence is not limited to violence involving physical contact but also includes threatening or intimidating behaviour and any other form of abuse which, directly or indirectly, may give rise to the risk of harm: see *Yemshaw v Hounslow London Borough Council* [2011] UKSC 3.

[134] Part IV of the 1996 Act was brought into force on 1 October 1997.

[135] [1993] 2 FLR 134.

against the father of three girls by the eldest girl who claimed that he had been abusing the three of them. The local authority successfully obtained leave to seek a prohibited steps order preventing the father from living in the household and from having contact with the girls. Ward J at first instance held that he was prevented by s 9(5) of the Children Act from making the orders and his decision was upheld by the Court of Appeal.

Sir Stephen Brown P held that in reality the effect of the prohibited steps order (if made) would be for the father to be ordered to have 'no contact' with the children and that a 'no contact' order was equivalent to a contact order. The authority was directly precluded from seeking such a contact order by the provisions of s 9(2) and indirectly by the provisions of s 9(5). From a broader policy perspective, the President said that 'the route chosen by the local authority in this case was wholly inappropriate'. He went on to criticise the authority for not taking steps under Part IV of the Children Act specifically to seek a supervision order to protect the children, and expressed deep concern at 'the absence of any power to direct this authority to take steps to protect the children'.

This decision did not prevent a prohibited steps order being subsequently made by the Court of Appeal (in a case in which the local authority had already obtained a care order in relation to one child and supervision orders in relation to the other children in the household) to restrain a man who was *not* living with the mother and the children from having or seeking to have, contact with the children.[136] The distinction drawn by Butler-Sloss LJ was essentially that this was to prevent an *external* threat to the children and that a 'no contact' order against the man could not be made since he did not live with the children. Local authorities also succeeded in a couple of reported decisions[137] in obtaining ouster orders by invoking the inherent jurisdiction, although the extent of this jurisdiction to protect children was not clear.[138] The distinctions drawn in these cases were often subtle and technical and it was a matter of some doubt whether they could be regarded as at all consistent from a policy perspective.

In 1992 the Law Commission considered the issue.[139] Having rejected the idea that undertakings could provide an adequate solution,[140] the Law Commission went on to recommend a new power for the court to make a short-term emergency ouster order when making an EPO or interim care order.[141] The

---

[136] *Re H (Prohibited Steps Order)* [1995] 1 FLR 638.
[137] *Re S (Minors) (Inherent Jurisdiction: Ouster)* [1994] 1 FLR 623 and *Devon County Council v S* [1994] Fam 169.
[138] See particularly *Pearson v Franklin* [1994] 2 All ER 137.
[139] Law Com Report No 207 *Domestic Violence and Occupation of the Family Home* (1992).
[140] Ibid, at para 6.15. The Law Commission was particularly bothered by the fact that, since proceedings for EPOs were usually ex parte, there would have to be an adjournment during which time the child might be exposed to risk. It also thought that a power of arrest could not very appropriately be attached to undertakings as opposed to orders.
[141] Law Com Report No 207 Domestic Violence and Occupation of the Family Home (1992), at para 6.18.

order would be dependent on proof of the criteria for these orders but there would also be additional criteria. First, it would have to be shown that there was reasonable cause to believe that the likelihood of harm to the child would not arise if the named person were to be removed from the household. Secondly, there would have to be another parent or other person in the household who was willing and able to provide reasonable care for the child and that that person consented to the order being made.[142] Importantly, the Law Commission also recommended that the court would have power to attach a power of arrest to the order to offer immediate protection to the child in the event of a breach.[143]

Part IV of the Family Law Act 1996

These recommendations have been substantially implemented by Part IV of the Family Law Act 1996.[144] Similar, but somewhat less restrictive, reforms were introduced into Scots law by the Children (Scotland) Act 1995.[145] In a text about children it is inappropriate to go into the intricacies of the scheme governing domestic violence and occupation of the family home. It is, however, possible here to sketch the principal features of the scheme and to draw attention to the way in which the law impacts on the protection of children and interacts with the emergency and short-term protective remedies which are the focus of this chapter.

Essential features of the scheme

Part IV of the Family Law Act 1996 repealed the various statutes which governed domestic violence and occupation of the family home[146] and gathered together in one place a consistent set of remedies obtainable on common criteria, under a concurrent jurisdiction exercised by the magistrates' (family proceedings) court, the county court and the High Court.[147] These courts may, at their discretion, make 'non-molestation orders' and 'occupation orders'.[148] The former protect from 'molestation' which, of course, includes violence but is a concept wide enough to cover a range of conduct which can broadly be described as 'pestering' or 'harassment'.[149] The Domestic Violence, Crime and

---

[142] Ibid, at para 6.20.

[143] Ibid, at para 6.22.

[144] For a detailed account, see S Gilmore and L Glennon *Hayes and Williams' Family Law* (Oxford University Press, 2012) ch 3. See also R Probert *Cretney and Probert's Family Law* (8th edn, Sweet & Maxwell, 2012), Pt 2.

[145] For a concise summary of the 'exclusion order' available to local authorities in Scotland, see E Sutherland 'Scotland: Child Law Reform – At Last!' in A Bainham (ed) *The International Survey of Family Law 1995* (Martinus Nijhoff, 1997), at pp 449–450.

[146] The Domestic Violence and Matrimonial Proceedings Act 1976, the Domestic Proceedings and Magistrates' Courts Act 1978 (to the extent that it governed these remedies) and the Matrimonial Homes Act 1983 (MHA 1983).

[147] In this respect it follows the pattern set by the Children Act 1989.

[148] In 2011 a total of 15,573 applications for non-molestation orders were made and a total of 5,098 applications for occupation orders: *Judicial and Court Statistics* 2011 (Ministry of Justice, 2012).

[149] It should be noted that the Protection from Harassment Act 1997 has created criminal offences

Victims Act 2004 inserted a new s 42A into the Family Law Act 1996, the effect of which is to make it a criminal offence to breach a non-molestation order.[150]

Standing to seek a non-molestation order depends on the applicant being 'associated' with the respondent, and the Act contains a definition of 'associated persons',[151] the effect of which is to extend essentially familial or domestic remedies to a very wide range of individuals not before treated as family members for other purposes by English law.[152] For present purposes it is sufficient to note that the definition of 'relevant child' in the legislation is drawn extremely widely and extends to many children who would not, for example, have been regarded as a 'child of the family' as required by some of the earlier legislation.[153] It is hard to visualise any children whose status would preclude the court from making a non-molestation order if it feels inclined to do so. Also of note is that the definition of 'associated persons' includes in relation to a child the two parents of that child, persons with parental responsibility and adoptive (or prospective adoptive) parents.[154] And the term 'relative', which also has the effect of rendering two people 'associated', can surely never have been so widely defined in legislation here or anywhere else.[155] So the scope for protective non-molestation orders being made in relation to children is very considerable. It should be remembered, however, that these orders can only be made on the application of a private individual, usually but not necessarily by the mother, and not by the local authority.[156]

Standing to seek an occupation order is exceedingly complex, as are the criteria which the court must apply. Pressures from the ultra-conservative wing of the Conservative party (then in government) and the tabloid press culminated in a

---

of 'harassment' and putting people in fear of violence. Where these offences are committed or threatened, the victim may have a civil remedy (damages and/or injunction) and a 'restraining order' may be made to prevent a recurrence of the behaviour. The remedies under this Act will be particularly useful where individuals fall outside the definition of 'associated persons' in Part IV of the Family Law Act 1996. The details of the 1997 legislation are beyond the scope of the present discussion, especially since they are more likely to be relevant to the protection of adults than the protection of children.

[150] For comment on the background, see H Conway 'The Domestic Violence, Crime and Victims Bill' [2004] Fam Law 132 and RN Hill 'The Effect of the Domestic Violence Bill on FLA 1996' [2004] Fam Law 442.

[151] Section 62(3).

[152] For commentary on the significance of this definition in the wider context of conceptual change in family law, see A Bainham 'Changing families and changing concepts: reforming the language of family law' [1998] CFLQ 1.

[153] 'Relevant child' is defined in s 62(2) as: '(a) any child who is living with or might reasonably be expected to live with either party to the proceedings;(b) any child in relation to whom an order under the Adoption Act 1976, the Adoption and Children Act 2002, or the Children Act 1989 is in question in the proceedings; and(c) any other child whose interests the court considers relevant'.

[154] Section 62(4) and (5).

[155] See s 63(1).

[156] Though there is nothing to preclude a parent from seeking a non-molestation order during the currency of care proceedings. To do so may demonstrate good faith in genuinely seeking to co-operate with the local authority by removing a risky individual from the vicinity of the children's home.

piece of legislation which seeks to draw distinctions between those who have a
property interest of some sort in the family home and those who do not; and
between spouses and cohabitants. It is a moot point, as Gillian Douglas has
observed, whether the purpose 'is as much to stress Parliament's concern for the
importance of property rights as it is to emphasise the importance of
marriage'.[157]

Either way, the Act draws distinctions between so-called 'entitled applicants'
and 'non-entitled applicants', the latter category being further sub-divided into
'former spouses or former civil partners' on the one hand and 'cohabitants' and
'former cohabitants' on the other. In essence, 'entitled applicants' are those with
'home rights' (which with very limited exceptions will include all spouses who
do not otherwise have a proprietary interest in the home) and those 'entitled to
occupy a dwelling house by virtue of a beneficial estate or interest or contract
or by notice of any enactment giving him the right to remain in occupation'.[158]
Entitled applicants may seek an occupation order where the home in question
has been the home of the applicant and an associated person or was intended
to be their home. Former spouses, cohabitants, and former cohabitants must
therefore apply as 'non-entitled' applicants unless they have an interest in the
property, and the overall effect in practice will be that the overwhelming
majority of spouses will be 'entitled' while very many of those who live
together outside marriage will be 'non-entitled'. The criteria for making
occupation orders differ depending on the category of the applicant as does the
potential duration of any order made.[159] The differential criteria may
conceivably be important to the question of the relative weight to be attached
to children's interests and we discuss this below in assessing the impact of
Part IV on children.

If made, an occupation order, as its name suggests, may regulate the occupation
of a home in various ways. In particular (and perhaps most relevant to the
current context of child protection), it may oust an alleged abuser from the
home, or may go further and exclude him from 'a defined area in which the
dwelling-house is included'.[160] An important change brought about by the Act
relates to powers of arrest. While it was the case that such powers could be
attached to orders under the previous legislation, judges were reluctant to do
this unless a pattern of flouting the court's orders had developed. Under the
1996 Act, the court must attach a power of arrest to the order if 'it appears to
the court that the respondent has used or threatened violence against the

---

[157] 'England and Wales: "Family Values" to the Fore?' in A Bainham (ed) *The International Survey
of Family Law 1996* (Martinus Nijhoff, 1998), at p 176.

[158] FLA 1996, s 33(1).

[159] As to duration, the essential difference is that an order of unlimited duration may conceivably
be made in relation to 'entitled applicants' whereas for 'non-entitled former spouses' there may
be successive six-monthly orders and for 'non-entitled cohabitants and former cohabitants' the
six-month order may be extended only once and is thus bound to be seen as a temporary and
not a permanent order.

[160] Section 33(3)(g).

applicant or a relevant child ... unless satisfied that in all the circumstances of the case the applicant or child will be adequately protected without such a power of arrest'.[161]

As in the case of 'non-molestation' orders, it should be carefully noted that occupation orders may be sought only by individuals, usually the mother of the children, and that the local authority has no standing under the legislation to make a 'free-standing' application.

The impact of Part IV on children

Undoubtedly the most innovative and potentially significant reform introduced by Part IV as it applies to children is the amendment of the Children Act to allow local authorities to seek 'exclusion requirements' as adjuncts to emergency protection orders and interim care orders. But before we consider these provisions it may be helpful to highlight two other ways in which the Act is arguably attaching greater weight to the interests of children to be protected. These are, respectively, the reformulation of the statutory criteria for occupation orders, and provision for applications by children themselves.

(i) Reformulation of criteria for occupation orders

One of the matters which caused the greatest amount of difficulty under the former jurisdiction to grant 'ouster orders' was the weight which the court should attach to the welfare of children vis-à-vis other factors, particularly the conduct of the respondent, in deciding whether to make the order. The Court of Appeal had been inconsistent in the guidance which it had given to the lower courts, and the issue eventually came before the House of Lords in *Richards v Richards*.[162] Here, it was held that the matter was governed by the criteria in the Matrimonial Homes Act 1983, which made reference to 'the conduct of the spouses in relation to each other and otherwise to their respective needs and financial resources, to the needs of any children and to all the circumstances of the case'.[163] Hence, it was not permissible for the court to treat the welfare of the children as the 'paramount', or even the 'first', consideration but rather it had to be taken into account alongside the other specified factors with no preconceived weighting as between them.

These criteria were substantially re-enacted in the Family Law Act 1996,[164] but, grafted onto them is a so-called 'balance of harm' test which the court must

---

[161] Section 47(2).

[162] [1984] AC 174.

[163] MHA 1983, s 1(3).

[164] The provision (s 33(6)) which applies to 'entitled applicants' and which, with some controversial additions, applies to the various categories of 'non-entitled' applicants (ss 35(6) and 36(6)) prescribes that the court must have regard to all the circumstances including: '(a) the housing needs and housing resources of each of the parties and of any relevant child; (b) the financial resources of each of the parties; (c) the likely effect of any order, or of any decision by the court not to exercise its powers, on the health, safety or well-being of the parties and of any relevant child; and (d) the conduct of the parties in relation to each other and otherwise'.

apply and which may appear to some to be tilting the balance in the direction of children's welfare vis-à-vis the respondent's conduct. It is provided, in the case of applications by 'entitled' applicants and by 'non-entitled former spouses', that where the applicant or any relevant child is likely to suffer significant harm attributable to the conduct of the respondent, the court *must* make the occupation order unless it appears to it that the respondent or any relevant child is likely to suffer significant harm if the order is made and that this harm is as great or greater than the harm attributable to the respondent's conduct if the order is not made.[165] This 'balance of harm' must also be considered on applications by 'non-entitled cohabitants and former cohabitants' but, in this case, there is no statutory presumption that the order will be made where the balance weighs on the side of the applicant or children.[166]

Not everyone agreed that the provisions of the Act as drafted would be effective if the intention was to emphasise welfare considerations at the expense of conduct in these cases of actual or threatened 'significant harm'. Stephen Cretney[167] argued that since it is only harm 'attributable to the respondent's conduct' which is taken into account under the test 'the effect seems to be to preserve the decision of the House of Lords in *Richards v Richards*'.[168] In other words, 'rubbishy' or 'flimsy' allegations of adverse conduct by the respondent (as occurred in that case) might not be enough to trigger effectively the balance of harm test, if the real problem is just relationship breakdown and/or poor housing conditions. This view certainly seems to be confirmed by the reported cases which have continued to emphasise the Draconian nature of occupation orders rather than the welfare needs of women and children. In *Chalmers v Johns*[169] Thorpe LJ said of the occupation order that it 'remains an order that overrides proprietary rights and ... it is an order that is only justified in exceptional circumstances'.[170] In this case the parties had a tempestuous relationship and the police had been called several times. But there was no evidence that the mother had not given as good as she had received in the matter of assaults.[171] The mother, having moved into temporary council accommodation with the seven-year-old daughter, sought to exclude the father. The Court of Appeal was unwilling to accept that there was a real risk of

---

[165] Sections 33(7) and 35(8).

[166] Section 36(7) and (8).

[167] SM Cretney *Family Law* (4th edn, Sweet & Maxwell, 2000), at p 125.

[168] The conduct in question is not, however, confined to *intentional* conduct, since it is the *effect* of the conduct on the applicant or child that is the important factor. See *G v G (Occupation Order: Conduct)* [2000] 2 FLR 36. In this case there was an atmosphere of tension and strain in the home after the wife issued divorce proceedings. The circuit judge, while recognising that this had been caused or contributed to by the husband's conduct, refused an occupation order on the basis that, since his conduct was unintentional, the likelihood of harm being suffered could not be attributed to him. The Court of Appeal held that he had erred in this respect but dismissed the mother's appeal on the basis that there was insufficient evidence justifying so Draconian an order.

[169] [1999] 1 FLR 392.

[170] Ibid, at 397.

[171] On three of the four occasions when the police were called to the home, it was to investigate an alleged assault by the mother on the father.

violence to the mother or child or that they were likely to suffer significant harm if the order were not made. The child had a longer journey to school but that could not amount to harm. There was insufficient evidence therefore to trigger the balance of harm test and, applying the ordinary criteria, the occupation order could not be justified.

This unwillingness to allow occupation orders to operate as a device for alleviating family discord or regulating a difficult housing situation is also evident in the decision of the Court of Appeal in *Re Y (Children) (Occupation Order)*.[172] Here there was a divided family under one roof with two teenage children each siding with one parent. There was some violence and the recorder concluded that harm was likely to be caused if they remained under the same roof. Taking into account the attitude of the local authority that they might more easily accommodate the mother and her (pregnant) 16-year-old daughter than the father and the 13-year-old child, he ordered the mother to vacate the home on the basis that greater harm would arise from not making the order. The Court of Appeal, however, found that there was insufficient misconduct on the part of the mother to justify the order and that there was no reason, pending divorce, why the matrimonial home could not reasonably be divided to meet the housing needs of all of them. Sedley LJ said that the purpose of an occupation order was 'not to break matrimonial deadlocks by evicting one of the parties, much less to do so at the expense of a dependent, and in this case a heavily pregnant, child'. And he went on: 'To use the occupation order as a weapon in domestic welfare is wholly inappropriate. Parliament has made provision for it as a last resort in an intolerable situation, not as a move in a game of matrimonial chess ...'.

Rather out of keeping with these decisions, *B v B (Occupation Order)*[173] is one decision which did appear to turn on the interests of a particular child and is one in which housing considerations had a decisive influence. Here the husband had been violent to the wife causing her to leave the family home, council accommodation, for temporary bed and breakfast accommodation provided by the council. She then sought a non-molestation order and an occupation order. The husband had with him in the home a child aged six from his previous marriage. The council's position was that, if excluded, he would be regarded as intentionally homeless and that it would have no duty to rehouse him. In contrast it was clear that the mother and baby would, as matters stood, be rehoused in suitable accommodation in a matter of months if not weeks. The judge made the occupation order, but the Court of Appeal allowed the husband's appeal, finding that the balance of harm test should be resolved in favour of the husband's child. If the father were evicted he would find himself in unsuitable temporary accommodation and the child might have to be separated from him by social services. The court was at pains to emphasise that the decision turned on the highly unusual position of the husband's child. The court emphatically did not wish to convey the message that men who subjected

---

[172] [2000] 2 FCR 470.
[173] [1999] 1 FLR 715.

their partners to domestic violence and drove them out could expect to remain in the previously shared accommodation.

Notwithstanding this decision, taken together, the reported cases do not represent the substantial tilting of the balance away from conduct and towards the welfare of mothers and children which appeared to have been the rationale for the introduction of the balance of harm test. As Cretney had astutely predicted, this remains an issue which is influenced more by considerations of the gravity, or otherwise, of misconduct in the family home.

(ii) Applications by children and legal representation

The 1996 Act provided for the first time that children themselves might bring applications for non-molestation orders and occupation orders. Hitherto they had in reality been dependent on applications being brought on their behalf – usually by their mothers. In many, perhaps most, cases of domestic violence, the mother will be seeking orders to protect herself and the children and their interests will coincide. But there may be instances in which they diverge. An extreme case might be where the mother is herself abusing the child or colluding in abuse by the father. Perhaps social services are unwilling or feel unable to intervene. In circumstances like this, the standing to bring proceedings might conceivably be very beneficial to a minority of children.

Where the child has attained the age of 16, he or she is able to seek a non-molestation order as an 'associated person'.[174] Where the child is under the age of 16, the 1996 Act follows the pattern of the Children Act 1989 and provides that such a child may not apply for a non-molestation or occupation order 'except with the leave of the court'.[175] Leave may only be granted for these purposes if the court is satisfied that 'the child has sufficient understanding to make the proposed application'.[176] We consider what is involved in this in the context of children's applications for private s 8 orders in chapter 14.

(iii) Action by the local authority: the exclusion requirements

We have seen that the local authority is precluded from applying for non-molestation or occupation orders under Part IV and to a large extent from resorting to the private s 8 orders of the Children Act. But, following the recommendations of the Law Commission, Part IV of the 1996 Act amended the Children Act to allow the court, in prescribed circumstances, to add 'exclusion requirements' to emergency protection orders and interim care orders.[177] While these requirements are likely to be specifically requested by the local authority concerned, there would appear to be no reason why the court should not insert such a requirement of its own volition. It is important to

---

[174] We looked at the definition of 'relevant child' in fn 153 on p 549 above.
[175] Section 43(1).
[176] Section 43(2).
[177] See ss 38A and 44A of the Children Act 1989.

appreciate that these requirements may only be inserted in the two orders in question and may not, for example, be included in child assessment orders.

The circumstances in which an exclusion requirement may be included in the above orders are:[178]

'(a) that there is reasonable cause to believe that, if a person ("the relevant person") is excluded from a dwelling-house in which the child lives, the child will cease to suffer, or cease to be likely to suffer, significant harm; and

(b) that another person living in the dwelling-house (whether a parent of the child or some other person) –

(i) is able and willing to give to the child the care which it would be reasonable to expect a parent to give him, and

(ii) consents to the inclusion of the exclusion requirement.'

The exclusion requirement may be one or more of the following:[179]

'(a) a provision requesting the relevant person to leave a dwelling-house in which he is living with the child;

(b) a provision prohibiting the relevant person from entering a dwelling-house in which the child lives; and

(c) a provision excluding the relevant person from a defined area in which a dwelling-house in which the child lives is situated.'

A power of arrest may be attached to the exclusion requirement.[180] The court may provide for this to have effect for a period shorter than the exclusion requirement itself.[181] Breach of the exclusion requirement will amount to contempt of court and may lead to imprisonment.[182]

The likely impact of these provisions is hard to assess since much depends on how far the local authority are prepared to use them. Two limitations on the use of the exclusion requirements should be noted. The first is that since they may only accompany emergency protection orders or interim care orders they are dependent on the authority being able to establish the grounds for those orders and they must cease to have effect when the principal orders themselves expire. They are thus by definition only temporary in nature, and this may give rise to anxiety that an alleged abuser may return to the home once the temporary exclusion requirement has expired. The second is that the

---

[178] Children Act 1989, s 38A(2). Section 44A(2) is in broadly similar terms.

[179] Ibid, ss 38A(3) and 44A(3).

[180] Children Act 1989, ss 38A(5) and 44A(5). For procedure, see FPR 2010, r 12.28(2); FJC Protocol of November 2011: *Process Servers: Non-Molestation Orders*.

[181] Children Act 1989, ss 38A(4) and 44A(4).

[182] For the procedural requirements in enforcing the exclusion requirement, see *Re W (Exclusion: Statement of Evidence)* [2000] 2 FLR 666. Here the father acted in clear breach of a requirement that he should not approach, enter or reside at the property where the mother and children were living. The magistrates made an order committing him to two months' imprisonment suspended for six months. Cazalet J reduced this to a suspended period of one month on the basis that the sentence was excessive. The judgment provides useful guidance on the appropriate formalities for seeking exclusion requirements.

requirements may not be included unless 'another person' in the home is able and willing to care for the child and consents to the inclusion of the requirement. Although this category is not confined to the child's parent, in the overwhelming majority of cases we are likely to be talking about the child's mother. There will be concern that the mother in some cases will not be willing to consent in view of the impact this might have on her marriage or relationship with the 'relevant person'.

These are genuine concerns but, it is submitted, they are capable of being exaggerated. Where an interim care order is made, although ultimately limited in time, the relevant person may be excluded for at least some months and in many cases this will help to resolve the problem. As to the mother's consent to the exclusion requirement, it needs to be appreciated that failure to consent may lead to the local authority pursuing a full care order with a view to removing the child from the home. Put crudely, the mother may in some cases have to decide whether she would prefer her husband or partner to be excluded or for her child to be removed. In these circumstances it seems likely that some mothers will be persuaded (albeit reluctantly) to consent. Indeed it is a common feature of care proceedings that mothers wishing to retain or regain the care of their children will need to be able to demonstrate that they have terminated their relationships with risky men.[183]

In this area, as in others, the division between voluntary co-operation and compulsion may be more apparent than real. So far as local authorities themselves are concerned, one attraction in seeking the exclusion requirements will surely be that there will be a considerable saving of hard-pressed resources if the abuser can be removed rather than if a care order, and the extensive ongoing responsibility that goes with it, has to be pursued.

POLICE PROTECTION

The police have important powers to protect children in cases of real urgency.[184] The raison d'être of these powers is that the police are able to act *immediately* without a court order where they find a child in need of protection. Thereafter, they must act expeditiously to pass responsibility for the child to the local authority which has the primary statutory responsibility for the child's welfare.

---

[183] For a classic example of the issues arising see *EH v Greenwich LBC* [2010] 2 FCR 106.

[184] Children Act 1989, s 46 and Home Office Circular 017/2008; and see for guidance *The Children Act 1989 Guidance and Regulations Vol 1 Court Orders* (TSO, 2008), at paras 4.64 et seq. For a particularly good example of the exercise of this power, see the facts of *Re M (A Minor) (Care Order: Threshold Conditions)* [1994] 2 AC 424, where the initial protective measures were taken by the police following the murder of the mother by the father. For an academic critique of the use of these powers, see J Masson 'Police Protection – Protecting Whom?' (2002) 24 JSWFL 1.

Direct action

Where a police constable has reasonable cause to believe that a child would otherwise be likely to suffer significant harm, he may remove the child to 'suitable accommodation' and keep him there. Alternatively, the constable may take reasonable steps to ensure that the child's removal from a hospital or other place in which he is accommodated is prevented.[185] In some cases it may be lawful for police protection to be used to protect a child immediately upon the child's birth, and without the mother being informed in advance of the intended use of the power. In *Re D (Unborn Baby)*[186] Munby J granted declaratory relief to a local authority indicating that such a plan would be lawful in the circumstances of the case. The test to be applied is a stringent one, namely: 'Is the step which the local authority is proposing to take, that is, the step of not involving the parents in its planning and not communicating to the parents its plan for immediate removal at birth, something which is justified by "the overriding necessity of the interests of the child" or something which is "essential to secure [the child's] safety"?'[187] On the facts of the case there was a real risk that the mother, who had talked disturbingly about the death of her children, would lash out at the baby once born.

The powers in s 46 mirror those conferred by an EPO but, here, the police may take direct action on the basis of their own belief. The powers do not include any rights of entry or search, so that if the police require these rights, they will have to apply to the court for an EPO, together with a warrant where appropriate.[188] These powers can, therefore, only relate to children who are found by the police. Such children are said to be in 'police protection' and may be kept there without legal challenge for up to 72 hours.[189] This is the same period of allowable detention as under an EPO before a discharge application can be made. It is a considerable reduction from the eight days allowed under the old law,[190] and is in keeping with the general policy to restrict the length of operation of emergency powers. At the end of this period, the child must either be released or detained further under the authorisation of an EPO.[191]

Obligations which the police must fulfil

As soon as practicable after a child is taken into police protection, the constable concerned must ensure that the case is inquired into by a senior officer appointed by the chief officer of the police area.[192] This officer is then known as the 'designated officer' and has independent statutory duties to those of the constable. The constable must, inter alia: inform the local authority of the

---

[185] Section 46(1).
[186] [2009] EWHC 446 (Fam), [2009] 2 FLR 313.
[187] Ibid, at para [11].
[188] Section 44(1) and s 48(9).
[189] Section 46(6).
[190] Children and Young Persons Act 1969, s 28(4).
[191] Children Act 1989, s 46(5).
[192] Ibid, s 46(3)(e).

situation; inform the child (where the child is capable of understanding) of the steps being taken, with reasons, and ascertain the child's wishes and feelings; ensure that where the child is not already in local authority accommodation or a refuge, that he is moved to such accommodation; and inform the parents, persons with parental responsibility or others with whom the child was living, of the steps that are being taken, with reasons.[193] The designated officer must inquire into the case. He may, where appropriate, apply for an EPO, whether or not the local authority agrees to it or is aware of it.[194] The *Guidance* states, however, that good effective channels of communication ought to mean that the police never find themselves in this position. No extension of an EPO obtained by the police is possible. The maximum period of police-instigated protection is, therefore, eight days. Thereafter the local authority must be involved if further protection is necessary. The *Guidance* emphasises the importance of inter-agency communication and co-operation between the police and the local authority. This ought to be reviewed and monitored at regular intervals. The aim is to ensure that no child taken into police protection need be accommodated in a police station and that his reception into local authority accommodation is achieved with the minimum of trauma.[195]

No parental responsibility

The police do not acquire parental responsibility where a child is in police protection. The designated officer is, however, required to do what is reasonable in all the circumstances for the purpose of safeguarding or promoting the child's welfare (having regard, in particular, to the length of time during which the child will remain under police protection).[196] Beyond the power of removal and detention, the powers of the police are, therefore, in essence, limited to those held by anyone with the de facto care of a child.[197] The designated officer must also allow prescribed individuals to have such contact with the child as is, in his opinion, reasonable and in the child's best interests.[198] Those concerned are the parents, or others with parental responsibility, contact orders or with whom the child was living before he was taken into police protection.[199] Again, contact under supervision may be the only realistic option during the first 72 hours of an emergency.

Relationship of police protection with EPO

In *Langley v Liverpool City Council*[200] the Court of Appeal considered the relationship between the police power in s 46 of the Act and emergency

---

[193] Section 46(3).
[194] Section 46(7) and (8).
[195] *The Children Act 1989 Guidance and Regulations Vol 1 Court Orders* (TSO, 2008), at para 4.71.
[196] Section 46(9)(b).
[197] Cf s 3(5) and the discussion in chapter 4 above.
[198] Section 46(10). Under s 46(11) this is the obligation of the local authority where a child taken into police protection is in local authority accommodation.
[199] Ibid.
[200] [2005] EWCA Civ 1173, [2006] 1 FLR 342.

protection under s 44. In that case parents of a child who was subject to an EPO challenged the lawfulness of use of police protection to remove a child from home where the local authority had already obtained an EPO but asked the police to bring the child into the local authority's 'care'. The Court of Appeal held there 'is nothing in the language of the Act which compels the conclusion that s 46 cannot be invoked where an EPO is in force',[201] but 'discretionary statutory powers must be exercised to promote the policy and objects of the statute'[202] and 'the statutory scheme clearly accords primacy to s 44'.[203] The court therefore held that 'where a police officer knows that an EPO is in force, he should not exercise the power of removing a child under s 46, unless there are compelling reasons to do so',[204] that is when it is not practicable to execute an EPO.[205] In practice many EPOs are sought after the child has initially been taken into police protection but where the authority may not yet be ready to issue its application for an interim care order. It should also be noted that a social worker may be present in some cases when the police take the child into their protection. What we can see in practice therefore is the police working in conjunction with children's services in cases of immediate urgency. These are cases of compelling risk of harm to children if action is not taken there and then.

ABDUCTION OF CHILDREN AND REFUGES FOR CHILDREN AT RISK

Runaways

The legal position of adolescents who run away has never been entirely clear, not least because the law has not set a definite age at which a young person may live independently.[206] Organisations such as the Children's Society, which have habitually given assistance to young runaways, particularly by providing them with temporary accommodation, until the Children Act had a dubious legal

---

[201] Ibid, at [30].

[202] Ibid, at [33], citing *Padfield and Others v Minister of Agriculture, Fisheries and Food and Others* [1968] AC 997, at 1030C.

[203] *Langley* [2005] EWCA Civ 1173, [2006] 1 FLR 342, at [38]. At [37] the court pointed to a number of important differences between the s 44 and s 46 regimes. They include the following. First, the court can give directions with respect to contact, examinations and assessments. This is a valuable power not available to the police. Secondly, an EPO gives the applicant parental responsibility, whereas while a child is being kept in police protection under s 46 neither the constable nor the designated officer has parental responsibility. Thirdly, no child can be kept in police protection for more than 72 hours, whereas an EPO may have effect for a period not exceeding 8 days (s 45(1)), and this period may be extended by up to 7 days (s 45(5)).

[204] Ibid, at [36].

[205] Ibid, at [40]. See for an example of when it was not practicable to execute an EPO and police protection was lawful, *A v East Sussex County Council and Chief Constable of Sussex Police*. [2010] EWCA Civ 743, [2010] 2 FLR 1596.

[206] For a discussion of the point, see A Bainham *Children, Parents and the State* (Sweet & Maxwell, 1988), at pp 63–64.

basis for doing so. The Children's Society, especially, was concerned to put its activities on a firmer legal footing and to counter any possible charge that they might constitute a criminal offence.

Criminal offence of abduction

The Children Act reaffirmed the criminal offence of abduction relating to children in care, but at the same time exempted from prosecution bona fide organisations, through a process of certification.[207] The starting point is s 49(1), which provides:

> 'A person shall be guilty of an offence if, knowingly and without lawful authority or reasonable excuse, he –
>
> (a)   takes a child to whom this section applies away from the responsible person;
> (b)   keeps such a child away from the responsible person; or
> (c)   induces, assists or incites such a child to run away or stay away from the responsible person.'

'Responsible person' for these purposes means any person who, for the time being, has care of the child by virtue of a care order, an emergency protection order, or as a result of the child being taken into police protection.[208] The offence is therefore concerned with children absconding from public care as opposed to fleeing the parental home. The court may make a 'recovery order' where it appears that a child has been taken or kept away from the responsible person unlawfully, where the child has run away, is staying away or missing.[209] Recovery orders may not be made in respect of children who are voluntarily 'looked after' by local authorities but authorities should report to the police immediately where these children abscond. The recovery order requires production of the child by any person able to produce him and disclosure of his whereabouts by any person with such information. It also authorises his removal, and authorises a police constable to enter specified premises and search for the child, using force if necessary.[210] The order may be sought by any person with parental responsibility for the child, under a care order or EPO, or by the designated officer where the child is in police protection.[211]

---

[207]   For the details see R White, P Carr and N Lowe *The Children Act in Practice* (4th edn, Butterworths, 2008).

[208]   Sections 49(2) and 50(2).

[209]   Section 51(1). For the first reported decision on the use of recovery orders, see *Re R (Recovery Orders)* [1998] 2 FLR 401, in which Wall J provides detailed guidance on the provisions of s 50. In this case, a recovery order was made where a boy aged 13 was the subject of a care order on the basis that he was beyond his mother's control. He refused to return to the boarding-school which he was required to attend as part of the care plan. The order was made and upheld after the local authority had revised the care plan nominating foster parents, rather than the boy's mother, to care for him during the holidays – thus making them 'responsible persons' for the purposes of a recovery order.

[210]   Section 50(3).

[211]   Section 50(4).

Exemption of children's refuges

The legislation exempts from all offences relating to the abduction or harbouring of children, voluntary or private children's homes which provide a refuge for children who appear to be at risk of harm and which have a certificate from the Secretary of State.[212] Local authority or voluntary organisation foster parents may also fall within the terms of the certificate where they provide a refuge.[213] The issue and withdrawal of certificates is governed by the Refuges (Children's Homes and Foster Placements) Regulations 1991.[214] It is not anticipated that such certificates will be readily granted to just *anyone* claiming to assist children, and it was said in Parliament that it would be necessary to separate the 'sheep' from the 'goats'. Without proper scrutiny, there would be a risk of exploitation of vulnerable adolescents by unscrupulous individuals. A key requirement is that, where any child is admitted to, or leaves, a refuge, the police must be notified.[215] Where a refuge fails to measure up to the required standards its certificate may be withdrawn and there is no right of appeal against this.[216]

---

[212] Section 51(1).
[213] Section 51(2).
[214] SI 1991/1507.
[215] Ibid, reg 3.
[216] Ibid, reg 4.

Chapter 12

CARE AND SUPERVISION

INTRODUCTION

It would be difficult to visualise a more striking failure of protection under the law than that which occurs when a defenceless young child is killed or seriously injured by an adult in the same household. However, it would be equally difficult to envisage a more serious invasion of family autonomy than that which arises where a child is unjustifiably removed from his family because of unwarranted suspicions of abuse. Here, then, is the dilemma for the law and for those, especially social workers, who have to apply it. The stakes could hardly be higher and, sadly, there have been plenty of examples (often attracting much media attention) of both kinds of failure. There has been a succession of public inquiries into apparent 'agency failure' to prevent the death or abuse of children who have been allowed to remain at, or return to, the family home.[1] In contrast, there have been a number of apparently over-zealous interventions in cases of suspected sexual abuse, most notably in Cleveland in 1987[2] and then in relation to alleged ritualistic abuse in Rochdale[3] and Orkney.[4]

Errors on either side of the line usually provoke public outrage, and the difficulty of formulating grounds and procedures which achieve the right balance for compulsory interventions in the family must be apparent to

---

[1] See, for example, the Victoria Climbié Inquiry chaired by Lord Laming and reporting in January 2003. A summary of the inquiry's findings appears at [2003] Fam Law 145. See also H Conway 'The Laming Inquiry – Victoria Climbié's Legacy' [2003] Fam Law 513.

[2] See the *Report of the Inquiry into Child Abuse in Cleveland 1987* ('the *Cleveland Report*') (1988) (Cmnd 412).

[3] *Rochdale Borough Council v A* [1991] 2 FLR 192; and see the guidelines established for the investigation of such cases in *Re A (Minors) (Wardship) (Child Abuse: Guidelines)* [1992] 1 All ER 153.

[4] As to which see R Brett 'Orkney – aberration or symptom?' (1991) 3 JCL 143; EE Sutherland 'The Orkney Case' (1992) *Juridical Review* 93; and A Bissett-Johnson 'Child Protection in Scotland – the Background to the Clyde Report' (1993) 5 JCL 28. The Orkney case was the subject of a major public inquiry: see *Report of the Inquiry into the Removal of Children from Orkney in February 1991* (the *Clyde Report*) (HMSO, 1992). Wide-ranging reforms have since been made to the child protection and children's hearings system in Scotland by Part II of the Children (Scotland) Act 1995. These include reforms which are similar, but not identical, to the reforms introduced in England by the Children Act 1989. The 1995 legislation, inter alia, abolished parental rights resolutions and place of safety orders and introduced child assessment orders, child protection orders and exclusion orders as alternative options for dealing with the short-term protection of children. For further discussion of the Scottish reforms, see EE Sutherland 'Scotland: Child Law Reform – At Last!' in A Bainham (ed) *The International Survey of Family Law 1995* (Martinus Nijhoff, 1997), p 435, at pp 444–452.

everyone. It is also an issue which has generated substantial academic disagreement. During the 1980s, a number of influential works were published which conveyed the central message that there had been an unacceptable escalation in State intervention which called for the imposition of greater legal controls on social services departments.[5] This view of child protection practice was seriously challenged by a study in three local authority areas which concluded that these charges were unsupported by hard empirical evidence.[6] The thrust of this research was that child protection agencies operated within a framework of cultural limitations which the authors called the 'rule of optimism'. They argued that the modus operandi of these agencies was to prefer the least coercive form of intervention in family life which was possible in the circumstances. On this analysis, parents would often be given the benefit of any doubt, and only the worst cases of abuse or neglect would be the subject of compulsory action.

The task for the reformers of child care law was to come up with a framework for compulsory action which offered sufficient protection to vulnerable children but which also respected the rights of family members, most obviously those of parents but, increasingly, those of children themselves.[7] The Children Act 1989 attempts to achieve this primarily by rationalising and unifying the statutory threshold for compulsory care or supervision of children, which is now set out in s 31 of the Children Act 1989. As we shall see, however, the introduction of this provision has not stemmed debate about the correct balance between child protection and family autonomy. The interpretation of the current law has proved controversial, particularly in so-called 'uncertain perpetrator' cases, in which a child has been harmed but it is unclear which of possible perpetrators perpetrated the harm. This chapter examines in detail the current law in Part IV of the Children Act 1989 which allows a local authority to protect children in the long-term by way of a care order or supervision order.

Emphasis on co-operation

The statutory emphasis for local authorities and other authorities to co-operate with each other has been noted, and 'partnership' has been identified as a central theme. The notion of partnership resurfaces here, with the expectation that lawyers, social workers, the police, the NSPCC, education and health personnel, health visitors, probation officers, representatives of voluntary organisations, and anyone else professionally involved with a child will pool their information and resources in the child's best interests.[8]

---

5   See, for example, H Geach and E Szwed (eds) *Providing Civil Justice for Children* (1983) and L
     Taylor, R Lacey and D Bracken *In Whose Best Interests?* (Cobden Trust, 1980).
6   R Dingwall, J Eekelaar and T Murray *The Protection of Children: State Intervention and
     Family Life* (Basil Blackwell, 1983).
7   The *Cleveland Report* drew public attention to violations of children's rights by child
     protection agencies, especially in the sphere of repeated medical examination.
8   See, generally, *Working Together to Safeguard Children: A guide to inter-agency working to
     safeguard and promote the welfare of children* (HM Government, 2013). For commentary on

Procedures before commencement of any action

The starting point for this discussion must be the realisation that compulsory action will not usually be commenced unless the option of voluntary assistance has first been explored. It is very much the philosophy of the legislation that the family should be supported in times of difficulty, that voluntary co-operation with parents is the preferred option, and that compulsory orders should be a last resort. The Departmental *Guidance* makes this plain when advising that 'voluntary arrangements for the provision of services to the child and his family including the consideration of potential alternative carers should always be fully explored prior to making an application under s 31, provided that this does not jeopardise the child's safety and welfare'.[9] The *Guidance* indicates that a family group conference 'can be an important opportunity to engage friends and members of the wider family at an early stage of concerns about a child, either to support the parents or to provide care for the child, whether in the short or longer term'.[10]

The procedures to be adopted by the local authority children's social care department and other relevant agencies in fulfilment of the local authority's duties to safeguard children are set out in *Working Together to Safeguard Children: A Guide to Inter-Agency Working to Safeguard and Promote the Welfare of Children*.[11] Within one working day of receipt of a referral, a local authority social worker should make a decision about the type of response that is required, namely immediate protection and urgent action; an assessment under s 17 of the Children Act 1989 because the child is in need; or enquiries under s 47 because there is reasonable cause to suspect that the child is suffering, or likely to suffer, significant harm. If the local authority's initial assessment of a child's situation suggests actual or likely significant harm, a s 47 investigation will be initiated following a strategy discussion. If there are concerns about a child's immediate safety at any stage, appropriate emergency action will be taken, as discussed in chapter 11. The s 47 investigation consists of a core assessment in accordance with local protocols, led by a social worker, with contributions from other relevant professionals. This should take no more than 45 working days. If concerns are substantiated a child protection conference will be convened by the social work manager.[12] The purpose is to 'bring together and analyse, in an inter-agency setting, all relevant information and plan how best to safeguard and promote the welfare of the child.' If the conclusion is that the child is likely to suffer significant harm in the future, the decision will be to provide inter-agency help and intervention through a formal child protection plan.[13] The conference will formulate an outline child

---

earlier editions, see B Lindley and M Richards 'Working Together 2000 – how will parents fare under the new child protection process?' [2000] CFLQ 213.

[9] *The Children Act 1989 Guidance and Regulations Vol 1 Court Orders* (TSO, 2008), at para 3. 7, and see also para 3.2.

[10] Ibid, at para 3.8.

[11] HM Government, March 2013.

[12] Within 15 days of the latest strategy discussion.

[13] In 2011, there were 42,700 children for whom child protection issues were recorded (18,700 for

protection plan, for which the local authority or the NSPCC carry statutory responsibility for the child's welfare. Ongoing assessment by a core group of professionals feeds in to refinement of the child protection plan. A child protection review conference is held within three months of the initial child protection conference and further reviews at intervals of not more than six months for as long as the child remains the subject of the child protection plan. At these various stages the local authority will be considering whether concerns about significant harm remain and what if any measures, including legal measures, need to be implemented.

Attendance of family members at child protection conferences

An issue which has caused some controversy is the attendance of parents at child protection conferences. It has been held that it is not a breach of natural justice for parents not to be invited to attend a child protection conference,[14] but the spirit of the Children Act requires a justification for excluding them.[15] The latest *Guidance* indicates that social work managers should 'ensure that the child and their parents understand the purpose of the conference and who will attend; and help prepare the child if he or she is attending or making representations through a third party to the conference' and give 'information about advocacy agencies and explain that the family may bring an advocate, friend or supporter'.[16] While parental involvement and the involvement of older children is a key feature of the legislation, so is the need to ensure that child protection agencies are not unduly inhibited in discharging their statutory functions. The shift brought about by the Children Act is that the onus now appears to be on those who would seek to deny participation since, as June Thoburn has put it:[17]

> 'Practice, wisdom and research lead to the conclusion that the maximum involvement of parents and older children in the work, and honesty at the investigation and case conference stage, can lead to the sort of working together between professionals and family members which is most conducive to the long-term welfare of the children.'

---

neglect, 12,100 for emotional abuse, 4,500 physical abuse, 2,300 sexual abuse, and 5,000 multiple categories) (figures from the NSPCC).

14   *R v Harrow London Borough Council, ex parte D* [1990] Fam 133; and see also *R v East Sussex County Council ex parte R* [1991] 2 FLR 358, and *R v Devon County Council ex parte L* [1991] 2 FLR 541.

15   For discussions of the issues involved in parents' attendance at conferences, see J Thoburn '"Working Together" and Parental Attendance at Case Conferences' (1992) 4 JCL 11, P Thomson 'Parents at Case Conferences – a Legal Advisor's Viewpoint' (1992) 4 JCL 15, and D Savas 'Parental Participation in Case Conferences' [1996] CFLQ 57. It has been held that a local authority may not adopt a rigid policy of restricting the participation of solicitors in the conference to reading out a prepared statement and of withholding minutes from parents. See *R v Cornwall County Council, ex parte LH* [2000] 1 FLR 236, discussed in chapter 10 above.

16   *Working Together to Safeguard Children: A guide to inter-agency working to safeguard and promote the welfare of children* (HM Government, 2013), at p 38.

17   J Thoburn (above), at p 14.

The importance of the child protection conference cannot be overstated. It has, in the recent past, been precisely the absence of this kind of co-ordinated approach and, in particular, the failure of agencies to pool vital information, which has led to some of the worst tragedies.

THE LEGAL BASIS FOR COMPULSORY ORDERS

Before the Children Act, there were many different routes by which a child might compulsorily enter the care of a local authority.[18] Broadly, these fell into three categories: cases in which children who were initially in voluntary care later became the subject of parental rights resolutions;[19] cases in which the local authority applied to the juvenile court for a care order under the Children and Young Persons Act 1969;[20] and cases where children were committed to care in family proceedings, most notably wardship, but also, for example, divorce, adoption or guardianship.[21] This system gave rise to a number of difficulties. The grounds for making a care order differed according to the proceedings in which it was sought,[22] the effects of each type of order were far from clear,[23] and there was growing concern that local authorities were beginning to rely too heavily on wardship. They were, in effect, invoking an extra-statutory basis for gaining compulsory control of a child where it was doubtful that the statutory grounds could be established.[24]

The Children Act met these difficulties head-on by enacting a single ground for all care or supervision orders, by making these orders available in all 'family

---

[18] For an excellent discussion of the old law, see S Maidment 'The Fragmentation of Parental Rights and Children in Care' [1981] JSWL 21. See also M Hayes 'Removing Children from their Families – Law and Policy before the Children Act 1989' in G Douglas and N Lowe *The Continuing Evolution of Family Law* (Family Law, 2009), ch 4.

[19] The grounds for passing resolutions were largely 'parent-centred' in that they concentrated on parental failings, such as unfitness arising from the parent's 'habits or modes of life' or consistent failure 'without reasonable cause to discharge the obligations of a parent'. See the Child Care Act 1980, s 3. For a critique of the former resolution procedure, see M Adcock, R White and O Rowlands *The Administrative Parent* (BAAF, 1983).

[20] These grounds were 'child-centred' in that they focused on the child's condition, as where the child was found to be 'exposed to moral danger', or his proper development was 'being unavoidably prevented or neglected' or he was 'beyond the control of his parent and guardian'. In each case there was a further test that the child was in need of care and control which he was unlikely to receive unless the order was made. See the Children and Young Persons Act 1969, s 1.

[21] Here, the test was whether there were 'exceptional circumstances making it impracticable or undesirable' for the child to be under the care of a parent or other individual. See, for example, the Matrimonial Causes Act 1973, s 43(1) and the Guardianship Act 1973, s 2(2)(b).

[22] See, generally, DHSS *Review of Child Care Law* (1985), ch 15.

[23] See the White Paper *The Law on Child Care and Family Services* (1987) (Cmnd 62), at para 7, which identified the lack of clarity in the mutual rights and responsibilities of parents and local authorities as the most striking defect of the law.

[24] On the other hand, a more positive view of this use of the wardship jurisdiction was that it was a necessary 'safety-net' underpinning the statutory regime. See, for example, N Lowe 'Caring for Children' (1989) 139 NLJ 87.

proceedings' and by closing-off wardship as an extra-statutory option.[25] The abolition of the resolution procedure meant that the new ground was also to be the sole basis for compulsorily *retaining* a child who was initially voluntarily accommodated, and this would also necessitate a court order. It should also be observed that there is no longer any legal means whereby parents may reach a voluntary arrangement that the child should enter the *care* of the local authority as opposed to merely being *looked after* by it. Since care proceedings are also 'family proceedings', the court is bound by the principles in Part I of the Children Act, although the manner of their operation in this child protection context is inevitably somewhat different from their undiluted application in private disputes.

The principle that delay is prejudicial also applies and, again, the court must draw up a timetable with a view to expediting matters.[26] Delay in care proceedings was a concern identified by the Family Justice Review, which found that care proceedings took an average of 61 weeks in care centres and that 20,000 children were waiting for a decision in public law cases.[27] The Family Justice Review recommended, *inter alia*, legislation to set a time limit on care proceedings of six months, with extension of time only exceptionally, and to regulate the use of expert evidence. The Government agreed to adopt measures to improve the management of public law cases as recommended. Clause 13 of the Children and Familes Bill, if enacted, will introduce tight controls on expert evidence, by providing that experts may only be instructed and expert evidence used with the permission of the court. Clause 14, if enacted, would amend s 32 of the Children Act to provide that the timetable for disposing of an application should seek to do so within twenty-six weeks beginning with the day on which the application was issued. Attempts have been made already to improve procedure, with a new Public Law Outline within a Practice Direction, and guidance.[28] The difficulties with delay are not aided by the fact that there appears to have been an increase in care proceedings in recent years.

In 2011 there were 29,492 children involved in public law applications made by local authorities, which represents a 13 per cent increase since 2009.[29] It is thought that the increase reflects publicity surrounding the handling by Haringey children's services of the case of baby P, who died in the care of his mother and her boyfriend, despite the fact that the authority and health services had been involved with the child. This may have led other authorities to be more proactive or, seen from another angle, defensive in their approach.

---

[25]   But not entirely the use of the inherent jurisdiction of the High Court. See s 100(3)–(5) of the Children Act 1989.

[26]   Sections 1(2) and 32.

[27]   Final Report, at para 3.2.

[28]   FPR PD12A, and see FPR 2010, r 12.25 on case management. The President of the Family Division has produced best practice guidelines on judicial continuity and case management: *Listing and Hearing Care Cases* (April 2011) and *President's Guidance in Relation to Allocation and Continuity of Case Managers in the Family Proceedings Courts* (see Part V) (July 2011).

[29]   Ministry of Justice, *Judicial and Court Statistics 2011* (28 June 2012), at p 21. The figure for 2009 was 19,760 and 25,810 for 2010.

Who may apply for an order?

It is the policy of the legislation to locate primary responsibility for child care in local authorities' children's social care departments. It is they who are under a statutory duty to investigate the circumstances of any child in their area, where they have reasonable cause to suspect that he is suffering, or is likely to suffer, significant harm,[30] and it is also they who may be directed by the court, in family proceedings, to conduct an investigation into a child's circumstances.[31] The court ought not to make such a direction, however, unless there is a reasonable prospect that a public law order might be made. In *Re L (Section 37 Direction)*[32] the child concerned had been well looked after by her maternal grandmother and there was no challenge to her as primary carer. The only issue was the amount of contact to be allowed to the father, mother and paternal grandmother. The Court of Appeal held, inter alia, that the judge had been wrong to make a s 37 direction in this case, since the case was nowhere near the threshold in which public law powers could be invoked.

The former power of the courts to make care orders of their own motion has been removed, except with respect to interim orders[33] in deference to this general principle of local authority responsibility. While the court may be concerned enough about a child to trigger an investigation, it is not for the court to usurp the functions of social services by dictating to the local authority, as it sometimes used to in wardship proceedings.[34] Similarly, while other agencies and individuals have their part to play in child protection work, they do not have legal responsibility for initiating action. There is no statutory duty in England which would require individuals to report suspected cases of abuse or neglect.[35]

---

[30]   Section 47, and see chapter 11.

[31]   Section 37, and A Bainham (above), at paras 5.57–5.61. In *Re H (A Minor) (Section 37 Direction)* [1993] 2 FLR 541, Scott-Baker J adopted a liberal construction of the section. In his view, the statutory phrase 'the child's circumstances' should be widely construed to include any situation which might have a bearing on the child being likely to suffer significant harm in the future. In this case (which involved a lesbian couple in an arrangement analogous to surrogacy) the court was entitled to have regard in particular to the long-term, as well as the short-term, future of the baby concerned. See also *Re CE (Section 37 Direction)* [1995] 1 FLR 26. But a s 37 direction should not be used as a device for appointing a children's guardian where there is no real prospect of a care or supervision order being made, and a local authority may not be made a party to a private law application if it decides, following its investigations, not to seek a public law order (see *F v Cambridgeshire County Council* [1995] 1 FLR 516).

[32]   [1999] 1 FLR 984.

[33]   Section 38 discussed below.

[34]   Particularly good examples of this are *Re E (SA) (A Minor) (Wardship)* [1984] 1 All ER 289, where the court directed a solution not sought by any of the parties; and *Re G-U (A Minor) (Wardship)* [1984] FLR 811, where the authority was reprimanded by the court for not referring back to it an abortion decision concerning a ward of court in its care. It has since been held that where the court is considering making an order not sought by the parties it must give them an opportunity to make submissions on the appropriateness of the order it is proposed to make. See *Devon County Council v S* [1992] 3 WLR 273 and *Croydon London Borough Council v A* [1992] 3 WLR 267.

[35]   There is such a mandatory reporting law in other jurisdictions, for example in the USA.

In keeping with this policy, only the local authority or an 'authorised person' may apply for a care or supervision order[36] and, for these purposes, only the NSPCC and its officers, with their historic and substantial contribution to child protection, have been authorised.[37] The police were formerly permitted to bring proceedings based on the so-called 'offence condition', but with the abolition of this ground and the redefinition of local authorities' responsibilities, it was no longer thought appropriate for them to retain the power.[38] Similarly, local education authorities, which used to be able to initiate proceedings based on truancy, are no longer empowered to do so following the abolition of this ground and its replacement with a new education supervision order.[39] Finally, there is no equivalent under the new law, to the former procedure whereby parents might require the local authority to bring proceedings in relation to a child who is beyond their control.[40] Proceedings must be brought by the 'designated authority', being the local authority in whose area the child is ordinarily resident or, where the child does not reside in any authority's area, the authority in whose area any circumstances arose in consequence of which the order is sought.[41] The Court of Appeal in *C (A Child) v Plymouth County Council*[42] has held that, in all but exceptional cases,[43] the appropriate authority should be determined by applying the simple rules of statutory construction. In this case the child was born and initially lived with her mother in Plymouth. She later spent time in a specialist unit in Cardiff and then lived with her paternal grandmother in Liverpool. At the care proceedings her father argued that Liverpool City Council, rather than Plymouth, should be responsible for any care order made. The judge and the Court of Appeal disagreed. Even if the

---

[36] Section 31(1).

[37] Section 31(9)(a).

[38] See, generally, DHSS *Review of Child Care Law* (1985), at paras 12.9–12.26.

[39] Section 36.

[40] Children and Young Persons Act 1963, s 3. But being beyond parental control remains an element in one of the alternatives under the statutory ground in s 31(2).

[41] Section 31(8). These provisions can give rise to legal wrangles between local authorities about which of them should be 'designated' and hence have the statutory responsibilities for a child who has moved between areas. See particularly *Re BC (A Minor) (Care Order: Appropriate Local Authority)* [1995] 3 FCR 598; *Gateshead Metropolitan Borough Council v L and Another* [1996] 2 FLR 179; *Re C (Care Order: Appropriate Local Authority)* [1997] 1 FLR 544; and *Re P (Care Proceedings: Designated Authority)* [1998] 1 FLR 80 (in which there were complications arising from the child spending a period of time in interim care); *Re C (Responsible Authority)* [2005] EWHC 2939 (Fam), [2006] 1 FLR 919; *Re D (Local Authority Responsibility)* [2012] EWCA Civ 627 [2012] 3 WLR 1468 (dispute between Surrey and Kent Councils) and *Re LM (A Child)* [2013] EWHC 646 (Fam) (a case involving transfer of proceedings from Ireland).

[42] [2000] 1 FLR 875.

[43] See *Northamptonshire County Council v Islington London Borough Council* [1999] 2 FLR 881 in which the Court of Appeal emphasised that the judge's function in designating the appropriate authority should involve a rapid and not over-sophisticated review of the child's history in order to make a purely factual determination. It was not to exercise a broad discretion. See also *Re H (Care Order: Appropriate Local Authority)* [2004] 1 FLR 534 and *London Borough of Redbridge v Newport City Council* [2004] 2 FLR 226. For commentaries on the issues, see V Smith 'Which Local Authority Gets the Care Order? The Simple Test' [2004] Fam Law 213, and J Hayes 'The Designated Local Authority in a Care Order: The Far-Reaching Consequences of *Re H*' [2004] Fam Law 511.

child's early life did not amount to ordinary residence in Plymouth, a new born baby's ordinary residence must be dependent on the mother's.

Which children?

Care or supervision orders may not be made in relation to a child who has reached the age of 17 years, or a married child who has attained 16 years of age.[44] While this corresponds with the old law, its effect is more dramatic, since there is no longer an option of warding children in this age group and securing care that way.[45] Opinion is divided on whether the removal of the power to take compulsory action, in relation to those older teenagers, was desirable. One view is that it leaves a potentially vulnerable group of adolescents unprotected.[46] An opposing view is that coercive orders grounded in non-criminal misbehaviour are open to civil libertarian objections and, in any event, would sit very uneasily with the philosophy of the legislation which finds expression in a number of other provisions.[47] This latter view is partly reinforced by provisions allowing troubled teenagers to seek a voluntary 'self-referral' into care,[48] unless, of course, it can be argued that some will lack the resourcefulness to engage in self-help. In any event, the Children Act is clear and the embargo on 'public' orders is in line with the corresponding embargo on 'private' orders in relation to this age group.[49] Where both the mother and baby are minors, as we have seen,[50] it is the *baby* whose welfare will be paramount in public law proceedings.[51]

Which proceedings and which orders?

It was observed above that care and supervision orders may be made in any family proceedings[52] and not only in what have traditionally been called 'care proceedings'. These latter proceedings, the sole purpose of which is to obtain a care or supervision order, are also now family proceedings for the purposes of the Children Act. Consequently, an application for these orders may be made

---

44 Section 31(3).
45 As occurred in *Re SW (A Minor) (Wardship Jurisdiction)* [1986] 1 FLR 24 where the girl in question was 17 years of age. It may, however, be possible for the local authority to exercise control over a 17-year-old by invoking, with leave, the inherent jurisdiction, but not to take the child into care. See below.
46 See, for example, N Lowe 'Caring for Children' (1989) 139 NLJ 87.
47 See, for example, J Eekelaar 'Parents' Rights to Punish – Further limits after Gillick' (1986) 28 *Childright* 9. See also the discussion of controversial uses of the inherent jurisdiction in relation to older teenagers below.
48 See chapter 10 above.
49 Contact, prohibited steps and specific issue orders may not usually be made in respect of children who have attained 16 years of age (s 9(6) and (7) and s 91(10)). Residence orders, however, do now last until the child's 18th birthday unless terminated earlier by court order. See chapter 5 above.
50 See chapter 2.
51 *Birmingham City Council v H (No 3)* [1994] 1 FLR 224 and *F v Leeds City Council* [1994] 2 FLR 60.
52 Section 8(3) and (4). We discuss the definition in chapter 2.

on its own or during the course of family proceedings which are brought for some other purpose.[53] This, to some extent, corresponds with the old law, except that there is now only one ground for an order, whatever the nature of the proceedings. The statutory test, or threshold criteria, must be crossed, whether an order is requested in care proceedings, divorce proceedings or any other kind of proceedings.

A complementary feature of the Children Act is that, just as 'public' orders may be sought in private family proceedings, so 'private' orders may be sought in public family proceedings.[54] Thus, the court considering an application for a care or supervision order must also consider the alternative of a s 8 order, especially a residence order. There are, however, limitations on the use of s 8 orders in public law proceedings, and local authorities will not be allowed to stretch the normal definition and use of such orders, especially where it would clearly be more appropriate for public law orders to be sought.[55] The court will also have at its disposal its general powers to attach conditions or give directions.[56] The court may also make s 8 orders, unlike care or supervision orders, whether or not they have been requested and, of course, it is not necessary for the statutory threshold criteria for care or supervision to be reached. It has been suggested that this power may be useful where there is doubt that the threshold criteria will be satisfied[57] but it is thought to be in the child's best interests that he lives away from his parents or, perhaps, to effect a 'phased rehabilitation' of the child with his family – a power which is not directly incorporated in the legislation.[58] In fact, it seems likely that the 'lesser' order (ie lesser in terms of its intrusion into family life) may prove valuable in cases at the margins of the statutory grounds.[59] A cautionary note should,

---

[53] Section 31(4).

[54] On the relationship between the public and private, see A Bainham 'Private and public children law: an under-explored relationship' [2013] CFLQ 138.

[55] It has, however, been held in *Croydon London Borough Council v A (No 1)* [1992] 2 FLR 341 that the court does not have power to make a prohibited steps order prohibiting a father from having contact with a mother in care proceedings, since contact between spouses is not 'a step which could be taken by a parent in meeting his parental responsibility for a child'. In principle, of course, in appropriate cases, prohibited steps orders are available in public law proceedings. But see also *Nottinghamshire County Council v P* [1993] 2 FLR 134, in which the Court of Appeal held that a local authority had erred in seeking a prohibited steps order instead of a care order in relation to two sisters at risk of sexual abuse by their father. The authority was in reality seeking to exclude the father. The effect of the order would be like that of a 'no contact' order which the authority was precluded from seeking under s 9(2).

[56] Section 11(7).

[57] An earlier edition of NV Lowe and G Douglas *Bromley's Family Law* (9th edn, Butterworths, 1998), at pp 562–563.

[58] This was the issue in the House of Lords decision in *Re E (SA) (A Minor) (Wardship)* [1984] 1 All ER 289.

[59] A further example, suggested by NV Lowe and G Douglas (above), is that of an alcoholic or drug-addicted parent. Where there is a relative who could look after the child they suggest that a residence order may be appropriate. But it should be noted that the courts will not, other than in exceptional circumstances, make a residence order in favour of someone who does not want it. In *Re K (Care Order or Residence Order)* [1995] 1 FLR 675, the local authority, having originally applied for a care order, wanted a residence order to be made in favour of the grandparents. The grandparents, however, were getting on in years and did not wish to be

however, be sounded. Too great a readiness in the courts to use s 8 orders in these circumstances could be interpreted as arrogating to themselves a wider power than Parliament intended. It could reopen all the old debates about wardship and its relationship to the statutory code – albeit in a rather different guise.[60]

It is one thing for a private individual to seek private orders, or for a court to make them of its own volition in public family proceedings, and quite another for the State in the guise of the local authority to be allowed to seek private orders. Here, the policy of the legislation is that the local authority should normally be obliged to go down the *public* route, satisfying the threshold criteria and seeking *public* orders. Where the authority has already obtained a care order, the scheme of the Act is that the authority is 'in the driving seat' with parental responsibility for the child and should not normally be allowed to pass this responsibility to the courts by seeking orders in relation to the child's upbringing. In limited circumstances, where the authority's statutory powers are inadequate and the child's welfare requires it, the authority may with leave seek the assistance of the High Court under its inherent jurisdiction. We discuss the inherent jurisdiction below. For the moment we are concerned with the restrictions which the legislation places on the making of private s 8 orders in favour of local authorities, and these are to be found in a cluster of provisions in s 9 of the Act.

First, where the child is already *in care* it is provided that no s 8 order may be made other than a residence order.[61] If a residence order were made in favour of an individual its effect would be to discharge the care order.[62] Such an application challenges the *source* of the authority's parental responsibility rather than its *exercise* and is not therefore inconsistent with the notion that the

---

exposed to the risk of private law proceedings being brought by the schizophrenic mother. Under a care order they would also be entitled to boarding-out allowances paid to local authority foster parents. Stuart-White J held that a care order was appropriate in these circumstances to provide the children with the required protection and security.

[60] The opposing arguments are extensively probed in Law Com Working Paper No 101 *Wards of Court* (1987), and see the discussion on the inherent jurisdiction below. In *Re RJ (Foster Placement)* [1998] 2 FLR 110 Sir Stephen Brown P refused to entertain an application for a residence order by foster parents, supported by the guardian ad litem, to preserve the status quo. The foster father was disqualified from acting as a foster parent by then newly implemented regulations protecting children from individuals convicted of or cautioned in relation to serious offences against children. He held that to have allowed the application would have been contrary to public policy. However, the Court of Appeal reversed this decision in *Re RJ (Fostering: Person Disqualified)* [1999] 1 FLR 605, taking the view that the court had jurisdiction to make a s 8 order and, in exercising its discretion, should weigh all relevant factors including public policy considerations. In an exceptional case such as this a private law application could prevail over a stated policy set out in regulations. The court made the children wards of court to preserve the status quo under which they could continue to live with the foster parents until the conclusion of the substantive hearing. One week later, in *Re RJ (Wardship)* [1999] 1 FLR 618, Cazalet J made an order arrived at by consent of all parties that the children should remain wards of court with care and control vested in the foster parents and a contact order in favour of the mother.

[61] Section 9(1).

[62] Section 91(1).

authority has parental responsibility under a care order. Secondly, no residence
or contact order may be made in favour of a local authority.[63] Here, the policy
is that if a local authority wishes to look after a child or have involvement with
a child it must do so, unless it can secure the voluntary co-operation of the
family, by means of the *public* care or supervision orders. As we have seen, a
residence order may, of course, be made in favour of an *individual* in care
proceedings. So far as contact is concerned, individuals must use the code in
s 34 and not seek s 8 contact orders in relation to a child in care. We discuss the
statutory contact regime below. Thirdly, no specific issue or prohibited steps
order may be made with a view to achieving a result which could be achieved
by making a residence or contact order or in any way which is denied to the
High Court (by s 100(2)) in the exercise of its inherent jurisdiction with respect
to children.[64] These provisions are complex and are not a good advertisement
for parliamentary draftsmanship. They have given rise to major difficulties of
interpretation, particularly in the case of *Nottinghamshire County Council v
P*.[65]

Perhaps the restrictions are best understood by concentrating on the limited
circumstances in which local authorities *may* seek s 8 orders rather than when
they may not seek them. The fact of the matter is that when all the restrictions
of s 9 are added together there is very little scope left for the granting of private
orders at the behest of the local authority. It is clear that residence and contact
orders may *never* be made in favour of the local authority and that specific
issue and prohibited steps orders may not be made where the child is *in care*.
The net result is that the latter two orders may be made in favour of a local
authority but not if their effect is to breach the embargo on making the former
two orders. They are thus likely only to be used to resolve 'single issues'. So, to
an appreciable extent, private s 8 orders are beyond the reach of the State.

All applications for care or supervision orders will be made, in the first
instance, at the magistrates' level to the family proceedings court, although
both the county court and the High Court now have concurrent jurisdiction.[66]
There is provision for proceedings to be transferred, vertically or horizontally,
to another court in appropriate cases.[67] As noted above this scheme will be
affected by the impending establishment of a single family court.

---

[63] Section 9(2).
[64] Section 100(2) precludes the court from exercising its inherent jurisdiction: '(a) so as to require
      the child to be placed in the care, or put under the supervision, of a local authority; (b) so as to
      require a child to be accommodated by or on behalf of a local authority; (c) so as to make a
      child who is the subject of a care order a ward of court; or (d) for the purpose of conferring on
      any local authority power to determine any question which has arisen, or which may arise, in
      connection with any aspect of parental responsibility for a child'.
[65] [1993] 2 FLR 134. Cf *Re H (Prohibited Steps Order)* [1995] 1 FLR 638. We considered these
      cases in the context of the discussion of excluding abusers from the family home in chapter 11.
[66] See chapter 2 above.
[67] ATPO 2008, arts 5, 9, and 14–19.

Deciding whether a care or supervision order can and should be made

There are two stages in the process by which a court decides whether to make a care or supervision order. First the court must be satisfied that the threshold for compulsory intervention by way of these orders is fulfilled. The *Review of Child Care Law*[68] that preceded the Children Act 1989 specifically rejected the idea that a simple welfare criterion could be adopted as the basis for compulsory action. The thinking was that this could give rise to widely differing interpretations of welfare and thus expose the family to unrestricted intervention. In short, it would give the State too open-ended a power, and might lead to children being removed from their families simply because someone else could do better in raising them. Instead, it was accepted that, subject to certain minimally acceptable standards, parents should be allowed to continue raising their children in their own way. The threshold for state intervention is now set out in s 31(2) of the Children Act 1989 which provides:

'A court may only make a care order or supervision order if it is satisfied –

(a)   that the child concerned is suffering, or is likely to suffer, significant harm; and
(b)   that the harm, or likelihood of harm, is attributable to:
    (i)   the care given to the child, or likely to be given to him if the order were not made, not being what it would be reasonable to expect a parent to give to him; or
    (ii)   the child's being beyond parental control.'

The first task for the judge is fact-finding, identifying agreed facts and adjudicating on those which are disputed. The judge must then decide whether, in light of the facts, the threshold is fulfilled or not. The Supreme Court has explained that this stage of the judge's task can be categorised as a value judgment,[69] an appraisal[70] or an evaluation.[71]

In many cases, however, it should be noted that the threshold conditions and indeed the court's order may be agreed by negotiation and the court's investigation of the facts more limited. There may be instances in which parents and others are willing to concede that the threshold criteria are met, thus averting the need for a lengthy trial of the issues. This does not mean, however, that the local authority will necessarily be precluded from leading, or the court from testing, the evidence relating to allegations of abuse. One reason for this is

---

[68]   DHSS *Review of Child Care Law* (1985), at para 15.10.
[69]   *In re B (A Child)* [2013] UKSC 33, at para 199 (Lady Hale), at para 44 (Lord Wilson), and para 56 (Lord Neuberger). See also Ward LJ in *Re MA (Care: Threshold)* [2010] 1 FLR 431, at para 56, and Black LJ in the Court of Appeal in *In re B* [2012] EWCA Civ 1475, at para 9.
[70]   *In re B (A Child)* [2013] UKSC 33, at para 109 (Lord Kerr).
[71]   Ibid, at para 56, per Lord Neuberger, citing Clarke LJ in *Assicurazioni Generali SpA v Arab Insurance Group* [2003] 1 WLR 577, at paras 16 and 17, which was cited with approval by the House of Lords in *Datec Electronics Holdings Ltd v United Parcels Service Ltd* [2007] 1 WLR 1325, at para 46.

that it may be important to establish whether or not the child has been the victim of a particular kind of abuse in taking future decisions relating to the care of the child. Thus, in *Re M (Threshold Criteria: Parental Concessions)*[72] the adoptive parents of three children conceded that the threshold criteria were met on the basis of their rejection of the child following allegations of sexual abuse by them, their use of inappropriate forms of punishment and their failure to pay reasonable attention to the children's emotional needs. Nonetheless, the authority was allowed to lead evidence of sexual abuse since the concessions made were different in kind and entirely different in importance from the abuse allegations. They did not meet the requirements of justice in this case, since there was the potential for future contact between the adoptive parents and the children. Any care plan, including therapy, ought to take account of the actual harm suffered by the children and any court considering contact should also be aware of it in deciding what approach to take.

If the threshold is fulfilled, the court has power to make a care order or a supervision order. However, the decision whether or not to make an order must then be considered applying the principles in s 1 of the Children Act 1989.[73] Thus the court must be guided by the child's welfare as the paramount consideration, must have regard to the factors in the checklist in s 1(3), and shall not make an order unless it is better for the child than making no order at all (s 1(5)). At the welfare stage the court must also engage in the 'vital judicial task' of considering the Convention rights of the adult members of the family and the children under Art 8 of the ECHR. The court is not empowered to sanction such an interference with family life unless it is satisfied that it is both necessary and proportionate and that no less radical form of order will achieve the essential aim of promoting the welfare of the children.[74] This issue is discussed in more detail below under the heading of the welfare stage.

Essentially, s 31(2) comprises two elements. The first is the presence or likelihood of significant harm to the child. The second is the attribution of this harm or likelihood of harm to parental upbringing or loss of parental control. We shall first outline these two elements and then consider the courts' interpretation of the words 'is suffering or is likely to suffer' and their proof.

---

[72]   [1999] 2 FLR 728.

[73]   The *Review of Child Care Law* had proposed the inclusion of a third element in the new ground: that the order would be 'the most effective means available to [the court] of safeguarding the child's welfare' (see DHSS *Review of Child Care Law* (1985), at para 15.24). In essence, this third element has been grafted on to the statutory ground through the application of the welfare principle in s 1 of the Children Act.

[74]   See for example the decision of the Court of Appeal in *Re B (Care: Interference with Family Life)* [2003] 2 FLR 813.

The first element – significant harm

What is harm?: the 'Russian doll' provision

The concept of 'harm' is very wide and is the cornerstone of the statutory ground. The legislation defines harm[75] as 'ill-treatment or the impairment of health or development' and then provides a definition of each of these components. 'Development' includes 'physical, intellectual, emotional, social or behavioural development'. 'Health' includes 'physical or mental health'. 'Ill-treatment' embraces 'sexual abuse and forms of ill-treatment which are not physical'. It is now provided that harm includes, by way of example, 'impairment suffered from seeing or hearing the ill-treatment of another'.[76] This is a welcome clarification of the doubt which existed about whether abusive actions had to be aimed at the child concerned. It is now clear that they do not. The amendment should bring within the concept of harm many instances of emotional harm to children where they witness domestic violence between adults in the same household.[77] The kinds of harm contemplated include neglect, physical injury, sexual abuse and emotional abuse.[78] These are defined in *Working Together*[79] and the definitions are used below to explain these concepts.

Neglect

Neglect is not, as such, mentioned in the Children Act but is subsumed within the idea of 'ill-treatment or the impairment of health or development'. Examples of neglect may be failure to summon essential medical attention,[80] failure to provide the child with sustenance or failure to prevent the child coming into contact with foreseeable hazards.

Working Together defines neglect as:

'the persistent failure to meet a child's basic physical and/or psychological needs, likely to result in the serious impairment of the child's health or development. Neglect may occur during pregnancy as a result of maternal substance abuse. Once a child is born, neglect may involve a parent or carer failing to:

- provide adequate food, clothing and shelter (including exclusion from home or abandonment);
- protect a child from physical or emotional harm or danger;

---

[75] Section 31(9).

[76] Section 31(9), as amended by the Adoption and Children Act 2002, s 120.

[77] For an example, see *Re M (A Minor) (Care Order: Threshold Conditions)* [1994] 2 FLR 577, discussed below.

[78] On the problems of defining child abuse, see C Wattam 'The social construction of child abuse for practical policy purposes – a review of *Child Protection: Messages from Research*' [1996] CFLQ 189, reviewing the Department of Health's overview of research findings (HMSO, 1995). See Department of Health *Child Protection: Messages from Research* (1995).

[79] See *Working Together to Safeguard Children: A guide to inter-agency working to safeguard and promote the welfare of children* (HM Government, 2013), at p 85 (Glossary).

[80] See chapter 8.

- ensure adequate supervision (including the use of inadequate care givers); or
- ensure access to appropriate medical care or treatment.

It may also include neglect of, or unresponsiveness to, a child's basic emotional needs.'

Physical injury and the problem of corporal punishment

Physical abuse may involve 'hitting, shaking, throwing, poisoning, burning or scalding, drowning, suffocating, or otherwise causing physical harm to a child. Physical harm may also be caused when a parent or carer fabricates the symptoms of, or deliberately induces illness in a child'. This latter situation is commonly described using terms such as factitious illness by proxy or Münchausen's syndrome by proxy.

Physical injury is understandable enough, but difficult questions can be asked about the line between corporal punishment and abuse. Some people would outlaw all corporal punishment (as, for example, in the Scandinavian countries, Austria and Cyprus) largely because of the danger that punishment can degenerate into abuse.[81] There is also an argument that to allow parental punishment of children violates Art 19 of the UNCRC, which, inter alia, protects the child from 'all forms of physical or mental violence'. Freeman's view is that 'nothing is a clearer statement of the position that children occupy in society, a clearer badge of childhood than the fact that children alone of all people in society can be hit with impunity'.[82]

The whole question of corporal punishment underwent close scrutiny by the Scottish Law Commission.[83] Although the Commission was not addressing the question of when it is or is not abuse, for the purposes of care proceedings, its conclusions were nonetheless an interesting barometer of Scottish public opinion.[84] This seemed to be that, while the spontaneous slap or smack by a loving parent was considered a legitimate exercise of parental control, the striking of a child of any age with an implement was not.[85] The Commission was not prepared to recommend the total abolition of the parental right to administer 'moderate and reasonable chastisement'.[86] We are concerned here

---

[81] This is MDA Freeman's view in *Children, Their Families and the Law* (Macmillan, 1992), at p 105. See also *The Moral Status of Children* (Martinus Nijhoff, 1997), especially at pp 116–117 and pp 131–132.

[82] (Above), at p 117.

[83] Scot Law Com Report No 135 *Family Law* (1992), at paras 2.67–2.105.

[84] The Commission conducted a survey through System Three Scotland in September 1991. The results of this are recorded at Scot Law Com Report No 135 (above), at paras 2.100–2.102.

[85] While, for example, 83 per cent thought that it ought to be lawful for a parent to smack a three-year-old, only 3 per cent thought that the use of a belt, stick or other object should be within the law.

[86] A test established in *R v Hopley* (1860) 2 F&F 202.

with the legality of parental corporal punishment, and the ECtHR had an opportunity to consider this in *A v United Kingdom (Human Rights: Punishment of Child)*.[87]

The step-father of a nine-year-old boy repeatedly beat him with a garden cane leaving linear bruises on his thighs and buttocks which remained for up to one week. This was held to amount to 'torture or inhuman or degrading treatment or punishment' contrary to Art 3 of the ECHR. The Court also unanimously held that the United Kingdom could be liable for its failure to take measures which could have prevented the beatings. Matters hinged on the fact that under English law, on a charge of assault, the defendant may rely on the defence of 'moderate and reasonable chastisement'. Where the defence is raised the burden of proof rests on the prosecution to establish that what occurred exceeded those limits. In *A v UK* the step-father was prosecuted for assault occasioning actual bodily harm but was acquitted on a majority verdict of the jury. The ECtHR took the view that the ECHR imposed on States an obligation to implement laws which provide sufficient protection to children and other vulnerable individuals 'in the form of effective deterrence, against such serious breaches of personal integrity'. This the UK had failed to do in making available a defence which could be successfully invoked in circumstances which involved 'punishment' at such a level of severity as to fall within the scope of Art 3.

The Government reacted to the ruling by issuing a Consultation Paper[88] and, for a while, it certainly looked as if it would take steps to legislate by defining more closely the legal limits of corporal punishment by parents. But it also made clear its view that it would not outlaw smacking because 'the overwhelming majority of parents know the difference between smacking and beating'. Others, however, argued strenuously that any attempt to define which applications of physical force to children were acceptable and which were not would be unworkable and argued instead for removal of the defence altogether. The key consideration for the abolitionists is the symbolic power of the law and the message which abolition would deliver in terms of children's rights and the need to remove the official justification for hitting children. It has also been pointed out that the experience in those countries which have taken this course has been that trivial assaults, such as smacking, would not lead to prosecution but that to make all corporal punishment unlawful can have a significant educative effect on social attitudes and promote alternative methods of discipline.

---

[87] [1998] 2 FLR 959. For commentary see C Barton 'The Thirty Thousand Pound Caning – an "English Vice" in Europe [1999] CFLQ 63, and A Bainham 'Corporal Punishment of Children: A Caning for the United Kingdom' (1999) CLJ 291. See also J Rogers 'A Criminal Lawyer's Response to Chastisement in the European Court of Human Rights' [2002] Crim LR 98.

[88] *Protecting Children, Supporting Parents: A Consultation Document on the physical punishment of children* (2000).

In the event the Government, to the surprise of many, decided not to legislate but to leave the matter in the hands of the judiciary.[89] It was left to the judges to make clear in their directions in individual cases what were the requirements of the ECHR in the light of the Court's ruling in *A v UK*. In *R v H (Assault of Child: Reasonable Chastisement)*[90] the Court of Appeal identified as factors, the nature of the defendant's behaviour, its duration, its physical and mental consequences in relation to the age and personal characteristics of the child and the reasons given by the defendant for administering punishment. Section 58 of the Children Act 2004 removed the defence of reasonable chastisement in any proceedings for an offence of assault occasioning actual bodily harm,[91] unlawfully inflicting grievous bodily harm,[92] causing grievous bodily harm with intent,[93] or cruelty to a child.[94] It also prevents the defence being relied upon in any *civil* proceedings where the harm caused amounted to actual bodily harm.[95] However, the defence would be available in relation to proceedings before a magistrates' court for common assault on a child. It is therefore effectively unlawful for a parent to cause anything more than temporary pain or discomfort to the child through the infliction of corporal punishment. Although there may clearly be some difficult line-drawing on the facts, smacking almost certainly does not amount to more than a common assault (and the defence of reasonable chastisement would therefore be available) whereas hitting a child with an implement of any kind may well fall on the wrong side of the line. The reform will not satisfy those children's rights advocates who believe philosophically that *any* form of hitting a child is morally wrong and should be unlawful. It seems clear that parents who operate within these limits[96] (vague though they are) will not have 'ill-treated' the child for the purposes of the legislation, whereas those who exceed them may well have done.

The issue of inappropriate corporal punishment has arisen in several reported care cases but the courts have been reluctant in those case to conclude that the level of gravity has been such as would justify the compulsory removal of those children.[97]

---

89   For a full discussion of the arguments, see J Fortin 'Children's Rights and the Use of Physical Force' [2001] CFLQ 243. See also R Smith '"Hands-off parenting?" – towards a reform of the defence of reasonable chastisement' [2004] CFLQ 261.
90   [2001] 2 FLR 431.
91   Offences Against the Person Act 1861, s 47.
92   Ibid, s 20.
93   Ibid, s 18.
94   Children and Young Persons Act 1933, s 1.
95   Children Act 2004, s 58(3).
96   Ibid, s 1(7), inter alia, excludes from the offence of cruelty the parental right to administer punishment to a child.
97   See for example *Re F (Interim Care Order)* [2007] 2 FLR 891 and *Re W (Care: Threshold Criteria)* [2007] EWCA Civ 102, [2007] 2 FLR 98.

Sexual abuse

Sexual abuse is included within the expression 'ill-treatment' but is not otherwise defined in the legislation. *Working Together* defines sexual abuse to include:

> 'forcing or enticing a child or young person to take part in sexual activities, not necessarily involving a high level of violence, whether or not the child is aware of what is happening. The activities may involve physical contact, including assault by penetration (for example, rape or oral sex) or non-penetrative acts such as masturbation, kissing, rubbing and touching outside of clothing. They may also include non-contact activities, such as involving children in looking at, or in the production of, sexual images, watching sexual activities, encouraging children to behave in sexually inappropriate ways, or grooming a child in preparation for abuse (including via the internet). Sexual abuse is not solely perpetrated by adult males. Women can also commit acts of sexual abuse, as can other children.'

It would be fair to say that this has been an area of great difficulty. Perhaps this is not so surprising since, as Freeman has pointed out,[98] the phenomenon was only recognised to exist at all comparatively recently. While the grosser forms of abuse (rape, and other offences of penetration) are easily recognisable as physical abuse, and serious criminal offences, there is much difficult line-drawing to be done over matters such as 'horseplay' between parents and children.[99] As we shall see in discussion of some of the case law below, the proof of sexual abuse is often difficult.[100] Moreover, the courts may be willing to continue contact arrangements even where sexual abuse is established.[101] The question of the criminal law as it applies to sexual offences, including those involving children, was the subject of a major Home Office Review published in 2000, which was followed by a White Paper in 2002. This culminated in the Sexual Offences Act 2003, which is considered in chapter 15.

Emotional abuse

Emotional abuse undoubtedly comes within the expression 'forms of ill-treatment which are not physical' and it was a recognised form of ill-treatment under the old law.[102] Again, it is not defined in the legislation, but it would seem that it is unlikely to be established without psychiatric evidence pointing to abnormal behaviour on the part of the child.[103] An example of

---

[98] MDA Freeman *Children, Their Families and the Law* (Macmillan, 1992), at p 93 referring to the DHSS circular in 1980 on registers which made no reference to it.

[99] In *C v C (Child Abuse: Access)* [1988] 1 FLR 462 the judge found the father to have indulged in 'vulgar and inappropriate horseplay' with his daughter.

[100] See, the discussion below of *Re H* [1996] 1 FLR 80 (HL).

[101] See chapter 5 above.

[102] *F v Suffolk County Council* (1981) 2 FLR 208. For a post-Children Act case of emotional abuse, see the facts of *Re M and R (Child Abuse: Evidence)* [1996] 2 FLR 195.

[103] Discussed further by MDA Freeman (above), at p 104.

emotional abuse may be the refusal to recognise a child's gender by making the child dress in the clothes of the opposite sex.[104]

Working Together defines emotional abuse as:

> 'The persistent emotional maltreatment of a child such as to cause severe and persistent adverse effects on the child's emotional development. It may involve conveying to children that they are worthless or unloved, inadequate, or valued only insofar as they meet the needs of another person. It may include not giving the child opportunities to express their views, deliberately silencing them or 'making fun' of what they say or how they communicate. It may feature age or developmentally inappropriate expectations being imposed on children. These may include interactions that are beyond a child's developmental capability, as well as overprotection and limitation of exploration and learning, or preventing the child participating in normal social interaction. It may involve seeing or hearing the ill-treatment of another. It may involve serious bullying (including cyber bullying), causing children frequently to feel frightened or in danger, or the exploitation or corruption of children. Some level of emotional abuse is involved in all types of maltreatment of a child, though it may occur alone.'

It goes without saying that the above categorisations should not necessarily be regarded as exhaustive since, sadly, the discovery of new forms of abuse,[105] or the rediscovery of old ones, cannot be discounted.

What is significant?

The immense variation in the forms which abuse or neglect can take means that the crucial issue is usually a question of *degree* rather than kind. How much does a child have to suffer, and how much society tolerate, before the 'private realm' of family life can be invaded? The answer given by the legislation is that the harm must be 'significant'.[106]

In *Humberside County Council v B*[107] Booth J accepted, indeed found 'very apt and helpful', counsel's submission that significant should be defined 'in accordance with dictionary definitions, first as being harm that the court should consider was either considerable or noteworthy or important'.[108] In *Re L (Care: Threshold Criteria)*[109] Hedley J explained that significant harm is 'fact specific and must retain the breadth of meaning that human fallibility may require of it'. He added, however, that for harm to be significant 'it must be something unusual; at least something more than the commonplace human

---

[104] MDA Freeman (above).

[105] Eg satanic or ritualistic abuse which, if it does exist, has only periodically been acted upon by child protection agencies.

[106] The question of significant harm must also be related to the likelihood of it occurring and vice versa. This is addressed below in discussion of the case of *In re B (A Child)* [2013] UKSC 33.

[107] [1993] 1 FLR 257.

[108] Ibid, at 265.

[109] [2007] 1 FLR 2050.

failure or inadequacy'.[110] He observed that as a matter of policy it is 'recognised in law, that children are best brought up within natural families'[111] and that it follows inexorably:[112]

> 'that society must be willing to tolerate very diverse standards of parenting, including the eccentric, the barely adequate and the inconsistent. It follows too that children will inevitably have both very different experiences of parenting and very unequal consequences flowing from it. It means that some children will experience disadvantage and harm, while others flourish in atmospheres of loving security and emotional stability. These are the consequences of our fallible humanity and it is not the provenance of the state to spare children all the consequences of defective parenting.'

In *Re K; A Local Authority v N and Others*[113] Munby J commented that 'the court must always be sensitive to the cultural, social and religious circumstances of the particular child and family'.[114] Endorsing the dicta of Hedley J and Munby J, Ward LJ in *Re MA (Care Threshold)*,[115] observed that, given the underlying philosophy of the Act, 'the harm must ... be significant enough to justify the intervention of the State and disturb the autonomy of the parents to bring up their children by themselves in the way they choose'.[116] In the Supreme Court in *In re B (A Child)*[117] Lady Hale commented that this definition is somewhat circular, but she noted that it 'serves to make the point that not all harm which children may suffer as a result of their parents' care falling short of what it is reasonable to expect is significant for this purpose'.[118] She found more helpful the dictionary definition as set out by Booth J. Lady Hale also set out, with apparent approval, the passage from Hedley J's judgment in *Re L (Care: Threshold Criteria)* above, as did Lord Neuberger, who described Hedley J's remarks as 'very wise'.[119]

---

[110] Ibid, at para [50].

[111] Citing Lord Templeman in *Re KD (A Minor: Ward) (Termination of Access)* [1988] AC 806 at 812: 'The best person to bring up a child is the natural parent. It matters not whether the parent is wise or foolish, rich or poor, educated or illiterate, provided the child's moral and physical health are not in danger. Public authorities cannot improve on nature'.

[112] [2007] 1 FLR 2050.

[113] [2005] EWHC 2956 (Fam), [2007] 1 FLR 399.

[114] Ibid, at para [26].

[115] [2009] EWCA Civ 853, [2010] 1 FLR 431, at [51]. For commentary on this case, see H Keating 'Re MA: The Significance of Harm' [2011] *Child and Family Law Quarterly* 115 and J Hayes, M Hayes, and J Williams '"Shocking" Abuse Followed by a 'Staggering Ruling': *Re MA (Care Threshold)*' [2010] Fam Law 166.

[116] [2009] EWCA Civ 853, [2010] 1 FLR 431, at [54].

[117] [2013] UKSC 33.

[118] Ibid, at para 185.

[119] Ibid, at para 67. Parts of Hedley J's judgment were also cited by Lord Wilson, at para 27, although he said that the Supreme Court should avoid attempting to explain the word 'significant', which would be a gloss which might lead the courts away from the word itself (at para 26). Lord Neuberger, at para 56 stated that Lord Wilson 'is rightly anxious not to encumber the comparatively simple wording of s 31(2) ... with too much judicial encrustation' but felt that some guidance was necessary, and had been provided by Lord Wilson, at paras 23–31, Lord Kerr, at para 108, and Lady Hale, at paras 179–193.

The Act also provides some guidance on when the requisite level will be reached. Section 31(10) states:[120]

> 'Where the question of whether harm suffered by a child is significant turns on the child's health or development, his health or development shall be compared with that which could reasonably be expected of a similar child.'

While there can be no precise way of measuring the extent of harm, it is agreed that not every minor deficiency in a child's health or development will constitute 'significant harm'. Indeed, it is clear that we are looking for some 'substantial deficit' in the standard of upbringing which could be expected for the child.[121] This can only be ascertained by making a comparison with the hypothetical 'similar child'. But what is a 'similar child' for these purposes? It is generally agreed that the expression was designed to incorporate any subjective or unusual characteristics of the child in question. Thus, disabled children require special care which children who are not disabled do not require. Yet even this may become problematic, and comparisons may need to be more sophisticated. It has been pointed out,[122] for example, that a deaf child of deaf parents may not be directly comparable to a deaf child of hearing parents.

Whether it is legitimate to go beyond the inherent characteristics of the child and explore his cultural or social background is more debatable and gave rise to an apparent difference of opinion between the Lord Chancellor and the Department of Health,[123] and some academic debate.[124] One view is that cultural pluralism ought to be relevant, especially since the legislation has an ideological commitment to this.[125] According to this view 'Muslim children, Rastafarian children, the children of Hasidic Jews may be different and have different needs from children brought up in the indigenous, white, nominally Christian culture'.[126] We have already noted above the view expressed by Munby J in *Re K; A Local Authority v N and Others*[127] regarding cultural

---

[120] On what is a 'similar child' in the context of truancy, see *Re O (A Minor) (Care Order: Education: Procedure)* [1992] 2 FLR 7.

[121] See the *Review* (above), at para 15(15).

[122] MDA Freeman *Children, Their Families and the Law* (Macmillan, 1992), at p 107.

[123] In the debates on the Children Bill, Lord Mackay LC suggested that background, as opposed to attributes, should be left out of account (House of Lords, Official Report, col 354). *The Children Act 1989 Guidance and Regulations Vol 1 Court Orders* (HMSO, 1991), at para 3.20, however, states that account may need to be taken of 'environmental, social and cultural characteristics of the child'.

[124] Freeman (above). Cf A Bainham 'Care after 1991 – A Reply' (1993) 3 JCL 99. For an extremely helpful discussion of the cultural question in the context of the competing philosophies of relativism, monism and pluralism, see M Freeman 'Children's Rights and Cultural Pluralism' in *The Moral Status of Children* (Martinus Nijhoff, 1997), ch 7. See also J Brophy '"Race" and Ethnicity in Public Law Proceedings' [2000] Fam Law 740; J Brophy 'Diversity and Child Protection' [2003] Fam Law 674; and J Brophy, J Jhutti-Johal and C Owen 'Assessing and Documenting Child Ill-Treatment in Ethnic Minority Households' [2003] Fam Law 756.

[125] This is Freeman's view, although he would discount social inequality arising from poor socio-economic status.

[126] Freeman (above), at p 153.

[127] [2005] EWHC 2956 (Fam), [2007] 1 FLR 399.

sensitivity. He added in that case that the 'court should, I think, be slow to find that parents only recently or comparatively recently arrived from a foreign country – particularly a country where standards and expectations may be more or less different, sometimes very different indeed, from those with which they are familiar – have fallen short of an acceptable standard of parenting if in truth they have done nothing wrong by the standards of their own community'.[128] The opposing view is that allowances for cultural background ought not to be made, except at the welfare stage of the court process,[129] since, by definition, the threshold criteria set minimally acceptable limits of behaviour towards children. As such, society has a right to expect everyone from whatever cultural background to comply[130] and, in any event, allowances for ethnic background take insufficient account of the widely divergent attitudes to child-rearing held among the indigenous population. In *Re D (Care: Threshold Criteria: Significant Harm)*,[131] Wilson J appeared to have greater sympathy for the second view. He made a care order in relation to the child of a Jamaican mother. Although the mother's positive qualities were noted, there had been a history of incidents which together evidenced repeated and gross suppression of the protective instinct at times of stress. These included holding the child out of a window, beating her with a belt which caused bruises and scratches and threatening her with eviction from the home. Wilson J had the following to say about cultural considerations: 'There are many real cultural differences even within ordinary white British society. Today in England and Wales we are not a collection of ghettoes, but one society enjoying the benefit of the composition of very many racial and cultural groups and one society governed by one set of laws. It would concern me if the same event could give rise in one case to a finding of significant harm and in another to a finding to the contrary'. He did, however, concede that 'if a child can say to himself or herself "my brothers, sisters, and friends are all treated in this way from time to time: it seems to be part of life" that child may suffer less emotional harm than a child who perceived himself or herself to be a unique victim'.

The second element: the attribution of significant harm

The second element has been described as 'causative'.[132] It has been argued, however, that a condition may be 'attributable' to some factor but not 'caused' by it.[133] Yet, the concept of causation in other areas of law is wide enough to embrace indirect influences which contribute to a situation.[134] What is agreed is that parental behaviour does not have to be the sole or direct cause of the

---

[128] Ibid, at para [26].

[129] Bainham (above), at p 103. In other words, culture should be relevant when the court decides what order is appropriate.

[130] Freeman himself would accept that practices such as female circumcision, excessive corporal punishment, refusal of essential medical aid on religious grounds, and so on, ought properly to be regarded as 'significant harm'.

[131] [1998] Fam Law 657.

[132] A Bainham 'Care After 1991 – A Reply' (1993) 3 JCL 99, at 101.

[133] MDA Freeman *Children, Their Families and the Law* (Macmillan, 1992), at p 150.

[134] A Bainham (above).

child's predicament, as long as it indirectly contributes to it.[135] This might occur as where, for example, a third party, such as a relative or baby sitter, causes harm to the child and the parents were aware of that party's unsuitability to undertake his care.

Parental upbringing

It must be shown that the harm the child is suffering, or is likely to suffer, is attributable to 'the care given to the child or likely to be given to him ... not being what it would be reasonable to expect a parent to give to him'.[136]

It was said by Lord Mackay LC, during the debates on the Children Bill,[137] that the underlying objective of this requirement is to strike a balance between the conflicting pressures of ensuring that intervention in the family occurs only in carefully defined circumstances, and allowing it where harm, or risk of harm, can be traced to a perceptible deficiency in parental care.

It must be shown first, that the harm or risk is indeed attributable, at least in part, to the standard or projected standard of parental care. The fact that the child has been injured while in parental care will not of itself fulfil the threshold; the local authority will usually have to prove non-accidental injury or neglect.[138] Harm caused solely by a third party is not caught by the threshold unless the entrusting of the child's care to the third party can be attributed to inadequate parental care. This might occur, for example, where a parent has a relationship with an undesirable adult, which exposes the child to contact with that person.[139]

It seems that the test of the adequacy of care is an objective one, although all the arguments about social or cultural background resurface again here.[140] The Court of Appeal has made clear that, in cases involving parents with learning disabilities, a care order is never made simply on the basis of the parent's learning disability[141] but there is also no issue of discrimination in judging a learning disabled parent by the standards expected of a non-disabled parent.[142]

---

[135] *Lancashire County Council v B* [2002] 2 AC 147 at 162, echoing Donaldson J in *Walsh v Rother District Council* [1978] ICR 1216 at 1220.

[136] Section 31(2)(b)(i).

[137] House of Lords, Official Report, 19 January 1989, col 355.

[138] *CL v East Riding Yorkshire Council, MB and BL (A Child)* [2006] EWCA Civ 49, [2006] 2 FLR 24, at para [52]. See also *Re J (Care Proceedings: Injuries)* [2009] 2 FLR 99 (FD) (Hogg J).

[139] A similar example was given by Lord Nicholls of Birkenhead in *Lancashire County Council v B* [2002] 2 AC 147 at 162.

[140] Freeman is in no doubt (above), at p 108, that social deprivation must be discounted: 'The care given to the child is not what it would be reasonable for this parent to give (in her high-rise flat, living on income support, with three children under five and a partner in prison), but what it would be reasonable to expect a parent to give'.

[141] *Re L (Children) (Care Proceedings: Significant Harm)* [2006] EWCA Civ 1282, [2007] 1 FLR 1068, at [52].

[142] *Re D (A Child) (Care Order: Evidence)* [2010] EWCA Civ 1000, [2011] 1 FLR 447. Note, however, Munby J's suggestion in *Re G (Care: Challenge To Local Authority's Decision)* [2003] EWHC 551 (Fam), [2003] 2 FLR 42, at [59] that a local authority may have to work harder to

Clearly, reasonableness must be assessed in relation to the particular child who is before the court, bearing in mind the needs of that child. The test is, therefore, what would a reasonable parent do for this child? Cultural considerations may well be relevant when the court has to apply the ultimate welfare test and decide on what order, if any, it should make. This is because the statutory checklist of factors applies and this includes a reference to the child's background.[143]

What is the position if it can be shown that the child is suffering significant harm which is attributable to a deficiency in care, but which cannot be conclusively attributed to either parent or to any other individual? This was the problem which the House of Lords had to address in *Lancashire County Council v B*.[144]

The case concerned two babies. Child A was looked after partly by her mother and father and partly by a child-minder. This child-minder was the mother of child B. A suffered serious non-accidental head injuries and it was established that these were caused by at least two episodes of violent shaking.[145] The child-minder lived with the father of B but he was exonerated from any blame. The finger of suspicion was therefore pointing at the other three adults in the caring arrangement but the evidence could not establish that any one of them was the perpetrator. The local authority sought care orders in relation to *both* A and B. The judge refused both applications but the Court of Appeal allowed the authority's appeal in relation to A. In the House of Lords there was no further argument about B because the authority accepted that in the absence of evidence establishing that B's mother (the child-minder) was responsible for the injuries to A, it could not be said that he had suffered significant harm or was at risk.

In relation to A, the parents argued in the House of Lords that the phrase 'care given to the child' could only refer to care given by *parents* or other *primary* carers and was not wide enough to cover care given by substitute carers such as a child-minder. Thus, if harm could not be attributed to the standard of care provided by the parents, the court would lack jurisdiction to make the care

---

fulfil its duty to ensure such parents understand the local authority's concerns. Furthermore, there may be a breach of Art 8 of the ECHR if consideration is not given to measures of support: see *Kutzner v Germany* (Application No 46544/99) [2003] 1 FCR 249, at para [75]. See also *Department of Health and Department for Education and Skills, Good Practice Guidance on Working with Parents with a Learning Disability* (London: TSO, 2007).

[143] Section 1(3)(d).

[144] [2000] 2 WLR 590. For commentary on the decision, see A Bainham 'Attributing Harm: Child Abuse and the Unknown Perpetrator' (2000) CLJ 458. See also A Perry '*Lancashire County Council v B:* Section 31 – threshold or barrier?' [2000] CFLQ 301.

[145] On the evidential difficulties of proving death or injury caused by the violent shaking of babies see *Re A (Non-Accidental Injury: Medical Evidence)* [2001] 2 FLR 657. In this case Bracewell J held that the presence of retinal haemorrhages in a child's body, even in the absence of cerebral haemorrhages, was sufficient for an expert to be able to say, on the balance of probabilities, that the child had suffered a non-accidental death. And see C Cobley and T Sanders '"Shaken Baby Syndrome": Child protection issues when children sustain a subdural haemorrhage' (2003) 25 JSWFL 101.

order. It was argued that this interpretation accorded with the non-interventionist philosophy of the Children Act, encapsulated in the no order principle in s 1(5),[146] and that the best interests of children were generally served by leaving them within the natural family unless it could be demonstrated that there was a serious deficiency in the standard of care *provided by those parents*.

The House of Lords disagreed. It held that the statutory language was wide enough to include situations in which the care of children was *shared*, as it was here between the parents and a child-minder (excluding purely temporary delegations of parental responsibility). Lord Clyde observed that the language of the statute did not expressly require identification of the author of the harm and that the phrase 'not being what it would be reasonable to expect a parent to give to him' merely referred to a *standard* or *level* of care and did 'not restrict the scope of the persons who may be responsible for the care given to the child in the particular case'.

This was the technical basis on which the House was able to find that jurisdiction existed to make the care order but policy justifications were also found for this comparatively liberal interpretation. First, it was said that Parliament could not possibly have intended that a child in the situation of A should remain unprotected. As Lord Nicholls said, a more restrictive interpretation 'would mean that the child's future health, or even her life, would have to be hazarded on the chance that, after all, the non-parental carer rather than one of the parents inflicted the injuries. Self-evidently, to proceed in such a way when a child is proved to have suffered serious injury on more than one occasion could be dangerously irresponsible'. These protective concerns outweighed the consideration that 'parents who may be wholly innocent, and whose care may not have fallen below that of a reasonable parent, will face the possibility of losing their child, with all the pain and distress this involves'. Secondly, Lord Clyde pointed out, as the House had done previously in *Re M (A Minor) (Care Orders: Threshold Conditions)*,[147] that the question before it was only a *jurisdictional* issue in the sense that the question was whether a care order *could* be made, not whether it *should* be made on the facts. Even if the threshold were crossed, the court would still at the welfare stage have to consider what was the appropriate order to make, if any. So, for Lord Clyde, it was 'reasonable to allow a degree of latitude in the scope of the jurisdictional provision, leaving the critical question of whether the circumstances require the making of an order to a detailed assessment of the welfare of the child'.

The decision again reveals the acute dilemma facing the courts, and indeed child protection agencies, in balancing the fundamental rights of family members, in this case the child A's right to protection as against the parent's right to family integrity.[148] A crucial factor here was that A had already been

---

[146] As to which see chapter 2 above.
[147] [1994] 2 AC 424.
[148] The House of Lords quickly dismissed the parents' argument that to continue care proceedings and leave A in foster care was a violation of their right to respect for family life under Art 8.

harmed whereas B had not, but the different treatment of the children is open to the objection that the authority ought not to have to wait for a child to be harmed before taking protective action. As discussed later in this chapter in a section below exploring proof of likely harm, the approach of the Court of Appeal in the *Lancashire* case in relation to the child-minder's child has now been endorsed by the Supreme Court.[149]

The question of the appropriate test to be applied when the court is considering potential perpetrators of non-accidental injury arose for decision in *North Yorkshire County Council v SA*.[150] The child, who was taken to hospital suffering from serious non-accidental injuries, had been injured twice – once within the last 14 hours and once on an earlier unspecified occasion. The judge was unable to establish the perpetrator of either injury, but applying a test that there was 'no possibility that the relevant person injured the child' did not exclude either parent, the maternal grandmother or the night nanny in relation to the latest incident, since all had taken care of the child in the previous 14 hours. Applying this test, there were a large number of possible perpetrators in relation to the earlier injury. The Court of Appeal held that the test the judge had applied was too wide since it could encompass all those who had even a fleeting contact with the child. The correct test, where there was insufficient evidence positively to identify the perpetrator on the balance of probabilities, was 'is there a likelihood or real possibility that A or B or C was the perpetrator or a perpetrator of the inflicted injuries?' Applying this test, the court was able to exclude the maternal grandmother and the night nanny, leaving the real possibility that either of the parents had caused both sets of injuries to the child.

In *Re O and N; Re B*[151] the House of Lords built on the *Lancashire* decision to hold that where the threshold is fulfilled but the court at the threshold stage was unable to identify which of *two* parents was the perpetrator, the court should proceed at the welfare stage on the basis that *each* of the parents was a possible perpetrator.[152] As Lord Nicholls of Birkenhead put it:[153]

> 'it would be grotesque if such a case had to proceed at the welfare stage on the footing that, because neither parent, considered individually, has been proved to be the perpetrator, therefore the child is not at risk from either of them. This

---

Lord Nicholls said that the action taken fell within the permitted exceptions under Art 8(2) as 'no more than … reasonably necessary to pursue the legitimate aim of protecting A from further injury'.

[149] *Re J (Care Proceedings: Possible Perpetrators)* [2013] UKSC 9, [2013] 1 FLR 1373.

[150] [2003] 2 FLR 849.

[151] [2003] 1 FLR 1169. For an evaluation of the decision of the Court of Appeal, see J Hayes and M Hayes 'Child Protection in the Court of Appeal' [2002] Fam Law 817. And for a commentary on the House of Lords decision, see E Ryder QC '*Re O and N* – Is My Likelihood Your Risk?' [2003] Fam Law 741 and M Hayes 'Uncertain evidence and risk-taking in child protection cases' [2004] CFLQ 63.

[152] See the House of Lords decision in *Re O and N; Re B* [2003] 1 FLR 1169.

[153] Ibid, at 1177.

would be grotesque because it would mean the court would proceed on the footing that neither parent represents a risk even though one or other of them was the perpetrator of the harm in question.'

Parental control

The alternative, in the second element, requires that the harm or risk to the child be attributable to 'the child's being beyond parental control'.[154] Under the old law, this was a freestanding ground for a care order, and the former power of parents to initiate proceedings indirectly has already been noted. This was, in essence, a 'status offence' and was open to the objection that compulsory action could be taken against a child for non-criminal misbehaviour. Under the Children Act, a care or supervision order may only be made where the child, being beyond parental control, is suffering significant harm or is exposed to the risk of doing so.[155] Whether the test is objective or subjective is not entirely clear[156] but the *Guidance* advises that it is not necessary to prove fault on the part of the parents.[157] It has been argued that the reference to 'parental' control is wide enough to include non-parents caring for a child, at least where they have parental responsibility.[158]

It is possible, but not necessary, for both alternatives to be satisfied at the same time. Indeed, in one reported case[159] the judge indicated that the circumstances established *either* a lack of reasonable parental care *or* the child being beyond parental control.

'Is suffering' and the temporal dimension

In *Newham London Borough Council v AG*[160] Sir Stephen Brown P expressed the hope that the courts would not be asked to perform in every case a strict legalistic analysis of the statutory meaning of s 31. Although the words of the statute had to be considered, Parliament could not have intended them to be unduly restrictive when the evidence clearly indicated that a certain course of action should be followed to protect a child. However, s 31(2) is a complex provision with many constituent elements, which prompted one commentator to warn:[161]

---

[154] Section 31(2)(b)(ii).

[155] This would seem to meet the above objections, especially since the order can only be sought in relation to younger teenagers, ie those under 16 years of age.

[156] See MDA Freeman *Children, Their Families and the Law* (Macmillan, 1992), at p 100.

[157] *The Children Act 1989 Guidance and Regulations Vol 1* (above), at para 3.25.

[158] Freeman (above), at p 100. This certainly seems to be confirmed by the decision in *M v Birmingham City Council* [1994] 2 FLR 141 where the teenager concerned was in local authority accommodation but held to be beyond the parental control of her mother and partner. Stuart White J took the view that the statutory conditions could include a state of affairs which might be in the past, present or future.

[159] *Re O (A Minor) (Care Order: Education: Procedure)* [1992] 2 FLR 7.

[160] [1993] 1 FLR 281.

[161] MDA Freeman 'Care After 1991' in D Freestone (ed) *Children and the Law* (Hull University Press, 1990), at p 135.

'Each of these elements will require considerable judicial exegesis. Almost every word will require interpretation and analysis. Argument on the meaning of the language contained here (as filled out by later subsections) is likely to rage for as long as this legislation remains in force.'

This prediction has proved only too true. As we shall see, the House of Lords or the Supreme Court has been called upon to interpret s 31(2) on eight occasions to date.[162] The resultant complexities now sit in some contrast to the hope of Sir Stephen Brown P.

The first case on s 31(2) to come before the House of Lords was *Re M (A Minor) (Care Order: Threshold Conditions)*.[163] It raised the meaning of the words 'is suffering', in particular their temporal dimension. Those words are in the present tense, the intention being to exclude harm which is purely historic, though local authorites habitually rely in part on historic allegations especially past involvement of the family with children's services. In *Re M* the father had murdered the mother in front of the children in particularly gruesome circumstances. The police took the children into emergency protection.[164] The father was convicted of the mother's murder and was serving a life sentence with a recommendation for deportation (he was Nigerian) on his eventual release. Three of the four children were placed with Mrs W, the mother's cousin, but initially she did not feel able to cope with the youngest child, M. So M, not yet four months old, was placed with a temporary foster mother. In due course, Mrs W wanted to offer M a home with his half-siblings. It should be noted in passing that there were several different fathers of the children but that the father of M was the mother's husband. Since he was married to her, he continued to retain parental responsibility and, indeed, sought to influence the decision from prison on what was to happen to M.[165] The local authority, the guardian for M and the father all wanted a care order to be made and for M to be placed for adoption outside the extended birth family.

---

[162] *Re M (A Minor) (Care Orders: Threshold Conditions)* [1994] 2 AC 424, [1994] 2 FLR 577; *Re H (Minors) (Sexual Abuse: Standard of Proof)* [1996] AC 563; *Lancashire County Council v B* [2000] 2 AC 147; *Re O (Minors) (Care: Preliminary Hearing)* [2003] UKHL 18, [2004] 1 AC 523, [2003] 1 FLR 1169; *Re B (Children) (Care Proceedings: Standard of Proof) (CAFCASS intervening)* [2008] UKHL 35, [2009] AC 11, [2008] 2 FLR 141; *Re S-B (Children) (Care Proceedings: Standard of Proof)* [2009] UKSC 17, [2010] 1 AC 678, [2010] 1 FLR 1161; *Re J (Care Proceedings: Possible Perpetrators)* [2013] UKSC 9, [2013] 1 FLR 1373; and *In re B (A Child)* [2013] UKSC 33.

[163] [1994] 3 WLR 558. For commentaries, see J Masson 'Social Engineering in the House of Lords: *Re M*' (1994) 6 JCL 170, J Whybrow '*Re M* – Past, Present and Future Significant Harm' (1994) 6 JCL 88, A Bainham 'The Temporal Dimension of Care' (1994) CLJ 458, and M Hayes 'Care by the Family or Care by the State?' (1995) 58 *Modern Law Review* 878.

[164] For the powers of the police to protect children in emergencies, see chapter 11.

[165] There is no statutory power to revoke the parental responsibility of a parent who is or was married to, or the civil partner, of the child's mother, short of the ultimate step of adoption. It is questionable whether a parent such as the father in these circumstances should be able to retain it at all.

At first instance, Bracewell J made the care order but the Court of Appeal allowed Mrs W's appeal and substituted a residence order in her favour.[166] The House of Lords restored the care order, although by the time of the hearing it was accepted on all sides that M had settled well with Mrs W and her family and should stay with her. The point of law was this: in considering whether a child 'is suffering significant harm' is it permissible to look backwards to the time when the initial protective measures were instigated (in this case police protection), or does this test have to be satisfied at the time of the hearing at which the application is being considered? The significance of the issue was, of course, that by the date of the hearing M was no longer suffering significant harm, nor was he 'likely' to suffer it because he was by this time properly looked after and the danger had passed.

The House of Lords held that there was jurisdiction to make a care order in these circumstances. Lord Mackay LC said that on a correct interpretation of s 31(2)(a) the court was entitled to have regard to the whole period from the instigation of the protective measures until the final disposal of the case. Thus, Bracewell J had been right to look back to the situation as it was when emergency protection was taken. She had been entitled to conclude that *at that time* M was suffering significant harm by being permanently deprived of the love and care of his mother and that this was attributable to the fact that the 'care' given by the parent (the father) was not what it would have been reasonable to expect a parent to give to him.[167] The only limitation on this retrospective process of looking backwards was that the initial protective arrangements had remained continuously in place. The local authority could not, for example, terminate a temporary foster placement, allow the child home and then, as it were, have a 'second bite at the cherry'. Lords Templeman and Nolan pointed out that to restrict evidence to that which was available at the hearing could mean that *any* temporary measures which removed the risk could preclude the court from making a final care order and that this could not have been Parliament's intention.

The decision raises a number of important questions of policy. First, the reader may wonder why, if the child M had settled happily with Mrs W, the local authority bothered to pursue the chance of obtaining a care order all the way to the House of Lords. Part of the answer to this was of course the need to obtain clarification of the important point of law about when precisely the threshold conditions must be proved to be satisfied. But there was more to it than this. The practical point of a care order in *Re M* itself was that it would enable social services to keep a 'watching brief' on M's situation and intervene quickly to remove him from Mrs W should the need arise. If the residence

---

[166] A particularly good example of the *private* s 8 order being made in *public* family proceedings. See, generally, chapter 2 for the scheme of the Children Act in this respect.

[167] A possible criticism of this logic, but not, it is submitted, a convincing objection, is that the father's behaviour, appalling though it was, had been directed towards the *mother* and not towards the child. However, following amendment by the Adoption and Children Act 2002 the concept of 'harm' for the purposes of the threshold now includes 'impairment suffered from seeing or hearing the ill-treatment of another'.

order in favour of Mrs W had stood, the authority would have had no such right, since parental responsibility would have vested in her and not in the authority. Secondly, there is the broader policy question, alluded to above, about whether the State should have the option of obtaining a compulsory order where the risk *in fact* has passed and there is no obvious future risk to the child. Surely the public law requirement of the Children Act is not intended to allow the State to remove children who are no longer at risk merely because it would have greater confidence in carers outside the family than those within it. The legislation is, after all, supposed to have a commitment to supporting the natural family, and reuniting the child with relatives, wherever possible.[168] In short, State intervention is not about finding the best available home for a child, and children are not to be taken into care merely because someone could make a better job of raising them than their own family.[169]

However, it should be remembered that to cross the threshold is not per se sufficient to found a care order. The court will still need to be convinced, at the welfare stage, that a care order is in the best interests of the particular child, and the authority will have to convince the court in its care plan that this is so. The court is not obliged to make a care order, supervision order or any other order if it sees no need for it at the date of the final hearing. While it is true that the potential contribution of the extended family must be properly explored, the authority will have to balance this with genuine anxieties it may have about whether the wider family, in which a parent has been shown to be unable to cope with a child, is actually the best environment in which that child should be raised.

Re M has been applied in several subsequent cases. In *Re K (Care Order or Residence Order)*,[170] it was held that the court had jurisdiction to make a care order even though, at the relevant time, the children were well looked after by their grandparents. Although the local authority no longer sought a care order, it had originally applied for one and there was no principle that a care order should only be made in the family context in exceptional circumstances. There would be cases (and this was one) in which a care order would be the only way of protecting from significant harm children placed with the extended family.

What if the initial 'protective measures' envisaged in *Re M* are taken under Part III of the Children Act, ie they are 'voluntary' measures in the sense that they are not opposed by anyone with parental responsibility? Two decisions make it plain that the provision of such services to children, particularly accommodation, may be sufficient to found a care order if in due course the authority feels that it needs the additional security of a care order. In *Re SH (Care Order: Orphan)*,[171] the child had had spells of voluntary accommodation with the local authority while his mother was in hospital. There had been

---

[168] See chapter 10.
[169] See the scathing criticism of the decision by J Masson 'Social Engineering in the House of Lords: *Re M*' (1994) 6 JCL 170.
[170] [1995] 1 FLR 675.
[171] [1995] 1 FLR 746.

allegations of sexual abuse of his half-brother in which the mother was implicated. The mother then died and within months the father also died. At that point, the local authority sought a care order which was opposed by the child's guardian on the basis that the threshold criteria were not satisfied and that, applying the 'no order' principle, the local authority had ample powers to continue to look after the child under Part III and particularly under its powers to accommodate under s 20. It was held that the words 'is suffering' in s 31(2) meant 'was suffering' significant harm at the time when the 'rescue operation' was instigated, provided that these measures were continuing at the time of the final hearing, and thus on the facts of the case the threshold criteria were fulfilled. The decision confirms that protective measures which start as voluntary accommodation, qualify as the necessary rescue operation. However, the finding that the threshold was fulfilled on the facts does not sit easily with the ruling in *Re M*, which seems to imply that the need for protective measures must be continuously in place between initiation of protection and the date of disposal. Once the parents were dead the risk of sexual abuse and the reason for the accommodation had gone. Having found the threshold fulfilled, the judge went on to make a care order. The order offered more than the continuation of voluntary accommodation since it gave the local authority parental responsibility and the legal standing to find an early adoption placement, to authorise medical procedures, to resist applications by relatives, etc. Its voluntary powers were inadequate for these purposes and neither was guardianship (which was the appropriate procedure where an individual wished to take over the care of an orphan) apposite in the case of a local authority.

A similar conclusion was reached in *Re M (Care Order: Parental Responsibility)*[172] which confirms that the threshold conditions may be satisfied in relation to an abandoned baby. Here, a baby of African-Caribbean origin was found abandoned on the steps of a health centre when a few days old. It proved impossible to trace the child's family and he was placed with foster parents. The baby was found to have developmental and other abnormalities and it was likely that medical intervention in the future would be necessary. The local authority was concerned that without a care order its powers were limited in relation, for example, to medical testing. It sought a care order with a view to placing the child for adoption and argued that there was a need for *someone* to have parental responsibility. Cazalet J held that the fact of abandonment, with all the risks it entailed, meant that the baby was suffering from significant harm immediately before he was found. Given his special needs, he was 'likely' to suffer significant harm in the future as a result of being abandoned. It was therefore necessary that someone should have parental responsibility and that the local authority should acquire this through a care order. By contrast with cases like this in which harm to the child can be shown, the mere fact that a child is an orphan will not satisfy the threshold.[173]

---

[172] [1996] 2 FLR 84.
[173] *Birmingham City Council v D; Birmingham City Council v M* [1994] 2 FLR 502 (Thorpe J).

The fact that the appropriate date for considering whether the threshold is crossed is the date when the authority first intervenes to protect the child does not mean that the authority may not rely on subsequent evidence or later events. In *Re G (Care Proceedings: Threshold Conditions)*[174] the Court of Appeal held that the authority was entitled to rely on information obtained after the date of intervention, in this case expert assessments, and on later events if those things were capable of *proving* the state of affairs which existed at the time of the protective action. Hale LJ emphasised that emergency and initial protection measures often had to be taken before the full picture emerged. As a practical matter the authority was bound to be able to rely at the hearing on matters which had come to light since protective action was taken. It did not have to be in possession of all the information on which it intended to rely when it initially intervened. As she put it:[175]

> 'Care cases, like all children cases, look to the future and not to the past. Things are changing all the time while the case progresses. The local authority is not required to plead their case at the outset or indeed at all.'

It seems clear that purely past conduct will not meet the statutory criteria unless, as discussed above, protective measures have been continuously in place since the conduct in question, or unless it also points to present or future harm.[176] This brings us to the alternative strand of the first limb of the threshold test, namely that the child 'is likely to suffer significant harm'.

The problem of the unborn child

One situation which has caused difficulty is that of the unborn child. Where the pregnant mother is already known to the children's social care department, perhaps because of drug or alcohol abuse, or previous difficulties with her other children, the local authority may be genuinely concerned about the welfare of the expected child. If the mother has a medical or psychiatric condition, the local authority may want to ensure that the mother co-operates in the provision of proper ante-natal care and that the birth itself should be under normal medical supervision. Whatever these anxieties, the legal position is that the foetus is not within the definition of 'child' which means 'a person under the age of eighteen'.[177] Moreover, the foetus may not be made a ward of

---

[174] [2001] 2 FLR 1111.

[175] [2001] 2 FLR 1111 at 1115. Hale LJ went on to point to the importance of parents being made aware of the case which they were required to answer by the date of the hearing and approved of the practice in many courts of requiring the authority, before the final hearing, to make a clear statement of the findings it is inviting the court to make and the basis on which it alleges the threshold is crossed.

[176] See for an example, *Re L (Children) (Care Proceedings: Significant Harm)* [2006] EWCA Civ 1282, [2007] 1 FLR 1068, remitting the case to Hedley J in *Re L (Care: Threshold Criteria)* [2007] 1 FLR 2050 (local authority could not rely on matters on which it had closed a file some two years previously for the purpose of the words 'is suffering'). Note, however, that the court may not be able to close its eyes to past events for the purpose of future harm and the words 'likely to suffer' in the statute. The issues were raised also by the pre-Children Act decision in *M v Westminster City Council* [1985] FLR 325.

[177] Section 105(1), and see chapter 1 above.

court.[178] All the authority can normally do is 'offer' voluntary assistance and 'keep its fingers crossed' that the birth will be trouble-free.[179] These limitations reflect, in part, the strong libertarian objections to the coercion of pregnant women who, it is often acknowledged, have complete autonomy over their own bodies. The legal and philosophical difficulty is how to balance any rights the foetus may have against such rights of the mother – an issue which has been hotly debated in the context of abortion.[180] As reflected in abortion law itself, it may well be that different considerations ought to apply to the later stages of pregnancy than in the first or second trimesters.[181] The case for ruling out all judicial intervention where a foetus is close to term is not, it is submitted, a strong one.

The position may, however, be different if the High Court is prepared to exercise its inherent jurisdiction in relation to *the mother herself*, as it did in a number of cases in order to authorise a Caesarean section in the face of opposition by a woman in labour.[182] The courts were careful to avoid saying explicitly that these interventions were designed to protect the health or life of the foetus, and the decisions are at least formally justified on the basis of the best interests of the patient herself. But the effect will nevertheless usually be to ensure the safe delivery of the child. It is now, however, necessary to distinguish between adults and adolescents as far as this issue is concerned. In the case of adults the Court of Appeal in *St George's Healthcare NHS Trust v S*[183] has made it plain that a competent adult patient has the absolute right to refuse a Caesarean even where to do so would jeopardise her own life as well as that of her child. However, where the patient is a minor, the courts have jurisdiction to intervene and may still do so. *A Metropolitan Borough Council v DB*[184] provides perhaps the best illustration of the court's willingness to intervene paternalistically to protect a young mother and her child in the period immediately before and after the birth. It also illustrates the use of the inherent jurisdiction in conjunction with statutory powers under the Children Act. Here,

---

[178] *Re F (In Utero)* [1988] Fam 122.

[179] The word 'offer' is used since it may well be that social services will attempt to exert pressure to co-operate.

[180] As to which, contrast J Jarvis Thomson 'A Defence of Abortion' and J Finnis 'The Rights and Wrongs of Abortion' both in RM Dworkin (ed) *The Philosophy of Law* (Oxford University Press, 1977).

[181] For a discussion of English abortion law, see G Douglas *Law, Fertility and Reproduction* (Sweet & Maxwell, 1991), ch 5. For a useful collection of materials on legal intervention, see J Bridgeman and S Millns *Feminist Perspectives in Law: Law's Engagement with the Female Body* (Sweet & Maxwell, 1998) especially at pp 352–379. See also for a thorough examination of the issues involved in balancing maternal rights and foetal welfare, M Brazier 'Parental responsibilities, foetal welfare and children's health' in C Bridge (ed) *Family Law Towards the Millennium: Essays for PM Bromley* (Butterworths, 1997), ch 8.

[182] See, for example, *Re S (Adult: Surgical Treatment)* [1993] 1 FLR 26, *Norfolk and Norwich Health Care (NHS) Trust v W* [1996] 2 FLR 613, and chapter 8 above.

[183] [1998] 2 FLR 728. See chapter 8 above. See also J Weaver 'Court-Ordered Caesarean Sections' in A Bainham, S Day Sclater and M Richards *Body Lore and Laws* (Hart Publishing, 2002), at p 229 and E Jackson *Regulating Reproduction: Law, Technology and Autonomy* (Hart Publishing, 2001), at pp 131–140.

[184] [1997] 1 FLR 767.

the mother was a 17-year-old crack-cocaine addict. She had a fear of doctors but her medical condition gave cause for concern since she had suffered eclamptic fits resulting from high blood pressure. A Caesarean section was performed under judicial authorisation, and an emergency protection order was then obtained in relation to the baby once born. The authority then successfully invoked the inherent jurisdiction to keep the mother in the hospital maternity ward, which for these purposes constituted 'secure accommodation', since she had threatened to discharge herself from the ward in life-threatening circumstances. In this case the court found her *incompetent* to consent to medical treatment but, as we have seen in chapter 8, the courts have reserved to themselves jurisdiction to intervene to protect even competent adolescents. It is therefore submitted that the result could well have been the same if she had been adjudged competent.

Before leaving the issue of the unborn child it should however be borne in mind that there is nothing to prevent a local authority from instigating a child protection plan prior to a child's birth where it has concerns thought to justify this. This is something which is very frequently done by local authorities, especially in situations where the prospective mother has had previous children removed into care. Moreover, it is not at all uncommon for such mothers to undergo pre-birth assessments arranged by local authorities. In reality therefore it is not correct to imply that authorites are powerless to act before the birth of a child. They may do so and indeed might be seriously negligent in some cases if they did not act. But they may not issue proceedings until the child is born.

Proof that the child 'is likely to suffer significant harm'

A major problem with the former conditions for care orders was that they generally required proof of *existing* harm. The local authority could not usually take a pre-emptive strike to protect a child from apprehended harm.[185] It is true that, in every case, the court had to make an evaluation of future risk when deciding whether to make a care order, but it could not make one *solely* on the strength of this.[186] This restriction caused problems in certain kinds of cases, as where a local authority wished to forestall the removal of a child from a stable foster home to an uncertain future with parents,[187] or where it wished to prevent a new-born baby leaving hospital with parents known to have a propensity for abuse or neglect.[188] The problem, in each case, was that it was very difficult to pin down existing harm, let alone attribute this to parental failings. These difficulties were occasionally circumvented by warding the child

---

[185] By way of exception to this, the old grounds did allow a care order to be made largely on the strength of the risk to one child in the family arising from previous abuse or neglect of *another* child in the household, or risk to the child occasioned by the presence in the household of a child offender. See the Children and Young Persons Act 1969, s 1(2)(b) and (bb).

[186] *Essex County Council v TLR and KBR (Minors)* (1978) Fam Law 15.

[187] As in the *Essex* case (above).

[188] Place of safety orders had, however, been granted, controversially, for this purpose for some considerable time before the Children Act. See MDA Freeman 'Removing Babies at Birth: A Questionable Practice' (1980) Fam Law 131.

or by straining the statutory language.[189] In principle the threshold in s 31 of the Children Act 1989 now makes it possible for cases like this to be resolved, if necessary, exclusively on the strength of the risk to the child's welfare as disclosed by all the surrounding circumstances.[190] Perhaps most cases of anticipated harm will arise where the child or another child has suffered significant harm at some time in the past in a particular circumstance and the child concerned is likely to do so again because of some recurring circumstance. Examples include:[191]

> 'where physical abuse of a child is associated with bouts of parental depression; or where a newly-born baby, because of the family history, would be at risk if taken home; or where the welfare of a child who was being looked after by the local authority under voluntary accommodation arrangements ... would be at risk if the parents went ahead with plans to return him to an unsuitable home environment.'

The interpretation of the words 'likely to suffer' in s 31(2) was considered by the House of Lords in *Re H and R (Child Sexual Abuse: Standard of Proof)*.[192] In that case, a 15-year-old girl alleged sexual abuse over a long period by her mother's cohabitant who was subsequently tried for rape but acquitted. The local authority nonetheless wanted to secure care orders in relation to the three younger girls in the household. They invited the judge to find that on the balance of probabilities (viz the lower civil, as opposed to criminal, standard of proof) the man concerned had indeed abused the eldest girl or that there was a substantial risk that he had done so and that, accordingly, the younger girls were 'likely to suffer significant harm' if a care order was not made. The judge was suspicious of abuse and recognised the real possibility that the eldest girl had given true evidence. But he dismissed the application for the care order holding that he could not be sure to the 'requisite high standard of proof' that this was so and that the threshold criteria were not therefore satisfied. The Court of Appeal by majority dismissed the authority's appeal, as did the House of Lords. The House of Lords found the issue sufficiently difficult that it was obliged to hand down a 3:2 majority decision.

The principal majority speech was given by Lord Nicholls (with whom Lord Goff and Lord Mustill agreed) but there were strong dissents by Lord Browne-Wilkinson and Lord Lloyd. The first point was unanimously accepted. Following the Court of Appeal's decision in the *Newham* case, the

---

189   See, for example, *D (A Minor) v Berkshire County Council* [1987] AC 317.
190   For a forceful dissent, see MDA Freeman 'Care after 1991' in D Freestone (ed) *Children and the Law* (Hull University Press, 1990). Cf A Bainham 'Care After 1991 – A Reply' (1991) 3 JCL 99.
191   As provided in an earlier version of Guidance: see The *Children Act 1989 Guidance and Regulations Vol 1 Court Orders* (HMSO, 1991), at para 3.22.
192   [1996] 1 FLR 80. For commentary, see H Keating 'Shifting Standards in the House of Lords' [1996] CFLQ 157; A Bainham 'Sexual Abuse in the Lords' (1996) CLJ 209; M Hayes 'Reconciling Protection for Children with Justice for Parents' (1997) 17 *Legal Studies* 1; I Hemingway and C Williams '*Re M and R: Re H and R*' [1997] *Family Law* 740; C Keenan 'Finding that a Child is at Risk from Sexual Abuse: *Re H (Minors) (Sexual Abuse: Standard of Proof*' (1997) 60 *Modern Law Review* 857.

House confirmed that in order to establish the prospective element in the statutory threshold it was *not* necessary to show that it was *probable* that the child would suffer significant harm in the sense of there being more than a fifty–fifty chance of it occurring. A child might need protection just as much where there was a *real possibility* of harm that could not sensibly be ignored having regard to the nature of the harm feared. Where the majority and minority views differed was in what was required in order to establish this real possibility of harm to the court's satisfaction.

It was further held that in assessing likelihood of harm the court had to determine disputed issues of fact. Suspicion was not enough since the foundation of care orders was 'the language of proof not suspicion'. In this respect, the evidence required to found a care order was greater than that required for short-term orders such as child assessment orders, emergency protection orders or interim care orders where, respectively, 'reasonable cause to suspect', 'reasonable cause to believe' or 'reasonable grounds for believing' that the child is likely to suffer significant harm will suffice.[193] In this case, in order to draw an inference that the younger children were likely to suffer harm, it first had to be proved that the eldest girl had been abused. The majority did, however, concede that there would be cases where, although the alleged maltreatment was not proved, the totality of proven facts established a combination of 'profoundly worrying features' which affected the care of the child within the family. It was possible that 'likelihood' of harm could be established in these circumstances even though it could not be said that the child was presently suffering it. In *Re H and R* itself, the difficulty was that the *only* relevant fact was the alleged abuse of the eldest girl, and it could not therefore be said that the younger girls were at risk unless this allegation could be proved. Parents, it was said, should not have their children taken away fom them solely on the basis of suspicion. The essential difference between the majority and the minority was that the latter, but not the former, were prepared to accept that the eldest girl's evidence remained *evidence* which could be taken into account in making the prognosis of risk. It was not essential to discount it if the truth of the allegations could not be substantiated. Thus, the judge's conclusion that there was a real possibility that her version of events was true was *not* a finding based on suspicion alone but on the *evidence*.

The approach to proof of likely harm set out in *Re H and R (Child Sexual Abuse: Standard of Proof)* applies equally at the welfare stage of care proceedings.[194] Having crossed the threshold and found either existing significant harm, or the risk of significant harm to the child, could it be argued that a lesser standard of proof should apply at the welfare stage, viz when the court is deciding whether or not it should make the care order? In *Re M and R*, the Court of Appeal emphatically rejected this argument, again holding that the court can only act on the basis of proven facts rather than suspicion. Here, the judge had made interim care orders on the basis of emotional abuse and

---

[193] See, respectively, s 43(1), s 44(1) and s 38(2). See also the discussion of the inherent jurisdiction below.

[194] *Re M and R (Child Abuse: Evidence)* [1996] 2 FLR 195.

neglect of the children but he found that serious allegations of sexual abuse of the children by the mother and two men had not been proved to the requisite standard. He thus refused to make a final care order but adjourned the case for three months. The Court of Appeal was not prepared to accede to the local authority's argument that, because the welfare of the child was paramount at the welfare stage, the establishment of likely harm should not need to be based on facts proved on the balance of probabilities. So again, the judge's finding of the real possibility of sexual abuse was not sufficient to found a full care order.

In *Re H and R* the House of Lords also held unanimously that the standard of proof is the ordinary civil standard of the balance of probabilities. However, more controversially, the majority took the view that, in applying this standard, the court should bear in mind that the more serious the allegations the less likely it was that the events had occurred and the stronger the evidence that would be required. The standard of proof itself was not higher in these cases but, since it was inherently unlikely that what was alleged had actually occurred, proportionately more cogent evidence would be required to overcome this improbability. Lord Lloyd, in the minority, commented adversely on the notion that because a risk is serious, it is less likely. As he put it, it 'would be a bizarre result if the more serious the anticipated injury, whether physical or sexual, the more difficult it became for the authority to ... secure protection for the child'. He was concerned that 'there is a danger that the repeated use of the words will harden into a formula, which, like other formulas (especially those based on a metaphor) may lead to misunderstanding'.

In *Re B (Children) (Care Proceedings: Standard of Proof) (Cafcass Intervening)*[195] the House of Lords observed that 'Lord Lloyd's prediction proved only too correct'.[196] Lord Nicholls' nuanced explanation became reduced to 'the more serious the allegation, the more cogent the evidence needed to prove it' and was misinterpreted in subsequent case law[197] as imposing a higher standard of proof than the simple balance of probabilities.[198] For this reason the House agreed that it was time to give Lord Nicholls' dictum 'its quietus'[199] and to announce 'loud and clear' that the

---

[195] [2008] UKHL 35, [2009] AC 11. For commentary, see J Hayes 'Farewell to the Cogent Evidence Test: *Re B*' [2008] Fam Law 859; H Keating 'Suspicions, Sitting on the Fence and Standards of Proof' [2009] CFLQ 230.

[196] Ibid, at [64].

[197] *R (McCann) v Crown Court at Manchester* [2003] 1 AC 787, at [37]. See also the ambiguity in Lord Bingham of Cornhill's opinion in *B v Chief Constable of the Avon and Somerset Constabulary* [2001] 1 WLR 340. The dicta in *McCann* and *B v Chief Constable* were applied in care proceedings by Bodey J in *Re ET (Serious Injuries: Standard of Proof) (Note)* [2003] 2 FLR 1205, until the Court of Appeal corrected the position in *Re U (A Child) (Department for Education and Skills intervening)* [2005] Fam 134, at [13]. [2008] UKHL 35, [2009] AC 11, at [5]–[12].

[198] Lord Nicholls' suggestion that the court should be 'more sure' in relation to serious allegations could be read as suggesting a higher standard than the simple preponderance of probabilities (see [2008] UKHL 35, [2009] AC 11, at [62] per Baroness Hale).

[199] Ibid, at [64].

standard of proof in care proceedings 'is the simple balance of probabilities, neither more nor less'.[200] Baroness Hale explained that:[201]

'Neither the seriousness of the allegation nor the seriousness of the consequences should make any difference to the standard of proof to be applied in determining the facts. The inherent probabilities are simply something to be taken into account, where relevant, in deciding where the truth lies.'

She pointed out that 'there is no logical or necessary connection between seriousness and probability,[202] and also emphasised that the context in which allegations are made is important.

In *Re B (Children) (Care Proceedings: Standard of Proof) (Cafcass Intervening)*[203] the facts and issue were similar to those in *Re H*.[204] The House unhesitatingly declined an invitation to depart from Lord Nicholls's reasoning in *Re H* which, the House said, remained 'thoroughly convincing'.[205] Baroness Hale explained that the threshold is there to protect both the children and their parents from unjustified intervention in their lives. It would provide no protection at all if it could be established on the basis of unsubstantiated suspicions; it would mean that the alleged perpetrator would have to prove that abuse did not take place.[206]

In *Re S-B (Children) (Care Proceedings: Standard of Proof)*,[207] the matter of the standard of proof arose again on the question of what standard was to be applied in identifying a perpetrator. A 4-week-old baby, J, had been found to have sustained non-accidental injuries in circumstances in which the judge could not rule out either parent as a possible perpetrator of the harm to J. The Supreme Court held that the correct standard of proof is the simple balance of probabilities and remitted the case for re-hearing as the judge had applied the wrong standard. The parents had separated during the proceedings and their younger child, W, was born before the hearing. The judge had also concluded

---

[200] Ibid, at [70].
[201] Ibid. Lord Hoffmann stated that having regard to the inherent probabilities was a matter required by common sense not law (see at [15]).
[202] Ibid, at [72]. Baroness Hale pointed out that, for example, murder is sufficiently rare to be inherently improbable in most circumstances, whereas some seriously harmful behaviour, such as alcohol or drug abuse, is all too common and not at all improbable.
[203] [2008] UKHL 35, [2009] AC 11.
[204] It was alleged that the father of a 9-year-old girl and a 6-year-old boy, had sexually abused their 16-year-old stepsister. Charles J was unable to conclude that there was no real possibility that the stepfather was guilty of abuse and therefore concluded that there was a real possibility that he did.
[205] [2008] UKHL 35, [2009] AC 11, at [54].
[206] She commented that it is difficult to see how reasons for interference with a child's right to respect for family life could be 'relevant and sufficient' as required by the European Court of Human Rights if unproven allegations are the only basis for inferring that the child is at risk of harm, citing for example *K and T v Finland* (2000) 31 EHRR 484; *Scozzari and Giunta v Italy* (2000) 35 EHRR 243; and *Kutzner v Germany* (2002) 35 EHRR 653.
[207] [2009] UKSC 17, [2010] 1 AC 678, [2010] 1 FLR 1161.

that the threshold was passed in respect of W. This was seen as another reason to remit the case. At para [49] of *Re S-B*, Lady Hale explained the court's reasoning as follows:

> 'The judge found the threshold crossed in relation to [W] on the basis that there was a real possibility that the mother had injured [J]. That, as already explained, is not a permissible approach to a finding of likelihood of future harm. It was established in *In re H* [1996] AC 563 and confirmed in *In re O* [2004] 1 AC 523 that a prediction of future harm has to be based upon findings of actual fact made on the balance of probabilities. It is only once those facts have been found that the degree of likelihood of future events becomes the 'real possibility' test adopted in *In re H*. It might have been open to the judge to find the threshold crossed in relation to [W] on a different basis but she did not do so.'

These arguably obiter comments, which were subsequently applied by the Court of Appeal in *Re F (Interim Care Order)*[208] caused 'consternation' amongst some practitioners and academics,[209] who were concerned that the ruling would leave some children at risk from possible perpetrators of proven harm.

The issue subsequently came before the Supreme Court for full argument and clarification in *Re J (Care Proceedings: Possible Perpetrators)*.[210] The case concerned three children, aged 7, 6, and 3 years who had been living in a family unit with adults DJ and JJ, respectively the father and mother of the household.[211] The local authority then formed a child protection plan in relation to the children which required JJ to move out of the family home. The local authority's concerns arose from findings in earlier care proceedings relating to JJ's second child, S, who had eventually been adopted outside his family. Those proceedings were brought because of the death of her first child, T-L, at three weeks old. The baby had been 'found to have multiple fractures to her ribs, caused on at least two occasions, bruising to her left jaw, right side of her face, left shoulder and left inner elbow, all caused non-accidentally, and serious and untreated nappy rash. She had died as a result of asphyxia caused either by a deliberate act or by SW [T-L's father] taking her to bed with him and JJ leaving her in SW's care'.[212] The judge had been unable to find who was the perpetrator, but both parents were held to have colluded to hide the truth.

The local authority issued care proceedings in respect of the three children relying solely on the fact that JJ was a possible perpetrator of harm to T-L, and not on her failure to protect the child or other adverse findings. The local

---

[208] [2011] EWCA Civ 258, [2011] 2 FLR 856.

[209] For comment, see M Hayes 'Why did the courts not protect this child? *Re SB* and *Re F*' [2012] Fam Law 169; I Goldrein QC 'There is Only So Much Juice in an Orange: *Re SB*' [2010] Fam Law 196; J Hayes 'Ensuring Equal Protection for Siblings' [2010] Fam Law 505.

[210] [2013] UKSC 9, [2013] 1 FLR 1373.

[211] It is convenient to refer to DJ and JJ as 'the parents', although the youngest child was the child of JJ and her former partner and the other children were DJ's children from a previous relationship. DJ and JJ had subsequently married and had a child together, born in December 2011, who was not a subject of the care proceedings.

[212] [2013] UKSC 9, [2013] 1 FLR 1373, at para [8].

authority took the view that other matters, such as her collusion, were not relevant to fulfilling the threshold now that JJ was with another partner who did not represent a risk to a subject child and from whom there was therefore no specific need for the child to be protected.[213] It should be noted, therefore, that the case had a certain artificiality about it, and that most cases will involve other facts upon which the local authority can rely, in addition to the fact of past possible perpetration of harm to another child. With regard to the local authority's pruned case, on a preliminary issue the judge, following *Re S-B*, held that the threshold could not be fulfilled solely on the basis of JJ's inclusion in a pool of possible perpetrators of harm to another child. The Court of Appeal[214] similarly found itself effectively bound by authority, although McFarlane LJ expressed the view that the approach in *Re S-B* might not be compatible with earlier House of Lords decisions,[215] which in his opinion 'indicated a different approach between cases where absolutely no past harm had been proved, and those where past harm is established but the identity of the actual perpetrator cannot be proved on the balance of probabilities'.[216] The Court of Appeal saw a pressing need for the issue to be determined by the Supreme Court[217] and gave the local authority permission to appeal.

It was contended that if, as per *Lancashire County Council v B*,[218] a parent can fall foul of the 'attribution criterion' when there is no more than a possibility that he or she has harmed the child, and if inclusion in a pool of possible perpetrators can be taken into account at the welfare stage (as held in *Re O*),[219] then inclusion in a pool of possible perpetrators could also be taken into account for the purpose of the likelihood criterion in s 31(2)(a).[220] Addressing those points, Lady Hale explained that *Lancashire County Council v B*[221] was concerned with paragraph (b), not paragraph (a), of s 31(2). It was not a case about the likelihood criterion.[222] Similarly, she found 'nothing in *Re O* to cast doubt upon the necessity for founding a prediction of future harm upon a

---

213 See, however, the comments of Lord Wilson, [2013] UKSC 9, [2013] 1 FLR 1373, at para [70], who was 'not at all sure that such findings become irrelevant just because the mother is now living with another partner ... for no doubt the child will continue to need protection from a variety of situations and from persons other than the new partner. More widely, such findings raise grave concerns about that mother's entire capacity for responsible care; and, if marshalled by a local authority as the factual foundation for the crossing of the threshold, they would need most carefully to be weighed against such evidence as indicated an improvement in her capacity for responsible care as at the relevant date'.

214 *Re J (Children) (Care Proceedings: Threshold Criteria)* [2012] EWCA Civ 380, [2012] 2 FLR 842 (McFarlane LJ, Lord Judge CJ, and Lord Neuberger of Abbotsbury MR).

215 *Lancashire County Council v B* [2000] 2 AC 147 and *Re O* [2003] UKHL 18, [2004] 1 AC 523, [2003] 1 FLR 1169.

216 *Re J (Children) (Care Proceedings: Threshold Criteria)* [2012] EWCA Civ 380, [2012] 2 FLR 842, at para [128].

217 Ibid, at para [131].

218 [2000] 2 AC 147.

219 [2003] UKHL 18, [2004] 1 AC 523, [2003] 1 FLR 1169. For comment, see M Hayes '*Re O and N; Re B* – uncertain evidence and risk-taking in child protection cases' [2004] CFLQ 63.

220 See [2013] UKSC 9, [2013] 1 FLR 1373, at paras [24] and [33].

221 [2000] 2 AC 147.

222 [2013] UKSC 9, [2013] 1 FLR 1373, at para [25].

proven factual basis'.[223] Lady Hale concluded that there is no inconsistency between para 49 of *Re S-B* [2010] 1 AC 678 and any of the earlier House of Lords authorities, with which it was entirely consistent in principle, and *Re S-B* should be followed as a correct statement of the law.[224]

Lady Hale added that 'no-one has suggested that the fact that a previous child has been injured or even killed while in the same household as the parent should be ignored'. She explained that such a fact 'normally comes associated with innumerable other facts which may be relevant to the prediction of future harm to another child'[225] and which 'must be set alongside other facts'.[226] She thus agreed entirely with McFarlane LJ that *Re S-B* is not authority for the proposition that 'if you cannot identify the past perpetrator, you cannot establish future likelihood'.[227] She continued:

> 'There may, or may not, be a multitude of established facts from which such a likelihood can be established. There is no substitute for a careful, individualised assessment of where those facts take one. But *In re S-B* is authority for the proposition that a real possibility that this parent has harmed a child in the past is not, by itself, sufficient to establish the likelihood that she will cause harm to another child in the future.'

---

[223] [2013] UKSC 9, [2013] 1 FLR 1373, at para [33].

[224] Ibid, at para [43]. Lady Hale also rejected Wall J's obiter conclusion in *Re B (Minors) (Care Proceedings: Practice)* [1999] 1 WLR 238, at 248 that a finding that there was a real likelihood that a mother caused harm to her baby could found the conclusion that there was a real likelihood that she would cause harm to a twin sibling. This, Lady Hale said, failed 'to distinguish between the degree of likelihood required by the word "likely" and the factual findings required to satisfy the court of that likelihood, a distinction which was clearly drawn by the House of Lords in the later case of *Re B* [2009] AC 11' ([2013] UKSC 9, [2013] 1 FLR 1373, at para [21]). Later in her judgment, Lady Hale stated that it was in the context of discussion of s 31(2)(b) that Lord Nicholls in the *Lancashire* case 'referred with apparent approval to what Wall J had said in *Re B (Minors) (Care Proceedings: Practice)* [1999] 1 WLR 238, 248' (see [2013] UKSC 9, [2013] 1 FLR 1373, at para [30]).

[225] Such as facts arising from the following questions, set out at [2013] UKSC 9, [2013] 1 FLR 1373, at para [52]: 'How many injuries were there? When and how were they caused? On how many occasions were they inflicted? How obvious will they have been? Was the child in pain or unable to use his limbs? Would any ordinary parent have noticed this? Was there a delay in seeking medical attention? Was there concealment from or active deception of the authorities? What do those facts tell us about the child care capacities of the parent with whom we are concerned?'

[226] Such as those arising from the following questions, set out at [2013] UKSC 9, [2013] 1 FLR 1373, at para [53]: 'What were the household circumstances at the time? Did drink and/or drugs feature? Was there violence between the adults? How have things changed since? Has this parent left the old relationship? Has she entered a new one? Is it different? What does this combination of facts tell us about the likelihood of harm to any of the individual children with whom the court is now concerned? Does what happened several years ago to a tiny baby in very different circumstances enable us to predict the likelihood of significant harm to much older children in a completely new household?'

[227] *Re J (Children) (Care Proceedings: Threshold Criteria)* [2012] EWCA Civ 380, [2012] 3 WLR 952, [2012] 2 FLR 842, at para [111], cited at [2013] UKSC 9, [2013] 1 FLR 1373, at para [54].

A majority of the court agreed with Lady Hale's reasoning.[228] Lord Hope, also expressing a majority view,[229] explained that if the possible perpetrators are still together, possible perpetration 'will be relevant, and may on its own be sufficient, to show that the threshold has been crossed'.[230] He declined to say that it would no longer be relevant if the parties have separated:[231]

> 'first because it is information which invites further inquiry as to whether the subsequent child is likely to suffer harm while in the care of X; and, second, because, in combination with other facts and circumstances that the inquiry reveals about X's attitude or behaviour, it may help to show that this threshold has been crossed. It may have a bearing on the weight of the evidence when looked at as a whole, including an assessment of the balance of probabilities.'

Lord Hope was clear that 'it will not on its own be sufficient' and 'cannot, and must not, be treated on its own as a finding of fact that it was X who caused or contributed to the injuries'.[232]

Lord Wilson, concurring in the disposal, held that, as a matter of logic, likely harm to the children in the new family unit could not be inferred from the mother's possible perpetration. In order to draw that inference it would be necessary to prove that the mother actually perpetrated the harm.[233] In Lord Wilson's opinion, the 'harm and the person's responsibility for it are the two planks on which any conclusion about likelihood must rest and they must be equally sturdy'.[234] Lord Wilson concluded that the mother's consignment to a pool of possible perpetrators of the injuries to T-L was *irrelevant* to whether the three subject children are likely to suffer significant harm, whether as a fact alone or taken together with other facts. In this latter respect, Lord Wilson's judgment (with which on this point Lord Sumption agreed) dissented from the majority.

Re J is clearly a controversial decision and some commentators have been critical of its reasoning and implications.[235] At the time of writing, an amendment to the Children and Families Bill has been laid before Parliament by Lord Lloyd of Berwick who, it will be recalled, was one of the dissenting judges in *Re H*. The amendment would have the effect of permitting judges, in an appropriate case, to find likely harm from the sole fact of past possible

---

228   Lord Hope, Lord Reed, Lord Carnwath, and Lord Clarke. Lord Sumption agreed in part.
229   Lord Reed, Lord Carnwath and Lord Clarke expressly agreed with his judgment.
230   Ibid, at para [87].
231   Ibid.
232   Ibid, at para [88], adding: 'A prediction of future harm based on what has happened in the past will only be justified if one can link what has happened in the past directly and unequivocally with the person in the new family unit in whose care the subsequent child is living or will now live'.
233   A majority of the court agreed with Lord Wilson on this point.
234   Ibid, at para [74].
235   S Gilmore '*Re J (Care Proceedings: Past Possible Perpetrators in a New Family Unit)* [2013] UKSC 9: Bulwarks and logic – the blood which runs through the veins of law – but how much will be spilled in future?' [2013] CFLQ 215; M Hayes 'The Supreme Court's failure to protect vulnerable children: *Re J (Children)*' [2013] Fam Law 1015.

perpetration, thus reversing the effect of *Re J*. Those who are critical of the decision have argued that the alleged inconsistency of *Re S-B* with earlier House of Lords' authorities was dismissed on a rather limited formal basis, which resulted in a failure to engage with the reasoning in those cases. Arguably the earlier authorities were not concerned with logic or the consistency of the authorities but with ensuring an interpretation of the threshold criteria which does not put children at risk. The policy consideration which weighed most heavily with the House of Lords in *Lancashire County Council v B* was child protection, even though it was appreciated that an injustice might be done to the parents concerned.[236] Especially in light of the approach already adopted in the *Lancashire* case, it could be argued that the court was not bound to apply the approach in *Re H* to the facts of *Re J* which, given the proven past harm to another child, were qualitatively different.

The court in the *Lancashire* case was also influenced by the fact that the threshold criteria are only jurisdictional requirements; their fulfillment merely allows the court to put in place some protection which is proportionate in all the circumstances. It by no means follows that a care order would be made, or indeed if one were made that the child would be removed from the parent thereunder. But the ruling in *Re J* means that the local authority cannot even obtain a supervision order to monitor the child's welfare. One solution to that problem might be to introduce a lower statutory threshold for the making of a supervision order.[237]

The implications of the decision might also be considered. Imagine if two possible perpetrators of harm resulting in the death of a baby split up and each is living with a baby in a new family unit; it is clear that one of the babies is living with a past perpetrator of serious harm, yet on the ruling in *Re J* neither child can be protected. Similar arguments would seem to apply to children in split residence or shared residence arrangements.[238] Thus possible perpetrators can frustrate state intervention by parting from each other. This may also affect the temporal dimension of the threshold as discussed earlier. If the possible perpetrators split up after initiation of protective measures but before disposal, it may be difficult to argue that the need for protective measures is continuously in force up to the date of disposal, since once the possible perpetrators split up, on the reasoning in *Re J* any child of the household is no longer at any relevant risk.

Some commentators, by contrast, will see *Re J* as holding the correct balance between child protection and unwarranted state intrusion in family life.[239] Advocates of the decision will no doubt point to the fact that had the Supreme Court not held as it did, no past possible perpetrator would ever be able to make a fresh start in a new family unit free from possible state intrusion.

---

[236] Ibid.

[237] As suggested by Bainham in his commentary on the decision. See A Bainham 'Suspicious minds: protecting children in the face of uncertainty' [2013] 72 *Cambridge Law Journal* 266.

[238] See Gilmore [2013] CFLQ 215, at 232–233.

[239] For a commentary largely supportive of the decision, see A Bainham (above).

Extreme examples can be given in an attempt to show how problematic this might be. Imagine, for example, a child who is injured while living in a commune of 12 individuals, all of whom are possible perpetrators of the harm. Should the State be able to intervene if one of the possible perpetrators leaves to set up home in a new family unit with children, even though in the example given the person concerned is only one of twelve possible perpetrators? Of course, a counter-example can be given: imagine that the injured child's sibling is still living in the commune. In this situation, on the reasoning in *Re J* the sibling cannot be protected even though he is living with eleven out of twelve possible perpetrators. Such 'statistical examples' must be treated with care, however, since for persons to be possible perpetrators it must have been shown in relation to each that there is a real possibility (a possibility that cannot sensibly be ignored) that he or she is the perpetrator.

One of the reasons that Lady Hale gave for her interpretation of the threshold was that there must be a clearly established objective basis for state interference, without which there would be no 'pressing social need' for the state to interfere in the family life protected by Art 8 of the European Convention for the Protection of Human Rights and Fundamental Freedoms 1950 (ECHR); and that reasonable suspicion cannot be a sufficient basis for the long term intervention entailed in a care order.[240] Lord Wilson considered that his interpretation was compelled in order to comply with Art 8 of the ECHR. On this point, however, a majority of the court, saw room for argument as to whether Art 8 'is engaged by a provision which merely confers upon the court the jurisdiction' and 'merely opens the way to the possibility that an order may be made'.[241] This issue was taken up in a subsequent Supreme Court decision *In re B (A Child)*,[242] which also made some important pronouncements regarding the meaning of 'likely' in s 31, and the standard for appellate review in care cases.

In re B (A Child) concerned a three year-old girl, Amelia, who at birth was placed with a foster mother. In subsequent proceedings under s 31 the judge made a care order with a view to the child's adoption outside the family, and the parents appealed, ultimately to the Supreme Court. Amelia's mother had had a dysfunctional upbringing, which included having had a child as a result of a sexual relationship with her stepfather, whose influence was described by Lord Wilson as 'malign in almost every sense'.[243] The mother was diagnosed with a somatisation disorder.[244] The father had a long criminal history.[245] Following removal of Amelia at birth the parents had been assiduous in attending contact sessions and reports as to the quality of contact were

---

[240]   Ibid, at para [44].
[241]   Ibid, at para [97], citing Lord Clyde in *Lancashire County Council v B* [2000] 2 AC 147, at p 170.
[242]   [2013] UKSC 33.
[243]   See para 8. The stepfather was described as egocentric, aggressive, domineering and dishonest.
[244]   A disorder characterised by recurring, multiple, clinically significant complaints about pain, gastrointestinal, sexual and pseudoneurologial symptoms.
[245]   He had spent about 15 years in prison, having been convicted of 52 offences between 1980 and 2008.

uniformly positive. However, the judge was concerned that, if brought up by the mother, Amelia might view the way the mother behaved as appropriate and might model herself upon it. All of the experts agreed that placement with the parents could only happen pursuant to a programme of multi-disciplinary monitoring and support which would require honest cooperation, and there were concerns, backed by a mass of evidence, that the parents were 'fundamentally dishonest, manipulative and antagonistic towards professionals'.[246] The judge concluded that the parents did not have the capacity to engage with professionals and that the only viable option for Amelia's future care was adoption. The Court of Appeal dismissed the parents' appeal, but Lewison LJ was concerned[247] that the judge might not have taken sufficient account of Hedley J's remarks in paras 50 and 51 of *Re L (Care: Threshold Criteria)*[248] concerning acceptance of diversity in parenting. The child had not suffered harm, had a warm and loving relationship with the parents, the threshold was arguably barely crossed and yet the order was the most extreme that could be made. Similarly, Rix LJ wondered whether the case illustrated 'a powerful but also troubling example of the state exercising its precautionary responsibilities for a much loved child in the face of parenting whose unsatisfactory nature lies not so much in the area of physical abuse but in the more subjective area of moral and emotional risk'.[249]

On appeal to the Supreme Court, counsel for the parents argued that the requirement in Art 8 of the ECHR of proportionality applied to whether harm was significant for the purpose of s 31(2), that there must be relevant and sufficient reason for crossing the threshold. The Supreme Court rejected this argument, holding that:[250]

> 'No interference occurs when a judge concludes that the threshold is crossed. The interference occurs only if, at the welfare stage, the judge proceeds to make a care or supervision order; and it is that order which must therefore fall foul of article 8.'

So the court must consider Convention rights when deciding whether to make the substantive order.[251]

The court went on to provide some guidance on the meaning of 'likely' within s 31.[252]

---

[246]   At para 19.
[247]   See [2012] EWCA Civ 1475, at para 147.
[248]   [2007] 1 FLR 2050, 2063
[249]   [2012] EWCA Civ 1475, at para 150.
[250]   *In re B (A Child)* [2013] UKSC 33, at para 29, per Lord Wilson. See also, agreeing, Lord Neuberger, at para 62, Lady Hale, at para 186, and Lord Clarke, at para 134. Lord Kerr, at para 129, tended to agree. Lady Hale added, however, that 'the reason why the threshold is crossed forms part of the court's reasons for making the order, and these must be "relevant and sufficient"'.
[251]   See per Lord Neuberger, at para 62.
[252]   At paras 188 and 189 per Lady Hale, which had the apparent approval of Lord Neuberger, at para 56 and Lord Wilson, at para 26.

Lady Hale explained that the reason for the comparatively low threshold of likelihood (that is, likely in the sense of a real possibility) is because 'some harm is so catastrophic that even a relatively small degree of likelihood should be sufficient to justify the state in intervening to protect the child before it happens'. She observed, however, that Lord Nicholls in *Re H* 'did not contemplate that a relatively small degree of likelihood would be sufficient in all cases. The corollary of "the more serious the harm, the less likely it has to be" is that "the less serious the harm, the more likely it has to be"'.[253] Lady Hale added that the Act 'does not set limits upon when the harm may be likely to occur and clearly the court is entitled to look to the medium and longer term as well as to the child's immediate future'.[254] She explained further that:[255]

> 'where harm has not yet been suffered, the court must consider the degree of likelihood that it will be suffered in the future. This will entail considering the degree of likelihood that the parents' future behaviour will amount to a lack of reasonable parental care. It will also entail considering the relationship between the significance of the harmed feared and the likelihood that it will occur. Simply to state that there is a "risk" is not enough. The court has to be satisfied, by relevant and sufficient evidence, that the harm is likely.'

There is thus an evident tension in the relationship between likelihood and magnitude of the harm, especially in uncertain perpetrator cases where there may be a proven risk of catastrophic harm which cannot sensibly be ignored, yet it is nevertheless not possible to prove likelihood within the meaning of the statute.

The Supreme Court held that on the facts that the threshold had been fulfilled.[256] As Lord Neuberger put it, 'the defective parenting that Amelia would undergo if she remained with her parents fell outside the wide spectrum of the acceptable "very diverse standards"[257] such as would justify the state stepping in'.[258] Emphasising that any order must be proportionate bearing in mind the requirements of Art 8 of the ECHR and that a care order in the circumstances of this case should only be made 'where nothing else will do', the court, by a majority (Lady Hale dissenting) upheld the judge's order on the basis that he had concluded on the evidence that it was 'the only viable option'.

---

[253] At para 188. Lord Wilson, at para 26 quoted *The Law on Child Care and Family Services*, Cm 62, January 1987, at para 60, which stated: 'It is intended that "likely harm" should cover all cases of unacceptable risk in which it may be necessary to balance the chance of the harm occurring against the magnitude of that harm if it does occur'. He commented: 'It follows that when, in *Re C and B (Care Order: Future Harm)* [2001] 1 FLR 611, Hale LJ (as my Lady then was) said, at para 28, that "a comparatively small risk of really serious harm can justify action, while even the virtual certainty of slight harm might not", she was faithfully expressing the intention behind the subsection'.

[254] At para 189.

[255] At para 193, per Lady Hale, citing *In re J* [2013] 2 WLR 649.

[256] See per Lord Wilson, at para 48, Lord Kerr, at paras 131–132, Lord Neuberger, at para 64, and Lady Hale, at paras 206–214 (with hesitation).

[257] Quoting Hedley J in *Re L (Care: Threshold Criteria)* [2007] 1 FLR 2050, 2063.

[258] *In re B (A Child)* [2013] UKSC 33, at para 69.

The welfare stage

As the case discussed above illustrates, once the court finds that the statutory threshold is crossed it must then go on to consider what kind of order, if any, is in the best interests of the child,[259] bearing in mind that human rights considerations require that the action taken should be *proportionate* and no more than is *necessary* to protect the welfare of the child. The order must comply with the requirements of the ECHR and with the extensive jurisprudence of the ECtHR in the field of child protection.[260] Any measures taken by the State which hinder the enjoyment of family life would amount to an interference with the rights protected by Art 8.[261] Such interferences clearly include compulsory removal of children from their parents under a care order[262] and later decisions relating to placement, contact and adoption. Given that all these major decisions amount to interferences with Convention rights, the focus must be on the *justifications* for such interferences provided by Art 8(2). The process is one of evaluating whether the particular form of intervention is *proportionate* and *necessary* to a *legitimate State aim*. The aims visualised by Art 8(2) are 'the protection of the rights and freedoms of others' and the 'protection of health or morals'. These aims must be 'necessary in a democratic society' which, according to the ECtHR, means that there must be a 'pressing social need' for the relevant interference. In determining this question, the ECtHR has applied the 'fair balance' test. This is that a fair balance must be struck between the legitimate aim and the means to achieve it. There are also procedural aspects to protection afforded by the ECHR. A failure to allow parents to be involved sufficiently in decisions affecting them may constitute a breach of Art 8 (right to respect for private life and family life) and/or Art 6 (right to a fair hearing).[263]

The application of these principles has been considered by the ECtHR in a raft of cases dealing with different decisions in the public law context. The ECtHR has acknowledged that States enjoyed a wide margin of appreciation in pursuing the legitimate aim of protecting the interests of children and assessing the necessity of taking children into care.[264] However, in the Court's view, taking a child into care should normally be regarded as a *temporary measure* to be discontinued as soon as circumstances permit. Moreover, any measures of

---

[259] It should be borne in mind that in practice the great majority of cases do not involve separate hearings, or even separate distinctive stages. The issue of whether and, if so, on what basis, the threshold is crossed is often determined following negotiations and subsequent judicial endorsement of an agreed or composite threshold document. This will usually take place in one and the same final hearing as the welfare determination is made. It is the welfare determination which, much more often than not, dominates that final hearing.

[260] See for discussion, S Choudhry and J Herring *European Human Rights and Family Law* (Hart Publishing, 2010), ch 7 (on child protection) and ch 8 (on adoption).

[261] See for examples *K and T v Finland* (2001) 36 EHRR 255, *R and H v United Kingdom* (2011) 54 EHRR 28, [2011] 2 FLR 1236, and *YC v United Kingdom* (2012) 55 EHRR 33 concerning the stringent requirements of the proportionality doctrine where family ties must be broken.

[262] Or indeed an EPO, discussed in chapter 11.

[263] *W v United Kingdom* (1987) 10 EHRR 29.

[264] See, for example, *Johansen v Norway* (1996) 23 EHRR 33.

implementation of temporary care should be consistent with the ultimate aim of reuniting the natural parent and the child. For example, in *Johansen v Norway*[265] decisions to remove a baby from her mother, removal of her parental rights, termination of access (contact) and a decision to place the baby for adoption, were found to violate Art 8 in the context of earlier successful contact between mother and child and improvement in the mother's lifestyle. The Court went on to hold that the deprivation of parental rights and access were far-reaching measures, totally depriving the mother of her family life with the child and inconsistent with the aim of reuniting them. Such measures, it was held, should be applied only in exceptional circumstances and could be justified only if they were motivated by an overriding requirement pertaining to the child's best interests. In *Olsson v Sweden*[266] the ECtHR said that good faith on the part of the State in its child protection procedures was not enough. The natural family relationship is not terminated by reason of the fact that a child is taken into public care. Splitting up a family was a very serious interference which must be supported by sound and weighty considerations in the interests of the child. In this case the three children were placed separately in homes and foster accommodation which was a long distance from the parents and each other and contact with the parents was limited. These measures were not supported by sufficient reasons and, in the Court's view, they were not proportionate to the legitimate aim pursued. In *Eriksson v Sweden*[267] the Court again found violations of the Convention arising from restrictions on access between a mother and daughter. The authorities in Sweden had placed a prohibition for an indefinite period on the removal of the child from foster care and had imposed restrictions on access. The Court held that the prohibitions and restrictions were inconsistent with the aim of reunifying parent and child contrary to Art 8. The inability of the mother to challenge the restrictions on access violated her right to a fair hearing under Art 6.

At the heart of these decisions is the obligation on the part of the State to promote reunification of parent and child. It must be emphasised that once the child is looked after away from home, the obligation on the State is a *positive* one, to promote reunification unless there is a very strong justification for not doing so. The whole question of the maintenance of contact between the child and the natural family where the child is looked after by the State is crucial to this reunification effort. We consider in depth below[268] what the ECtHR has had to say about this and also examine the statutory regime applying to contact with children in care under s 34 of the Children Act 1989.

Another aspect of the ECHR's requirements in the context of public care is the requirement in Art 6 that parents and others be granted a fair hearing in care procedures. We noted above the violation of Art 6 in *Eriksson v Sweden*. The matter arose again in the important case of *P, C and S v United Kingdom*.[269] In

---

[265] Ibid.
[266] (1988) 11 EHRR 259.
[267] (1989) 12 EHRR 183.
[268] See pp 624 et seq.
[269] [2002] 2 FLR 631. For the facts and the aspect of the case relating to the emergency removal of

this case the ECtHR found violations of *both* Art 6 and Art 8 where parents were insufficiently able to protect their interests in care proceedings and freeing for adoption proceedings. The Court's decision was based to an appreciable extent on the parents' lack of legal representation in these proceedings. It is not inevitable under the ECHR that publicly funded legal representation should always be made available where Convention rights are at stake. Article 6 does not necessarily guarantee a right to legal aid. But the ECtHR had previously held in *Airey v Ireland*[270] that there might be an obligation on the State to provide it, since the complexity of the issues might make it necessary in order to provide effective access to the courts. In *P, C and S* the Court unanimously held that the complexity of the case, the importance of what was at stake and the highly emotive subject-matter led to the conclusion that the principle of effective access to the court and fairness required that the mother should have received the assistance of a lawyer. The importance of providing this effective access to the courts cannot be under-estimated for the self-evident reason that Convention rights are seriously undermined where there is a lack of an effective remedy.

Almost all of the above decisions have been concerned with protecting the rights of the natural family from unwarranted intrusion by the State and requiring the State to demonstrate strong justifications for taking or keeping a child away from home. It should not be forgotten, however, that there is another equally important side to Convention rights in this public law context. This is that the *child* also has rights to be protected from abuse and neglect. Where the State fails negligently to intervene to protect a child there may be a breach of the child's Convention rights, especially under Arts 3 and 8. We considered this aspect of human rights in chapter 11 but it should be borne in mind when considering the difficult balancing exercises which the Convention requires.

The requirement that the State provide adequate protection for the child from abuse or neglect is enshrined in Art 19 of the UNCRC. This provides:

> '1. States Parties shall take all appropriate legislative, administrative, social and educational measures to protect the child from all forms of physical or mental violence, injury or abuse, neglect or negligent treatment, maltreatment or exploitation, including sexual abuse, while in the care of parent(s), legal guardian(s) or any other person who has the care of the child.'

At the same time, there is recognition of the need for family support as well as adequate investigative procedures:

---

the child, see chapter 11 above. For an article which focuses especially on the participation issue and Art 6 rights, see D Casey, B Hewson and N Mole 'Effective Participation and the European Court' [2002] Fam Law 755. See also *L v Finland* [2000] 2 FLR 118 in which a violation of Art 6 was also found.

[270] (1979) 2 EHRR 305.

'2. Such protective measures should, as appropriate, include effective procedures for the establishment of social programmes to provide necessary support for the child and for those who have the care of the child, as well as for other forms of prevention and identification, treatment and follow-up of instances of child maltreatment described heretofore, and, as appropriate, for judicial involvement.'

In *Re G (A Child)*[271] the Court of Appeal held that the approach set out by the Supreme Court in *Re B (A Child)*[272] requiring a careful assessment of proportionality in the context of intervention by adoption, 'must similarly apply to lesser forms of intervention'.[273] The Court of Appeal considered how the exercise in considering proportionality is to be carried out in a child care case in which a choice falls to be made between two or more options. McFarlane LJ, delivering the Court's judgment, explained that the exercise:[274]

'should not be a linear process whereby each option, other than the most draconian, is looked at in isolation and then rejected because of internal deficits that may be identified, with the result that, at the end of the line, the only option left standing is the most draconian and that is therefore chosen without any particular consideration of whether there are internal deficits within that option.'

Instead the judge must undertake a 'global, holistic evaluation of each of the options'.[275] The Court held that:[276]

'What is required is a balancing exercise in which each option is evaluated to the degree of detail necessary to analyse and weigh its own internal positives and negatives and each option is then compared, side by side, against the competing option or options.'

In *Re G* the Court of Appeal overturned a District Judge's linear approach whereby the judge ruled out the prospect of the child being placed with the mother and thus concluded, without further consideration, that the only viable option was long-term fostering under a care order. The judge had failed to contemplate, as required by *Re B (A Child)*, why permanent separation of mother and child was 'necessary' on the basis that it was the 'last resort' and 'nothing else will do'. The judge gave no consideration, for example, to whether a supervision order might be made.[277]

---

[271] [2013] EWCA Civ 965 (McFarlane LJ, Davis and Longmore LJJ agreeing).

[272] [2013] UKSC 33.

[273] [2013] EWCA Civ 965, at para [32]. The significance of *Re B* (above) was also emphasised by Black LJ in *Re P (A Child)* [2013] EWCA Civ 963, at para [102], and by the Court (Lord Dyson MR, Sir James Munby P, and Black LJ) in *Re B-S (Children)* [2013] EWCA Civ 1146 (17 September 2013).

[274] Ibid, at para [49].

[275] Ibid, at para [51].

[276] Ibid, at para [53].

[277] Ibid, at para [62].

Care plans

In order to enable the court to make an informed choice as between care, supervision, a s 8 order or no order at all, it is necessary for the local authority to have a care plan to put before the court. The 1987 White Paper[278] acknowledged the importance of care plans. Care plans were placed on a statutory footing by the Adoption and Children Act 2002[279] which amended the Children Act 1989, inserting a new s 31A. This provides that where any application is made on which a care order might be made, the appropriate local authority must, within such time as the court directs, prepare a care plan for the future care of the child.[280] While the application is pending the authority must keep the care plan under review and where it is of the opinion that some change is required it must revise the plan or make a new one.[281] The prescribed information to be included in the plan and the manner in which it is to be presented are set out in regulations.[282] None of these requirements applies to *interim* care orders.[283]

Care plans, human rights and the courts

Since the implementation of the Children Act 1989 there have been disputes about the extent to which the courts are, or should be, able to control aspects of the care plan. Controversies about the proper balance of decision-making between local authorities and the courts have centred on this issue. In a number of cases[284] the courts have exhibited frustration at their inability to direct local authorities to take action in certain circumstances where the authorities concerned were reluctant to do so, but where the court in question felt that action was warranted in the best interests of the children. The matter has been complicated by the issue of the allocation of scarce resources and whether the court or the local authority is best placed to determine these priorities. An authority may, for example, be resisting an expensive assessment of the child and parents at the interim stage of care proceedings because it may feel that it would involve a disproportionate commitment of resources to one family and one or more children. On the other hand, the court may feel that a decision on whether or not a care order should be made should largely rest on such an assessment. Questions like this have been given an even sharper focus with the advent of the HRA 1998. Here the essential argument is that an 'unreviewable'

---

278 *The Law on Child Care and Family Services* (Cm 62), at para 10, where it was said that the 'amount of detail in the plan will vary from case to case depending on how far it is possible for the local authority to foresee what will be best for the child at that time'.

279 Section 121.

280 Section 31A(1). The plan is to be known as a 's 31A plan' (s 31A(6)).

281 Section 31A(2). It is normal for there to be an interim care plan, often successively numbered interim care plans, culminating in a final care plan before the final hearing in public law proceedings.

282 Section 31A(3), the Care Planning, Placement and Case Review (England) Regulations 2010 (SI 2010/959) and the Fostering Services (England) Regulations 2011 (SI 2011/581).

283 Section 31A(5).

284 See especially *Nottinghamshire County Council v P* [1993] 2 FLR 134 and *Re C (Interim Care Order: Residential Assessment)* [1996] 3 WLR 1098, discussed at length below.

care order, or an absence of judicial control over any major decisions taken in relation to children by local authorities, may breach the rights of children, parents or both under Arts 6 and 8 of the ECHR. Since most such decisions will relate to matters in the care plan, the content and implementation of the plan became a focal point for human rights arguments.

These arguments have so far fixed particularly on two questions. The first is the legitimate extent of the court's control at the interim stage. How far may courts control aspects of the proposed care plan *before* a care order is made by prolonging matters until they are completely satisfied, through the device of successive interim orders? The second issue relates to judicial control over the *implementation* of the care plan *after* a care order has been made. Given the theory and philosophy of the Children Act, that the local authority should be exclusively responsible for the child and not subject to judicial interference once the care order is made,[285] is it consistent with this that parents and others should be able to return to court to challenge what the authority has decided? But again, is it consistent with their Convention rights to respect for family life and a fair hearing that they should *not* be able to do so?

Matters came to a head in 2002 in *Re S (Minors); Re W (Minors)*.[286] These two cases, the facts of which were unremarkable and not especially unusual, exemplify the two problems identified above.

In *Re W* the care plan was 'inchoate' or, in simple terms, incomplete. At the interim stage of care proceedings, the future of two boys was rather uncertain. Their mother suffered from mental health problems. There was some prospect, however, of rehabilitation with her, but not for 12–18 months. In the meantime there was the prospect that the grandparents might come from the USA to the UK to look after them in the interim period. Could an interim care order be made and continued in these circumstances? The judge, who wanted to make an interim order, felt bound by authority to make a *final* care order, but the Court of Appeal reversed this decision on the basis that interim orders were available to achieve the required flexibility. This ruling resulted in a change of heart by the grandparents so that, by the time the case reached the House of Lords, they had decided not to come to England, and final care orders were made with the consent of all concerned.

Re S was very different in that a care order had already been made in respect of two children, but similar to the extent that eventual rehabilitation with the mother was also visualised as part of the care plan. The attempt at

---

[285] See chapter 2 above. Note that judicial control of contact and the use of secure accommodation, together with judicial control over the making and discharge of care orders, were exceptions to the general principle.

[286] *Re S (Minors) (Care Order: Implementation of Care Plan); Re W (Minors) (Care Order: Adequacy of Care Plan)* [2002] 1 FLR 815. For an extremely helpful critique of the House of Lords decision which concentrates, on the human rights implications see R Tolson QC *Care Plans and the Human Rights Act* (Family Law, 2002). See also J Herring 'The Human Rights of Children in Care' (2002) 118 LQR 534; and J Harwin and M Owen 'The implementation of care plans and its relationship to children's welfare' [2003] CFLQ 71.

rehabilitation was to be effected by a package of support measures but, in the event, the authority had failed to deliver on these because of its views of its priorities regarding competing resources. By the time the case reached the House of Lords it was implementing the care plan as it had promised to do.

The underlying issues were therefore whether the use of interim orders was a legitimate exercise of judicial control *before* the making of the final care order where the care plan was incomplete and whether there was an adequate mechanism under the Children Act for controlling the implementation of a care plan *after* the making of a care order. It was argued by the respective appellants that, unless the interpretation and application of the Children Act were modified, the Act was incompatible with the ECHR. The Court of Appeal dismissed the appeal in *Re S*, but allowed the appeal in *Re W*. It held that two adjustments were required in the construction and application of the Children Act in order to avoid risking a breach of Convention rights. The first was that judges should enjoy a wider discretion to make interim care orders as opposed to final care orders. The second was that the 'essential milestones' in a care plan should be identified at trial and elevated to starred status. Where the local authority failed to achieve a starred milestone within a reasonable time, this would reactivate the interdisciplinary process which contributed to the creation of the care plan. As a minimum requirement, the children's guardian would be informed of the failure, and either the guardian or the local authority would then have the right to apply to the court for further directions.

The House of Lords dismissed the mother's appeal against the care order in *Re W*, but allowed the authority's appeal against the proposed 'adjustments' but not against the substantive orders in *Re S*. On the two core issues, the House unanimously held as follows.

(1) Interim orders were a legitimate exercise of the court's discretion in some cases where there were uncertainties within care plans which needed to be resolved before a final care order could be made. It was, however, a question of balance, since some other uncertainties could only be resolved after a care order had been made. Interim care orders were not intended to be used as a means by which the court might continue to exercise a supervisory role over the local authority where it was determined that it was in the best interests of a child that a care order should be made. The court needed always to maintain a proper balance between the need to satisfy itself about the appropriateness of a care plan and the avoidance of over-zealous investigation of matters which fell within the responsibility of the local authority. Lord Nicholls considered that this was already established law and did not amount to a 'major innovation' as the Court of Appeal had appeared to think it was.

(2) 'Starring', on the other hand, was an illegitimate practice, since it crossed the line between what was perfectly proper statutory interpretation and a 'judicial innovation' going well beyond that. In the words of Lord Nicholls it would have 'constituted amendment of the Children

Act'. Where a care order was made it was the clear intention of Parliament that responsibility for the child should be with the local authority rather than the court. There was no provision in the Children Act which required starring. Although s 3 of the HRA 1998 required primary legislation to be read and given effect in a way which was compatible with Convention rights, so far as possible, the system of starred milestones would contravene a clear and cardinal principle of the Children Act which could not be interpreted in that way. A declaration of incompatibility could not therefore be made. On the other hand, the House of Lords, crucially, acknowledged the existence of a 'lacuna' or gap in the statutory scheme under the Children Act which could lead to breaches of Convention rights under Arts 6 or 8 and could trigger recourse to the remedies under ss 7 and 8 of the HRA 1998. In particular, the requirements of Art 6 regarding a fair hearing might not be satisfied in relation to 'questions of a fundamental nature regarding the child's future' which 'attract a high degree of judicial control'. Lord Nicholls went on to say that 'one of the questions needing urgent consideration is whether some degree of court supervision of local authorities' discharge of their parental responsibilities would bring about an overall improvement in the quality of child care provided by local authorities'.

The House also noted a problem familiar to family lawyers. This was that there was an absence in the statutory scheme of an effective means of instigating proceedings to protect the civil rights of *young* children, who were unable to engage a lawyer themselves and who had no parent, guardian or other interested adult willing to vindicate their rights on their behalf. But this too was a lacuna and did not mean that the Children Act was thereby incompatible with the ECHR. In the case of both parents and children,[287] the House of Lords urged the Government to address the pressing need to attend to the serious practical and legal problems which the starring system had tried to address. There followed an amendment to s 26 of the Children Act 1989, together with regulations, to ensure that care plans are kept under review. Independent reviewing officers are employed to monitor the process and are able to refer appropriate cases to CAFCASS. CAFCASS officers are then able to initiate proceedings on the child's behalf under s 7 of the Human Rights Act 1998 or by way of judicial review.

There is no reason in principle why all decisions, whether made before or after a final care order, should not be open to challenge where it is alleged that they have violated Convention rights. Such a case was *Re G (Care: Challenge to Local Authority's Decision)*.[288] Here Munby J emphasised that Art 8 of the ECHR offered not merely substantive protection of rights to respect for family life, but also procedural safeguards. This procedural protection was, moreover,

---

[287] Specifically in relation to young children Lord Mackay said that he did not see 'how a child who has no person to raise the matter on his behalf can be protected from violation of his or her human rights conferred on him or her by our domestic law, other than by reliance on an effective means by which others bring the violation to notice'.

[288] [2003] 2 FLR 42.

not confined to the trial process but extended to all stages of the decision-making process including the implementation of the care order. Parents had to be properly involved in the decision-making process before, during *and after* care proceedings. Where therefore the authority sought to make significant changes to the care plan (in this case a decision that the children should be removed from parental care), it was under a duty to inform the parents and to give[289] the parents an opportunity, inter alia, to respond to allegations and to make representations. The remedies under the HRA 1998 may be increasingly invoked and we may see many such challenges in the coming years.[290]

Controverisally, however, following recommendations in the Family Justice Review that the courts should not scrutinise the detail of care plans and focus instead only on the so-called 'core issues', the Children and Families Bill 2013 seeks to implement this approach. If the relevant clause[291] is enacted the Court will be required only to consider, before making a care order, the 'permanence provisions' of the plan and not the rest of it. The permanence provisions relate to the long-term plan for the child's placement and upbringing. The threefold choice is essentially: firstly, that the child will live with a parent or member of the extended family; second, placement for adoption; and third, other long-term care which would principally be either long-term foster care or some form of residential care. Not everyone is convinced by these proposals. District Judge Nicholas Crichton who, as the senior judge at the Inner London Family Proceedings Court, has had more involvement with judicial scrutiny of care plans than most had this to say:[292]

'It is not my experience in public law cases that the courts spend an inordinate amount of time scrutinising care plans ... My experience is that in almost every case sensible discussion with the Children's Guardian leads to helpful and significant improvement in the care plan. I consider it part of my responsibility to oversee that process.'

It would seem that this wisdom has fallen on deaf ears.

CARE ORDERS

In some respects, there is considerable similarity between the respective legal positions of those children who are voluntarily accommodated by local authorities and those in care. They are all 'looked after' by the local authority

---

[289] See the discussion of the role of the court in the Family Justice Review, Final Report, at paras 3.12–3.44.

[290] Procedurally, where care proceedings are still afoot, human rights complaints should normally be dealt with in the context of those proceedings. Where they have come to an end, a 'freestanding' application under s 7(1)(a) of the HRA 1998 is the appropriate remedy. See *Re L (Care Proceedings: Human Rights Claims)* [2003] 2 FLR 160, an approach confirmed by the Court of Appeal in *Re V (Care Proceedings: Human Rights Claims)* [2004] 1 FLR 944.

[291] Clause 15.

[292] Comment: The Family Justice Review (2012) *Family Law* 3.

whose general and specific duties apply to both groups.[293] Yet there are also important distinctions. This section looks at the distinctive legal effects of a care order and at the special regime which applies to contact with children in care.

The legal effects of a care order

Section 33 of the Children Act spells out the legal effects of a care order. There is now only one set of criteria for care orders and uniform legal effects whatever the proceedings in which the order was made. One important feature is that the court, having made the care order, retains no residual control over the management of the child's case. The *Review* recommended that the local authority should be able to take a grip on the case by taking firm and early decisions, and should resist the temptation of passing responsibility to another body.[294] Accordingly, the former power of certain courts to give directions to the local authority about strategic plans for the child has been removed.[295] The court has the more limited power of directing an investigation in family proceedings, but it may not act of its own volition in making a care order or dictate to the local authority once an order is made.

Local authorities must receive and keep a child in their care

The first effect of a care order is to require local authorities 'to receive the child into their care and to keep him in their care while the order remains in force'.[296] Although parents do not lose their parental responsibility when a care order is made, they must not exercise this in a way which is incompatible with any order of the court.[297] Thus, they may not remove a child who is subject to a care order, since this would contravene the effect of that order.

Local authorities must assume/share parental responsibility

The second consequence of a care order is prescribed in s 33(3) and is more controversial. It provides:

> 'While a care order is in force with respect to a child, the local authority designated by the order shall –
>
> (a)   have parental responsibility for the child; and
> (b)   have the power (subject to the following provisions of this section) to determine the extent to which
>   (i)   a parent, guardian or special guardian of the child; or
>   (ii) a person who by virtue of section 4A has parental responsibility for the child,

---

[293] See chapter 10 above.
[294] DHSS *Review of Child Care Law* (1985), at para 2.24.
[295] Powers used most frequently, but not exclusively, in wardship.
[296] Section 33(1).
[297] Section 2(8).

may meet his parental responsibility for him.'

The local authority, therefore, has parental responsibility by virtue of the care order and is not dependent, as where a child is voluntarily accommodated, for its legal powers on parental delegation. However, parents do not lose their parental responsibility merely because the local authority also acquires it.[298] Most other people who hold parental responsibility when a care order is made will lose it, since the effect of the order is to revoke a residence order.[299] The effect of s 33(3) is that the local authority must *share* parental responsibility with the parents. This was not the intention in the *Review* or the White Paper which, as Eekelaar has observed, clearly contemplated that a care order would involve a transfer of parental responsibility from the parents to the local authority.[300] It was, for Eekelaar, the Law Commission, which in 1988 'struck out in a new direction'. This sharing of parental responsibility, where the child is in care, has been the subject of trenchant criticism[301] on the ground that it dilutes the local authority's control over the child. In contrast to this, there has also been criticism that parents' participatory rights have been threatened by a late amendment to s 33(3), discussed below.

Sharing parental responsibility

What then does sharing entail? The theory is clear enough. Parents maintain an *equal* say in matters of upbringing and may exercise all aspects of parental responsibility, including, of course, the right of independent action, when the child is with them. But since the child will usually *not* be with them, all of this theory probably adds up, in practice, to little more than a right of consultation.[302]

While the Children Bill was progressing through Parliament, concern began to be expressed that parents might use the opportunity, where a child was allowed home, to act in ways contrary to the wishes of the local authority.[303] In consequence, an amendment was introduced which is now s 33(3)(b). The intention was to try to ensure that, despite the notional equality of parents and the local authority and the idea of partnership, the local authority would

---

[298] Section 2(5) and (6). The central effect of a care order is to give the local authority the power to regulate the management of the child's life in care except insofar as the statutory regime makes express contrary provision – for example, in relation to contact or the use of secure accommodation or where respect for rights under the ECHR require it. See the discussion of care plans and contact with children in care below.

[299] Section 91(2). A care order will also automatically revoke a supervision order (s 91(3)), wardship (s 91(4)), or a school attendance order under the Education Act 1996, s 437(2) (s 91(5)).

[300] J Eekelaar 'Parental Responsibility: State of Nature or Nature of the State?' (1991) JSWFL 37, at 43.

[301] Ibid, especially at pp 41–42.

[302] Section 22(4) and (5), and see chapter 10 above. It would not appear that parents are under a concomitant duty to consult the authority and that this is one reason why s 33(3)(b) is required.

[303] There could, for example, be arguments about whether what parents proposed to do was incompatible with the care order.

remain in effective control of the situation. Thus, the Children Act gives the local authority power to control the *exercise* of parental responsibility by parents if this would undermine its plan for the child. It allows the local authority to impose its will. As Freeman has put it, 'the local authority has the whip hand'.[304] He is scathing about what he sees as a largely illusory retention of parental responsibility by parents:[305]

> 'There is concern that we are saying parents have responsibility but giving them no way of challenging the exercise by a local authority of its discretion to take that responsibility away'.

It was envisaged that the power would only be exercised sparingly, and it *can* only be exercised where it is necessary to safeguard or promote the child's welfare.[306] Also, it cannot prevent a parent or guardian with physical care of a child from doing what is reasonable in all the circumstances, for the purpose of safeguarding or promoting that child's welfare.[307]

It can be argued that the very idea of sharing parental responsibility, where a child has been compulsorily removed because of parental failings, is an unacceptable intrusion into the managerial control of the local authority. On this view, the concept of a partnership between children's services and, for example, parents who are responsible for serious abuse, may be ill-conceived.[308] It is difficult to resist the conclusion that the provision was an unhappy compromise, cobbled together at the eleventh hour, which satisfies neither local authorities nor the advocates of parents' rights. On the other hand, the continuing involvement of parents through the sharing of parental responsibility may be thought consistent with the ultimate aim of reunification of parent and child, something required by the ECHR.

How much parental responsibility does the local authority acquire?

The parental responsibility which the local authority acquires is not quite as extensive as that of parents since there are some express statutory limitations. The general principle, which also applies to non-parents with parental responsibility,[309] is that those legal incidents which are fundamental to the relationship of parent and child ought not to pass to others by any means short of adoption. The powers in question are to agree or refuse to agree to the making of an adoption order, or an order under s 84 of the Adoption and Children Act 2002 with respect to the child, and the right to appoint a guardian.[310] None of these powers pass under a care order. There are also restrictions on changing the child's name and removing him from the country

---

[304] See MDA Freeman *Children, The Family and the Law* (Macmillan, 1992), at p 121.
[305] Ibid.
[306] Section 33(4).
[307] Section 33(5), which mirrors s 3(5) in relation to de facto carers.
[308] This certainly seems to be the thrust of Eekelaar's position in 'Parental Responsibility: State of Nature or Nature of the State?' (1991) JSWFL 37.
[309] See chapter 4 above.
[310] Section 33(6)(b).

which correspond broadly with those restrictions which apply where a residence order is made.[311] The restriction on changing the child's name will not necessarily apply where the child wishes the change. In *Re S (Change of Surname)*[312] the father of two girls was prosecuted, but acquitted, on sexual abuse charges involving them. He admitted the physical abuse of one of them. The girls, who by this time were the subject of care orders, sought leave of the court to change their surname from that of their father to that of their maternal family. The judge allowed the change only in relation to one of them. The appeal of the other was allowed by the Court of Appeal, which emphasised that, although the welfare principle applied, the judge should give very careful consideration to the wishes, feelings, needs and objectives of the applicant child. The court attached significance to the fact that the young woman was *Gillick*-competent and that a reconciliation with the father was unlikely. It has also been held by Dame Elizabeth Butler-Sloss P in *Re D, L and LA (Care: Change of Forename)*[313] that no foster parent or carer should unilaterally change the forename of a child in their care. If the child should subsequently be adopted, however, the adoptive parents would, of course, acquire that right.

In addition, the local authority must not 'cause the child to be brought up in any religious persuasion other than that in which he would have been brought up if the order had not been made'.[314] In *Re A and D (Local Authority: Religious Upbringing)*[315] a Muslim father contended that s 33(6)(a) means that a child must be brought up in the religion to which he 'belonged' at the time of the making of the care order, and that to place his child with Catholics was a breach of his rights under Arts 8 and 9 of the ECHR. Rejecting these contentions, Baker J observed that both parents might change religion after a care order was made, and that the nature of a child's religious persuasion, and parental control over it, evolves as the child matures.[316] Thus s 33(6) requires a 'subtle and careful interpretation, rather than the inflexible, and … unworkable, interpretation for which the father contends'.[317] Section 33(6) is subject to the local authority's overriding duty under s 17(1) and s 22(3) to safeguard and promote the child's welfare.[318] The child's mother was now a Catholic, having converted from Islam, and Baker J held that the local authority was entitled, and correct, to adopt its policy of trying to ensure that the child was bought up with an understanding of his mixed and varied heritage, and given the opportunity to develop his own thinking.

---

[311] Section 33(7) and (8). But the child may be allowed to leave the jurisdiction in accordance with arrangements made under Sch 2, para 19.
[312] [1999] 1 FLR 672.
[313] [2003] 1 FLR 339.
[314] Section 33(6)(a).
[315] [2010] EWHC 2503 (Fam), [2011] 1 FLR 615.
[316] Ibid, at [73].
[317] Ibid, at [74].
[318] Ibid, at [75].

Contact with children in care

The background

There is no question that the issue of contact between a child in care and parents or relatives has generated more complaints and litigation than any other issue in this area of the law. No doubt this was, in part, a reflection of the largely unrestrained power which local authorities used to wield over contact arrangements. The absence of effective mechanisms of redress led to a clamour in the early 1980s which culminated in successful challenges under the ECHR[319] and domestic legislation.[320] This legislation provided for judicial control over decisions to 'refuse' or 'terminate' access (as it then was). The current legislation builds on these foundations but goes much further. In particular, it shifts the onus from aggrieved parents to local authorities where local authorities wish to refuse contact to a prescribed category of individuals.

Before turning to the current regime it is as well to put the contact question into perspective. It should be seen alongside the principles of parental responsibility for children, partnership, and the statutory responsibilities of local authorities to endeavour to effect a reunification of the child with his family and, to this end, to promote contact.[321] The contact code in s 34 must be seen in this wider context. The hope is that it will not have to come into play at all, since questions of the nature or extent of contact arrangements will be resolved at the time the care order is made and indeed during the currency of care proceedings. Indeed, the court is specifically empowered to make a contact order when it makes a care order.[322] More importantly, it must, before making a care order:[323]

> '(a) consider the arrangements which the authority have made, or propose to make, for affording any person contact with a child ... and
>
> (b) invite the parties to the proceedings to comment on those arrangements.'

Proposals for contact should, therefore, be an important element in the authority's care plan for the child which it puts before the court. The function of the contact code, constituted by s 34 and regulations[324] is, therefore, to resolve disputes and to make the local authority accountable for the discharge of its statutory duties.

---

[319] *R v The United Kingdom* [1988] 2 FLR 445.
[320] Health and Social Services and Social Security Adjudications Act 1983, s 6 and Sch 1, adding ss 12A–12G to the Child Care Act 1980.
[321] Particularly Sch 2, para 15.
[322] Section 34(10).
[323] Section 34(11).
[324] Care Planning, Placement and Case Review (England) Regulations 2010 (SI 2010/959).

Contact in care and human rights

The question of the promotion of contact and preservation of contact between a child in care and his natural family is all part of the general aim of reunification which, as we saw, is mandated by the ECHR. The right to contact in this context is a Convention right which both parent and child have as an aspect of the right to respect for their family life together. This implies a continuing relationship between them. Interference with this right must be based on reasons which are relevant and sufficient.

It is important to grasp that the ECtHR has in a number of cases, including *S and G v Italy*[325] and *K and T v Finland*[326] emphasised that it is *more difficult* for the State to justify decisions which would curtail or terminate contact between parent and child than it is to justify the initial decision to take a child into care. 'Very strict scrutiny' is required of decisions which would have this effect. Thus there was a violation of Art 8 in *K and T v Finland* where the State had failed to take sufficient steps to effect a reunification of the family. In *S and G v Italy* the children had been placed in a community which opposed contact and in which two of the community leaders had convictions for sexual offences against children. The ECtHR found a violation of Art 8 on account of the delays and limited number of contact visits the mother was allowed with her children and because the community in question failed to promote the re-establishment of contact between them.

We now turn to the statutory regime under the Children Act governing contact with children in care.

The presumption of reasonable contact

The Children Act broke new ground by creating, for the first time, a presumption of reasonable contact with a child in care. This is in favour of a parent, guardian, any person who by virtue of s 4A has parental responsibility for him, any person who held a residence order or person who had the care of a child under an exercise of the inherent jurisdiction, immediately before the care order was made.[327] The local authority may refuse contact to these individuals only in very limited circumstances, ie where:[328]

---

[325] [2000] 2 FLR 771.
[326] [2000] 2 FLR 79. The case was referred to a Grand Chamber of the ECtHR. The decision of the Grand Chamber is reported at [2001] 2 FLR 707. See also *KA v Finland* [2003] 1 FLR 696 in which the ECtHR emphasised again the *positive* duty on the State to take measures to facilitate family reunification as soon as reasonably feasible. This duty began to weigh on the responsible authorities with 'progressively increasing force' from the commencement of the period of care, subject always to being balanced against the duty to consider the best interests of the child. In this case there had been a categorical statement by one social worker to the parents to the effect that 'they would not get their children back'. The Court took the view that the restrictions on contact, and the failure of the welfare authorities to review them genuinely and sufficiently frequently, not only did not facilitate reunification but contributed to hindering it.
[327] Section 34(1).
[328] Section 34(6).

'(a) they are satisfied that it is necessary to do so in order to safeguard or promote the child's welfare; and

(b) the refusal –

(i)   is decided upon as a matter of urgency; and
(ii) does not last for more than seven days.'

If the local authority then wishes to continue to disallow contact, it must get the court's authorisation, and the onus is on the local authority to bring the application.[329] The court has power to authorise or refuse contact.[330] This is a major shift of emphasis from the pre-Children Act position. Under the old law, the local authority's initial obligations were limited to giving notice of an intended refusal or termination of access. Now there are automatic restraints on the local authority's power to refuse contact and it is incumbent on the local authority, subject to emergencies, to justify this to the court. Orders refusing contact under s 34(4) are exceptional but not rare. A strong justification will be required.[331] Where, in contrast, an order *for* contact is made under s 34(3) it has been held that a failure to comply on the part of the local authority could result in committal proceedings.[332]

There is undoubtedly a tension between the two principles: (1) that the courts are *not* allowed under the statutory regime to interfere with the implementation of the local authority's care plan, and (2) that they *are* authorised to regulate the question of contact with a child in care. The short point is that the question of contact with the family is itself a very important integral part of the care plan. The reported cases have given guidance on the proper relationship between these two principles. First, the court must have regard to the authority's care plan before making a care order.[333] If, therefore, the court is not happy with what is proposed concerning contact, one obvious solution will be for it to refuse to make the care order in the first place.[334] Secondly, once the child is actually subject to a care order, the courts have made it plain that Parliament has given them the right and duty to determine the question of contact in the event of a dispute. Where, therefore, there are any prospects of

---

[329]   Section 34(4). On such an application, the parent must be permitted to call such evidence as he or she sees fit, provided that this is presented in a professional and responsible manner. See *H v West Sussex County Council* [1998] 1 FLR 862.

[330]   Section 34(2) and (4). The court does not, however, have jurisdiction to make a prohibitory order which would prohibit the authority from exercising its discretion to allow staying contact with a parent. See *Re W (Section 34(2) Orders)* [2000] 1 FLR 502. For a decision illustrating the complex relationship between contact and the overall care plan, see *L v London Borough of Bromley* [1998] 1 FLR 709. For some research findings about efforts to promote contact between children looked after by local authorities and their families, see J Masson 'Restoring Contact and Rebuilding Partnerships' [1998] Fam Law 142.

[331]   For one such exceptional case see *Re K (Contact)* [2008] EWHC 540 (Fam), [2008] 2 FLR 581.

[332]   *Re P-B (Contact: Committal)* [2009] 2 FLR 66.

[333]   *Re J (Minors) (Care: Care Plan)* [1994] 1 FLR 253.

[334]   *Re T (A Minor) (Care Orders: Conditions)* [1994] 2 FLR 423.

the link between the child and the family being meaningfully maintained, it falls to the court to decide the reasonableness of continuing contact and either to authorise it or refuse it.[335]

Applications for contact

The category of those who benefit from the presumption of contact is limited. Others, such as grandparents or other relatives, may apply, with leave of the court, for a contact order.[336] In *Re M (Care: Contact: Grandmother's Application for Leave)*,[337] the Court of Appeal set out in some detail the principles to be applied where the applicant for leave to apply for contact with a child in care is not in the category of those who benefit from the presumption (in this case a grandparent). The court said that, as in private law, grandparents are not entitled to reasonable contact as of right. At the same time, the special place of relatives was acknowledged in the legislation, and grandparents should have a special place in any child's affections. Contact between the child and the birth family should be assumed to be beneficial and the local authority should file evidence to justify why it would not be consistent with the child's welfare to promote contact with relatives. The court went on to hold that, by analogy with private law applications for contact, the criteria in s 10(9)[338] governing applications for leave in that context, were apposite on applications for leave to seek contact under the public regime. The local authority's general duty to promote contact with the child also extends to 'any relative, friend, or other person connected with him'.[339] It should not, therefore, be difficult for relatives to surmount the leave hurdle, where the application is genuine.[340] It may prove more difficult for those with a less obvious connection with the child. The main

---

[335] See, particularly, the judgment of Hale J in *Berkshire County Council v B* [1997] 1 FLR 171. See also *Re B (Minors) (Termination of Contact: Paramount Consideration)* [1993] Fam 301, *Re T (Termination of Contact: Discharge of Order)* [1997] 1 FLR 517, and *Re D and H (Care: Termination of Contact)* [1997] 1 FLR 841. The court must not, however, attempt to control contact in a way which strikes at the heart of the local authority's care plan. For a case in which the court trespassed unjustifiably on the 'forbidden territory' of the care plan itself, see *Re S (A Minor) (Care: Contact Order)* [1994] 2 FLR 222. For commentary, see C Smith 'Parental powers and local authority discretion – the contested frontier' [1997] CFLQ 243.

[336] Under s 34(3)(b) 'any person' may apply with leave.

[337] [1995] 2 FLR 86.

[338] See chapter 5.

[339] Schedule 2, para 15(1)(c).

[340] The leave requirement was considered necessary to prevent a 'free for all' which could inhibit the authority in executing its plans for children in care. However, in *F v Kent County Council* [1993] 1 FLR 432, Sir Stephen Brown P said that the court should be slow to exercise its discretion under s 91(14) of the Children Act which enables it, on disposing of an application, to order that no application for an order of a specified kind be made without leave of the court. In this case the justices had made an order restricting applications by the parents for contact or discharge of the care order. This had been an improper exercise of their discretion since there was no evidence suggesting that the parents had behaved unreasonably or that their previous applications were vexatious or frivolous. Cf *Cheshire County Council v M* [1993] 1 FLR 463 for a case in which the circumstances justified a refusal to allow a father to seek a contact order where the children were in care. For the operation of s 91(14) in the context of applications for leave to seek private orders, see chapter 5 above.

difference between this group and those entitled to the presumption of contact is that the onus here is on the applicant and not on the local authority.

Where the issue is not the complete refusal of contact, but rather the level or nature of contact being allowed, the onus will always be on the person affected by the decision to bring the matter to court. The court may then specify the time, place and frequency of contact.[341] Those entitled to the presumption of reasonable contact, together with the local authority and the child, are entitled to apply without leave for defined contact.[342] Others require leave. This power to define contact is again wider than that which existed before the Children Act. Under the old law, the local authority had power to curtail access drastically, perhaps with a view to phasing it out completely, and this was not susceptible to challenge.[343] This is precisely what had happened in the leading wardship case *A v Liverpool City Council*[344] in which a mother's access had been cut to one hour's supervised visit per month at a day nursey. Decisions on the amount of contact are now opened up to judicial scrutiny.

The local authority might itself find it advantageous to apply to the court to define contact where it is anticipating a dispute which could inhibit its ability to make positive plans for the child. The child's standing to make an application may be important, not merely to establish or increase contact but, perhaps more significantly, where the child wishes to have it terminated.[345] When making its orders, the court, as usual, has flexible powers to impose such conditions as it thinks fit.[346]

Changes to contact arrangements

The court may vary or discharge a contact order on an application by the local authority, child, or person named in the order.[347] But the effect of s 34(8) and the regulations[348] is that the local authority can depart from the order with the agreement of the person in whose favour the order is made, provided that any child, being of sufficient age and understanding, also agrees.[349] Again, the principle is that it is better to arrive at voluntary arrangements wherever possible. Judicial intervention should be a last resort.

---

[341] Section 34(3) allows the court to 'make such order as it considers appropriate'.

[342] Section 34(2) and (3)(a).

[343] Under the Child Care Act 1980, s 12B(4) it was expressly provided that the authority was not to be taken to have terminated access where it proposed to substitute new arrangements for existing ones.

[344] [1982] AC 363.

[345] This is an especially pertinent point in the light of the sudden glut of cases in Autumn 1992 in which several children took to the courts in an attempt to secure the right to live apart from their parents. See chapter 14 below.

[346] Section 34(7).

[347] Section 34(9).

[348] Care Planning, Placement and Case Review (England) Regulations 2010 (SI 2010/959).

[349] See ibid, reg 8(4).

Application of the welfare principle

Since contact proceedings are proceedings under Part IV, the principles in s 1 apply. Thus the court must apply the welfare principle and the statutory checklist, together with the no order principle.

SUPERVISION

Supervision orders were traditionally used for two distinct purposes. One was to provide a measure of local authority control over a family situation, where there was concern that a child might be at risk, but a care order was not thought necessary. The other was to provide short-term assistance to parents, following separation or divorce. The Law Commission wanted to make this distinction clear. Thus the second type of order has now been replaced by the family assistance order, discussed earlier.[350] The first type of order remains as an alternative to a care order and is regulated by s 35 and Parts I and II of Sch 3 to the Children Act. We also discussed earlier the fact that truancy used to be a ground for a care order.[351] The *Review* and the White Paper did not think it an appropriate use of care proceedings where absence from school was the *sole* reason for bringing them, although a care order could remain appropriate where absenteeism represented part of a wider family problem.[352] The 'education supervision order' was introduced to deal with truancy as such. Educational supervision will be looked at in the context of education generally.[353] The concern, for the moment, is with the more traditional use of supervision in care proceedings, itself the subject of significant reform.[354]

When may a supervision order be made?

A supervision order may be used as an alternative to a care order[355] or may be made on discharging a care order.[356] The threshold criteria of s 31(2) must be satisfied in the ordinary way. Although supervision might be viewed as a less Draconian intervention in the family, the *Review* took the position that nothing less than the minimum conditions for a care order could justify compulsion, even at this lower level.[357]

---

[350] See chapter 5 above.

[351] Children and Young Persons Act 1969, s 1(2)(e).

[352] DHSS *Review of Child Care Law* (1985), at para 15.26, and the White Paper *The Law on Child Care and Family Services* (1987) (Cmnd 62), at para 59.

[353] See chapter 17 below.

[354] See, generally, the *Review* (above), at paras 3.87–3.97.

[355] Section 31(1)(b). On the circumstances in which a supervision order can be replaced by a care order, see *Croydon London Borough Council v A (No 3)* [1992] 2 FLR 350.

[356] Section 39(4).

[357] *Review* at para 18.18. But for an argument that there is a need for an intermediate order between the two in care proceedings, see A Gillespie 'Establishing a third order in care proceedings' [2000] CFLQ 239. The debate about the threshold for supervision has been brought into sharper focus recently by the decision of the Supreme Court in *Re J (Care Proceedings: Possible Perpetrators)* [2013] UKSC 9, [2013] 1 FLR 1373, discussed above.

Although the threshold conditions for care and supervision orders are identical, the distinction between the legal effects of the two orders becomes crucial at the welfare stage when the court has to consider which order (if any) to make.[358] We discuss the effects of supervision orders in more detail below. As between a care order or supervision order, the central question for the court will be whether the level of protection which can be offered to the child under a supervision order will be adequate or whether it is necessary to go further and make a full care order.[359] The reported cases provide illustrations of instances in which the courts have felt it necessary to impose a care order and others in which they have decided a supervision order would suffice.

Re V (Care or Supervision Order)[360] is perhaps the best illustration of the first type of case. It reveals that one reason why a care order may be necessary is that it gives to the local authority parental responsibility which it will not acquire under a supervision order. This is also a frequently used rationale for the making of an interim care order rather than an interim supervision order. The case concerned an adolescent boy approaching his seventeenth birthday (the age beyond which it becomes impossible to obtain a care order). He suffered from cerebral palsy, had spastic quadriplegia and learning disabilities. His father and mother quarrelled over the specialist school which he attended. The local authority was concerned at his absences and, fearing that his condition was regressing, sought a care order. The judge found that the threshold criteria were satisfied but refused to make the care order on the basis of the strain which this might place on the parents' marriage. Instead, he made a supervision order and attached conditions to it which, inter alia, required the boy to continue to attend the school as a weekly boarder.

The Court of Appeal allowed the guardian ad litem's appeal and substituted a care order. It was held that supervision orders with conditions do not fit into the framework of the Children Act. Requirements and directions in supervision orders could not be enforced other than by returning to court. Supervision orders depended rather on consent and co-operation, failing which the ultimate sanction was a care order. In this case, the risk to the parents' marriage was outweighed by the risk of harm to the boy if he was deprived of the specialist facilities at the school.

An example of the second type of case is *Re O (Care or Supervision Order)*.[361] Here, the proceedings concerned six children aged between nine and two.

---

[358] For a careful judicial analysis of the differences, see *Re S (J) (A Minor) (Care or Supervision Order)* [1993] 2 FLR 919 (FD), especially 947–951.

[359] A supervision order will also frequently be made at the end of care proceedings where the child is to remain in, or return to, the care of a parent. The purpose is to enable the local authority to go on monitoring the child's welfare, usually for 12 months.

[360] [1996] 1 FLR 776. See also *Re S (Care or Supervision Order)* [1996] 1 FLR 753 in which the Court of Appeal held that the judge, in making a supervision order, had not properly adverted to the difference between this and a care order. In this case, the risk of the possibility of sexual abuse of the child justified the making of a care order.

[361] [1996] 2 FLR 755. See also, in similar vein, *Re B (Care or Supervision Order)* [1996] 2 FLR 693 and *Oxfordshire County Council v L (Care Order or Supervision Order)* [1998] 1 FLR 70, in

Health professionals and social workers had long been concerned about the children's development and about the neglect of certain specific health needs. On the other hand, it was accepted that their educational needs were largely being met, that their parents loved them and that present standards in the home were satisfactory. The local authority went to the family proceedings court for a supervision order to enable it to monitor the children's progress and continue to work with the family but the guardian ad litem wanted a care order so that the local authority, while leaving the children at home, could share parental responsibility with the parents. The justices made the care order but Hale J allowed the parents' appeal and substituted supervision orders in relation to all the children. She held, inter alia, that the justices had given insufficient weight to the improvements which had taken place in relation to the children's condition, the co-operation of the parents, the intensification of the local authority's efforts and how best to develop that co-operation further. They ought to have looked more carefully at the effect of supervision orders before going on to the most Draconian order (the care order) permitted under the legislation.

The courts must now take account of Convention rights under the Human Rights Act 1998, which requires that any order made be a proportionate response. An example is provided by *Re C and B (Care Order: Future Harm)*.[362] The parents had four children. The two older children were taken into care under orders which were based on actual harm to the elder child and the likelihood of such harm to the younger child. An interim care order was then made in the relation to the third child on the basis of likelihood of significant harm in the future even though all the available evidence was that he was currently doing well. When the fourth child was born, an EPO was made the same day and the two younger children were placed together with foster parents. The local authority was given permission to refuse contact between the parents and any of the children and an order was made under s 91(14) prohibiting any applications by the parents for contact or discharge of the care orders for a two-year period without the court's permission. The Court of Appeal upheld the orders in relation to the two older children on the basis of past difficulties with contact and the parents' inability to understand the problems which had arisen. But the court had no difficulty in finding that the orders in relation to the two younger children were a disproportionate reaction to their situation. Although there was a real possibility of future harm to them, there were no long-standing problems of the sort which interfere with the capacity to provide adequate parenting, and the authority could have taken time to explore other options. The principle of proportionality meant that the

which Hale J sets out in some detail the reasons why a care order might be preferred over a supervision order and emphasises that although the court is empowered to make an order other than that sought by the local authority it should not make a more Draconian order unless there are cogent and strong reasons for doing so. In this case, the local authority wanted supervision orders while the guardian ad litem pressed for care orders. On the facts, supervision orders were considered sufficient and were substituted for the care orders made by the justices.

362 [2001] 1 FLR 611.

authority was obliged to work to support and eventually reunite the family unless the risks were so high that the child's welfare required alternative care. The care orders were therefore discharged and the case remitted for re-hearing before a High Court judge. In the court's view, the younger children ought never to have been removed on an interim basis and, accordingly, they were allowed home under an interim supervision order.

This decision was followed in *Re O (Supervision Order)*,[363] a case in which the mother had mental health problems and there was some risk of sexual abuse of the children by the father. The parents had, however, been co-operating by residing with the child (the mother's fifth child) in a residential assessment facility. The judge had made a supervision order but the local authority appealed wanting a care order. The Court of Appeal upheld the supervision order. The risk to the child was at the lower end of the spectrum, and a supervision order was the proportionate response. The court emphasised that where this was so the supervision order could and *should* be made to work. There was an obligation on the local authority to deliver the services that were needed and to ensure that other agencies, such as the health services, played their part. The parents also, under a supervision order, were required to co-operate fully.

What is the effect of a supervision order?

A supervision order will automatically terminate any existing supervision or care order.[364] It lasts, in the first instance, for one year but may be extended for up to three years from the date on which it was made[365] and will, in any event, terminate when the child attains 18 years of age.[366] The initial time-limit is designed to enable the court to control the effectiveness of the order.

The chief effect of a supervision order is to place the child under the supervision of a designated local authority.[367] Parental responsibility does not pass to the local authority, as under a care order, but remains exclusively with the parents or those who currently have it. The order places certain duties on the supervisor, the child and, for the first time under the Childen Act, the 'responsible person'.[368]

---

[363] [2001] 1 FLR 923. See also *Re C (Care Order or Supervision Order)* [2001] 2 FLR 466 which was also adjudged to be a low risk case in which a supervision order rather than a care order was the proportionate response. For a case in which the court considered whether a supervision order was required at all, as opposed to no order, see *Re K (Supervision Order)* [1999] 2 FLR 303.

[364] Schedule 3, para 10.

[365] Schedule 3, para 6.

[366] Section 91(13).

[367] Section 31(1)(b). The selection of supervisor is governed by Sch 3, para 9.

[368] 'Responsible person' is defined in Sch 3, para 1 as '(a) any person who has parental responsibility for the child; and (b) any other person with whom the child is living'.

Role of the supervisor

The supervisor has three duties:[369]

'(a) to advise, assist and befriend the supervised child;

(b) to take such steps as are reasonably necessary to give effect to the order; and

(c) where –

(i)   the order is not wholly complied with; or
(ii) the supervisor considers that the order may no longer be necessary, to consider whether or not to apply to the court for its variation or discharge.'

The purpose of the second two duties is to try to prevent the situation of 'drifting' which arose under the old law and tended to discredit supervision orders for their ineffectiveness. Under the Children Act, the supervisor's duties are more specific, and he is obliged to take positive action where the order is proving ineffective. The hope is that local authorities will come to see supervision as a real alternative to care.

Making supervision work

The legislation provides that the order may empower the supervisor to give a range of directions to the child which may include where he is to live for specified periods, requiring him to present himself to a specified person or to take part in specified activities at particular places or times.[370] One of the main difficulties in making supervision work has been that parents or other carers could not be made to comply with the order. The position now is that the court may impose obligations on them but only with their consent. This sounds contradictory, but it should be remembered that supervision depends on co-operation, and, as Freeman has pertinently observed, it is likely that consent 'will be readily obtained where it becomes apparent that the alternative is a care order'.[371] Supervision is only one possible solution, the alternatives being care or, at the other end of the spectrum, voluntary assistance. The order may require the responsible person to take reasonable steps to ensure that the child complies with any requirement in the order or the various directions of the supervisor.[372] It may also require the responsible person to keep the supervisor informed of his own address where it differs from that of the child, and allow the supervisor to visit the child at the address where the child lives.[373] The supervisor has no power to direct the child to undergo medical or psychiatric examination or treatment.[374] The court may do so, subject to the general principle that where a child is capable of giving an informed consent, this must

---

[369] Section 35(1).
[370] Schedule 3, para 2.
[371] MDA Freeman *Children, Their Families and the Law* (Macmillan, 1992), at p 130.
[372] Schedule 3, para 3(1).
[373] Schedule 3, para 3(3).
[374] See chapter 11 and below for further discussion of the issues.

be obtained.[375] Other than in relation to this one matter, the child's consent is not required under the regime of supervision.

'Enforcement'

The 'enforcement' of supervision has always been problematic and, in some ways, it is a contradiction even to talk of enforcement of what is an essentially co-operative programme. However, failure to allow a supervisor access to the child could be a serious matter and, where this happens, the supervisor may apply to the court for a warrant or possibly take other emergency action, which was discussed in the previous chapter. Of course, every effort should be made to secure cooperation in advance of taking further action.

PROCEDURAL FEATURES AND OTHER ORDERS

The minutiae of the procedural rules governing care and related proceedings are beyond the scope of this work.[376] The procedural peculiarities of care proceedings were the source of much discontent and certainly contributed to the impetus for reform. These peculiarities derived from the Children and Young Persons Act 1969 – a piece of legislation which governed both care proceedings and criminal proceedings arising from juvenile delinquency. Most of the defects of care proceedings were the result of the adoption of a quasi-criminal procedure, arguably suited to delinquency cases but certainly not appropriate in cases of alleged abuse or neglect. Under the procedure, only the child and the local authority had party status. Parents were not parties but, initially, might represent the child.[377] This was wholly inappropriate since, by definition, it was their upbringing of the child which was usually in issue.[378] The local authority had no right to appeal against the refusal to make a care order and would sometimes seek to circumvent this restriction by using wardship as an extra-statutory avenue of appeal.[379] Neither did parents have any right of appeal against the making of a care order, at least in their own right.[380]

---

[375] Schedule 3, paras 4 and 5.

[376] The leading practitioner works are *Clarke Hall and Morrison on Children* (LexisNexis) now in looseleaf format, and D Hershman and A McFarlane *Children Law and Practice* (Family Law) also in looseleaf format.

[377] Provision for separate representation for children in care proceedings was first recognised in the Children Act 1975 but those provisions were not brought fully into force until some years after that.

[378] Parents themselves had only limited rights of participation in the proceedings, falling short of party status, and this initially meant that they were unable to obtain legal aid (*R v Worthing Justices, ex parte Stevenson* [1976] 2 All ER 194). Under the Children and Young Persons (Amendment) Act 1986, parents did become entitled to party status but only where there had been an order for separate representation of the child.

[379] See, for example, *Hertfordshire County Council v Dolling* (1982) 3 FLR 423 and *Re R (A Minor) (Discharge of Care Order: Wardship)* [1987] 2 FLR 400.

[380] Although they could exercise the child's right of appeal on his behalf (*B v Gloucestershire County Council* [1980] 2 All 746) but not where a formal order for separate representation of the child had been made (*A-R v Avon County Council* [1985] Fam 150).

The changes made by the Children Act sought to emphasise the *civil* nature of care and supervision proceedings by procedural changes and also by abolishing the use of care orders in criminal proceedings[381] and the 'offence condition' in care proceedings.[382] We will now look briefly at these changes and at the central features of the law under the Children Act as it applies to interim orders and the discharge and variation of existing orders for care and supervision.

Procedural changes

Parties

As well as the child and the local authority, parents and others with parental responsibility now automatically have party status in care proceedings.[383] *Anyone* else may apply to the court to be joined as a party.[384] The White Paper had recognised the potential contribution which others might have to make in care proceedings.[385] The most likely candidates are grandparents, foster parents or members of the extended family, but there is no restriction on those who may be joined. The child has a right to attend court by virtue of his party status, and the court has power to order attendance, where necessary, by authorising the police to bring the child to court.[386] In many cases, however, particularly those involving young children, the child will not attend but will almost invariably be represented by a children's guardian.

Representation of the child

Since the Children Act 1975, provision has been made for the separate representation of children in public proceedings.[387] The Children Act extended and reinforced the system of representation by a guardian ad litem (GAL), now known as a 'children's guardian'. The court is now required in care and supervision proceedings[388] to appoint a children's guardian for the child 'unless satisfied that it is not necessary to do so in order to safeguard his interests'.[389] A solicitor will also represent the child. In contrast to private proceedings, independent representation of children is therefore the norm in public proceedings.

---

[381] Section 90(2).
[382] Section 90(1).
[383] FPR 2010, r 12.3.
[384] FPR 2010, r 12.16.
[385] The White Paper *The Law on Child Care and Family Services* (1987) (Cmnd 62), at paras 55–56.
[386] Section 95, but this may often be inappropriate. See *Re G* (1992) *The Times*, November 19.
[387] Ie care and related proceedings.
[388] And in a range of other 'specified proceedings'. See s 41(6).
[389] Section 41(1).

Disclosure of evidence and discovery of documents

The *Review* recommended that there should be more advance disclosure and discovery of documents in care proceedings.[390] Care proceedings formerly always took place at the level of magistrates' courts (in the juvenile court), and evidence was oral rather than written. This could take parties by surprise, and it was felt that families should know in advance the essential nature of the case for a care order. Now written statements of the substance of the oral evidence which a party intends to adduce at the hearing must be submitted in advance, and the same applies to copies of any documents upon which a party intends to rely, including experts' reports.

Appeals

It was a logical consequence of the peculiar rules which governed party status in care proceedings that appeal rights were very restricted. Only the child had a right of appeal as such, although, initially, parents could (very inappropriately) exercise this on the child's behalf. This right was later removed where there had been an order for the separate representation of the child at first instance,[391] but one effect of this was to deny parents any right of appeal *at all* since they had no right independent of the child's.

The Children Act removed these restrictions at a stroke, by ushering in a new rule that *any* party to care proceedings should have an automatic right of appeal.[392] In keeping with the new civil character of care proceedings, the appeal now lies from the family proceedings court (ie the magistrates' court) to a county court[393] and not as before to the Crown Court, with its almost exclusively criminal jurisdiction. Parents, local authorities and all other parties thus now have *independent* rights of appeal.

The legislation makes provision for preserving the status quo, pending an appeal against the court's refusal to make (or decision to discharge) a care or supervision order. The objective is to avoid the risk of unnecessary disruption to the child's current living arrangements. Where the child is already the subject of an interim order (a necessary pre-condition), the court may order that he remain in care or supervision for the 'appeal period'.[394]

---

[390] DHSS *Review of Child Care Law* (1985), ch 16, especially at paras 16.2–16.29.

[391] Ibid.

[392] Section 94(1), which provides for an appeal against the making or refusing of any order under the Children Act by magistrates.

[393] Ibid. FPR 2010, Pt 30 and PD30A. The Crime and Courts Act 2013 creates a new family court with judges at all levels, so in future appeals will be heard at the appropriate level within that framework. See Joint Statement by the President of the Family Division and the HMCTS Family Business Authority (April, 2013). Specifically on how the reorganisation will affect the London region see the Joint Statement at [2013] Fam Law 740.

[394] Section 40. The 'appeal period' is either the period between the making of the decision and the determination of the appeal or the period during which an appeal might be made against the decision (s 40(6)).

Standard for appellate review

As we saw above, the first stage in care proceedings is the threshold stage which involves an evaluation by the judge. In *In re B (A Child)*[395] the Supreme Court held that in respect of an appeal against a finding that the threshold is crossed, the question for the court is simply whether the judge's decision was wrong.[396] In respect of any appeal against the court's ultimate decision at the welfare stage, an appellate court is not required by the Human Rights Act 1998 to assess the question of proportionality for itself *de novo*.[397] An appellate court should not interfere with a judge's decision on proportionality unless it decides that that conclusion is wrong.[398]

Interim orders

The old law governing interim orders was criticised in the *Review* for several reasons.[399] First, the orders were apparently routinely granted as part of the package of care proceedings and, in some cases, there could be many such orders before the final care hearing took place. This could result in the child being kept away from home for an indefinite and potentially unlimited time without proof of one of the grounds for a care order. Secondly, the test for granting interim orders was imprecise and inconsistently applied and amounted to no more than showing a prima facie case for a care order. Thirdly, the orders were often made by single justices without an adequate opportunity for parents, or others affected, to be heard.

The Children Act now prescribes the circumstances under which the order may be made,[400] restricts their maximum duration[401] and requires them to be sought

---

[395] [2013] UKSC 33.

[396] Ibid, at para 44 (Lord Wilson), para 56 (Lord Neuberger), para 139 (Lord Clarke), and paras 110 and 113 (Lord Kerr).

[397] Ibid, at para 36 (Lord Wilson), at para 83 (Lord Neuberger), at para 136 (Lord Clarke); Lady Hale (at paras 204–205) and Lord Kerr (at paras 116–127) dissented on this point.

[398] Lord Neuberger was concerned that otherwise the appellate court will have some sort of half-way house role between review and reconsideration: see para 89.

[399] See DHSS *Review of Child Care Law* (1985), ch 17.

[400] Under s 38(1) this is where proceedings for a care or supervision order are adjourned or where the court directs an investigation of the child's circumstances under s 37(1). The court must be satisfied under s 38(2) that there are reasonable grounds for believing that the threshold criteria in s 31(2) are satisfied in relation to the child. The test of whether there are 'reasonable grounds to believe' does not require the court to be satisfied that the threshold conditions are met or to make final findings. See *Oxfordshire County Council v S* [2004] 1 FLR 426. For an application of the test and its relationship to the principles in s 1, see *Humberside County Council v B* [1993] 1 FLR 257. Guidelines on the handling of applications for interim orders were given by Cazalet J in *Hampshire County Council v S* [1993] 1 FLR 559. See also *Re B (A Minor) (Care Order: Criteria)* [1993] 1 FLR 815 especially on the attribution of harm or likely harm at the interim stage.

[401] Under s 38(4) this is eight weeks in the first instance, and there are complex rules governing the maximum duration of subsequent orders. A second or subsequent interim order may only last for 'the relevant period' which is defined as eight weeks from the date of the original order or four weeks from the date of a subsequent order, whichever is the longer (s 38(4) and (5)). On

before a properly constituted court.[402] In keeping with the new image of supervision, it became possible for the court under the Children Act, for the first time, to make an *interim* supervision order. It *must* do so when making a residence order in care or supervision proceedings, unless it is satisfied that the child's welfare will be satisfactorily safeguarded without the order.[403] The making of the interim order does not prejudge the case;[404] the objective is to 'establish a holding position pending a full hearing'[405] and it is 'an essentially impartial step, favouring neither one side nor the other, and affording no one, least of all the local authority in whose favour it is made, an opportunity for tactical or adventitious advantage'.[406]

The Court of Appeal has held that separation of a child from a parent is only to be ordered if the child's safety demands immediate separation.[407] The concept of safety is not confined to physical safety and includes the child's emotional safety or psychological welfare.[408] The risks of removal must also be considered.[409] In *Re B (Interim Care Order)*[410] the Court of Appeal said that the question for the court could be put as follows: 'whether the continued removal of the child from the care of the parents is proportionate to the risk of harm to which she will be exposed if she is allowed to return to her parents' care?'[411] Clearly there will be cases which fall either side of the line.[412] More recently the Court of Appeal has emphasised in *Re B (Refusal to Grant Interim Care Order)*[413] that the issue of whether the interim threshold is crossed is quite distinct from whether removal of the child is warranted. In this case the judge

---

the duration of subsequent interim care orders, see *Gateshead Metropolitan Borough Council v N* [1993] 1 FLR 811. See also *Re C (A Minor) (Interim Care Order)* [1994] 1 FCR 447 for some of the difficulties which have arisen.

[402] This is implicit in s 38(1). It was held in *W v Hertfordshire County Council* [1993] 1 FLR 118 that the justices must give reasons when making or refusing interim orders. In *S v Oxfordshire County Council* [1993] 1 FLR 452 it was similarly held that reasons must be given when making a supervision order rather than a care order, especially where this conflicts with the recommendations of the child's guardian.

[403] Section 38(3).

[404] See *Re G (Interim Care Order: Residential Assessment)* [2006] 1 AC 576, at [57]: 'This does not pre-judge the eventual outcome of the case'.

[405] *Re GR (Care Order)* [2010] EWCA Civ 871, [2011] 1 FLR 669, at [35].

[406] *Re G (Minors) (Interim Care Order)* [1993] 2 FLR 839 (CA), at 845, and endorsed in *Re B (Care Proceedings: Interim Care Order)* [2009] EWCA Civ 1254, [2010] 1 FLR 1211, at [52] and [53].

[407] *LA (Care: Chronic Neglect)* [2009] EWCA Civ 822, [2010] 1 FLR 80, and see also *Re H (A Child) (Interim Order)* [2002] EWCA Civ 1932, [2003] 1 FCR 350, at [39] and *Re K and H* [2006] EWCA Civ 1898, [2007] 1 FLR 2043, at [16].

[408] *Re GR (Care Order)* [2010] EWCA Civ 871, [2011] 1 FLR 669, at [42] drawing on *Re B (Care Proceedings: Interim Care Order)* [2009] EWCA Civ 1254, [2010] 1 FLR 1211.

[409] *Re M (Interim Care Order: Removal)* [2005] EWCA Civ 1594, [2006] 1 FLR 1043.

[410] [2010] EWCA Civ 324, [2010] 2 FLR 283.

[411] Ibid, at [21], drawing on in *Re B (Care Proceedings: Interim Care Order)* [2009] EWCA Civ 1254, [2010] 1 FLR 1211.

[412] *Re K and H* [2006] EWCA Civ 1898, [2007] 1 FLR 2043, *Re F (Care Proceedings: Interim Care Order)* [2010] EWCA Civ 826, [2010] 2 FLR 1455, cases where safety did not demand removal; and compare *Re B (Interim Care Order)* [2010] EWCA Civ 324, [2010] 2 FLR 283 (risk from domestic violence).

[413] [2013] 2 FLR 153.

had been wrong to conclude that the threshold had not been crossed but right to conclude that removal was not justified as the risks did not present as immediate.

Concern has been expressed[414] that chronic situations and long-term neglect cases sit uncomfortably with the current test for interim removal and children in such situations are unlikely to be protected. By contrast, it can also be argued that in some cases interim care orders are made too readily by lower courts.[415] A common practice is to obtain an agreed order where the parents neither consent to nor oppose it, yet the lack of opposition is likely to be because of pressures such as the perception of the need to cooperate to achieve reunification with the child, and a wish to avoid an interim court ruling on the threshold criteria. The Court of Appeal's characterisation of interim care orders as 'neutral' holding orders is thus not a credible view from the perspective of such parents. It has been suggested[416] that one way of achieving the local authority's wish to have parental responsibility at the interim stage without the juggernaut of care starting to roll by way of an interim care order, might be for Parliament to extend availability of the parental responsibility orders and agreements to local authorities, provided they have already instituted care proceedings. Alternatively, it might be possible to introduce a new, intermediate order, with new nomenclature which avoids at the interim stage the pejorative connotations which entering care has for many parents.

The court has an important power when making an interim order to direct medical or psychiatric examination or other assessments of the child or to prohibit them.[417] This power is, again, subject to the mature child's right of objection.

Difficult questions have arisen concerning the extent to which the courts may direct local authorities to do certain things at the interim stage. The proper division of responsibility between the courts and local authorities under the Children Act is the general context in which this issue has been debated, and there has been speculation about whether the court's function in public cases is meant to be 'adjudicative' or 'participative'.[418] Sometimes the focus of tension between the courts and children's services has been the use of limited resources. The authority may be resisting a particular course of action because it does not believe the cost is justifiable in the light of its competing priorities. Is it then open to the court to order it to conduct an expensive investigation against its better judgment? If a full care order has already been made the management of the child's care is a matter for the local authority and not for the court. But does this logic hold good for the interim stage? The legal effect of an interim care order is to place the child in care with the legal effects of a care order –

---

[414] D Howe 'Removal of Children at Interim Hearings: Is the Test Now Set Too High?' [2009] Fam Law 320.

[415] A Bainham 'Interim Care Orders: Is the Bar Set Too Low?' [2011] Fam Law 374.

[416] Ibid.

[417] Section 38(6) and (7).

[418] See J Dewar 'The Courts and Local Authority Autonomy' [1995] CFLQ 15.

most notably that the authority acquires parental responsibility.[419] On the other hand, the court still has to be satisfied about whether the conditions are made out for a full care order.

The question of the court's powers at the interim stage fell to be determined by the House of Lords in *Re C (Interim Care Order: Residential Assessment)*.[420] The narrow issue in this case was a matter of the correct technical interpretation of two subsections of the Children Act, but the broader issue was nothing less than the appropriate balance of power between the courts and local authorities at the interim stage.

The provisions in question (so far as they are relevant) were as follows. Section 38(6) of the Children Act provides:

'Where the court makes an interim care order, or interim supervision order, it may give such directions (if any) as it considers appropriate with regard to the medical or psychiatric examination or other assessment of the child ...'

Section 38(7) provides:

'A direction under subsection (6) may be to the effect that there is to be –

(a) no such examination or assessment; or
(b) no such examination or assessment unless the court directs otherwise.'

The facts were that the local authority had obtained an emergency protection order and interim care order in relation to a baby taken to hospital with serious non-accidental injuries. The parents were very young (father 16, mother 17). Social workers, a clinical psychologist and the child's guardian all favoured an in-depth assessment of parents and child together at a residential unit. The local authority disagreed. The initial objection appeared to be on the basis of cost which was projected at between £18,000–£24,000. Later, the Assistant Director of Social Services put it differently to the court, arguing that the

---

[419] Section 31(11).
[420] [1996] 3 WLR 1098. For commentary, see A Bainham 'Authority Over the Authority' [1997] CLJ 267. The issue had come before the courts on a number of previous occasions. See, for example, *Re C (Minors) (Care: Procedure)* (1993) Fam Law 288, which held that a local authority might be directed by the court to arrange for a child to be assessed by a suitably qualified social worker. Without this direction, there might have been substantial delay because of pressure on the authority's resources. The court's power to direct assessment by a *named* social worker has also been confirmed by the Court of Appeal in *Re W (Assessment of Child)* [1998] 2 FLR 130. The court held, however, that this should not be encouraged since the court had no means of forcing an unwilling individual to act. The court should take into account the resources of the local authority employing the social worker and any difficulties there might be regarding its responsibility for and duty to supervise that individual. The better direction would be that an assessment be carried out by a 'suitably qualified social worker'. See also *Re O (Minors) (Medical Examination)* [1993] 1 FLR 860 in which Rattee J held that the court had power on making an interim care order to direct the local authority to have the children medically tested for HIV.

assessment would expose the child to an unacceptable level of risk. The authority instead pressed for a final care order with a view to adoption.

The judge directed the residential assessment but the Court of Appeal reluctantly allowed the authority's appeal following its own earlier decision in *Re M (Interim Care Order: Assessment)*.[421] The House of Lords allowed the parents' appeal and ordered the assessment.

On the proper construction of s 38(6), the Court of Appeal had adopted a narrow interpretation of the court's power to direct an assessment. It had held that the words 'other assessment of the child' had to be construed *ejusdem generis* with 'medical or psychiatric examination'. It also attached importance to the fact that the statute made no reference to the assessment of anyone other than the child (specifically not the parents), and it thought that to direct the child's residence would be to usurp the local authority's powers to regulate where the child was to reside.

The House of Lords preferred a broader, more purposive interpretation to give effect to the underlying intentions of Parliament. The House accepted that a child in interim care was subject to control by the local authority and that the court had no power to interfere except where specified in the legislation. But the subsections in question created exceptions to this principle. Their purpose was to enable the court to obtain the information necessary for its final decision as to whether the threshold was crossed and a care order was required. The court therefore had power to override the authority to the extent that it was necessary to enable it to reach this decision. It was not for the authority to decide what evidence was to go before the court, and the court should not allow the authority by administrative decision to pre-empt its own judicial decision. Moreover, the prohibition of assessments under subs (7) must have been intended to extend to the prohibition of assessment of *parents* as well as children so that, by analogy, subs (6) ought also to cover assessments of parents.

Re C has been followed or distinguished in a number of cases concerned with what may or may not be within the jurisdiction of the court to order at the interim stage. In *Re B (Psychiatric Therapy for Parents)*[422] the Court of Appeal allowed the local authority's appeal against a judge's order that the authority should be required to support and fund a therapeutic programme for parents recommended by a psychotherapist engaged by the children's guardian as an expert. The court distinguished between an *assessment* and something more appropriately described as *treatment* or *therapy*, and between matters which involved the child alone or the parent–child relationship and those which concerned the parents alone. Since what was proposed was only directed to addressing the parents' disabilities rather than assessing anything in relation to the child, the direction fell outside the scope of s 38(6). The projected cost here

---

[421]   [1996] 2 FLR 464.
[422]   [1999] 1 FLR 701.

was £86,360 and the authority would also have to rent a house. The court held that it would be an order of last resort to impose on the authority an obligation to spend over £100,000 on a single child where the authority was resolutely opposed to this course. Similarly, in *Re D (Jurisdiction: Programme of Assessment or Therapy)*[423] the Court of Appeal held that the judge had lacked jurisdiction to impose on the authority a programme of treatment for a drug-dependent mother at a residential unit since its *primary* aim was treatment for the mother and not an assessment of her parenting abilities. The court acknowledged, however, that a programme in which the primary aim was *assessment* could be authorised under s 38(6) notwithstanding that it could include a large element of therapy for a parent.

These decisions reveal a sensitivity to the problems which local authorities face in allocating scarce resources, and there can be little doubt that cost was an important factor in all these cases as well as what may be a difficult distinction to draw in practice between assessment and treatment. The desire on the part of the courts to strike a balance between these competing considerations is apparent in *Re M (Residential Assessment Directions)*.[424] Here Holman J directed the authority to participate in and to fund a residential assessment of the mother and her younger child but limited to eight weeks and at a cost of about £14,000. He accepted that at the end of this period the programme would shift to *treatment* as opposed to assessment and that he had no power to direct this treatment or its funding, even if at the end of the eight-week assessment period there was a good prospect of permanent rehabilitation of mother and child. In *Re B (Interim Care Order: Directions)*[425] the Court of Appeal allowed the appeal of parents against the refusal of the judge to direct a residential placement and assessment of the mother and her newborn baby. The authority had previously removed no less than six children from the parents and also wished to remove the seventh permanently when born. The court held that the proposed placement for mother and baby would clearly involve assessment not only of the mother but also the child and therefore fell within the court's jurisdiction. It represented the best course for management of the case in the context of a series of simultaneous assessments designed to illuminate the court's ultimate conclusion.[426] The House of Lords has now confirmed that interim orders are a legitimate exercise of judicial discretion where the care plan is incomplete.[427]

In *Re G (A Minor) (Interim Care Order: Residential Assessment)*[428] the House of Lords considered again the nature of s 38(6). The House concluded that the purpose of the provision is 'not only to enable the court to obtain the information it needs, but also to enable the court to control the

---

[423] [1999] 2 FLR 632.
[424] [1998] 2 FLR 371.
[425] [2002] 1 FLR 545.
[426] As we have noted, the separation of mother and baby at birth is now inevitably sensitive owing to human rights requirements.
[427] See pp 614 et seq above.
[428] [2006] 1 AC 576.

information-gathering activities of others'.[429] There is nothing in the Act which permits a court to order the provision of services to anyone[430] and it 'cannot be a proper use of the court's powers under s 38(6) to seek to bring about change'.[431] What is directed under s 38(6) must be:[432]

'an examination or assessment of the child, including where appropriate her relationship with her parents, the risk that her parents may present to her, and the ways in which those risks may be avoided or managed, all with a view to enabling the court to make the decisions which it has to make under the Act with the minimum of delay. Any services which are provided for the child and his family must be ancillary to that end. They must not be an end in themselves.'

Discharge of care orders and discharge or variation of supervision orders

The defects in the old law which applied to interim orders also applied to care and supervision orders. Only the child or the local authority could apply for a discharge order. The parents had no right to do so except on behalf of the child[433] and this despite a clear conflict of interest between them. After all, what was usually at stake was the question of parental fitness to resume care of the child and the adequacy of the home environment. Recognising these conflicts of interest and providing for separate representation of the child did not offer a complete solution either, since this raised difficult issues about the parents' relationship with the child's guardian. It was not clear how far parents might pursue a discharge application where the guardian opposed it,[434] and it was held that parents had no right to exercise the child's appeal against refusal to discharge a care order where the guardian refused to do so.[435] The grounds for discharge were vague. The court simply had to be satisfied that it was 'appropriate' and there was a distinct feeling that the courts were more concerned with issues of parental fitness than with the broader question of the child's welfare.[436]

The Children Act increased the category of those persons who are eligible to apply for discharge and made children rather than parents the focus of attention through the application of the welfare principle.

---

[429] Ibid, at [64].
[430] Ibid, at [65].
[431] Ibid, at [67].
[432] Ibid, at [69].
[433] Section 21(2) of the Children and Young Persons Act 1969.
[434] *R v Wandsworth West Juvenile Court ex parte S* [1984] FLR 713.
[435] *A-R v Avon County Council* [1985] Fam 150.
[436] See DHSS *Review of Child Care Law* (1985), at paras 20.11 et seq.

Discharge of care orders

The child himself, the local authority, and anyone with parental responsibility may now apply for discharge of a care order.[437] Variation of care orders (except, indirectly, by substituting supervision orders) is not permitted since this would conflict with the principle that management of the child's case is under the control of the local authority. Parents with parental responsibility[438] and guardians (viz guardians taking office on the death of a parent) thus now have independent rights to apply for discharge.[439] Those who do not have parental responsibility may not apply, but may instead apply for a residence order, the effect of which would be to discharge the care order.[440] As part of its statutory obligations, the local authority must keep under regular review the care of all children looked after by it.[441] An aspect of these reviews is to consider specifically whether an application should be made to discharge a care order.[442]

Discharge applications are now governed by the welfare principle and by the other principles in Part I of the Children Act.[443] It should be emphasised that, in contrast to the position where a care order is *sought*, the discharge of a care order is an undiluted application of the welfare principle, and the threshold criteria have no part to play. Indeed, it is expressly provided that the statutory criteria do not have to be proved again where the court wishes to substitute a

---

[437] Section 39(1). It has been established that a child (in this case a 14-year-old boy) has a statutory right to seek discharge of a care order, and does not require leave as is the case with private law applications for a s 8 order. See *Re A (Care: Discharge Application by Child)* [1995] 1 FLR 599.

[438] Parents *without* parental responsibility should, under the Family Procedure Rules, be joined as parties to applications to discharge care orders but the court also has a discretion to discharge any party from the proceedings. In *Re W (Discharge of Party to Proceedings)* [1997] 1 FLR 128, the father was serving a life sentence for the murder of his step-daughter. The mother, who was seeking to discharge a care order in relation to their two children, successfully applied to have the father discharged from the proceedings to prevent him from having any involvement.

[439] Non-parents by definition are ineligible since they cannot hold parental responsibility while a care order is in operation. They could only derive it from a residence order, and a care order revokes a residence order (s 91(2)). It is, however, provided that a person to whom an exclusion requirement in an interim care order applies, where not qualified to apply for discharge of the interim order itself, may apply for it to be varied or discharged insofar as it imposes the exclusion requirement (s 39(3A)). The court may also, on the application of such person, vary or discharge the order insofar as it confers a power of arrest (s 39(3B)).

[440] Where someone qualifies to apply for either discharge *or* a residence order, the only advantage of the latter would appear to be where there is disunity between two or more eligible applicants such as estranged parents. The residence order would not simply discharge the care order but would also determine the child's residence.

[441] Section 26(2), and Care Planning, Placement and Case Review (England) Regulations 2010 (SI 2010/959).

[442] Section 26(2)(e), and Care Planning, Placement and Case Review (England) Regulations 2010 (SI 2010/959).

[443] This is because Part I applies to proceedings under Part IV of the Children Act. In *Re C (Care: Discharge of Care Order)* [2009] EWCA Civ 955, [2010] 1 FLR 774 the Court of Appeal upheld discharge of the care order because of its ineffectiveness – the child concerned kept absconding back to his mother. The Court observed that in such a case the order's lack of effect needed to be balanced against the potential advantages under the leaving care provisions of preserving the order.

supervision order for the existing care order.[444] Conversely, the substitution of a supervision order with a care order *does* necessitate proof of the threshold criteria, since this involves a higher level of intervention.

The Children Act provisions do not expressly allow a 'phased return' of the child. This was an issue which led to litigation before the Children Act.[445] There has been speculation that, where a phased rehabilitation is considered desirable, the court may be able to sanction this indirectly through its power to control contact decisions,[446] or to attach conditions or give directions when making s 8 orders.[447] It would have been preferable if the legislation had confronted the issue directly, both because it is an important matter and because failure to do so may push applicants into inappropriate discharge applications.[448]

A final matter is that, where an application (the 'previous application') for discharge of a care or supervision order, or for the substitution of a supervision for a care order, has been disposed of, no further application can be made until six months have elapsed.[449] Again, the thinking is that the local authority should be given a reasonable chance of implementing its plans for the child without the constant interference of court applications.

Variation or discharge of supervision orders

A supervision order may be varied or discharged on the application of the child himself, any person with parental responsibility, or the supervisor.[450] It is also provided that a person who is not entitled to apply for discharge may apply for variation where the child is living with him and where the supervision order imposes a requirement which affects that person.[451] This reflects the obligations

---

[444] Section 39(4). In *Manchester City Council v Stanley* [1991] 2 FLR 370 this was done where the local authority had mismanaged the care of two girls committed to its care in wardship proceedings. See also *Re O (Care: Discharge of Care Order)* [1999] 2 FLR 119 where the judge discharged a care order and substituted supervision and residence orders on the basis that the children concerned should not be removed from their mother. The authority's decision to remove them had been shaped by advice based on inaccurate and misleading information. The mother had co-operated with the care plan to the best of her ability, and the major factor in its breakdown had been the authority's failure to provide the agreed support, involving shared care and therapy for the children. There had been a long period with minimal professional input. In these circumstances the care order amounted to an unjustified level of intervention and a supervision order was more appropriate. It might be added, by way of commentary, that the care order in this case would almost certainly not have complied with the requirements of the ECHR.

[445] See, particularly, *Re J (A Minor) (Wardship: Jurisdiction)* [1984] 1 WLR 81. Cf *Re M (A Minor)* [1985] Fam 60.

[446] Under s 34.

[447] Under s 11(7). See NV Lowe and G Douglas *Bromley's Family Law* (9th edn, Butterworths, 1998), at p 580.

[448] This might occur where, for example, parents are unhappy with the pace of a rehabilitative programme.

[449] Section 91(15).

[450] Section 39(2).

[451] Section 39(3).

which the legislation imposes on 'responsible persons'.[452] Applications in relation to the discharge or variation of supervision orders are also governed by the welfare principle.

WARDSHIP AND THE INHERENT JURISDICTION

One of the aims of the Children Act was to render wardship less necessary by incorporating its more valuable features into the statutory code. The flexible powers given to the court in family proceedings, especially those relating to specific issues and prohibited steps, are designed to have this effect. We have already commented on the possible future use of wardship in private cases.[453]

We now turn our attention to the relationship between wardship or the inherent jurisdiction of the High Court and the public law embodied in the Children Act. The effect of the legislation is greatly to reduce the possibilities for recourse to these jurisdictions but, whereas wardship and local authority care are now virtually incompatible, local authorities may still, in limited circumstances, be able to invoke the inherent jurisdiction. What then is the difference between these two jurisdictions? It should be said immediately that wardship is itself one manifestation of the inherent jurisdiction. In essence, the distinction is this: where the court is exercising its wardship jurisdiction, but not where it is otherwise exercising its more general inherent jurisdiction, the court has 'custody' of the child (in the old terminology) or 'parental responsibility' for the child (in the new terminology).[454] As such, the court has all-embracing, automatic and ongoing control of major issues in the child's life which have to be referred back to the court. This is not the case where the court exercises its inherent jurisdiction in relation to children who are *not* wards of court.

Wardship and local authorities

Wardship proceedings are 'family proceedings' (as are all proceedings under the inherent jurisdiction) for the purposes of the Children Act.[455] It therefore follows that there is no reason, in principle, why the court in wardship proceedings should not make a care or supervision order. But it may *not* do so otherwise than in accordance with the statutory criteria in s 31(2). It is the

---

[452] See p 631 above.
[453] Chapter 5 above. There is an extremely informative and detailed discussion of wardship in NV Lowe and G Douglas *Bromley's Family Law* (10th edn, OUP, 2007), ch 16. See also chapter 6 above for the use of wardship in cases of child abduction which is today, at least numerically, by far the most important use of the jurisdiction. For two recent examples of the value of wardship in a small number of difficult domestic cases see *T v S (Wardship)* [2012] 1 FLR 230 and *Re K (Children with Disabilities)* [2012] 2 FLR 745.
[454] Of necessity, the physical 'care and control' of the child has to be delegated to an individual by the court.
[455] Section 8(3).

wider basis for committing wards to care, based on broad welfare considerations, which had proved so popular with social services, which was abolished by the legislation.

This result was achieved in a number of ways. Where a ward is committed to care, properly applying the statutory criteria, the care order will terminate the wardship.[456] The former power under s 7(2) of the Family Law Reform Act 1969, to place a ward of court in care or under supervision, was repealed,[457] as was the court's inherent power to do so.[458] Conversely, no child who is already in care may be made a ward of court.[459] Neither may the inherent jurisdiction be used to require a local authority to accommodate a child,[460] nor to confer on it any power to decide questions concerned with any aspect of parental responsibility for the child.[461] These restrictions apply equally to wardship and other exercises of the inherent jurisdiction. The common reasoning behind the restrictions is that local authorities, the courts and everyone else must operate within, rather than outside, the carefully established statutory parameters for compulsory intervention.

It must be emphasised that these restrictions apply only where the child is *in care*. They do not apply where the child is merely 'accommodated'. In principle, wardship is not incompatible with voluntary accommodation arrangements, but it cannot be used initially to bring about such an arrangement.[462] Whether the courts will be prepared to entertain applications to ward accommodated children is highly questionable. There are perhaps two reasons for this. The first reason is that the *Liverpool* principle had been extended by the courts to voluntary cases,[463] and it is likely that the courts would follow a similar policy under the Children Act. The second reason is that the courts are very unlikely to allow wardship to be used where they think the purpose can be achieved under the statutory code itself. The important consideration here is that s 8 orders, especially specific issue and prohibited steps orders, are available.[464] It is therefore unlikely that the courts will allow wardship to be used by or against local authorities in voluntary accommodation cases. One view is therefore that

---

[456] Section 91(4).

[457] Section 100(1).

[458] Section 100(2)(a).

[459] Section 100(2)(c).

[460] Section 100(2)(b).

[461] Section 100(2)(d).

[462] Section 100(2)(b). Once a child is accommodated, accommodation and wardship, unlike care and wardship, are not incompatible.

[463] *W v Nottinghamshire County Council* [1986] 1 FLR 565.

[464] The restrictions in s 9(1) apply only where the child is in care. For an exceptional case in which wardship was continued and a combination of public (supervision) and private (residence) law orders were made at the final hearing of care proceedings, see *Re M and J (Wardship: Supervision and Residence Orders)* [2003] 2 FLR 541. In this case Charles J held that as a matter of principle the court should utilise the statutory scheme under the Children Act 1989 wherever possible rather than retreat to an exercise of the inherent jurisdiction. However, there could be exceptional cases such as this in which the structure of wardship, with the opportunity to return to court and the combination of orders, would provide the best solution.

wardship as such is redundant in public law cases.[465] This view has, however, been challenged by White, Carr and Lowe[466] who point out that s 8 orders do not cover every situation in which a local authority may be concerned about a child's welfare. They argue that wardship may still be useful to local authorities in those cases in which it is thought to be desirable for the court to exercise a continuing control which is perhaps the hallmark of the wardship jurisdiction. In support they cite cases in which a local authority used wardship to protect a teenage girl from an undesirable relationship with an older man.[467] Other possible uses, they argue, could include protecting 17-year-olds where the normal public law options do not exist, or orphans, and restraining harmful publicity. It should be emphasised again, however, that if the child is in care any such protections could only be obtained either by seeking prohibited steps or specific issue orders[468] or by invoking the inherent jurisdiction, as distinct from wardship, and only then with leave of the court.[469]

The inherent jurisdiction and local authorities

The realisation that the High Court has a more general inherent jurisdiction to protect children outside wardship appears to be a comparatively recent phenomenon. The effect of invoking the inherent jurisdiction is not to trigger the extremely wide-ranging effects of wardship but rather to invite the High Court to determine certain specific issues of difficulty. It is in effect a 'single issues' jurisdiction. Local authorities, but not others, require leave for this purpose. It is, prima facie, inconsistent with their primary responsibilities that local authorities should wish to hand over a decision affecting a child in their care. A limited exception to this principle has been allowed because it was appreciated that there can be some particularly sensitive or complex questions where it may be appropriate for local authorities to seek the assistance of the courts.[470]

---

[465] See chapter 10 for possible alternatives to wardship. For a good example of the flexibility which can now be achieved in public cases under the Children Act, see *C v Solihull Metropolitan Borough Council* [1993] 1 FLR 290, in which Ward J indicated that a conditional residence order could be made alongside the interim supervision order. This could avoid the two extremes of a final supervision order or a care order. The court could, in effect, continue to preserve a degree of control over the child's situation where it thought this necessary, by an imaginative use of its statutory powers. But it should be noted that there are *some* limits to the flexibility of the statutory scheme. Thus it was made plain by Booth J in *Hounslow London Borough Council v A* [1993] 1 FLR 702 that care orders and residence orders are incompatible. Where, therefore, the justices had made a care order they were deemed to have dismissed the father's application for a residence order. The proper course, where there remained some uncertainty about the father's role, would have been for the justices to have made an interim care order and adjourned both applications until the authority had had a chance to assess the father as carer.

[466] R White, P Carr and N Lowe *The Children Act in Practice* (4th edn, Butterworths, 2008).

[467] *Re R (A Minor) (Contempt)* [1994] 2 All ER 144.

[468] See chapter 5 above.

[469] Discussed below.

[470] But the Court of Appeal has held that county courts do *not* have an inherent jurisdiction to grant injunctions to supplement public law orders in favour of local authorities. See *Devon County Council v B* [1997] 1 FLR 591.

The Children Act allows the inherent jurisdiction to be invoked by local authorities with leave.[471] This will be granted where the court is satisfied that:

(a)   the result which the authority wishes to achieve could not be achieved through the making of any other order available to the authority under the legislation; and

(b)   there is reasonable cause to believe that, if the inherent jurisdiction is not exercised, the child is likely to suffer significant harm.[472]

There are, thus, two key elements in obtaining leave. The first ought not to be difficult to satisfy since, where the child is in care, the legislation prevents the courts from making specific issue or prohibited steps orders.[473] The inherent jurisdiction will probably be the only mechanism where the local authority wishes to obtain the court's ruling on a 'single issue'. The second requirement is the familiar 'significant harm' test which applies elsewhere in the legislation.[474] Its suitability here as a pre-condition for leave has been thought by some commentators to be unnecessarily restrictive.[475] On the other hand, it might be argued that it is unduly liberal since it effectively lowers the statutory threshold for State intervention.

What kind of circumstances then might justify leave? It seems to be agreed that the most likely issues will revolve around serious medical procedures,[476] restricting harmful publicity[477] or restraining other harmful interferences with

---

[471]   Section 100(3), and see JM Masson 'Leave, Local Authorities and Welfare' [1992] Fam Law 443. For an illustration of the use of the inherent jurisdiction in this context, see *Nottingham City Council v October Films Ltd* [1999] 2 FLR 347 where the authority sought to restrain the further filming for a Channel 4 documentary of several delinquent children who were either in the care of, or accommodated by, the council. Sir Stephen Brown P, balancing freedom of the press with the need to support caring professionals working with delinquent children, accepted undertakings from the film company in lieu of injunctions restraining its activities which he would otherwise have granted. For commentary, see L Wood 'Freedom of expression and the protection of minors' [2001] CFLQ 470. Cf *Medway Council v BBC* [2002] 1 FLR 104 in which Wilson J refused the authority leave to apply for an injunction restraining the BBC from broadcasting a short interview with a child who had been the subject of an anti-social behaviour order under the Crime and Disorder Act 1998. Significantly, he emphasised that, since the coming into force of the HRA 1998, restrictions on the right to freedom of expression guaranteed by Art 10 of the ECHR had to be based on a strong and pressing social need which did not exist in this case. For a case exploring the child's own rights under Arts 8 and 10 of the ECHR in relation to publicity, see *Re Roddy (A Child) (Identification: Restriction on Publication)* [2004] 2 FLR 949.

[472]   Section 100(4).

[473]   Section 9(1).

[474]   Ie in Parts IV and V. But note that whereas under s 31(2) the court must be satisfied that *the child is suffering, or likely to suffer, significant harm*, under s 100(3) it need only be satisfied that *there is reasonable cause to believe* that if the inherent jurisdiction is not exercised with respect to the child, the child is likely to suffer significant harm.

[475]   See, for example, A Bainham *Children: The New Law* (Family Law, 1990), at para 8.55, and J Eekelaar and R Dingwall 'The Role of the Courts under the Children Bill' (1989) 139 NLJ 217.

[476]   See chapter 8 for examples.

[477]   As in *Re L (A Minor) (Wardship: Freedom of Publication)* [1988] 1 All ER 418. See also *Re Z (A Minor) (Freedom of Publication)* [1996] 1 FLR 191. It appears that leave may not be

the child.[478] There is some doubt as to the precise extent of the court's powers but the view has been expressed judicially that they are co-extensive with the court's powers in wardship.[479] Clearly, these powers extend beyond the court's statutory powers under the Children Act and also exceed the power of a natural parent.[480] In *Re (Wardship: Peremptory Return)*[481] the Court of Appeal held that leave might be granted to an authority to make the child a ward of court where the child had been lawfully taken from the jurisdiction by her mother and this was the only basis upon which (absent abduction) the child could be peremptorily returned.[482]

It is fair to say that in recent years there have been some controversial uses of the inherent jurisdiction by local authorities which have led to suggestions that it is being used in a way which subverts the intentions of Parliament. It is sufficient to note that one area of difficulty has concerned the refusal of consent to treatment or medical procedures by young people who have attained the age of 16 but are below the age of majority. We discussed the leading case of *Re W (A Minor) (Medical Treatment: Court's Jurisdiction)*[483] in chapter 8. This case was followed by the decision of Wall J in *Re C (Detention: Medical Treatment)*,[484] another case involving a 16-year-old suffering from anorexia nervosa who was refusing all treatment. Here, it was held that the inherent jurisdiction might be exercised at the behest of the local authority not merely to authorise treatment but also to restrain the young patient in a secure unit.[485]

Cases like this raise serious questions about the autonomy aspect of children's rights[486] but they also provoke consideration of the limits of State paternalism under the legislation. Superficially it might appear that intervention via the inherent jurisdiction is, because of the requirement of leave, just as constrained by the threshold test of 'significant harm' to the child as is intervention by means of a care or supervision order. Yet this is not really the case and the decision of the House of Lords in *Re H and R (Child Sexual Abuse: Standard of Proof)*[487] makes this clear. In that case, the House was at pains to emphasise the difference between proof of the statutory threshold conditions and the kind

---

required where the court can exercise its powers to grant injunctions under the Senior Courts Act 1981, s 37. See *Re P (Care Orders: Injunctive Relief)* [2000] 2 FLR 385. In that case Charles J granted the local authority injunctions ancillary to a care order requiring the parents to allow the child to attend a sixth-form college without interference and permitting the authority to monitor the family.

[478] As in *Re JT (A Minor) (Wardship: Committal to Care)* [1986] 2 FLR 107.

[479] *Re W (A Minor) (Medical Treatment: Court's Jurisdiction)* [1993] Fam 64.

[480] A point made plain in relation to wardship in *Re R (A Minor) (Wardship: Consent to Treatment)* [1992] Fam 11, discussed in chapter 8 above.

[481] [2010] EWCA Civ 465.

[482] On the facts the Court held that the child's welfare did not demand her peremptory return.

[483] [1993] Fam 64. See also *A Metropolitan Borough Council v DB* [1997] 1 FLR 767.

[484] [1997] 2 FLR 180.

[485] He also held that the secure unit in this case did not amount to 'secure accommodation' under s 25 of the Children Act so as to require an application for a 'secure accommodation order' under that section.

[486] See chapters 7 and 8 above.

[487] [1996] 1 FLR 80 (discussed above).

of reasonable suspicions of harm which would be sufficient to found emergency protection orders or interim care orders. When we turn to s 100(4), which governs the criteria for granting leave to invoke the inherent jurisdiction, we find that it is *not* satisfaction of the threshold criteria which is required but *reasonable cause to believe* that the child would otherwise be likely to suffer significant harm. It might be replied that where we are concerned only with a 'single issue' and not with removal of the child from the family, a less stringent test for intervention is justified. But it is also legitimate to reflect on whether the State, through the High Court, is effectively arrogating to itself a wider power of compulsory intervention than that envisaged when the public law affecting children was reformed.

Chapter 13

PERMANENCE FOR CHILDREN: ADOPTION AND SPECIAL GUARDIANSHIP

INTRODUCTION

Adoption in English law is distinguishable from all other forms of social parenthood. It is with a limited legal exception the only legal mechanism for terminating the legal status of parent and the parental responsibility which goes with it.[1] Adoption is in effect a 'legal transplant' involving the total replacement of one family with a new substitute family. The adoptive parents step into the shoes of the birth parents. Unlike the residence order under the Children Act 1989 (now the primary order giving parental responsibility to social parents) adoption is permanent and, with rare exceptions, irrevocable. Although its general effect may easily be described, the purposes of adoption are far from easy to state. First, it is clear that adoption has served different needs at different times[2] and these have differed markedly from society to society. Thus, for example, Duncan[3] notes that in Roman law and in the Code Napoleon of 1804, the primary purpose of adoption was to ensure the continuation of the family line. In the Hindu tradition, adoption was mandated by the need for a child to perform certain spiritual tasks for the parent. When adoption was first introduced in England,[4] it served the dual purpose of offering a discreet way out of the stigma and economic hardship faced by unmarried mothers and meeting the needs of childless couples. Historically, it can be said that the emphasis in adoption was on satisfying adult needs of one kind or another. The major shift in thinking which has occurred in modern adoption law is that adoption is now supposed to be a 'child-centred' process, a means of finding a family for a child and not a child for a family.[5] The circumstances in which adoption is used also differ widely and there were major

---

[1] The other mechanism for achieving this in cases of assisted reproduction is s 54 of the Human Fertilisation and Embryology Act 2008 or its predecessor s 30 of the Human Fertilisation and Embryology Act 1990.

[2] For historical background to adoption law, see S Cretney *Family Law in the Twentieth Century – A History* (Oxford University Press, 2003), ch 17; NV Lowe 'English Adoption Law: Past, Present and Future' in S Katz, J Eekelaar, and M Maclean (eds) *Cross-Currents: Family Law and Policy in the US and England* (Oxford, Oxford University Press, 2000), ch 14.

[3] W Duncan 'Regulating Intercountry Adoption – an International Perspective' in A Bainham, DS Pearl and R Pickford (eds) *Frontiers of Family Law* (2nd edn, John Wiley and Sons, 1995), ch 3.

[4] By the Adoption of Children Act 1926.

[5] Nonetheless, there remains considerable anxiety, especially in the context of intercountry

changes in the role and incidence of adoption in the last few decades of the twentieth century.[6] Lowe[7] notes that there was a sharp increase in the use of adoption in England between 1927 and 1968 and then a dramatic decline in the last quarter of the twentieth century. Adoption figures reached a peak of 25,000 per year in 1968 but by 1990 had declined to 10,000 and by 1998 to under 5,000. Lowe[8] goes on to distinguish between three sorts of adoption cases as follows.

(1) *Adoption of babies*, viz children under the age of 12 months.[9] In 1968 there were over 12,000 such adoptions representing 51 per cent of the total. By 1998 there were just 195, or 4 per cent of the total. In other words there had been by the 1990s a virtual disappearance of baby adoption in England. Only 60 babies were adopted in 2012.[10] The factors contributing to this dramatic decline include the greater effectiveness and availability of contraception, the increase in abortion, the much greater incidence and acceptability of birth outside marriage and the explosion in unmarried cohabitation and births into that situation. These demographic and social changes also largely account for the high demand in the West for babies from the under-developed world and Eastern Europe.

(2) *Step-parent adoption.* There was a sharp increase in the adoption of children by their step-parents between 1951 and 1968. This reflected in large measure the growth in the number of step-parents following the liberalisation of divorce and the consequential increase in remarriage. In 1968 there were about 4,500 step-parent adoptions. By 1998 this had almost halved to about 2,300. The Houghton Report in 1972 officially discouraged step-parent adoption because of its effect of terminating the legal relationship between the now-divorced parent, usually the father, and the child. The Children Act 1975, later consolidated in the Adoption Act 1976, introduced directives that the courts should give specific consideration to alternative solutions in these cases. Step-parent adoptions still account for a substantial proportion of all adoptions although it remains to be seen whether the provision for step-parents to acquire parental responsibility by agreement or court order will lead to a decline in the use of adoption by step-parents.

---

adoption, that the process can still be used to prioritise adult needs without proper regard for the interests of the children involved and their birth families.

[6] For an account, see J Lewis 'Adoption: The Nature of Policy Shifts in England and Wales, 1972–2002' (2004) 18(2) *International Journal of Law, Policy and the Family* 235.

[7] NV Lowe 'English Adoption Law: Past, Present and Future' in S Katz, J Eekelaar and M Maclean (eds) *Cross Currents: Family Law and Policy in the US and England* (Oxford University Press, 2000), ch 14.

[8] Ibid, at pp 316–323.

[9] Success in such adoptions is quite usual: see J Castle, C Beckett, and C Groothues 'Infant Adoption in England: A Longitudinal Account of Social and Cognitive Progress' (2000) 24 *Adoption and Fostering* 26.

[10] Department for Education *An Action Plan for Adoption: Tackling Delay* (March 2012), Ministerial foreword.

(3) *Public law adoption.* The proportion of adoptions which are public law adoptions is increasing. While in 1968 these represented only 8.7 per cent of the total, they now account for over one-third of all adoptions, although the numbers of children adopted from care has been going down in recent years.[11]

As Nigel Lowe[12] has argued, the adoption of children from state care is very different from the one-off gift/donation model of baby adoption. It might rather be characterised as a contract/services model in which the adopters are providing a service to the local authority in circumstances which may require considerable post-adoption support to adopters in their role.

In the light of the shifting circumstances which may lead to adoption, it has become increasingly evident that a single model of adoption cannot be appropriate in all cases. In particular, there has been a growing appreciation that the traditional 'exclusivity' and secrecy of the adoption process must give way to a more flexible approach which admits of greater 'openness' and *inclusive* relationships. Increasingly, especially since implementation of the Human Rights Act 1998, account has had to be taken of human rights obligations, which again militate towards a more inclusive approach. The central question in the context of human rights will be whether it can be convincingly demonstrated that adoption can offer the child something which cannot be offered by the various alternative legal mechanisms at the court's disposal.[13] It was against all of this changing background that the current law of adoption was enacted in the Adoption and Children Act 2002.[14]

THE ADOPTION AND CHILDREN ACT 2002: BACKGROUND

The law on adoption is to be found in the Adoption and Children Act 2002,[15] which constituted a major reform of the law. It was the culmination of a long

---

11 Just 3,050 children found new homes through adoption in 2011 – the lowest number since 2001: see Department for Education, *An Action Plan for Adoption: Tackling Delay* (March 2012), at para 5.

12 N Lowe 'The Changing Face of Adoption – The Gift/Donation Model versus the Contract/Services Model' [1997] CFLQ 371.

13 See, for example, C Dance and A Rushton 'Predictors of Outcome for Unrelated Adoptive Placements made During Middle Childhood' (2005) 10 *Child and Family Social Work* 269. Disruptions for adolescents are even higher: see, for example, D Howe, D Shemmings, and J Feast 'Age at Placement and Adult Adopted People's Experience of Being Adopted' (2001) 6 *Child and Family Social Work* 337.

14 The Act is supplemented by statutory guidance: see Department for Education *Statutory Guidance on Adoption For local authorities, voluntary adoption agencies and adoption support agencies* (July 2013).

15 On the Act generally see C Bridge and H Swindells QC *Adoption: The Modern Law* (Family Law, 2003). For other detailed accounts of the law, see JM Masson, R Bailey-Harris and RJ Probert *Cretney's Principles of Family Law* (8th edn, Sweet and Maxwell, 2008) ch 22; S Gilmore and L Glennon *Hayes and Williams' Family Law* (3rd edn, Oxford University Press, 2012), ch 11. For brief overviews, see D Cullen 'The Adoption and Children Act 2002' [2003]

process of review beginning in the early 1990s.[16] When the Children Act 1989 reformed most of the private and public law affecting children, adoption was not included and continued to be governed by its own separate legislation, then the Adoption Act 1976.[17] A major interdepartmental *Review of Adoption Law* (hereafter the 'Adoption Review') was published in 1992. This was followed by a White Paper in 1993 and a subsequent consultative document, which incorporated a draft Adoption Bill, was presented in March 1996. Some aspects of this Bill proved controversial and it failed to be introduced into Parliament in the latter days of the Government at the time.

Following a change of Government, it did not look as if adoption reform was one of the Government's priorities but then, in February 2000, the Prime Minister at the time, Tony Blair, announced that he would personally lead a thorough review of adoption policy. The Performance and Innovation Unit of the Cabinet was commissioned and reported in July 2000.[18] This was quickly followed by a White Paper, *Adoption: A New Approach*, which was published in December of that year.[19]

The content of the Adoption and Children Act 2002 is therefore the result of two major influences – the Review of the 1990s and the policy initiatives which have resulted from the Prime Ministerial Review and which were embodied in the White Paper. It is fair to say also that certain key provisions in the Act were significantly affected by political pressures during the parliamentary passage of the Bill, none more so than the provisions governing those who are entitled to

---

Fam Law 235 and S Mahmood 'Adoption and Children Act 2002: Where Are We So Far?' [2004] Fam Law 449. For some commentaries on the background to the 2002 Act, see C Bridge 'Adoption Law: A Balance of Interests' in J Herring (ed) *Family Law: Issues, Debates, Policy* (Willan Publishing, 2001); C Barton 'Adoption: The Prime Minister's Review' [2000] Fam Law 731 'Adoption Strategy' [2001] Fam Law 89 and 'Adoption and Children Bill – Don't let them out of your sight' [2001] Fam Law 431; and S Harris-Short 'The Adoption and Children Bill – A Fast Track to Failure?' [2001] CFLQ 405. For a critique of the political influences on the reforms and of the central policy to increase the use of adoption for children in long-term substitute care, see J Eekelaar 'Contact and the Adoption Reform' in A Bainham, B Lindley, M Richards and L Trinder (eds) *Children and Their Families: Contact, Rights and Welfare* (Hart Publishing, 2003), and I Dey 'Adapting Adoption: A Case of Closet Politics?' (2005) 19(3) *International Journal of Law, Policy and the Family* 289. For an assessment of the Act's impact on the scheme of the Children Act 1989, see J Masson 'The Impact of the Adoption and Children Act 2002, Part I – Parental Responsibility' [2003] Fam Law 580 and 'Part II – The Provision of Services for Children and Families' [2003] Fam Law 644.

[16] The principal reports and White Papers were Department of Health and Welsh Office, Report to Ministers of the Interdepartmental Working Group *Review of Adoption Law* (1992); Department of Health and Welsh Office, Home Office, Lord Chancellor's Department *Adoption: The Future* (1993) (Cm 2288); Department of Health and Welsh Office *Adoption: A Service for Children, Draft Bill* (1996); and Department of Health *Adoption Now: Messages from Research* (1999).

[17] The law under the Adoption Act 1976 is described in chapter 7 of the second edition of this work and is referred to here only to the extent that it is necessary for an understanding of the current law.

[18] Performance and Innovation Unit *Prime Minister's Review: Adoption: Issued for Consultation* (Cabinet Office, July 2000).

[19] Department of Health *Adoption: A New Approach: A White Paper* (2000) (Cm 5017).

adopt.[20] The influence of the HRA 1998 and the ECHR must also be taken into account in attempting to understand the legislation, and the Act's compatibility with the Convention is something which has exercised the courts.

Perhaps the salient feature of the reforms which is most attributable to the earlier Adoption Review is the attempt to harmonise the principles of adoption law with those of the Children Act 1989. This was, in a sense, a task left over from the earlier wholesale reform of children law in 1989. Accordingly, we discuss below the new central principles which govern adoption law. While, however, these are derived largely from the Children Act 1989 it should be borne in mind that they are tailored in some cases to the special case of adoption. Neither should it be thought that the transplanting of the Children Act principles into the new adoption law is uncontroversial. The application of the welfare principle to the question of dispensing with consent to adoption is especially problematic and gives rise to very real tensions with human rights obligations.[21]

The White Paper had a very specific agenda – one which focused especially on one type of adoption, public law adoption, or the adoption of children being looked after by local authorities. The Government saw it as the clear responsibility of the State to provide permanent alternative homes for children who were unable to return to their birth parents and that adoption was the most important vehicle for this.[22] Although the White Paper and the Act visualised a role for alternative options for permanence, such as long-term fostering and the new status of special guardianship,[23] adoption received the emphasis, with the Government's stated intention of increasing significantly the number of adoptions of looked after children.[24]

There are two fundamental criticisms which can be made of this approach. The first is that adoption is *only one* of the various mechanisms for providing for children who are looked after on a long-term basis by local authorities, and there is a lack of clear empirical evidence demonstrating that children who are adopted in such circumstances fare better than those who are not adopted.[25] Other European countries resort to adoption much less frequently in such cases and have a stronger commitment of resources to family support and foster care.

---

[20]   Another influence was undoubtedly the report of the Waterhouse Inquiry into the abuse of children in children's homes in North Wales. See *Lost in Care – Report of the Tribunal of Inquiry into the Abuse of Children in the Former County Council Areas of Gwynedd and Clwyd since 1974* (2000).

[21]   We have already seen that the application of the welfare principle generally does not sit easily with the new human rights obligations. See chapter 2 above.

[22]   At para 1.13 of the White Paper it is stated that 'the government believes that more can and should be done to promote the wider use of adoption for looked after children who cannot return to their birth parents'.

[23]   See White Paper, ch 5.

[24]   The Government's stated intention was to invest £66.5 million in the improvement of adoption services over a three-year period following enactment of the 2002 Act and if possible to achieve a 50 per cent increase in adoptions of looked-after children.

[25]   For a review of the evidence see *Adoption Now: Messages From Research* (above) and Eekelaar (above).

Secondly, and more importantly, adoption represents the most drastic of all interferences with family life under Art 8 of the ECHR and, as such, requires a much stronger justification. As we have seen, the emphasis of the Convention in relation to children and families in difficulty is on family support services, temporary accommodation away from home where necessary and strong duties to attempt to reunify the child with the family. Where the child *does* need to be away from home permanently, there remain strong human rights obligations to maintain an ongoing link between the child and the birth family. This suggests, contrary to the emphasis in the White Paper, that those measures which will preserve the legal relationship and contact between the child and the birth family should usually be the *preferred* course of action. Adoption should be seen as a *last resort*, rather than the option of choice, after all other attempts to meet the needs of the child have failed. It is only in those circumstances that it can be said with confidence that adoption will pass the test of being 'necessary' and 'proportionate' as required by the Convention.

Those provisions in the legislation which are therefore designed to facilitate or speed up adoption need to be examined with a critical eye for compliance with the ECHR. This is an issue which will arise both at the placement stage and when the court has to consider whether to make an adoption order in the face of an objecting parent. Even in those cases in which adoption does ultimately prove to be in the best interests of the child, there are still important questions relating to the child's identity rights which need to be accommodated. This may imply a more 'open' system of adoption than has traditionally been the case in England and ongoing contact of some sort with the birth family.

This chapter attempts to set out the essential features of adoption law and to identify the core issues. We begin with a discussion of the central principles under the Adoption and Children Act 2002.[26]

CENTRAL PRINCIPLES OF ADOPTION LAW

The central principles of the legislation are set out in s 1 of the Adoption and Children Act 2002 and are reminiscent of those in s 1 of the Children Act 1989.[27] They apply 'whenever a court or adoption agency is coming to a decision relating to the adoption of a child'[28] and as such will apply, for example, at both the placement stage and when the court is considering whether or not to make an adoption order.

---

[26] For an account of the law on the controversial topic of international adoption, see R Cabeza, A Bhutta and J Braier *International Adoption* (Family Law, 2012), and see also K O'Halloran *The Politics of Adoption: International Perspectives on Law, Policy and Practice* (2nd edn, Vienna, Springer, 2009).

[27] As to which see chapter 2 above.

[28] Section 1(1). (References within this chapter are to the Adoption and Children Act 2002 unless otherwise stated.)

The welfare principle

Section 1(2) provides that 'the paramount consideration of the court or adoption agency must be the child's welfare, throughout his life'. This brings adoption law into line with both the Children Act 1989 and the UNCRC, Art 21 of which requires States parties that 'recognise and/or permit the system of adoption to ensure that the best interests of the child shall be the paramount consideration'. This is contrary, however, to a long tradition in English adoption law which acknowledged the child's welfare to be the 'first' but not 'paramount' consideration for courts and adoption agencies.[29]

There was some disagreement under the old law about whether these apparently different weightings of the child's welfare in the adoption process made any practical difference. The purpose of the 'first consideration' criterion was, however, reasonably clear. It was that the total severance of the parent–child relationship ought not to occur without a thorough examination of the *parent's* claims and interests as well as those of the child. The welfare principle, as interpreted by the English courts, subsumes any such parental claims into the overall inquiry into the child's welfare.[30] On the contrary, the 'first but not paramount' formulation meant that while the child's welfare was the single most important consideration, it could conceivably be outweighed, at least in theory, by other factors.

In practice, the only context in which this distinction was a serious issue was where the court was considering whether to dispense with a parent's consent to adoption. The Adoption Review recommended that the welfare principle should be extended to adoption law generally to bring it in line with other family proceedings, but this was subject to the important qualification that the child's welfare ought *not* to be paramount in determining this one crucial issue of whether or not adoption should be granted against a parent's wishes. At the time it was put this way:[31]

> 'We are concerned that at present insufficient weight is given to a parent's lack of agreement. Where it is decided that adoption is in a child's interests, there is in practice very little room left for the court to decide to give any weight to parental views. This cannot be regarded as satisfactory in relation to an order which irrevocably terminates a parent's legal relationship with his or her child.'

The test favoured by the Adoption Review was that the court should be 'satisfied that the advantages to a child of becoming part of a new family and having a new legal status are so significantly greater than the advantages to the child of any alternative option as to justify overriding the wishes of a parent or guardian'.[32]

---

[29] Section 6 of the Adoption Act 1976.
[30] This is the effect of Lord MacDermott's long-accepted interpretation of the welfare principle in *J v C* [1970] AC 668 discussed in chapter 2 above.
[31] Adoption Review, at para 12.1.
[32] Ibid, at para 12.6.

This test, if enacted, would have captured the essence of what is required under the ECHR in that it would have required a clear demonstration that adoption was *necessary* and *proportionate* and that the child's best interests could not be served by some alternative form of protection which keeps alive the child's legal links with the birth family. It is, however, the undiluted welfare test which has been favoured by Parliament to apply throughout adoption law and which has also been expressly extended to the question of dispensing with parental consent, whether at the placement stage or at the stage when the court is considering whether to make an adoption order. We consider this all-important issue further below.

It should also be noted that the new test refers to the child's welfare 'throughout his life'. This enables the court or adoption agency to have regard to the benefits of adoption which may extend to the child in adulthood and this is also reflected in the statutory checklist of factors which we discuss below. The essential point is that since adoption entails membership of a new family, the new family links which it generates will not be broken on the attainment of majority. The child will remain a member of the adoptive family for his or her life. All of us remain 'children' of our parents though no longer minors but adults.

The statutory checklist of factors

Section 1(4) contains a statutory checklist of factors to which the court or adoption agency must have regard. Most of these reflect the checklist in s 1 of the Children Act[33] but there are important modifications and additions which adapt the list of factors to the special circumstances of adoption. The list is as follows:

'(a) the child's ascertainable wishes and feelings regarding the decision (considered in the light of the child's age and understanding);

(b) the child's particular needs;

(c) the likely effect on the child (throughout his life) of having ceased to be a member of the original family and become an adopted person;

(d) the child's age, sex, background and any of the child's characteristics which the court or agency considers relevant;

(e) any harm (within the meaning of the Children Act 1989) which the child has suffered or is at risk of suffering;

(f) the relationship which the child has with relatives, and with any other person in relation to whom the court or agency considers the relationship to be relevant, including:

---

[33] Children Act 1989, s 1(3), as to which see chapters 2 and 5 above.

(i) the likelihood of any such relationship continuing and the value to the child of its doing so;

(ii) the ability and willingness of any of the child's relatives, or of any such person, to provide the child with a secure environment in which the child can develop, and otherwise to meet the child's needs;

(iii) the wishes and feelings of any of the child's relatives, or of any such person, regarding the child.'

It should be noted that, unlike the position in many other jurisdictions, there is no requirement as to the *consent* to adoption of a child who has attained a particular age, such as 12.[34] The Adoption and Children Act 2002 merely gives to children themselves qualified autonomy to the extent that their wishes are to be taken into account, commensurate with their age and understanding. This formula is, of course, consistent with the general approach of the Children Act 1989 but, again in the special context of adoption, it is open to doubt whether it ought to be possible to make such an order against the express wishes of, for example, a teenager. Factors (c) and (f) are tailored to adoption and require the court or adoption agency to apply their minds to the specific question of what the child may *lose*, as well as what the child may *gain*, from moving, legally, from one family to another. They must consider the value of preserving the child's existing relationships and whether such relationships would be likely to continue if adoption were granted. Specific thought must be given to the resources of the wider family in meeting the child's needs and to the wishes of relatives. In some jurisdictions, notably New Zealand, considerable weight is given to the question of the possibility of the child being looked after by the wider family before adoption by strangers is countenanced.

As in the case of the Children Act checklist, the enumerated factors are not exhaustive. The court or agency must have regard to them 'among others'. Failure to take proper account of a factor in the checklist would, however, constitute a ground of appeal. The application of the welfare principle does mean that nothing is in principle excluded from consideration. None of the factors specifically mentioned is weighted more strongly than any other, so that the points made earlier about the wide discretion which this leaves are as valid here as they are in relation to Children Act jurisdictions.

Culture and religion

It is expressly provided in s 1(5) that 'in placing the child for adoption, the adoption agency must give due consideration to the child's religious persuasion, racial origin and cultural and religious background'. This is again consistent with the Children Act and the duty placed on local authorities, under s 22(5) of that Act, in relation to children looked after by them, which is in exactly similar terms. It is especially important in the context of adoption, indeed crucial where international adoption is contemplated, since the risk to the child of the loss of cultural, linguistic and religious background is all too obvious where the

---

[34] The position in Scotland under the Age of Legal Capacity (Scotland) Act 1991, s 2(3).

child moves from one family to another permanently. The threat to the child's identity rights, protected by Arts 7 and 8 of the UNCRC, is palpable.

In relation to domestic adoptions, however, following recommendations in the Narey report, the Children and Families Bill 2013[35] will controversially repeal this requirement in the legislation to give due consideration to ethnicity. The reasoning is that some children have languished too long in care while too much effort has been made to find an ethnically appropriate match.

The no delay principle

Section 1(3) enshrines the no delay principle of the Children Act. It is provided that 'the court or adoption agency must at all times bear in mind that, in general, any delay in coming to a decision is likely to prejudice the child's welfare'.

The White Paper was especially concerned about what were seen as delays and inconsistencies in the practice of local authorities and courts at all stages of the adoption process. The Government's conclusion was that for too many children the operation of the system as it was did not provide a chance for a long-term family life.[36] Its proposed solution has a number of aspects to it. First, performance targets would be set for local authorities designed to increase sharply the number of adoptions in relation to children looked after by them. This would be supported by central government investment of £66.5 million over three years to secure sustained improvement in adoption services. It was said that those councils which consistently failed to provide a reasonable level of service on adoption would risk a range of sanctions.[37] Secondly, the Act established a new Adoption and Children Act Register which contains details of children suitable for adoption and of approved prospective adopters.[38] The intention is to enable suitable 'matches' to be made on a national level and thus overcome the problems which can arise where such a match cannot be made within a reasonable time at the local level. Thirdly, National Adoption Standards[39] were established, the purpose of which was set out in the White Paper in the following terms:[40]

> 'The National Standards set out what children, prospective adopters, adoptive parents, and birth families can expect from the adoption process, and the responsibilities of adoption agencies and councils, so that all parties receive a fair and consistent service wherever they live. They are underpinned by a set of values,

---

[35] Clause 2.

[36] White Paper, at paras 1.15 et seq.

[37] Ibid, at paras 7.21–7.23.

[38] Section 125. The Register should not be confused with the Adopted Children Register or with the Adoption Contact Register, both discussed below. It accounts for around 12 per cent of matches each year: see Department for Education *An Action Plan for Adoption: Tackling Delay* (March 2012), at para 65.

[39] See now, Department of Education *Adoption: National Minimum Standards* (March 2011), issued by the Secretary of State under ss 23 and 49 of the Care Standards Act 2000.

[40] White Paper, at para 4.5.

which stress the importance to each child of having a permanent family, where they are safe. They put the child's needs at the centre of the adoption process.'

A central feature of the standards is that they include 'timescales within which decisions for most children should be reached and action taken, to ensure that children are not kept waiting for a family'.[41] The reforms resulted in an initial upsurge in adoptions of children in care, but over time concerns about delay were not resolved.

In recent years, the Government has again focused on tackling delay in the adoption process. The case for radical reform of the adoption system was put back on the agenda by Martin Narey who, as Ministerial Advisor on Adoption, has been responsible for driving through reforms. The Government's concern is that there are looked after children for whom adoption is the best option for alternative care but that they are not being adopted or adopted in timely fashion, which has implications for child well-being.[42] The Government issued revised statutory guidance, which emphasises the need to avoid delay, and in March 2012 published *An Action Plan for Adoption: Tackling Delay*. This identified that the average time between a child entering care and moving in with their adoptive family is one year and nine months.[43] The *Action Plan* commented that 'all but a small handful of local authorities fail on average to meet the timescales that statutory guidance sets out for the different parts of the assessment process' with 'huge variation between local authorities' and many 'fall short by a significant margin, with the very slowest local authorities taking an average of nearly three years for a child to go from entering care to being placed for adoption'.[44] The *Action Plan* indicated several measures by which the Government intends to tackle the perceived delay. First it was recognised that there was a need to recruit a greater number of prospective adopters[45] and it was recommended that there be a 'national Gateway to adoption' as a consistent source of advice and information for those thinking about adoption. This, operating as *First4Adoption*, was launched in April 2013 as a first point of contact for anyone interested in adoption.[46] The *Action Plan* also suggested that the adopter assessment process be speeded up, including a fast track process for those who have adopted before or who are foster carers wishing to adopt a child in their care. These recommendations were implemented by regulations. The Government also indicated that it would 'require swifter use of the national Adoption Register in order to find the right adopters for a child wherever they might live'; 'encourage all local authorities

---

[41]   Ibid, at para 4.6.
[42]   On the implications of delay, see: J Selwyn, W Sturgess, D Quinton and C Baxter *Costs and outcomes of non-infant adoptions* (British Association for Adoption and Fostering, 2006) and H Ward, R Brown and D Westlake *Safeguarding Babies and Very Young Children from Abuse and Neglect* (Jessica Kingsley Publishers. 2012).
[43]   Department for Education *An Action Plan for Adoption: Tackling Delay* (March 2012), at para 9.
[44]   Ibid, at para 96.
[45]   Ibid, at para 17.
[46]   See also the *Adoption Passport*, setting out in one place the help and support that is available to adopters.

to seek to place children with their potential adopters in anticipation of the court's placement order'; and 'legislate to reduce the number of adoptions delayed in order to achieve a perfect or near ethnic match between adoptive parents and the adoptive child'.[47] Finally, the Government intends to measure improvements in tackling delay through the introduction of performance score cards. These will measure the average time it takes for a child who goes on to be adopted from entering care to moving in with his or her adoptive family; identify the proportion of children who wait longer for adoption than they should; and the speed and effectiveness of family-finding. It will measure the average time it takes for a local authority to match a child to an adoptive family once the court has formally decided that adoption is the best option. The Government will set a performance threshold (minimal expectations) for the child's journey overall. This has initially been set at twenty one months but, within four years, it is set to go down to fourteen months. Another threshold, for the family finding indicator, will be seven months initially, moving down to four months within four years.

The avoidance of delay in the adoption process, once a decision has been taken to plan for adoption, should not be confused, however, with the process leading up to that decision. It should be remembered that the overwhelming majority of looked after children return home within a short time and that, for those who do not, there are other alternatives to adoption which will need to be carefully explored at the periodic reviews. Indeed, any principle which led to adoption being viewed as the *first* option would be contrary to the ECHR and it is precisely this rush to adoption which has led to multiple violations of the human rights of parents and children in the context of international adoption. Delay, in the sense of a measured consideration of the proportionate response to the child's needs, is therefore not only appropriate but mandated by human rights obligations.

The no order principle

Section 1(6) of the Act enacts the so-called 'no order principle'. As in the Children Act, it provides that 'the court must not make any order under this Act unless it considers that making the order would be better for the child than not doing so'. We considered the interpretation of the principle in the context of the Children Act[48] and there is little to add here except to make the rather obvious point that, given the extreme effect of a placement order or adoption order, the need to demonstrate conclusively that such orders are better for the child than not making them is that much stronger. Along with the requirement

---

[47] Having regard to research evidence: see J Selwyn et al *Pathways to Permanence for Black, Asian and Mixed Ethnicity Children* (British Association for Adoption and Fostering, 2010); Evan B. Donaldson Institute, *Finding Families for African American Children* (2009) www. adoptionistitute.org; D Quinton *Matching In Adoptions From Care: A Conceptual And Research Review* (British Association for Adoption and Fostering, 2012).
[48] See chapter 2 above.

to have regard to the range of powers at the court's disposal, this principle really requires that the least intrusive action which is consistent with the best interests of the child should be taken.

The range of powers

Section 1(6) also requires the court or adoption agency to 'consider the whole range of powers available to it in the child's case (whether under this Act or the Children Act 1989)'. Thus, in addition to considering whether or not to make *any* order in accordance with the no order principle, courts and adoption agencies must have express regard to *which* powers or *which* orders are the most appropriate in the individual case. Specifically this requires the court to have regard to the whole range of alternatives to adoption including, especially, the making of a residence order, an order for special guardianship or, in the case of step-parent applications, a parental responsibility order. We consider below some of the reported cases, before and after implementation of the HRA 1998, in which the courts have concluded that some 'lesser' form of order than adoption is the right course of action.

LEGAL CONTROL OF ADOPTION SERVICES AND PLACEMENTS

If adoption is viewed as a process of providing children with the love and security of a family, it follows that great care needs to be taken to ensure the suitability of placements. The process of selection and matching of children with prospective adopters is therefore tightly controlled. This is achieved partly by prohibiting private placements and private arrangements relating to adoption and partly by trying to ensure that a comprehensive adoption service is provided by properly approved adoption agencies.

Prohibition of private adoption

The Act contains a cluster of provisions which prohibit the various kinds of private activities that might occur in connection with the adoption of children.[49] It is a criminal offence for someone other than an adoption agency to be involved in arrangements relating to adoption.[50] This extends to asking a person other than an adoption agency to provide a child, or prospective adopters for a child, offering to find a child for adoption or receiving or handing over a child with a view to adoption. Taking part in negotiations relating to any of those things is also prohibited.[51] The Act prohibits the preparation of reports about the suitability of a child for adoption or of a person to adopt a child or about the adoption or placement of a child, by those

---

[49]   See particularly ss 92–97 and ss 123 and 124.
[50]   Section 92.
[51]   Section 92(2).

unauthorised to do so under the legislation.[52] The restrictions on advertisements of children for adoption other than those placed by adoption agencies, which were also a feature of the previous law, have been extended by making it explicit that the prohibitions extend to publishing or distributing information to the public by electronic means including, specifically, the internet.[53]

There are offences relating to any form of financial reward in connection with the adoption of children. In essence, it is an offence to give or receive any payment in consideration of the adoption of a child, or to obtain a consent to adoption or to remove a child who is a Commonwealth citizen or habitually resident in the UK to a place outside the British Isles for the purposes of adoption.[54] This latter prohibition is complemented by an offence of bringing into the UK children habitually resident overseas for the purposes of adoption or children adopted by British residents overseas other than in accordance with the Conventions to which the UK is party.[55] There are certain 'excepted payments' which are allowable and which amount to the reimbursement of 'reasonable expenses' incurred by a registered adoption society, such as legal or medical expenses associated with the making of applications for placement or adoption orders.[56] The experience with international adoption and with surrogacy arrangements reveals all too clearly the problematic nature of the concept of 'reasonable expenses' which can be distorted and exceeded in a way that disguises an element of profit.

The provisions raise the difficult problem of how to deal with breaches of these prohibitions in a way which is consistent with giving effect to the best interests of the child. Under the old law the court had express power to authorise retrospectively what had been illegal payments if, in the court's opinion, making the adoption order was nevertheless, by that time, in the best interests of the child. This is what happened in *Re C (Adoption: Legality)*.[57] A 39-year-old woman, separated and childless, was rejected as a suitable adopter by two social services departments and one independent adoption agency. She applied to adopt a baby from Guatemala whom she had never seen. She had never been to Guatemala but had arranged a private placement and made illegal payments to Guatemalan lawyers. Johnson J nonetheless made the adoption order on welfare grounds despite these irregularities. The problem has been endemic in international adoption and we discuss it further below.

The adoption service and adoption agencies

The corollary of the prohibitions on private activities relating to adoption is the requirement, which originally followed the recommendations of the Houghton

---

52 Section 94.
53 Section 123, especially s 123(4).
54 Section 95.
55 Section 83.
56 Section 96.
57 [1999] 1 FLR 370.

Report,[58] that every local authority should provide a comprehensive adoption service designed to meet the needs of children who have been or may be adopted, their parents or guardians and prospective adopters. Local authorities and voluntary adoption societies have long worked in partnership and co-operation to meet local needs in relation to adoption. Some of these societies, such as Barnado's, are national societies while others operate only at local level. The Adoption and Children Act 2002 sets out the extent of the service which must now be provided in relation to adoption and especially perhaps in the new requirements to provide 'adoption support services'.[59]

The core obligation under the Act is that every local authority:[60]

> 'must continue to maintain within their area a service designed to meet the needs, in relation to adoption, of:
>
> (a)   children who may be adopted, their parents and guardians;
> (b)   persons wishing to adopt a child; and
> (c)   adopted persons, their parents, natural parents and former guardians,
>
> and for that purpose must provide the requisite facilities.'

Local authorities provide this service in conjunction with registered adoption societies. These are voluntary organisations registered under Part 2 of the Care Standards Act 2000. Collectively, the services provided by the local authority and these agencies are known under the Act as 'the Adoption Service'[61] and either a local authority or an adoption society may be referred to as an 'adoption agency'.[62] Each local authority must provide the requisite facilities for making and participating in arrangements for the adoption of children and for the provision of adoption support services.[63] The idea of adoption support services is an innovation of the Act and includes such services as advice and counselling, health, education and cultural services. The local authority *must* carry out an assessment of the needs for adoption support services of those mentioned above if requested to do so.[64] Before the Act there was criticism of some councils for unfairly rejecting some would-be adopters on inadequate grounds and of the review mechanisms applying to such decisions. The Act therefore makes provision for the independent review of such determinations.

---

[58]   *Report of the Departmental Committee on the Adoption of Children* ('the Houghton Report') (1972) (Cmnd 5107).

[59]   See White Paper, ch 6.

[60]   Section 3(1). The details of the support services to be provided by local authorities are beyond the scope of the present work but governed by the Adoption Support Services (Local Authorities) (England) Regulations 2003 (SI 2003/1348).

[61]   Section 2(1).

[62]   Ibid.

[63]   Section 3(2).

[64]   Section 4(1).

Those in relation to whom a 'qualifying determination' has been made by an adoption agency have the right to apply to an independent panel for review of that determination.[65]

We have already noted the establishment of the Adoption and Children Act Register and the introduction of National Adoption Standards which together are designed to facilitate the adoption process and to achieve consistency of practice between local authorities.

QUALIFICATIONS FOR ADOPTION

The question of who may adopt a child was a controversial issue during the passage through Parliament of what became the Adoption and Children Act 2002. The arguments raged around the central question of whether the necessary link between marriage and adoption should be preserved or severed. The legislation broke this connection and enabled, for the first time, unmarried couples whether heterosexual or same-sex couples, in principle, to adopt a child together. We consider first which children may be adopted and then turn to this more complex and controversial question of who is eligible to be an adoptive parent.

Which children may be adopted?

English law, unlike that of some other European jurisdictions, does not have a concept of 'adoptable' children so that in principle any child may, with very limited exceptions, be adopted. It should be said that English law, again unlike the law in some jurisdictions, does not permit the adoption of adults except now in the very limited circumstances of an 18-year-old where the proceedings were commenced before his or her eighteenth birthday. Under the old law an adoption could not be granted after the child had attained majority although, because of the benefits of the adoptive status in adulthood, there were occasions when it was thought appropriate to grant an adoption in relation to a child approaching majority. Two reported cases illustrated the advantages of adoption in adulthood.

In *Re D (A Minor) (Adoption Order: Validity)*[66] a severely mentally incapacitated child was adopted six days before his eighteenth birthday. The long-term foster parents felt harassed by the natural mother who argued that adoption was not necessary to promote the welfare of the child throughout his childhood. The Court of Appeal upheld the judge's adoption order. There was no requirement that benefits during minority were a prerequisite of adoption. It was open to the court to take into account benefits which would accrue to the child after attaining majority and for the rest of his life. Adoption, it was thought, would cement the young man's relationship with his foster parents. It

---

65   Section 12.
66   [1991] 2 FLR 66.

will be recalled that the checklist of factors now requires the court to take into account the effects of adoption throughout the child's life and not merely during minority. In *Re B (Adoption Order: Nationality)*[67] a teenager from Jamaica was adopted by her grandparents in the UK. Her father was dead and her mother lived in impoverished circumstances back in Jamaica. The House of Lords reinstated the judge's adoption order. Although the courts would not allow adoption to be used as a device for obtaining nationality and the right of abode, in this case the grandparents had assumed parental responsibility, and the girl was doing well in school. The court could not ignore these benefits to her of adoption despite the fact that she was close to majority.[68]

The Adoption and Children Act 2002 now provides that the child must be under the age of 19 and must not have been married[69] or a civil partner.[70] As noted above, an adoption order may be made notwithstanding the child's attaining majority provided that the proceedings were commenced, but not concluded, before the child's eighteenth birthday.[71] An adoption order may be made even if the child to be adopted is already an adopted child.[72]

Who may adopt?

The rules governing eligibility in applying to adopt a child are now set out in ss 50 and 51 of the Act. The rules distinguish between adoption by a couple and adoption by one person.

Adoption by a couple

Where a couple apply to adopt both must normally have attained the age of 21 years but, where one of the couple is the mother or father of the child to be adopted, it is sufficient if that parent has attained the age of 18 and the other member of the couple has attained the age of 21.[73] So far as age is concerned English law contains no statutory requirement, such as exists in many jurisdictions, that there should be a minimum age disparity between the child and the adoption applicants.

A couple is defined for the purpose of the Act as:[74]

'(a) a married couple, or

(aa) two people who are civil partners of each other, or

---

[67] [1999] 1 FLR 907.
[68] See also *Re S and J (Adoption: Non-Patrials)* [2004] 2 FLR 111 where Bodey J reached a similar conclusion in relation to two teenage boys from Bangladesh.
[69] Section 47(8) and (9).
[70] Section 47(8A).
[71] Section 49(4) and (5).
[72] Section 46(5).
[73] Section 50(1) and (2).
[74] Section 144(4).

(b) two people (whether of different sexes or the same sex) living as partners in an enduring family relationship.'

No period is specified for the length of the relationship, merely that it is 'enduring' – a condition which implies stability without telling us how exactly that stability is to be measured. The concept of what amounts to an 'enduring family relationship' thus requires judicial interpretation. For example, is it necessary that adopters are living together for this provision to apply? This question was addressed in *Re T and M (Adoption)*[75] in which two women wanted to adopt although their circumstances were such that they had to live in two separate households nearby each other. Hedley J held that the words 'living as partners in an enduring family relationship' were 'no doubt chosen so as not to require the residence of both in the same property', which he did not see as unusual given that many a parent has had to work abroad leaving the rest of the family at home. He held that what is required is 'first, an unambiguous intention to create and maintain family life, and secondly, a factual matrix consistent with that intention',[76] which 'is clearly a question of fact and degree in each case'.[77]

This provision represented a major break with traditional adoption law, which was only prepared to countenance joint applications by couples who were married to each other.[78] The Adoption Review had recognised that *some* unmarried couples might make suitable adopters but felt that, on balance, the security and stability required by adopted children was more likely to be met by those who had made the publicly recognised commitment of marriage and who had legal responsibilities to each other.[79] This, of course, was not perceived as a fair argument in relation to same-sex couples who, being unable to marry in law, could not give a public commitment through marriage.[80] That argument was to some extent addressed by the Civil Partnership Act 2004, and the law is now clear that it would be unlawful to discriminate against prospective adopters solely on the basis of marital status[81] or sexuality.[82] Of course, the question of whether any *specific* couple should be allowed to adopt a particular child will always ultimately rest on the court's view of the best interests of that child.

---

[75] [2010] EWHC 964 (Fam), [2011] 1 FLR 1487 (Hedley J).
[76] Ibid, at [16].
[77] Ibid. See also under the old legislation, *Re WM (Adoption: Non-Patrial)* [1997] 1 FLR 132 (FD) (order in respect of married couple who had separated).
[78] Adoption Act 1976, ss 14 and 15.
[79] Adoption Review, at paras 26.9 et seq.
[80] For an excellent critique of the provision removing the bar on adoption by same-sex couples, which traces the legislative history and also looks at the reform in the context of other legal developments affecting same-sex relationships, see A Marshall 'Comedy of Adoption – When is a Parent not a Parent?' [2003] Fam Law 840.
[81] *Re P* [2008] UKHL 38.
[82] *EB v France* (Application No 43546/02) [2008] 1 FLR 850, ECtHR. For comment on this case, see I Curry-Sumner '*EB v France*: A Missed Opportunity?' [2009] CFLQ 356. Note also the Equality Act 2010, ss 12 and 29.

Adoption by a single applicant

There are several different sets of circumstances set out in the Act in which a single applicant may apply to adopt a child, as follows.

First, there is the general rule that an adoption order may be made on the application of one person who has attained the age of 21 years and is *not* married or not a civil partner.[83]

Secondly, an adoption order may be made in favour of one applicant who *is* married where the court is satisfied that his or her spouse cannot be found, they have separated and the separation is likely to be permanent, or the other spouse is by reason of ill health, whether physical or mental, incapable of making an application for an adoption order.[84] There is a similar provision in relation to the applicant's civil partner.[85] Unless these circumstances apply, the expectation is that a step as serious as adoption must be undertaken by two spouses together. It is perhaps slightly inconsistent with this notion that there would appear to be nothing in principle to prevent a single application by a member of an unmarried couple, however much the other member of that couple might disapprove of it. In such a situation the court might in its discretion decide that the adoption was not in the best interests of the child.

Thirdly, the partner of a parent of the child concerned may apply as a sole applicant.[86] This overcomes the previous requirement that a step-parent adoption should necessarily involve a joint application by both spouses, since all applications by married couples had to be joint applications. The unfortunate result was that a natural parent was required to adopt his or her own child. The change in the law means that the application for adoption may now be brought by the step-parent alone. It should be noted that there is again no requirement that the parent and partner should be married so that the unmarried cohabitant of a parent is also eligible to adopt as a sole applicant. This rule may be thought somewhat inconsistent with the new rules governing the acquisition of parental responsibility by step-parents by agreement or court order.[87] In that case the new provisions only apply to step-parents and not to the cohabitants or partners of parents.

Finally, in very limited circumstances, one natural parent may apply to adopt his or her own child to the exclusion of the other parent. If granted, the effect of this type of adoption is to take away rather than give, since the focus is on the *termination* of the parental status of the other parent. The circumstances in which such an order may be made are where the court is satisfied that:

(a)   the other natural parent is dead or cannot be found;

---

[83]   Section 51(1).
[84]   Section 51(3).
[85]   Section 51(3A).
[86]   Section 51(2).
[87]   Section 112, inserting s 4A into the Children Act 1989. See chapter 4 above.

(b)   there is no other parent by virtue of s 28 of the HFEA 1990 or ss 34–47 of the Human Fertilisation and Embryology Act 2008;[88] or

(c)   there is some other reason justifying the child's being adopted by the applicant alone.[89]

In the case of a successful application the court must record that it is satisfied as to the facts in (a) or (b), and where some other reason is thought to justify the application it must record that reason.[90]

The corresponding provision under the Adoption Act 1976[91] came up for interpretation by the Court of Appeal and then the House of Lords in one of the most remarkable adoption cases in recent decades. It is a case which raises profound questions about the place of adoption in the modern law and its relationship with human rights. As such we devote considerable space to it and focus more particularly on the decision of the Court of Appeal which, although reversed by the House of Lords, engages more convincingly with the human rights issues presented by the case.

Re B (Adoption: Natural Parent)[92] is one of a number of reported cases in which a woman has become pregnant, not informed the genetic father of the pregnancy or birth and wanted essentially to give the child up for a secret or confidential adoption. In this case there was a sexual relationship lasting less than a year. When the baby was born, the mother did not look at her and said that she had no maternal instincts. She had previously given up another daughter for adoption. She told the local authority that the father was working abroad when in fact he was in England. There was then a chance recognition of the father's name in the adoption papers by a secretary working for the local authority. The authority then contacted the father who gave up work to look after the child and in due course wanted to adopt her to the exclusion of the mother. The mother was not opposed to the adoption. She had no direct contact with the child and did not want any beyond an annual photograph and progress report. The judge granted the adoption on the basis that the mother had rejected the child and cited that as the reason. The Official Solicitor appealed on the basis that it was not in the child's best interests for the adoption order to exclude the mother.

The Court of Appeal set aside the adoption order and substituted a residence order in favour of the father to run on to the child's eighteenth birthday. It also gave him power to apply for a passport for the child without the mother's

---

[88]   Disregarding ss 39, 40 and 46 of the 2008 Act.
[89]   Section 51(4).
[90]   Ibid.
[91]   Adoption Act 1976, s 15(3).
[92]   *Re B (Adoption: Natural Parent)* [2002] 1 FLR 196 (HL); [2001] 1 FLR 589 (CA). For more detailed comment, see A Bainham 'Unintentional Parenthood: the Case of the Reluctant Mother' [2002] CLJ 288. See also S Harris-Short 'Putting the child at the heart of adoption?' [2002] CFLQ 325.

consent and an unfettered right to take the child abroad. The mother was prohibited from applying for orders under the Children Act 1989 without the leave of the court. This package of orders was designed to give the father security against possible interference by the mother, which seemed very unlikely but which bothered the father. Specifically on the adoption question, however, the Court of Appeal took the view that it was generally in the best interests of children to have two legal parents and two legal families and that the exclusion of one could only be justified, under Art 8(2) of the ECHR, if necessary in a democratic society. Hale LJ said that the relationship of mother and child was in itself sufficient to establish 'family life' even where the two were separated at birth. The carrying of and giving birth to a child brings with it a relationship between mother and child which is entitled to respect. Were it otherwise, she said, the State could always interfere without fear of contravening Art 8 by removing children the moment they were born. That only needed stating for it to be clear how wrong that would be. Adoption here would therefore be a disproportionate response to the child's current needs, since to deprive the child entirely of a legal relationship with the mother was not necessary when a package of other measures could achieve the desired result. Under the various orders the court made, the mother would be left with only the remnants of parental responsibility which would come into play only if something serious happened in the father's life and if the court approved the mother's involvement at that stage.

The House of Lords reversed the Court of Appeal's decision and reinstated the adoption order on the narrow, but well-established, ground that the Court of Appeal ought not to have interfered with the exercise of the judge's discretion.[93] In this case it could not be said that the judge had misdirected herself on the proper interpretation of the legislation or that her decision was manifestly wrong. There was no reason for importing into the legislation a requirement that the 'reason' for allowing a sole adoption by one parent must be comparable to the death or disappearance of the other parent. It had therefore been open to the judge to conclude that the child's best interests required adoption. The father's anxiety about the mother's continuing status could perpetuate insecurity for him and potentially affect the child's stability. There was moreover no inconsistency between the kind of balancing exercise under the ECHR which required that interferences be proportionate. The judge's determination that the child's best interests required adoption identified a pressing social need, and the adoption complied with the principle of proportionality.

This decision raises fundamental questions about human rights in the context of adoption. First, it exposes a distinction in the circumstances in which 'family life' may be said to arise between mother and child on the one hand and father and child on the other. Hale LJ, in the Court of Appeal, was at pains to emphasise the fundamental bond between mother and child which arises at

---

[93] A rule firmly established by the House of Lords in *G v G (Minors: Custody Appeal)* [1985] 1 WLR 647.

birth and amounts to family life and also to highlight the importance of this for the creation of kinship links between the mother's wider family and the child. It is therefore worth speculating on whether she would have taken the same position if this case had involved the *mother* trying to adopt to the exclusion of the father. How would the bond between the genetic father and child have been viewed in those circumstances and could distinctions sensibly be drawn between the child's interest in the *maternal* family and in the *paternal* family?

Secondly, the case again prompts an evaluation of the theory of intentional parenthood.[94] The corollary of the theory that parentage should be recognised, or parental responsibility awarded, on the basis of a person's *intention* to perform the social role of parent is that parentage should be lost and parental responsibility removed where someone is *unwilling* to perform that social role. The Court of Appeal's approach in this case could be viewed as an emphatic rejection of any such theory. What the Court of Appeal seemed to be saying was that, in the light of human rights considerations, the law ought not to allow a parent simply to drop out of parenthood because that is what that parent wishes to do. Such an approach if carried to its logical conclusion does suggest that the mother's traditional right to give up her child for adoption, which indeed was an important influence on the introduction of adoption in England in the Adoption of Children Act 1926, may be about to be seriously eroded. This case, along with others which we discuss below, challenges the right of mothers to arrange the confidential adoption of their children as a potential breach of both the child's and father's Convention rights, or, conceivably, the Convention rights of the wider maternal or paternal family.

Finally, the case demonstrates again the importance, from a human rights perspective, of balancing the extreme solution of adoption with other less drastic alternatives which may equally well achieve the result needed to protect the welfare of the child but which do not ignore or devalue adult claims. It is submitted that the approach of the Court of Appeal showed a much more sophisticated appreciation of the need to demonstrate that adoption was better than other solutions, and therefore proportionate, than did either the judge or the House of Lords.

The probationary periods

In addition to the above qualifications for applicants, English law also requires the child to live with the prospective adopters for a specified period of time.[95] The prescribed periods vary markedly depending on the class of applicant. In each case the court must be satisfied that there have been sufficient opportunities to see the child and the applicant/applicants in the home

---

[94] As to which see especially C Barton and G Douglas *Law and Parenthood* (Butterworths, 1995).
[95] Adoption and Children Act 2002, s 42. This was also the case under the previous legislation in s 13 of the Adoption Act 1976.

environment[96] together afforded to the adoption agency, or, where the child was not placed by an adoption agency, the local authority within whose area the home is.[97]

The requisite periods are as follows.

(1) Where the child was placed by an adoption agency or under the authority of the High Court, the child must have had his home with the applicant/applicants at all times during the period of *ten weeks* preceding the application.[98]

(2) Where the applicant, or one of the applicants, is the partner of a parent of the child, the period is *six months*.[99]

(3) For local authority foster parents the period is *one year*,[100] a requirement which is consistent with the new period for eligibility, in their case, to seek leave for a s 8 order under the Children Act 1989.[101]

(4) In all other cases, which are perhaps most likely to involve relatives of the child, the period is *three years* whether continuous or not during the period of five years preceding the application.[102] This is a very significantly longer period than the corresponding period under the Adoption Act 1976 which was 13 weeks.[103] The reasoning is that it may be more appropriate in such cases for some other order to be sought. Where an adoption order is granted in favour of a relative, such as a grandparent, the effect may be to distort family relationships – in that example by making the grandmother legally the mother of the child, the natural mother the sister, and so on in relation to wider kinship relationships with the extended family. It was for this reason that such adoptions have been discouraged since the Houghton Report, although granted in a minority of appropriate cases. The three-year residence requirement will operate as an automatic break on such adoptions and, where such applications are made, the court will need to consider carefully the other options for permanence such as the making of a residence or special guardianship order.

In all of the above cases, the court may give leave for an application to be made notwithstanding the failure of the applicant to satisfy the relevant probationary

---

[96] Home is not defined geographically, and could be a home abroad: see *Re A (Adoption: Removal)* [2009] EWCA Civ 41, [2010] Fam 9.
[97] Section 42(7).
[98] Section 42(2).
[99] Section 42(3).
[100] Section 42(4).
[101] Section 113, amending s 9(3) of the Children Act 1989. See chapter 5 above.
[102] Section 42(5).
[103] Adoption Act 1976, s 13(1).

period.[104] Probationary periods like this are by no means universally required. The absence of such requirements in the case of jurisdictions which send children for the purposes of international adoption is a continuing cause of concern given the importance of being satisfied that an appropriate matching of adoptive parents and child has been made.

THE PLACEMENT REGIME

The Adoption and Children Act 2002 abolished the former process of 'freeing for adoption' under the Adoption Act 1976 and replaced it with a wholly new placement regime. Placement of a child for adoption is possible only with parental consent or where the court is prepared to dispense with that consent and certain other conditions are satisfied.[105] The purpose of having a legal process at the stage of placement is essentially twofold. First, it is intended to reduce the uncertainty for prospective adopters who might otherwise face a contested hearing at the stage of the final hearing for an adoption order. Secondly, it is intended to reduce the extent to which birth families are presented with a fait accompli at the final hearing where the child has been placed with prospective adopters for some time. The former process of freeing for adoption had similar aims but was ineffective in achieving them and widely criticised.[106]

The two routes for placement

An adoption agency wishing to place a child for adoption may only do so *either* where each parent or guardian of the child consents *or* where the court makes a placement order.[107] Placement orders are a new type of order introduced by the Act. So far as placement with parental consent is concerned, the provisions which govern the giving of consent to placement are similar to those which determine the relevant consents and how they must be given in relation to adoption itself, and we consider them below in that context.[108] At this stage we focus only on the placement order route.

The placement order is an order 'authorising a local authority to place a child for adoption with any prospective adopters who may be chosen by the

---

[104] Section 42(6). See, for example, *ASB and KBS v MQS (Secretary of State for the Home Department Intervening)* [2009] EWHC 2491 (Fam).

[105] This marks a significant departure from the old law under which there was no such restraint on placing children for adoption and under which the freeing for adoption procedure was only *one* route by which a local authority might seek to arrange the adoption of a child.

[106] For discussion of the difficulties with freeing for adoption, see the third edition of this book, at p 281.

[107] Adoption and Children Act 2002, s 18(1). The decision to place must comply with regulations: see *Re B (Placement Order)* [2008] EWCA Civ 835, [2008] 2 FLR 1404. Contrast *Re P-B* [2006] EWCA Civ 1016, where the agency's failure to fulfil its statutory duty was undiscovered until after the making of the placement order.

[108] Consent to placement is governed by s 19.

authority'.[109] The circumstances in which the court may make a placement order require the satisfaction of two separate conditions. The first is as follows:

(a) that the child is in the care of the local authority under a care order; or

(b) that the court is satisfied that the threshold conditions for making a care order under s 31(2) of the Children Act 1989 are met; or

(c) that the child has no parent or guardian.[110]

The second condition is:

(a) that the parent or guardian has consented to placement and that consent has not been withdrawn; or

(b) that the court should dispense with that consent.[111]

The Act therefore brings under one umbrella the threshold conditions for compulsory State intervention through a care order with the legal requirements for dispensing with parental consent to adoption. It cannot be emphasised strongly enough that, where a parent or guardian does *not* consent to placement, a placement order may only be made where *both* conditions are satisfied.[112] Thus the threshold conditions must be fulfilled as well as the quite separate grounds for dispensing with consent to adoption. As we shall see, this really amounts to a determination at that stage that adoption is in the best interests of the child. We consider the grounds for dispensing with consent in the context of the adoption order itself below.

There are prescribed circumstances in which the local authority *must* seek a placement order where it is satisfied that the child ought to be placed for adoption.[113]

A placement order will remain in force until it is revoked, an adoption is made, or the child marries or attains the age of 18 years.[114] A local authority or the child (or a person acting on behalf of the child) may apply to revoke a

---

[109] Section 21(1).

[110] Section 21(2).

[111] Section 21(3).

[112] This was not reflected in the original Bill as drafted but, following widespread criticism, the Bill was amended to make it plain that a local authority should not be able (through the vehicle of a placement order) to obtain compulsory care of a child without meeting the normal threshold conditions.

[113] Section 22. It has been held that a local authority can be satisfied that the child ought to be placed for adoption within the meaning of s 22(1)(d) 'even though it recognises the reality that a search for adoptive parents may be unsuccessful and that, if it is, the alternative plan will have to be for long-term fostering', ie, there is 'no objection in principle to dual planning in appropriate cases': see *Re P (Placement Orders: Parental Consent)* [2008] EWCA Civ 535, [2008] 2 FLR 625 at [137].

[114] Section 21(4).

placement order at any time. Others, including most obviously parents, may only apply for revocation with the leave of the court where the child has not yet been placed for adoption.[115] Leave will only be granted where the court is satisfied that there has been a change of circumstances since the order was made.[116] The matter is not governed by the welfare principle. The child's welfare has to be weighed with the prospects of successful revocation. The correct question to be asked therefore is whether there is a real prospect of success of revocation.[117]

The legal effects of placement

Parental responsibility

Whether the child is placed by consent or under a placement order, parental responsibility is given to the adoption agency (which will be the local authority or, where placement is by consent, a registered adoption society).[118] While the child is placed with prospective adopters, parental responsibility is also given to them.[119] In each case, the parents retain parental responsibility up to the time an adoption order is made. The adoption agency, however, 'may determine that the parental responsibility of any parent or guardian, or prospective adopters, is to be restricted to the extent specified in the determination'.[120] This provision is analogous to s 33 of the Children Act 1989 which applies where a child is in care.[121] Its purpose is to ensure that, notwithstanding the sharing of parental responsibility under the placement regime, the adoption agency remains 'in the driving seat' and able to fulfil its plans for the child without being constantly frustrated in these by the parents or prospective adopters. Where such a determination is made, the retention of parental responsibility may amount to little more than a right of consultation.

Contact

The whole question of contact in the context of adoption has been and remains a hugely debated issue which has been heightened by the greater emphasis which the law now attaches to the rights of the child specifically and to human rights in general. We consider below the question of post-adoption contact. For the moment we are concerned only with contact after a placement order has been made. The hope is that this will be agreed with the local authority and its final care plan should set out what is proposed. Where, however, it is not

---

[115] Section 24(1) and (2). It is critical whether the child has yet been placed or not. On when a child is placed as a matter of law see *Re S (Placement Order: Revocation)* [2008] EWCA Civ 1333, [2009] 1 FLR 503 and *Coventry City Council v O (Adoption)* [2011] EWCA Civ 729, [2011] 2 FLR 936.

[116] Section 24(3).

[117] *M v Warwickshire County Council* [2008] 1 FLR 1093 and *NS-H v Kingston upon Hull City Council and MC* [2008] EWCA Civ 493; [2008] 2 FLR 918.

[118] Section 25(2).

[119] Section 25(3).

[120] Section 25(4).

[121] See chapter 12 above.

agreed, there is provision for a 'freestanding' application for contact under ss 26 and 27 which constitute a discrete contact code applying only after the making of a placement order.

The effect of a placement order will be to terminate any existing contact order made under the Children Act,[122] and any other s 8 order, and to *suspend* any existing care order.[123] The broad effect of these provisions as they apply to contact is that applications for contact, after the making of a placement order, must be made as an integral part of the placement regime, and not by way of applying for a private contact order under s 8 or a public contact order under s 34 where the child is in care. Subject to that, the provisions governing contact in the placement context are again modelled on the contact code where the child is in care. Where a contact order is sought at the same time as an application for a final adoption order, a s 8 contact order may be made.[124]

The reality in practice of contact after a placement order has been made is as follows. The local authority will implement a gradual reduction in contact between the birth parents and the child which will be substantially less than the often quite high level of contact during the care proceedings. A search will begin for family finding. Once a placement has been identified, the birth parents will usually be offered a final contact with the child, sometimes euphemistically described as a 'wishing you well' contact and sometimes (perhaps more accurately) described as a 'goodbye' contact. The great majority of birth parents can expect no more than 'letterbox' contact once the child has been placed.

Restrictions on removal of children during placement

Under the placement regime, there is a general prohibition on removing a child who is placed for adoption from the prospective adopters and this will apply even where the parent has withdrawn his or her consent.[125] Where, however, a child is placed by consent, and that consent is then withdrawn, the prospective adopters are required to return the child to the adoption agency.[126] This is distinguishable from the situation following a placement order. Here there is no automatic right for parents to recover their child, and only the local authority is empowered to remove the child where there has been a withdrawal of parental consent.[127] Where a child is being accommodated before any placement order has been made, the agency must return the child to the parents on request within seven days unless an application for a placement order has been made

---

[122] Any contact activity direction (see Children Act 1989, s 11A) relating to contact with the child is also discharged.

[123] Section 26(1).

[124] Section 26(5).

[125] Section 30(1). The previous law contained prohibitions on the removal of 'protected children' while an adoption application was pending: see Adoption Act 1976, s 27 et seq.

[126] Section 32.

[127] Section 34.

and not yet concluded.[128] Once an application for an adoption order has been made, the child may not be removed by anyone without the leave of the court.[129]

CONSENT TO ADOPTION

The question of consent has always been central to the adoption process and, more than anything else, the feature which has distinguished adoption from other legal procedures relating to children.[130] The Adoption and Children Act 2002 made radical changes to the legal requirements for consent in a number of ways. It makes provision for the giving of an 'advance consent', requires the issue of consent to be addressed in all cases before a child is placed for adoption and, most controversially, openly places the welfare principle at the heart of the judicial decision to dispense with parental consent. In one respect, however, the legislation is less radical than might have been expected in that the consent of *the child*, however old, has not been made a formal legal requirement, despite hints during the long reform process that it would be, as in other jurisdictions, notably Scotland.[131] The issue of consent will arise in most cases at the placement stage, but there will continue to be cases – where, for example, the application is by relatives with whom the child has been living – where it will not arise until the application for the adoption order itself. First, we consider the essential conditions in the new legislation regarding consent, including the question of whose consent is legally required. We then consider the grounds for dispensing with consent.

The essential conditions

One of three conditions as to consent must be satisfied before the court may make an adoption order.[132] Only the first two conditions are relevant to a book on English law, since the third relates solely to children who have been freed for adoption under orders made in Scotland or Northern Ireland. The first two conditions are as follows.

The first condition is:

(a)   that the parent or guardian consents to the making of the adoption order;

(b)   that the parent or guardian has consented under s 20 (and has not withdrawn the consent) and does not oppose the making of the adoption order; or

---

[128]   Section 31(1) and (2).

[129]   Section 37.

[130]   For background discussion see E Cooke 'Dispensing with parental consent to adoption – a choice of welfare tests' [1997] CFLQ 259.

[131]   See Age of Legal Capacity (Scotland) Act 1991 s 2(3).

[132]   Section 47.

(c)   that the parent's or guardian's consent should be dispensed with.[133]

The second condition is:

(a)   that the child has been placed for adoption by an adoption agency with the prospective adopters in whose favour the order is proposed to be made; and

(b)   that either:

(i)   the child was placed for adoption with the consent of each parent or guardian, and the consent of the mother was given when the child was at least six weeks old; or

(ii)   the child was placed for adoption under a placement order; and

(c)   that no parent or guardian opposes the making of an adoption order.[134]

These are therefore two *alternative* conditions, the first focusing on the issue of consent where the child has not been placed for adoption under a placement order, and the second dealing with cases where there has been a placement under the placement regime and the parent or guardian does not oppose the adoption. It should be noted that the requirements set out in the first condition are *alternative* requirements whereas those in the second condition are *cumulative* requirements, apart from requirement (b) which deals with the alternatives of placement by consent or placement under a placement order.

Several features relating to the nature of giving consent should be observed. First, it is provided, as it was under the previous law, that the consent of a mother to an adoption order is ineffective if given less than six weeks after the birth of the child.[135] This is in part to comply with the requirements of the European Convention on the Adoption of Children 1967. It would appear that the mother may consent to the *placement* of the child for adoption within six weeks of the child's birth but that, if she were to do so, this would be ineffective for the purposes of the adoption order and consent would need to be given again to adoption itself.[136] The purpose of the restriction is to enable the mother to recover from the effects of giving birth and to receive appropriate counselling. The question of early consent to adoption is an especially controversial one in the context of international adoption where, in some countries, there is clear evidence that expectant mothers have been put under pressure to give up their children for adoption at, or soon after, birth.

Secondly, and not unrelated to the first point, it must be established that consent is given 'unconditionally and with full understanding of what is involved'. The consent need not, however, involve knowing the identity of the

---

[133]   Section 47(2).
[134]   Section 47(4).
[135]   Section 52(3).
[136]   *A Local Authority v GC* [2008] EWHC 2555 (Fam); [2009] 1 FLR 299.

prospective adopters.[137] The previous legislation required that consent be given 'freely'.[138] This term does not appear in the 2002 legislation although, clearly, it is still implied that the parent must give consent free from external pressure. The explanation for the change given in the White Paper was that the 'decision to agree to adoption is often a very difficult one' and that to say that a parent was agreeing 'freely' might not reflect this. The new wording is supposed to reflect better 'the reality that birth parents have agreed to the adoption on the basis that it is in the best interests of the child'.[139] It is a pity, it is submitted, that it is not made explicit, as it was in previous legislation, that consent must be freely given and this adds to the concern that there may be something of a devaluation of parental rights in the legislation. The giving or withdrawing of consent has, however, been formalised and must be given in a form prescribed by rules made under the legislation.[140] It is the responsibility of CAFCASS officers to advise parents on the implications of giving consent and to ensure that the formalities are properly observed.

Thirdly, the legislation provides, for the first time, for the giving of an advance consent. The Act allows a parent or guardian who consents to a child being placed for adoption by an adoption agency to give an advance consent to an adoption order.[141] He or she may therefore give consent at the same time as consenting to placement, or at any subsequent time, to the making of a future adoption order. The consent may be either in relation to *specific* prospective adopters or to *any* prospective adopters who may be chosen by the agency.[142] This advance consent may subsequently be withdrawn by giving notice to the agency in the prescribed form.[143] This may not be done, however, if by that time an application for an adoption order has already been made.[144] It is possible also to give notice that he or she does not wish to be informed of any application for an adoption order but such a statement may also subsequently be withdrawn.[145]

The Act also contains provisions designed to deal with the question of a 'change of heart' by the parent following placement of the child or the giving of an advance consent. In each case it is provided that the parent or guardian concerned may only oppose the making of the adoption order with the leave of the court,[146] which may only be granted where the court is 'satisfied that there has been a change in circumstances since the consent of the parent or guardian was given or, as the case may be, the placement order was made'.[147] Given the policy of the legislation to deal expeditiously with the issue of consent, in the

---

[137] Section 52(5).
[138] Adoption Act 1976, s 16(1)(b)(i).
[139] White Paper, at paras 8.27 and 8.28.
[140] Section 52(7).
[141] Section 20(1).
[142] Section 20(2).
[143] Sections 20(3) and 52(8).
[144] Section 52(4).
[145] Section 20(4).
[146] Section 47(3)–(5).
[147] Section 47(7).

interests of certainty, at an earlier stage of the adoption process, it is unlikely that leave will be readily given to oppose adoption at the eleventh hour. Indeed the Court of Appeal has said that such an application 'is an absolute last ditch opportunity and it will only be in exceptionally rare circumstances that permission will be granted after the making of the care order, the making of the placement order, the placement of the child, and the issue of the adoption order application'.[148] The applicant will need first 'to establish the necessary change of circumstances'[149] and 'then to satisfy the court that, in the exercise of discretion, it would be right to grant permission' and then 'persuade the court at the opposed hearing to refuse the adoption order and to reverse the direction in which the child's life has travelled since the inception of the original public law care proceedings'.[150] In *Re P (A Child) (Adoption: Leave Provisions)*[151] the Court of Appeal held that s 1 of the 2002 Act applies to the question of leave, and in *Re W (Adoption Order: Set Aside and Leave to Oppose)*[152] the Court of Appeal held that a 'judge must have great regard to impact of the grant of permission on the child within the context of the adoptive family'[153] and should only grant leave if the prospects of success of the application have substance or solidity.[154]

In *Re B-S (Children)*[155] the Court of Appeal considered s 47(5) once again and in particular Thorpe LJ's comment in *Re W* that a stringent approach is required and 'it will only be in exceptionally rare circumstances that permission will be granted'.[156] The Court commented that:[157]

'use of the phrase "exceptionally rare circumstances" carries with it far too great a potential for misunderstanding, misapplication and indeed injustice for safety. The same, if in lesser measure, applies also to the word "stringent". Stringent, as we have said, is a word that appropriately describes the test that has to be surmounted before a non-consensual adoption can be sanctioned. It is not a word that comfortably describes the test that a parent has to meet in seeking to resist such an adoption.'

And the court added:

'Parliament intended section 47(5) to provide a real remedy. Unthinking reliance upon the concept of the "exceptionally rare" runs the risk – a very real and wholly unacceptable risk – of rendering section 47(5) nugatory and its protections illusory. Except in the fairly unusual case where section 47(4)(b)(i) applies, a parent

---

[148] *Re W (Adoption Order: Set Aside and Leave to Oppose)* [2010] EWCA Civ 1535, [2011] 1 FLR 2153, at para [17].
[149] Ibid, at para [18]
[150] Ibid. Fresh evidence may not constitute a change of circumstances, see *Re M (Adoption: Leave to Oppose)* [2010] 1 FLR 238 (HHJ Newton sitting as judge of the High Court).
[151] [2007] EWCA Civ 616, [2007] 2 FLR 1069, at [55].
[152] [2010] EWCA Civ 1535, [2011] 1 FLR 2153.
[153] Ibid.
[154] Ibid.
[155] [2013] EWCA Civ 1146.
[156] See also *Re C (A Child)* [2013] EWCA Civ 431, at paras 29–30.
[157] [2013] EWCA Civ 1146, at para [70].

applying under section 47(5) will always, by definition, be faced with the twin realities that the court has made both a care order and a placement order and that the child is now living with the prospective adopter. But, unless section 47(5) is to be robbed of all practical efficacy, none of those facts, even in combination, can of themselves justify the refusal of leave.'

The Court of Appeal set out in detail the proper approach.[158] The court explained that:[159]

'the judge must consider very carefully indeed whether the child's welfare really does necessitate the refusal of leave. The judge must keep at the forefront of his mind the teaching of *Re B*, in particular that adoption is the "last resort" and only permissible if "nothing else will do" and that, as Lord Neuberger emphasised, the child's interests include being brought up by the parents or wider family unless the overriding requirements of the child's welfare make that not possible. That said, the child's welfare is paramount.'

The court must assess the pros and cons of each option, and this close focus on the circumstances requires that the court has proper evidence.[160] In addition the court observed that:

'As a general proposition, the greater the change in circumstances (assuming, of course, that the change is positive) and the more solid the parent's grounds for seeking leave to oppose, the more cogent and compelling the arguments based on the child's welfare must be if leave to oppose is to be refused.'

And:

'The mere fact that the child has been placed with prospective adopters cannot be determinative, nor can the mere passage of time. On the other hand, the older the child and the longer the child has been placed the greater the adverse impacts of disturbing the arrangements are likely to be.'

The judge must always bear in mind that what is paramount in every adoption case is the welfare of the child 'throughout his life'.

As far as arguments about the adverse impact on the prospective adopters, the court indicated that the argument must not be trivialised in its impact upon a child but also judges must be careful not to give it too much weight. The court urged judges to bear in mind 'the wise and humane words of Wall LJ in *Re P*, para 32' that 'the test should not be set too high, because ... parents ... should not be discouraged either from bettering themselves or from seeking to prevent the adoption of their child by the imposition of a test which is unachievable.'

---

158   Ibid, at paras [72]–[75].
159   Ibid, at para [74].
160   Ibid.

Whose consent is required?

Whether consent is to placement or to adoption, s 52 of the Adoption and Children Act 2002 governs the question of whose consent is required and these provisions also call for some comment on whose consent is *not* required.

Those *required* to consent are parents and guardians.[161] The expression 'guardian' now includes the 'special guardian'[162] appointed by the court under the new regime of special guardianship introduced by the Act, as well as the more obvious guardian who takes over on the death of a parent and whose status is governed by the Children Act 1989.[163] The inclusion of the special guardian among those whose consent is required underlines the superior status involved and further distinguishes the special guardian from other substitute carers, especially from those holding residence orders whose consent is *not* required to the child's placement or subsequent adoption. It should not be thought, however, that the inclusion of the special guardian in this privileged category for the purposes of adoption is uncontroversial since, it will be recalled, the other central feature of special guardianship is that it enables the child's legal link with the birth family to be preserved. The effect of adoption is, of course, to extinguish that connection. It should, however, be understood that the consent of the special guardian would not *by itself* be sufficient if the child also has a parent or parents. Their consent would also have to be obtained or the court would have to take the decision to dispense with it.

It should also be noted that the child's consent is *not* required. The Adoption Review had accepted the principle that an adoption order ought not to be made without the consent of a child who had attained the age of 12, an age at which children are required to consent in a number of other jurisdictions including Scotland. It is, of course, the case that the adoption agency and the court are required to ascertain and have regard to the child's wishes, in the light of the child's age and understanding, in accordance with the general principles in the Act.[164] There is no doubt that the wishes of an older child will be highly relevant to the decision and have probably been the decisive factor in the exercise of the court's discretion in some cases.[165]

The expression 'parent', as under the Adoption Act 1976, 'means a parent having parental responsibility'.[166] That will clearly include all legal mothers, whether married or not, fathers married to the mother and unmarried fathers who have taken steps to acquire parental responsibility under one of the statutory mechanisms. The change brought about by the Act, whereby parental responsibility may be acquired automatically on registration as the child's father, will (as noted earlier) result in the great majority of unmarried fathers

---

[161] Section 52(1).
[162] Section 144(1).
[163] Children Act 1989, s 5; and see chapter 4 above.
[164] Section 1(4)(a).
[165] See particularly *Re M (Adoption or Residence Order)* [1998] 1 FLR 570.
[166] Section 52(6).

acquiring parental responsibility as opposed to the situation before the Act when the vast majority did not. The Adoption and Children Act 2002 goes on to provide for the situation where an unmarried mother has already given consent to placement of the child for adoption and, subsequently, the legal father acquires parental responsibility. In these circumstances he will be treated as having, at that time, given consent 'in the same terms in which [the mother] gave consent'.[167] The idea is to prevent the father from frustrating or obstructing the arrangement which the mother has entered into with the adoption agency.

The definition of 'parent' thus continues to exclude from the consent requirements a category of unmarried fathers who have not acquired parental responsibility. This does not mean, any more than it did under the old law, that these men will necessarily have no standing in adoption proceedings and no say in the outcome. Indeed, in a whole string of cases since the implementation of the HRA 1998, it has been asserted that human rights obligations require that the father without parental responsibility be notified of the proceedings and allowed to participate in them. In *Keegan v Ireland*[168] the ECtHR signalled its general view on this question when it found Irish law in breach of the father's rights under the Convention by in effect allowing a 'secret' adoption of a child born out of wedlock. Whether a parent who is not married to (or the civil partner of) the mother has family life within the meaning of Art 8 of the ECHR depends on the circumstances, including the nature of the relationship between the natural parents and the demonstrable interest in and commitment by the natural father to the child both before and after the birth.[169] It can be established, therefore, where there are sufficiently close *de facto* family ties, for example arising through cohabitation,[170] and even in the case of a potential relationship, provided the father has had some relationship with the mother and expressed his commitment to the child in some way, even if there was no cohabitation.[171] In some circumstances, intended family life may be enough to establish a right to respect for one's family life.[172]

The reported cases have been concerned with much the same scenario as in *Keegan v Ireland* with variations on the facts. What usually happens is that there is a relatively brief sexual relationship, even a casual encounter in some cases, which results in the pregnancy. The mother decides to give birth but not to inform the genetic father of either the pregnancy or the subsequent birth.

---

[167] Section 52(9) and (10).
[168] (1994) 18 EHRR 342.
[169] See *Rozanski v Poland* (Application No 55339/00) [2006] 2 FLR 1163.
[170] It need not involve cohabitation: see *Söderbäck v Sweden*: family life where only small amount of contact between father and daughter.
[171] *Nylund v Finland* (Application No 27110/95) (unreported) 29 June 1999; cf *G v Netherlands* (Application No 16944/90) (1993) 16 EHRR CD 38; see *Re C* at [31]. See also *Gorgülü v Germany* (family life where significant relationship ending before father aware of pregnancy).
[172] *Pini v Romania* (2005) 40 EHRR 132, [2005] 2 FLR 596, at para 143: although holding that there was no family life in the case of persons who had obtained adoption orders but had not had care of the children concerned, the Court indicated that the requirement for de facto ties 'does not mean that all intended family life falls entirely outside the ambit of Art 8'.

Later, when adoption is under consideration, either the father becomes aware of the situation and wishes to establish some sort of relationship with the child or the adoption agency or local authority are concerned about pressing ahead with adoption with the mother's consent without exploring any possible contribution the father might make to the life of the child.

An adoption agency is under a duty to compile considerable information about the child, including information about the child's parents and relatives,[173] and difficulties can thus arise where the mother wishes to conceal her pregnancy from her family or will not disclose who the father is. In *Re L (Adoption: Contacting Natural Father)*[174] the mother requested her child be adopted without her family knowing[175] and maintained that she was unable (or as professionals suspected, unwilling) to disclose the father's identity. The local authority, with whom the child was accommodated, sought leave to invoke the inherent jurisdiction of the High Court for orders that it need not take further steps to identify the child's father nor inform or consult members of the maternal family concerning the intended adoption. Munby J, held that respecting the mother's wishes was lawful.[176] He was of the view that the court had the necessary power under the inherent jurisdiction to order the mother to disclose the father's identity, but he found it deeply unattractive,[177] and that it would be wrong to coerce the mother in this way.[178] Where the father's identity is known, a local authority is able to ask the High Court for directions on the need to give a father who does not have parental responsibility notice of the intention to place a child for adoption. The court has power to direct that a father be joined as a party to adoption proceedings. Equally, however, the child can be placed for adoption and an adoption order could be made without notice to a father. In *Re A (Father: Knowledge of Child's Birth)*[179] the Court of Appeal upheld the judge's refusal of a declaration that the mother's husband (the child's father) not be told of the child's birth. The father suffered mental health problems and was prone to unpredictable, frightening behaviour, including domestic violence but the expert evidence did not support the mother's case that knowledge of the child would be adverse to the father's equilibrium.[180] Reviewing earlier authorities the court concluded that 'the court will not be persuaded to sanction the withholding of information about the existence of a child from that child's parent or to dispense with service on him of proceedings relating to the child in anything other than exceptional circumstances where there are ... strong countervailing factors'.[181] However,

---

[173] As set out in Sch 1 to the Adoption Agencies Regulations 2005, especially para 3.
[174] [2007] EWHC 1771 (Fam), [2008] 1 FLR 1079.
[175] For another example, see *Z County Council v R* [2001] 1 FLR 365.
[176] At [11], drawing on Holman J's judgment in *Z County Council v R* [2001] 1 FLR 365, at 367.
[177] Ibid, at [38].
[178] Ibid, at [41].
[179] [2011] EWCA Civ 273, [2011] 2 FLR 123.
[180] [2011] EWCA Civ 273, [2011] 2 FLR 123, at [16].
[181] [2011] EWCA Civ 273, [2011] 2 FLR 123, at [37]. See also *Re B (Adoption by One Natural Parent: Exclusion of Other)* [2001] 1 FLR 589, *Re H and G (Adoption: Consultation of Unmarried Fathers)* [2001] 1 FLR 745 at [48]; *Re C (Adoption: Disclosure to Father)* [2005] EWHC 3385 (Fam), [2006] 2 FLR 589, at [17] ('very compelling reasons'); *Birmingham City*

every case is different.[182] In some cases notification may result in a catastrophic destruction of the family so as to warrant hiding the truth.[183] In *Re H; Re G (Adoption: Consultation of Unmarried Fathers)*[184] Butler-Sloss P gave further examples of countervailing circumstances, such as rape or other serious domestic violence that placed the mother at serious physical risk,[185] although there is no 'requirement of significant physical risk'.[186] An example is provided by *Re M (Adoption: Rights of Natural Father)*;[187] Bodey J held on the facts that any such interference with the rights of the father would be justified by the proper and legitimate aim of protecting the physical and emotional welfare of the mother and child and the protection of the child's right to family life.

In *Re H; Re G (Adoption: Consultation of Unmarried Fathers)*[188] the respective mothers had placed their children for adoption with the local authorities concerned on the understanding that their confidentiality would be respected. Neither mother was put under pressure to disclose the identity of the father and in neither case had the father acquired parental responsibility but, beyond that, the circumstances were quite different. In the first case there had been cohabitation between the mother and father and indeed they had an elder child together. Nonetheless the pregnancy had been concealed from the father and his family. The mother was concerned that information about the adoption might damage the relationship which she had built up with the father. The local authority sought guidance on whether the father should be joined as respondent and the court held that steps should be taken to identify and consult him. Here there had been cohabitation for several years and a continuing commitment by the father to the elder child. There could therefore be a breach of his Art 8 rights if the child were to be placed for adoption without giving the father notice of this and an opportunity to be heard. In contrast, in the second case the mother and father had never cohabited. They had been engaged at one point but the relationship had broken down and they had lost touch. The mother did not want the father, who was from another country but training for a profession in the UK, to be identified and she did not want her family to know of the birth. In this case, the court confirmed in the inherent jurisdiction that it was lawful for the local authority to place the child for adoption without consulting the natural father. They had not cohabited and their relationship did not show the constancy which was necessary to establish

---

Council v S, R and A [2006] EWHC 3065 (Fam), [2007] 1 FLR 1223, at [73] ('cogent and compelling grounds'). For a review of some of the case law, see A Bainham 'Can We Protect Children and Protect Their Rights?' [2002] Fam Law 279.

[182] *Re L (Adoption: Contacting Natural Father)*,2007] EWHC 1771 (Fam), [2008] 1 FLR 1079, at [25].

[183] See, for example, *Re X (Care: Notice of Proceedings)* [1996] 1 FLR 186.

[184] [2001] 1 FLR 745, at [48].

[185] See also *Z County Council v R* [2001] 1 FLR 365 (relatives suffering illness which made it impossible for them to care for the child).

[186] *Re A (Father: Knowledge of Child's Birth)* [2011] EWCA Civ 273, [2011] 2 FLR 123, at para [45].

[187] [2001] 1 FLR 745.

[188] [2001] 1 FLR 646. See also *Re R (Adoption: Father's Involvement)* [2001] 1 FLR 302.

de facto family ties. Hence 'family life' for the purposes of Art 8 had not been shown to exist between the father and the child.

In *Re C (A Child) (Adoption: Duty of Local Authority)*[189] an unmarried mother concealed her pregnancy from her family and placed her baby (conceived as a result of a one-night stand) for adoption. The mother did not want her family to care for the child. The judge held that the local authority was under a duty to inform itself of as much of the child's background as it was able. However, the Court of Appeal held that the judge had been wrong in principle and set aside his exercise of discretion. The court held that s 1 of the 2002 Act applied, and that there is no duty to make enquiries which are not in the interests of the child to make, and enquiries 'are not in the interests of the child simply because they will provide more information about the child's background'.[190] Arden LJ commented:

'I do not consider that this court should require a preference to be given as a matter of policy to the natural family of a child. Section 1 [of the 2002 Act] does not impose any such policy. Rather, it requires the interests of the child to be considered. That must mean the child as an individual. In some cases, the birth tie will be very important, especially where the child is of an age to understand what is happening or where there are ethnic or cultural or religious reasons for keeping the child in the birth family. Where a child has never lived with her birth family, and is too young to understand what is going on, that argument must be weaker. In my judgment, in a case such as this, it is (absent any application by any member of the family, which succeeds) overtaken by the need to find the child a permanent home as soon as that can be done.'

Arden LJ concluded that the father had no Art 8 right which could be violated by adoption of the child without his knowledge. Lawrence Collins LJ observed that even if Art 8 were engaged, it would be difficult to envisage a situation in which there could be an interference with the exercise of that right where the father does not know (or care) about the existence of the child. Moreover, he took the view that the protection of the rights of the mother and child would plainly justify the interference with any such right.[191]

In *Re A (Father: Knowledge of Child's Birth)*[192] the decision in *Re C* was not perceived as contemplating a radical departure from the earlier authorities. The Court of Appeal said that Arden LJ had recognised that the circumstances in which a father would remain in ignorance about the child would be exceptional.[193]

---

[189] [2007] EWCA Civ 1206, [2008] Fam 54. For comment, see B Sloan '*Re C (A Child) (Adoption: Duty of Local Authority)* – Welfare and the Rights of the Birth Family in "Fast Track" Adoption Cases' [2009] *Child and Family Law Quarterly* 87.

[190] [2007] EWCA Civ 1206, [2008] Fam 54, at [3].

[191] *Re C* at [55].

[192] [2011] EWCA Civ 273, [2011] 2 FLR 123 (Black LJ, at [40], Longmore LJ agreeing).

[193] See *Re C* [2007] EWCA Civ 1206, [2008] Fam 54, at [24].

This is one aspect of adoption law, among others, which will continue to give rise to challenges based on human rights arguments. The desire of the courts to exclude from participation in adoption proceedings the man who represents a danger to the mother and the child is understandable enough and consistent with the general approach taken to the refusal of contact. The decisions in the other category of case, in which the father has been unable to establish a relationship with the child because his own relationship with the mother broke down before the child was born, are much more difficult to justify in terms of human rights. It may very well be that the decision to break the relationship in at least some of these cases was the mother's, and that the father, if informed, might have indicated a strong desire to exercise responsibility for the child from the start.

Dispensing with consent

The question of dispensing with consent has been at the heart of the conflict which can arise between the professional view of the best interests of the child and the fundamental rights which attach to the relationship of parent and child. While parents might understand that they are unable to look after a child themselves and might be prepared to have the child looked after by others, they might not be willing to accept the complete termination of their legal relationship with the child. Traditionally English law has viewed this as a question which involves the rights of parents and has made provision, through the statutory consent requirements, for the proper accommodation of those rights. Put another way, the approach under previous legislation has been to deny that the welfare of the child should be the sole criterion for determining whether or not an adoption should be granted. This was reinforced by the requirement that consent be either given by the parent or dispensed with on one of the grounds set out in the legislation. The major change brought about by the 2002 Act is that the welfare of the child has, controversially, been placed centre stage – both by its application throughout the new law and, more specifically, by making it one of only two conditions for dispensing with parental consent and, of these two, by far the more significant. This has led to quite legitimate speculation about what has happened to the rights of parents in the adoption process and may give rise to challenges under the ECHR.

The Adoption and Children Act 2002 catapults the welfare principle into the middle of this hugely problematic question. It abolishes all the previous grounds for dispensing with parental consent except for one and replaces them with the undiluted welfare principle which applies elsewhere in the Act.[194]

The all-important provision is now s 52(1), which provides:

---

[194] For discussion of the grounds under the previous legislation, see the third edition of this book, at pp 291–294.

'The court cannot dispense with the consent of any parent or guardian of a child to the child being placed for adoption or to the making of an adoption order in respect of the child unless the court is satisfied that –

(a)   the parent or guardian cannot be found or is incapable of giving consent, or
(b)   the welfare of the child requires the consent to be dispensed with.'

Condition (a) is the one ground for dispensing with consent which has been preserved from the old law. It was not much used and is unlikely to be used very often under the new law, but there has been a reported case involving the use of this ground. In *Re A (Adoption of a Russian Child)*[195] the mother was in Russia and had agreed to the adoption in Russia within six weeks of the child's birth. Her consent was insufficient for the English adoption of the child but the Russian authorities would not co-operate in locating her to obtain her consent to this. The court held in these circumstances that the phrase 'cannot be found' meant that all practicable means must have been employed and all reasonable steps taken to find and communicate with the parent. Charles J was in the circumstances prepared to dispense with her consent on the basis that she could not be found.

Condition (b) is now the major ground for dispensing with parental consent and will apply in all but a small number of cases. It raises the serious question of what weight, if any, is to be given to parental interests or rights in preserving their legal relationship with the child. What is clear is that if the court's view is that adoption is in the child's best interests, then whether or not the parent is behaving reasonably in objecting to this will have no bearing on the decision. If parental claims are to be fed into this process at all, then it is going to have to happen as an integral part of applying the welfare test as in other contexts in which the welfare principle applies.

In *Re P (Placement Orders: Parental Consent)*[196] the Court of Appeal gave guidance on the approach to be taken to dispensing with consent. The court said that judges approaching the question of dispensation under s 52(1)(b) should 'apply the statutory language with care to the facts of the particular case'.[197] Dispensing with parental consent is a decision relating to the adoption of a child, and accordingly s 1(2) of the 2002 Act requires the court to treat 'the child's welfare throughout his life' as its 'paramount consideration'.[198] Welfare is to be determined having regard to the matters set out in s 1(4) of the 2002 Act, which provides a far wider checklist of factors than that provided in s 1(3) of the Children Act 1989.[199] The court highlighted that the focus on the child's welfare 'throughout his life' emphasises that adoption has lifelong implications, and therefore a judge exercising his powers under s 52(1)(b) 'has to be satisfied that the child's welfare now, throughout the rest of his childhood, into

---

[195]   [2000] 1 FLR 539.
[196]   [2008] EWCA Civ 535, [2008] 2 FLR 625.
[197]   Ibid, at [117].
[198]   Ibid, at [114].
[199]   [2008] EWCA Civ 535, [2008] 2 FLR 625, at [115].

adulthood and indeed throughout his life, requires that he or she be adopted',[200] as reinforced by s 1(4)(c) and by s 1(4)(f).

The court commented that 'the word "requires" in s 52(1)(b) is a perfectly ordinary English word',[201] but it must be understood in its context, that is addressing the question whether the child's situation requires *adoption* rather than something short of adoption.[202] The Strasbourg jurisprudence also provides the context in which the word 'requires' is used.[203] Reviewing the main principles on state interference with the rights of children and parents under Art 8 of the ECHR (which will usually be engaged in this context),[204] the court explained that intervention must represent a proportionate response to achieving the legitimate aim (in this context, protection of the child's welfare).[205] In assessing what is proportionate the judge must always bear in mind that adoption without parental consent is the most extreme interference with family life, and therefore cogent justification must exist.[206] Thus, the court held that, viewed from this perspective, the word 'requires' has 'the connotation of the imperative, what is demanded rather than what is merely optional or reasonable or desirable'.[207] The court emphasised the 'need for care, sensitivity and intellectual rigour on the part of judges hearing applications for placement orders'.[208] The judge must not apply s 1(4) simply as a mantra, nor act as a rubber stamp; the 'underlying facts, properly analysed, must support the judicial conclusion'.[209] This is a valiant attempt, within the constraints of the paramountcy principle as interpreted by the House of Lords/Supreme Court, to emphasise the child's interest in his birth family not being disintegrated by adoption. However, for some it will be a pale substitute for the more full-blooded protection historically afforded by English law to the parents' rights and interests. Under the former law, notwithstanding the prominence of the child's welfare, the parental decision (provided it fell within a reasonable band of decisions) could be effective as a veto.[210]

---

[200]   Ibid, [128]. For an example, see *Re Q (Adoption)* [2011] EWCA Civ 1610.

[201]   Ibid.

[202]   Ibid, at [126].

[203]   Ibid, at [125].

[204]   Ibid, at [119].

[205]   Any interference must be in accordance with the law, pursue a legitimate aim, and be necessary in a democratic society (implying the existence of a 'pressing social need'). See the discussion at [119]–[124], citing *Re C and B (Children) (Care Order: Future Harm)* [2000] 2 FCR 614, at [33]; *Haase v Germany* [2004] 2 FLR 39, at [93]; *Re O (A Child) (Supervision Order: Future Harm)* [2001] EWCA Civ 16, [2001] 1 FCR 289, at [28]; *Re B (Children) (Care: Interference with Family Life)* [2003] EWCA Civ 786, [2004] 1 FCR 463, at [34]; *Re O (Minors) (Care or Supervision Order)* [1997] 2 FCR 17, at 22; *Johansen v Norway* (1996) 23 EHRR 33, at para 78.

[206]   See [2008] EWCA Civ 535, [2008] 2 FLR 625, at [124].

[207]   Ibid, at [125].

[208]   Ibid, at [132].

[209]   Ibid, at [131].

[210]   C Bridge and H Swindells QC (above), at paras 8.44–8.45. On the previous law, see s 16(2)(b) of the Adoption Act 1976, *Re W (An Infant)* [1971] 2 All ER 49, [1971] AC 682, and Lord Wilberforce's parent '(hypothetically) endowed with mind and temperament capable of making reasonable decisions' – see *Re D (Adoption: Parent's Consent)* [1977] 1 All ER 145, at 130, [1977] AC 602, at 625.

In *Re B-S (Children)*[211] the Court of Appeal expressed 'real concerns, shared by other judges, about the recurrent inadequacy of the analysis and reasoning put forward in support of the case for adoption, both in the materials put before the court by local authorities and guardians and also in too many judgments'.[212] The court insisted that it was necessary to call a halt to this state of affairs. The court indicated that adoption orders must be made on proper evidence by the local authority and guardian and 'sloppy practice must stop'.[213] In addition, judgments must be adequately reasoned, applying a 'global, holistic evaluation'[214] as explained by McFarlane LJ in *Re G (A Child)*,[215] the judicial task being 'to evaluate *all* the options, undertaking a global, holistic and (see *Re G* para 51) multi-faceted evaluation of the child's welfare which takes into account *all* the negatives and the positives, *all* the pros and cons, of *each* option'.[216] Clearly this requirement may lead to a greater burden on judges and lawyers than some apparently had been assuming before, and the Court of Appeal commented on how it sits with the Revised Public Law Outline and reforms to the family justice system. The court explained:

> 'We do not envisage that proper compliance with what we are demanding, which may well impose a more onerous burden on practitioners and judges, will conflict with the requirement, soon to be imposed by statute, that care cases are to be concluded within a maximum of 26 weeks. Critical to the success of the reforms is robust judicial case management from the outset of every care case. Case management judges must be astute to ensure that the directions they give are apt to the task and also to ensure that their directions are complied with. Never is this more important than in cases where the local authority's plan envisages adoption. If, despite all, the court does not have the kind of evidence we have identified, and is therefore not properly equipped to decide these issues, then an adjournment must be directed, even if this takes the case over 26 weeks. Where the proposal before the court is for non-consensual adoption, the issues are too grave, the stakes for all are too high, for the outcome to be determined by rigorous adherence to an inflexible timetable and justice thereby potentially denied.'

THE LEGAL EFFECTS OF ADOPTION

General effects

Adoption fundamentally affects the legal *status* of the child. The Adoption and Children Act 2002 provides that 'an adopted person is to be treated in law as the child of the adopters or adopter'.[217] He or she will also be the 'legitimate'

---

[211] [2013] EWCA Civ 1146.

[212] Ibid, at para [30], and citing by way of recent examples four cases: *Re V (Children)* [2013] EWCA Civ 913 (judgment of Black LJ), *Re S, K v The London Borough of Brent* [2013] EWCA Civ 926 (Ryder LJ), *Re P (A Child)* [2013] EWCA Civ 963 (Black LJ) and *Re G (A Child)* [2013] EWCA Civ 965 (McFarlane LJ).

[213] Ibid, at para [40].

[214] Ibid, at paras [41]–[46].

[215] See [2013] EWCA Civ 965, at paras 49 et seq.

[216] [2013] EWCA Civ 1146, at para [44].

[217] Section 67(1).

child of the adopter or adopters and, if adopted by a couple or one of a couple under s 51(2), is to be treated as the child of the relationship of the couple in question.[218] The child is then *not* to be treated in law as the child of anyone else except where legislation refers to a person's 'natural parent' or to any other 'natural relationship'.[219] Relationships which are created by adoption may be referred to as 'adoptive relationships',[220] an adopter may be referred to as 'an adoptive parent' or (as the case may be) an 'adoptive father or mother' and other relatives following adoption may be referred to as 'adoptive relatives' of the relevant degree, for example brother or aunt. Where, however, the adoption has occurred in the context of a same-sex relationship the expressions 'adoptive father' and 'adoptive mother' are not thought apposite and instead any reference in that case will instead be to the child's 'adoptive parents'.[221] An adoption order will also operate to extinguish the parental responsibility which anyone other than the adopter or adopters had for the child immediately preceding the making of the order.[222] It will also terminate, as from the date of the adoption order, any maintenance duty in relation to the child whether made by agreement or under a court order.[223] There are rules which govern the interpretation of instruments concerning the disposition of property which are beyond the scope of the present work.[224]

Adoption is therefore different from other court orders affecting children, for example s 8 orders under the Children Act, in that it is a legal transplant. Not only does it terminate existing parental responsibility and transfer this to the adoptive parents, it also terminates the very legal relationship of parent and child and the wider family relationships which derive from the relationship of parent and child and replaces these with new parental and family relationships. In short it replaces one legal family with another. There are certain limited exceptions to the transplant principle where the child's relationship with his or her birth parents will continue to be of relevance, the most important of which is that the child remains within the natural family for the purposes of the prohibited degrees of marriage and for the purposes of certain sexual offences within the family.[225] The reasoning here is that the rationale for these prohibitions is largely the perceived genetic objections to intermarriage and sexual relations between close blood relatives. So far as the former is concerned, it should be noted that marriage is prohibited also between the adopted child and his or her adoptive parent but marriage with other adoptive relatives is

---

[218] Section 67(2).
[219] Section 67(3).
[220] Section 68.
[221] Section 68(3).
[222] Section 46(2)(a).
[223] Section 46(2)(d).
[224] Sections 69–73. For a discussion of these rules, see Bridge and Swindells (above), at paras 10.85–10.88.
[225] Section 74 which states that s 67 does not apply to a number of enactments including the table of kindred and affinity in Sch 1 to the Marriage Act 1949, nor to certain sexual offences. Neither does s 67 apply for the purposes of the British Nationality Act 1981 or the Immigration Act 1971.

permitted.[226] So far as the latter is concerned, the principal offence has been incest in its various forms. It should be noted, however, that the Sexual Offences Act 2003 abolished incest and replaced this offence with new sexual offences which reflect the changing nature of modern families and which take greater account of the need to prevent sexual coercion within the context of adoptive relationships. These new offences do shift the focus somewhat from the genetic concerns of the past – though these still exist – towards the problem of abuse of power in familial relationships. That being the case, the protection afforded to an adoptive person may need to be as strong as that afforded to a natural relative in certain cases.

Setting aside an adoption order

Given that the purpose of adoption is to effect a permanent change of family, the making of an adoption order is seen as final, and it is thus very rare for an adoption order to be set aside.[227] In *Re B (Adoption: Jurisdiction to Set Aside)*[228] the Court of Appeal held that there was no general inherent power to set aside an adoption order on the basis of a mistake. B was the child of an Arab father and Roman Catholic mother and had been adopted and raised in the Jewish faith by an orthodox Jewish couple. On investigating the background, B discovered the truth and, now an adult, sought to have the adoption order set aside. While expressing sympathy for his position, the court thought that its ultimate imperative must be the inviolability of the adoption system.

This public policy consideration means that an adoption order will not necessarily be set aside even where natural parents have suffered a serious injustice.[229] In *Webster v Norfolk County Council and the Children (By Their Children's Guardian)*[230] three children were taken into care because of what was thought to be non-accidental injury to one of the children who had suffered fractures. Expert evidence subsequently suggested that the fractures were caused by a rare case of scurvy as a result of the child's diet which had been recommended by doctors. The Court of Appeal refused the parents leave to appeal out of time to have the adoptions set aside, having regard to the social importance of not undermining the irrevocability of adoption orders, and the interests of the children. By the time of the application, the children had been settled with the adoptive parents for four years.

---

226 Marriage Act 1949, Sch 1, as amended.

227 The imposition of conditions on adoption will be very rare too. See *Re S (A Minor) (Adoption: Blood Transfusion)* [1995] 2 FCR 177 (CA) (refusing to impose a condition on adoptive parents who were Jehovah's Witnesses obliging them to involve the High Court if the child required a blood transfusion).

228 [1995] 2 FLR 1. See also *Re PJ (Adoption: Practice on Appeal)* [1998] 2 FLR 252 where, despite finding that a step-parent adoption ought not to have been granted, the Court of Appeal refused to set it aside.

229 *Webster v Norfolk County Council and the Children (By Their Children's Guardian)* [2009] EWCA Civ 59, [2009] 1 FLR 1378 at [148].

230 [2009] EWCA Civ 59, [2009] 1 FLR 1378.

Re K (Adoption and Wardship)[231] provides a rare example of an adoption order being set aside. In *Re K*, the English foster parents had adopted a Muslim Bosnian baby found under a pile of bodies during the conflict in the former Yugoslavia. There had, however, been fatal flaws in the adoption process including failure to appoint a guardian ad litem, failure to contact the baby's appointed guardian in Bosnia, failure to serve notice of the proceedings on the Home Office, and the provision of inadequate evidence of the death of the natural parents. The Court of Appeal held that this was a denial of natural justice to the Bosnian guardian and, through him, to the natural parents. The adoption order was therefore set aside and the case remitted for rehearing.[232] At the rehearing in wardship proceedings, care and control was given to the foster parents, the child was to remain a ward of court and the foster parents were required to cause the child to receive appropriate instruction in the Bosnian language and Muslim religion. They were also required to report every three months to the Official Solicitor as to the progress of contact with the natural family back in Bosnia. The case shows the continuing value of wardship in some cases, especially where ongoing judicial control of a situation is thought desirable, and the inter-relationship of legal procedures affecting children.

Open adoption?

The Adoption Review recognised the argument for a system which would allow more 'open' adoption while preserving secrecy and confidentiality in those cases in which this was thought appropriate.[233] It was concerned that adoption law and procedure assumed 'a closed model of adoption where this was not always the case, nor always appropriate'. Accordingly, it made a cluster of recommendations to promote openness at different stages of the adoption process. These included the proposal that the child should have a statutory right to know that he or she is adopted; that the courts should continue to have power to make a contact order in conjunction with an adoption order;[234] that birth parents' wishes and feelings about such matters as race, religion, language and culture should be taken into account more than had been the case in the past;[235] and that adoption agencies should have power to be proactive in contacting adopted adults and birth relatives to ask whether they would agree to identifying information being passed on to each other.[236]

The Adoption and Children Act 2002 does not embody any clear directives as far as open adoption is concerned. The messages are mixed at best and any policy favouring a more open system of adoption, insofar as it may exist, is implicit rather than explicit. In terms of the provision of identifying

---

[231] [1997] 2 FLR 221.
[232] See also *Re M (Minors) (Adoption)* [1991] 1 FLR 458 (adoption set aside where father agreed to adoption in ignorance of the mother's terminal cancer).
[233] Adoption Review, at para 4.2.
[234] Ibid, at para 5.5.
[235] Ibid, at para 28.2.
[236] Ibid, at para 31.7.

information, there is much in the Act which does appear to support greater openness. But this needs to be set against the absence of any express statutory encouragement of post-adoption contact, although the power to make contact orders is preserved. More significantly, perhaps, the effective removal of the parental veto to adoption noted above and the official policy of driving up the adoption figures in relation to children in long-term care will be seen by some as less than unequivocal support for the preservation of the child's links with the birth family.

We focus here on two aspects of the open adoption question: post-adoption contact and the issue of identity.

Adoption and contact

The whole question of contact with parents and other birth relatives in the context of adoption has long been a controversial one[237] and it is fair to say that it continues to be an issue which provokes significant disagreement and, for that reason, some uncertainty in the attitude which the law is taking to the question.[238] In *Down Lisburn Health and Social Services Trust v H*[239] Lord Carswell noted that:[240]

> 'There have been some differences of opinion in the published literature about the desirability of contact, which is propounded by some as universally beneficial, while others are more cautious and urge a degree of flexibility of approach and avoidance of doctrinaire policies. They point out that in the wrong case contact can lead to disturbance of the children and impose a significant burden on the adopting parents. There is, however, general agreement that in appropriate cases contact can contribute to reassurance and security and a feeling of identity for adopted children and help to dispel feelings of rejection.'

---

[237] See D Quinton, A Rushton, C Dance, and D Mayes 'Contact Between Children Placed Away from Home and Their Birth Parents: Research Issues and Evidence' (1997) 2(3) *Clinical Child Psychology and Psychiatry* 393; M Ryburn 'In Whose Best Interests? – Post-Adoption Contact with the Birth Family' [1998] *Child and Family Law Quarterly* 53; D Quinton, J Selwyn, A Rushton, and C Dance 'Contact with Birth Parents in Adoption – A Response to Ryburn' [1998] *Child and Family Law Quarterly* 349.

[238] On the question of post-adoption contact, see J Eekelaar 'Contact and the Adoption Reform' in A Bainham, B Lindley, M Richards and L Trinder *Children and Their Families: Contact, Rights and Welfare* (Hart Publishing, 2003); C Bridge 'Adoption and Contact: The Value of Openness' [1994] JCL 147; Casey and Gibberd 'Adoption and Contact' [2000] Fam Law 39; J Masson 'Thinking about contact – A social or legal problem' [2000] CFLQ 15; C Smith and J Logan 'Adoptive parenthood as a "legal fiction" – its consequences for direct post-adoption contact' [2002] CFLQ 281; and E Neil 'Post-Adoption Contact and Openness in Adoptive Parents' Minds: Consequences for Children's Development' (2009) 39 *British Journal of Social Work* 303.

[239] [2006] UKHL 36, [2007] 1 FLR 121, a case on appeal from Northern Ireland.

[240] Ibid, at [44]. See Department of Health *Adoption Now: Messages from Research* (Chichester: Wiley, 1999) for an overview of research findings in this context.

He went on to say that 'courts must exercise care in assessing the effect which contact is likely to have on the particular child in the particular circumstances of the case, bearing in mind the paramountcy of the welfare of the child'.[241]

The traditional view of English adoption law was that post-adoption contact was contrary to the very nature of adoption, which severs irrevocably the tie between the natural family and the child, that there should be continuing contact between the child and the birth family. This was the view which largely prevailed in the courts before the passing of the Children Act 1989. Some relaxation in this position was evidenced by the House of Lords decision in *Re C (A Minor) (Adoption Order: Conditions)*.[242] Here it was held that there was power under the adoption legislation, in appropriate circumstances, to attach conditions to an adoption order and one of those conditions could be designed to preserve contact between the child and the child's siblings. A feature of this decision was, however, that all parties were in agreement and this was to become an important factor, perhaps even the decisive factor, in later cases which considered post-adoption contact.

Under the Children Act 1989 adoption proceedings fall within the definition of 'family proceedings', and the courts have therefore had jurisdiction to make a s 8 contact order when making an adoption order. So far as the underlying policy is concerned, the question of post-adoption contact came to be seen as an important, but by no means the only, aspect of the emerging notion of 'open adoption'. This was rapidly taking the place of the previous closed model of adoption in which secrecy and confidentiality at all stages of the process were the hallmark. It would no longer necessarily be assumed that contact with the birth family was incompatible with the nature of an adoption order. Cases then began to be reported in which such orders were made, but they were characterised by a high level of co-operation between the birth parents and the adoptive parents. In that event, it was recognised that there could be benefits to the child in preserving contact, albeit much more limited contact than the kind associated, for example, with divorce, but it remained open to doubt whether the courts would ever *impose* a contact order against the wishes of adoptive parents.

Thus, in *Re T (Adoption: Contact)*[243] the Court of Appeal was at pains to emphasise, in a case in which adoptive parents had agreed to allow the natural mother some contact, that the mother's security resided in the trust she had in the adopters and not in any court order. The onus should not therefore be on the adoptive parents to go to court in the event of disagreement over contact but should be on the mother who could go back to court with leave. On the other hand, once there has been agreement for some contact, the courts might expect the adoptive parents to adhere to that agreement. Thus, in *Re T (Adopted Children: Contact)*[244] the adoptive parents had resiled from an

---

241   [2006] UKHL 36, [2007] 1 FLR 121, at [44].
242   [1988] 2 FLR 159.
243   [1995] 2 FLR 251.
244   [1995] 2 FLR 792.

undertaking to provide annual reports to the adopted child's half-siblings via social services. The Court of Appeal allowed the half-sister's appeal against refusal to grant her leave to seek a contact order. The court took the view that if adoptive parents changed their minds about an informal agreement for contact they ought to give reasons for doing so and that their decision was open to challenge in the courts.

The Adoption and Children Act 2002 is largely silent on the question of post-adoption contact. By no stretch of the imagination can this be said to have been trumpeted either in the White Paper or in the Act itself. About the closest the White Paper came to mentioning it is a reference in two paragraphs to 'Links with the Birth Family'. The first of these paragraphs is concerned with supporting birth families and keeping them fully informed through the adoption process.[245] The second refers to a statement in the then draft Adoption Standards that 'a child's needs to maintain links to their birth family including parents, grandparents, brothers, sisters and other significant people should always be considered'.[246] This is scarcely a ringing endorsement of either open adoption generally or post-adoption contact more particularly. In the light of this it is not perhaps surprising that the power to make post-adoption contact orders is tucked away in a fairly obscure subsection of the Act.

Section 46(6) provides that 'before making an adoption order, the court must consider whether there should be arrangements for allowing any person contact with the child; and for that purpose the court must consider any existing or proposed arrangements and obtain any views of the parties to the proceedings'. There is therefore a statutory *duty* to address the question of contact and to have regard to any existing contact arrangements. In addition, as we have seen, the statutory checklist of factors requires the court to consider the child's existing relationships, the likelihood of their continuing and the value in their doing so. Moreover, it is expressly provided that there is a right, as at present, to apply for a s 8 contact order to be heard together with the application for the adoption order.[247] Yet none of this adds up to *encouragement* of post-adoption contact and there is no implication that, for example, all other things being equal, continuing contact with birth relatives is a good thing which is receiving official approval. This would have been possible, just as the Family Law Act 1996 incorporated a set of principles emphasising Parliament's expectation that contact with both parents should continue post-divorce.[248] Post-adoption contact receives no such official imprimatur.

Indeed in *Re R (A Child) (Adoption: Contact)*[249] the Court of Appeal expressed the view that under the Children Act 1989 the imposition of contact arrangements on unwilling adoptive parents will be extremely unusual, and this

---

[245] White Paper, at para 6.42.
[246] Ibid, at para 6.43.
[247] Section 26(5).
[248] Family Law Act 1996, s 1(c), and see chapter 5 above.
[249] [2005] EWCA Civ 1128, [2007] 1 FCR 149, at para [49].

view was affirmed by the Court of Appeal in *Oxfordshire County Council v X, Y and J*.[250] In that case the adoptive parents objected to the parents retaining a photograph of the child, fearing it might be placed on the internet to trace the child. The judge at first instance, assessing the risk of disruption to the placement as very small, granted the application, but the Court of Appeal overturned it. The judge had failed to apply the correct approach as set out in *Re R*. The 'essential question was whether the adoptive parents' fear had no reasonable basis'[251] since the court's focus had to be on the child's welfare and the court saw a clear link between the fears of the adoptive parents, and their sense of security, and the welfare of their daughter.[252] The court commented that it was far from obvious that the natural parents can have any Art 8 rights at all vis-à-vis a child who is no longer their child,[253] but in any event those rights would not have sufficed to tip the balance in their favour.[254]

How consistent the courts' approach to post-adoption contact is with human rights obligations is as questionable as are the provisions which facilitate dispensing with parental consent. Writing around the time of enactment of the 2002 Act, Bridge and Swindells offered the rather damning assessment that the 2002 Act 'does appear to be giving out the signal that the traditional approach of the clean break under the controlling hands of the adoptive parents is intended to stay' and that 'the suspicion is that the Government's "target" approach to adoption ... may have weakened any earlier resolve to change the climate of the closed adoption to a more open approach in the interests of the older child'.[255] It is difficult to disagree with this evaluation and there has more recently been little, if any, change. Indeed, the Children and Families Bill 2013[256] contains provisions which may be thought to erode further the commitment to more open adoption at least as far as post-adopton contact is concerned. Under the new provisions the Court may, inter alia, of its own volition *prohibit*, as well as allow, contact between the child and the individuals named in the statute.

The issue of identity

As we have seen, the child's identity rights are asserted by Arts 7 and 8 of the UNCRC.[257] Article 8 in particular is concerned with *preservation* of the child's

---

[250] [2010] EWCA Civ 581, [2011] 1 FLR 272. For comment, see K Hughes and B Sloan 'Post-Adoption Photographs: Welfare, Rights and Judicial Reasoning' [2011] *Child and Family Law Quarterly* 393.

[251] Ibid, at [28].

[252] Ibid, at [29].

[253] Ibid, at [43]. The position in the Strasbourg jurisprudence is rather unclear; see for discussion K Hughes and B Sloan 'Post-Adoption Photographs: Welfare, Rights and Judicial Reasoning' [2011] CFLQ 393.

[254] [2010] EWCA Civ 581, at [43]. For criticism, see K Hughes and B Sloan 'Post-Adoption Photographs: Welfare, Rights and Judicial Reasoning' [2011] CFLQ 393.

[255] Bridge and Swindells (above), at para 11.18.

[256] Clause 8.

[257] Chapter 2 above. For discussions of the child's right to know genetic origins, see T Callus 'Tempered Hope – A Qualified Right to Know One's Genetic Origins' (2004) 67 MLR 658, and

identity 'including nationality, name and family relations'. This issue of identity has surfaced in a number of different contexts including, for example, disputes over paternity and, as we have just seen, the question of post-adoption contact. It also arises where a child was conceived by donated gametes and the issue is whether the child has any right to information concerning the gamete donor who is, of course, the genetic parent.[258] Where the child is adopted, similar concerns arise about the extent to which the adopted person may have access to hitherto confidential information relating to the birth family which was obtained during the adoption process. The issue also arises as to whether members of the birth family should also be able to have access to information about the adopted person. These questions now have to be addressed bearing in mind the identity rights which are internationally protected.

Adoption self-evidently threatens identity rights because its purpose has been to terminate a person's link with one family and replace it with another. Traditionally the adoption process has been a secretive one and it has been usual to preserve the anonymity of adoptive parents and often to shield the child from knowledge about, or contact with, the natural family. Adoption proceedings are heard in private and adoption applicants have been able to apply for a serial number so that birth parents are prevented from discovering their identity.[259] Information collected during the adoption process is confidential and designed to prevent anyone from linking the child's identity before and after adoption. Gradually this view of adoption gave way to recognition, acknowledged in the Adoption Review, that 'a child's knowledge of his or her background is crucial to the formation of positive self-identity, and that adoptive families should be encouraged to be open about the child's adoptive status and the special nature of the adoptive relationship'.[260] It has also begun to be appreciated more that there are serious medical issues about information relating to the birth family where, for example, there is a risk of hereditary disease.

Legislation began incrementally to make greater provision for openness in adoption. Following the recommendations of the Houghton Committee, the Children Act 1975 (quickly consolidated in the Adoption Act 1976) enabled an adopted person over the age of 18 years for the first time to obtain a copy of his or her original birth certificate.[261] The Children Act 1989 then took the process of disclosure a stage further by establishing an adoption contact register, the purpose of which was to enable adopted persons to discover

---

J Wallbank 'The Role of Rights and Utility in Instituting a Child's Right to Know Her Genetic History' (2004) 13 *Social and Legal Studies* 245.

[258] As to which see S Maclean and M Maclean 'Keeping Secrets in Assisted Reproduction – the Tension between Donor Anonymity and the Need of the Child for Information' [1996] CFLQ 243, and J Feast and G Brasse 'Embryological Secrecy Syndrome' [2000] Fam Law 897.

[259] The details of adoption procedures are beyond the scope of the present work but are discussed in C Bridge and H Swindells (above), at pp 256 et seq.

[260] Adoption Review, at para 4.1.

[261] Adoption Act 1976, s 51(1).

whether attempts to contact relatives would be welcome and, where this was the case, to provide them with factual information which might enable them to do so.[262]

The Adoption and Children Act 2002 built on these earlier legislative initiatives by placing the primary responsibility for the collection and disclosure of confidential information on adoption agencies, but it also makes provision for restricting disclosure in circumstances which are not thought to be appropriate.[263] The statutory scheme is complex and the details are beyond the scope of the present work.[264] What follows is a description of the salient features relating to disclosure of information under the 2002 Act. The Act distinguishes between adoptions which take place before and after implementation of the Act, but the following discussion is confined to the scheme which applies in relation to adoptions which take place under the 2002 Act.

The Registers

The Adopted Children Register

The Registrar-General must continue to maintain at the General Register Office a register of adopted children together with an index.[265] The Register is *not* open to public inspection but any person may search the index and have a certified copy of any entry made in the Register.[266] The Act places a duty on the Registrar-General to make necessary connections between the register of live births under the Births and Deaths Registration Act 1953 and other records in which the person concerned has been marked 'Adopted' and the Adopted Children Register.[267] In other words, the legislation requires the preservation of connecting information which makes traceable the link between birth records and the later adoption of a child. One of the most important reasons for these statutory duties is to enable an adopted adult to obtain access to his or her original birth certificate. The means of access has, however, changed under the 2002 legislation. When exercising this right under the Adoption Act 1976, the adopted person applied directly to the Registrar-General.[268] Now, under the 2002 Act, adoption agencies are usually to be the gateway for all confidential information held by the Registrar-General, the court involved in the adoption or the agency itself. Accordingly, the application for access to the original birth certificate will now be made to the adoption agency, and the Registrar-General is obliged to give the necessary connecting information to an adoption agency

---

[262] Ibid, s 51A, as inserted by Sch 10, para 21 to the Children Act 1989.
[263] The principal provisions are ss 56–65 and ss 77–79, but much of the detail is consigned to regulations.
[264] For a more detailed discussion, see Bridge and Swindells (above), ch 12.
[265] Sections 77(1) and 78(1).
[266] Section 78(2).
[267] Section 79(1).
[268] Adoption Act 1976, s 51(1).

in relation to any person whose birth record is kept by the Registrar-General.[269] Provision is made for informing the applicant about the availability of counselling before taking this step.[270]

The statutory 'right' to obtain access to the original birth certificate has never been absolute. An adopted person has, prima facie, the right to receive from the appropriate adoption agency:

(a)   any information which would enable him to obtain a certified copy of the record of his birth, and

(b)   any prescribed information disclosed to the adopters by the agency.[271]

This is subject to any order to the contrary made by the High Court on application to the court by the adoption agency.[272] Such an order may be made by the High Court if it is satisfied that the circumstances are exceptional.[273] An illustration of what is likely to amount to exceptional circumstances occurred under the old law in the remarkable case of *R v Registrar General, ex parte Smith*.[274] Here the Court of Appeal upheld the decision of the Registrar-General to refuse access to a Broadmoor patient who had killed his cellmate in Wormwood Scrubs in the mistaken belief that he was killing his adoptive mother. The court held that access to his original birth certificate could be refused on the grounds of public policy if there was evidence to suggest that the applicant might use the information to harm his natural mother.

A number of limitations to this process of disclosing birth records should be noted.

First, the legislation confers no statutory right to be told that one is adopted, despite recommendations in the Adoption Review that there should be such a right. Clearly, it remains possible that an adopted person may go through life in ignorance of the fact that he or she is not the natural child of his or her parents. The problem is even more acute for children conceived by donated gametes who are statistically much less likely to be informed of the true position than are adopted children. It has been good practice in adoption for some time for children to be told of their adoptive status, and the expectation is that the overwhelming majority of adopted children will be told and will thus be able to take advantage as adults of the above tracing procedures. This does, of course, still leave the unanswered question of whether these 'rights' to knowledge of origins should be postponed until adulthood, and what rights, if any, children should have to information *as children* while they grow up. Clearly this issue lies

---

[269]   Adoption and Children Act 2002, s 79(5).
[270]   Section 63.
[271]   Section 60(2).
[272]   Ibid.
[273]   Section 60(3).
[274]   [1991] 2 QB 393.

at the heart of the debates about when it is appropriate for courts to direct tests in paternity disputes, whether there should be immediate post-adoption contact, and so on. The short point is that, if there is a right to knowledge of origins, there is a serious question about when that right should bite. And of course it is all too obvious that relationships which might have been encouraged and nurtured *during childhood* will be likely to be that much more difficult, if not impossible, to re-establish in adulthood.

Secondly, there is a limited right for those under the age of 18 but of an age at which they have the capacity to marry, that is 16 and 17, to be given information about whether or not it appears from the information contained in the relevant birth records that the applicant and the intended spouse may be within the prohibited degrees of relationship.[275] Similar rights are conferred on those conceived by donated gametes under the Human Fertilisation and Embryology Act 1990, as amended.[276]

Thirdly, these rights of access do not extend to a birth parent wishing to obtain the converse information about the adoption of their natural child. In *D v Registrar General*,[277] a mother was seeking to trace her daughter. The Court of Appeal held that only in truly exceptional circumstances would confidential information held by the Registrar-General be ordered to be given to a birth parent. On the other hand, natural relatives, although lacking a statutory right to connecting information, may in some cases be contacted by adopted persons under the scheme in the Adoption Contact Register and may also be able in appropriate circumstances to obtain confidential information from the relevant adoption agency. Thus, in *Gunn-Russo v Nugent Care Society and Secretary of State for Health*[278] there was a successful application for judicial review of an adoption agency's refusal to disclose confidential information in the adoption file it was holding on the applicant. Here the passage of time was an important factor. The claimant had been adopted as long ago as 1948, had managed to trace her natural parents, her adoptive parents were now dead and more than half a century had passed since the adoption. In these circumstances the court's view was that the agency's policy of non-disclosure was too inflexible.

The Adoption Contact Register

As noted above, this was an innovation of the Children Act 1989. The Adoption and Children Act 2002 requires the Registrar-General to continue to maintain this register.[279] The register is in two parts. Part I contains the names and addresses of adopted persons over 18 years of age who have obtained the

---

[275] Section 79(7).
[276] Discussed in chapter 3.
[277] [1997] 1 FLR 715.
[278] [2002] 1 FLR 1.
[279] Section 80(1). For research on use of the register, see J Haskey and E Errington 'Adoptees and Relatives Who Wish to Contact One Another: The Adoption Contact Register' (2001) 104 *Population Trends* 18.

copies of their birth certificates and who may wish to contact a relative.[280] Part II contains details of the name and present address of any relative who would like to contact an adopted person.[281] 'Relative' for these purposes includes, in relation to an adopted person, 'any person who (but for his adoption) would be related to him by blood (including half-blood) or marriage'.[282] Regulations will govern the disclosure of information where there is a 'match' on the register, and information must not be disclosed except in accordance with these regulations.[283] These provisions therefore go further than mere disclosure of the original birth certificate since they are designed to enable adopted persons and birth relatives to be given sufficient information to enable them to make contact with one another where they both want this.

Under the old law the adopted person, but not the relative, might be given the requisite information.[284] Thus, it was for the adopted person to decide whether or not to seek contact. Regulations made under the Act endorse this approach. The Adoption Review recommended and the Draft Adoption Bill of 1976 provided that adopted persons and relatives should be able to register their wish *not* to be contacted where that is the case.[285] The Adoption Act 1976 had provided only for those who positively wanted to make contact, although there was provision for cancellation of an entry in the register where the relevant person gave the appropriate notice.[286] The Review recognised that it might be deeply disappointing for the adopted person but it was also acknowledged that some birth mothers have suffered grave distress when traced by adopted children, or at the prospect of such an approach being made. While there is no express provision in the Act for registering a desire not to be contacted, the wording, it is submitted, is wide enough to include this situation. The Act talks of adopted persons and relatives 'expressing their wishes *as to* making contact'[287] and not their wishes *for* making contact.

Disclosure of information relating to a person's adoption

The Adoption and Children Act 2002 contains a cluster of provisions in ss 56–65 which regulate, in much greater depth than has been the case under previous legislation, the provision of, or refusal to provide, information relating to a person's adoption. There is a great deal of detail in the Act about this but what follows is no more than a description of some of the salient features of the statutory scheme.[288]

---

[280] Section 80(2).
[281] Section 80(4).
[282] Section 81(2).
[283] Sections 80(6) and 81(3).
[284] Adoption Act 1976, s 51A(9).
[285] Adoption Review, at para 31.5, and Draft Adoption Bill 1996, cl 65.
[286] Adoption Act 1976, s 51A(7).
[287] Section 80(2) and (4).
[288] For a closer analysis of the details see Bridge and Swindells (above), at paras 12.31–12.64.

Information about the adoption of a person and the various parties involved is held in three separate places – by the Registrar-General, by the court which granted the adoption and by the adoption agency. The policy of the Act is to make the adoption agency in future the principal 'gateway' for access to information from these three sources.[289] The policy has been influenced by human rights concerns about privacy, data protection considerations and by the awareness that the adoption agency is best placed to have access to the detailed information about the adoption which goes beyond some of the basic information held by the Registrar-General or the court. The agency is equally the best place to contact those concerned and to arrange for counselling. The Act therefore introduces a scheme whereby the adoption agency will act as the intermediary for disclosure of the information from these three sources. Information is then divided into different categories which *must* or *may* be disclosed depending on the type of information and the person seeking disclosure. Broadly, these categories are as follows:

(a)   information which an adoption agency *must* keep in relation to a person's adoption (this includes identifying information and is known as 'protected information');[290]

(b)   information which an adoption agency *must* disclose to an adopted adult on request;[291]

(c)   information which an adoption agency *must* disclose to a prescribed person (this is information which must be released to adoptive adults and adopted persons on request and is essentially s 56 information which is *not* protected information such as background information about the child);[292]

(d)   information which adoption agencies *may* disclose to any person in accordance with prescribed arrangements.[293]

In all these cases much of the detail is consigned to secondary legislation.

SPECIAL GUARDIANSHIP

In its White Paper which preceded the radical reform of adoption law effected by the 2002 Act, the Government recognised the need to provide a range of options for giving children who are unable to live with their parents a permanent and secure family life.[294] The 2002 Act amended the Children Act 1989 to streamline the procedures whereby step-parents and local authority

---

[289]   White Paper, at paras 6.44–6.46.
[290]   Section 56.
[291]   Section 60.
[292]   Section 58(3).
[293]   Section 58(2).
[294]   *Adoption: A New Approach* (above), ch 5.

foster parents respectively may acquire parental responsibility for a child where it is clear that the child is to remain with them on a long-term basis. Another change, applicable to all social parents, was the extension of residence orders to the child's eighteenth birthday. However, a residence order can be a less than perfect solution for those wishing to provide a permanent home for a child, for several reasons. First, parental responsibility, although acquired under the order, is *shared* with others already holding it – most obviously the parents. Secondly, residence orders are *revocable*,[295] in particular on the application of a parent. This is one of the key distinctions between a residence order and an adoption order, which is *irrevocable* other than in wholly exceptional circumstances. It explains why in the past some foster parents would be inclined to fight tooth and nail for an adoption order rather than a residence order, because of their perception of the threat of disruption to their family life which may be caused by successive applications to court by parents.[296] Restricting further applications without the leave of the court[297] could provide a partial but not completely satisfactory solution to these nagging feelings of insecurity.[298]

The White Paper recognised that there was 'no status which provides legal permanence, but lacks the complete legal break with birth parents of adoption'.[299] A special guardianship order (conferring the status of special guardianship) was designed to fill that gap with 'a new legislative option to provide permanence short of the legal separation involved in adoption'[300] and to tackle the problems of insecurity with residence orders identified above.[301] On the spectrum of legal substitute arrangements a special guardianship order thus sits somewhere between a residence order and an adoption order.

In its White Paper the Government identified a number of situations in which it was thought adoption could be inappropriate to the child's situation. These included the position of older children who might not wish to be legally separated from their birth families;[302] some children being cared for on a permanent basis by members of the wider birth family;[303] some children in minority communities which have religious and cultural difficulties with legal

---

[295] Section 8(2) defines all s 8 orders in such a way as to include orders 'varying or discharging' such orders.

[296] In *Re M (Adoption or Residence Order)* [1998] 1 FLR 570 the foster parents went so far as to refuse to continue to look after the child unless they were allowed to adopt the child.

[297] Under s 91(14). See chapter 5 above.

[298] This was ultimately part of the package of measures produced by the court in *Re M* (above) but had previously been rejected by the foster parents as an unsatisfactory outcome for them.

[299] White Paper, at para 5.2.

[300] Ibid, at para 5.9.

[301] For discussion, see L Jordan and B Lindley (eds) *Special Guardianship: What Does it Offer Children Who Cannot Live with Their Parents?* (London: Family Rights Group, 2006).

[302] For a critique of the assessment of birth families as carers themselves in the light of the new special guardianship provisions, see C Talbot and P Kidd 'Special Guardianship Orders – Issues in Respect of Family Assessment' [2004] Fam Law 273.

[303] Adoption by relatives has the added disadvantage of the distortion of existing family relationships.

adoption;[304] and asylum-seeking children who, while needing secure, permanent families, have strong attachments to their families abroad.[305] The Government's hope for the new option of special guardianship was that it would give clear responsibility for all aspects of upbringing; provide a firm foundation on which to build a lifelong permanent relationship between the carer and the child or young person; be legally secure; preserve the basic legal link between the child and the birth family; and be accompanied by proper access to a full range of support services including, where appropriate, financial support.[306]

The law governing special guardianship

The regime of special guardianship is set out in ss 14A–14G of the Children Act 1989.[307] A 'special guardianship order' may appoint 'one or more persons' to be the child's 'special guardian'.[308] They must be aged 18 or over and must not be a parent of the child.[309]

As with s 8 orders, certain categories of applicant may apply for the order *as of right*, while all other applicants may do so only *with leave* of the court.[310] Those qualified to seek an order as of right are guardians, holders of residence orders, those with whom the child has lived for at least three years, or who have the consent of those with parental responsibility or, where the child is in care, the consent of the local authority.[311] The restrictions on applications by local authority foster parents which apply to s 8 orders also apply to applications for special guardianship.[312] The order may be made in any 'family proceedings'[313] in which a question arises with respect to the welfare of a child either on application or of the court's own volition.[314]

---

[304] Islamic law in particular does not recognise the concept of adoption and has its own related institution of Kafala recognised by Art 20(3) of the UNCRC.

[305] White Paper, at para 5.8.

[306] Ibid, at para 5.10.

[307] Inserted by the Adoption and Children Act 2002, s 115. The provisions are supplemented by the Special Guardianship Regulations 2005 (SI 2005/1109), and with guidance: see Department for Children, Schools and Families *The Children Act 1989 Guidance and Regulations Volume 1: Court Orders* (London: TSO, 2008), at paras 2.59–2.66. A similar concept, custodianship, had been introduced by the Children Act 1975, following a recommendation of the Houghton Committee's Report (Cmnd 5107, 1972). For the history, see S Cretney *Family Law in the Twentieth Century – A History* (Oxford University Press, 2003), chs 17 and 20. The provisions were elaborate and little used and were not implemented until 1988, by which time the adoption provisions of the 1975 Act had been consolidated in the Adoption Act 1976: see *Re S (Adoption Order or Special Guardianship Order)* [2007] EWCA Civ 54, [2007] 1 FLR 819, at [5]–[9].

[308] Section 14A(1).

[309] Section 14A(2).

[310] Section 14A(3).

[311] Section 14A(5).

[312] Section 14A(4) and (5).

[313] For the definition of 'family proceedings', see Children Act 1989, s 8(3) and (4), and chapter 2 above.

[314] Section 14A(6).

Applicants are required to give at least three months' notice of their intention to apply to the relevant local authority which is looking after the child or in whose area the applicant resides.[315] The authority must then investigate and report to the court on the suitability of the applicant to be a special guardian and other relevant matters.[316] It is anticipated that this responsibility will fall on an officer of CAFCASS, and the court is precluded from making a special guardianship order unless it has received such a report.[317] The court is also expressly required, before making the order, to consider whether, if the order were made, a contact order should be made and whether any existing s 8 order should be varied or discharged.[318] This is a clear reflection of the consideration that special guardianship orders will often be expected to be made alongside the preservation of contact with members of the birth family. This is not to say, of course, that such orders for contact will always be appropriate nor that they will be inappropriate if, instead of special guardianship, an adoption order is made. The court may also give leave for the child to be known by a new surname[319] or for the special guardian to take the child out of the jurisdiction generally or for specified purposes since, without leave, a special guardian will not have authority to do these things without the consent of all those with parental responsibility.[320]

The effect of a special guardianship order is set out in s 14C. The special guardian will have parental responsibility for the child and, importantly, will be able to 'exercise parental responsibility to the exclusion of any other person with parental responsibility for the child (apart from another special guardian)'.[321] This right to act exclusively, often referred to in practice as 'overriding responsibility', does not affect those rules of law or statutory provisions which require the consent of everyone with parental responsibility such as those above, other issues such as circumcision discussed earlier,[322] or a parent's rights in relation to adoption or placement for adoption.[323]

Special guardianship orders may in principle be varied or discharged on the application of a special guardian, parent, guardian, holder of a residence order, person with parental responsibility before the order was made, the child himself[324] or the local authority designated in a care order with respect to the child.[325] The court may also vary or discharge the order of its own motion.[326]

---

[315] Section 14A(7).
[316] Section 14A(8).
[317] Section 14A(10) and (11), and see *Re S (Adoption Order or Special Guardianship Order) (No 2)* [2007] EWCA Civ 90, [2007] 1 FLR 855, at [14] and [15].
[318] Section 14B(1)(a).
[319] See, for example, *Re L (Special Guardianship: Surname)* [2007] EWCA Civ 196, [2007] 2 FLR 50 (a case in which grandparents were not granted leave).
[320] Sections 14B(2) and 14C(3).
[321] Section 14C(1).
[322] See chapters 4 and 5.
[323] Section 14C(2).
[324] Where the court is satisfied that he has sufficient understanding (s 14D(4)).
[325] Section 14D(1).
[326] Section 14D(2).

But it is crucial to note that there are significant restrictions on the circumstances in which an application to vary or discharge may be made and on the circumstances in which the court is permitted to grant the application. These restrictions are a cardinal feature of the new status of special guardian. The first restriction is that, most unusually in family proceedings, there is a general requirement that the leave of the court is necessary for the application. This applies not only to those who are not closely related to the child but also to, inter alia, the parents.[327] Moreover, when the court comes to consider the application for leave, it must *not* grant it (unless the applicant is the child himself) 'unless it is satisfied that there has been a significant change in circumstances since the making of the special guardianship order'.[328] These restrictions create in effect a presumption against variation, with the onus on the applicant to demonstrate a change of circumstances warranting disruption of what is conceived to be a permanent arrangement. In *Re G (Special Guardianship Order)*[329] the Court of Appeal held that the 'significant change of circumstances' test is similar to that in s 24(3) of the 2002 Act and accordingly the test should be the same, namely a weighing of the child's welfare and the prospects of success of the application as in in *M v Warwickshire County Council*.[330]

Sections 14F and 14G are concerned with support services for special guardianship. The details are beyond the scope of this work but the essential features are as follows. Every local authority is required to provide such services which include counselling, advice and information about special guardianship.[331] The authority may, and in prescribed cases must, carry out an assessment of the needs of individuals, including particularly children themselves and their special guardians, for these support services.[332] Where, as a result of an assessment, the authority concludes that a person has such needs, it must then decide whether to provide any such services to that person[333] and, where it does, it must in prescribed circumstances prepare and keep under review a plan for the provision of such services.[334] The Secretary of State is given power to make provisions in regulations concerning assessments, preparing and reviewing plans which may cover matters prescribed in the legislation.[335] The legislation also requires local authorities to establish a procedure for considering representations, including complaints, made by any person to whom they may provide such services.[336]

---

[327] Section 14D(3).
[328] Section 14D(5).
[329] [2010] EWCA Civ 300, [2010] 2 FLR 696.
[330] [2007] EWCA Civ 1084, [2008] 1 FLR 1093.
[331] Section 14F(1).
[332] Section 14F(2) and (3).
[333] Section 14F(4).
[334] Section 14F(5).
[335] Section 14F(6) and (7).
[336] Section 14G.

So what is special about special guardianship?

The obvious question which arises is what precisely is the difference between being appointed special guardian and, on the one hand, holding a residence order (now extended to the child's majority) and, on the other hand, adopting the child?

So far as residence orders are concerned, the key differences lie in the provisions relating to the exercise of parental responsibility and the circumstances under which orders for variation or revocation can be made. The special guardian will be 'in the driving seat' as far as decisions on the upbringing of a child are concerned and the parent, who it will be recalled retains parental responsibility, will be very definitely in the back seat at best. While this may already be true to an extent in practice with a residence order, it is more explicit in relation to special guardianship. There is perhaps an analogy here with the provision which restricts the exercise of parental responsibility by parents where a child is in care.[337] The objective there is also to prevent interference by the parent with matters relating to the child's upbringing. Yet the special guardianship provision is stronger. It not only gives the special guardian a right to restrict the parent's exercise of parental responsibility; it makes it plain that parental responsibility is to be *exclusively* exercised by the special guardian. The restrictions on variation of the special guardianship order are perhaps even more significant in insulating the special guardian from subsequent challenges by the parent to terminate the arrangement. This will only be allowed under the legislation where there is a clear change of circumstances which makes it reasonable to entertain such a proposal. This contrasts greatly with the residence order regime whereby parents and certain others may apply for variation or discharge of the order *as of right* unless there is a good reason for imposing on them what may be seen as the draconian s 91(14) order. Perhaps, therefore, the real distinction lies in a shift in the requirement that the court be satisfied that a restriction on further applications is justified, to an onus on the parent, in special guardianship cases, to demonstrate a very good reason for disturbing a largely secure and permanent arrangement.

What then is the distinction between special guardianship and adoption? The major difference of course is that adoption *terminates* one set of legal family relations and replaces them with another. It is a legal transplant in every sense. Special guardianship in contrast *preserves* such relationships. Succession rights between family members are, for example, unaffected by special guardianship. Despite the restrictions on revocation of special guardianship orders, it is still the case that they are revocable while an adoption order is intended to be irrevocable. At the same time, where an 'open adoption' is contemplated, in which the child will continue to have some limited contact with the birth family, the distinction between special guardianship and adoption may not be huge on

---

[337] Children Act 1989, s 33(3)(b), which allows the local authority to 'determine the extent to which a parent or guardian of the child may meet his parental responsibility for him'.

the ground. It is, however, fair to say that the assumption of continued contact with the birth family is perhaps stronger in the case of special guardianship than it is in the case of adoption. The adoption legislation is indeed (controversially) rather silent on that issue.

In *Re S (Adoption Order or Special Guardianship Order)*[338] the Court of Appeal provided some general guidance on the nature and use of special guardianship orders,[339] and particularly the choice between adoption and special guardianship.[340] The court first pointed out that:[341]

> 'special guardianship is an issue of very great importance to everyone concerned with it, not least, of course, the child who is its subject. It is plainly not something to be embarked upon lightly or capriciously, not least because the status it gives the special guardian effectively prevents the exercise of parental responsibility on the part of the child's natural parents, and terminates the parental authority given to a local authority under a care order (whether interim or final).'

The court added that:[342]

> 'There is nothing in the statutory provisions themselves which limits the making of a special guardianship order or an adoption order to any given set of circumstances. The statute itself is silent on the circumstances in which a special guardianship order is likely to be appropriate, and there is no presumption contained within the statute that a special guardianship order is preferable to an adoption order in any particular category of case. Each case must be decided on its particular facts; and each case will involve the careful application of a judicial discretion to those facts.'

The court drew attention to the distinctions between the status of children who are adopted and those who are subject to a special guardianship order,[343] and also to the equally fundamental differences between the status and powers of

---

338 [2007] EWCA Civ 54, [2007] 1 FLR 819.

339 The guidance was endorsed by the then President of the Family Division, Sir Mark Potter, and also incorporated in, and endorsed by the judges in, two other cases: *Re M-J (Adoption Order or Special Guardianship Order)* [2007] EWCA Civ 56, [2007] 1 FLR 691 and *Re AJ (Adoption Order or Special Guardianship Order)* [2007] EWCA Civ 55, [2007] 1 FLR 507. For discussion of the case law, see A Hall 'Special Guardianship – Themes Emerging from Case-Law' [2008] Fam Law 244.

340 For the merits of foster care rather than adoption, see *Re F (Adoption: Welfare of Child: Financial Considerations)* [2004] 2 FLR 440 and *Re P (Adoption: Breach of Care Plan)* [2004] 2 FLR 1109.

341 Repeating what the court had said at [78] in *Birmingham City Council v R* [2006] EWCA Civ 1748, [2007] 1 FLR 564.

342 *Re S (Adoption Order or Special Guardianship Order)* [2007] EWCA Civ 54, [2007] 1 FLR 819, at para [47]. There are thus no routine solutions: see ibid, at para [43]. See, however, the findings in A Hall 'Special Guardianship and Permanency Planning: Unforeseen Consequences and Missed Opportunities' [2008] *Child and Family Law Quarterly* 359 and 'Special Guardianship: A Missed Opportunity – Findings from Research' [2008] Fam Law 148 that aspirations for reducing the number of looked after children may not have been met.

343 *Re S (Adoption Order or Special Guardianship Order)* [2007] EWCA Civ 54, [2007] 1 FLR 819, at [44].

adopters and special guardians.[344] The court recognised that 'it is a material feature of the special guardianship regime that it is "less intrusive" than adoption'[345] and does not distort relationships as does adoption, but also material that special guardianship does not always provide the same permanency of protection as adoption'.[346] This 'is a factor, which, in a finely balanced case, could well tip the scales in favour of adoption'.[347] Thus in *Re M-J (Adoption Order or Special Guardianship Order)*[348] and *Re AJ (Adoption Order or Special Guardianship Order)*[349] adoption orders rather than special guardianship orders in favour of relatives were upheld where the children had not been looked after by their respective parents since they were babies, and where the adoption met the children's long-term needs for security and stability. By contrast, in *Re S (Adoption Order or Special Guardianship Order)*[350] the Court of Appeal upheld a judge's decision to make a SGO in favour of the child's foster mother rather than an adoption order because of the close relationship between the 6-year-old child and the natural mother, rejecting the foster mother's argument that special guardianship orders are usually made in cases of proposed adoption by relatives when adoption may distort family relationships. The Court of Appeal emphasised that each case must be decided on its facts and not by reference to categories of case.

It is clear, however, that adoption must be seen as a measure of last resort. The approach under the ECHR requires that for adoption to be justified, and for the interference with Art 8 rights which undoubtedly occurs, it must be a necessary and proportionate response to the child's situation. Put simply, if another alternative will equally well serve the child's interests, adoption would be an unnecessary and disproportionate response and would violate both the Convention rights of the child and those of the parent.[351] In *Re I (Adoption: Appeal: Special Guardianship)*[352] the Court of Appeal emphasised that it was not possible for a judge to decide that the child's welfare *required* adoption unless the judge had given active and detailed consideration to the pros and cons of special guardianship as an alternative disposal.

---

[344] Ibid, at [46]. For a full account of the differences, see the table set out in *Re AJ (Adoption Order or Special Guardianship Order)* [2007] EWCA Civ 55, [2007] 1 FLR 507, at 524–525.

[345] *Re S (Adoption Order or Special Guardianship Order)* [2007] EWCA Civ 54, [2007] 1 FLR 819, at [49].

[346] Note, however, that a restriction under Children Act 1989, s 91(14) could be imposed: see eg *Re K (Special Guardianship Order)* [2011] EWCA Civ 635.

[347] *Re S* above, at [68].

[348] [2007] EWCA Civ 56, [2007] 1 FLR 691.

[349] [2007] EWCA Civ 55, [2007] 1 FLR 507.

[350] [2007] EWCA Civ 54, [2007] 1 FLR 819.

[351] As emphasised by the Supreme Court in *In re B (A Child)* [2013] UKSC 33. See, for example, at para [130], citing *R and H v United Kingdom* (2011) 54 EHRR 28, [2011] 2 FLR 1236 and *YC v United Kingdom* (2012) 55 EHRR 33.

[352] [2012] EWCA Civ 1217; (2012) Fam Law 1461.

INTERCOUNTRY ADOPTION

Introductory background[353]

The significant decline in the number of babies available for adoption in developed countries has resulted in a situation in which demand from childless couples vastly outstrips the supply. One consequence of this is that there has been an upsurge in applications for intercountry adoption.[354] The figures for abandoned children across the world, particularly in Latin America, Asia and Africa, have reached staggering proportions.[355] As the *Adoption Review*[356] noted, it is scarcely surprising that some people, especially those unable to have children, should wish to combine the needs of destitute children with their own desire to have a family. Yet fears have been expressed across the international community that many of these adoptions have not been child-centred but have had, instead, as their main objective, the satisfaction of adult needs. Often they have been arranged privately and without the professional supervision, support and safeguards which characterise many domestic adoption laws including English adoption law. At their worst, some unregulated adoptions have

---

[353] See JL Gibbons and K Smith Rotabi (eds) *Intercountry Adoption: Policies, Practices, and Outcomes* (Ashgate, 2012); K O'Halloran *The Politics of Adoption: International Perspectives on Law, Policy and Practice* (2nd edn, Springer, 2009). For a critique of the ability of the Hague Convention to protect children, see D Watkins 'Intercountry adoption and the Hague Convention: Art 22 and limitations upon safeguarding' [2012] CFLQ 389, and, for an assessment of the Hague Convention, see L Silberman 'The Hague Children's Conventions' in SN Katz, J Eekelaar and M Maclean (eds) *Cross Currents* (Oxford University Press, 2000), at p 589, pp 606–615. For the process in England and Wales, see Naomi Angell 'Intercountry adoption and the court process in England and Wales' [2012] IFL 422. See also, DFE *Consultation on the Review of Intercountry Adoption Legislation* (11 October 2011). For some earlier accounts of the topic, see W Duncan 'Regulating Intercountry Adoption – an International Perspective' in A Bainham, DS Pearl and R Pickford (eds) *Frontiers of Family Law* (2nd edn, John Wiley & Sons, 1995); C Bridge 'Reforming Intercountry Adoption' (1992) 4 JCL 116; W Duncan 'Hague Convention on the Protection of Children and Co-operation in respect of Intercountry Adoption (29 May 1993)' [1999] *International Family Law* 31; C Bridge and H Swindells *Adoption: The Modern Law* (Family Law, 2003), ch 14. Much useful information on the position of children in sending States is to be found in ED Jaffe (ed) *Intercountry Adoptions: Laws and Perspectives of 'Sending' Countries* (Martinus Nijhoff, 1995).
[354] Selman estimated that by 2010 there would be about a million intercountry adoptions: see P Selman 'Intercountry Adoption in Europe 1998–2008 Patterns, Trends and Issues' (2010) 34(1) *Adoption and Fostering* 4. The trend is most dramatically illustrated by the upsurge in the aftermath of the Romanian revolution: see W Duncan 'Regulating Intercountry Adoption – an International Perspective' (above), at p 43. And for a review of the position in the former Soviet Union, see OA Dyuzheva 'Adoption and the Abandonment of Children in the former Soviet Union' [1992] Fam Law 389. For illustrations of the kinds of difficulties which can arise in practice concerning overseas adoptions, see *Re WM (Adoption: Non-Patrial)* [1997] 1 FLR 132 and *Re K (Adoption and Wardship)* [1997] 2 FLR 221. For the immigration difficulties which can occur, see *Re J (Adoption: Non-Patrial)* [1998] 1 FLR 225. Cf *Re B (Adoption Order: Nationality)* [1998] 1 FLR 965. The correct test appears to be whether the adoption is genuinely justified as in the best interests of the child as opposed to a 'status device' designed purely to confer British nationality and the right of abode on the child. The appellate decisions are, however, by no means easy to reconcile on their facts. See the comment by S Cretney at [1998] Fam Law 385.
[355] See W Duncan 'Regulating Intercountry Adoption – an International Perspective' (above).
[356] Paragraph 46.2.

involved corruption, child-stealing and trafficking.[357] Added to this, there is a further controversy about whether transracial adoptions are in children's best interests.

Some of these problems surfaced in the High Court in *Re M (Adoption: International Adoption Trade)*.[358] The facts of the case, shocking as they are, deserve extensive citation. A white British couple paid £18,500 (of which only US $1,000 was paid to the American birth parents) to adopt a black child. The rest of the money was paid to the lawyers involved, to an American adoption agency, and to the British so-called 'independent social worker'. The 'home study report' supported the adoption, despite the fact that the adoptive mother had been divorced four times and had six children by four different fathers. One of her children had been on the child protection register, she herself had been diagnosed with cancer and had attempted suicide more than once. Both Barnado's and the local authority had concluded that she was unsuitable to adopt. Despite all this, the adoption went ahead in the USA. Within five months the adoptive parents had separated and three months after that the adoptive mother committed suicide. The adoptive father then abandoned the child, who was placed with foster parents.

The birth parents sought return of the child to the USA but Munby J concluded that she would be exposed to the risk of significant emotional and possibly physical harm if returned. Instead he made an order freeing her for adoption in the UK. But he went much further than this in his criticisms both of what happened in this case and of the international adoption system more generally. First, he held that the adoption should never have happened. Secondly, the 'independent social worker', Jay Carter, had committed criminal offences under ss 11 and 57 of the Adoption Act 1976, which prohibit private adoptions and illegal payments. Thirdly, the 'home study reports' were deeply flawed, inadequate, positively and dangerously misleading. They rendered the author unfit ever to be involved in such work again. Accordingly, copies of the judgment were to be sent to the Director of Public Prosecutions and the Attorney-General with a view to criminal proceedings. And his verdict on the way in which some international adoptions are carried out was as follows:

'It is high time that this evil and exploitative trade was stamped out. It is a trade because, however it is dressed up, it involves the buying and selling of babies by intermediaries who pocket most of the large sums of money which change hands during the course of the transaction. It is evil and exploitative because it battens on would-be adopters who, unable to adopt through more conventional channels, are induced in their desperation to part with large sums of money to intermediaries whose motives are purely mercenary; because it battens on the emotional turmoil of disadvantaged and desperately vulnerable birth mothers who are induced to part with their babies within days of birth, who see little of the large sums of money paid to the intermediaries by the adopters and who too

---

[357] See Watkins' concerns that the responsibilities of central authorities can be delegated to profit making organisations: D Watkins 'Intercountry adoption and the Hague Convention: Art 22 and limitations upon safeguarding' [2012] CFLQ 389.

[358] [2003] 1 FLR 1111.

often, as in the present case, soon come to regret their hasty and ill-considered decision; and because it can cause untold harm to children, untold misery to their birth mothers and untold heartache to adopters.'

In an effort to meet these concerns, and to facilitate intercountry adoption only when it is in the best interests of the child concerned, the Hague Conference on Private International Law set up, in 1990, a Special Commission to develop an international Convention on intercountry adoption.[359] The Convention was finalised in May 1993. The principal aims and features of the Convention are considered below, but first we look briefly at the terms of the UNCRC and the recommendations of the *Adoption Review* as they applied to intercountry adoption.

The United Nations Convention

The Hague Convention takes, as its starting point, the principles of the UNCRC, and these must also be the yardstick for evaluating domestic law and practice. The all-important provision is Art 21, the relevant part of which requires Member States to:

'(b) recognise that inter-country adoption may be considered as an alternative means of a child's care, if the child cannot be placed in a foster or an adoptive family or cannot in any suitable manner be cared for in the child's country of origin;

(c) ensure that the child concerned by inter-country adoption enjoys safeguards and standards equivalent to those existing in the case of national adoption;

(d) take all appropriate measures to ensure that, in inter-country adoption, the placement does not result in improper financial gain for those involved in it;

(e) promote, where appropriate, the objectives of this article by concluding bilateral or multi-lateral arrangements or agreements and endeavour, within this framework, to ensure that the placement of the child in another country is carried out by competent authorities or organs.'

The Adoption Review

The *Adoption Review*[360] recognised that intercountry adoption, while not a solution to problems arising from world poverty, might, in some cases, represent the *only* opportunity for some children to have a stable home life. Accordingly, those applicants who were assessed as being suitable to offer a home to a child from overseas should be allowed to do so. At the same time, the *Review* took the view that the practice of intercountry adoption should be regulated to ensure that it only takes place where it is in the interests of the child concerned and with safeguards to protect the welfare of the child and to

---

[359] See, generally, W Duncan (above).
[360] Paragraph 47.1.

eliminate corrupt practices.[361] The system, it was said, should reflect certain fundamental principles accepted in international statutory instruments. In particular, intercountry adoption should operate as a child-centred service and *not* a child-finding service for adults. It should be allowed only in relation to those children who could not be suitably cared for in their own countries.[362] Other significant recommendations were as follows. It was proposed that children should be admitted to the UK only where authorisation had been granted by the responsible authority in the UK that the adoption proceed, subject to immigration requirements being met.[363] It was also proposed that local authorities should have a duty to provide services in connection with intercountry adoption, or arrange for them to be provided by approved adoption societies. They should be responsible for supervising the placement of children from overseas from the time of their arrival in the UK.[364] Once the new system had been properly developed, it was proposed that it should be a criminal offence to bring a child to the UK for adoption without having obtained the prior authorisation of the relevant authority to proceed.[365]

The Hague Convention came into force in the UK on 1 June 2003. The enabling legislation was the Adoption (Intercountry Aspects) Act 1999.[366] Most of the provisions of the 1999 Act were incorporated into the Adoption and Children Act 2002.[367] The main provisions of the 1999 Act enabled the UK to ratify the Convention; amended the Adoption Act 1976 to place local authorities under a duty to provide, or arrange to provide, an intercountry adoption service; enabled certain children who are the subject of a Convention adoption to receive British citizenship; and enabled those who adopt children in accordance with the Hague Convention or from a designated country[368] to apply to register the adoption at the Office of the Registrar General for England and Wales. There is a list of designated countries in the Adoption (Designation of Overseas Adoptions) Order 1973, as amended. Adoption orders made in these countries are automatically recognised in the UK. Following a recent consultation, the Government proposes to amend the Order only to recognise adoptions made in a country which has implemented the Hague Convention or which has signed (but not yet implemented) the Hague Convention *and* with whom the United Kingdom has a bilateral agreement.

---

[361] *Adoption Review*, at para 47.1.

[362] Ibid, at para 47.2.

[363] Ibid, at para 47.3.

[364] Ibid, at para 53.

[365] *Adoption Review*, at para 56.2.

[366] See D Ranton 'Striking the Balance – Intercountry Adoption in England and Wales' [2001] *International Family Law* 35.

[367] The position is also regulated by The Adoptions with a Foreign Element Regulations 2005 (SI 2005/392) as amended by the Adoptions with a Foreign Element (Amendment) Regulations 2009 (SI 2009/2563).

[368] There is a list of designated countries in the Adoption (Designation of Overseas Adoptions) Order 1973, as amended. Adoption orders made in these countries are automatically recognised in the UK.

The effect of the amendments made by the Adoption and Children Act 2002 is to extend the restrictions on bringing children into the UK in connection with intercountry adoption, and regulations made thereunder require prospective adopters to have their eligibility and suitability to adopt approved and to meet other prescribed conditions.[369] This is backed up by criminal sanctions with a maximum of 12 months' imprisonment and/or an unlimited fine on conviction.

The fundamental objective of the primary and secondary legislation is to try to ensure that the same adoption practice and professional standards are applied to both intercountry and domestic adoptions. Hence, the same requirement to provide an adoption service, specifically in this case for intercountry adoption, is imposed on local authorities and there are similar prohibitions on private adoptions.[370] Only local authorities and voluntary adoption agencies (VAAs) may 'make arrangements' for adoption, and it is made explicit that any arrangement for the assessment of a person's child is considered to fall within this expression.[371] The effect is that home study assessments and reports on the suitability of a person to be an adoptive parent may only be arranged and produced by a local authority or VAA which is registered. Other duties imposed on local authorities include the duty to monitor placements for adoption once they have been notified of a prospective adopter's intention to adopt, to prepare reports for courts considering applications for adoption and to report any breach, or suspected breach, of the legal requirements to the police for investigation. Prospective adopters must also give notice of their intention to adopt or not to give the child a home within 14 days of their return to the UK unless they have a recognised adoption order from a designated country.

Where the UK is the State of origin and it is proposed to take a child who is a Commonwealth citizen out of the British Isles with a view to an adoption overseas, those wishing to do so must apply for and obtain a court order authorising a proposed foreign adoption and conferring parental responsibility on them.[372]

Therefore, to summarise, where the UK is a 'receiving State' in connection with intercountry adoption, the precise legal regime governing such adoptions will depend on the status of the country of origin. First, there will be adoptions of children from the Hague Convention countries, which must comply with the requirements of the Hague Convention and regulations[373] Secondly, there will be adoptions from designated countries, which must comply with the relevant

---

[369] The Adoptions with a Foreign Element Regulations 2005 (SI 2005/392).

[370] See above.

[371] Adoption Act 1976, s 72, as amended.

[372] See the Adoptions with a Foreign Element Regulations 2005 (SI 2005/392). Clearly there are likely to be far fewer instances in which the UK is the 'sending State' rather than the 'receiving State'. There is a detailed academic analysis of intercountry adoption in Europe and the potential contribution of the ECHR in regulating it in C Fenton-Glynn *Children's Rights in Intercountry Adoption: A European Perspective* (as yet unpublished PhD thesis, University of Cambridge, 2013).

[373] See the Adoptions with a Foreign Element Regulations 2005 (SI 2005/392) and the

conditions. Thirdly, where adoption orders have been made in countries which are neither party to the Hague Convention, nor designated countries, it will be necessary to obtain an adoption order in a UK court having first complied with the above regulations.

The Hague Convention

Objectives

The objects of the Convention[374] are threefold. They are:

(1)   to establish safeguards to ensure that intercountry adoptions take place in the best interests of the child and with respect for his or her fundamental rights as recognised in international law;

(2)   to establish a system of co-operation amongst contracting States to ensure that those safeguards are respected and thereby prevent the abduction, the sale of, or traffic in children;

(3)   to secure the recognition in contracting States of adoptions made in accordance with the Convention.

Encouraging adoption of children within their country of origin

The Convention contains a number of fundamental provisions. One of these, which requires special mention, derives from the important principle of *subsidiarity* in Art 21(b) of the UNCRC.[375] This is that an intercountry adoption should only take place once the competent authorities in the State of origin have determined, after possibilities for placement of the child within the State of origin have been given due consideration, that an intercountry adoption is in the child's best interests.[376] This is, in many ways, the crux of the matter. The chief concern of the international community is that priority should be given to the fostering of child care services in the developing countries and that, wherever possible, children in difficulty should be kept in their families and, failing that, be placed with families in their own communities.

The purpose of the Hague Convention is, therefore, not simply to facilitate intercountry adoption but to regulate it so that it only takes place when the possibilities for substitute care in the child's country of origin have been exhausted. The difficulty is that, in many developing countries, inadequate

---

Intercountry Adoption (Hague Convention) Regulations 2003. There are also guidelines: see the UN Guidelines for the Alternative Care of Children, A/RES/64/142.

[374]   Article 1.
[375]   Discussed above.
[376]   Article 4(b).

child care services exist. Duncan[377] has noted how difficult it is for the child-centred approach to be maintained when, on the international scene, the supply of children available for adoption vastly exceeds the demand. It was his view[378] that the success of the Convention might ultimately be measured 'as much by what it does to encourage and stimulate the growth of child care services in countries of origin as by the number of intercountry adoptions effected under it'.

Once intercountry adoption has been approved

Assuming that it is determined by the State of origin that an intercountry adoption *is* in the child's best interests, the Convention contains a number of other fundamental provisions including the following.

(1) The competent authorities of the State of origin must ensure that the child is adoptable, that all relevant consents (including the child's consent where appropriate) have been given freely and unconditionally after appropriate counselling, and that they have not been induced by payment or compensation.[379]

(2) The competent authorities of the State of origin must also ensure, having regard to the age and degree of maturity of the child, that his or her consent has been given freely and unconditionally after appropriate counselling, where the child's consent is required, and that, where it is not, consideration has been given to the child's wishes and opinions.[380]

(3) The competent authorities in the receiving State must determine that the prospective adopters are eligible and suited to adopt and that the child will be authorised to enter and reside permanently in that State.[381]

(4) There should be no unsupervised contact between the prospective adopters and the natural parents until the fundamental requirements for intercountry adoption have been satisfied.[382] The purpose of this provision will be to prevent economic and other pressure being brought to bear on the birth parents.

(5) Transfer of the child to the receiving State is prohibited, until it has been verified by the competent authorities of both States that no bars exist to the adoption under the respective laws of those States and that a

---

[377] W Duncan 'Regulating Intercountry Adoption – an International Perspective' in A Bainham, DS Pearl and R Pickford (eds) *Frontiers of Family Law* (2nd edn, John Wiley & Sons, 1995), at pp 42–43.

[378] Ibid, at p 51.

[379] Article 4(a) and (c).

[380] Article 4(d).

[381] Article 5.

[382] Article 29.

permanent placement has been agreed. This is to avoid the situation of 'legal limbo' in which some children arriving in another State currently find themselves.[383]

Designation of a Central Authority

Another important feature of the Convention is the requirement that the contracting States designate a Central Authority to discharge their obligations under the Convention.[384] These Central Authorities are expected to co-operate with one another, especially in the exchange of information and in monitoring the operation of the Convention. Some of their functions may be delegated to 'accredited bodies', which are expected to be, for the most part, approved adoption agencies.[385] Finally, the Convention provides for the automatic recognition in all contracting States of adoptions certified by the competent authority of the State in question as having been made in accordance with the Convention.[386]

Recognition of Convention adoptions

Art 23 provides that an adoption certified by the competent authority of the State of the adoption as having been made in accordance with the Convention must be recognised by operation of law in all the contracting States. Such recognition may only be refused if the adoption is 'manifestly contrary to [that State's] public policy, taking into account the best interests of the child'.[387]

Romania: a test case for intercountry adoption?

No country epitomises the controversies surrounding intercountry adoption more, perhaps, than does Romania.[388] Before 1990 international adoption from Romania was a very rare occurrence. Then, following the fall of Ceaucescu in December 1989, the world became aware of the situation of large numbers of

---

[383] Articles 17–19.
[384] Article 8. Cf the role of Central Authorities in relation to the international Conventions on Child Abduction, discussed, at pp 750 et seq.
[385] See Articles 6–13.
[386] Article 23.
[387] Article 24.
[388] One of the authors, Andrew Bainham, acted as Special Adviser to Baroness Nicholson of Winterbourne MEP, in her capacity as rapporteur for Romania in the European Parliament. For the author's views on the issues surrounding international adoption from Romania in greater depth, see A Bainham 'International Adoption from Romania: Why the moratorium should not be ended' [2003] CFLQ 223. See also A Bainham 'Child Protection, Adoption and the Moratorium: An Important Crossroads for Romania' (2003) 3 *Romanian Journal of Society and Politics* 54. For a detailed exploration of the issues surrounding the practice of international adoption more generally, see S Dillon 'Making Legal Regimes for Intercountry Adoption Reflect Human Rights Principles: Transforming the United Nations Convention on the Rights of the Child with the Hague Convention on Intercountry Adoption' (2003) 21 *Boston University International Law Journal* 179.

so-called 'orphans' in large State-run institutions, in many cases in highly unsatisfactory circumstances. In 1990 the international adoption system was liberalised in Romania and this was accompanied by a new law passed in 1993[389] which facilitated declarations of 'abandonment', thereby in effect freeing up large numbers of children for adoption. A child looked after by the State could henceforth be declared abandoned where the parents were found not to have contacted the child within a period of six months. It is well-documented and accepted that throughout the 1990s a market in children sprung up in Romania. After 1997 the Romanian authorities made a 'constant offer' of children available for international adoption by maintaining a database. Children on this database would be allocated to agencies specialising in international adoption on a 'points system'. During this period *domestic* adoption was deliberately suppressed and 'fast-track' procedures operated to speed up *international* adoptions. The 'entrustment' or probationary period during which the child should live with the prospective adopters was waived for international, but not for domestic, adoptions. Large sums of money found their way into the pockets of unscrupulous intermediaries arranging such adoptions.

It is worth pausing to reflect on some of the worst excesses of this regime. An Independent Group for International Adoption Analysis[390] was set up by the Prime Minister of Romania and reported on these abuses in March 2002. It highlighted the creation of 'adoption pools' whereby children would be plucked from institutions by agencies, how documents were falsified and how expectant mothers in maternity hospitals had been coerced into surrendering newborn babies at birth. It reached the damning conclusion that Romanian law 'under the appearance of complying with international treaties would stimulate abandonment and financial profit from international adoption'.[391] The point about stimulation of abandonment is critical to an understanding of the argument for *prohibiting* intercountry adoption. The statistical evidence exists which establishes a clear association between the availability of intercountry adoption and the abandonment of children in Romania.[392] In other words, it needs to be understood that there is a strong likelihood that a significant number of children would not have been 'abandoned' and would not have been institutionalised at all but for the existence of the international adoption market.

In October 2001, the Romanian government imposed a moratorium on international adoption from the country other than for a category of special cases. Despite this, abuses continued to surface. In January 2004 it was widely reported that 105 children had been despatched to Italy in breach of the

---

[389] Law 47/1993.
[390] The IGIAA Report *Re-Organising the International Adoption and Child Protection System* (2002).
[391] Ibid, at p 26.
[392] The author was provided with statistics from the judets of Cluj and Valcea which show the abandonment rates sharply falling back after the imposition of the moratorium on international adoption from Romania in October 2001.

various applicable international Conventions following a visit to the country by the Italian Prime Minister.[393] At about the same time a criminal investigation was launched at the Ploiesti Maternity Hospital where it was alleged that the parents of certain babies were informed, without having had an opportunity to see them, that they were stillborn when in fact a number were reported to have been found alive and well several months later.

Romania's response to these abuses involved maintaining the moratorium while, at the same time, embarking on a wide-ranging reform of its entire child protection system, its child protection laws and its laws on adoption[394] in order to comply with the UNCRC, the ECHR and the conditions for Romania's accession to the European Union. Under its new child protection system there is a primary focus on preventive services for the family, closure of the large-scale institutions and their replacement with more suitable 'family-based' alternatives such as smaller family-type homes and the placement of children with 'maternal assistants' (foster carers). The new laws, inter alia, prohibit the placement of a child under two years old in an institution and give priority to placement with the extended family or, failing that, foster care. There are new measures to ensure birth registration and to combat the problem of 'abandonment' of babies by their mothers in maternity hospitals, backed up by criminal sanctions.

Since the Western media is fond of continuing to emphasise the predicament of children in large-scale institutions, despite all the progress made in Romania, it is important to set out the facts on de-institutionalisation.[395] The total number of institutionalised children fell by 34 per cent between January 2001 and December 2003. The number of large-scale institutions (with more than 100 children in care) dropped from 205 at the beginning of 2001 to 85 in December 2003. By the end of December 2003 some 537 alternative services had been created to prevent the separation of children from their families and to support children's re-integration into their birth or extended families.

Romania has, since the commencement of the moratorium, been under relentless political pressure to return to becoming a 'sending State' for the purposes of international adoption. Much of this pressure has emanated from the powerful adoption lobby in the USA and from certain other Western European countries. Often these are countries which are strongly opposed to *domestic* adoption and strongly committed to reunification of children looked after by the State with their birth families, but which have failed (apparently) to see the double standard involved in undermining Romania's own efforts to achieve the same for *its* children. Serious questions must be asked about

---

[393] See 'Child traffickers prey on Romania' *The Sunday Times*, 9 May 2004. The same incident was reported in *Ziua*, a leading Romanian newspaper, on 11 May 2004.

[394] These laws were passed by the Romanian Parliament in June 2004 and are due to come into force early in 2005.

[395] Statistics contained in a paper entitled 'Child Protection in Romania – Accomplishments and Challenges' prepared by the National Authority for Child Protection and Adoption and made available to the author at a conference in Targu Mures in May 2004.

whether this pressure was 'children-driven' and borne of a desire to help Romanian families and their children, or whether it was 'adult-driven' and has been about finding attractive European children for would-be adopters who have often not been accepted as suitable adopters by their own domestic authorities. If the latter is the correct interpretation, then such pressure runs counter to the whole spirit of modern adoption law. This is about the rights of the child and finding a family for a child. It is not about finding a child for a family, however much sympathy might be felt for those who long for a child.

The Romanian experience raises the fundamental question whether intercountry adoption is better *regulated* (as it is by the Hague Convention) or *prohibited*. While it should be acknowledged that there are of course instances in which children are truly 'orphaned' or 'abandoned', for example in circumstances of war or famine, international obligations require Romania (and those other countries in Eastern Europe which are members of the Council of Europe and either members of, or aspiring to be members of, the European Union) to operate effective child protection systems which enable them properly to look after all those children who may be in difficulty. The phenomenon of intercountry adoption from such countries is nothing less than an admission of failure on the part of the State to achieve this goal. It is something which, more often than not, under the imprimatur of the Hague Convention, masks multiple breaches by the State concerned of the UNCRC and the ECHR.

CONCLUDING COMMENTS

Arguably there has been too much concern in the context of intercountry adoption for the regulation of *individual* adoptions and of safeguarding the welfare of the individual children involved (although it is certainly not conceded that the Convention has been successful in this respect), and too little concern for the *collective* interests of children and birth families in the country of origin. The fact that an individual institutionalised child might conceivably benefit from adoption abroad must be weighed against the perpetuation of a system which can be operated to the detriment of the domestic child protection system in the country of origin. The very existence of intercountry adoption may divert valuable resources, human and financial, into a system which at best can only assist a tiny minority of children in difficulty.

Within England and Wales there has been considerable emphasis in recent policy debate surrounding adoption on ensuring that children who are 'looked after' by local authorities and who would benefit from the stability and nurture of an adoptive family, are offered this possibility and offered it without unnecessary delay. Care will need to be taken, however, to ensure that this policy, and any resulting swiftness with which the adoption process takes place, does not ride roughshod over the interests of birth parents, and the interests that some children may have in retaining family life with their birth families. There is always a danger that a 'pushing' of the option of adoption, by targeting a substantial increase in its use, can mutate subtly to the idea of adoption as the *preferred* option for children in long-term care. Such a policy sits very uneasily with the approach of the ECtHR and it will fall to the judiciary to ensure that adoption takes place only where other measures of family support and substitute care will not adequately safeguard the child's welfare and that, even where adoption proves necessary, care is taken to preserve the child's identity rights and interest in maintaining some connection with the birth family.

As Patrick Parkinson[396] has observed there is great potential for debates surrounding adoption for children in need of protection to become polarised, emphasising *either* family support and 'partnership' *or* adoption[397] as the preferred form of permanency planning and something to be championed in the name of children's rights. However, as he points out:

> 'the notion that children's rights can be pitted against parents' rights is altogether too simplistic. Families, even dysfunctional and abusive ones, have complex patterns of interrelatedness which make it problematic to conceive of the situation in terms of sharp lines or to conceptualise the issues in oppositional terms'.[398]

When decision-making about the future of individual children is at stake, 'it is important that such political initiatives are scrutinised carefully in the light of human rights instruments and available research'.[399]

---

[396] P Parkinson 'Child Protection, Permanency Planning and Children's Right to Family Life' (2003) 17 *International Journal of Law, Policy and the Family* 147.

[397] A pro adoption policy was taken, for example, in the USA by the Adoption and Safe Families Act 1997 (For a penetrating critique of the Act, see B Bennett Woodhouse 'The Adoption and Safe Families Act: A Major Shift in Child Welfare Law and Policy' in A Bainham (ed) *The International Survey of Family Law (2000 Edition)* (Family Law, 2000), at p 375) but in a number of major European States such as France, Sweden and the Netherlands, and in Australia and New Zealand much greater emphasis has been placed on family support and reunification. For comparison, see A Warman and C Roberts *Adoption and Looked After Children – an International Comparison* Working Paper 2003/1, Oxford Centre for Family Law and Policy, Department of Social Policy, University of Oxford (2003).

[398] Parkinson (above), at p 167.

[399] Ibid.

Part IV

CHILDREN AND SOCIETY

Part IV of this book is concerned primarily with issues which arise in relation to the child's activities outside the family. This is not an easy distinction to make since the family is often (if not always) affected by these activities. But such a distinction can be made for the purposes of exposition and analysis. It is certainly the case that, whereas Parts II and III have been principally concerned with what might be described as 'mainstream family law', the subjects under discussion in Part IV take the family lawyer into other legal spheres. And whereas Parts II and III have been predominantly concerned with the statutory code constituted by the Children Act 1989, Part IV involves an examination of many other pieces of legislation, common law rules and international instruments.

Chapter 14 highlights an issue crucial to the position of children in the legal system – their standing before the courts. This chapter concentrates on the two issues of representation and evidence in children cases including the evidence of children themselves. Chapter 15 discusses the position of children, or more accurately children and young persons, under the criminal law. Chapter 16 does the same in relation to the civil law concentrating, particularly, on the two great areas of the common law, contract and tort, but also pausing to look at the thorny issues surrounding children's employment. Both of these chapters identify, as central features of the law applying to children, the twin concepts of protection and responsibility. Chapter 17 examines education law, so crucial to the rights of both children and parents.

Chapter 14

CHILDREN IN COURT

INTRODUCTION

The greater awareness of the independent interests and capacities of children, noted elsewhere in this work, has also manifested itself in changes to the legal standing of children in the courts.[1] Indeed, without these changes it might have been difficult to speak with any conviction about children's rights. Rights are arguably of little value, and certainly of less value, where the machinery does not exist for their enforcement.[2] In the case of children, there is an initial difficulty in that the protection of their rights or interests is usually dependent on the intervention of interested adults, most obviously their parents. Children generally suffer from a natural disability, reflected in a legal disability, which prevents them from bringing legal proceedings on their own account. In the case of young children, this factual dependency on adults is self-evident. It is less so in the case of older children, especially adolescents. But whatever the age of the child there is an ever-present danger that there may be a conflict of interest between the child and the adult on whom he or she is dependent for taking action. As has been seen,[3] this became apparent in public law cases in the 1970s when the Children Act 1975 first provided for the separate representation of children in care proceedings.

This dependency on adults is illustrated by many features of the legal procedures which govern children cases. In ordinary civil litigation, children are usually required to commence and conduct proceedings through an adult known for these purposes as a 'litigation friend'.[4] In private family proceedings, children are rarely parties, and their independent interests are usually represented, if at all, through welfare reports by children and family reporters (formerly known as court welfare officers).[5] No public official is charged generally with the responsibility of bringing proceedings on behalf of

---

[1]   The representation of children and reports in proceedings involving children are now governed by Part 16 of the Family Procedure Rules 2010 (hereafter the 'FPR') and by Practice Direction 16A – *Representation of Children* (hereafter 'PD16A'). For a general evaluation of the position of children in family proceedings, drawing on empirical research, see N Lowe and M Murch 'Children's Participation in the Family Justice System – Translating Principles into Practice' [2001] CFLQ 137.

[2]   This is not to deny the value of international normative standards as reflected in Conventions like the UNCRC, as to which see chapter 2 above.

[3]   In chapter 12 above.

[4]   See FPR, Chapter 5 and PD16A, Part 2.

[5]   FPR, Chapter 10 and PD16A, Part 6.

children.[6] Moreover, rules of evidence relating to child witnesses traditionally incorporated warnings about placing too much reliance on children's evidence and were, on the whole, unsympathetic to the special difficulties which they faced when confronting the intimidating environment of the courts.[7]

A new philosophy: the importance of children's views

The new philosophy of the Children Act 1989, with its emphasis on the importance of children's views[8] and the primacy of their interests, necessitated change on several fronts. The Act allows children to commence and conduct certain types of family proceedings in their own right in specified circumstances; they are given party status in a wider range of proceedings and there is much greater provision for their separate representation. Changes to the law of evidence (some in the Children Act and some outside it) were designed to give greater credence to the evidence of children and to make the process of giving evidence a less stressful one for them.

These changes are best seen as incremental. In particular, the greater representation of children in the public sphere has not been extended in a major way to private law cases, although the Family Law Act 1996 did empower the Lord Chancellor to provide by regulations for the separate representation of children in certain specified proceedings.[9] The Adoption and Children Act 2002[10] amended the Children Act 1989 to enable proceedings for the making, variation or discharge of s 8 orders to be included in the list of 'specified proceedings' which may be added by rules of court. There are some who think that the changes to the law of evidence which have been made fall well short of tackling the fundamental problem as they see it – that children should not appear as witnesses in court at all.[11] It is fair to say, however, that the Youth Justice and Criminal Evidence Act 1999 introduced substantial further reforms, especially by empowering the courts to make 'special measures directions' in children cases.[12]

This chapter highlights these changes. We begin by considering briefly the human rights requirements and international obligations which may bear on the general question of children's access to the courts and representation. We then look at the rules governing the way in which legal proceedings involving children are commenced and conducted. We then turn to the crucial question

---

[6] It is not, for example, the function of the Official Solicitor to *initiate* wardship proceedings but only to act in existing proceedings. See Heilbron J's remarks in *Re D (A Minor) (Wardship: Sterilisation)* [1976] Fam 185, at 197.

[7] Again wardship, with its inquisitorial approach, has been something of an exception.

[8] See chapter 2 above. But for a case evincing a more cautious attitude to the significance of children's views in care proceedings, see *Re C (A Minor) (Care: Child's Wishes)* [1993] 1 FLR 832. See also the cases granting leave to children to commence proceedings, at pp 733 et seq.

[9] Section 64.

[10] Section 122(1)(b), inserting s 41(6A) into the Children Act 1989.

[11] See, for example, JR Spencer 'Child Witnesses, Video-Technology and the Law of Evidence' [1987] Crim LR 76.

[12] See pp 760 et seq below.

of representation and conclude with a section on the rules applying to child witnesses in legal proceedings both civil and criminal.

INTERNATIONAL OBLIGATIONS AND HUMAN RIGHTS IN THE COURT PROCESS

We noted that one of the most important Articles in the UNCRC is Art 12. This enshrines the right of 'the child who is capable of forming his or her own views ... to express those views freely in all matters affecting the child, the views of the child being given due weight in accordance with the age and maturity of the child'.[13] Article 12 goes on to be more explicit about the child's right to be heard in the court process, providing that 'the child shall in particular be provided the opportunity to be heard in any judicial and administrative proceedings affecting the child, either directly, or through a representative or an appropriate body, in a manner consistent with the procedural rules of national law'.[14]

These are statements of broad principle indicating the international community's commitment to the importance of listening to the child's views in court as elsewhere. It should be noted that the commitment is to a *qualified*, not absolute, level of autonomy. Children have a right to be heard and to have their views taken seriously, but not to take decisions which are properly left to the courts to make in the light not only of the child's views but also of the child's welfare.[15] There is a lack of detail in Art 12 about how precisely the child's views should be presented to the court and what level of representation is mandated. The Council of Europe has attempted to flesh out these procedural obligations towards children in a Convention directly concerned with the *exercise* of children's rights.

The European Convention on the Exercise of Children's Rights 1996

The European Convention on the Exercise of Children's Rights[16] is, as its title suggests, not concerned with creating substantive rights for children but with the practical implementation of their rights.[17] The Convention is the response of the Council of Europe to the perceived need for an instrument to

---

¹³ Article 12(1).
¹⁴ Article 12(2).
¹⁵ See also chapter 5.
¹⁶ At the time of writing the Convention had been ratified by some 17 European states but not by the United Kingdom. A detailed evaluation of the Convention is to be found in J Fortin, *Children's Rights and the Developing Law* (3rd edn, Cambridge University Press, 2009), at pp 236–239.
¹⁷ For commentary on the Convention, see M Freeman *The Moral Status of Children* (Martinus Nijhoff, 1997), at pp 57–59; G Van Bueren 'Annual Review of International Family Law' in A Bainham (ed) *The International Survey of Family Law 1995* (Martinus Nijhoff, 1997), at pp 5–8; M Killerby 'The Draft European Convention on the Exercise of Children's Rights' (1995)

supplement the UNCRC, Art 4 of which requires States parties to 'undertake all appropriate legislative, administrative and other measures for the implementation of the rights recognised in [that] Convention'.[18]

The object of the 1996 Convention is set out in Art 1(2) and is:

'... in the best interests of children, to promote their rights, to grant them procedural rights and to facilitate the exercise of these rights by ensuring that children are, themselves or through other persons or bodies, informed and allowed to participate in the proceedings affecting them before a judicial authority.'

The subject-matter of the Convention is therefore procedural rights. It is about the participation of children in family proceedings affecting them – in short, their right to be heard – and, as indicated above, it builds upon Art 12(2) of the UNCRC.

Scope of the Convention

The Convention applies to children under the age of 18.[19] It is concerned with 'family proceedings' before a judicial authority which, for these purposes, includes an administrative authority having equivalent powers. The Convention contains no definition of 'family proceedings' but it is made explicit that the expression includes 'those involving the exercise of parental responsibilities, in particular, residence and access to children'.[20] Each State is required to specify at least three types of family proceedings before a judicial authority to which the Convention is to apply.[21] As Freeman has rightly pointed out, it would be much easier for English law to comply with the Convention's requirements in those family proceedings in which care or adoption issues arise than in relation to 'private' family proceedings such as divorce or freestanding applications for residence or contact,[22] although later provisions in the Adoption and Children Act 2002 have led to increased representation of children in private proceedings.[23]

What then are the requirements of the Convention? The key provisions are Arts 3 and 4. Article 3 gives to the child 'considered by internal law as having sufficient understanding' the rights:

(a)   to receive all relevant information;

International Journal of Children's Rights 127; and C Sawyer 'One Step Forward, Two Steps Back – The European Convention on the Exercise of Children's Rights' [1999] CFLQ 151.

[18]   For a more detailed discussion of the initiatives of the Council of Europe in the area of children's rights, see J Fortin *Children's Rights and the Developing Law* (3rd edn, Cambridge University Press, 2009), at pp 72–73.

[19]   Article 1(1).

[20]   Article 1(3).

[21]   Article 1(4).

[22]   M Freeman *The Moral Status of Children* (above), at p 58.

[23]   See below.

(b)   to be consulted and express his or her views; and

(c)   to be informed of the possible consequences of his or her wishes and the possible consequences of any decision.

Article 4 relates to separate representation of children in cases of conflicts of interest which preclude the 'holders of parental responsibilities' from representing the children themselves. It provides that, in these circumstances, the child concerned 'shall have the right to apply in person or through other persons or bodies for a special representative'.[24] Other principles under the Convention strike a chord with English family legislation. There is, for example, a duty on the part of judicial authorities 'to act speedily to avoid any unnecessary delay and procedures [must] be available to ensure that [their] decisions are rapidly enforced'.[25] In urgent cases, judicial authorities are to have power to take decisions which are immediately enforceable and to act of their own motion in 'serious cases' where the welfare of the child is in danger.[26] There is encouragement of mediation but, as Freeman comments, the Convention curiously 'does not extend the procedural rights just listed to this method of dispute resolution'.[27] The position of children in the mediation process remains a matter of considerable uncertainty.[28] A Standing Committee was established to keep under review problems relating to the Convention, to consider any relevant questions concerning its interpretation or implementation, to propose amendments and to provide advice and assistance to the national bodies having functions under the Convention.[29]

Assessment of the Convention

The Convention has not had an enthusiastic reception from commentators who have been quick to draw attention to its limitations. Van Bueren regrets that more was not done to encourage States 'to begin to develop innovative methods of child participation in family proceedings' and considers some of the language used in the Convention to be unduly restrictive.[30] Freeman describes it as a 'weak document' and thinks it 'toothless' when compared with the ECHR.[31] Fortin[32] has highlighted the restrictive nature of the requirement of 'understanding' on the part of the child when compared with the more liberal requirement in Art 12 of the UNCRC that the child should merely be 'capable of forming his or her own views' on the matter in question. She sees this as having the potential for seriously undermining the requirement of the UNCRC and draws attention also to the problems of formally demonstrating a conflict

---

[24]   Under Art 4(2), States are free to limit this right to children who are considered by internal law to have sufficient understanding.

[25]   Article 7. Cf the 'no delay' principle under the Children Act 1989 discussed in chapter 2.

[26]   Articles 7 and 8.

[27]   Article 13, and M Freeman (above), at p 58.

[28]   See chapter 5 above.

[29]   Articles 16 et seq.

[30]   G Van Beuren 'Annual Review of International Family Law' (above).

[31]   M Freeman (above), at p 39.

[32]   *Children's Rights and the Developing Law* (3rd edn, Cambridge University Press, 2009), ch 7.

of interest between the child and others for the purpose of demanding separate representation. She concludes that 'the Convention appears to be gathering dust, not without reason'. At the same time, there is general acknowledgement that the Convention has a symbolic significance in drawing the attention of States to the procedural rights of children and in recognising that without effective remedies the assertion of rights may be little more than empty rhetoric.

The European Convention on Human Rights

Since the implementation of the HRA 1998, there has also been concern that failure to ensure adequate participation and representation of children in legal proceedings might lead to breaches of the ECHR, especially of Art 6 which guarantees the right to a fair hearing in civil, as well as criminal, proceedings. In principle this applies equally to children as persons under the Convention.[33]

There has as yet been little testing of the extent of the obligations under the ECHR to provide representation for children.[34] There has been an indication by the Grand Chamber of the ECtHR that it would be going too far to say that domestic courts should always hear evidence from a child in court on the question of access (contact). In the cases in question[35] one of the children had been five years old at the relevant time, and the Court held that the German court had been entitled to rely on the findings of an expert whose competence there had been no reason to doubt. There had been no direct contact between the other child and the German court which had been well placed to evaluate her statements and establish whether or not she had been able to make up her own mind. On the other hand, in the criminal context, the ECtHR has emphasised the procedural rights of young children to a fair hearing.[36]

As we shall see, the extensive provision for the separate representation of children in public law proceedings in England almost certainly complies with the requirements of Arts 6 and 8. The doubts revolve around the adequacy of participatory rights in private law children cases in which there is a conflict of interest between them and the adults involved.[37]

---

[33] For discussion of the requirements of Arts 6 and 8 in terms of children's access to the courts and representation see S Choudhry and J Herring *European Human Rights and Family Law* (Hart Publishing, 2010), at pp 239–241.

[34] But for an evaluation of what might be required under the ECHR, see J Munby 'Making Sure the Child is Heard – Part 2 – Representation' [2004] Fam Law 427.

[35] *Sahin v Germany*; *Somerfeld v Germany* [2003] 2 FLR 671.

[36] *V and T v United Kingdom* (1999) 30 EHRR 121.

[37] See pp 748 et seq below and the discussion of *Re A (Contact: Separate Representation)* [2001] 1 FLR 715.

COMMENCING AN ACTION

Traditional procedure

The basic rule of civil litigation is that a child is a person under a 'disability'. As such:[38]

> 'A child must have a litigation friend to conduct proceedings on his behalf unless the court makes an order ... permitting the child to conduct proceedings without a litigation friend.'

It is one of the incidents of parenthood that a parent has the prima facie right to act as the child's litigation friend and the duty to act as his guardian ad litem (GAL) in legal proceedings.[39] An obvious example might be where the child has allegedly been injured by the negligence of some third party. The court does, however, have power to remove a parent and substitute another adult as litigation friend or GAL where a parent is acting improperly or against the child's best interests.[40]

Exceptions under the Children Act 1989

This normal rule of civil proceedings applies also in 'family proceedings' but is subject to significant exceptions introduced by the Children Act 1989 and the rules of court made under it.[41] The starting point is r 16.5(1) of the FPR which provides, subject to exceptions, that where a child is a party to proceedings, but not the subject of those proceedings, the child must have a litigation friend to conduct proceedings on the child's behalf. The exceptions are in FPR, r 16.6 providing that children may conduct proceedings under the Children Act 1989, proceedings relating to Part 4A of the Family Law Act 1996, applications in adoption, placement and related proceedings, or the inherent jurisdiction of the High Court[42] *without* a litigation friend or children's guardian in two alternative sets of circumstances. These are either:

(1)   where the permission of the court is obtained; *or*

(2)   where a solicitor:

  (a)   considers that the child is able, having regard to the child's understanding, to give instructions in relation to the proceedings; *and*

---

[38]   CPR 1998 (SI 1998/3132), r 21.2(2) and (3).
[39]   *Woolf v Pemberton* (1877) 6 Ch D 19.
[40]   *Re Birchall, Wilson v Birchall* (1880) 16 ChD 41; *Re Taylor's Application* [1972] 2 QB 369.
[41]   FPR, Chapter 4.
[42]   FPR, r 16.6(3).

(b) has accepted instructions from that child to act for him in the proceedings and, if the proceedings have begun, the solicitor is already acting.[43]

The rules go on to provide that a minor may apply for leave to remove an existing litigation friend or children's guardian where he wishes to conduct the remaining stages of the proceedings himself.[44]

This ability of the child to commence proceedings without a litigation friend is most likely to become relevant where the child obtains the leave of the court to seek a s 8 order. The Act allows a child to seek leave to apply for *any* s 8 order.[45] This may be granted by the court where 'it is satisfied that he has sufficient understanding to make the proposed application'.[46] The same test of 'sufficient understanding' also governs the court's decision whether to allow the child to appear without a litigation friend or children's guardian[47] and is generally thought to be a statutory application of the *Gillick* test.[48] Where leave is refused, the child may be able to persuade an interested adult to apply for the order. Where leave is given, the child may wish to seek: a residence order preserving his existing home or authorising him to live somewhere else;[49] a contact order or an order prohibiting contact with a relative he does not wish to see; or, perhaps, a prohibited steps or specific issue order to regulate areas of disagreement with his parents or other carers. In this connection, it should be recalled that *Gillick*, subject to its controversial interpretation by the Court of Appeal,[50] appears to support the right of the competent child to decide matters within his capacity, thus overriding parental views.

When can a child invoke these procedures?

There has been much speculation about the circumstances in which children might be allowed to invoke these procedures. There was concern that there might be an abuse of the procedures by young people who, following some

---

[43] On how solicitors go about the task of assessing a child's competence, see C Sawyer 'The competence of children to participate in family proceedings' [1995] CFLQ 180.

[44] FPR, r 16.6(5). For the principles to be applied on such an application by a child, see *Re S (A Minor) (Independent Representation)* [1993] 2 FLR 437 discussed at p 737 below. See also *Re K (Replacement of Guardian ad Litem)* [2001] 1 FLR 663 in which a father applied unsuccessfully for removal of the child's GAL; and see especially the Court of Appeal decision in *Mabon v Mabon* [2005] EWCA Civ 634, [2005] 2 FLR 1011.

[45] Section 10(2)(b).

[46] Section 10(8).

[47] FPR, r 16.6 (6), requiring that the court grant leave 'if it considers that the minor concerned has sufficient understanding to conduct the proceedings concerned or proposed without a litigation friend or children's guardian'.

[48] *Gillick v West Norfolk and Wisbech Area Health Authority* [1986] 1 AC 112. See, particularly, chapter 8 above and the cases discussed below for what is involved.

[49] On this question, it should also be remembered that minors who have reached 16 years of age may effectively seek a 'self-referral' into local authority accommodation (s 20(3) and (11)), and see chapter 10 above.

[50] In *Re R (A Minor) (Wardship: Consent to Treatment)* [1992] Fam 11 and *Re W (A Minor) (Medical Treatment: Court's Jurisdiction)* [1992] 3 WLR 758, as to which see chapter 8 above.

temporary tiff with their parents, seek a 'divorce' from them.[51] On the other hand, it is not difficult to visualise circumstances in which children who are the alleged victims of physical or sexual abuse could find these procedures an invaluable self-help mechanism. The same might be said of the right of children to seek orders in cases of domestic violence under Part IV of the Family Law Act 1996 which was discussed in the previous chapter.

On the whole, it is the first view which seems to have characterised the reported decisions of the courts.[52] The case-law has made it plain that even where the court finds that the child has the requisite understanding that is not the end of the matter. The court still retains a discretion in deciding whether or not to grant leave, and the key question has been whether this residual discretion should be exercised restrictively or liberally. Unlike in the case of adults where the Act[53] specifies the criteria the court is to apply, the Act is silent on the considerations which should govern children's applications for leave.

In *Re C (A Minor) (Leave to Seek Section 8 Orders)*,[54] a 14-year-old girl who did not get on with her parents went to stay with a friend's family and did not want to return. With the consent of the friend's father, she sought leave to apply for a residence order to enable her to continue living with the family and a specific issue order to allow her to take a holiday with them in Bulgaria. Johnson J refused leave on the specific issue application and adjourned the application relating to residence. In his view, there was no advantage in an order being made at that time in relation to a matter which should be resolved internally within the family. He also took the view that Parliament had intended the jurisdiction only to be exercised in relation to matters of importance and that the issues here were not serious enough to warrant judicial orders. Controversially, he also held that the question of leave was governed by the central principles of the Children Act including the welfare principle. The effect of applying a welfare test to the issue of leave would be, as here, to reserve to the court a wide discretion to refuse leave and to filter out applications by children thought by the courts to be against their best interests. In contrast, two subsequent decisions of the Family Division have held that, on children applications, as on adult applications, for leave to seek s 8 orders, the welfare principle does *not* govern the issue.

---

51 In fact, the idea is not such a revolutionary one. Legal procedures have long existed in certain jurisdictions, particularly in the USA, for the legal emancipation of certain children, but usually only those who had already achieved de facto independence from their parents. On the doctrine of emancipation, see A Bainham *Children, Parents and the State* (Sweet & Maxwell, 1988), at pp 67–69 and the sources cited there. For an analysis of the phenomenon of 'divorcing parents', see M Freeman 'Can Children Divorce Their Parents?' in *The Moral Status of Children* (Martinus Nijhoff, 1997), ch 11 which also cites many useful sources dealing with the position in North America.

52 For a general commentary, see A Bainham '"See you in Court, Mum": Children as Litigants' (1994) 6 JCL 127. For a more recent and detailed evaluation, see J Fortin *Children's Rights and the Developing Law* (3rd edn, (Cambridge University Press, 2009), at pp 264–273.

53 Section 10(9).

54 [1994] 1 FLR 26.

In *Re SC (A Minor) (Leave to Seek Residence Order)*,[55] another adolescent girl wanted to live with a friend's family but her circumstances were very different. She had been in care for many years and had suffered a number of breakdowns in foster placements. Her mother was opposed to her obtaining a residence order and wanted her to remain in care, even though she was herself unable to provide a home. Booth J granted the child leave to seek a residence order. In her view, assuming the child passed the test of understanding (which she did here) the court in exercising its discretion should then simply have regard to the likelihood of success of the substantive application. It should be satisfied that this was not a 'non-starter' doomed to failure. She further held that the child's welfare was *not* paramount on the leave question since the issue of the child's upbringing did not arise at that stage. This case also confirmed that a child was capable of seeking a residence order in favour of an adult since it was Parliament's intention that all s 8 orders should, in principle, be available to children even though the residence order, because of its form, could not be framed in favour of the child herself.

This decision was followed in *Re C (Residence: Child's Application for Leave)*.[56] Here, there had been a long history of proceedings between the two parents since they had separated. The child, another 14-year-old girl, felt that her views had never been properly represented by the court welfare officer. She had a fervent wish to live with her mother but felt under pressure from her father. Stuart-White J held that the welfare principle did not govern the leave question but that applications for leave by children should be treated cautiously. Making a child party in proceedings between warring parents might, for example, expose the child to the evidence of the parents and to matters which it might be better for the child not to hear. However, in this case, he held that the girl had the necessary understanding and leave should be granted. Her application concerned an important matter and it had a reasonable prospect of success.

These latter two decisions perhaps illustrate a more relaxed judicial attitude to children applications, certainly where the issues raised are undeniably serious. On the other hand the courts are likely to refuse leave where they can see no positive benefit to the child in direct involvement in the proceedings. In *Re H (Residence Order: Child's Application for Leave)*,[57] for example, a 12-year-old boy applied for leave to seek a residence order in his parents' divorce proceedings. Johnson J found, on the evidence of the solicitors consulted by the boy and that of an educational psychologist, that he had the requisite understanding to instruct a solicitor independently. However, he held, refusing leave, that there would be no advantage to him in doing so and that there could be considerable disadvantages to his being a party. He wanted to live with his father and his wishes in this respect were conveyed to the court in the court welfare officer's report. There was no issue between the wishes of the child and

---

55 [1994] 1 FLR 96.
56 [1995] 1 FLR 927.
57 [2000] 1 FLR 780.

his father, and Johnson J was satisfied that the judge who ultimately decided where the boy should live would be required under the legislation to take full account of his wishes.

It remains the case, of course, that the child concerned must pass the preliminary test of understanding. The leading authority on what is required in this respect was *Re S (A Minor) (Independent Representation)*,[58] a case in which a boy aged 11 sought to 'sack' the Official Solicitor who was acting as his guardian in acrimonious proceedings concerned with whether he should live with his father or his mother. Sir Thomas Bingham MR said that the Children Act required a judicious balance to be struck between two considerations. The first was that children were human beings with individual minds, wills, views and emotions which should command serious attention. They should not be discarded merely because they were children. The second was that a child is, after all, a child. The law should be sensitive to the need to protect children who were likely to be vulnerable and impressionable, lacking the maturity to weigh the longer term against the short term amongst other things. In this case, the court concluded that the judge's ruling to the effect that the child lacked sufficient understanding to participate as a party without representation by a guardian, in what were emotionally complex and highly fraught proceedings, was impregnable.[59]

Re S has now to a degree been overtaken by a seminal decision of the Court of Appeal in *Mabon v Mabon*.[60] The case involved the three eldest children of six who were caught up in proceedings between their parents in which their mother was seeking a residence order. There had been a welfare report and they were also represented by what used to be known as a 'rule 9.5 guardian' viz a guardian appointed in private law proceedings. The three boys were respectively 17, 15 and 13 and were articulate. They wanted to instruct their own solicitor but the judge refused to allow them to do so. The Court of Appeal allowed the appeal and ordered separate representation, but also made wide-ranging remarks about the need to recognise the growing autonomy of children in the light of international obligations, specifically Art 12 of the UNCRC. The Court's view was that it was unthinkable that young men of such ability and maturity should be excluded from knowledge of, and participation in, legal proceedings which affected them so fundamentally. Thorpe LJ said that courts must in the case of articulate teenagers accept that their right to freedom of expression outweighed the paternalistic judgment of welfare.

---

[58] [1993] 3 All ER 36.
[59] See also *Re HB (Abduction: Children's Objections)* [1998] 1 FLR 422 which demonstrates the negative aspects of direct involvement by children in proceedings between parents.
[60] [2005] EWCA Civ 634, [2005] 2 FLR 1011.

REPRESENTATION
Background

English law has not traditionally given minors a generalised right to representation in legal proceedings or any automatic party status. The process of conferring statutory rights in this area has been an evolutionary one and the changes in the Children Act were another stage in this process. Traditionally, it has been more usual for courts to call for welfare reports on children's 'best interests' rather than for the children themselves or their views to be represented as such. This duty to provide reports has in the past fallen on different people depending on the nature of the proceedings. The welfare test is, as has been seen,[61] an indeterminate one, and it has been said that 'the approach taken in each child's case could be as different as the people called upon to discharge the task of representing them to the court'.[62] The notion of more comprehensive reform requiring *every* court in *all* kinds of proceedings to consider whether children should be separately represented or joined as parties has been mooted for a considerable period of time. It was the subject of an abortive private member's Bill introduced by Dr David Owen (later Lord Owen) in the mid-1970s. The idea was closely associated with the establishment of a family court and an independent court welfare service.[63]

Current trends

This did not materialise, largely, it appears, because of its resource implications, and there remains a patchwork of different kinds of representation. The trend, however, is undoubtedly towards *more* representation.[64] The effect of the reforms first begun in the Children Act 1975 and built upon in the 1989 Act is to increase, very substantially, the provision for representation of children in *public* law cases. The essential feature of child representation in the modern law is that in *public* law cases it is the rule rather than the exception while in *private*

---

[61] See chapter 2 above.

[62] CM Lyon 'Safeguarding Children's Interests? – Some Problematic Issues Surrounding Separate Representation in Care and Associated Proceedings' in MDA Freeman (ed) *Essays in Family Law* (University College, London, 1985), at p 1. Lyon's essay is an excellent introduction to the law on representation of children's interests before the reforms of the Children Act. See also I Robertson 'Acting in Children's Cases – The Future of Specialisation' [1993] Fam Law 103, indicating that the admission of solicitors to The Law Society's Children Panel is carefully controlled to ensure suitability. See further PM Harris 'Procedural problems in representing children' (1995) JCL 49. See also J Masson 'Representations of Children' (1996) *Current Legal Problems* 245, J Fortin *Children's Rights and the Developing Law* (3rd edn, Cambridge University Press, 2009), ch 7, and J Masson and M Winn Oakley *Out of Hearing: Representing Children in Care Proceedings* (John Wiley & Sons, 1999). More recently see M Thorpe and J Cadbury (eds) *Hearing the Children* (Family Law, 2004). Much useful information on the practical concerns involved in representing children may be found in the quarterly journal *Representing Children* (formerly *Panel News*) published by the National Youth Advocacy Service.

[63] CM Lyon (above), at p 2.

[64] For a useful article exploring the adequacy of the representation of *parents'* views in the family justice system, see J Whybrow 'The Judge, the Lawyer and CAFCASS' [2004] Fam Law 251.

law cases it has until now been the exception rather than the rule,[65] although there is at least some increased representation of children in private cases.[66] The effect of this divergent policy is to preserve, at least on this issue, a distinct dichotomy of public and private children cases. This might be thought rather contrary to the general thrust of the legislation which has been to harmonise the two through common procedures and common principles.[67] It is thus necessary to take public and private law separately for the purposes of this discussion.

CAFCASS – the reorganisation of representation in family proceedings

Before 2001 there were three separate systems in place for the provision of representation of children in family proceedings which applied in three different contexts. First, there was the Family Court Welfare Service which was responsible for providing welfare services, including welfare reports, conciliation (mediation) and advice in private law cases. 'Court welfare officers' were provided by the Probation Service whose much greater function related to criminal proceedings. The civil court aspect of the work of the Probation Service was under-resourced and jarred somewhat with its principal function in the criminal courts. Secondly, there was the provision of guardians ad litem and reporting officers through local GALRO panels[68] who were appointed in public law and adoption cases. GALs were either self-employed social workers or self-employed probation officers. One of the principal concerns was whether they were sufficiently independent of the local authorities whose responsibility it was to establish these panels, but who were themselves of course involved in child care proceedings, and because the service was partially funded by those authorities.[69] Thirdly, in a small minority of sensitive or complex children cases, the Official Solicitor's Department might provide representation and this could be in either public[70] or private law[71] cases in the High Court or county court.

---

65 The term 'representation' is used here to refer to representation of the *child* as such rather than investigations into the child's *interests*.

66 See p 748 below.

67 See chapter 2 above.

68 For discussion of the GAL panel service, see the second edition of this work at pp 453–454.

69 See, for example, *R v Cornwall County Council ex parte Cornwall and Isles of Scilly Guardians ad Litem and Reporting Officers Panel* [1992] 1 WLR 427.

70 For discussion of the Official Solicitor's former involvement in public law cases, see the second edition of this work at pp 449–450. The lawyers and civil servants who took part in these cases were not qualified social workers (as were GALS) but did have a particular expertise in certain types of case, such as those with a foreign element. For a comparison of the work of the Official Solicitor's staff with that of panel guardians in public law cases, see J Masson 'The Official Solicitor as the child's guardian ad litem under the Children Act 1989' (1992) 4 J Ch L 58.

71 For a discussion of the Official Solicitor's Role in pre-CAFCASS private law cases, see the second edition of this work at pp 457–458. It was not uncommon for the Official Solicitor to be involved in wardship cases and cases under the inherent jurisdiction. Good examples of the kind of cases in which this might occur were disputes over serious medical procedures

The advent of CAFCASS

There was a perceived need to provide a more rational and integrated system for delivering welfare services to the courts, including representation, in the various kinds of children proceedings. This led to the establishment in April 2001 of CAFCASS – the Children and Family Court Advisory and Support Service.[72] This was set up under the Criminal Justice and Court Services Act 2000[73] and is a non-departmental public body, centrally funded, originally accountable to the Department of Constitutional Affairs and now accountable to the Department of Education. In Wales CAFCASS is the responsibility of the National Assembly for Wales. It brings together in one service the previous three disparate forms of provision discussed above, together with some significant changes in terminology. Generically, those providing services under the CAFCASS regime are referred to as 'officers of the service'.[74] This umbrella term now includes 'child and family reporters' who undertake the work formerly done by 'court welfare officers' in private law cases;[75] 'children's guardians' appointed in public law cases to perform the role formerly undertaken by panel guardians (GALs); and 'CAFCASS Legal Services' which have largely, although not entirely, taken over the role of the Official Solicitor's Department in the kinds of difficult children cases in which that Department had previously been involved and in which the child will usually be made a party to the proceedings.[76]

The early problems of the new service were legion and were very publicly aired.[77] They included a damaging dispute over the contractual arrangements for guardians, most of whom were self-employed but who were effectively told that self-employment in any form was not compatible with a managed service. This dispute ultimately had to be resolved by the courts.[78] Other problems

---

involving children (see, for example, *Re HG (Specific Issue Order: Sterilisation)* [1993] 1 FLR 587) or cases in which a parent who was herself a minor was seeking an order in relation to her child.

[72] The Service has a website at www.cafcass.gov.uk.

[73] Sections 11–17 and Sch 2.

[74] See, for example, the amended s 41 of the Children Act 1989 which, although concerned with the appointment and role of children's guardians, refers throughout to 'an officer of the service', meaning CAFCASS.

[75] Although local authority social workers may continue to provide welfare reports in some cases.

[76] It was envisaged that the Official Solicitor's Department would have a residual ongoing role in some children cases. In areas of doubt and, in order to avoid duplication, the staff of CAFCASS Legal are expected to liaise with the Official Solicitor's office to ensure that the most suitable arrangements are made. See *CAFCASS Practice Note (Officers of CAFCASS Legal Services and Special Casework: Appointment in Family Proceedings)* [2001] 2 FLR 151.

[77] They were the subject of an investigation by the Constitutional Affairs Select Committee. The Government then published a response to this Committee's report. See *The Response of the Government and the Children and Family Court Advisory and Support Service to the Constitutional Affairs Select Committee's Report on Children and Family Court Advisory and Support Service (CAFCASS)* (Cm 6004) (2003).

[78] *The Queen on the Application of National Association of Guardians ad Litem and Reporting Officers v Children and Family Court Advisory and Support Service* [2002] 1 FLR 255. See also *R v Children and Family Court Advisory and Support Service* [2003] 1 FLR 953 in which Charles J dismissed an application in judicial review that CAFCASS was legally obliged to make an

included an unrealistically short timetable for establishment of the service, unacceptable delays, and a shortage of qualified staff and confused lines of accountability between the then Lord Chancellor's Department and the service. These problems were highlighted in a report by the House of Commons Select Committee on CAFCASS.[79]

More recently, in *R and Others v Cafcass*[80] the Court of Appeal upheld the decision of the Divisional Court refusing a declaration that CAFCASS had acted unlawfully and in breach of its statutory duty by failing to allocate a guardian sooner than it did in four test cases. The Court held that the legislation established a general framework for the operation of CAFCASS and did not create duties to individuals. The obligation was confined to appointing a guardian 'as soon as reasonably practicable'. Neither was there a breach of Arts 6 or 8 of the ECHR since the procedural requirements of those articles could not be interpreted to require the appointment of a guardian 'immediately at the very start of the proceedings'.

In response to the many criticisms levelled at the service,[81] CAFCASS introduced National Standards relating to its work with children and families in family proceedings, implemented as from April 2003. These were revised, after consultation, in June 2007. These are said to incorporate a 'rigorous complaints procedure to ensure that issues regarding the service are reviewed and resolved transparently and efficiently'. It remains to be seen whether the quality of performance can be raised sufficiently to enable the proper discharge of the service's responsibilities. A key ongoing question is whether the service will be able to cope adequately with what is likely to be an expansion in the separate representation of children in private proceedings alongside the already onerous provision of tandem representation (see below) in public law proceedings. A further issue may be the impact of the expected rise in litigants in person following the substantial withdrawal of legal aid in private law cases from April 2013.

Public law children proceedings

An earlier chapter[82] considered the background to the provision of separate representation for children in care proceedings. The Children Act significantly

---

officer of the service immediately available to act as guardian on receiving a request from the court for it to do so. The relevant statutory provisions, he held, implied that CAFCASS should respond as soon as possible but there could lawfully be a gap between the request and an appointment.

[79] A convenient summary of the findings of this report is set out at [2003] Fam Law 626–627 with a comment by the Right Honourable Alan Beith MP, at p 625.

[80] [2012] EWCA Civ 853, [2012] 2 FLR 1432.

[81] As to which see the views of Jonathan Tross, then Chief Executive of CAFCASS in 'CAFCASS – Moving Forward' [2002] Fam Law 829 and, reviewing the next two years of CAFCASS, J Tross 'CAFCASS Present and Future' [2004] Fam Law 731. For the statistics of involvement of CAFCASS in various types of children proceedings between April 2003 and March 2004, see the CAFCASS Annual Report summarised at [2004] Fam Law 760.

[82] Chapter 12 above.

increased this in two ways. First, it created a presumption of appointment of a GAL (now known as a 'children's guardian' and hereafter referred to as such) in 'specified proceedings' and, secondly, it enlarged the range of proceedings in which the presumption of appointment applies. The child will also automatically be a party in such proceedings.

Appointment of a separate representative

Where the child is separately represented, this is sometimes referred to as 'tandem representation' since it will usually be by a children's guardian and a solicitor. The relationship between these two kinds of representative is discussed below. The concern for the moment is with the circumstances of appointment.

Appointment of a children's guardian

Section 41(6) of the Children Act 1989 and the accompanying rules of court[83] specify a long list of proceedings in which the court *must* appoint a children's guardian for the child 'unless satisfied that it is not necessary to do so in order to safeguard his interests'.[84] It was envisaged by the Lord Chancellor, during the passage of the Children Bill, that an appointment would need to be made in the vast majority of cases falling within the specified proceedings.[85] The wording of the legislation is a reformulation of the former statutory language and was designed to remove the wide discretion which the courts previously had in deciding whether to appoint a children's guardian.[86] The small minority of cases in which a children's guardian is not appointed are likely to be mainly those in which the child wishes to instruct his own solicitor and is found to be competent to do so. In 'specified proceedings' the child is automatically entitled to be a party[87] and may instruct a solicitor where he has sufficient understanding and wishes to do so.[88] In 'non-specified proceedings', which

---

[83] FPR, r 16.3 and PD16A, Part 3.

[84] Section 41(1). On the appointment and functions of children's guardians generally, see *The Children Act 1989 Guidance and Regulations Vol 7 Guardians ad Litem and other Court Related Issues* (HMSO, 1991).

[85] House of Lords Official Report, Vol 503, col 408 (19 January 1989). But for a case in which the court held that the appointment of a children's guardian in specified proceedings was unnecessary on the facts, see *Re J (A Minor) (Change of Name)* [1993] 1 FLR 699. Here, a 12-year-old girl in care and living with long-term foster parents wished to use their name. This was not opposed by the Official Solicitor and there was no longer any contact between the girl and her natural parents following a history of severe abuse. Booth J said that a children's guardian could not have said any more than counsel for the local authority and there was no conflict of interest. Neither was it appropriate here to serve either the parents or the girl or for her to be present in court.

[86] In some courts, appointments were evidently made in only a small proportion of cases. See *R v Plymouth Juvenile Court ex parte F and F* [1987] 1 FLR 169 at 178.

[87] FPR, r 16.2.

[88] Section 41(3), (4)(b).

expression includes mainly private law cases under the Children Act,[89] the child is not usually a party but the court has a discretion to join him at his request and also to appoint a children's guardian or solicitor.[90] As we shall see, it may be expected that the representation of children in certain private law cases will increase in the future.[91]

What are 'specified proceedings'?

Essentially, specified proceedings are all proceedings which involve public intervention in the family.[92] They include, most obviously, applications for care or supervision orders and, significantly since the Children Act, applications for the short-term remedies of EPOs and CAOs. Other proceedings included are: those in which a s 37 direction has been made or the court is considering whether to make an interim care order; applications for discharge or variation of care or supervision orders; and applications for residence or contact orders where a child is in care; and appeals against the making or refusal of these orders. In addition, children's guardians will continue to be appointed in adoption proceedings under the Adoption and Children Act 2002.

Although the appointment of a children's guardian can be made at any stage of the proceedings, the rules require the court to make the appointment as soon as possible after the commencement or transfer of the proceedings.[93] Children's guardians should thus be involved at an early stage and consequently should be able to advise the court about short-term orders, such as EPOs and interim orders, and directions the court may wish to make in the initial stages of protective intervention.[94] In practice however, because of the shortage of resources, it has been common for a guardian not to have been appointed when the first hearing takes place. The child is then usually represented by the duty guardian at court until a more formal appointment of a guardian can be made.

Appointment of a solicitor

It is not the function of the children's guardian to represent the child at the hearing in court. This is undertaken, as one would expect, by a solicitor and,

---

[89] 'Relevant proceedings' for these purposes are any proceedings under the Children Act, under any statutory instrument made under it or any amendment made by the Children Act in any other enactment (s 93(1)–(3)).

[90] FPR, r 16.4 and PD16A, Part 4. See, for example, *Re CE (Section 37 Direction)* [1995] 1 FLR 26 where a children's guardian appointed following a s 37 direction by a district judge continued to represent a 14-year-old child (who had left her parents to live with her boyfriend's family) even though the local authority decided not to seek a public law order following its investigations. Section 37 should not, however, be used purely as a device to secure the appointment of a children's guardian since the normal course is for the child's views to be presented by the court welfare officer in private proceedings. Neither should wardship be used for the purpose of foisting a children's guardian on a child. See *Re CT (A Minor) (Wardship: Representation)* [1993] 2 FLR 278.

[91] See below.

[92] Children Act, s 41(6).

[93] FPR, r 12.6.

[94] As to which see chapter 11 above.

where appropriate, counsel.[95] Where a solicitor has not already been appointed, one of the functions of the children's guardian is to appoint one and thereafter give instructions to him. We consider below the problem of what happens where the instructions of the children's guardian do not accord with the wishes of the child. Where no solicitor has been appointed, the court may itself make an appointment where:

(1)   no children's guardian has been appointed for the child;

(2)   the child has sufficient understanding to instruct a solicitor and wishes to do so; and

(3)   it appears to the court that it would be in the child's best interests for him to be represented by a solicitor.[96]

The appointed solicitor must then represent the child in accordance with rules of court.[97]

Public funding is available for proceedings under the Children Act 1989[98] and this includes the representation of children. The normal 'means and merits' test does not apply to certain 'special Children Act proceedings'.[99] In these cases, children have a right to non-means, non-merits-tested funding or 'free legal aid'. Legal aid is now under the control of the Legal Aid Agency which has replaced the former Legal Services Commission.

The specialised nature of the work involved in representing children is recognised by The Law Society which has established a Children Panel, also known as the Children Law Accreditation Scheme, with regional branches, in an effort to ensure that solicitors chosen to represent children will have the necessary expertise.

The role of the children's guardian

General

Children's guardians are individuals with qualifications in social work who are required to have a thorough knowledge of both social work theory and child care law. The principal function of the children's guardian system is to ensure that 'the court is fully informed of the relevant facts which relate to the child's

---

[95]   There is much valuable information about the nature of the solicitor's role in representing children in P King and I Young *The Child as Client* (Family Law, 1992).

[96]   Section 41(3) and (4).

[97]   Section 41(5), and FPR, chapter 8.

[98]   Access to Justice Act 1999.

[99]   See Community Legal Service (Financial) Regulations 2000, reg 3(1)(c), and section 2.2 of the Funding Code made under the Access to Justice Act 1999.

welfare and that the wishes and feelings of the child are clearly established'.[100] They were described by the initial *Guidance* under the Children Act[101] as having a 'proactive role' in relation to the conduct of the proceedings, including timetabling and advising the court on the range of orders available. The general duty of the guardian, as expressed in the Children Act, is 'to safeguard the interests of the child' in the manner prescribed by rules of court.[102] It should be noted that these rules only govern guardians appointed in 'specified' Children Act proceedings. The rules[103] spell out in some detail the more specific duties of children's guardians in public law proceedings.

The importance of the role of the guardian in public law proceedings cannot be over-estimated. As well as representing the interests of the child and conveying (where appropriate) the child's wishes, the children's guardian occupies a pivotal position and weilds considerable influence over the course of the proceedings. Where the guardian does not support the authority's care plan, this is something which cannot be sensibly ignored by the social work team concerned. Conversely, no parent seeking reunification with a child can afford to be without the support of the children's guardian. In this sense, the guardian often holds the balance of power between the local authority and the other parties, notably the parents.

Specific duties

The children's guardian is required to attend all directions, appointments and hearings, unless excused by the court, and to advise the court on the following matters:[104]

'(a) whether the child is of sufficient understanding for any purpose including the child's refusal to submit to a medical or psychiatric examination or other assessment that the court has power to require, direct or order;

(b) the wishes of the child in respect of any matter relevant to the proceedings, including his attendance at court;

(c) the appropriate forum for the proceedings;

(d) the appropriate timing of the proceedings or any part of them;

(e) the options available to it in respect of the child and the suitability of each such option including what order should be made in determining the application;

---

[100] *Children Act Advisory Committee Annual Report 1992/3* (Lord Chancellor's Department, 1993), at p 14. See also D Dinan-Hayward 'The Changing Role of the Guardian ad Litem' [1992] Fam Law 555.

[101] *The Children Act 1989 Guidance and Regulations Vol 7 Guardians ad Litem and Other Court Related Issues* (HMSO, 1991), at para 2.2.

[102] Section 41(2).

[103] FPR, Chapter 6 and PD16A, Part 3.

[104] FPR, r 16.20 and PD16A, para 6.6.

(f) any other matter on which the court seeks his advice or on which the children's guardian considers that the court should be informed.'

In addition to this advisory role, the guardian must[105] make such investigations as are necessary to carry out the children's guardian's duties and must, in particular:

(a) contact or seek to interview such persons as the children's guardian thinks appropriate or the court directs; and

(b) obtain such professional assistance as is available when the children's guardian thinks appropriate or which the court directs to be obtained.

The guardian must also:

(a) appoint a solicitor for the child unless a solicitor has already been appointed;

(b) give such advice to the child as is appropriate having regard to that child's understanding; and

(c) where appropriate instruct the solicitor representing the child on all matters relevant to the interests of the child arising in the course of proceedings, including possibilities for appeal.

Regarding the inspection of records, the Children Act, as amended by the Courts and Legal Services Act 1990,[106] gives the guardian access to the records of children's services departments which may be inspected and copies taken. This right does not, however, extend to the records of health authorities, except where health records form part of the local authority's own records.[107] As regards the guardian's report, the Act provides that the court may take account of any statement made by the guardian in the report and any evidence given in respect of matters referred to in it where, in its opinion, these are relevant to the issue it is considering.[108] The broad effect of this provision was to disapply the hearsay rule, reflecting the inquisitorial nature of children proceedings.[109] Children cases are, however, no longer distinctive in relation to the hearsay rule since, under the Civil Evidence Act 1995, hearsay has been admissible in civil proceedings generally and its relevance is now only to weight and not to admissibility.

---

[105] FPR, r 6.1 and 6.2 and PD16A, Part 2 and Part 4.

[106] Section 42(1), and the Courts and Legal Services Act 1990, Sch 16, para 18.

[107] For further analysis of s 42, see MDA Freeman *Children, Their Families and the Law* (Macmillan, 1992), at p 169.

[108] Section 41(11).

[109] On the shift towards inquisitorial procedures in children cases under the Children Act, see chapter 2 above.

Tandem representation: relationship between the guardian and the child's solicitor

The guardian and the child's solicitor are required to work closely together in the child's best interests.[110] It will usually be the guardian who appoints and instructs the solicitor. Although the solicitor presents the child's case in court, he must act on the guardian's instructions in determining the manner of presentation.[111] Difficulties can arise where the views of the guardian diverge from those of the child, especially if he or she is an older teenager who disagrees strongly with the guardian's view of his or her welfare. A particular problem may be a difference of opinion between the guardian and the solicitor about the competence of the child. It has been suggested[112] that this can lead to acute problems, for example in sexual abuse cases. Here, the solicitor may wish to take instructions from the child direct if, having taken into account the guardian's views and any court directions, he considers that the child wishes to give instructions which conflict with those of the guardian and he has sufficient understanding to do so. The rules allow him to deal directly with the child in these circumstances.[113] In this eventuality, the guardian remains in office and will continue to discharge all his duties other than instructing the solicitor.[114] There is also provision for a children's guardian to seek to terminate the appointment of the child's solicitor.[115]

The child's ability to instruct a solicitor was considered in *Re H (A Minor) (Care Proceedings: Child's Wishes)*.[116] In that case, Thorpe J emphasised that a child must have sufficient understanding and rationality and that this may not be so where the child is suffering from intense emotional disturbance. Where there is any issue as to the child's rationality, the question should be the subject of specific expert opinion from experts already involved in the case. There is

---

[110] See, generally, P King and I Young *The Child as Client* (Family Law, 1992), ch 7, and MR Bell and R Daley 'Social Workers and Solicitors: Working Together?' [1992] Fam Law 257. For a more recent commentary, see J Fortin *Children's Rights and the Developing Law* (3rd edn, Cambridge University Press, 2009), at pp 273–284. For a summary of research exploring lawyers' views on their relationship with guardians in public law proceedings see G Timmis 'Lawyers' Perspectives on Public Law Cases' [2003] Fam Law 174. For a discussion of the relationship between social workers and lawyers in children cases, see J Dickens 'Risks and Responsibilities – the role of the local authority lawyer in child care cases' [2004] CFLQ 17.

[111] Detailed guidance on the role of solicitors in public law proceedings, especially where a guardian has not yet been appointed for the child, has been issued by the Law Society. See 'Representation of Children in Public Proceedings: Notice to Children Panel Members Issued by the Law Society, September 2002' [2002] Fam Law 930.

[112] MDA Freeman *Children, Their Families and the Law* (Macmillan, 1992), at p 168.

[113] FPR, r 16.29(7).

[114] He is entitled to legal representation but not to public funding for this purpose. See *The Children Act Advisory Committee Annual Report 1992/3* (Lord Chancellor's Department, 1993), at p 29. It is for the court to decide how the child should be represented in these circumstances and to rule on any dispute between the guardian and solicitor about whether the child has the necessary capacity to instruct the solicitor. See *Re M (Minors) (Care Proceedings: Child's Wishes)* [1994] 1 FLR 749.

[115] FPR, r 16.29(8).

[116] [1993] 1 FLR 440.

evidence that in practice, notwithstanding these provisions, there is a reluctance to accept that children may be able to instruct solicitors independently and that this rarely happens.[117]

Private law children proceedings

The contrast between representation for children in public law and private law proceedings could hardly be more striking.[118] The issue can be disposed of much more quickly in the private context, since representation of the child, as such, occurs in only a tiny minority of cases. Objective assessments of the child's best interests through welfare reports take place in a much larger number of cases, but the proportion of the total is still very small, principally because of the large number of divorce cases in which there is no dispute over children and no need for a court order. Sometimes children's interests are very intimately involved and there is no better illustration of this than divorce. There can be few matters which have the potential for affecting children so deeply as the breakdown of their parents' marriage, yet they are rarely represented in divorce proceedings, and welfare reports are usually ordered only in the small minority of cases in which there is a real contest over the arrangements for the children.[119] In certain other jurisdictions, there is a more systematic investigation of children's interests in private proceedings,[120] and there is no doubt that the lack of provision for representation in English law has been influenced, to some extent, perhaps heavily, by resource implications – a fact indirectly acknowledged by the Law Commission[121] in its report which formed the basis of the private law in the Children Act. It is, perhaps, a fair question to pose whether there is any justification, other than pressure on resources, for the preservation of the current distinctions between public and private law on this

---

[117] J Masson and M Winn Oakley *Out of Hearing: Representing Children in Care Proceedings* (John Wiley & Sons, 1999). See also *Re C (Secure Accommodation Order: Representation)* [2001] 2 FLR 169. Here a secure accommodation order was upheld on appeal despite the very limited opportunities which the 15-year-old child had been given to instruct her solicitor whom she had engaged after being dissatisfied with the children's guardian's approach to her case.

[118] There is an extensive discussion of the issues surrounding the representation of children in private proceedings in J Fortin *Children's Rights and the Developing Law* (3rd edn, Cambridge University Press,, 2009), at pp 256–273. For an evaluation of the appointment of guardians for children in private proceedings (which takes account of recent practice directions and notes by, respectively, the President of the Family Division and CAFCASS), see J Whybrow 'Children, Guardians and Rule 9.5' [2004] Fam Law 504. See also the views of Munby J on the lack of appropriate support and representation where *administrative* decisions are being taken in relation to children in 'Making sure the Child is Heard' (2004) 17 *Representing Children* 10, especially, at pp 21–22. For the results of some research on the extent to which children's wishes were heard and were influential in residence and contact disputes, see V May and C Smart 'Silence in Court? – hearing children in residence and contact disputes' [2004] CFLQ 305.

[119] The court is not, however, confined to contested cases. See chapter 5 above.

[120] See, for example, the role of the family advocate in South Africa in I Schäfer 'The Family Advocate in South Africa' in A Bainham, DS Pearl and R Pickford (eds) *Frontiers of Family Law* (2nd edn, John Wiley & Sons, 1995), at p 30.

[121] See Law Com Report No 172 (1988), at para 6.15, where the Law Commission recognised that welfare officers' time was limited and 'must be targeted on the cases in which it will be most valuable'.

issue. On the other hand it could be said that in public law proceedings the conflict of interest, or at least potential conflict, between parent and child is palpable. The proceedings are about the alleged parental failure to care properly for the child. This conflict of interest is much less obvious in private law proceedings where there may very well be something approaching an identity of interests between the child and one or other parent. Independent representation of the child in private law proceedings therefore requires more specific justification.

In recent years there has been increasing pressure from children's rights organisations for the creation of greater opportunities for the representation of children in private family proceedings. This pressure lead to the insertion of an empowering provision in the Family Law Act 1996.[122]

There remains the broader policy question of exactly how far it is desirable for children to be independently represented in such proceedings. *L v L (Minors) (Separate Representation)*[123] is a good illustration of the circumstances in which there is a need for the separate representation of children in private law proceedings. Here, the parents and three children aged respectively 14, 12 and 9 were Australian. The parents had separated, the mother having formed a new relationship, and the children remained with their father. There was some suggestion that they might be taken back to Australia. There was a dispute as to residence and the amount of contact with the mother. The children expressed their view to the court welfare officer that existing contact with their mother was inadequate. The welfare officer took the position that she could not adequately reflect the views of the children in court, and the judge therefore ordered the children to be separately represented by a solicitor from the child care panel. The Court of Appeal upheld this decision and also directed that the children be joined as parties to the proceedings. In the later case of *Re A (Contact: Separate Representation)*[124] the Court of Appeal allowed a mother's appeal against the judge's refusal to grant leave for the child's separate representation in private proceedings between her parents who had separated. The mother, inter alia, raised allegations of sexual abuse of the child and approached the charity, the National Youth Advocacy Service (NYAS), which sought leave to intervene and act as guardian to the child. The mother was opposed to contact between the father and the child. The Court of Appeal transferred the case to London but invited the Official Solicitor, rather than NYAS, to act as guardian since the father might have perceived NYAS (albeit wrongly) as acting on the mother's behalf. The court's view was that separate representation was appropriate given the problems facing both parents, the sexual abuse allegations and the potential conflict of interest between each

---

[122] Section 64.
[123] [1994] 1 FLR 156. See also *Re C (Prohibition on Further Applications)* [2002] 1 FLR 1136 where CAFCASS Legal was directed to represent two younger daughters of four children in a protracted contact dispute.
[124] [2001] 1 FLR 715.

parent and the child. Dame Elizabeth Butler-Sloss P remarked that, following the HRA 1998, there would be likely to be an increased use of guardians in private law cases.[125]

Other instances in which children might appropriately be parties and separately represented spring to mind. Clearly, this would be so where a child is the applicant for an order under Part IV of the Family Law Act 1996 where, as previously discussed, the division between what is 'public' and what is 'private' is in any event artificial. In acrimonious divorce proceedings in which there is a bitter ongoing battle over the children, it is equally clear that the case for separate representation, which acknowledges the conflict of interest between the parents and the children, is also very strong. But these cases are exceptional. The overwhelming majority of divorce cases are not like this. There is not usually a dispute over the children and in a very high proportion of cases an order in relation to the children is neither sought nor necessary.[126] It would therefore seem right that, unlike in public proceedings in which a conflict of interest between parents and children is rightly presumed, in private proceedings independent representation should continue to be regarded as the exception rather than the rule but nevertheless important in the minority of cases in which there is a real dispute and real conflict.

Guardians appointed in private law proceedings are now known as 'rule 16.4 guardians' (formerly 'rule 9.5 guardians' under the Family Proeedings Rules 1991). Their appointment is now governed by chapter 7 of the FPR and Part 4 of the PD16A. The key guidance in the rules is that: 'Making a child a party to the proceedings is a step that will be taken only in cases which involve an issue of significant difficulty'.[127] The Rules go on to list guidance on the kinds of cases in which such an appointment might be justified.[128] They are similar to the instances referred to above. The Rules set out the duties of a children's guardian so appointed.[129]

---

[125] For a very helpful article discussing the circumstances under which children have been made parties to private law proceedings and guardians appointed for them in one region (Leeds), see C Bellamy and G Lord 'Reflections on Family Proceedings Rule 9.5' [2003] Fam Law 265. The authors identify on the basis of their research a number of factors tending to be relevant to the question of independent representation in private proceedings. These were intractable cases; a significant foreign, ethnic or cultural element; significant health problems; violence and/or sexual abuse; and complex family relationships. The circumstances under which children should be made a party to proceedings which are not specified proceedings and a guardian appointed were the subject of a Direction by the President of the Family Division. See *President's Direction: Representation of Children in Family Proceedings Pursuant to Family Proceedings Rules 1991, rule 9.5* [2004] 1 FLR 1188.

[126] See chapter 4 above.

[127] PD16A, para 7.1.

[128] PD16A, para 7.2.

[129] PD16A, para 7.6 provides: 'It is the duty of a children's guardian fairly and competently to conduct proceedings on behalf of the child. The children's guardian must have no interest in the proceedings adverse to that of the child and all steps and decisions the children's guardian takes in the proceedings must be taken for the benefit of the child.'

Welfare reports in private law proceedings

Some of the principles applying to welfare reports have already been noted[130] and they will not be repeated here. Instead, we will focus briefly on the essential differences between representation by a children's guardian in public law proceedings and the involvement of the child and family reporters[131] in private law cases.[132] We also touch upon the role of the Official Solicitor in wardship proceedings, which is somewhat different from that of either guardians or child and family reporters.

The first point to emphasise is that a child and family reporter is *not* the child's representative, and his role is not to represent the child's interest. Rather, it is to provide the court with an objective evaluation, through a report, of the child and his background. There is no reason, in principle, why the court should not appoint a children's guardian *and* seek a welfare report, but the Court of Appeal has warned against unnecessary duplication which might occur where two reports are obtained.[133] Such cases are therefore likely to be rare.

The duty of the child and family reporter is to conduct a thorough investigation of the child's circumstances and prepare a written report for the court. This investigation must extend beyond the child himself, to all other members of the child's family and adult figures in the child's life. This entails interviewing all relevant parties and, perhaps also, inquiries among relatives, the child's school or health authorities. Conciliation is not part of the child and family reporter's function and should not be undertaken.[134] The child and family reporter must consider whether it is in the best interests of the child for the child to be made a party to the proceedings.[135] Where he thinks it is, he must notify the court with reasons.[136] When his investigations are completed, the officer produces a report which must be filed in the time prescribed by the court or, in any event, within 14 days of the hearing.[137] This will then be served on the parties, and on the guardian, where one is appointed. Only the parties, their legal representatives, the guardian, the Legal Aid Agency, the child and family reporter and an expert whose instruction has been authorised by the

---

[130] Section 7, and chapter 5 above.

[131] Where the officers of local authorities provide reports they are to be known as 'local authority officers'.

[132] Governed now by FPR, chapter 10 and PD16A, Part 6. Such a reporter is known as 'the officer' in the rules.

[133] *Re S (A Minor) (Guardian ad Litem/Welfare Officer)* [1993] 1 FLR 110, a *public law* case concerning the question of whether an additional report from a welfare officer should be obtained where an appointed guardian already had responsibility to provide a report. Cf *Re W (Welfare Reports)* [1995] 2 FLR 142, which confirms that the court has an unfettered discretion to order more than one welfare report where it considers this appropriate. For a general comparison of the respective roles of the court welfare officer and the guardian, see C Jackson 'Reporting on Children: The Guardian ad Litem, the court welfare officer and the Children Act 1989' [1992] Fam Law 252.

[134] *Scott v Scott* [1986] 2 FLR 320, and *Re H (Conciliation: Welfare Reports)* [1986] 1 FLR 476.

[135] PD16A, para 9.4(d).

[136] Ibid.

[137] Ibid, para 9.4(e).

court are entitled to have access to the report, without the leave of the court. In due course, the child and family reporter must, unless excused by the court, attend the hearing, and may be questioned about the report by the court or the parties.[138] The influence of welfare reports on the ultimate decision of the court was considered previously.[139]

What are the salient differences between the process of obtaining welfare reports and representation by a guardian? In essence, the child and family reporter is an officer of the court with an investigative and reporting role. He is in no sense a representative or witness for the child or any other party. There are, of course, some similarities in what child and family reporters and guardians do, but the functions of the latter are much wider than just investigation and report. It is the representative element of their duties which is the real point of distinction. Apart from the small proportion of private law cases in which children are actually joined as parties, as the law stands, they will be unrepresented either by a children's guardian or a solicitor. A further point of distinction is that there is no *presumption* of welfare involvement in private law cases which corresponds to the statutory presumption of representation by a children's guardian in public law cases. It is certainly arguable that more still needs to be done to ensure an adequate voice for the child and representation of his independent interests and views in the private law sphere.

EVIDENCE

How is evidence obtained in children cases? Are children themselves competent to give evidence and, if so, ought their evidence to be given the same weight as that of adults, or ought allowances to be made for the age of the child witness? Should the legal system make special arrangements for accommodating child witnesses to counteract the ordeal of a court appearance, often arising in connection with alleged abuse of the child concerned? Ought children to attend court at all? These are some of the questions which law reform agencies have had to face.[140] In considering the answers which the legal system currently gives to these questions, it is necessary to distinguish between *civil* and *criminal* proceedings.

---

[138] PD16A, para 9.4(a) and FPR, r 16. 33(5).

[139] At chapter 5 above.

[140] A useful up-to-date account of the law of evidence is to be found in IH Dennis *The Law of Evidence* (5th edn, Sweet & Maxwell, 2013) especially ch 13, at paras 20 et seq on children's competence, and ch 15, at paras 20 et seq on special measures directions. For an account of relevant psychological research and forensic practice, see ME Lamb, DJ La Rooy, LC Malloy and C Katz (eds) *Children's Testimony: A Handbook of Psychological Research and Forensic Practice* (2nd edn, Wiley, 2011). For a collection of essays critically examining the law, including perspectives from some other jurisdictions, see JR Spencer and ME Lamb (eds) *Children and Cross-Examination: Time to Change the Rules?* (Hart Publishing, 2012). A comprehensive treatment of issues relating to children's evidence can be found in JR Spencer and R Flin *The Evidence of Children* (2nd edn, Blackstone Press, 1993), although this book is now somewhat dated on the law. See also for earlier resources which may provide useful background on the law: H Dent and R Flin (eds) *Children as Witnesses* (1992), especially JR

Family proceedings are civil proceedings, and the dominant principle is that the importance of the child's welfare requires the court to have regard to *all* available evidence.[141] This gave rise to a substantial relaxation in the ordinary rules of evidence, most particularly the hearsay rule. While this had long been a feature of some children proceedings, especially wardship, the effect of the Children Act was to extend the principle more generally to civil cases involving children.

In contrast, in criminal proceedings, the primary focus is not on the welfare of the child victim or witness but on the issue of the guilt or innocence of the accused. That being the case, a balance has to be struck between the needs of children in court as witnesses, whether victims or not, and the traditional safeguards afforded the accused by English criminal procedure, especially the right to confront his accusers through cross-examination. Moreover, these safeguards are now reinforced by Art 6 of the ECHR and the HRA 1998 which require that even more caution be taken in achieving the correct balance.[142] This involves weighing the potential benefits to children of being spared certain aspects of the ordeal of appearing in court against possible prejudice to the accused which might thereby be occasioned. The current law reflects an appreciation that justice is not served if children are so intimidated by the legal process that their evidence is rendered less reliable or, more seriously, that they feel unable to give evidence at all. The result of excluding the evidence of children may be to deny the court access to the only available evidence of certain offences against children themselves or other children and to allow the perpetrator to escape justice and to continue to represent an ongoing threat to other children.

The Youth Justice and Criminal Evidence Act 1999, building on previous legislative initiatives, seeks to make available a raft of measures designed to facilitate the reception of evidence by children. It does this particularly by allowing the court to make 'special measures directions' to lessen what would

---

Spencer 'Reforming the Law on Children's Evidence in England: The Pigot Committee and After', ch 7; JR Spencer, G Nicholson, R Flin and R Bull (eds) *Children's Evidence in Legal Proceedings* (1990), distributed by the Faculty of Law, University of Cambridge; The Royal College of Psychiatrists *The Evidence of Children* (1996) Council Report CR 44. See also A Levy QC 'Children in Court' in J Fionda (ed) *Legal Concepts of Childhood* (Hart Publishing, 2001), at p 99. Specifically on the changes brought about by the Youth Justice and Criminal Evidence Act 1999, see D Birch and R Leng *Blackstone's Guide to the Youth Justice and Criminal Evidence Act 1999* (2000).

[141] For an illustration of this principle, see *Re S (Contact: Evidence)* [1998] 1 FLR 798, where the Court of Appeal granted leave to issue a subpoena duces tecum to compel production of video evidence held by the police. The father wished to challenge allegations of sexual abuse of his five-year-old daughter with whom he had hitherto enjoyed extensive contact but which was now under threat. The court held that it had a duty to decide whether the allegations were true and could not allow the local authority or the police to decide the case. The court needed to have access to the best available evidence, and the parents had to have the opportunity of considering it.

[142] Although in *Doorson v The Netherlands* (1996) 22 EHRR 330, the ECtHR accepted that some modification of the normal principle that all evidence should be presented publicly in the presence of the accused was permissible in the case of vulnerable witnesses.

otherwise be the ordeal of appearing in an ordinary court, daunting enough for adults and, in many cases, impossibly daunting for children. In some cases the accused may be a child, whose defence may be inhibited unless some assistance in giving evidence is provided, and amendments were made to the 1999 Act by the Coroners and Justice Act 2009 to address the fact that the 1999 Act's provisions initially did not apply to the accused.[143]

Criminal proceedings

The issues relating to child witnesses in criminal proceedings are *competence, compellability, credibility* and *stress*.[144]

Competence

The question of children's competence to give evidence in criminal proceedings is governed by the Youth Justice and Criminal Evidence Act 1999.[145] The Act incorporates a general presumption of competence. All persons are (whatever their age) competent to give evidence at any stage of criminal proceedings.[146] This may be rebutted in the case of an individual, however:[147]

'if it appears to the court that he is not a person who is able to –

(a) understand questions put to him as a witness, and
(b) give answers to them which can be understood.'

Whether or not a child is capable of giving intelligible evidence is a simple test well within the capacity of a judge or magistrate and it does not require any input from an expert,[148] although expert evidence may be received on the issue.[149] In *R v Barker*[150] the Court of Appeal explained that the 'provisions of the statute are clear and unequivocal, and do not require reinterpretation'.[151] The court explained:

'The question is entirely witness or child specific. There are no presumptions or preconceptions. The witness need not understand the special importance that

---

143 Inserting ss 24(1A) and (1B), 33A, 33B, and 33BA, and amending s 21, discussed below. The provisions do not equalise the position of the accused child and other child witnesses: see for criticism LCH Hoyano 'Special Measures Directions Take Two: Entrenching Unequal Access to Justice?' [2010] Crim LR 345.

144 Competence, credibility and stress are identified as the major issues by R Flin 'Child Witnesses: The Psychological Evidence' (1988) 138 NLJ 608.

145 For a comprehensive analysis of the Act, see D Birch and R Leng *Blackstone's Guide to the Youth Justice and Criminal Evidence Act 1999* (2000).

146 Youth Justice and Criminal Evidence Act 1999, s 53(1).

147 Ibid, s 53(3). This is effectively a re-enactment of an earlier test in the Criminal Justice Act 1988.

148 *G v DPP* [1997] 2 All ER 755.

149 Section 54(5).

150 [2010] EWCA Crim 4.

151 Ibid, at para [38]. *R v MacPherson* [2006] 1 CAR 30; *R v Powell* [2006] 1 CAR 31; *R v M* [2008] EWCA Crim 2751; and *R v Malicki* [2009] EWCA Crim 365.

the truth should be told in court, and the witness need not understand every single question or give a readily understood answer to every question. Many competent adult witnesses would fail such a competency test. Dealing with it broadly and fairly, provided the witness can understand the questions put to him and can also provide understandable answers, he or she is competent. If the witness cannot understand the questions or his answers to questions which he understands cannot themselves be understood he is not'.[152]

The court added that 'the age of a witness is not determinative on his or her ability to give truthful and accurate evidence' and 'the child witness starts off on the basis of equality with every other witness'.[153] In *R v Barker* the defendant was convicted of the rape of a three-year-old child on testimony given by her when aged four-and-a-half.[154] In the case of unsworn evidence, there is no requirement that the child understand the duty to tell the truth, or the difference between truth and falsehood.[155]

Where the issue of competence of a child is raised by either a party or the court, the onus to prove competence on the balance of probabilities will be on the party calling the witness and will be for the court to determine.[156] For the purpose of assessing competence, the court must treat the witness as having the benefit of any 'special measures directions' which the court has given, or proposes to give to assist the child in giving evidence.[157] Thus, for example, in the case of a child who has difficulty speaking clearly, the child's competence could be determined bearing in mind that the child might be assisted by an intermediary who understands the child's speech, or a computer as an aid to communication. Any hearing to determine competence will take place in the absence of a jury (if there is one),[158] expert evidence may be received[159] and any questioning of the witness by the court must take place in the presence of the parties.[160]

The competency test 'may be re-analysed at the end of the child's evidence' and if the child witness was unable to give intelligible evidence, the evidence could be excluded by the judge as unfair under s 78 of the Police and Criminal Evidence Act 1984.[161] In *R v Malicki*[162] the complainant was 4 years 8 months

---

[152] [2010] EWCA Crim 4, at para [38].

[153] Ibid, at para [40]. For an earlier expression of this view, see *DPP v M* [1997] 2 All ER 749.

[154] The appellant was one of those charged with causing or allowing the death of Peter Connelly, in the highly publicised case known in the media as 'Baby P' or 'Baby Peter', contrary to s 5 of the Domestic Violence, Crime and Victims Act 2004.

[155] *R v MacPherson* [2006] 1 Cr App R 30.

[156] Youth Justice and Criminal Evidence Act 1999, s 54(1) and (2).

[157] 'Special measures directions' are governed by ss 19 et seq of the Act and discussed, at pp 759 et seq below.

[158] Ibid, s 54(4).

[159] Ibid, s 54(5).

[160] Ibid, s 54(6).

[161] *R v Barker* [2010] EWCA Crim 4, at para [43], and see *R v MacPherson* [2006] 1 Cr App R 30; *R v Powell* [2006] 1 Cr App R 31; *R v M* [2008] EWCA Crim 2751; and *R v Malicki* [2009] EWCA Crim 365; cf *DPP v R* [2007] EWHC 1842 (Admin).

[162] [2009] EWCA Crim 365. See for another example, *R v Powell* [2006] 1 Cr App R 31.

at the date of the alleged indecent assault and video interviews suggested she was competent. After cross-examination, however, the question of her competence was re-visited since it was impossible to discern whether she was actually remembering the incident which had taken place some 14 months earlier, or simply recalling her video, which she had just seen twice shortly before cross-examination. The court concluded that the evidence should have been excluded under s 78 of the 1984 Act.

A child under the age of 14 may not give sworn evidence.[163] For sworn evidence the child must be older than this and it must be shown that 'he has a sufficient appreciation of the solemnity of the occasion and of the particular responsibility to tell the truth which is involved in taking an oath'.[164] Those over 14 who are able to give 'intelligible' testimony will be presumed to have a sufficient appreciation of those matters if no evidence is adduced to the contrary.[165] The Act also preserves the rule that those under 14 (and others) who are competent to give evidence but not able to take an oath may give it unsworn.[166] The difference between sworn and unsworn evidence lies in the consequences of giving false evidence. In the case of evidence given under oath, this constitutes the offence of perjury, which is an indictable offence, whereas giving false evidence unsworn is a summary offence.[167] A child giving unsworn evidence will receive an admonition from the court in the following terms: 'Tell us all you can remember of what happened. Don't make anything up or leave anything out. This is very important'.[168]

Compellability

If a child is a competent witness, the next question that arises is whether the child should be compelled to give evidence. The general rule is that a competent witness is compellable, and thus a child *can* be compelled to attend and give evidence in any criminal trial. A child's failure to give evidence would, at least in theory, amount to contempt of court unless the child was aged under 10 and thus below the age of criminal responsibility. However, in deciding whether to

---

[163] Youth Justice and Criminal Evidence Act 1999, s 55(2)(a). In the past, a child under 14 years of age could give evidence either sworn or unsworn by virtue of the Children and Young Persons Act 1933, s 38, but the law was amended by the Criminal Justice Act 1991, s 52, inserting s 33A into the Criminal Justice Act 1988, and further amended by the Criminal Justice and Public Order Act 1994 by Sch 9, para 33, inserting s 33A(2A) of the 1988 Act. This introduced an intelligibility test: 'A child's evidence shall be received unless it appears to the court that the child is incapable of giving intelligible testimony'. This was a less rigorous test of competence than that derived from s 38 of the 1933 Act in that it removed 'the need to determine on a question of competence, whether a child knows the difference between truth and a lie and the importance of speaking the truth', the opinion expressed in *R v Hampshire* [1995] 2 All ER 1019 (CA), agreeing with the view of John Spencer in *Archbold News* (1994) issue 6. See also M Childs 'Children's Evidence in Criminal Cases' [1996] CFLQ 81.

[164] Ibid, s 55(2)(b).

[165] Ibid, s 55(3).

[166] Ibid, s 56(1) and (2).

[167] Ibid, s 57.

[168] For further discussion of the background to this admonition, see Birch and Leng (above), at p 140.

issue a witness summons against the child, the court must balance the interests of justice and fairness to the accused against the possible detriment to the child in having to appear.

In *R v Highbury Corner Magistrates' Court ex parte D*[169] the defendant to an assault charge relating to his former cohabitant sought to have a witness summons issued against their nine-year-old son who saw the incident. The materiality of the witness was accepted but the metropolitan magistrate refused to issue the summons taking the view that the detriment to the boy's welfare if he were obliged to give evidence outweighed the interests of the defendant. His judgment was set aside in judicial review proceedings on the basis that it was premature. The balancing act, it was held, should be performed at the court of trial when the moment arose and a decision had to be taken on whether to call the child. Schiemann LJ pointed out that, by that stage, the picture may have become clearer since something might, or might not, be admitted. It is also evident from the tenor of the judgment that the court in criminal cases should take into account not merely the welfare of children but also their *duties* as citizens to society to an extent appropriate to their age and understanding.[170] This suggests that a witness summons is perhaps more likely to be issued against a child in criminal than in civil proceedings.[171]

Credibility

Having admitted the evidence of a child, the next question is how credible is it? At common law, the judge was required to warn the jury about convicting on the strength of a child's uncorroborated evidence. Similar warnings were, until recent years, given in sexual cases whether the alleged victim was a child or an adult.

The Pigot Committee, reporting in 1989,[172] was highly critical of the corroboration rules in sexual offence cases and recommended their abolition. It disapproved of the underlying assumption that women or children were more likely to be untruthful than the ordinary experience and knowledge of jurors might suggest. The corroboration rule as it applied to children was grounded in the notion that children have a propensity for imagining things, lack moral responsibility, have weaker powers of observation and recollection, and are more likely to be open to suggestion. On the last point, similar claims were made for many years in family proceedings and have been used as a reason for discounting, or treating with suspicion, the views of children on residence or

---

[169] [1997] 1 FLR 683.
[170] On the concept of children's duties, see chapter 7. See also *Re F (Specific Issue: Child Interview)* [1995] 1 FLR 819 and the remarks of Lord Donaldson in *Re R (A Minor) (Wardship: Witness in Criminal Proceedings)* [1991] 2 FLR 95 on which the court relied.
[171] Although as we shall see below the approach to calling children to give oral evidence in care proceedings was, to some extent, relaxed by the Supreme Court in *Re W*.
[172] *The Report of the Advisory Group on Video Evidence* (Home Office, 1989), as to which see, generally, J McEwan 'In the Box or on the Box? The Pigot Report and Child Witnesses' [1990] Crim LR 363.

contact questions.[173] These claims did not appear to be substantiated by the psychological evidence. Thus, it was asserted by some psychologists[174] that moral understanding is not proved to be a reliable predictor of honesty in *adults* (and hence should not be seen as such for children either), and that moral knowledge should not be equated with intelligence. Moreover, it was said that comparisons between children and adults were often founded on an exaggerated view of adult competence.

The Criminal Justice Act 1988[175] went some way towards meeting these objections, by abolishing the corroboration rule in relation to children. It is provided that:[176]

> 'Any requirement whereby at a trial on indictment it is obligatory for the court to give the jury a warning about convicting the accused on the uncorroborated evidence of a child is abrogated in relation to cases where such a warning is required by reason only that the evidence is the evidence of a child.'

The effect of this reform is that it is at least possible for a conviction to be sustained solely on the basis of the unsworn evidence of a single child, and it also allows the unsworn evidence of one child to be corroborated by the evidence of another child. The 1988 Act did not, however, strike at the rule requiring an official warning regarding the uncorroborated evidence of a *sexual* complainant. In many cases the child might well be the victim of a sexual offence. However, the former mandatory requirement of a warning in sexual cases was abolished by s 32 of the Criminal Justice and Public Order Act 1994.

The effect of the reforms is to remove the obligatory judicial warnings and to leave the question of what warning (if any) is appropriate to the judge's discretion. The Court of Appeal (Criminal Division)[177] has said that whether the judge chooses to give a warning and in what terms will depend on the circumstances of the case, the issues raised, the context and quality of the witness's evidence and whether there is any evidential basis for suggesting that the evidence of the witnesses may be unreliable. Thus Dennis[178] suggests that where there is evidence supporting an allegation that the child's evidence may be fabricated or a fantasy on the part of the child, the judge might think it appropriate to direct the jury to view the child's evidence with caution and to look for supporting evidence. Moreover, where such a warning is given the judge should give it as part of his general review of the evidence and his comments to the jury on how they should evaluate it. Any warning should not be delivered in the traditional manner used when corroboration warnings were mandatory.

---

[173] See chapter 5 above.
[174] See, for example, R Flin 'Child Witnesses: The Psychological Evidence' (1988) 138 NLJ 608.
[175] Section 34(2).
[176] The provision applies only to 'trials on indictment'. *Quaere* whether magistrates have to apply it by implication.
[177] *R v Makanjuola; R v Easton* [1995] 3 All ER 730.
[178] (Above), ch 13, para 025.

Stress and special measures directions

The background

Anyone who has been a witness in court will know that it can be a stressful and worrying experience. These natural anxieties can be magnified in the case of children to such an extent that they may break down in the witness box or become unable to continue at all. Many of the cases will involve highly distasteful sexual allegations. The prospect of the child having to relive the experience in the presence of the alleged offender will be harrowing. It is one reason why many prosecutions for sexual offences against children have in the past either failed to get off the ground at all, collapsed, or resulted in acquittals.

The courts have over the years tried to mitigate the problem through a number of ad hoc devices. As long ago as 1919, in *Smellie's* case,[179] the defendant was required by the judge to sit on the stairs leading out of the dock, out of sight of his 11-year-old daughter whom he was alleged to have beaten for stealing.[180] The Court of Appeal dismissed *Smellie's* appeal, rejecting arguments by defence counsel that the girl might be inclined to say untrue things which she would not have said in her father's presence, and that the jury might be adversely influenced by his removal. Lord Coleridge LCJ laconically responded that there was nothing to prevent the judge from securing the ends of justice by removing the accused from a witness he might intimidate.

Subsequently, the courts introduced the use of screens in court to screen the witness from the accused, and the advent of video technology increased the options open to the courts, the use of which was put on a statutory footing,[181] and reinforced by another provision which prohibited cross-examination by an unrepresented defendant of a child under 14 years, where the offence was one of violence, or a child under 17 years, where it was a sexual offence.[182] The child might be either the victim or simply a witness to the commission of the alleged offence. The use of video technology was the subject of a report by the Pigot Committee in 1989,[183] which recommended that all of children's evidence, whether examination-in-chief or cross-examination, should be video recorded.

---

[179] (1919) 14 Cr App R 128.

[180] The actual conviction was for 'assaulting, ill-treating and neglecting' his daughter.

[181] The position is now governed by the Youth Justice and Criminal Evidence Act 1999, as amended by the Coroners and Justice Act 2009, but formerly the Criminal Justice Act 1988, s 32 allowed children under 14 years of age to give evidence from outside the courtroom via closed-circuit television, in sex, cruelty and assault cases. This age-limit was raised to accommodate those under 15 years for offences of violence, and those under 18 years in sex cases, by the Criminal Justice Act 1991, s 54(7).

[182] Criminal Justice Act 1991, s 55.

[183] For some of the earlier writings on the introduction of video technology see *The Report of the Advisory Group on Video Evidence* (Home Office, 1989). See also: JR Spencer 'Child Witnesses, Video-Technology and the Law of Evidence' [1987] Crim LR 76; G Smith 'Good practice or yet another hurdle: video recording children's statements' (1993) 5 JCL 21; J Aldridge and K Freshwater 'The preparation of child witnesses' (1993) 5 JCL 25; and J McEwan 'Where the prosecution witness is a child: the memorandum of good practice' (1993) 5 JCL 16. For a discussion of the implications of video technology for *civil* cases, see PM Smith 'Child

The Youth Justice and Criminal Evidence Act 1999 brought together under one statute, and extended, the range of measures designed to assist vulnerable and intimidated witnesses in giving evidence in criminal proceedings.[184] Although the 1999 Act now provides a statutory code for such measures, known as 'special measures directions', it should be noted that the Act expressly provides that nothing in the Act is to be regarded as affecting any power of a court to make an order or give leave of any description, in the exercise of its inherent jurisdiction or otherwise in relation to a witness who is not eligible for a special measure under the Act, or in relation to an eligible witness where the order is made or the leave is given otherwise than by reason of the fact that the witness is an eligible witness.[185] In what follows, therefore, we outline the provisions of the Act, but also at relevant points discuss the relevant common law, including cases which have interpreted the Act itself.

The Youth Justice and Criminal Evidence Act 1999 – special measures directions

The 1999 Act followed a Home Office report, *Speaking Up for Justice*, published in June 1998[186] and is concerned with other categories of vulnerable witnesses apart from children, as well as those eligible for assistance on the grounds of fear or distress about testifying. Its provisions were amended and extended by the Coroners and Justice Act 2009. We are concerned here only with the provisions as they relate to children.

The Act lists a total of eight special measures which may be directed by the court and which may be directed singly or in combination. The first six measures may be directed in relation to other vulnerable witnesses[187] as well as children, but the final two relate only to witnesses under the age of 17.

Witnesses: Implications for Civil Proceedings' [1993] Fam Law 110. For later evaluations of the video-link facilities, see G Davis, C Wilson, R Mitchell and J Milson *Videotaping Children's Evidence: An Evaluation* (Home Office, 1995), *The Child, the Court and the Video* (Social Services Inspectorate, 1994), and H Wescott and J Jones *Perspectives on the Memorandum* (Arena, 1997).

[184] See Birch and Leng (above), chs 4 and 5, and Dennis (above), ch 15. See also D Birch 'A Better Deal for Vulnerable Witnesses' [2000] Crim LR 223; L Hoyano 'Striking a Balance between the Rights of Defendants and Vulnerable Witnesses' (2000) Crim LR 948; and L Hoyano 'Special Measures Directions Take Two: Entrenching Unequal Access to Justice?' [2010] Crim LR 345.

[185] Youth Justice and Criminal Evidence Act 1991, s 19(6).

[186] *Speaking Up for Justice, the Report of the Home Office Interdepartmental Working Group on the Treatment of Vulnerable and Intimidated Witnesses in the Criminal Justice System* (1998).

[187] The Act (ss 16 and 17) identifies four other categories: witnesses suffering from mental disorder; witnesses significantly impaired in relation to intelligence and social functioning; physically disabled witnesses; and witnesses suffering from fear or distress in relation to testifying in the case.

The special measures

Special measures in brief are as follows.

(1) Screens[188]

Screens may be used to shield the witness from the defendant. This practice had been used by the courts for many years.[189] The screen or other arrangement must not, however, prevent the witness from being able to see, and be seen by, the judge, justices, or jury, legal representatives or any interpreter or other person appointed to assist the witness.[190]

(2) Evidence by live link[191]

This enables the witness to give evidence during the trial from outside the courtroom by means of a televised link to the courtroom. This may take place either within the court building or outside it. The witness must be able to see, and be seen by, those mentioned in (1) above.[192] The direction for live link may also provide for a specified person to accompany the witness while the witness is giving evidence by live link.[193] In determining who may accompany the witness, the court must have regard to the wishes of the witness.[194] The live link has been used especially for cross-examination of child witnesses. The argument for use of a live link is that it ameliorates the child's ordeal without an unacceptable risk of prejudice to the defendant. Although the system is recognised to have drawbacks for children,[195] there is some evidence that children are less likely to break down under cross-examination and less likely to refuse to

---

[188] Youth Justice and Criminal Evidence Act 1999, s 23.

[189] See, for example, *R v X; R v Y; R v Z* [1990] Crim LR 515 in which the Court of Appeal approved the use of wooden screens to conceal the victims from the defendants during the victims' evidence. In this case, the children in question were alleged to have been abused 'in almost every permutation of sexual perversion'. Counsel could plainly see the children, and the judge expressly warned the jury not to allow the mere presence of the screen to prejudice them in any way against the defendants. In refusing leave to appeal, the court emphasised that the trial judge had to see that justice was done. This meant that he had to ensure that the system operated fairly, not only to the defendants, but also to the prosecution and the witnesses. It was a matter of the balance of fairness, and the judge had been right to conclude that the necessity of trying to ensure that the children were able to give evidence outweighed any possible prejudice to the defendants.

[190] Youth Justice and Criminal Evidence Act 1999, s 23(2).

[191] Ibid, s 24.

[192] Ibid, s 24(8).

[193] Ibid, 24(1A). It is unclear quite how far the decision in *R v Smith* [1994] Crim LR 458 will be applied to this provision. In that case a social worker had sat beside the victim of sexual abuse and comforted her and talked quietly to her when she broke down while giving evidence. The Court of Appeal said that in future it was important that anyone providing comfort or support to a child witness should not talk to the child while she is giving evidence and that this should be made clear publicly. To do otherwise would arouse suspicions that something was being said about the evidence. It was therefore desirable that anyone performing that role should say as little as possible to the witness and preferably nothing.

[194] Ibid, s 24(1B).

[195] By increasing their feeling of isolation, by being intimidated or distracted by the camera or by having difficulty concentrating on a face or voice speaking over a television monitor.

give evidence in the first place.[196] It was held in *R v Ukpabio*[197] that the use of a live link is now exclusively regulated by the 1999 Act and there was thus no common law power to order evidence to be given by a defendant in this way. However, s 33A of the Act, inserted by the Coroners and Justice Act 2009, now provides for live link to be given by accused children. The court may, on the application of the accused, give a live link direction if it is satisfied that it is in the interests of justice for the accused to give oral evidence through a live link and that (a) his ability to participate effectively in the proceedings as a witness giving oral evidence in court is compromised by his level of intellectual ability or social functioning, and (b) use of a live link would enable him to participate more effectively in the proceedings as a witness (whether by improving the quality of his evidence or otherwise).[198]

(3) Evidence given in private[199]
The court may direct the exclusion of members of the public and press (except for one named person to represent the press) in proceedings relating to a sexual offence or where there are reasonable grounds for believing that there is a risk of intimidation of the witness.[200] The accused, legal representatives and any interpreter or other person appointed to assist the witness may not be excluded.[201]

(4) Removal of wigs and gowns[202]
The court may direct that wigs and gowns be dispensed with by judges and barristers during the giving of the witness's evidence.

(5) Video-recorded evidence-in-chief[203]
The court may direct that a video-recording of an interview with the witness be admitted as evidence-in-chief of the witness.[204] It will not be admitted, however, if the court is of the opinion, having regard to all the circumstances of the case, that in the interests of justice the recording or part of it should not be admitted.[205] Thus, a recording might be excluded if it was of poor quality or, more importantly, if the rules of evidence had been violated in making it – for example, by the interviewer asking too

---

[196] G Davies and E Noon *An evaluation of the live-link for child witnesses* (Home Office, 1991).
[197] [2007] EWCA Crim 2108, [2008] 1 Cr App R 6, approving *R (S) v Waltham Forest Youth Court* [2004] EWHC 715 (Admin), [2004] 2 Cr App R 21.
[198] Youth Justice and Criminal Evidence Act 1999, s 33A(2) and (4).
[199] Ibid, s 25.
[200] Ibid, s 25(4).
[201] Ibid, s 25(2).
[202] Ibid, s 26.
[203] Ibid, s 27.
[204] Ibid, s 27(1).
[205] Ibid, s 27(2).

many leading questions of a child.[206] The court must balance any possible prejudice to the accused against the desirability of showing the whole or part of the interview.[207]

(6) Video-recorded cross-examination or re-examination[208]

The Act makes video-recorded cross-examination or re-examination admissible where there has been a direction for a video-recording to be admitted as evidence-in-chief. Again the video may be excluded if the rules have not been followed in making it. Sometimes known as 'Full Pigot', this is the most significant of the measures introduced by the 1999 legislation. It overcomes the restriction in previous legislation that video-evidence was limited to evidence-in-chief and that the witness had to be available for cross-examination at the trial, if necessary by live television link.

(7) Examination of the witness through an intermediary[209]

This is an innovation of the 1999 legislation which applies only to witnesses under the age of 17 and those suffering from incapacity. It enables the court to appoint an interpreter or other person to assist the witness in giving evidence in court. The possibility of use of an intermediary was extended to accused children by s 33BA of the 1999 Act, which was inserted by the Coroners and Justice Act 2009.[210] This direction in favour of the accused may be made where it is necessary to ensure that the accused receives a fair trial and the accused's ability to participate effectively in the proceedings as a witness giving oral evidence in court is compromised by the accused's level of intellectual ability or social functioning.[211]

(8) Aids to communication[212]

This enables the court to direct that a witness may, while giving evidence, be provided with 'such device as the court considers appropriate with a view to enabling questions or answers to be communicated to or by the witness despite any disability or disorder or other impairment which the witness has suffered from'. This again applies to witnesses on grounds of age or incapacity.

---

[206] The Department of Health issued a *Memorandum of Good Practice in Video Recorded Interviews with Child Witnesses* in 1992. This has now been superseded by *Achieving Best Evidence in Criminal Proceedings: Guidance for Vulnerable or Intimidated Witnesses including Children* (2007).

[207] Youth Justice and Criminal Evidence Act 1999, s 27(3).

[208] Ibid, s 28. This provision has yet to be fully implemented. See D Cooper 'Pigot Unfulfilled: Video-recorded Cross-Examination under s 28 of the Youth Justice and Criminal Evidence Act 1999' [2005] Crim LR 456.

[209] Ibid, s 29.

[210] Such power is also available at common law: see *R (C) v Sevenoaks Youth Court* [2009] EWHC 3088 (Admin), and *R v Cox* [2012] EWCA Crim 549, [2012] 2 Cr App R 6.

[211] Youth Justice and Criminal Evidence Act 1999, s 33BA(2) and (5).

[212] Ibid, s 30.

Eligibility for special measures directions

As noted above, the 1999 Act divides witnesses into two categories for the purposes of eligibility for special measures directions. We are concerned only with the rules which govern the first category, namely those eligible for assistance on the grounds of age or incapacity.[213] Those under the age of 17 at the time of the hearing are automatically eligible for assistance.[214] The general test or 'primary rule' which the court must apply in exercising its discretion on whether it should direct special measures is set out in s 19(2). Where the court is satisfied that a witness is eligible for assistance it must 'determine whether any of the special measures available in relation to the witness (or a combination of them) would, in its opinion, be likely to improve the quality of evidence given by the witness' and then go on to direct them as appropriate.

This primary rule is, however, augmented by special provisions in s 21 in the case of child witnesses which have the broad effect of creating presumptions that certain special measures will be directed. The scheme of s 21 as initially enacted was described as 'labyrinthine',[215] and was amended by the Coroners and Justice Act 2009 to simplify it. The provision is still complex, and what follows is a brief description of the essential distinctions drawn in the Act.

In the case of any child witness the court must first have first have regard to subss (3)–(4C) of s 21. These provide that the primary rule is that the child should give evidence-in-chief by way of video recording and other evidence by live video link.[216] Qualifications to this rule are that such measures are available and that the interests of justice do not dictate that the pre-recorded evidence should not be admitted.[217] The primary rule also does not apply if the witness informs the court of the witness's wish that the rule should not apply or should apply only in part, to the extent that the court is satisfied that not complying with the rule would not diminish the quality of the witness's evidence; and the rule does not apply 'to the extent that the court is satisfied that compliance with it would not be likely to maximise the quality of the witness's evidence so far as practicable'.[218] If as a result of the above provisions the child will be giving testimony in court, then the court must give a special measure direction making provision as described in s 23 (screened evidence),[219] except where the witness informs the court that this should not apply and the court is satisfied that not complying with it will not diminish the quality of the witness's evidence, or the requirement does not apply because the court is satisfied that making such a provision would not be likely to maximise the quality of the witness's evidence

---

[213] Ibid, s 16.

[214] Ibid, s 16(1)(a).

[215] Dennis (above), at p 516.

[216] Youth Justice and Criminal Evidence Act 1999, s 21(3).

[217] Ibid.

[218] Whether because the application to that evidence of one or more other special measures available in relation to the witness would have that result or for any other reason.

[219] Section 21(4A).

so far as practicable.[220] In deciding, for the purpose of the above-mentioned provisions, whether the court is satisfied that the quality of the child's evidence will not be diminished, the court must take into account the following factors and any others it considers relevant: (a) the age and maturity of the witness; (b) the ability of the witness to understand the consequences of giving evidence otherwise than in accordance with the primary rule or without screens as the case may be; (c) the relationship (if any) between the witness and the accused; (d) the witness's social and cultural background and ethnic origins; (e) the nature and alleged circumstances of the offence to which the proceedings relate.[221]

The general effect of s 21 therefore is that the court does not have to apply the normal rule in s 19(2) which would require it to evaluate whether videoed evidence would be likely to improve the quality of the child's evidence. This is presumed to be the case. The court must then also apply s 19(2) and consider whether any other special measures should be directed as likely to improve the quality of the child's evidence. The normal course will therefore be for evidence-in-chief to be by video-recording but cross-examination via live-link unless, applying s 19(2), the court decides that a video-recording would be likely to improve the quality of the child's evidence. It has been held that these provisions do not in any way breach Art 6 of the ECHR.[222]

Civil proceedings

There are perhaps three major issues concerning civil proceedings. The first is the question of the *competence* of child witnesses and the weight to be attached to their *own* evidence. The second is the question whether a child is *entitled* to attend court or can be *compelled* to attend as a witness. The third is how *other* evidence is obtained.[223]

Children as witnesses: competence

The difficulty with the rules on competence of child witnesses before the Children Act was that the common law required them to understand the nature of an oath before being allowed to give evidence. While this was usually assumed in the case of an adult, this was not so with a child. The court would inquire into the *competence* of a child under the age of 14 years who was to be sworn in. The leading case was *R v Hayes*, in which Bridge LJ identified the important consideration as being:[224]

---

[220] Section 21(4B).
[221] Section 21(4C).
[222] *R (D) v Camberwell Green Youth Court* [2005] UKHL 4, [2005] 2 Cr App R 1.
[223] For extensive treatment of evidence in family proceedings affecting children, see R White, P Carr and N Lowe *The Children Act in Practice* (4th edn, LexisNexis, 2008), ch 11.
[224] [1977] 1 WLR 234 at 237.

'whether the child has a sufficient appreciation of the solemnity of the occasion and the added responsibility to tell the truth, which is involved in taking an oath, over and above the duty to tell the truth which is an ordinary duty of normal social conduct.'

The problem with this test was that, while some children may make competent and credible witnesses,[225] they will not necessarily understand abstract concepts like an oath or 'the truth' or the technicalities of the legal system. Dennis[226] has described the *Hayes* decision as 'a policy decision to secularise the common law test'. It was the specifically religious basis of the common law oath which presented a problem to children since it involved an appreciation of the existence of God and the possibility of divine, as well as secular, sanctions for deliberately lying. In *Hayes* itself this would have presented an insurmountable problem since the two boys concerned, aged 11 and 13, both claimed to be ignorant, to have no knowledge of the existence of God and to have received no religious instruction. Rhona Flin has given some colourful illustrations, from a study of child witnesses, of some of the misconceptions which children have about 'law'.[227] Thus, a six-year-old child offered the view that judges 'teach people dancing'; a 10-year-old child said of a jury, 'They ask the criminal questions, then he gives up and they sit down'; an eight-year-old child thought that a lawyer 'gives money to the poor'; and some children in a similar US study thought that a lawyer 'loans money', 'sits around', 'plays golf ' or 'lies'.[228]

The Children Act 1989 sought to overcome these difficulties, by admitting the *unsworn* evidence of children, subject to a different test. This test, which formerly governed the admission of unsworn evidence of children of 'tender years' in *criminal* proceedings,[229] is based on more general powers of understanding. It allows children with the requisite level of understanding to give unsworn evidence which is not dependent on appreciation of an oath. It provides that a child's evidence may be heard, notwithstanding the child's inability to understand the nature of an oath, where the court is of the opinion that:[230]

'(a) he understands that it is his duty to speak the truth; and

(b) he has sufficient understanding to justify his evidence being heard.'

This provision applies only where a child is, in fact, incapable of understanding an oath under the *Hayes* test. Thus, children may now conceivably give sworn *or* unsworn evidence in civil proceedings depending on their level of understanding. This test of competence in civil proceedings appears to be more

---

[225] As to which see JR Spencer and R Flin *The Evidence of Children* (2nd edn, Blackstone Press, 1993), ch 11, and R Flin 'Child Witnesses: The Psychological Evidence' (1988) 138 NLJ 608.

[226] IH Dennis *The Law of Evidence* (5th edn, Sweet & Maxwell, 2013), ch 13, para 021.

[227] R Flin 'Child Witnesses: The Psychological Evidence' (above).

[228] R Flin (above), at p 610.

[229] Children and Young Persons Act 1933, s 38.

[230] Section 96(1) and (2).

stringent than the test in criminal proceedings in two respects. First, the requirement of 'understanding' seems to ask more of the child than the test of 'intelligibility' applying in the criminal law. Secondly, in the civil but not the criminal context, the child concerned must still be capable of understanding the duty to tell the truth. Dennis[231] speculates that this may lead to the exclusion of evidence of very young children in civil cases, which might be admitted in a criminal case. However, this may be counter-balanced to some extent by the admission of hearsay and other evidence whereby the evidence of those children may be heard more indirectly. It is younger children who are more likely to give evidence unsworn. There remains the question of the credibility and weight which ought to be attached to the evidence of particular child witnesses, but this is also an issue in relation to adults.

Attendance at court and compellability

There are really two sides to this question. The first is whether children are *entitled* to attend family proceedings affecting them when they wish to do so. The second is whether they can be *compelled* to attend as witnesses where they do *not* wish to do so. These issues have been addressed mainly in the context of care proceedings.

It used to be the case that children over the age of five were required to attend care proceedings if an interim care order was to be made.[232] However, now, under the Children Act[233] the court has a discretion which can mean that they may be required to attend where they do *not* wish to do so or may not be allowed to attend where they *do*. The higher courts have generally discouraged the attendance of children, which they generally believe to be a potentially damaging experience to be avoided where possible and prefer to rely on obtaining evidence about the child's situation from adults.[234]

Exclusion of children from civil proceedings has been criticised by Masson,[235] who contrasts the position with the shift in social work practices towards the participation of children in meetings and case conferences and with the requirement that the child must attend criminal proceedings. She finds it 'paradoxical that children should be excluded when the "benign jurisdiction" is being exercised but required to attend in the punitive atmosphere of the criminal courts'. This is an issue which has arisen in a number of cases in which the courts have been considering whether to make a secure accommodation order under s 25 of the Children Act 1989.[236] These are cases in which the child's liberty is directly threatened, however welfare-based may be the

---

[231] Above, at ch 13, para 026.

[232] Children and Young Persons Act 1969, s 22.

[233] Children Act 1989, s 95(1).

[234] See, for example, *Re C (A Minor) (Care: Child's Wishes)* [1993] 1 FLR 832 and *Re W (Secure Accommodation Order: Attendance at Court)* [1994] 2 FLR 1092.

[235] J Masson 'Representations of Children' (1996) *Current Legal Problems* 245, at pp 259–262.

[236] See, for example, *Re W (A Minor) (Secure Accommodation Orders: Attendance at Court)* [1994] 2 FLR 1092.

objective of containing the child. As such they have as much, if not more, in common with criminal proceedings as they do with civil proceedings. In this context the initial judicial refusal to allow the attendance at these hearings has given way to an appreciation that, in view of what is at stake for the child, it is normal that the child should attend and be represented.[237]

So far as compelling children to attend as witnesses is concerned, the courts have made it plain that a party may not demand as of right that a child attend to give evidence. As Butler-Sloss LJ has explained in the context of a case of alleged sexual abuse of a child:[238]

> 'Research has shown the adverse effects upon some children of the requirement to give evidence in cases of sexual abuse. In cases of young children, such harm may well be inferred. ... The introduction of the Order of 1990 [now the Children (Admissibility of Hearsay Evidence) Order 1993, SI 1993/621] clearly envisages an alternative to oral evidence and cross-examination and to make it possible for children making allegations of, inter alia, sexual abuse to do so without the additional stress of a court hearing. The philosophy behind the Children Act 1989 would be thwarted by the abuser himself being able to require the attendance of the child at court.

The leading decision on how the courts should approach the question of the child giving oral evidence in family proceedings is the Supreme Court's decision in *Re W (Children) (Abuse: Oral Evidence)*.[239] In that case the appellant challenged the approach, which had been established in several earlier cases, whereby the court's starting point was that it was undesirable that a child should have to give evidence in care proceedings and that a particular justification would be required before that course was taken and such cases would be rare.[240] Effectively, the courts had put in place a presumption against children giving oral evidence in care proceedings. The Supreme Court held[241] that that approach could not 'be reconciled with the approach of the European Court of Human Rights, which always aims to strike a fair balance between competing European Convention rights. Article 6 requires that the proceedings

---

[237] See, for example, *Re C (Secure Accommodation Order: Representation)* [2001] 2 FLR 169, *Re K (Secure Accommodation Order: Right to Liberty)* [2001] 1 FLR 526, and *Re AS (Secure Accommodation Order: Representation)* [1999] 1 FLR 103.

[238] *R v B County Council, ex parte P* [1991] 1 WLR 221.

[239] [2010] UKSC 12, [2010] 1 FLR 1485, and see *Re W (Children) (Abuse: Oral Evidence)* [2010] EWCA Civ 57, [2010] 2 FLR 256. For commentary, see A Bainham 'Child Witnesses in Family Proceedings' (2010) 69(3) *Cambridge Law Journal* 458–460; M Hall 'The misfortune of being straightforward? The impact of *Re W* on children giving evidence in care proceedings' [2010] CFLQ 499.

[240] See, for example, *LM (By Her Guardian) v Medway Council, RM and YM* [2007] EWCA Civ 9, [2007] 1 FLR 1698, at para [44], per Smith LJ: 'The correct starting point ... is that it is undesirable that a child should have to give evidence in care proceedings and that particular justification will be required before that course is taken. There will be some cases in which it will be right to make an order. In my view they will be rare'. See also *R v B County Council ex parte P* [1991] 1 WLR 221, [1991] 1 FLR 470; and *Re P (Witness Summons)* [1997] 2 FLR 447. Endorsed in *SW v Portsmouth City Council; Re W (Care Order: Sexual Abuse)* [2009] EWCA Civ 644, [2009] 2 Cr App Rep 384, [2009] 2 FLR 1106.

[241] At para [22].

overall be fair and this normally entails an opportunity to challenge the evidence presented by the other side'. The court pointed out that striking 'that balance in care proceedings may well mean that the child should not be called to give evidence in the great majority of cases, but that is a result and not a presumption or even a starting point'.[242]

The court explained that:[243]

'When the court is considering whether a particular child should be called as a witness, the court will have to weigh two considerations: the advantages that that will bring to the determination of the truth and the damage it may do to the welfare of this or any other child.'

In weighing the advantages that calling the child to give evidence may bring, the court will have to look at several factors, including the issues it has to decide in order properly to determine the case; the quality of the evidence it already has,[244] as will be the nature of any challenge which the party may wish to make;[245] the age and maturity of the child and the length of time since the events in question.[246]

The Supreme Court indicated that the age and maturity of the child are also relevant to the risk of harm to the child, as is 'the support which the child has from family or other sources, or the lack of it, the child's own wishes and feelings about giving evidence, and the views of the child's guardian and, where appropriate, those with parental responsibility,' and the risk of delay.[247] A court is also:[248]

'entitled to have regard to the general evidence of the harm which giving evidence may do to children, as well as to any features which are particular to this child and this case. That risk of harm is an ever-present feature to which, on the present evidence, the court must give great weight. The risk, and, therefore, the weight,

---

[242] Ibid.
[243] Ibid, at para [24]. The court added that the hearing 'cannot be fair to them unless their interests are given great weight'.
[244] Including the quality of any Achieving Best Evidence interview which will be an important factor. In *Re W*, at para [10], Lady Hale commented that '"Achieving Best Evidence" (ABE) interviews are routinely used in care proceedings if they are available. The near-contemporaneous account, given in response to open-ended questioning, in relaxed and comfortable surroundings, is considered inherently more likely to be reliable than an account elicited by formal questioning in the stressful surroundings of a courtroom months if not years after the event. Unlike criminal proceedings, however, it is "rare" for the child to be called for cross-examination in family proceedings'.
[245] Ibid, at para [24]: 'The court is unlikely to be helped by generalised accusations of lying, or by a fishing expedition in which the child is taken slowly through the story yet again in the hope that something will turn up, or by a cross-examination which is designed to intimidate the child and pave the way for accusations of inconsistency in a future criminal trial. On the other hand, focused questions which put forward a different explanation for certain events may help the court to do justice between the parties'.
[246] Ibid, at para [25].
[247] Ibid, at para [26].
[248] Ibid.

may vary from case to case, but the court must always take it into account and does not need expert evidence in order to do so.'

The court will also need to be mindful that 'the family court has to give less weight to the evidence of a child because she has not been called, then that may be damaging too'.[249] The Supreme Court was clear that an unwilling child should rarely, if ever, be obliged to give evidence.[250]

The court must also 'factor in what steps can be taken to improve the quality of the child's evidence and at the same time to decrease the risk of harm to the child,'[251] and in this regard the court is not limited to applying by analogy the special measures directions available in criminal proceedings.[252]

The Supreme Court indicated that in principle the approach in private family proceedings should be the same, but added that 'there are specific risks to which the court must be alive'.[253] The court explained:[254]

> 'Allegations of abuse are not being made by a neutral and expert local authority which has nothing to gain by making them, but by a parent who is seeking to gain an advantage in the battle against the other parent. This does not mean that they are false but it does increase the risk of misinterpretation, exaggeration or downright fabrication. On the other hand, the child will not routinely have the protection and support of a Cafcass guardian. There are also many more litigants in person in private proceedings. So if the court does reach the conclusion that justice cannot be done unless the child gives evidence, it will have to take very careful precautions to ensure that the child is not harmed by this.'

The court predicted that 'the consequence of the balancing exercise will usually be that the additional benefits to the court's task in calling the child do not outweigh the additional harm that it will do to the child', adding that the 'rarity should be a consequence of the exercise rather than a threshold test'.[255]

Accordingly, the case was remitted to the judge to consider the matter of the child's oral evidence in light of the Supreme Court's guidance. In light of concerns about the courts' previous practice and the Supreme Court's new approach, a Working Party of the Family Justice Council produced *Guidelines in relation to Children Giving Evidence in Family Proceedings*[256] which, *inter alia*, provide[257] that if the Court decides a child should give oral evidence, the Court and all parties should take into account the Good Practice Guidance in managing young witness cases and questioning children.[258]

---

[249] Ibid.
[250] Ibid.
[251] Ibid, at para [27].
[252] Ibid, at para [28].
[253] Ibid, at para [29].
[254] Ibid.
[255] Ibid, at para [30].
[256] December 2011.
[257] At para 19.
[258] Joyce Plotnikoff and Richard Woolfson, *Measuring up? Evaluating implementation of*

In *SMBC v PR (SR Intervening) (Care Proceedings: Children's Evidence) (No 2)*[259] the High Court held that the approach in *Re W* applied also to an alleged child perpetrator of harm to the child concerned. Therefore in concluding that a perpetrator, who had already given evidence in criminal proceedings and objected to giving oral evidence, should not give oral evidence in care proceedings the court took account of the proposition that an unwilling child should rarely, if ever, be required to give evidence. The court also indicated that the child's unwillingness was especially important if the child had already given evidence in a criminal trial.[260]

Several cases have applied the guidance in *Re W*.[261] In *Re J (Child Giving Evidence)*[262] a teenage child, who was considered by the guardian to have appropriate maturity, who wished to give evidence to the court so that the judge could 'hear his truth' (as he put it to the guardian) was permitted by the judge to give oral evidence. By contrast, in *Re X (A Child: Evidence)*,[263] Theis J refused an application for a 17 year-old young man to give evidence. The child had Asperger's Syndrome and while this did not prevent him from giving evidence per se, on the facts and circumstances of the case the balance tipped in favour of him not giving evidence. The evidence was not crucial, there was 'real doubt whether he fully understood the consequences of giving evidence as well as the adverse risks to his welfare if the evidence did not go the way he expected, which could adversely affect the effectiveness of emotional support that he would be able to receive, which would be contrary to his welfare',[264] and his giving evidence would result in delay contrary to the welfare of the child concerned in the care proceedings.[265] The case might be compared with *Re G and E (Vulnerable Witnesses)*[266] in which the High Court concluded that a 17 year-old girl with significant learning difficulties should give oral evidence within public law proceedings as to allegations of sexual abuse against her father. Experts agreed that the girl should give evidence and that various measures would be appropriate so as to enable G to make the best of her opportunity to tell her story.

Government commitments to young witnesses in criminal proceedings: Good practice guidance in managing young witness cases and questioning children (Nuffield and NSPCC, July 2009), as endorsed by the Judicial Studies Board, the Director of Public Prosecutions, the Criminal Bar Association and the Law Society, and the President of the Family Division: see http://www.nspcc.org.uk/Inform/research/findings/measuring_up_guidance_wdf66581.pdf.

[259] [2012] 1 FLR 852.

[260] Ibid, especially at paras [14], [17], [21]–[23].

[261] For a case in which post *Re W* a judge's decision, erroneously applying the presumption, was upheld by the Court of Appeal because the judge's decision would not have been different had a presumption not been applied, see *Re H (Abuse: Oral Evidence)* [2011] EWCA Civ 741, [2012] 1 FLR 186.

[262] [2010] EWHC 962 (Fam), [2010] 2 FLR 1080.

[263] [2011] EWHC 3401 (Fam), [2012] 2 FLR 456.

[264] Ibid, at para [33].

[265] Ibid.

[266] [2011] EWHC 4063 (Fam).

Other evidence in family proceedings

Hearsay

The key feature of civil proceedings involving children is now the disapplication of the hearsay rule, although under the Civil Evidence Act 1995 it has now been disapplied more generally in civil cases. This general rule of evidence, where it applies, renders inadmissible as proof of facts evidence given by someone as to what someone else said or did. If applied in children cases it could prevent the court from relying on evidence in welfare reports and the reports of children's guardians about what children said to the writer of the report, perhaps concerning incidents of abuse.

The rule was abolished in all *civil* proceedings affecting children[267] before its more general abolition in civil proceedings, the result being that the court can admit a wide range of documentary evidence[268] and simultaneously avert the need for the child to attend court and give oral evidence. While the grounds for challenging the *admissibility* of hearsay have thus been removed, the *weight* to be given to hearsay evidence is a matter within the discretion of the judge, and it is even open to him to disregard it completely.[269] Such weight may well diminish in the case of second or even more remote hearsay. Where it is the child's hearsay evidence, the court will need to take into account factors such as the child's age, the context and circumstances in which the statement was made, the child's previous behaviour, etc. It may also take account of the child's opportunities to have acquired the information elsewhere, and any predilection he may have for fantasising or telling untruths.

The rules admitting hearsay are very important in care and other public law proceedings. Prior to the Children Act 1989, care proceedings took place exclusively in the juvenile court – a specialised magistrates' court.[270] Magistrates, subject to limited exceptions, had to apply the hearsay rule and refuse to admit hearsay statements and documentary evidence, such as reports, as evidence of the facts to which they related. The *Review of Child Care Law* recommended an extension of the rules of civil evidence to care proceedings.[271] The broad effect of s 96 of the Children Act was to apply the new rules in *all* civil proceedings affecting children,[272] including care proceedings.

---

[267] Children (Admissibility of Hearsay Evidence) Order 1993 (SI 1993/621), made under the Children Act, s 96(3).

[268] Formerly this was largely proved by means of affidavits but these have now been displaced by written statements.

[269] See *Re W (Minors) (Wardship: Evidence)* [1990] 1 FLR 203 and *R v B County Council ex parte P* [1991] 1 FLR 470.

[270] Now replaced by the youth court. The civil side of the former juvenile court's work has now been taken over by the family proceedings court. On the implications of the change from the juvenile court to the youth court, see the research of C Ball 'Youth justice and the youth court – the end of a separate system?' [1995] CFLQ 196.

[271] DHSS *Review of Child Care Law* (1985), at paras 16.30–16.38.

[272] The rule is thus also disapplied in civil proceedings which fall outside the definition of family proceedings in the Children Act.

The relaxation of the rules of evidence in children cases has other implications. The courts have made it clear that normal rules of evidence applicable in an adversarial legal system do not necessarily apply in children cases.[273] This is especially so regarding the disclosure of documents.[274] Thus, parents are required to disclose to the court all the documents in their possession, including expert reports commissioned by them, even if they are not favourable to their case.[275] Likewise, the local authority must disclose to the parents all relevant documents in its possession.[276]

---

[273] For a general discussion of these developments, see C Tapper 'Evidential privilege in cases involving children' [1997] CFLQ 1, L Mendoza 'Confidentiality in Child Proceedings' [1998] Fam Law 30, and J McEwan 'The privilege of parents and the protection of the child – where do priorities lie?' in C Bridge (ed) *Family Law Towards the Millennium: Essays for PM Bromley* (Butterworths, 1997), ch 5.

[274] The issue of disclosure has involved the courts in a delicate balancing exercise involving conflicting considerations of public policy. For particularly good illustrations of the difficult balance which must be struck and how the courts go about it, see *A County Council v W and Others (Disclosure)* [1997] 1 FLR 574 and *Re R (Disclosure)* [1998] 1 FLR 433.

[275] See *Oxfordshire County Council v M* [1994] 2 All ER 269 and *Re L (Police Investigation: Privilege)* [1996] 1 FLR 731.

[276] *R v Hampshire County Council, ex parte K* [1990] 2 All ER 129.

Chapter 15

CHILDREN AND THE CRIMINAL LAW

INTRODUCTION

Children's relationship to and within the criminal law has long been a complex one that has both reinforced and been influenced by social constructions of childhood.[1] On the one hand, the child as victim aligns with the image of children as vulnerable and dependent (an 'image' that is nonetheless based on a real lack of physical, economic, political and legal power);[2] on the other, the child as offender challenges prevailing notions of childhood innocence and plays into adult fears and anxieties.[3] The duality of the criminal law's approach towards children – the angel/devil dichotomy[4] – appeared particularly marked at the time that the last edition of this book was published (2005). The protective reach of the criminal law was extending further into children's lives, with new (at that time) legislation safeguarding children from sexual exploitation[5] but which also (some commentators argued)[6] constituted an intrusion into normal sexual relations between teenagers. At the same time as the protective function of the criminal law highlighted children's immaturity and vulnerability, children in conflict with the law experienced 'adulterisation';[7] with legal reforms creating a framework that allowed for greater responsibility and more punitive punishment.[8]

Since 2005, neither the protective aspects of the criminal law nor those processes designed to hold children criminally responsible have undergone the overhaul of previous decades. Changes, where they have occurred, have been more incremental. Nonetheless, although the differences in how we perceive the child as victim and the child as offender persist, there does appear to be less of a dichotomy than was the case eight years ago. One reason for this may be the growing influence of children's rights in criminal law, policy and practice. Children have at their disposal legal tools which allow them to argue both for

---

[1]   J Fionda 'Youth and Justice' in J Fionda (ed) *Legal Concepts of Childhood* (Hart Publishing, 2001).

[2]   See for example, R Dixon and M Nussbaum 'Children's Rights and a Capabilities Approach' (2012) 97 *Cornell Law Review* 549–594.

[3]   Because they 'challenge both social identity and a stable social order'; J Fionda *Devils and Angels: Youth Policy and Crime* (Hart Publishing, 2005), at p 27.

[4]   Fionda (2001), above.

[5]   Sexual Offences Act 2003.

[6]   JR Spencer 'The Sexual Offences Act 2003: (2) Child and Family Offences' (2004) Crim LR 347.

[7]   Fionda (2005), above.

[8]   Specifically under the Crime and Disorder Act 1998.

their equality with adults and for their difference from them. The former can be achieved by appealing to the European Convention on Human Rights and the equal status that children have to protection for those rights. In the criminal law, this might play out in terms of arguments for protection from physical chastisement (and respect for bodily integrity under Arts 3 and 8 ECHR) or respect for the child's private life so that sexual experimentation is not unnecessarily criminalised. Such arguments may not always be successful (see below) but they are being argued, and they alter how the law perceives children. The UN Convention on the Rights of the Child (UNCRC) gives children the mechanism by which to emphasise their distinctiveness from adults, and to argue for rights that *all* children have, even those who offend. The European Court of Human Rights has been influenced by the UNCRC and together the emphasis on *children's* rights has perhaps allowed us to consider the vulnerabilities – and not just the responsibilities – of children in conflict with the law.

However, any movement towards a convergence in the social construction of child victims and child offenders is less obvious from the language used in the law. In the civil law anyone below the age of majority is a 'child' or a 'minor'[9] and in the UNCRC a child is defined as a person under the age of 18. In criminal justice legislation, at least until 1998, a distinction was drawn between minors under the age of 14 years who were defined as 'children' and those over 14 but under 18 years who were referred to as young persons.[10] This mirrored the presumption of competence vis à vis criminal responsibility: those aged 14 and over were conclusively presumed to have sufficient capacity to be held criminally responsible, whilst those aged 10–13 were protected by the rebuttable presumption of doli incapax; the prosecution had to prove in addition to the elements of the offence that the child knew that what she did was seriously wrong.[11] The Crime and Disorder Act 1998 abolished the presumption of doli incapax for the under 14s. Since then the legal differentiation between the two age groups has diminished[12] and the major pieces of criminal justice legislation have referred instead to all minors over the minimum age of criminal responsibility as 'young offenders' or 'offenders under 18'.[13] However, despite

---

[9]　There are, of course, many age-related rules which distinguish between children of different ages for specific purposes.

[10]　The principal legislation where the distinction is drawn is the Children and Young Persons Acts of 1933, 1963 and 1969, the Criminal Justice Act 1991, the Criminal Justice and Public Order Act 1994, and the Crime and Disorder Act 1998.

[11]　Also, one of the main distinctions between 'children' and 'young persons' was that it had been intended, under the Children and Young Persons Act 1969, to abolish criminal prosecutions of 'children' and, instead, to deal with young offenders below the age of 14 years through the more welfare-orientated care procedures. In fact, this never happened (see Children and Young Persons Act 1969, s 4, now repealed by s 72 of the Criminal Justice Act 1991).

[12]　Though there are other distinctions drawn on the basis of age; for example in relation to sentencing certain sentences are not available for those under 12, and stricter conditions are in place for those under 15 (see below).

[13]　There has not, as far as the author is aware, been an explicit rejection of the legal distinction between the two age groups, but it has not been replicated in recent legislation. See for example the Youth Justice and Criminal Evidence Act 1999, the Criminal Justice Act 2003, the Criminal Justice and Immigration Act 2008 and the Legal Aid, Sentencing and Punishment of Offenders

the language used, it is important to remember that children in conflict with the law *are* children and have many of the same vulnerabilities and needs as those children who are victims of crime (indeed, there is significant overlap between the cohorts).

It is not possible, in a general introductory work of this nature, to do justice to the multifarious aspects of the criminal justice system as it applies to children. The focus of this chapter is therefore on understanding the various ways in which the criminal law treats children *differently* from adults.[14] It does so by examining how children are protected by the criminal law and how they are held responsible before it.

PROTECTION

This section is concerned with crimes *against* children which, for the purposes of exposition, can conveniently be put into three categories: those which relate to violence and physical harm; sexual offences; and special offences designed to eradicate or control activities which are thought to be harmful to children. There is a good deal of overlap between these categories. Sexual offences, for example, frequently involve violence and physical harm. Many of the special offences in the third category also involve physical harm but are distinctive in that they are ad hoc legislative responses to particular dangers for children which arise from time to time.

It should be noted at the outset that a high proportion of crimes against children are committed by members of the same family or household. Most instances of child abuse or neglect also involve criminal offences so that, to some extent, child protection agencies face a choice about whether to prosecute or to invoke the civil remedies.[15] In some cases, it may be necessary to take action on both fronts. However, the threat of the criminal law, and the potential criminalisation of a parent, can hinder the ability of the civil law to protect the child[16] and can inhibit the older child's willingness to seek help.[17] There have

---

Act 2012 (hereafter the Legal Aid Act). One exception is s 107 of the Legal Aid Act which, in the context of remands to custody, refers to 'children'; indicative perhaps, of a view that prior to conviction minors are children, and after conviction they instead become offenders.

[14] For a detailed look at these issues see Fionda (2005), above; J Fortin *Children's Rights and the Developing Law* (3rd edn, Cambridge University Press, 2009), chs 17 and 18. For a theoretical rights-based perspective on juvenile crime, see MDA Freeman *The Rights and Wrongs of Children* (Frances Pinter, 1983). For more historical perspectives, see J Fionda 'Youth Justice' in J Fionda (ed) *Legal Concepts of Childhood* (Hart Publishing, 2001) and HK Bevan *Child Law* (Butterworths, 1989), chs 9, 10, 12 and 13.

[15] See chapters 11 and 12 above.

[16] See C Cobley 'Working Together? Admissions of Child Abuse in Child Protection Proceedings and Criminal Prosecutions' (2004) 16 (2) CFLQ 175–187 and L Hoyano and C Keenan *Child Abuse: Law and Policy Across Boundaries* (Oxford University Press, 2007) who, at p 122 quote the comments of McLaughlin CJ in the Canadian Supreme Court that 'The criminal law ... is a blunt instrument whose power can also be destructive of family and educational relationships'.

[17] Hoyano and Keenan, ibid, at p 122.

also been, until recently, difficulties in bringing a successful prosecution, especially in cases of sexual abuse, because of the restrictive rules regarding children's evidence. The reforms in this area[18] now render prosecution a more realistic option and it has been argued that in some cases prosecution may serve to remove an abuser (rather than the child) from the family home – and is, in that sense, consistent with the thinking in the Children Act 1989.[19]

The Children Act supports the primary responsibility of parents to raise children, and the principle that the relationship between children and parents should be fostered, except where this is outweighed by considerations of harm to the child. In many cases, child abuse will be the result of stress on parents who themselves have inadequate family backgrounds and who lack sufficient understanding of child development or basic child care techniques. In cases like these, social work support and education may be a more appropriate response than either prosecution or care proceedings.[20] It may also be in the child's best interests for the family unit to be preserved, despite the instances of abuse, and for residential or foster care to be avoided. The backward looking criminal law may not, therefore, be the best tool to protect the future interests of children.[21] However, in other cases, the abuse may be so serious or abhorrent as to necessitate a prosecution in the public interest. In such cases, it may, in any event, be difficult to conceive of any possible benefit to the child in preserving her 'relationship' with the adult concerned.[22] The broad question, in any given case, must be whether the beneficial consequences of criminal proceedings are likely to outweigh the potential harm to the child and the family.[23]

Violent crimes and physical harm

Homicide

The statistics on child homicide are, as Herring comments, 'chilling'.[24] In 2010/11, 56 children under the age of 16 were killed and children under the age of one are more likely to be the victims of homicide than any other age group.[25]

---

18 See chapter 14 above.

19 C Cobley 'Child Abuse, Child Protection and the Criminal Law' (1992) 4 JCL 78. The removal of the alleged abuser is possible under the powers to add 'exclusion requirements' to EPOs and interim care orders under ss 44A and 38A of the Children Act 1989 (inserted by s 52 and Sch 6 to the Family Law Act 1996), and this may well represent a better alternative than prosecution in some cases. See chapter 11.

20 See, eg, JG Hall and DF Martin 'Crimes Against Children' (1992) 142 NLJ 902. See also A Wilczynski and A Morris 'Parents who kill their children' [1993] 1 Crim LR 31, and R Mackay 'The consequences of killing very young children' [1993] 1 Crim LR 21.

21 Hoyano and Keenan, above, at p 122.

22 The female pronoun is used throughout this chapter for simplicity (except where the male pronoun is used in legislation or quotes, or reference is made to specific cases or people).

23 See, for example, C Cobley's argument in 'Child Abuse, Child Protection and the Criminal Law' (1992) 4 JCL 78 at 80, that prosecutions in cases of intra-familial sexual abuse may not always be justified either in the public interest or in the interests of the child victim.

24 J Herring 'Familial homicide, failure to protect and domestic violence: who's the victim?' [2007] Crim L R 923.

25 There were 18 children under the age of one killed in 2010/11. See K Smith (ed) S Osborne, I

The law governing murder and manslaughter applies just as much to child victims[26] but there are features in relation to children that deserve special attention. These are the unborn child and the law of homicide, infanticide, deaths of children as a result of neglect or omission, and familial homicide.

The unborn child and the law of homicide

A charge of murder or manslaughter may only be brought in relation to 'any reasonable creature in rerum natura'[27] or, in other words, a human being. There can be some difficult line-drawing for these purposes. The essential test is that the child should have 'an existence independent of its mother'. This involves expulsion from the mother's body, an independent circulation and breathing after birth.[28] Any killing of a foetus before this constitutes (if anything) the offence of child destruction or falls within the abortion laws. Detailed discussion of the status of the 'unborn child' and the criminal law is beyond the scope of the present work.[29]

On the other hand, there may be liability for the homicide of a child where the injury is inflicted on the foetus before birth, the child is born alive and then subsequently dies as a result, at least in part, of the injury. The Court of Appeal so held in *Attorney-General's Reference (No 3 of 1994)*[30] through an ingenious use of the doctrine of transferred malice.[31] In this case, the accused had stabbed his girlfriend, who was 26 weeks' pregnant, cutting the abdomen of the foetus. The child was born prematurely, survived 120 days and then died as a result of stress from operations and immaturity. The accused was acquitted on a charge of murder by direction of the trial judge. The Court of Appeal held that this direction was wrong since the foetus could be regarded as part of the mother's

---

Lau, and A Britton *Homicides, firearm offences and intimate violence 2010/11: supplementary volume 2 to Crime in England and Wales 2010/11* (Home Office, 2012).

[26] For a general analysis of the law of homicide, see Smith and Hogan *Criminal Law* (13th edn, Oxford University Press, 2011), chs 14 and 16, J Herring *Criminal Law* (7th edn, Palgrave Macmillan, 2011), ch 9, and MJ Allen *Textbook on Criminal Law* (10th edn, Oxford University Press, 2011), ch 8. For an incisive academic critique of the underlying principles, see A Ashworth *Principles of Criminal Law* (6th edn, Oxford University Press, 2009), ch 7. For its more specific application to child victims, see Hoyano and Keenan *Child Abuse*, at pp 133–147. Hoyano and Keenan provide an interesting discussion in particular of the difficulty in proving the requisite mens rea for murder where a child dies as a result of repeated physical attacks, and the application of defences of provocation and diminished responsibility in the case of the killing of a child.

[27] Coke, 3 Inst 47.

[28] For further discussion of the point, see Smith and Hogan (above), at pp 602–603. See also the discussion of the offence of concealment of birth under s 60 of the Offences Against the Person Act 1861, which essentially makes it an offence to conceal the dead body of a child after birth: ibid, at pp 581–582.

[29] But see Smith and Hogan (above).

[30] [1996] 2 FLR 1. For commentary, see J Keown 'Homicide, Fetuses and Appendages' (1996) CLJ 207.

[31] On the doctrine of transferred malice, see Smith and Hogan (above), at pp 212–13, and for commentary on this case, see J Beaumont 'The Unborn Child and the Limits of Homicide' (1997) 61 JCL 86.

body. An intention to cause serious harm to the mother was an intention to cause serious harm to part of the mother. This could be transferred and there was no requirement that the person to whom it was transferred had to be in being at the time of infliction of the injury. The 'malice' towards the mother could thus be transferred to the child at the point where the child was born and became an independent person. The House of Lords[32] subsequently rejected the application of the doctrine of transferred malice in the circumstances of this case, but held that liability could instead lie in constructive manslaughter. The mother and foetus were to be regarded as 'two distinct organisms living symbiotically, not a single organism with two aspects'. But the child, once born, could be regarded as falling within the defendant's mens rea when he stabbed the mother. The decision appears somewhat strained in terms of principle in order to arrive at what was thought to be the right conclusion on policy grounds.[33] In particular, the House declined to hold that murder, rather than manslaughter, could be an appropriate charge.

Infanticide

Where a child was killed by her mother within a short time of birth there was a traditional reluctance on the part of juries to convict her of murder, and public and professional disapproval of treating these cases as ordinary murders, particularly given a conviction would result in the mandatory sentence of death.[34] Many such cases arose, historically, through the fear of unmarried mothers of the stigma of giving birth to an illegitimate child.

Infanticide is both a partial defence to murder[35] and a substantive offence[36] which applies where, but for the infanticide provisions, a woman would otherwise be charged with murder or, since 2010, manslaughter.[37] The offence is committed in the following circumstances:[38]

> 'Where a woman by any wilful act or omission causes the death of her child being a child under the age of twelve months, but at the time of the act or omission the balance of her mind was disturbed by reason of her not having fully recovered from the effect of giving birth to the child or by reason of the effect of lactation consequent upon the birth of the child.'

---

[32] [1998] AC 245.
[33] See J Keown 'Homicide by Prenatal Assault Revisited' (1998) CLJ 240.
[34] See D Seaborne-Davies 'Child-killing in English Law' (1937) 1 MLR 203.
[35] Infanticide Act 1938, s 1(2).
[36] Infanticide Act 1922, s 1(1).
[37] Infanticide was extended to manslaughter by s 57 of the Coroners and Justice Act 2009 (amending the Infanticide Act 1938) following recommendations of the Law Commission. In any event, an earlier Court of Appeal decision appeared 'to have moved the law in this direction [extending infanticide to manslaughter] by judicial interpretation'. See A Ashworth 'Infanticide: whether mens rea of infanticide consists of an intention to kill or cause grievous bodily harm', discussing the decision in *R v Gore (Lisa Therese)(Deceased)* [2007] EWCA Crim 2789, [2008] Crim LR 388.
[38] Infanticide Act 1938, s 1(1); s 1(2) provides for an identical definition in relation to a defence to murder.

A woman convicted of infanticide is to be dealt with as if she had been convicted of manslaughter and thus the maximum available punishment is a life sentence. Nonetheless, in most cases a conviction for infanticide results in a non-custodial sentence.[39] There are a number of difficulties in justifying the retention of the offence in the modern law:[40] the causal link between the mother's mental imbalance and the killing may not be easy to establish;[41] it is gender-specific[42] and is not available to fathers or other carers of the child;[43] and it seemingly reinforces stereotypes, particularly the medicalisation/pathologisation of women.[44] Moreover, the availability of the offence/defence could be seen to devalue the lives of children under the age of one.[45] Given the availability of the defence to murder of diminished responsibility infanticide is arguably no longer necessary or suitable. However, the Law Commission did not reach this conclusion when it reviewed the laws of homicide in 2006,[46] and instead recommended the retention of infanticide in the existing form,[47] citing in support of its decision medical evidence that some women are more vulnerable to psychiatric disorder following childbirth.[48] The only resulting change therefore was to extend its availability from murder to manslaughter.[49]

Death by neglect or omission

As a general proposition, admittedly subject to significant exceptions, the criminal law does not punish for omission or inactivity.[50] The point was

---

[39] See The Law Commission *Murder, Manslaughter and Infanticide* (2006) Law Com No 304; HC 30, Appendix D: RD MacKay 'Infanticide and Related Diminished Responsibility Manslaughters – An Empirical Study' (2006).

[40] See Smith and Hogan (above), at p 594. See also D Maier-Katkin and R Ogle 'A rationale for infanticide laws' [1993] Crim LR 903; R Mackay 'The consequences of killing very young children' [1993] Crim LR 19; K Brennan 'Beyond the Medical Model: A Rationale for Infanticide Legislation' (2007) 58 NILQ 505, at p 506.

[41] Although the killing need not be causally linked to the disturbance of mind; only a temporal connection is required. On the medical foundation of infanticide more generally see Brennan, ibid.

[42] Contrary to the trend regarding other criminal offences in the era of human rights equality. See A Ashworth *Principles of Criminal Law* (6th edn, Oxford University Press, 2009), at pp 267–269.

[43] The Law Commission (above) received evidence that men who kill their own babies do so in very different circumstances than mothers, and the offence/defence should not therefore be extended to fathers or other carers.

[44] However, this criticism was strongly refuted by the Law Commission (above, at para 8.39) who stated that there is only 'the surface appearance of discrimination: the substantive offence ensures substantive justice'.

[45] See Brennan (above) citing C Damme 'Infanticide: The Worth of an Infant Under Law' (1978) 22 *Medical History* 1.

[46] Partly because there would be increased difficulties for mothers to discharge the burden of proof if infanticide was brought into diminished responsibility. See Law Commission (above).

[47] The Commission's earlier consultation paper (*A New Homicide Act for England and Wales? A Consultation Paper* (consultation paper no 177)) had provisionally proposed the removal of the reference to lactation and raising the age limit to two years but in the final report these were rejected.

[48] Law Commission (above).

[49] Coroners and Justice Act 2009, s 57.

[50] Discussed, generally, in Smith and Hogan (above).

graphically made by Stephen[51] who said that no offence was committed by a person who could save someone from drowning merely by holding out her hand. Morally reprehensible though it would undoubtedly be, it seems that failure to rescue a drowning child from a shallow pool is not homicide on the part of the bystander. However, where a *duty* to act can be established, the criminal law applies.[52] In the case of parents, this duty of protection is an incident of parental responsibility but others who have 'responsibility' for children, in the less technical sense of assuming their physical care, are also bound by this duty.[53] Thus, as long ago as 1918,[54] a conviction for murder was upheld where a female cohabitant withheld food from her male cohabitant's child resulting in the child's death. She was held to have assumed responsibility for the child by living with the man and accepting from him money for food. In most cases, manslaughter is more likely to be the charge, but where an *intention* to kill or cause grievous bodily harm can be established, it is murder, in the absence of an exculpatory defence.[55]

Familial homicide

The Domestic Violence, Crime and Victims Act 2004, s 5 created a familial homicide offence to deal with the situation where a child dies as a result of an unlawful act by one of the child's carers, but it is unclear who in the household caused the child to die.[56] Prior to this legislation, where a child died at the hands of her parents or carers but it could not be established who in the household was criminally responsible then all of the carers (including the unknown perpetrator) had to be acquitted.[57] The 2004 Act addresses this mischief[58] by creating an offence that carries a maximum sentence of 14 years imprisonment and applies where:

'(a) a child or vulnerable adult ("V") dies as a result of the unlawful act of a person who –

(i) was a member of the same household as V, and

---

[51]   *Digest of Criminal Law* (4th edn, 1887), Art 212.

[52]   The imposition of liability for inactivity more generally in the criminal law has been the subject of more than one theory, but the duty theory is probably the most convincing and was the basis of the decision in *R v Miller* [1983] 2 AC 161.

[53]   See below for those who have potential liability for neglect under the Children and Young Persons Act 1933, s 1.

[54]   *R v Gibbins and Proctor* (1918) 13 Cr App Rep 134.

[55]   The leading cases are now *R v Hancock* [1986] AC 455, *R v Moloney* [1985] AC 905, *R v Nedrick* [1986] 3 All ER 1, and *R v Woollin* [1999] AC 82.

[56]   See J Herring 'Familial homicide, failure to protect and domestic violence: who's the victim?' [2007] Crim LR 923; S Morrison 'Allowing the Death of a Vulnerable Child' [2009] LQR 570 and Hoyano and Keenan (above), at pp 158ff. The Act was amended in 2012 to include cases where the child suffers serious physical injury but does not die. See below.

[57]   *R v Lane* (1986) 82 Cr App R 5 (CA).

[58]   The issues were considered in depth by the Law Commission, which reported in September 2003. See Law Com Report No 282 *Children: Their Non-Accidental Death or Serious Injury (Criminal Trials)* (2003).

(ii)   had frequent contact with him,[59]

(b) D was such a person at the time of that act,

(c) at that time there was a significant risk of serious physical harm being caused to V by the unlawful act of such a person, and

(d) either D was the person whose act caused V's death or –

(i)   D was, or ought to have been, aware of the risk mentioned in paragraph (c),
(ii)   D failed to take such steps as he could reasonably have been expected to take to protect V from the risk, and
(iii) the act occurred in circumstances of the kind that D foresaw or ought to have foreseen.'[60]

The provisions under the 2004 Act apply not only to cases where it is unclear who killed the child but can also be used to punish another member of the household (usually the perpetrator's partner) for failing to protect the child.[61] As Hoyano and Keenan note, this provision therefore 'reflects a growing recognition in the law that in cases where an adult is a child's only hope of protection, the failure of that adult to effect an easy rescue of the child from the violence the child is suffering, can be as culpable as the person who inflicts the blows which kill the child'.[62] The difficulty of this is that it can facilitate the punishment, rather than protection, of (usually) mothers who are themselves victims of domestic violence at the hands of their partners.[63] The provision may be further criticised as an example of the imposition of serious criminal liability on the basis of negligence rather than on the basis of mental capacity required by proof of intention or recklessness.

Non-fatal offences

Assaults under the Offences Against the Person Act 1861

The Offences Against the Person Act 1861 still governs the various criminal offences arising from assault. The main offences are assault occasioning actual bodily harm,[64] and wounding or grievous bodily harm with[65] or without intent.[66] Where an injury is intentionally or recklessly inflicted on a child by an outsider who does not have responsibility for her, one of these charges will be

---

59   On the proper directions to be given to the jury, and the meaning of frequent (albeit in the context of the death of a vulnerable adult) see *R. v Khan (Uzma)* [2009] EWCA Crim 2, [2009] 1 WLR 2036 (CA (Crim Div)).
60   This is the original version of the Act. As noted, it now applies also where the child suffers serious physical injury.
61   J Herring (2007), above.
62   Above, at p 177.
63   See J Herring (2007), above.
64   Offences Against the Person Act 1861, s 47.
65   Ibid, s 18.
66   Ibid, s 20.

appropriate, depending on the extent of the injury and the mental state of the assailant. Again, as with homicide, these are general offences which are not confined to child victims.

Cruelty to children under 16 years of age

Where, as is more likely, the injury to the child has been caused by one of her 'carers', the offence in s 1(1) of the Children and Young Persons Act 1933 will apply.[67] However, the offence is a good deal wider in its coverage than simply assaults. It extends to various forms of neglect, ill-treatment, abandonment and exposure, as well as to physical assaults.[68] The offence is committed by 'any person who has attained the age of sixteen years' who 'has responsibility for any child or young person under that age'. The concept of 'responsibility' reflects the change of terminology in the Children Act 1989 and replaces the former expressions 'custody, charge or care'.[69] The general idea is of either someone who has parental responsibility formally, most obviously a parent or someone with a residence order, but also anyone else who is de facto looking after the child at the relevant time, for example a relative, babysitter or foster parent.

This potential liability for failure to care adequately for the child is really the obverse of s 3(5) of the Children Act which, as we saw,[70] gives to such de facto carers the power to take necessary action to promote the child's welfare. It is also plain that someone who does, formally, have parental responsibility cannot 'contract out' of liability under this offence by delegating responsibility to someone else[71] but, where proper care has been taken to ensure the adequacy of a substitute caring arrangement, it would be unlikely that the parent would have the requisite mens rea. Similar problems as those described above in relation to familial homicide can arise where the child suffers harm but it does not result in death; that it may be clear that a person with responsibility has caused the child's injury but it is unclear which person has done it.[72] There is authority that the court may be able to infer that they are jointly responsible[73]

---

[67] For a more comprehensive discussion than space allows here see Hoyano and Keenan (above), at pp 178ff.

[68] For discussion of the offence in the context of failure to summon medical aid for the child, see chapter 8 above. Hoyano and Keenan suggest that the offence of ill-treatment and neglect should be considered one of the worst offences against children, since it breaks their spirit and damages the fundamental trust they have in others (resulting in damaging long term consequences). Hoyano and Keenan above, at p 178.

[69] On the interpretation of these expressions, see HK Bevan *Child Law* (Butterworths, 1989), at paras 9.48–9.55.

[70] At chapter 4 above.

[71] Children Act 1989, s 2(11).

[72] There may be difficulty here also for the purposes of care proceedings. See the discussion of *Lancashire County Council v B* [2000] 2 WLR 590 in chapter 12.

[73] *R v Gibson and Gibson* [1984] Crim LR 615. Cf *R v Aston and Mason* [1991] Crim LR 701. In *R v Young* (1993) 97 Cr App R 280, the Court of Appeal held that as long as the jury were unanimous that cruelty in the sense alleged by the prosecution had been established, it was not necessary for them to agree on the specific evidence which led to a finding of guilt. They might legitimately differ on the emphasis to place on different incidents. Lloyd LJ said that it might,

and, where the child suffers 'serious physical harm', the provisions in s 5 of the Domestic Violence, Crime and Victims Act 2004, outlined above, will apply.[74]

What is wilful neglect?

The Children and Young Persons Act 1933 goes on to create certain presumptions of neglect which can be applied to parents, guardians and persons who are legally liable to maintain the child. Such persons will be deemed to have neglected the child 'in a manner likely to cause injury to his health' where they have failed 'to provide adequate food, clothing, medical aid or lodging' or have failed to take steps to procure these things for the child.[75] All forms of conduct or omission envisaged by the offence must be committed 'wilfully'. It has been held by a majority of the House of Lords that this requires intention or subjective recklessness.[76] The unintelligent or inadequate parent who does not appreciate, as would an average person, the health and other needs of the child, will not be liable.[77]

How far can parental discipline go?

An issue which arises in relation to offences against children is how far a parent might be able to rely on the defence that the conduct in question was a proper exercise of parental discipline. The defence of reasonable chastisement has long existed in the common law.[78] However, following adverse decisions in the European Court of Human Rights,[79] and repeated criticism by the UN Committee on the Rights of the Child, s 58 of the Children Act 2004 limited the availability of the defence to cases of common assault only; it is no longer available for offences falling within ss 18, 20, or 47 of the Offences Against the Person Act nor for offences committed under s 1 of the Children and Young

---

however, be wrong for the jury to be given the impression that they could convict if some of them were satisfied that *neglect* was established while others were satisfied of *assault* or *ill-treatment*. But there was no evidence in this case that the jury had been given that impression.

[74] Domestic Violence, Crimes and Victims (Amendment) Act 2012. The amendments came into force on 2 July 2012.

[75] Section 1(2)(a) of the Children and Young Persons Act 1933. Section 1(2)(b) also deals with the death of an infant under three years of age by suffocation. Where the suffocation was not caused by disease or a foreign body in the throat or air passages of the infant, and the infant was at the time in bed with someone over 16 years of age, that person is, if he was under the influence of drink when he went to bed, 'deemed to have neglected the infant in a manner likely to cause injury to its health'.

[76] *R v Sheppard* [1981] AC 394.

[77] For a criticism of the case, see HK Bevan *Child Law* (Butterworths, 1989), at para 9.37. Note also that the offence will be committed where there is a failure to summon medical aid even if in fact there was no help which a doctor could have given (*R v S and M* [1995] Crim LR 486). See chapter 8 above.

[78] The defence was established in *R v Hopley* (1860) 2 F&F 202 and placed on a legislative basis in s 1(7) Children and Young Persons Act 1933.

[79] *A v United Kingdom* [1998] 2 FLR 959.

Persons Act 1933.[80] The issue has already been discussed in the context of 'significant harm' in care proceedings[81] and is discussed in the context of intentional torts in chapter 16 below.

Prosecutions

Before 1988, prosecutions for wilful neglect were uncommon.[82] This doubtless reflected, in part, the low maximum punishment which, in 1988, was two years' imprisonment. The Criminal Justice Act 1988[83] raised this to 10 years, and there were immediate signs that prosecutions were increasing. 10 years is the maximum sentence and, of course, within it, actual sentences will vary depending on such factors as the extent of the child's injuries and the circumstances surrounding the conduct in question. Where poverty and social deprivation have played a part, this may be expected to have an influence, but not necessarily so in the most atrocious cases of abuse. It has been observed that where a mother and step-father are jointly charged, the tendency has been to impose a more severe sentence on the step-father.[84]

Sexual offences

General considerations

The law governing sexual offences was completely reformed by the Sexual Offences Act 2003.[85] Before the 2003 Act, there were already a great many sexual offences on the statute book, but the effect of the Act is nonetheless to increase the number of offences.[86] While the Act does bring about some much needed reforms, it also introduces a great deal of complexity and, more alarmingly, extends the reach of the criminal law to many activities which are

---

[80]   The UN Committee has remained critical of the UK even after the 2004 Act limited physical chastisement. The UN Committee has called for the prohibition of *all* corporal punishment. See UN Committee on the Rights of the Child 'Concluding Observations on the United Kingdom of Great Britain and Northern Ireland' Forty-ninth session, CRC/C/GBR/CO/4 (October 2008), at para 42.

[81]   At chapter 12 above.

[82]   In 1987, only 145 persons were sentenced for the offence while, by 1989, 189 women and 192 men were prosecuted and 105 women and 107 men were convicted. See JG Hall and DF Martin 'Crimes Against Children' (1992) 142 NLJ 902.

[83]   Section 45.

[84]   A point made by HK Bevan (above), at para 9.57, citing as an example the *Jasmine Beckford* case where the step-father received a 10-year sentence for manslaughter, to run concurrently with an eight-year sentence for cruelty, while the mother was sentenced to only 18 months' imprisonment for wilful neglect. See also A Morris and A Wilcynski 'Parents Who Kill Their Children' [1993] *Criminal Law Review* 31 who note similar patterns.

[85]   For more detailed treatment of the Act, see R Card, A Gillespie, M Hirst *Sexual Offences: The New Law* (Jordan Publishing, 2008). For a shorter commentary on its principal provisions, see B Brooks-Gordon and A Bainham 'Reforming the Law on Sexual Offences' in B Brooks-Gordon, L Gelsthorpe, M Johnson and A Bainham (eds) *Sexuality Repositioned: Diversity and the Law* (Hart Publishing, 2003). Specifically on the offences relating to children, see J Spencer 'The Sexual Offences Act 2003: Child and Family Offences' [2004] *Criminal Law Review* 347 and Hoyano and Keenan (above), at pp 192ff.

[86]   For a critique, see Spencer (2004), above.

arguably innocuous, or at least ought not to be the business of the State. This is perhaps especially true of the new offences relating to sexual activity with children which are the concern of this chapter.

The Sexual Offences Act 2003 followed two Reviews by the Home Office – the *Review of Part I of the Sex Offenders Act 1997*[87] and *Setting the Boundaries*,[88] published in 2000. These Reviews were followed by a White Paper, *Protecting the Public*.[89] Part II of the Act re-enacts with modifications the law designed to protect the public from sexual offenders. This is beyond the scope of the present work except to note that the Act introduced two new kinds of orders – the sexual offences prevention order[90] and the risk of sexual harm order.[91] The latter order is designed to protect children from coming into contact with paedophiles.[92] It enables the police to apply to the magistrates' court for an order prohibiting an adult from doing certain things where this is 'necessary for the purpose of protecting children generally or any child from the harm of the defendant'.[93] The order may be made where it appears to a chief officer of police that the individual concerned has, on at least two occasions, done certain prescribed acts and 'there is reasonable cause to believe that it is necessary for such an order to be made'.[94] The specified acts are:

(a)   engaging in sexual activity involving a child or in the presence of a child;

(b)   causing or inciting a child to watch a person engaging in sexual activity or to look at a moving or still image that is sexual;

(c)   giving a child anything that relates to sexual activity or contains a reference to such activity; and

---

[87]   Home Office *Consultation Paper on the Review of the Sex Offenders Act 1997* (July 2001).

[88]   Home Office *Setting the Boundaries: Reforming the Law on Sexual Offences* (2000). For a critique of the Home Office Review, see N Lacey 'Beset by Boundaries: The Home Office Review of Sex Offences' (2001) *Criminal Law Review* 3.

[89]   Home Office *Protecting the Public: Strengthening Protection against Sex Offenders and Reforming the Law on Sexual Offences*.

[90]   For judicial guidance on the wording of Sexual Offences Protection Order, to ensure they are necessary and proportionate, see *R v Smith* [2011] EWCA Crim 1772, [2012] 1 WLR 1316 and for commentary see A Gillespie 'Terms of a Sexual Offences Prevention Order' [2011] *Journal of Criminal Law* 462. See also Home Office *Guidance on Part Two of the Secual Offences Act 2003* (2012).

[91]   See ss 104–113 (sexual offences prevention orders) and ss 123–129 (risk of sexual harm orders). For commentary, see S Shute 'The Sexual Offences Act 2003: (4) New Civil Preventative Orders: Sexual Offences Prevention Orders; Foreign Travel Orders; Risk of Sexual Harm Orders' (2004) *Criminal Law Review* 417.

[92]   See also the Criminal Justice and Immigration Act 2008, s 140 which amended the Criminal Justice Act 2003, by introducing s 327A. This provides for a 'Sarah's Law' allowing the disclosure to any other particular person of information about a person's previous convictions for child sex offences. There is a presumption of disclosure where the child is at risk from the individual and disclosure is necessary to protect the child (s 327A(2), (3)).

[93]   Sexual Offences Act 2003, s 123(6).

[94]   Ibid, s 123(1).

(d) communicating with a child, where any part of the communication is sexual.[95]

As with so many of the provisions of the Sexual Offences Act 2003, while the motivation for the powers was clear and laudable, the provision is drawn so widely that it is capable of operating oppressively and is also founded on the same erroneous assumption which pervades the Act – that all sexual activity involving children is wrong. Our principal concern here, however, is with Part I of the Act and the new sexual offences which it introduces. What follows is a necessarily selective account of the principal features of the new code, concentrating on those offences which specifically relate to children and young people. It should, of course, be borne in mind that the major sexual offences such as rape,[96] assault by penetration[97] and sexual assault[98] apply as much to child victims as they do to adult victims. We comment here on these general sexual offences only insofar as there may be special considerations where the victim is a child. One of the unsatisfactory features of the new legislation is that there appears to be a good deal of overlap, or as it has been put by Spencer, 'overkill',[99] and the boundaries between the various offences are not always clear.

Before coming to the offences themselves, it is worth noting a number of general aspects of the legislation. First, with few exceptions, consent will generally be a defence to adult sexual offences,[100] whereas the consent of a child will not normally be effective to prevent the commission of an offence. In effect, children under 16 are regarded as incapable of giving a valid consent to sexual activity and, in relation to some offences, and despite the age of consent generally being fixed at 16, there are some instances where the relevant age is 18 and not 16.[101] Important exceptions, however, are rape, the new offence of assault by penetration, and sexual assault where the essence of these extremely serious offences[102] is that the victim did not consent. Here it is necessary to

---

[95] Ibid, s 123(8).

[96] Sexual Offences Act 2003, s 1.

[97] Ibid, s 2.

[98] Ibid, s 3.

[99] Above (2004) at 352.

[100] There are two exceptions: first the new offence of 'sex with an adult relative' in s 64, an offence involving penetrative sexual activities between related adults and replacing the former offence of incest; and second, since 2010, paying for the sexual services of a prostitute subject to force (see s 53A introduced following amendment by the Policing and Crime Act 2009).

[101] This is so in relation to the new abuse of trust offences and familial child sex offences discussed below.

[102] Rape, for example, is now defined as follows;
'(1) A person (A) commits an offence if –
(a) he intentionally penetrates the vagina, anus or mouth of another person (B) with his penis,
(b) B does not consent to the penetration, and
(c) A does not reasonably believe that B consents.
(2) Whether a belief is reasonable is to be determined having regard to all the circumstances, including any steps A has taken to ascertain whether B consents'.
The consent and mens rea elements are essentially replicated for assault by penetration (s 2) and sexual assault (s 3).

distinguish between children *over* the age of 13 and those *under* that age. In relation to those *over* 13, the consent of the child to sexual intercourse, or to penetration with some object other than the penis, will prevent liability for these offences – although some activity will undoubtedly amount to one of the less serious child sex offences *despite* the child's consent. Where, however, the child is *under* the age of 13, the broad effect of ss 5–8 of the Act is to remove the relevance of the child's consent and to create a separate category of offences, of equal seriousness and carrying the same maximum punishments.[103]

Second, the view was taken in *Setting the Boundaries* that a coherent and fair code, which had proper regard for human rights, should also be gender-neutral and ought not to discriminate between men and women, boys and girls, whether as victims or perpetrators of sexual offences, unless there was a good reason for doing so.[104] The 2003 Act gives effect to this principle. It represents a major change from the old law where specific offences relating to children[105] generally applied only to under-age girls and where there was not a single sexual offence specifically enacted to protect boys. In contrast, the child sex offences and familial child sex offences under the Sexual Offences Act 2003 apply equally to boys and girls, young men and young women.

Setting the Boundaries also concluded that the law should reflect the 'looser structure of modern families' and, accordingly, the former offence of incest[106] is replaced by 'familial child sex offences'.[107] The key change is that the post 2003 offences move beyond prohibiting sexual activity between blood relations (to which the objections have traditionally been eugenic) to include sexual activity between a range of 'family members' more widely defined. In particular they include step- and foster relationships and also situations where those concerned have lived in the same household as the victim.

A final general feature of the law which ought to be highlighted is the distinct shift throughout the Sexual Offences Act 2003 in the direction of criminal liability based on *negligence* rather than on *intention* or *recklessness* which constituted the minimum mental requirement for most sexual offending before the Act. Thus, in relation to the principal offences of rape, assault by penetration and sexual assault, there is now a requirement of *reasonable* belief in the victim's consent, as opposed to a merely genuine, but unreasonable,

---

[103] Life imprisonment in the case of rape and assault by penetration, and 14 years' imprisonment in the case of sexual assault.

[104] A good reason was thought to exist in relation to rape which, although gender-neutral as to the victim, remains gender-specific as to the perpetrator since it is an offence grounded in the concept of *penile* penetration.

[105] Especially unlawful sexual intercourse with a girl under 16 (Sexual Offences Act 1956, s 6) or under 13 (Sexual Offences Act 1956, s 5). Boys were protected as children, but not gender-specifically as boys, under the general law of indecent assault and the Indecency with Children Act 1960.

[106] Governed by ss 10 and 11 of the Sexual Offences Act 1956 and discussed in the second edition of this work, at pp 480–481.

[107] Sexual Offences Act 2003, ss 25–29.

one.[108] A similar relaxation in the mental requirement is also apparent in relation to the child sex offences and familial child sex offences where a mistake as to the child's age must also be *reasonably* held.[109] Where the child is under the age of 13, it is a strict liability offence and no mistake as to age, whether reasonable or not, exculpates the accused.[110]

Rape and other offences against children under 13

It is an offence where the accused 'intentionally penetrates the vagina, anus or mouth of a child under 13 with his penis'.[111] This offence mirrors the re-definition of rape which also includes forced fellatio. Yet, this offence is rather misleadingly referred to as 'rape' in that, first, as noted above, and contrary to the essence of adult rape, the child's consent to the penetration is irrelevant and, secondly, it covers much of the ground previously occupied by the offence of unlawful sexual intercourse with a girl under the age of 13. It is, of course, much broader in that the new offence includes non-vaginal penetration and is gender-neutral and, thus, equally applicable to girls and boys.

It is an offence also to assault by penetration a child of this age.[112] This is an offence that again mirrors the adult offence, except that consent is again irrelevant. These offences are designed to reflect the gravity of non-penile penetrations carried out by insertion in the vagina, anus or mouth of such objects as fingers or bottles. These violations are considered to be as serious and repugnant as rape and, as with rape, there is a maximum punishment of life imprisonment. Then come the offences of sexual assault of a child under 13[113] and causing or inciting a child under 13 to engage in sexual activity.[114] The concept of sexual assault replaced the former notion of 'indecent assault'.[115] We discuss below the concept of what is 'sexual' for the purposes of the Act. Much of the ground covered by the former offence is duplicated by the lesser offence of 'sexual activity with a child', and the latter offence may be committed also in relation to children over 13, but under the age of 16. The significance of the separate offence seems therefore to turn only on the fact that there is strict liability as to the child's age where that child is under 13. This means that it is irrelevant to criminal liability that a defendant thought that the child was over 13.

---

[108] Thus overruling the long-standing authority of *DPP v Morgan* [1976] AC 182. See J Temkin and A Ashworth 'The Sexual Offences Act 2003: (1) Rape, Sexual Assaults and the Problem of Consent' [2004] Crim LR 328.

[109] Sexual Offences Act 2003, ss 9–12.

[110] See below.

[111] Ibid, s 5.

[112] Sexual Offences Act 2003, s 6.

[113] Ibid, s 7.

[114] Ibid, s 8.

[115] Contrary to ss 14 and 15 of the Sexual Offences Act 1956. The leading authority on the interpretation of indecency was *R v Court* [1988] 2 All ER 221, discussed in the second edition of this work, at pp 481–482.

The issue of strict liability vis à vis sexual activity with a child under the age of 13 arose in *R v G* when a 15-year-old boy was convicted of rape for having sexual intercourse with a 12-year-old girl.[116] One argument made by G was that the strict liability aspect of the offence was a breach of Art 6(2) ECHR as it offended the principle of the presumption of innocence. This was rejected by the House of Lords on the basis that Art 6 must be read as a whole and that when it is it is clear that it is concerned with the procedural aspects of the criminal justice process not with the substantive elements of the offence.[117] The European Court of Human Rights later agreed with this outcome.[118] Ashworth is critical of the decision because it focuses on the *child* victim but fails to consider the impact on prosecuting a *child*, particularly when a lesser offence was available.[119] However, Baroness Hale was particularly forceful on this point, and held that G's age is relevant to the sentence (which was lenient)[120] but it did not alter the fact that he should not have done what he did. As she quite bluntly put it:[121]

> 'every male has a choice about where he puts his penis. It may be difficult for him to restrain himself when aroused but he has a choice. There is nothing unjust or irrational about a law that says if he chooses to put his penis inside a child who turns out to be under 13 he has committed an offence (though the state of his mind may again be relevant to sentence).'

Child sex offences

Sections 9–15 of the Sexual Offences Act 2003 contain the so-called 'child sex offences'. The principal offence is that of 'sexual activity with a child'.[122] This is committed where a person aged 18 or over (A):

> '(a) intentionally touches another person (B);
>
> (b) the touching is sexual; and
>
> (c) either –

---

[116] [2008] UKHL 37, [2009] 1 AC 92 and see the commentary by A Ashworth 'Sexual offences: Sexual Offences Act 2003, s 5 – rape of child under 13 – defendant under 18' [2008] *Criminal Law Review* 818. On Art 8 more generally including a discussion of this case see R Buxton 'Private Life and the English Judges' OJLS 2009, 29(3), 413–425.

[117] See Lord Hope of Craigshead at [2008] 1 AC 92 at 103A.

[118] In an admissibility decision. See *G v United Kingdom (Admissibility)* (Application No 37334/08) [2012] Crim LR 46 (ECHR).

[119] A Ashworth 'Human Rights: Presumption of innocence: Art 6(2)' *Criminal Law Review* [2012] 47.

[120] On the relevance of mistaken belief as the child's age on sentencing (as mitigation) see (inter alia) *R v Corran* [2005] EWCA Crim 192, [2005] 2 Cr App R (S) 73; *R v Charles (Ashley Dwayne)* [2011] EWCA Crim 2153, [2012] 1 Cr App R (S) 74 (CA (Crim Div)); and for commentary of relevant cases see D Selfe 'Sentencing for rape of a child under thirteen' [2012] *Criminal Lawyer* 3.

[121] Baroness Hale, at p 110.

[122] Sexual Offences Act 2003, s 9.

(i)   B is under 16 and A does not reasonably believe B is 16 or over, or

(ii)   B is under 13.'

The offence carries a maximum punishment of six months' imprisonment but, where it involves penetration, the maximum punishment is increased to 14 years.

A good deal of criticism may be made of this offence. At one end of the spectrum it catches all the conduct which would have fallen within the former offences of indecent assault and indecency with children, but it also represents a potentially enormous extension of the range of activities which may now be regarded as criminal. It is capable of prohibiting the sort of innocuous, some may even think desirable, sexual experimentation between adolescents which is a normal part of growing up.[123] This is because it is backed up, as are the other child sex offences, by a provision which makes it plain that all of these offences may be committed not merely by adults against children (where the very age disparity may automatically give cause for concern) but also between children and young persons themselves where there is little or no difference in age. Section 13 blandly states that 'a person under 18 commits an offence if he does anything which would be an offence under any of ss 9–12 if he were aged 18'. In *R v G* (discussed above), in addition to the Art 6(2) point, G also argued that the decision to charge him under s 5 (rape) rather than the similar but lesser offence under s 13 (child sex offences committed by a young person under 18) constituted a violation of his Art 8 ECHR right to a private and family life. This right was engaged, it was argued, because the conviction would affect his ability to form future relationships and the decision to charge under s 5 was unnecessary (because s 13 would provide the same protective function for potential victims) and disproportionate (because of the stigma, punishment and practical consequences that accompanied the rape conviction). This argument was rejected by a majority in the House of Lords, who held that the offence fell within s 5 and that Parliament had clearly intended that a child under 13 could not consent to sex. Lords Hope and Carswell dissented, holding that where the issue of charge was one of prosecutorial discretion those decisions had to be compatible with the ECHR, and that as the offence fell within s 13 it was disproportionate to continue with the prosecution.[124]

A particular problem with the Sexual Offences Act 2003 – particularly in how it applies between children – is that the concept of what is 'sexual' is very widely

---

[123]   For a defence of the right of adults to have normal associations with children, which may be seen as threatened by the new law, see F Bennion *Sexual Ethics and the Criminal Law: A Critique of the Sexual Offences Bill 2003* (Lester Publishing, 2003).

[124]   On prosecutorial policy and Art 8 see B Malkani 'Article 8 of the European Convention on Human Rights, and the decision to prosecute' [2011] Crim LR 943.

drawn, as is the notion of 'touching'.[125] 'Sexual' is perhaps the central concept throughout the Sexual Offences Act and is defined as follows:[126]

> 'For the purposes of this part of the Act ... penetration, touching or any other activity is sexual if a reasonable person would consider that –
>
> (a)   whatever its circumstances or any person's purpose in relation to it, it is because of its nature sexual, or
> (b)   because of its nature it may be sexual and because of its circumstances or the purpose of any person in relation to it (or both) it is sexual.'

This puts the 'objective' view of the magistrates or jury centre stage. Essentially, that which is sexual is that which a reasonable person, rather than the accused, would deem to be sexual. This is open to the criticism that, along with other provisions in the legislation, it makes criminal liability for sexual offending dependent on negligence alone. It does not require mental culpability as was normally the case before the 2003 Act. It is moreover questionable whether the new notion of what is 'sexual' is an adequate replacement for 'indecency' as the chief component in this type of offence. The point is surely that 'indecency' implies wrongdoing whereas 'sexual' is morally neutral and, in many contexts, has a positive connotation.

Yet the message of the legislation is that all sexual activity involving children is by definition wrong. It was believed (apparently) by the Government that it is only by criminalising all sexual activity involving children that the law will be sufficiently effective in facilitating the prosecution of paedophiles.[127] Thus, for example, in cases where (for example) two 15-year-olds engage in consensual sexual activity (which may merely involve kissing or petting), the Sexual Offences Act creates a legal framework that constructs one or both of the parties as the perpetrator of sexual exploitation.[128] Further, in some instances

---

[125]   'Touching' as defined by the Sexual Offences Act 2003, s 79(8) includes:
'touching –
(a) with any part of the body;
(b) with anything else,
(c) through anything,
and in particular includes touching amounting to penetration.'

[126]   Ibid, s 78. See F Bennion 'The Meaning of "Sexual" in the Sexual Offences Bill' (2003) 167 *Justice of the Peace* 764. On how a jury should be directed to answer the second part of the question (s 78(b)) see Lord Woolf CJ in *R v H* [2005] 1 WLR 2005 as summarised by A Gillespie in 'Indecent Images, Grooming and the Law' [2006] Crim LR 412 at 415: '1. Would a jury, as 12 reasonable people, consider that because of its nature [the activity] that took place in the particular case could be sexual? 2. If the answer to (1) is "Yes", then in view of the circumstances and/or the purpose of any person in relation to the [activity] was it in fact sexual?'

[127]   See J Chalmers 'Regulating Adolescent Sexuality: English and Scottish Approaches Compared' [2011] 23 CFLQ 450.

[128]   However, it should be noted that prosecutions are highly unlikely in such scenarios. See the CPS Guidance on the Sexual Offences Act 2003: 'it is not in the public interest to prosecute children who are of the same or similar age and understanding that engage in sexual activity, where the activity is truly consensual for both parties and there are no aggravating features, such as coercion or corruption. In such cases, protection will normally be best achieved by

both parties engaged in the sexual activity are victims of abuse but the law wrongly constructs one as the perpetrator. This was the case in *R (E) v DPP*[129] when a 14-year-old girl, who was 12 when the offences took place, was charged under the Sexual Offences Act after she filmed herself engaging in sexual activities with her two sisters who were aged two and three at the time.[130] The older child had herself been groomed over the internet by an adult male and yet, despite the views of most of the parties of the multi-agency strategy group (convened to discuss the safeguarding of the girls) that it was not in the best interests of *any* of the children to bring a prosecution (the police being the only dissenters), she was in fact charged and was to be brought to trial (in the crown court) for the offences.[131] In her judicial review claim against the decision, E unsuccessfully argued that the CPS guidance was unlawful for failing to give sufficient attention to cases where the child is both victim and offender. The court rejected this argument on the basis that it was for the CPS to determine its prosecution policy, not the courts. However, E's claim that the CPS had failed to take into account the best interests of the children (contrary to its own guidance) was held to be unlawful and the decision quashed. Hoyano criticises the decision to bring criminal proceedings against a 12-year-old in this situation because it treats her as a paedophile when she herself was a victim. It also delayed the availability of therapeutic treatment for all three girls in order to preserve the fairness of the trial proceedings.[132] The decision to prosecute in this case seems particularly bizarre given that the Sexual Offences Act regards children under 13 as incapable of ever consenting to sexual activity and as being victims in all cases involving sexual activity regardless of actual consent.

The requirement of reasonableness of belief regarding consent in the context of adult sex offences was noted above. Consent is irrelevant in relation to child sex offences, but the issue of negligence raises its head here too. This is because any belief that the child concerned was over the age of 16 must now be *reasonably* held. This effectively overruled two decisions of the House of Lords heard only a short time before the 2003 Act[133] where it had held that a presumption of mens rea applied, although this was not expressly stated in the legislation. Thus an honest or genuine belief that the girls in question were over age for the purposes of the offences was a defence and it was not necessary to show that

---

[129] providing education for the children and young people and providing them and their families with access to advisory and counselling services. This is the intention of Parliament' (available at http://www.cps.gov.uk/legal/s_to_u/sexual_offences_act/#Charging_practice_5, last accessed 23 August 2012).

[129] [2011] EWHC 1465 (Admin), [2012] 1 Cr App R 6.

[130] See the commentaries of L Hoyano 'Decision to prosecute: whether decision of defendant to prosecute a child for alleged sexual abuse by her of her two younger sisters amenable to judicial review' [2011] Crim LR 39, and JR Spencer 'Controlling the discretion to prosecute' [2012] CLJ 27.

[131] The trial was adjourned pending the outcome of the judicial review application.

[132] See the discussion in Hoyano (2011), above.

[133] *B (A Minor) v DPP* [2000] 2 AC 428. See generally J Horder 'How Culpability Can, and Cannot, be Denied in Under-age Sex Crimes' (2001) *Criminal Law Review* 15 and *R v K (Age of Consent: Reasonable Belief)* [2002] 1 AC 462 (indecent assault on a 14-year-old girl).

such belief was reasonable. This is no longer the case, placing the Sexual Offences Act 2003 at odds with jurisprudential developments.[134]

Other child sex offences included in the 2003 legislation include causing or inciting a child to engage in sexual activity,[135] engaging in sexual activity in the presence of a child,[136] causing a child to watch a sexual act,[137] arranging or facilitating the commission of a child sex offence[138] and meeting a child following sexual grooming.[139] The latter offence is designed principally to meet the modern menace of attempts by paedophiles to seduce children through the internet. It is committed where a person aged 18 or over (A):

'(a) having met or communicated with another person (B) on at least two earlier occasions ...

(i)   intentionally meets B, or
(ii)   travels with the intention of meeting B in any part of the world or arranges to meet B in any part of the world,
(iii)   B travels with the intention of meeting A in any part of the world.

(b) A intends to do anything to or in respect of B, during or after the meeting mentioned in paragraph (a)(i) to (iii) and in any part of the world, which if done will involve the commission by A of a relevant offence,

(c) B is under 16, and

(d) A does not reasonably believe that B is 16 or over.'

'Relevant offence'[140] is defined to include all the offences under the Sexual Offences Act 2003 and some others.

Again, while the mischief which the offence is trying to address is all too obvious, the breadth of the offence is quite staggering. It must give rise to serious concerns about the extension of criminal liability to situations in which no harm has yet occurred and in which there may be a good deal of equivocality or ambiguity in what may have occurred.

Abuse of a position of trust

The Sexual Offences Act 2003 in ss 16–24 builds on offences relating to the abuse of positions of trust which were introduced by the Sexual Offences (Amendment) Act 2000. The 2003 offences follow the same pattern as child sex

---

[134] See also *R v G and another* [2003] UKHL 50 where the House of Lords overruled the long standing *Caldwell* objective recklessness test and replaced it with a subjective test.

[135] Sexual Offences Act 2003, s 10.

[136] Ibid, s 11.

[137] Ibid, s 12.

[138] Ibid, s 14.

[139] Ibid, s 15 as amended by the Criminal Justice and Immigration Act 2008. See further A Gillespie 'Indecent Images, Grooming and the Law' [2006] Crim L R 412.

[140] Ibid, s 15(2)(b).

offences in that there are specific offences again of sexual activity with a child,[141] causing or inciting a child to engage in sexual activity,[142] sexual activity in the presence of a child[143] and causing a child to watch a sexual act.[144] What distinguishes these offences is that they are committed by someone in a 'position of trust' in relation to the child and that they apply to young people under the age of 18 and not, as in the case of child sex offences, under 16. Again, any mistake as to age, in this case 18, must be reasonably held for it to operate as a defence. For the purposes of these offences, 'position of trust' is defined to include situations where A 'looks after persons under 18' in various specified institutions including educational establishments, hospitals and certain residential homes.[145] The extension of the previous offence to 16- and 17-year-old 'victims' has been criticised by Spencer[146] as having the sole purpose of criminalising consensual sexual acts between schoolteachers and sixth formers who are over the normal age of consent and whose relationships may sometimes endure and even end in marriage. In his view, these involvements, even if 'unwise and reprehensible, do not look like criminal behaviour punishable with five years' imprisonment'.

Familial child sex offences

The 2003 Act creates two 'familial child sex offences' which replaced incest insofar as that offence applied to children as opposed to sexual activity between adult relatives. These are sexual activity with a child family member[147] and inciting a child family member to engage in sexual activity.[148] The relevant age of the child is again under 18 but the offence may also be committed by a family member who himself or herself is also under 18. The key feature of these offences is that the activity takes place between two people who are in a 'family relationship' as defined by the Act.[149] This includes the relationship of 'parent, grandparent, brother, sister, half-sister, aunt or uncle'. It also includes foster parents and former foster parents, together with those 'who live or have lived in the same household' or where the accused 'has been regularly involved in caring for, training, supervising, or being in sole charge of' the young person concerned. Step-relationships are included as are relationships between cousins.

The new offences may also be criticised for much the same reasons – they are over-broad, overlap with other offences and catch consensual activity between older teenagers which perhaps should not be the business of the law at all.

---

[141] Sexual Offences Act 2003, s 16.
[142] Ibid, s 17.
[143] Ibid, s 18.
[144] Ibid, s 19.
[145] Ibid, ss 21 and 22.
[146] Above (2004).
[147] Sexual Offences Act 2003, s 25. On sentencing pursuant to s 25 see *R v Thomas* [2005] EWCA Crim 2343, [2006] 1 Cr App R 101.
[148] Ibid, s 26.
[149] Ibid, s 27.

Other offences involving children

We should note briefly several other offences in the Sexual Offences Act 2003 which have a specific application to children. First, s 45 amends the Protection of Children Act 1978 (which governs the taking of indecent photographs of children) so that it applies now to children under the age of 18 as opposed to 16 under the previous law. This means that 16- and 17-year-olds can consent to sexual intercourse but not to being the subject of pornographic photographs.[150]

Secondly, ss 47–51 of the Sexual Offences Act 2003 created a number of offences relating to the abuse of children through prostitution or pornography.[151] These include paying for the sexual services of a child (s 47), causing or inciting child prostitution or pornography (s 48), controlling a child prostitute or child involved in pornography (s 49) or arranging and facilitating child prostitution or pornography (s 50). Each of these offences apply where a child is under 18 and where the defendant does not reasonably believe the child is over 18, and to a child under 13 (again, it is a strict liability offence). Amendments to the law relating to prostitution have been introduced by s 14 of the Policing and Crime Act 2009 (which inserts s 53A into the Sexual Offences Act 2003). This provision creates a new criminal offence in England and Wales of paying for the sexual services of a prostitute who is, or has been, subject to force (specifically through exploitative conduct used to induce or encourage the person to engage in the sexual activity). It is a strict liability offence – s 53A(2)(b) states that it is irrelevant whether the person paying for the sex is or ought to have been aware that the person selling sex was being exploited. The definition of prostitution in the Act is not age specific and it therefore protects children who are subject to sexual exploitation or who have been trafficked as well as adults.[152] Therefore, where a defendant reasonably believes the child (aged over 13) from whom he is buying sex is over 18 (thus escaping liability under s 47), he would nonetheless be caught by s 53A, if force is involved.[153]

Concluding remarks

For all its good intentions, the Sexual Offences Act 2003 is a flawed piece of legislation as it applies to children. It is, as it was put by Dominic Grieve MP at the Committee stage of the Bill,[154] 'a blunderbuss', a strikingly illiberal piece of legislation which rests on the philosophy that to prosecute successfully harmful

---

[150] See A Gillespie 'The Sexual Offences Act 2003: (3) Tinkering with "child pornography"' [2004] *Criminal Law Review* 361. Section 1A introduces exceptions where the child and the person charged with the offence are married or living together in an enduring family relationship. However, the exception does not extend to one-night stands. See *R v M* [2011] EWCA Crim 2752.

[151] See further Department for Children Schools and Families *Safeguarding Children and Young People from Sexual Exploitation: Supplementary Guidance to Working Together to Safeguard Children* (2009).

[152] See Department for Education and Home Office *Safeguarding Children who may have been Trafficked: Practice Guidance* (2011).

[153] Though the use of term 'prostitute' to describe such children appears inappropriate.

[154] House of Commons Standing Committee B, 18 September 2003.

sexual misconduct in relation to children it is necessary to criminalise *all* sexual contact, whatever the circumstances. John Spencer has rightly lampooned such an approach as 'bad news for Adrian Mole'. Among those activities between consenting teenagers which will now be caught by the Act and its penalties, he identifies 'mouth to mouth kissing', or minor acts of sexual exploration between two 14 or 15-year-olds (five years); two boys giving themselves a sexual thrill by looking at a dirty book (five years); and 'rude games' between two 10-year-olds (14 years, maybe life).[155] It is, of course, argued by the Government that there is a prosecutorial discretion and that, in practice, prosecutions will not be brought and maximum penalties not imposed except in truly serious cases.[156] This, however, fails to meet the essential requirement of 'fair labelling' in the criminal law or, to put it as strongly as Spencer does, it is an approach which 'runs contrary to the notion of the rule of law'.[157]

Special offences relating to children

Restrictions and prohibitions on sale of harmful goods

There are numerous statutory offences regulating various activities which may cause harm to children. Some of these are in the Children and Young Persons Act 1933, while others are scattered about the statute book. Little purpose would be served by reproducing a catalogue of these offences[158] but it is important to get a sense of the breadth of coverage of the criminal law. The offences include, most obviously, restrictions on the sale of alcohol[159] and tobacco,[160] and road safety regulations.[161] These are widely known to the general public. Also well-known are those offences relating to firearms,[162] crossbows[163] and explosives, including fireworks.[164] The rationale of these offences is partly to protect the children themselves and partly to protect society from the anti-social conduct which might result from allowing children and traders complete freedom of action.

Offences centred on protection

Other offences are more overtly centred on protection of children. The prohibition on tattooing of minors,[165] the restrictions on the employment of children[166] and the offence relating to the exposure of children under 12 years

---

[155] J Spencer 'The Shameful Sex Crimes of Adrian Mole aged 13¾' *The Times*, 7 October 2003.
[156] See again the CPS Guidance, above.
[157] Above (2004).
[158] They are examined extensively in HK Bevan *Child Law* (Butterworths, 1989), chs 9 and 10, and in D Bedingfield *The Child in Need* (Family Law, 1998) especially at paras 5.198–5.216.
[159] Licensing Act 2003, ss 145–154.
[160] The Children and Young Persons Act 1933, s 7 (as amended most recently by the Children and Young Persons (Sale of Tobacco etc) Order 2007 (SI 2007/767), art 2(a) (October 1, 2007)).
[161] Thus, persons under 17 years of age are not allowed to drive motor vehicles on public roads.
[162] Firearms Acts 1968 and 1982.
[163] Crossbows Act 1987.
[164] Explosives Act 1875, as amended by the Explosives (Age of Purchase etc) Act 1976.
[165] Tattooing of Minors Act 1969.
[166] Mainly in the Children and Young Persons Act 1933. See chapter 16 below.

to the risk of burning[167] would all seem to fall into this category. A more recent example is the creation of an offence of selling aerosol spray paints to children under 16 by the Anti-social Behaviour Act 2003.[168] The objective is to reduce the incidence of criminal damage caused by acts of graffiti.

Restriction of children's liberty

A feature of many of these special statutory offences is that they restrict not only the activities of adult society towards children but also the liberty of children themselves. This raises the general issue of how far the State has a legitimate interest in imposing these restraints. One of the freedoms which adults enjoy is the right to make mistakes. Many adults are not, for example, conspicuously competent drivers or noted for their restraint with alcohol, tobacco or in sexual matters. Yet the law generally does not step in to prevent them from behaving contrary to their own interests, objectively judged. What then is the case for denying children the right to make mistakes? The justification would seem to reside in the overriding obligation of the State to uphold the public interest in the well-being of children. But ultimately the view which is taken of the proper limits of State paternalism depends on the individual's own stance on the general question of children's rights.[169]

CHILDREN'S RESPONSIBILITY

As noted at the beginning of this chapter, nowhere in the legal system is the complexity and inconsistency in the societal and legal treatment of children more evident than in the criminal law. In the previous section we saw that the vulnerability and immaturity of children was emphasised to justify the protection – and within the context of the Sexual Offences Act 2003 arguably the *over*-protection – of children. In this section, the view of children as vulnerable has often been set aside in favour of an emphasis on the competence of children and their responsibility.

The current Youth Justice System in England and Wales is the product of a major overhaul by the Labour Government in 1998 and a number of additional, and often incremental, changes brought in over the past 15 years. Many of the key themes of New Labour's reforms – prevention, increased responsibilisation of children, and increased responsibility of parents – have become entrenched and on the whole the institutional structure introduced by Labour's key piece of criminal justice legislation, the Crime and Disorder Act 1998, remains in place.[170] However, reforms to the processes of youth

---

[167] Children and Young Persons Act 1933, s 11, as amended. Another example of such legislation is the Horses (Protective Headgear for Young Riders) Act 1990. The Confiscation of Alcohol (Young Persons) Act 1997 enables a police constable to confiscate intoxicating liquor from young persons under the age of 18 in prescribed circumstances.

[168] Section 54.

[169] See chapter 7 above.

[170] On the reforms from 1998 see (inter alia) L Gelsthorpe and A Morris 'Much Ado About

justice, and particularly pre-court orders and sentencing disposals, have been subject to reform on a fairly regular basis since 1997, including most recently the proposals introduced by the Conservative-Liberal Democrat Coalition Government. There have also been a number of key legal decisions which have helped to emphasise the status of children in conflict with the law as vulnerable children who need support, and not just as offenders deserving of punishment.

Responsibility for children involved in offending: institutional structures and aims

Institutional structures

The Crime and Disorder Act 1998 brought in wide changes to the institutional structure of the youth justice system. First, an executive non-departmental public body, the Youth Justice Board (YJB), was established under Part III of the Act. The functions of the YJB include monitoring the operation of the youth justice system, advising the Secretary of State, promoting best practice across the sector, commissioning research, and the management of the juvenile 'secure estate'.[171] The YJB falls under the responsibility of the Ministry of Justice, following a brief period – prior to the election of the Coalition Government – when it was jointly under the remit of the Home Office and the Department for Children, Schools and Families.[172] In 2010, the newly elected Coalition Government introduced proposals to abolish the YJB as part of its 'bonfire of the quangos'.[173] However, the proposal was widely criticised and the Government in the end accepted a House of Lords amendment to remove the YJB from the Bill. The opposition to the abolition of the YJB came from a wide-range of organisations, many of whom emphasised the independent and child-centred approach that the YJB brings to the youth justice system.[174] It seems that the YJB has become an integral part of a 'distinct and separate youth system', as required by the UNCRC.[175]

Nothing – a Critical Comment on Key Provisions Relating to Children in the Crime and Disorder Act 1998' (1999) 11 CFLQ 209; C Piper 'The Crime and Disorder Act 1998: Child and Community "Safety' (1999) 62 MLR 397; B Goldson (ed) *The New Youth Justice* (Russell House Publishing Ltd, 2000); and J Fionda (2005), above.

[171] Crime and Disorder Act 1998, s 41.

[172] The YJB's joint responsibility to the Home Office and the DCSF appeared to be indicative of a move to a focus more on young offenders as *children*. The DCSF did not, however, survive the election of the Coalition Government.

[173] See the Public Bodies Bill 2010 (as introduced). The proposed abolition was justified on the basis that the YJB failed to meet the generic three-pronged survival test for public bodies and because the Government claimed that placing the YJB's functions within the Ministry of Justice would increase accountability.

[174] It can, however, be difficult for the YJB to assert its independence. See the comments of Professor Rod Morgan, the former head of the YJB, since he left the post in 2007 (for example see R Morgan 'Axing the Youth Justice Board could be a bold step' in *JoePublicBlog, The Guardian* at http://www.guardian.co.uk/society/joepublic/2010/oct/26/youth-justice-reform-bold-steps (last visited 4 October 2012)).

[175] Article 40(3).

The second structural change brought about by the Crime and Disorder Act 1998 was the requirement that each local authority ensure the availability of appropriate youth justice services, and also that police authorities, probation committees and health authorities co-operate in securing that such services are available.[176] The Act goes on to specify and define the meaning of 'youth justice services'.[177] In particular, each local authority must establish one or more multi-agency youth offending teams (YOTs),[178] which include representatives from the different partner organisations.[179] YOTs are therefore responsible for delivering youth justice services. However, it is important to note that local authority children's services departments continue to have general responsibilities to all children (and their families) in their area,[180] with particular responsibilities to children in need, looked after children and care-leavers.[181] In addition, local authorities are under a specific duty to take reasonable steps designed to reduce the need to bring criminal proceedings against children, to encourage children in their areas not to commit crime, and to avoid the need for children to be placed in secure accommodation.[182]

The principal aim of the youth justice system: prevention of offending

Some of the trends that emerged from the Labour Government's reform of the youth justice system are likely to be reversed as a result of changes introduced by the current Government.[183] However, one thing that remains – and will do so unless statutory amendments are made – is the emphasis on prevention of

---

[176] Crime and Disorder Act, s 38.

[177] Sections 38–40.

[178] Section 39 CDA 1998. On multi-agency working in YOTs see R Burnett and C Appleton 'Joined-Up Services to Tackle Youth Crime' (2004) 44 *British Journal of Criminology* 34.

[179] Home Office *No More Excuses: A New Approach to Tackling Youth Crime in England and Wales* (Home Office, 1997) sets out the main framework for the legislation that followed (the Crime and Disorder Act 1998) and *New National and Local Focus on Youth Crime: A Consultation Paper* (Home Office, 1997) set out the proposals for reforming the national and local structures for the delivery of work with young offenders.

[180] Principally under the Children Act 1989 and Children Act 2004. See chapter 10.

[181] See chapter 10. These duties continue when children are sentenced to custody. See the decision of Mr Justice Munby in *R (Howard League for Penal Reform) v Secretary of State for the Home Department* [2002] EWHC 2497 (Admin), [2003] 1 FLR 484 and the discussion below. On young people in care and offending see generally C Taylor *Young People in Care and Criminal Behaviour* (Jessica Kingsley Publishers, 2006).

[182] Schedule 2, para 7 to the Children Act 1989. See R Arthur 'Youth Crime Prevention – the Role of Children's Services' in Z Davies and W McMahon (eds) *Debating Youth Justice: From Punishment to Problem Solving?* (Centre for Crime and Justice Studies, 2007).

[183] In particular, there is a move away from centralist managerialism towards de-regulation and localism, with the reduction of nationally set guidance and the delivery of services by the third sector as part of the 'Big Society' agenda. On the the New Labour reforms see the references in fn 171 and generally J Muncie *Youth and Crime* (Sage, 2004) and L Gelsthorpe 'Recent Changes in Youth Justice Policy in England and Wales' in I Weijers and A Duff (eds) *Punishing Juveniles: Principle and Critique* (Hart Publishing, 2002). For a discussion of the potential impact of the recent reforms on children's rights see K Hollingsworth 'Youth Justice in the Big Society' (2012) 34 JSWFL 241.

offending.[184] Section 37 of the Crime and Disorder Act 1998 introduced as the principal aim of the youth justice system the prevention of offending by children and young persons. The aim applies throughout the youth justice system and in 2009 was formally extended to sentencing.[185] Section 37 also requires that all those carrying out functions in relation to the youth justice system must have regard to this aim including, presumably, those from the third sector who are set to have an increasing role in the delivery of criminal justice.[186]

Preventing children from offending underpins how minors are dealt with once they are within the criminal justice system, and it is also the raison d'etre for a number of pre-crime initiatives aimed at keeping children away from crime – 'nipping offending in the bud' – in the first place. Some of these initiatives are non-statutory (such as the Safer Schools Initiative, the Youth Inclusion Programme, Youth Inclusion and Support Panels and, more recently, the 'Troubled Families' programme)[187] but in addition prevention also provides (at least some of) the justification for a number of statutory orders introduced by the Crime and Disorder Act 1998. These include the child safety order,[188] the parenting order,[189] and the anti-social behaviour order.[190] Preventing children from offending is, on the face of it, a laudable aim for the youth justice system; one which protects the interests of the community *and* the child. However, it

---

[184]   On the original proposals regarding the principal aim see Home Office *Preventing Children Offending: A Consultation Document* (Home Office, 1997).

[185]   Criminal Justice and Immigration Act 2008, s 9 introduced s 142A into the Criminal Justice Act 2003. This sets out the aims of sentencing of juveniles (see below). This provision has not yet been brought into force but nonetheless, the Sentencing Guidelines Council's (SGC) guidance on the overarching principles to govern the sentencing of youths – to which sentencing courts must have regard (Criminal Justice Act 2003 Act, s 172) –identifies the principal aim as one of the principles of sentencing. See Sentencing Guidelines Council (2009) *Overarching Principles – Sentencing Youths*, at para 2.6, issued pursuant to s. 170(9) Criminal Justice Act 2003.

[186]   See Ministry of Justice *Breaking the Cycle: Effective Punishment, Rehabilitation and Sentencing of Offenders* (Ministry of Justice, 2010) and *Breaking the Cycle: The Government Response* (Ministry of Justice, 2011). In particular, see the introduction of the 'Youth Justice Reinvestment Pathfinder Initiative' which confers upon local authorities a grant that can be used to invest (inter alia) in preventative schemes. If custody reduction targets are subsequently met then the local authority can keep the grant; if not, some must be repaid. See further Hollingsworth (above, 2012) and the discussion below.

[187]   See the press release about the launch of the Tackling Troubled Families programme on 15 December 2011 (http://www.communities.gov.uk/news/corporate/2052302, last visited 24 August 2012). On specific family interventions aimed (inter alia) at preventing youth crime see Department for Education *Monitoring and evaluation of family intervention services and projects between February 2007 and March 2011* (2011). Also see the earlier *Youth Crime Action Plan* from 2008 which proposed targeted support of 110,000 so-called 'high risk families' whose children are considered to be 'identifiably at risk of becoming prolific offenders'.

[188]   Crime and Disorder Act 1998, s 11. See below.

[189]   Section 8. See below.

[190]   Section 1. ASBOs are available for use against adults and children but in practice approximately 50 per cent have been used against those aged under 18. On the proposals to replace the ASBO, see Home Office *Putting victims first: more effective responses to anti-social behaviour* (Home Office, 2012), Cm 8367 and the subsequent Anti-social, Crime and Policing Bill 2013–2014.

cannot be assumed that interventions (before or after offending) aimed at the prevention of offending or anti-social behaviour are, in fact, in the child's best interests especially where the child experiences a corresponding restriction of her rights. One example of this is the powers of the police to enforce child curfews and to remove children to their home when they are in a 'dispersal' zone. The concept of the child curfew was first introduced for the under 10s in the Crime and Disorder Act 1998[191] and quickly extended to all those under 16 in 2001.[192] Almost identical powers were then introduced in 2003, giving the police the power to remove an unaccompanied child to her home if she was in a dispersal zone between 9pm and 6am.[193] The question of whether removal powers allow the police to take a child home against her will or only with her consent was the subject of a judicial review in 2006.[194] At first instance, the High Court held that the powers were *not* coercive; that only a consenting child could be taken home. However, the Court of Appeal held, on the basis of statutory interpretation, that the powers were intended to be coercive (there would be little point in them otherwise), and thus overturned the decision of the High Court. The Court of Appeal did not directly engage with the question of whether the statutory powers were consistent with the child's rights under the ECHR (especially Arts 8 and 11), but it did state that the police must (of course) exercise their removal powers in accordance with the Human Rights Act 1998.[195] In 2012, as part of a wider review of anti-social behaviour, the Government set out its plans to replace the police power to disperse with a similar 'police directions power'.[196] The proposed power differs from its predecessor in a number of ways.[197] The Anti-social Behaviour, Crime and Policing Bill 2013–14 still requires that the powers be exercised within a specified locality but the maximum period for the authorisation of the powers reduces from six months to 48 hours.[198] However, the consent of the local authority is no longer necessary before an authorisation is made, and there is no requirement for it to be publicised; therefore providing a more readily available police power. The general power to exclude persons from an area set out in clause 33 of the 2013–14 Bill applies to children over the age of criminal responsibility (10 years old), and where the constable issuing the direction reasonably believes the person is under 16, she or he may remove the child ('person' in the Bill) to a place where she lives 'or a place of safety'.[199] Thus, the removal of the child is linked to the giving of the direction, which is turn can be imposed if the person's behavior has contributed or 'is likely to contribute' to

---

[191] Section 14.

[192] Criminal Justice and Police Act 2001.

[193] Anti-Social Behaviour Act 2003, Part IV and especially s 30(6).

[194] See *R (W) v Metropolitan Police Commissioner and another* [2006] EWCA Civ 458, [2006] 3 All ER 144 and see further K Hollingsworth 'R (W) v Commissioner of Police for the Metropolis; the London Borough of Richmond-upon-Thames* – interpreting child curfews: a question of rights?' (2006) 18 CFLQ 253.

[195] On the use of the dispersal powers see A Crawford and S Lister *The use and impact of dispersal orders: Sticking plasters and wake-up calls* (The Policy Press, 2007).

[196] Home Office (2012), above.

[197] See Anti-social Behaviour, Crime and Policing Bill 2013–14, Part 3.

[198] At the time of writing the Bill had gone through Committee stage in the House of Commons.

[199] Clause 33(7).

members of the public in the locality being harassed, alarmed or distressed or the occurrence of crime and disorder; and that the power is necessary to remove or reduce the likelihood of such events.[200] Therefore, the curfew type power, that could previously be employed between 9pm and 6am if the child was not under the 'effective control' of a responsible adult, is not replicated in the Bill. Nonetheless, a failure to comply with a direction will be a criminal offence for anyone over the age of criminal responsibility.

Also included in the Anti-social Behaviour, Crime and Policing Bill are provisions that will replace the existing ASBO and anti-social behaviour injunctions with a new injunction and new criminal behaviour order. The injunction can be imposed by the Youth Court against children from the age of 10 upon application by a wide range of organisations[201] if two conditions are met:

> (2) The first condition is that the court is satisfied, on the balance of probabilities, that the respondent has engaged or threatens to engage in conduct capable of causing nuisance or annoyance to any person ("anti-social behaviour").

> (3) The second condition is that the court considers it just and convenient to grant the injunction for the purpose of preventing the respondent from engaging in anti-social behaviour.

An injunction will therefore be available in wide ranging circumstance including where the behaviour is *annoying;* a much wider definition of anti-social behaviour than that in the 1998 Act. If the court is satisfied beyond reasonable doubt that a child over 14 has breached an injunction, the Bill allows a detention order to be imposed for up to three months. Injunctions will also be available without notice, and the reporting restrictions that ordinarily apply in the youth court pursuant to s 49 of the Children and Young Persons Act 1933 will not apply.[202] The Criminal Behaviour Order will be available upon criminal conviction where:[203]

> the court is satisfied that the offender has engaged in behaviour that caused or was likely to cause harassment, alarm or distress to one or more persons not of the same household as the offender.

> (4)   The second condition is that the court considers that making the order will help in preventing the offender from engaging in such behavior.

Breach of the criminal behavior order is a criminal offence with a maximum custodial sentence of five years. The potential restriction of children's rights in the name of prevention – including short-term custodial sentences for potentially low-level bad behavior – therefore continues despite the change of Government. This is evident from other recent changes too, including the

---

[200] Clause 33(2), (3).
[201] Clause 4.
[202] Clause 17.
[203] Clause 21(3) and (4).

introduction of gang injunctions for 14–17-year-olds, the breach of which – as with the earlier ASBO – is to be backed up by penal sanctions.[204]

Perhaps not surprisingly given the criminological evidence,[205] the identification of prevention as the principal aim of the youth justice system does not necessarily lead to a decrease in the numbers of children coming into contact with criminal justice agencies. Indeed, in the decade following the Crime and Disorder Act, the number of first time entrants into the youth justice system and the number of children sentenced to custody increased significantly.[206] Both trends have seen a reversal in the past three years, and in the most recent white paper the Government expressed its concern not to use preventative powers such as gang injunctions and the ASBO replacements (the injunctions and criminal behaviour orders described above)[207] to unnecessarily criminalise young people. However, the existence of such orders nonetheless creates a framework within which attempts to prevent children from offending actually results in their criminalisation; an argument perhaps, for a greater focus on local authorities' general duties to children in their area under the Children Acts 1989 and 2004 which can, and should, be used to prevent children from engaging in criminal behavior.[208]

The responsibility of parents for the offending behaviour of their children[209]

The financial responsibility of parents for their child's offending

The responsibility of parents for the offending behaviour of their children has a long history in English law, one that Arthur traces back to the nineteenth century.[210] Until the 1990s, that responsibility had largely been financial.[211] For

---

204 Again, these apply to adults too. For their application to children see the Policing and Crime Act 2009, s 34(1) as amended by the Crime and Security Act 2010 (and see SI 2011/3016).

205 See L McAra and S McVie 'Youth Justice?: The Impact of System Contact on Patterns of Desistance from Offending' (2007) 4 *European Journal of Criminology* 315.

206 E Solomon and R Garside *Ten Years of Labour's Youth Justice Reforms: An Independent Audit* (Centre for Crime and Justice Studies, 2008). The increase in the figures was attributable to a combination of factors, including the introduction of an 'offence brought to justice target' within the police.

207 For critiques of earlier versions of these orders see A Ashworth 'Social Control and "Anti-Social Behaviour": the Subversion of Human Rights' (2004) 120 LQR 263; E Burney *Making People Behave: Anti-social Behaviour, Politics and Policy* (Willan Publishing, 2009); J Rodger *Criminalising Social Policy: Anti-social Behaviour and Welfare in a De-Civilised Society* (Willan Publishing, 2008); and A Millie *Anti-social behaviour* (Open University Press, 2009).

208 See Arthur (above).

209 Some of the discussion in this part of the chapter is based on K Hollingsworth 'Responsibility and Rights: Children and their Parents in the Youth Justice System ' (2007) 21 IJLPF 191.

210 R Arthur 'Punishing Parents for the Crimes of Their Children' (2005) 44 *The Howard Journal of Criminal Justice* 233. See also L Gelsthorpe and A Morris 'Juvenile Justice: 1945–1992' in M Maguire, R Morgan and R Reiner (eds) *The Oxford Handbook of Criminology* (Oxford University Press, 1994).

211 Though the Children and Young Persons Act 1933, s 24, Children and Young Persons Act 1963, s 25 and the Criminal Justice Act 1991, s 56 also required parents to accompany their child to court.

children under 16 years of age, the court has a duty to order that a fine, compensation, or costs be paid by a parent or guardian, unless it is satisfied that the parent or guardian could not be found or the order would be unreasonable in the circumstances.[212] For a child over 16 years (and under 18), the duty of the court becomes a power.[213] This reflects a presumption that many young people in this age group will have de facto independence from their parents and should therefore be responsible for their own financial penalties. The Criminal Justice Act 1991 extended these provisions from parents to local authorities where a child under the age of 18 who is looked after by them is convicted of an offence.[214] In 2005, parental compensation orders (PCOs) were introduced.[215] A PCO requires a parent to pay compensation where a child *under* 10 (which is below the minimum age of criminal responsibility) has taken or caused loss or damage to property in the course of acting in either an anti-social manner, or in a way which if she were over 10 would be a criminal offence; provided that it would be desirable to do so in the interests of preventing a repetition of the behaviour in question.

The imposition of responsibility on parents for their children is not simply intended to recoup money for the public purse or for victims in lieu of the child being able to pay himself. These provisions have, since at least 1980, also been underpinned by the aim of encouraging 'courts to assert the duty of parents to act responsibly towards their children and take all steps within their power to prevent them committing criminal offences'.[216] This aim is even more explicit in the context of non-financial responsibilities.

---

[212] Children and Young Persons Act 1933, s 55 and the Criminal Justice Act 1982, s 26. There is some evidence that these powers were rarely used. See JG Hall and DF Martin 'Child Delinquency and Parental Responsibility' (1990) JPN 604 and D Boyd 'Blaming the Parents' (1990) 2 JCL 65. On the current financial responsibility of parents see Powers of Criminal Courts (Sentencing) Act 2000, s 137 as amended. Parents must pay fines, compensation orders, costs and surcharges (the latter as a result of the Criminal Justice Act 2003, s 161A). On the meaning of when it is 'unreasonable' to impose a compensation order see *R (M) v Inner London Crown Court* [2003] EWHC 301 (Admin) and *R v J-B* [2004] EWCA Crim 14, and see N Stone 'Financial Orders Against Parents: Falling Down on Obligations?' (2004) 4 *Youth Justice: An International Journal* 133.

[213] Powers of Criminal Courts (Sentencing) Act 2000, s 137 as amended.

[214] Criminal Justice Act 1991, s 57, inserting a new s 55(5) into the Children and Young Persons Act 1933 and effectively reversing the decision in *Leeds City Council v West Yorkshire Metropolitan Police* [1983] 1 AC 29. The liability of the local authority will turn in individual cases on whether it has behaved reasonably and properly in its efforts to control the child. See *D (A Minor) v DPP* [1995] 2 FLR 502 and *Bedfordshire County Council v DPP* [1995] Crim LR 962.

[215] Serious Organised Crime and Police Act 2005, s 144 and Sch 10, amending the Crime and Disorder Act 1998, ss 13A–13E. The provisions are only partially in force, in certain areas.

[216] See Home Office, Welsh Office, Department of Health and Social Security *Young Offenders* (Home Office, 1980) at para 54 and Home Office *Crime, Justice and Protecting the Public* (Home Office, 1990), at para 8.8.

Non-financial responsibility for the child's offending

The power to bind-over

In 1990, the then Conservative Government turned its focus to the accountability of parents for their child's offending and suggested the introduction of an offence for parents failing 'to prevent their children from committing offences'.[217] Not surprisingly this proposal was heavily criticised (by, among other, the Magistrates' Association) and was subsequently dropped.[218] Instead, the notion of parental responsibility was strengthened by the Criminal Justice Act 1991 which provided the criminal courts with powers to bind-over a parent upon the conviction of her child.[219] In 2000, the provisions of the 1991 Act were repealed but the powers to bind-over were retained under the Powers of Criminal Courts (Sentencing) Act 2000.[220] The provisions are largely similar to the earlier ones and require that where the child is under 16 years the court *must* impose a bind-over if satisfied, in the circumstances, that the exercise of this power 'would be desirable in the interests of preventing the commission by him of further offences'; and if the court is not so satisfied, it must give reasons in open court. The court is prohibited from using the bind-over where a child's conviction results in a referral order,[221] but in all other cases there is an apparent presumption that it will be used. The maximum period for the bind-over is three-years or until the child reaches 18, and if parents refuse to consent to it, they may be fined £1000. The bind-over requires the parent to take proper care and exercise proper control, and where the child has received a youth rehabilitation order the court may require the parent to ensure that her child complies with the requirement of the order.[222]

It is not at all clear how well the idea underpinning the bind-over accords with the civil concept of parental responsibility under the Children Act or how far it acknowledges the conflict of interest which may arise between the child and the parent who has done everything in her power to control the child but has failed. The trend in the civil law since *Gillick* has been very much away from the notion of parental control and towards independence for adolescents. The binding-over power seems to jar with this, although figures reported by the Home Office in 2003 suggest that it is not frequently used by the courts.[223] The

---

[217] Home Office (1990, ibid). See L Gelsthorpe 'Youth Crime and Parental Responsibility' in A Bainham, S Day Sclater and M Richards (eds) *What is a Parent? A Socio-Legal Analysis* (Hart Publishing, 1999). For criticisms of the idea see Hall and Martin, and Boyd (above).

[218] See Hall and Martin (above) for a summary of the criticisms.

[219] Section 58. Prior to 1991, limited powers to bind-over the parents of a child brought before the juvenile court existed in the Children and Young Persons Act 1933, s 62(1)(c). On its use see *Bowers and Anor* [1953] 1 WLR 297. See also Home Office (1980 and 1990 above) both of which refer to pre-existing powers of the court to bind-over parents.

[220] Section 150.

[221] Powers of Criminal Courts (Sentencing) Act 2000, s 19(5). A referral order is the usual sentence where a child is convicted of her first offence. See below.

[222] The YRO is the main community order a child receives upon conviction and was first introduced by the Criminal Justice and Immigration Act 2008. See below.

[223] There was a steady increase in the use of bind-overs between 1992 (91) and 1999 (4066) but a

reason for the decline in the use of the bind-over may be due to the introduction of the parenting order by New Labour.

Parenting orders and contracts

The Labour Government introduced the parenting order in the Crime and Disorder Act 1998. Its reasons for doing so were set out in two 1997 White Papers: *No More Excuses* and *Preventing Children Offending: A Consultation Document*. In justifying the introduction of the orders, the Government relied on research that showed a correlation between inadequate parental supervision and the offending behaviour of children.[224] It was thought that the courts required more powers to help parents effectively keep their children out of trouble. Therefore, although the Labour Administration stopped short of holding parents directly accountable for the crimes of their children, it continued the trend set by the preceding Conservative Government to demand greater responsibility for them.

Since 1998, the circumstances in which parenting orders are available has extended. Section 8 of the Crime and Disorder Act 1998 provides that an order can be imposed where a child safety order, a parental compensation order, a sex offender order or ASBO has been made in relation to a child or young person, where a child has been convicted of an offence, or where a person is convicted of either failing to comply with a school attendance order or failing to secure the child's regular attendance at school under ss 443 and 444 (respectively) of the Education Act 1996. The Crime and Security Act 2010, s 41 provided for the insertion of a new s 8A into the Crime and Disorder Act which, if brought into force,[225] will impose a duty on the court to make a parenting order in the case of a child under the age of 16 who breaches an anti-social behaviour order unless there are 'exceptional circumstances' that would make the order inappropriate.

In all cases, a parenting order can only be made where the 'relevant condition' is met: that is, where the order is desirable in the interests of preventing a repetition of the behaviour by the child or young person that led to the making of the original order, to prevent further offending by the child, or to prevent a further offence under ss 443 and 444 of the Education Act. For the most part, the court's power to make a parenting order is discretionary. However, where a child is under 16 and has been convicted of an offence or issued with an ASBO,[226] and the relevant condition is satisfied, the court *must* make an order unless the child is before court for the first time and has received a referral

---

decline then followed. In 2001 the figure was down to 1471. See Home Office *Bind Overs: A Power for the 21st Century. A Consultation Document* (Home Office, 2003).

[224] J Graham and B Bowling *Young People and Crime* (Home Office, 1995) cited in Home Office *Preventing Children Offending* (1997), above.

[225] The Coalition Government has proposed the abolition of the ASBO so this provision is likely to be subject to amendment or repeal.

[226] Amended by the Anti-social Behaviour Act 2003, s 85.

order, in which case a parenting order is discretionary.[227] The court must also consider information about the person's family circumstances and the likely effect of the order on those circumstances before imposing the order.

Section 8 of the Act empowers the court to make an order for up to 12 months, compelling a parent or guardian to comply with the requirements in the order.[228] This can include exercising specific functions relating to their child (for example, ensuring the child attends school, is home at certain times, and refrains from associating with certain people), but the primary purpose of parenting orders is to compel parents to attend a 'counselling or guidance programme' – in effect parenting classes – for up to three months.[229] Since the 2003 Anti-social Behaviour Act, this can include attendance on a residential course.[230] A person who fails to comply with a parenting order is criminally liable and can be fined.[231] As with ASBOs and non-molestation orders, this is an example of a civil order that gives rise to criminal sanctions in the event of a breach of the conditions imposed.[232] Nonetheless, in *R (M) v Inner London Crown Court*[233] the High Court dismissed the claim of a mother that a heightened burden of proof – similar to the criminal standard – should apply. The civil standard was deemed adequate because the role of the court was one of evaluation and assessment (would a parenting order help prevent the child from behaving in a particular way in future) rather than the determination of a particular fact. Nor was the court willing to hold that the scheme in s 8 was incompatible with Art 8 ECHR; the restriction to private and family life was necessary and proportionate. Nonetheless, the decision to impose a parenting order must, of course, comply with the requirements of the Human Rights Act 1998, and in particular Art 8, as well as the common law judicial review principles.[234]

No other legal challenges have been made to the parenting order scheme, but it is worth noting that their scope and applicability has expanded since the decision in *M*. The Anti-social Behaviour Act 2003 provides for a stand-alone

---

[227] CDA 1998, s 9(1). See Criminal Justice Act 2003, s 234 and Sch 34.

[228] No definition of 'parent' is given in the Act but a circular issued in 2004 defines parent as under Family Law Reform Act 1996, s 1 (the child's natural parents) and guardian as under CYPA 1933, s 107 which includes anybody who in the opinion of the court has for the time being the care of the child. This would include step parents.

[229] CDA 1998, ss 8(4)(b) and (5), amended by the Anti-social Behaviour Act 2003.

[230] CDA 1998, s 8(7A). The residential courses usually take place over a weekend.

[231] CDA 1998, s 9(7).

[232] See respectively, CDA 1998, s 1(10) and Domestic Violence, Crime and Victims Act 2004, s 1 which inserted s 42A into Family Law Act 1996. All of these are strict liability offences. For an early evaluation of parenting orders see D Ghate and M Ramella *Positive Parenting: The National Evaluation of the Youth Justice Board's Parenting Programme* (Youth Justice Board; Policy Research Bureau, 2002). For an overview of the problems with parenting orders as a solution to deficits in parenting skills and as a technique to prevent children offending, see L Gelsthorpe and E Burney 'Do We Need a Naughty Step: Rethinking Parenting Orders After Ten Years' (2008) 47 *Howard Journal of Criminal Justice* 470, at pp 475–479.

[233] [2003] EWHC 301, [2003] 1 FLR 994.

[234] See *R (M) v Inner London Crown Court* (above) where the court held that in that case the decision to impose a parenting order was irrational.

order to be made where a child has been excluded from school on disciplinary grounds or engaged in behaviour that could warrant her exclusion, or he has been referred to a YOT and the court is satisfied the child has engaged in criminal or anti-social behaviour. In the case of exclusion, the order can be applied for by the local authority or a school governing body, and in the case of bad behaviour, a YOT. In both instances, the court must be satisfied that the child has engaged in the requisite behaviour and that the making of the order would be desirable in the interests of improving her behaviour.[235] The Police and Justice Act 2006 further provides that a local authority or a relevant housing authority can apply for a parenting order where the child has engaged in anti-social behavior.[236] The circumstances in which these rather heavy-handed orders can be applied for are therefore extensive.

However, at the same time as extending the availability of parenting orders, the 2003 Anti-social Behaviour Act also introduced parenting *contracts*, into which parents can 'voluntarily' enter.[237] This consists of a statement by the parent that s/he agrees to comply with the requirements in the contract for a specified period (which may include attendance on a counselling or guidance programme) and a statement by the school, LEA, or youth offending team (as the case may be) that it will provide or arrange support to the parent to help her comply with the requirements. Parenting contracts are available to the same bodies as can apply for parenting orders (LEAs, School Governing bodies, YOTs, local authorities, relevant housing providers) but are available in much wider circumstances. For example, a parenting contract is available where in the case of the child's bad behaviour at school she has caused or 'is likely to cause' significant disruption to the education of other pupils or significant detriment to the welfare of the child himself or other pupils or to the health and safety of any staff, or it forms a pattern of behaviour which if continued will give rise to a risk of future exclusion. And local authorities, YOTs and housing providers can apply for a parenting contract where the child is 'at risk' of engaging in anti-social behaviour. Given the wide definition of anti-social behaviour[238] this is potentially an unlimited power.[239] The parenting contract is of course less coercive than the parenting order and breach of the contract does not result in legal liability.

---

[235] Anti-social Behaviour Act 2003, ss 20 and 26 respectively.

[236] Also see the Education and Skills Act 2008, ss 40–44 of which extend the availability of parenting orders and contracts to the parents of 16–17-year-old children who are failing in their (the child's) duty under s 2 of the Act to be in full-time education, training or employment. These provisions have not yet been brought into force at the time of writing. See chapter 17.

[237] Sections 19, 25, 25A and 25B. These provisions simply formalise what many agencies already do. As they are 'voluntary' they do not require a legislative basis.

[238] See s 1 Crime and Disorder Act 1998. What is anti-social behaviour is 'determined by a series of factors including context, location, community tolerance and quality of life expectations'. S Harradine, J Kodz, F Lemettiet and B Jones *Defining and Measuring Anti-social Behaviour* (Home Office, 2004), at p 3.

[239] For the wider landscape of 'contractual governance' see A Crawford '"Contractual Governance" of Deviant Behaviour' (2003) 30 JLS 479.

Parenting orders and contracts are just one part of a much wider system of voluntary parental support for parents whose children are at risk of or engaged in anti-social and criminal behaviour. Research conducted by Gelsthorpe and Burney into the use of parenting orders by four YOTs found that 81 per cent of parenting interventions were voluntary, compared with 7 per cent contracts and 12 per cent parenting orders.[240] They therefore conclude that such a heavy legal instrument as the parenting order is unnecessary in light of the amount of voluntary support that is available to, and engaged with by, parents. The current legislative framework remains in place however, and despite a promised increase in the voluntary support for families,[241] the coercive backdrop of parenting orders remains.

THE CRIMINAL RESPONSIBILITY OF CHILDREN

The minimum age of criminal responsibility (MACR) in England and Wales is 10: those below it cannot be held responsible in the criminal courts; those above it are held accountable for their offending behaviour in much the same way as adults. Susceptibility to the criminal law is therefore based on chronological age rather than developmental capacity. However, a number of caveats need to be made to this rather broad statement. First, the offending behaviour of children under the age of 10 years is not ignored by the state; in England and Wales, young children have increasingly been subject to regulation and risk-management. Secondly, the police and prosecution service retain considerable discretion *not* to bring proceedings against children whom they deem to lack sufficient capacity to be held to account. Third, there remain mechanisms within criminal justice processes, in particular the requirements of a fair trial, that allow some account to be taken of the developing capacity of children. And finally, criminal justice processes and the length and types of punishment available for children differ – though not always[242] – from adults. These issues will be explored in subsequent sections.

Children under 10 years of age

Children under the age of 10 are conclusively presumed to be doli incapax ('incapable of evil') and therefore are presumed to lack the capacity necessary for criminal responsibility.[243] These children cannot be prosecuted. The setting of a 'bright line' age threshold for criminal responsibility is in line with the

---

[240] Above, at p 483.
[241] The Coalition Government has promised an extra £448 million to provide additional support to 120,000 of the most 'troubled families', which it is hoped will help address the bad behaviour of the children in those families. Whether this is sufficient additional investment remains to be seen however, given the cost of the most effective family intervention projects.
[242] For example, children can be referred to the adult crown court if they are jointly charged with an adult or the offence of which they are accused is sufficiently serious.
[243] Children and Young Persons Act 1933, s 50, as amended by Children and Young Persons Act 1963, s 16. The minimum age of criminal responsibility has increased from seven (under the common law), to eight (in 1933) and then to 10 in 1963.

requirements of Art 40(3)(a) of the UNCRC.[244] The Convention does not prescribe a minimum age of criminal responsibility (MACR) but Rule 4.1 of the Beijing Rules requires state members to bear in mind 'the facts of emotional, mental and intellectual maturity'. The UN Committee on the Rights of the Child has been more prescriptive than both the Convention and the Rules. In General Comment No 10, the Committee states that an MACR below 12 is 'internationally unacceptable'[245] and so, unsurprisingly, the UK has come in for criticism from the Committee in its Concluding Observations on the Rights of the Child in the UK.[246] However, although the MACR in England and Wales appears to fall foul of the standards of the United Nations, it has not been held to breach the child's rights under Art 3 of the European Convention on Human Rights (freedom from degrading and inhuman treatment). In *V v UK* the European Court on Human Rights concluded that given the wide disparity in the MACR across European states, the setting of the minimum age of criminal responsibility was an issue which rightly falls within a country's margin of appreciation.[247] It is noteworthy however that the MACR in England and Wales is lower than most other European jurisdictions.[248]

However, just because a child falls below the minimum age of criminal responsibility, this does not mean that the state ignores entirely her behaviour that would, if she were over the age of 10, be deemed criminal. Instead, children can be dealt with through the public law procedures of the Children Act 1989. In many cases, this would involve social services providing the family with voluntary assistance. As has been seen,[249] the abolition of the 'offence condition' means that proceedings for compulsory care or supervision may no longer be instigated simply on the strength of delinquency. It has to be shown that the child is also at risk of 'significant harm', applying the statutory criteria and, at the welfare stage, the welfare principle. In particular, the harm must be

---

[244] Which requires 'the establishment of a minimum age below which children shall be presumed not to have the capacity to infringe the penal law'.

[245] UN Committee on the Rights of the Child *General Comment No 10: Children's Rights in Juvenile Justice* (CRC/C/GC/10, 25 Apr 2007).

[246] See for example UN Committee on the Rights of the Child *Concluding Observations of the Committee on the Rights of the Child on the United Kingdom of Great Britain and Northern Ireland* CRC/C/15 Add 188, 2002 and CRC/C/GBR/CO/4, 2008. In Scotland the MACR is currently eight but is to be increased to 12. However, it is difficult to compare England and Wales with Scotland, given the very different systems that operate in the jurisdictions. In Scotland, the Children's Hearing System operates as a welfare-based system. See inter alia The Committee on Children and Young Persons Scotland *Children and Young Persons, Scotland (The Kilbrandon Report)* (Committee on Children and Young Persons Scotland, 1964); A Lockyer and F Stone (Eds) *Juvenile Justice in Scotland: 25 Years of the Welfare Approach* (T&T Clark Ltd, 1998); C McDiarmid 'Welfare, Offending and the Scottish Children's Hearing System' (2005) 27 JSWFL 31 and E Sutherland 'The Child in Conflict with the Law' in A Cleland and E Sutherland *Children's Rights in Scotland.* (W Green, 2009).

[247] See *V v United Kingdom* (1999) 30 EHRR 121. However, prosecuting children of a young age may fall foul of the Art 6 requirement of effective participation. See below. For a very comprehensive examination of children's rights and the age of criminal responsibility see D Cipriani *Children's Rights and the Minimum Age of Criminal Responsibility* (Ashgate, 2009).

[248] Ibid, ch 5.

[249] Section 90(1) of the Children Act 1989.

attributable to either the child not receiving care that it is reasonable to give, or the child being 'beyond parental control'.[250]

The options for dealing with the behaviour of children under the age of 10 that would, but for their age, constitute criminal activity were extended by New Labour through non-statutory risk-based interventions[251] and the statutory-based child safety order.[252] The child safety order (CSO) is aimed at preventing the offending behaviour of children under the age of 10 and was a response to the Labour Government's view that childhood offending must be 'nipped in the bud'.[253] However, as Piper notes, the order was justified on the basis of 'protecting' children, and was accordingly seen as being in the child's best interests, thus detracting from its coerciveness.[254] A CSO can be made by a magistrate in family proceedings, following a request by a local authority, where a child has committed an act which would have constituted an offence if she had been over 10; or where the CSO is necessary in order to prevent a child from committing such an act; and where the child has acted in a way that constitutes anti-social behaviour.[255] A CSO will set out a number of requirements with which the child must comply and place the child under the supervision of the 'responsible officer' – a social worker or a member of the YOT.[256] The requirements in the order must be considered 'desirable' by the court in the interests of '(a) securing that the child receives appropriate care, protection and support and is subject to proper control; *or* (b) preventing any repetition of the kind of behaviour which led to the child safety order being made'.[257] In practice, orders include curfews, restrictions on the people with whom the child associates, requirements to attend school and so on.[258] The maximum length of an order is 12 months,[259] and if it is breached the court is empowered to issue a parenting order.[260]

---

[250] Section 31(2)(b)(i) and (ii) Children Act 1989 respectively. See further chapter 12.

[251] Specifically the youth inclusion support panels which could address the behaviour of children from 8 years old.

[252] Powers to impose curfews on children under the age of 10 were also introduced; first under s 14 of the Crime and Disorder Act 1998 (which empowers local authorities to establish child curfew schemes where it is necessary for the purpose of maintaining order) and secondly, almost identical powers were included in s 30(6) of the Anti-Social Behaviour Act 2003 which gave the police the power to remove a child to her home if she is unaccompanied by an adult and in a dispersal zone. s 14 of the Crime and Disorder Act was repealed by Policing and Crime Act 2009, Sch 8, Pt 13, para 1. On the removal powers in the Anti-social Behaviour 2003 and the proposed replacement powers see above.

[253] Crime and Disorder Act 1998, s 11.

[254] Piper (1999), above.

[255] Crime and Disorder Act 1998, s 11(3).

[256] Section 8. Piper notes that a trained social worker will probably supervise the child and thus it 'might be seen as alarmist to view such orders as heralding an Orwellian state'. Piper (above, at p 406).

[257] Section 11(5).

[258] See Home Office Guidance (http://www.homeoffice.gov.uk/cdat/csorddft.htm).

[259] Section 11(4). This was extended from three months by the Children Act 2004.

[260] When CSOs were first introduced, a breach could result in a care order but this provision was (rightly, in order to be consistent with the principles of the Children Act 1989) repealed by the Children Act 2004.

The CSO appears to blur the boundary between how children above and below the age of 10 are perceived in terms of their ability to be held criminally to account and has led some commentators to argue that through this order 'the age of criminal responsibility becomes meaningless'.[261] It should be noted however that CSOs have rarely been used in practice.[262] This is perhaps indicative of a difference in approach and perception of the 'problem' of the under 10s between central government (who initiate the legislation) and local government (who utilise it).

Children over 10 years of age

Prior to 1998, a 'buffer' zone existed for children aged 10–13 years old. These children were presumed to be *doli incapax* unless the prosecution proved beyond reasonable doubt that they knew that what they did was 'seriously wrong'[263] in addition to establishing that the elements of the offence were met. In 1994, in the wake of the murder of James Bulger by two 10-year-old boys, there was an attempt by the Divisional Court in *C v DPP*[264] to abolish the common law presumption on the basis that it was out-dated. However, the House of Lords[265] subsequently held that, although reform was desirable, this was a matter for Parliament and not for the courts. It therefore reasserted the existence of the common law presumption only for the Labour Government to incorporate its abolition as part of a wider package of measures to tackle youth crime in the 1998 legislation.

As noted above, the introduction of a clear age threshold for criminal responsibility is in-keeping with the UNCRC. However, although the attainment of legal certainty is usually welcomed, the abolition of the presumption left very young children exposed to what was an increasingly (particularly in the wake of the moral panic following the death of James Bulger) punitive youth justice system. It also appeared to be out of line with the notion of gradual or gathering independence of children which underpins parts of the law elsewhere, and in particular the *Gillick* competence test.[266] As Tony

---

[261] Gelsthorpe and Morris (above, 1999).

[262] Figures provided to the author from the YJB indicate that one or two CSOs are used nationally on an annual basis. Some years show a high use of the orders in one or two authorities (namely 44 in 2004/05 and 26 in 2006/07) but the two authorities concerned have disputed these figures (in correspondence with the author).

[263] For a detailed history on the common law interpretation of the term 'doli incapax' see T Crofts *The Criminal Responsibility of Children and Young Persons: A Comparison of English and German Law* (Ashgate, 2002) and Cipriani (above).

[264] [1994] 3 WLR 888, and for commentary on the Divisional Court's decision, see ATH Smith 'Doli Incapax Under Threat' (1994) CLJ 426. Also see Fionda (2005), above for a criticism of the presumptions upon which Mr Justice Laws based his decision.

[265] [1995] 2 WLR 383. For commentary, see ATH Smith 'Reshaping the Criminal Law in the House of Lords' (1995) CLJ 486. For a wider critique of the doli incapax presumption, see G Douglas 'The Child's Right to Make Mistakes: Criminal Responsibility and the Immature Minor' in G Douglas and L Sebba *Children's Rights and Traditional Values* (Ashgate, 1998), ch 15.

[266] See H Keating 'The 'Responsibility' of Children in the Criminal Law' (2007) 19 CFLQ 183.

Smith put it, referring to the earlier decision of the Divisional Court in *C v DPP*, 'we now have a law which holds that a person is completely irresponsible on the day before his tenth birthday, and fully responsible as soon as the jelly and ice-cream have been cleared away the following day'.[267] However, Stokes has suggested that the presumption was easily rebutted and therefore it merely perpetrated the fiction of protection when in practice it offered little.[268]

In 1999, Nigel Walker put forward the argument that s 34 of the Crime and Disorder Act 1998 succeeded only in abolishing the *presumption* of doli incapax but left in place the possibility that a defence of incapacity remained for those aged 10–13.[269] Walker's argument gained some support from Lady Justice Smith in her obiter dicta comments in *Crown Prosecution Service v P*;[270] however, this interpretation of s 34 was conclusively rejected by the House of Lords in *R v JTB* on the grounds that Parliament clearly intended to repeal both the presumption and the defence of doli incapax.[271]

CHILDREN AND THE CRIMINAL PROCESS

Each year thousands of children are brought into the youth justice system, and a considerable number are deprived of their liberty when they are sentenced to detention.[272] Children who are brought into the criminal justice process will come into contact with a number of agencies all of whom are bound by the obligation under ss 10 and 11 of the Children Act 2004 to make arrangements to promote co-operation to discharge their functions 'having regard to the need to safeguard and promote the welfare of children'. Additionally, and in line with the civil context,[273] inter-agency working is a key feature of the criminal processes (especially since the introduction of YOTs in the Crime and Disorder Act 1998). Local authorities' social services departments have statutory obligations to provide support services to children and families.[274] As noted above, these include a duty to take reasonable steps designed to reduce the need to bring criminal proceedings against children, to encourage children within their areas not to commit crime, and to avoid the need for children to be placed

---

[267]   ATH Smith 'Doli Incapax Under Threat' (1994) CLJ 426 at 427.

[268]   E Stokes 'Abolishing the Presumption of Doli Incapax: Reflections on the Death of a Doctrine' in J Pickford (ed) *Youth Justice: Theory and Practice* (Cavendish Publishing, 2000).

[269]   See N Walker 'The End of an Old Song' (1999) 149 *New Law Journal* 64.

[270]   [2007] EWHC 946 (Admin), [2007] All ER (D) 244. See M Telford 'Youth Justice: new shoots on a bleak landscape – *Director of Public Prosecutions v P*' (2007) 19 CFLQ 505.

[271]   [2008] EWCA Crim 815, [2009] 1 AC 1310. For commentary see F Bennion 'Mens Rea and Defendants Below the Age of Discretion' (2009) Crim LR 757 and N Stone 'Old heads upon young shoulders: "compassion to human infirmity" following *R v T*' (2010) 32 JSWFL 287.

[272]   However, there has been a noteworthy decrease in both sets of figures since 2008. Nonetheless, in 2010/11 there were 45,510 first time entrants into the youth justice system and over 85,000 people supervised by youth offending teams and just over 2000 children are in custody. See Ministry of Justice, Home Office, YJB *Youth Justice Statistics 2010–122 England and Wales* (2012).

[273]   See chapters 11 and 12.

[274]   See chapter 10.

in secure accommodation.[275] Early local authority involvement is also secured by requiring the prosecuting authorities (the police and CPS) to give notice of any decision to prosecute a juvenile to the relevant local authority. While this ought to, and often will, involve co-operation and consultation *before* the decision to prosecute is taken, there is no statutory requirement to this effect. In practice, there is usually close liaison between the police, social services, education authorities and the probation service.[276]

Diversion

Diverting children away from the formality of criminal court proceedings allows for a more proportionate response to what are often minor and/or first offences for young people, it decreases the likelihood of later offending,[277] and also helps to ensure compliance with Art 40(3)(b) of the UNCRC.[278] The system of diversion in England and Wales was overhauled in 1998 as part of New Labour's reforms to youth justice, and a statutory diversionary scheme introduced reprimands and final warnings to replace the old system of cautions.[279] The Crime and Disorder Act limited the use of diversion to two occasions (first a reprimand, then a final warning),[280] after which the child would usually be subject to prosecution. The statutory scheme was supplemented by Home Office circulars[281] and a Gravity Factor Scheme which guided police as to whether a child should be reprimanded, warned or charged.[282] A reprimand or warning was not without consequence for the child and could, for example, be cited in court if a child later appeared for another

---

[275] Schedule 2, para 7 to the Children Act.

[276] See for example, the case of *R (E) v DPP* discussed above in relation to the Sexual Offences Act 2003.

[277] L McAra and S McVie (2007) 'Youth Justice?: The Impact of System Contact on Patterns of Desistance from Offending' 4 *European Journal of Criminology* 315.

[278] Which provides that State Parties should promote 'whenever appropriate and desirable measures for dealing with such children without resorting to judicial proceedings, providing that human rights and legal safeguards are fully respected'. See also Rule 11 of the Beijing Rules.

[279] See Crime and Disorder Act 1998, ss 65–66. The use of cautions had been subject to criticism because of the geographical disparity and the alleged high use of repeat cautions. See Audit Commission *Misspent Youth* (Audit Commission, 1996). For an overview see B Goldson 'Wither Diversion? Interventionism and the New Youth Justice' in B Goldson (ed) *The New Youth Justice* (Russell House Publishing Ltd, 2000), at p 35.

[280] They could only be used if the conditions in s 65(1) were met, including the child's admission to the offence, the child's lack of criminal record, and a realistic prospect of conviction. A final warning was usually accompanied by a programme of intervention (a 'rehabilitation programme'). See s 66(2)(b).

[281] Home Office/Youth Justice Board Guidance on the Final Warning Scheme November 2002 and Home Office Circular 14/2006.

[282] See S Field 'Early Intervention and the "New" Youth Justice: a Study of Initial Decision-Making' (2008) *Criminal Law Review* 177; V Kemp and L Gelsthorpe 'Youth Justice: Discretion in Pre-Court Decision-Making' in L Gelsthorpe and N Padfield (eds) *Exercising Discretion: Decision-making in the Criminal Justice System and Beyond* (Willan Publishing, 2003); and R Evans and K Puech 'Reprimands and Warnings: Populist Punitiveness or Restorative Justice?' (2001) *Criminal Law Review* 794.

offence.[283] In *R (R) v Durham Constabulary* a judicial review claim was made, challenging the decision of the police to issue a final warning against a 14-year-old boy without his prior consent, which he claimed breached his rights under Art 6(1) ECHR.[284] The Divisional Court allowed the claim and, quashing the police decision, held that as the consequences of a final warning were punitive it constituted a public pronouncement of guilt. The process was therefore deemed to amount to the determination of a criminal charge and Art 6(1) was thus engaged. Since the police had investigated the offence they were not an independent and impartial tribunal (as required by Art 6(1)) and, in the absence of the boy's written consent (which would have had the effect of waiving the rights), there was a breach of the due process rights protected by the ECHR. However, the House of Lords disagreed with the High Court and overturned the decision. Lord Bingham held that the processes of diversion for children were preventative, designed to promote the child's welfare and could not be regarded as punitive: Article 6 was not, therefore, engaged. Lord Bingham did not articulate what he meant by 'welfare' in this context, but he seemed to accept the Government view that preventing a child from offending is in her best interests; though whether inclusion on the Police National Computer and the Sex Offender's Register – two of the outcomes of the final warning for R – are consistent with the child's welfare is questionable.

As well as being subject to critique from a children's rights-perspective,[285] the statutory scheme introduced in 1998 was criticised for restricting the discretion of the police and for leading to an increase in the numbers of children being brought into formal criminal justice processes and escalating them through it more quickly.[286] The Coalition Government reformed the system of diversion in response to such concerns, including the 'rapid expansion' of diversionary mechanisms,[287] And the reprimand and warning scheme has now been replaced with the youth caution.[288] The new caution sits alongside the youth conditional caution which was introduced by the last Labour Government and extended to children in 2008.[289] The youth caution must be accompanied by a rehabilitation

---

[283] Other out of court disposals – other than diversion – also exist. Penalty Notices for Disorder allow the police to issue on the spot fines for example. See A Crawford 'Governing through anti-social behaviour: regulatory challenges to criminal justice' (2009) 49 BJC 810. The Coalition Government has pledged to abolish these for young people.

[284] [2005] UKHL 21, [2005] 1 WLR 1184. See A Gillespie 'Reprimanding Juveniles and the Right to Due Process' (2005) 68 MLR 1006.

[285] See Gillespie Ibid, and also K Hollingsworth 'Judicial Approaches to Children's Rights in Youth Crime' (2007) 17 CFLQ 42.

[286] Office of Criminal Justice Reform *Initial findings from a review of the use of out-of-court disposals* (2010). Other factors are also relevant to the increase in first time entrants, including offence brought to justice targets.

[287] Ministry of Justice *Breaking the Cycle*, above. See further Hollingsworth (2012), above.

[288] Legal Aid Act 2012, ss 135, amending the Crime and Disorder Act 1998 by introducing a new s 66ZA, in force since 8th April 2013. Informal disposal mechanisms are also to be promoted. See Ministry of Justice (above).

[289] Conditional cautions were introduced by Part 3 of the Criminal Justice Act 2003 and extended to children in the Criminal Justice and Immigration Act 2008, s 48 and Sch 9. For a critique of conditional cautions see I Brownlee 'Conditional Cautions and Fair Trial Rights in England and Wales: Form Versus Substance in the Diversionary Agenda?' [2007] Crim LR 129.

programme unless the YOT considers it inappropriate or it is the first caution the child has received, in which case the imposition of a rehabilitation programme is discretionary.[290] Further, that a child has earlier received a youth caution can be cited in criminal proceedings and thus, like the final warning, the new form of diversion is not without consequence for the child.

Overruling decisions on prosecution

An issue which has come before the courts is whether the decision of the prosecuting authorities is final or susceptible to judicial review. Several cases have established that judicial review could lie in respect of decisions *not* to prosecute. In *R v Chief Constable of Kent*[291] the question was whether a decision to continue a prosecution, against the advice of the local Juvenile Offender Liaison Team, could be impugned. The Home Office criteria for cautioning were satisfied, but the police, nevertheless, decided to go ahead with the prosecution on the basis that the injuries sustained exceeded the usual incidents of juvenile violence and that it was therefore in the public interest to prosecute.[292] This decision received the endorsement of the Crown Prosecution Service (CPS). The Divisional Court held that a decision of the CPS to continue or discontinue criminal proceedings was, in principle, susceptible to judicial review but only in very restricted circumstances.[293] It would have to be shown that the decision contravened a settled policy of the DPP, evolved in the public interest. Such instances of a complete disregard of public policy would be rare. The reluctance of the courts to interfere with prosecutorial decision-making continued in relation to the statutory scheme of reprimands and warnings. Thus, even where a child was prosecuted for an offence that would have ordinarily resulted in a final warning under the Gravity Factor Scheme, the court refused to overturn the decision of the prosecuting authorities.[294] However, more recently in *R (E) v DPP* (discussed above), a 14 year-old girl brought a successful judicial review claim against the CPS for its decision to prosecute her under the Sexual Offences Act 2003.[295] E argued that the Code of Crown Prosecutors and the relevant guidance[296] were unlawful for they failed to address the special case where a child is both victim and offender.

---

[290] Section 66ZB.

[291] *R v Chief Constable of Kent and Another ex parte L* [1991] Crim LR 841. See the commentaries on the case in C Eades 'The Decision to Prosecute Juveniles – No Review of the Actions of the Police and Crown Prosecution Service' (1991) JPN 358, and S Uglow, A Dart, A Bottomley and C Hale 'Cautioning Juveniles – Multi-Agency Impotence' [1992] Crim LR 632.

[292] The victim had sustained a fracture to the maxillary spine of his nose and had been knocked to the ground. As he lay there it was alleged that the accused had kicked him in the head.

[293] It was held that the initial decision of the police was not susceptible to judicial review since their power to prosecute had been severely limited by the setting up of the CPS.

[294] See *R (Harvey) v London Bus Services Ltd* [2002] EWHC 224 (Admin). Also see *R (F) v Crown Prosecution Service* [2003] EWHC 3266 (Admin) and *R (A) v South Yorkshire Police* [2007] EWHC 1261 (Admin).

[295] See the discussion above.

[296] CPS *Sexual Offences and Child Abuse by Young Offenders*, April 2010.

However, the court would not question the CPS guidance and it was successful only because the CPS had failed to take into account relevant considerations specific to the case.[297]

The question whether prosecutorial decisions may engage Art 8 ECHR was considered by the House of Lords in the case of *R v G* (discussed above). The House was split on whether Art 8 was engaged where a 15-year-old boy was charged with rape (of a child under 13) under s 5 of the Sexual Offences Act 2003, rather than the lesser offence under s 13. Three of the five judges held that Art 8 was engaged but only Lords Hope and Carswell held that G's right was disproportionately restricted.[298]

The investigative process

In general, the powers of arrest and detention that the police have are governed by the Police and Criminal Evidence Act 1984 (PACE 1984), and the accompanying Codes of Practice which regulate the detention, treatment and questioning of persons by police officers.[299] The police must also exercise those powers compatibly with the ECHR; Arts 5 and 6 are of particular relevance.[300] Given that children can experience difficulty asserting their rights – especially in stressful situations and when dealing with authority figures[301] – and given that they are more susceptible to making false confessions and self-incriminatory statements than adults,[302] the existence of special support for young suspects when detained and questioned by the police is crucial. In England and Wales this type of support is provided by the requirement in PACE that a child be accompanied by an appropriate adult who should 'safeguard the interests of children and young people detained or questioned by police officers'. However, the special protections afforded to children in police custody apply only to children *under* the age of 17. The Government had proposed to extend the provision to 17-year-olds, thus bringing the legislation and accompanying codes into line with the UNCRC (where a child is defined as person under 18) and the rest of the youth justice system,[303] but these were scrapped.[304] In 2013, a legal challenge was brought against the Secretary of

---

[297] See above.

[298] See the discussion above of the decision of the ECtHR in *G v United Kingdom* (Application No 37334/08) [2011] ECHR 1308.

[299] Police and Criminal Evidence Act 1984, s 66.

[300] On the relevance of the Human Rights Act see F Brookman and H Pierpoint 'The Implications of the Human Rights Act for Young Suspects and Remand Prisoners in England and Wales' (2002) 46 *Journal of the Institute of Justice and International Studies* 45.

[301] B Feld 'Juveniles' Waiver of Legal Rights: Confessions, *Miranda*, and the Right to Counsel' in T Grisso and R Schwatz (eds) *Youth on Trial: A Developmental Perspective on Juvenile Justice* (Chicago University Press, 2000).

[302] D Dixon 'Juvenile Suspects and the Police and Criminal Evidence Act' in D Freestone *Children and the Law: Essays in Honour of Professor HK Bevan* (Hull University Press, 1990) and see PACE Code of Practice C, Note 11C.

[303] Including the jurisdiction of the Youth Court and (since the Legal Aid Act 2012) the provisions relating to remand.

[304] See Nick Herbert MP, answer to written question on 16 July 2012, Hansard Col 549W.

State's decision not to amend PACE in order to bring 17-year-olds within the protective framework available to other children. In *R (HC) v Secretary of State for the Home Department*[305] it was held that the failure to either provide the 17-year-old applicant with the support of an appropriate adult or to inform his mother that he had been arrested was a breach of Art 8 which, following the decision in *ZH (Tanzania)*, required his best interests to be a primary consideration in line with Art 3 of the UNCRC. Since the UNCRC defines a child as a person under the age of 18, this included 17-year-olds, and giving primary consideration to the child's best interests required differential treatment from adults.[306] Treating 17-year-olds as adults upon arrest was therefore unlawful.

Where a juvenile is arrested, the arresting officer must, where practicable, ascertain the identity of the person responsible for that juvenile's welfare and must notify that person of the arrest.[307] This will normally be the juvenile's parent or guardian or, perhaps, social services, where he is being looked after by the local authority.[308] If the juvenile is then held in custody he must be told of her rights to have someone informed of her whereabouts and he has the right to a solicitor.[309] The appropriate adult must then generally be present at any interview with the juvenile,[310] when she is asked to sign a written statement, told of her rights, subject to an identification procedure, subject to an intimate strip search, asked to provide an intimate sample, or issued with a youth caution.[311] The juvenile must not be detained in a police cell without good reason and must not be allowed to come into contact with adult suspects.[312] As soon as practicable after the arrest, the 'custody officer'[313] must determine whether or not there is sufficient evidence to charge the juvenile. If not, she

---

[305] [2013] EWHC 982 (Admin).

[306] At the time of writing, PACE has not been amended to reflect the judgment but immediately after the judgment was handed down ACPO issued guidance that appropriate adults should be made available to 17-year-olds.

[307] Children and Young Persons Act 1933, s 34(2) and (3). See again HC (above) on the definition of 'juvenile' for these purposes.

[308] Ibid, s 34(5)(b) refers to 'any other person who has for the time being assumed responsibility for his welfare'.

[309] PACE 1984, ss 56 and 58.

[310] See the *Code of Practice for the Detention, Treatment and Questioning of Persons by Police Officers (Code C)*, at para 11.15–17.

[311] See Codes C and D. Failure to comply with these requirements may result in any evidence obtained during them being excluded from being used in court pursuant to PACE, s 78. For critiques of the practice relating to the use of appropriate adults, see J Williams 'The Inappropriate Adult' (2000) 22 JSWFL 43; H Pierpoint 'How appropriate are volunteers as "appropriate adults" for young suspects? The appropriate adult system and human rights' (2000) 22 JSWFL 383; H Pierpoint 'Reconstructing the Role of the Appropriate Adult in England and Wales' (2006) 6 *Criminology and Criminal Justice* 219; and H Pierpoint 'Extending and professionalising the role of the appropriate adult' (2011) 33 JSWFL139.

[312] Children and Young Persons Act 1933, s 31, which also prescribes that a girl should be under the care of a woman.

[313] The 'custody officer' is a designated police officer who is charged with the responsibility of ensuring that the statutory requirements and Code of Practice under PACE 1984 are observed. See PACE 1984, s 36(3), which provides that the officer appointed must be of at least the rank of sergeant.

must be released, with or without bail, unless her further detention is necessary: (1) to secure or preserve evidence relating to an offence for which he is under arrest; or (2) to obtain such evidence by questioning her.[314] The maximum period of detention without charge is 24 hours, but this may be extended on the authority of a superintendent or the court.[315]

Further detention of a juvenile

Where the juvenile is charged and further detention is necessary, PACE 1984,[316] as amended, imposes important duties on the custody officer. Ordinarily a child should be bailed until he is due to appear in court, but bail can be refused if one of the specified grounds in PACE is met.[317] Where a juvenile is charged and is to be detained, he ought, in all but exceptional circumstances, to be looked after by social services in local authority accommodation and not held in police custody.[318] This was the original intention reflected in PACE 1984 but there was evidence that the practice of police forces throughout the country differed significantly. The purpose of the amendments made by the Criminal Justice Act 1991 was to reinforce the policy of passing responsibility for the juvenile's accommodation to the local authority.[319]

Where the custody officer authorises an arrested juvenile to be kept in police detention, he must now secure that the juvenile is moved to local authority accommodation, unless he certifies:

(1) that, by reason of specified circumstances, it is impracticable for him to do so; or

(2) in the case of an arrested juvenile who has attained the age of 12 years, that no secure accommodation is available and that keeping him in other local authority accommodation would not be adequate to protect the public from serious harm from him.[320]

A report published in 2011 by the Howard League for Penal Reform, based on a series of Freedom of Information requests, suggests that considerable numbers of children are in fact held in cells overnight.[321] However, the courts are reluctant to hold that a failure to place a child in local authority

---

[314] PACE 1984, s 37(2).

[315] Ibid, ss 41, 42 and 43.

[316] Ibid, s 38(6).

[317] Section 38(1)(a) and (b).

[318] Section 38(6) PACE. See also s 21(2)(b) of the Children Act 1989.

[319] For further discussion, see C Bell 'New Criminal Justice Act amends PACE on detention of juveniles' (1991) 79 *Childright* 7.

[320] PACE 1984, s 38(6), as amended by the Criminal Justice Act 1991, s 59.

[321] Howard League for Penal Reform *The Overnight Detention of Children in Police Cells* (2011) (available http://www.howardleague.org/overnight-detention-research/, last visited 28 August 2012). The report found that 53000 children under the age of 16 had been detained overnight between 2008–2009.

accommodation is unlawful. In *R (M) v Gateshead MBC*[322] the Court of Appeal held that '[i]t is wholly unrealistic to expect local authorities to be able to guarantee that they will provide secure accommodation for children whenever a request is received from the police for such accommodation'[323] and a failure on the part of the local authority to provide such accommodation would be unlawful only where it had no arrangements in place at all, or the decision was *Wednesbury* unreasonable.

Remand and committal

Where a court remands a child or young person charged with or convicted of one or more offences, or commits her for trial or sentence, and she is not released on bail, he may be remanded to either non-secure or secure accommodation. In 1991, the Criminal Justice Act amended s 23 of the Children and Young Persons Act 1969 and prohibited the use of custodial remand for the under 17s, and required instead that all children under that age were to be remanded to local authority accommodation.[324] This could include the use of secure accommodation for 15–16-year-olds (but only in certain limited conditions)[325] and later, from 1994, the availability of secure accommodation was extended to 12–14-year-olds.[326] The arrangements for juvenile remand were complicated by the Crime and Disorder Act 1998. This Act limited the application of the Criminal Justice 1991 Act (the prohibition of custodial remand) to boys aged 12–14 years and girls aged 12–16.[327] Therefore, the legal prohibition on remand to *custody* no longer applied to 15–16-year-old boys, and instead a modified version of s 23 was introduced which allowed remand to local authority accommodation *only* if the boy is vulnerable and a place is available. Thus, there were two types of secure remand currently available: 'court ordered secure remand' was used for girls aged 12–16, boys aged 12–14 and 15–16-year-old vulnerable boys where a place is available in local authority accommodation; and remand to custody was used for all other 15–16-year-olds boys. Seventeen-year-olds were treated as adults for the purposes of remand.

The Legal Aid, Sentencing and Punishment of Offenders Act 2012 has amended this complex and seemingly discriminatory[328] framework.[329] The 2012 Act brings 17-year-olds within the remand system for juveniles (thus ensuring compliance with the UNCRC), and it introduces one secure remand order;

---

[322] [2006] EWCA Civ 221, [2006] QB 650.

[323] Ibid, at para 48.

[324] Section 23(1) Children and Young Persons Act 1969.

[325] Set out in the statute.

[326] Criminal Justice and Public Order Act 1994.

[327] See Secure Remands and Committals (Prescribed Description of Children and Young Persons) Order 1999 (SI 1999/1265).

[328] Though see *R (SR) v Nottingham Magistrates' Court* [2001] EWHC 802 (Admin) which held that the discrimination between girls and boys was legitimate and proportionate under the ECHR.

[329] See ss 91–107 of the Legal Aid Act 2012, which came into force in December 2012.

remand to youth detention accommodation.[330] The provisions apply equally to boys and girls over the age of 12, and the legislation tightens up the criteria that must be met before a child is remanded to detention.[331] The other significant aspect of the new legislation is that 'looked after' status is to be extended to *all* children remanded to youth detention accommodation.[332] Further, the cost for remand placements is to be transferred to local authorities. There will thus be some incentive on local authorities to keep children out of custodial remand.[333] In 2010–11, only 39 per cent of children who were placed in custodial remand went on to receive a custodial sentence and of the others, 29 per cent were acquitted and 32 per cent received a community or other sentence.[334] Attempts to reform the system of remand are therefore to be welcomed if they reduce the numbers of children unnecessarily detained.

Criminal courts

The UN Convention on the Rights of the Child requires a separate system of criminal justice for children.[335] This ensures that children do not come into contact with adult offenders whilst awaiting trial, during the trial, or whilst detained. But, as importantly, a separate youth justice system also helps to ensure that children are dealt with throughout the criminal justice processes in an age appropriate way, that takes account of their (usually) more limited capacity than adults and their (usually) greater vulnerabilities compared to adults. The establishment of a juvenile or youth court helps to achieve both of those aims. In England and Wales, a juvenile court with civil and criminal jurisdiction was first established by the Children Act 1908 which, since 1989, has been a criminal court only. In 1991, the remit of the Court was extended to include 17-year-olds[336] and its name changed to the 'youth court'.

The trials of most children charged with a criminal offence are heard in the youth court but there are about 2900 children per year committed to the adult crown court.[337] The youth court and the crown court are both bound by the duty in s 44(1) of the Children and Young Persons Act 1933 that regard must be had to the child's welfare. This is a weaker obligation than both the paramountcy principle under the Children Act 1989 and the primacy given to the child's 'best interests' by Art 3 UNCRC. This is because there are other considerations for the court to consider in criminal trials, including the interests

---

[330] Which can be a secure children's home, a secure training centre or a youth offender institution.
[331] A stricter definition of 'necessity' is required. See further, Hollingsworth (2012) above.
[332] Section 104 of the Legal Aid Act. On the disparities relating to care status within the pre-reformed system see J Driscoll and K Hollingsworth 'Accommodating Children in Need: *R (M) v Hammersmith and Fulham London Borough Council*' (2008) 20 CFLQ 522 and on the potential limits of the new reforms see Hollingsworth (2012) above.
[333] For example, by ensuring there is sufficient suitable non-secure accommodation.
[334] See YJB Statistics 2010–11 (12 January 2012).
[335] Article 40(3).
[336] Criminal Justice Act 1991, s 68.
[337] This is the data for 2011. Figures obtained by the author from the YJB.

of justice and the need to protect the public. Nonetheless, welfare is a principle that should inform the treatment of children during the trial process and sentencing.

Youth court

The youth court is a branch of the magistrates' court[338] made up of specially qualified and trained magistrates. The physical environment of the court is designed to be less intimidating and more inclusive than the crown court, for example magistrates do not wear wigs, the bench is not raised, and the accused child is not in a 'dock' but instead sits with her parents. To ensure that children and adults are kept separate the court cannot sit in a room which is used for normal criminal proceedings within one hour either side of those proceedings.[339] There are strict limits on public access to the court[340] and the reporting of the proceedings.[341] All of these various protections have led the High Court to conclude that the Art 6 rights of children, and specifically the right to 'effective participation', are satisfactorily protected in the youth court.[342]

Crown court

Although most children are tried in the youth court, about 3–5 per cent are committed for trial in the crown court.[343] A child can be referred to the crown court only in the circumstances set out in the Magistrates' Court Act 1980.[344] These include children who are jointly charged with an adult, and children who are charged with the most serious criminal offences. In most cases, the committal is at the discretion of the youth court, and the court must take

---

[338] On the history of the juvenile justice system and the juvenile court see M May 'Innocence and Experience: The Evolution of the Concept of Juvenile Delinquency in the Mid-Nineteenth Century' (1973) 17 *Victorian Studies*: 7, A Morris and H Giller, et al *Justice for Children* (The Macmillan Press Ltd, 1980); and W Cavenagh *Juvenile Courts, the Child and the Law* (Penguin Books, 1967).

[339] Children and Young Persons Act, s 47(2).

[340] Those allowed are members and officers of the court, the parties, their lawyers and others directly concerned with the case, witnesses, bona fide representatives of newspapers or news agencies and others specially authorised by the court. This contrasts with the position where the juvenile is tried in an adult magistrates' court or crown court. The hearings will normally be in open court, although there is power to clear the court in sensitive cases (Children and Young Persons Act 1933).

[341] Children and Young Persons Act 1933, s 47. The media must not name the juvenile or report identifying information, although there is power for the court to lift this restriction in order to avoid injustice to the juvenile or where he is unlawfully at large and charged with a violent or sexual or other serious offence (Children and Young Persons Act 1933, s 49). The converse is true in the adult magistrates' court or crown court, where the juvenile may be named unless the court orders otherwise.

[342] *R (TP) v West London Youth Court* [2005] EWHC 2583 (Admin). See *A Good Practice Guide for the Youth Court* (2001)(Home Office, Lord Chancellor's Department).

[343] Home Office *Youth Justice – The Next Steps* (Companion Document to *Every Child Matters*) (Home Office, 2003) and data obtained by the author from the YJB.

[344] Section 24 as amended by Criminal Justice Act 2003 (not yet fully in force).

account of the child's welfare. A child is usually only sent to the crown court if the youth court's own sentencing powers are inadequate.[345]

The decision to commit a child for trial in the crown court is significant not only because it opens up sentencing powers not available to the youth court[346] but also because the protections afforded to children are weaker. The use of crown court proceedings for children came under the spotlight as a result of the trial of 11-year-old Jon Venables and Robert Thompson for the murder of James Bulger in 1993[347] where the trial was conducted with only minor concessions to the children's age. After the conviction, the boys argued before the European Court of Human Rights that the trial process breached their Art 6 rights, in particular the right to effective participation. The court agreed and held that where a child is charged with a grave offence, and where there are high levels of media and public interest, the hearing must be conducted in a way which reduces, as far as possible, the child's feelings of intimidation and inhibition.[348] Following this ruling, Lord Bingham of Cornhill CJ issued a Practice Note[349] that implemented forthwith changes to the practice of the crown courts' conduct of the trials of children and young persons. The overriding principle is now that 'all possible steps should be taken to assist the young defendant to understand and participate in the proceedings' and that 'the ordinary trial process should so far as necessary be adapted to meet these ends'. It is explicitly reasserted that regard must be had to the young defendant's welfare as required by s 44 of the Children and Young Persons Act 1933. Among the changes required are that the trial be held, as far as practicable, in a courtroom in which all the participants are on the same or almost the same level; that a young defendant should be free to sit with a member of her family or others and in a place which facilitates easy, informal communication with legal representatives and others; that robes and wigs should not be worn; that the timetable for the trial should allow for frequent and regular breaks; and that those allowed to attend and report on the trial should be restricted.

However, despite these changes – which are certainly more than cosmetic – the UN Committee still considers the crown court to be an inappropriate place for children and that they should never be tried as adults in the ordinary courts.[350]

---

[345] See *R (H, A and O) v Southampton Youth Court* [2004] EWHC 2912 (Admin).

[346] Specifically custodial sentences over two years long. See below.

[347] On the murder and the trial see B Morrison *As If* (Granta Publications, 1997); D Smith *The Sleep of Reason* (Century, 2000), D Haydon and P Scraton 'Condemn a Little More, Understand a Little Less: The Political Context and Rights Implications of the Domestic and European Rulings in the Venables-Thompson Case' (2000) 27 JLS 416.

[348] See *V v United Kingdom* and *T v United Kingdom* (2000) 30 EHRR 121.

[349] [2000] 1 Cr App R 483.

[350] UN Committee on the Rights of the Child (2008), above.

Sentencing

The sentences that are available in relation to children and young persons have undergone quite significant changes over the last 14 years; first in the Crime and Disorder Act 1998, then the Youth Justice and Criminal Evidence Act 1999 and most recently the Criminal Justice and Immigration Act 2008. The changes that have taken place over the past 50 years in the context of sentencing are reflective of broader trends in youth justice and the movement along the welfare-justice spectrum.[351] During the 1960s, within the wider context of the welfare state, it seemed that the welfare model was in the ascendant and, although it can be argued that an increasingly punitive approach was taken in the following decades, there was still, in the 1970s and 1980s, an emphasis on diversion from the criminal courts and a preference for community-based rather than custodial sentences.[352] In the 1990s, however, there was a distinctly authoritarian shift, and the sentencing of juveniles took on an increasingly punitive ethos. Once again, juvenile crime was seen predominantly as a matter of personal responsibility, rather than principally the product of adverse social conditions or a disadvantaged family background. This appeared to be the philosophical basis of the Crime and Disorder Act 1998 although there were also aspects of this legislation that were grounded in the notion of 'restorative justice'.[353] Community sentences were rationalised in 2008 with the introduction of the youth rehabilitation order, and the formalisation of 'alternatives to custody' that had developed over the previous five years, such as intensive supervision and surveillance and intensive fostering. The most recent changes to the sentencing framework appear to mark a shift away from custody for young people, evidenced in part by the declining use of detention for young people.[354]

When sentencing juveniles, the courts must take account of a number of factors. First, there is a general instruction that a custodial sentence may be imposed where the offence is 'so serious' that only a custodial sentence can be justified[355] and, where a community sentence is proposed, it must be shown that the offence is 'serious enough' to warrant such a sentence.[356] Secondly, some sentences are limited to offenders over a particular age threshold, or by

---

[351] The history of youth justice shows some oscillation between welfare (focusing on the child's needs and characterised by discretion, an individual approach and rehabilitation) and justice (a focus on due process and proportionality of sentence) approaches.

[352] On the 'justice' versus 'welfare' debate, see C Ball 'Young Offenders and the Youth Court' [1992] Crim LR 277.

[353] The central tenet of restorative justice has been described as being that 'crime should be seen primarily as a matter concerning the offender and victim and their immediate families and thus should be resolved by them through constructive effort (restorative measures) to put right the harm that has been done'. See L Gelsthorpe 'Recent Changes in Youth Justice Policy in England and Wales' in I Weijers and A Duff *Punishing Juveniles: Principle and Critique* (Hart Publishing, 2002), at p 57.

[354] See Ministry of Justice, Home Office, and YJB *Youth Justice Statistics: 2010/11: England and Wales* (available at http://www.justice.gov.uk/downloads/statistics/youth-justice/yjb-statistics-10–11.pdf, last visited 24 August 2012).

[355] Criminal Justice Act 1991, s 1(2).

[356] Ibid, s 6(1).

maximum and minimum sentences set out in statute. Thirdly, the purposes of sentencing juveniles are set out in s 142A of the Criminal Justice Act 2003 (inserted by s 9 of the Criminal Justice and Immigration Act 2008). This provision structures the discretion of the sentencing courts (beyond the legislative upper and lower limits of sentencing) by providing a list of factors that should inform their decisions. These are similar to the factors that guide the sentencing of adults and include the punishment of offenders, reform and rehabilitation of offenders, protection of the public, and reparation by offenders to victims. There is one factor on the adult list that is not included however – 'reduction of crime (including its reduction by deterrence)'. This omission suggests that deterring others should not be relevant to the sentencing of children.[357] Section 142A of the Criminal Justice Act 2003 also instructs the courts to have regard to both the principal aim of the youth justice system to prevent offending and to the welfare of the child in accordance with s 44(1) of the Children and Young Persons Act 1933. Section 142A has not yet been brought into force but nonetheless the Sentencing Guidelines Council's guidance for the sentencing of juveniles places a strong emphasis on the welfare of the child and on preventing her offending.[358]

First tier sentences

First tier sentences are used for minor or first time offending. These include a deferred sentence, an absolute or conditional discharge, a fine, a compensation order, a reparation order, or the referral order.

Discharges

In cases which are perceived by the courts to be at the least serious end of the spectrum, they may either discharge the offender absolutely, or discharge him subject to a condition that he commits no further offences during a specified period not exceeding three years.[359] If he then re-offends, he will be in breach of the order, and may be brought back before the court and dealt with as the court had power to do originally. Discharges have the advantage that they do not count as convictions against the child or young person, except for limited purposes.[360]

---

[357] A Ashworth *Sentencing and Criminal Justice* (5th edn, Cambridge University Press, 2010).
[358] See above.
[359] Under the PCC(S)A 2000, s 12, the court may grant a discharge where it is of the opinion 'having regard to the circumstances including the nature of the offence and the character of the offender, that it is inexpedient to inflict punishment'. When the referral order was introduced (see below) if the referral conditions were met and the court did not intend to use an absolute discharge or imprisonment then the referral order was mandatory – conditional discharge was not available. This has been amended by the Legal Aid Act 2012 but the provision is not yet in force.
[360] PCC(S)A 2000, s 14.

Fines

Magistrates' courts and youth courts may impose fines subject to maximum levels prescribed by the statutes which create the various offences. The particular fine within the appropriate scale is then fixed in accordance with standard scales. This involves taking into account the gravity of the offence, the means of the person responsible for payment and any mitigating circumstances.[361] Where a juvenile is fined in the magistrates' or youth court there is a maximum fine of £1,000 where he is under 18, and £250 is the maximum in relation to a child aged under 14.[362] As noted above, parents may be required to pay the cost of the fine.

Compensation orders

Instead of, or in addition to, dealing with the offender in any other way, the court may order him to pay compensation to the victim for any personal injury, loss, or damage resulting from the offence, or any other offence taken into account.[363] As with other financial orders, parents may be required to pay the cost of the compensation order.

Reparation order

The court may order the child to make reparation (other than compensation) to the victim or the community at large where it is not proposing to order a custodial sentence, a youth rehabilitation order or a referral order.[364] The reparation must be proportionate to the offence or offences, and cannot exceed 24 hours aggregate of unpaid work.[365]

Referral order

The Youth Justice and Criminal Evidence Act 1999 introduced the referral order as an additional community sentence to be used in the youth court for most young people pleading guilty to their first offence.[366] The referral order was initially a mandatory order for all those children and young people pleading guilty to their first offence, where the offence was neither sufficiently serious to merit a custodial sentence, nor sufficiently minor to warrant an

---

[361] Criminal Justice Act 2003, s 164.

[362] PCC(S)A 2000, s 135. On defaulting on paying a fine, see s 39 Criminal Justice and Immigration Act 2008 which allows an unpaid work requirement (for those aged 16–17), an attendance centre requirement or a curfew requirement to be used when a child defaults (not yet in force).

[363] Ibid, s 130.

[364] PCC(S)A 2000, s 73.

[365] PCC(S) A 2000, s 74.

[366] The provisions in the 1999 legislation have now been replaced by the Powers of Criminal Courts (Sentencing) Act 2000, Part III, as amended by the Criminal Justice Act 2003, the Criminal Justice and Immigration Act 2008 and the Legal Aid Act 2012. For a critique of the original legislation see C Ball 'The Youth Justice and Criminal Evidence Act 1999 – Part I: A Significant Move Towards Restorative Justice, or a Recipe for Unintended Consequences?' (2000) Crim LR 211.

absolute discharge.[367] However, the Criminal Justice Act 2003 limited the circumstances in which the order is compulsory.[368] A referral order is now only mandatory where it is the young person's first conviction and the offence is one punishable by a custodial sentence; for all other offences it is discretionary (though it is still envisaged that the referral order will be the primary sentence used).[369] Amendments introduced by the Criminal Justice and Immigration Act 2008 have extended the availability of the discretionary order to those young people who have either already been convicted of an offence on one previous occasion but were not referred to a youth offender panel,[370] or who have been referred on only one previous occasion.[371] The Legal Aid Act 2012 extends it even further and remove entirely the limits on the number of times a referral order can be used.[372] The order is unavailable where a young person pleads not guilty to all the charges brought and is later found guilty.[373]

The effect of the order is to refer the young person to the youth offender panel. Panels provide an opportunity for the victim, the community (represented by two community panel members), the young person, and her parent(s),[374] to discuss the impact of the offending behaviour, to explore why it took place, and to draw up a contract, setting out the conditions that must be met by the young person to restore the harm caused and to prevent the young person from re-offending. It is one part of the youth justice system where restorative justice methods are employed.[375] The order can run from 3–12 months and conditions in the contract can include direct reparation to the victim (for example, an apology or compensation) or indirect reparation to the community (for example, painting and decorating, conservation work), work with the YOT (for example, on issues such as peer pressure, drug and alcohol misuse, victim

---

[367] Powers of Criminal Courts (Sentencing) Act 2000, ss 16 and 17. The referral order is not to be used where the young person has ever been bound over or where the offence has a fixed sentence in law, or where the child has been given a hospital order. Where a young person is charged with more than one offence, and pleads guilty to one but not guilty to one or more others, the power of the court to make a referral order is discretionary. See Powers of Criminal Courts (Sentencing) Act 2000, s 17(2). The Legal Aid Act 2012 allows a child to be conditionally discharged instead of a referral order being made.

[368] See Sixth Standing Committee on Delegated Legislation, 5 June 2003, col 3 and the resulting Referral Order (Amendment of Referral Conditions) Regulations 2003 (SI 2003/1605) which amends Powers of Criminal Courts (Sentencing) Act 2000, s 17.

[369] Ibid, as amended by the Coroners and Justice Act 2009, Sch 17.

[370] Section 17(2B) Powers of Criminal Courts (Sentencing) Act 2000 (as amended).

[371] In this case, the YOT worker or probation officer must recommend the order and the court consider there to be exceptional circumstances for its use. See s 17(2C) of the 2000 Act. In both of these cases, the previous conviction can have been either in a UK court or a court in another member state. See amendments introduced by the Coroners and Justice Act 2009.

[372] Section 79. These provisions are not yet in force at the time of writing.

[373] On an early evaluation of the referral order see A Crawford and T Newburn *Youth Offending and Restorative Justice: Implementing Reform in Youth Justice* (Willan Publishing, 2003).

[374] The court can order a parent to attend, and this will usually be the case if the child is under 16. Powers of Criminal Courts (Sentencing) Act 2000, s 20.

[375] Though on the difficulty of achieving restorative justice aims through youth offender panels see A Newbury 'I Would Have Been Able to Hear What They Think': Tensions in Achieving Restorative Outcomes in the English Youth Justice System' (2011) 11 *Youth Justice: An International Journal* 250.

awareness, anger management), or a requirement to attend school or work or to stay away from specified persons or places. A panel can refer a young person back to court if she fails to attend the meeting, if no agreement can be reached on the terms of the contract, or if the young person 'unreasonably' refuses to sign the contract after agreement is reached. A progress meeting can be held where the panel believes the young person has failed to comply with the terms of the contract.

Community sentence: the youth rehabilitation order

The Crime and Disorder Act 1998 introduced a wide range of new community orders for juveniles.[376] However, the Criminal Justice and Immigration Act 2008 sought to rationalise the community sentences for children through the introduction of a single community sentence: the youth rehabilitation order (YRO).[377] The YRO is a generic order which allows a court to choose from a 'menu' of specific requirements in determining the most appropriate response to the child's offending. The maximum length of the YRO is three years, and it can be used multiple times for the same offender, with the sentencing court determining on each occasion the most suitable components. As noted above, the court must consider the offence serious enough to warrant a YRO, and the restriction of liberty involved must be proportionate to seriousness of offence.[378] However, in contrast to adult offenders, a YRO can – in most cases – be imposed regardless of whether the offence is an imprisonable one.[379]

---

[376] These provisions were repealed and replicated in the Powers of the Courts (Sentencing) Act 2000.

[377] As amended by the Legal Aid Act 2012. The older provisions continue to apply to young people who committed offences prior to the new legislation coming into force (November 2009). See the previous edition of this book for details of those sentences which included (a) community rehabilitation order; (b) community punishment order; (c) community punishment and rehabilitation order; (d) curfew order; (e) supervision order; (f) attendance centre order; (g) drug treatment and testing order; and (h) action plan order.

[378] Sections 147–148 CJA Act 2003.

[379] See sentencing guidelines council, overarching guidance (above), at para 10.5. The exceptions are the intensive fostering requirement and the ISSP.

The requirements that are available for inclusion in the YRO replicate some of the community sentences introduced by the Crime and Disorder Act; others replicate non-statutory interventions.[380] The 18 different requirements are the:[381] activity requirement;[382] curfew requirement;[383] exclusion requirement;[384] local authority residence requirement;[385] education requirement;[386] mental health treatment requirement;[387] unpaid work requirement (16/17 years);[388] supervision requirement;[389] electronic monitoring requirement;[390] prohibited activity requirement;[391] drug treatment requirement and intoxicating substance treatment requirement;[392] drug testing requirement;[393] residence

---

[380] The provisions came into force in November 2009.

[381] See s 1(1)(a)–(o) Criminal Justice and Immigration Act 2008.

[382] Paragraph 6 of Sch 1 to the Criminal Justice and Immigration Act 2008. This requires the sentenced child to engage in prescribed activities for a period of days up to a maximum of 90.

[383] This can be used to require that the child remain in a particular place for periods of between 2–12 hours at a time (para 14) and is monitored through the use of electronic tagging, which must accompany the order (Sch 1, para 2).

[384] This order is used to prevent the child from certain places or areas for up to 3 months, and for the times specified in the order (para 15) and must be accompanied by an electronic tag (Sch 1, para 2).

[385] This requires the child to reside in local authority accommodation, but it can only be included in a YRO where the court is satisfied that the behaviour which constituted the offence was due to a significant extent to the circumstances in which the offender was living, and that the imposition of that requirement will assist in the offender's rehabilitation. Parents or guardians must be consulted, though neither their consent nor that of the child is necessary before it is used (Sch 1, para 16). The maximum period the child can be required to reside in local authority accommodation is six months, and this period cannot extend beyond the child's 18th birthday. This requirement can only be imposed where the child has been legally represented (Sch 1, para 19).

[386] This requires the child to attend education as arranged by her parents and approved by the local authority, but only if 'arrangements exist for the offender to receive efficient fulltime education suitable to the offender's age, ability, aptitude and special educational needs (if any), and (ii) that, having regard to the circumstances of the case, the inclusion of the education requirement is necessary for securing the good conduct of the offender or for preventing the commission of further offences' (Sch 1, para 25).

[387] This order can be used to require the child to undergo mental health treatment, including treatment in a residential hospital, though it can only be used if the child has shown a 'willingness' to comply with the requirement and only if the mental condition of the offender is such as requires and may be susceptible to treatment (Sch 1, para 20).

[388] This requires the child to work for between 40–240 hours.

[389] This requires the child to meet with the 'responsible officer' (usually a YOT worker) as and when required by the order (Sch 1, para 9).

[390] This order allows for the tagging of children when used in conjunction with other requirements.

[391] The court can prohibit the child from engaging in activities for a day or days specified, or for a specific period. There are no limits on these prohibitions, but the court does have to exercise its powers in accordance with the ECHR and Arts 8, 10 and 11 would be particularly pertinent (Sch 1, para 13).

[392] Where a child offender is dependent on, or has a propensity to misuse, drugs or other intoxicating substances, and the offender's dependency or propensity is such as requires and may be susceptible to treatment then a drug treatment/intoxicating substance requirement can be imposed, which can include residential treatment (para 22 and para 24 respectively).

[393] A child who is willing can be required to comply with drug testing where she is also undergoing drug treatment as part of the YRO (para 23).

requirement;[394] programme requirement;[395] and attendance centre requirement.[396] Two final components are specifically alternatives to custody: intensive supervision and surveillance and intensive fostering.

Intensive supervision and surveillance

This part of the order puts on a statutory basis what was previously the intensive supervision and surveillance programme. It comprises an extended activity requirement of between 90–180 days and a curfew and electronic monitoring (tagging). The ISS is an alternative to custody and thus it can only be imposed if the offence for which the child is being sentenced is an imprisonable one and but for the use of ISS a custodial sentence would be 'appropriate'; and, if the child is under the age of 15, he is a persistent offender.[397] Interestingly, although a custodial sentence cannot be imposed by the youth court for a child under the age of 12,[398] the ISS – an 'alternative' to custody – can be used for the 10–11 year age group.

Intensive fostering

The court can require intensive fostering provided the same conditions are met as are required for ISS (though the two orders are mutually exclusive and cannot be imposed in conjunction with one another), and also if the court is satisfied:(a) that the behaviour which constituted the offence was due to a significant extent to the circumstances in which the offender was living; and (b) that the imposition of a fostering requirement would assist in the offender's rehabilitation.[399] Before an intensive fostering requirement is imposed, the consent of the child's parents and the relevant local authority that will place the child must be obtained. Although the child is being removed from her parents and placed into the care of the state the protections of the Children Act 1989 do not apply.[400] However, there is a requirement that the child must have had legal representation before this element is imposed (similarly with the local authority residence requirement), recognising at least partially the impact of the order on the child's rights (especially Art 8 ECHR). The child can only be fostered for up to 12 months, and if a foster placement is not available she will be subject instead to the local authority residential requirement.[401]

---

[394] This order can be used to require a 16–17-year-old to reside with a particular person, with that person's consent (para 15).

[395] This requires the child to participate in a programme of activities which may be residential (para 10 of Sch 1).

[396] The child must attend for the requisite number of hours (but no more than three hours in any one day) an attendance centre. For children under 14, the maximum number of hours is 12, for those aged 14–15, the order should be between 12–24 hours, and for those aged 16–17 the attendance is for 12–36 hours.

[397] Section 1(4) Criminal Justice and Immigration Act 2008.

[398] See below regarding the detention and training order.

[399] Paragraph 4 of Sch 1 to the Act.

[400] For a critique of this see K Hollingsworth 'Children's Rights at the Margins of Youth Justice'(2008) *Youth Justice: An International Journal* 229.

[401] Paragraph 18 of Sch 1.

In deciding which of the components to include within an order *and* the length of the order, the Sentencing Guidelines Council instructs sentencing courts that the key factors are the assessment of the seriousness of the offence, the objective(s) the court wishes to achieve, the risk of re-offending, the ability of the offender to comply, and the availability of requirements in the local area. The introduction of risk of re-offending in the length of the sentence, as well as its content, appears to move away from a retributive 'just deserts' approach to sentencing young people.[402] There is a considerable amount of discretion placed on sentencing courts and on YOTs who compile the pre-sentence reports which make the recommendations to the court as to the child's risk and the availability of certain programmes and so on within their area. Some of the components of the YRO are clearly very intrusive into the child's life, including her private and family life and her right to liberty where residential requirements are imposed. The courts must however, exercise its powers in compliance with the ECHR.

Custodial sentences

The UN Convention on the Rights of the Child requires that custody is used only as a last resort[403] but the high rates of custody for juveniles in England and Wales, especially up until 2008, have resulted in criticism from the UN Committee on the Rights of the Child. Throughout the late 1990s and most of the first decade of the 21st century, England and Wales had one of the highest rates of juvenile custody in Europe. However, in the last 4 years, the YJB's annual statistics show that custodial sentences for juveniles are declining, with the average population in custody in 2010–11 down to 2040 from a highpoint of approximately 3000 in 2002–03.[404]

The statutory framework for custodial sentences is both permissive and restrictive. The Criminal Justice Act 1991[405] limited the use of custodial sentences generally by establishing a threshold for their use, and this applied as much to young offenders as it did to adults. The conditions are now contained in the Powers of the Criminal Courts (Sentencing) Act 2000.[406] The key concept is that of *proportionality*. Before making a custodial sentence the court must be satisfied that either:

(a)   the offence, or the combination of the offence and one or more offences associated with it, was *so serious* that only such a sentence can be justified for it; or

---

[402]   On the potential limitations of this, and the impact on children's rights, see T Bateman 'Punishing Poverty: The "Scaled Approach" and Youth Justice Practice' (2011) 50 *The Howard Journal of Criminal Justice* 171.

[403]   Article 37.

[404]   YJB statistics 2010–11, 12 January 2012.

[405]   Criminal Justice Act 1991, s 1(2).

[406]   Section 79.

(b) that the offence is a violent or sexual offence, and that only such a sentence would be adequate to protect the public from serious harm from the offender.

Assuming this threshold is crossed, a custodial sentence can be used.

Children who are sentenced to custody are placed in one of three types of secure accommodation:[407] youth offender institutions (YOIs), secure training centres (STCs) and local authority secure children's homes (LASCHs).[408] YOIs are prison-type accommodation, run by the Prison Service and regulated by prison service rules. YOIs accommodate 80 per cent of juveniles held in the secure estate, and these are usually those young offenders who are older and less vulnerable.[409] LASCHs are run by local authorities and typically house only a small number of children; they are governed by the Care Standards Act 2000 and the Children's Home Regulations 2001.[410] There are four privately run STCs, subject to the STC rules. The decision to place a child in one particular type of institution over another is a matter of discretion for the YJB and (in the case of those sentenced in the crown court) the Secretary of State. Given the very different ethos and care provided in the three types of institution, it is unsurprising that placement decisions have occasionally been subject to judicial review challenge, but they are rarely successful.[411] More successful have been the challenges to the policies and rules that apply within the institution and which affect the way in which children are treated therein. For example, in 2002 the landmark decision by Mr Justice Munby in *R (Howard League for Penal Reform) v Secretary of State for the Home Department* held that the obligations placed on local authorities by the Children Act 1989 to children in need in their area continue to apply when the child is in a YOI. Additionally, local authorities have responsibility for children in custody who prior to sentence were subject to a care order under s 31 of the Children Act 1989, or who are care leavers. Children who are 'looked after' children because they are voluntarily accommodated under s 20 of the Children

---

[407] The first penal institution used exclusively for children was Parkhurst prison for boys in 1838. Since then, various types of penal institutions have been used to house children and young people: reformatories, industrial schools, Borstals, approved schools, detention centres, and youth custody centres. See B Goldson 'New Punitiveness: The Politics of Child Incarceration' and J Muncie 'Failure Never Matters: Detention Centres and the Politics of Deterrence' both in J Muncie, G Hughes, E McLaughlin (eds) *Youth Justice: Critical Readings* (Sage Publications, 2002).

[408] The YJB commissions places in secure children's homes, where children in 'criminal justice' beds are cared for alongside children in 'welfare' beds (ie those children accommodated under s 25 Children Act 1989). The YJB has decommissioned the number of places in LASCH's in recent years in response to the decrease in the numbers of children sentenced to custody. This decision was subject to an unsuccessful judicial review challenge in *R (Secure Services Ltd and others) v Youth Justice Board and others* [2009] EWHC 2347 (Admin).

[409] B Goldson 'Damage, Harm and Death in Child Prisons in England and Wales: Questions of Abuse and Accountability' (2006) 45 *Howard Journal for Criminal Justice* 449.

[410] The regulations apply to all children accommodated by local authorities, whether through the criminal justice route or the care and protection route.

[411] See for example, *R v Secretary of State for the Home Department, ex parte J; R v Same, ex parte B* (The Independent, 20 July 1998).

Act 1989 lose that status upon entering custody, but since April 2011 duties are also now imposed on local authorities towards this group of 'former looked after children'.[412] The increased duties regarding the provision of education and training for children subject to youth detention, contained within the Apprenticeships, Skills, Children and Learning Act 2009,[413] is further recognition of the specific obligations that the state has towards detained children *qua* children. However, safeguarding of children in custodial institutions continues to be a particular concern, and has been highlighted in a number of prison inspection reports. Children sentenced to custody have very high levels of prior disadvantage,[414] which can be compounded by their experiences in custody. It is not unusual for children in detention to die,[415] as exemplified by the cases of Adam Rickwood and Gareth Wyatt who both died in STCs (the other deaths have been in YOIs).[416] One of the contributing factors in Adam's death was the treatment he received at the hands of those charged with his 'care' and specifically the use of painful restraint techniques for 'good order and behaviour'. These techniques were only outlawed following the decision in *R (C) v The Secretary of State for Justice* when the Court of Appeal held that the STC rules which allowed painful restraint techniques to be used against children for the purposes of good behaviour and order constituted a breach of Art 3 ECHR, and were thus unlawful.[417]

The trends towards improving the conditions within custodial institutions is to be welcomed, as is the improvement in alternatives to custody and the drops in the rates of detention for children. However, there remains a long way to go before the juvenile custodial estate in England and Wales fully complies with the requirements of the UNCRC. The next sections set out the framework for sentencing children to custody.

Detention and training order (DTO)

The detention and training order was introduced by the Crime and Disorder Act 1998.[418] It is the principal custodial sentence for offenders between the ages of 12[419] and 17 and replaces the former detention in a young offender institution (for 15–17-year-olds) and the secure training order (which was

---

[412]   Children Act 1989, s 23ZA and SI 2010/2797 (England) and SI 2011/699 (Wales).

[413]   See chapter 17.

[414]   J Jacobson, B Bhardwa, T Gyateng, G Hunter, and M Hough *Punishing disadvantage: a profile of children in custody* (Prison Reform Trust, 2010).

[415]   There have been 33 deaths of young people in custody since 1990, including two deaths in January 2012. See T Bateman 'Two more children die in English Prisons' (2012) 12 *Youth Justice* 146.

[416]   Ibid.

[417]   [2008] EWCA Civ 882, [2009] QB 657. See also *Children's Rights Alliance for England v Secretary of State for Justice* [2013] EWCA Civ 34 [2013] HRLR 17 where an unsuccessful argument was made that the Secretary of State had a duty to inform children who had been unlawfully subject to restraint that they had a potential claim for damages.

[418]   Sections 73–79, and now governed by PCC(S)A 2000, ss 100–107.

[419]   The DTO does not currently extend to 10–11-year-olds but the Secretary of State has the statutory power to extend it if she so wishes.

available in relation to children aged between 12 and 14 years).[420] There are limits to the use of a DTO: it can only be used where the offence is one for which an adult could be imprisoned and the offence is so serious that only a custodial sentence is justified[421] and in relation to an offender under the age of 15 at the time of conviction, the order may be made only where the court is satisfied that she is 'a persistent offender'.[422]

The legislation is quite specific about the possible length of order which may only be for 4, 6, 8, 10, 12, 18 or 24 months.[423] Half of this period is spent in custody, detention and training while the other half is spent in the community under the supervision of a probation officer, social worker or a member of the youth offending team.

Most children sentenced to custody receive a detention and training order but 19 per cent are serving long-term sentences under ss 90 and 91 of the Powers of Criminal Courts (Sentencing) Act 2000.

Custodial sentences for serious offences (s 91)

Section 91 of the Powers of Criminal Courts (Sentencing Act) 2000 is used only when a sentence of over two years is expected and which can only be imposed by the crown court. This often marks the threshold for the child being tried or sentenced in the crown court.[424]

Detention during Her Majesty's pleasure

Children or young persons convicted on indictment for murder *must* be sentenced to detention during Her Majesty's pleasure.[425] The young person concerned must have been under 18 at the time of the commission of the offence. This power has been the subject of extensive criticism and litigation before both the English courts and the ECtHR.[426] The central issue has been the essential indeterminacy of such orders and, as a result of actions brought under the ECHR, the British Government was required to amend the law. A

---

[420] Prior to this children under 15 could only be sentenced to custody in the crown court for very serious offences.

[421] Powers of Criminal Courts (Sentencing) Act 2000, s 100(1)(b).

[422] PCC(S)A 2000, s 100(2)(a). There is no statutory definition for this term but see the Sentencing Guideline Councils' guidance (see above). The DTO can be used for 10–11-year-olds but only if it is necessary to protect the public and the Secretary of State has appointed a date after which it can be so used (which s/he has not, as noted above).

[423] Ibid, s 101.

[424] See above.

[425] Ibid, s 90, formerly Children and Young Persons Act 1933, s 53(1).

[426] See particularly, *Hussain v United Kingdom* (1996) 22 EHRR 1, *R v Secretary of State for the Home Department ex parte Thompson and Venables* [1997] 2 FLR 471 and *V and T v United Kingdom* (2000) 30 EHRR 121. For a more detailed discussion of these cases, see the second edition of this work, at pp 502–503, and J Fortin *Children's Rights and the Developing Law* (2nd edn, Butterworths, 2003), at pp 580–583.

particularly notorious case, which provided the focal point for these concerns, was that of Thompson and Venables, the two young boys convicted of murdering two-year-old James Bulger.

Before the matter was challenged in the courts, children detained under this provision were detained subject to a minimum initial 'tariff' period followed by a 'post-tariff' period. The period of detention would be reviewed and an assessment of the risk to the public made. The length of both the tariff and the post-tariff periods was ultimately decided by a politician, the Home Secretary, and not by a judge or the Parole Board. As a result of the successful challenge in *Hussain v United Kingdom* the post-tariff period and the question of final release were shifted from the Home Secretary to the Parole Board.[427] Then the decision of Michael Howard, the then Home Secretary, to increase the initial tariff period in the case of Thompson and Venables was quashed by the House of Lords, which took the view, inter alia, that the approach to the tariff in the case of young offenders was not to be equated with the approach in the case of adults. The policy had to be sufficiently flexible that it could take into account, by continuing review, any progress or development of the child in addition to considerations of retribution, deterrence and risk – in other words, welfare considerations. Finally, the decision on the tariff period was wrested from the control of the Home Secretary and given to the judges by the decision of the ECtHR in *V and T v United Kingdom*.[428] However, as Jane Fortin notes,[429] the consequence has not been a less punitive approach, in that judges must now, when sentencing children convicted of murders, operate a presumption or starting point of a tariff of 12 years which may be increased or reduced depending on the circumstances. Whether this is compatible with the 'last resort' principle of the UNCRC remains to be seen.

Sentences for dangerous offences

The Criminal Justice Act 2003 provides additional sentencing powers for both adults and children where either a serious offence,[430] or a specified offence,[431] is committed and the court considers there is a significant risk that the offender will commit another specified offence causing serious harm.[432] Section 226 provides that where the offence carries a life sentence under s 91 of the 2000 Act then that *must* be imposed if the seriousness of the offence justifies it,[433] and if not, the court *may* impose a sentence of detention for public

---

[427] In order to comply with Art 5(4) ECHR.

[428] Above. See C McDiarmid 'Children Who Murder: What is Her Majesty's Pleasure?' 2000 Crim LR 547.

[429] Above, fn 426, at p 836.

[430] Defined as a serious sexual or violent offence, specified in Sch 15, which carries a maximum sentence of 10 years or more (for children, see s 226, the detention for life and public protection sentence).

[431] In Sch 15 (for children it applies to s 228, the extended sentence).

[432] Serious harm is defined in s 224(3) as meaning 'death or serious personal injury, whether physical or psychological'.

[433] This applies to serious offences *other* than murder. Those convicted of murder are sentenced to detention during her Majesty's pleasure. See below.

protection.[434] These are indeterminate sentences.[435] If a child under 18 is convicted of a specified offence, and the risk criteria are met and where the sentence for life does not apply, the court *may* impose an extended sentence under s 228.[436] The provisions thus provide for longer sentences on the basis of risk relating to the offender's dangerousness, as perceived at the time of sentencing.[437]

Return to the community

Children on DTOs serve half of the sentence in custody and half in the community under supervision. For children sentenced for dangerous offences or detained during her majesty's pleasure then an application for release is made to the Parole Board. The Parole Board must comply with principles of fairness in its decision-making, as it must for all prisoners seeking release. However, in *K v Parole Board*, Mr Justice McCombe held that the Parole Board is 'obliged to be particularly scrupulous in observing its obligations of fairness in a case considering the liberty of one so young',[438] this might include, for example, the assistance of an adult in preparing a representation and an oral hearing.

When children leave custody, their resettlement back into the community is principally the responsibility of the youth offending team. Resettlement support for children has improved over the past decade as a result of increased funding and a concerted effort on the part of the YJB. The support now mirrors, in some ways, that provided to children leaving care.[439] However, unlike the leaving care provisions under the Children Act 1989,[440] resettlement support is not founded in primary legislation but in soft law such as Prison Service Instructions, YJB polices, and the National Standards for Youth Justice.[441] Where child custody-leavers fall into the category of child in need, looked after child or care-leaver, local authorities Children's Services departments must meet their obligations to them under the Children Act 1989.

---

[434] Where the notional minimum term is at least two years. This provision has been repealed by the Legal Aid Act 2012, Sch 19(1), para 17 but the repeal has not yet come into force. See DA Thomas 'The Legal Aid, Sentencing and Punishment of Offenders Act 2012: the sentencing provisions' (2012) Crim LR 572.

[435] On the role of the Parole Board see Howard League 'Parole 4 Kids: A Review of the Parole Process for Children in England and Wales' (Howard League for Penal Reform, 2007) and see below.

[436] As amended by the Criminal Justice and Immigration Act 2008.

[437] On the meaning of dangerous, see *R v Lang* [2005] EWCA Crim 2864.

[438] [2006] EWHC 2413 (Admin), at para 28. See further K Hollingsworth 'Protecting the rights of children leaving custody: *R (K) v Parole Board* and *R (K) v Manchester CityCouncil*' (2007) *Journal of Social Welfare and Family Law* 163.

[439] See chapter 10.

[440] As amended by the Children (Leaving Care) Act 2000.

[441] See further K Hollingsworth 'Securing Responsibility, Achieving Parity? The Legal Support for Children Leaving Custody' (2013) *Legal Studies* 22.

In particular, where a child leaving custody is homeless she will be a child in need[442] and the duty to accommodate under s 20 of the Children Act 1989 applies.

Conclusion

The shape of the youth justice system in England and Wales remains based on the reforms of New Labour which brought an emphasis on prevention and responsibility, including the increased responsibility of parents. However, the deregulation and 'Big Society' agenda of the current Coalition Government is resulting in some piecemeal reform. This includes changes to the system of diversion, increased devolution of responsibility to local authorities for custodial placements, and the introduction of payment by results in some parts of the youth justice system. These changes – especially when coupled with shrinking budgets – may help to consolidate the downward trends in the numbers of children being brought into the criminal justice system and the use of custody for minors. This may, in turn, help to bring an alignment with the principles of the rights of children in conflict with the law, as set out in the UN Convention on the Rights of the Child.[443]

---

[442] *R (G) v Barnett Borough Council* [2003] UKHL 57, [2004] 1 FLR 454.
[443] See Hollingsworth (2012) above.

Chapter 16

CHILDREN AND THE CIVIL LAW

INTRODUCTION

We now turn our attention from the criminal law to the civil law. Family law, with which most of this book is concerned, is itself a branch of the civil law but we are concerned in this chapter with those areas which are not directly related to the child's position in the family. We are dealing primarily with those legal issues which can arise from the child's activities outside the home. We have already seen[1] that young people do not acquire capacities and responsibilities all at once, on attaining majority, but at different ages, depending on the activity in question,[2] and it has been noted that this can give rise to difficult questions about the relationship between the child's own capacities and the responsibilities of parents.[3] We now concentrate on three key and related areas of the civil law – the law of tort, contract and employment. Little is written on these subjects as they affect children beyond what can be gleaned from the standard texts.[4] Useful comparisons can, however, be made with Scots law where, following a wide-ranging report on the legal capacities and responsibilities of minors and pupils in 1987, there was legislation on the subject in 1991.[5]

The central themes of the civil law, like those of the criminal law, are *protection and responsibility*. What special protections are afforded children where they are injured by the actions of third parties or where children purport to enter into contracts (whether of employment or otherwise) which are, objectively judged, not in their best interests? To what extent are children responsible for their own actions which lead to the injury of third parties or to commercial loss, as where a trader has dealt fairly with a minor who then defaults? The answers which the law gives reflect a compromise between the desire to protect children, either

---

[1] At chapter 8 above.

[2] For a good review of the various age limits, see *At What Age Can I?* published periodically by the Children's Legal Centre.

[3] See especially chapter 8 above in relation to medical issues where most of the difficulties have arisen.

[4] An exception is Roderick Bagshaw's excellent treatment of children in the law of torts. See R Bagshaw 'Children Through Tort' in J Fionda (ed) *Legal Concepts of Childhood* (Hart Publishing, 2001). For the liability of local authorities towards children in their care or for failure to take action to prevent abuse or neglect, see chapter 10 above.

[5] Scot Law Com No 110 *Report on the Legal Capacity and Responsibility of Minors and Pupils* (1987) implemented by the Age of Legal Capacity (Scotland) Act 1991. For commentary on the Act, see JM Thomson *Family Law in Scotland* (6th edn, Bloomsbury Professional Ltd, 2011), ch 10.

from themselves or from the exploitation of others, and the need to avoid unnecessary hardship to those who deal with children in good faith.

CHILDREN AND THE LAW OF TORT

There are two broad aspects of the law of tort which affect children. The first is the question of civil liability for interferences with, or injuries to, children by third parties or by their carers. The second is the issue of the liability which children themselves have for their own tortious acts. In each case, difficult questions arise about the extent of the parental duty to *protect*.[6] Where a child is injured at home, this may be the result of negligence by the parent or other carer or it may be a pure accident. Essentially, this turns on what ought to have been expected of the reasonably prudent parent.[7] Where a child is injured outside the home, this may again be attributable to the negligence of the carer, that of a third party or the negligence of both of them, but again, it may be an accident for which no one is to be held responsible. Conversely, where a child causes injury to someone, this may be solely the responsibility of the child, the result of negligence by the carer or, again, just accidental.

The extent of control, as an aspect of parental responsibility, is also a central feature of the so-called 'intentional torts' involving trespass to the person whether by assault, battery or false imprisonment. It is accepted that the right to control and discipline the child is an element of parental responsibility and, indeed, a failure to exercise that responsibility might conceivably give rise to an action in negligence against the parent. But how far does this go? As the child gets older, the *Gillick* case and the Children Act 1989[8] both support the notion of a gradual relaxation of parental authority and control. Thus, certain purported exercises of parental discipline may themselves be tortious, if they exceed the bounds of reasonableness. A related issue here is the extent to which (if at all) a third party may be held liable for interfering with parents in the discharge of their responsibilities.

Protection of children

Torts based on negligence

The tort of negligence is committed where a duty of care is owed, there is a breach of that duty, and someone (a child for present purposes) is injured as a result.[9] In order to establish this, it needs to be proved, on the balance of

---

6   The duty which is recognised by implication in the Children and Young Persons Act 1933, s 1, as to which see chapter 15 above.

7   It is of course the case that prolonged negligence of the child's needs at home or inadequate supervision which places a child at risk may result in action by a local authority. Indeed, cases of neglect are numerically the most significant basis for care proceedings by some distance. See chapter 12 below.

8   See chapter 8.

9   See, generally: WHV Rogers *Winfield and Jolowicz on Tort* (18th edn, Sweet & Maxwell, 2010),

probabilities, that the defendant failed to avoid acts or omissions which were foreseeably likely to injure the child. The child will then have a claim for damages.

As a general proposition, the standard of care required towards children is higher than that towards adults.[10] Conversely, children themselves (especially young children) are not expected to exercise the same degree of care as adults.[11] While these are general principles of the law of negligence, they have been applied more specifically by statute in the context of occupiers' liability. This legislation governs the liability of 'occupiers'[12] for injuries caused to those on land or structures under their control. The natural curiosity of children and their propensity for straying into hazardous environments has generated a mass of reported cases over a substantial period of years.[13]

The chapter begins by looking at the principles which have emerged in this area of applied negligence. It then considers the tort of negligence itself, in its application to parental failings.

Occupiers' liability

The liability of occupiers is governed by the Occupiers' Liability Acts of 1957 and 1984. The extent of the duty owed depends on whether the injured person was a 'visitor' (the 1957 Act) or a 'non-visitor' (the 1984 Act). Essentially, the distinction is between those persons who were invited onto the property or were otherwise there with the express or implied permission of the occupier, and those who were not – usually, but not always, trespassers.[14] In the case of

---

ch 5; P Giliker and S Beckwith, *Tort* (4th edn, 2011), ch 2. For a substantial collection of cases and materials with commentary see J Steele, *Tort Law: Text, Cases and Materials* (2nd edn, Oxford University Press, 2011), ch 3.

10 The general standard of care was summed up by Alderson B in *Blyth v Birmingham Waterworks Co* (1856) 11 Ex 781 at 784 where he said: 'Negligence is the omission to do something which a reasonable man, guided upon those considerations which ordinarily regulate the conduct of human affairs, would do, or doing something which a prudent and reasonable man would not do'. Clearly, a reasonable man would appreciate the need for greater caution where children are concerned. An obvious example is child pedestrians.

11 See below. On children's duties generally, see chapter 7 above.

12 Essentially, the concept of 'occupier' is related to control rather than ownership of property although the two will frequently coincide. The test is laid down in *Wheat v Lacon & Co Ltd* [1966] AC 552.

13 For an excellent, albeit now somewhat dated, review, see R Kidner 'The Duty of Occupiers Towards Children' (1988) 139 *Northern Ireland Legal Quarterly* 150.

14 The Occupiers' Liability Act 1957 abolished the former distinction between 'invitees' and 'licensees'. See *Winfield and Jolowicz on Tort* (18th edn, Sweet & Maxwell, 2010), at pp 445 et seq, Giliker and Beckwith, op cit n 9, ch 8 and Steele, op cit n 9, ch 12. In fact, the position is somewhat more complex than this since there is a category of those who enter by virtue of a legal right, such as the use of a public right of way, who are neither visitors nor trespassers. The effect of the House of Lords ruling in *McGeown v Northern Ireland Housing Executive* [1995] 1 AC 233 is that there is no liability for negligent non-feasance in these circumstances. Thus the occupier is under a duty not to add to the danger but not to take positive steps to avoid it. In this case there was no liability for failure to keep a footpath in good repair.

children, the distinction is not as marked as with adults and many of the cases have, for obvious reasons, involved at least technical trespasses by children.[15]

Children as visitors – the Occupiers' Liability Act 1957

The 'common duty of care' owed to visitors is 'a duty to take such care as in all the circumstances of the case is reasonable, to see that the visitor will be reasonably safe in using the premises for the purposes for which he is invited or permitted by the occupier to be there'.

The duty is, therefore, not an unlimited one, but is only to take such precautions as are *reasonable*. In deciding whether there has been a breach of duty, account must be taken of the degree of care, or want of care, which would ordinarily be looked for in the visitor.[16] For these purposes, the Occupiers' Liability Act 1957 singles out children as a special case and provides that 'an occupier must be prepared for children to be less careful than adults'.[17]

What then is the requisite standard of care? It is first established that allowances must be made for the greater vulnerability of children. Something which would not be a danger to an adult might be a danger to a child. This is illustrated by *Moloney v Lambeth Borough Council*[18] where a four-year-old child fell through a balustrade protecting a staircase leading from a ground-floor to a first-floor flat. The gaps in the railings were not wide enough for an adult to fall through but were wide enough for a child of the age and size of the plaintiff. The defendant council was held liable on the basis that it ought to have anticipated that young children would use the staircase when unaccompanied by adults. The design of the staircase did not conform with the council's common duty of care owed to a child of that age. A second, long-established, principle is that an occupier may be liable where he has created, or is aware of, an 'allurement' to children, but fails to guard against it. Over 90 years ago, Glasgow Corporation fell foul of this principle.[19] It was held liable to the father of a deceased seven-year-old child who had eaten poisonous 'deadly nightshade' berries from a shrub in public gardens controlled by the Corporation. The berries were attractive and accessible to children, and the Corporation was aware that the area was frequented by them. Yet it took no steps either to fence off the shrub or warn of the danger.

The courts have had to confront the difficulty in the case of young children that virtually anything can be a danger. Is there then an obligation on occupiers to make their premises as safe as a nursery? The courts have avoided this extreme conclusion, first by finding that children were trespassers in some

---

[15] See, for example, *Glasgow Corp v Taylor* [1922] 1 AC 44.

[16] Occupiers' Liability Act 1957, s 2(3).

[17] Ibid, s 2(3)(a).

[18] (1966) LGR 440.

[19] *Glasgow Corp v Taylor* [1922] 1 AC 44. The concept of allurement could have the effect of preventing the child being regarded as a trespasser.

circumstances where unaccompanied by adults,[20] and secondly, more realistically, by limiting occupiers' duties to take into account parents' own responsibilities to young children. The essential point is that where a young child comes into contact with a man-made or natural hazard this may be at least as much the fault of the parent, for failing to supervise the child, as it is the fault of the occupier.

In *Phipps v Rochester Corporation*,[21] a boy aged five years, out picking blackberries with his seven-year-old sister, broke his leg when he fell into a trench which his sister had safely negotiated. The trench was part of a building site adjoining the plaintiff's home. In exonerating the council, Devlin J held that the council would discharge its duty of care if it reduced the dangers present to those which would either be obvious to a parent or, if not obvious, it warned against them. He emphasised the primary duty of parents to ensure that young children did not wander about on their own or that, if they did, they were allowed to go only to safe places. If, on the other hand, an occupier ought to have anticipated the presence of young unaccompanied children, this could impose a duty to take appropriate precautionary measures.

These principles were applied to natural hazards in *Simkiss v Rhondda Borough Council*.[22] Here, the seven-year-old plaintiff slid down a Welsh mountainside on a picnic blanket. The mountain had a bluff or steep slope which became very steep at the bottom. The plaintiff sustained a fractured skull when she fell 30 to 40 feet onto the road below. The Court of Appeal held that the council was not obliged either to fence the mountain or to warn of the sharp drop, despite the evidence that unaccompanied children were known to play in the vicinity. The prudent parent, it was said, would warn his children of such natural hazards.[23] As Dunn LJ remarked, an occupier was not bound to fence every tree simply because a child might climb it and fall out of it. It should be remembered, however, that this principle applies only to those hazards, natural or unnatural, which would be obvious to a prudent parent. Where the danger is latent or concealed, the duty is squarely on the occupier, if he knows of it, to take precautions. A recent tragic example in similar vein is the decision of the Court of Appeal in *Bourne Leisure Limited v Marsden*[24] where Matthew Marsden, aged two and a half, drowned in a pond in the holiday park operated and occupied by the defendant company. The Court of Appeal allowed the occupiers' appeal against the judge's finding that they had breached their duty of care to visitors. Matthew had wandered away from his mother's care in a moment as she was distracted by talking to a neighbour at his caravan. The Court found that it was not a breach of duty for the occupiers to fail to give a

---

[20] The so-called 'conditional licence'.
[21] [1955] 1 QB 450.
[22] (1983) 81 LGR 460.
[23] The responsibilities of parents to take reasonable steps to prevent accidents, in this case to a baby, also arose in *B v Camden London Borough Council* [2001] PIQR 9. Here, a landlord was held not liable under s 4 of the Defective Premises Act 1972 where a baby fell out of bed and was burnt on uncased heating pipes, in part because the risk was small and in part because the mother should have prevented the accident.
[24] [2009] EWCA Civ 671.

specific warning about the location of the particular pond and the access which might be gained to it. The parents were aware that there were ponds and other dangers to small children on the site and these dangers were obvious. That was not to say that someone, be it the parent or the occupier, was bound to be at fault since, as Stanley Burnton LJ put it, 'accidents may and do happen to young children without anyone being at fault'.

Where the plaintiff is an older child, the occupier's duty will be discharged more easily and the standard of care owed to adolescents may not differ markedly (if at all) from that owed to adults.[25] Nonetheless, even in a case involving teenage children, Lord Hoffmann has said that 'their ingenuity in finding unexpected ways of doing mischief to themselves and others should never be under-estimated'.[26] The case was *Jolley v Sutton London Borough Council*,[27] which raised the issue of whether the kind of accident, and not merely the injury, to befall the child must be a reasonably foreseeable consequence of the defendant's negligence or breach of statutory duty as an occupier. The defendant council had failed to remove an abandoned and derelict boat from land adjoining a block of flats owned by the council. It was aware of the boat's presence and had made plans to remove it. Two boys aged 13 and 14 began to repair it using a car jack and some wood to prop it up. One of the boys suffered serious spinal injuries, resulting in paraplegia with major complications, when the boat fell off the prop and crushed him. The council argued that the manner of the accident was not foreseeable, despite the fact that it was foreseeable that children might play on the boat and be injured. The claimant's accident, it was argued, was of a different kind from that which was foreseeable. This argument prevailed in the Court of Appeal but not in the House of Lords. The risk that had been created and had been conceded by the council was one of injury to children if rotten planking gave way beneath them. The wider risk of more serious injury being caused to children by the condition of the boat fell within its duty of care and the accident which had occurred fell within the general description of the risk.

The case can usefully be contrasted with the decision of the High Court in *Baldacchino v West Wittering Estate plc*.[28] Here a teenage boy sustained a neck injury when he dived into the sea off the Defendant's navigation beacon. There was no warning sign in the vicinity, but HHJ Stuart Baker held that this should not be interpreted as an implied permission. Accordingly the young man was not the Defendant's visitor for the purposes of the 1957 Act and the defendant was not liable.

Children as trespassers - the Occupiers' Liability Act 1984

At common law an occupier was not liable at all to trespassers, except where the injury was caused deliberately or maliciously. No distinction was made

---

[25] See, for example, *Titchener v British Railways Board* [1983] 3 All ER 770.

[26] *Jolley v Sutton London Borough Council* [2000] 1 WLR 1082, at 1093.

[27] Ibid.

[28] [2008] EWHC 3386 (QB).

between adults and children, and the rule could operate very harshly, as it did in *Addie v Dumbreck*.[29] Here, a four-year-old boy was crushed in the wheel of a haulage system operated at a colliery. The wheel was in a field known to be frequented by children. It was attractive to them but inadequately protected. The House of Lords held that, since the child had no express or implied permission to be on the premises, he had to be classed as a trespasser and hence no duty of care was owed to him. The harshness of the rule was mitigated over the years by several devices, including the concepts of allurement and the implied licence, before a more generalised duty of 'common humanity' towards trespassers was fashioned by the House of Lords in *British Railways Board v Herrington*.[30] This extended beyond the duty merely to refrain from deliberately causing injury to a duty to take precautionary measures where there was knowledge of the circumstances of the danger and the actual or likely presence of trespassers. The duty to 'non-visitors', including trespassers, is now contained in the Occupiers' Liability Act 1984.[31] The test for liability now comprises three elements as follows:

(1) the occupier must be aware of the danger or have reasonable grounds to believe it exists;

(2) he must have known, or had reasonable grounds to believe, that the non-visitor was in, or might have come into, the vicinity of the danger; and

(3) the risk of injury must have been one against which, in all the circumstances, the occupier might have been expected to offer the non-visitor some protection.

The duty is then 'to take such care as is reasonable in all the circumstances of the case to see that [the non-visitor] does not suffer injury on the premises by reason of the danger concerned'.[32] The circumstances which give rise to a duty of care do, therefore, have elements of subjectivity and it is also provided that the duty may be discharged in appropriate cases by giving a warning.[33] However, it has been doubted whether, in its application to children, there is any appreciable difference from the common duty of care owed to child visitors. Clearly, the precautions which might be expected of occupiers towards child trespassers are greater than those one would expect for burglars. And it is unlikely that the duty could be discharged merely by giving a warning since this might well be incomprehensible to young children.

---

[29]   *Robert Addie and Sons (Collieries) Ltd v Dumbreck* [1929] AC 358.
[30]   [1972] AC 877.
[31]   Occupiers' Liability Act 1984, s 1(3).
[32]   Ibid, s 1(4).
[33]   Ibid, s 1(5).

Negligence of parents and other carers

As was seen above, the duties of the prudent parent to protect his child might absolve a third party from liability, but under what circumstances might a parent *himself* be liable for the child's injuries, arising from failure to take proper care of him?[34] There is no reason, in principle, why a child should not sue his parent,[35] although he would need, as in other ordinary civil actions, to act by a 'litigation friend'.[36] However, since the child and his parent will usually be part of a family which constitutes a single economic unit, there will seldom be any point in suing, unless the parent is insured. That exception will, of course, apply where a child is injured through the negligent driving of his parent.[37] Where the child is injured in a road accident caused by the negligence of a third party, a parent may be liable to make a contribution to the child's damages if there is contributory negligence.[38]

Some case-law has been concerned with the liability of foster parents but the principles can be extrapolated to parents and other carers. Accidents frequently occur at home and the question is: what standard of care is it reasonable to expect the ordinary parent to achieve in the domestic context? The matter arose in *Surtees v Kingston-upon-Thames Borough Council*,[39] where the two-year-old plaintiff, while a foster child, suffered serious foot injuries from immersion in hot water. The facts were disputed, but the court accepted the version of the

---

[34] See, generally, C McIvor 'Expelling the Myth of the Parental Duty to Rescue' [2000] CFLQ 229, advocating that the law should distinguish more clearly between situations in which the parent has, by his or her conduct, contributed positively to the harm suffered by the child and cases of mere omission. According to this thesis there would be liability in the former situation but not in the latter.

[35] Although it was apparently assumed by the House of Lords in *Barrett v Enfield London Borough Council* [1999] 2 FLR 426 that a child could not sue his parent in relation to care-giving decisions. This view has been hotly disputed by Michael Freeman, who questions why there should not be 'an actionable duty of care against a mother who decides to live with a known sex abuser or against parents who smoke in the presence of an asthmatic child or against a mother with HIV who insists on breastfeeding her baby'. See M Freeman 'The End of the Century of the Child?' (2000) 53 *Current Legal Problems* 505, at pp 543–544. Cf R Bagshaw (above), at p 135, who rehearses the concerns, from a public policy perspective, about tortious actions between parents and children.

[36] See chapter 14 above. The child's parent will normally act as litigation friend although this will clearly be impossible where the parent is the defendant.

[37] This is also the one exceptional situation in which a child may sue his mother in relation to congenital defects caused before birth. See the Congenital Disabilities (Civil Liability) Act 1976, s 2.

[38] In the recently reported case of *Williams v the Estate of Dayne Joshua Williams (Deceased)* [2013] EWCA Civ 455 the Court of Appeal upheld the judge's finding of contributory negligence by a genuinely caring and devoted mother. She had negligently placed her child, then aged three years and two months, in a booster seat rather than in another car seat which had a five point harness. In doing so, she had failed to heed the manufacturers' warnings about weight, height and age of children using the seat. The child was badly injured in a collision caused entirely by the negligent driving of an 18-year-old (killed in the accident) who had consumed alcohol and drugs. The fact that many other parents were said to have moved their children prematurely to booster seats, did not absolve the mother of negligence or prevent her liability to make a 25 per cent contribution to the child's damages.

[39] [1991] 2 FLR 559.

foster parents that, while the foster mother was absent from the bathroom, the child contrived to stick her foot into the wash basin and to turn on the hot water tap. It was not disputed that the foster mother sought immediate medical attention for the child. A majority of the Court of Appeal held that an injury of the kind suffered was not foreseeable, taking into account the foster mother's domestic circumstances. The court was mindful of the need to avoid imposing too high a standard of care, given the stress and preoccupation with household tasks which usually characterise parents' domestic circumstances.[40]

The decision of the Court of Appeal in *Perry v Harris*[41] is not a case about alleged negligence by parents but rather concerns the adequacy of supervision of children playing together by a third party. It is nonetheless a useful modern authority on the standard of care to be expected of parents in this situation since the decision applies that standard in determining the liability of the third party. The case concerns a tragic accident on that modern day favourite attraction at children's events – the bouncy castle. The claimant child was aged 11 when he sustained an injury of 'horrifying severity'. He suffered a depressed skull fracture and subdural haematoma which would result in severe, permament cognitive, behavioural, emotional and social consequences. This happened when he was struck in the forehead by the heel of a somersaulting 15-year-old boy who had been permitted to go onto the castle. The inflatable, one of two hired by the defendants, Mr and Mrs Perry, for their children's party, was being supervised by Mrs Perry. The somersaulting occurred while her back was turned and her attention was being given to the other inflatable, a bungee run. The judge had found the defendants liable in negligence but the Court of Appeal, allowing the appeal, held that the judge had imposed an unreasonably high standard of care in, inter alia, requiring 'constant surveillance' and 'uninterrupted supervision'. The Court's view was that the standard of care was 'that appropriate to protect children against a foreseeable risk of physical harm that fell short of serious injury'. In applying the test of what care a reasonable parent would have taken the Court did not think that this turned on expert evidence or special knowledge. Instead the Court had to place themselves 'in the shoes of the defendant and consider the adequacy of her conduct from that viewpoint and with the knowledge that she had'.[42] The Court's conclusion was that the accident was a freak and tragic accident but one which had occurred without fault.

Clearly, the line must be drawn somewhere, but it ought to be remembered that parents and others with responsibility may be criminally liable for cruelty or neglect and that the circumstances which suffice for this would, almost by

---

[40]   Sir Nicolas Browne-Wilkinson V-C said that the court should be wary to hold parents in breach of a duty of care owed to their children. The duty owed by a foster parent to a child in care was the same as that owed by the ordinary parent to his or her own children. There were, he thought, very real public policy considerations to be taken into account if the conflicts inherent in legal proceedings were to be brought into family relationships. But see the dissent of Beldam LJ.

[41]   [2008] EWCA Civ 907, [2009] 1 WLR 19.

[42]   Per Lord Phillips of Worth Matravers, delivering the judgment of the Court, at para 47.

definition, also be enough for civil liability.[43] This would also be the case if parents failed to ensure the suitability or adequacy of substitute carers such as babysitters, and the child came to harm as a result.[44] Where the child is injured, partly as a result of the negligence of a third party, and partly as a result of the contributory negligence of a carer, it has been held that the child's damages should not be reduced.[45] Where, of course, the negligence of the carer is the major cause of the child's injury, the court may conclude that the third party is not negligent at all.

Intentional torts

Children, as persons, are protected from civil wrongs in the ordinary way, just as they are protected by the criminal law.[46] In the context of the intentional torts of assault, battery and false imprisonment, special considerations apply to parents and others who exercise lawful authority over children. In short, certain bodily interferences with children which would, without doubt, be tortious if carried out on adults *may* be justifiable if they can be regarded as proper acts of parental discipline. Yet, especially after *Gillick*, there are limits to this principle.[47] The responsibility of parents to control the actions of their children also raises the question of whether a third party may commit a tort against the *parent* by interfering.

The limits of parental discipline

Parents will have a defence to the torts of assault and battery where they can show that physical 'touchings' were proper exercises of parental discipline being moderate and reasonable. Young children, especially, often have to be restrained physically by parents from placing themselves in danger, and some parents resort, however controversially, quite lawfully to low-level corporal

---

[43] For a New Zealand decision in which negligence was established against a parent, see *McCallion v Dodd* [1966] NZLR 710 and the analysis of the case in *Bromley's Family Law* (10th edn, Oxford University Press, 2007), at pp 383–384. See also *S v Walsall Metropolitan Borough Council* [1986] 1 FLR 397 in which the Court of Appeal upheld the liability of a foster mother for severe burns to the soles of a child's feet caused by her negligence. The council was held not to be liable since the foster parents could not be regarded as agents of the local authority. In *S v W and Another (Child Abuse: Damages)* [1995] 1 FLR 862 the 29-year-old plaintiff succeeded in an action for damages against her mother arising from her mother's breach of duty in failing to protect her, while a child, from repeated physical and sexual abuse by her father. Her claim against her father himself (which was based on trespass to the person) was statute-barred. She succeeded against her mother on the basis that she could take advantage of the longer limitation period applicable to negligence claims under the Limitation Act 1980, s 11.

[44] See the Children Act 1989, s 2(11).

[45] *Oliver v Birmingham and Midland Omnibus Co Ltd* [1933] 1 KB 35.

[46] See, generally, *Winfield and Jolowicz on Tort* (18th edn, Sweet & Maxwell, 2010), ch 4 and J Steele *Tort Law: Text, Cases and Materials* (2nd edn, Oxford University Press, 2010), ch 2.

[47] *Gillick v West Norfolk and Wisbech Area Health Authority* [1986] 1 AC 112. On the specific issue of consent and potential tortious liability in medical matters, see chapter 8.

punishment, such as smacking. If this does not become excessive, whatever the morality of the practice, it is not tortious.[48]

Following decisions of the European Court of Human Rights and domestic decisions, the law is now contained in s 58 Children Act 2004. This provides that in relation to criminal offences against the person which involve wounding, grevious (serious) bodily harm[49] and actual bodily harm[50] or child cruelty[51] battery of a child cannot be justified on the ground that it constituted reasonable punishment. It is also provided that such acts involving actual bodily harm cannot be justified in any civil proceedings on the same basis. The broad effect is to criminalise and render tortious most purported acts of discipline by parents which exceed the level of causing transient pain or discomfort. Smacking, unless excessive and resulting in injury, is therefore legally the right side of the line though it would constitute common assault were it not for the parent and child relationship. Many advocates of children's rights continue to argue that all forms of hitting children should be unlawful.[52]

Parents are also known to confine children to the home, or perhaps a bedroom, for misbehaviour. Their special authority deriving from parental responsibility is, again, a defence to what might otherwise amount to false imprisonment.[53]

It is equally well established that, in principle, a parent behaving unreasonably may be criminally liable and, by deduction, liable also in tort. In *R v D*,[54] the House of Lords held that a parent might be guilty of the common law offence of kidnapping and, in *R v Rahman*,[55] a father who tried to take his teenage daughter, by force, to Bangladesh, had his conviction for the common law offence of false imprisonment upheld. Lord Lane CJ said that a parent could act unlawfully where the detention of the child was 'for such a period or in such circumstances as to take it out of the realm of reasonable parental discipline'. The circumstances of the case are instructive and suggest that physical restraints and punishments of older children, especially teenagers, may at best be inappropriate and at worst positively unlawful.

It should also be noted that in 2007 Parliament acted to prevent the specific mischief of forced marriages by enacting the Forced Marriage (Civil Protection) Act 2007. While instances of persons being compelled to undergo marriage are clearly not confined to minors, many of them have involved children and young people and the compulsion often extends to attempting to

---

48   We consider the connection between corporal punishment and the threshold for care proceedings in chapter 12.
49   Sections 18 and 20 Offences against the Person Act 1861.
50   Section 47 Offences against the Person Act 1861.
51   Section 1 Children and Young Persons Act 1933.
52   See particularly the campaign of the 'Children are Unbeatable' alliance.
53   For a detailed academic analysis of the parental use of force on children, whether physical punishment or restraint, see J Fortin 'Children's rights and the use of physical force' [2001] 13 CFLQ 243.
54   [1984] AC 778.
55   (1985) 81 Cr App R 349.

send them to another country for the purposes of marriage. Parents who attempt to force their children into such marriages may now be prevented by a forced marriage protection order.[56] In deciding whether to make such an order the court must have regard to 'all the circumstances including the need to secure the health, safety and well-being of the person to be protected'.[57] In ascertaining that person's well-being the court must have regard to her wishes and feelings to the extent that they are ascertainable and the court considers appropriate in the light of her age and understanding.[58]

Powers of control and discipline are also exercised by schools, for the purposes of maintaining good order, but these were severely curtailed as regards the use of corporal punishment by legislation in 1986. In *Campbell and Cosans v United Kingdom*,[59] the UK was found to be in breach of the ECHR by failing to respect the philosophical convictions of certain Scottish parents who were opposed to the use of corporal punishment on their children. As a result, corporal punishment was prohibited in all State schools and in relation to State-funded pupils in independent schools[60] by s 47 of the Education (No 2) Act 1986. Although it remained lawful in independent schools, the Guidance under the Children Act[61] indicated that its continued use should be regarded as exceptional and that it should not be used for trivial offences or applied indiscriminately to whole classes of children. It was advised that it should normally only be administered by the head teacher, and should be properly recorded in the school punishment book.[62]

Then, in *Costello-Roberts v United Kingdom*,[63] the ECtHR, by a narrow 5:4 majority, held that corporal punishment inflicted on a seven-year-old pupil in a private boarding school was not a violation of the ECHR. The boy had been struck three times on the buttocks with a rubber-soled gym shoe. The court held that this did not reach the required minimum threshold of severity as to constitute degrading punishment under Art 3 of the Convention. The narrowness of the result and the tone of the judgments, however, necessitated amending legislation which made it explicit that, insofar as corporal punishment was still used in the independent sector, it could not be administered in a way which was 'inhuman or degrading' since this would be in breach of the Convention.[64] The way was paved for the total abolition of

---

[56] The provisions are contained in Part 4A of the Family Law Reform Act 1996.
[57] Section 63A(2).
[58] Section 63A(3).
[59] (1982) 4 EHRR 293.
[60] Education (No 2) Act 1986, s 47 applied to all maintained schools (including special schools), grant-maintained schools, non-maintained special schools, independent schools for 'assisted places' pupils and other pupils whose fees were partly or entirely paid out of public funds.
[61] *The Children Act 1989 Guidance and Regulations Vol 5 Independent Schools* (HMSO, 1991), at paras 3.9.1 et seq.
[62] Ibid, at para 3.9.5.
[63] [1994] ELR 1.
[64] The original provision in the Education Act 1993 was later consolidated in the Education Act 1996, s 584(2). It was also provided in s 549(3) that, in applying the test of whether the punishment was inhuman or degrading, regard was to be had to 'all the circumstances of the

corporal punishment in independent schools, and this was achieved by an amendment to the Labour Government's School Standards and Framework Act 1998.[65] The abolition of corporal punishment in the independent sector was subsequently challenged unsuccessfully in the House of Lords in *R (Williamson) v Secretary of State for Education and Employment*.[66] The House acknowledged that the ban did interfere with the rights relating to freedom of religion and philosophical convictions of the parents concerned under Art 9 and Art 2 of Protocol 1, but it was held that it did not violate them as it was a proportionate interference. The change in the law was in pursuit of a legitimate aim, the protection of children and promotion of their well-being. It was an issue of broad social policy and appropriate for Parliament to decide that a universal ban was preferable to a selective one.

Interference with parental responsibility

If parents have primary responsibility for the care and upbringing of their children (and usually are the only people formally vested with parental responsibility) can it be tortious for an outsider to intervene in their affairs? It might be thought that, since only the persons with parental responsibility have legal authority to take decisions in relation to the child,[67] another person trying to frustrate this would be acting unlawfully as that person would have no legal basis for doing so. Yet, in *F v Wirral Metropolitan Borough Council*,[68] the Court of Appeal denied that parents had *independent* rights which were capable of being infringed.[69] The former action which a parent could bring for loss of his child's services[70] had become anachronistic and was abolished by the Administration of Justice Act 1982. Any right a parent possessed, therefore, was subordinate to the welfare of the child. There was no tort of interference with parental rights known to the law.

It should be noted, however, that it may in certain circumstances be possible for what is in reality a financial loss to the parent to be recovered as an element in the child's damages. Thus, in *Donnelly v Joyce*,[71] the child's injuries required regular re-bandaging which would normally have been undertaken by a nurse but which was in fact carried out by his mother, herself a nurse. The Court of Appeal allowed the child to recover in damages the cost of the wages which his mother lost by devoting an hour a day to her son's special care. The result could

---

case, including the reason given for it, how soon after the event it is given, its nature, the manner and circumstances in which it is given, the persons involved and its mental and physical effects'.

65 Section 131, now contained in s 548 Education Act 1996.
66 [2005] UKHL 15, [2005] 2 FLR 374.
67 Children Act 1989, ss 2 and 3, and see chapter 4 above. It should be remembered of course that de facto carers have a limited amount of authority under s 3(5).
68 [1991] Fam 69.
69 For a critique of the decision see A Bainham 'Interfering with Parental Responsibility – A New Challenge for the Law of Torts?' (1990) 3 JCL 3.
70 The former action is discussed at length in *Bromley's Family Law* (6th edn, Butterworths, 1981), at pp 329 et seq.
71 [1974] QB 454.

be achieved only by the rather artificial characterisation of the child's loss as the existence of the need for care, rather than the incurring of nursing expenses and this reasoning has been criticised as unconvincing by the House of Lords.[72]

Any tortious action by a parent against a third party must, therefore, be grounded in a tort against the child and not against the parent. In the case of physical touchings, it may be possible to establish an infringement of the child's rights[73] but this will be very difficult where the complaint is merely that an outsider is acting contrary to parental wishes and encouraging the child to do likewise.[74] In this situation the only option would seem to be for the parent to seek a 'prohibited steps' order under the Children Act or an analogous order under the inherent jurisdiction. But each of these actions would depend on the exercise of the court's discretion in determining what is in the child's best interests; the court would not seek to enforce any independent parental claim. As the law stands, the onus would seem to be on the parent to commence legal action. Arguably, the third party interference should be prima facie unlawful, so that the onus of proof is shifted onto the outsider.

Fatal accidents constitute something of an exception. Where a third party has unlawfully brought about the death of a parent or a child, the survivor will have a claim for damages under the Fatal Accidents Act 1976.[75]

Congenital Disabilities (Civil Liability) Act 1976

Children born disabled as a result of injuries before their birth caused to their parents may have a cause of action under the Congenital Disabilities (Civil Liability) Act 1976.[76] The action is 'derivative' in that the child must establish that the defendant would have been actually or potentially liable to the *parent* in respect of the injury,[77] but it is not necessary to show that the parent did, in fact, sustain injury. Thus, if a pregnant mother takes a negligently

---

[72] See *Hunt v Severs* [1994] 2 AC 350. If the parent should also be the tortfeasor the effect of this decision is that the child would be unable to recover the cost of nursing by that parent.

[73] See the discussion in the medical context in chapter 8 above.

[74] An example would be various advice agencies. There is nothing tortious about giving advice (unless it amounts to negligent misstatement), but a parent might wish to stop the child from visiting whatever agency it is. See the discussion in chapter 17 below of the former Conservative Government's circular on sex education and advice given by teachers to individual pupils about sexual matters.

[75] Section 1, as substituted by s 3(1) of the Administration of Estates Act 1982.

[76] This Act followed the Law Com Report No 60 *Injuries to Unborn Children* (1974). See, generally, *Winfield and Jolowicz on Tort* (18th edn, Sweet & Maxwell, 2010), at pp 1109 et seq. The common law position was uncertain until 1992 when, in *Burton v Islington Health Authority* [1993] QB 204, the Court of Appeal held that an action lay at common law for injuries caused to an unborn child by negligence. The action crystallises on the birth of the child. In practice, the common law action will only need to be utilised in respect of births before 1976 since the 1976 legislation governs births after that time. The so-called action for 'wrongful life', where the claimant contends that he or she should never have been born at all, is beyond the scope of the present work but is discussed in *Winfield and Jolowicz* (above), at pp 1112 et seq.

[77] Congenital Disabilities (Civil Liability) Act 1976, s 1.

manufactured drug which causes her child, when born, to be disabled, an action will lie against the manufacturer, even though the mother suffers no ill-effects.[78] The mother herself is not generally liable where, for example, she neglects her own body through alcohol or drug abuse while pregnant.[79] The exception is where she is driving a car in which case the real defendant will be the insurers. The father does not have the same immunity, and may be liable if, for example, he assaults the mother while she is pregnant. However, it has been pointed out that the mother might be unenthusiastic or unwilling about acting as the child's litigation friend in an action against the father.[80]

Since an action under the 1976 Act is derivative in nature, the child's claim may be defeated or reduced by defences available to the parent. Thus, there is no liability for an occurrence preceding the time of conception if, at that time, either or both of the parents knew the risk of the child being born disabled.[81] Similarly, where the responsibility for the child being born disabled is shared by the parent and the defendant, the damages may be reduced as the court thinks just and equitable having regard to the extent of the parent's responsibility.[82] Finally, any term of a contract excluding or restricting liability to the parent binds the child.[83]

A major problem for many children who are born disabled is to establish causation and prove that the congenital defects were actually brought about by negligence. The Pearson Committee[84] thought that the Congenital Disabilities (Civil Liability) Act 1976 would benefit only a minute proportion of children born with these defects. Some attention has been focused on group actions by children alleged to have suffered birth defects or developed childhood diseases as a result of local environmental factors.[85]

Responsibility for children's acts

Two general principles govern liability for tortious acts committed by children. The first principle is that children themselves are prima facie liable and there is no defence of minority as such.[86] A minor is therefore as liable to be sued as an adult. The second principle is that parents (and others exercising parental responsibility) are not usually liable for torts committed by children.[87] Both of these principles require qualification.

---

78 The example given in *Winfield and Jolowicz on Tort* (above), at p 1110.
79 But this might lead to local authority intervention especially perhaps making the unborn child the subject of a child protection plan which is frequently done in practice. See *D (A Minor) v Berkshire County Council* [1987] 1 All ER 20, and chapter 12 above.
80 HK Bevan *Child Law* (Butterworths, 1989), at para 9.83.
81 Congenital Disabilities (Civil Liability) Act 1976, s 1(4).
82 Ibid, s 1(7).
83 Ibid, s 1(6).
84 *Compensation for Personal Injuries* (1978) (Cmnd 7054).
85 For a good discussion of the issues, see E Palmer 'Children and Toxic Torts' (1992) 4 JCL 156.
86 See, for example, *Gorely v Codd* [1967] 1 WLR 19.
87 For a useful Australian perspective on the limits of parental liability see, S Yeo 'Am I my child's keeper? Parental liability in negligence' (1998) 12 *Australian Journal of Family Law* 150. Yeo's

Liability of children

The standard of care required for the tort of negligence is that of the reasonable person. Some torts require proof of malice. In either case, the age of a child may be relevant to show that the child did not possess the requisite mental state. Most of the reported cases have been concerned with the issue of contributory negligence. In many such cases, children have been found not to be negligent where, in similar circumstances, adults would have been. The test appears to be the degree of care for his own safety which it would have been reasonable to expect a child of the particular age reasonably to take.[88] It is not clear whether this test is entirely objective or whether the child's subjective characteristics, such as maturity and understanding, may be taken into account.[89]

The standard of care expected of children is illustrated by the Australian case of *McHale v Watson*[90] where a boy of 12 years of age threw a piece of steel welding rod, sharpened to a spike, at a post. The spike glanced off the post hitting a nine-year-old girl who was standing nearby, causing injuries to her eye. It was established that the boy had no intention of hitting the girl or frightening her. The High Court of Australia upheld the judge's decision that this did not amount to negligence, applying the standard of care reasonably to be expected of a child of the same age, intelligence and experience. As Kitto J put it:

'It is, I think, a matter for judicial notice that the ordinary boy of 12 suffers from a feeling that a piece of wood and a sharp instrument have a special affinity. To expect a boy of that age to consider before throwing the spike whether the timber was hard or soft, to weigh the chances of being able to make the spike stick in the post, and to foresee that it might glance off and hit the girl, would be, I think, to expect a degree of sense and circumspection which nature ordinarily withholds till life becomes less rosy.'

Until comparatively recently, there was no direct English authority on the standard of care required of children, but in *Mullin v Richards*[91] the Court of Appeal addressed the issue and substantially adopted the reasoning of the High Court of Australia in *McHale v Watson*.

Teresa and Heidi were 15-year-old Birmingham schoolgirls. At the end of a maths lesson they were engaged in a mock 'sword-fight' with plastic rulers when tragedy struck. One of the rulers snapped and a fragment of plastic entered Teresa's eye causing her to lose all useful sight in it. Teresa sued Heidi,

---

central argument is that there are sound policy reasons why parental liability should generally be limited to acts of commission rather than acts of omission.

[88] *Yachuk v Oliver Blais Co Ltd* [1949] AC 396.

[89] Such authority as there is suggests that, although a child's age may be taken into account, the test is otherwise entirely objective. See *Watkins v Birmingham City Council* (1976) 126 NLJ 442.

[90] [1966] ALR 513. On the standard of care expected of children, see Winfield and Jolowicz (above), at p 1116; Giliker and Beckwith (above), at para 5.017 and Steele (above) which has particularly useful extracts, at pp 121–128.

[91] [1998] 1 All ER 920.

together with Birmingham City Council, alleging negligence on the part of Miss Osborne, the maths teacher. The judge found that the latter had not been negligent and dismissed the claim against the education authority. But he found that both the girls had been negligent and that Teresa's injury was the foreseeable result. Accordingly, he awarded damages subject to a 50 per cent reduction for contributory negligence.

Allowing the appeal, the Court of Appeal held that where the defendant was a child the test was not that of the ordinary prudent and reasonable adult but that of the ordinary prudent and reasonable child of the same age as the defendant in the defendant's situation. The judge had indeed referred to the fact that the girls were aged 15 but there had been insufficient evidence to justify his conclusion that the accident was foreseeable. There was no evidence of the propensity of such rulers to break, that the practice of playing with rulers was frowned upon or barred by the school or that either of the girls had used excessive or inappropriate violence. All that had occurred was a schoolgirls' game and there was no justification for attributing to the girls foresight of any significant risk of likelihood of injury. Butler-Sloss LJ referred with approval to the judgment of Kitto J in *McHale v Watson* where it was said that 'children, like everyone else, must accept as they go about in society the risks from which ordinary care on the part of others will not suffice to save them. One such risk is that boys of 12 may behave as boys of 12'. And she added that 'girls of 15 playing together may play as somewhat irresponsible girls of 15'.[92]

One of the reasons why there is a shortage of English authority on the standard of care required of children, at least outside the context of contributory negligence, is that a child will generally not be worth suing.[93] One way around this problem, in an appropriate case, is to sue the child's parent or, perhaps, the education authority, where an accident was near the child's school.

Liability of parents and other carers

There are two recognised exceptions to the rule that parents are not liable for the torts of their children. The first exception is where they have specifically authorised the child's actions, or where the child is employed by them. Here, they will be vicariously liable. A similar principle applies to contracts authorised by parents.[94]

---

[92] Later cases applying *Mullin v Richards* are *Blake v Galloway* [2004] 1 WLR 2844 (where a 15-year-old boy also suffered a serious injury to his eye arising from 'horseplay' with twigs) and *Orchard v Lee* [2009] EWCA Civ 295 (where the Court of Appeal held there was no breach of duty of care to an adult playground supervisor when a 13-year-old boy injured him by running backwards during a game of tag between a group of friends).

[93] This is not, however, inevitably so since the child is capable of owning substantial personal property. See chapter 9 above.

[94] For the child's *own* contractual capacity and liability, see pp 859 et seq below.

The second, and more significant, exception arises where the parent himself is found to be negligent in failing to prevent the act or omission of the child which has injured a third party.[95] A number of the reported cases have concerned firearms. Thus, a father was held liable where he gave his 15-year-old son an air gun and allowed him to keep it after he had smashed a neighbour's window with it. The son then went on to injure the eye of another boy with the gun.[96] However, a father was held not liable where his 13-year-old son resiled on a promise never to use an air rifle outside the house and did so injuring the plaintiff. It was accepted that the father had taken all reasonable precautions and the son's disobedience was unforeseeable.[97]

Similar principles apply to school authorities where the standard of care is that of the reasonably prudent parent.[98] The leading case is the decision of the House of Lords in *Carmarthenshire County Council v Lewis*.[99] Here, the local authority was held liable for the lack of supervision at a nursery school. This led to a young child, not yet four years of age, running out of school and into the road, which caused the death of a lorry driver in the accident which followed. School authorities may also be liable where the child is injured owing to their negligence.[100]

It would seem fair to conclude that anyone who has assumed responsibility for a child, such as a child-minder taking a child to or from school, could be liable on similar principles if either a child or a third party is injured as a result of

---

[95] As to liability to pay the child's fines and other responsibility for children's crimes, see chapter 15 above and *TA v DPP* [1997] 2 FLR 887 where on the facts a parent was held to be not liable as she was not exerting control over a child accommodated by the local authority at the time of the relevant offence.

[96] *Bebee v Sales* (1916) 32 TLR 413. Liability was also established in *Newton v Edgerley* [1959] 1 WLR 1031.

[97] *Donaldson v McNiven* [1952] 2 All ER 691.

[98] *Ricketts v Erith Borough Council* [1943] 2 All ER 629.

[99] [1955] AC 549.

[100] As in *Barnes v Hampshire County Council* [1969] 1 WLR 1563. Here, school children were let out of school five minutes earlier than was the normal practice. A five-year-old child was injured when she wandered into the street, her mother having not yet arrived. The local education authority was held responsible, since the injury was foreseeable. Cf *Wilson v Governors of Sacred Heart Roman Catholic School* [1998] 1 FLR 663. Here, a nine-year-old boy was injured at the end of the school day when he was hit in the eye by a coat which had been deliberately whirled around like a lasso by another pupil. The Court of Appeal allowed the school's appeal against a finding of negligence arising from alleged failure to supervise children leaving through the school gates. Supervision was in fact provided during the lunch break when large numbers of children were in the playground. But the lunch period was contrasted with the very short period in which, and very short distance over which, children were engaged in leaving the school. It was not standard procedure to supervise children leaving school and the need for such supervision was not demonstrated. Contrast also *Nwabudike v Southwark London Borough Council* [1997] ELR 35 (where liability was not established on the basis that reasonable precautions to prevent accidents had been taken) with *J v North Lincolnshire County Council* [2000] ELR 245 (where liability was established on the basis that a vulnerable exit gate had not been protected).

their lack of supervision.[101] The employer of someone who injures a child may also vicariously liable if that person was acting within the scope of his or her employment.[102]

CHILDREN AND THE LAW OF CONTRACT

Trietel has observed that the law governing minors' contracts is based on two principles.[103] The first principle is that 'the law must protect the minor against his inexperience, which may enable an adult to take unfair advantage of him, or to induce him to enter into a contract which, though in itself fair, is simply improvident'. The second principle is that 'the law should not cause unnecessary hardship to adults who deal fairly with minors'.

The result of attempting to follow a policy which embraces these two, somewhat conflicting, principles is that the law is complex and, in some respects, quite vague. Some contracts are valid, others are voidable, and yet others are completely unenforceable against the minor. The first principle underlies the general rule that a minor is not bound by his contracts. But this principle is only one of 'qualified unenforceability' since, under the second principle, the minor will be liable under certain types of contract from the outset, while others will bind him unless he takes steps to repudiate them. He may also incur some liability in tort, restitution, or under the Minors' Contracts Act 1987.[104] This section examines the current state of English law regarding the various kinds of contract which a minor may purport to make.[105]

It should be appreciated that the practical significance of the issue diminished when the age of majority was lowered from 21 to 18 years of age, by the Family Law Reform Act 1969.[106] Many of the older cases related to young people in this age group such as, for example, undergraduates at the universities of

---

[101] The principle may extend to failure to control teenagers where there is an expectation of supervision. See *Home Office v Dorset Yacht Co* [1970] AC 1004.

[102] See *Lister v Hesley Hall Ltd* [2002] 1 AC 215 where the House of Lords held that a children's home could be liable for the acts of its warden in abusing children in the home. The defendants had assumed responsibility for the care of the children when they placed them in the home and had entrusted their care to the warden. There was therefore a sufficiently close connection between the actions of the warden and the nature of his employment that the defendants should be liable. For the liability of local authorities for failing to prevent abuse, see chapter 10 above. A good collection of materials is to be found in Steele (above), at pp 414–425.

[103] E Peel *Treitel: The Law of Contract* (13th edn, Sweet & Maxwell, 2011), at pp 539–557. See also J Beatson, A Burrows and J Cartwright *Anson's Law of Contract* (29th edn, Oxford University Press, 2010), at pp 232–246 and M Furmston *Cheshire, Fifoot and Furmston's Law of Contract* (16th edn, Oxford University Press, 2012), at pp 537–553.

[104] Following Law Com Report No 134 *Minors' Contracts* (1984).

[105] For a discussion of minors' capacity to obtain housing and to rent accommodation, see D Cowan and N Dearden 'The Minor as (a) Subject: the Case of Housing Law' in J Fionda (ed) *Legal Concepts of Childhood* (Hart Publishing, 2001).

[106] Following *Report of the Committee on the Age of Majority* (the Latey Committee) (1967) (Cmnd 3342).

Oxford and Cambridge.[107] Such people are now young adults with full contractual capacity.[108] Having said that, we are witnessing in other areas of the law a gradual emancipation of older minors,[109] and there are certain areas, such as entertainment and sport, in which minors regularly do enter into contracts. Children, sometimes quite young, also routinely engage in everyday transactions, such as purchasing sweets, which, although trivial, have contractual implications.

A comparatively recent example from the sporting world is the case of Manchester United and England footballer, Wayne Rooney.[110] When he was just 15 years of age and an apprentice at Everton, he entered into a 'representation agreement' with the claimant company. He later gave notice to the claimant that he would not renew this agreement on its expiry. Shortly after it expired he entered into a different agreement with the defendants. The claimant sued the defendants for unlawful interference with and/or the procuring of the breach of the earlier agreement. HH Judge Hodge QC held that there could be no liability for inducing or facilitating the breach of a voidable contract with a minor. Giving summary judgment for the defendants it was held that the representation agreement was not within the class of contracts analogous to necessaries, contracts of employment, apprenticeship or education which were enforceable against a minor. Wayne Rooney was already with a football club at the time he entered into the representation agreement (which entailed the claimant acting as his executive agent). The agreement did not involve the claimant undertaking matters essential to the player's training or livelihood, nor did the agreement enable him to earn a living or advance his skills as a professional footballer.

We conclude this section with a brief look at the position in Scotland where, following a wide-ranging report by the Scottish Law Commission,[111] statutory reforms to Scots law have simplified the law on minors' contracts and other civil law capacities. We pose the question whether English law should not be similarly reformed, in pursuit of what the Scottish Commission identified as a

---

[107] *Nash v Inman* [1908] 2 KB 1 concerned an action by a Savile Row tailor against a Cambridge undergraduate with respect to 11 fancy waistcoats. The action failed since he had not adduced sufficient evidence that the clothes were suitable to the condition in life of the minor or that he was not already adequately supplied with clothes. By contrast, Viscount Middleton, during the second reading of the Infants Contracts Bill 1874, referred to the decisions of juries at Oxford which had found, inter alia, that champagne and wild ducks and studs of emeralds set in diamonds were necessaries for Oxford undergraduates! See (1874) *Hansard*, Vol 219, Ser 3, col 1225.

[108] And with full civil capacities for other legal purposes such as making a will or owning real property.

[109] See chapter 8 above.

[110] *Proform Sports Management Limited v Proactive Sports Management Limited* [2006] EWCA Civ 52, [2007] 3 All ER 946.

[111] Scot Law Com No 110 *Report on the Legal Capacity and Responsibility of Minors* (1987).

third central principle which ought to inform the law: 'that the law should be clear and coherent and should accord with modern social and economic conditions.'[112]

Valid contracts

Two kinds of minors' contracts have long been recognised as exceptions to the principle of unenforceability. They are contracts for 'necessaries' and contracts of service. In each case they are only binding on the minor if, on balance, they are *beneficial* to him. Beyond these two special kinds of contract there is no wider principle that a minor is bound by beneficial contracts. Thus, it is equally well established that trading contracts are not binding on a minor, however beneficial the terms might be for him.[113]

Contracts for necessaries

A minor is liable to pay for necessaries, whether goods or services, which have been supplied to him under a contract. The concept of necessaries clearly includes the essentials of life such as food, clothing and lodging, but it is wider than this. It extends to what is appropriate to maintain the *particular* minor in his ordinary way of life and this can vary, depending on the lifestyle to which he is accustomed. What are considered necessaries is clearly capable of evolving with the times. O'Sullivan and Hilliard, for example, speculate on whether today they might include mobile phones![114] Pure luxuries are not included, but some of the older cases recognised as necessaries luxurious articles which were also articles of utility.[115] In the case of goods, there is a statutory definition of necessaries, namely 'goods suitable to the condition in life of the minor ... and to his actual requirements at the time of sale and delivery'.[116] The latter part of the definition makes it plain that, as well as being capable of being regarded as necessaries in law, the minor must actually have had need of the items in question.[117]

The contract will be enforceable against the minor only if it does not contain harsh or onerous terms so that it is, on balance, substantially for his benefit.[118]

---

[112]   Ibid, at para 2.12. The other two principles broadly corresponded with those identified by GH Treitel (above):
   '(a) that the law should protect young people from the consequences of their immaturity without restricting unnecessarily their freedom of action;
   (b) that the law should not cause unnecessary prejudice to adults who enter into transactions with young people.'

[113]   See, for example, *Cowern v Nield* [1912] 2 KB 419, although there may be some liability in restitution (see below).

[114]   J O'Sullivan and J Hilliard, *The Law of Contract* (4th edn, Oxford University Press, 2010) p 309.

[115]   See *Chapple v Cooper* (1844) 13 M&W 252.

[116]   Sale of Goods Act 1979, s 3(3).

[117]   Thus, in *Nash v Inman* (above) there was no evidence that the minor did not already possess sufficient waistcoats.

[118]   See *Roberts v Gray* [1913] 1 KB 520.

The concept of necessaries has now been abandoned in Scotland and replaced by a less technical and more wide-ranging notion of 'ordinary transactions' being everyday transactions commonly entered into by a child of the transacting child's age.[119]

Contracts of service

It is established that a minor is bound by contracts of apprenticeship or service[120] on the basis that it is 'to his advantage that he should acquire the means of earning his livelihood'.[121] Again, as with necessaries, this will be so only where the contract, construed as a whole, is beneficial to the minor. Where it is not, he is free to repudiate it. The issue is again a question of balance, and the minor will not be able to escape liability merely because some of the terms of the contract are onerous. The standard texts[122] contrast two cases.

De Francesco v Barnum[123]

This case is an example of the oppressive sort of contract which is not binding on minors. Here, a 14-year-old girl entered into an apprenticeship deed to be taught stage dancing for seven years. The agreement prevented her from marrying during the apprenticeship, or from accepting professional engagements without the plaintiff's permission. However, the obligations were one-sided, since the plaintiff did not bind himself to provide the girl with professional engagements or to maintain her, if unemployed, and the stipulated remuneration was very poor. Fry J found the terms of the deed unreasonable and unenforceable since the girl was at the complete disposal of the plaintiff without commensurate obligations on his part.

Clements v London and North Western Railway Co[124]

This case illustrates the kind of contract of service which is regarded as broadly beneficial to minors and hence enforceable. The minor entered the service of the Railway Company as a porter, agreeing to join the company's insurance scheme and to relinquish his right to sue for personal injury under the Employers' Liability Act 1880. This occupational insurance scheme was more favourable to the minor than the statutory scheme, since it provided for compensation in a greater range of accidents but, on the other hand, it fixed a lower scale of compensation. Overall, it was held that the agreement was to the minor's advantage and thus binding on him.

---

[119] Age of Legal Capacity (Scotland) Act 1991, s 2(1)(a).
[120] E Peel, *Treitel: The Law of Contract* (13th edn, Sweet & Maxwell, 2011), at pp 571–573, and *Cheshire, Fifoot and Furmston's Law of Contract* (16th edn, Oxford University Press, 2012), at pp 541–543.
[121] Cheshire et al (above).
[122] Treitel (above), at p 571, and Cheshire et al (above), at p 542.
[123] (1890) 45 Ch D 430.
[124] [1894] 2 QB 482.

It has also been held that where a term of the contract is repugnant but severable, it may be severed leaving intact the remainder of the contract which is of benefit to the minor.[125]

Voidable contracts

Voidable contracts are those which are valid and binding on minors, unless they repudiate them during minority or within a short time of attaining majority. Four types of such contract have been recognised to exist, namely: contracts concerning land; the acquisition of shares in companies; partnership agreements; and marriage settlements.[126] The basis for placing these contracts in a separate category is not clear. The view of the commentators is that the common factor is the quality of relative permanence which attaches to them. They are all contracts under which the minor acquires an interest in some subject-matter, ie a subject-matter to which continuous or recurring obligations are incident.[127] As such, the obligations continue, unless and until the minor decides to put an end to them. It would then be unjust to allow him to retain his interest in the subject-matter without carrying out his own obligations. Where the minor repudiates the contract in time, he will be freed from future liabilities under it but cannot recover money paid over unless there has been a total failure of consideration.[128]

The continued existence of this exceptional category of contracts has been questioned, for it has been said that special treatment has been based on 'social and economic factors which have long since passed away'.[129]

Unenforceable contracts: liability under the Minors' Contracts Act 1987, in restitution or in tort

Where a contract does not fall within any of the categories mentioned above, it is unenforceable against the minor. This does not necessarily mean that it has no legal effect. First, the other party remains bound by it and then certain legal consequences for the minor may also flow from it.

Liability under the Minors' Contracts Act 1987

Where the contract is partially carried out, property may pass to the minor under the ordinary principles of contract of sale. It would be unjust to allow

---

[125] *Bromley v Smith* [1909] 2 KB 235.
[126] See Treitel (above), at pp 573–575, and Cheshire et al (above), at pp 543–549.
[127] Cheshire et al (above), at p 543.
[128] *Steinberg v Scala (Leeds) Ltd* [1923] 2 Ch 452.
[129] E Peel, *Treitel: The Law of Contract* (13th edn, Sweet and Maxwell, 2011), at p 577.

the minor to retain this property where he has resiled from his part of the bargain. The issue is now governed by s 3 of the Minors' Contracts Act 1987.[130] This provides:

> '(1) Where –
>
> (a)   a person ("the plaintiff") has after the commencement of this Act entered into a contract with another ("the defendant") and
> (b)   the contract is unenforceable against the defendant (or he repudiates it) because he was a minor when the contract was made, the court may, if it is just and equitable to do so, require the defendant to transfer to the plaintiff any property acquired by the defendant under the contract, or any property representing it.
>
> (2) Nothing in this section shall be taken to prejudice any other remedy available to the plaintiff.'

Most obviously, this provision can catch a minor who has obtained goods on credit and is now refusing to pay for them, but the remedy is discretionary and there is no guarantee that the court will order the transfer of the property. Moreover, the remedy is limited to the property itself transferred under the contract, or 'any property representing it'. In other words, the court does not have carte blanche to order the minor to pay the price of the goods or otherwise to pay out of his wider assets. There may be some difficult 'tracing' issues about whether property really does represent that which was originally transferred.[131] The reasoning for the restriction is that to allow the minor's wider assets to be touched would be to enforce indirectly an unenforceable contract. It has been suggested that, in exercising its discretion, the court will probably wish to take into account the intrinsic fairness of the original contract, such as the price the minor was required to pay. Where this was unreasonable, the court might order the minor to return the property unless he pays a reasonable price for it, fixed by the court.[132]

Liability in restitution

The Minors' Contracts Act 1987 preserves any other legal remedy available to the plaintiff. Under the equitable doctrine of restitution, a minor who has obtained goods by fraud may be obliged to disgorge them, if they are still in his possession, on the basis of unjust enrichment. This remedy is not available where the minor has already disposed of the goods and, in this respect, it is more limited than the statutory remedy which allows limited tracing.[133] Moreover, the statutory remedy, unlike the equitable one, is not dependent on proof of fraud.

---

[130]   For a concise review of the Act, see J Holroyd 'The Minors' Contracts Act 1987' (1987) 84 LS Gaz 2266.

[131]   These are explored with examples in Treitel (above), at pp 580–585.

[132]   Suggested in Treitel (above), at p 582.

[133]   The limitations of the doctrine of restitution are well illustrated by *Leslie Ltd v Sheill* [1914] 3 KB 607.

Liability in tort

The issue here is whether a minor could incur tortious liability for acts directly connected with unenforceable contracts. The general principle is that an unenforceable contract may not be indirectly enforced against a minor by framing the cause of action in tort. Where, however, the wrongful event can be sufficiently divorced from the contract that it can be regarded as an independent wrong, the minor may not escape tortious liability. Two old cases, both involving horse-riding, resulted in different conclusions on this point.

In *Jennings v Rundall*,[134] it was held that the minor was not liable in the tort of negligence where he hired a mare for riding and injured her through excessive and improper riding. However, in *Burnard v Haggis*,[135] the opposite conclusion was reached where, contrary to the express instructions of the horse's owner, the minor injured the horse while jumping her, having hired her simply for riding. The point of distinction is elusive but is thought to turn on whether or not the wrongful act was contemplated by the contract. In the first case, riding clearly was contemplated (albeit not excessive riding) while, in the second case, jumping was positively excluded under the agreement.

A Scottish solution for England?

The English Law Commission, over 30 years ago, considered the possibility of simplifying the law by adopting a general rule that minors of 16 years or over should be fully liable on *all* contracts while those under that age would be immune from liability.[136] In the event, it opted for more limited reforms which found their way into the Minors' Contracts Act 1987.[137]

Meanwhile, in Scotland, the Scottish Law Commission had embarked on a major examination of the legal capacities and responsibilities of minors and pupils in Scots law.[138] Its review included, but was considerably wider than, the contractual capacity of young people. Its concern was with what, in Scots law, was termed 'active' capacity to perform civil acts having legal effect as opposed to 'passive' capacity simply to hold rights.[139] This active capacity included the

---

[134] (1799) 8 Term Rep 335.

[135] (1863) 14 CB(NS) 45.

[136] Law Com Working Paper No 81 *Minors' Contracts* (1982) Part XII.

[137] One of these was that minors' contracts should generally be capable of being ratified by the minor on attaining majority.

[138] Before the Age of Legal Capacity (Scotland) Act 1991, Scots law distinguished between 'minors' who were boys between the ages of 14 and 18 years and girls between 12 and 18 years and 'pupils' who were boys under 14 and girls under 12 years. For further discussion of the Scottish Law Commission's work and the 1991 legislation, see A Bainham 'Growing Up in Britain: Adolescence in the Post-Gillick Era' (1992) *Juridical Review* 155, at pp 169–172, and JM Thomson *Family Law in Scotland* (6th edn, Bloomsbury Professional Ltd, 2011), ch 10. See also E Sutherland *Child and Family Law* (2nd edn, Thomson, W Green, 2008), ch 7, at para 7.038 et seq.

[139] Scot Law Com No 110 *Report on the Legal Capacity and Responsibility of Minors* (1987), at para 3.22.

capacity 'to enter contracts, make promises, grant conveyances or discharges, make a will, give consent, participate in court proceedings or perform any act of legal significance in the field of private law'.[140] After an extensive consultation, the Scottish Law Commission proposed a two-tier system of legal capacity. Children from the age of 0 to 16 years would, subject to limited but important exceptions, have no legal capacity,[141] while those young people from the age of 16 to 18 years would, subject to limited protections, enjoy full legal capacity for all those acts listed above.[142] Transactions purportedly entered into by those under 16 years of age would be void, unless ratified on attaining 16 years, but there would be an important exception, whereby they would have capacity to engage in 'ordinary transactions' – being reasonable transactions of a kind commonly entered into by a child of the same age and circumstances provided the terms of the contract were not unreasonable.[143] Transactions entered into by those over 16 years of age would be valid, but the court would have a discretion to set a transaction aside on a young person's application made before attaining 21 years of age, if satisfied that it had caused or was likely to cause him 'substantial prejudice' and was not of a kind 'which a reasonably prudent person acting in the same circumstances, would have entered into'.[144] These recommendations were implemented by the Age of Legal Capacity (Scotland) Act 1991.[145]

Effects of the reformed Scots law

The broad effect of the new law was to draw a reasonably clear line for contractual (and other civil) capacity at 16 years of age. This is subject to the very significant exception for 'ordinary transactions'.[146] The gist of this is that the legal capacity of children to do those things which children habitually do is legally recognised, and this varies, depending on the age of the child. The Scottish Law Commission gave the examples of the five-year-old child buying sweets and the 15-year-old child purchasing a cinema ticket. Neither of these examples comes within the traditional category of necessaries, but ought to be placed, the Commission thought, on a proper legal footing.[147] The advantage of the 'ordinary transactions' formula was thought to be that it would be flexible enough to cater for children at the two extremes of the age group. Thus, a child of five years would have the capacity to engage in transactions appropriate to his age group, but not those appropriate to an older child. Accordingly, the rule would have built-in recognition of the different levels of

---

[140] Ibid.
[141] Ibid, at paras 3.21 et seq.
[142] Ibid, at paras 3.97 et seq.
[143] Ibid, at paras 3.41–3.51.
[144] Ibid, at paras 3.102 et seq.
[145] This Act received Royal Assent on 25 July 1991 and came into force on 25 September 1991.
[146] Section 2(1) of the Age of Legal Capacity (Scotland) Act referring instead to 'common' transactions provides that 'a person under the age of 16 years shall have legal capacity to enter into a transaction – (a) of a kind commonly entered into by persons of his age and circumstances and (b) on terms which are not unreasonable'.
[147] Scot Law Com Report No 110 *Report on the Legal Capacity and Responsibility of Minors* (1987), at para 3.41.

understanding of children of different ages.[148] The Commission acknowledged that there might be an element of vagueness, but thought that this would be no worse than that which surrounded the concept of necessaries. It believed that the new formula could cover, inter alia: small shopping transactions; payment of bus or train fares; payment for skating lessons or a haircut; Saturday or holiday jobs; booking accommodation at a Youth Hostel; and the operation of bank deposit accounts.[149]

The new scheme also made it possible to sweep away, at a stroke, the existing rules governing the exceptional cases of valid contracts. It thought that it was unnecessary to retain contracts for necessaries as an exception to the general rule of incapacity. It also thought that these items would usually be provided by the parent or guardian and that, where they were not, they would be covered by the ordinary transactions rule.[150] Similarly, the Commission thought that there should be no exemption relating to employment or trading contracts since, where appropriate, they too would fall within the general exception – the most obvious examples being contracts for Saturday or holiday jobs.[151]

Reform for England?

Whether such a scheme would be suitable for England is legitimately the subject of debate, but there is no question that Scots law now has a more coherent and rational system. Reform along the lines of the Scottish legislation would also be consistent with the changes in the Children Act 1989 regarding young people over 16 years of age.[152] A comprehensive review of the legal capacities and responsibilities of children and young people in English law is overdue.

THE EMPLOYMENT OF CHILDREN AND YOUNG PERSONS

It has been seen that a minor may enter into a valid contract of employment, or other contract whereby he makes a living professionally, if it is substantially for his benefit, but the contractual rules are subject to extensive and complex legislation which places restrictions on the employment of children. Some of these restrictions are general, while others relate to specific kinds of employment.[153]

---

[148] Ibid, at para 3.42.

[149] Ibid, at para 3.48.

[150] Ibid, at paras 3.87–3.88.

[151] Ibid, at para 3.92.

[152] See chapter 5 above.

[153] See S Deakin and G Morris, *Labour Law* (6th edn, Hart Publishing, 2012), at para 4.93. See also N Selwyn, *Selwyn's Law of Employment* (16th edn, Oxford University Press, 2011), at paras 2.103–2.106.

Historical background

Legislative intervention can be traced back to the early nineteenth century and was a response to the appalling working conditions and long hours which prevailed in factories, mines and shops during the industrial revolution. This legislation began to impose controls over the hours which children and young people (and women) were permitted to work, at first in textile factories, and later underground or as shop assistants. Other early legislation dealt with health and safety, dangerous and unhealthy industries, and the education of children.

A comprehensive review of this legislation is beyond the scope of the present work[154] but the following were some of the principal landmarks in the nineteenth century. The Factory Act 1833 prohibited the employment of children under nine years of age in textile factories and regulated the employment of older children. The Factory Act 1847 imposed a maximum daily limit of 10 hours' work for women and young persons employed in textile factories. The Factory and Workshop Act 1878, following the report of a Royal Commission, extended the protections to all factories, raised the minimum age of employment to 10 years of age, and limited the hours of children under 14 years of age to half the normal day. The Education Act 1880 introduced compulsory school attendance up to 10 years of age, and this was extended to 13 years of age for those with poor attendance records. The connection between compulsory education and the restrictions on employment is an obvious and significant one and remains a feature of the law today.[155]

Further protective legislation continued to be introduced from time to time throughout the twentieth century.[156] The Employment of Women, Young Persons and Children Act 1920, for example, prohibited (with limited exceptions) the employment of women and young persons at night in industrial undertakings and established 14 years of age (the then school leaving age) as the minimum age for employment in such undertakings. The Children and Young Persons Act 1933 imposed the general restrictions on the employment of children under 13 years of age which continue to apply today, although the age restriction has now been raised to 14. The Mines and Quarries Act 1954 consolidated previous legislation regulating the employment of women and children underground in mines, or above ground in quarries, and the Shops Act 1950 was a similar consolidation of legislation, mainly controlling the hours of work of young people in shops. The Education Act 1944 raised the compulsory school leaving age to 15 and this was subsequently raised to 16 (or just under) in 1972, where it remains at the time of writing.[157] More recently,

---

[154] There is a detailed review of this legislation in the Department of Employment's Consultative Document *Restrictions on Employment of Young People and the Removal of Sex Discrimination in Legislation* (1987).

[155] See also chapter 17 below.

[156] A selective approach is necessary here, but for a full review see the Consultative Document (above), at paras 2.6 et seq.

[157] Raising of the School Leaving Age Order 1972 (SI 1972/444). The Government has however

the Employment Act 1989 brought about a substantial 'deregulation' of the employment of young persons (as opposed to children) by sweeping away most of the protective employment legislation applying to this age group. However, in 1994, the Council of the European Union issued a Directive on the Protection of Young Persons at Work[158] which necessitated some reform of domestic employment legislation affecting children and young people.

International obligations regarding the employment of children and young people

Various international instruments impose obligations on the UK regarding the employment of children and young persons which have as their common themes the objectives of protecting children from economic exploitation, prohibiting the employment of children (with limited qualifications) and ensuring safe and proper conditions of work where they are employed. This is an area in which theory appears to be quite divorced from practice and in which there is an absence of reliable data regarding the actual employment of children and young persons. The detailed provisions are beyond the scope of the present work. What follows is a sketch of the principal instruments.[159]

The UNCRC

Article 32 of the UNCRC protects children against economic exploitation. It asserts 'the right of the child to be protected from economic exploitation and from performing any work that is likely to be hazardous or to interfere with the child's education, or to be harmful to the child's health or physical, mental, spiritual, moral or social development'.[160] In particular, States parties are required to provide for a minimum age or minimum ages for admission to

---

legislated in the Education and Skills Act 2008 to raise the school leaving age to 17 from 2013 and then to 18 from 2015. This will not however mean that young people are required to remain at school as training is to be an authorised alternative to education. See below.

[158] The Young Workers Directive, Council Directive No 94/33/EC of 22 June 1994. For a critique of the Directive and of English legislation as it applies to the employment of children in 'family work', see A Bond 'Working for the family? Child employment legislation and the public/private debate' (1996) JSWFL 291. For a review of the issues surrounding children's work in the UK, see B Pettitt (ed) *Children and Work in the UK: Reassessing the Issues* (CPAG, 1998).

[159] For more extensive discussion see U Kilkelly 'Economic Exploitation of Children' [2003] *Saint Louis University Public Law Review* 321. This article looks at the issue of the economic exploitation of children from a European perspective. It reviews the provisions of the major international instruments and considers compliance with the relevant standards across the countries of Western and Eastern Europe. See also C Hamilton and B Watt 'The Employment of Children' [2004] CFLQ 135. This article looks at the major international obligations but also includes discussion of the position under English domestic legislation.

[160] Article 32(1).

employment; appropriate regulation of hours and conditions of employment and appropriate penalties or other sanctions to ensure effective enforcement of these obligations.[161]

European Union Council Directive on the Protection of Young Persons at Work

This Council Directive[162] imposed a wide range of obligations on Member States relating to prohibitions on work by children and the conditions of work affecting young persons. It incorporated into English law some of the central requirements of the EU Charter of Fundamental Rights and Freedoms.[163] The following are among the more important provisions. Member States are required to adopt the measures necessary to prohibit work by children and to ensure that the minimum working or employment age is not lower than the compulsory school leaving age or 15 years in any event.[164] 'Children' are defined as persons below the minimum school leaving age or 15 years whichever is the higher. 'Young persons' (described as 'adolescents' in the directive) are therefore aged between 15 or the minimum school leaving age and 18 years.

Member states are obliged to ensure that work by adolescents is strictly regulated and that employers guarantee that young persons have working conditions which suit their age. They must also ensure that young persons are 'protected against economic exploitation and against any work likely to harm their safety, health or physical, mental, moral or social development or to jeopardise their education'.[165]

There are limited exceptions to the prohibitions on employment of children which allow Member States to permit the employment of children aged 13 or 14 in 'light work' and in certain authorised 'cultural or similar activities'.[166] The work undertaken by these children must not be likely to be harmful to their safety, health or development or their attendance at school or participation in vocational guidance or training programmes.

The Directive goes on to impose obligations on employers to take the necessary measures to protect the health and safety of young persons. They must assess the hazards before young persons begin work, inform the young persons of them and of the measures adopted concerning their safety and health. They must undergo a similar assessment wherever there is any major change in working conditions.[167] Other provisions of the Directive prohibit employing

---

[161] Article 32(2). See also the International Labour Organization, Convention No 138 on the Minimum Ages for Employment, discussed by Hamilton and Watt (above), at pp 138–139.
[162] Council Directive 94/33/EC.
[163] See Article 32 of the Charter.
[164] Council Directive 94/33/EC, Art 1(1).
[165] Ibid, Art 1(2) and (3).
[166] Ibid, Arts 3, 4 and 5.
[167] Ibid, Art 6.

young persons in work which represents a risk to their safety, health and development;[168] limit the number of hours of work for both children and adolescents;[169] subject to limited exceptions, prohibit night work (defined as between the hours of 8 pm and 6 am for children and 10 pm and 6 am or 11 pm and 7 am for adolescents);[170] and require minimum rest periods, annual rest and minimum break periods.[171] The Working Time Regulations 1995 implement the 1994 Directive and, perhaps confusingly, refer to neither 'young persons' nor 'adolescents' but 'young workers'. The Management of Health and Safety at Work Regulations 1999 also require employers to undertake a risk assessment before employing a young person and to 'ensure that young persons are protected at work from any risks to their health and safety which are a consequence of their lack of experience, absence of awareness of risks and lack of maturity'.[172]

The Council of Europe: the European Social Charter

Article 7 of the European Social Charter governs child labour and has detailed provisions designed to protect children from exploitation. Among the more important obligations which it imposes on the contracting parties are the following:[173]

(i)   a minimum age for employment set at 15, subject to exceptions for children employed in light work which does not harm their health, morals or education;

(ii)   a higher minimum age of admission to prescribed occupations regarded as dangerous or unhealthy;

(iii)   a prohibition on work which would deprive a person still in full-time education of the full benefit of that education;

(iv)   a limit on the working hours of those under 16 bearing in mind their developmental needs and their need for vocational training;

(v)   the duty to recognise the right of young workers and apprentices to a fair wage or appropriate allowances.

Other provisions, similar to those of the EU Directive above, regulate such matters as annual holidays and restrictions on night work.

---

[168]   Ibid, Art 7.
[169]   Ibid, Art 8.
[170]   Ibid, Art 9.
[171]   Ibid, Arts 10, 11 and 12.
[172]   See N Selwyn *Selwyn's Law of Employment*, at para 2.104.
[173]   There is an extensive and detailed discussion of Art 7 and its requirements in Kilkelly (above), at pp 334–346.

English law: the current situation

The key distinction in current employment law is between 'children' and 'young persons'. This is not, however, the same distinction which has existed historically for the purposes of the criminal law where, as was seen,[174] those under 14 years of age were 'children' while those over 14 years of age were 'young persons'. In the employment sphere, the crucial divide is the compulsory school leaving age: those below it are 'children' while those above it are 'young persons'.[175] It would be convenient, for the student's purposes, if a precise age were fixed in this respect, but the position is not quite as straightforward as this. Although 16 years of age is the benchmark, the school leaving age fluctuates slightly depending on the date of the individual pupil's birthday and its relationship to the statutory school leaving dates. In practical terms, this means that it may apply to someone as young as 15 years and eight months or as old as 16 years and seven months.[176] In 2007 the government signalled its intention to raise the school leaving age to 18. The education leaving age will rise to 17 from the academic year beginning in September 2013 and to 18 from 2015.[177] The change will not however compel young people to remain at school. Alternative options will be to attend college, take up an apprenticeship or part-time training course. Employers of young people are placed under statutory duties to enable young people who are in their employment to participate in education or training.

The distinction between children and young persons remains important since there are extensive restrictions on the employment of children but practically none on the employment of young persons.

The employment of children

Restrictions on the employment of children may be divided into two categories – general restrictions and specific restrictions.[178]

General restrictions

The general restrictions are contained in the Children and Young Persons Act 1933, as amended.[179] This provides that children may not be employed:

---

[174] In chapter 15.

[175] Under the Education Act 1996, s 558, any person who is not for the purposes of the Act over compulsory school age is deemed to be a child for the purposes of any enactment relating to the prohibition or regulation of the employment of children or young persons.

[176] Education Act 1996, s 8, and the Education (School Leaving Date) Order 1997 (SI 1997/1970). On compulsory attendance at school, see chapter 17 below.

[177] Part I Education and Skills Act 2008.

[178] For a discussion based on the ages of the children, see Hamilton and Watt (above), at pp 141–146.

[179] Children and Young Persons Act 1933, ss 18–21, as amended by the Children (Protection at Work) Regulations 1998 (SI 1998/276). The Regulations, which came into force on 4 August 1998, made various amendments to the 1933 Act and the Children and Young Persons

(1) who are under the age of 14 years;

(2) to do any work other than light work;

(3) before the close of school hours on any school day (except where leave to be absent can be, and is, given);

(4) before 7 am or after 7 pm on any day;

(5) for more than two hours on any school day;

(6) for more than two hours on any Sunday;

(7) for more than eight hours or, if the child is under the age of 15 years, for more than five hours in any day:

    (i)   on which he is not required to attend school, and
    (ii) which is not a Sunday;

(8) for more than 35 hours or, if the child is under the age of 15 years, for more than 25 hours in any week in which he is not required to attend school; or

(9) for more than four hours in any day without a rest break of one hour; or

(10) at any time in a year unless at that time he has had, or could still have, during a period in the year in which he is not required to attend school, at least two consecutive weeks without employment.

These restrictions may be augmented by other restrictions imposed by local authority bye-laws. Conversely, such bye-laws may allow children under 14 years of age to be employed in limited circumstances.[180] Under the unimplemented Employment of Children Act 1973, the Secretary of State has wide powers to regulate the employment of children, the intention being to remove regional variations and impose uniform standards. It is a criminal offence for an employer to engage a child in breach of any of the above restrictions, but he will have a defence where it can be shown that the

---

Act 1963 to implement in relation to children the EC Directive on the Protection of Young Persons at Work. In particular, they raised from 13 to 14 years the age at which a child may be employed in any work other than as an employee of his parent or guardian in light agricultural or horticultural work on an occasional basis. So far as the latter work is concerned, the relevant age at which children may be employed in such work was raised from 10 to 13 years by the Children (Protection at Work) Regulations 2000 (SI 2000/1333) and the Children (Protection at Work) (No 2) Regulations 2000 (SI 2000/2548).

[180] Children and Young Persons Act 1933, s 18(2).

contravention was due to the act or default of some other person and that he himself used all due diligence to secure compliance with the statutory requirements.[181]

Specific restrictions

Various pieces of legislation impose specific restrictions on children participating in particular kinds of employment. Thus, no child may be employed in an industrial undertaking,[182] factory,[183] mine or quarry,[184] in a shop,[185] or aboard a UK registered ship.[186]

Children may not, generally, be employed in street-trading,[187] but local authorities are empowered to make bye-laws which authorise children of 14 years or over (but not younger children) to be employed by their parents in street-trading to a specified extent. The bye-laws may provide for the granting of licences and specify conditions relating to their issue, suspension and revocation. In particular, the bye-laws may determine the days, hours and places during which the children concerned may take part in street-trading.[188]

The employment of children in entertainment and performances is strictly regulated by the Children and Young Persons Acts of 1933 and 1963. Detailed discussion of the minutiae of these provisions is not appropriate here.[189] Suffice it to note that the 1933 Act prohibits the participation by children in dangerous public performances.[190] The training of children to take part in dangerous performances or to be employed outside the UK in singing, playing, performing or being exhibited for profit is controlled by local authority licences.[191] The 1963 Act extended the licensing system to performances more generally, including those on film, television or in broadcasting. Again, a local authority licence must be obtained. This will not be granted unless the authority is satisfied that the child is fit to take part in the performance, that proper provision has been made to secure his health and kind treatment, and that his education will not suffer.[192] These licences apply to all children, namely those under school leaving age, but there are further restrictions on the granting of licences in relation to those under 14 years of age.[193]

---

[181] Ibid, s 21(1).
[182] Employment of Women, Young Persons and Children Act 1920, s 1(1).
[183] Factories Act 1961, s 167.
[184] Mines and Quarries Act 1954, s 124.
[185] Shops Act 1950, s 74(1) and Part II.
[186] Merchant Shipping Act 1995, s 55.
[187] Children and Young Persons Act 1933, s 20(1).
[188] Ibid, s 20(2).
[189] But such a discussion may be found in HK Bevan *Child Law* (Butterworths, 1989), at paras 11.71–11.76. Such children must have attained the age of 12 years to be so trained.
[190] Children and Young Persons Act 1933, s 23, as amended, refers to any performance in which the child's 'life or limbs are endangered'. And see also the Children (Performance) Regulations 1968.
[191] Ibid, s 24. For a more up-to-date discussion see Hamilton and Watt (above) pp 142–143.
[192] Children and Young Persons Act 1963, s 37(4).
[193] Ibid, s 38. Essentially, such a licence may not be granted unless it is for acting or performing in

Enforcement of restrictions

Local education authorities are empowered to institute proceedings in respect of offences under Part II of the Children and Young Persons Act 1933.[194] They may also prohibit or restrict the employment of children where it appears to them that a child is 'being employed in such a manner as to be prejudicial to his health or otherwise to render him unfit to obtain the full benefit of the education provided for him'.[195] The parent or employer may also be required to provide information necessary to ascertain whether the child is being employed in that manner.[196] Failure to comply with a local authority's request for information, or notice of prohibition, constitutes a criminal offence.[197]

There is substantial evidence that enforcement of the statutory restrictions is ineffective and that there is widespread contravention of the law.[198] A report by the Low Pay Unit, following a National Child Employment Study,[199] found a vast amount of illegal employment of children in Birmingham and concluded that large numbers of children were at risk of economic exploitation, physical risk and educational disadvantage. Among the report's more significant findings were that 43 per cent of children between the ages of 10 and 16 years of age had some sort of job: 74 per cent of these were illegally employed, of which one-quarter were under 13 years of age, and many were employed in work prohibited for children or were working illegal hours; 35 per cent had had an accident including cuts, burns, broken bones and assault; and children were generally underpaid with one-quarter of them earning less than £1 per hour. The report called for immediate implementation of the Employment of Children Act 1973, a thorough review of all employment legislation affecting children, minimum wage protection for children and young persons and action, at a European level, to provide greater protection for children at work under the European Social Charter.

Family decisions and the employment of children

Children are, of course, members of families as well as individuals, and this raises issues about the application of family law principles in the context of the employment of children.[200] Two problematic and inter-related issues may be identified. The first issue is the impact of parental responsibility on

---

a ballet or opera. It will need to be established that the particular part to be played by the child could not be taken except by a child of about that age.

[194] Ibid, s 98.
[195] Education Act 1996, s 559(1).
[196] Ibid, s 559(2).
[197] Ibid, s 559(3).
[198] See the assessment of Hamilton and Watt (above), at pp 145–149.
[199] C Pond and A Searle *The Hidden Army: Children at Work in the 1990s* Low Pay Pamphlet No 55, and see the summary at (1991) 76 *Childright* 17.
[200] For a damning critique of the law relating to the employment of children by their families, see A Bond 'Working for the Family? Child employment legislation and the public/private divide' (1996) JSWFL 291.

employment decisions. The second issue is the relationship between child autonomy or '*Gillick* competence' and the restrictions on employment.

Employment and parental responsibility

Bevan has noted how, historically, the absolute nature of parental rights was used as a justification for child slavery, whereby a father sold his child to an employer. This influence of parental rights, according to Bevan, also contributed indirectly to the wretched conditions of apprenticeship in the nineteenth century. The father–child and master–servant relationships were considered so closely analogous that, just as the father could make unrestricted demands on the services of his child, so also could the master or employer – thus giving the barbaric conditions of apprenticeship 'an aura of respectability'.[201]

Parental rights, now responsibilities, are no longer absolute, as has been shown, but an unresolved question is how far a parent might legally be able to interfere with the relationship of child and employer which does not contravene the statutory restrictions. What, for example, is the legal position if a 14-year-old agrees to take a Saturday job but his parents object? Can they prohibit the potential employer from engaging the child? The one point which is clear is that, if the employer should decide to flout the parents' wishes, no action would lie against him in tort.[202] From a practical point of view this may be all that we need to know, but the theoretical question remains. Does the parent, or the child acting in conjunction with the employer, have the right to decide? The answer would again appear to turn on the uncertain interpretation of *Gillick*. The later Court of Appeal decisions in *Re R* and *Re W* suggest that the employer, if satisfied that the child is '*Gillick*-competent', would be acting lawfully either in deciding to employ the child or in following the parents' wishes and deciding not to do so.[203] Any disputes could, at least theoretically, be resolved by application to the court, with leave, for a s 8 order.

Gillick competence and employment restrictions

A respectable argument can be mounted for saying that those children who have acquired *Gillick* competence should be liberated from the statutory restrictions on employment and the corresponding requirements of compulsory education. Why should such children not decide to work rather than stay on in school? This is an argument which undoubtedly appeals to some advocates of the liberationist school of children's rights.[204] The opposing argument, in favour of the employment restrictions and compulsory education, is that the

---

[201] HK Bevan *Child Law* (Butterworths, 1989), at para 11.67.

[202] *F v Wirral Metropolitan Borough Council* [1991] Fam 69.

[203] *Gillick v West Norfolk and Wisbech Area Health Authority* [1986] 1 AC 112, *Re R (A Minor) (Wardship: Medical Treatment)* [1992] Fam 11, and *Re W (A Minor) (Medical Treatment: Court's Jurisdiction)* [1993] Fam 64. And see chapter 8 above.

[204] See also the discussion in MP Grenville 'Compulsory School Attendance and the Child's Wishes' [1988] JSWL 4.

child's 'developmental' and 'basic' interests require that he receive a certain level of education and be protected from premature exposure to work.[205] The essence of this argument is that it is only through proper education that a child can acquire the capacity for meaningful independence later in life, and this justifies imposing statutory restrictions before he matures into adulthood.

The employment of young persons

Until comparatively recent years, there were innumerable statutory provisions regulating the employment of young persons.[206] Most of these related to night work in industrial undertakings and the number of hours which young people were permitted to work in specified occupations, mainly related to the delivery of goods and the running of errands.[207]

Abolition of most protective legislation

The Employment Act 1989[208] swept away practically all the protective legislation applying to young persons as distinct from children. Only a few restrictions which were considered necessary, on health and safety grounds, remain. The legislation involved denunciation of part of the European Social Charter, the main provision being Art 7(8) governing night work, which requires contracting parties 'to provide that persons under 18 years of age shall not be employed in night work with the exception of certain occupations provided for by national laws and regulations'. The power of local authorities to make bye-laws governing the employment of young persons was removed, while the Secretary of State was given wide powers to repeal or amend other relevant statutory provisions. The Employment Act 1989 was part of a wider government policy for the 'deregulation' of the labour market by the removal of discriminatory and protective legislation and the relaxation of certain employment protection rights.[209] The position is, for the present, very straightforward. There is effectively no special protective employment legislation and no general legal restrictions on the employment of young persons.

The legislation was controversial and followed a Consultative Document issued by the Department of Employment in 1987. This contended that there was 'no evidence that long hours, shift work or night work have a different effect on young people than on adults'.[210] Another argument in favour of deregulation was that the existing regulations were piecemeal, complex and difficult to

---

[205] See A Bainham *Children, Parents and the State* (Sweet & Maxwell, 1988), at pp 166–169.
[206] As to which see HK Bevan (above), at para 11.81.
[207] The principal legislation was the Employment of Women, Young Persons and Children Act 1920 and the Young Persons (Employment) Acts 1938 and 1964.
[208] Employment Act 1989, s 10 and Sch 3.
[209] For a critique of the Employment Act 1989, see S Deakin 'Equality Under a Market Order: The Employment Act 1989' (1990) 19 *Industrial Law Journal* 1.
[210] Department of Employment's Consultative Document *Restrictions on Employment of Young People and the Removal of Sex Discrimination in Legislation* (1987), at para 1.8.

understand. As such, they constituted an administrative and clerical burden for employers. It was also said that the legislation was selective in its coverage, without any evidence of greater exploitation in the protected spheres than in the unprotected ones.[211] It was conceded that some form of regulation might need to be retained, on health and safety grounds, or on 'moral' grounds as, for example, to protect young people from exposure to drinking and gambling.[212] The employment of young persons over the age of 16 but under 18 is now subject to special requirements relating to health and safety at work.[213] The regulations require the prospective employer of a young person of that age to undertake a risk assessment relating to his or her health or safety if employed. The regulations specify the factors that must be taken into account in carrying out or reviewing the assessment and these include 'the inexperience, lack of awareness of risks and immaturity of young persons'. The employer must then ensure that such young persons are protected from such risks at work.

Deakin[214] has criticised the legislation for taking away the, admittedly selective, protections for young workers, without making more general provision for maximum hours of work, rest periods and working at weekends. While conceding that there may be no evidence of an extra risk to the health and safety of young workers in the 16–18-year age group, Deakin put forward a more compelling reason for restricting their hours of work, namely 'to facilitate their integration into society'.[215] This, he argued, required that they have positive incentives to train and pursue their education in the transitional period between leaving school and entering fully waged work. The legislation, in his view, 'contributes further to the undervaluing of youth training and education which began with the linking of YTS to a policy of disguising unemployment and coercing the young unemployed into work through cuts in social security'.[216] He concluded that government employment policy in the UK was increasingly out of step with international and European domestic labour standards, which recognise 'that a high level of social protection is a pre-condition of a fair and efficient labour market'.[217] It should be noted that the European Directive applies to 'adolescents' as well as to children, although its requirements are understandably less exacting in relation to the latter. 'Adolescent', for these purposes, is defined by Art 3 as 'any young person of at least 15 years of age but less than 18 years of age who is no longer subject to compulsory full-time schooling under national law'. The Directive prescribes maximum daily working times for adolescents and a prohibition on night work which, despite a partial opt-out for the UK, should require a significant reform of English legislation.

---

[211] Department of Employment's Consultative Document (1987) (above).
[212] Ibid, at para 1.6.2.
[213] Health and Safety (Young Persons) Regulations 1997 (SI 1997/135).
[214] S Deakin (above), at pp 18–19.
[215] Citing the Council of Europe *Nightwork, Comparative Study of Legislation and Regulations, Problems and Social Repercussions* (1981), at p 48.
[216] These wider aspects of employment policy are beyond the scope of this work.
[217] S Deakin (above), at p 19.

The near abolition of protective legislation applying to young persons and the signal failure to enforce that which applies to children presents us with a curious paradox – that the area of law in which there has perhaps, historically, been the largest amount of legislative intervention is also the one in which the legal system has most emphatically failed to protect children and young people.

Chapter 17

CHILDREN AND EDUCATION

'The last duty of parents to their children is that of giving them an education suitable to their station in life: a duty pointed out by reason, and of far the greatest importance of any. For... it is not easy to imagine or allow, that a parent has conferred any considerable benefit on a child, by bringing him into the world, if he afterwards entirely neglects his culture and education, and suffers him to grow up like a mere beast, to lead a life useless to others, and shameful to himself.'

So wrote William Blackstone in his *Commentaries on the Laws of England* (1765–1769) after outlining the law governing parents' duties to maintain and protect their children, hence this being the 'last' of the duties to which he was referring.[1] The position as articulated by Blackstone represents merely a distant echo in our legal history and we are likely to baulk at key aspects of his, and the then law's, approach to the status of children. After all, his chapter on parents and children classified the latter into 'two sorts; legitimate, and spurious, or bastards'. In any event the law at that time did not to any meaningful extent seek the enforcement of parents' natural responsibility, as Blackstone saw it, regarding the child's education. Blackstone noted that in most countries 'municipal laws ... seem to be defective in this point, by not constraining the parent to bestow a proper education upon his children'; and he declared that the shortcomings of English Law in that regard 'cannot be denied'.[2] Today, the law of education is one of the most extensive and highly developed areas of the law affecting children. Nevertheless, Blackstone's emphasis on the importance of education itself, in terms of its contribution to the individual's intellectual and social development, and thus of the obligation to educate, has lost none of its original validity. Yet one of key differences from that time is the role played by the state in guaranteeing the education of all children and providing institutions and other resources to that end. Parental responsibility for a child's education remains, but it is overshadowed by the wide-ranging public responsibility in this sphere.

Under the modern law the functions of educating children and young people are, in effect, covered by a joint or shared responsibility between parent and state, often described (in somewhat idealistic terms) as a 'partnership'. The state's role in educational provision became dominant during the twentieth century, albeit retaining the involvement of religious bodies, which had played the leading educational role in the nineteenth century. Nevertheless, the parent's statutory duty to cause a child of compulsory school age to receive an 'efficient full-time education suitable to his age, ability, and aptitude, either by regular

---

1   W Blackstone *Commentaries on the Laws of England* (1765–1769) Book 1, chapter 16.
2   Ibid.

attendance at school or otherwise'[3] – described by a leading commentator immediately prior to its enactment in the Education Act 1944 as 'bring[ing] the parent right into the front of the picture'[4] – continued. Moreover, from the 1960s onwards the state education system increasingly looked to parents to support its role by participating in their children's education. Today many areas of educational practice seek to harness parental involvement, which is underpinned by numerous parental rights of participation in decision-making, albeit that their practical realisation is experienced unevenly, particularly across social divides.[5]

Among many parents their personal wishes and aspirations for their children represent a powerful motivating force for action and involvement. In seeking to harness such parental instincts, governments from the 1980s onwards were identifying considerable political capital in the advancement of parental rights in education. It also served the ideological interests of the Conservative government throughout that decade in developing a market approach to educational provision based on parental choice and competition between schools.[6] Choice in education remains potent politically today and continues to feature prominently in much of the policy rhetoric in this field and in a range of legislative provisions. Across important areas such as school admissions, the status of a school as an academically-selective grammar school, educational provision for children with learning difficulties, school inspections, and the school curriculum, parents have acquired statutory rights affording them a degree of influence over their child's education. Beyond the area of choice, parental rights have encompassed opportunities to, for example: make representations in connection with the assessment of their child's special educational needs; gain access to information; and complain and/or, in specific circumstances,[7] to appeal or seek a review of a decision. Additionally, the notion of home-school 'partnership', which had gained currency in educational theory and practice, was reinforced statutorily by the requirement that schools offer parents the opportunity to sign a home-school agreement specifying the school's aims and values, its responsibilities and those of the parent, and the 'school's expectations of its pupils'.[8] This was to have been taken a stage further by the introduction of the 'parent's guarantee' concerning aspects of their child's schooling under the relevant provisions of Labour's Children, Schools and Families Bill, although they were contained in clauses which were among those jettisoned in order to facilitate the passage of the rest of the Bill before the general election in May 2010.

---

[3]   Education Act 1944, s 36.

[4]   H C Dent *The New Education Bill. What it Contains. What it Means. Why it Should be Supported* (University of London Press Ltd, 1944), 4.

[5]   See generally N Harris 'Playing catch-up in the schoolyard? Children and young people's "voice" and education rights in the UK' *International Journal of Law, Policy and the Family* (2009), 23(3) 331–366; N Harris *Education, Law and Diversity* (Hart Publishing, 2007).

[6]   See M Flude and M Hammer (eds) *The Education Reform Act 1988. Its origins and implications* (Falmer, 1990); N Harris, *Law and Education: Regulation, Consumerism and the Education System* (Sweet & Maxwell, 1993).

[7]   Ie, in the areas of admissions, permanent exclusions and special educational needs.

[8]   School Standards and Framework Act 1998, ss 110 and 111.

Of course, the rationale for giving parents a greater input into their children's education rests in large part on the potential benefits for the children. Parental rights in this field are indeed premised primarily on the principle that a parent (or other carer) is particularly well placed to know the child's various needs, although the importance of upholding religious and culturally based preferences reflective of the family's values and beliefs is also recognised,[9] being underpinned by the Human Rights Act 1998's incorporation of ECHR Art 2, Protocol 1, discussed more fully below:

> 'No-one shall be denied the right to education. In the exercise of any functions which it assumes in relation to education and to teaching, the State shall respect the right of parents to ensure such education and teaching in conformity with their own religious and philosophical convictions.'

Nevertheless, in relation to the independent rights of children themselves, the pervasiveness of parental rights and obligations within key areas of educational practice and decision-making, discussed in this chapter, could be seen as having negative implications. The emphasis on parental rather than children's rights has repeatedly prompted commentators to focus on the contrast, under domestic law, between the law of education and other key areas of the law concerned with children.[10] It remains a valid concern notwithstanding an increasing recognition of children's autonomy interests and independent rights in this field,[11] often linked to the notion of 'evolving capacities' of young people, which has wide application.[12] The issue was highlighted in a report by the UN's Special Rapporteur on the Right to Education when she visited the UK in 1999. She noted that the underlying conceptual basis to the provision of schooling was seen by government as 'a contract between school and parents' and that children were, in contrast, 'absent as actors in this process although it is aimed at their learning'.[13] Small advances were, however, being made at that time, such as the inclusion of a discretion for school governing bodies to permit the child to sign a home-school agreement, subject to a competency test that the pupil was considered to have a 'sufficient understanding' of the agreement 'as it relates to him' – although such participation was on the somewhat one-sided basis that the child 'acknowledges and accepts the school's expectations of its pupils'.[14] This provision is still in force. Since that time, as discussed below, some real progress has been made; but the broad conclusion remains valid.

---

9   See L Lundy 'Family Values in the Classroom? Reconciling Parental Wishes and Children's Rights in State Schools' (2005) 19 *International Journal of Law, Policy and the Family* 346; and Harris (2007) n 5 above.

10 See N Harris 'Playing catch-up in the schoolyard? Children and young people's "voice" and education rights in the UK' *International Journal of Law, Policy and the Family* (2009), 23(3) 331–366, at 334–335.

11 Ibid.

12 See in particular references to Art 12 of the UN Convention on the Rights of the Child below.

13 UN Commission on Human Rights *Report submitted by Katarina Tomaševski, Special Rapporteur on the Right to Education, Addendum. Mission to the United Kingdom 18–22 October 1999*, E/CN.4/2000/6/Add 2 (2000), at para 31.

14 School Standards and Framework Act 1998, s 110(5).

The other central and related point made by the UN Rapporteur concerned the failure to adopt within English law the rights-based approach reflected in the UN Convention on the Rights of the Child (discussed below). Instead, English law maintained 'the inherited legal status of the child as the object of a legally recognised relationship between the school and the child's parents rather than the subject of the right to education and of human rights in education'.[15] Again, as explained below, progress is being made in addressing this shortcoming. The issue remains important, given the critical role that education is expected to play in children's development as they progress towards adult citizenship, a process involving growing independence and autonomy. It would be entirely inconsistent with that function of education if the law failed to recognise children's autonomic interests. A modern Blackstone may therefore focus rather more on how access to education forms part of an 'empowerment right' for children and young people – as so described by, amongst others, the UN Committee on Economic, Social and Cultural Rights[16] – aiming to ensure that they are equipped with the knowledge, skills and qualifications necessary for social participation and for the advancement of their own, as well as society's, interests.

THE RIGHT TO EDUCATION UNDER INTERNATIONAL LAW

In order to bring out fully the contrast between English education law's somewhat limited recognition of children as independent holders of rights and the position under international law it is necessary to survey the international framework on the right to education and other rights associated with it. The right to education per se is in fact incorporated into a wide range of key international instruments, reflecting its significance as a fundamental human right. The principal provisions comprise:

- The UN Declaration on Human Rights (1948), Art 26;[17]

---

[15] Note 13 above, at para 90.

[16] *Implementation of the International Covenant on Economic, Social and Cultural Rights. General Comment No. 13. The right to education.* E/C.12/1999/10 (UN Economic and Social Council, 1999), at para 1.

[17] '(1) Everyone has the right to education. Education shall be free, at least in the elementary and fundamental stages. Elementary education shall be compulsory. Technical and professional education shall be made generally available and higher education shall be equally accessible to all on the basis of merit.

(2) Education shall be directed to the full development of the human personality and to the strengthening of respect for human rights and fundamental freedoms. It shall promote understanding, tolerance and friendship among all nations, racial or religious groups, and shall further the activities of the United Nations for the maintenance of peace.

(3) Parents have a prior right to choose the kind of education that shall be given to their children.'

- The European Convention for the Protection of Human Rights and Fundamental Freedoms (ECHR) (1950), Art 2 of Protocol 1;[18]

- The European Social Charter, (1961, revised 1996), Arts. 15, 17 and 30;[19]

- The International Covenant on Economic, Social and Cultural Rights (ICESCR) (1966), Arts 13 and 14;[20]

- The UN Convention on the Rights of the Child (CRC) (1990), Arts 28[21] and 29;[22] and

---

18 See p 883 above.
19 Article 15, covering the 'right of persons with disabilities to independence, social integration and participation in the life of the community', requires the taking of measures 'to provide persons with disabilities with ... education'. Article 17, requires that children should receive 'the education and training they need', in particular through the provision of suitable institutions for that purpose and 'a free primary and secondary education'; and should 'encourage regular attendance at schools'. Article 30 includes education among the matters to which efforts should be made to ensure that those at risk of social exclusion or poverty have access.
20 Article 13.1 provides for recognition of everyone's right to education and specifies various matters towards which education should be directed, including 'the full development of the human personality and the sense of its dignity' and the promotion of 'understanding, tolerance and respect' among people of different characteristics or backgrounds. Article 13.2 sets out various institutional requirements for the realisation of the right, such as free and compulsory primary education and the general availability of secondary education. Article 13.3 confers a liberty for parents to choose schools outside the state system, while Art 13.4 upholds the liberty of individuals to establish and direct an educational institution provided the principles in Art 13.1 are observed and the institution meets at least the minimum standards laid down by the state. Article 14 calls for a plan for the progressive implementation within a reasonable space of time of free compulsory primary education where not provided in the state. ICESCR, a 'specialised international instrument in the field of education', is 'in an appropriate case, [to] be taken into consideration by the court': *R (Hurley and Moore) v Secretary of State for Business, Innovation and Skills* [2012] EWHC 201 (Admin) [2012] ELR 297, per Elias LJ, at [43].
21 Article 28.1 provides for the right to education and access to various forms of it, including free and compulsory primary education. Article 28.2 requires States parties to 'take all appropriate measures to ensure that school discipline is administered in a manner consistent with the child's human dignity and in conformity with the present Convention'. Article 28.3 provides for international co-operation in matters relating to education.
22 Article 29.1 sets out matters towards which the child's education should be directed:
'(a) The development of the child's personality, talents and mental and physical abilities to their fullest potential;
(b) The development of respect for human rights and fundamental freedoms, and for the principles enshrined in the Charter of the United Nations;
(c) The development of respect for the child's parents, his or her own cultural identity, language and values, for the national values of the country in which the child is living, the country from which he or she may originate, and for civilizations different from his or her own;
(d) The preparation of the child for responsible life in a free society, in the spirit of understanding, peace, tolerance, equality of sexes, and friendship among all peoples, ethnic, national and religious groups and persons of indigenous origin;
(e) The development of respect for the natural environment.'
Article 29.2 makes similar provision on the right to establish and direct educational institutions to that in Art 13.4 of ICECSR (note 20 above).

- The Charter of Fundamental Rights of the European Union (2000), Art 14.[23]

Other international provisions which lay down obligations relevant to the right to education include the UN Convention on the Rights of Persons with Disabilities, ratified by the UK, which calls on States Parties to accord recognition to the right to education of persons with disabilities and, to this end 'ensure an inclusive education system at all levels'.[24] In addition, general provisions providing for the equal enjoyment of the various rights regardless of personal characteristics such as gender, ethnicity and disability[25] will apply and are of particular importance where education is concerned (see below). A range of other human rights variously protected by the above instruments, such as the right to privacy and family life (Art 8) and freedom of religious expression (Art 9) under the ECHR,[26] have been seen to have a particular relevance to the field of education.[27] Indeed, education has been one of the key testing areas for human rights protection in the changing social environment of the past 30 years. Across most western states there has been an increase in social and cultural diversity and in citizens' awareness of their rights and willingness to assert them – particularly in a field where parents' sensitivity to the potential impact of professionals' and administrators' decisions on their child's welfare increases the risk that disagreements will be transformed into disputes.[28]

From the various instruments we can discern certain essential features of the right to education which are common to most of them, either expressly or when read with their general equality provisions. In particular, the rights conferred should be enjoyed *universally* and *equally* within states. The right to education is generally expressed to be a right available to all and, as the CRC puts it: 'on the basis of equal opportunity' (Art 28.1). Many of the cases about the right to education under the ECHR that have come before the European Court of Human Rights (and, in the past the European Commission of Human Rights) have concerned discrimination under Art 14 of the ECHR. This provides that Convention rights and freedoms –

---

[23]   This includes the right to education and to have access to vocational and continuing training, the 'possibility to receive free compulsory education', the 'freedom to found educational establishments with due respect for democratic principles', and a requirement that 'the right of parents to ensure the education and teaching of their children in conformity with their religious, philosophical and pedagogical convictions shall be respected, in accordance with the national laws governing the exercise of such freedom and right'. See, as regards the effect of the special protocol (protocol 30) on the UK's (and Poland's) obligations under the Charter: S Peers 'The "Opt-out" that Fell to Earth: The British and Polish Protocol Concerning the EU Charter of Fundamental Rights' HRLR (2012) 12(2), 375–389.

[24]   Article 24.1.

[25]   Such as Art 14 of ECHR and Art 2 of the CRC.

[26]   Both set out and explained below.

[27]   N Harris *Education, Law and Diversity* (n 5 above), chs 2 and 7.

[28]   See N Harris and S Riddell *Resolving Disputes about Educational Provision* (Ashgate, 2011), ch 2.

'shall be secured without discrimination on any ground such as sex, race, colour, language, religion, political or other opinion, national or social origin, association with a national minority, property, birth or other status.'

Read with Art 2 of the First Protocol (A2P1) it in effect provides for equality of access to education. However, discrimination will not violate the Convention where it can be shown to have an objective or reasonable justification by being in pursuit of a legitimate aim and being effected in a way that is proportionate to that aim. In some cases this has meant that state social policies which are discriminatory, for example treating some groups less favourably than others, may be justifiable in order to target state support where it is considered to be most needed.[29] For example, Art 14 was held not to be violated in *Angeleni v Sweden*,[30] where atheists were not excused from school religious knowledge lessons, which had a Christian focus, whereas children of non-Christian faiths could be exempted at the parents' request. The rationale for the difference of treatment was that the latter group would learn about religion from their own faith communities but atheists would not and so needed to be exposed to religious knowledge in these classes. The Commission of Human Rights held that the arrangements had a legitimate aim, to ensure that all children had sufficient knowledge of religion, and that the discrimination had an objective and reasonable justification.[31] Justification was also found by the Court in *Belgian Linguistics* (above) for the requirement that all children be taught in Flemish-speaking schools. The Court regarded it as consistent with a legitimate aim of ensuring linguistic unity in that state, thereby justifying the denial of mother tongue teaching in French to the complainants' children.

It should be stressed, however, that a relatively higher threshold has been set for justification relating to matters of race or ethnicity than for other forms of discrimination. This was re-emphasised by the Grand Chamber of the Court in *DH v Czech Republic*:[32]

'Where the difference in treatment is based on race, colour or ethic origin, the notion of objective and reasonable justification must be interpreted as strictly as possible.'[33]

In this important case, 18 Czech national children of Roma origin were, on the basis of test scores, placed in special schools for children with learning difficulties. The tests could not be carried out without the consent of the parents' legal representative. The complaint was that there was a violation of A2P1 since the practice had led to a form of segregation and discrimination on the basis of race, with Roma children disproportionately sent to special schools.

---

[29] See *Carson v United Kingdom* (2009) 48 EHRR 41; and *R (RJM) v Secretary of State for Work and Pensions* [2008] UKHL 63.

[30] Application No 10491/83, (1988) 10 EHRR CD 123.

[31] Ibid, at para 4. The Commission also rejected the argument that by being exposed to Christian-focused religious knowledge the complainants' children were subjected to religious indoctrination.

[32] Application No 57325/00 (Grand Chamber, 13 November 2007) [2008] ELR 17.

[33] Ibid, at para 196.

The Grand Chamber found that there were questions concerning the reliability of the tests; and that while consent to discriminatory treatment by those affected (that is, the parents) could operate as a waiver to the right under Art 14, that did not apply where that consent was not properly informed. The Czech Republic was found to be attempting to find a suitable solution to meeting the needs of Roma children, and enjoyed the margin of appreciation accorded to states in doing so. But it had placed Roma children at a disadvantage by being at a school for those with mental disabilities who followed a more basic curriculum and it had separated them from other children. The difference in treatment was not objectively justified.[34] There have been two other similar cases, one involving Croatia and the other Greece, where such a violation has been found to occur.[35]

Equality in practice cannot be taken for granted. Indeed, the redistributive effect associated with social and economic rights[36] is undermined by the structural inequalities within societies which have the effect of limiting the enjoyment of such rights among the least advantaged. In relation to education, there may be social or economic barriers to accessing the provision that these rights are meant to guarantee – or, at least, to the degree of choice or to ensuring access to better quality services. While rights convey an egalitarian and universalist message, the extent to which they are enjoyed by individuals in practice may of course vary in accordance with their personal resources and capacities and their socio-economic position.[37]

Often the right to education as set out in the various international instruments refers to specific levels of education – such as primary, secondary, and tertiary/ higher education. Generally it is provided that primary education should be free to all, but (with the exception of the CFREU) that the provision of free secondary education is a goal. Another important principle in some of the instruments, notably the ECHR and the UN Declaration, is that of parental choice, as in the requirement in the ECHR A2P1 that respect is paid to parents' right for the child to be educated in accordance with 'their own religious and philosophical convictions'. In similar vein, Art 26(3) of the UN Declaration provides that '[p]arents have a prior right to choose the kind of education that shall be given to their children'.

---

[34]   The Court awarded €4,000 in respect of non-pecuniary losses to each of the applicants and a joint award of €10,000 in costs.

[35]   *Oršuš v Croatia*, (Application No 15766/03), 16 March 2010 (Grand Chamber); *Sampanis and Others v Greece* (Application No 32526/05), 5 June 2008.

[36]   D Feldman, *Civil Liberties and Human Rights in England and Wales* (2nd edn, Oxford University Press, 2002), 13–14. Fredman, however, regards education as falling on both sides of the line between, on one side, civil and political rights, and on the other, socio-economic rights, citing in relation to the former the right not to be denied education and the restraint on the state from interfering with respect for religious and philosophical preferences under the ECHR Art 2 of the First Protocol: S. Fredman *Human Rights Transformed. Positive rights and positive duties* (OUP, 2008), at p 215.

[37]   See generally Harris, n 5 above.

We also see in the instruments that in some cases discipline is specifically included as a matter governed by the right to education. Article 28 of the UNCRC, for example, requires among other things that school discipline is to be 'administered in a manner consistent with the child's human dignity'. In other cases, as under the ECHR, issues arising in connection with discipline or other facets of school life may fall implicitly within the scope of the right to education: thus the state's obligation under ECHR to respect parents' religious or philosophical convictions in relation to the teaching of the child, noted above, has been held in the case of *Campbell and Cosans* to extend to discipline in school.[38] However, discipline is also relevant, for the purposes of the ECHR, to issues such as 'inhuman or degrading treatment or punishment' (Art 3),[39] interference with private and family life (Art 8),[40] and, where it clashes with religious or philosophical convictions, freedom of religion (Art 9),[41] all of which have formed the basis of challenges via the Strasbourg court (and, as discussed later, the courts in the UK). Indeed, the European Court of Human Rights has repeatedly emphasised the need for these rights and the right to education under A2P1 to be read in the light of each other.[42] School attendance is also addressed, in the UNCRC (Art 28.1(e)), which provides that States Parties must 'Take measures to encourage regular attendance at schools and the reduction of drop-out rates.'

In addition, the General Comment on Art 13 of the ICESCR sets out a basic framework of four 'interrelated and essential features' that are regarded as a useful basis for analysing the content of the right to education, although the Comment recognises that the precise basis on which educational provision will be made in a particular state may depend on the prevailing conditions (economic, political or social). The four elements are:

(a) *Availability*
This refers to the need for 'functioning educational institutions and programmes ... available in sufficient quantity within the jurisdiction of the State party' and sufficient trained teachers and library, computing and other facilities.

(b) *Accessibility*
This refers to the accessibility of institutions and programmes to everyone, without discrimination. Both physical/geographical and economic accessibility are referred to.

(c) *Acceptability*

---

[38] *Campbell and Cosans v United Kingdom* (1982) 4 EHRR 293.
[39] Eg *Costello-Roberts v United Kingdom* (Case No 89/1991/341/414) [1994] ELR 1.
[40] Ibid.
[41] Eg *Valsamis v Greece* (Case No 74/1995/580/666) (1997) 24 EHRR 294, [1998] ELR 430; *Şahin v Turkey* (Application No 44774/98), 10 November 2005; *Dogru v France* (Application No 27058/05) [2009] ELR 77.
[42] Eg *Kjeldsen, Busk Madsen and Pedersen v Denmark* (1979–80) 1 EHRR 711, at [52]; *Costello-Roberts* (n 39 above), at [27]; *Dojan and Others v Germany* (Application Nos 391/08, 2455/08, 7908/10, 8152/10 and 8155/10) [2011] ELR 511.

This refers to the form and substance of education, including curricula and teaching methods, which must be 'acceptable (e.g. relevant, culturally appropriate and of good quality) to students and, in appropriate cases, parents; this is subject to [certain educational objectives required by Art 13] and such minimum educational standards as may be approved by the State'; and

(d)   *Adaptability*
This refers to the need for education 'to be flexible so it can adapt to the needs of changing societies and communities and respond to the needs of students within their diverse social and cultural settings.'

However, as the content of Art 13 of ICESCR itself suggests, the state has considerable flexibility in how it meets its broad obligations and this includes the allocation of resources to that end. The state is generally acknowledged to have a responsibility to manage and allocate resources in a way that supports collective interests such as meeting particular social/educational goals within budgetary constraints. One of the problems with social rights such as the right to education relates to the resource-dependency of the public services that are responsible for ensuring social entitlement. It limits the guarantees that are provided and reinforces the difficulty in enforcing the rights – rights which are not absolute, whose limitations are underlined by their contingency and which are mostly expressed in open-textured and fairly imprecise language.

This limitation was confirmed by the European Court of Human Rights in *Belgian Linguistics*, referred to above, when deciding that the Belgian state was, essentially, not acting in conflict with A2P1 in refusing to provide French-medium schooling at the state's expense in a Flemish speaking part of the country despite parental claims that their linguistic preference for the use of the French language in teaching fell within the scope of the right to education. The Court noted that:[43]

'the Contracting Parties do not recognise such a right to education as would require them to establish at their own expense, or to subsidise, education of any particular type or at any particular level.'

This conclusion was influenced by the negative formulation of the first sentence of the Article, in the sense that it was premised on the authority of the individual state to decide on the nature of its education system.[44] But it should also be noted that the UK entered a reservation to the second sentence of the Article. The reservation provides that the right of parents for their children's

---

[43]   *Belgian Linguistics (No 2)* 1 EHRR 252 (1979–80), at para 3.
[44]   The *travaux preparatoires* note that the proponents of a negative formulation, led by the British delegation on the Committee of Experts, feared that 'if the right to education were stated positively, it might be interpreted as imposing on the governments the obligation to take effective measures to ensure that everybody could receive the education which he desired': Council of Europe, *Travaux preparatoires de l'article 2 du Protocole additionnel à la Convention* (1967), Report of the Committee of Experts to the Committee of Ministers, 24 February 1951 (Doc. CM/WP VI (51) 7, Doc. CM/WP I (51) 4C; A 4024), at p 128.

education to be in accordance with the parents' convictions is accepted only to the extent that it is compatible with the provision of efficient instruction and training and the avoidance of unreasonable public expenditure. Even without this reservation, the Strasbourg case law shows that rights of choice under A2P1 are relatively weak in the light of the state's freedom to determine how educational provision is to be made in the wider collective interest of citizens. Individual rights therefore often have to give way in the face of national or local priorities, for example with regard to the type of institution in which the child is to be educated (although domestic law may provide a stronger guarantee: see below). As a result, the respect to be paid to parents' philosophical or religious convictions will offer protection against the indoctrination of their children; but public authorities' power to make policy and resource decisions regardless of the limiting effect on parental choice is otherwise not cut down.[45] However, it is also the case that sometimes parental wishes may play against the state's broader role in supporting a free society and preparing children for it.

For example, in *Kjeldsen* the European Court of Human Rights held that compulsory sex education in schools in Denmark did not infringe the rights of the parents, who had strict Christian views and were opposed to sex education in school. This was because, inter alia, the education provided was 'objective, critical and pluralistic' and did not amount to indoctrination.[46] Similarly in *Dojan and Others v Germany*[47] the Court concluded that the refusal of the authorities to permit the parents, who were members of the Christian Evangelical Baptist Church and were opposed to aspects of sex education at school, to withdraw their children from lessons did not give rise to a breach of A2P1. The Court found consonant with the Article the approach of the German state towards sex education for the fourth grade pupils in question, as it was objective and aimed to educate 'responsible and emancipated citizens capable of participating in the democratic processes of a pluralistic society' and 'avoid the formation of religiously or ideologically motivated "parallel societies"'.[48] In another case, *Konrad and Others v Germany*,[49] where the parents who belonged to a Christian community and wanted to educate their children at home because they disagreed profoundly on religious grounds with various aspects of school education, including sex education and the inclusion of content which made reference to mythical creatures such as witches and dwarfs in fairytales, the Court held that compulsory school education did not violate their rights under the Article. It found that the domestic courts'

---

[45] See e g *Belgian Linguistics* n 43 above. See also *Horváth and Kiss v Hungary* (Application No 11146/11) [2013] ELR 102, at para 103, the Court stating that while 'respect' connotes a positive obligation on the state, the state's obligation arising from it varied 'considerably from case to case' given the diversity of practices and circumstances in individual states, and states enjoyed 'a wide margin of appreciation in determining the steps to be taken to ensure compliance ... with due regard to the needs and resources of the community and of individuals'. But see *Catan v Moldova and Russia* (Application Nos 43370/04 and 18454/06).

[46] *Kjeldsen, Busk Masden and Pedersen v Denmark* (1979–80) 1 EHRR 711.

[47] Application Nos 391/08, 2455/08, 7908/10, 8152/10 and 8155/10 [2011] ELR 511.

[48] Ibid, at [2].

[49] *Konrad and Others v Germany* (Application No 35504/03) [2007] ELR 435.

conclusion, that the goals of primary education in ensuring integration into and first experiences of society could not be met via home education, was consistent with the ECHR and its own jurisprudence. It took a similar view to that taken subsequently in *Dojan* (above) with regard to the state's aim of avoiding the development of 'parallel societies' and stressing the importance of integrating minorities.[50] A further issue, considered by the Commission of Human Rights in *Leuffen v Germany*,[51] is whether the education provided by the parent at home would result in a denial of the child's right to education. In that case the Commission found that the authorities had concluded that the education to be provided at home by the mother, who resisted her child's compulsory kindergarten attendance due to what she perceived as an academic and moral decline in state schools and the potential exposure of the child to violent and immoral influences there, would be 'damaging for the child'. The Commission stated that 'parents may not refuse the right to education of a child on the basis of their convictions'.[52]

On the other hand, in *Folgerø v Norway*,[53] the Court considered that the line had been crossed by the inclusion in the school curriculum of a subject known as 'Christianity, Religion and Philosophy' (or KRL) which was objected to by humanist parents. Partial exemptions were granted by the state but the court considered them to be insufficient in the light of the considerable emphasis given to Christianity and the risk that although parents would not have to reveal intimate details of their own religious or philosophical convictions in order to claim exemption, they might feel compelled to do so in order to fulfil the condition of showing reasonable grounds. Although the parents in Norway (where private schools were funded to the tune of 85 per cent by the state) had the option of private education, 'the existence of such a possibility could not dispense the state from its obligation to safeguard pluralism in state schools which are open to everyone'.[54] The curriculum arrangements were therefore incompatible with A2P1 because the Norweigan state did not take 'sufficient care that information and knowledge in the curriculum was conveyed in an objective, critical and pluralistic manner for the purposes of [the Article]'.[55]

Once one moves away from the curriculum per se the claim of indoctrination is harder to sustain. In *Lautsi v Italy*,[56] for example, the Grand Chamber of the European Court of Human Rights considered that the hanging of crucifixes on the walls of classrooms in state schools in Italy did not amount to indoctrination of children such as to give rise to an infringement of A2P1 by

---

[50]　The Court also considered that interference with the Art 8 and 9 rights of the parents was justified under Art 8(2) and 9(2) respectively due to being 'provided by law and necessary in a democratic society in view of the public interest in ensuring children's education' (ibid (ELR) at 443).

[51]　Application No 19844/92 (9 July 1992).

[52]　For the purposes of Art 8(2), the interference with rights under Art 8 was provided for by law and necessary for the protection of the child's right to education.

[53]　Application No 15472/02 [2007] ELR 557.

[54]　Ibid, at para 101.

[55]　Ibid, at para 102.

[56]　Application No 30814/06 [2011] ELR 176.

conflicting with the religious and philosophical convictions of a parent who favoured secularism. Among other things, the court did not consider that there was anything to suggest an intolerance of pupils from other or no religions or that the crucifixes tended to encourage proselytising.[57] The crucifix was seen as a 'passive symbol' consistent with the requirement of neutrality in the approach to education. It could not be 'deemed to have an influence on pupils comparable to that of didactic speech or participation in religious activities'.[58] A further factor in this decision was the continuing right of the applicant (a mother of a pupil) to impart her own beliefs to the child away from school:[59]

> 'the parent retained in full her right as a parent to enlighten and advise her children, to exercise … her natural functions as educator and to guide them on a path in line with her own philosophical convictions.'

This further illustrates the shared parent-and-state responsibility for a child's education referred to earlier. Another illustration is the case of *Valsamis v Greece*[60] where the court held that the required participation of children in the school parades to mark the successful resistance of Greece to Italy in the Second World War could not 'offend the applicants' pacifist convictions to an extent prohibited by [Article 2 of the First Protocol]',[61] particularly since the parents, who were Jehovah's witnesses, could promote their pacifist values to the children at home.

The Court has also refused to specify beyond a few very basic matters – namely access to educational institutions established or supported by the state, certification of qualifications obtained and teaching via the national language or one of the national languages[62] – what obligations rest with the state to ensure the right to education is not denied. However, in *Ali v United Kingdom*,[63] the European Court of Human Rights made reference to access to the national curriculum. The court held that while arrangements for a child's education following temporary exclusion from school may not necessarily violate the right to education even if they did not provide access to the national curriculum, 'the situation may well be different if a pupil of compulsory school age were to be permanently excluded from one school and were not able to secure full-time education in line with the national curriculum at another school'.[64]

A majority of the formulations of the right to education under international law are clearly parent-orientated. The relevant provisions of the CRC are an obvious exception, although even here it is acknowledged (in Art 5) that in the exercise of these rights children may need 'appropriate direction and guidance'

---

[57] Ibid, at [74].
[58] Ibid, at [72].
[59] Ibid, at [75].
[60] *Valsamis v Greece* (Case No 74/1995/580/666) (1997) 24 EHRR 294.
[61] Ibid, at para 31.
[62] *Belgian Linguistics* n 43 above, at para 3.
[63] Application No 40385/06 [2011] ELR 85.
[64] Ibid, at [60].

from their parents, taking account of the 'evolving capacities of the child'. The European Court of Human Rights, referring to A2P1 to the ECHR, has declared that:[65]

> '[i]t is in the discharge of a natural duty towards their children – parents being primarily responsible for the education and teaching of their children – that parents may require the state to respect their religious and philosophical convictions.'

Yet it is clear that children are not merely vicarious beneficiaries of education rights held by parents. A2P1 ECHR (above) has been described by the European Court of Human Rights as being 'dominated by its first sentence' ('no-one shall be denied the right to education'),[66] which may be regarded as concerned with a right of the *child*, although there is a clear *parent* orientation to the second sentence, which refers to teaching in conformity with the parent's religious or philosophical convictions. Indeed, in a number of education cases decided by the Court, although not all concerned with this Article specifically, the complainant has been a child/young person[67] and no-one, including the Court, appears to have suggested that, on that basis, the judges have lacked jurisdiction.[68] It should also be noted that in the UK courts litigant children have a clear right to invoke the Convention provisions in addition to provisions of domestic law in support of a legal claim and this has happened repeatedly.[69] (Of course, legal aid eligibility will more easily be established in the case of a child, who is more likely than an adult to satisfy the relevant means test.)

For most children it may seem reasonable to recognise parental responsibility over education as in the case of other areas linked to children's development, such as religion[70] and culture. Nevertheless, there are concerns. Can it reasonably be assumed that parents will know what arrangements are most appropriate educationally for the child or will act sensibly, rationally and in the child's best interests and without some other motive at heart? Will the upholding of parents' rights mean that children's wishes and feelings, which may be the key to understanding what form of education or setting would be the most effective for them (and are meant to be given consideration, in 'all matters affecting the child', under Art 12 of the CRC[71]), are overlooked? Given the recognition under the CRC and in the post-*Gillick* era of children's

---

[65]   *Dojan and Others v Germany*, n 47 above, at [2].

[66]   *Oršuš v Croatia*, European Court of Human Rights (Application No 15766/03) [2008] ELR 619, at para 57.

[67]   *Dogru v France*, n 41 above.

[68]   But see J Fortin, *Children's Rights and the Developing Law* (3rd edn, Cambridge University Press, 2009), at pp 67–69 as regards the failure by the Strasbourg judges to focus adequately on the child's position.

[69]   See e g the case of *Begum*, discussed below.

[70]   Note the parent's right to withdraw the child from religious education or collective worship at school: pp 928 and 929 below.

[71]   Provided the child is 'capable of forming his or her own views' he or she is to have a right to express them freely on such matters; and the views are to be given 'due weight in accordance with the age and maturity of the child': Art 12(1). See also Art 12(2) as regards the right to be heard in judicial and administrative proceedings. See further pp 920 and 929 below.

'evolving capacities' as they develop and mature, is it appropriate for many areas of domestic education law to offer parental rights exclusively rather than conferring rights on mature and capable adolescents?

A final point about the right to education under international law that one should not lose sight of is that, in the less developed world, the effective realisation of this right cannot be taken for granted, particularly in the case of girls in general or children with disabilities. The UN Special Rapporteur on the Right to Education has, for example, noted 'a marked disparity between rich countries and poor countries with regard to the conditions in which persons with disabilities are educated in schools'.[72]

THE RIGHT TO EDUCATION UNDER DOMESTIC LAW

Does domestic law embody a 'right to education' per se?

The law of education in England or Wales does not provide an express 'right to education' in the way that, for example, the law in Scotland does.[73] Instead, the right to education under domestic law derives from statutory duties imposed on parents and the state. By virtue of the Human Rights Act 1998, s 6, public authorities (which term includes a state school[74]) in the UK must not act in a way that is incompatible with the main Convention obligations including those relating to the right to education in ECHR Art 2 of the First Protocol (above). However, as we have seen, it is clear that the Convention's right to education is weak, offering no guarantee of access to any particular institution and a right only to 'a minimum level of education'.[75] Consequently, the Article itself has added little additional protection to that already afforded by domestic legislation. This is also true of the other key provisions of the Convention that are of particular relevance to education, notably Arts 8 and 9. The latter is discussed in more detail below.

In the case of Art 8 (the right to respect for private and family life), the UK courts have rejected claims arising in a wide range of educational contexts, such as exclusion from school[76] (including an appeal[77]), special educational needs,[78]

---

[72]   Human Rights Council, *The right to education of persons with disabilities Report of the Special Rapporteur on the right to education, Vernor Muñoz*, A/HRC/4/29, 19 February 2007, at para 74.

[73]   See the Standards in Scotland's Schools Act 2000, s 1, headed 'Right of child to school education': 'It shall be the right of every child of school age to be provided with school education by, or by virtue of arrangements made, or entered into, by, an education authority'.

[74]   *Ali v Headteacher and Governors of Lord Grey School* [2006] UKHL 14, [2006] ELR 223, at 79 (per Baroness Hale).

[75]   Ibid, per Lord Hoffmann, at para 61. Case law on A2P1 is reviewed in Lord Bingham's judgment.

[76]   *R (B) v Head Teacher of Alperton Community School; R v Head Teacher of Wembley High School Ex p T; R v The Governing Body of Cardinal Newman High School Ex p C* [2001] ELR 359; and *R (LG, Mother and Litigation Friend of V) v Independent Appeal Panel for Tom Hood School and Others* [2009] ELR 248.

school transport,[79] admission to school (where one sibling was refused a place at a school to which the other sibling had been admitted),[80] and restrictions on what pupils may wear at school.[81] Generally this is because education decisions by their nature will impinge upon family autonomy and the courts accept the basic precept that 'the sending of a child to school necessarily involves some interference with his or her private life'.[82] There is in any event the authority in Art 8(2) to interfere with the Art 8 right where it is:[83]

> 'in accordance with the law and is necessary in a democratic society in the interests of national security, public safety or the economic well-being of the country, for the prevention of disorder or crime, for the protection of health or morals, or for the protection of the rights and freedoms of others.'

In one case where a parent of a child with profound bilateral hearing loss objected to the child's placement in a boarding school the court accepted that such a decision gave rise to a prime facie interference with family life. However, the judge nevertheless considered that as there was no other identified school closer to the family home which could meet the child's needs, which were severe and complex, the interference was justified by Art 8(2).[84]

One measure that would have given domestic law more of a rights orientation in England was the Children, Schools and Families Bill published in November 2009. In addition to the proposed 'parent guarantee' referred to in the introduction to this chapter the Bill also made reference to a 'pupil guarantee',[85] a component which also failed to survive in the Bill's frantic final stages prior to the 2010 general election. Under the Bill the pupil guarantee was to be 'framed with a view to realising the pupil ambitions'. The 'ambitions' (but not the guarantee itself) were set out in the Bill and included that all pupils should 'go to schools were there is good behaviour, strong discipline, order and safety' and where they are taught 'a broad, balanced and flexible curriculum' and acquire 'skills for life'. There was also reference to schools teaching pupils 'in ways that meet their needs', checking their progress and promoting their health and well-being. The matters set out in the guarantee largely replicated

---

[77]   *H v Tomlinson* [2009] ELR 14 CA.

[78]   *A v Essex County Council; J v Worcestershire County Council; S v Hertfordshire County Council; B v Suffolk County Council* [2007] EWHC 1652 (QB); *CB v Merton LBC and the Special Educational Needs Tribunal* [2002] ELR 441.

[79]   *R (R and Others) v Leeds City Council/Education Leeds* [2006] ELR 25.

[80]   *R (O) v St James RC Roman Catholic Primary School Appeal Panel* [2001] ELR 469. But note the comment by Collins J in *R (K) v London Borough of Newham* that school admission policies' tendency to prioritise siblings of existing pupils was 'rendered all the more necessary because of the provisions of Art 8 of the Convention': [2002] ELR 390, at para [39].

[81]   See *R (Watkins-Singh) v Governing Body of Aberdare Girls' High School and Rhondda Cynon Taf Unitary Authority* [2008] ELR 561 – concerning the wearing of the Kara, a bangle worn by Sikhs. The girl in question was nevertheless successful with the discrimination aspect of her claim – see pp 911–913 below.

[82]   *Costello-Roberts v United Kingdom* [1994] ELR 1, at [36].

[83]   ECHR Art 8(2).

[84]   *CB v London Borough of Merton and SENT* [2002] ELR 441.

[85]   Children, Schools and Families Bill, as first published (November 2009), clause 1.

existing (and somewhat vague) entitlements derived from duties spanning wide areas of education law,[86] thereby perhaps justifying the Opposition's criticism that the Bill was offering nothing new. The pupil guarantee itself appeared mostly to be aimed at reassuring parents. Nevertheless, it placed a focus on the entitlement of the child and thus reinforced the idea that education rights are children's rights. Even so, one should note that although it was aimed at conferring benefits on pupils, the pupil guarantee was to be enforceable via *parental* complaint.[87]

Ensuring the child's access to education

In the absence of an explicit right to education under domestic law, children's right to education derives in part from a parental duty to ensure that the child, if of compulsory school age, receives an efficient full-time education and, if the child is enrolled at a school, attends regularly.[88] This duty was originally laid down in the Education Act 1944 and was subsequently consolidated within the Education Act 1996.[89] The question of whether child's right to education might also be reinforced by placing a responsibility on children themselves to attend school, is discussed later, but it may be noted that as a result of the Education and Skills Act 2008 young people aged 16–18 will progressively be placed under a duty to participate in education, training or an apprenticeship; provision, not yet introduced, is made for those who fail to comply with any attendance notice served on them for not participating to be fined.[90] Within this post-compulsory school age group the 'participation age,' as it is known, will effectively be 17 for the first cohort of young people affected, from the summer of 2013, and will rise to 18 from summer 2015.[91] This is happening at a time when financial support to facilitate participation by this age group, through an educational maintenance allowance (EMA) for those from families on low incomes, has been phased out and replaced by a bursary scheme for the most vulnerable 16–19-year-olds. The bursary scheme is more restricted than the EMA scheme

---

[86] As acknowledged by the then Secretary of State, Mr Ed Balls: HC Debs, vol 503, col 433, 11 January 2012.

[87] DCSF Press Release 'Your child, your schools, our future. Building a 21st century schools system', 30 June 2009.

[88] The basic age range of compulsory school age is 5 to 16: Education Act 1996, s 8, as amended by the Education Act 1997, s 52. See also the Education (Start of Compulsory School Age) Order 1998 (SI 1998/1607). The school leaving date (SLD), which is prescribed (the last Friday in June: Education (School Leaving Date) Order 1997 (SI 1997/1970)), is important. A child reaching the age of 16 before the SLD remains of compulsory school age until after that date. A child reaching 16 between the SLD and the start of the next school year officially ceases to be of compulsory school age with effect from the end of SLD. Note that school admission authorities must act in accordance with the School Admissions Code (Department for Education, 2012) (School Standards and Framework Act 1998, s 84, as amended), which facilitates admission of four-year-olds to school by stating (at para 2.16) that the authorities must 'provide for the admission of all children in the September following their fourth birthday'.

[89] Education Act 1996, ss 7, 444, 444A. See below.

[90] Education and Skills Act 2008, ss 51 and 55.

[91] See the Education and Skills Act 2008, Part 1 and s 173 (as amended by the Education Act 2011, s 74). See further pp 960–961 below.

and is giving rise to government expenditure only one-third as high as that on EMAs.[92] The element of coercion introduced by the 2008 Act reform perhaps places this promotion of participation in education or similar activities outside the rights paradigm. This is particularly so if one accepts the conclusion of the Parliamentary Joint Committee on Human Rights that it constitutes a potential interference with the right to respect for private or family life for the purposes of Art 8 of the ECHR.[93]

The other main way in which the child's right to education is recognised is through the wide-ranging obligations placed on local authorities, formerly known, in connection with their education duties, as 'local education authorities' (or LEAs).[94] In particular, local authorities have a broad statutory duty to:[95]

> 'contribute towards the spiritual, moral, mental and physical development of the community by securing that efficient primary, secondary and further education are available to meet the needs of the population in their area.'

The orientation of this requirement is essentially collective rather than focussed on the position of the individual child.

There is, however, more of an individual focus to at least the third head of the separate duty resting with local authorities, under the Education Act 1996, s 14, to exercise their relevant education and training functions, so far as they can be, with a view to:[96]

> '(a) promoting high standards, (b) ensuring fair access to opportunity for education and training, and (c) promoting the fulfilment of learning potential by [amongst others, every person aged under 20].'

Section 14 also contains a very important local authority duty to ensure that 'sufficient' schools for primary and secondary education are available for providing all pupils with 'the opportunity of appropriate education' (namely education which is sufficiently varied as to cater for the different ages, abilities, aptitudes and special educational needs of pupils).[97] Local authorities in

---

92   Noted in Department for Employment and Learning (Northern Ireland) (DELNI), *Future of the Education Maintenance Allowance Scheme* (DELNI, 2012), at para 5.3. The new bursary scheme in England is in two parts: a guaranteed payment for a small number (12,000) of the most vulnerable young people; and a discretionary fund provided to colleges for them to distribute.

93   Parliamentary Joint Committee on Human Rights, Ninteenth Report of Session 2007–08, *Legislative Scrunity: Education and Skills Bill*, HL paper 107, HC 553 (The Stationery Office, 2008).

94   The Education Act 1944 created 'local education authorities', but as a separate legal entity they have ceased to exist, being replaced across education legislation by 'local authority' from April 2010 under the Education and Inspections Act 2006, s 162.

95   Education Act 1944, s 7, now the Education Act 1996, s 13(1).

96   Education Act 1996, s 13A(1) and (2), as substituted by the Apprenticeships, Skills, Children and Learning Act 2009, Sch 2.

97   Education Act 1996, s 14(1)–(3).

England have also recently been placed under (i) a duty to ensure that there is 'enough suitable education and training' in their area to meet the 'reasonable needs' of people who are above compulsory school age but under 19 and those of 19–24-year-olds who are subject to learning difficulty assessment, and (ii) a separate equivalent duty in respect of the reasonable needs of 16–18-year-olds subject to youth detention; the latter duty also applies in respect of children subject to youth detention, save that it relates to educational provision only (not training).[98]

The 'sufficient' schools duty in s 14 was held in the case of *Ali and Murshid* in 1990 to be a 'target duty', not an absolute one.[99] The local authority was considered to be doing all it could to ensure provision was available for every child in the area in question, in East London, following an influx of population, and not to be in breach of its duty when due to a combination of budget constraints and teacher shortages it was unable one year to make available for all children sufficient primary school places. However, as previously mentioned, ensuring the availability of a sufficient quantity of functioning educational institutions is a requirement identified by the Committee on Economic, Social and Cultural Rights as integral to the state's obligations under Art 13 of ICESCR. Indeed one might assume that in the era of the Human Rights Act 1998 some form of provision would now be necessary in a case such as *Ali and Murshid*, if a denial of the right to education under Art 2 of the First Protocol is not to occur. Yet the case law of the past decade might suggest otherwise.

In particular, in *A v Essex County Council*[100] a boy who had special educational needs due to autism, epilepsy and a range of other factors was left without a suitable educational placement for eighteen months before being placed, at the local authority's considerable expense, at a suitable residential school. The court accepted that the delay in settling his educational placement had resulted from the authority's lack of resources to conduct the necessary medical assessment combined with the absence of a suitable school place. Lord Phillips confirmed that during that period the boy's right to education under Art 2 of the First Protocol (A2P1) had not been denied, since that right had to have regard to such a limitation in available facilities and 'to the limited resources actually available to deal with his special needs'.[101] In the light of this ruling one might expect a similar view to be taken in a case such as *Ali and Murshid* if fought under the Human Rights Act.

---

[98]   Education Act 1996, ss 15ZA, 15ZB and 18A, all inserted by the Apprenticeships, Skills, Children and Learning Act 2009. Note that a 'learning difficulty assessment' is an assessment of a young person's learning difficulties arranged by the local authority (or Welsh Ministers in Wales) under the Learning and Skills Act 2000, s 139A (or s 140 in Wales) either in the last year in which he or she is of compulsory school age or at any time after the young person has ceased to be of compulsory school age and is below the age of 25: Education Act 1996, s 13(4) and (5) as inserted by the 2009 Act Sch 2, para 2(3).

[99]   *R v Inner London Education Authority ex p Ali and Murshid* [1990] 2 Admin LR 822.

[100]   [2010] UKSC 33, [2010] ELR 531.

[101]   Ibid, at [86].

The further important instance in which the local authority's duty to ensure suitable provision for a child was tested against the ECHR was the case of *Ali v Headteacher and Governors of Lord Grey School*.[102] This case concerned the legality of action taken by a school in relation to a boy who had been excluded due to being suspected of committing arson on the premises which was being investigated by the police. Under the Education Act 1996, s 19 a local authority must make arrangements for suitable educational provision for children, at school or elsewhere, if they are of compulsory school age and 'by reason of illness, exclusion from school or otherwise, may not for any period receive suitable education unless such arrangements are made for them'.[103] This is a mandatory duty (although it is only a discretion in relation to young people who are over compulsory school age[104]); it is clear, for example, that a local authority cannot rely on budget constraints to justify a failure to meet this obligation.[105] In the Court of Appeal in this case Sedley LJ commented that 'it is the [local authority's] obligation to ensure that no child falls out of the education system, even if excluded from school'.[106] However, the House of Lords held (by a 4–1 majority)[107] that the fact that a child's exclusion from his or her school is unlawful under domestic law (in this case because the child had been subjected to indefinite exclusion, which domestic education law does not sanction[108]) does not in itself mean the child is being subjected to a denial of the right to education for the purposes of ECHR A2P1, provided a sufficient form of suitable alternative educational provision is made available. Here the school had set work to be done at home by the boy in question. A meeting had been arranged at the school with the parents to attempt to resolve matters, while the family had also been offered a place for him (which they had declined) at a pupil referral unit (in furtherance of the local authority's s 19 duty). Lord Hoffmann said that for a denial of the Article to have occurred there would have to have been 'a systemic failure of the educational system which resulted in the respondent not having access to a minimum level of education', which he concluded had not happened in this case.[109] Lord Bingham, also with the majority, took a similar view, noting that the right in A2P1 was 'a weak one, and deliberately so', offering 'no Convention guarantee of compliance with domestic law' and 'no guarantee of education at or by a particular institution'.[110] He said that denial of the right to education would rest on the question 'have the authorities of the state acted so as to deny a pupil effective access to such educational facilities as the state provides for such pupils?'[111] The

---

[102] *Ali v Headteacher and Governors of Lord Grey School* [2006] UKHL 14, [2006] ELR 223.

[103] Education Act 1996, ss 19(1). See also subss (3A), (3B). See also the Education (Provision of Full-time Education for Excluded Pupils) (England) Regulations 2007 (SI 2007/1870). As regards compulsory school age, see n 88 above.

[104] Education Act 1996, s 19(4).

[105] *R v East Sussex County Council ex p T* [1998] AC 714, [1998] 2 WLR 818.

[106] *A v Head Teacher and Governors of Lord Grey School* [2004] ELR 169, at para 6 (per Sedley LJ).

[107] Note 102 above.

[108] Education Act 2002, s 51A – or s 52 in Wales.

[109] See n 102 above, at [61].

[110] Ibid, at [24].

[111] Ibid.

question, he felt, was to be answered in the negative in the circumstances of the particular case. Only Baroness Hale felt unable to support the majority view on this issue, concluding that the boy had had a 'right not to be denied education which the established system had provided for him', a right denied by his unlawful exclusion.[112]

Protecting the right to education of an excluded child is particularly important, since in the past there has been much evidence of excluded children falling out of the system and local authorities failing to meet their needs. The law has been tightened up by removing the option for local authorities of making only part-time provision for such children under s 19, although the courts have held that this may be legitimate in cases where it is for a temporary period while the child has to be reintegrated into school gradually.[113] In addition, the period of interruption of the child's education is to be limited since both the governing body of the school, in the case of a fixed period exclusion, and the local authority, in the case of a permanent exclusion, must ensure that education is provided to the child from the *sixth day* following the exclusion.[114] Moreover, during the first five days after exclusion, the parent would commit an offence if the child is of compulsory school age and is found in a public place during normal school hours.[115]

Access and equality

Domestic law also seeks to guarantee freedom from discrimination by the local authority and school in the child's enjoyment of the right to education. The Equality Act 2010, the relevant provisions of which came into force in October 2010, follows its predecessor legislation[116] in specifically proscribing, in the context of education, direct or indirect discrimination, victimisation and harassment related to any one of the prescribed 'protected characteristics' – sex, sexual orientation, gender reassignment, pregnancy, race/ethnicity, disability and religion/belief (but not in respect of age or marriage/civil partnership). The areas of education specifically covered by the non-discrimination duty are admission to school,[117] access to the benefits or

---

[112] Ibid, at [81].

[113] See *The Queen on the application of B v Head Teacher of Alperton Community School and Others; The Queen v Head Teacher of Wembley High School and Others ex p T; The Queen v Governing Body of Cardinal Newman High School and Others ex p C* [2001] ELR 359, Admin Ct. But see *R (M) v Worcestershire CC* [2005] ELR 48, in which provision totalling two and a half days per week was found to be insufficient.

[114] Education (Provision of Full-time Education for Excluded Pupils) (England) Regulations 2007 (SI 2007/1870). See further n 619 below.

[115] Education and Inspections Act 2006, ss 103 and 104.

[116] The Sex Discrimination Act 1975, the Race Relations Act 1976, the Disability Discrimination Act 1995 and the Equality Act 2006.

[117] Specifically, in '(a) in the arrangements it makes for deciding who is offered admission as a pupil; (b) as to the terms on which it offers to admit the person as a pupil; (c) by not admitting the person as a pupil' (Equality Act 2010, s 85(1)).
Schools, or more specifically the 'responsible body', must not harass any pupil or person who

facilities provided by schools,[118] and exclusion from school and subjection to 'any other detriment'.[119] The Act also incorporates pre-existing statutory duties in the area of disability. They include a duty resting with the governing body or proprietor to make 'reasonable adjustments' to practices and arrangements in a school in order to prevent a person being at a substantial disadvantage due to their disability – a failure to make such adjustments amounts to unlawful discrimination.[120] They also include requirements for local authorities to have accessibility strategies for increasing disabled pupils' participation in the school curriculum and for improving the physical environment of the school in order to increase such pupils' ability to take advantage of the education and other services provided; and for the school governors or proprietor to prepare an accessibility plan with the same objectives.[121] More generally, there is also a 'public sector equality duty' requiring public authorities, in exercising their functions, to have due regard to the need to eliminate discrimination prohibited by the 2010 Act, advance equality of opportunity between people with, and those who do not have, a particular protected characteristic under the Act, and increase equality of opportunity.[122]

There are some exceptions regarding the non-discrimination duties specifically concerning education (above), also continued from the previous legislation.[123] First, there is a general exception for 'anything done in connection with the

---

seeks admission as a pupil and must not victimise a person in relation to admission or over the above actions relating to access to education (Ibid, s 85(4) and (5)).

[118] Specifically, '(a) in the way it provides education for the pupil; (b) in the way it affords the pupil access to a benefit, facility or service; (c) by not providing education for the pupil; (d) by not affording the pupil access to a benefit, facility or service' (Equality Act 2010, s 85(2)).

[119] Equality Act 2010, s 85(2)(e) and (f). See further the discussion of exclusion below.

[120] Under s 21 of the 2010 Act, a failure to comply with the first, second or third requirement in s 20 amounts to a failure to make reasonable adjustments and constitutes unlawful discrimination. The requirements in s 20 (in subs (3)–(5)) are: '(3) The first requirement is a requirement, where a provision, criterion or practice of A's puts a disabled person at a substantial disadvantage in relation to a relevant matter in comparison with persons who are not disabled, to take such steps as it is reasonable to have to take to avoid the disadvantage. (4) The second requirement is a requirement, where a physical feature puts a disabled person at a substantial disadvantage in relation to a relevant matter in comparison with persons who are not disabled, to take such steps as it is reasonable to have to take to avoid the disadvantage.(5) The third requirement is a requirement, where a disabled person would, but for the provision of an auxiliary aid, be put at a substantial disadvantage in relation to a relevant matter in comparison with persons who are not disabled, to take such steps as it is reasonable to have to take to provide the auxiliary aid'. However, *schools* are bound to meet the *first* and *third* requirements only, and only in respect of deciding who is offered admission as a pupil and provision of education or access to a benefit, facility or service: see Sch 13, para 2. While non-discrimination requirements apply to local authorities exercising functions under the Education Acts they are not under a duty to 'remove or alter a physical feature': Sch 3, para 10(1), read with s 29. On the meaning of 'physical feature', see s 20(10).

[121] Equality Act 2010, s 88 and Sch 10, which also provides for a power of enforcement (by direction) in the event of failure or for acting or proposing to act unreasonably with regard to the duty.

[122] See the Equality Act 2010, s 149(1) and (3).

[123] Ibid, s 89 and Sch 11.

content of the curriculum'.[124] The Department for Education's guidance on the 2010 Act offers a rationale for this exception, referring to the desirability of a liberal and pluralistic approach:[125]

> 'Excluding the content of the curriculum ensures that schools are free to include a full range of issues, ideas and materials in their syllabus, and to expose pupils to thoughts and ideas of all kinds, however challenging or controversial, without fear of legal challenge based on a protected characteristic.'

The *delivery* of the curriculum is, however, covered by the non-discrimination duty. Thus 'schools will need to ensure that the way in which issues are taught does not subject individual pupils to discrimination'.[126] The guidance gives a range of hypothetical examples of complaints that would fall outside the protection of the legislation: they include a complaint that having to study Shakespeare's *The Taming of the Shrew* is discriminatory on the grounds of sex or that the inclusion of *The Merchant of Venice* on the curriculum is discriminatory as regards Jewish pupils.[127] On the other hand, prohibiting girls from taking design technology or discouraging boys from doing food technology, for example, would be unlawfully discriminatory as being 'not intrinsic to the curriculum itself but to the way in which education is made available to pupils'.[128]

The other exceptions to protection against discrimination in education relate to sex discrimination; religion and belief; and disability discrimination.[129] In relation to sex discrimination,[130] the sex equality duty concerning admission is dis-applied in the case of single sex schools. Single sex boarding arrangements and transitional arrangements where a school is turning co-educational are also exempt. Discrimination on the grounds of religion or belief is permitted in relation to admission to schools designated as having a religious character or to acts of worship or observance at a school.[131] In relation to disability,[132] selective admission arrangements, whereby pupils are admitted on the basis of their academic ability, are also exempt if approved – for example, where a school is a grammar school or if it is an independent school whose admission arrangements are aimed at 'admitting only pupils of high ability or aptitude'.[133]

Complaints of disability discrimination lie to the county court with the exception of those alleging discrimination by schools, which (apart from cases arising out of admission – see below) fall within the jurisdiction of the

---

[124] Ibid, s 89(2).
[125] Department for Education, *Equality Act 2010. Advice for school leaders, school staff, governing bodies and local authorities* (Department for Education, 2012), at para 2.9.
[126] Ibid.
[127] Ibid, at para 2.10.
[128] Ibid, at para 2.12.
[129] Equality Act 2010, Sch 11.
[130] Ibid, Sch 11, Part 1.
[131] Ibid, Sch 11, Part 2.
[132] Ibid, Sch 11, Part 3. See also the Equality (Disability) Regulations 2010 (SI 2010/2128).
[133] Ibid, at para 8(2)(c).

First-tier Tribunal (Health, Education and Social Care Chamber), the body which also has jurisdiction vis-à-vis special educational needs appeals.[134] As discussed below in the section on special educational needs, consideration has been given to giving children and young people in England an independent right to bring a complaint of disability discrimination in respect of schools, such as has been introduced in Wales. This right is proposed for those aged 16 or over in draft legislation in England (although, once a proposed pilot is completed, may be extended to younger pupils). At present such a claim may only be made by the parent,[135] which contrasts with the position in Scotland where the claim may be brought by the parent or by the pupil if he or she 'has capacity to make the claim'.[136] Under the proposed right in England the young person only would have this right. In cases concerning discrimination arising in connection with admission to or *permanent* exclusion from school, the complaint of disability discrimination has had to be pursued within the appeal processes governing those respective areas.[137] However, following the introduction in England of a review process in place of an appeal for exclusion cases, under the Education Act 2011, discrimination complaints in connection with exclusion, whether permanent or fixed term, will fall within the First-tier Tribunal's jurisdiction.[138]

Over the years there have been a number of key rulings concerning discrimination against or affecting children in the specific context of education.[139] Although mostly decided under the pre-Equality Act 2010 law, they have continuing relevance. Those of particular significance include the decision of the House of Lords in *Mandla v Dowell Lee*,[140] where it was held that a school rule which had the effect of prohibiting the wearing of a turban by a Sikh pupil, thereby preventing his admission to the school, gave rise to unlawful indirect race discrimination. The school's argument that its policy of prohibiting cultural/religious dress was intended to promote racial harmony by downplaying differences between pupils was not considered to provide justification for the discrimination that arose. More recent was the House's rather controversial decision (by a majority of 5–4) in *R(E) v Governing Body of JFS*[141] concerning the admission policy at an Orthodox Jewish school. The school was held to have practised unlawful direct discrimination related to ethnic origins by refusing the admission of a child not recognised as Jewish by the Office of the Chief Rabbi (OCR). A child would be recognised as Jewish if he or she had a Jewish mother, but in this case the mother was not regarded as Jewish by the school as although she had converted to Judaism her conversion had not been in a manner approved by the OCR.

---

134   Equality Act 2010, s 114 and 116 and Sch 17, as amended by the Education Act 2011 Sch 1 (see n 138 below).
135   Ibid, Sch 17, para 3.
136   Ibid, para 8.
137   Ibid, paras 13 and 14.
138   Education Act 2011, Sch 1, paras 11–13, amending Equality Act 2010, Sch 17, para 14.
139   See generally Harris, *Education, Law and Diversity*, n 5 above, ch 4.
140   [1983] 2 AC 548.
141   *R (E) v Governing Body of JFS and Others; R (E) v The Office of the Schools Adjudicator* [2009] UKSC 15, [2009] WLR (D) 298, [2010] ELR 26.

Generally a child must be admitted to a school if it has a place available.[142] In one important case, *Cleveland*,[143] a local authority had upheld a parent's preference for the transfer of her child from one of its primary schools to another. At the child's initial school there had been a number of pupils of Asian origin and the school provided for the singing of what the child's mother referred to as 'Pakistani songs'. The mother requested that her child be transferred from this school to one with, as she saw it, more of a Christian character. The local authority was held not to have infringed its duties under race discrimination law (then the Race Relations Act 1976) by agreeing to the transfer. This was because it had been acting in furtherance of a mandatory duty (then within the Education Act 1980) to uphold parental choice of school. In another admission case, *Sikander Ali*,[144] it was alleged that the Bradford local education authority's secondary school admissions policy unlawfully discriminated against Asian people. The policy excluded from one school's catchment area (the residents of which had priority for admission to the school) a part of the city, Manningham, which had a particularly high number of residents of Asian origin compared to others. The court held that since a white person living in Manningham would be similarly disadvantaged under the policy it was not unlawfully discriminatory on the grounds of race or ethnicity.

In the area of sex discrimination, access to single sex schooling has been the main subject of litigation. The courts have confirmed that the local authority's duty to ensure sufficient schools,[145] noted above, has to be exercised in a way that conforms to the sex equality duty. Consequently, if an area has fewer places overall at single sex schools for girls than are available at boys' schools, or vice versa, a breach of that duty may arise,[146] although such disparity may be excused if it arises from a necessary closure of a school than has ceased to be viable.[147] The House of Lords confirmed in *Equal Opportunities Commission v Birmingham City Council*[148] that the disadvantage generated by the discrimination arises not so much from any notion that single sex schooling is inherently better than mixed schooling but rather from the reduced opportunity to select single sex schooling by choice.

Disability discrimination in relation to schooling is an area in which there can be now expected to be the greatest number of discrimination cases. Not only are the duties on schools and local authorities more onerous than in relation to the other spheres of disadvantage, as noted above, but also the opportunity to pursue a complaint to the First-tier Tribunal and on appeal from there to the Upper Tribunal increases the likelihood of claims in this area. Perhaps the most

---

[142] See the School Standards and Framework Act 1998, s 86(2).

[143] *R v Cleveland LEA and Others ex p Commission for Racial Equality* [1994] ELR 44 (CA).

[144] *R v City of Bradford Metropolitan Council ex p Sikander Ali* [1994] ELR 299.

[145] Education Act 1996, s 14 and before that the Education Act 1944, s 8.

[146] *R v Secretary of State for Education and Science ex p Keating* (1985) 84 LGR 469.

[147] *R v Northamptonshire County Council and the Secretary of State for Education ex p K* [1994] ELR 397.

[148] [1989] 1 All ER 769 HL. See also *R v Birmingham City Council ex p Equal Opportunities Commission (No 2)* [1994] ELR 282 (CA).

important case to date has been *R (N) v London Borough of Barking and Dagenham Independent Appeal Panel*.[149] It concerned the approach to be followed in determining whether a disabled pupil whose disability causes him to misbehave is unlawfully discriminated against[150] when he or she is excluded for some act or acts of misbehaviour which, if committed by a non-disabled pupil, would result in exclusion. In this case the boy who was excluded was suffering from Attention Deficit Hyperactivity Disorder. The Court of Appeal concluded that for the purposes of assessing whether there had been disability discrimination in such a case one had to compare the disabled person who behaved in a particular way with the non-disabled person who behaved the same way. If their treatment would be the same then the disabled person was not subject to the exclusion on the basis of their disability and thus could not have suffered unlawful discrimination.

Another important element in the promotion of equal access is the range of measures designed to target socio-economic disadvantage, such as provision of free school meals – currently one in six children is eligible for them[151] – and free transport to and from school.[152] Additionally, the School Admissions Code, with which those responsible for decisions on admissions are required to act in accordance,[153] has for around the past five years provided that schools should ensure that they do not have practices or policies that put applicants from more deprived backgrounds at a particular disadvantage – such as where a school adopts a uniform that is particularly expensive or where an application form asks about a parent's occupation.[154] The law was also amended in 2006 to prevent state maintained schools from interviewing applicants and their families, since that was considered to facilitate a form of covert selection on the basis of social class.[155] A further reform designed to promote equity is that 'looked after children', who are often the most disadvantaged children, must be

---

[149] [2009] ELR 268.

[150] Under the Disability Discrimination Act 1995, ss 28A(4) and 28B(1); see now the Equality Act 2010, ss 15 and 85(2)(e).

[151] Department for Education, *Consultation on school funding reform: proposals for a fairer system* (DfE, 2011), at para 8.6. These are pupils whose disadvantaged background entitles the school to receive additional funds in the form of a 'pupil premium' – see n 337 below.

[152] Education Act 1996, s 509 as amended. See N Harris *Education, Law and Diversity* (Hart Publishing, 2007), ch 4.

[153] School Standards and Framework Act 1998, s 84(3) as amended by the Education and Inspections Act 2006, s 40.

[154] Department for Education, *School Admissions Code* (2012) at https://www.education.gov.uk/publications/eOrderingDownload/DFE-00013-2012.pdf (last accessed 30 May 2012) which, for example states (at para 1.8): 'Admission authorities **must** ensure that their arrangements will not disadvantage unfairly, either directly or indirectly, a child from a particular social or racial group, or a child with a disability or special educational needs, and that other policies around school uniform or school trips do not discourage parents from applying for a place for their child' (original emphasis). See also, eg, the now superseded 2010 Code, at para 1.78 which proscribed the use by admission authorities of supplementary application or information forms asking for parents' 'marital, occupational or financial status' or 'parents' achievements, educational background ....'

[155] School Standards and Framework Act 1998, s 88A, inserted by the Education and Inspections Act 2006, s 44.

given priority for admission under state school admission policies.[156] Additionally, academies (including free schools) may, if their funding agreement with the Department for Education permits it, give admissions priority to children entitled to free school meals.[157] Although independent schools are covered by anti-discrimination law (above), they are not subject to the School Admissions Code or any of the above restrictions on admission arrangements, illustrating how the private-public split within the education system continues to effect social division among children.

School dress and the right to education

There is a potential conflict between a school's policy on the uniform to be worn by pupils – including any restrictions on jewellery, hair-style, and make-up and other adornments – and the religious beliefs and cultural traditions of a pupil, his or her family and the religious and cultural group to which they belong. This conflict may pose a threat to the enjoyment of the right to education, since there may be family or peer pressure as well as personal inner feelings that might prevent a pupil's adherence to the policy, with the result that some form of disciplinary sanction is incurred, including an exclusion from the school. In the wider European context this conflict has been at the heart of several important cases concerned primarily with Art 9 of the ECHR, although also variously engaged with the right to education in Art 2 of the First Protocol (A2P1) (especially the recognition of religious and cultural preferences under the second sentence) and with Art 14 (freedom from discrimination).

Article 9, as noted earlier in the chapter, protects the individual's 'right to freedom of thought, conscience and religion', and freedom to 'manifest his religion or beliefs', the latter freedom stated, under Art 9(2), to be:

> 'subject only to such limitations as are prescribed by law and necessary in a democratic society in the interests of public safety, for the protection of public order, health or morals, or for the protection of the rights and freedom of others.'

Article 9(2) effectively mandates the balancing of individual religious freedom with the authority of the state to have regard to wider social interests in regulating conduct related to religion and belief.[158] Thus in one of the leading cases, *Leyla Şahin v Turkey*,[159] the European Court of Human Rights Grand Chamber found no violation of Art 9 read with A2P1 arising from a ban on the wearing of the hijab at Instanbul University. It considered that, inter alia, while the complainant's right to manifest her religion had been violated: the ban was

---

[156] School Standards and Framework Act 1998, s 88B and the School Admissions (Admission Arrangements) (England) Regulations 2008 (SI 2008/3089), reg 7.

[157] School Admissions Code (2012), n 154 above, at p 10 n 22. Note that the basis for paying the pupil premium has widened in 2012 to include children for whom there has been free school entitlement at any time in the past 6 years: see n 337 below.

[158] See generally D McGoldrick *Human Rights and Religion* (Hart Publishing, 2006).

[159] Application No 44774/98, 10 November 2005, [2006] ELR 73.

in accordance with Turkish law; Turkish courts had acknowledged that a right to wear the hijab would be inconsistent with the principle of neutrality applied to state education in the country; and Art 9(2) gave justification to the ban which sought to pursue the legitimate aim of protecting the rights and freedoms of others in an environment in which there was a risk of students being pressured by fundamentalists.[160] The ban itself was considered to be proportionate to the realisation of this aim.[161] The court was mindful of the margin of appreciation that it was necessary to apply in relation to a States Party's approach to the relationship between religion and the state. It said that '[t]his will notably be the case when it comes to the wearing of religious symbols in educational institutions'.[162]

A similar approach was followed by the court in *Dogru v France*.[163] A Muslim girl, then aged 11, attended physical education and sports classes wearing her headscarf even though it was banned under the internal rules for reasons of health and safety. She was not allowed to take part in those classes and was later excluded from the school for non-participation in those parts of the curriculum. The exclusion was upheld by the administrative court and by the Nantes Court of Appeal, the latter concluding that the complainant had overstepped the limits of her right to express her religion and manifest her beliefs at school. The European Court of Human Rights found that the interference with her Art 9 right was 'prescribed by law' for the purposes of Art 9(2) (above). It also found it to be foreseeable by virtue of being consistent with a well established opinion by the Conseil d'Etat as to the wearing of religious symbols in school and the policy of secularism, and with the school rules, which were signed by the applicant when she enrolled at the school. Furthermore, the interference with religious expression was in pursuit of the legitimate aim of protecting both the rights and freedoms of others. It was 'necessary in a democractic society' to achieve those aims and states had an entitlement to set their own frameworks in limiting freedom of religion in order to ensure 'public order, religious harmony and tolerance in a democratic society'.[164] The Court did not consider the penalty of exclusion to be disproportionate, especially as the girl was able to continue her schooling via correspondence classes.

Therefore it is clear that any individual state may regulate pupils' dress at school provided it has legal authority for doing so and does it in pursuit of a legitimate aim and in a way that is proportionate to such an aim. In England, there is no national policy on school uniform (although there is official

---

[160] See ibid, at [81], [99] and [111].

[161] Ibid, at [115]–[122].

[162] Ibid, at [109]. See also *Dahlab v Switzerland* (Application No 42393/98) which concerned the refusal to permit a teacher of a class of young children to wear the Islamic headscarf, a ban upheld by the court on the basis that due to the prosletysing effect of wearing it the restriction was justified as a means of protecting the rights and freedom of others.

[163] Application No 27058/05 [2009] ELR 77. The case was decided under Art 9. There was also an A2P1 head, but the court decided that in view of its conclusions on Art 9 it was not necessary to reach a conclusion on it.

[164] Ibid, at [62].

guidance) and school governing bodies are expected to determine their own policy for their school under the terms of their general responsibility for the conduct of the school.[165] Enforcement of the policy would seem to fall within the scope of the disciplinary roles of the governing body[166] and head teacher.[167] Only in relatively recent years has school uniform policy in the UK been subjected to ECHR challenges or claims under domestic anti-discrimination law. Clearly a combination of the extension of the latter to include discrimination on the basis of religion or belief and the introduction of the Human Rights Act 1998, in 2000, has opened a door for what has been a rash of cases since the mid-2000s. However, it is also symptomatic of a stronger public focus on religious and cultural identity, including various policy initiatives at national level, some of which are concerned with education specifically, designed to limit the effects of social segregation along religious, cultural and ethnic divides.[168]

The first case to come to judgment in this specific context was *Begum*,[169] a very important decision which has attracted considerable attention. Here a Muslim girl attended a non-denominational state secondary school which had pupils from a diverse range of backgrounds; nearly 80 per cent classed themselves as Muslims. The school's policy on uniform permitted girls to wear the shalwar kameez but not the jilbab, a full-length tunic covering the legs and arms. The school uniform policy was partly premised on the need to prevent pupils from feeling pressured to adopt a strict form of dress. After two years as a pupil there, during which she wore the shalwar kameez, Ms Begum decided to wear the jilbab to school. When prohibited from doing so by the school she stayed away and claimed that in effect she had been excluded. Her case was that she had been denied her right to education under A2P1 and her right to freedom of religious expression under Art 9. Bennett J rejected her claims, holding that the policy was supported by a justification based on protecting the rights and freedoms of others, for the purposes of Art 9(2). He also held that Ms Begum had not been denied the right to education since the school was willing to have her as a pupil as long as she wore an approved form of dress and she could in any event pursue her education at a nearby school which permitted the wearing

---

[165] Education Act 2002, s 21, as amended. As regards the official guidance, see n 190 below.

[166] In particular, the duty to 'ensure that policies designed to promote good behaviour and discipline are pursued at the school': Education and Inspections Act 2006, s 88(1).

[167] See ibid, s 89(1), referring to the head teacher's duty to determine the measures to be taken with a view to, inter alia, 'promoting, among pupils, self-discipline and proper regard for authority' and 'encouraging good behaviour and respect for others on the part of pupils' (including 'preventing all forms of bullying among pupils'). See further p 966 below.

[168] For example, the attempts to ensure that denominational schools take a proportion of pupils of other or no faiths (the 2005–2010 Labour Government had planned to set such a quota at 25 per cent although was persuaded to abandon it due to religious bodies' objections and after assurances that the Church of England was adopting a similar policy for its schools), and the introduction of a new duty on school governing bodies in England to 'promote community cohesion' in the course of discharging their functions in relation to the conduct of the school: Education Act 2002, s 21(5)(b) inserted by the Education and Inspections Act 2006, s 38(1).

[169] R *(Begum) v Headteacher and Governors of Denbigh High School* [2006] UKHL 15, [2006] ELR 273.

of the jilbab.[170] This ruling was overturned by the Court of Appeal,[171] which focussed on the procedure followed by the school in devising its policy, finding that the school had not given sufficient consideration to factors such as whether there would be an interference with Ms Begum's Art 9 right and whether there was justification for such interference for the purposes of Art 9(2). The court also held that Ms Begum was correct in her assertion that she had been excluded from school. However, the House of Lords rejected these conclusions. It held by a 3–2 majority that there had been no interference with her Art 9 right: the majority considered that she could indeed manifest her religion by attending a different school which permitted the wearing of the jilbab. All five members of the court agreed that the school uniform rules, on which there had been prior consultation by the school with the local community and which, as noted above, aimed to prevent young girls from being pressured into wearing more extreme forms of religious dress by others, gave rise to an interference that was justifiable for the purposes of Art 9(2). They also held that the girl had not been excluded from school, because she could return provided she complied with the policy on uniform.

A second case in which a rule restricting the wearing of Islamic dress at school and in which again a major element was the question of justification for Art 9(2) purposes is *R (X) v Y School*,[172] decided a year after *Begum*. Here X, a Muslim girl aged 12, was a pupil at Y school, a single sex grammar school, and wished to wear the niqab (a veil covering the entire face apart from the eyes) at school when taught by male teachers or when otherwise in the presence of men. The school informed her that she would be excluded from school if she wore the niqab and so she stayed away. She was offered a place at another grammar school, involving a journey of 25 minutes from home, at which she would be permitted to wear the niqab, but the offer was rejected. X's three elder sisters had each attended Y school previously and been permitted to wear the niqab. X claimed, inter alia, that the ban on the niqab violated her ECHR Art 9 rights.[173] She also contended that the change of policy on uniform had no objective justification. Silber J held that Art 9 was engaged but the right had not been interfered with since X had had an opportunity to go to an alternative school which had a good academic record. Considering the effect of Art 9(2), the judge found that the policy on uniform which had been adopted had been properly grounded as had its application in the present case. In particular, there were: educational factors related to the inability of a teacher to see the pupil's face; the importance of the uniform policy in the promotion of 'unformity and an ethos of equality and cohesion'; security factors; and a wish to avoid pressure on girls to wear the niqab.[174] As in *Begum* there had been local consultation over the uniform policy. Silber J concluded that 'the measures adopted by the school in prohibiting the wearing of the niqab were rationally

---

[170] [2004] EWHC (Admin) 1389, [2004] ELR 374.
[171] [2005] EWCA Civ 199, [2005] ELR 198.
[172] [2007] EWHC 298 (Admin), [2007] ELR 278.
[173] She also advanced the ground that she had a legitimate expectation that she would be permitted to wear the niqab; this was rejected by the court.
[174] See n 172 above, at [64].

connected to the school's objectives' and did no more than was necessary to achieve them.[175] The policy met the test of proportionality.[176]

In both *Begum* and *X* Art 9 was engaged since both claimants' freedom to manifest their religion was clearly at issue. In two other cases, however, this was a more contentious question. In *Playfoot*[177] a girl aged 16 when the matter came before the court complained that her school's decision to subject her to a disciplinary sanction for wearing a 'purity ring' on her finger in contravention of school rules prohibiting the wearing of most forms of jewellery violated her right to manifest her religion or beliefs under Art 9. The ring was worn to signify a belief in abstinence from sexual intercourse before marriage. The girl contended that wearing the ring was a manifestation of her Christian belief. The High Court rejected this argument, finding that wearing the ring was not 'intimately linked' to a belief in chastity before marriage and was not a requirement of her belief or religion. Moreover, the girl could signify her belief by displaying the ring in other ways, such as on a keychain or by attaching it to a bag. The court considered that, in any event, the policy had justification under Art 9(2). It had a legitimate purpose in meeting a number of objectives similar to those in the two above cases, such as fostering social cohesion and reducing social pressure. In addition, the policy sought to minimise the risk of bullying and there were health and safety arguments for restricting the wearing of jewellery. By this time the Government had issued draft guidelines to schools on uniform and the aims of the school's policy were considered to be consistent with them. The judge also rejected the claim of discrimination contrary to Art 14. That claim was based on the contention that as Muslim girls were permitted to wear a headscarf and Sikh girls the Kara bangle the claimant should have been permitted to wear the purity ring. The court held that the school had based its policy on whether a restriction would, in its view, conflict with a faith requirement, a description that could not be applied to the purity ring.

At the time of *Playfoot* the draft central guidance on school uniform made no explicit reference to the Kara, but the case of *Watkins-Singh*[178] soon brought this symbol into focus. A Sikh girl was told by her school that she could not wear the Kara in school as it was contrary to the school's policy on uniform. In a very careful judgment Silber J explained why being prevented from wearing this religious symbol constituted a particular disadvantage or detriment to the girl. The importance of this symbol to the girl herself but also, in terms of its religious significance, to Sikhs as a group, were critical considerations. Silber J found that it was, to the girl's reasonable belief, a matter of 'exceptional importance to ... her racial identity or religious belief' and it was objectively of

---

[175] Ibid, at [76] and [78].

[176] Ibid, at [93].

[177] *R (Playfoot) v Governing Body of Millais School* [2007] EWHC 1698 (Admin), [2007] ELR 484.

[178] *R (Watkins-Singh) v Governing Body of Aberdare Girls' High School and Rhondda Cynon Taf Unitary Authority* [2008] ELR 561, [2008] EWHC 1865 (Admin).

'exceptional importance to ... her religion or race'.[179] The court also distinguished between, on the one hand, the highly visible jilbab, niqab and purity ring that had justified many of the reasons underlying the uniform policy in *Begum*, *X* and *Playfoot* respectively, and, on the other, the largely concealed and 'unostentatious' Kara.[180] Silber J also rejected the arguments that the ban was justified by the need to prevent bullying and that permitting it would be difficult to explain to pupils and parents given other restrictions on dress set out in the policy. He said that the school had a statutory duty[181] to have regard to the need to eliminate unlawful race discrimination and promote equality of opportunity and had a race equality policy that included a commitment to fostering respect for people of all cultural backgrounds. He also said that a school was under a very important obligation 'to ensure that its pupils are first tolerant as to the religious rites and beliefs of other races and other religions and second to respect other people's religious wishes'.[182] Rather than seeking to remove a possible cause of tension within the school it should have 'taken steps to ensure that the other pupils understood the importance of wearing the Kara to the claimant and to other Sikhs so that they would then tolerate and accept the claimant when wearing the Kara'.[183] While the school's policy prohibited the wearing of the crucifix, Silber J did not consider that the crucifix had the same significance for Christians that the Kara had for Sikhs.[184] Although this issue was decided under domestic equality law[185] the court applied the principles in the above Art 9 cases whilst, as noted above, distinguishing them on the basis of the nature of the symbol worn. The ECHR did come into direct consideration in this case, however, as the claimant also contended, unsuccessfully as it turned out, that the school's decision to teach her in seclusion from other pupils when wearing the Kara infringed her right to private and family life contrary to Art 8.

Unlawful discrimination under domestic law was also at issue in the case of *G v The Head Teacher and Governors of St Gregory's Catholic Science College*,[186] which concerned an 11-year-old boy of African-Caribbean origin who wore 'cornrows' (or braids) in his hair. The boy was due to start his secondary education but was unable to take up his place at his school, a Catholic college, because his manner of wearing of his hair conflicted with the school's policy on uniform and appearance. He claimed that the policy gave rise to unlawful race and sex discrimination. The school stated that its policy was in part aimed at ensuring that the local gang culture was kept out of the school as well as promoting the school's Catholic ethos, and that if it was discriminatory the discrimination was therefore justifiable. For the complainant it was contended that he belonged to a group of people who would suffer a particular

---

179   Ibid, at [56A] and [56B].
180   Ibid, at [78].
181   Under the Race Relations Act 1976, s 71.
182   See n 178 above, at [84].
183   Ibid, at [85].
184   Ibid, at [78].
185   At that time, the Race Relations Act 1976 and the Equality Act 2006.
186   [2011] ELR 446.

disadvantage by not being permitted to wear the cornrows. Collins J accepted that there were among people of African-Caribbean ethnicity those who regarded the cutting of hair as wrong so that it needed to be worn in cornrows. Counsel for the school sought to argue, inter alia, that the wearing of the cornrows by the boy did not meet the test of being of 'exceptional importance' to the complainant laid down in *Watkins-Singh* (above). But Collins J considered that 'the need to show exceptional importance puts the threshold too high' and he preferred the test of 'particular importance'.[187] But he said that whichever test was right, the boy had met the threshold.[188] Collins J also rejected the argument that the policy had justification on the basis that permitting one exception to the rules on hairstyles would make it more difficult to apply a 'zero tolerance' approach to other hairstyles, such as those linked to the gang culture, since any exception would have to be based on 'genuine cultural and family practice'.[189] Finally, whilst upholding the claim of race discrimination, Collins J rejected the claim of sex discrimination, confirming that different hairstyle requirements for boys and girls were lawful if based on a 'conventional standard of appearance' for the sex in question. The school had not been wrong to regard the wearing of cornrows by boys as not conventional. It may be noted that the revised version of the Department for Education's guidance on school uniform now includes a reference to a ban on 'cornrow' hairstyles as an illustration of potential indirect race discrimination.[190]

There are inherent dangers in the apparent distinctions drawn by the courts between children's different religious or cultural backgrounds in relation to whether restrictions on dress for school are legally justified. While each of the above decisions ought to be evaluated on an individual basis, particularly since uniform policies are specific to individual schools (albeit that there will be commonalities in relation to their content and the underlying rationale for them), there is a risk that somewhat simplistic comparisons will be made between the judgments in order to suggest that the law is inconsistent. Yet this is not the fault of the judges, who have approached the issues with care and concern to reflect, in particular, the balance inherent in the ECHR (and the Strasbourg jurisprudence pertaining to it) as well as domestic legislation. The current non-statutory Department for Education guidance to schools on school uniform attempts to reflect the legal position in the light of these cases, explaining the various considerations that schools need to be mindful of in order to ensure that policies do not infringe pupils' rights under human rights and anti-discrimination law.[191] In doing so it reveals the somewhat delicate path

---

[187] Ibid, at [37].

[188] Ibid, at [38].

[189] Ibid, at [47] and [48]. Presumably the two elements are to be considered conjunctively in this context: surely 'family practice' per se would not necessarily need to be respected.

[190] 'An example of indirect discrimination could be a school that bans "cornrow" hairstyles. As these are more likely to be seen as part of a family's custom and practice and therefore constitute part of a person's ethnicity (sic). Banning this type of hairstyle without justification could constitute indirect racial discrimination': Department for Education *School Uniform – A guide for Head Teachers, Governing Bodies, Academy Trusts, Free Schools and Local Authorities* (2012), at p 4.

[191] Ibid.

that schools governors and head teachers must now tread. The guidance does not, for example, tell schools how to determine whether a particular hairstyle or item of clothing reflects 'genuine cultural and family practice', which may well be an important consideration when framing a policy on uniform.

EDUCATIONAL PROVISION IN ENGLAND

Schools and alternative arrangements

Official statistics covering the position in January 2013 (the most recent available at the time of writing)[192] reveal that the state education system in England is based around 21,915 state schools catering for around 7.5 million pupils, comprising approximately 93 per cent of the school population as a whole. There is significant social and cultural diversity across the state school population: 28.5 per cent of pupils in state-funded primary schools and 24.2 per cent of those in state-funded secondary schools were identified as being of minority ethnic origin. For a fairly large number of children attending such schools their first language is not English: this was the case for 18.1 per cent of pupils in state-funded primary schools and 13.6 per cent in secondary schools. Some 579,680 pupils attend the 2,413 independent schools in England. There are in addition a small number of children who are educated at home (see below), either under arrangements made by the parents[193] or through provision by the local authority, such as via a tutor or tutors. All children of compulsory school age should have a school place available to them, because, as discussed earlier in the context of the right to education, local authorities must ensure the availability in their area of sufficient schools – sufficient in 'number, character and equipment' – to meet local educational needs and in particular provide appropriate education for all children.[194] However, some children are unable due to physical or mental illness to attend either a school or an alternative form of provision such as a pupil referral unit.[195] The official statistics (above) show that nearly 13,000 children (over two-thirds of whom were males) attended a pupil referral unit.

The precise number of children of compulsory school age who are being educated at home is not recorded. It was estimated, in England, at 12,000 in 1999, 21,000 in 2004 and 20,000 in 2009, while the officially recorded total in Wales for 2011/12 was 986.[196] Research in 2007 found indications that home

---

[192] All the figures quoted in this paragraph are taken from Department for Education, Statistical First Release SFR 13/2013, *Schools, Pupils and their Characteristics, January 2013* (DfE, 2013).

[193] Home education is permitted since parents' duty to ensure their child receives an efficient full-time education refers to education 'at school *or otherwise*': Education Act 1996, s 7 (emphasis added). See further p 949 below.

[194] Education Act 1996, ss 13, 13A and 14. However, if financial shortages result in under-provision, the local authority may not necessarily be in breach of this duty: see *R v ILEA of parte Ali and Murshid* [1990] 2 Admin LR 822 discussed on p 900 above.

[195] Provision made under the duty to make alternative arrangements for those unable to attend school due to illness, exclusion etc (Education Act 1996, s 19) – see pp 900–902 above.

[196] L Rogers 'Number of children taught at home soars' *The Sunday Times*, 26 June 2005; House

schooling was increasing but that published estimates varied very widely and that the true figure in England appeared to lie somewhere between 45,250 and 150,000.[197] Unfortunately this research also concluded that it was not feasible to ascertain the extent of home education through surveys of local authorities or home education support organisations. As parents have not been under a specific legal duty to notify the state that they are home educating their child, the child may be unknown to the local authority particularly where he or she has never before been enrolled at a school.[198] This will hinder the local authority in meeting its statutory duty to identify children who are not registered at a school and are not receiving suitable education elsewhere than at a school.[199]

Home education may be 'not necessarily less favourable to the pupil' than school education, as a judge commented in one case a few years ago.[200] However, there has been considerable concern that arrangements for home schooling may be insufficiently well policed. There is a possible risk that the parents' right to educate the child away from school provides an opportunity for the covering up of abuse due to the child's isolation from potential scrutiny by teachers and others. In the face of such concerns an attempt was made by the Labour Government through the Children, Schools and Families Bill in 2010 to establish a better framework for the regulation of home education. It would have involved a registration scheme to be operated by local authorities (as had been recommended by the Government-commissioned *Report to the Secretary of State on the Review of Elective Home Education in England* by Graham Badman of Kent County Council in 2009). Authorities would have had to make arrangements for ascertaining whether the education provided to the child who was identified on the register was suitable, what the child's wishes and feelings were about it, and 'whether it would be harmful for the child's welfare for the child to continue to be a home-educated child'. Local authorities would have had to identify any child aged 5–16 who was being home educated but was not on the home education register, or who was not being home educated, nor registered at a school or receiving suitable education. A parent would only have fulfilled his or her duty to ensure the child received 'suitable' education[201] in respect of a home educated child if the child was on the home education register. Unfortunately the Labour Government was running out of Parliamentary time prior to the general election in 2010 and had to abandon these proposed requirements, although in September 2012 the

---

of Commons Children, Schools and Families Committee, Second Report, Session 2009–2010, *The Review of Elective Home Education*, HC 39-I (The Stationery Office, 2009), at para 52; Welsh Government, *Consultation Document. Registering and monitoring home-based education* (Welsh Government, 2012), at para 7.

[197] V Hopwood, L O'Neill, G Castro and B Hodgson *The Prevalence of Home Education in England: A Feasibility Study* Research Report RR827 (Department for Education and Skills, 2007).

[198] Ibid, at para 1.9.

[199] Education Act 1996, s 436A as inserted by the Education and Inspections Act 2006, s 4.

[200] Stanley Burnton J in *VK v Norfolk County Council and the Special Educational Needs and Disability Tribunal* [2005] ELR 342, at para 47.

[201] Per the Education Act 1996, s 7.

Welsh Government published proposals to introduce such a scheme in Wales.[202] Nevertheless, it is important to note that it is still the law under the Education Act 1996, s 7, that the education provided to the child who is home educated must be efficient and full-time as well as 'suitable' for the child, a condition attached to the parent's home education right that underscores its position as a facet of parental responsibility. It does so in a way that, as Monk explains,[203] is consistent with the European Commission of Human Rights' decision in the *Leuffen* case, which was discussed above.[204] Local authorities are still responsible for ensuring that home education arrangements are scrutinised, for example via inspection visits, although there are doubts regarding the effectiveness of this process particularly at a time when these authorities are under such great resource pressures. Research has shown that local authorities regard the test as to 'efficient' and 'suitable' education in the 1996 Act as too vague and imprecise, making it difficult to assess whether the home education being provided to a child is appropriate.[205]

With regard to schools, where most children receive their formal education, the state system in England is in fact rapidly changing at present.[206] The essential features of what is an increasingly diverse state system, are that schools are partly classifiable broadly by the age range they cover – nursery schools (for children under compulsory school age), primary schools (mostly for those aged 11 or under), and secondary schools (11–16 or 11–18), plus 'special schools' for children of various ages with various forms of learning difficulty. In January 2013 there were 3,281 state-funded secondary schools, nearly 17,000 state-funded primary schools and just over 1,000 special schools of which over 90 per cent were in the state sector.[207] One further complication is that most, although not quite all, secondary schools have 'specialist' school status, which was first introduced under the Labour Government, covering a wide range of curriculum specialisms.[208] State schools are also classifiable with reference to their religious denomination (ie designated as having a religious character, as 'voluntary' and religious 'foundation' schools) or lack of one (community schools and some foundation schools). The most recent available statistics on schools' religious character, from January 2011, show that approximately 30 per cent of primary school pupils and just under 20 per cent of secondary

---

[202] Welsh Government, *Consultation Document. Registering and monitoring home-based education* (Welsh Government, 2012).

[203] D Monk 'Problematising home education: challenging "parental rights" and "socialization"' (2004) *Legal Studies*, 24(4), 568–598.

[204] *Leuffen v Federal Republic of Germany* (Application No 00019844/92); see p 892 above.

[205] V Hopwood, L O'Neill, G Castro and B Hodgson *The Prevalence of Home Education in England: A Feasibility Study* Research Report RR827 (DfES, 2007).

[206] It is not possible in this chapter to discuss the institutional structure in great detail. See further N Harris *Education, Law and Diversity* (Hart Publishing, 2007), ch 3 and Idem 'Local Authorities and the Accountability Gap in a Fragmenting Schools System' (2012) 75(4) MLR 511–546.

[207] Department for Education, Statistical First Release: note 192 above. In addition there are sixth-form colleges for those aged above compulsory school age.

[208] Specialist status is based on official recognition of at least one curriculum specialism.

school pupils attended a school with a religious character.[209] Of the 6,834 'faith' schools (as they are also known) in January 2011, 4,605 were Church of England schools, 2,001 were Roman Catholic schools, 26 were Methodist schools, 130 represented other Christian denominations, 39 were Jewish schools, 11 were Muslim schools and there were 4 Sikh schools.[210] There were also 18 representing various other faiths (unspecified in the official statistics).

A further way in which schools they are classified relates to their funding and control arrangements: in particular, some are local authority maintained, receiving a delegated budget from the local authority, whilst others receive their funding direct from the Department for Education (via the Education Funding Agency). Academies,[211] including 'free' schools[212] (which are classed as academies), fall into the latter category, receiving their funds under their agreement with the Department.[213] By January 2013 there were 2,644 academies, 1,638 of which were secondary schools (meaning that approximately half of all state secondary schools held academy status).[214] New forms of school have also come into existence in recent years, such as University Technical Colleges, which are sponsored institutions catering for the 14–19 age groups and providing vocational education combined with work experience.

The conduct and governance of schools: pupil participation and 'voice'

Schools must have governing bodies which are responsible for conducting them and, in most cases, for their financial management, although head teachers or principals play a key role in the exercise of day-to-day management responsibilities. The constitution of governing bodies is governed by legislation (or in the case of academies by a governance model to which they are bound under their agreement with the Department for Education), although following the Education Act 2011 there is more flexibility than previously.[215] Since the Education Act 1980 there has been mandatory parental representation on state

---

[209] Department for Education, Statistical First Release SFR 12 2011, *Schools, Pupils and their Characteristics, January 2011* (DfE, 2011).

[210] Ibid.

[211] Academies are either established as new schools by private promoters or, more commonly, are pre-existing schools which have converted to academy status. They operate under an agreement with the Department for Education. See further the Academies Act 2010.

[212] Free schools, based on a model developed in Sweden, are state schools established by parents, community groups, teachers or existing education providers. In 2011–12 there were 24 of these schools and approval was granted for a further 55 to open in September 2012. A further 114 have been approved to open in or after 2013: DfE Press Notice '55 new Free Schools to open this month – twice as many as last year', 3 September 2012.

[213] See Harris (2012), n 206 above.

[214] DfE First Statistical Release (2013), n 192 above.

[215] Education Act 2002, s 19 (as amended by the Education Act 2011, s 38) and the School Governance (Constitution) (England) Regulations 2012 (SI 2012/1034), applicable from 1 September 2012 but only if the school's instrument of government is made or varied after that date (otherwise, see the School Governance (Constitution) (England) Regulations 2007 (SI 2007/957), as amended.

school governing bodies, through elected parent governors. There is, however, no requirement for school governing bodies in England to include one or more pupil representatives. In Wales, which also has no provision for pupil governors and where the minimum prescribed age for being a school governor is set at 18 (as it is in England),[216] there is recognition of the contribution that pupils can make to the effective governance of a school.[217] In particular, head teachers are placed under a duty to ensure that their school council (which is made up of pupils at the school: see below) has the opportunity to nominate two of its members to be 'associate pupil governors' on the school's governing body.[218] However, associate pupil governors have no voting rights at meetings of the governing body and may be excluded from meetings concerning a range of prescribed matters including staff appointments or pay, individual pupil discipline, and the budget and financial commitments of the governing body.[219] These restrictions and the age limit clearly limit significantly the influence that pupil governors are likely to be able to have on the operation or policy of a school.

School councils – in practice most schools in England now have such a council although they are not legally required – have been one of the ways in which the issue of ensuring that pupils have a collective voice within schools has received increasing attention. School councils do not hold any power but enable pupils to share their views on school issues that affect them and communicate them to the adults who are responsible for the governance of the school. In Wales, where they have been compulsory since November 2006,[220] their prescribed purpose is 'to enable pupils to discuss matters relating to their school, their education and any other matters of concern or interest and to make representations on these to the governing body and the head teacher'.[221] The head teacher and the governing body of the school are under a duty to have regard to the school council's views and provide a response to any issue the council has raised.[222] Welsh school councils must consist exclusively of pupils and be comprised of at least one representative of each year group from year 3 upwards.[223] Although school councils are advocated by the UN Committee on the Rights of the Child,[224] among others, there is a risk that the lack of any

---

[216] See the Government of Maintained Schools (Wales) Regulations 2005 (SI 2005/2914) (W 211), as amended.

[217] See Governors Wales, Fact File 02/08, *Pupil Participation, Associate Pupil Governors and School Councils* (Governors Wales, 2008), at http://www.governorswales.org.uk/media/files/documents/2008-11-24/English_version.pdf (last accessed 2 July 2013).

[218] The School Councils (Wales) Regulations 2005 (SI 2005/3200) (W 236), reg 7(1). The governing body must accept the nomination unless the pupil in question is disqualified for membership under the school government regulations. That would appear to rule out any pupil aged under 18 from serving. See also the Government of Maintained Schools (Wales) Regulations 2005 (SI 2005/2914) (W 211), as amended, reg 12A and Sch 5.

[219] Government of Maintained Schools (Wales) Regulations 2005, n 218 above, reg 44A and 46.

[220] The School Councils (Wales) Regulations 2005 (SI 2005/3200 (W 236)), as amended.

[221] Ibid, reg 3(1).

[222] Ibid, reg 3(3).

[223] Ibid, reg 4.

[224] *Concluding Observations of the Committee on the Rights of the Child: United Kingdom*, CRC/C/15/Add 188 (Centre for Human Rights, 1995), at para 30.

guaranteed collective influence for them over decisions that affect pupils might lead to cynicism among pupils that these councils are merely tokenistic. Young people have criticised them for being 'just for show' and for the way that pupils' suggestions tend to be ignored.[225] In one survey only 39 per cent of pupils considered that their school council was effective in listening to their ideas concerning the school, whilst 27 per cent took the opposite view and around 33 per cent were unsure.[226] A separate survey showed that a majority of teachers in England favour making school councils compulsory.[227]

The UK Children's Commissioners have stated that '[w]hilst structures such as Schools Councils have been established... there is a need to embed children's participation in all aspects of learning and school'.[228] The imperative for this lies not only in the educational and managerial benefits of involving children in decisions and policies concerning their education – a practice that has received stronger encouragement in relation to some areas of education, such as the formulation of a school's behaviour policy, than others, such as the school curriculum.[229] It also stems from Art 12 of the UNCRC, whose principle of participation is particularly relevant to many aspects of education decision-making and practice and whose realisation requires a multi-faceted response.[230] Its implementation in the specific context of education in the UK has received considerable attention from the UN Committee on the Rights of the Child in its periodic reports. A particular concern has been that insufficient opportunities are created for pupils to be consulted on a systematic basis over school matters that affect them.[231] A statutory duty, introduced in 2003 under s 176 Education Act 2002, has required local authorities and school governing bodies to have regard to any guidance issued by the Secretary of State (or Welsh Assembly in relation to Wales) about consulting individual pupils over decisions affecting them. Such guidance is required to 'provide for a pupil's

---

[225] See L Pople, *The Good Childhood Inquiry. Learning: A summary of themes emerging from children and young people's evidence* (Children's Society, 2009), 26.

[226] Office of the Children's Commissioner/NfER, *Children and young people's views of education policy* (Office of the Children's Commissioner, 2011), at para 2.4.

[227] G Whitty and E Wisby, DCSF Research Report DCSF-RR001 *Real Decision Making? School Councils in Action* (DCSF, 2007).

[228] UK Children's Commissioners, *The Story so Far. The Report. UK Children's Commissioners' Midterm Report to the UK State Party on the UN Convention on the Rights of the Child* (UK Children's Commissioners, 2011), at p 8.

[229] See N Harris 'Playing Catch-up in the Schoolyard? Children and Young People's "Voice" and Education Rights in the United Kingdom' (2009) *International Journal of Law, Policy and the Family*, 23(3), 331–366 at 344 and 348.

[230] See L Lundy '"Voice" is not enough: conceptualising Art 12 of the United Nations Convention on the Rights of the Child' *British Educational Research Journal* (2007), 33(6), 927–942. See further p 895 above and p 929 below.

[231] See e g Committee on the Rights of the Child, *Concluding Observations of the Committee on the Rights of the Child: United Kingdom*, CRC/C/15/Add 188 (Centre for Human Rights, Geneva, 2002), at para 29.

views to be considered in the light of his age and understanding'.[232] Whilst the statutory duty appears to focus on the individual pupil, the guidance itself also covers collective participation.[233]

Further advances have come, first, with the inclusion of pupils in the categories of interested parties whose views, if expressed, school inspectors must take into account when carrying out a statutory inspection of a school.[234] Secondly, a requirement has been placed on school governing bodies to consult pupils (among others) before making or revising the required statement of general principles on behaviour and discipline at the school.[235] Nevertheless, it was only the enactment of a new duty on school governing bodies in 2008 to 'invite the views of pupils about prescribed matters' and to consider such views, having regard to the age and understanding of the pupils who expressed them,[236] that raised the prospect of schools having to have regard to pupils' collective voice more generally. However, this duty, which was set to replace the duty under s 176 of the 2002 Act (above),[237] had not been brought into effect by the time of the 2010 general election and it remains unimplemented. This is unfortunate, since although in its 2008 observations on the UK the UN Committee on the Rights of the Child welcomed the new opportunities for pupil participation in the context of school inspections and the formulation of behaviour policies, noted above, the Committee was more generally 'concerned that there has been little progress in enshrining Art 12 in education law and policy'.[238]

The School Curriculum

Regulation of the content of children's education

The content of children's education, at least in the state sector, is to a large extent centrally regulated. Religious education has always been determined locally and this was also the case with regard to the secular curriculum until the 1980s, when central government decided to remove it from local authority control, leaving local authorities merely with a duty to maintain a statement of policy on it.[239] There was a shift in curricular responsibility towards governing bodies. They had to have their own statement of curriculum policy to which the head teacher had to have regard when carrying out his or her responsibility for the 'determination and organisation of the secular curriculum'.[240] In relation to

---

[232] Education Act 2002, s 176(1) and (2).

[233] Department for Education and Skills *Working Together: Giving children and young people a say* DfES guidance 0134/2004 (DfES, 2004).

[234] Education Act 2005, s 7(f).

[235] Education and Inspections Act 2006, ss 88 and 89.

[236] Education and Skills Act 2008, s 157, inserting Education Act 2002, s 29B.

[237] Under amendments to be made via s 158 of the 2008 Act, the duty in s 176 of the 2002 Act was to be confined to Wales.

[238] *Concluding Observations: United Kingdom of Great Britain and Northern Ireland, CRC/C/GBR/CO/4* (Centre for Human Rights, Geneva, 2008), at para 32.

[239] Through the repeal of the Education Act 1944, s 23.

[240] Education (No 2) Act 1986, ss 18 and 19.

one specific matter, sex education, the governing body had authority to determine whether it should form part of the school's curriculum.

Government concern to rein in pedagogic freedom in order to prevent bias and limit iconoclastic approaches to the curriculum led, at this time, to the first elements of central regulation over the content of the secular curriculum. First, a duty was imposed on schools to ensure that when sex education was given to pupils, this should be 'in such manner as to encourage those pupils to have due regard to moral considerations and the value of family life'.[241] Secondly, head teachers and governing bodies were placed under a duty to prevent various forms of political bias or indoctrination in the school, including a duty to ensure that 'where political issues are brought to the attention of pupils ... they are offered a balanced presentation of opposing views'.[242] In a case in 2007 it was held that there was unlawful political bias in the teacher's pack accompanying the distribution to schools by the Department for Education and Skills of the film *An Inconvenient Truth* (whose subject was that of global warming) for showing to pupils.[243] These requirements on political issues and the approach to sex education remain part of the present law;[244] indeed, the 'family life' aspect of sex education has been reinforced.[245]

The Conservative Government's moralistic concern over lesson content and supposed bias in teaching led also to the notorious 'clause 28' which became s 28 of the Local Government Act 1988.[246] It was originally proposed via a backbench amendment but as Meredith explains 'was enthusiastically adopted by the then Conservative government as part of a broader campaign to underpin traditional family values in education'.[247] It prohibited local authorities from intentionally promoting homosexuality or publishing material with that intention and from promoting the teaching in any state-maintained school 'of the acceptability of homosexuality as a pretended family relationship'. As Bibbings put it, this reflected 'negative views of lesbians and gay men'.[248] After a protracted campaign by various groups to remove this provision, its repeal was finally brought about by the Local Government Act 2003.[249]

---

[241] Ibid, s 46.

[242] Ibid, s 45.

[243] *Dimmock v Secretary of State for Education and Skills (Now Secretary of State for Children, Schools and Families)* [2007] EWHC 2288 (Admin), [2008] ELR 98.

[244] Education Act 1996, ss 403, 404 and 407.

[245] One of the required aims which must underpin the design of central guidance on sex education (see below) is that pupils 'learn the nature of marriage and its importance for family life and the bringing up of children': Education Act 1996, s 403(1A), inserted by the Learning and Skills Act 2000, s 148.

[246] Inserting s 2A into the Local Government Act 1986. See further n 277 below.

[247] P Meredith 'Some shortcomings in the provision of sex education in England', in N Harris and P Meredith (eds) *Children, Education and Health – International Perspectives on Law and Policy* (Ashgate, 2005), 105–128, at 119.

[248] L Bibbings 'Gender, sexuality and sex education', in N Harris (ed), *Children, Sex Education and the Law* (National Children's Bureau, 1996), 70–86, at 79.

[249] Section 122.

The significant but relatively small scale statutory incursions into local autonomy over sex education and political content were followed by the wholesale capture by central government of secular curriculum territory with the enactment of the Education Reform Act 1988. This Act laid down basic curricular aims and prescribed for the first time in England and Wales a national curriculum comprised of core subjects (English, mathematics and science, plus Welsh in Welsh-speaking schools in Wales) and other foundation subjects for each 'key stage' (KS) of children's education, broadly thus:

- KS1: ages 6–7

- KS2: ages 8–11

- KS3: ages 12–14

- KS4: ages 15–16.

The introduction of a national curriculum aimed to correct the absence of clear and consistent approaches towards the curriculum across the schools system and to address shortfalls in standards of education. It also sought to increase schools' accountability to parents for what was taught to their children. The national curriculum was intended to provide a 'framework not a straitjacket' for teachers.[250] The legal framework is now in the Education Act 2002, Part 6 (as amended) and in myriad statutory instruments covering content and assessment at the various KSs. Since its introduction the national curriculum has been slimmed down several times, but there is still concern that it hinders teachers' creativity and imposes too great an administrative burden on them, as well as placing the focus of teaching on outputs (especially national test results) alone. This is despite the fact that national tests for 14-year-olds were abolished post 2008, after problems with the external marking made a system which was already criticised as overly burdensome for schools and for placing undue strains on individual pupils, impossible to defend.[251]

The Coalition Government now argues that '[t]o too great an extent, the National Curriculum has been over-prescriptive, has included material that is not essential and has specified teaching method rather than core knowledge'.[252] It has therefore instituted a review of the national curriculum in England and further changes are in prospect. They include (i) the possible introduction of compulsory foreign language teaching at the age of 7 rather than KS3 at present and (ii) for the school year 2013–14, in the run-up to a new national

---

[250] Department for Education and Science and the Welsh Office, *The National Curriculum 5-16 – A Consulation Document* (DES/Welsh Office, 1987), 5.

[251] See eg, R Garner 'National tests for 14-year-olds are scrapped after marking chaos' *The Independent* 15 October 2008. http://www.independent.co.uk/news/education/education-news/national-tests-for-14yearolds-are-scrapped-after-marking-chaos-961393.html [last accessed 8 June 2012].

[252] Department for Education, *The Importance of Teaching. The Schools White Paper 2010*, Cm 7980 (The Stationery Office, 2010), at para 4.8.

curriculum framework (due to be published in the autumn of 2013 and implemented from September 2014), the disapplication of the prescribed programmes of study, attainment targets and programmes of study for core and foundation subjects across all KSs (with some exceptions, such as the core subjects at KS1) – although the subjects themselves would still have to be taught.[253] In relation to the assessment arrangements, the Government has expressed a particular concern about the tests at the end of KS2, i.e. at the end of primary education, where:

> 'there is excessive test preparation – with some children practising test questions for many weeks in advance of the tests. This is poor practice... We want to see whether there can be improvements... so that parents have the information they want and schools can be properly accountable for pupil progress, without encouraging over-rehearsal of test questions.'[254]

The raw data for 2011 at least indicated a small overall improvement in the proportion of pupils who reached the expected level of achievement, level 4, for the end of KS2 (English 82 per cent, Reading 84 per cent, Writing 75 per cent, Mathematics 80 per cent), although in most subjects there was a slight fall in the proportion exceeding the expected level.[255] However, the gap in attainment of level 4 in both mathematics and English between those in receipt of free school meals and others was 20 percentage points, underlining the continuing association between social deprivation and low educational attainment despite the recommendation to the UK by the UN Committee on the Rights of the Child in 2008 that it should 'strengthen its efforts to reduce the effects of the social background of children on their achievement at school'.[256] Following an independent review of the assessment arrangements by Lord Bew,[257] commissioned by the Government, some changes are being made, including a greater emphasis on pupil progress. Nevertheless, KS2 assessment will continue.[258] With regard to assessment at age 14, after national tests at the end

---

[253] National Curriculum (Exceptions for First, Second, Third and Fourth Key Stages) (England) Regulations 2013 (SI 2013/1487). The disapplication also extends to the core subjects in parts of KS2. Also, at KS4 the programmes of study for the core subjects are to be disapplied in 2014–2015. A report commissioned from an expert panel had recommended, inter alia, changes to the KSs (including a division of KS2 into two separate stages) and greater breadth at KS4: T Oates (Chair, Expert Panel), *The Framework for the National Curriculum. A report by the Expert Panel for the National Curriculum review* (Department for Education, 2011). The disapplications of the elements of the national curriculum are explained in DfE *Consultation on (i) the Order for replacing ICT with computing and (ii) the regulations for disapplying aspects of the existing National Curriculum* (Department for Education, 2013). The rationale for the disapplications is to enable schools to adapt their curricula pending the changes, such as by introducing elements of the new framework early.

[254] See n 252 above, at para 4.43.

[255] Department for Education, SFR 31/2011, Statistical First Release. *National Curriculum Assessments at Key Stage 2 in England, 2011 (Revised)* (DfE, 2011).

[256] *Concluding Observations: United Kingdom of Great Britain and Northern Ireland, CRC/C/GBR/CO/4* (Centre for Human Rights, Geneva, 2008), at para 67.

[257] Lord Bew, *Independent Review of Key Stage 2 testing, assessment and accountability. Final Report* (Department for Education, 2011).

[258] Department for Education, *Independent Review of Key Stage 2 testing, assessment and accountability. Government Response* Cm 8144 (Department for Education, 2011).

of KS3 were abolished they were replaced by teacher assessment. However, a new testing agency is being asked to prepare a 'suite of national tests' for this stage in order to give schools a 'national benchmark', although these tests will be 'entirely voluntary' for schools.[259]

The 2002 Act added a new 'Foundation Stage' prior to KS1 with flexible 'areas of learning' (such as 'personal, social and emotional development', 'mathematical development' and 'knowledge and understanding of the world') rather than prescribed subjects. This reflected the post-1997 Labour Government's recognition of the importance of early years education, the quality of which 'has been shown to have a major impact on [young people's] achievements at 16 and their wider social skills'.[260] Subsequently the Foundation Stage was replaced by the Early Years Foundation Stage (EYFS),[261] based on 'learning and development requirements'[262] and 'welfare requirements', applicable to both schools and childcare providers, reflecting the more integrated approach to education and child welfare that the Labour Government adopted.[263] An independent review of the EYFS by Dame Clare Tickell,[264] commissioned by the present Government, has painted a generally positive picture but has recommended a slimming down including a reduction in the number of learning goals (from 69 to 17), a simplification of the assessment of 5-year-olds and a more simply worded framework to make it more accessible.

There is only limited scope for some pupils' education to be excepted from conformity with the national curriculum in its entirety, such as in certain cases where a child has special educational needs or it is otherwise not appropriate given the pupil's particular circumstances.[265] Indeed, there is no basic statutory right for either parents or children and young people themselves to opt out of elements of the national curriculum. Neither has the Human Rights Act 1998 offered much prospect that in any conflict between parents and the state over the secular curriculum primacy should be given to parental choice. As discussed above, the Strasbourg case law permits parental wishes to be overridden in this context provided the curriculum to which children are subjected is objective, critical and pluralistic in its approach and content.[266] Indeed, it is unlikely that the unconditional right of parents to withdraw their

---

[259] Department for Education, *The Importance of Teaching. The Schools White Paper 2010*, Cm 7980 (The Stationery Office, 2010), at para 4.46.

[260] Department for Education and Employment, *Excellence in Schools* Cm 3681 (The Stationery Office, 1997), at p 15, para 2.

[261] Childcare Act 2006, ss 39–48 and Sch 1.

[262] But see the exemptions in the Early Years Foundation Stage (Exemptions from Learning and Development Requirements) Regulations 2008 (SI 2008/1743), as amended.

[263] See eg the Children Act 2004 which, in effect, combined the education and children's services executive functions of local authorities.

[264] Dame Clare Tickell, *The Early Years: Foundations for life, health and learning* (DfE, 2011) and *The Early Years Foundation Stage (EYFS) Review. Report on the evidence* (DfE, 2011), at http://www.education.gov.uk/tickellreview (last accessed 18 December 2012).

[265] Education Act 2002, ss 91–95.

[266] *Folgerø v Norway* (n 53 above) being an exceptional case in that regard.

child from sex education at school,[267] first introduced when sex education was made part of the statutory basic curriculum in England (see below), is in fact necessary to ensure conformity with the ECHR given the approach taken by the European Court of Human Rights in *Kjeldsen*[268] and *Dojan*[269] noted earlier. The basic duty on the Secretary of State and local authorities, in performing their education functions, to 'have regard to the general principle that pupils are to be educated in accordance with the wishes of their parents ...'.[270] is, as noted above, only a general principle to be taken into account and affords no firm guarantees.[271] Effectively, therefore, those from minority cultural/religious backgrounds who object to elements of the secular curriculum other than sex education would be faced with the choice of withdrawing their child from the state system of education altogether.[272]

The national curriculum is part of the 'basic curriculum' that all state schools, apart from academies (including 'free' schools) must provide. The curricular freedom enjoyed by academies has been sought to be justified by government as providing greater scope for schools to innovate and raise standards through tailoring the curriculum to the needs of their pupils;[273] but there is a strong argument that if it carries such benefits other state schools should also have it. The other elements of the basic curriculum are, first, sex education (which first became part of it under the Education Act 1993), but only in the case of pupils attending a secondary school or receiving secondary education in a special school, and secondly, religious education (RE).[274] The fact that sex education is only part of the basic curriculum and usually taught via the non-statutory personal health and social education (PHSE) rather than forming part of the national curriculum,[275] has been a cause of criticism. There are concerns about its uneven quality, partly attributable to the lack of prescription as to content (which it has been argued is significantly motivated by a wish to avoid causing offence to some groups[276]), notwithstanding the 'moral values' requirement and the introduction of national guidance to which schools must have regard.[277]

---

[267] Education Act 1996, s 405.

[268] See n 42 above.

[269] See n 47 above.

[270] Education Act 1996, s 9.

[271] See further *Watt v Kesteven County Council* [1955] 1 QB 408 and *Wood v Ealing LBC* [1967] Ch 364.

[272] The problem of how the state education system should respond to the diverse interests within a multi-cultural society is discussed in detail in N Harris, *Education, Law and Diversity* (Hart Publishing, 2007), ch 7.

[273] House of Commons Children, Schools and Families Committee, Third Report of Session 2008–09, *National Curriculum: Government Response to the Committee's Fourth Report of Session 2008–09* HC 645 (The Stationery Office, 2009), 7.

[274] Education Act 2002, s 80.

[275] Note that the basic biological facts of human reproduction are covered in national curriculum science.

[276] A point made by Meredith (2005), n 247 above.

[277] Education Act 1996, s 403(1B)–(1D). The fact that the guidance must be 'designed to secure that when sex education is given to registered pupils at maintained schools' they 'are protected from teaching and materials which are inappropriate having regard to the age and religious and cultural background of the pupils concerned' (ibid, subs (1A)) shows the concern to respect

Given these concerns and the huge importance of sex education for young people in relation to health and reducing the incidence of adolescent pregnancy there is a case for making it, or PHSE as a whole, part of the national curriculum, as was recommended by an External Steering Group review of sex education in 2008.[278]

In addition to the 'basic curriculum' above, the law continues to set out broad aims which are reflected in rather wide duties. Local authorities have retained a duty from the Education Act 1944 to, as noted above, 'contribute towards the spiritual, moral, mental, and physical development of the community by securing efficient education' throughout the 'three progressive stages' – primary, secondary and further education.[279] Also noted earlier is their duty to promote each child's fulfilment of his or her 'learning potential'.[280] In turn, school governing bodies, head teachers, local authorities and the Secretary of State have duties, originally (in a slightly different form) in the 1988 Act and considered at that time to reflect the notion of a 'whole curriculum'. They must ensure that the curriculum of each school is 'balanced and broadly based' and both 'promotes the spiritual, moral, cultural, mental and physical development of pupils at the school and of society' and 'prepares pupils at the school for the opportunities, responsibilities and experiences of later life'.[281] The latter duty is arguably reinforced by the inclusion of 'Citizenship' as a national curriculum foundation subject for the 11–16 age group from 2000 onwards, albeit that there is evidence that it has not been universally well taught.[282] Changes such as facilitating work experience and vocational education in the form of various diploma courses post the age of 14 have also been aimed at better preparation

---

minority groups' sensibilities and avoid causing offence. The current guidance dates from 2000: Department for Education and Skills *Sex and Relationship Education Guidance*, DfES 0116 2000 (DfES, 2000).

[278] External Steering Group, *Review of Sex and Relationship Education in Schools* (Department of Children, Schools and Families, 2008). See also n 245 above.

[279] Education Act 1944, s 7; see now Education Act 1996, s 13(1).

[280] Education Act 1996, s 13A.

[281] Education Act 2002, s 78(1) and 79. Academy schools are not covered by these statutory requirements, but it is a condition of an academy agreement (which sets out the conditions attached to state funding for the academy) that the body responsible for the school enters into an undertaking with the Secretary of State to ensure that the school meets them: Academies Act 2010 s 1A, inserted by the Education Act 2011, s 53(7).

[282] See N Harris *Education, Law and Diversity* (Hart Publishing, 2007), at p 380. Note that the House of Commons Education and Skills Committee has classed citizenship education as providing an opportunity for extending pupil participation in schools: Second Report, Session 2006–07, *Citizenship Education*, HC 147 (The Stationery Office, 2007), at para 53. With its focus on promoting an understanding of rights and responsibilities, Citizenship would also provide an opportunity to contribute to compliance with the CRC's requirement that the CRC's principles and provisions are made widely known to children (and adults): CRC Art 42. However, the CRC is not referred to specifically in the current programmes of study (part of the prescribed curriculum content) for national curriculum Citizenship. Nevertheless, the guidance (QCA, *Citizenship. Programme of study for key stage 4*, (QCA: 2007)) refers specifically to human rights: 'Human rights are part of national and international law. Students should explore the roles of the United Nations and the European Union in securing human rights and learn that International Humanitarian Law aims to provide protection for victims of armed conflict and children caught up in fighting.'

of pupils for entry to employment, although following the highly critical review of 14–19 vocational education by Wolf the Government conceded that '[f]ar too many 14–16-year-olds are doing courses with little or no value because performance tables incentivise schools to offer these inadequate qualifications'.[283] Indeed, at the end of 2012 it was announced that 14–16-year-olds are to be permitted to attend further education colleges. In any event, the 'whole curriculum' duties do not provide any specific guarantees to children. Nevertheless, they do reflect an holistic view of education and its wider 'affective' curriculum that tends to be overlooked as a result of the almost exclusive policy and legal focus on formal curriculum content.

Finally, mention must be made of the requirement, introduced under the Education Reform Act 1988, that in community and secular foundation schools pupils should take part in an act of collective worship each day which is 'wholly or mainly of a broadly Christian character', that is, reflecting 'the broad traditions of Christian belief without being distinctive of any particular denomination'.[284] Provision was made for the possible lifting or modification of the requirement from the school or class/year group on the application of the head teacher, in the light of factors such as pupils' family backgrounds and thus cultural traditions.[285] Moreover, parents have a long-standing right to withdraw their child from individual (or all) acts of collective worship (and/or RE) at the school.[286] It was also clearly stated that 'most' (and therefore not all) acts of collective worship had to meet the 'broadly Christian' requirements.[287] Nevertheless many minority faith/cultural groups have regarded these provisions on collective worship as discriminatory. Despite this they continue under the present law,[288] although as noted below sixth-formers now have an independent right to opt of collective worship.[289] In practice a majority of schools fail to ensure the provision of a daily act of collective worship, leading to arguments from, among others, a former Chief Inspector of Schools, that the requirements are outdated and should be repealed.[290] In a survey

---

[283] A Wolf, *Review of Vocational Education – The Wolf Report* (Department for Education, 2011), Foreword by Michael Gove MP, Secretary of State for Education. Note that 'work-related learning' has now ceased to be a required element of KS4, as per s 85 of the Education Act 2002 (substituted by the Education and Inspections Act 2006, s 74 and amended by the Education (Amendment of the Curriculum Requirements for Fourth Key Stage) (England) Order 2012 (SI 2012/2056)), although schools retain the power to facilitate it: see further Department for Education, *Wolf Review of Vocational Education. Government Response* (Department for Education, 2012), at p 12.

[284] Education Reform Act 1988, ss 7(1)–(2). The requirement for a daily act of religious worship per se in schools dates back to the Education Act 1944.

[285] Education Reform Act 1988, s 12.

[286] Ibid, s 9(3).

[287] Ibid, s 7(3).

[288] School Standards and Framework Act 1998, ss 70 (requirement for daily act of collective worship) and 71 (right to opt out) and Sch 20, paras 3 (requirement as to 'broadly Christian character' in respect of 'most' acts of collective worship) and 4 (where permission for exemption from para 3 requirement has been granted – under Education Act 1996, s 394).

[289] Introduced via amendments to s 71 of the 1998 Act made by the Education and Inspections Act 2006, s 55: see p 930 below.

[290] See N Harris *Education, Law and Diversity* (Hart Publishing, 2007), at p 440.

commissioned in 2011 by the BBC 64 per cent of parents said that their child did not take part in a daily act of collective worship at school and 60 per cent of adults did not believe that the law should be enforced.[291]

Children's rights and the curriculum

One of the concerns about the curriculum, its formulation and the assessment arrangements that are attached to it, is the absence of a focus on children's rights. A persuasive case in this regard is advanced by Ellwood and Lundy in analysing assessment arrangements in England.[292] They point to the relevance to such arrangements of children's rights under international legal obligations, especially those in the CRC, not merely in the principles of best interests of the child (CRC Art 3) and freedom from discrimination (CRC Art 2) but also others, including rights of participation per Art 12.[293] Under Scottish legislation an education authority must 'secure that education is directed to the development of the personality, talents and mental and physical abilities of the child or young person to their fullest potential,' the wording reflecting CRC Art 29(1)(a), which is concerned with the empowering of individual young people through learning. In addition, in carrying out this duty, it:[294]

'shall have due regard, so far as is reasonably practicable, to the views (if there is a wish to express them) of the child or young person in decisions that significantly affect that child or young person, taking account of the child or young person's age and maturity.'

There is nothing equivalent to this duty in England. The Scottish legislation acknowledges that children and young people have an independent stake in the content of their education. Ellwood and Lundy, noting that Art 12 appears to have had little impact in the area of assessment in England, argue that the Article gives rise to a need, as yet unmet, 'to consult directly with children in relation to the processes and products of assessment, acknowledging children's roles as definitive stakeholders in these matters'.[295] Consulting with young people over the content of the curriculum also needs to be better promoted, as the External Steering Group on sex and relationships education (SRE) recommended, in its proposal that steps should be taken to involve young people in the design of SRE programmes.[296]

So the domestic law of education provides only limited guarantees that children and young people will have an opportunity to influence the content of their

---

[291] BBC News 'State schools "not providing group worship"' http://www.bbc.co.uk/news/uk-england-14794472 (last accessed 27 July 2012).

[292] J Ellwood and L Lundy 'Revisioning assessment through a children's rights approach: implications for policy, process and practice' *Research Papers in Education* (2010), 25:3, 335–353.

[293] See pp 894, 920 and 929 above.

[294] Standards in Scotland's Schools Act 2000, s 2.

[295] Ellwood and Lundy, n 292 above.

[296] External Steering Group, *Review of Sex and Relationship Education (SRE) in Schools* (Department for Children, Schools and Families, 2008), at para 46.

education. However, it should be stressed that, as we have seen, despite the principle in the Education Act 1996 that 'children are to be educated in accordance with the wishes of their parent' and the state's duty under the ECHR A2P1 to give respect, in the context of education, to parents' philosophical and religious convictions, parents' ability to control the content of their child's education is similarly limited. Parents do, at least, have unconditional statutory rights to withdraw their child from sex education, RE or acts of collective worship at school, as noted above.[297] This however begs the question of why young people themselves have not been given equivalent rights, especially more mature pupils who meet the *Gillick* test of competency.[298] In the case of collective worship there was government resistance to applying such a test. It was regarded as impracticable since each child's competency would have to be separately assessed. Instead, an independent right of withdrawal from collective worship at school was conferred on sixth-formers (as noted above), from September 2007.[299] Yet that effectively, for example, denies many 15- and 16-year-olds from exercising choice over participation in an act of religious worship. Indeed, the Joint Committee on Human Rights (JCHR) has argued that an administrative burden, such as would be involved in applying a *Gillick*-competency test, would not provide a basis for interfering with a pupil's Art 9 rights (to freedom to manifest their religion or beliefs) on the grounds of necessity under Art 9(2).[300] Whether such an age limit would meet the test of proportionality linked to justification for discrimination for the purposes of Art 14 of the ECHR, noted above, might also be open to debate.

The Government's case for denying pupils an independent right of withdrawal from RE was based in part on the benefits to 'community cohesion' of ensuring that all pupils learn about faiths of others; and partly on the contention, clearly at odds with the view of the JCHR on the matter,[301] that appropriate teaching of RE combined with the parental right of withdrawal made it 'unlikely' that pupils' Art 9 freedoms would be denied.[302] An attempt during the Parliamentary stages of the Education and Skills Bill in 2008 to extend the collective worship opt-out right to any *Gillick*-competent child and to include religious education in it failed due to lack of government support.[303]

Concerning the parental right to withdraw their child from sex education at school, the author has argued elsewhere[304] that to deny young people an

---

[297] Education Act 1996, s 405 (sex education); School Standards and Framework Act 1998, s 71(1) (religious education and collective worship).

[298] See chapter 8 above.

[299] School Standards and Framework Act 1998, s 71(1C), inserted by the Education and Inspections Act 2006, s 55.

[300] JCHR, Nineteenth Report of Session 2007–08, *Legislative Scrutiny: Education and Skills Bill*, HL paper 107, HC 553 (The Stationery Office, 2008), at para 1.45. For the content of Art 9(2), see p 908 above.

[301] JCHR, Twenty-eighth Report of Session 2005–2006, *Legislative Scrutiny: Fourteenth Progress Report*, HL Paper 247, HC 1626 (The Stationery Office, 2006), at paras 2.2–2.4.

[302] HC Debs, 2 November 2006, col 502, per Mr Jim Knight (Minister for Schools).

[303] See Harris (2009), n 229 above, at 343–344.

[304] Ibid, at 341.

independent right to decide for themselves whether they should receive sex education might at least engage Art 8 of the ECHR (right to privacy and family life). Indeed, case law suggests that the parent's own right under Art 8 over a matter affecting their child may fall away once the child is *Gillick*-competent.[305] But in any event, as we have seen, Art 8 rights are able to be cut down by the grounds for interference set out in Art 8(2); and in this context the need to protect health and perhaps also morals (note the moral dimension required for sex education in England, noted above), both of which are within the grounds in Art 8(2), could be invoked. Moreover, in *Kjeldsen* the European Court of Human Rights confirmed that 'the setting and planning of the curriculum fall in principle within the competence of the Contracting States' and involved 'questions of expediency on which it is not for the Court to rule', although (as noted above) required that 'information or knowledge included in the curriculum [be] conveyed in an objective, critical and pluralistic manner'.[306] That interpretation, for the purposes of A2P1, was held to be consistent with Art 8.[307] Moreover, in *Dojan*, the European Court of Human Rights held that mandatory attendance of pupils at sex education lessons was justified under Art 8(2) as being 'provided for by law and necessary in a democratic society in view of the public interest in ensuring children's education'.[308]

Therefore to deny a right of withdrawal is unlikely, in the context of sex education in England, to be inconsistent with Art 8. As with RE and Art 9 above, it is also unlikely that Art 14 is violated by restricting any right of withdrawal to parents only, at least where less mature children are concerned. The need to protect such children from harmful consequences of an autonomous decision is likely to be regarded as providing sufficient justification in this context. When the sex and relationships guidance was reviewed by an External Steering Group in 2008 the issue of whether the right to withdraw should be extended to pupils themselves was not explored; the Group did consider whether the parental right should continue and found 'no clear consensus on this point' although suggested that it would need further government consideration if the status of PSHE was altered to make it statutory as part of the national curriculum at key stages 1–4.[309]

Complaints

Finally, in relation to the curriculum, there is the question of whether pupils have any independent rights to utilise the various statutory mechanisms for complaints about the curriculum and its delivery in schools. One is referring here to mechanisms other than those concerned with discrimination cases,

---

[305] *R (Axon) Secretary of State for Health and the Family Planning Association* [2006] EWHC Admin 37, per Silber J at 132. *Axon* is discussed at pp 392–393 above.

[306] *Kjeldsen, Busk Masden and Pedersen v Denmark* (1979–80) 1 EHRR 711, at [53], noted at p 891 above.

[307] Ibid.

[308] *Dojan and Others v Germany* Application Nos 391/08, 2455/08, 7908/10, 8152/10 and 8155/10 [2011] ELR 511, at [3]. See p 892 above.

[309] External Steering Group, *Review of Sex and Relationship Education (SRE) in Schools* (Department for Children, Schools and Families, 2008), at paras 1 and 59.

which were discussed earlier, although it will in any event be recalled that in relation to schools the Equality Act 2010 Part 6 excludes discrimination complaints about 'anything done in connection with the content of the curriculum'.[310]

The Education Reform Act 1988 made provision for a local process for complaints concerning the way that the local authority or the school governing body carried out their duties concerning the school curriculum, including religious education.[311] Complaints that could not be resolved informally would be dealt with by the governing body and, if the complainant remained dissatisfied, the complaint could be referred for determination by the local authority.[312] The idea was, in part, to enable complaints about these matters to be resolved locally rather than being made directly to the Department for Education (DfE), which had (and retains) general default powers exercisable against schools and local authorities.[313] Since August 2012 this local curriculum complaints procedure has only applied in Wales: see below.

A separate complaints process was established, via the Education and Inspections Act 2006, involving the Office for Standards in Education, Children's Services and Skills (Ofsted). The Chief Inspector of Schools (who is the head of Ofsted) has a power to investigate written complaints by parents once they have been considered by the governing body.[314] However, the process is not concerned with any matter relating to an individual child. It is limited to specific matters relating to the school – such as the quality of educational provision, the effectiveness of leadership and management, and the school's contribution to the well-being and development of pupils and to community cohesion.[315] Its purpose seems to be more that of enabling Ofsted to carry out investigations as part of its wider role of assessing standards of provision across schools, since no remedies for individuals are prescribed. The investigatory process may involve a meeting with parents at the school, to which all parents must be invited, if Ofsted considers this appropriate.[316]

---

[310] See p 902 above.

[311] Education Reform Act 1988, s 23, subsequently re-enacted in the Education Act 1996, s 409. It also covered complaints about the provision of information.

[312] Complaints about the local authority, however, would not go to the governing body first.

[313] Education Act 1944 ss 68 and 99, since re-enacted in the Education Act 1996 ss 496 and 497. The powers can be invoked in respect of failures of duty or *Wednesbury* unreasonableness in the performance of duties or exercise of statutory powers. See *Secretary of State for Education and Science v Tameside Metropolitan Borough Council* [1976] 3 All ER 665; *Meade v Haringey London Borough Council* [1979] 2 All ER 1016; *R v Inner London Education Authority ex parte Ali and Murshid* [1990] 2 Admin LR 822. Complaints on matters falling within the jurisdiction of the local procedure are statutorily barred from being dealt with by the DfE unless first taken through the local process: Education Act 1996, s 409(4).

[314] Education Act 2006, s 160, inserting Education Act 2005 ss 11A–11C; and see also the Education (Investigation of Parents' Complaints) (England) Regulations 2007 (SI 2007/1089), as amended.

[315] Ibid.

[316] Education Act 2005, s 11B.

Neither of the above complaints processes make any reference to complaints by children themselves. This contrasts with complaints relating to welfare services provided by local authorities.[317] The UN Committee on the Rights of the Child was critical of the fact that '[t]he right to complain regarding educational provisions is restricted to parents, which represent (sic) a problem especially for looked after children for whom local authorities have, though mostly do not use, parental authority'.[318] After the UN Committee's report the Government held out the promise of an independent right for every child to complain under a new process involving the investigation of school complaints by the Local Government Ombudsman (LGO).[319] Measures were set in place to enable individual complaints to be brought to the LGO where parents or pupils asserted that they had 'sustained injustice in consequence of – an act of the governing body of the school; or (b) an exercise of, or failure to exercise, a prescribed function of the head teacher of the school'.[320] Obviously this was much broader in potential scope than the complaints process concerning the curriculum – indeed, the only school matters specifically excluded were those concerned with admissions and those where a right of appeal existed.[321] Nevertheless, it may reasonably be assumed that with the exception of disciplinary matters a child's complaint is perhaps most likely to concern some aspect of the curriculum or its delivery by a teacher. That the child was being given an independent right to complain was, the Government stated, merely consistent with the existing position under the LGO's general complaints handling role (under the Local Government Act 1974) under which it investigates complaints of maladministration.[322] While support for this new independent right was not universal among those consulted in advance of the new legislation, those in favour outnumbered dissenters.[323] The process enabled a complaint to be investigated by the LGO once it had been considered by the governing body.[324] The implication therefore was that pupils themselves could initiate a complaint at school level. However, the Government's proposals failed to state clearly how any disagreement between parent and child over a complaint should be resolved, merely indicating that it was a matter for the discretion of the complaints handlers although in determining their approach they should take account of the child's age and understanding.[325]

There was a clear benefit to having a complaints handling process operated by an independent body, especially one with an established record in calling public

---

[317] Under the Children Act 1989, s 26.

[318] *Concluding Observations: United Kingdom of Great Britain and Northern Ireland, CRC/C/GBR/CO/4* (Centre for Human Rights, Geneva, 2008), at para 66.

[319] Apprenticeships, Skills, Children and Learning Act 2009, Part 10, Chapter 2.

[320] Ibid, s 206(2).

[321] Ibid, s 206(3).

[322] Department for Children, Schools and Families *A New Way of Handling Complaints about School Issues* (DCSF, 2008), at para 40.

[323] Department for Children, Schools and Families *A New Way of Handling Parents' Complaints About School Issues: Consultation Outcome* (DCSF, 2009), at para 9.

[324] Apprenticeships, Skills, Children and Learning Act 2009, s 207.

[325] Department for Children, Schools and Families *A New Way of Handling Complaints about School Issues* (DCSF, 2008), at para 40.

authorities into account and that was able to recommend remedies to complainants. Therefore, even though the LGO's investigations can take many months to be completed, its involvement was very much to be welcomed. The previous Government introduced the new procedure on a pilot basis in April 2010, initially in four areas but then, while still in office, made provision for extending it to ten others from September 2010.[326] Take-up of the process was low. It has not been disclosed how many, if any, of the 150 complaints in the pilot areas which were received in the first 12 months were made by pupils. The Coalition Government decided that because of the small number of cases and the cost of the process (£2–£6m per annum[327] – rather higher than the previous government's estimate of £1.65m[328]) it should be withdrawn.[329] This is especially so in view of the failure to set in place an alternative independent complaints route for pupils themselves. The planned extension of the pilot in September 2010[330] was cancelled and the LGO school complaints jurisdiction as a whole was brought to an end in August 2012,[331] before it had been rolled out nationally. At the same time, the local curriculum complaints process first established under the 1988 Act (above) was abolished in England.[332] Such complaints now fall within the general complaints jurisdiction of governing bodies of schools under the Education Act 2002.[333] Interestingly, the legislation does not specify the complainant, thereby not restricting this process to parents. Indeed, the DfE's 'toolkit' on these complaints mirrors the legislation in that regard but acknowledges complaints by pupils will fall within this process.[334] Few children might, however, be expected to bring complaints in their own right. It is not clear how far pupils are made aware of the process and shown how to use it. But that the opportunity exists should at least partly meet the concern expressed by the UN Committee on the Rights of the Child, noted above.[335]

---

[326] Apprenticeships, Skills, Children and Learning Act 2009 (Commencement No 3 and Transitional and Transitory Provisions) and (Commencement No 2 (Amendment)) Order 2010 (SI 2010/1151).

[327] Education Bill, Explanatory Notes (2011), at para 344.

[328] C Gillie and S Hubble *Apprenticeships, Skills, Children and Learning Bill: Provisions for Children, Education and Learners,* Research Paper 09/15 (House of Commons Library, 2009), at p 127.

[329] See the Education Act 2011, s 45.

[330] See the Apprenticeships, Skills, Children and Learning Act 2009 (Commencement No 3 (Amendment)) Order 2010 (SI 2010/1702), made in June 2010.

[331] Education Act 2011 (Commencement No 4 and Transitional and Savings Provisions) Order 2012 (SI 2012/1087).

[332] It continues in Wales: see the Education Act 2011, s 45(2).

[333] Education Act 2002, s 29(1) and (2).

[334] Department for Education, *School Complaints Procedure 2011* (DfE, 2011), Annex B, which sets out an example of a possible procedure. It says: 'Extra care needs to be taken when the complainant is a child. Careful consideration of the atmosphere and proceedings will ensure that the child does not feel intimidated. The panel needs to be aware of the views of the child and give them equal consideration to those of adults'. However, it contemplates parental guidance playing a role: 'Where the child's parent is the complainant, it would be helpful to give the parent the opportunity to say which parts of the hearing, if any, the child needs to attend.'

[335] Above at p 931.

Responding to special educational needs

Children vary in their capacity to learn and achieve educationally, but it should be a standard aim of any education system to ensure that all children are helped to maximise their individual potential, as reflected in the state's obligation under Art 29(1) of the CRC.[336] There are many social and economic barriers to children's educational achievement and the institutional framework can be adapted to ameliorate some of them – for example, by targeting resources on schools in more deprived communities as the previous government did through its 'education action zones' and the present Coalition Government seeks to do through the 'pupil premium' paid to schools.[337] Yet for some children the barriers they face are the result of inherent problems often related to a physical or mental disability. Such factors may affect their capacity to learn in a way that demands a specific level of help, including the targeting of resources on them individually. Additionally, certain types of physical or mental problems which affect learning may most efficiently and effectively be responded to through education in specialist settings, especially 'special schools' which are established to make provision for children with specific kinds of difficulties. As noted above, there are around 1,000 special schools, but an increasingly smaller proportion of children with such problems are attending them, for reasons outlined below.

The law, which is currently planned for reform (from September 2014) under Part 3 of the Children and Families Bill,[338] adopts a pivotal definition in identifying children with such problems. Such identification is a necessity if the children are to be provided with the kind of educational arrangements that match their requirements. When it was first introduced under the Education Act 1981 the definition marked a shift from a medically based categorisation of children 'requiring special treatment'[339] to one related specifically to how far the child's learning capacity was hampered by their inherent problems. The definition – which is set to be retained, in substance, under the planned reforms[340] – is that of having 'special educational needs' (SEN), which means

---

[336] See n 22 above.

[337] The premium is set at £900 per disadvantaged pupil in 2013–14. This amount is paid to a school in respect of each of its pupils who has been entitled to free school meals within the previous six years and any child looked after by the local authority within the previous six months: in total, some 1.8m children in 2012: DfE Press Notice 'Cash boost for disadvantaged school children', 24 September 2012.

[338] The law is contained in Part 4 Education Act 1996 but the Government presented to Parliament in September 2012 its draft statutory provisions which will replace it: Secretary of State for Education, *Draft legislation on Reform of provision for children and young people with Special Educational Needs* Cm 8438 (The Stationery Office, 2012). The relevant draft provisions were incorporated into the Children and Families Bill, which had its First Reading in the House of Commons in February 2013 and reached the House of Lords in June 2013. References to the planned reforms are included in the ensuing discussion. Regulations will add further specific requirements. For a detailed reference work on the provision made by the 1996 Act and regulations made under it, see S Oliver and P Clements *Special Educational Needs and the Law* (2nd edn, Jordan Publishing, 2007).

[339] See the repealed Education Act 1944, s 33(1).

[340] The House of Commons Education Committee favours retention of the terminology 'in the

having a 'learning difficulty which calls for special educational provision to be made for [the child]'.[341] The Education Act 1996 defines learning difficulty as arising where a child:[342]

'(a) ... has a significantly greater difficulty in learning than the majority of children his age,

(b) ... has a disability which either prevents or hinders him from making use of the educational facilities of a kind generally provided for children of his age in schools within the area of the local authority, or

(c) ... is under the age of five years and is, or would be if special educational provision were not made for him, likely to fall within paragraphs (a) or (b) when over that age.'[343]

Thus 'learning difficulty' is in part a relativistic concept identified through comparison between the capacity of the child in question and that of a notional 'majority' of children, and in part a defined consequence of disablement in terms of its impact on the child's ability to make use of standard educational facilities. However, the legislation provides that a child cannot have SEN simply by virtue of there being a difference between the language used in the child's home and that used in teaching him or her.[344]

To have SEN also requires that, as stated above, the child's learning difficulty 'calls for special educational provision to be made for him' – and this is not set to change under the new Bill. The 1996 Act says that if the child is under the age of 2 *any* educational provision that he or she requires is special educational provision, whereas for a child aged 2 or over it is:[345]

'educational provision which is additional to, or otherwise different from, the educational provision made generally for children of his age in schools maintained by the local authority (other than special schools) in their area.'

Some kinds of provision made to support children in school, such as nursing care[346] or the provision of a lift,[347] have been held to fall outside the definition

---

absence of any consensus or strong support for change': Sixth Report Session 2012–2013, *Pre-legislative scrutiny: Special Educational Needs* (The Stationery Office, 2012), at para 37.

[341] Education Act 1996, s 312(1).

[342] 'Child' is defined for SEN purposes as 'any person who has not attained the age of 19 and is a registered pupil at a school': Education Act 1996, s 312(5). This has proved problematic in relation to young people continuing at school beyond the age of 18 and seeking the same level of support from the local authority as they enjoyed before then: see *Essex County Council v Williams* [2011] EWCA Civ 1315, [2012] ELR 1 (CA).

[343] 1996 Act, s 312(2), as amended.

[344] Ibid, subs (3). This is retained, under the Children and Families Bill.

[345] Ibid, subs (4). Again, the substance of this definition is essentially retained under the Children and Families Bill.

[346] *City of Bradford Metropolitan Council v A* [1997] ELR 417, QBD.

[347] *R v London Borough of Lambeth ex p MBM* [1995] ELR 374.

of special educational provision. That effectively means that the local authority or school will be under no duty under Part 4 of the 1996 Act to arrange for it.[348]

Although schools and local authorities have the Special Educational Needs Code of Practice[349] to guide them in identifying children with SEN and making suitable arrangements for them – indeed they are under a duty to have regard to the Code's provisions[350] and this will continue under the planned reforms although a revised code is expected (see below) – there is scope for interpretation. The courts have, for example, resolved the question of whether certain common areas of learning difficulty, namely dyslexia[351] and a need for speech therapy,[352] are covered (holding that they are). Judgments have also dealt with whether a child's religious or cultural needs or domestic problems could give rise to a special educational need (holding that they generally will not do so).[353] Uncertainty has also arisen over the position of gifted children, meaning those with exceptional ability who learn far more quickly than other children and for whom standard lessons may therefore be unsuitable. It has been contended that giftedness or exceptionally high intelligence can constitute a special educational need, on the basis that a child with that level of capacity may find it difficult to learn if participating in lessons designed for non-gifted children. In the Hampshire dyslexia case cited above Taylor J had said that '[t]he fact that [a child] has a very high intelligence and may therefore be able to some extent to compensate for [dyslexia] is neither here nor there'.[354] The child's needs were related exclusively to dyslexia, although it was also noted by Taylor J that the interaction of the child's high intelligence and dyslexia caused him to be depressed and frustrated. The statistics on children with SEN show that a small proportion of the pupils who are identified as having SEN are also classed as 'gifted and talented'.[355] In *R v Secretary of State for Education*

---

[348] The governing body and, in the case of a maintained nursery school, the local authority must, for example, use their 'best endeavours' to ensure that a child with SEN receives the special educational provision their learning difficulty calls for: 1996 Act, s 317(1). Special educational provision must be included in a child's 'statement' of special educational needs, if one is required, maintained by the local authority and the authority must normally arrange for it to be made for the child: ibid, s 324(5)(a). But these duties only apply to special educational provision, as defined.

[349] Department for Education and Skills 2001.

[350] Education Act 1996, s 313(1). Note that in the case of academies this duty and others relating to children with SEN under Part 4 of the Education Act 1996 described below apply to them under the academy arrangements (comprising the agreement or terms of financial assistance between the Secretary of State and the body responsible for the academy): see the Academies Act 2010, s 1. Under the Children and Families Bill, however, academies will be fully included in the legislation alongside local authority maintained schools.

[351] *R v Hampshire Education Authority ex parte J* (1985) 84 LGR 547.

[352] *R v Lancashire CC ex p CM (A Minor)* [1989] 2 FLR 279 (CA).

[353] *G v London Borough of Barnet and the SENT* [1998] ELR 480; *A v SENDIST and London Borough of Barnet* [2004] ELR 293 (religious background); *G v Wakefield Metropolitan Borough Council* 29 January, 1998 (unreported) (domestic background).

[354] See n 351 above, at 555.

[355] In 2011, of the primary school pupils with SEN 3.7 per cent were classed as gifted and talented, as were 4.7 per cent of secondary pupils with SEN: Department for Education, Statistical First Release SFR 14/2011, *Special Educational Needs in England, January 2011*

ex p C[356] Schiemann J (as he then was) held that the Secretary of State's conclusion that C, a gifted child, did not have a learning difficulty despite having memory problems, was not contrary to Taylor J's conclusion in the Hampshire case. Subsequently, in *R v Portsmouth City Council ex p F*,[357] Tucker J confirmed that in the light of *ex p C* one could not say that 'giftedness' of itself could constitute a learning difficulty. While having SEN is not incompatible with being gifted and talented, a child will not, merely by virtue of being gifted and talented, have SEN. Indeed, in *S v Special Educational Needs and Disability Tribunal and Oxfordshire CC*[358] Elias J considered that there was insufficient flexibility in the statutory definition of SEN to extend it to exceptionally able pupils. While he nevertheless accepted that there was an argument that gifted children had a status for the purposes of protection from discrimination, under Art 14 of the ECHR, any discrimination they were suffering in relation to their right to education under Art 2 to the First Protocol to the Convention (see above) was capable of being justified by the need to target (state) resources on those who were the least rather than the most able.

Therefore there have been some difficulties in determining whether some children have SEN, albeit that these marginal cases represent a minority of those where a decision about SEN has to be made. A broader problematic issue is the labelling of children as 'SEN' in the way that the legislation and policy framework provides for. It may be helpful if it means that their educational needs can be properly identified and responded to, but there are disadvantages in terms of the assumptions that arise from a single categorisation.[359] For example, in 2006 the House of Commons Education and Skills Committee argued powerfully that:[360]

> 'There is an underlying problem, in that the premise on which SEN provision is based – that there exists a single category of children with SEN – is fundamentally flawed. Children exist on a broad continuum of needs and learning styles but do not fit into neat categories of different sorts of children – those with and those without SEN. The category of "SEN" is an arbitrary distinction that leads to false classifications ...'

Another issue is whether SEN should be considered separately from other needs that are related to a child's welfare. In Scotland the broader concept of

---

(DfE, 2011), table 10. The 2012 statistical release stated that such information 'is no longer collected': Department for Education, Statistical First Release SFR 14/2012, *Special Educational Needs in England, January 2012* (DfE, 2012), Technical Notes, at para 7.

[356] [1996] ELR 93.

[357] [1998] ELR 619.

[358] *S v Special Educational Needs and Disability Tribunal and Oxfordshire County Council* [2005] ELR 443.

[359] For further discussion, see D Monk 'Theorising Education Law and Childhood: Constructing the Ideal Pupil' (2000) 21(3) *Br Jnl Sociology of Education* (2000), 21(3), 355–370; M King and D King 'How the law defines the special educational needs of autistic children' CFLQ (2006), 18(1), 23–42.

[360] Third Report, Session 2005–6, *Special Educational Needs* HC 478-I (The Stationery Office, 2006), at para 34.

'additional support needs' is used;[361] the adoption of a similar categorisation, based on having 'additional needs' rather than SEN per se, is under consideration in Wales, the rationale being the need for an integrated, multi-agency approach to 'support [children] in the journey through education and their life choices'.[362] As discussed below, reform in England is focusing on this need for integrated support. But it does not appear to involve a move away from the notion of SEN.

In 2012, 19.8 per cent of children in schools in England had SEN,[363] although the proportion varied across the country and there was a marked disparity between the genders, with almost twice as many boys than girls classed as having SEN.[364] The reasons for the regional variations are not entirely clear although there is a link to social deprivation levels. The proportion of children identified as having SEN tends to be above average in the more socio-economically deprived areas.[365] Although Ofsted has stated, controversially, that SEN classification tends to include children whose needs are 'no different to those of most other pupils',[366] the Government seems to see the problem not so much in terms of a flawed definition but rather an over-identification which leads to lower expectations from some children so that their lack of progress is seen as less problematic.[367] Moreover, there seems to be an incentive for schools to over-identify, since identifying a child as having SEN may be a way of 'evading responsibility for low standards that might relate to poor teaching or other problems'; and the 'concept of "special educational need" risks allowing schools to use "needs" as an excuse for poor provision'.[368] In any event, the kinds of needs that children are identified as having vary widely. The needs most commonly identified fall within the categories behaviour/emotional/social difficulties (BESD); speech, language and communication needs; 'moderate learning difficulty'; 'specific learning difficulty' (the category covering dyslexia); and autistic spectrum disorder. Visual and hearing difficulties are somewhat less common.[369]

---

[361] Education (Additional Support for Learning) (Scotland) Act 2004 as amended. See further N Harris and S Riddell, *Resolving Disputes about Educational Provision* (Ashgate, 2011), ch 4.

[362] Welsh Government, *Consultation Document, Forward in partnership for children and young people with additional support needs* (Welsh Government, 2012), at para 4.

[363] Department for Education, Statistical First Release SFR 14/2012, *Special Educational Needs in England, January 2012* (DfE, 2012), Tables 1A–1C.

[364] Ibid, Tables 5A–5D. Variations on the basis of ethnicity are small, with the exception of Irish Traveller and Gypsy/Roma categories, which have a much higher incidence of SEN although the DfE urges the figures for these groups to be viewed with caution due to the small numbers recorded: Ibid, at p 3 and Tables 8A–8D.

[365] See Harris and Riddell n 361 above, at p 55.

[366] Ofsted, *Special educational needs and disability review – a statement is not enough*, ref 090221 (Ofsted, 2010), 9.

[367] See DfE, *Support and Aspiration: A new approach to special educational needs and disability. A consultation* Cm 8207 (DfE, 2011), at para 3.40.

[368] M Farrell *Educating Special Children* (2nd edn, Routledge, 2012), 21.

[369] Department for Education, Statistical First Release SFR 14/2012, *Special Educational Needs in England, January 2012* (DfE, 2012), Charts A and B and Table 10A.

Following its review of SEN in 2011 the Government is proposing to revise the Code of Practice with a view to ensuring a more effective and consistent identification of SEN and to streamline the way pupils are categorised for help at school level, both of which could lead to fewer children being identified as having SEN.[370] However, one cannot see any departure from the Code's essential message that early identification is important and that both primary and secondary schools have a key responsibility to monitor pupils' progress. This will involve their special educational needs co-ordinator (SENCO)[371] in determining the needs of a particular child who appears to have difficulty. A failure to offer an appropriate professional response to a child's special educational needs, in terms of identification and referral of a child for assessment and the provision of careful and effective advice to parents, could constitute a breach of the duty of care, particularly in the light of the decisions in *X (Minors)*[372] and *Phelps*[373] in the House of Lords and having regard to other, subsequent cases.[374]

For the majority of children with SEN the arrangements to meet their educational needs will be set out in 'individual education plans' (IEPs) drawn up by the school. The contents of an IEP are not, however, enforceable and therefore there have been concerns that this leaves children and parents with an insufficient guarantee that the child's education rights will be properly protected.[375] It is partly for this reason that parents may press for their child's needs to be formally assessed under the statutory process which, currently, can lead to the making of a 'statement of special educational needs' for the child, although a more broadly based 'education, health and care plan' (EHCP) (which unlike the statement could run until the young person is 25) will replace it under the planned reforms.[376] In January 2012 there were just over 226,000

---

[370] See n 367 above paras 3.43 and 3.44 and DfE, *Support and Aspiration: A new approach to special educational needs and disability. Progress and next steps* (DfE, 2012), at para 3.34 and p 37. The idea is to replace the separate categories of 'School Action' and 'School Action Plus'. School Action arises where the school is able to make arrangements for the child's educational needs to be met from its own resources and without the need for outside help. School Action Plus involves a need to bring in outside support and advice, albeit on the basis that the school's own resources can cover the arrangements.

[371] The governing body of the school must designate a member of staff as the school's SENCO 'having responsibility for co-ordinating the provision for pupils with special educational needs': Education Act 1996, s 317(3A), inserted by the Education and Inspections Act 2006, s 173.

[372] *X (Minors) v Bedfordshire County Council; v Clwyd CC; G v London Bromley LBC; Jarvis v Hampshire CC* [1995] ELR 404.

[373] *Phelps v London Borough of Hillingdon; Anderton v Clwyd County Council; G v London Borough of Bromley; Jarvis v Hampshire County Council* [2000] ELR 499.

[374] See especially *Robinson v St Helens MBC* [2002] ELR 681 CA; *Carty v London Borough of Croydon* [2005] EWCA Civ 19, [2005] ELR 104; *Skipper v Calderdale Metropolitan Borough Council and the Governors of Crossley Heath School* [2006] EWCA Civ 238, [2006] ELR 322; *Smith v Hampshire County Council* [2007] EWCA Civ 246, [2007] ELR 321 CA. See further Oliver and Clements, n 338 above, at 323–331 and Harris and Riddell, n 361 above, at 92–95.

[375] See L Lundy 'Stating a case for the unstatemented – children with special educational needs in mainstream schools' (1998) 10(1) CFLQ 39–51.

[376] The statement will only run until a pupil is 19: see *Essex County Council v Williams* [2012] ELR 1.

children in England with a statement of SEN, representing 2.8 per cent of the school population (a proportion that has remained fairly constant in recent years).[377]

The statement is a document, prepared on the basis of the assessment (and with the professional opinions prepared as part of the process appended to it), that sets out the child's SEN, the special educational provision required to meet them, the name or type of school or placement considered suitable for the child, and any non-educational needs or provision that may be considered appropriate.[378] Any special educational provision specified in a statement must be made for the child (the local authority will be expected to fund it) and any school named in the statement as the child's placement must admit the child.[379] The decision on whether to make a statement hinges, under the statute, on the question whether, following the assessment of the child's needs and in the light of any representations by the parent, it is 'necessary' for the authority to determine the special educational provision needed for the child.[380] In practice the decision is meant to be based primarily on the capacity of the school to make such provision from its own resources.[381] If it cannot do so, a statement would be needed. (The test for making an ECHP under the planned legislation will similarly be based on the necessity for special educational provision to be made for the child.)

One of the most contentious issues in the field of SEN is the specificity of statements; local authorities may resist the detailed specification of educational provision in the statement, particularly where it refers to a set number of hours of specialist input, because it will mean that the local authority will be bound to fund it in order to guarantee its provision. Judicial guidance has clarified the degree of specificity required, emphasising the need for a balance between flexibility – so that provision can be altered in accordance with the child's changing needs without having to go through the formal statutory process of statement amendment – whilst ensuring that provision is sufficiently detailed to show how the child's identified needs will be met.[382]

One of the key features of the assessment and statementing processes is the involvement of the parent. Across the field of education as a whole the area of

---

[377] Department for Education, Statistical First Release SFR 14/2012, *Special Educational Needs in England, January 2012* (DfE, 2012), Table 1A.

[378] Education Act 1996, ss 323 and 324 and Schs 26 and 27, as amended.

[379] Ibid, s 324(5).

[380] Ibid, s 324(1).

[381] Department for Education and Skills, *Special Educational Needs Code of Practice* (DfES, 2001), at para 8:2.

[382] See *R v Secretary of State for Education ex p E* [1992] 1 FLR 377; *R v Cumbria County Council ex p P* [1995] 337; *L v Clarke and Somerset CC* [1998] ELR 129; *S v City and Council of Swansea* [2000] ELR 315; *J v Devon County Council and Strowger* [2001] EWHC 958 (Admin); *E v Rotherham Metropolitan Borough Council* [2002] ELR 266; *E v Flintshire CC and the SENT* [2002] 378; *E v LB Newham and SENT* [2002] ELR 453, QBD [2003] ELR 286 (CA); *R (Wiltshire County Council) v YM and SENDIST* [2006] ELR 56; *T v Devon County Council and SENDIST* [2007] ELR 79; *R (N) v North Tyneside Borough Council* [2010] ELR 312 (CA); and *CL v Hampshire County Council* [2011] UKUT 468 (AAC), [2012] ELR 110.

SEN is the one in which the rights of parents are most fully developed. This is a consequence of the priority accorded to them by the Warnock report,[383] as adopted in the Education Act 1981, on whose central principles the present system still rests. Parents must, for example, be given notice of the assessment and permitted to submit written evidence, a right which under the planned legislation will be extended to the young person him/herself if above compulsory school age. They also have a right to: attend the examination of their child; receive a copy of any draft statement made; make representations to the local authority about the contents of the statement; call for a meeting with an officer of the local authority to discuss the statement; and express a preference for a maintained school[384] to be named in the statement.[385] The law contains a presumption that the preference regarding the child's school will be upheld, subject to: (a) the school not being unsuitable in respect of the child's age, ability or aptitude or his/her special educational needs, or (b) the child's attendance there not being incompatible with either the provision of efficient education for the other children or the 'efficient use of resources'.[386] The planned reforms will operate a similar presumption in relation to the naming of a school in an education, health and care plan. Often it is the relative cost of the placement (for the purposes of (b)) that is in issue; disputes frequently arise over the calculation of the cost of a placement preferred by the parent and one specified by the local authority.[387] The parent must also be consulted over any decision of the local authority to make the relevant special educational provision for the child 'otherwise than in a school'.[388]

Some parents may want a mainstream placement for their child, whilst others may feel that their child's needs are best met in a specialist setting, for example one that offers a so-called '24 hour curriculum'. The law has long incorporated a basic presumption, as originally proposed in the Warnock report, that children with SEN should receive the provision they need in a *mainstream* school. The policy of the previous Labour Government supported a strengthening of this presumption of 'inclusion' and this was put into effect under the Special Educational Needs and Disability Act 2001. As amended under that Act, the law states that if a child does not have a statement he or she

---

[383] M H Warnock *Special Educational Needs. Report of the Committee of Enquiry into the Education of Handicapped Children and Young People* Cmnd 7212 (HMSO, 1978).

[384] If the preference is for an independent school, the parent would only be able to rely on the broad (and weak and difficult to enforce) principle in the Education Act 1996, s 9, outlined above, that children are to be educated in accordance with their parents' wishes. Three recent cases, between them, contain a useful review of the case law on s 9 in this context: *K v London Borough of Hillingdon* [2011] UKUT 71 (AAC), [2011] ELR 165; *AM v Kent County Council* [2011] UKUT 51 (AAC), [2011] ELR 287; and *CM v London Borough of Bexley* [2011] UKUT 215, [2011] ELR 413.

[385] Education Act 1996, s 323(1) and Schs 26 and 27.

[386] Ibid, Sch 27, para 3(3).

[387] Transport costs in particular can be an important consideration: see *Dudley Metropolitan Borough Council v Shurvington and Others* [2012] EWCA Civ 346, [2012] ELR 206, in which the Court of Appeal reviews the case law. See also their relevance to cost comparisons made for the purposes of s 9 of the Act when the parent prefers an independent school: eg *EH v Kent County Council* [2011] EWCA Civ 709, [2011] ELR 433.

[388] Education Act 1996, s 319. See *TM v London Borough of Hounslow* [2011] ELR 137.

'must be educated in a mainstream school'.[389] Even for those who do have a statement, placement must be in a mainstream school unless that would be incompatible with the wishes of the parent or with the provision of education for other children.[390] Additionally, schools have long been under a duty to ensure that, so far as is practicable, every child with SEN 'engages in the activities of the school together with children who do not have special educational needs', provided this is compatible with (i) the child receiving the special educational provision he or she needs, (ii) other children's education, and (iii) the efficient use of resources.[391] The proportion of children with statements who were placed in mainstream schools rose from 54 per cent in 1995 to 61 per cent in 2000, but perversely the trend has reversed since the 2001 Act. In 2005 the proportion was down to 60 per cent, in 2010 it was just under 55 per cent and in 2011 it was back to where it was a decade and half earlier, at slightly over 54 per cent.[392] By 2012 it had declined further, to 53.7 per cent.[393] Under the planned reforms to the law, the above requirements and presumptions in respect of inclusion are to be broadly retained (albeit with some alterations) for children or young people who do or do not have education, health and care plans.

Human rights challenges to SEN placements, based on a philosophical preference for or opposition to a particular form of placement (for example, a belief in favour of inclusive education), have foundered to date.[394] But there is at least a right of appeal over, inter alia, the contents of the statement, including the placement, as well as against a local authority's refusal to conduct an assessment or make a statement.[395] Appeals lie to the First-tier Tribunal (Health, Education and Social Care Chamber) and from there, on a point of law, to the Upper Tribunal (Administrative Appeals Chamber).[396] Statementing decisions are prominent among appeals; indeed, over half of all appeals concern the contents of statements.[397] Placement decisions often have

---

[389]   Ibid, s 316(1) and (2) as inserted by the 2001 Act, s 1.

[390]   1996 Act, s 316(3), inserted by the 2001 Act, s 1.

[391]   Ibid, s 317(4).

[392]   DfES, First Release *Special Educational Needs in England: January 2005* SFR 24/2005 (DfES, 2005), Table 1a; DfES, First Release *Special Educational Needs in England: January 2011* SFR 14/2011 (DfES, 2011), Table 1a.

[393]   Department for Education, Statistical First Release SFR 14/2012, *Special Educational Needs in England, January 2012* (DfE, 2012), at p 2.

[394]   See in particular *Simpson v UK* (1989) 64 DR 188; *Graeme v UK* (1990) 64 DR 158; and *R (JW) v The Learning Trust* [2009] UKUT 1997 (AAC), [2010] ELR 115. See further N Harris *Education, Law and Diversity* (Hart, 2007), 335–340.

[395]   Education Act 1996 ss 325 (decision not to make a statement); s 326 (decision to make, amend or not to amend a statement); 328 (decision not to grant a request by a parent of a child with a statement that he or she be further assessed); 328A (a decision, following a review of the child's needs, not to amend a statement); 329 (decision not to grant a parent's request for an assessment of a non-statemented child); 329A (refusal to grant head teacher's request that pupil's needs be formally assessed); Sch 27 para 8 (refusal to agree to change of school for naming in a statement); and Sch 27 para 11 (decision to terminate a statement).

[396]   First-tier Tribunal and Upper Tribunal (Chambers) Order 2008 (SI 2008/2684).

[397]   Based on appeals statistics for 2008–09, the most recent available showing the subject matter of appeals: Tribunals Service, *Special Educational Needs and Disability Tribunal Annual Report 2008–2009* (Tribunals Service, 2009), at paras 1.7 and 1.8.

significant cost implications for the local authority, particularly if the parents want an independent school to be named, which is why appeals in such cases tend to be vigorously contested. In addition to the right of appeal, there is a right, albeit somewhat under-utilised, to request mediation; the local authority is required to make arrangements for it.[398] The Government is keen to promote greater use of mediation in this area. It has rejected abolition of the right of appeal,[399] but at the same time proposed initially that participation in mediation in connection with the dispute should be a pre-condition to an appeal, save in certain cases. The exceptions would comprise appeals concerning the name or type of school or other institution to be stated in the education, health and care plan or the failure of the draft plan to name a school or other institution. Currently, parents always have a choice about entering into mediation and even if they take this option, which relatively few parents do, they may simultaneously pursue an appeal in the tribunal. A Parliamentary Committee found there was much opposition to making mediation 'compulsory' for SEN disputes; the Committee only supported compulsory attendance by parents at an information meeting about the process.[400] The Government subsequently modified its proposals. Under the Children and Families Bill an appeal will only (subject to the same categories of exception as originally proposed) be possible if the would-be appellant has received information and advice about mediation from a mediation adviser and has informed the adviser either (i) that he or she does not wish to participate in mediation or (ii) that he or she wishes to take part in it (and in the case of (ii), subsequently does so).

The Children and Families Bill will also extend to young persons over compulsory school age the above rights of appeal (with the conditions relating to receiving information about mediation) and to bring a complaint of disability discrimination in relation to a school. These changes would represent a significant advance in young people's rights in this field. The rights would only apply to the parent in the case of a child, to be defined in this context as a person of compulsory school age. The Government had previously intended merely to pilot an extension to pupils of the right of appeal and the right to bring a complaint of disability discrimination in a small number of local authorities.[401] The draft legislation has clearly gone further than this and so only needs to (and does) make provision for pilots in respect of those who are of compulsory school age. It also empowers the Secretary of State subsequently to confirm children's appeal and complaint rights. Such an extension of children's procedural rights would represent an important if somewhat belated response[402] to the many calls to facilitate their participation

---

[398] Education Act 1996, s 332B.

[399] DfE *Support and Aspiration: A new approach to special educational needs and disability. Progress and next steps* (DfE, 2012), at paras 2.42 and 2.43.

[400] House of Commons Education Committee, Sixth Report Session 2013–2013 *Pre-legislative scrutinty: Special Educational Needs* (The Stationery Office, 2012), at para 110.

[401] See n 399 above, at paras 2.46 and 2.47.

[402] Wales set out on this course four years ago: see Welsh Assembly Government, *Voices and Choices. A proposed right for children to appeal to the Special Educational Needs Tribunal in*

rights in this area. It would be in tune with the principle adopted in the SEN Code of Practice itself that children, with their 'unique knowledge of their own needs and circumstances... should, where possible, participate in all the decision-making processes that occur in education...'.[403] It is also noteworthy that the Children and Families Bill as currently drafted sets out a general principle regarding provision for those with SEN, that local authorities must have regard to 'the views, wishes and feelings of the child and his or her parent, or the young person'. The planned extension of appeal rights to young people will particularly benefit looked-after children, who have effectively been denied a right of appeal because the local authority is their 'parent' for the purposes of the Education Acts.[404] In the case of those under compulsory school age it is quite likely that the overwhelming majority of appeals would be brought by parents, but it could at least mean that more attention is given to enhancing children's participation in other ways, such as by ensuring that their wishes are communicated and taken into account.[405] The tribunal rules permit the child to attend an appeal hearing and provide that he or she may be permitted to give evidence to the tribunal,[406] but currently there is relatively little involvement of children in either the appeal or mediation processes.[407]

These recent developments in the recognition of children's independent rights in the field of SEN go some way at least towards addressing the concern that the emphasis on parental rights in this area has prejudiced the best interests principle in Art 3 of the CRC as well as denying the child's rights under Art 12.[408] Yet one should perhaps recognise that, regardless of whose rights are in issue, it will in practice be parents who will normally be seeking to engage

---

Wales Doc 051/2008 (Welsh Assembly Government 2008); Idem, *Education (Wales) Measure. Explanatory Memorandum* (Welsh Assembly Government, 2009). The law is contained in the Education (Wales) Measure 2009 nawm 5, and gives young people rights of appeal under Part 4 of the 1996 Act (inserting s 332ZA into the 1996 Act) and a separate right to bring a complaint of disability discrimination (under the Equality Act 2010, Part 1, Chapter 6 and Sch 17, para 3A). In both cases the rights are stated to be 'exercisable concurrently' with the parent's rights. The law only came into force in March 2012 and only to an extent to enable these new rights to be piloted in two areas (Carmarthenshire and Wrexham), although it is intended to roll them out nationally: see the Education (Wales) Measure 2009 (Commencement No 3 and Transitional Provisions) Order 2012 (SI 2012/320) (W 51); and the Education (Wales) Measure 2009 (Pilot) Regulations 2012 (SI 2012/321) (W 52).

[403] DfES, *Special Educational Needs Code of Practice* (DfES, 2001), at para 3:2.

[404] See Harris, n 229 above, at 355–356. Foster parents count as parents for this purpose: *Fairpo v Humberside County Council* [1997] 1 All ER 183.

[405] Within the appeal process the local authority's written response to an appeal must currently set out, inter alia, 'the views of the child about the issues raised by the proceedings, or the reason why the respondent has not ascertained those views': First-tier Tribunal (Health, Education and Social Care Chamber) Rules 2008 (SI 2008/2699), r 21(2)(e). The Practice Direction stipulates that if the child's views were not available by the time of sending the response, 'the views of the child about the issues raised by the proceedings' must be provided to the tribunal: *Practice Direction, Health and Social Care Chamber, Special Educational Needs or Disability Discrimination in Schools Cases* (2008), at para 15c.

[406] Ibid, (SI 2008/2699), r 24(b).

[407] Harris and Riddell, n 361 above, ch.3.

[408] C O'Mahoney 'Special Educational Needs: Balancing the interests of children and parents in the statementing process' (2008), CFLQ 20, 199–218.

with the various decision making and appellate processes. The evidence is that the experience for parents can be highly fraught and involve a fight. The report of the inquiry led by Sir Brian Lamb set out by the previous government referred to the 'battle' that parents often experience in seeking to secure the provision they feel their child needs. Its recommendations placed a strong emphasis on improved support and information for parents as well as a much closer and more constructive relationship between parents and schools/local authorities.[409] The Lamb report has informed some of the present government's thinking on the reform of SEN, including its proposal to give parents 'better support and more control'[410] and to make the system 'less adversarial'.[411] One of the key reforms, involving the replacement of statements by education, health and care plans, which was noted above, will involve bringing together support arrangements across those three areas. An improvement in agency co-operation and co-ordination in meeting needs is hoped for. The agencies would be expected to 'agree their support with parents'.[412]

Other reforms to SEN currently proposed by the Government, designed to make the system less difficult for parents to participate in and more supportive of families, include tackling the problem of delay. This problem has long been evident in the process of assessment and statementing, creating uncertainty for parents and children and causing children to have to wait too long for necessary improvements to their educational arrangements. There is currently a statutory time limit of 26 weeks from consideration of the need for an assessment through to the making of the statement[413] and the Government says it is looking at ways to reduce it.[414] Other proposed changes include the making by local authorities of a 'local offer' to parents concerning the provision, in terms of education and other services relevant to the needs of children with SEN and disabilities, that is expected to be available;[415] the provision of information for parents that is more transparent than at present; the provision of 'personalised funding' for parents who want it for their child (the Bill calls it

---

[409] Sir B Lamb *Lamb Inquiry, Special Educational Needs and Parental Confidence* (DCSF, 2009).

[410] DfE *Support and Aspiration: A new approach to special educational needs and disability. A consultation* Cm 8207 (The Stationery Office, 2011), at p 42.

[411] DfE *Support and Aspiration: A new approach to special educational needs and disability. A consultation* Cm 8207 (The Stationery Office, 2011), at para 1.46.

[412] Ibid. Extensive provision on agency co-operation is made in the draft legislation.

[413] There are separate time limits for each stage: Education (Special Educational Needs) (England) Consolidation Regulations 2001 (SI 2001/3455). A decision on whether an assessment is needed must be made within six weeks. Within 10 weeks from a decision that an assessment is needed the assessment must be carried out. If a statement may be required a draft must be issued for consultation within 2 weeks of the assessment. There is a time limit of a further 8 weeks for the statement to be finalised and issued. Thus the whole process from start to finish should not exceed 26 weeks.

[414] DfE *Support and Aspiration: A new approach to special educational needs and disability. Progress and next steps* (DfE, 2012), at para 1.38.

[415] 'The Local Offer is ... of crucial importance in outlining what is ordinarily available in schools and what will be provided as additional above and beyond this': House of Commons Education Committee Sixth Report Session 2012–13 *Pre-legislative scrutiny: Special Educational Needs* (The Stationery Office, 2012), at para 136.

a 'personalised budget'), so that they will be able to decide how the needs of the child should be addressed; and offering parents a 'clear choice of school',[416] including a choice of a free school or academy, although, as the above discussion showed, it is now clear that this 'clear choice' will only involve a presumption of preference for parents almost identical to that operating currently.[417] It remains to be seen whether these changes will work in practice and deliver the hoped for benefits for parents and children. The idea that parents will be 'empowered' by these reforms as the Government has suggested[418] is perhaps over-stating the position, since although parents will be better informed and in some cases have a more direct input into decisions, there are for the most part no real guarantees of additional resources or significantly enhanced choice.[419]

APPROPRIATE ENGAGEMENT WITH EDUCATION

This section looks at how the law seeks to ensure that children are properly engaged with education by attending school (in most cases) and by contributing to the school community through behaviour which is conducive to a good learning environment. Effectively, it considers a different aspect of inclusion to that outlined in the previous section on special educational needs. The contribution of truancy and exclusion from school to social exclusion is well understood and indeed formed the subject of the first report by the Social Exclusion Unit set up by the post 1997 Labour Government.[420] Policy emphasis continues to be placed heavily on parental responsibility in relation to these areas and on the use of ever more forceful measures to ensure compliance with the expected norms of attendance and good behaviour among pupils. The recent reinforcement of schools' disciplinary powers[421] and suggestions by government that the sanction of forfeited child benefit may be considered in cases of persistent truancy are illustrative of this approach.

School attendance

It was noted earlier that the child's right to education under domestic law derives in part from the enforcement of the parental obligation to ensure that

---

[416] DfE *Support and Aspiration: A new approach to special educational needs and disability. Progress and next steps* (DfE, 2012), at para 2.17.

[417] In particular, choice will be guaranteed unless it would be: unsuitable to the child's age, aptitude, ability or SEN; incompatible with the education of other children; or constitute an inefficient use of resources.

[418] See n 416 above, at para 2.1.

[419] One exception perhaps is the proposed new right of parents to express a preference for an academy or free school place within the process, which they cannot do at present.

[420] Social Exclusion Unit, *Truancy and School Exclusion* Cm 3957 (The Stationery Office, 1998). See also J Fortin *Children's Rights and the Developing Law* (3rd edn, Cambridge University Press, 2009), at p 206.

[421] See Education Act 2011, Part 2.

the child receives education.[422] As the ensuing discussion will show, new powers to enforce this obligation, such enforcement being a responsibility of local authorities, have been introduced over the past few decades. Yet the problem of unauthorised absence from school (or 'truancy') has not diminished.[423] The Coalition Government has repeated the commitment made by the predecessor Labour governments to combat truancy.[424] Whether it will succeed remains to be seen, but one of the shortcomings of past government policies aimed at tackling the problem is that they appear to be guided more by political or ideological agendas than a desire to address truancy's underlying causes. It is true that the previous Labour government had a commitment to reducing social exclusion to which truancy contributes by maximising the educational opportunities for those from disadvantaged backgrounds. This included, for example, placing state schools' governing bodies under a duty to set targets for reducing levels of truancy at their school.[425] Nevertheless, the major influence on policy in this area was the idea that the relationship between citizens' rights and responsibilities needed to be re-balanced, with an increased weighting to be given to the latter. Thus in the context of schooling, parental obligations needed to be re-emphasised.[426]

The Secretary of State for Education has referred to the 'truancy tragedy'[427] represented by persistent unauthorised absence from school. The Government has launched a review of the sanctions that can be imposed where truancy occurs. The message it is sending out is that the current sanctions are ineffective largely because the policing of them is 'weak'. It is not yet known what new measures will be taken to strengthen the control of truancy. One proposal that has been mooted is the withholding of child benefit from parents who fail to pay fines in truancy cases.

The scale of the problem of truancy

There is a distinction between *authorised* absence, for example due to illness, a medical/dental appointment or religious observance (see below), and *unauthorised* absence, which occurs where there is no lawful excuse for

---

[422] See p 898 above.

[423] See, for example, G Attwood and P Croll 'Truancy in secondary school pupils: prevalence, trajectories and pupil perspectives' (2006) *Research Papers in Education*, 21(4) 467–484; J Donoghue 'Truancy and the Prosecution of Parents: An Unfair Burden on Mothers?' (2011) 74(2) MLR 216–244.

[424] Department for Education and Skills *Higher Standards, Better Schools for All*, Cm 6677 White Paper (The Stationery Office, 2005), at para 7.33: 'We will clamp down on truancy'. See further pp 948–949 below.

[425] School Standards and Framework Act 1998, s 63, as amended by the Education Act 2002, s 53. See also the Education (School Attendance Targets) (England) Regulations 2007 (SI 2007/2261), as amended.

[426] Department for Education and Skills *Higher Standards, Better Schools for All* Cm 6677 (The Stationery Office, 2005), at paras 7.32 and 7.33.

[427] Michael Gove, Secretary of State for Education, speech at Durand Academy, London, 1 September 2011, at http://www.education.gov.uk/inthenews/speeches/a00197684/michael-gove-to-the-durand-academy (last accessed 28 June 2012).

non-attendance. According to the latest available statistics, covering 2011/12,[428] around one per cent of all half-days of schooling were lost due to unauthorised absence, which means that on each school day an average of approximately 60,000 pupils were absent from school without a lawful excuse. This represents a small decrease over the previous year, when the total was similar to the record level of 2008/09. The level of authorised absence, on the other hand, fell in 2011/12 from the previous year's rate of 4.7 per cent to 4.1 per cent and, indeed, has been steadily falling since 2000–2001. Boys and girls have similar rates of unauthorised absence. Rates are highest among pupils aged approximately 13–16. There is an association between social deprivation (relative poverty) and truancy: the rate of unauthorised absence among those with an entitlement to free school meals was more than one and a half times the overall rate; there is a similar correlation between severe special educational needs and increased rates of unauthorised absence.[429]

What the Government refers to as 'persistent absenteeism' is seen as the greatest problem. The Secretary of State has referred to a link with poor behaviour: 'a child who is persistently absent is currently 23 times more likely to end up excluded than other children'.[430] The Department for Education bases the categorisation as 'persistently absent' on the extent to which pupils miss a significant proportion of schooling: in 2009/10 persistent absenteeism was defined as occurring when 64 or more half-days of schooling are missed, that is around 20 per cent of the annual total.[431] Since 2010/11 it has been defined as missing 15 per cent of the total of school half-days, so more pupils than under the past definition are likely to be classed as persistently absent, although persistent absenteeism has declined a little over the past few years.[432] Unauthorised absence is particularly associated with persistent absence.

Education 'at school or otherwise'

Under the Education Act 1996 the central obligation resting with the parent, as noted above,[433] is to ensure that a child who is of compulsory school age[434] receives an:[435]

---

[428] Department for Education, Statistical First Release *Pupil Absences in Schools in England, including Pupil Characteristics: 2011/12,* SFR 10/2013 (Department for Education, 2013); Department for Education, Statistical First Release *Pupil Absence in Schools in England, including Pupil Characteristics: 2010/11,* SFR 04/2012 (Department for Education, 2012).

[429] Ibid (both 2012 and 2013 statistics).

[430] Michael Gove, Secretary of State for Education, speech at Durand Academy, London, 1 September 2011, at https://www.gov.uk/government/speeches/michael-gove-to-the-durand-academy (last accessed 1 July 2013).

[431] DfE (2012), n 428 above, Technical Note 7.

[432] Ibid and DfE (2013), n 428 above.

[433] See p 897 above.

[434] See n 88 above.

[435] Education Act 1996, s 7.

'efficient full-time education suitable ... to his age, ability and aptitude, and ... to any special educational needs he may have, either by regular attendance at school or otherwise.'

Therefore it is clear that the parent may discharge that obligation either by sending the child to school or arranging for him or her to be suitably educated away from school, for example at home.[436] As noted in the discussion of home education earlier, there are no official figures on the precise number of children of compulsory school age being educated at home, but it was estimated at 12,000 in 1999 and 21,000 in 2004[437] and considered in 2007 to be increasing and to lie somewhere between 45,250 and 150,000.[438] Few parents have the desire or capacity to undertake home schooling of their children. Therefore, save in exceptional cases, such as where the local authority provides a home tutor for a child who is unable to attend school for a health or psychological reason, under the authority's statutory duty to make such alternative arrangements,[439] the parent must fulfil his or her statutory parental duty by ensuring their child attends a school.[440]

School attendance orders

If the parent is not fulfilling his or her duty under the 1996 Act (above) to ensure the child's receipt of suitable education, the local authority should enforce this duty by serving a 'school attendance order' on the parent requiring the child to attend a specified school.[441] If the parent fails to comply with the order and does not cause the child to receive suitable education anywhere else, the parent commits a criminal offence.[442] The maximum penalty that can be imposed by the magistrates in such a case is a level 3 fine of up to £1,000. The proceedings are brought by the local authority, but before it institutes them it must consider whether it would be appropriate, as an alternative or additional step, to apply for an 'education supervision order' (ESO).[443] This is a civil order made under the Children Act 1989 enabling the child to be supervised by a officer of the local authority's children's services with the aim of establishing why the child is not attending school and working with the family to ensure the child's successful resumption (or commencement) of regular schooling. The ESO process is discussed further at p 955 below.

---

[436] For critical analysis of this parental right, see D Monk 'Problematising home education: challenging "parental rights" and "socialization"' (2004) 24(4) LS 568–598.

[437] L Rogers 'Number of children taught at home soars' *The Sunday Times*, 26 June 2005.

[438] V Hopwood, L O'Neill, G Castro and B Hodgson, *The Prevalence of Home Education in England: A Feasibility Study* Research Report RR827 (Department for Education and Skills, 2007).

[439] Education Act 1996, s 19.

[440] Local authorities are under a duty to ensure the availability in their area of sufficient schools to meet local educational needs and in particular the provision of appropriate education for all children: ibid, ss 13, 13A and 14. See also n 194 above.

[441] 1996 Act, s 437.

[442] 1996 Act, s 443.

[443] 1996 Act, s 447.

School attendance duty

Once the child is registered at school the parent is under a duty to ensure that the child's attendance is regular, unless one or more of the lawful excuses apply (see below). There are two separate offences under the 1996 Act for failure in this duty. They also apply in cases where the child is absent from alternative educational arrangements not at a school or the child's home which have been made for him or her by the local authority or the school's governing body.[444] Research has shown that there is some variation across the local authority sector in the level of non-attendance which triggers the use of attendance enforcement measures, ranging per authority from 10 per cent to 20 per cent plus.[445]

The first of the offences, under s 444(1), is that of not ensuring that such a child attends school regularly.[446] Commission is not dependent on the parent's knowledge or condonation of the child's failure to attend. The offence carries a maximum penalty of a £1,000 fine, although generally the fine imposed will be much lower than this.[447] The courts have confirmed that this is a strict liability offence.[448] Moreover, as Richards J said in one case:[449]

> 'The subsection looks not to the conduct of the parent or even to the parent's failure to act, but simply to whether the child has failed to attend regularly at school and whether the defendant is the parent of that child.'

While strict liability in this context may seem harsh in the case of a parent who has no knowledge that their child has truanted, the courts have acknowledged the importance of the underlying objective of the law in reinforcing parents' responsibility.[450] In *Barnfather*,[451] however, the court was asked to declare this strict liability offence to be in conflict with Art 6(2) of the European Convention on Human Rights, which provides: 'Everyone charged with a criminal offence shall be presumed innocent until proven guilty according to law'. The court held that s 444(1) did not impose a burden on the accused to establish their innocence; it was still incumbent on the prosecution to show that

---

[444] 1996 Act, s 444ZA as inserted by the Education Act 2005, s 116 and amended by the Education and Skills Act 2008, s 155.

[445] K Crowther and S Kendall *Investigating the use of Parental Responsibility Measures for School Attendance and Behaviour: Final Report*, DfE Research Report DFE-RR041 (DfE, 2010), at para 40.

[446] Prosecution can only be brought by the local authority: Education Act 1996, s 446. 'Regular' attendance means attendance at the times prescribed by the authorities, so that an offence may be committed not only due to the child's absence but also if the child is frequently late: *Hinchley v Rankin* [1961] 1 All ER 692. In *London Borough of Bromley v C* [2006] EWHC 1110 (Admin), [2006] ELR 358 it was held that a child who had had unauthorised absences from school on 9 days out of 57 had not been attending regularly.

[447] See p 952 below.

[448] *Crump v Gilmore* (1970) 68 LGR 56; *Hampshire County Council v E* [2008] EWHC 2584 (Admin), [2008] ELR 260.

[449] *Hampshire County Council v E*, ibid, at para 10.

[450] See in particular Davis J, *R v Leeds Magistrates Court and Others* [2005] EWHC 1479 (Admin), [2005] ELR 589, at para 23.

[451] *Barnfather v London Borough of Islington* [2003] EWHC 418 (Admin), [2003] ELR 263.

the accused had committed the offence. That meant that Art 6(2) had no relevance. Nevertheless the two judges commented on the strict liability issue, but they disagreed profoundly with each other. Elias J said that strict liability was disproportionate to the objective behind the offence and could result in an 'innocent' parent acquiring a conviction carrying a 'real stigma' and connoting 'indifference to one's children, or incompetence at parenting, which in the case of a blameless parent will be unwarranted'.[452] Maurice Kay J, however, saw strict liability as reasonable and proportionate given the legislation's general context and considered that 'the wholly ignorant and blameless parent in respect of a child who does not attend school regularly ought to be an extreme rarity'.[453] In another case the parent attempted to rely on a general criminal defence of 'duress of circumstances'.[454] Her son was 15, violent and disposed to consuming alcohol and taking controlled drugs. His mother said that she feared a risk of death or serious injury to herself or the boy's sister if she and the sister attempted to force the boy to attend school. Although the magistrates' court upheld the defence of 'duress of circumstances' the divisional court held that it was not available in respect of a s 444(1) offence and that in any event there was insufficient evidence that the mother and sister were objectively at risk of death or serious injury.[455]

The other offence, under s 444(1A), is committed when the parent 'knows that his child is failing to attend regularly at the school' and is not able to prove he or she had 'a reasonable justification' for not causing him or her to attend.[456] The onus of proving 'reasonable justification' is now therefore on the parent, whereas prior to its amendment in 2006 the position was that if the parent put forward evidence in support of such a claim the burden of proof would lie with the prosecutor to show that there was no such justification.[457] The penalty for breach of a subs (1A) offence will be a fine at level 4 (up to £2,500) or a term of imprisonment not exceeding three months, or both.[458] In July 2008, for example, a mother in Oxfordshire, aged 41, was imprisoned for two months; she had previous convictions for a child's non-attendance.[459]

A parent's acquittal in respect of a subs (1A) offence does not preclude his or her conviction of the strict liability offence under s 444(1) on the same facts.[460]

---

[452] Ibid, at para 57.

[453] Ibid, at paras 30 and 31.

[454] *Hampshire County Council v E*, n 448 above.

[455] The magistrates were also criticised for failure to consider whether a reasonable person would have responded to the threat posed by the pupil by allowing the child not to attend school.

[456] Education Act 1996 s 444(1A) (as introduced via an amendment made by the Criminal Justice and Court Services Act 2000 and amended by the Education and Inspections Act (EIA) 2006) and (1B) (as introduced by the EIA 2006, s 109).

[457] *R (P) v Liverpool City Magistrates* [2006] ELR 386.

[458] Education Act 1996, s 444(8A). Note that an amendment enabling the maximum penalty for this offence to be increased to 51 weeks' imprisonment has been waiting since 2003 to be brought into force: Criminal Justice Act 2003, s 280 and Sch 26, para 49.

[459] See http://news.bbc.co.uk/1/hi/england/oxfordshire/7514768.stm (last accessed 28 June 2013).

[460] Education Act 1996, s 444(8B).

In *R (P) v Liverpool City Magistrates*[461] the child had 99 unauthorised absences out of 122 possible attendances and although the mother had tried to ensure the child attended school, including on one occasion trying to drag him there (despite his being much larger than she was), she had not been successful. She was convicted by the magistrates under s 444(1A), but her conviction was quashed on appeal. Although the court accepted that there was a breach of the s 444(1) offence it in fact declined in the interests of justice to refer the case back to the magistrates to consider that offence.[462]

Fines are the most common penalty: in 2005–06 most fines for parents convicted of a truancy offence were set at £50 or £100, but the average fine imposed in such cases in 2010 was £165.[463] Research suggests that mothers are more likely than fathers to be prosecuted even though both could fall within the definition of 'parent' under the 1996 Act. An important factor is the greater likelihood that the child will live with the mother and that the mother will hold de facto parental responsibility.[464]

Permitted reasons for non-attendance

There are statutory excuses in respect of non-attendance. If any of them applies the child is not to be treated as failing to attend regularly and the absence would be classed as authorised. They are:

(i)   where the child's absence is due to the granting of leave of absence by the school;[465]

(ii) when a day of absence is one 'exclusively set apart for religious observance by the religious body to which his parent belongs';[466]

(iii) if the parent proves that at the relevant time 'the child was prevented from attending by reason of sickness or other unavoidable cause'.[467] Unlike the religious observance ground above, this must relate specifically to the child

---

[461]   Note 457 above.

[462]   Ibid, at paras [23]–[25]. Cf *West Sussex County Council v C* [2013] EWHC 1757 (Admin).

[463]   House of Commons Committee of Public Accounts *Department for Education and Skills: Improving school attendance in England*, Eighteenth Report of Session 2005–06, HC 789 (The Stationery Office, 2006), at para 13; C Taylor *Improving attendance at school* (Department for Education, 2012), at para 24.

[464]   See J Donoghue 'Truancy and the Prosecution of Parents: An Unfair Burden on Mothers?' (2011) 74(2) MLR 74 216–244.

[465]   Education Act 1996, s 444(3)(a). Under rules in force until 1 September 2013 leave could only be granted by the proprietor or other authorised person. If it related to a holiday, leave could be granted for up to ten days only, in any school year, save in exceptional circumstances: Education (Pupil Registration) (England) Regulations 2006 (SI 2006/1751), reg 7. From 1 September 2013, however, leave *for any purpose* can only be granted where the person authorising it considers that due to 'exceptional circumstances' it should be granted: ibid, as amended by the Education (Pupil Registration) (England) Regulations 2013 (SI 2013/756).

[466]   Education Act 1996, s 444(3)(c).

[467]   Ibid, s 444(2A), inserted by the Education and Inspections Act 2006 s 109(4).

and generally not to his or her parent;[468] so where, in one case, a child did not attend school in order to look after the parent, who was infirm, it was not an 'unavoidable cause'.[469] Such a cause is not that easy to establish. For example, in two cases involving 15-year-old girls where, in the first, the girl had left home to live with her boyfriend and did not tell her mother where she was, and, in the second, the girl who lived with her mother traced her father and truanted without the mother's knowledge to visit him and his family and had a 'chaotic lifestyle', the judges found no unavoidable cause for absence from school.[470] In another case also concerning a 15-year-old girl it was asserted that the girl's absence from school was due to the bullying of her by other pupils which had made her depressed, indeed suicidal. The magistrates did not, however, find a significant risk of suicide and Davis J held that they had been entitled to reject a claim of 'unavoidable cause';[471]

(iv) where the parent proves that the school is not within walking distance (as defined) of the home and the local authority has failed to make suitable arrangements for transport or to enable the child to attend a nearer school or to reside at the school.[472]

No other excuses are permitted. The prescribed excuses 'cover quite a wide field for exemption from responsibility to attend' and the legislation 'does not ... leave it open to ... consider matters other than those which are set down'.[473]

These excuses do not apply where a child has 'no fixed abode'; but it is a defence if the parent of such a child proves (thus placing an onus on the person accused of the offence to establish the 'defence') certain matters.[474] They are that the parent is engaged in a trade or business which requires travelling from place to place, that the child has attended as a registered pupil at a school 'as regularly as that trade or business permits', and that in the case of a child aged six or over, at least 200 school sessions (half days) have been attended by the child in the 12 months prior to the institution of proceedings.[475] This therefore provides a basis for a person with an itinerant lifestyle to escape liability for their child's non attendance. However, such is the concern about the

---

[468] 'Generally' because in *R v Leeds Magistrates' Court and others* [2005] ELR 589 Davis J departed a little from the previous jurisprudence and acknowledged that the parent's circumstances might in some cases impact on the child. This could mean that unavoidable cause might be accepted where, for example, the mother flees the area due to a violent partner and takes the child with her.

[469] *Jenkins v Howells* [1949] 2 KB 218.

[470] *Bath v North-East Somerset District Council v Warman* [1999] ELR 81 and *West Sussex County Council v C* [2013] EWHC 1757 (Admin), in which Hallett LJ confirmed (at para 26) that 'unavoidable cause' should be given a 'strict interpretation' and 'must amount to something of an emergency'. See also *London Borough of Islington v D* [2011] EWHC 990.

[471] *R v Leeds Magistrates' Court and others*, n 468 above.

[472] Education Act 1996, s 444(4) and (5).

[473] See *Spiers v Warrington Corporation* [1954] 1 QB 61, per Sellers J, at 69.

[474] Education Act 1996, s 444(6) (as amended by the Education and Inspections Act 2006 s 109(6)).

[475] Ibid.

educational under-achievement of such children, and in particular children of Gypsy, Roma and Traveller communities, that the Government is at the time of writing consulting over the abolition of this defence, while nevertheless seeming to recognise that such a change in the law (which would take effect in 2014) may not be consistent with the culture and practices of travelling communities.[476]

The effectives of prosecution and use of alternatives in non-attendance cases

In a recent report the Government's advisor on school attendance and behaviour asserted that 'the process of taking a parent to court is cumbersome and expensive' and can take up to six months.[477] However, many cases are now dealt with through a 'fast track' system which enables parents of persistent truants to be brought before the court more rapidly. In the fast track process the local authority sets a review date at six weeks thereafter. The local authority gives notice to the parent and at the same time serves a prosecution summons and requests a court hearing date to be fixed for 6 weeks after the review date. If child's attendance has improved by the review date (as would be hoped) the case will not proceed to court. If it has not, the scheduled hearing will go ahead. Official figures reveal that, in 2009–10, 46,848 cases entered the fast track process and 5,346 cases were prosecuted, whereas in 2011–12 the number entering the process fell significantly to 36,687 but there was a small increase in the number of prosecutions, to 5,606.[478]. Thus a higher proportion of fast track cases resulted in a prosecution in 2011–12, the reason for which is unclear.

The conviction rate is high in school attendance prosecution cases, at 80 per cent.[479] As a tool for improving attendance, prosecution appears to be most effective in cases concerning non-attendance of children of primary school age and in cases where truancy is not too severe, is relatively new and the family is not one facing a complexity of social issues.[480] It works less well where the parents have difficulty with managing their lives. Families that are burdened by various social problems – in particular, exceptional pressures caused by unemployment, poverty, illness and family responsibilities – are particularly

---

[476] Department for Education *Improving educational outcomes for children of travelling families* (Department for Education, 2012). See also, more generally, A Wilkin et al *Improving the outcomes for Gypsy, Roma and Traveller pupils: final report* (Research Report DFE-RR043) (Department for Education, 2010).

[477] C Taylor *Improving attendance at school* (Department for Education, 2012), at para 21.

[478] Department for Children, Schools and Families *2010 Parental Responsibility Measures Data* (DCSF, 2010) and Department for Education *Parental Responsibility Measures Data for Academic Year 2011/12,* both at http://www.education.gov.uk/schools/pupilsupport/behaviour/attendance/a0010302/parental-responsibility-data (both last accessed 20 September 2013).

[479] National Audit Office *Improving School Attendance Cases in England* HC 212 (The Stationery Office, 2005), at para 3.24, citing research by NFER.

[480] K Halsey, N Bedford, M Atkinson, R White and K Kinder *Evaluation of Fast Track to Prosecution for School Non-Attendance*, RR567 (Department for Education and Skills, 2004); S Kendall, R White, K Kinder, K Halsey and N Bedford (eds), *School Attendance and the Prosecution of Parents: Effects and Effectiveness.* LGA Research Report 2/04 (NFER/LGA 2004).

likely to be unable to secure their child's regular attendance at school.[481] Prosecution can merely exacerbate these problems for families with a child who is habitually truanting and is beyond the parent's effective control.[482] From a local authority perspective, many authorities regard the small fines and limited custodial sentences that are imposed as undermining the value of prosecution.[483] In any event, some local authorities consider that if prosecution is to be effective it needs to be instituted quickly. Indeed while official guidance indicates that alternatives to prosecution should be considered in some cases and that prosecuting should be seen as a last resort, in others it 'may be the only appropriate response where acting early will prevent problems from worsening'.[484] The 'fast track' process, outlined above, can obviously support the early intervention approach. Research has shown that local authorities consider it the most effective means of improving school attendance over the longer term, at least in cases where truancy is not too entrenched.[485]

Local authorities are also aware that some of the alternatives to prosecution will only work with the co-operation of the parents. A good example is the *Education Supervision Order* (ESO), referred to earlier. ESOs are made under the Children Act 1989. They provide for the supervision of the child by a supervisor who will 'advise, assist and befriend and give directions' to secure that the child is 'properly educated'.[486] The official guidance emphasises that an ESO will not be suitable if the parents are hostile to the involvement of local children's services.[487] The local authority will, however, still have the option of bringing a prosecution if the ESO is not working.[488] In any event, the supervisor can give directions to the family; breaches would give rise to criminal liability.[489] Supervision under an ESO enables the causes of the truancy to be explored, involving the family in seeking to address them. Children's services can link up with other agencies, especially schools, a multi-agency approach which Newvell describes as being 'ahead of its time' when it was first introduced two decades ago.[490] Unfortunately this level of support is relatively expensive for local authorities. Indeed, the use of ESOs seems to have become increasingly less popular: since 1992 there has been a

---

481 P Carlen *Truancy: The Politics of Compulsory Schooling* (Open University Press, 1992), at p 137.

482 National Audit Office *Improving School Attendance in England* HC 212 (The Stationery Office, 2005).

483 K Crowther and S Kendall *Investigating the use of Parental Responsibility Measures for School Attendance and Behaviour: Final Report*, DfE Research Report DFE-RR041 (DfE, 2010), at para 5.72.

484 Department for Children, Schools and Families *Ensuring Children's Right to Education* (DCSF, 2008), at para 1.

485 K Crowther and S Kendall, n 483 above, at paras 6.29–6.31.

486 Children Act 1989, Sch 3, para 12.

487 Department for Education and Employment *DfEE guidance on Education Supervision Orders (Children Act 1989)* (DfEE, 1991), at p 2.

488 *Graves v London Borough of Islington* [2004] ELR 1.

489 Children Act 1989, Sch 3, para 18. Prosecutions for such breaches are most uncommon.

490 J Newvell *Multi-agency Interventions with Poor School Attenders: Education Supervision Orders – developing effective practice* (National Children's Bureau, 2008), at p 3.

steady decline in orders.[491] Note that if truancy is but one of a number of problems affecting the child which are due to parental neglect, the local authority would be expected to intervene under its more general child protection duties in the Children Act 1989. The ESO has, however, made it extremely unlikely that this general welfare framework would be used where truancy is the only difficulty.[492]

The Anti-social Behaviour Act 2003 brought in several new alternatives to prosecution that are still in use. *Penalty notices* are one,[493] and they also depend on parental co-operation if they are to succeed. They are available in England, but the Welsh Government is currently consulting on their introduction in Wales.[494] An 'authorised officer', including a head teacher, who has reason to believe that a parent has committed a school attendance offence under s 444(1) (above) may serve a penalty notice on that person.[495] The notice requires the person to pay to the local authority, within 28 days (it was 42 days prior to 1 September 2013), the prescribed penalty, which was increased in September 2012 from £50 to £60. If the payment is not made within 21 days (previously 28 days) the penalty will rise to £120 (increased from £100).[496] Payment of the penalty will prevent the parent from being convicted of the offence or of an offence under s 444(1A) (above) arising out of the same circumstances.[497] The increases in the penalty were recommended by the Government's advisor.[498] However, it is not yet clear whether his accompanying recommendation that non-paid fines should be recouped from the parent's child benefit[499] will also be adopted. That would require new legislation but it is bound to be opposed on the basis that it will only exacerbate the difficulties faced by families in deprived circumstances among whose members truants are particularly likely to be found and that it is therefore likely to be counter-productive. The official guidance indicates that the decision to use a penalty notice will depend on the perceived likelihood of its effectiveness in securing the child's attendance at school or in alternative provision (such as a pupil referral unit). This will in turn hinge on whether the parent who has failed to respond to pressure or guidance is nevertheless 'judged capable of securing their child's regular

---

[491] Ibid.

[492] But it would still be possible: see *In Re O (A minor) (Care proceedings: education)* [1992] 4 All ER 905.

[493] Education Act 1996, ss 444A and 444B, inserted by the Anti-social Behaviour Act 2003, s 23.

[494] Welsh Government, *Penalty notices for regular non-attendance at school* (Welsh Government, 2012).

[495] Authorised for this purposes would be a police constable; an officer of the local authority; or an authorised staff member (the head teacher or a deputy or assistant head authorised to issue penalty notices): 1996 Act s 444B and the Education (Penalty Notices) (England) Regulations 2007 (SI 2007/1867), as amended from 1 September 2012 by the Education (Penalty Notices) (England) (Amendment) Regulations 2012 (SI 2012/1046).

[496] Education (Penalty Notices) (England) Regulations 2007 (SI 2007/1867), as amended by SI 2012/1046 (see n 495 above) and the Education (Penalty Notices) (England) (Amendment) Regulations 2013 (SI 2013/757).

[497] Education Act 1996, s 444A(4).

[498] C Taylor, *Improving attendance at school* (Department for Education, 2012), R 11.

[499] Ibid.

attendance'.[500] Local authorities have varying views regarding the utility of these notices, whereas schools seem to favour their use but are unwilling to issue them themselves.[501]

The use of penalty notices has increased in the years since their introduction in 2004. In the first four years to 2008 a total of 48,549 were issued, but there were 25,659 in 2009–10 alone and 41,224 in 2011–12. The proportion of penalties paid within 28 days steadily increased, from 38 per cent in 2004–08 to 46 per cent in 2009–10 and 53 per cent in 2011–12, and the proportion not paid at all within 42 days progressively fell across these three periods, from 40 per cent to 28 per cent and then to 21 per cent.[502] This trend arguably gives more encouragement to the use of these notices, particularly as they do appear to be quite effective in avoiding the need for a prosecution. But it is important to assess the deterrent effect of a notice as compared with prosecution in relation to repetition of truancy by a child. Research has shown that penalty notices generally lead to a short term improvement in attendance but that it tends to fall away over the longer term; across eight case studies, the improved level of attendance was only sustained beyond three months in two cases and the researchers concluded that in cases where there were 'underlying family issues or where attendance issues were more entrenched' penalty notices were 'less effective'.[503]

The Anti-social Behaviour Act 2003 also brought in *parenting contracts and parenting orders* for truancy (and exclusion) cases.[504] Parenting orders have been in use in the criminal courts as a means of attempting to harness parental responsibility to control lawless behaviour among young people. A court may now impose such an order, to last for up to 12 months, as an ancillary order following a truancy conviction. The idea is that the parent will be ordered to attend classes designed to inculcate effective parenting skills. The order would require attendance once per week for up to three months and any breach of it would give rise to criminal liability (penalised by a fine of up to £1,000).[505] Parenting contracts have a similar objective but are voluntary and not legally binding. The contract is to include a statement by the parent agreeing to particular action. It must also incorporate a statement by the local authority or school indicating that they will provide support to aid the parent's compliance

---

[500] Department for Children, Schools and Families (DCSF) *Guidance on Education-Related Parenting Contracts, Parenting Orders and Penalty Notices* (DCSF, 2007), at paras 183 and 184.

[501] M Zhang 'School Absenteeism and the Implementation of Truancy-Related Penalty Notices' *Pastoral Care in Education* (2007), 25(4), 25–34.

[502] Department for Children, Schools and Families *Parental Responsibility Data. Data on Penalty Notices, Fast-track to attendance, Parenting Orders and Parenting Contracts cumulative data for period September 2004 – August 2008* (DCSF, 2008) http://media.education.gov.uk/assets/files/pdf/s/parental%20responsibility%20data%20september%202004%20%20%20august%202008.pdf (last accessed 1 July 2013); DCSF, *2010 Parental Responsibility Measures Data* (2010) and DfE, *Parental Responsibility Measures* (2013), both n 478 above.

[503] Crowther and Kendall, n 483 above, Executive Summary paras 52–53.

[504] Anti-social Behaviour Act 2003, s 19, amending the Crime and Disorder Act 1998, s 8.

[505] Crime and Disorder Act 1998, s 9. See also n 500 above, Part 4.

with the contract.[506] The premise behind parenting contracts is that some parents wish to address their child's non-attendance at school but need help in doing so. Help would include advice and information about voluntary organisations or local authority services, plus 'family group conferencing, peer mentoring, parenting classes, literacy classes, [social security] benefits and drugs/alcohol advice, provision of a key link worker for the parent and help with transport to and from school'.[507]

Some 25,852 parenting contracts were proposed by local authorities in 2009–10, of which 77 per cent were accepted by parents, and there were 360 parenting orders, most of which were implemented; but fewer contracts (20,019) were offered in 2011–12 (of which 73 per cent were accepted) and there was also a fall in the number of parenting orders (to 335), 87 per cent of which were implemented.[508] Overall the use of parenting orders in truancy cases seems to be declining, perhaps due to the relative popularity of parenting contracts but also the mixed views of local authorities as to the orders' effectiveness.[509] Zhang found that 'a significantly high proportion of local authorities' saw the parenting contract as 'an effective measure for their schools to address attendance problems', many reporting 'improvement in school attendance after issuing and implementing parenting contracts'.[510] Research by Crowther and Kendall revealed a similar view of parenting contracts among local authorities; more than three-quarters of those surveyed reported that the contracts were either very or fairly successful in improving the rate of attendance.[511] The researchers also found that the attendance rate among truanting pupils who were made the subject of a parenting contract rose from an average of 48 per cent before the contract to 78 per cent after it had been in place for three months.[512] They also found, perhaps not surprisingly, that local authorities were less sure about the effectiveness of parenting contracts in cases where parents were unwilling to engage with the process or where truancy was more entrenched or severe.[513]

Local authorities also operate *truancy 'sweeps' (patrols)* as a means of combating truancy in their area. A team typically comprising a local authority welfare officer and a police officer will patrol shopping malls, town or city centres or other public places during school hours looking for children who, due to their age, might be expected to be in school. Any such child who is found and any accompanying adult will be asked the reason for the child's absence from school. There is a power under the Crime and Disorder Act 1998 for a police officer who 'has reasonable grounds for believing the child is of compulsory school age and is absent from school without lawful authority' to

---

[506] See n 500 above, at para 36.
[507] Ibid, at para 62.
[508] DCSF *2010 Parental Responsibility Data* and DfE *Parental Responsibility Measures* (2013) both n 478 above.
[509] K Crowther and S Kendall, n 483 above, at para 6.36.
[510] Zhang, n 501 above, at p 34.
[511] K Crowther and S Kendall, n 483 above, at para 6.12.
[512] Ibid, at para 6.13.
[513] Ibid, at para 6.17.

'remove the child... to designated premises, or to the school from which he is so absent'.[514] A national survey in late 2006 covering three weeks of truancy sweeps found that across 126 local authorities there were 1,100 truancy patrols; 11,713 children were stopped in the period; nearly 5,000 of them did not have a valid reason for being away from school; 77 per cent of the truants were of secondary school age, 60 per cent were boys and 37 per cent were accompanied by an adult.[515] While the extent of their use varies across the country, truancy sweeps are employed to a significant degree. It is unclear, however, how much use is made of the power to 'remove' a truanting child to school or another designated place. In a survey of education welfare officers reported by the National Audit Office in 2005, 51 per cent of the officers considered that truancy sweeps were effective and only 16 per cent thought they were not, although 38 per cent considered that the sweeps were not cost effective.[516] The Labour Government advocated their further use in urban areas[517] and this seems to have materialised.

Should young people be given legal responsibility for their own attendance?

There is a continuing legal and policy emphasis on parental responsibility in the sphere of school attendance and it may, even if not directly aimed at doing so, reinforce the child's right to education. At the same time the idea of promoting among the group associated with the highest levels of truancy, adolescents, a sense of personal responsibility has tended to be ignored. Parental responsibility has important protective and developmental roles in the critical area of education. Nevertheless, children and young people's understanding of their position as holders of both rights and responsibilities is important and is, for example, an aim of citizenship education programmes which, as noted above, are now compulsory in schools in England and have been shown to make pupils more engaged in their schools and the learning process.[518] Therefore there may be a case for further emphasising pupils' responsibilities in relation to attendance, provided it is not at the expense of agency support for those for whom truancy is a symptom of deeper problems.

For young people above compulsory school age there has recently been established a so-called 'participation age' through measures set out in the Education and Skills Act 2008.[519] There are provisions in the Act which aim to promote young people's participation in either appropriate full-time education

---

[514] Crime and Disorder Act 1998, s 16.

[515] DCSF figures cited at the National Youth Agency website http://www.nya.org.uk/enjoying-and-achieving (last accessed 28 June 2013).

[516] National Audit Office *Improving School Attendance in England* HC 212 (The Stationery Office, 2005), at para 3.19.

[517] DfES, *Higher Standards, Better Schools for All*, Cm 6677 (The Stationery Office, 2005), at para 7.33.

[518] See for example K Covell, R B Howe and J K McNeil "' If there is a dead rat, don't leave it'. Young children's understanding of their citizenship rights and responsibilities' *Cambridge Journal of Education*, (2008) 38(3), 321–329.

[519] Part 1 of the 2008 Act, comprising 67 sections.

or training or an apprenticeship contract. Local authorities must (since 28 June 2013) promote the fulfillment by young people who are above compulsory school age by not more than 12 months and who do not have a level 3 qualification of their duty to participate in education or training.[520] This covers 17-year-olds initially, but it will be extended to 18-year-olds in 2015. If or when implemented in full, however, the relevant part of the 2008 Act will provide for enforcement via parenting contracts or parenting orders (as above – presumably only in respect of young people under 18), but additionally there would be the possibility of an attendance notice served on the young person himself or herself by the local authority, with a right of appeal to an 'attendance panel' against the notice or the education or training specified in it. Non-compliance with the notice without reasonable excuse would be an offence (level 1) although only after a penalty notice has first been issued and not complied with.[521] The Government has said, however, that it wishes 'to avoid criminalising young people' and 'will legislate to allow the enforcement process to be introduced progressively over a longer period'.[522]

Leaving aside the social and educational undesirability of trying to coerce independent minded young people into an activity to which they may be antipathetic, it is the case that many young people reach the age of 17 with an established record of truancy; they are the ones who are likely to be most resistant to the participation policy, a fact which on the one hand justifies a tough approach but which at the same time shows why it might well be unsuccessful. This conclusion is reinforced by research for the Brookings Institution in the United States, where, in his State of the Union address in 2012, President Barack Obama proposed that 'every state, every state, requires that students stay in high school until they graduate or turn 18', because 'students... not allowed to drop out, do better'. The Brookings research found that raising the compulsory school attendance ('CSA') age to 18 could induce some potential dropouts to remain in school until the legal leaving age and thereby bring 'positive long-term effects, e.g on employment and college-going' for them, but that in general it would not increase school graduation rates

---

[520] 2008 Act ss 1–10 (as variously amended by the Apprenticeships, Skills, Children and Learning Act 2009 (Consequential Amendments to Part 1 of the Education and Skills Act 2008) Order 2013 (SI 2013/1242)) and 173(9) and (10) (as substituted by the Education Act 2011, s 74). See also the Duty to Participate in Education or Training (Alternative Ways of Working) Regulations 2013 (SI 2013/1243) and the Duty to Participate in Education or Training (Miscellaneous Provisions) Regulations 2013 (SI 2013/1205). The local authority must also make arrangements to identify non-participating young people: 2008 Act s 12. See also the 2008 Act ss 13 and 14 as regards information about non-participation which is to be supplied by the relevant education institutions to the local authority. Local authorities already had a separate duty, introduced by the Apprenticeships, Skills, Children and Learning Act 2009, to encourage participation in education or training by young people aged 16 and 17 and by those with a learning difficulty who were aged 19–24: Education Act 1996 s 15ZC, inserted by the 2009 Act s 42. Level 3 qualifications include, for example, A levels and certain diplomas.

[521] As regards the right of appeal to the attendance panel against a penalty notice, see the Education and Skills Act 2008, s 54.

[522] Department for Education *The Importance of Teaching, The Schools White Paper 2010* Cm 7980 (The Stationery Office, 2010), at para 4.55.

among potential dropouts: '"compulsory" is a misnomer with regards to the CSA age in that large numbers of students do not feel compelled to obey the law.'[523]

Behaviour and discipline issues

Schools and teachers are now increasingly being judged with reference to how well they manage the behaviour of pupils. For example, one of the specific factors which reports of Ofsted inspections of schools must address is 'the behaviour and safety of pupils at the school'.[524] In addition, one of the new Teachers' Standards which came into effect in September 2012 concerns being able to 'manage behaviour effectively to ensure a good and safe learning environment'.[525] The standards provide benchmarks for qualified teacher status and are to be used in assessing the performance of teachers for the purposes of the prescribed appraisal arrangements. The importance attached to good behaviour among pupils is borne out of its clear benefits to the learning environment in schools. The Practitioners' Group on School Behaviour and Discipline chaired by Sir Alan Steer stated as a principle that 'Poor behaviour cannot be tolerated as it is a denial of the right of pupils to learn and teachers to teach'.[526] Promoting good behaviour forms part of the 'affective' or 'hidden' curriculum in schools through which positive values are sought to be imparted to pupils and which aims to help to prepare them for later life in the community and workplace. Equally, the deleterious impact of bad behaviour by some towards others, not merely on their learning but also their psychological well-being, such as where there is bullying (especially sexual, racial or homophobic bullying and/or where it is related to disability), is well known and schools have been recognised as having a legal duty to prevent or ameliorate it, as discussed below.

Over the years, various reports, the most notable being Elton in 1989[527] and Steer in 2005,[528] have examined the management of pupil behaviour and the disciplinary framework. Discipline problems in schools have been pervasive and each era seems to generate a new impetus to tackle them – for example, by strengthening the powers and duties on schools and improving the guidance

---

[523] GJ(R) Whitehurst and S Whitfield *Compulsory School Attendance. What Research Says and What it Means for State Policy* (Brown Center on Education Policy, The Brookings Institution, 2012), at p 5.

[524] Education Act 2005, s 5(5A)(d), inserted by the Education Act 2011, s 41 with effect from November 2011.

[525] Department for Education *Teachers' Standards* (DfE, 2012), at pp 7–8.

[526] A Steer, *Learning Behaviour. The Report of the Practitioners' Group on School Behaviour and Discipline* (Department for Education and Skills, 2005), at p 2.

[527] Lord Elton *Discipline in Schools. Report of the Committee of Enquiry Chaired by Lord Elton* (HMSO, 1989). See N Harris 'Discipline in Schools: The Elton Report' (1991)(2) JSWFL 110–127.

[528] A Steer (2005), n 526 above. See also the follow-up report by Steer, *Learning Behaviour: Lessons Learned* (Department for Children, Schools and Families 2009). https://www.education.gov.uk/publications/eOrderingDownload/DCSF-Learning-Behaviour. pdf

and training issued to staff.[529] Government has placed an ever-increasing emphasis on improving pupil behaviour and discipline as a key to raising overall standards of achievement among pupils.[530] Detailed guidance is made available to schools by the Department for Education but, more importantly, a wide range of statutory obligations and powers has been set in place. The contribution that these powers may have made to the maintenance of good behaviour in schools is, however, difficult to gauge. The skill of managing pupil behaviour involves a whole range of strategies and techniques. The use of disciplinary powers is but one element of this. Nevertheless, it is perhaps regrettable that the present government's 'Behaviour Czar', Charlie Taylor, did not make any reference in his recommendations on improving the training of trainee teachers in behaviour management[531] to ensuring an effective understanding of the statutory disciplinary powers. These powers enable teachers to interfere in very significant ways with the liberty and privacy of individual pupils, making it vitally important that teachers know how to use them in an appropriate manner. Steer's follow-up report in 2009 nevertheless identified a need for a 'dissemination strategy' to raise understanding and awareness among teachers of their powers relating to discipline.[532]

Media coverage of schools tends to contribute to a general impression that they are fairly violent places where unruly behaviour is the norm.[533] Marked governmental emphasis over the years on the need to improve discipline and behaviour tends to fuel this perception. Indeed, the Coalition Government's schools White Paper emphasised the impact of poor behaviour among pupils as a factor in teachers leaving the profession or in graduates deciding not to join it.[534] Yet there is evidence indicating that while bad behaviour and worrying levels of disruption and violence among pupils are present in a number of schools, the overwhelming majority of schools are predominantly places where discipline levels are high. In the 2005 schools White Paper the Labour Government cited Ofsted figures showing that 74 per cent of secondary schools had 'good or better behaviour', 20 per cent had 'satisfactory' behaviour and 6 per cent had behaviour that was 'unsatisfactory or worse'.[535] Since then, there

---

[529] See the report by Charlie Taylor, *Improving teacher training for behaviour* (Teaching Agency, 2012). See also his 'checklist' on behaviour for schools: DfE, *Getting the simple things right: Charlie Taylor's behaviour checklists* (DfE, 2011).

[530] See for example, the White Papers in 2005 and 2010, which each devote an entire chapter to discipline and behaviour: DfES, *Higher Standards, Better Schools for All* Cm 6677 (The Stationery Office, 2005), chapter 7; and DfE (2010) n 522 above, ch 3.

[531] *Improving teacher training for behaviour* (Teaching Agency, 2012).
http://media.education.gov.uk/assets/files/pdf/i/improving_teacher_training_for_behaviour.pdf

[532] Steer (2009), n 528 above, at p 32.

[533] See, eg, A Kershaw 'Primary school pupil behaviour becomes more violent, according to new figures' *The Independent (online)*, 25 July 2012.

[533] http://www.independent.co.uk/news/education/education-news/primary-school-pupil-behaviour-becomes-more-violent-according-to-new-figures-7976140.html (last accessed 3 July 2013). See also DfE, Statistical First Release SFR 17/2012, *Permanent and Fixed Period Exclusions from Schools and Exclusion Appeals in England, 2010/11* (DfE, 2012), table 11.

[534] DfE (2010), n 522 above, at para 3.2.

[535] DfES, *Higher Standards, Better Schools for All* Cm 6677 (The Stationery Office, 2005), at para 7.6.

seems to have been an improvement. In 2009 the Steer follow-up report found 'strong evidence' that the overall standard of behaviour in schools was 'good and has improved in recent years'.[536] Moreover, the Chief Inspector's annual report for 2010–11 records that only 2 per cent of secondary schools were classed by Ofsted as having 'inadequate' behaviour[537] and that, across all the schools sector as whole, '[t]he large majority... are orderly places where pupils' behaviour is at least good'; and pupils' behaviour was considered 'good or outstanding in 87 per cent of all schools inspected'.[538]

Nevertheless, the House of Commons Education Committee reports evidence from among the teaching profession that the picture presented by Ofsted and Steer does not reflect the reality of what teachers experience at first hand in schools.[539] So it is difficult to get a true sense of how bad a problem indiscipline in schools really is. In any event, much of the concern seems to be directed towards primary schools, reinforced, first, by evidence of a perception among teachers that there has been a marked deterioration in the level of behaviour among some pupils in these schools,[540] and, secondly, by the numbers of exclusions for violent or threatening behaviour towards other pupils or staff.[541]

The general disciplinary framework

The law divides up responsibility for pupil behaviour in schools between local authorities, governing bodies, head teachers and teachers, as described below. In addition, parental responsibility for their children's behaviour has increasingly been emphasised. The Derrington report on *Behaviour in Primary Schools* found that more than half of teachers placed much of the blame for poor pupil behaviour in the classroom on parents.[542] For some years now government too has been keen to hold parents to account in this context. For example, parents who have signed a home-school agreement, for which statutory provision has been made although there is no compulsion to sign, have thereby recorded 'that they... accept the parental responsibilities and the

---

[536] A Steer (2009), n 528 above, at p 4.

[537] Ibid.

[538] Ofsted *The Annual Report of Her Majesty's Chief Inspector of Education, Children's Services and Skills 2010/11* HC 1633 (The Stationery Office, 2011), at p 12.

[539] House of Commons Education Committee *Behaviour and Discipline in Schools*, First Report of Session 2010–11, Vol.1, HC 516-I (The Stationery Office, 2011), at paras 11 and 15.

[540] C Derrington *Behaviour in Primary Schools* (2008), available at: www.channel4.com/ . . ./Dispatches_Behaviour%20in%20Primary%20Schools_%20Survey.doc (last accessed 2 July 2013). The report is stated to have been commissioned by True Visions Productions for Channel 4 and supported by the NASUWT.

[541] See n 533 above. The DfE figures show that in 2010–11 there were nearly 400 permanent exclusions from primary schools for physical assault, verbal abuse/threatening behaviour or sexual misconduct and over 20,000 fixed period exclusions on such grounds. Most primary school exclusions appear to be imposed on children over the age of 7: see Ofsted *The exclusion from school of children aged four to seven* (Ofsted, 2009).

[542] Derrington (2008), n 540 above, at p 5.

school's expectations of its pupils',[543] which are defined as 'the expectations of the school as regards the conduct of such pupils while they are registered pupils there'.[544]

Regardless of whether they have signed a home-school agreement, parents may be asked to sign a parenting contract or may have a parenting order imposed on them under the Anti-social Behaviour Act 2003. The nature of parenting contracts and parenting orders was discussed earlier in relation to truancy (p 957 above). In the disciplinary context, their use has been extended as a result of amendments made by the Education and Inspections Act 2006 (the 2006 Act) in furtherance of the post 2005 Labour Government's commitment to strengthen the legal framework on discipline in schools. There was a promise to 'allow parenting contracts to be used earlier in order to tackle poor behaviour before exclusion occurs'.[545] A parenting contract may be entered into by the local authority or school governing body with the parent whose child has been excluded from school for a fixed period or permanently. It may also be entered into, following the 2006 Act reforms, where a child is believed to have engaged in behaviour connected with the school[546] which (a) has caused or is likely to cause 'significant disruption to the education of other pupils' or 'significant detriment' to the child's welfare or that of other pupils or to the safety of staff; or (b) forms part of a pattern of behaviour whose continuation would create a risk of future exclusion from school on disciplinary grounds.[547] Provision for parenting orders, which as noted earlier are made by a magistrates' court, was also extended by the 2006 Act to cover not merely cases where the pupil has been excluded but also where he or she has misbehaved in a way that would warrant his or her exclusion and the court considers that 'the making of the order would be desirable in the interests of improving the behaviour of the pupil'.[548] The idea behind this extension was therefore to enable parents to 'take responsibility for their child's bad behaviour at school' in order to avoid the imposition of exclusion.[549] The 2006 Act also gave school governing bodies the authority, previously enjoyed only by the local authority, to apply for an order.

---

[543] School Standards and Framework Act 1998, s 110(2).

[544] Ibid.

[545] DfES (2005), n 535 above, at para 7.11.

[546] This can include behaviour away from school 'in circumstances in which it would be reasonable for the school to regulate his conduct': Anti-social Behaviour Act 2003, s 19(1B), inserted by the Education and Inspections Act 2006, s 97(2).

[547] Anti-social Behaviour Act 2003, s 19 (as amended by the Education and Inspections Act 2006, s 97). See also ss 21 (as amended) and 22A (the latter inserted by the 2006 Act s 99).

[548] Anti-social Behaviour Act 2003, s 20 (as amended by the Education and Inspections Act 2006, s 98). See also ss 21 (as amended) and 22A (the latter inserted by the 2006 Act s 99). The application for the order must be made within 40 days of the misbehaviour in question (or last act of it) or within 6 months of the entering into of a parenting contract, whichever expires later: the Education (Parenting Contracts and Parenting Orders) (England) Regulations 2007 (SI 2007/1869), regs 5 and 6. See also the same (Wales) Regulations 2010 (SI 2010/2954 (W 246)).

[549] DfES (2005), n 535 above, at para 7.11.

Official statistics show that only *one* application was made by a local authority for a parenting order following exclusion in England in 2009–10[550] and *none* were applied for in the period 2004–08.[551] They do not show the number of orders made in cases where exclusion has not occurred, but it seems reasonable to assume that few if any pre-exclusion applications were made. Research has revealed that a lack of resources or funding is the main reason for the failure to invoke this measure for behaviour cases.[552] Parenting contracts were used in a number of cases, however. Some 1,910 were agreed to by parents in 2009–2010 out of 2,169 proposed by local authorities.[553]

Of course, the responsibility for enforcing discipline within schools lies with those responsible for running them. Local authorities have little responsibility for discipline in schools, having only intervention powers in extreme cases where disciplinary authority at a school has collapsed or is set to do so. In particular, they have a general reserve power to 'take such steps ... as they consider are required' to prevent a breakdown or continuing breakdown of discipline at a school[554] and a power to issue a warning notice to a school where the safety of pupils or staff is threatened by, inter alia, a breakdown of discipline.[555] Since the 1980s general responsibility for discipline in a school has been placed on the school's governing body whilst the head teacher has been responsible for determining measures to promote appropriate behaviour and regulate the conduct of pupils, having regard in doing so to any general principles laid down by the governing body.[556] Much of classroom teachers' disciplinary authority, which was derived from the common law principle *in loco parentis* (based on implied parental delegation of authority to punish),[557] was incrementally replaced by new statutory powers and consolidated under the 2006 Act.

Under the present legal framework, therefore, the school governing body is under a duty to ensure that the school pursues policies which are 'designed to

---

[550] DCSF *2010 Parental Responsibility Data* (DCSF, 2010).

[550] http://media.education.gov.uk/assets/files/pdf/2/2010%20parental%20responsibility%20 measures%20data.pdf (last accessed 20 September 2013). It is not clear whether governing bodies applied for any such orders – this seems very unlikely however.

[551] Cited in K Crowther and S Kendall, n 483 above, Executive Summary, at para 34.

[552] Ibid, at para 35.

[553] DCSF *2010 Parental Responsibility Data* (DCSF, 2010) http://media.education.gov.uk/assets/files/pdf/2/2010%20parental%20responsibility%20 measures%20data.pdf (last accessed 20 September 2013). The figures do not show if any were proposed by school governing bodies. If they were, but are not included in the figures, then the actual total would obviously be higher.

[554] School Standards and Framework Act 1998, s 62.

[555] Education and Inspections Act 2006, s 60. If the notice is not properly complied with by the school's governing body the local authority has various powers open to it such as to appoint additional governors to the school or suspend the school's control of its own delegated budget: see ibid, ss 63–66.

[556] Education (No 2) Act 1986, ss 16 and 22, as amended by the Education Act 1993 and, following consolidation into the Education Act 1996, replaced by provisions within the 2006 Act, below.

[557] See N Harris, *The Law Relating to Schools* (2nd edn, Tolley, 1995), at pp 313–314.

promote good behaviour and discipline' among pupils.[558] The governing body has a duty to prepare a statement of general principles to guide the head teacher in determining the measures to give effect to the school's behaviour policy; and pupils are among those with whom the governing body must consult before making this statement of principles.[559] As discussed below, the governing body also has a role in relation to exclusion.[560] So far as the school's behaviour policy is concerned, the head teacher is to be the central figure. He or she must determine measures concerning pupil behaviour and set them out in a written document, which must be made known within the school and to parents.[561] The measures must be directed at: regulating the conduct of pupils and promoting self-discipline among them; promoting pupils' 'proper regard for authority'; ensuring that pupils' standard of behaviour is 'acceptable' (as defined by the head teacher, so far as it is not determined by the governing body); securing the completion by pupils of tasks reasonably assigned to them; and encouraging 'good behaviour and respect for others' among pupils, 'and, in particular, preventing all forms of bullying among pupils'.[562]

Bullying is a huge problem among school pupils and a subject of considerable concern.[563] The availability and use of mobile phones and social networking sites has precipitated the phenomenon of 'cyber bullying' directed at individual pupils.[564] Bullying on racist grounds is common,[565] making the current paucity of exclusions relating to racist abuse (see below) somewhat surprising. So is bullying related to sexuality: two-thirds of gay, lesbian and bisexual pupils are reported to have experienced it.[566] Bullying can be hugely damaging to the victim's mental health; indeed, it is implicated in a number of cases of child suicide.[567] Ensuring that reasonable steps are taken to protect children from it when they are either at school or under the school's supervision is considered to

---

[558] Education and Inspections Act 2006, s 88(1).

[559] Ibid, s 88(2) and (3). The governing body must, in turn, have regard to guidance given by the Secretary of State: ibid, subs (4).

[560] See pp 972–982 below.

[561] Including rules on disciplinary penalties and identifying items for which a search may be made.

[562] Education and Inspections Act 2006, s 89(1), (3), (4), (4A) (inserted by the 2011 Act, s 2(7)) and (6).

[563] See N Harris 'Pupil Bullying, Mental Health and the Law in England', in N Harris and P Meredith (eds) *Children, Education and Health. International perspectives on law and policy* (Ashgate, 2005), 31–58, which, at pp 36–38 reports on a range of surveys of bullying; see also J Fortin *Children's Rights and the Developing Law* (3rd edn, Cambridge University Press, 2009), 201–203.

[564] Ofsted *Children on Bullying. A Report by the Children's Rights Director for England* (Ofsted, 2008), at pp 14–15.

[565] For example, in one survey of teachers almost half reported that it was problem in their school: BBC News 'Teacher report "racist bullying"' 23 April 2009, http://news.bbc.co.uk/1/hi/education/8014880.stm (last accessed 31 July 2012). Analysis of returns by head teachers disclosed some 87,900 incidents involving racism across schools in Britain between 2007 and 2011: BBC News 'More than 87,000 racist incidents recorded in schools', BBC News 23 May 2012, at http://www.bbc.co.uk/news/education-18155255 (last accessed 31 July 2012).

[566] R Hunt and J Jensen *The School Report: The Experiences of Young Gay People in Britain's Schools* (Stonewall, 2007), cited in DfE (2010), n 522 above, at para 3.19.

[567] See research by the organisation 'Beatbullying' indicating that 44 per cent of suicides among

fall within the scope of the school's duty of care.[568] The Government's current guidance to schools on tackling bullying stresses that an incident of bullying should be dealt with as a child protection concern for the purposes of the Children Act 1989, so staff should alert the local authority's children's services of its occurrence when there is 'reasonable cause to suspect that a child is suffering, or is likely to suffer, harm'.[569]

The 2006 Act sets out a general framework governing the lawfulness of any disciplinary penalty[570] to be imposed on a pupil, aside from exclusion. It requires any such penalty to meet each of three conditions.[571] First, the penalty must not be in breach of any statutory requirement or prohibition and must be 'reasonable in all the circumstances'. Secondly, it must be imposed by a paid member of school staff, or by any other member of staff reasonably authorised to impose it. Thirdly, the decision to impose the penalty must be made, and action to implement that decision taken, on the school's premises or elsewhere at a time when the pupil is under the lawful control or charge of the staff. Clearly the most contentious issue will be whether the imposition of a penalty is 'reasonable'. The legislation attempts to aid the interpretation of this condition by indicating that account must be taken of the proportionality of the punishment having regard to the particular circumstances of the case and any special circumstances relevant to the pupil which are known to the person imposing the punishment, in particular the child's age, any SEN, any disability and any religious requirements to which he or she may be subject.[572]

With regard to corporal punishment, the 2006 Act[573] expressly excludes its use from the scope of lawful disciplinary authority, but it was already effectively outwith the disciplinary powers of staff in any school in the UK. This is because s 548 Education Act 1996[574] provides that corporal punishment by a member of staff in relation to a child at a school or in alternative educational arrangements cannot, in any proceedings, be considered to be justified as being given under a right enjoyed by the person concerned by virtue of his or her position. Effectively that means that there is no defence, in any civil litigation, of lawful chastisement when corporal punishment has been inflicted on a pupil. An attempt to challenge s 548 as being in conflict with the ECHR failed in

---

10–14-year-olds between 2000 and 2008 were related to bullying: http://archive.beatbullying. org/dox/media-centre/press-releases/June%202010/bullying-accounts-44percent-suicides.html (last accessed 2 July 2013).

[568] See in particular *Bradford-Smart v West Sussex County Council* [2002] ELR 139 and *Faulkner v London Borough of Enfield and Lea Valley High School* [2003] ELR 426.

[569] Department for Education *Preventing and Tackling Bullying. Advice for School Leaders, Staff and Governing Bodies* (DfE, 2011), at p 2.

[570] Defined as a penalty imposed on a pupil by a school 'where his conduct falls below any standard which could reasonably be expected of him (whether because he fails to follow a rule in force at any such school or an instruction given to him by a member of its staff or for any other reasons)': Education and Inspections Act 2006, s 90(1). It can include conduct not on the school premises if it is reasonable in the circumstances for it to be included: ibid, s 90(2).

[571] Education and Inspections Act 2006, s 91.

[572] Ibid, s 91(6) and (7).

[573] Ibid, s 91(10).

[574] As substituted by the School Standards and Framework Act 1998, s 131.

Williamson.[575] The applicants were head teachers, teachers and parents of pupils at independent schools which wished to retain the use of corporal punishment. They contended that its use was a manifestation of their Christian beliefs. The House of Lords accepted that s 548 interfered with the parents' rights under Art 9 (freedom of religion) and Art 2 of the First Protocol (A2P1) (right to education through teaching which respects parents' religious and philosophical convictions). However, the court considered that the ban on using corporal punishment was, for the purposes of Art 9, in pursuit of a legitimate aim covered by Art 9(2) (that of protecting children from distress, pain and other harmful effects through the infliction of physical violence); the means employed were not disproportionate in relation to their effects on the parents; and the issue of corporal punishment was one particularly suited to decision by Parliament. The A2P1 claim was rejected for the same reasons.[576] Baroness Hale emphasised that 'If a child has a right to be brought up without institutional violence, as he does, that right should be respected whether or not his parents and teachers believe otherwise'.[577]

If the disciplinary penalty involves detention outside school hours, specific conditions will apply to its imposition.[578] Firstly, the pupil must be under 18. Secondly, the head teacher must have established detention outside school sessions as a disciplinary measure in the school and made the measure known to parents and within the school. Thirdly, the detention must, in relation to any pupil affected, be on a 'permitted day of detention', which could include not only a school day but also a Saturday or Sunday during school term (but not one at the end or beginning of a half-term break). A fourth condition, requiring parents to be given at least 24 hours' notice in writing of a detention, has been removed in relation to England by the Education Act 2011.[579] The rationale presented for this change is that teachers 'should be able to punish unacceptably poor behaviour immediately in the way that they think most appropriate, using their professional judgement and understanding of the child concerned'.[580] However, teachers will still need to consider the reasonableness of a detention (per the first of the general conditions above), as with the application of any other disciplinary penalty. Such reasonableness will need to be judged with reference to whether suitable travel arrangements can be made[581] along with factors such as the child's age and special needs and/or disability.[582] Any of those factors could militate against a same day detention. The wider issue of whether detention of groups or pupils or a whole class can

---

[575] R *(Williamson)* v *Secretary of State for Education and Employment and Others* [2005] UKHL 15, [2005] 2 AC 246.
[576] Ibid, per Lord Nicholls, at [52].
[577] Ibid, at [86].
[578] Education and Inspections Act 2006, s 92.
[579] Education Act 2011, s 5, which came into force on 15 January 2012.
[580] DfE (2010), n 522 above, at para 3.8.
[581] Education and Inspections Act 2006, s 92(5).
[582] Ibid, s 91(6).

be justified when the culprit for any particular misbehaviour is not identified is uncertain.[583] There must surely be serious questions about its proportionality in the majority of such cases.

The use of 'reasonable' force

The Education Act 1997 introduced for the first time a statutory power for a member of staff of a school to use reasonable force against a pupil in prescribed circumstances, although not for the purposes of inflicting corporal punishment.[584] The relevant section was headed 'Power of member of staff to restrain pupils', reflecting its emphasis on preventing a pupil from committing an offence, causing injury to anyone or their property, or engaging in behaviour considered 'prejudicial to the maintenance of good order and discipline at the school...'. It was re-enacted, with only very minor changes, in the 2006 Act.[585] The purpose remains that of reinforcing teachers' capacity to intervene physically in certain situations, in the interests of pupils, without the inhibiting fear of allegations of abuse. However, it may not have achieved its objective, since evidence suggests that teachers have remained reticent about restraining pupils for fear of complaint or litigation. An ESRC-funded survey in 2006, cited in the 2010 White Paper, found that around half of schools had 'over-cautious' 'no-touch' policies.[586] A survey by the Association of Teachers and Lecturers, which was reported in early 2010, revealed that half of student, newly qualified and probationer teachers felt that they had not received sufficient guidance on restraining pupils who were behaving violently.[587]

The Government issued fresh guidance on the use of reasonable force in schools in April 2010[588] and in a speech that month to the NASUWT[589] the Secretary of State for Education tried to reassure teachers. He argued that their fears and uncertainties over the legal power to use physical force to restrain pupils were misplaced; and he reportedly told the conference that 'A no-contact policy is not required by law, and is not good leadership'.[590] However, the 2010 White Paper issued by the Coalition Government stated, in relation to the power to use force, that 'many teachers fear the rules are not strong enough to support them'.[591] The Government promised to increase teachers' confidence

---

[583] The DfE's guidance makes no reference to it: see DfE *Behaviour and Discipline in Schools. A guide for head teachers and school staff* (DfE, 2012), at paras 22–29.

[584] Education Act 1997, s 4, inserting a new s 550A, Education Act 1996.

[585] Education and Inspections Act 2006, s 93.

[586] *Touchlines: the Problematics of 'Touching' Between Children and Professionals* (2006) http://www.esrc.ac.uk/search/search-page.aspx?q=Touchlines (last accessed 2 July 2013).

[587] The survey figures were released to the BBC: News item 'Teachers "lack violence training"', 6 February 2010 at http://news.bbc.co.uk/1/hi/education/8501202.stm (last accessed 2 July 2013).

[588] *The Use of Reasonable Force to Control or Restrain Pupils: Guidance for Schools in England* (DCSF-00368-2010).

[589] National Union of Schoolmasters and Union of Women Teachers.

[590] Quoted in R Williams 'Teachers can use physical restraint, says Ed Balls' *The Guardian online* 5 April 2010 http://www.guardian.co.uk/education/2010/apr/05/teachers-can-use-force-says-balls (last accessed 2 July 2013).

[591] DfE (2010), n 522 above, at para 3.9.

by strengthening the rules and issuing new 'robust' guidance.[592] This guidance was issued in March 2012.[593] Teachers may well find it reassuring to learn from the guidance that the Department accepts that, for example, a pupil may well be injured as an unfortunate consequence of a legitimate intervention by a member of staff. But the bottom line for any teacher is that, as the guidance also says, 'the decision on whether or not to physically intervene is down to the professional judgement of the staff member concerned and should always depend on the individual circumstances'. This ultimately puts the risk onto the teacher in making a split-second decision, underlining the impossibility of providing the complete reassurance that many teachers would wish for.

Searching and seizing possessions

The statutory measures sanctioning searches and the seizure of pupils' possessions which have been introduced in recent years represent a response to the perceived challenging behavioural environment in some schools and reflect wider concerns about knife crime, the illicit use and selling of drugs, and other social problems, among young people. The previous Labour Government put forward a policy of 'zero tolerance' of this kind of conduct within schools[594] and included in its Violent Crime Reduction Act 2006 amendments to education legislation in England and Wales to strengthen head teachers' powers to carry out searches and seize various items.[595] More detailed legislation was introduced in its place in England in September 2010 via the Apprenticeships, Skills, Children and Learning Act 2009[596] and the powers have been extended further via amendments brought into effect in April 2012 under the Education Act 2011. Perhaps most controversial are, first, those enabling an individual school's rules to identify items which, in addition to those specifically listed in the legislation (such as offensive weapons, see below), may be searched for and possibly seized; and, secondly, those sanctioning searches of data or files on an electronic device which has been seized as a prohibited item.[597]

The basic power to search a pupil or his or her possessions is available to the head teacher or other member of staff authorised by the head. It may be exercised where the relevant person has 'reasonable grounds for suspecting that a pupil ... may have a prohibited item with him or her or in his or her

---

[592] Ibid.

[593] Department for Education *Use of Reasonable Force. Advice for head teachers, staff and governing bodies* (DfE, 2012, updated April 2013). http://www.education.gov.uk/aboutdfe/advice/f0077153/use-of-reasonable-force/use-of-reasonable-force—advice-for-school-leaders-staff-and-governing-bodies (last accessed 2 July 2013). Note that this is non-statutory guidance.

[594] DfES *Higher Standards, Better Schools for All* Cm 6677 (The Stationery Office, 2005), at para 7.5.

[595] Education Act 1996 s 550AA, inserted by the Violent Crime Reduction Act 2006, s .44.

[596] Education Act 1996 ss 550ZA–550ZD, inserted by the 2009 Act, s 242(1).

[597] Amendments made by the Education Act 2011, s 2. In the case of a school which is an academy, it is effectively for the principal to identify the items which, in addition to those which are specifically prescribed by the legislation, are to be prohibited under the school's disciplinary measures: see the School Behaviour (Determination and Publicising of Measures in Academies) Regulations 2012 (SI 2012/619).

possessions'.[598] The search may be conducted where the head or authorised person and the pupil are on the school premises or where the pupil is under the lawful control or charge of the relevant member of staff.[599] The list of 'prohibited items' includes knives/blades, offensive weapons, alcohol, unlawfully possessed controlled drugs, stolen articles, articles prescribed by regulations (tobacco and cigarette papers, fireworks, and pornographic images have been prescribed[600]), and, as noted above, items identified for this purpose by the individual school's rules. Schools' power to prescribe items as prohibited means that, for example, they could decide not to permit pupils to have mobile phones in their possession within the school. The Joint Committee on Human Rights expressed concerns about the width of this provision which, it considered, might be in conflict with the right to respect for private life under Art 8 of the ECHR; it therefore recommended firm statutory guidance to indicate the purpose(s) for which the power should be used.[601] The 2011 Act has also added to the list of prohibited items an article that the member of staff reasonably suspects has been or is likely to be used to commit an offence or to cause damage to person or property.[602] It has also defined 'offence' for this purpose as including anything which would be an offence but for the minimum age of criminal responsibility (someone under the age of ten is classed as incapable of committing an offence),[603] a definition which seems to reflect concern about behaviour in primary schools, which was noted earlier.

Searching pupils clearly raises all kinds of concerns about invasions of privacy and risk of abuse allegations, so staff authorised to conduct searches would need to exercise this power with care. However, although prescriptive, the law leaves a certain amount to the exercise of judgment by teachers. For example, 'such force as is reasonable in the circumstances' may be used in conducting a search,[604] appearing to warrant the application of an objective test rather than one related to the subjective belief of the authorised member of staff. One clear stipulation is that the pupil may not be made to remove any clothing other than outer clothing (as defined).[605] Additionally, there is a basic rule that the person conducting the search must be of the same sex as the pupil and may only carry out the search in the presence of another member of staff whom he or she must

---

598   Education Act 1996, ss 550ZA(1) and (2) and 550ZB(1).

599   Ibid, s 550ZB(4).

600   Education (Specification and Disposal of Items) Regulations 2012 (SI 2012/951).

601   House of Lords/House of Commons Joint Committee on Human Rights *Legislative Scrutiny: Education Bill; and other Bills*, Thirteenth Report of Session 2010–12, HL Paper 154, HC 1140 (The Stationery Office, 2011), at para 1.15. The guidance was published in 2012: Department for Education *Screening, searching and confiscation. Advice for head teachers, staff and governing bodies* (DfE, 2012). It states, inter alia, that a school exercising its statutory powers properly 'should have no difficulty in demonstrating that it has also acted in accordance with Article 8'.

602   Education Act 1996, s 550ZA(3) as amended by the 2011 Act, s 2(2).

603   Ibid (1996 Act), s 550ZA(4A), inserted by the 2011 Act, s 2(2).

604   Ibid, s 550ZB(5).

605   Ibid, s 550ZB(6)(a). Outer clothing is defined for this purpose as 'any item of clothing that is being worn otherwise than wholly next to the skin or immediately over a garment being worn as underwear' or 'a hat, shoes, boots, gloves or a scarf': ibid, s 550ZB(8).

ensure is of the same sex as the pupil.[606] However, in relation to both these cases there is exception to the basic rule where, for example, the search is needed very urgently due to a risk of serious harm if delayed.[607] Where the pupil's possessions are being searched the pupil and another member of staff must be present, again subject to exceptions.[608]

Alongside the powers of search are those concerning the seizure of items which the searcher has reasonable grounds for suspecting are prohibited items (as defined above) or are something which the searcher has reasonable grounds for suspecting constitute evidence of an offence.[609] Knives/blades, offensive weapons[610] and material which may be evidence of an offence, and extreme or child-related pornographic images, must in all cases by delivered to a police constable as soon as is reasonably practicable.[611] This is also required if the material seized is a controlled drug, although it may instead be disposed of if the member of staff considers there is 'good reason to do so'.[612] The same applies if it is a stolen item, although such an item may be disposed of in other ways (including returning it to the owner) if there is considered to be 'good reason to do so'.[613] In the case of an article that the member of staff reasonably suspects has been or is likely to be used to commit an offence or to cause damage to person or property, delivery to a police constable is but one of the prescribed options.[614] In the case of items prescribed by the school as prohibited there is no requirement to hand them to the police; instead they may be returned to the owner, retained or disposed of.[615] Thus, the relevant member of staff has a degree of discretion over the action to be taken in many of these cases, although he or she is required to have regard to any guidance issued by the Secretary of State.[616] Such guidance must also be taken into account in the exercise of the new power to view data or files on an electronic device which has been seized due to its being reasonably suspected of being used to commit an offence or cause damage to person or property or because its possession by a pupil is proscribed under school rules.[617] This power also includes that of

---

[606]   Ibid, s 550ZB(6).
[607]   Ibid, s 550ZB(6A), inserted by the 2011 Act s 2(3).
[608]   Ibid, s 550ZB(7). The exceptions are the need for urgency due to risk of harm if there is a delay, or that in the time available another member of staff cannot reasonably be brought in to observe: ibid, susbs (7A).
[609]   Ibid, s 550ZC(1).
[610]   Defined with reference to the Prevention of Crime Act 1953.
[611]   Education Act 1996, s 550ZC(8) and the Education (Specification and Disposal of Items) Regulations 2012 (SI 2012/951), reg 4.
[612]   Education Act 1996, s 550ZC(4).
[613]   Ibid, s 550ZC(5).
[614]   Ibid, s 550ZC(6A), inserted by the 2011 Act, s 2(4). The others are to return the item to its owner, retain the item, or dispose of it.
[615]   Ibid, s 550ZC(6B), inserted by the 2011 Act, s 2(4).
[616]   Ibid, s 550ZC(6) and (6C), the latter inserted by the 2011 Act, s 2(4). The current guidance is DfE *Screening, searching and confiscation. Advice for head teachers, staff and governing bodies* (DfE, 2012).
[617]   Ibid, s 550ZC(6D), (6E) and (6G), inserted by the 2011 Act, s 2(4).

erasing any data or files from the device, whether the device is retained by the school, disposed of or returned to the owner.[618]

The new statutory powers on search, seizure and disposal of prohibited items in schools are unprecedented in the UK. They do give rise to legitimate concerns about civil liberties and the risk that security and control alter the internal character of schools. On the other hand, no-one could deny the importance of preventing violence and criminality which threaten the well-being and safety of pupils. Whether these powers, most of which have been in force for not more than a few years and whose operation has yet to be assessed, prove effective in this regard, something which in turn will depend on the capacity and willingness of staff to utilise them in the ways which may be intended, remains to be seen.

Exclusion from school

Exclusion remains the most severe sanction that can be imposed on a pupil by a school. Although its consequences for the pupil, in terms of missed schooling, have been ameliorated to some extent by the tightening up of the duty to make arrangements for an excluded child's education[619] and by efforts to improve both the management of pupil referral units, which some excluded pupils attend, and the provision made by them,[620] it still disrupts their education and carries a psychological impact through the stigma for some and the isolating effects of segregation. Moreover, concerns arise from the disproportionate incidence of exclusion among particular social or ethnic groups. For example, the latest official statistics (at the time of writing) show that in 2010/11 boys were three times more likely than girls to be excluded (whether permanently or for a fixed term); pupils with a statement of special educational needs (SEN) were nine times more likely to be excluded than those without SEN, and pupils with SEN received 74 per cent of the permanent exclusions while representing 19 per cent of the school population; pupils eligible for free school meals were four times more likely to be permanently excluded than other pupils; and the

---

[618] Ibid, s 550ZC(6F), inserted by the 2011 Act, s 2(4).

[619] Under the Education Act 1996, s 19, as amended, which was discussed above, at pp 901 and 902. Amendments to s 19 by the Education and Inspections Act 2006, s 101(2), read with the Education (Provision of Full-time Education for Excluded Pupils) (England) Regulations 2007 (SI 2007/1870), mean that normally the local authority is under a duty to ensure that a child of compulsory school age who is permanently excluded from school receives full-time education from the sixth school day of their exclusion, as noted above. In the case of a child of compulsory school age who is excluded for a fixed period, the 2006 Act also (read with the 2007 Regulations above, reg 3), introduced (in s 100) a duty whereby the governing body must normally make arrangements for him or her to receive suitable education from the sixth school day of the exclusion.

[620] The Government also wants to extend the range of providers (see DfE (2010), n 522 above, at paras 3.33 and 3.34, and DfE *Reform of Alternative Provision* (DfE, 2012)). For example, provision is now made for pupil referral units to operate as 'alternative provision Academies,' which are 'principally concerned with providing full-time or part-time education for children of compulsory school age who, by reason of illness, exclusion from school or otherwise, may not otherwise receive suitable education for any period': Academies Act 2010, s 1C, inserted by the Education Act 2011, s 53(7).

rate of permanent exclusion among pupils of black Caribbean origin was three times higher than across the school population as a whole (although it was four times higher in 2009–10).[621]

In the 1990s, government encouragement of improvements to the disciplinary environment in schools, together with the continuing pressure on schools to be called to account for overall pupil performance levels, led to a significant increase in the use of the power of permanent exclusion, which peaked at 12,665 exclusions in 1996–97.[622] While those influences have continued, government guidance to schools since the late 1990s has sought to discourage permanent exclusion from school save in the most serious cases of misbehaviour, in recognition of the contribution of permanent exclusion to social exclusion more generally. In furtherance of the Labour Government's policy of promoting early intervention in relation to pupils at risk of being excluded, the Education and Skills Act 2008 introduced a new power for the governing body to require any of its registered pupils to 'attend at any place outside the school premises for the purpose of receiving educational provision which is intended to improve the behaviour of the pupil'.[623] This power, which did not come into force until September 2010, is seemingly far reaching. However, some safeguards against its misuse have been incorporated, such as that any arrangements must be reviewed – review meetings must be held which the parent or (if aged 18+) the pupil may attend – and there is a prescribed maximum duration for any requirement to attend elsewhere.[624]

---

[621] DfE, Statistical First Release SFR 17/2012 *Permanent and Fixed Period Exclusions from Schools and Exclusion Appeals in England, 2010/11* (DfE, 2012).

[622] See N Harris and K Eden, with A Blair *Challenges to School Exclusion. Exclusions, Appeals and the Law* (Routledge Falmer, 2000).

[623] Education Act 2002, s 29A inserted by the Education and Skills Act 2008, s 154; and the Education (Educational Provision for Improving Behaviour) Regulations 2010 (SI 2010/1156), as amended by the Education (Educational Provision for Improving Behaviour) (Amendment) Regulations 2012 (SI 2012/2532). For background, including a summary of the consultation responses to the original proposals on this power and process, see Department for Children, Schools and Families (DCSF) *Explanatory Memorandum to the Education (Educational Provision for Improving Behaviour) Regulations 2010* (2010) http://www.legislation.gov.uk/uksi/2010/1156/pdfs/uksiem_20101156_en.pdf (last accessed 21 August 2012). Section 444 of the Education Act 1996 (offences for non-attendance) is extended to cover pupils being educated under such special arrangements: see s 444ZA of that Act, as inserted by the Education Act 2005, s 115 and amended by the Education and Skills Act 2008, s 115. For Labour Government policy on early intervention and alternative educational arrangements, see DCSF *Back on Track: A strategy on modernising alternative provision for young people*, Cm 7410 (The Stationery Office, 2008).

[624] There must be not more than 30 days' interval between review meetings: ibid (2010 Regulations) reg 4. The requirement may, however, have effect until the end of the last school day of the school year in which it was imposed: ibid, reg 3(5). Additionally, under an amendment from January 2013, a review meeting may be requested by the parent, pupil (if aged 18 or over) or (in the case of a child with SEN) the local authority and such a meeting must be convened provided one has not been held within the previous 10 weeks: ibid, reg 4A, inserted by the Education (Educational Provision for Improving Behaviour) Amendment Regulations 2012 (SI 2012/2532).

Rates of permanent exclusion have fallen dramatically in recent years, as the table below indicates, with a fall each year over the seven years from 2004–05 and an overall decline from 9,440 that year to 5,080 in 2010–11.

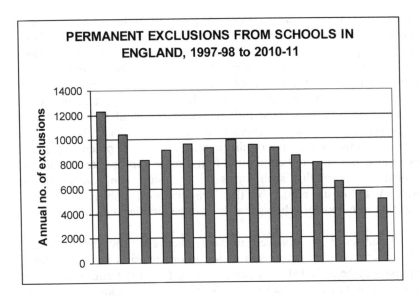

Source: DfE, Statistical First Release SFR 17/2012, Permanent and Fixed Period Exclusions from Schools and Exclusion Appeals in England, 2010/11 (DfE, 2012), table 1

The present government, while emphasising the authority of head teachers to exclude where they feel there is no alternative, seems keen to reduce the number of such exclusions still further. It is proposing that schools which permanently exclude pupils should be given the responsibility held by local authorities at present to arrange alternative provision for permanently excluded pupils and that the achievements of excluded children should count in a school's performance tables; it says that this would create 'a strong incentive for schools to avoid exclusion where possible' and 'ensure that where it does happen it is appropriate and pupils receive good alternative provision'.[625]

The imposition of fixed-term (temporary) exclusions, which are sometimes referred to as 'suspensions' although this description is not used in the law, has also decreased, but to much smaller extent: between 2006–07 and 2010–11 the annual number of fixed-term exclusions fell from 425,600 to 324,110, with a decrease occurring each year and across primary, special and secondary schools.[626] In 2010–11, 97 per cent of such exclusions were for 5 school days or

---

[625] DfE (2010), n 522 above, at paras 3.38–3.39. Funds to pay for the alternative provision would effectively be devolved from local authorities to schools for this purpose.

[626] DfE, Statistical First Release SFR 17/2012 *Permanent and Fixed Period Exclusions from Schools and Exclusion Appeals in England, 2010/11* (DfE, 2012), Table 2. On the factors which lie behind the (relatively rare) exclusion of those aged seven or under, see Ofsted (2009) n 541 above.

less – indeed, 81 per cent were for between 1–3 days.[627] A longer period may be considered justified where the pupil has already been subjected to such exclusions and in the light of the severity of the misbehaviour.[628]

Various practices involving illegal, unofficial forms of exclusion have come to light, highlighted in reports by the Children's Commissioner in England, following an inquiry on school exclusions, and in Wales.[629] Such exclusions typically occur where a school asks a pupil to leave the premises but does not record this as an exclusion. For example, the pupil is told to go home so he or she can 'cool off'. Exclusion may also be hidden where the parents of a child are persuaded or perhaps coaxed into removing the child from the school thereby preventing a formal exclusion from taking place. The English Children's Commissioner's report distinguishes such a practice from a 'managed move' designed to help a pupil find a more appropriate educational environment. It argues that such forms of 'exclusion' can and should be prevented. A follow-up report by the Commissioner, published in 2013, calculates that hundreds of schools may be involved in illegal excluding.[630]

The law,[631] substantially amended in September 2012 by the Education Act 2011, sanctions either permanent exclusion or exclusion for a fixed-term, but no pupil may be excluded for a fixed-term, or for fixed terms, in excess of 45 days in total in any one school year.[632] The power to exclude rests with the head teacher or, in the case of an academy, the principal.[633] As noted earlier, although any other exclusion, such as where it is imposed for an indefinite period, would be unlawful under domestic law that fact alone does not

---

[627] Ibid (DfE, 2012), Table 7.

[628] See, for example, *R (K) v The Governors of Tamworth Manor High School* [2005] ELR 192, where exclusion for a fixed period of 16 days imposed a pupil who had a past record of one or two day exclusions and had deliberately exposed his buttocks on the school playing field was considered not unreasonable.

[629] Children's Commissioner (England) *'They never give up on you'. Office of the Children's Commissioner School Exclusions Inquiry* (Office of the Children's Commissioner, 2012); Children's Commissioner for Wales *Report on Unofficial Exclusions* (Children's Commissioner's Office, 2007).

[630] Children's Commissioner (England) *Always Someone Else's Problem' Office of the Children's Commissioner's Report on Illegal Exclusions* (Office of the Children's Commissioner, 2013), at p 7.

[631] Note that the law here applies to state schools. In the case of private (independent) schools the exclusion of a child will have a contractual basis, thus challenges would be expected to be pursued as contractual disputes: see e.g. *R v Fernhill Manor School ex parte A* [1994] ELR 67. Nevertheless, in *Gray v Marlborough College* [2006] EWCA Civ 1262 [2006] ELR 516 the Court of Appeal emphasised that the exercise of the contractual power of exclusion needs to be undertaken fairly and that the statutory (and public law) requirements applicable to the state sector may be considered to 'provide a starting point or indications of principle as to what is required from an independent school head teacher in deciding how and whether to exercise a contractual power of exclusion' (per Auld LJ at [41]).

[632] Education Act 2002, s 51A(1) (inserted by the Education Act 2011, s 4(2)) and the School Discipline (Pupil Exclusions and Reviews) (England) Regulations 2012 (SI 2012/1033), reg 4. The head of a pupil referral unit has the same power of exclusion: 2002 Act, s 51A(2).

[633] The School Discipline (Pupil Exclusions and Reviews) (England) Regulations 2012 (SI 2012/1033), regs 4 and 22.

necessarily give rise to a denial of the child's right to education for the purposes of Art 2 of the First Protocol to the ECHR.[634]

While the decision to exclude and other decisions related to a case – such as whether reinstatement is warranted – will involve the exercise of discretion and judgment, there is official guidance, revised in 2012,[635] to which head teachers and others involved in taking decisions about exclusions (such as school governing bodies and review panels: below) must have regard.[636] It is clear that the decision to exclude is not to be taken lightly. In relation to decisions to exclude the guidance emphasises the need to exercise this power proportionately[637] and only when there really is no alternative. The basic advice has remained constant in the various versions of the guidance issued over the past decade, namely that exclusion should be considered only for serious and/or persistent breaches of the school's behaviour policy and where allowing the pupil to remain at school would seriously harm his or her education or welfare or that of others at the school.[638] Nevertheless, the latest guidance is considerably less prescriptive than in the past in relation to particular circumstances which might warrant exclusion.

The official statistics reveal the bases for the exclusions which have been imposed.[639] They show that in 2010–11 around one-third of permanent

---

[634]   *Ali v Headteacher and Governors of Lord Grey School* [2006] UKHL 14, [2006] ELR 223; see pp 899–901.

[635]   Department for Education *Exclusion from maintained schools, Academies and pupil referral units in England. A guide for those with legal responsibilities in relation to exclusion* (DfE, 2012), at https://www.gov.uk/government/uploads/attachment_data/file/18078/DFE-00042-2012_Statutory_Guidance_-_exclusion_from_1_Sep_2002_-_june.pdf (last accessed 28 June 2013).

[636]   School Discipline (Pupil Exclusions and Reviews) (England) Regulations 2012 (SI 2012/1033), reg 9.

[637]   This could mean, where there are other culprits, having regard to how they are being treated: see *R v Governors of Bacon's City Technology College ex part W* [1998] ELR 488, where Collins J said that 'there may be unfairness if one is picked out and others are not' (at 500).

[638]   Guidance, n 635 above, at para 15. In *R (A) v Head Teacher and Governing Body of North Westminster Community School and the City of Westminster Exclusion Appeal Panel* [2002] EWHC 2351 (Admin), [2003] ELR 378, for example, a pupil had been permanently excluded after being found with fireworks in school, with one witness having seen him throw a firework in the playground. Newman J upheld the decision of the independent appeal panel (IAP), which had confirmed the exclusion on the grounds of the seriousness of the incident, the potential health and safety risk to pupils of the conduct concerned and the potentially deleterious impact on other pupils of allowing the pupil to remain in school in the light of what he had done, in breach of the school's disciplinary code. In *G v IAP of London Borough of Bexley* [2009] ELR 100, [2008] EWHC 3051 (Admin), the court held that the IAP had been entitled to hold that the throwing of a wad of wet tissues which hit a teacher in the eye was a serious act of violence and that permanent exclusion was a proportionate penalty given that fact and the potential impact of violence on the school and on the pupils and its staff, notwithstanding the fact that it was a one-off incident. Persistent misbehaviour over a period of time can also justify permanent exclusion even if the act or incident which finally triggers it is not in itself all that serious: see *R v Staffordshire County Council Education Appeals Committee ex parte Ashworth* (1997) 9 Admin LR 373 per Turner J, at 395F–395G.

[639]   DfE, Statistical First Release SFR 17/2012 *Permanent and Fixed Period Exclusions from Schools and Exclusion Appeals in England, 2010/11* (DfE, 2012), table 11. The factors behind

exclusions from primary schools and special schools were mainly due to physical assault against an adult. A further one third in primary schools, and a similar proportion in the case of secondary schools, were mainly due to 'persistent disruptive behaviour'. Across all three categories of schools bullying was the reason for only 80 of the 5,080 cases of permanent exclusion in that year, almost all of which related to secondary schools. Racist abuse accounted for just 10 cases. It is, of course, likely that some of the cases of 'verbal abuse/threatening behaviour' against a pupil also involved racist abuse. They may also have included cases of homophobic abuse, about which no separate statistics seem to be kept. Physical assaults against another pupil account for very similar proportions of exclusions across primary, secondary and special schools, at approximately 15 per cent of cases in each of these categories.

In terms of the establishment of the facts before making the decision to exclude, the official guidance reflects an accumulation of case law which indicates the need for head teachers to investigate the circumstances thoroughly[640] and to ensure that, wherever possible, the pupil him or herself is given an opportunity to provide an explanation of his or her behaviour in relation to an alleged incident.[641] The standard of proof to be adopted by the head teacher is the balance of probabilities,[642] the normal standard of proof in civil cases. This is also the case if the governing body or an exclusion review panel are dealing with a case (see below).[643]

There is a set procedure to be followed by a school after a decision to exclude has been made. The following represents the basis position in maintained

---

exclusions from primary schools are explored in Ofsted, *The exclusion from school of children aged four to seven* (Ofsted, 2009) http://www.ofsted.gov.uk/resources/exclusion-school-of-children-aged-four-seven (last accessed 4 August 2012). An article highlighting this report had a somewhat sensionalised headline: N Woodcock and A Fishburn 'Teachers struggle with sex and aggression in children aged 7' *The Times*, 24 June 2009, at p 9. Nevertheless, as the article indicates, violent behaviour is occurring in primary schools.

[640] See e g *R v Solihull Borough Council ex parte W* [1997] ELR 489; *R v Roman Catholic Schools ex parte S* [1998] ELR. 304; *R v Headteacher and Independent Appeal Committee of Dunraven School ex p B* [2000] ELR 156, QBD and CA; and *The Queen on the application of C v Sefton Metropolitan Council Independent Appeals Panel and the Governors of Hillside High School* [2001] ELR 393.

[641] *R v Headteacher and Independent Appeal Committee of Dunraven School ex p B* [2000] ELR 156, QBD.

[642] School Discipline (Pupil Exclusions and Reviews) (England) Regulations 2012 (SI 2012/1033), reg 10.

[643] The standard of proof has been somewhat problematic in exclusion cases, with the courts variously suggesting a heightened standard of proof in cases where the conduct is particularly serious, especially where it is akin to criminal behaviour: see in particular *R (S) v Governing Body of YP School* [2004] ELR 37 and *R (H) v The Independent Appeal Panel for Y College* [2005] ELR 25. It was also argued that the civil standard of proof, as prescribed in regulations, was ultra vires due to conflict with Art 6(2) ECHR and its presumption of innocence, a view rejected by the Court of Appeal in *R (LG) v The Independent Appeal Panel for Tom Hood School and (as Interested Party) the Secretary of State for Children, Schools and Families* [2010] EWCA Civ 142, [2010] ELR 291 (CA), along with the broader claim that a criminal standard of proof should have been applied in relation to the claimant's conduct, involving the alleged possession and brandishing of a knife and threatening of a teacher, which had resulted in his exclusion.

schools; separate, broadly equivalent, provisions apply to pupil referral units and academies.[644] If the exclusion is for a fixed period the head teacher must without delay notify the parent (or pupil if aged 18 or over) in writing of the exclusion and reasons for it and also of the right to make representations to the governing body, including the right of the pupil him/herself (regardless of age) to 'be involved in the process of making representations' and how the pupil may be involved.[645] Such information must also be sent to the parent of a pupil excluded permanently, or for a period which would result in his/her being excluded for more than five days in any term or losing an opportunity to take a public examination or sit a national curriculum test. But in addition, the parent must be told about any right to attend a meeting with the governing body[646] at which they may be represented (at their own expense) and/or accompanied by a friend. This meeting of the governing body is to consider whether or not the pupil should be reinstated and if so whether reinstatement[647] should be immediate or by a fixed date. The regulations spell out the matters to be taken into account by the governing body, including the interests and circumstances of the excluded pupil, the interests of other pupils and those working at the school, and any representations which have been made.[648] The head teacher, the parent and a representative of the local authority have a right to attend this meeting and make representations. The pupil has no right to attend but could be called as a witness, although the guidance states that the parent's consent would be needed. The guidance nevertheless requires the governing body to 'identify the steps they will take to enable and encourage the excluded pupil to attend the meeting and speak on his/her own behalf ... taking into account the pupil's age and understanding'.[649]

The guidance states that in coming to its decision the governing body 'should consider whether the decision to exclude the pupil was lawful, reasonable and

---

[644] School Discipline etc Regulations, n 642 above, Parts 2, 3 and 4 respectively.

[645] The head teacher is also under a duty to inform the parent, without delay and no later than the end of the afternoon session of the first day of the exclusion, of the first day on which the appropriate authority will make provision for full-time education of the pupil following his/her exclusion and of the days on which the parent will be under a duty to ensure their child is not present in a public place during school hours (which duty applies in respect of the first five days of a period of exclusion): Education (Provision of Full-time Education for Excluded Pupils) (England) Regulations 2007 (SI 2007/1870) as amended (in particular by the School Discipline etc Regulations 2012, n 642 above, Sch 2, para 8), read with the Education and Inspections Act 2006, ss 103 and 104.

[646] But this will only apply where the total periods of exclusion would exceed 5 days in the term and the parents have made representations, or where the pupil would miss 15 school days in the term or an opportunity to take a public examination or sit a national curriculum test.

[647] The reinstatement of an excluded pupil does not necessarily have to involve their return to the class of which they were a member before they were excluded. A school may be entitled, in the exercise of its managerial authority, to make different educational arrangements for the pupil on his or her return to the school to those which applied prior to the exclusion. See *Re L* [2003] UKHL 9, [2003] ELR 309; *P v National Association of Teachers/Union of Women Teachers* [2001] ELR 607 (CA); *P v National Association of Teachers/Union of Women Teachers (NASUWT)* [2003] UKHL 8 [2003] ELR 357; and *R (O) v Governing Body of Park View Academy* [2007] ELR 388 (QBD) and [2007] EWCA Civ 592, [2007] ELR 454 (CA).

[648] School Discipline etc Regulations 2012, n 642 above, reg 6(3).

[649] Guidance, n 635 above, at para 58.

procedurally fair, taking account of the head teacher's legal duties'.[650] Nevertheless, research has indicated that governing bodies are generally reluctant to overturn an exclusion, because to do so may be seen as undermining the head teacher's managerial authority.[651] A direction by the governing body that the pupil should be reinstated is binding on the head teacher.[652] If the governing body decides against reinstatement it must inform the parent (or pupil if aged 18 or over[653]) of their right to apply for a review of the decision by a review panel and to require the local authority to appoint an SEN expert to advise the panel.

The review panels replaced the independent appeal panels (IAPs) in September 2012 under the Education Act 2011.[654] The constitution of the review panels is very similar to that of IAPs and the members will be appointed by local authorities, as was the case with IAPs.[655] It is the limited extent of their powers that is the main concern about them. The IAP could issue a binding direction that a pupil be reinstated,[656] but the new panel has no such power. The Government argued that the appeal process could become 'unduly adversarial' and that the possible reinstatement of a pupil directed by an IAP 'however rarely this happens – can undermine the head teacher's authority'.[657] The reference to rarity alludes to the fact that, for example, in 2010–11, of the 450 appeals heard just 120 succeeded (26.5 per cent) and reinstatement of the excluded pupil was directed in only 40 of these cases.[658] As cases of reinstatement therefore constituted less than 0.8 per cent of the 5,080 cases where there was a permanent exclusion that year, it is difficult to view this as amounting to an undermining of head teachers' authority in general. The Government contended that despite the small numbers 'each case can create significant problems for the school'.[659] Even if that is the case, however, it hardly helps to counter the rather more compelling arguments supporting the continuation of the appeal process put forward by, among others, the Children's Commissioner for England[660] and the Administrative Justice and Tribunals Council, which criticised the erosion of appeal rights 'given the serious consequences for pupils of being excluded from school'.[661] The Government also chose to ignore the conclusion of the House of Commons

---

[650] Ibid, at para 67.

[651] N Harris and K Eden with A Blair *Challenges to School Exclusion. Exclusion, Appeals and the Law* (Routledge Falmer 2000).

[652] School Discipline etc Regulations 2012, n 642 above, reg 6(5).

[653] But note that 'less than five' pupils excluded in 2010–2011 were aged 18 or over: DfE, Statistical First Release SFR 17/2012 *Permanent and Fixed Period Exclusions from Schools and Exclusion Appeals in England, 2010/11* (DfE, 2012), Table 3.

[654] Education Act 2011, s 4.

[655] In the case of academies the members are appointed by the proprietor.

[656] Education (Pupil Exclusions and Appeals) (Maintained Schools) (England) Regulations 2002 (SI 2002/3178), reg 6(6).

[657] DfE (2010), n 522 above, at para 3.29.

[658] DfE, Statistical First Release SFR 17/2012, n 653 above, Table 13.

[659] House of Lords, Grand Committee, Education Bill, third day, 4 July 2011, col.GC21.

[660] See *'They never give up on you' Office of the Children's Commissioner School Exclusions Inquiry* (Office of the Children's Commissioner, 2012).

[661] AJTC, Education Bill – letter to the Secretary of State, March 2011, at www.ajtc.org.uk.

Education Committee that the appeal process should be retained in view of the evidence of 'very strong support' for its continuation.[662] Additionally, the Joint Committee on Human Rights concluded that the reform conflicted with Art 6 of the ECHR, which provides for a right to have a civil right determined before an impartial tribunal.[663] The Committee disagreed with the Government's view that an exclusion decision is not concerned with a 'civil right' and so the Article is inapplicable.[664] It also considered that the possibility of pursuing a separate judicial review application in order to challenge an exclusion decision was not sufficient to ensure respect for the Art 6 right.

The review panel may either (i) uphold the governing body's decision; (ii) recommend that the governing body reconsiders the matter; or (iii) if it regards the governing body's decision to be 'flawed when considered in the light of the principles applicable on an application for judicial review', quash the decision and direct the governing body to reconsider the matter.[665] There must, however, be doubt as to whether it is realistic to expect lay review panels, under (iii), to be able to apply judicial review principles to the cases that come before them. The governing body must reconvene to re-consider the exclusion, when recommended or directed to do so, within 10 school days of being notified of the review panel's decision.[666] Although, under (iii), the governing body may ultimately choose not to reinstate the pupil, they could incur a cost; this is because the review panel has a power to order the local authority to adjust the school's budget share (downwards) by £4,000 during the relevant funding period if the governing body decides, after reconsidering the decision which has been quashed, not to reinstate the pupil.[667]

The parent's right to request (in writing) that an SEN expert be appointed at the local authority's expenses for the review process[668] is also new. This right applies regardless of whether the pupil has actually been diagnosed as having SEN. The SEN expert's role in a case will not, however, include that of assessing whether the child has SEN.[669] Rather, he or she will be expected to provide the review panel with 'impartial advice on how [SEN] may be relevant to the decision to exclude the pupil permanently',[670] as though an 'expert witness'.[671] There is clearly a somewhat fine line between advising the panel

---

[662] House of Commons Education Committee *Behaviour and Discipline in Schools*, First Report of Session 2010–11, Vol.1, HC 516-I (The Stationery Office, 2011), at paras 73 and 76.

[663] Joint Committee on Human Rights, Thirteenth Report Session 2010–12, *Legislative Scrutiny: Education Bill and other Bills*, HL Paper 154, HC 1140 (The Stationery Office, 2011), at paras 1.37–1.43.

[664] In its conclusion on Art 6 the Committee argued that *Oršuš v Croatia*, European Court of Human Rights (Application No 15766/03) [2008] ELR 619 was authority for the application of that article to education disputes.

[665] Education Act 2002, s 51A(4), inserted by the Education Act 2011, s 4(2).

[666] School Discipline etc Regulations 2012, n 642 above, reg 8.

[667] Ibid, reg 7(5). This 'penalty' can also be attached to a failure to reconsider the decision within the prescribed time limit for doing so: ibid, read with reg 8(1).

[668] Ibid, regs 7(1)(a) and 16(1)(a).

[669] Ibid, Sch 1, para 18.

[670] Ibid, regs 7(1)(b) and 16(1)(b).

[671] Guidance n 635 above, at para 155.

that the pupil has SEN, which is not within the remit of the expert, and that of indicating that the way a pupil has behaved might be typical of a person with, say, emotional and/or behavioural problems (a category of SEN). Furthermore, part of the SEN expert's role is to indicate to the panel, in a case where he or she thinks that the school has not dealt with a pupil in a way that was 'legal, reasonable and procedurally fair with respect to identification of any [SEN] the pupil may potentially have', the contribution that that treatment might have made to the child's exclusion.[672] In other words, the expert could be expected to indicate to the panel that although the pupil has not been classed as having SEN, the school may not have been led to exclude the pupil had it investigated whether the pupil did have such needs. Again this is tantamount to saying the pupil is likely to have SEN, potentially taking the expert outside his or her intended remit.

Despite these ambiguities in the role of the SEN expert this reform represents a welcome development, since the association between SEN and exclusion is well established and is indicated clearly in the exclusion statistics cited earlier (see p 974 above). Indeed, previously arguments have been presented for exclusion appeals to brought within the jurisdiction of the First-tier Tribunal (Health, Education and Social Care Chamber), which deals with SEN appeals, due to this association and the tribunal's expertise in SEN, a position consistently supported by the Administrative Justice and Tribunals Council among others.[673] In any event, parents challenging a permanent exclusion now have the additional option of bringing a complaint of disability discrimination relating to the exclusion to the First-tier Tribunal,[674] whereas previously it would have had to be pursued via the (now abolished) appeal process.[675] An artificial procedural distinction between cases of fixed-term and permanent exclusion has thus been removed, but it means there is a twin-track towards potential redress in some cases.[676]

Some will find it regrettable, particularly having regard to the principle in Art 12 of the CRC,[677] that the Government has not conferred an independent right to apply for an exclusion review on pupils under the age of 18. In relation to exclusion appeals, pupils in Scotland and Wales have an independent right of appeal at the age of 16, with pupils under that age (down to 11 in Wales and

---

[672] Ibid, at para 157.

[673] See eg Administrative Justice and Tribunals Council, written evidence to the Joint Committee on Human Rights, in Joint Committee on Human Rights, n 663 above, at pp 66–67; Harris and Eden (2000), n 622 above, at pp 171–172.

[674] Equality Act 2010, Sch 17, para 14, amended by the Education Act 2011, Sch 1, paras 11–13. See p 904 above.

[675] Anomalously, discrimination relating to fixed term exclusions, not justiciable under the appeal process, could be pursued before the tribunal.

[676] Note that if a review has not been requested within the normal 15 day time limit it can still be pursued once the disability discrimination case before the tribunal is determined, since in such cases the time limit will run from the date of the tribunal's determination: see the School Discipline (Pupil Exclusions and Reviews) (England) Regulations 2012 (SI 2012/1033), Sch 1 para 2.

[677] See pp 895, 920 and 929 above.

generally 12 in Scotland) having a right in common with their parents.[678] The UK Children's Commissioners recommended in 2008 that the position in England be brought into line with that in these jurisdictions[679] and the Labour Government subsequently reported that consideration was being given to doing that and that it would consult on the matter,[680] although the outcome of the consultation on this issue is not known. The present government agreed to pilot a right of appeal for young people in SEN cases and disability discrimination cases before the First-tier Tribunal, as noted above, after consultation found support for such a right.[681] It remains to be seen whether the same will happen in the case of exclusion reviews.

CONCLUDING COMMENTS

The law governing education is probably the most complex and detailed of all areas of particular relevance to children. Given the degree of central regulatory control over education and the prominence government tends to give to education policy and to the continual introduction of new initiatives and adjustments to the system, it is not surprising that education law itself, as an instrument of policy and regulation, is also in a constant state of flux. One of the reasons for the legal complexity in this field is that the frequent legal changes very often involve intricate amendments to already elaborate and highly technical legislative provisions. Given this and the large number of statutory instruments specifically governing education that are made each year, typically in the region of around 100, it can be very difficult to ascertain the current law with precision in order to apply it to individual circumstances. This is a matter of some concern given the overwhelming importance of education to the lives and futures of young people and the wide range of key responsibilities placed upon the professionals who are involved in providing it. It can also exacerbate the difficulties faced by parents seeking to negotiate the system and its various processes in the exercise of the various opportunities the law provides for them to participate in decisions. As one author has commented with reference to one of the principal education statutes, the Education Act 1996, 'there is very little evidence of the Act's intended audience being children and their parents'.[682] Both children themselves, where the law guarantees or facilitates their participation – for which a real commitment among policy makers and legislators is still lacking despite some progress in

---

[678] See Harris (2009), n 229 above, at 350.

[679] UK Children's Commissioners *UK Children's Commissioners Report to the UN Committee on the Rights of the Child* (2008) http://www.childcomwales.org.uk/uploads/publications/61.pdf (last accessed 31 July 2012).

[680] HL Debs, 30 October 2008, col 1826, per Baroness Morgan of Drefelin (Parliamentary Under-Secretary, DCSF).

[681] See p 944 above. As noted, however, under the Children and Families Bill young people over compulsory school age are to be given independent SEN appeal and disability discrimination complaint rights, and piloting would only cover those who are of compulsory school age.

[682] C F Huws 'The Language of Education Law in England and/or Wales' (2012) *Statute Law Review* 33(2), 252–280 at 254.

recognising children's independent rights – and their parents need far more help than is available to them at present if more of them are to be able to assert their rights effectively.

INDEX

References are to page numbers.